A HISTORY OF UKRAINE:
THE LAND AND ITS PEOPLES

Second, Revised and Expanded Edition

First published in 1996, *A History of Ukraine* quickly became the authoritative account of the evolution of Europe's second-largest country. In this fully revised and expanded second edition, Paul Robert Magocsi takes into account both the recent developments in the country's history as well as the information and insights found in the vast body of recent publications. Included in this revised edition are three new chapters that deal with the Crimean Khanate in the sixteenth and seventeenth centuries, the reaction of Ukraine's other peoples to the post-World War I revolutionary era, and the developments in Ukraine since it obtained independent statehood in 1991.

Other issues not dealt with in the first edition are now given the attention they deserve, including the role of music and opera in the nineteenth-century Ukrainian national awakening, socialist realism in the early Soviet period, and the Polish-Ukrainian conflict at the close of World War II. The number of text inserts, an extremely useful and enjoyable feature of the first edition, has been increased; new topics covered include the pre-historic Trypillians, the Italianate Crimea and the Black Death, the Karaites, Ottoman and Crimean slavery, Soviet-style ethnic cleansing, and the Orange Revolution. The maps have been revised and three new ones added. Finally, the "For Further Reading" section has been expanded significantly.

In keeping with the innovative approach of the first edition – the emphasis on the multicultural reality of past and present Ukraine – much new information has been added on the experience of Ukraine's Russians (including Old Believers), Poles, Greeks, Romanians, and Crimean Tatars, as well as on those peoples who were absent in the first edition: Bulgarians, Czechs, and Moldovans. Comprehensive, innovative, and geared towards teaching, the second edition of *A History of Ukraine: The Land and Its Peoples* is ideal for both teachers and students.

PAUL ROBERT MAGOCSI, a fellow of the Royal Society of Canada, is professor of History and Political Science and holds the Chair of Ukrainian Studies at the University of Toronto. He is the author of twenty books, including *Historical Atlas of Central Europe*, *The Roots of Ukrainian Nationalism*, and *Ukraine: An Illustrated History*.

A History of *Ukraine*

The Land and Its Peoples

Second, Revised and Expanded Edition

Paul Robert Magocsi

UNIVERSITY OF TORONTO PRESS
Toronto Buffalo London

© University of Toronto Press 1996, 2010
Toronto Buffalo London
www.utppublishing.com
Printed in the U.S.A.

First edition published 1996, reprinted in paper 2000
Second edition published 2010, reprinted 2012

ISBN 978–1–4426–4085–6 (cloth)
ISBN 978–1–4426–1021–7 (paper)

Printed on acid-free paper

Library and Archives Canada Cataloguing in Publication

Magocsi, Paul R.
    A history of Ukraine : the land and its peoples / Paul Robert Magocsi. – 2nd ed.

Includes bibliographical references and index.
ISBN 978-1-4426-4085-6 (bound). – ISBN 978-1-4426-1021-7 (pbk.)

1. Ukraine – History.   I. Title.

DK508.51.M34 2010   947.7   C2009-906664-5

University of Toronto Press acknowledges the financial assistance to its publishing
program of the Canada Council for the Arts and the Ontario Arts Council.

  Canada Council   Conseil des Arts    ONTARIO ARTS COUNCIL
for the Arts   du Canada   CONSEIL DES ARTS DE L'ONTARIO

University of Toronto Press acknowledges the financial support for its publishing
activities of the Government of Canada through the Canada Book Fund.

For Tinka

Contents

Part Seven: Ukraine in the Austrian Empire

List of Maps

List of Tables

Preface to the Second Edition

Fifteen years have gone by since *A History of Ukraine* was first published. During that time, much has happened in the evolution of Europe's second largest country. No less impressive has been the virtual explosion of scholarship published about various aspects of Ukraine's distant and more recent past.

This fully revised and expanded second edition of what is now entitled *A History of Ukraine: The Land and Its Peoples* takes into account both the recent developments in the country's history as well as the information and insights found in the vast body of recent publications. Included in this revised edition are three new chapters that deal with the Crimean Khanate in the sixteenth and seventeenth centuries, the reaction of Ukraine's other peoples to the post–World War I revolutionary era, and the developments in Ukraine since it obtained independent statehood in 1991. Other issues not dealt with in the first edition are now given the attention they deserve, including the role of symphonic music and opera in the nineteenth-century Ukrainian national awakening, socialist realism and work competition in the early Soviet period, and the Polish-Ukrainian conflict at the close of World War II. The number of text inserts, which proved to be an extremely useful and enjoyable aspect of the first edition, has increased by seven to a total of seventy-two. Among the new topics covered are the pre-historic Trypillians, the Italianate Crimea and the Black Death, the Karaites, Ottoman and Crimean slavery, Soviet-style ethnic cleansing, and the Orange Revolution. All the maps have been significantly revised and three new ones added for a total of forty-six. Finally, the "For Further Reading" section has been expanded by one-third more than what it was in the original edition.

In keeping with the innovative approach of the first edition, the emphasis on depicting the multicultural reality of past and present Ukraine has been maintained, and reflected in the newly added sub-title of the book. Much new information has been added on the experience of Ukraine's Russians (including Old Believers), Poles, Greeks, Romanians, and Crimean Tatars, as well as on those peoples who were absent in the first edition: Bulgarians, Czechs, and Moldovans. Another consequence of the multinational approach is to accept the reality of Ukraine's other diasporas, so that the fully revised text insert on that topic now includes an expanded discussion of Russians, Jews, and Poles, as well as Carpatho-

Rusyns, Crimean Tatars, Germans, and Mennonites from Ukraine whose communities live in several countries abroad and who have at times influenced developments in their ancestral homeland.

Aside from the addition of factual data, this second edition of a *A History of Ukraine* argues for a new conceptual approach aimed, in particular, at reconfiguring our understanding of developments before the eighteenth century. In that regard, the third phase in Ukrainian historical development is referred to here as the Lithuanian-Polish-Crimean period, in order to emphasize that the Crimean Khanate (which for centuries ruled nearly one-third of present-day Ukraine) should be moved from the periphery and treated as an integral part of the Ukrainian historical narrative.

Whatever improvements may be found in this revised edition are in no small measure due to the comments by a whole host of colleagues (including reviewers) and students who have used the first edition of the *A History of Ukraine*. I am particularly grateful to other colleagues who more recently have generously devoted their time to review certain parts of the revised edition before publication. Among them are the cohort of Ottoman and Crimean specialists led by Victor Ostapchuk (University of Toronto) and his graduate students Maryna Kravets and Murat Yasar. Other sections of the work were read critically by Doris Bergen, Peter Galadza, Roman Serbyn, and Stephen Velychenko. The chapter on independent Ukraine benefited enormously from the information provided by Taras Kuzio and the critical comments of Serhiy Bilenky.

Preparation of this second edition posed some new challenges, which modern technology did not substantially alleviate. Thanks to the efforts of Gabriele Scardellato, the text of the first edition was "electronically recovered" and the burden of preparing a revised index was rendered less time consuming. The coordination between the author and publisher necessary to make this large-scale project possible was graciously provided by the University of Toronto Press editor Richard Ratzlaff. Rendering with consistency place names and proper names from other languages into English was once again a challenge. Most place and geographic names follow the preferred (first) form given in *Merriam-Webster's Geographical Dictionary*, 3rd ed. (Springfield, Mass. 2001). Maryna Kravets kindly prepared a list of modified Turkish spellings for names/terms that are originally in Crimean Tatar, Ottoman Turkish, and modern Turkish. Most of the names/terms referring to Jewish matters are based on those used in an outstanding new resource on the subject, compiled under the direction of Gershon David Hundert, *The YIVO Encyclopedia of Jews in Eastern Europe*, 2 vols. (New Haven and London 2008).

I am deeply grateful to all these colleagues, but most of all to Nadiya Kushko, a daughter and patriot of the land of Ukraine, whose vast knowledge of pre-historic and historic times as well as insights into Soviet life have truly enriched and made this revised edition better than it could ever have been without her. Of course, whatever shortcomings may still exist are mine alone.

Paul Robert Magocsi
Toronto, Ontario
February 2010

Preface to the First Edition

In 1991, a newly independent country came into being – Ukraine. It was one of many new states formed or reconfigured in the wake of the Revolution of 1989, perhaps the most influential event in Europe's political evolution since the French Revolution two centuries before. Ukraine may have achieved independence only in 1991, but it was hardly a new country. For thousands of years, prehistoric and historical civilizations had flourished on Ukrainian territory. Even the idea and realization of Ukrainian statehood was nothing new: it had existed, albeit briefly, during the second decade of the twentieth century.

Despite these realities, the world has generally known little of Ukraine. And what it has learned and remembered seems to be associated only with tragedy, whether the nuclear disaster at Chornobyl' in 1986, the Nazi massacre of civilians at Babi Yar in 1941, the death of millions of Ukrainian peasants in the Great Famine of 1933, or the pogroms against Jews in 1919. Yet there is certainly more to Ukraine than tragedy, and there is as well more to Ukraine than Ukrainians.

Ukraine is, after all, a land of many peoples and many cultures. It is the place where much of the treasure of Scythian gold was created during the half millennium before the common era; where Borodin's imagined Polovtsian dances were performed before the twelfth-century Kievan Rus' prince Ihor; where Gogol's Cossack, Taras Bul'ba, and the darling of the Romantic era, Ivan Mazepa, carried out their exploits; where Florence Nightingale did her early nursing work and Lord Tennyson found the subject for one of his most famous poems; where the Nobel Prize laureate and Polish novelist Henryk Sienkiewicz set his trilogy about the decline of Poland in the second half of the seventeenth century; where life in the Galician countryside provided Leopold von Sacher-Masoch with lurid tales that became the source for the concept of masochism; where the Jewish Hasidic movement was born; and where the writer Shalom Aleichem re-created late nineteenth-century life in a Jewish *shtetl,* in a work that North Americans later came to know as *Fiddler on the Roof.* The contexts for these and many other stories are what is to be found on the pages of this book.

Until now, most histories of Ukraine have told the story of the Ukrainian people. While this book also traces the evolution of ethnic Ukrainians, it tries as well to give judicious treatment to the many other peoples who developed within the borders of Ukraine, including Greeks, Crimean Tatars, Poles, Russians, Germans, Jews, Mennonites, and Romanians. Only through an understanding of all their cultures can one hope to gain an adequate introduction to Ukrainian history. In other words, this book is not simply a history of ethnic Ukrainians, but a survey of a wide variety of developments that have taken place during the past two and a half millennia among all peoples living on territory encompassed by the boundaries of the contemporary state of Ukraine.

This book began as long ago as 1980–1981, in the form of a lecture course at the University of Toronto on Ukraine from earliest times to the present. The work has retained the structure of a textbook that can be used in a university survey course, whether a full-year course or two half-year courses. There are ten sections of roughly five chapters each, for a total of fifty chapters. The arrangement is essentially chronological, from the first millennium before the common era to the declaration of Ukrainian independence and its confirmation by national referendum during the second half of 1991. Within each of the ten sections, there has been an attempt to provide an equally balanced discussion of political, economic, and cultural developments. Dispersed throughout the narrative are sixty-six textual inserts that contain the texts of important documents, contemporary descriptions, or explanations of specific events, concepts, and historiographic problems. Unless otherwise indicated, the texts of documents and other cited material have been translated by the author. Interspersed as well are nineteen statistical tables and forty-two maps depicting the historical evolution of all or part of Ukraine.

In works about multicultural countries like Ukraine, it is impossible to avoid the problem of which linguistic form to use for personal names and place-names. For personal names, spellings are in the language of the nationality with which the person generally identified. In the case of individuals in the medieval period who were of East Slavic background, the modern Ukrainian spelling of their names is used. Transliterations from languages using the Cyrillic alphabet follow the Library of Congress system; names of Jewish figures follow the spellings used in the *Encyclopedia Judaica*. For towns, cities, provinces, and regions, the language used is determined by present-day international boundaries – thus, the Ukrainian form for L'viv, in Ukraine; the Belarusan form for Polatsk, in Belarus; and the Polish form for Przemyśl, in Poland. In general, historic names are used on maps covering earlier periods: for example, Akkerman (today Bilhorod), Theodosia/ Caffa/Kefe (today Feodosiia), Iuzivka/Stalino (today Donets'k), and Katerynoslav (today Dnipropetrovs'k). A few Ukrainian geographic names and place-names are rendered in their commonly accepted English forms, such as Bukovina, Dnieper, Galicia, Podolia, Pripet, Volhynia, and Zaporozhia (for the historic region, but Zaporizhzhia for the modern city). Since the writing of this book, the government of Ukraine has adopted the form Kyiv as its official transliteration for the country's capital city. The more traditional English form, Kiev, is used here.

No individual could hope to be fully informed about the entire range of Ukrainian history, which is vast in chronological and thematic scope. I am, therefore, deeply indebted to many colleagues who at different times during the past decade have read all or parts of the various drafts of this work: Henry Abramson (University of Toronto), Karel C. Berkhoff (University of Toronto), Bohdan Budurowycz (University of Toronto), John-Paul Himka (University of Alberta), Stella Hryniuk (University of Manitoba), Iaroslav Isaievych (Shevchenko Scientific Society, L'viv), Ivan S. Koropeckyj (Temple University), Lubomir Luciuk (Royal Military College of Canada), James Mace (University of Illinois), Alexander Motyl (Columbia University), and Stephen Velychenko (University of Toronto).

I am also grateful to the many persons who contributed to preparing the manuscript for publication, including, at the first stage, the typists Maureen Harris, Nadia Diakun, Florence Pasquier, and Cindy Magocsi; and, at the latter stage, Darlene Zeleney of the University of Toronto Press and, in particular, Tessie Griffin, who did an outstanding editorial job. Special appreciation as well to Karel Berkhoff for his accuracy in preparing the index, and to Byron Moldofsky and his staff at the Cartographic Office of the University of Toronto for their elegant drafting of the maps. While the counsel and constructive criticism of all these persons have helped greatly to improve the text, I alone am responsible for the interpretations and for whatever factual errors may remain.

Paul Robert Magocsi
Toronto, Ontario
December 1995

PART ONE

Introduction and Pre-Kievan Times

1

Ukraine's Geographic and Ethnolinguistic Setting

Territory and geography

Ukrainian territory can be defined in basically two ways. First, there is the territory as delimited by the political boundaries of a Ukrainian state that evolved in the twentieth century. Second, there is Ukrainian ethnolinguistic territory. An ethnolinguistic group consists of people who speak the same language or, more properly, varying dialects of one language, and who have common ethnographic characteristics. Accordingly, Ukrainian ethnolinguistic territory, is made up of the contiguous lands where ethnic Ukrainians live that are both within and beyond the boundaries of the Ukrainian state.

The state of Ukraine comprises 232,200 square miles (603,700 square kilometers) and is thus larger than any European country except Russia. Put another way, Ukraine is roughly the size of Germany and Great Britain combined, of the states of Arizona and New Mexico combined, or of the province of Manitoba in Canada. Ukrainian ethnolinguistic territory (which includes most, though not all, of Ukraine) comprises 288,800 square miles (750,800 square kilometers). This is approximately the size of Germany, Austria, and Italy combined, or of Texas in the United States.

The geographic setting for both Ukraine and the ethnolinguistic territory inhabited by Ukrainians is not complex. Almost the entire land mass in question consists of vast plains and plateaus which seldom rise more than 1,600 feet (500 meters) above sea level. These include coastal lowlands along the northern shores of the Black Sea and Sea of Azov, a vast plain to the east of the Dnieper River, a low marshy plain in the northwest, and somewhat higher plateaus with slightly rolling hills toward the west and in the far east. Outside the borders of Ukraine but still within Ukrainian ethnolinguistic territory, that is, in the region east of the Sea of Azov, the geography consists of a continuation of a flat lowland similar to that north of the Black Sea. Thus, the plain and slightly higher plateau are the predominant and somewhat monotonous features of the Ukrainian landscape. This fact prompted the Ukrainian geographer Stepan Rudnyts'kyi, at the beginning of the twentieth century, to comment, "Nine-tenths of Ukrainians have certainly never seen a mountain and do not even know what one looks like."[1]

MAP 1

GEOGRAPHIC FEATURES

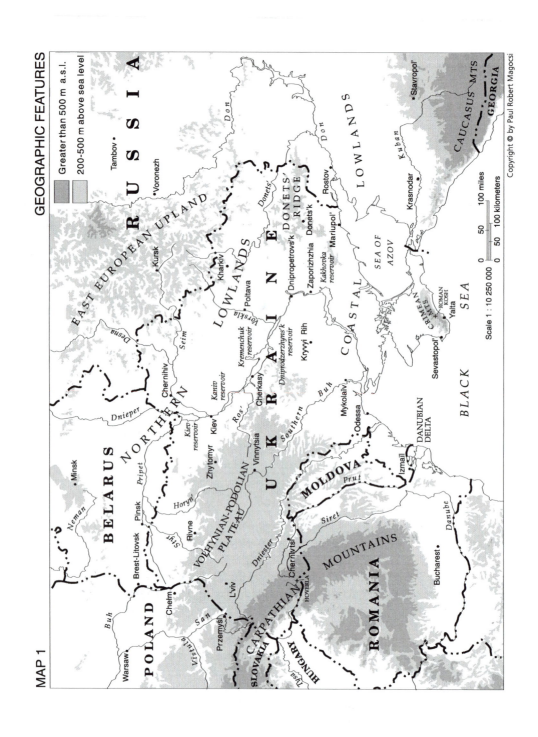

Greater than 500 m a.s.l.

200-500 m above sea level

Scale 1 : 10 250 000

0   50   100 miles

0   50   100 kilometers

Copyright © by Paul Robert Magocsi

There are mountains within Ukraine, but they are along the extreme edges of its territory. In the far west are the north-central ranges of the Carpathians, whose highest peak (Hoverla) reaches 6,760 feet (2,061 meters). At the southern tip of the Crimean Peninsula – actually outside Ukrainian ethnolinguistic territory – are the Crimean Mountains, whose highest peak (Roman Kosh) is 5,061 feet (1,543 meters). Just beyond the very southern fringes of Ukrainian ethnolinguistic territory in the southeast are the Caucasus Mountains, whose highest peaks reach well over 16,400 feet (5,000 meters). Thus, the only "Ukrainian" mountains are one portion of the Carpathian range, which comprises no more than five percent of all Ukrainian territory.

Dominated as it is by open plains and plateaus, Ukraine lacks any real natural boundaries. Even the Carpathian Mountains, which in any case cover a very small area of Ukraine, contain several passes through which communication has been maintained. Lacking any natural geographic barriers, Ukraine has historically been open to all peoples, friendly or unfriendly, who might wish to come there.

Throughout Ukraine's broad plains and plateaus, a rather well knit network of rivers has facilitated north-south travel and communication. Most of these rivers are part of the Black Sea or Pontic watershed. The major rivers run essentially in a north-southeasterly or north-southwesterly direction, emptying into the Black Sea or its subsidiary, the Sea of Azov. From west to east, the major rivers are the Dniester (Ukrainian: Dnister), Southern Buh (Pivdennyi Buh), Dnieper (Dnipro) – all of which empty into the Black Sea – and the Donets', a tributary of the Don, which in turn empties into the Sea of Azov. In the far southwest, Ukrainian territory is bounded by the mouths of the Danube River as they empty into the Black Sea; in the far southeast, the Kuban River descends from the Caucasus Mountains, flowing westward through Ukrainian ethnolinguistic territory before reaching the Sea of Azov. Only along the very western edge of Ukrainian territory are there a few rivers that are not part of the Pontic watershed. These include the Buh (Western Buh) and San, which flow north into the Vistula as part of the Baltic watershed. Finally, there is the Tysa/Tisza River, south of the Carpathians, which flows westward and then southward across the Hungarian Plain into the Danube.

The Baltic and Pontic watersheds are rather closely interrelated in western Ukraine, where for centuries they have been part of an important communication network. This network links the Baltic Sea to the Black Sea via the Vistula, Buh, San, and Dniester Rivers. Of even greater historical significance has been the Dnieper River, which connects Belarusan and Russian cities in the north with the Black Sea in the south, and from there beyond to the straits of the Bosporus, which connect to the Aegean and Mediterranean Seas.

Climate

Just as its landscape has few extremes, so the temperature throughout Ukraine is relatively moderate, the yearly average for the vast majority of the territory being between +43° and +48° F (+6° and +9°C). Only the very extreme ends of Ukrainian territory have higher temperature averages – these being along the Black Sea coast, with Odessa having +50°F (+9.8°C) and Yalta, in the Crimea, +56°F (+13.4°C).

The Ukrainian average of +43° to +48°F (+6° to +9°C) is considerably lower than average temperatures in central or western Europe. For instance, London, which is at a latitude farther north than any city in Ukraine except Chernihiv, has a yearly average temperature of +51°F (+10.3°C). The more severe winters account for the lower Ukrainian readings. As the following comparison with western European cities reveals, Ukrainian cities have considerably colder average winter temperatures with slightly warmer summer averages:

	January	July		January	July
L'viv	+24°F (−4.6°C)	+64°F (+18°C)	London	+38°F (+3.5°C)	+64°F (+17.9°C)
Kiev	+21°F (−6.2°C)	+66°F (+19.2°C)	Brussels	+36°F (+2°C)	+64°F (+18°C)
Kharkiv	+18°F (−8.3°C)	+70°F (+20.9°C)	Frankfurt	+33°F (+0.7°C)	+64°F (+18.7°C)

From the standpoint of temperature, most of Ukraine – with a January mean temperature of +23°F (−5°C) and a July mean of +68°F (+20°C) – is more like Toronto, Canada, than western Europe.

Natural resources

Because of the large expanse of plains and the relatively moderate continental temperatures with adequate rainfall, Ukraine has traditionally been a rich agricultural region. As much as two-thirds of the country's surface land consists of the so-called black earth (*chornozem*), a resource that has made Ukraine one of the most fertile regions in the world and famous as the "breadbasket" of those states which in the past ruled the country, whether the Polish-Lithuanian Commonwealth, the Russian Empire, or the Soviet Union. Ukraine has always had an abundance of truck-farming produce, industrial crops (hemp, sunflower, sugar beets), and grains – wheat, corn, rye, and barley. On the eve of World War I, for instance, Ukraine accounted for 98 percent of all the wheat exports from the Russian Empire, and produced 84 percent of its corn, 75 percent of its rye, and 73 percent of its barley. Historically, however, the ease in obtaining a harvest has played a role in preventing progress and inventiveness in farming methods, which have traditionally come from areas much less richly endowed with favorable natural conditions.

Ukraine is also rich in minerals. Salt, used as a preservative since medieval times, contributed to the wealth of Galicia and the Crimea, where it was found. Beginning in the late nineteenth century, rich deposits of coal, iron ore, and manganese, found especially in the south-central and eastern parts of the country; that is, the Dnieper industrial region (within the triangle formed by the cities of Kryvyi Rih-Dnipropetrovs'k-Zaporizhzhia), and in Donbas (encompassing the Donets' Ridge and lower Donets' valley). Since the early twentieth century, these two regions have been among the world's major centers of heavy industry.

Administrative and ethnolinguistic divisions

Ukraine is divided into twenty-four regions, called oblasts, and one autonomous republic – Crimea. With few exceptions, the oblasts do not coincide with the historical regions of the country, even if some might use historical names. It is, however, the historical regions which will be mentioned most often in this text. Among these, from west to east, are Transcarpathia, Bukovina, Galicia, Podolia, Volhynia, Chernihiv, Poltava, Sloboda Ukraine, Zaporozhia, the Donbas, the Black Sea Lands, the Crimea, and the Kuban Region.

Ukrainian ethnolinguistic boundaries do not coincide with the boundaries of Ukraine. This makes Ukraine similar to many other states in the world, which often have (1) a dominant ethnolinguistic group (also known as a titular nationality) within their own borders as well as members of the same group living on contiguous territory in neighboring states, and (2) one or more ethnolinguistic groups that are different from the titular and often numerically dominant nationality.

Ukrainian is one of the fourteen Slavic languages, which are grouped into West Slavic (Polish, Kashubian, Sorbian, Czech, Slovak), South Slavic (Slovenian, Croatian, Serbian, Macedonian, Bulgarian), and East Slavic (Russian, Belarusan, Ukrainian, Carpatho-Rusyn). As an East Slavic language, Ukrainian is structurally closest to Belarusan and Russian, although some dialects, especially in western Ukraine, have been heavily influenced by either Polish or Slovak.

Linguists generally refer to three major Ukrainian dialectal groups: (1) northern dialects, which are spoken in Polissia, northern Volhynia, the northern Kiev region, and the Chernihiv region; (2) eastern dialects, which are spoken in a vast territory east and south of a line running roughly from Zhytomyr to Odessa; and (3) western dialects, which are spoken in southern Volhynia, Podolia, Galicia, northern Bukovina, and Transcarpathia. In a sense, the Ukrainian language reflects the geographic makeup of the country, with its vast stretches of plains and plateaus. That is, there is little variation in dialects and subdialects throughout the northern, the eastern, and even most of the western dialectal regions. Only in the far west on both sides of the Carpathian Mountains – in Transcarpathia and the East Slavic-inhabited lands of southeastern Poland and northeastern Slovakia – do the number and degree of differences among local dialects increase substantially, so much so that there has often been considerable debate among scholars and the people themselves as to whether they should be considered ethnically Ukrainian or a distinct people called Carpatho-Rusyns.

There are, of course, numerous other languages spoken both in the past and present by several peoples, many of whom – given the fact that they have lived on Ukrainian lands for centuries – can be considered among the country's indigeneous inhabitants. Languages from virtually all of Europe's linguistic families are represented: Slavic (Russian, Belarusan, Carpatho-Rusyn, Polish, Bulgarian); Germanic (German and Yiddish); Romance (Romanian and Moldovan); Turkic (Crimean Tatar, Gagauz, Azerbaijani/Azeri); Finno-Ugric (Hungarian); Greek; and Armenian. Quite often these peoples speak a form of language that differs considerably from the literary norm, such as *surzhyk* (an uncodified mixture of

MAP 2

UKRAINIAN ETHNOLINGUISTIC TERRITORY

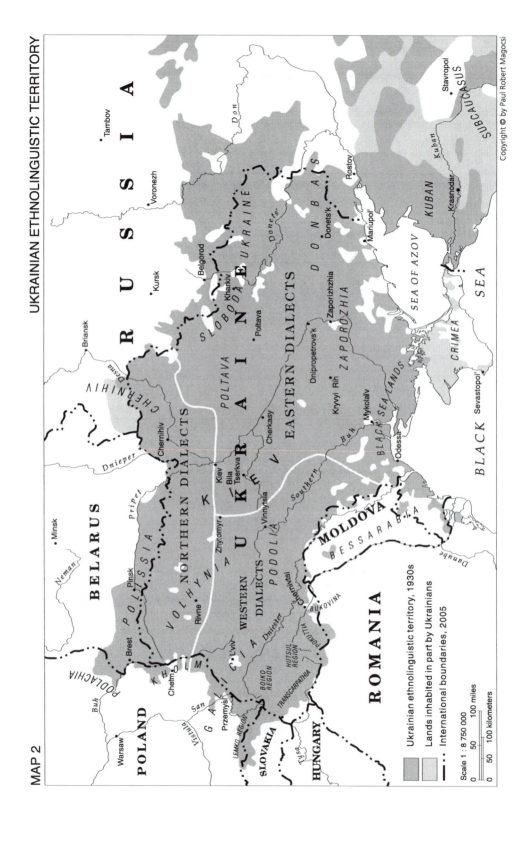

Ukrainian ethnolinguistic territory, 1930s

Lands inhabited in part by Ukrainians

International boundaries, 2005

Scale 1 : 8 750 000

0   50   100 miles

0   50   100 kilometers

Copyright © by Paul Robert Magocsi

TABLE 1.1
Nationality composition of Ukraine, 2001[2]

Nationality	Number	Percentage
Ukrainians	37,542,000	77.8
Russians	8,334,000	17.3
Belarusans	276,000	0.6
Moldovans	259,000	0.5
Crimean Tatars	248,000	0.5
Bulgarians	205,000	0.4
Magyars/Hungarians	157,000	0.3
Romanians	151,000	0.3
Poles	144,000	0.3
Jews	104,000	0.2
Armenians	100,000	0.2
Greeks	92,000	0.2
Tatars	73,000	0.2
Roma (Gypsies)	48,000	0.1
Azerbaijanis	45,000	0.1
Georgians	34,000	0.1
Germans	33,000	0.1
Gagauz	32,000	0.1
Others	177,000	0.4
TOTAL	48,241,000	99.4

Russian and Ukrainian) among Russian speakers, Tatar Greek among some Greek speakers, and *Plattdeutsch* (Low German) among some German speakers.

Population

According to the census of 2001, there were 48.2 million people living in Ukraine. Over three-quarters, or 37.5 million inhabitants (77 percent), were ethnic Ukrainians, while the remaining 11 million inhabitants (23 percent) belonged to several ethnolinguistic or national minorities (see table 1.1). Although ethnic Ukrainians have traditionally made up the majority of the country's population, in the last two centuries there has been a great discrepancy between their numbers in rural and in urban areas. For instance, in 1897, ethnic Ukrainians made up only 30 percent of the urban population of Ukraine, a percentage that has steadily increased since then, reaching 67 percent in 2001. As for other peoples, the Russians live primarily in the urbanized industrial regions of eastern Ukraine, the Jews and Belarusans in urban areas throughout the country, and the Crimean Tatars mostly in cities and towns of the Crimea. The remaining groups mostly inhabit rural areas: the Moldovans live in areas adjacent to Moldova; the Poles in islets scattered throughout Volhynia and eastern Galicia; the Bulgarians in southern Bessarabia; the Magyars in southern Transcarpathia; the Romanians in northern Bukovina; and the Greeks along the shores of the Black Sea (near Odessa) and the Sea of Azov (near Mariupol').

Aside from the 37.5 million ethnic Ukrainians within the boundaries of

TABLE 1.2
Ukrainians beyond Ukraine[3]
on contiguous ethnolinguistic territory, 2001

Russia (Kursk, Belgorod, Voronezh, Rostov, Krasnodar oblasts)	617,000
Moldova	600,000
Belarus (Brest and Homel oblasts)	108,000
Romania	52,000
Slovakia	11,000
Poland	6,000
TOTAL	1,394,000

Ukraine, in 2001 there were another 1.4 million Ukrainians living on contiguous ethnolinguistic territory in bordering countries (see table 1.2).

In Belarus, Ukrainians live within the marshland of the Pripet River valley; in Poland, along its eastern border in the Podlachia, Chełm, San, and Lemko regions; in Slovakia, in the far northeast known as the Prešov region; in Romania, in the Maramureş district, southern Bukovina, and the Danube Delta; in Moldova, along its northern and eastern border; and in Russia, along the Don and Kuban River valleys.

Aside from Ukrainians living in areas contiguous to Ukraine, there are still another estimated 6.2 million Ukrainians in other parts of the former Soviet Union and the world (see table 1.3). They are the descendants of ethnic Ukrainians who migrated to those areas in the course of the nineteenth and twentieth centuries.

The above statistics indicate that there are 45.1 million Ukrainians worldwide. Other sources suggest the figure might be as high as 51.8 million.

Nomenclature

Many different names have been used to designate the inhabitants and territory known today as Ukrainians and Ukraine. Indeed, it is not uncommon for any territory in Europe or elsewhere to have had different names for its inhabitants and its homeland in the past. The very question of nomenclature is frequently an integral part of a given nationality's historical development. It is not surprising, therefore, that the names used to designate Ukrainians and Ukraine in the distant and not so distant past have often been chosen to reflect a certain political stance, and sometimes even to deny the very existence of ethnic Ukrainians as a distinct nationality.

Until recently, knowledge of Ukraine in other parts of the world derived from Russian secondary sources. After the second half of the seventeenth century, when Muscovy and, later, the Russian Empire came to control most Ukrainian territory, Russian writers included Ukraine within Russian history. As part of this accommodation, old terms took on new meanings. Medieval *Kievan Rus'* became *Kievan Russia*, its culture and inhabitants *Kievan Russian* or *Old Russian*. For later periods, Ukraine was referred to in whole or in part as *Little Russia, South Russia, West Russia* (together with Belarus), or *New Russia* (the steppe and Black Sea coastal

TABLE 1.3
Ukrainians beyond their contiguous ethnolinguistic
territory, ca. 2000[4]

Russia	2,350,000
Kazakhstan	896,000
Uzbekistan	154,000
Kyrgyzstan	108,000
Tadjikistan	41,000
Turkmenistan	36,000
Latvia	70,000
Estonia	29,000
Lithuania	22,000
Belarus	129,000
Poland	25,000
Czech Republic	8,000
Serbia	5,000
Hungary	5,000
Bosnia-Herzegovina	4,000
Croatia	2,000
Other European countries	93,000
Canada	1,100, 000
United States	893,000
South America	170,000
Australia	20,000
TOTAL	6,174,000

regions), and its indigenous East Slavic inhabitants as *Little Russians*. In those parts of Ukraine not ruled by Muscovy or Russia, the territory was at times called *Ruthenia* and the East Slavic inhabitants *Ruthenians*.

The geographic names and ethnonyms, *Kievan Russia/Old Russian, Little Russia/Little Russian, Ruthenia/Ruthenian,* are still found in older and even in some contemporary publications about Ukraine written by authors from Europe, North America, and other parts of the world. In this volume, which is concerned primarily with the historical evolution of territory within the boundaries of present-day Ukraine, the term *Ukraine* will be used to designate the territory and *Ukrainians,* or *ethnic Ukrainians* to designate the major nationality inhabiting that territory. When discussing the medieval period, that is, approximately from the eighth to the fourteenth century, the terms *Rus'* or *Kievan Rus'* will be used for the territory and the *Rus'* or the *Rus' people* for its inhabitants. The progressive use of *Rus'/Ukraine* and *Rus'/Ukrainian* people in this volume is analogous to the use of *Franks/French,* or *Romans/Italians* in volumes surveying the history of France or Italy.

2

Historical Perceptions

Ukraine has been under the rule of foreign powers, especially Poland and Russia, for long periods of time. As a result, in historical writings Ukraine has often been treated not as an entity unto itself, but rather as a sort of appendage to a larger state structure, whether the old Polish-Lithuanian Commonwealth, the Russian Empire, or the Soviet Union. For instance, it was common for Russian or Polish historians writing in the nineteenth century to fit into their respective national historical narratives all territories that were at one time or another part of Russia or Poland. The result was that certain areas such as Ukraine and Belarus became in many Russian, Polish, and, subsequently, Western-language accounts countries without a history.

From such a perspective, the history of Ukraine was associated solely with the growth of the Ukrainian national idea, which skeptics argued could be dated only from the beginning of the nineteenth century at the earliest. Such perceptions of the historical past led to questions about the present and future. Faced with the existence of a Ukrainian national movement, those unsympathetic to Ukrainian distinctiveness would ask: If there was no Ukrainian state and therefore no Ukrainian history before the nineteenth century, on what grounds can one justify the creation of a sovereign state in the future? Because of the political implications as well as the scholarly significance of historical writings, it seems important that the reader be familiar with at least the main outlines of the various perceptions of the history of Ukraine. These may be classified as the Russian, Polish, Ukrainian, and Soviet viewpoints.

The Russian historical viewpoint

The various perceptions actually reflect a serious debate concerning the history of eastern Europe as a whole, or, more specifically, of the East Slavic peoples – the Russians, Belarusans, and Ukrainians. By the late eighteenth and early nineteenth centuries, when the first scholarly histories of eastern Europe began to be written, the only East Slavic state in existence was the Russian Empire. This state was headed by an all-powerful monarch, or tsar, of the Romanov dynasty, which had ruled

WHAT IS EASTERN EUROPE?

The term *eastern Europe* is difficult if not impossible to define with precision. Logically, one might assume that the term refers to the eastern half of the European continent. After World War II, however, it came to have more a political than a geographic meaning: *eastern Europe* referred to the territory encompassed by the new postwar boundaries of those countries (East Germany, Poland, Czechoslovakia, Hungary, Romania, Yugoslavia, Bulgaria, and Albania) that had just come under Communist rule and that were at one time or another closely allied, if not subordinate, to the Soviet Union.

Such a definition produced obvious geographic anomalies. Greece and Austria were excluded simply because they were non-Communist, regardless of the fact that both were as far east as or even farther east than some of the other "eastern" European states. Such an illogical conceptualization of eastern Europe is no longer defensible, on what were anyway rather tenuous post–World War II political grounds. This has become the case especially since 1989, as the former "eastern" European countries have abandoned Communist rule and as the Soviet bloc and the Soviet Union itself have ceased to exist.

Accordingly, use of the term *eastern Europe* in this book will be based solely on geographic criteria. Since Europe as a continent stretches from the coasts of Ireland and Portugal in the west to the Ural Mountains in the east, the west–east geographic divide is roughly along the 25°E longitudinal line, which runs very near the present-day western border of Belarus and Ukraine. It is interesting to note that the exact north–south as well as west–east geographic mid-point of the European continent – one that was carefully calculated in the second half of the nineteenth century – is actually on Ukrainian territory, near the village of Dilove (formerly Trebushany), in the southeastern corner of the Transcarpathian oblast.

This means that geographic eastern Europe is made up of virtually all of Belarus and Ukraine, Russia west of the Urals, Moldova, most of Finland, Estonia, Latvia, and Lithuania, and half of Romania and Bulgaria. Hence, if geographic and historical criteria are combined, eastern Europe can be said to coincide in the main with the homelands of the East Slavs – Russians, Belarusans, and Ukrainians – and it is in this context that the term will be used here. The term *central Europe* as used in this volume will refer to territory encompassed by the present-day countries of Poland, eastern Germany, the Czech Republic, Slovakia, Austria, Slovenia, Croatia, Hungary, and western Romania.

from Moscow and, later, St Petersburg since the early seventeenth century. Not surprisingly, both the Romanov dynasty and the Russian imperial state it represented encouraged the publication of works presenting a historical scheme that justified their existence. Among these works were the first two histories of Russia, by the eighteenth-century authors S.O. Mankeev (1715, published 1770) and Vasilii M. Tatishchev (1739, published in five volumes, 1768–1818). Both were elaborate tracts justifying the existence of absolute rule under the Romanov dynasty.

The best example of the dynastic approach to Russian history was the monumental twelve-volume *Istoriia gosudarstva rossiiskago* (History of the Russian State, 1818–29), by Nikolai M. Karamzin. Karamzin brought his historical coverage from earliest times to 1613 – that is, to the founding of the Romanov dynasty. He portrayed the Muscovite tsardom from the fourteenth to the late sixteenth century as coincident with the era of Russia's greatest well-being, especially because it was a time when autocratic rule was supposedly at its height. "Delivered by the princes of Moscow from the disaster of internecine wars as well as from a foreign yoke ... and satisfied with the uses of authority, the people did not argue over rights. ... In the end, all Russians began to look upon the tsar as a terrestrial god."[1] The direct implication was that Russia's nineteenth-century tsars should follow the autocratic example of their Muscovite predecessors.

An indispensable part of glorifying any state or monarchy is proving its proper genealogical lineage and descent. This is what in our times Bernard Lewis has so aptly called the foundation myth: the need for countries and peoples and powers – most of whom "arise from humble origins" – "to improve or conceal their undistinguished beginnings and attach themselves to something older and greater."[2] In this regard, Russian historians could draw on a conceptual framework developed in the fourteenth century by medieval churchmen. At that time, when the Muscovite state was in its early stage of development, monastic scribes recopied earlier historical chronicles, which they then "improved" and expanded in order to show the descent of their own secular rulers, the Muscovite princes, from the rulers of Kievan Rus', who belonged to a dynasty that could be traced back to the ninth-century semi-legendary ruler of Novgorod, Riuryk. The Muscovite princes were ostensibly the direct descendants of the Riuryk dynasty, which after the early seventeenth century was continued by the Romanovs. The Riurykid genealogical scheme, which argued for the historical continuity of Kievan Rus', Muscovy, and the Russian Empire, was also given a prophetic ecclesiastical twist in the early sixteenth century, when a monk named Filofei sought an explanation for the capture by Muscovy (1510) of his native western Russian city of Pskov. In the wake of the earlier fall of Constantinople, the capital of the Eastern (second) Roman Empire, to the Ottoman Turks (1453), Filofei was content to explain that event and the catastrophe that later beset his native city as part of God's larger plan: "All Christian empires will come to an end and, in accordance with the prophetic books, will merge with the empire of our sovereign, that is, the Russian tsardom. For two Romes have fallen, and a third [Muscovite Russia] still stands, but a fourth shall never be."[3]

By the nineteenth century, secular historians had begun to explain Russia's manifest destiny in eastern Europe not with genealogical or religious criteria, but rather in terms of political and sociodemographic patterns. This new trend had already been heralded in Karamzin's multivolume history. Karamzin believed in the unity of all the East Slavs, whom he referred to as the Russian people and whose first political center was Kiev. After the Mongol invasion of the mid-thirteenth century and the destruction of Kiev, the political and religious center of the "Russian" people shifted north, first to Vladimir-na-Kliazma, then to Moscow, and finally, in the early eighteenth century, to St Petersburg. This became in Russian history what might be called the theory of the displacement of political centers. The "mother of Russian cities," according to the popular image, was Kiev, and it was the duty of the descendants of that mother to ensure that one day all the lands that were once part of Kievan "Russia" would again be part of a unified Russian state. Since the Muscovite princes were considered the rightful heirs of the Kievan inheritance, their survival ensured that the historical destiny of the Russian people would be fulfilled. That destiny was the unification of *Veliko-Rus'* "Great Russia," *Belo-Rus'* "White Russia," and *Malo-Rus'* "Little Russia" – the biblical three in one.

Although Karamzin believed that the inhabitants of what he called Great, White, and Little Russia constituted a single Russian people, by the early nineteenth century, linguistic and ethnographic research, together with the publication of contemporary descriptions and travel accounts, was forcing many scholars to realize that there were, indeed, considerable differences among the various components of the so-called one Russian people, in particular between the Great Russians and the Little Russians, or Ukrainians. The confirmation of such differences not only would undermine the idea of a single Russian people, but also might threaten the link between medieval Kiev and Moscow and thus render precarious the whole framework upon which the Russian imperial conception of history was built. Hence, a suitable explanation for this potentially dangerous discrepancy had to be found.

The explanation was provided in the writings of Mikhail D. Pogodin, an influential nineteenth-century historian and publicist for the Russian version of Pan-Slavism. In 1856, Pogodin put forth his depopulation theory, according to which the ancestors of the Muscovites had supposedly lived in the central (Dnieper-Ukrainian) lands of Kievan Rus' from the tenth through the twelfth century, but had fled to the north after the Mongol invasion of the mid-thirteenth century. Later, in the thirteenth and, especially, fourteenth centuries, peasants from Polish- and Lithuanian-controlled areas in the west came into barren Ukraine. This new immigrant population represented the ancestors of the present-day Ukrainians. Thus, to Karamzin's theory of the displacement of political centers was added Pogodin's theory of shift in population.

This conception of the history of the East Slavs was adopted by perhaps the most influential of all Russian historians, Sergei M. Solov'ev, in his twenty-nine volume *Istoriia Rossii s drevnieishikh vremen'* (History of Russia from Earliest Times, 1851–79) and by Solov'ev's student Vasilii Kliuchevskii in his even more widely read five-volume *Kurs russkoi istorii* (Course of Russian History, 1904–21). According to Solov'ev, "At the end of the twelfth century [Kiev] ... revealed its incapacity to develop any solid foundations for a single state. Following a definite path from the beginning, all the best elements of the land poured out of the southwest toward the northeast. Settlement moved in the same direction and with it the course of history."[4] Solov'ev's deterministic view was complemented by Kliuchevskii's stress on supposed psychological change:

As soon as the population of northern Rus' felt that Moscow was capable of becoming the political center around which could unite its forces to struggle against the foreign enemy, that the Moscow prince could be a national leader in this struggle, a drastic change took place in the minds of people and in their relations. ... All the suppressed and inarticulate national and political aspirations of the Great Russian race, aspirations that had so long and so successfully sought means of self-expression, then met with the dynastic ambitions of the grand duke of Moscow and carried him to the exalted height of national sovereign of Great Russia.[5]

The Russian conception of eastern Europe's history, as presented most elegantly in the works of Solov'ev and Kliuchevskii, continues to dominate most histories of Russia. It was the conception put forward by Russian émigré historians, the most influential of whom were George Vernadsky and Michael Florinsky, and it has been repeated in most textbooks of Russian history published in western Europe and North America during the twentieth century. Consequently, in these works the history of Ukraine, if considered at all, is treated as the history of one of Russia's provinces. Moreover, since the Kievan period is treated as an integral part of Russian history, Ukrainian history per se is considered to have begun in the fourteenth century at best, or in the seventeenth century. For some Russian writers, the very concept of Ukrainian history is illogical, since it is considered simply a political idea born in the nineteenth century – an idea, moreover, which was used by foreign powers like Germany and Austria to undermine the unity of the Russian state.

Finally, there is the view that the very idea of Russia without Little Russia, or Ukraine, is inconceivable. The dean of twentieth-century Russian specialists of Kievan Rus', Dmitrii Likhachev, best summed up this attitude: "Over the course of the centuries following their division into two entities, Russia and Ukraine have formed not only a political but also a culturally dualistic unity. Russian culture is meaningless without Ukrainian, as Ukrainian is without Russian."[6]

The Polish historical viewpoint

Somewhat related to the classic Russian conception of eastern European history, although clearly having other goals, is the traditional approach of Polish writers to the history of Ukraine. During the nineteenth century, Poland did not exist as an independent state. In such circumstances, Polish political commentators and writers frequently looked to the historical past in an attempt to explain why they had lost their statehood and perhaps to discover what should or should not be done to regain independence in the future. In their search through Poland's past, most frequently it was the seventeenth century and the problem of the Cossacks in what was then Polish-ruled Ukraine that was considered the crucial turning point and beginning of the decline of Poland.

The Polish perception of Ukrainian history was greatly influenced in the decades before World War I by Aleksander Jabłonowski in his seven volumes of historical studies (*Pisma*, 1910–13) and his *Historya Rusi Południowej do upadku Rzeczypospolitej Polskiej* (History of Southern Rus' until the Fall of the Polish Commonwealth, 1912). Despite his relative sympathy for Ukrainian national strivings in the late nineteenth century, Jabłonowski concluded that historically the Ukrainian lands had never constituted a distinct entity nor the population of Ukraine a distinct people. Rather, in the sixteenth century, when Poland annexed Ukraine, Poles discovered an uncivilized frontier, into which they brought culture and state formations. While they recognized there had been a high level of culture during the period of Kievan Rus', they did not consider it specifically Ukrainian. Moreover, because Polish and Kievan princely families intermarried, and because Poland controlled parts of the Rus' federation (especially its western borderlands) and even the city of Kiev itself during certain periods, there arose the view, especially after Poland's incorporation of most of the Ukrainian lands in 1569, that the Poles had a legal and historical right to the Kievan inheritance.

Polish writers also implicitly accepted the theory of the Russian writer Pogodin about the depopulation of Ukraine (southern Rus') after the mid-thirteenth-century Mongol invasion. Into this supposedly barren wilderness of the Ukrainian steppe (Polish: *Dzikie Pola* "Wild Fields") came settlers from the Polish- and Lithuanian-controlled lands of Galicia and Volhynia. Even if most of these people were East Slavs, they were under the organizational leadership of the Polish state and manorial nobility. Moreover, the cultural, linguistic, and religious diversity of the populations that came under Polish rule was tolerated in what Polish writers were fond of referring to as the democracy of the republic of nobles and commonwealth headed by kings of the Jagiellonian dynasty.

The era of Jagiellonian rule, which lasted from 1385 to 1572, was considered to epitomize the ideal Polish system of government, supposedly characterized by democratic institutions and, in general, by religious and national tolerance. Assuming the existence of such an ideal state, Polish writers quite naturally stressed that the country's inhabitants, whatever their religious or cultural background, eagerly strove to identify themselves as free citizens of the Polish commonwealth. Within such a constellation, Ukraine, together with neighboring Belarus and Lithuania, was viewed simply as part of the eastern *kresy*, or borderlands, which had been fortunate enough to be included within that bastion of Western and Catholic civilization, Poland.

To be sure, there were times when these apparently peaceful and productive "borderlands of western civilization" (to quote the popular twentieth-century Polish-American historian Oscar Halecki) were struck by disturbances. Taking their cue from several monographs on the Cossacks and their most famous leader, Bohdan Khmel'nyts'kyi, by the early twentieth-century historian Franciszek Rawita-Gawroński, Polish authors generally have presented these disturbances as little more than barbaric outbreaks caused by destructive elements among the uncivilized Ukrainian masses. Sometimes the outbreaks would result in major upheavals, as during the Khmel'nyts'kyi revolution of the mid-seventeenth century or the haidamak uprisings of the eighteenth century. After they were put down and foreign (Turkish, Tatar, or Muscovite) intervention was repelled, the Ukrainian frontier was rightfully restored to Poland as part of its cultural and political patrimony. This pattern lasted until the late eighteenth century, when Poland's Ukrainian lands were forcibly annexed by Russia and Austria, who joined with Prussia eventually to remove all of Poland from the map of Europe.

In essence, Ukrainian lands, especially those west of the Dnieper River (the Right Bank, Volhynia, Galicia), were considered an integral part of Poland. Hence, when the nineteenth-century efforts to restore a Polish state finally came to fruition in 1918, it was expected that its boundaries would "quite naturally" encompass Ukrainian and other eastern borderland territories in a reincarnation of the Jagiellonian state that would stretch from the Baltic to the Black Sea. As it turned out, such territorial designs proved impossible to achieve when Europe's boundaries were being redrawn after World War I. A quarter century later, however, most Poles did expect that the Ukrainian-inhabited lands (eastern Galicia and western Volhynia) ruled by Poland during the interwar years would be returned to the reconstituted country at the close of World War II. Some Polish circles, especially among political exiles in the West, even kept alive the idea of reviving a Poland from the Baltic to the Black Sea.

Whereas the peripheral nature of Ukrainian developments was generally accepted in traditional Polish historical and popular perceptions before World War II, after that time Polish historians, initially under the impact of Soviet political influence in east-central Europe and the dominance of the Marxist approach to scholarship, considerably reassessed their views. The Cossack period continued to be of primary interest, but in the writings of postwar historians like Leszek Podhorodecki, Władysław Serczyk, and Zbigniew Wójcik, Ukraine is no longer treated simply as an appendage to Poland, but rather as a country with a distinct historical process from earliest times to the present. This positive reassessment of Ukraine – in part reflective of Polish post-Communist political accommodation to, and support for, its large eastern neighbor – is evident in recent surveys of Polish history by Jerzy Topolski and Marek Borucki, among others. Nevertheless, it takes time for new attitudes to permeate any society, and still today it is not uncommon to find in Polish public opinion the conviction that whatever was positive in the Ukrainian past came not from indigenous forces but solely from the country's association with the ostensibly civilizing influence of Poland.

The Ukrainian historical viewpoint

The beginnings of a specifically Ukrainian perception of eastern Europe's historical development can be said to coincide with the appearance of the first general histories of Ukraine in the eighteenth century. Despite their titles, which referred to the works as general histories of Little Russia, they were in fact accounts of the Zaporozhian Cossacks during the sixteenth and, especially, seventeenth centuries. The Zaporozhians and Ukraine were also the subject of works by Alsatian French (Jean-Benoît Scherer, 1788), German (Karl Hammerdörfer, 1789), and Austro-Hungarian (Johann Christian von Engel, 1796) authors.

The first half of the nineteenth century saw the appearance of the first multivolume histories of Ukraine, by Dmitrii Bantysh-Kamenskii (1822) and Mykola Markevych (1842–43), both of whom stressed the role of the Zaporozhian Cossacks in the Ukrainian historical process. The most influential work of the period, however, was the *Istoriia Rusov* (History of the Rus' People, 1846), of uncertain authorship, which first appeared in an unpublished form in the late 1820s. The popularity and influence of this work were perhaps due to the fact that it was more a political tract than a history. The *Istoriia Rusov* was one of the first works to treat Ukraine not as a province of Russia or Poland, but rather as an independent country deriving from Kievan times. Ukraine attained its greatest heights during the Cossack era, and it began to decline only in the eighteenth century after coming increasingly under Muscovite, later Russian, rule. The ability of the *Istoriia Rusov* to provide a clear sense of historical continuity for Ukraine was to have an enormous impact on historians as well as on the poets, folklorists, and language enthusiasts active in the slowly emerging Ukrainian national revival.

The first half of the nineteenth century was also a time when the Romantic movement reached Ukraine. Both professional and, in particular, amateur historians were receptive to Romanticism's emphasis on the distinctive genius of individual peoples as an alternative to the previous and often exclusive emphasis on dynasties and state structures as the driving force of the historical process. Adopting such populist-Romantic attitudes, a new generation of scholars led by Mykhailo Maksymovych, Mykola Kostomarov, and, at least initially, Panteleimon Kulish saw the Cossacks as the quintessential expression of the supposedly democratic and egalitarian ideals of the Ukrainian people. The new tone was set as early as the 1840s in the political program of the St Cyril and Methodius Society, published under the title *Knyhy bytiia ukraïns'koho narodu* (Books of Genesis of the Ukrainian People). This book, authored by Kostomarov, presented a personified Ukraine that "loved neither the tsar nor the [Polish] lord and established a Cossack Host … in which Cossacks were all equal amongst themselves." Moreover, "day after day the Cossack Host grew and multiplied and soon people in Ukraine would all have become Cossacks, that is, all free and equal."[7] This idyllic scenario did not work out, according to Kostomarov, because of the intervention of outside forces – Polish landlords, Muscovite tsars, Catholic popes, and Jesuits.

The view that the people were the driving force in history also led populist writers to try to discover the peculiar genius of ethnic Ukrainians, and by so doing arrive at both their uniqueness and their difference from Russians and Poles. Again, Kostomarov best summed up this approach in an article "Dvie russkii narodnosti" ("Two Rus' Nationalities," 1861), which subsequently came to be regarded as the gospel of Ukrainian nationalism.

Besides striving to depict the uniqueness of Ukrainians, an effort which undermined the conceptual unity of the East Slavs, Ukrainian scholars began chipping away at another aspect of the Russian historical conception, the ostensible link between medieval Kievan Rus' and Muscovy. In response to Pogodin's argument that the population of the Kiev region moved north after the thirteenth-century Mongol invasion, Mykhailo Maksymovych (1857) undertook research that was continued later by Volodymyr Antonovych (1882) and Mikhail Vladimirskii-Budanov (1890 and 1893), and that seemed to prove convincingly that central Ukraine was not depopulated in the fourteenth century, but rather that a society continued to

KOSTOMAROV ON UKRAINIANS, RUSSIANS, AND POLES

The following excerpts are from Mykola Kostomarov's 1861 article "Dvie russkii narodnosti" ("Two Rus' Nationalities"), published in the short-lived St Petersburg journal *Osnova*.

The Southern Rus' [Ukrainians] are characterized by individualism, the Great Rus' [Russians] by collectivism. ... In the political sphere, the Southern Rus' people were able to create among themselves free forms of society which were controlled no more than was required for their very existence, and yet they were strong in themselves without infringing on personal liberties. The Great Rus' people attempted to build on a firm foundation a collective structure permeated by one spirit. The striving of the Southern Rus' was towards federation, that of the Great Rus' towards autocracy and a firm monarchy.

The Great Rus' element has in it something grand and creative: the spirit of totality, the consciousness of unity, the rule of practical reason. The Great Rus' can live through all adversities and select the hour when action is most fitting and circumstances most favorable.

The Southern Rus' people lack such qualities. Their free spontaneity led them either to the destruction of social forms or to a whirlpool of striving which dissipated national efforts in all directions. Such testimony about these two peoples is provided by history. ...

The relations between the Southern Rus' and the Poles are quite different. If, linguistically, the Southern Rus' are less close to the Poles than they are to the Great Rus', in national character they are more akin to the Poles. ...

To be sure, there is a deep gulf which separates the Poles and the Southern Rus', a gulf which may never be bridged. The Poles and Southern Rus' are like two branches growing in opposite directions; one is pruned and has born refined fruit – the nobility; the other produced a peasantry. To put it more bluntly: the Poles are aristocratic while the Southern Rus' [Ukrainians] are a democratic people. Yet these two labels do not reflect the histories of the two peoples: Polish aristocracy is very democratic; that of the Southern Rus' is very aristocratic. The Polish nobility has tried to remain within the limitations of its own class; in Ukraine, on the other hand, the people have equal status and rights and often produce individuals who climb much higher and attain more for themselves, but in turn are again absorbed by the mass of the people from which they stem. Here and there this struggle often weakens the social structure, providing an opportunity for another people, who know the value of a strong community, to seize it.

SOURCE: Based on the English translation (with emendations for ethnonyms) in Dmytro Doroshenko, *Survey of Ukrainian Historiography/Annals of the Ukrainian Academy of Arts and Sciences*, Vol. V–VI (New York 1957), pp. 137–139.

function there until the Cossacks created new social and governmental structures in the sixteenth and seventeenth centuries. Despite such seeming flaws in the traditional Russian conception of eastern European history, the overall framework still seemed plausible.

The first serious challenge to the Russian conception came at the beginning of the twentieth century, from the pen of Mykhailo S. Hrushevs'kyi. In 1904, Hrushevs'kyi published an article entitled "The Traditional Scheme of 'Russian' History and the Problem of a Rational Organization of the History of the Eastern Slavs." Continuing in the tradition of the *Istoriia Rusov*, he not only pointed out what he considered the illogical aspects of the Russian conception of the eastern European historical process, but also provided a framework for a Ukrainian historical continuum that according to him began even earlier than the Kievan period and lasted past the Cossack era.

Even before the appearance of his seminal article, Hrushevs'kyi had begun to elaborate his framework for Ukrainian historical continuity in what was to become the monumental ten-volume *Istoriia Ukraïny-Rusy* (History of Ukraine-Rus', 1898–1937). Although the ten-volume work reached only the year 1658, Hrushevs'kyi also prepared several one-volume historical surveys which covered developments from pre-Kievan times to the struggle for a "renewed" independent Ukrainian state just after World War I. Thus, in his article "The Traditional Scheme" and his popular one-volume histories – all backed up by the erudition of his ten-volume scholarly magnum opus – Hrushevs'kyi provided, for the first time, a Ukrainian conception of eastern European history that could rival the dominant Russian one. While subsequent Ukrainian historians such as Dmytro Doroshenko and Viacheslav Lypyns'kyi may have challenged many of the populist inclinations of Hrushevs'kyi in favor of a more statist approach to the past, Ukrainianists outside the borders of the former Soviet Union – in interwar Galicia, later in western Europe and North America, and more recently in post-Soviet Ukraine – have followed Hrushevs'kyi's framework for the continuity of a distinct Ukrainian historical process that begins in pre-Kievan times and lasts until the present.

The Soviet historical viewpoint

The Bolshevik Revolution of 1917 and the subsequent creation of the Soviet Union in 1922 changed the course of Russian historical scholarship. The change did not come immediately, however, and at least during the 1920s both Marxist and non-Marxist approaches appeared in historical publications. The work of a few non-Marxist Russian historians such as Aleksander Presniakov (1918) and Matvei K. Liubavskii (1929) was in part influenced by the arguments of Hrushevs'kyi. Consequently, they began to seek the origins of the Muscovite Russian state not in Kiev but in the northeastern lands of Rostov, Suzdal', and Vladimir. On the other hand Russian émigré historians, led by George Vernadsky, continued to work within the framework of the nineteenth-century Russian historical conception of Solov'ev and Kliuchevskii.

In Soviet Ukraine as well, both Marxist and non-Marxist historians were able to research and publish, at least during the 1920s. The Hrushevs'kyi school continued under the historian's personal direction (he had returned from exile in the West to Kiev in 1924). Hrushevs'kyi's basic framework was retained even by Soviet Ukrainian Marxist historians like Matvii Iavors'kyi, who otherwise was concerned with emphasizing socioeconomic developments and the class struggle in Ukrainian history.

Beginning in the 1930s, however, when Stalin decided to eliminate all vestiges of any ideology that was not in keeping with his Great Russian Bolshevik version of Marxism, most of the members of the Ukrainian historical school, including Hrushevs'kyi, were exiled or imprisoned, and effectively silenced. Those who survived were expected to accept the new interpretation of eastern European history. That new interpretation as it applied to the non-Russian nationalities of the Soviet Union was epitomized by the so-called lesser-evil formula.

In the new Bolshevik state, founded as it was on Marxist ideological principles adjusted to local conditions by Lenin and Stalin, the nationality problem was an issue of primary concern. Leninist nationality policy did not permit the excesses of tsarist Russian nationalism, which had denied the very existence of Ukrainians as a distinct nationality. While the Bolsheviks recognized Ukrainians as a nationality, they nonetheless expected them to live with Russians in the same state. Hence, the old Leninist revolutionary slogan that tsarist Russia was a "prison of peoples" had to be adjusted. A solution to this seemingly contradictory state of affairs was the theory of the "lesser evil," summed up by the former Soviet historian Konstantin Shteppa in the following manner: "Although the annexation of non-Russian peoples to Russia was an evil – particularly when annexation meant the loss of their national independence – it was a lesser evil by comparison with that which could be expected to have resulted from their annexation to some other large state. Thus, Ukraine's annexation to Russia in the seventeenth century had to be regarded, according to this theory, as an evil, but a somewhat lesser evil than absorption by Poland, Turkey or – later – Sweden would have been."[8]

To diminish even further the negative impact of this "lesser evil," Soviet Russian and Soviet Ukrainian historians emphasized, whenever and wherever possible, the friendship between the two peoples, their relationship being presented – because Russia had always been stronger and thus the "elder brother" – as having been particularly beneficial to Ukrainians. The most outstanding example of this friendship between the "brotherly Russian and Ukrainian peoples" was the so-called act of union reached at Pereiaslav in 1654, in which the Cossack leader Bohdan Khmel'nyts'kyi pledged his loyalty to the tsar. In honor of its 300th anniversary in 1954, the Pereiaslav act was celebrated with great pomp in the Soviet Union by means of various popular and scholarly events and numerous publications. The depiction of the act in Soviet textbooks graphically reveals the evolution of Soviet Marxist historical perceptions, as in the following summary.

In 1928, a brief history of Ukraine by Matvii Iavors'kyi proclaimed that seventeenth-century Ukrainians "did not know that a fate worse than that under the [Polish] *szlachta* [nobility] awaited them in the future at the hands of the Muscovite *dvorianstvo* [nobility] and its autocrat – the 'white tsar'."[9] In 1940, however, a textbook of Soviet history concluded that "Ukraine's incorporation into the Russian state was for her a lesser evil than seizure by Poland of the lords or Turkey of the sultans."[10] Finally, by the 1950s, incorporation purely and simply "signified a reunion of two great brotherly peoples which was to save Ukraine from seizure by Poland and Turkey."[11] The fact that the 1654 act was being hailed 300 years later as an act of "reunification" rather than union reveals how Soviet scholarship had returned to a variant of the pre-revolutionary Russian framework for understanding the history of eastern Europe.

According to the accepted Soviet historical framework, which was clung to as a kind of dogma until the 1980s, Kievan Rus' was the common cradle of all the East Slavs. The political and cultural traditions of that medieval entity were subsequently carried on most forcefully by the "elder brother" – the Russians – first through their Muscovite state, later through the Russian Empire, and most recently by its Soviet successor state. As for the common Kievan patrimony, it was inhabited by what is described as the "Old Russian nationality" (and its inhabitants ostensibly spoke the Old Russian language). Moreover, it was not until after the Mongol invasion in the mid-thirteenth century, when the southern and western Rus' lands were "torn away" from the rest of old Rus', that the Ukrainian and Belarusan territories began to develop separate existences while under the control of Lithuania and, later, Poland. Thus, according to the Soviet historical framework, the Ukrainian and Belarusan nationalities (and languages) began to be formed sometime between the fourteenth and sixteenth centuries. Suggestions of a separate Ukrainian development before that time (whether in politics, language, or national distinctiveness) were condemned as "bourgeois nationalist" ideology. Such an ideology reflected the views of Hrushevs'kyi, whose historical scheme was considered "hostile," "reactionary," and a "threat" to another Soviet dogma – the centuries-old unity and friendship between the Russian and Ukrainian peoples.

In summation, present-day perceptions of the history of eastern Europe and in particular of Ukraine derive largely from historical frameworks formulated in the nineteenth century. These differ in varying degree according to whether authors wrote from a Russian, Polish, Ukrainian, or, by the twentieth century, Soviet perspective. The Russian perception stresses a pattern of steady political growth, which begins in so-called Kievan Russia in medieval times and subsequently is continued by the displacement of political centers and population to the north – first to Vladimir-na-Kliazma, then to Moscow and St Petersburg, and finally back to Moscow under the hegemony of the Soviet state. In such a framework, Ukraine has no independent historical existence.

The traditional Polish perception also fails to allow for a distinct Ukrainian historical process, since Ukraine is considered to be no more than a borderland of Polish civilization. Most of Ukraine, especially the territories west of the Dnieper River, is viewed as an integral part of Poland in which the only redeeming political and cultural developments of the past were those undertaken by the "defenders of western civilization," the Poles.

The Ukrainian perception sees the formation of a Ukrainian ethos even before the ninth century and the beginning of medieval Kievan Rus'. Moreover, Kiev's population was not entirely dispersed after the mid-thirteenth-century Mongol invasion, a time when Rus' civilization shifted only slightly westward, to Galicia and Volhynia, before returning to Dnieper Ukraine in the form of a Cossack political entity in the seventeenth and eighteenth centuries. Rus'-Ukrainian civilization was subsequently continued in the form of a national revival in the nineteenth century and the achievement – albeit short-lived – of independence in the twentieth century.

After World War II, the Soviet view became a variant of the pre-revolutionary Russian view. Kievan Rus' came to be seen as the cradle of all the East Slavs, although the Russian branch was depicted as the elder protector of the other two (the Belarusan and the Ukrainian) against the imperialistic tendencies of Poland and the Ottoman Empire before the eighteenth century and against western European powers, especially Germany, in the twentieth century.

Scholars in the West, particularly in the United States, have essentially adopted the traditional Russian view of the history of eastern Europe. Kievan Rus', Muscovy, the Russian Empire, and the Soviet Union are all seen as part of a single historical continuum and are referred to in popular and often in professional literature simply as Russia. Those who accept the traditional Russian view are, in turn, quick to dismiss the framework of Ukrainian history formulated by Hrushevs'kyi and his successors with arguments that Ukrainian writings are suspect because they serve the political interests either of former anti-Soviet cold warriors or of extreme anti-Russian local nationalists. The rest of this volume will be less concerned with adopting or denying any of the existing frameworks than with trying to present in a basically chronological sequence the events that have taken place from roughly the first millennium before the common era (BCE) to the present on the territory of what, since December 1991, is the independent republic of Ukraine.

3

The Steppe Hinterland and the Black Sea Cities

The first period of Ukrainian history, or, more precisely, prehistory, lasted from about 1150 BCE to CE 850. These twenty-one centuries of human development on Ukrainian territory witnessed the slow evolution from primitive agricultural and nomadic civilization to more advanced societies that attempted to create centrally organized state and socioeconomic structures. During these millennia, Ukrainian territory was divided into two rather distinct spheres: (1) the vast steppe and forest-steppe zones of the hinterland, and (2) the coastal regions of the Black Sea and Sea of Azov. While in each of these spheres there were quite different socioeconomic and political structures, the two were closely linked in a symbiotic relationship based on a high degree of economic interdependence.

In general, the hinterland was inhabited by sedentary agriculturalists ruled by different nomadic military elites who most often originated from the steppes of Central Asia. The Black Sea coast, on the other hand, was characterized by the establishment of Greek and, later, Romano-Byzantine cities that either functioned as independent city-states or joined in federations that had varying degrees of independence or that were dependent on the Greek, Roman, or Byzantine homelands to the south. In effect, the Black Sea coastal cities functioned for over two millennia as appendages or dependencies, whose economic, social, and cultural orientation was toward the classical civilizations of the Aegean and Mediterranean Seas.

The steppe hinterland

The earliest information about the steppe hinterland and its inhabitants comes from contemporary Greek, Roman, Byzantine, and Arab writers, who almost invariably painted negative descriptions of fierce barbarians from the east whose only purpose in life was to destroy the achievements of the civilized world as represented by Greece and, later, Rome and the Byzantine Empire. The few written sources from this early era give a general picture of an unending swarm of "barbaric" Asiatic peoples with strange-sounding names such as Cimmerians, Scythians, Sarmatians, Alans, Huns, Avars, Bulgars, and Khazars, who successively ruled the steppe hinterland before being driven out by the next nomadic invaders. Recent archaeological discoveries, especially during the twentieth century, have revealed that these nomadic peoples were neither as uncivilized nor as exclusively bent on destruction as the classical Greek and Romano-Byzantine writers made them out to be. In fact, the civilizations established by these nomads from the east were often directed to maintaining a stable environment that would allow their income from trade and commerce to increase.

Before turning to the chronological evolution during these two millennia (1150 BCE to CE 850), a few general caveats should be kept in mind. When considering the various nomadic groups and their invasions of the Ukrainian steppe, the reader may form the impression – and misconception – that the fierce warriors coming from Central Asia belonged to compact tribes each made up of a particular people. Moreover, it might seem that these nomads entered territory north of the Black Sea that was uninhabited, and that a particular tribe remained as the sole inhabitants until pushed out by another nomadic tribe, which, in turn, took their place and began the demographic cycle all over again. Such a scenario does not reflect what really occurred.

First of all, the Ukrainian steppe was never virgin uninhabited land into which nomadic hordes poured. Archaeological evidence has shown that the steppe and, for that matter, all Ukrainian territories were inhabited throughout the Stone Age, from its earliest (the Paleolithic, ca. 200,000–8000 BCE) to its most recent (the Neolithic, ca. 5000–1800 BCE) period. Stone Age settlements have been uncovered along the middle Dnieper River (the Kiev region and near the rapids of Zaporozhia) and the Middle Dniester River (near Bukovina); the oldest known site (about 1 million years old) is at Korolevo along the Tysa River in Transcarpathia. The most important change during these hundreds of millennia occurred at the beginning of the Neolithic period (ca. 5000 BCE), when the inhabitants of Ukraine, at least west of the Dnieper River, changed their means of livelihood from hunting and mobile food-gathering to the cultivation of cereals and the raising of livestock. This sedentary and agricultural way of life continued generally without interruption through the Neolithic period, which on Ukrainian territory largely coincides with the era of Trypillian culture (ca. 4500–2000 BCE).

Events during the late Neolithic or Copper Age were to upset the relatively stable and isolated existence of Trypillian sedentary communities in Ukraine. This change took place because during the second millennium BCE, Ukrainian lands were exposed to the movement of peoples from central Europe, to the arrival of traders from the Aegean and Oriental lands, and, finally, to the disrupting invasions of steppe peoples from the east. Nonetheless, both before and during the period 1150 to 850 BCE there were always fixed settlements throughout Ukrainian territory inhabited by people who derived their livelihood from agriculture and the raising of livestock and, secondarily, from hunting and fishing.

The other misconception about this period concerns the nomadic invaders. Despite the fact that authors from the Greek and Romano-Byzantine worlds gave names such as Cimmerians, Scythians, Sarmatians, and so on to these groups, none was ever composed of a culturally or ethnolinguistically unified people. Rather,

TRYPILLIANS AND UKRAINIANS

Of all the archeological cultures in Ukraine, it is the Trypillian which has perhaps received the most attention by archeologists. More recently, and in particular since Ukraine gained its independence in 1991, the Trypillians have attracted the attention of popular writers and civic promoters who have used this pre-historic culture to propagate their own brand of modern Ukrainian patriotism.

The culture derives its name from a site uncovered in 1898 near the village of Trypillia, just southwest of Kiev, by the Czech archeologist active in Ukraine, Vikentii Khvoika (Chvojka). Subsequent archeological research determined the chronological and geographic extent of Trypillian culture. It lasted over two millennia from about 4500 to 2250 BCE, and at its farthest extent covered, in modern-day terms, Ukraine west of the Dnieper River, most of Moldova, and Romania east of Carpathians. Western literature refers to the same phenomenon as the Cucuteni-Tripolye culture. Cucuteni, a village in present-day eastern Romania (near Iaşi) and the first site in the western portion of the Trypillian sphere, was discovered in 1884 and excavated during the first decade of the twentieth century by the German archeologist Hubert Schmidt. The greatest concentration of Trypillian sites have been found along the upper and middle Prut and Seret rivers (northeastern Romania and northern Moldova) and in Ukraine along the middle Dniester River (southeastern Galicia and western Podolia), the triangle between the middle Southern Buh (east of Vinnytsia) and Syniukha rivers, and the region surrounding Kiev.

Scholars point to three periods of the development of Trypillian culture, which are characterized by an increase in the size of population that practiced primitive agriculture and animal husbandry. It seems that the social structure was characterized by a matriarchal-clan order in which women were responsible for agricultural work, for the production of pottery and cloth, and for playing a leading role in social life.

In the early period, extended families shared a single dwelling, but later nuclear families had their own dwellings. The result was an enormous growth of large multi-roomed buildings as well as individual dwellings whose solid construction reflected a concern for maintaining good hygienic conditions. Concentrations of population could range from 500 to several thousand inhabitants. During the middle and later periods, the Trypillians had large ground-floor workshops and they developed specialized manufactories for pottery and eventually for metal-working in copper. The most widespread artifacts that have come down to us are examples of ceramic pottery (with painted spiral and meander decorations of often high aesthetic quality) and small-scale stone figurines probably linked to an agrarian cult of fertility and prosperity.

Since the 1990s several writers (and some professional archeologists) have elaborated further on the artifacts that date from the Neolithic period and that are connected with Trypillian culture. There is even a Kolo-Ra Society based in Kiev that organizes tourist visits and that carries out archeological research and projects for the reconstruction of Trypillian sites. The archeological finds connected with Trypillians are likened to those of pre-historic Troy and Mycenae. The Trypillian "people" are credited with creating a male-female egalitarian society, inventing the wheel, domesticating the horse, and producing highly advanced metallurgical products. Their large settlements, among the most extensive of which was Talianky near the upper Syniukha River (with 15,000 inhabitants living in 3,000 houses), are described as towns, or even proto-cities, with two-story apartment-like buildings larger than residences in the better-known ancient civilizations of Mesopotamia and Egypt.

An excess of enthusiasm has often gotten the better of those who are promoting the Trypillian "cause." There are writers who are convinced of a direct connection between the Trypillians and modern Ukrainians and Ukraine. The archeologist Viktor Petrov is among the leading proponents of the view that Trypillians are the ancestors of ethnic Ukrainians. And even those skeptical of such claims seem willing to accept that the basic features of Trypillian culture are reflected in the way houses were built and decorated by ethnic Ukrainians in later times and in the symbology and designs still found in Ukrainian embroidery and on painted Easter eggs. Some patriotic writers (Iurii Kanyhin's 1997 book *Shliakh ariïv/The Arian Way* being the most widely read example) go further, arguing that the Trypillia zone coincides with the "state" of Arrata, mentioned in ancient Mesopotamian (Sumerian) records from the third millennium BCE. Consequently, the earliest genealogy for modern Ukrainian statehood should begin not with ninth-century Kievan Rus', nor even with the fourth-century Antaen tribal federation, but rather with the four- to five-thousand-year-old "state" of Arrata-Trypillia.

these groups were made up of various nomadic tribes that were sometimes united under the leadership of one tribe that gave its name to (or had its name adopted by classical authors for) the entire group. The sedentary agricultural or pastoral settlers already living on Ukrainian lands were also subsumed under the name of the nomadic group that had come to rule over them. It is in this more complex sense that the names Scythian, Sarmatians, and Khazars must be understood.

The nomads of the steppe hinterland

The first of these nomadic civilizations on Ukrainian territory about which there is information, albeit limited, was the Cimmerian. The Cimmerians seem to have been an Indo-European group that came to dominate Ukrainian lands north of the Black Sea between 1150 and 950 BCE, a period that coincides with the late Bronze Age. Most of what we know about the enigmatic Cimmerians comes from archaeological finds consisting of bronze implements and the remains of bronze

NOMADIC CIVILIZATIONS ON UKRAINIAN TERRITORY

Cimmerians	1150–750 BCE
Scythians	750–250 BCE
Sarmatians	250 BCE–CE 250
Roxolani	
Alans	
Antes	
Goths	250–375 CE
Huns	375–550 CE
Kutrigurs	
Utigurs	
Avars	550–565 CE
Bulgars	575–650 CE
Khazars	650–900 CE

foundries. The Cimmerian era lasted on Ukrainian territory about four centuries, and it is only from the last two of these centuries (900–750 BCE) that there exist archaeological remains, of bronze implements and weapons, along the lower Dnieper River near Nikopol' (the Mykhailivka treasure) and from the region just south of Kiev (the Pidhirtsi treasure).

Around the middle of the eighth century (750 BCE), the Cimmerian era came to end. The Cimmerian leadership seems to have fled westward (across the Carpathians to Pannonia) and southward (to the Crimea and on to Thrace and Asia Minor) in the face of a new invasion of nomads from the east – the Scythians. The Scythians were known in the classical world for their fierceness as warriors, but this one-sided image has been tempered by archaeological discoveries which have unearthed numerous examples of finely wrought sculpture, ornamentation, and jewellery, primarily in gold. The Scythians actually formed a branch of the Iranian people – more specifically, that branch which remained in the so-called original Iranian country east of the Caspian Sea (present-day Turkestan), as distinct from their Medean and Persian tribal relatives, who established a sedentary civilization farther south on the plateaus of Iran.

Between 750 and 700 BCE, the Scythians moved westward toward Ukraine, and eventually they settled for the most part first in the Kuban Region and Taman Peninsula (700–550 BCE) and later along the Dnieper River in south-central Ukraine (550–450 BCE), where their civilization reached its peak between 350 and 250 BCE. Classical sources tell us that Scythian society was composed of four groups: royalty, notables (steppe nomads), agriculturalists (*georgoi*), and ploughmen (*aroteres*). Actually, only the first two groups – the royalty and notables – were made up of migrants from the east. This ruling elite, of nomadic origin and way of life, dominated the sedentary agriculturalists living under their control and the residents of the cities. Both these groups, together with their rulers, were known to the outside world as "Scythians."

The mention of cities may seem confusing, since this discussion of the steppe hinterland has focused so far on nomads and the sedentary agricultural dwellers under their control. In fact, it seems that the Scythian ruling elite – the royalty and their notables – virtually lived on horseback, roaming the steppes while hunting for food or engaging in war with neighboring tribes. One might speak, however, of mobile Scythian cities, that is, huge caravans of tribes which moved from one place to another. Nonetheless, there were a few cities – or, more properly, fortified centers with permanent settlers engaged in activity other than agriculture – within the Scythian sphere. These were so-called Oriental-type cities, owned by Scythian royalty and notables and inhabited by remnants of the Cimmerians and other peoples, who paid tribute to their Scythian overlords. Among the more important Scythian hill-forts (*horodyshche*) were Kam'ianka on the lower Dnieper River, Bil's'k (Gelonos/Helon) in the far northeast, and the later capital of Scythia Minor, Neapolis, in the Crimea.

The Greeks of the coastal region

The few Scythian settlements were in no way as important as the Greek trading cities along the shores of the Black Sea and Sea of Azov. Not long after the Scythians began to enter Ukraine from the east, in the eighth century BCE, colonists fleeing civil strife in Greece arrived from the south, especially from Miletus, in Asia Minor. As a result, between the seventh and fifth centuries BCE several prosperous Greek cities came into being along the shores of the Black Sea, the Straits of Kerch, and the Sea of Azov. Among the first to be established were Tiras at the mouth of the Dniester River and Olbia at the mouth of the Southern Buh, then Chersonesus at the southwestern tip of the Crimean Peninsula and Theodosia farther east on the Crimean Peninsula, and Panticapaeum (Bospor) and Phanagoria on the west and east banks respectively of the Straits of Kerch.

The Greek homeland along both shores of the Aegean Sea was composed of individual city-states, each of which jealously guarded its independence. By the fifth century BCE, however, they had come to form a united civilization whose achievements set a standard for culture in the civilized world that was to outlast the city-states themselves. Like the Aegean homeland, the Greek colonies along the northern Black Sea coast at least initially remained independent of each other, though they were economically and politically dependent on the city-state which founded them – generally either Miletus, along the Aegean coast in Asia Minor, or Megara, just west of Athens. There were also periods when the Black Sea colonies were completely independent, or when they united into federations or states.

The most important instance of a federation came into being about 480 BCE, when the Greek cities near the Straits of Kerch began to unite under the leadership of Panticapaeum in what became known as the Bosporan Kingdom. The Bosporan Kingdom became independent of the Greek homeland, and under its

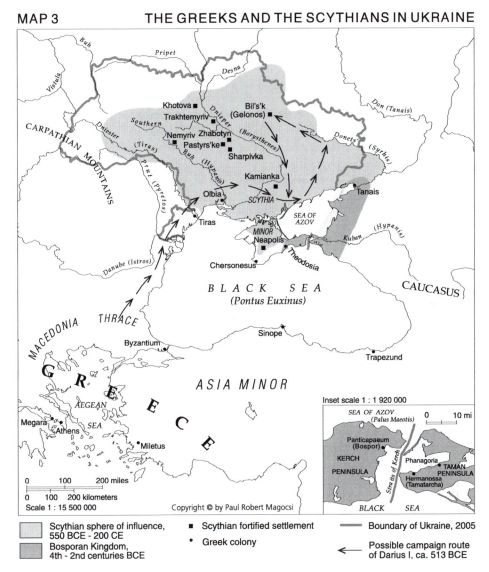

MAP 3   THE GREEKS AND THE SCYTHIANS IN UKRAINE

Scale 1 : 15 500 000
Copyright © by Paul Robert Magocsi

Inset scale 1 : 1 920 000

| | Scythian sphere of influence, 550 BCE - 200 CE | ■ Scythian fortified settlement | ⸺ Boundary of Ukraine, 2005 |
| | Bosporan Kingdom, 4th - 2nd centuries BCE | • Greek colony | ← Possible campaign route of Darius I, ca. 513 BCE |

dynamic king Levkon I (reigned ca. 389–348 BCE) came to control all of the Kerch and Taman Peninsulas as well as the eastern shore of the Sea of Azov as far as the mouth of the Don River, where the city of Tanais was established (ca. 375 BCE) The Bosporan Kingdom included not only Greek cities, but also the regions around the Sea of Azov inhabited by Scythians and related tribes. Until the second century BCE, the kingdom flourished as a center of grain trade, fishing, wine-making, and small-scale artisan craftsmanship, especially metalworking. The following century was to witness a period of political instability and the consequent loss of Bosporan independence. Finally, in 63 BCE, the Bosporan Kingdom together with other Hellenic states around the Black Sea came under the control of the Roman Empire.

The Pax Scythica, the Sarmatians, and the Pax Romana

During the nearly five centuries from 700 to 250 BCE, the Greek cities along the Black Sea littoral, in the southern Crimean Peninsula, and in the Bosporan Kingdom all developed a kind of symbiotic relationship with the Scythian hinterland. By about 250 BCE, the center of Scythian power had come to be based in the region known as Scythia Minor (Mala Skifiia), between the lower Dnieper River and the Black Sea, as well as in the northern portion of the Crimean Peninsula (beyond the mountains), where the fortified center of Neapolis was located. The symbiotic relationship had three elements: (1) the Scythian-controlled Ukrainian steppe, (2) the Black Sea Greek cities, and (3) the Greek city-states along the Aegean Sea.

Bread and fish were the staples of ancient Greece, and the increasing demand for these foodstuffs was met by markets in the Black Sea Greek cities. These and other food products came from Ukrainian lands, which already in ancient times had a reputation for natural wealth. In the fourth book of his *History*, the Greek historian Herodotus, who had lived for a while in Olbia, wrote the following description of the Dnieper River, or, as he called it, "the fourth of the Scythian rivers, the Borysthenes": "It has upon its banks the loveliest and most excellent pasturages for cattle; it contains an abundance of the most delicious fish; ... the richest harvests spring up along its course, and where the ground is not sown, the heaviest crops of grass; while salt forms in great plenty about its mouth without human aid."[1] In this region, the Scythians exacted grain and fish from the sedentary populations under their control and traded these commodities in the Greek coastal cities along with cattle, hides, furs, wax, honey, and slaves. These products were then processed and sent to Greece. In turn, the Scythians bought from the Greeks textiles, wines, olive oil, art works, and other luxury items to satisfy their taste for opulence.

As a result of these economic interrelations, the Greeks brought to the world the earliest and still the primary information about the Scythians. Herodotus, in particular, left a detailed description of the geography, way of life, and often cruel customs of the Scythians and of the lands under their control. The other source of information about the Scythians, which corroborates much of what Herodotus wrote, concerns their numerous royal burial mounds, spread throughout south-central Ukraine and uncovered in the course of excavations that have been going on systematically since the late nineteenth century. These burial mounds (known as *kurhany*, or barrows) have preserved for posterity that for which the Scythians are most famous: their small-scale decorative art, which consisted primarily of finely balanced renderings of a host of animal forms in gold and bronze.

It is not certain whether this art was produced by the Scythians for themselves, or, more likely, commissioned from Greek artisans living in the cities. Nevertheless, its themes reflect the violent world inhabited by Scythians, and its forms show the high level of technology their civilization was able to foster and appreciate. Also associated with the Scythian and subsequent Sarmatian eras are more modest grave-markers, which took the form of stone statues of standing or sitting females ranging from one to four meters (three to twelve feet) in height. Hundreds of these stone statues, popularly known as *skifs'ki baby* (Scythian older women), have

Scythian Customs

Among the various customs practiced by the Scythians, those associated with their reputation as fierce warriors made an especially strong impression on the classical Greek world. In the fourth book of his *History*, Herodotus writes:

The Scythian soldier drinks the blood of the first man he overthrows in battle. Whatever number he slays, he cuts off all their heads, and carries them to the king; since he is thus entitled to a share of the booty, whereto he forfeits all claim if he does not produce a head. In order to strip the skull of its covering, he makes a cut round the head above the ears, and, laying hold of the scalp, shakes the skull out; then with the rib of an ox he scrapes the scalp clean of flesh, and softening it by rubbing between the hands, uses it thenceforth as a napkin. The Scythian is proud of these scalps, and hangs them from his bridle-rein; the greater the number of such napkins that a man can show, the more highly is he esteemed among them. Many make themselves cloaks, like the capotes of our peasants, by sewing a quantity of these scalps together. Others flay the right arms of their dead enemies, and make of the skin, which is stripped off with the nails hanging to it, a covering for their quivers. Now the skin of a man is thick and glossy, and would in whiteness surpass almost all other hides. Some even flay the entire body of their enemy, and stretching it upon a frame carry it about with them wherever they ride.

The skulls of their enemies, not indeed of all, but of those whom they most detest, they treat as follows. Having sawn off the portion below the eyebrows, and cleaned out the inside, they cover the outside with leather. When a man is poor, this is all that he does; but if he is rich, he also lines the inside with gold: in either case the skull is used as a drinking-cup. They do the same with the skulls of their own kith and kin if they have been at feud with them, and have vanquished them in the presence of the king. When strangers whom they deem of any account come to visit them, these skulls are handed round, and the host tells how that these were his relations who made war upon him, and how that he got the better of them; all this being looked upon as proof of bravery.

SOURCE: Herodotus, *The History*, translated by George Rawlinson, Great Books of the Western World, Vol. VI (Chicago, London, and Toronto 1952), pp. 134–135.

been uncovered throughout the southern Ukrainian steppe from the Dniester River eastward to the Donets' and well beyond.

The Scythians brought a period of peace and stability to Ukrainian territories which lasted for about 500 years and which has come to be known as the Pax Scythica, or Scythian Order. During the Pax Scythica, the Scythians promoted trade and commerce with the Greek cities along the Black Sea, which in turn supplied Greece with needed foodstuffs and raw materials. The Scythians also successfully fought off other nomadic peoples from the east, and they even defeated the powerful king of ancient Persia Darius I ("the Great," reigned 522–486 BCE). After adding Thrace to his realm, Darius launched a campaign northward against the Scythians in an attempt persianize their land, which he considered to be "outer

Iran" and part of his own patrimony. His efforts against the Scythians were unsuccessful, but the incursion of Darius, which began in 513 BCE and which covered most of the Black Sea steppe and area east of the Dnieper River as far as Gelonos/Helon (perhaps Bil's'k) became the first major historical event involving Ukrainian territory recorded in written documents.

It would be some time before long-term stability like that created by the Pax Scythica was reestablished in Ukraine. Around 250 BCE, nomads related to the Scythians and known as Sarmatians appeared in the Ukrainian steppe. The Sarmatians were typical of the civilizations under discussion in that they were not a homogeneous people, but rather made up of several tribes, each of which led an independent existence. Those most directly associated with developments in Ukraine were the Roxolani and, in particular, the Alans.

At least during the first two centuries of the Sarmatian presence, that is, from 250 to 50 BCE, the relative stability and resultant economic prosperity that had previously existed between the Scythian hinterland and the Greek cities of the coast was disrupted. Pressed by the Sarmatians in the steppe, the Scythian leaders fled to the Crimea, where they were forced to consolidate their rule over a smaller region that included the Crimean Peninsula north of the mountains and the lands just to the north between the peninsula and the lower Dnieper River. This new political entity, which, with its capital at Neapolis (modern-day Simferopol'), was known as Scythia Minor (Mala Skifiia), lasted from about 250 BCE to 200 CE. Initially, the Scythian leadership in Neapolis tried to continue its traditional practice of exacting tribute and goods from the Greeks. But because they no longer controlled the resources of the steppes, they had little to give the Greeks in return. The result was frequent conflict between the Scythians of the Crimea and the Greek cities along the coast and in the Bosporan Kingdom.

This era of instability, which affected not only the Sarmatian-controlled hinterland but also the Black Sea cities, came to an end along the coastal region after 63 BCE. Beginning in that year, the Roman Empire succeeded in extending its sphere of influence over the independent Greek cities as well as over those within the Bosporan Kingdom. With the presence of Roman legions and administrators in the region, peace and stability were restored. The new Pax Romana reduced the friction between the Scythians and the Greeks in the Crimea, and the Sarmatian tribes in the hinterland also realized the advantages to be accrued from some kind of cooperation with the Roman world. Reacting to the stabilizing presence of the Romans, one Sarmatian tribe, the Alans, renewed the Scythian tradition of trade with the Greco-Roman cities. Before long, a Greek-Scythian-Sarmatian hybrid civilization evolved within the Bosporan Kingdom, which itself was revived, this time under the protection of Rome. The resultant trade and commerce between the steppe hinterland and the Mediterranean world brought a renewed prosperity to the Bosporan Kingdom that lasted for over two centuries.

The third century CE, however, ushered in a new era of instability, especially in the steppe hinterland, that was to last until the seventh century. During these four centuries, Ukrainian territory was subjected to the invasions of several new nomadic warrior tribes who were bent on destruction and plunder of the classical world as represented by the Black Sea and Bosporan coastal cities. With few exceptions, the nomads were not interested – as the Scythians and even the Sarmatians had been before them – in settling down and exploiting by peaceful means the symbiotic relationship of the steppe hinterland and coastal cities. Between about 250 and 650 CE, several nomadic groups – the Goths, Huns, Kutrigurs, Utigurs, Avars, Bulgars – came and went across parts of Ukrainian territory. It was not until the arrival of the Khazars in the seventh century that stability was restored north of the Black Sea.

The four centuries of strife between 250 and 650 CE began not with the arrival of nomads from Central Asia, but rather with the arrival in the mid-third century of Alans from the region just north of the Caucasus, and Germanic tribes known as Goths from northern Europe. The Alans were a Sarmatian tribal group who moved into the Crimea. They settled both in the mountainous region, where they were among the first inhabitants in the hilltop town of Kirk Yer (later Çufut-Kale), as well as along the Black Sea coast, where they are considered by some scholars to have founded in 212 CE the town of Sugdeia (today's Sudak). They engaged in agriculture, cattle-breeding, and handicrafts. After arriving in the Crimea the Alans adopted Christianity; this was one of the reasons they were able to assimilate easily with other Christian inhabitants, resulting within a few centuries in their disappearance as a distinct people in the peninsula.

The Goths were originally from what is today Sweden, but about 50 BCE they moved to the southern shores of the Baltic Sea (i.e., modern day Poland). It was from there that toward the end of the second century CE they moved south into Ukraine, where they broke the Sarmatian dominance of the steppe hinterland and came into contact with the Roman world along the northern shores of the Black Sea. The Goths had by this time split into two branches. Those that remained in Ukraine came to be known as Ostrogoths, or East Goths. After 250 CE, they captured Olbia and Tiras from the Romans, with the result that during the following century the remaining Greco-Roman cities as well as the Bosporan Kingdom were drawn, together with the steppe hinterland, into the sphere of the Ostrogothic Kingdom.

Ostrogothic rule in southern Ukraine and the Crimea reached its apogee under King Ermanaric (reigned 350–375). It was toward the end of Ermanaric's reign, ca. 370, that a new nomadic people, this time from Central Asia, arrived in the steppes of Ukraine. These were the Huns, who easily subjected the Ostrogoths and then moved quickly westward toward the Roman provinces in the Balkan Peninsula and Pannonia (modern-day Hungary). By the 420s these fierce nomads made the Hungarian plain their base, and after 435 under their talented leader Attila they launched repeated attacks against various cities throughout the Roman Empire. Following the unexpected death of Attila in 453, the "Hunnic empire," which stretched from the Caspian Sea westward through Ukraine to the heart of central Europe, rapidly disintegrated. Some of the Huns remained in Pannonia as did most of the Ostrogoths whom they had brought with them. Other Hunnic tribes returned to the steppes of Ukraine, including the Utigurs who made their new home the steppeland in the northern Crimea. Those Ostrogoths who were not taken by the Huns westward to Pannonia remained in the Crimea, where they were concentrated in the mountainous back country away from the coast.

The Crimean Goths, as they came to be known, were anxious to maintain good relations with the Eastern Roman, or Byzantine Empire, represented by officials in its administrative and trading center at the port city of Chersonesus in the far southwestern corner of the Crimean peninsula. To assure that their allies could protect the coastal regions from further nomadic attacks out of the north, Byzantine engineers assisted the Crimean Goths and Alans in fortifying several "cave towns' on the top of mountain cliffs and promontories, which in some cases rose up to 200 meters (600 feet) above the surrounding valleys. Despite the popular designation given to them, the inhabitants of these naturally fortified sites did not live in caves but rather in structures built from wood and stone on the top of the caves (usually used for storage or as a part of the defense system) and along the table-top promontories that in some cases covered tens of acres of territory. It was only somewhat later that true cave dwellings came into being in the form of monasteries built by Orthodox Christian monks along the sheer faces of mountain cliffs. Among the largest of the hill-top "cave towns" were Mangup, Kirk Yer, and Eski Kermen located in the back country east of Chersonesus; the best known cave-monasteries were at Kaçi-Kalyon, Kalamita/Inkerman and the Dormition monastery (still functioning) near Bakhchysarai. The Crimean Gothic center was a place called Doros/Dory, most likely at what later became known as Mangup, located about halfway between Chersonesus and the Scythian center at Neapolis.

In the course of the fourth century, the Ostrogoths accepted Christianity according to the Eastern Byzantine rite, although they adopted the teaching of Arius (who denied Christ's divinity in favor of his humanity). The Goths of Crimea were to remain Arians even after that sect was declared heretical. More important was the fact that the Christian connection cemented Crimean Gothic relations with the Byzantine Empire. By the outset of the fifth century (ca. 400 CE), their center of Doros was made the seat of the Eparchy of Gothia. Gothia's first bishop was appointed by the Patriarch of Constantinople, who at the time was the influential church father, St John Chrysostom. The Crimean Goths had, therefore, become part of the Byzantine political and cultural sphere, and for the next five centuries they functioned as a protective shield for the Greco-Byzantine cities along the coast against further invasions by nomads from the north.

Meanwhile, the Ukrainian steppe hinterland north of the Crimean peninsula and Black Sea continued to be subjected to a series of invaders: the Hunnic Kutrigurs and Utigurs in the fifth century, the Avars in the sixth century, and the Bulgars in the seventh century. More often than not, the presence of these groups in steppe Ukraine was short-lived. This was because they were in search of the richer sources of booty to be found along the borders of the Roman Empire in central Europe (the Pannonian Plain) or along the trade routes between the Black and Caspian Seas. During periods when one nomadic group had departed and another had not yet arrived, the power vacuum was sometimes filled by the local population. One such case was that of the Antae, a tribe of Sarmatian (Alanic) and possibly Gothic elements which by the third century had organized the sedentary agricultural population of south-central and southwestern Ukraine into a powerful military force that stood up to the Goths, the Byzantine Empire, and the Huns.

Because this sedentary population, which the Antae led and to which they gave their name, was probably composed of Slavs, the group is of particular interest with respect to subsequent developments in Ukraine (see chapter 4).

The Byzantines and the Khazars

While the Ukrainian steppe and hinterland were experiencing frequent disruptions between 250 and 650 CE, the coastal region along the Black Sea and Sea of Azov was undergoing another revival. This time the stabilizing factor was the Eastern Roman, or Byzantine Empire, which reached its greatest territorial extent and political influence during the sixth-century reign of Emperor Justinian (reigned 527–565). Under Justinian, the Black Sea coastal cities received Byzantine garrisons, their walls were fortified, and Chersonesus became the region's Byzantine administrative center. Byzantine Greek culture in the form of Eastern Christianity also was strengthened, with the result that Chersonesus, with its ten churches and chapels (including St Peter's basilica) and a fortress and monastery built in caves in the face of cliffs at nearby Kalamita (today Inkerman), was to become an important center from which Christian influence was subsequently to radiate throughout Ukrainian territory and among the East Slavs. Byzantine influence was also strong at the eastern end of the Crimea, where the Bosporan Kingdom was revived, this time as a colony of Byzantium.

While it is true that direct Byzantine political control over the Crimean cities and the Bosporan Kingdom was frequently interrupted, economic, social, and cultural ties in the form of Byzantine Orthodox Christianity were to last until at least the thirteenth century. It was during the era of Roman and Byzantine control of the Bosporan Kingdom, moreover, that Hellenic Jews settled in the region's coastal cities. And it is from these cities that Jewish contacts across the Straits of Kerch were, by the seventh century, to reach the realm of the Khazars, a new nomadic civilization that was beginning to make its presence felt.

Not long after the rise of Byzantine influence along the coast, which began in earnest during the late sixth century, a group of nomads arrived from the east whose presence was to have a profound impact on the region both north and east of the Black Sea. These were the Khazars, a Turkic group who originally inhabited the westernmost part of the Inner Asian Türk Empire. Unlike most of their predecessors during the preceding three centuries, the Khazars preferred diplomacy to war. Soon after their arrival along the Black Sea, they signed a treaty (626) with the Byzantine Empire. The Byzantines, ever anxious about their own eastern frontier with the Persians and about potential invaders from the east who might threaten their Black Sea possessions, welcomed the seeming willingness of the Khazars to fit into the plans of Byzantium's northern diplomacy.

The appearance of the Khazars in the seventh century proved to be of great significance for developments in eastern Europe in general and in Ukraine in particular. The Khazars continued the tradition established by the Scythians (750–250 BCE) and continued by the Sarmatians (50 BCE to CE 250) whereby nomads from the east would gain control over the sedentary population of the steppe hinterland, keep in line recalcitrant nomadic tribes, protect trade routes, and foster commercial contacts with the Greco-Roman–Byzantine cities along the Black Sea coast. The age-old symbiotic relationship between the coast and the steppe hinterland was to be restored under the hegemony of the Khazars. The resultant Khazar Order, or Pax Chazarica, which lasted approximately from the mid-seventh to the mid-ninth century, did in fact cushion Ukrainian lands from further nomadic invasions from the steppes of Central Asia in the east as well as from incursions by the Persians and, later, the Arabs from the south. Because of the Khazars' role in protecting the eastern and southern frontiers of the European continent, some writers have compared them to Charles Martel and the Franks in western Europe. The Pax Chazarica also provided at least two centuries of peace and stability during which sedentary peoples living within the Khazar sphere of influence were allowed to develop. Among those peoples, within and just beyond the northwestern edge of the Khazar sphere, were the Slavs.

4

The Slavs and the Khazars

The origins of the Slavs

The origins and early development of the Slavs are, like those of other peoples,
clouded in uncertainty. The few written references to the Slavs from the earliest period, together with extensive archaeological evidence uncovered in the
nineteenth and twentieth centuries, are still insufficient for modern scholarship
to provide conclusive answers to many thorny questions concerning their origin, location, way of life, and sociopolitical organization. The written evidence
about the early Slavs is scanty and consists of little more than brief descriptions of
them by the Greek historian Herodotus in the fifth century BCE and by Byzantine
(Procopius) and Gothic (Jordanes) historians in the sixth century CE. Moreover,
despite the best efforts of some scholars, the link between the growing body of
archaeological data from these early centuries and any particular tribe of people
is still a matter of speculation. The only thing that seems certain is that the Slavic
peoples and their Proto-Slavic ancestors were present in eastern Europe from at
least the first millennium BCE. Precisely where in eastern Europe the Slavs had
their origin is a question that will probably continue to remain a topic of debate
among specialists.

The current consensus suggests that the original homeland of the Slavs was
located somewhere north of the Carpathian Mountains within a territory stretching from the upper Oder River valley in the west through the upper Vistula and
Buh Rivers on to the middle Dnieper River in the east. In modern terms, this
means that the original Slavic homeland included some parts or all of central and
eastern Poland, southern Belarus, and northwestern Ukraine.

In terms of geography, the Slavic homeland was clearly north of the line that
divided the mixed forest-steppe zone from the open steppe farther south – a line
that ran diagonally across Ukraine from the lower Prut and Dniester Rivers in the
southwest to the upper Donets' River in the northeast. In the mixed forest-steppe
zone north of that line, the sedentary agricultural Slavs found a modicum of protection from the aggressive nomadic peoples of the open steppe.

MAP 4

THE ORIGINAL HOMELAND OF THE SLAVS

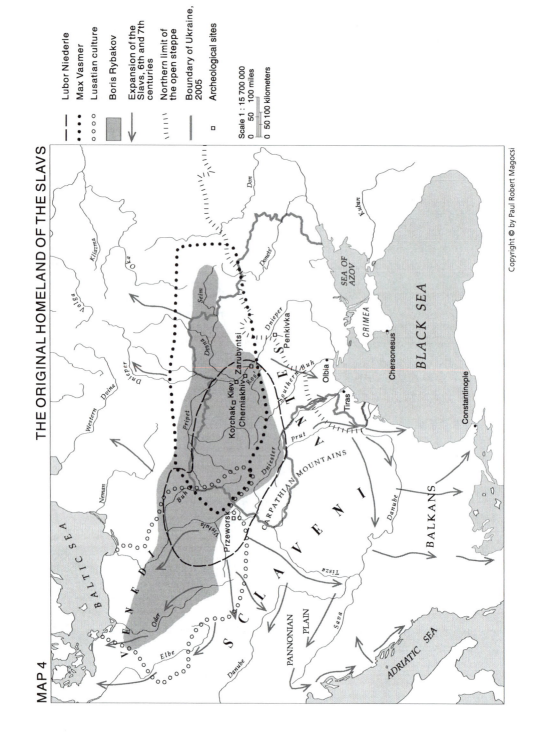

Lubor Niederle

Max Vasmer

Lusatian culture

Boris Rybakov

Expansion of the
Slavs, 6th and 7th
centuries

Northern limit of
the open steppe

Boundary of Ukraine,
2005

Archeological sites

Scale 1 : 15 700 000

0   50   100 miles

0 50 100 kilometers

THE ORIGINAL HOMELAND OF THE SLAVS

Among the first historical accounts to define the original homeland of the Slavs is the early medieval Rus' *Primary Chronicle* (Slavonic: *Poviest' vremennykh liet*). It states that the Slavs first "settled beside the Danube, where the Hungarian and Bulgarian lands now lie," that is, along the middle and lower Danube valley, from the Pannonian Plain to the Black Sea. This view was accepted for many centuries, but later was replaced by the so-called Sarmatian theory, which considered the Slavic homeland to be on the Don River, thereby placing the Slavs in close relationship with the Iranian Scythians and Sarmatians. In the nineteenth century, scholars began to argue that the original Slavic habitat was either in the Carpathian Mountains or farther north, along the marshes of the Pripet River. Today, four views are current.

(1) The Czech archaeologist Lubor Niederle (1902) defined the Slavic homeland as centered in northwestern Ukraine, encompassing the upper Vistula and Buh valleys, the Pripet Marshes, and Right Bank Ukraine bounded by the Dnieper River in the east and the crest of the Carpathians in the south.

(2) The Slavic linguist Max Vasmer (1941) fixed the Slavic homeland somewhat farther east, centering it in north-central Ukraine where the Pripet and Desna Rivers meet the Dnieper. This territory includes, in the west, the Pripet Marshes and Right Bank as far as the upper valley of the Southern Buh River, and, in the east, the region of the upper Donets' and upper Don valleys.

(3) Several interwar and postwar Polish archaeologists – Jan Czekanowski, Tadeusz Lehr-Spławinski, Leon Kozłowski, Józef Kostrzewski, and Tadeusz Sulimirski – argued that the original Slavic homeland coincides with the area of the so-called Lusatian culture, which, on the evidence of archaeological finds, they identified as having been located between the Elbe River in the west and the Buh River in the east, and as spreading from the crest of the Carpathians northward all the way to the Baltic Sea. This territory coincides largely with the present-day boundaries of Poland.

(4) Post–World War II Soviet archaeologists (Petr N. Tret'iakov, Boris Rybakov), joined by Polish (Konrad Jażdżewski) and Czech archaeologists (Jan Filip, Jiří Horák, and Zdeněk Váňa), argued that the area of Lusatian culture was only one part of the Slavic homeland, and the westernmost one at that, and that the territory should therefore be extended eastward as far as the lower Desna and Seim Rivers.

Whereas their emphases may differ slightly, most modern scholars seem to maintain the common premise that the original homeland of the Slavs was north of the Carpathian Mountains and north of the line that divided the mixed forest-steppe from the open steppe. This territory extended from the middle Vistula River in the west across the Buh, Pripet, middle Dnieper, and Desna Rivers in the east; in contemporary terms: north-central and western Ukraine, southwestern Belarus, and south-central and southeastern Poland.

Nevertheless, other views about the original Slavic homeland continue to be put forward. Some archeologists have argued for Bohemia (Ivan Borkovský) or Pannonia (Josip Korošec); others have gone back to the earlier theories of the lower Danube (Florian Curta), or the Pripet valley marshes along the present Belarus-Ukrainian border (Irena Rusanova), or the Carpathian Mountains, specifically its northern foothills on both sides of the present Polish-Ukrainian border in historic Galicia (Volodymyr Baran).

The migrations of the Slavs

By the middle of the first millennium BCE, the Slavs had begun to move slowly in various directions from their original homeland. This gradual process of outward migration was to last a millennium. It was especially pronounced toward the south, into the middle Dniester and Southern Buh valleys of southwestern Ukraine. The Slavs and, for that matter, other peoples were drawn to Ukraine because of its natural wealth and the possibility for trade with the Greek and, later, Roman cities along the coasts of the Black Sea and Sea of Azov.

It was inevitable that the Slavs would come into contact with the nomadic and semi-sedentary civilizations that held sway over Ukrainian territory. This was the case with the Scythians, who after 750 BCE controlled the steppe area north of the Black Sea. It seems that the agriculturalists and certain that the so-called ploughmen of Scythian society were at least to some degree made up of Slavs. The subordinate position of the Slavs at first was maintained under the Sarmatians, who displaced the Scythians after 250 BCE.

Information about the Slavs on Ukrainian territory during the Sarmatian era comes from the sixth-century Goth and Byzantine historians Jordanes and Procopius. They were the first writers to describe the Slavs in any detail. Jordanes divided them into three groups: (1) the Venedi, living along the Baltic Sea and the lower valleys of the Elbe, Oder, and Vistula Rivers; (2) the Antae, living along the Black Sea between the Prut and the Southern Buh Rivers; and (3) the Sclaveni, living north of the Danube, in both Moravia and the Carpathian Basin as well as in Walachia and Moldavia. The second of these groups, the Antae, are of particular interest with respect to the developments in Ukraine.

The Antae

Because of the limited and conflicting written evidence (in contrast to Jordanes, Procopius does not classify the Antae as Slavs) and the inconclusive nature of archaeological data, there remains much controversy about the Antae (Ukrainian: Anty). It is agreed that their presence derives from the Sarmatian era. The most important Sarmatian tribe on Ukrainian territory were the Alans, and one group of the Alans were known as the Antae. It seems that after their arrival in the Ukrainian steppe during the first two centuries CE, the Alanic Antae (like other Sarmatian tribes of Iranic origin) began to organize the Slavic and other tribes living in their midst. Initially centered on lands between the Prut and the lower Dniester Rivers during the fourth century CE, the Antaen power base moved progressively northward: first to the upper valley of the Southern Buh; then, in the fifth and sixth centuries, to Volhynia; and later to the middle Dnieper region. Eventually, as they moved farther north beyond the open steppe into the more heavily Slavic-populated areas, the name Antae came to be used for the upper echelons as well as the Slavs under their control. At the same time, the Slavs themselves gradually replaced the original group of Irano-Alanic conquerors and military elite from whom they had acquired the Antae name.

By the fourth century CE, the Antae had evolved into a powerful tribal league with effective military units. Their reputation as a potent fighting force was still evident in the sixth century, when Jordanes described them as "the bravest of these peoples dwelling in the curve of the Sea of Pontus [Black Sea], spread from the Dniester to the Dnieper."[1] The Antae were able to undertake successful raids against the Byzantine Empire and to resist the Goths, who after 250 CE had established a power base in the Crimea and southern Ukraine. It is from the Gothic-Antaen conflicts that descriptions of powerful military leaders like the fourth-century Antaen "king" Boz have come down to us.

The fifth century marked the apogee of Antaen power on Ukrainian territories. At that time, the Antae were able to fill a power vacuum that had been left in the region west of the Dnieper River. This occurred after the Gothic supremacy in the area was undermined by the Huns in the late fourth century during the latter's westward advance across Ukraine toward the Pannonian Plain beyond the Carpathian Mountains. Within the Antaen sphere, based in north-central and north-western Ukraine, a sedentary civilization consisting of numerous villages in which agriculture and cattle breeding were the primary occupations came into being.

The sedentary Antae also established several hill forts, known as *horodyshcha* or *horody*, where artisans produced metalwares and pottery. Remnants of these items have been uncovered by archaeologists, who describe their findings as belonging to what they call the Cherniakhiv and Pen'kivka cultures. Among the more important of the fortified centers were Volyn' in the far west and Kiev along the middle Dnieper, from which the Antae carried on a brisk local and international trade reaching the markets of the Roman and Byzantine empires.

Whereas the existence of the Antae somewhere on Ukrainian territory between the third and seventh centuries is recognized, the nature of their society and the extent of their rule remain a source of controversy. Some scholars believe the Antae were Slavic or partly slavicized tribal groups who from time to time were able to join together to create tribal leagues with their own military forces. Others suggest that the Antaen tribal league evolved into "statehood," which would make them the creators of one of the earliest Slavic states. Francis Dvornik even speaks of an Antaen "empire" stretching virtually the full extent of the original Slavic homeland from the Oder River in the west to the upper Donets' and Oka Rivers in the east. Most writers, however, limit the Antaen sphere to the East Slavs: non-Soviet Ukrainian authors (Hrushevs'kyi, Polons'ka-Vasylenko) consider them creators of the first Ukrainian state; Soviet authors (Grekov, Rybakov) see them as an indigenous Slavic group who formed the first East Slavic state, based in the sixth

ARCHAEOLOGY IN UKRAINE

Historical accounts frequently describe the first period of Ukrainian history or prehistory (ca. 1150 BCE to CE 850) in terms of the succession of nomadic peoples, from the Cimmerians to the Khazars, who invaded Ukrainian territory and controlled it for varying periods of time. Archaeological accounts, however, describe these same two millennia, as well as previous eras, in terms of cultures whose characteristics are arrived at on the basis of the remains found in archaeological digs. Such remains include dwellings, household implements, military equipment, burial sites, coins, and, especially, pottery. These archaeological data tell us more about the material way of life of the sedentary agricultural population than do the scattered accounts by classical authors, who at best left sketchy descriptions of the ruling nomadic peoples.

Archaeologists have uncovered the presence of more than one culture on Ukrainian territory during any given period. These cultures, moreover, may have been geographically displaced and may have lasted longer in a new place than in their places of origin. The names given to the cultures frequently are derived from sites where the first archaeological discovery was made in the late nineteenth or early twentieth century (Trypillia, Zarubintsiv, Cherniakhiv) or from the style of the pottery (*shnurova* "line") or burial pattern (catacomb) adopted by the given culture.

Many cultures from the prehistoric and historical eras have been distinguished by archaeologists on Ukrainian territory. Among the best known are the Trypillian culture (ca. 4500–2000 BCE), which witnessed the transition from nomadic pastoralism to sedentary agriculture; the Bilohrudivka culture (1350–800 BCE), which coincided in part with the Cimmerian presence; and the Srubna culture (1200–600 BCE), toward the end of which the Scythians made their appearance.

By the beginning of the common era, several new cultures had emerged, although there is on-going debate among scholars whether archaeological finds can be classified and then related to specific historical cultures and peoples. The problem of relating archaeology to history is particularly marked with regard to the ethnogenesis of the Slavs.

The first of these new cultures was the Zarubynets' (named for a site near Pereiaslav), which flourished from about 200 BCE to CE 200, particularly in northwestern (Volhynia and the Pripet Marshes) and north-central (the Kiev region) Ukraine. This culture was that of an agricultural people living in small dwellings along protected banks of rivers. They were noted for excellent iron production. The Zarubynets' culture coincides with the Sarmatian period, although it probably included several peoples (Baltic, Scythian, Pomeranian), of whom the Slavs may have been one.

In about 200 CE, the so-called Cherniakhiv culture (named for a burial ground near Kiev discovered in 1899 by V. Khvoika) emerged in both the mixed forest-steppe and open steppe geographic zones covering most of Ukraine, Moldova, and eastern Romania. This area included hundreds of settlements scattered in narrow strips, sometimes nearly two-thirds of a mile (one kilometer) in length, along river banks. Gray or black polished pottery, iron tools, and metal ornaments of a high standard are associated with the Cherniakhiv culture, and, as is evident from remains, the inhabitants of the settlements also carried on trade with the Roman world to the south. Their spiritual life is revealed through several stone statues of pagan idols, three to ten feet (one to three meters) in height, found at various sites in the middle Dniester River valley and dating from the second to the fifth century. Scholars disagree as to what tribal groups created the artifacts related to Cherniakhiv culture, although it seems to be the result of several, including the Dacians, Sarmatians, Germans, Scythians, and Antae. Whatever its ethnic composition, the Cherniakhiv culture seems to have come to a sudden end around 400 CE, probably the victim of the invasion of the nomadic Huns.

Almost simultaneously with the Cherniakhiv culture arose the Pen'kivka culture (named for a site near the middle Dnieper River now under the Kremenchuk reservoir), which was initially based in the region between the Dnieper, Southern Buh, and lower Dnieper Rivers. The Pen'kivka culture seems to have represented the remnants of the Sarmatian presence in Ukraine, whose Iranian inhabitants had become slavicized and who were later described in historical records as the Antae. This agriculture-based culture was marked by small settlements along river banks, made up of semi-subterranean dwellings, each with a stone oven. The Pen'kivka culture associated with the Antae flourished from the fourth century CE until the Avar invasion of the early seventh century. The Avars may have reduced the power of the Antae' military forces, but they did not destroy the way of life characteristic of the Pen'kivka culture, which continued to survive, especially in northwestern and north-central Ukraine.

century among the Dulibians in Volhynia and in the seventh and eighth centuries among the Polianians in the middle Dnieper region near the Ros' River.

Whether the Antae created a state structure or existed simply as tribal groupings, their influence was broken after the arrival of the Avars during the second half of the sixth century. With the Avar presence, the Antae disappeared; they are last mentioned in historical sources at the beginning of the seventh century (602).

The Pax Chazarica

Aside from the disappearance of the Antae, the seventh century proved to be an important turning point in the history of Ukraine. By the middle of that century, the warlike Avars had moved out of Ukrainian lands and westward across the Carpathians into the Pannonian Plain, while a new Turkic people, the Khazars, were

MAP 5

THE EAST SLAVIC TRIBES AND THE KHAZARS

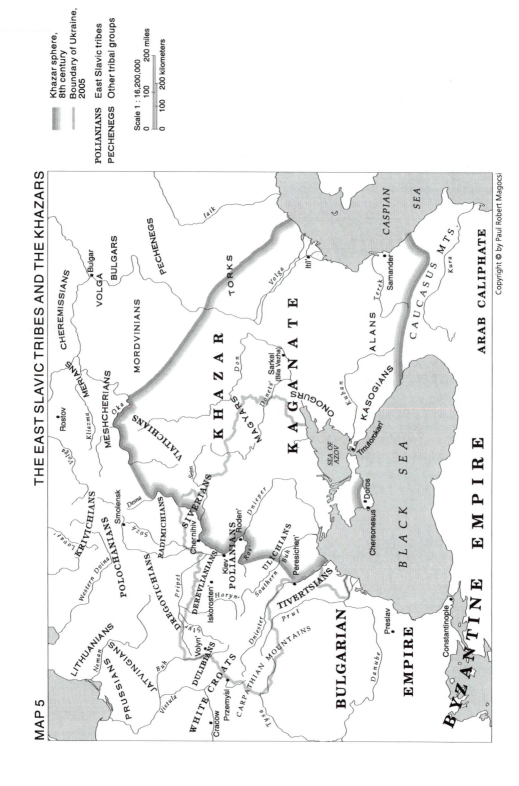

Khazar sphere, 8th century
Boundary of Ukraine, 2005

POLIANIANS   East Slavic tribes
PECHENEGS   Other tribal groups

Scale 1 : 16,200,000

0   100   200 miles

0   100   200 kilometers

PRUSSIANS

LITHUANIANS

JATVINGIANS

Niman

Buh

Vistula

DULIBIANS

WHITE CROATS

Cracow

Przemyśl

Tysa

CARPATHIAN MOUNTAINS

Dniester

Prut

Volyn'

Horyn'

Styr

DEREVLIANIANS

Iskorosten'

Pripet

DREGOVICHIANS

POLOCHANIANS

Western Dvina

Lovať

KRIVICHIANS

Smolensk

Sozh

Desna

Sem

RADIMICHIANS

SIVERIANS

Chernihiv

Kiev

POLIANIANS

Roden'

Ros'

Dnieper

ULICHIANS

Southern Buh

Peresichen'

TIVERTSIANS

Volga

Kliazma

Rostov

MERIANS

MESHCHERIANS

VIATICHIANS

Oka

CHEREMISSIANS

MORDVINIANS

Bulgar

VOLGA

BULGARS

PECHENEGS

Iaik

TORKS

Volga

Don

Donets'

Sarkel
(Bila Vezha)

MAGYARS

K H A Z A R

K A G A N A T E

ONOGURS

Tmutorokan'

SEA OF
AZOV

Kuban

ALANS

Terek

Samander

KASOGIANS

Itil

CASPIAN

SEA

Kura

CAUCASUS MTS.

ARAB CALIPHATE

B L A C K   S E A

Chersonesus

Doros

Preslav

BULGARIAN

E M P I R E

Danube

Constantinople

B Y Z A N T I N E   E M P I R E

Copyright © by Paul Robert Magocsi

establishing a powerful political and commercial center just east of Ukrainian territory between the lower Don, lower Volga, and Kuban-Terek River valleys. As for the East Slavic tribes, some went west beyond the Carpathians with the Avars. In Ukraine, the Dulibian tribal union in Volhynia dissipated and was replaced by a new tribal union among the Polianians and Siverians along the middle Dnieper valley. Scholars maintain either that the Polianian-Siverian union, with centers such as Roden', at the conjunction of the Ros' and Dnieper Rivers, continued the tradition of East Slavic statehood (Soviet authors spoke of an early Rus' state in this region), or that it functioned as a tribal unit within the Khazar sphere.

The Khazar sphere was concentrated within the triangle formed by the lower Don, lower Volga, and Kuban-Terek Rivers. But Khazar influence was felt far beyond as well. By the early ninth century, several East Slavic tribes to the northwest (the Polianians, Radimichians, Siverians, Viatichians), and other peoples, including the Mordvinians, Cheremissians, and Volga Bulgars in the north, and the Magyars, Onogurs, Kasogians, and Alans in the south, were all under the hegemony of the Khazar Kaganate, or empire. From the eighth century, the Khazars also controlled much of the Crimea, where the Crimean Goths with their center at Doros came under their domination as well.

Within this vast territory were to be found some of the most lucrative international trading routes, especially the northern branch of the silk route from China, which passed the Aral Sea and skirted the northern Caspian Sea, ending in the Khazar capital of Itil', near the mouth of the Volga. From Itil', the Khazars traded southward across the Caspian Sea to Baghdad and the Persian, later Arab, Middle East, or westward down the Don River and across the Black Sea to Byzantium. Trade and commerce were of the greatest concern to the Khazars, and the control and protection of commercial routes was the highest priority of the empire's military forces. Customs duties levied on goods passing along the trade routes under their control provided the main source of Khazar wealth, which was supplemented by taxes collected from various peoples under their hegemony. In return for this lord-vassal relationship, the Khazars provided peace and stability in the region as well as possibilities for trade. These were the main characteristics of the new order known as the Pax Chazarica.

Because of their interest in trade and commerce, the Khazars, unlike their nomadic predecessors and successors, preferred diplomacy and peace to war and plundering. Accordingly, in the north, even after the Volga Bulgars had become independent in the mid-eighth century, the Khazars maintained friendly relations with them. Toward the south, after a fierce struggle with the Persian Empire and, later, the Arab Caliphate during the seventh and eighth centuries, in about 750 the antagonists agreed it was useless to continue fighting. Both powers decided that the Caucasus Mountains should serve as their "natural" frontier.

Relations with Byzantium, the region's major commercial emporium, were very favorable from the time of the initial rise of Khazar power in the seventh century. The Khazars served as allies of Byzantium, first against the Persians and later against the Arabs. The only potential threat to peaceful ties was in the Crimean Peninsula, where the Bosporan Kingdom had been under Byzantine hegemony since the sixth century. The Khazars built a fortress, Tmutorokan', at the site of the Greco-Bosporan city Hermanossa (Tamatarcha), on the eastern shore of the Straits of Kerch. Taking advantage of civil strife between the Crimea and the Byzantine capital, the Khazars took control of most of the peninsula at the very end of the seventh century. It was not long, however, before the Khazars assuaged Byzantine fears. They agreed to divide the Crimea into a Byzantine sphere along the coast and a Khazar sphere in the hinterland behind the mountains.

Byzantine-Khazar relations were further strengthened in the eighth century by marital diplomacy (several Khazar princesses became wives of Byzantine emperors) and in the ninth century by a common defense against the increasingly restless nomadic Magyars and the newly arrived Varangian Rus'. The common defense took the form of the construction in the 830s by Byzantine architects of a second Khazar capital on the Don River at Sarkel (in Slavic, Bila Vezha) and the dispatch to the Khazars in the 860s of a "cultural" mission headed by the Byzantine Christian missionaries Constantine and Methodius.

The international commercial relations emphasized by the Khazars also transformed their empire into a fertile ground for cultural development, especially for religion. The Khazars were originally believers in Shamanism of the Altaic variety, but their ruling elite was receptive to other more advanced religions. In fact, all three great religions were received favorably by the Khazar leadership: (1) Islam, via Arab traders in the seventh century; (2) Judaism, via Jewish missionaries, among them Isaac Sangari in 767; and (3) Christianity, via Constantine and Methodius from Byzantium, the future "Apostles to the Slavs," who lived in the Khazar capital of Sarkel in 860 and 861. Between 789 and 809, the Khazar ruler (kagan) and nobility embraced Judaism, and later, during the first half of the tenth century, the kaganate became a refuge for Jews fleeing persecution by the Byzantine emperor (Romanus Lecapanus, reigned 919–944). Although eventually the Khazar Kaganate was most influenced by Islam, it nonetheless is the only state in history to have converted to Judaism, for however brief a time. Its conversion has given rise to Jewish legend and to theories (the most recent treatment being Arthur Koestler's *The Thirteenth Tribe*) adopted by various authors to prove that eastern Europe's Jews are descendants of the Khazars.

The Khazars are important because for two centuries – ca. 650 to 850 – their state fostered stability within a wide region, one surrounded by several cultures, between the Black Sea, the Caspian Sea, and the Caucasus Mountains. While the Khazar Kaganate was never the kind of impenetrable "bulwark of the steppe" against the East that is often suggested in traditional literature, it nonetheless served as a power center around which nomadic tribes and federations (the Bulgars, Alans, Magyars, East Slavs) gravitated and in which they found it more advantageous to trade and to live in peace than to provoke war and conflict.

The Slavic tribes in the shadow of the Khazars

The Slavic inhabitants of central and southwestern Ukraine, protected by the Pax Chazarica, were able to move south along water routes as far as the Black Sea and to expand east of the Dnieper River. Out of the old Antae federation, several distinct Slavic tribes evolved on Ukrainian territory: the Siverians, in the northeast along the lower Desna and upper Seim and Sula Rivers; the Polianians (plains people), along the Dnieper River between Kiev and Roden'; the Derevlianians (forest dwellers), bounded by the Pripet and Horyn' Rivers; the Dulibians, in Volhynia, along the upper valleys of the Vistula, Buh, and Styr' Rivers; the White Croats, north of the Carpathian Mountains; the Ulichians, on the left bank of the Southern Buh River; and the Tivertsians, between the Dniester and Prut Rivers near the Black Sea.

As during the period of the Antaen tribal leagues, the centers for these various Slavic tribes were hill forts known as *horodyshcha* or *horody*. At first, these were no more than stockades encircled by moats and ramparts where the surrounding agricultural population came for protection in times of danger. Eventually, the *horody* became towns where artisans produced wares and merchants conducted trade. By the ninth century, there were an estimated 400 *horody* in the Kiev area, 350 in Volhynia, 250 in Podolia, and 100 in Galicia. Among the more important were Kiev, the center for the Polianians, founded by their semi-legendary leader Kii (ca. 560); Chernihiv, the center for the Siverians; Iskorosten' (Korosten'), for the Derevlianians; Volyn' (now Horodok, on the Buh), for the Dulibians; Przemyśl, for the White Croats; and Peresichen', for the Ulichians. Initially, the tribal organization was in the hands of representatives of those families who had secured positions of power and influence on the basis of wealth, military prowess, or personal qualities. These representatives met in a council (*viche*) to decide important issues, and from time to time the most powerful of them became leaders or princes for the tribal group as a whole.

The primary livelihood of the Slavic tribes was agriculture and cattle raising. They harvested several different grains, fished, hunted wild animals, and collected honey and wax from bees. These were some of the goods they traded in the *horody*, where artisans had well-developed pottery, weaving, and metal industries, especially in iron. Besides supporting local commerce, Ukrainian lands became an important component of the Khazar international trading network.

In the early centuries of Khazar rule, the major trade route connecting Central Asia, the Arab world, and Byzantium with northern Europe passed through the Khazars' territory – Khazaria – up the Volga River, then crossed several lakes to the Gulf of Finland and the Baltic Sea (see map 6). The initiators of this northern trade were the Varangians, who, from their home base on the western shores of the Baltic Sea and outposts in northern (Staraia Ladoga) and north-central (Rostov) Russia, began during the eighth century to descend the Volga River to Khazaria. By the ninth century, a shorter route, from the Baltic through several lakes and rivers directly southward to the Dnieper River on to the Black Sea and Byzantium, had been opened. Not wanting to be outdone by what later became famous as the great waterway "from the Varangians to the Greeks," the Khazars strengthened their presence in the middle Dnieper with a garrison at Kiev, which in turn was connected by an east-west overland route to the Khazar capitals at Sarkel and Itil'. The result was that Kiev became the axis for major north–south and east–west trade routes along which goods flowed to and from Central Asian, Arabic, Byzantine, and Balto-Scandinavian markets. Along these and subsidiary routes, the East Slavic tribes in Ukraine exchanged their grain, wax, honey, and, sometimes, fur and slaves for fine cloth, gold, silver objects, wine, and pottery.

Although there were several Slavic tribes, they had much in common with regard to their basically agricultural way of life and their mythology or system of belief. Scattered in small groups across the vast plains and forests, the Slavs responded to their isolation and fear before the mysteries of nature by formulating divinities who peopled the clouds and the earth, the forests and the rivers, and their own fields and stables. In personifying nature, they were attempting to communicate with it in "human" terms and thereby to reduce the terror of the unknown. Since their system of beliefs is not set forth in a body of written texts, what we know of it derives from descriptions by antagonistic Christian writers and from latter-day folk customs that are presumed to retain remnants of pre-Christian Slavic mythology.

There seem to have been two categories of gods: major ones, who had control over the forces of nature; and minor ones, who inhabited local woods, fields, and rivers. The major gods included Svaroh, the sky, who gave birth to two children – Dazhboh, the sun, and Svarozhych, fire. Also of importance were Perun, the god of thunder, and Volos, the god of the animals. In the second, minor category were a whole host of spirits who inhabited forests (*lesky*), bogs (*bisy*), fields (*pol'ovyky*), and bodies of water (*rusalky*). Others were associated with human emotion, such as Iarylo, the god of springtime regeneration and sexual passion, and Kupalo, the god of water, herbs, and flowers with their purifying powers. Sacrifices were made and rituals performed in the service of all these gods.

In general, however, the system of belief among the Slavs was personal, with no temples, statues, or priests. There were two exceptions, however, found among Slavs on the island of Rügen in the Baltic Sea, and in Kiev. Both places had effigies of mythic gods. In Kiev, there was a large wooden statue of Perun, who as the personification of thunder became the god of war to whom Kiev's earliest rulers and first Rus' princes paid tribute, as they did also to Volos, the god of beasts, before going off to war. On the island of Rügen, the Slavic Ranians had an even more elaborate ritual and temple-like setting for their "god of gods," Svantovit. Svantovit's influence seemed to be widespread as well among West Slavic tribes north of the Carpathians, and an eight-foot (two-and-a-half-meter) statue believed to depict him was found in the mid-nineteenth century along the banks of the Zbruch River, in western Ukraine. With the coming of Christianity, the major Slavic gods and their statues were destroyed, but belief in the minor ones throughout rural areas remained strong – often flourishing through amalgamation with Christian beliefs – until as recently as the twentieth century.

Living within the protective shadow of the Pax Chazarica, the Slavic tribes on Ukrainian lands were spared for a while the worst nomadic invasions from the east, and, as a result, between the seventh and ninth centuries they were able to expand their agricultural and trading activities. But despite such protection, some Slavic princes began to resent their vassal-like relationship to the Khazar rulers. For the longest time, however, the Slavs were not united, and no individual tribe had the strength to confront the Khazar Kaganate. Building up the necessary strength became a possibility only in the mid-ninth century, with a new development in the region of Kiev. This development combined local forces with a group of leaders from Scandinavia – the Varangians – and the result was the eventual consolidation of a new power known as Rus'. How did this new phenomenon arise? Or, to cite the opening passage of the *Primary Chronicle*, the most famous discussion of the subject, what was "the origin of the land of Rus', [and of] the first princes of Kiev, and from what source did the land of Rus' have its beginning?"[2]

PART TWO

The Kievan Period

5

The Rise of Kievan Rus'

Our knowledge of the earliest developments on Ukrainian lands is based on scanty historical evidence and is riddled with uncertainties. There is no question, however, that a political entity known as Kievan Rus' began its existence sometime in the late ninth century and lasted until the mid-fourteenth century on the lands inhabited by the East Slavs. The political and cultural center of Kievan Rus' was in the middle Dnieper region of Ukraine, although the sphere of Kievan rule eventually extended far north of Ukrainian lands. This and the next four chapters will survey the rise, consolidation, decline, and transformation of Kievan Rus' during four periods: (1) the 870s to 972, the era of growth and expansion; (2) 972 to 1132, the era of consolidation; (3) 1132 to 1240, the era of disintegration; and (4) 1240 to 1340, the era of political transformation.

The origin of Rus'

While it is true that in comparison with the Khazar and early Slavic eras there is more historical data available about Kievan Rus', its first century is still shrouded in uncertainty and controversy. Among several problematic issues is the question of the origin of Rus'. Who were the Rus', and what were the beginnings of the state structure known as Kievan Rus'? These are among the most disputed and certainly most written about questions in the history of eastern Europe. Admittedly, the ongoing and often passionate debate that these questions have provoked among scholars and publicists frequently reflects less the actual issues of early medieval eastern European historical development than the needs of subsequent generations to find in their past an appropriate "foundation myth" that will both explain the origin of their people and provide for an appropriate degree of national pride. Did the East Slavs create their own state, or did they need outsiders to do it for them? In other words, was Kievan Rus' the first state on East Slavic territory, or was it just a successor to earlier ones? Finally, who were the Rus': Scandinavian outsiders, indigenous East Slavs, or both?

The controversy surrounding these questions derives from the different interpretations given to certain passages in the opening pages of one of the oldest and best-known written sources for the early history of the East Slavs, the *Rus' Primary*

THE GREAT DEBATE: THE ORIGIN OF RUS'

The invitation to the Varangians and the problem of the origin of Rus' have provoked a controversy that has been raging for over two centuries. The principal schools of thought on these questions have come to be known as the Normanist and anti-Normanist.

It could be said that the Normanist position was first presented in the oldest historical chronicles from Kievan times, the *Novgorod First Chronicle* and the *Rus' Primary Chronicle* (also known by its opening phrase as the *Poviest' vremennykh liet*, "Tale of Bygone Years"). *The Novgorod First Chronicle* dates from 1071, and despite subsequent modifications it is the earliest historical compilation available. The *Primary Chronicle* was begun even earlier, in the mid-eleventh century. Although it was subsequently copied and revised several times, its present form reflects a version prepared by the Kievan monk Nestor at the beginning of the twelfth century and subsequently reworked twice by his monastic colleagues (ca. 1118 and 1123). Both the *Novgorod First Chronicle* and the *Primary Chronicle* relate the story of the invitation to the Varangians and in various places associate them with the Rus'. Consequently, the Varangians are considered to have played a determining role in the establishment of Kievan Rus'.

With the advent of critical historical writing about eastern Europe in the eighteenth century, two German historians in the service of the Russian Empire, Gottlieb Bayer and Gerhard F. Müller, set the Normanist tone. They and their nineteenth-century successors (A. L. Schlözer, E. Kunik, V. Thomsen) claimed that most features of early Kievan Rus' civilization – its political and legal structure, religion, and art – owed their origin and subsequent development to Scandinavian influences. Although later research undermined many of these original Normanist assertions, one seemed irrefutable: the chronicle's "invitation to the Varangians" and the association of them with the Rus'.

A revised Normanist understanding of early Rus' history was adopted by the leading nineteenth- and twentieth-century historians of Russia (N. Karamzin, M. Pogodin, S. Solov'ev, V. Kliuchevskii, P. Miliukov, M. Pokrovskii) and their successors in the West (M. Florinsky, F. Dvornik, D. Obolensky), as well as by some Ukrainian historians (M. Kostomarov, P. Kulish, V. Antonovych, S. Tomashivs'kyi). The chronicle's association of the Varangians with the Rus' having been accepted, a quest using linguistic evidence was undertaken to find the original Rus' homeland. The hypothesis of Ernst Kunik and Vilhelm Thomsen that the original homeland was the Swedish maritime district of Uppland, along the Baltic Sea north of present-day Stockholm, was a view accepted by many leading Slavic philologists (F. Miklošić, I. Sreznevskii, V. Jagić, A. Shakhmatov, A. Brückner). According to linguistic criteria, the name *Rus'* reflects the Finnic tribes' description of these "newcomers from overseas." Consequently, *Rus'* derives either (1) from *Ruotsi*, the Finnish designation for Sweden, especially the coastal region just north of Stockholm known as Roslagen, inhabited by the *rospiggar* (pronounced *ruspiggar*), or (2) from *ropsmenn* or *ropskarlar*, old Nordic designations meaning seafarers or rowers, a group the Finns thought to be a nationality and whose name they preserved in the first syllable of their terms for Sweden (*Ruotsi*) and Swedish (*ruotsalaiset*).

An anti-Normanist reaction had already been expressed by the eighteenth-century Russian author Mikhail Lomonosov, but his defense of the "Russian nation" and of the East Slavs in general was not really developed until the nineteenth century. Since then, the first serious anti-Normanists, Dmitrii Ilovaiskii and Stepan Gedeonov, have been joined by a host of other scholars (I. Filevich, M. Hrushevs'kyi, P. Golubovskii, G. Vernadsky, H. Paszkiewicz, M. Tikhomirov, B. Grekov, B. Rybakov), who have either criticized particular aspects of the Normanist position or, often with the use of archaeological evidence, constructed new schema to explain the early development of East Slavic state structures in which the Varangian invitation is treated as a mere episode.

According to the anti-Normanists, the name *Rus'* was originally associated not with Varangians in the Novgorod and other northern regions around Lake Ladoga, but rather with a tribe much farther south, either along the middle Dnieper region just below Kiev or, in the opinion of one author (Vernadsky), east of the Sea of Azov. In the middle Dnieper region, a Slavic tribe known as the Ros (*rosy/rodi*) lived in the valley of the Ros' River, a tributary of the Dnieper south of Kiev. From their center at Roden', the Ros united the surrounding Slavic peoples into a tribal alliance in the sixth century. That union was subsequently enlarged and strengthened when the Ros merged with the Polianians of the Kiev region as well as with the Siverians of the Chernihiv region to form a new tribal union along the middle Dnieper valley that was called *Rus'*.

Making use of such – some would say hypothetical – information, Soviet historians (B. Grekov, B. Rybakov) became especially adamant anti-Normanists. They based their position in particular on twentieth-century archaeological discoveries which supposedly proved the existence of East Slavic state structures well before the Varangians appeared in eastern Europe. These "states" included a Dulibian tribal alliance based in Volhynia and a Rus' alliance based in the middle Dnieper region (made up of the Polianians, Siverians, and Ulichians). Both alliances are considered continuations of the earlier Antean "Slavic state." It was the expansion of the Rus' northward from Kiev and their increasing control over other East Slavic tribes (and not the arrival of Varangians) that in the late ninth and early tenth centuries led to the formation of Kievan Rus'.

The anti-Normanists argue further that no people known as Rus' or any variant thereof was ever mentioned in old Scandinavian sources. They point out that some ninth-century Islamic writers, furthermore, speak of the Rūs as a tribe of Slavs and even make reference to three East Slavic states: Kuyaba, Slava, and Arta. The anti-Normanists argue, moreover, that the traditional association of Slava (Slavia) with Novgorod is incorrect, and that the names refer simply to Kiev (Kuyaba) and two of its satellite towns, Pereiaslav (Slavia) and Roden' (Arta). As for the supposedly indisputable evidence of the invitation to the Varangians and their identification with the Rus' found in the chronicles, the anti-Normanists dismiss it as a latter-day interpolation. The story of the "invitation" was added by copyists who, as loyal monarchists, hoped to legitimize the Riuryk dynasty (a fourteenth-century concept) by arguing for its descent from Riuryk, the eldest of the Varangian warriors invited to the Novgorod region and the supposed first ruler of the Rus' state. The anti-Normanists also dismiss the supporting evidence that the Rus' envoys to Byzantium clearly had Scandinavian names, arguing that they were simply hirelings of Slavic Rus' princes sent on their missions because they were specialists in commercial and diplomatic matters.

An attempt to break the Normanist–anti-Normanist controversy was put forth in 1929 by the lawyer and Ukrainian civic activist Serhii Shelukhyn, living at the time as an émigré in Prague. Shelukhyn developed what he called "the theory of the Celtic origin of Kievan Rus' from France." Among the Celtic tribes of Gaul conquered by Rome under Julius Caesar in 58–51 BCE were the Rutheni, who lived west of the Rhône River in, and just to the north of Narbonne, that is, the first Roman colony west of the Alps encompassing the regions of Languedoc and Auvergne in present-day southern France. Half a millennium later, during the fifth-century CE dispersal of populations in Europe caused by the Hunnic invasions, the Rutheni moved eastward and settled in the Roman provinces of Rhaetia, Noricum, and Pannonia (present-day Austria and western Hungary). It was not long, however, before the Rutheni rebelled against Roman rule. Among their leaders was Odoacer, described in sources as "king of the Ruthenians" (*Rex Ruthenorum*). Odoacer was the very same military leader of Germanic origin who brought about the fall of Rome in 476 CE.

As for the Celtic Rutheni, Shelukhyn argues, they continued to live in Rhaetia, Noricum, Pannonia, and coastal Illyria (present-day Croatia and Slovenia), where they mixed with the local population, including Slavs. Sometime in the seventh century CE, the Rutheni again moved eastward. A small number went northeastward to the Carpathian region in far western Ukraine, where they left their names of alleged Celtic origin: *Rutheni* (Slavic: Rus'/Rusyn) and *Galicia* (Slavic: Galich/Halych). A larger number traveled southeastward, along the Danube River to its delta, and then across the steppes of Ukraine until settling along the eastern shores of the Sea of Azov, in particular in the Taman Peninsula on the eastern banks of the Straits of Kerch. There they established a Ruthenian/Rus' center at Tamarcha/Tmutorokan'. From Tmutorokan' some of the Rus' went north to Kiev where they mixed with the local East Slavic Polianians to whom they bequeathed the name Rus'. Eventually, the Rus' spread from Kiev northward to Novgorod.

Another explanation that keeps the Celtic ("French") factor in mind has been made by the Ukrainian-American historian Omeljan Pritsak. He agrees with the Normanists that the Varangian Rus' came from abroad and that they were instrumental in organizing the first lasting East Slavic state. The Rus', moreover, were already established among the Finnic and East Slavic tribes in the north at the beginning of the ninth century, their power base being the region around Rostov. Nonetheless, these early Varangian Rus', as well those who responded to the later famous "invitation," according to Pritsak represented no particular ethnic group – neither Scandinavian, nor Slavic, nor Celtic, nor Iranian (as Vernadsky asserts). Rather, they were an international trading company made up of peoples of various origins who plied the North Sea and the Baltic (or Varangian) Sea. As for the mid-ninth-century invitation to the Varangian Riuryk and his brothers, Pritsak agrees with the anti-Normanists that the emphasis on this episode is a latter-day interpolation by copiers of the chronicles. He also agrees with their rejection of the theory that the Rus' were ethnically Scandinavian, although he denies that the origin of the term has anything to do with the Ros tribe, the Ros' River, or any Slavic state on Ukrainian lands before the ninth century. Instead, he proposes that the word *Rus'* is derived from *Rūti/Rūzzi*, the Middle German equivalent of Middle French *Rusi*, which in turn refers to *Ruteni/Rutena* – the old Celtic polity in south-central France, where in the town of Rodez (whose inhabitants to this very day call themselves *rutenois*) an international Ruteno-Frisian trading company was based.

Despite the seemingly persuasive arguments of proponents of the various theories, there still is no definitive answer to the question of the origin of Rus', and the debate goes on.

Chronicle. After the typical descriptions of the biblical flood and the dispersion of Noah's descendants throughout the earth, the *Primary Chronicle* provides a list of East Slavic tribes and places special emphasis on the Polianians. The Polianians are presented as a "gentle and peaceful" people whose chief, Kii, not only was cofounder of Kiev but also was strong enough to visit and be received with "great honor" by the Byzantine emperor. The clear implication in the *Primary Chronicle* is that well before the ninth century there were several powerful East Slavic tribes or tribal leagues with their own chiefs or princes. By the ninth century, however, the Polianians and other East Slavic tribes in the middle Dnieper region had become vassals of the Khazars, while the Slavic and neighboring Finnic tribes farther north, inward from the Gulf of Finland, had become vassals of the Varangians, or Varangian Rus', "from overseas."

Sometime in the mid-ninth century (the *Primary Chronicle* says 860; the older *First Novgorod Chronicle* indicates 854), the Slavs (Slovenians and Krivichians) and the Finnic Chud, Vepsians, and Merians, all of whom were vassals of the Varangians, "drove [them] away overseas and did not give them tribute. And they themselves began to rule among themselves."[1] The Slavs and Finnic peoples in the north, it seems, were incapable of ruling themselves, with the result that "kin rose against kin" and they "began to raid against one another." In such circumstances, says the *Primary Chronicle*, the former Slavic and Finnic vassals "said to each other, 'Let us seek out a prince for ourselves, one who might rule us and keep order according to law.' And they went overseas to the Varangians, to the Rus'. … The Chud, Slavs, and Krivichians, and the Vepsians said to the Rus': 'Our land is big and fertile, but there is no order in it. Come to be prince and rule us'."[2] In response, the Varangian Rus' sent three brothers, Hroerkr/Riuryk, Sineus, and Truvor, who settled respectively in Staraia Ladoga (the *First Novgorod Chronicle* says Novgorod), Beloozero, and Izborsk. It is because of "these Varangians" in the Novgorod region "that the land of Rus' was named," even though previous to their arrival the inhabitants were Slavs. The *Primary Chronicle* seems, therefore, to distinguish the Varangian Rus' newcomers and the indigenous Slavs as two different groups.

Soon after, the story goes, two of the Varangian brothers died, leaving Hroerkr/Riuryk in control of the Novgorodian land of Rus'. Two of Hroerkr/Riuryk's military servitors, Askol'd and Dir, were permitted to go to Constantinople, but on their way down the Dnieper River, which was to become part of the famed great waterway "from the Varangians to the [Byzantine] Greeks," they stopped at Kiev, which at the time, together with the surrounding Polianian countryside, was in vassalage to the Khazars. While it is not clear whether or not they were asked to do so by the people of Kiev, Askol'd and Dir "remained in this town, and they collected many Varangians and began to rule the land of the Polianians, while Riuryk was ruling as a prince in Novgorod."[3]

Seemingly entrenched in Kiev, the emboldened Askol'd and Dir continued their journey to Constantinople, and in 860, with 200 ships, they attacked the capital of the Byzantine Empire. Although Askol'd and Dir were able to defeat the powerful Byzantines, they proved less successful against their fellow Varangians. In 880–882, the new Varangian ruler of Novgorod, Helgi/Oleh, came to Kiev from the north with a large army, killed Askol'd and Dir, and "settled as prince in Kiev." Pleased with his achievement, Helgi/Oleh declared that Kiev should "be the mother of towns of Rus'."[4] He then proceeded to force the other East Slavic and Finnic tribes to recognize his authority.

Thus, according to the *Primary Chronicle*, the various East Slavic tribes, in particular the Polianians, had from earliest times strong military forces and princely leaders. By the mid-ninth century, however, they were in vassalage to either the Varangians or the Khazars. A brief attempt at self-rule proved abortive, and therefore an invitation was sent to the foreigners known as the Varangians or Rus' from Scandinavia to rule over them in the region of Novgorod. Not long after, the new Varangian sphere of influence had spread southward to Kiev and its immediate environs. At first, there were two separate Varangian spheres, one under Riuryk in the Novgorod region, the other under Askol'd and Dir in the Kiev region. By the 880s, these had been brought under the hegemony of one ruler, Helgi/Oleh, who proceeded to unite the other East Slavic tribes. With Helgi/Oleh, the rise of Kievan Rus' had begun. In order to reconstruct the historical record from the sketchy and at times contradictory information of the *Primary Chronicle*, it is first necessary to examine the situation in Europe as a whole during the ninth century and to see how events at seemingly far distances had a direct and indirect impact on developments among the East Slavs and on Ukraine in particular.

Europe in the ninth century

The ninth century witnessed profound changes throughout Europe, from the

Scandinavian north to the Mediterranean south, and from the far eastern steppes of the Khazar Kaganate to the heart of the Continent, which was experiencing the disintegration of Charlemagne's empire and the destructive multidirectional invasions of the Norsemen, Arabs, and Magyars. The result of these changes was the rise of new political alignments not only in the east but also throughout Europe.

In the Scandinavian north, political and demographic changes led to a steady outward migration of warriors, traders, and adventurers, who, beginning in the last decade of the eighth century, invaded and pillaged large parts of Europe. To the inhabitants of northern Germany, Britain, and Ireland, they were known as Vikings; to the inhabitants of France, Spain, and Italy, as Norsemen or Normans; and to the Slavs and Finns in eastern Europe, as Varangians (from the Old Norse name *Vaeringjar,* "one who has taken an oath"). Throughout the ninth century, the Vikings/Norsemen/Varangians descended from the Scandinavian north in relentless attacks upon the cities and countryside of large portions of the Continent and the British Isles.

The causes of the Scandinavian expansion were complex, but the most important cause seems to have been political. In Denmark, and to a lesser degree in Norway and Sweden, kings were beginning to consolidate larger territories under their rule and to maintain firmer control over a traditionally freebooting population of subsistence farmers and fishermen. During this period of transition to more centralized authority, petty tribal leaders and rebellious subjects were forced into exile. One result of political consolidation was greater security and stability, which in turn promoted a prosperity and population increase that soon grew beyond what the meager natural resources of the mountainous Scandinavian landscape could support. It was this combination of population pressure and internal political consolidation that provided the manpower and leaders for the Viking raids. The result is a classic example of what may be called the safety-valve theory in history. Had the Vikings had nowhere to go, civil war between a centralizing power and discontented elements in the population might have become widespread. During the ninth century, however, the European continent was itself passing through a series of crises, and it became a kind of safety valve through which Scandinavian pressure could be released.

In the heart of the Continent, the empire of Charlemagne (reigned 768–814) restored a measure of stability to large parts of central and western Europe both north and south of the Alps, a stability which had been unknown since the days of the Roman Empire. Soon after Charlemagne's death in 814, however, dissension among his successors led to the breakup of his empire and to internecine war between various Christian kings and princes. Farther south, the Mediterranean sphere had come to be dominated by the Islamic Arabs. From its base in the Middle East, the Arab Caliphate had brought all of northern Africa and most of the Iberian Peninsula (Spain and Portugal) under its control by the second half of the eighth century. Then, during the ninth century, the Arabs (or Saracens, as they were known) moved from their bases in northern Africa to acquire Sicily, Sardinia, Corsica, and southern Italy. Most of the Mediterranean and its trade routes were in Arab hands.

At the far southeastern end of the European continent, the Khazar Kaganate and the stability it had created within its large sphere of influence began to break down. A violent civil war took place during the 820s, and although the kaganate's strength was restored a decade later, certain results of the conflict would have serious implications in the future. The losers in the internal political struggle, known as Kabars, fled northward to the Varangian Rus' in the upper Volga region, near Rostov, and southward to the Magyars, who formerly had been loyal vassals of the Khazars. The presence of Kabar political refugees from Khazaria among the Varangian traders in Rostov helped to raise the latter's prestige, with the consequence that by the 830s a new power center known as the Rus' Kaganate had come into existence. The acceptance of the Kabar rebels by the Magyars, however, turned the latter into enemies of the new rulers of Khazaria.

Finally, a fierce warrior nomadic people, the Pechenegs (Patzinaks), began to move out of their abode north of the Caspian Sea in Khazaria. The Pechenegs displaced the Magyars from their homeland (Levedia) between the Don and Donets' Rivers. This forced the Magyars to move westward and, in about 840–850, to settle in the Ukrainian steppe between the Dnieper and Prut Rivers. From their new homeland (Etelköz) in Ukraine, the Magyars came into direct contact with the East Slavic Polianians living in the middle Dnieper region just to the north of them. The Magyars also began the first of their raids farther westward into the Balkans and central Europe. All these political changes and tribal displacements led to military clashes and disruption in trade, which had the overall effect of producing instability within the Khazar Kaganate and the Ukrainian steppe.

In fact, during the troubled ninth century, the only European power to maintain and even to increase its influence was the Byzantine Empire. That empire had itself just survived a profound internal cultural and political upheaval known as the iconoclast controversy, which lasted through most of the eighth and first half of the ninth centuries. Beginning in 843, Byzantium entered a golden age that continued until the first quarter of the eleventh century and witnessed the greatest extension of its territory and expansion of its commercial and cultural influence it was ever to achieve. Nonetheless, though the empire survived onslaughts from the Arab-dominated Middle East, its access to western Europe was cut off by Arab control of the Mediterranean during the ninth and much of the tenth centuries. In temporary isolation from the west and the south, therefore, Europe's greatest trade and commercial emporium was forced to strengthen further its relations with the Khazar Kaganate and with the regions north and east of the Black Sea. The traditional close relations between the Byzantines and the Khazars were threatened, however, by the arrival of a new element in the eastern European world, the Varangians of Scandinavia.

The Varangians in the east

Whereas initially the Scandinavian marauders were content with hit-and-run raids on undefended coastal ports or with attacks on towns and monasteries along rivers navigable from the sea, they soon began to realize the advantages of settling down and establishing rudimentary administrations to control and exploit for longer periods the population in regions under their authority. In this way, they took over and developed entities such as Normandy in France, the Norman Kingdom of Two Sicilies in southern Italy, and Kievan Rus' in the east.

In the east, the Scandinavians already had a long though interrupted tradition of contact going back to the beginning of the first millennium BCE, especially along the eastern shores of the Baltic Sea (modern Estonia and Latvia). The earliest Scandinavians along those shores had been absorbed by the indigenous Baltic and Finnic populations within a few centuries.

By the sixth and seventh centuries CE, traders from Scandinavia, who had come to be known as Varangians, were back again along the eastern shores of the Baltic Sea. As they gradually pushed farther inland, they heard stories from the local Baltic and Finnic peoples about the riches of Khazaria on the lower Volga and the lucrative commerce of the kaganate with the Arab Caliphate and Byzantine Empire farther south and southwest. Spurred on by such tales, the Varangian traders and marauders grew anxious to tap the Khazarian market. By the eighth century, they had established the so-called Saracen route, which brought them from Birka along Sweden's east coast, across the Baltic Sea and on through the Gulf of Finland, and then over land, rivers, and lakes (Ladoga, Onega, and White) to the upper Volga, whose course brought them southward to the heart of Khazaria. Along this route, the Varangians set up trading outposts and, eventually, centers of settlement. Three became especially important during the eighth century: Staraia Ladoga (called Aldeigjuborg in Icelandic sagas), on the southern shore of Lake Ladoga; Beloozero, on the southern shore of the White Lake; and Rostov, in the triangle between the upper Volga and Kliazma Rivers. From these trading posts in the north, the Varangians carried slaves and furs and other valuable skins, which they exchanged for spices, metalwares, cloth, and silver from the Arabic and Central Asian trade routes that converged in Khazaria.

Products from Central Asia and the Far East were still in demand in Byzantium and western Europe, but access to them via Baghdad and the ports of the eastern Mediterranean was closed off in the eighth century as a result of the Byzantine-Islamic wars and subsequent Arab control of the Mediterranean. The Khazar Kaganate accordingly became the new intermediary for Byzantium's eastern commercial interests. The Varangians initially seemed content to join the Khazarian trade nexus, transferring products from Khazarian markets along the Volga River to the Baltic Sea and eventually to northern and western Europe. This mutually beneficial relationship was upset, however, after the 820s, in consequence of the internal disturbances in and external threats to the Khazar Kaganate discussed above. In conjunction with the disruption of the Pax Chazarica, the restless Pecheneg and Magyar tribes hampered trade along the Volga and forced the Varangians to look for alternative routes. Moreover, if the Khazars could not serve as effective intermediaries between the Orient, Byzantium, and northern Europe, perhaps the Varangians themselves could replace them in that role.

These are the factors which soon after the mid-ninth century led the Varangians to develop an alternative trade route that began at the eastern Swedish ports of Birka and Sigtuna. After crossing the Baltic (Varangian) Sea, they traveled up

MAP 6

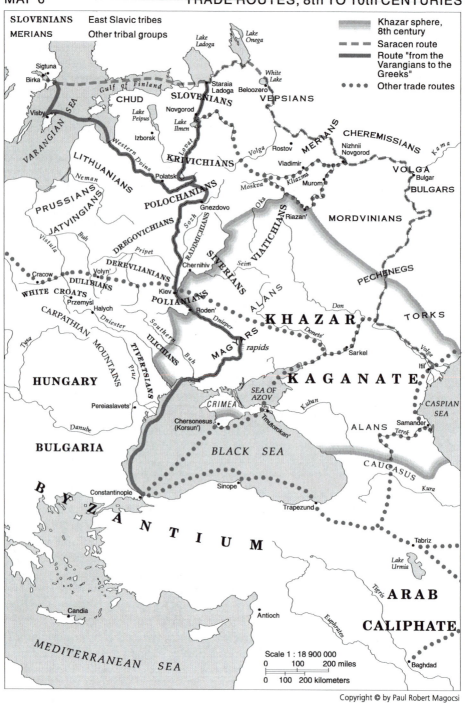

Copyright © by Paul Robert Magocsi

the Western Dvina River virtually to its source. From there they followed the small tributary southward and then carried their boats over land (the so-called portage) to the upper reaches of the Dnieper River, where they established an outpost at Gnezdovo (just west of present-day Smolensk). The Varangians could also cross the Baltic Sea and sail through the Gulf of Finland, reaching their outpost at Staraia Ladoga, and from there go directly south in the direction of Lake Ilmen', not far from which they set up the outpost of Gorodishche (Scandinavian: Holmgarthr), later Novgorod. Crossing Lake Ilmen', they proceeded in a southerly direction up the Lovat' River to a point near its source. From there it was a short distance carrying their boats (the first portage) to the Western Dvina River and from there on to Gnezdovo. They then sailed down the Dnieper to the Khazar outpost of Kiev. From Kiev the Varangians could travel eastward by overland route to the Donets' River and Khazar capital of Itil', or they could sail farther south along the Dnieper (again carrying their boats past that river's impassible rapids) to the Black Sea and on directly to Constantinople. The route that began in Birka or Sigtuna – and that traversed the Baltic Sea, several rivers to the Dnieper, and from the Dnieper's mouth across the Black Sea, ending in Constantinople – came to be known as the great waterway "from the Varangians to the [Byzantine] Greeks."

The potential wealth to be accrued from international trade along the Baltic–Dnieper–Black Sea route is what accounts for the increased Varangian presence in eastern Europe. The Varangian task was made easier by the weakening of the Khazar Kaganate, which in the mid-ninth century was losing control of its western borderland. By then the nomadic Magyars dominated the Dnieper steppe region, and the neighboring East Slavic tribes (the Polianians, Severians, etc.) were becoming restless in the face of the increasingly ineffective Pax Chazarica. In the far north, the Varangians controlled the trade routes until their local Finnic and East Slavic vassals temporarily drove them away. This was the discord and war of "one against another" that set the stage for the mid-ninth-century "invitation to the Varangians" described in the opening pages of the *Primary Chronicle*.

It is precisely the implications of the "invitation" that have caused such controversy in the historiography of eastern Europe. Of the two basic schools of thought, one accepts the tale of the invitation from the *Primary Chronicle*, thereby attributing the creation of the Kievan state to Scandivanians known as the Varangian Rus'. The other school minimizes the role of the Varangians, considers the Rus' to have been an East Slavic, not Scandinavian, people, and sees Kievan Rus' essentially as the creation of East Slavs who may simply have hired a Varangian military retinue to serve them. Perhaps the most balanced explanation of the problem is to be found in a commentary by twentieth-century scholars on the well-known tenth-century historical tract *De Administrando Imperio*, by the Byzantine historian and emperor Constantine Porphyrogenitus (reigned 913–959):

It is now, indeed, widely recognized that the Kiev state was not born *ex nihilo* with the advent of the Varangians in the ninth century; but that its social and economic foundations were laid in the preceding period, during which the Slavs in the Dnieper basin played an active part in the political and commercial life of the west Eurasian and Pontic steppes; and that a pre-existing Slavonic land-owning aristocracy and merchant class remained the mainstay of the country's territorial stability and economic growth under its Viking overlords. It is equally clear, however, that it was the Scandinavian invaders who in the second half of the ninth century united the scattered tribes of the Eastern Slavs into a single state based on the Baltic–Black Sea waterway, to which they gave their Rus' name.[5]

The era of growth and expansion

Regardless of the uncertainties surrounding the origin of Rus', with Helgi/Oleh (reigned 878–912) we have a known historical figure credited with building the foundations of a Kievan state. His reign begins the era of the growth and expansion of the Kievan realm that was to last for approximately a century, until 972. During this first stage in Kievan Rus' history, Helgi/Oleh and his three successors – Ingvar/Ihor, Helga/Ol'ha, and Sveinald/Sviatoslav – faced two basic challenges: (1) to acquire control of the disparate East Slavic and Finnic tribes who lived along trade routes the Varangians hoped to control; and (2) to establish a favorable relationship with the nomads of the steppe and a positive military and economic position vis-à-vis the two strongest powers in the region, Byzantium and Khazaria.

With Oleh's invasion of Kiev and the assassination of Askol'd and Dir in 882, the consolidation of the East Slavic and Finnic tribes under the authority of the Varangian Rus' had begun. According to the *Primary Chronicle*, Oleh made himself "prince of Kiev and ... said, 'Let this be the mother of the towns of Rus'."[6] The Slovenians, Krivichians, and Merians, who had been under his control in the north, continued to pay him tribute, as did the Polianians, over whom he ruled directly in Kiev. With the far north and the middle of the Dnieper region in Varangian Rus' hands, Oleh turned to the other East Slavic tribes, and between 883 and 885 he brought the Derevlianians, Siverians, and Radimichians under his hegemony. The Ulichians and Tivertsians, living farther south, took longer to subdue, but control of them was finally accomplished in the course of Varangian steppe politics in the 890s. Thus, by the end of the ninth century, Helgi/Oleh the empire builder – as he is sometimes described – had from his capital in Kiev gained control over most of the East Slavic tribes from the Black Sea coast and Danube Delta in the south to the Gulf of Finland and upper Volga in the far north.

Such rapid expansion inevitably brought him into conflict with Khazaria and Byzantium. Having been shaken by the internal upheavals during the 820s and the subsequent movement of the Magyars and Pechenegs in the steppe, the Khazars were in no position seriously to challenge the loss of their former East Slavic vassals – the Siverians and Radimichians – to the Varangian Rus'. Moreover, as part of the volatile nature of steppe politics during Oleh's reign, the Magyars were forced by Pecheneg pressure to move even farther westward – to leave Ukraine entirely. They crossed the Carpathians, and, by the beginning of the tenth century, had settled in the Danube-Tisza Plain, which was to become their final homeland, eventually known as Hungary. The Ukrainian steppe was now left open to the Pechenegs, who could raid it at will from their new base between the Volga and Don Rivers.

Oleh's relations with the Byzantine Empire were more complex and reflected commercial and cultural as well as military concerns. The very rise of Kievan Rus' depended on the opening of the great Baltic-Dnieper-Black Sea commercial route "from the Varangians to the Greeks," and its wealth and income depended on favorable trade relations with Byzantium. For their part, the Byzantines were forced to reckon with the Rus' after the unexpected attack on their capital led by Askol'd and Dir in 860. The initial Byzantine response was to strengthen ties with its traditional Khazar allies (hence the mission of Constantine and Methodius to Khazaria in 860–861) and to try to entice the Rus' into their Christian sphere. In this they were successful. The envoys of Askol'd and Dir were baptized, a Christian mission was established in Kiev in the late 860s, and as part of a Rus'-Byzantine treaty of 874, a Byzantine archbishop was sent to reside probably in Tmutorokan'.

These favorable Byzantine-Rus' relations were brought to an end, however, when Oleh drove out Askol'd and Dir and took over Kiev. After Oleh completed the subjugation of the East Slavic tribes, his Rus' armies were dispatched in a new attack against the Byzantine capital in 907. This successful invasion forced the Byzantines to sign a treaty in 911 that exempted Rus' traders from customs duties and provided them with a special place of residence (with free lodging for up to six months) during their trading missions in the Byzantine capital. With this treaty the financial basis of the new Kievan state was assured, since the Rus' were thereby given preferential rights in their commerce with Byzantium, the richest power in the region. In return for furs, wax, honey, and slaves, the Rus' received "gold, silk fabrics, fruit, and all manner of finery," which their own ruling elite either retained for themselves or sold for a profit to merchants who plied the Dnieper River en route to the Baltic Sea and to northern and western Europe. By the time of Oleh's death in 912, he had succeeded in expanding the sphere of Kievan Rus' over an extensive territory and in neutralizing the most powerful states in the region, Khazaria and Byzantium.

The favorable position of Kievan Rus' was maintained, though with great difficulty, by Oleh's succesor, Ingvar/Ihor (reigned 912–945). The East Slavic tribes began to resent the manner in which the Varangian rulers exacted tribute (*poliudie*) from them. The payments, which included dues to support the prince and his retinue as well as contributions in kind (furs, wax, honey), were collected from each homestead by fiscal agents. In practice, the process of collection was not much different from organized robbery, with the proceeds going to support the opulence of the Varangian ruling elite. This state of affairs prompted several revolts during Ihor's reign, most notably by the Ulichians and Derevlianians.

External relations also suffered a setback. While the Khazar Kaganate proved not to be a particular threat, the Pechenegs were a problem. They returned to the Ukrainian steppe and, in 915 and 920, undertook at least two major attacks against Kievan Rus'. Relations with Byzantium also deteriorated, and prompted by some misunderstanding with Rus' trading missions in Constantinople, Ihor decided in 941 to undertake a punitive attack on the imperial capital. This time the Rus' were defeated, and although a new commercial treaty was signed in 944, it gave Kiev much less favorable terms.

Relations with Byzantium and the internal situation in Kievan Rus' improved after Ihor's widow succeeded him in 945. The new ruler, Helga/Ol'ha (reigned 945–962), came to the throne unexpectedly, after her husband was assassinated during one of the Rus' ruler's foraging trips for tribute from the nearby Derevliani-ans. The *Primary Chronicle* describes in some detail Ol'ha's brutal revenge against the Derevlianians for her husband's death, but one result of the assassination was a change in the manner in which the Rus' exacted tribute from the various East Slavic tribes. Ol'ha reformed the collection practices by replacing the arbitrary visitations from Rus' central authorities or their appointed representatives with a system whereby payments were organized by local agents operating from specific posts throughout the land.

Ol'ha is best remembered for her interest in improving relations with Byzan-tium. In 957, she went to Constantinople, but unlike each of her Kievan Rus' predecessors, who sent armies to attack the imperial capital, she went on a mission of peace. Ol'ha was even accepted into the imperial fold, which became possible following her conversion to Christianity and adoption of a new name, Helena. This move not only enhanced Byzantine-Rus' relations but also strengthened the earlier Christian presence in Kiev, which had been largely eliminated after Oleh came to power in the 880s and only slightly restored under Ihor. Nonetheless, despite Ol'ha/Helena's conversion, neither the Varangian Rus' elite nor her son accepted Christianity. Satisfied with their own pagan rituals, they tolerated and even seemed amused by the new faith.

Ol'ha/Helena's reign came to an end in 962, when her twenty-one-year-old son Sveinald/Sviatoslav began to rule in his own right. During his decade of rule, Sviatoslav returned to the expansionist tendencies of Oleh. Like the many "barbar-ians" before him, Sviatoslav was attracted to the riches of Byzantium and wanted to be as close as possible to the radiance of the imperial capital. His first concern was the north and east. He succeeded in bringing the Viatichians, the last of the East Slavic vassals, within the Rus' sphere. Then, when the Khazars asked the Rus' for help against the Pechenegs, his response was to attack the kaganate, capture its capital of Sarkel in 965, and refashion it into the far eastern Rus' outpost of Bila Vezha. That same year, Sviatoslav subdued the Khazars' other allies, the Volga Bulgars, and then he returned to Khazaria, looting its old center at Itil'. By the late 960s, Sviatoslav's forces had destroyed the Khazar Kaganate and with it the last remnants of the Pax Chazarica.

Sviatoslav was now ready to turn to what he considered the ultimate prize, Byzan-tium. The Byzantines had already realized that their traditional Khazar allies were no longer dependable, and they sought new ones, therefore, among the Rus'. The somewhat naive Sviatoslav allowed himself to become a pawn of Byzantine north-ern diplomacy. The main players in this diplomatic chess game were the Rus', the Bulgarian Empire along the lower Danube River, and the Pechenegs of the steppe, each of whom the Byzantines were ready to play off against the others. For his part, Sviatoslav hoped to gain a foothold in the Balkans at the expense of the Bulgar-ians. He even dreamed of transferring his capital from Kiev to Pereiaslavets', near the mouth of the Danube. In the end, he was forced to give up his dream and, in 971, to sign an unfavorable peace treaty with Byzantium. A year later, while returning to Kiev, he fell in an ambush by Pecheneg warriors, who had probably been informed of his movements by his erstwhile Bulgarian and/or Byzantine allies.

The death of Sviatoslav in 972 marks the end of the first century of Kievan Rus'. Under the leadership of military lieutenants and descendants of the Varangian leader Riuryk, who had been invited to the Novgorod region in the second half of the ninth century, a new power was created in eastern Europe. Centered after the 880s in Kiev, the Rus' princes were able to bring under their control several East Slavic and Finnic tribes within less than a century. Carrying on the tradition of the Viking/Varangian marauders who had ravaged Europe throughout most of the ninth century, Kiev's new leaders, especially Oleh and Sviatoslav, dreamed of an empire that would dominate the trade routes from the Baltic to the Black and Caspian Seas. In the rush to expand their frontiers, however, they hastened the demise of their commercial rival in the east, the Khazar Kaganate. This upset the centuries-old Pax Chazarica, which had provided a measure of peace among the steppe peoples and had blocked new nomadic invasions. The qualified success of the Rus' princes in the east was counterbalanced, moreover, by the failure of expansionist programs with respect to Bulgaria and Byzantium. While it is true that during the first century of growth and expansion the Varangian Rus' were able to establish their hegemony over a larger territory in eastern Europe, the Kievan realm still had much more internal consolidation to achieve before it could hope to become an enduring political force in the region.

6

Political Consolidation and Disintegration

Following the untimely death of Sviatoslav in 972, his successors were left with an enormous territorial expanse stretching from the edge of the Ukrainian steppe in the south to the Gulf of Finland and lake region of Russia in the north. In the course of the next century and a half – from 972 to 1132 – the rulers of Kievan Rus' were to consolidate control over this territory, making it one of the strongest and most influential powers in early medieval Europe. This era of consolidation was marked in particular by the successful rule of three charismatic leaders: Volodymyr/Volodimer "the Great," Iaroslav "the Wise," and Volodymyr/Volodimer Monomakh. It is their reigns as grand princes of Kiev, which spanned more than half the era in question (84 of 160 years), that will be of particular concern in this chapter. During the era of consolidation (972–1132), Kiev's grand princes were preoccupied with two problems: (1) to create an administration that could effectively unite and control the vast and expanding territory of Kievan Rus'; and (2) to protect the realm from the threat of external invasion, especially by the nomads of the steppe.

General success in these two areas lasted, albeit with interruptions, until about 1132. Thereafter, internal divisiveness and external threats increased, with the result that Kievan Rus' entered a period of disintegration and gradual diffusion of political authority. The era of disintegration was to last just over a century, culminating during the Mongol invasions of 1237–1240 and the subsequent realignment of political power within the Kievan realm.

The six years between the death of Sviatoslav and the accession of the first of the charismatic leaders, Volodymyr the Great, revealed one of the fundamental problems of Kievan Rus', namely, the transfer of power from one grand prince to the next. Traditionally, the Varangian Rus' rulers treated the lands they controlled as their private property, passing it on to their male offspring. The eldest son, as grand prince, received Kiev; the younger sons, other cities and lands. In order to function, this rudimentary system assumed that the brothers would respect one another's individual patrimonies, and the younger brothers the hegemony of their elder, the grand prince. Instead, conflict between family members proved to be the rule, resulting in internecine warfare following the death of virtually each grand prince. Such conflict took place upon the death of Sviatoslav, and it was to become a typical feature of Kievan political life during the era of so-called consolidation as well as during that of disintegration.

Of Sviatoslav's three sons, Iaropolk, Oleh, and Volodymyr, the eldest, Iaropolk, became grand prince (reigned 972–980). Iaropolk's rule witnessed frequent conflict between him and his brothers, however, resulting in the death in 977 of Oleh, who had been assigned to rule the Derevlianians. Oleh's murder frightened the youngest brother, Volodymyr, who was ruling in Novgorod. Fearing for his own life, Volodymyr fled to Scandinavia. He returned in 980 with a Varangian army, reestablished himself in Novgorod, then turned southward and drove Iaropolk out of Kiev. That same year, Volodymyr had Iaropolk killed and began his long reign as grand prince, until 1015. In the absence of rival claimants to the grand princely throne, Kievan Rus' was spared internecine warfare for nearly four decades.

Volodymyr the Great

Volodymyr I ("the Great," reigned 980–1015) was able to extend the territorial sphere of Kievan Rus' and to enhance its internal cohesion. In contrast to his father, Sviatoslav, who had been interested in expanding southward into the Balkans, Volodymyr concentrated on the lands of the East Slavs, subduing the Viatichians and Radimichians. He also strengthened his realm's frontiers by defeating the Volga Bulgars in the east, by capturing Cherven', Przemyśl, and other borderland cities from the Poles in the west, and by holding back advances from the north by the Jatvingians (Slavic: Iatvigians), a Baltic people related to the Lithuanians living along the Neman River.

In the Varangian tradition, Volodymyr used his numerous legitimate and illegitimate sons as personal representatives throughout his far-flung Kievan patrimony. It was, in fact, during Volodymyr's reign that Kievan Rus' reached its greatest territorial extent, an achievement that prompted the chroniclers to describe his military activity in poetic terms as the "gathering of the lands of Rus'." By Volodymyr's time, the Rus' lands no longer coincided with the homelands of the various East Slavic tribes, but rather with the spheres of influence of the leading commercial and military-political centers, from which they often derived their names. Thus arose the eight lands of Pereiaslav, Chernihiv, Galicia, Volhynia, Polatsk, Smolensk, Rostov-Suzdal', and Novgorod. All were satellites of Kiev and its grand prince, who assigned his offspring to rule as local princes over them. In this regard, Kievan Rus' was not a unified state, but rather a typical medieval conglomerate of various lands or principalities based on a common familial relationship to the grand prince ruling in Kiev (see map 7).

The idea that the realm of Rus' as a whole formed a single entity began to take hold during the reign of Volodymyr the Great, at least among the princely, military, and commercial elite of Kievan society. The very term *Rus'*, which until then had been associated simply with the Varangian princes, now began to take on a new connotation. Rus' came to mean the territories and their inhabitants living under the rule of Volodymyr the Great and his filial representatives. Because of

THE MEANING OF RUS'

Whereas controversy continues to rage over the origin of the term *Rus'*, there is some consensus as to how the term came to be applied to the territory and inhabitants of the Kievan realm. Initially, the term *Rus'* was associated with the ruling Varangian princes and the lands under their control. This meant, in particular, the cities of Kiev, Chernihiv, and Pereiaslav together with the surrounding countryside. The lands within this larger Kiev-Chernihiv-Pereiaslav triangle became the Rus' land par excellence.

Beginning with Volodymyr the Great in the late tenth century and, especially, Iaroslav the Wise in the eleventh century, there was a conscious effort to associate the term with all the lands under the hegemony of Kiev's grand princes. To the concept of Rus' as the territory of Kievan Rus' was added another dimension by the Christian inhabitants' description of themselves collectively as Rus' (the singular of which term was *rusyn*, sometimes *rusych*). Nevertheless, while political and cultural leaders from the various principalities (Galicia-Volhynia, Novgorod, Suzdal', etc.) may have spoken of their patrimonies as part of the land of Rus', they often referred to Rus' in a narrower sense; that is, the triangular area east of the middle Dnieper River surrounding the cities of Chernihiv, Kiev, and Pereiaslav.

Following the end of Kievan Rus' in the second half of the fourteenth century, the successor states which fought for control of the former realm often used the term *Rus'* to describe all the lands that had once been under Kiev's hegemony. The Lithuanians claimed for themselves and conquered what they described as the Rus' lands from Polatsk and Smolensk in the north, to Volhynia and Turaŭ-Pinsk in the center, to Kiev, Chernihiv, Pereiaslav, and beyond in the south. Analogously, the Poles designated Galicia, their mid-fourteenth-century acquisition, as the Rus' land or Rus' palatinate (*Ziemia Ruska* or *Wojewódzówo Ruskie*). By the late sixteenth century, Rus' had come to mean all the Orthodox faithful and the lands they inhabited in the Belarusan and Ukrainian palatinates of the Polish-Lithuanian Commonwealth. Finally, the rulers of the principality of Vladimir-Suzdal' and then Muscovy fused the concept of the Rus' land with the idea of their own Riuryk dynasty (ostensibly descended from the ninth-century Varangian leader Riuryk). For them, Rus' meant not only all the lands already under Muscovy's control, but also other parts of the Kievan heritage that awaited acquisition in the future. In short, by the fifteenth and sixteenth centuries, the idea that Rus' coincided with all the lands of the former Kievan realm of Iaroslav the Wise and his descendants had become firmly entrenched in the political mind-set of eastern Europe.

Another perspective was that of the Orthodox Church and the Byzantine world, of which Kievan Rus' was a part. From the time of the first appearance of Christianity among the Rus', the Byzantine Orthodox Church recognized the office of the Metropolitan of Kiev and All Rus', by which title was meant all the lands of Kievan Rus'. When, in the fourteenth century, Byzantium agreed to the establishment of a second Rus' metropolitanate (the Metropolitanate of Halych in Galicia) to complement that of the Kiev metropolitan, by then resident in Moscow, terms were needed to distinguish the two jurisdictions. The region closest to Constantinople, the Galician metropolitanate, with its six eparchies on the southern Rus' or Ukrainian lands, was called in Byzantine Greek *Mikrā Rosiia* – inner or Little Rus'; the more distant Muscovite jurisdiction, with its twelve eparchies, became *Megalē Rosiia* – outer or Great Rus'.

These distinctions were maintained during the political expansion of Muscovy. Beginning in the early fourteenth century, Muscovite rulers styled themselves grand princes, then tsars, of all Rus' (*vseia Rusii*), and after the mid-seventeenth century their title was reformulated as Tsar of All Great, Little, and White Rus' (*vseia Velikiia i Malyia i Belyia Rusii*). During the first half of the eighteenth century, the old term *Rus'* was transformed into Russia (*Rossiia*), when Tsar Peter I transformed the tsardom of Muscovy into the Russian Empire. Henceforth, the terms *Little Russia* (*Malorossiia*) and *Little Russians* were used to describe Ukraine and its inhabitants under Russian imperial rule.

As for the original term *Rus'*, it was really maintained only in Ukraine's western lands, Galicia, Bukovina, and Transcarpathia, all of which after 1772 were under Austrian rule. The Greek Catholic Church in the Austrian Empire used the term in the title of the restored Metropolitanate of Halych and Rus' (1808). Even more widespread was the use of the term by the East Slavic inhabitants of Galicia, Bukovina, and Transcarpathia, who until well into the twentieth century continued to call themselves the people of Rus', or of the Rus' faith, that is, Rusyns (*rusyny, rusnatsi*).

Besides the Greco-Byzantine term *Rosia* to describe Rus', Latin documents used several related terms – *Ruscia, Russia, Ruzzia* – for Kievan Rus' as a whole. Subsequently, the terms *Ruteni* and *Rutheni* were used to describe Ukrainian and Belarusan Eastern Christians (especially members of the Uniate, later Greek Catholic, Church) residing in the old Polish-Lithuanian Commonwealth. The German, French, and English versions of those terms – *Ruthenen, ruthène, Ruthenian* – generally were applied only to the inhabitants of Austrian Galicia and Bukovina and of Hungarian Transcarpathia. For the longest time, English-language writings did not distinguish the name *Rus'* from *Russia*, with the result that in descriptions of the pre-fourteenth-century Kievan realm the conceptually distorted formulation *Kievan Russia* was used. In recent years, however, the correct terms *Rus'* and *Kievan Rus'* have appeared more frequently in English-language scholarly publications, although the corresponding adjective *Rus'/Rusyn* has been avoided in favor of either the incorrect term *Russian* or the correct but visually confusing term *Rus'ian/Rusian*.

Volodymyr's ability to demand and obtain the respect of his sons, Kievan Rus' experienced a marked degree of political unity for most of his reign.

The efforts toward political unity based on familial ties to the Kievan grand prince were complemented on the ideological front as well. In contrast to his predecessors, who seemed to show only a passive allegiance to their traditional paganism and therefore a general tolerance of differing religions, Volodymyr decided to make religion an affair of state and, by means of it, he hoped, to make his subjects ideologically united and therefore more loyal to Kievan rule. Such a policy was adopted early in his reign, when he established an animistic pantheon based on gods already familiar to the East Slavs (headed by Perun and including Khors, Dazhboh, Striboh, and Mokosh), which he intended to serve as the official state religion. Simultaneously with this development, Kiev witnessed religious discrimination, as Christians and others who were not loyal pagans became subject to persecution.

While the idea of a state religion seemed politically wise, the choice of paganism proved inappropriate. All the surrounding powers with which Volodymyr was familiar had more advanced systems of religious belief and ritual, whether Christianity among the Byzantine Greeks in the southwest and Poles in the west, Islam among the Volga Bulgars in the east, or Judaism among the Khazars in the southeast. The existence of these faiths among neighboring and often militarily strong entities could not help but have an influence on the politically ambitious and astute Volodymyr.

Christianity and the baptism of Rus'

Of the three systems of belief, Christianity was perhaps best known. There was already a strong Christian presence on Ukrainian lands (especially in the Crimea) going back to the fourth century, and in Kiev, Christianity struck roots during the rule of the first Varangians, Askol'd and Dir, in the second half of the ninth century. After a lull in its development, Christianity was revived a century later by Ol'ha/Helena and her immediate entourage, but it was her grandson Volodymyr who was to establish the new religion permanently in Kievan Rus'.

Notwithstanding the medieval chronicles, whose clerical authors emphasized the spiritual conversion of Volodymyr, politics as much as personal inclinations prompted him to reject the recently established pagan pantheon in favor of the relatively more complex Eastern Christianity from Byzantium. At issue for Volodymyr was the possibility of raising the international prestige of Kievan Rus', of developing further commercial and diplomatic links with Byzantium, and of consolidating his own rule over a Slavic-Varangian realm through common loyalty to a church of which he would be the secular guardian. The decision to accept Christianity occurred sometime in the late 980s, following a complex series of events over which there is still disagreement regarding the exact timing and sequence.

In late 987, Volodymyr agreed to come to the aid of the Byzantine emperor, whose throne was being threatened by internal revolt. In return for Rus' military assistance, the Kievan grand prince was to receive a singular honor, the hand in

CHRISTIANITY IN UKRAINE

The famed baptism of Rus' by which Grand Prince Volodymyr the Great accepted Christianity as the official religion of his realm sometime in the late 980s does not mark the first appearance of that religion on Ukrainian territory. The *Primary Chronicle* dates the beginnings of Christianity in Ukraine to apostolic times. According to the chronicle, during the early decades of the common era, St Andrew included in his missionary itinerary a visit to Chersonesus, in the western Crimea, and from there he is said to have traveled up the Dnieper River through Scythia to the hills upon which Kiev was subsequently built.

Whether or not the story of St Andrew is true, written evidence and archaeological remains reveal that Christianity was well established as one of the many religions flourishing in the coastal cities along the northern Black Sea and Sea of Azov during the first century CE. The Crimea and the revived Bosporan Kingdom under Roman hegemony in particular became a refuge for Christians fleeing from persecution. The most famous of these refugees was the fourth pope, St Clement I, who in the year 92 was banished to Chersonesus. He found several thousand Christians in the city and converted many more people to Christianity before he was put to death in 101 on the orders of the Roman emperor. Clement's memory remained alive in Rus' lands, and in 860 his remains were exhumed by the Byzantine missionary Constantine and sent to Rome. Then, in 989, when Grand Prince Volodymyr the Great was baptized and married, Clement's head was sent as a relic to the newly Christianized Rus' leader, whose successors preserved it as a sacred treasure for the next several centuries.

After Clement, Christianity continued to flourish in the coastal cities and the steppe hinterland. The Germanic Gothic tribes who invaded Ukrainian lands in the third century had already accepted some form of Christianity – the Visigoths Arianism, and the Ostrogoths Eastern Byzantine Christianity. Christianity survived on southern Ukrainian lands even after the dispersion of the Goths in 375 by the Huns. Those Goths who remained after the Hunnic onslaught – the Byzantine Christian Ostrogoths – retreated to the Crimean Peninsula. They came to be known as the Crimean Goths, and their capital of Doros, in the central Crimea, became in about 400 CE the seat of the Christian Eparchy of Gothia. Under the jurisdiction of the patriarch in Constantinople, the Eparchy, later the Metropolitanate of Gothia and Caffa, was to survive on the peninsula until the end of the eighteenth century.

Christianity flourished to an even greater degree after the sixth century, when the Crimean coastal cities came under direct Byzantine control. The local Byzantine administrative center, Chersonesus, was the site of many churches, and the whole coastal region became a refuge for Christian dissidents, including Pope Martin I. At the height of the iconoclast controversy, which gave rise to profound political and cultural disruptions in the Byzantine Empire during the eighth and early ninth centuries, many more discontented bishops, monks, and clergy arrived in the Crimea. It was during this expansion of Christianity that in Tamatarcha (later Tmutorokan'), on the eastern shore of the Straits of Kerch, a bishopric was established sometime in the 730s under the jurisdiction of the Archbishop of Gothia at Doros, which was in turn subordinate to Constantinople. Although the Tamatarcha bishopric is not mentioned again until the 970s, in the interim it had come to be inhabited by the Varangian Rus', a development prompting some writers to consider Tmutorokan' the first Rus' eparchy.

With the arrival of the Varangian Rus' in Kiev and their early contacts with Byzantium, Christianity was established in the middle Dnieper region. Following the Varangian attack on Constantinople led by Askol'd and Dir in 860, their Rus' ambassadors to Byzantium were baptized, and they brought the new faith back to Kiev. It is not clear whether Askol'd and Dir themselves ever converted, but the Byzantine patriarch Photius announced in 867 that the formerly feared Rus' were now Christian "subjects and friends" living under the spiritual authority of the Byzantine Empire. In consequence, in 874 the patriarch assigned an archbishop to Rus' (probably to Tmutorokan'). These promising beginnings of Christianity among the Rus' in the Kiev region ended during the reign of Helgi/Oleh in the 880s. Nonetheless, some remnants of the community seem to have survived and even to have grown in the mid-tenth century, a growth culminating in 957 in the baptism of the Rus' ruler Helga/ Ol'ha as the Christian Helena.

Aside from the long-term Christian presence in the southern Ukrainian lands (the Crimea) and the appearance of the faith in the Kiev region during the 860s, Christianity also made inroads in far western Ukraine. This development was related to the activity of the "Apostles to the Slavs," the Byzantine envoys Constantine/Cyril and Methodius, whose mission at various times between 863 and 885 in Moravia, in the heart of central Europe, coincided with the political influence of the Great Moravian Empire. By the second half of the ninth century, the sphere of influence of that empire included far western Ukrainian lands, where the eparchies of Przemyśl (Peremyshl') in Galicia and of Mukachevo in Transcarpathia are reputed to have been established by the Byzantine missionaries in the 890s or, in the more questionable case of Mukachevo, as early as the 860s.

All these observations lead certain authors (M. Chubaty, P. Bilaniuk) to maintain that there has been an unbroken Christian presence on Ukrainian territory from apostolic times, through the official "baptism of Rus'" in about 988, to the present. Accepting this premise, they argue that the Ukrainian church is an apostolic one whose origins go back to the very beginnings of Christianity.

marriage of the Byzantine emperor's sister. Nor was the prize to be just any royal offspring, but one born in the royal bedchamber, literally born into the imperial purple (porphyrogenesis), who might be described more prosaically as someone of "blue blood." Before the marriage could take place, Volodymyr had to be bap-tized and agree to bring his entire realm into the Christian sphere of Byzantine influence.

The sequence of these events has remained a source of controversy to this day. Some scholars argue that local Kievan influences may have prompted Volodymyr to accept Christianity even without Byzantium's political incentive. Moreover, he may have been baptized already, before agreeing to be "re-baptized" in response to Byzantine demands. Finally, there is a question as to whether these events took place in 987, 988, or 989. What we do know is that in 988 Volodymyr supplied mili-tary aid to the Byzantine emperor, who was consequently able to retain his throne. We also know that the Rus' captured the Byzantine city of Chersonesus in the Crimea, an action which probably encouraged the emperor to live up to his side of the political bargain. In the end, Volodymyr the Great returned triumphantly to Kiev in 990, accompanied by his new bride "born of imperial purple."

Volodymyr seems to have wasted little time in exchanging the recently estab-lished pagan state religion for the Christian one. Over a century later, the *Primary Chronicle* described in dramatic detail how the pagan idols were "cast down," some "chopped up and others put in the fire," and how the citizens of Kiev were brought en masse to the Dnieper River to mark the symbolic baptism of Rus'.[1] The construction of numerous churches followed; priests and church books were brought from Byzantium and, later, its other Slavic cultural satellite, Bulgaria; and the Byzantine model of church administration was set up – the basic unit being the eparchy (usually headed by a bishop), with a number of eparchies joined together in a metropolitan province (headed by a metropolitan). Missionary activity began as early as 990, and although there was often fierce local resistance to the new faith, seven new eparchies were established within the next century and a half – Novgorod, Bilhorod, Chernihiv, Turaŭ, Volodymyr-Volyns'kyi, Rostov, and Polatsk (see map 7).

In order to finance this new venture, Volodymyr assigned one-tenth of the state's income to the Christian church. As a result of his activity on behalf of Christianity, Volodymyr the former "libertine" (reputed to have had 800 concubines, accord-ing to the *Primary Chronicle*), together with his no less worldly grandmother Ol'ha, was especially venerated by the Rus' church, and both were consecrated as saints in the thirteenth century. In most subsequent Rus' writings, St Ol'ha/Helena and St Volodymyr have been considered "equals to the apostles."

Despite the aggressive efforts at proselytization begun under Volodymyr the Great, the acceptance of Christianity by the inhabitants of Kievan Rus' spread only gradually. The faith may have taken hold early on in Kiev and other urban centers, but it was to be several more centuries before it took root in the countryside, where pagan traditions continued to flourish. Nonetheless, Volodymyr began a process that provided, via Christianity, an ideological mortar which enhanced the unity of Kievan Rus'. Thus, at the same time that the concept of Rus' was being associated with the territory and inhabitants of the Kievan realm, it was also beginning to take on a religious connotation. In short, being Rus' and being of the Orthodox Christian faith came to denote the same thing.

The association with Christianity served Kievan Rus' well also in its foreign affairs. Because they now shared the same faith and Christian culture and, in theory, recognized the authority of the same "god-anointed" temporal ruler, the Byzantine emperor, the Rus' were finally accepted into the larger sphere of the East Roman, or Byzantine Empire. Closer to home, the introduction of a unified ideology in the form of Christianity helped in the defense against the Pechenegs, who renewed their attacks from the steppes on several occasions toward the end of the century (988, 992, 996, and 997). In the end, Volodymyr turned the Pecheneg threat into a political advantage, by seizing the opportunity to call upon the Christian Rus' people to struggle against the infidels. The inhabitants of Kievan Rus' now had a sense of common purpose – to protect the Rus' nation and faith.

By the time of the death of Volodymyr the Great in 1015, Kievan Rus' had increased its political and ideological control over the various territories of the realm and had enhanced its relationship with Byzantium while protecting and even expanding its borders in the face of conflict with its neighbors to the west, east, and south. But the problem of succession had not been resolved, and conflict among Volodymyr's several sons was to rage for nearly a decade. In this new round of internecine struggle, two of his sons played a role that was to become immortalized in Rus' and East Slavic culture. These were Borys/Boris and Hlib/ Gleb, true Christian believers who, following the principle of non-violence, refused to resist the assassinations carried out against them in 1015 by another of their brother's soldiers. As a result of an unwillingness "to resist evil with evil," the martyrs Borys and Hlib became the first Rus' Christians to be canonized.

Iaroslav the Wise

After nearly a decade of internal conflict, stability returned to Kievan Rus'. Two of the brothers, Iaroslav and Mstyslav, emerged as the strongest contenders. Although Volodymyr's oldest surviving son, Iaroslav, had held the title of grand prince of Kiev since 1019, he had preferred to remain in the north, in Novgorod, where he had ruled during his father's lifetime. Initially, Iaroslav and Mstyslav clashed over control of Kiev and the southern Rus' lands, but in 1026 they reached an agreement and, henceforth, remained at peace, dividing the realm into two spheres of influence roughly along the Dnieper River. Working together, they recaptured the western borderlands (lost during the internecine struggle after Volodymyr's death) from the Poles, and they increased trade with Byzantium. It was also during this period that Tmutorokan' (part of Mstyslav's patrimony) came to play an important role in Kievan Rus' history. As long as the Dnieper trade route was threatened in the open steppe region by the Pechenegs, Kiev's economic prosperity suffered. Consequently, Novgorod and Chernihiv were able for a while to increase their own trade at Kiev's expense. Chernihiv was itself linked to a trade route that went up the Desna and Seim Rivers and across a land portage to the upper Don River. From there, traders could descend the Don, pass through the Rus' fortress at Bila Vezha, and continue across the Sea of Azov to Rus' Tmutorokan', which itself, located on the strategic Straits of Kerch, lay at the juncture of several commercial routes extending eastward to Central Asia and Transcaucasia, and southwestward to Constantinople.

The unity of the Kievan realm was further strengthened in 1036, when Mstyslav suddenly died. Iaroslav now became in fact as well as in name the grand prince and undisputed sovereign of all of Rus', from Novgorod to Tmutorokan'. Known to history as Iaroslav I ("the Wise," reigned 1036–1054), he decided to leave Novgorod and make Kiev once again the realm's political and cultural capital. His first step was to secure the city against the Pechenegs, who in the interim had become victims of the traditional nomadic fate on the steppes. Since the late ninth century, the Pechenegs had been the dominant force in the open steppe between the lower Don and lower Danube Rivers, but now they were being forced out by the Torks, who in turn were being pressured by new invaders from the east – the Polovtsians (also known as the Cumans or Kipçaks/Qipçaqs).

In the face of Tork pressure, the frightened Pechenegs moved north and attempted to capture Kiev itself, but they were defeated in 1036 by a Rus' army led by Iaroslav. This victory over the Pechenegs was to be memorialized in a special way: it was supposedly on the battle site that, in commemoration of an earlier victory in 1019 (also over the Pechenegs), Iaroslav began construction of Kiev's monumental Cathedral of the Holy Wisdom, or Cathedral of St Sophia. As for the formerly feared Pechenegs, some moved farther south and attacked the Byzantine Empire. In 1091, the Pechenegs were crushed by a Byzantine army (in alliance with the Polovtsians), and soon they disappeared as a distinct political force. Some Pechenegs had remained along the Ros' River south of Kiev, which served as the frontier with the steppe. There they joined with the remnants of the Torks and other Turkic groups (driven from the steppe by the Polovtsians) to form a new confederation known as the Karakalpaks. Referred to in the Rus' chronicles as *Chorni Klobuky* (Black Caps), the Karakalpaks along the Ros' River frontier were to remain allies of the Rus' princes.

The Karakalpak experience reveals a lesser-known aspect of Kievan Rus' society. Although the Kievan historical chronicles (and subsequent historians and belletrists) invariably paint the steppe nomads in the darkest of colors as the pagan enemies of the Christian Rus', more often than not the two groups cooperated and interacted at many levels. Certain nomads like the Karakalpaks not only protected the frontier principalities (especially Pereiaslav and Chernihiv) against the attacks of their fellow Turkic Polovtsians, but also played an important role in Rus' politics by marrying into Rus' princely families and serving as mercenaries for various sides in the interprincely feuds that racked the Kievan realm.

In addition to the southern steppe frontier, Iaroslav was concerned with the northwest. There he subdued the Mazovians and Jatvingians, and his son Volodymyr, who replaced him in Novgorod, brought several of the Finnic groups directly under Rus' hegemony. In the far south, however, Iaroslav was less successful. Increased trade with Byzantium caused commercial rivalry and sometimes conflict between Rus' merchants and Byzantine officials. In an attempt to resolve these disputes, in 1043 Iaroslav sent a large fleet to attack Constantinople, but it met an ignominious defeat.

MAP 7

KIEVAN RUS', circa 1054

Rus' land, ca. 800

Sphere of Kievan Rus', 1054

Boundary of Ukraine, 2005

⊙ Seat of principality

‡ Orthodox metropolitan seat

‡ Orthodox eparchial seat

Lake Onega

Lake Ladoga

Gulf of Finland

BALTIC SEA

White Lake

Ladoga

CHUDS

ROSTOV-SUZDAL

Lake Peipus

Novgorod

Lake Ilmen

Pskov

Volga

LITHUANIANS

NOVGOROD

Western Dvina

Rostov

Suzdal'

Neman

Vladimir

Polatsk

SMOLENSK

Kliazma

Murom

IATVIGIANS

POLATSK

Smolensk

Oka

Riazan

Sozh

CHERNIHIV

MAZOVIANS

Buh

K I E V

Pinsk

Turaŭ

Desna

Novhorod-Sivers'kyi

POLAND

Volodymyr

Cracow

Cherven'

VOLHYNIA

Liubech

Seim

Chernihiv

PEREIASLAV

Przemysl

Bilhorod

Kiev

Pereiaslav

Zvenyhorod

Iur'iev

Ros'

GALICIA

Terebovlia

KARAKALPAKS

Dnieper

Don

Mukachevo

CARPATHIAN MOUNTAINS

Southern Buh

POLOVTSIANS

Tysa

Dniester

TORKS

Donets'

HUNGARY

Prut

Bila Vezha

PECHENEGS

SEA OF AZOV

Kuban

Danube

CRIMEA

Tmutorokan'

Doros

Chersonesus (Korsun')

Preslav

BLACK SEA

BYZANTINE EMPIRE

Constantinople

Scale 1 : 14 400 000

0   50   100 miles

0   50 100 kilometers

Whether or not Iaroslav was always successful against his foreign neighbors, he consistently carried out a policy of marital diplomacy. His western European ties were especially strong. His second wife, Ingigard, was the daughter of the king of Sweden (Olaf); of his daughters, Anastasia was married to the king of Hungary (András I), Elizabeth to the king of Norway (Harold the Stern), and Anna to the king of France (Henry); and of his sons, Iziaslav was married to the daughter of the king of Poland, Sviatoslav to the sister of the bishop of Trier, in Germany, and Vsevolod to a Byzantine imperial princess. By means of these marital ties, Kievan Rus' became well known throughout Europe.

Iaroslav is remembered not only for his military victories and diplomatic initiatives but also for the beautification of Kiev. During his reign, five major buildings were erected: a new citadel with its monumental entrance, the Golden Gate; three churches (the Annunciation above the Golden Gate, St George, and St Irene); and, most important in the whole medieval cityscape of Kiev, the Cathedral of the Holy Wisdom, or Cathedral of St Sophia. Finally, Iaroslav enhanced the sense of unity throughout Kievan Rus' that had begun to develop under his father, Volodymyr the Great. He did so by means of the church, creative writing, and law.

In negotiations with Byzantium, Iaroslav was able to secure from the ecumenical patriarch in Constantinople – the ultimate authority in the Eastern Christian world – the appointment of a metropolitan (initially all were Byzantine Greeks) to head the Rus' church based in Kiev. In contrast to previous decades, there does exist concrete documentary evidence about three prelates who held the office of Metropolitan of Rus' (Greek: Rhōsia) during the period of Iaroslav's reign. Kiev's metropolitan was also given two assistant bishops (based in the new eparchies of Iur'iev and Bilhorod, near Kiev), and another eparchy was created in Pereiaslav. The Byzantine-Rus' war that began in 1043 had an effect on church relations, however, and Iaroslav felt obliged to challenge the jealously guarded influence of the Byzantium Empire as exerted through its ecclesiastical representatives. In 1051, the grand prince successfully arranged for the election of Ilarion, a loyal Kievan intellectual, as the first native of Rus' to become metropolitan.

To promote Rus' intellectual life as well as to instill a sense of political unity, Iaroslav commissioned the preparation of historical chronicles tracing the history of his realm from earliest times to the present. A further sense of common social order throughout the Kievan realm was encouraged by his commissioning the preparation of a law code. Known as the *Ruskaia Pravda/Pravda Russkaia*, or *Rus' Law*, this compilation of mostly common law was, in an otherwise brutal era, noted for its mild punishments, which consisted of various kinds of payment instead of imprisonment or death. Because of his diplomatic skills, cultural interests, and codification of the first written law code in any Slavic land, Iaroslav came to be known in Rus' history as "the Wise."

Iaroslav hoped to impart some of his wisdom to future generations, and in the last years of his life he tried to put some order into the process of the succession and transfer of political power, the settling of which had destabilized Kievan Rus' following the death of each grand prince. His solution was to group the lands of

THE KIEVAN SYSTEM OF POLITICAL SUCCESSION

From the time of their very first appearance in eastern Europe, the Varangians treated the regions that came under their control as private property to be passed on to their offspring. Although in theory priority was given to the eldest son, in practice brother fought against brother until the strongest won. Scholars have debated what the actual system of succession was or whether there was any system at all.

Grand Prince Iaroslav the Wise tried to lessen familial antagonism by defining the order in which his successors should follow him. According to his testament, recorded in the *Primary Chronicle*, he assigned to each of his surviving sons in the order of their age (and therefore of their prestige) one or more of the Kievan Rus' lands as his patrimony. The most important were (1) Kiev and Novgorod, for the eldest son, Iziaslav, who became grand prince; (2) Chernihiv (together with Tmutorokan'), for Sviatoslav; (3) Pereiaslav and Rostov-Suzdal', for Vsevolod; (4) Smolensk, for Viacheslav; and (5) Volhynia, for Ihor. Not mentioned in Iaroslav's testament were two other lands: Polatsk, which had been ruled by Iaroslav's older brother (Iziaslav) and which continued to be ruled by his descendants; and Galicia, which was eventually ruled by the Rostyslav dynasty, that is, the descendants of Iaroslav's grandson Rostyslav. In each of the lands or groups of lands, Iaroslav's "sons and grandsons" created local dynasties and power bases, while at the same time expecting to become the grand prince when their turn came in the order of lateral succession.

Lateral succession meant that at the death of the grand prince, the Kievan seat did not go to the eldest son of the grand prince, but rather to his first brother according to the order of rank in the list of seven principalities. In theory, only after all the brothers from one generation had passed from the scene did the next generation have its turn, beginning with the eldest son of the original grand prince. The principle of lateral or horizontal succession to the Kievan realm as a whole clashed, however, with the practice of vertical succession from father to son that was followed in each of the local principalities, where a prince more often than not strove both to retain his individual patrimony and to obtain the title of grand prince of Kiev.

The confusion and conflict between the principles of lateral and of vertical succession prompted Grand Prince Volodymyr Monomakh to convene in 1097 a conference of princes at Liubech. The conference abandoned the complex principle of lateral succession and accepted the practice of vertical succession, essentially transforming Kievan Rus' into a federation of independent principalities. Yet even this agreement was soon challenged, since Monomakh himself, whose own patrimony was Pereiaslav, crossed dynastic lines and accepted in 1113 the grand princely throne of Kiev. In effect, he returned to the old ideal of establishing a single (Monomakh) dynasty, as most of the principalities of Kievan Rus' were ruled directly either by him or by his offspring. Upon the death of the charismatic Monomakh in 1125 and his eldest son in 1132, however, the absence of any strong grand prince saw Kievan Rus' revert to a state of affairs in which brother fought brother and nephew fought uncle in a vain attempt to gain political and military superiority in an environment that continued to be without any orderly principle of political succession. By the era of disintegration beginning after 1132, whatever tenuous political unity still existed in Kievan Rus' was based on the fact that each of the realm's component parts (the number of lands had increased from nine at the death of Iaroslav the Wise in 1054 to twelve in the twelfth century) was ruled by a descendant of one of the many branches of the family of Iaroslav the Wise.

Only much later, in the late fourteenth century, did the concept of a single Riuryk dynasty (the Riurykids or Riurykovyches) begin to be discussed. The Riurykid concept was evolved by Muscovite chroniclers who were anxious to prove that the Muscovite branch of the family was descended in a direct line from Riuryk, the semi-legendary ninth-century "founder" of the dynasty, through Iaroslav the Wise, Volodymyr Monomakh, and the junior branch of the Monomakh dynasty, whose princes (Iurii Dolgorukii and Andrei Bogoliubskii) ruled what had become the Grand Duchy of Vladimir-Suzdal'. Eventually, that duchy was replaced by one of the younger cities on its territory, which became the new center of the Riuryk dynasty, Moscow. Despite this framework for explaining the transfer of political-dynastic power, it should be remembered that the concept of a Riuryk dynasty was never considered in Kievan times. The rulers of Kievan Rus' spoke of themselves simply as the sons, grandsons, and great-grandsons of the eleventh-century grand prince Iaroslav the Wise.

Kievan Rus' into five patrimonies, each to be assigned to one of his sons, with a sixth land (Polatsk) ruled by his brother. The eldest son became the grand prince of Kiev, to be followed after his death by the other sons in a defined order of succession. At the same time, each of the sons built up his own dynasty on the lands given to him as his patrimony.

Despite Iaroslav's admonishment to his sons that they "love one another" and "dwell in amity" under the direction of the eldest, Grand Prince Iziaslav I (reigned 1054–1078), and despite his efforts at establishing a system of succession, conflicts arose among Iaroslav's descendants almost immediately. Those conflicts were to disrupt the Kievan realm for nearly a half century. The situation was only made worse by the appearance of a new threat from the south, the Polovtsians, who had dominated the steppe since driving out the Pechenegs earlier in the century. Aware of the dissension among the Rus' princes (in which the nomads themselves were often allied with one Rus' prince against another), in 1061 the Polovtsians decided to attack Kiev directly. For nearly a decade, they were able to roam at will and to ravage the Kievan Rus' countryside, especially the border regions of the Pereiaslav and southern Kiev principalities. Not only did the Polovtsian attacks ruin the agricultural base of the economy in the borderlands (whose population was either killed or deported as slaves), by the end of the eleventh century they had effectively cut off Kievan trade with Byzantium, whether down the Dnieper River or down the Donets' River and via Tmutorokan'. After 1094, Tmutorokan' and after 1117 Bila Vezha were permanently severed from the Rus' lands to the north. Both came under Polovtsian and Byzantine influence until destroyed by the Mongols in the thirteenth century.

The conference of Liubech and Volodymyr Monomakh

The Polovtsian danger and the inconclusive results of the continuing interprincely feuds prompted five of the Rus' princes to meet in 1097 at Liubech, a small town north of Kiev. There, at what came to be known as the conference of Liubech, the princes agreed to recognize the existing assignment of lands to their present rulers and offspring. In the words of the *Primary Chronicle*, each prince swore to "hold his own patrimony" and not to cross over local dynastic lines, while together they were to "preserve the land of Rus" and defend it against the Polovtsians.[2] They also agreed to hold future councils to decide on subsequent differences that might arise among them.

In the spirit of cooperation called for at Liubech, and under the leadership of the dynamic prince of Pereiaslav, Volodymyr Monomakh, the Rus' princes were able to defeat the Polovtsians on three occasions between 1103 and 1111. As a result of these victories, the Polovtsian threat was eliminated for the next half century. The Liubech example also served as a model for the resolution of interprincely quarrels at similar conferences that were held from time to time.

Nevertheless, despite the best intentions, the order agreed to at Liubech, whereby each prince would remain within his own domains, was short-lived. In 1113, following the death of Grand Prince Sviatopolk II (reigned 1093–1113), the city assembly (*viche*) of Kiev decided to invite the hero of the wars against the Polovtsians, Volodymyr Monomakh of Pereiaslav, to rule over them. At first he hesitated, for fear of disrupting the dynastic agreements reached at Liubech, which he himself had supported. But after riots broke out in Kiev that threatened the wealthy social strata, the monasteries, and the deceased ruler's widow, he accepted the offer and he ruled as grand prince Volodymyr II Monomakh (reigned 1113–1125). After acquiring the title of grand prince, whose realm included the principalities of Kiev, Turaŭ-Pinsk, and Novgorod, Monomakh still retained his original patrimony of Pereiaslav and through his offspring ruled in Smolensk and Rostov-Suzdal'. In effect, most of the principalities of Kievan Rus' were under the control of one ruler.

Volodymyr Monomakh was the last of the three outstanding, charismatic rulers of Kievan Rus' during the era of consolidation. In an effort to strengthen his authority in the city of Kiev and throughout the Rus' realm, Monomakh did away with the practice of charging excessive interest rates and codified the Expanded Version of the *Rus' Law* of Iaroslav the Wise. Also, like Iaroslav the Wise, Monomakh extended his own family's ties to western Europe (his wife was a daughter of the last independent Saxon king in England), and he improved relations with Byzantium, which had worsened in recent decades. All these factors, combined with the peace on the Polovtsian steppe, contributed to make the reign of Volody-myr Monomakh one of the last periods of stability in Kievan Rus'.

Monomakh hoped to retain the unity of the Rus' realm by returning to the pre-Iaroslav system of succession, that is, by placing his eldest son on the throne of Kiev and his younger sons in other principalities. Initially, this approach worked. His successor, Mstyslav I (reigned 1125–1132), not only maintained order through-out Kievan Rus' but even increased the realm's influence, especially in the Baltic region. After Mstyslav's death in 1132, however, the reign of his brother Iaropolk II (reigned 1132–1139) was marked by a renewal of the internal strife that had already characterized certain periods of Kievan history. The periods of decline in central authority, which during the era of consolidation generally had lasted only a few years between the long reigns of strong rulers like Volodymyr the Great, Iaro-slav the Wise, and Volodymyr Monomakh, grew into decades, until they became the norm during the era of disintegration, which was to last from 1132 to 1240.

The era of disintegration

A symbolic indication of political disintegration was the frequency with which the title of grand prince changed hands. For instance, whereas during the first two and a half centuries of Kievan Rus' (878–1132) there were fourteen grand princes, in the initial three decades of the era of disintegration (1132–1169) there were eighteen. The new era witnessed esssentially two trends: (1) the gradual decline of Kiev as a political and economic center, and (2) the diffusion of power to cent-ers in other parts of the realm. This meant that as Kiev declined three new power centers began to take its place: Galicia-Volhynia in the southwest, Vladimir-Suzdal' in the northeast, and Novgorod in the far north.

In 1136, Novgorod revolted and became independent of the Kiev principal-ity, to which it had previously belonged. Subsequently known as Lord Novgorod the Great, the independent city-republic directed its mercantile interest westward toward the Baltic Sea and northward toward the sparsely inhabited forest regions. On the other hand, Rostov (later, Vladimir-Suzdal') and Galicia-Volhynia partici-pated actively in the struggle for control of Kiev and the grand princely title. Yet while each of the principalities had its own charismatic leader capable of attack-ing and controlling Kiev, those leaders were more interested in remaining within their own domains than residing in the weakened seat of the grand prince. In this regard, the activity of the grandson of Monomakh, Andrei Bogoliubskii, is often considered to epitomize the new era. As ruler of Vladimir-Suzdal', in 1169 he organized a coalition of Rus' princes, who marched on Kiev, captured the city, pillaged and burned many of its churches and monasteries, and killed many of its inhabitants. Indeed, warring Rus' princes had fought for control of Kiev before, but none had treated it as a foreign city in the way Andrei Bogoliubskii did. He shunned the title of grand prince, and unlike most of his predecessors who had sought and gained the prize of Kiev, Bogoliubskii was content at leaving the city to someone else whom he could manipulate, preferring instead to reside in his native principality of Vladimir-Suzdal' in the north.

MAP 8

Sphere of Kievan Rus', 1240
Boundaries of Ukraine, 2005
⊙ Seat of principality and grand duchy
✕ Major Rus'-Polovtsian battle

Lake Ladoga

Lake Onega

Gulf of Finland

BALTIC SEA

White Lake

N O V G O R O D

Lake Peipus

Novgorod

Pskov

Lovat'

V L A D I M I R - S U Z D A L'

• Rostov

Volga

Suzdal'
Vladimir •

Kliazma

LITHUANIA

Western

Dvina

S M O L E N S K

Moskva

Moscow • Murom

Neman

Polatsk

Smolensk

MUROM-
RIAZAN'

POLATSK

Oka

Riazan' •

Buh

Sozh

C H E R N I H I V

POLAND

TURAŬ-PINSK

Pinsk

Desna

Vistula

Styr

Pripet

Turaŭ

Novhorod-Sivers'kyi

San

Horyn'

Chernihiv

Seim

Volodymyr ⊙

Kiev

P E R E I A S L A V

P O L O V T S I A N S

Halych

GALICIA-VOLHYNIA

K I E V
Torchesk

⊙ Pereiaslav

Ros'

• Sharukan'

Dniester

CHORNI KLOBUKY

Dnieper

Balin

Donets'

CARPATHIAN MOUNTAINS

Southern

1111

✕1185

Buh

1103

✕

Don

P O L

Danube

SEA OF AZOV

Kuban

HUNGARY

CRIMEA

Doros

Tmutorokan'

Chersonesus
(Korsun')

BULGARIA

B L A C K   S E A

N I C A E A

Constantinople

SELJUKS OF RUM

Scale 1 : 13 900 000
0   50   100 miles
0 50 100 kilometers

Struggling for Kiev but ruling it from afar was repeated in the first half of the thirteenth century and became the pattern. For instance, Roman of Volhynia gained hegemony over the city in 1200 but remained in his Volhynian homeland. It was during his absence that in 1203 a combined force of lesser Kievan and Chernihiv princes, in alliance with the Polovtsians, attacked Kiev and plundered it so mercilessly that the chroniclers were prompted to report, "Such great evil had not been seen in the Rus' land since the Christianization of Kiev."[3] At the very end of the era of disintegration, Danylo of Galicia captured Kiev (1239–1240), but he too preferred to remain in his native principality, especially in the face of the Mongol threat to the region.

External invasions from the steppe hastened the disintegration of whatever the interprincely warfare had left of Kievan unity. Ever since their three defeats at the hands of Volodymyr Monomakh, the Polovtsians had not dared to attack the Rus'. In the 1160s, however, under their new dynamic leader Khan Konçak, the Polovtsians renewed their raids against the southern principalities, especially Pereiaslav, Chernihiv, and Novhorod-Sivers'kyi. Also from this period dates the 1185 expedition against the Polovtsians led by Prince Ihor of Chernihiv, who was immortalized in the literary work *Slovo o polku Ihorevi*, or the *Lay of Ihor's Campaign*. After the death of Khan Konçak in 1187, many of the Polovtsians moved farther west toward Bulgaria; those who remained in the steppes drew closer to the Rus', serving with them in their interprincely battles and becoming integral (by many marriages, as well as in other ways) in Kievan dynastic politics.

Yet even with the Polovtsian danger eliminated or neutralized, the steppe remained a potential source of danger unless a strong defense could be mounted by a unified Kievan realm. By the first half of the thirteenth century, however, this seemed no longer possible. The decline of the grand prince's authority and the diffusion of political and economic power, especially toward three peripheral regions – Galicia-Volhynia, Vladimir-Suzdal', and Novgorod – had proceeded so far that any return to the era of Volodymyr Monomakh or Iaroslav the Wise seemed impossible. The full transformation of Kievan Rus' into a new alignment of political forces was not to occur until the appearance in 1237 of a new factor in eastern Europe – the Mongols. But before turning to the role of the Mongols in hastening the realignment of Rus' politics, it is necessary to examine socioeconomic and cultural developments in Kievan Rus' from its early years to the mid-thirteenth century.

7

Socioeconomic and Cultural Developments

The political history of Kievan Rus' outlined in the last two chapters emphasized as much the disunity as the unity of the realm. During its first three stages of development, the first (the 870s–972) witnessed the slow growth of the realm outward from the Kiev and Novgorod regions, while the third (1132–1240) witnessed the steady breakdown of any effective political authority over Kievan Rus' as a whole. Only during the second stage, the era of consolidation (972–1132), was there a semblance of political unity, especially during the long reigns of three charismatic grand princes: Volodymyr I the Great (978–1015), Iaroslav I the Wise (1019–1054), and Volodymyr II Monomakh (1113–1125).

The era of consolidation was clearly an exception. It could therefore be argued that most of Kievan Rus' history during its first three stages, and certainly during its fourth stage (1240–1349), is not that of a unified realm or state. Rather, it is the history of several individual lands or principalities, each with its own ruler and each vying for greater independence vis-à-vis its neighbors and vis-à-vis the so-called senior ruler, the grand prince in Kiev. Aside from the general absence of political unity, Kievan Rus' encompassed a vast territory, with regions that differed greatly in geography and in the language of the inhabitants. Tribal distinctions going back to the era of the dispersion of the Slavic peoples also persisted into the Kievan era. All these factors have prompted certain historians and linguists to see already in the Kievan Rus' period of eastern European history a clear indication of territorial differentiation that should be considered as the first stage in the subsequent distinct evolution of the Ukrainian, Belarusan, and Russian peoples.

Notwithstanding certain periods of political unity, therefore, the modern-day observer might legitimately ask why writers continue to discuss the historical experience of Kievan Rus' as a whole instead of tracing the histories of each of its component parts. In a word, is there any justification for considering Kievan Rus' as a single historical unit? Indeed, from the political and perhaps the linguistic standpoint, it may be difficult to do so, but other factors do make it possible to speak of Kievan Rus' as a whole. Despite its geographic extent and internal diversity, Kievan Rus' was remarkably homogeneous with regard to its social structure, legal system, economic order, and cultural life.

Demography and social structure

It is estimated that by the late twelfth and early thirteenth centuries the total population of Kievan Rus' was approximately seven to eight million people. At about the
same time in western Europe, territorially much smaller Germany (the Holy Roman
Empire) also had approximately eight million people, and France about fifteen million. Thus, the population density of Kievan Rus' was very low compared with that
of western Europe. On the other hand, nearly a million people lived in towns and
cities. This meant that 13 percent of Rus' inhabitants were urban dwellers, a percentage much higher than in any contemporary western European country.

    Historians still debate whether it was international trade or the needs of the
internal local economy that caused the rise of towns in Kievan Rus'. There is no
question, however, that their numerical growth was rapid. For instance, whereas
in the ninth and tenth centuries the chronicles refer to only twenty-three towns in
Kievan Rus' (thirteen of them located in Ukrainian lands), by the mid-thirteenth
century there were close to 300. These numbers made an impression on outsiders, with the result that Scandinavian sources refer to Kievan Rus' as the "land of
fortified towns" (*Gardariki*). The vast majority of these towns contained no more
than 1,000 inhabitants, although a few (Chernihiv, Volodymyr, and Halych in
Ukrainian lands; Novgorod, Vladimir-na-Kliazma, Polatsk, and Smolensk farther
north) may have reached between 20,000 and 30,000 inhabitants by the early thirteenth century. By far the largest city was Kiev, which at the height of its economic power during the twelfth century had 8,000 dwellings and 40,000 inhabitants.
This was decidedly more than any other European city. By comparison, western
Europe's largest city, London, did not attain a population of 40,000 until the fourteenth century.

    As for its social structure, the population of Kievan Rus' was essentially divided
into six strata, most of which included several subgroups. Of the six categories,
three could be considered the ruling elite: the grand prince and his family; the
druzhyna and boyars; and the church people. The other three, subordinate strata
were the townspeople, peasants, and slaves.

    It should be kept in mind that the references to these various social strata are to
women as well as to men. Both customary and written law in Kievan Rus' protected
a woman's right to property within the context of the family unit and accorded
her personal protection equal to that accorded men. As a result, women not only
worked alongside men as artisans and farmers, but in the absence of their husbands enjoyed legal rights to administer shops and fields – not to mention the
leadership roles played by women in the princely social strata, who often functioned as regents and, in the case of Ol'ha, as grand prince in her own right.

The ruling social strata

The grand prince of Kiev and his offspring throughout the realm were originally of
Scandinavian origin, as is evident in the names of the earliest rulers – Helgi (Oleh),
Ingvar (Ihor), Helga (Ol'ha), Sveinald (Sviatoslav). By the late tenth century,

The Social Structure of Kievan Rus'

THE RULING SOCIAL STRATA

1 **Princes** (*kniazi*)
the grand prince and his family
regional princes and their families

2 **Prince's retinue** (*druzhyna*) and **boyars**

3 **Church people**
hierarchs
clergy (priests, monks, deacons)
church employees

THE SUBORDINATE SOCIAL STRATA

4 **Townspeople**
merchants
artisans
unskilled workers

5 **Peasants**
freepersons (*smerdy*)
half-free persons (*zakupy*).

6 **Slaves** (*cheliad'/kholopy*)

OTHER SOCIAL STRATA

7 *Izgoi* (persons whose social status had changed)

8 **Frontier military settlers** (Karakalpaks/*Chorni Klobuky*)

the princely strata had intermarried with notables in the local Slavic population with the result that the Varangian element was rapidly assimilated.

At the same time, the number of princes and their families increased. The increase was a result of the practice of dividing the realm among the sons and younger brothers of the grand prince, a practice that took greater hold following the reign of Iaroslav the Wise, when distinct dynasties were established in each of the lands or groups of lands of Kievan Rus'. The princely stratum was made up of all persons who were of royal blood. According to terminology that was to be developed in the fourteenth century and applied retrospectively, this meant persons who were descendants of the semi-legendary Riuryk/Hroerkr and therefore part of the house of Riuryk – the Riurykids or the Riurykovyches.

As a result of intermarriage with members of the local Slavic elite as well as with Byzantine and, later, Polovtsian royal families, the pure Varangian element among the Rus' princes progressively decreased. Nonetheless. Kiev's princes retained the traditional Varangian attitude that the Rus' realm – or, more precisely, that part of it they were able effectively to control – was their hereditary possession (*votchina*), to be exploited for whatever riches it might yield. It is not surprising, therefore, that the early Varangian rulers and their retainers lived apart from the rest of the population, which, like the countryside it inhabited, was perceived as an object for the exaction of tribute and for exploitation. The princes also took an active role in the economy, in regulating weights and measures, and in holding a direct or indirect monopoly over certain industries or trade. Further sources of income included fees for judicial services, customs and transit duties connected with domestic and international commerce, and sales taxes on certain products such as salt. Accordingly, the struggle for control of the various princely posts – in particular the grand prince's throne in Kiev – was often motivated by the desire not only for political prestige, but also for concrete economic advantages.

The next ruling stratum of Rus' society comprised the *druzhyna* and boyars, who formed two distinct groups in the early centuries but became merged into one over time. The *druzhyna*, or prince's retinue, was made up of the leading Varangian warriors, who were closely connected with the Kievan realm. The Varangian element among the *druzhyna* was often renewed as a result of the practice followed by rival claimants to the Kievan throne, especially during the tenth and early eleventh centuries, of inviting soldiers from Scandinavia to participate in the interprincely conflicts. The *druzhyna* might also include local Slavs as well as individuals from the Magyar, Turkic, and other steppe peoples who found favor with Rus' princes. In the second half of the eleventh century, the *druzhyna* began to merge with the boyars, the traditional elite of the local East Slavic population. This merger also coincided with the trend of the *druzhyna* to move away from the princely centers to the countryside, where they acted as administrative officials for and representatives of the ruling princes.

The boyars are described in the early sources as the *luchshie liudi* "better people" or *muzhi narochitie,* "prominent men." They were descended from the ruling groups within the local East Slavic tribes, or were persons who by their wealth or service to the Varangian princes were recognized as among the leaders of society. With the merger of the originally Scandinavian *druzhyna* and the Slavic boyars in the second half of the eleventh century, the group formed a stratum of great landowners. Although the land they acquired was frequently given to them as a reward or payment for services rendered the prince, the boyars had full title to the land as personal property (*votchina*) and were not required to render further service to retain it. A lord-vassal relationship similar to that in some parts of western Europe therefore did not exist between princes and boyars throughout most of Kievan Rus'. Only in the far western Rus' land of Galicia-Volhynia did the pattern exist whereby boyars formed a defined social group bound by mutual agreement in vassalage to the prince, who often granted them lands as fiefdoms. Consequently, a strong boyar class evolved in Galicia-Volhynia that frequently challenged the authority of the princes. In Kievan Rus' as a whole, however, boyar strength depended not on a particular legal arrangement, but on the ability to acquire landed wealth, sometimes along with castles (as in Galicia), fortresses, and armed retinues. In the princely centers, boyar councils (*boiars' ki dumy*) were called from time to time, although they were only consultative bodies that met at the discretion of the prince.

The third ruling stratum consisted of church people. They included not only the clergy, but all those who in some way served the church or its institutions – church singers, candle extinguishers, wafer makers, physicians, and other personnel in hospitals and homes for the aged or for pilgrims. The clergy proper consisted of both the black clergy (monks) and the white clergy (parish priests and deacons).

The church that was established in Kievan Rus' after the official acceptance of Christianity at the end of the tenth century followed the Byzantine model. Initially, most of the clerical personnel at all levels was of Byzantine origin, and the heads, or metropolitans, of the Kievan church were, with few exceptions, also Byzantines. Among the Byzantine features of church organization established in Kievan Rus' were juridical autonomy, the tradition of asylum for persons who lost their social status (the so-called *izgoi*), and, most important, the right of church hierarchs and monasteries to own and exploit landed property. From the outset, the bishops and some monastic communities played an important role in the economic life of towns and cities, often sharing (or challenging) princely prerogatives over the control of weights and measures or over monopolies in the production or processing of certain goods. By the twelfth century, as a result of the growth of the monastic movement and its colonizing efforts throughout the vast Kievan countryside, the church had become one of the leading landowners in Kievan Rus'. During the fourth stage of Kievan Rus' history, under Mongol hegemony (1240–1349), the church increased its wealth even further with the approval of the Mongol rulers, who often chose cooperation with the stabilizing force of the church (whose clergy the Mongols enriched further) rather than with the potentially disruptive secular Rus' princes.

The subordinate social strata

Below the ruling strata were the townspeople, peasants, and slaves. Each of these strata had, in turn, several subgroups. As centers of political as well as economic and religious power, the towns included members of both the ruling and the subordinate strata. Among the ruling groups were the local prince and/or his representatives, boyars, church hierarchs, and rich merchants (*gosti*) of local Rus' or foreign origin (Armenian, Greek, German, and Jewish in Kiev; mostly German in northern Rus' cities).

Most of the townspeople, however, were artisans and workers of various kinds (the so-called *molodshie liudi*, "younger people"). There was also a smaller number of well-to-do people (*zhit'i liudi*) who derived their status from the ownership of artisanal enterprises and who might also be in the service of the princely court. In subsequent writings, these workers and artisans have generally been described as the middle classes. In order to protect their economic interests, they organized into guilds which frequently corresponded with certain sections or streets in the city.

To express their views on political issues, townspeople spoke out at the *viche*, or public town meeting. Meetings took place in the open air of the town square whenever the need arose. While the *viche* never became a permanent or organized body with a fixed number of members, as a political body it played a decisive role at times in the chief cities of Kievan Rus'. For instance, some say it was the *viche* in Kiev that invited Askol'd and Dir to rule over the city in the mid-ninth century, just as it was the *viche* in Kiev that called upon Volodymyr II Monomakh to become grand prince in 1113. The existence of the *viche* and its increasing influence during the twelfth century in the leading cities of Kiev and Novgorod has given rise to subsequent descriptions of Kievan Rus' as a democratic society. In practice, however, the *viche* often became the instrument of only the most powerful elements in the city, the rich merchants. Similarly, the leading urban official, the *tysiats'-kyi*, fluctuated between supporting the interests of the ruling authorities and supporting those of the urban masses. As commander of the city militia (as distinct from the troops of the prince's retinue), the *tysiats'kyi* was originally elected by the townspeople of each city, although eventually the holder of the post was appointed (except in Novgorod) by the local prince, usually from among the boyars.

The largest number of inhabitants in Kievan Rus' were the peasants, who lived in the countryside and were divided into several groups differentiated by their legal status. The so-called *smerdy*, or rural freepersons, lived on their own land or on the land of the princes. They engaged in agriculture and cattle raising. All paid taxes to the prince. Those settled on the prince's land were also expected to provide horses for his troops and to supply men for his army in time of war. The *smerdy* often lived in large communal settlements.

In the pre-Varangian and early post-Varangian eras, these communal units were composed of extended families called *zadruga*, but by the tenth or the eleventh century the familial units had been transformed into territorial units in which the members were united by common social and economic interests. These territorial units came to be known as the *verv* in the southern Rus' lands and as the *mir* in Novgorod and the north. Living in unprotected rural areas, the *smerdy* were the group who most often felt the brunt of the nomadic invasions and, perhaps even more destructive for them, the interprincely feuds. By the time of the era of disintegration (1132–1240), it had become common for a Rus' prince, when attacking his rival, to destroy the rival's livestock, grain stores, and villages and to carry off his peasants, making them slaves and settling them on his own lands or selling them to the Polovtsians. Even the most benevolent of the princes, Volodymyr II Monomakh, was not averse to such practices. Besides the ravages of the Rus' princes and the nomads, local boyars – themselves interested in expanding their landholdings and controlling the rural population – often took advantage of economic or other crises to gain full or partial control over the peasantry. In this way, the interprincely wars and the economic greed of the boyars combined to reduce many *smerdy* from the status of rural freepersons to some degree of servitude or to full slavery.

Among those whose status changed were the so-called *zakupy*, or half-free persons. They included persons, some of whom were peasants, temporarily deprived of their freedom. The reason was often indebtedness, although they could regain the status of freepersons by paying a fee. The numbers of *zakupy* fluctuated. They generally rose during periods of declining economic conditions, which were caused, in part, by the interprincely wars and nomadic invasions. Such periods of economic decline also coincided with efforts on the part of the local boyars to increase the profits from their own landholdings by keeping control over the productive capacity of the *zakupy*. Their control made it even harder for the *zakupy* to attain emancipation or to return to the *smerd*, or freeperson, category.

At the bottom of the social order were the slaves, known originally as *cheliad'* and later as *kholopy*. They were the outright property of their owners and had no rights. Owners were not even held liable for killing slaves. A person other than the owner who killed a slave was liable only to pay the owner a monetary fee, as one would for an animal. The greatest source of slavery was the frequent conflict among boyars and princes, in which the victors often gained warriors captured in battle as well as peasants taken from the lands of the defeated belligerent. The existence of these two kinds of slave contributed to the evolution of temporary and permanent slavery. Captured warriors were considered temporary slaves, whose freedom could be obtained by political agreement. The stolen peasants became permanent slaves with no legal rights unless as individuals they were granted freedom or somehow were able to purchase it from their owner.

Other social strata

At least two groups did not fit into any of the strata in the social order of Kievan Rus'. One of these consisted of the so-called *izgoi*, a heterogeneous body of people, including princes without territory, sons of priests who could neither read nor write, merchants who had gone bankrupt, and slaves who had bought their freedom. In short, the *izgoi* were people whose social status had changed and who therefore did not fit into the existing social order. The *izgoi* often found refuge on church lands.

The other group outside Kiev's social structure were the *Chorni Klobuky*, or Black Caps. These were Turkic peoples from the steppes, such as the Pechenegs, Berendei, and Torks, who had been pushed out of their homeland by the arrival of the Polovtsians in the eleventh century. The Polovtsians, or Kipçaks, set up their own nomadic-sedentary state known as Desht-i- Qipçak (The Steppe of the Kipçaks). It was based in the region between the Donets' and Don Rivers, from which, between the mid-eleventh and mid-thirteenth centuries, the Polovtsians were able to control the Ukrainian steppe as far west as the lower Danube River and Carpathian Mountains. Despite their nomadic lifestyle, the Polovtsians established towns such as Sharukan,' Sugrov, and Balin along the Donets' River, from where they maintained trade and other relations with Kievan Rus'. The Pechenegs, Berendei, and Torks, who were sworn enemies of the Polovtsians, sought refuge in the Rus' lands. Known as the *Chorni Klobuky*, the refugees later formed the Karakalpak federation, which remained loyal to the Rus' princes. These "loyal Turks," referred to in the chronicles as "our pagans" (*svoi paganye*), settled along the southern frontier of Kievan Rus', in the valley of the Ros' River, near the outpost of Torchesk. The *Chorni Klobuky* also had a permanent garrison stationed in Kiev, which together with their frontier forces came to play an important role in Kievan Rus' society, often intervening in interprincely succession disputes and civil wars. The *Chorni Klobuky* along the southern frontier of the Kiev principality, like the politically strong boyars in Galicia-Volhynia, were exceptional phenomena, since most lands throughout Kievan Rus' had the same social structure.

The legal system

Another integrating feature of Kievan Rus' society was the legal system. A legal code was written down in the eleventh century, and it became the standard used by all courts throughout the realm. The result was that, through the legal system, the inhabitants of Kievan Rus' – regardless of which principality they resided in or which prince controlled it at a given time – acquired or were able to recognize a common tradition in which there were certain recognized norms of behavior.

In this regard, the most important development was the codification known as the *Ruskaia Pravda/Pravda Russkaia*, or *Rus' Law*, which was first compiled at Iaroslav the Wise's behest during the mid-eleventh century (the Short Version, with forty-three sections). The code was later supplemented by his successors, especially Volodymyr Monomakh, during the twelfth century (the Expanded Version). The large number of copies of the *Rus' Law* that have subsequently been uncovered suggests that it was widely used and served the practical purpose of allowing judges to render decisions on the basis of commonly accepted norms. In effect, the *Rus' Law* was a compilation of (1) customary law preserved in the form of oral tradition that had been in use in Rus' territory since pre-Varangian times, and (2) princely decrees (in the Expanded Version) formulated in response to specific cases that therefore became supplementary to customary law. The *Rus' Law* contained provisions for civil law (concerning property, obligations, family) and criminal law. The most notable aspect of the criminal provisions was that punishments took the form of seizure of property, banishment, or, more often, payment of a fine. Even murder and other severe crimes (arson, organized horse thieving, robbery) were settled by monetary fines. Although the death penalty had been introduced by Volodymyr the Great, it too was soon replaced by fines.

The *Rus' Law* also reflected the generally equal status accorded women in Kievan Rus' society. The murderer of a woman, for instance, was treated in the same manner as the murderer of a man. In contrast to the practice in several other contemporary European societies, if a wife in Kievan Rus' survived her husband, she was not assigned a legal guardian, but functioned as head of the family and determined (unless it was otherwise stated in her husband's will) when to grant sons their patrimony. When family property was divided, the wife kept and administered her own share.

The economic order

The very rise of Kievan Rus' was directly related to the needs of international commerce. The Varangian princes, beginning with Oleh in the last decades of the ninth century, were primarily concerned with securing control over the lands immediately adjacent to the lucrative north–south trade route, the great waterway "from the Varangians to the Greeks." With this goal in mind, Oleh's successors continued to subdue and periodically to reassert their authority over the various East Slavic tribes along the routes that connected the Baltic Sea to the Black Sea. Accordingly, the importance of international trade as an integrating factor in early Kievan Rus' seems indisputable.

As for the realm's subsequent development, historians so far have been unable to resolve the question of whether international trade (V. Kliuchevskii) or agriculture (B. Grekov) was the mainstay of economic life. Whereas both factors were present throughout Kievan economic evolution, their respective importance varied along with local and, especially, international political conditions. In a real sense, the Varangian Rus' were the successors of the Khazars, in that they continued the tradition of international commerce that linked Central Asia and the Middle East with the markets of Byzantium and Europe. Like the Khazars, the Rus' gained control of the international trade routes, from which they derived income in the form of customs duties paid by merchants and traders. Also, like the Khazars and even the Scythians before them, the Rus' dominated the local East Slavic and Finnic populations, from whom they exacted tribute (especially furs and hides) and, later, taxes.

The products of this international trade remained essentially the same from the time of the Scythians to that of the Khazars and the Varangian Rus'. From the lands of Kievan Rus' came honey, wax, flax, hemp, hides, sometimes grain, and the particularly valuable furs and slaves. These were exchanged for wines, silk fabrics, naval equipment, jewelry, glassware, and art works (especially icons, after the introduction of Christianity) from Byzantium, and for spices, precious stones, silk and satin fabrics, and metal weapons from Central Asia and the Arab Middle East. The basic pattern thus saw Kievan Rus' as a supplier of raw materials, for which manufactured goods, especially luxury items, were received in return.

Trade routes did change, however. The so-called Saracen route along the Volga River, used by the Varangians to connect their bases in the Rostov-Suzdal' region with the Khazar Kaganate and from there farther south across the Caspian Sea to the Middle East, by the late ninth century had been replaced in importance by the Baltic–Black Sea trade route. The goal of the new route, which passed through Kiev, was Byzantium. In good conditions, the trip by boat from Kiev to Constantinople took six weeks.

Beginning in the tenth century, when the Dnieper and Volga trade routes were increasingly threatened by the Pechenegs, and then in the twelfth century, when they were cut off by the Polovtsians, the international trade pattern of Kievan Rus' shifted. Novgorod turned its attention away from the south and toward the economic sphere of the Baltic Sea, trading the products of the far northern Rus' lands (especially furs) directly to northern and western Europe. In the south, the east–west overland route to Galicia increased in significance, especially because Kiev came to depend on Halych for the valuable medieval commodity salt (the basic preservative of food), which after the twelfth century could no longer effectively be brought up the Dnieper River from the Crimea. Aside from its east–west salt route, Galicia was crossed by several international trade routes that connected

The Voyage from Kiev to Constantinople

The exceedingly important political, socioeconomic, and cultural relations between Kievan Rus' and the Byzantine Empire were made possible by the famous great waterway "from the Varangians to the Greeks," which connected Kiev with Constantinople along the Dnieper River and Black Sea. The Byzantine emperor Constantine VII Porphyrogenitus (reigned 913–959) left for his son and successor an invaluable "instructional manual" on how to rule – *De Administrando Imperio* – in which the following description of the Scandinavian-Rus' warrior-traders and their voyages is given:

The *monoxyla* which come down from outer Rus' [i.e., northern Rus'] are from Novgorod, where Sviatoslav, son of Igor, prince of Rus', had his seat, and others from the city of Smolensk and from Teliutsa and Chernihiv and from Vyshehrad. All these come down the river Dnieper, and are collected together at the city of Kiev, also called Sambatas. Their Slav tributaries, the so-called Krivichians and the Lenzanenes and the rest of the Slavonic regions, cut the *monoxyla* on their mountains in time of winter, and when they have prepared them, as spring approaches, and the ice melts, they bring them to the neighboring lakes. And since these lakes debouch into the river Dnieper, they enter thence on to this same river, and come down to Kiev, and draw the ships along to be finished and sell them to the Rus'. The Rus' buy these bottoms only, furnishing them with oars and rowlocks and other tackle from their old *monoxyla*, which they dismantle; and so they fit them out.

And in the month of June they move off down the river Dnieper and come to Vytychiv, which is a tributary city of the Rus', and there they gather during two or three days; and when all the *monoxyla* are collected together, then they set out and come down the said Dnieper River. And first they come to the first barrage [rapid], called Essoupi, which means in the Rus' and Slavonic languages: 'Do not sleep!'; the barrage itself is as narrow as the width of the Polo-ground [a great stadium in Constantinople]; in the middle of it are rooted high rocks, which stand out like islands. Against these, then, comes the water which wells up and dashes down over the other side, with a mighty and terrific din. Therefore, the Rus' do not venture to pass between them, but put in to the bank hard by, disembarking the men on to dry land leaving the rest of the goods on board the *monoxyla*; they then strip, feeling with their feet to avoid striking on a rock. This they do, some at the prow, some amidships, while others again, in the stern, punt with poles; and with all this careful procedure they pass their first barrage, edging round under the river-bank. When they have passed this barrage, they re-embark the others from the dry land and sail away, and come down to the second barrage, called in Rus' Oulvorsi, and in Slavonic Ostrovouniprach, which means 'the Island of the Barrage.' This one is like the first, awkward and not to be passed through. Once again they disembark the men and convey the *monoxyla* past, as on the first occasion. Similarly they pass the third barrage also, called Gelandri, which means in Slavonic 'Noise of the Barrage,' and then the fourth barrage, the big one, called in Rus' Aeifor, and in Slavonic Neasit, because the pelicans nest in the stones of the barrage. At this barrage all put into land prow foremost, and those who are deputed to keep the watch with them get out, and off they go, these men, and keep vigilant watch for the Pechenegs.

The remainder, taking up the goods which they have on board the *monoxyla*, conduct the slaves in their chains past by land, six miles, until they are through the barrage. Then, partly dragging their *monoxyla*, partly portaging them on their shoulders, they convey them to the far side of the barrage; and then, putting them on the river and loading up their baggage, they embark themselves, and again sail off in them. When they come to the fifth barrage, called in Rus' Varouforos, and in Slavonic Voulniprach, because it forms a large lake, they again convey their *monoxyla* through at the edges of the river, as at the first and second barrages, and arrive at the sixth barrage, called in Rus' Leanti, and in Slavonic Veroutsi, that is 'the Boiling of the Water,' and this too they pass similarly. And thence they sail away to the seventh barrage, called in Rus' Stroukoun, and in Slavonic Naprezi, which means 'Little Barrage.' This they pass at the so-called ford of Vrar, where the Khersonites cross over from Rus' and the Pechenegs to Kherson; which ford is as wide as the Hippodrome, and, measured upstream from the bottom as far as the rocks break surface, a bow-shot in length. It is at this point, therefore, that the Pechenegs come down and attack the Rus'.

After traversing this place, they reach the island called St Gregory, on which island they perform their sacrifices because a gigantic oak-tree stands there; and they sacrifice live cocks. Arrows, too, they peg in round about, and others bread and meat, or something of whatever each may have, as is their custom. They also throw lots regarding the cocks, whether to slaughter them, or to eat them as well, or to leave them alive. From this island onwards, the Rus' do not fear the Pechenegs until they reach the river Selinas. So then they start off thence and sail for four days, until they reach the lake which forms the mouth of the river, on which is the island of St Aitherios. Arrived at this island, they rest themselves there for two or three days. And they re-equip their *monoxyla* with such tackle as is needed, sails and masts and rudders, which they bring with them. Since this lake is the mouth of this river, as has been said, and carries on down to the sea, and the island of St Aitherios lies on the sea, they come thence to the Dniester River, and having got safely there they rest again.

But when the weather is propitious, they put to sea and come to the river called Aspros, and after resting there too in like manner, they again set out and come to the Selinas, to the so-called branch of the Danube River. And until they are past the river Selinas, the Pechenegs keep pace with them. And if it happens that the sea casts a *monoxylon* on shore, they all put in to land, in order to present a united opposition to the Pechenegs. But after the Selinas they fear nobody, but, entering the territory of Bulgaria, they come to the mouth of the Danube. From the Danube they proceed to the Konopas, and from the Konopas to Constantia, and from Constantia to the river of Varna, and from Varna they come to the river Ditzina, all of which are Bulgarian territory. From the Ditzina they reach the district of Mesembria, and there at last their voyage, fraught with such travail and terror, such difficulty and danger, is at an end.

SOURCE: Constantine Porphyrogenitus, *De Administrando Imperio*, translated by R.J.H. Jenkins, 2nd rev. ed. (Washington, D.C. 1967), pp. 59–63.

Kievan Rus' with Poland and central Europe toward the west and, across the Carpathians, with Hungary toward the south.

International trade was generally controlled and exploited by the princes and rich merchants. But Kievan Rus' also had a flourishing domestic commerce, one that initially served the rich urban dwellers and the ruling strata, but later attracted peasants from the countryside, who exchanged their agricultural products, cattle, and honey in the local town markets for cloth, metal implements from the local iron industries, and salt from the Crimea and, later, Galicia. The number of domestic handicraft industries continued to grow (scholars debate their number, as being from forty to sixty-four distinct industries), with particular emphasis on building products, military hardware, household implements, religious wares, and the arts.

The relationship between international trade and local agricultural production as the basis of the Kievan economy was directly affected by the changing international situation. In a real sense, Kievan Rus' had become economically and politically important because the traditional trade routes connecting Byzantium and Europe to Central Asia and the Orient through the eastern Mediterranean were disrupted by the rise of Islam and Arab control of the Middle East beginning in the last decades of the seventh century. In this situation, a northern route that connected Byzantium and the Middle and Far East with northern and western Europe was made possible by the Khazars and their successors, the Rus'.

By the twelfth century, however, Arab control over the eastern Mediterranean was ending. The main reasons for the end of Arabic hegemony were internal dissension and the impact of the Crusades, whose leaders in the course of the eleventh century established a European outpost on the eastern shores of the Mediterranean in the form of the Kingdom of Jerusalem. As a result, nearby Antioch and other eastern Mediterranean ports, with their products from the Orient and Middle East, were once again open directly to Byzantium and to western Europe. Italian merchants from Genoa, Pisa, and, especially, Venice (to whom Byzantium gave its trade monopoly in 1082) became the primary beneficiaries of the new international trading pattern. In this sense, regardless of the mid-eleventh-century Polovtsian presence on the Ukrainian steppe that disrupted trade along the Dnieper River, the Baltic–Black Sea route would have declined in importance as a source of wealth for Kievan Rus'.

It is no mere coincidence that the period of disintegration in Kievan Rus' (1132–1240) coincided with the changing pattern of international trade. Faced with this new situation, the ruling strata in Kievan Rus', in particular the boyars, attempted to derive new wealth by controlling larger and larger tracts of agricultural land, the products of which could be sold in the cities and traded for whatever practical and luxury items might be manufactured in the growing domestic industries of Kievan Rus', or might still be imported, especially from central Europe via Galicia. This desire for more land had two effects: (1) a struggle between the boyars and the princes that contributed to general instability and the enslavement of free peasants (*smerdy*), and (2) a slow but inevitable transformation of the economy of Kievan Rus' from one which depended primarily on international trade to one which was based more and more on agriculture.

Byzantine cultural influences

The third and perhaps most influential of the integrating factors in Kievan Rus' was culture. And when speaking of culture it is essential to recall the role of the Eastern Roman, or Byzantine Empire. In a real sense, Kievan Rus' was the cultural child of Byzantium. For the Varangian and East Slavic Rus', as for the many other sedentary and nomadic civilizations in the Balkans and north of the Black Sea, Byzantium was a magnet attracting all those who hoped to capture the imperial capital, New Rome – Constantinople, or to trade with it and live within its culture and economic orbit.

During its more than a thousand years of existence from the fourth to the mid-fifteenth century, the political fortunes of the Byzantine Empire changed many times. After a profound internal crisis (the iconoclast controversy) and the external threat posed by the Islamic Arabs in the east and the First Bulgarian Empire in the Balkans during the eighth and first half of the ninth centuries, the empire's strength was restored, and it entered a new period of revival and prosperity during the second half of the ninth century. The period of revival lasted for almost two centuries (843–1025) and has come to be known as Byzantium's golden age. The empire's territorial extent was stabilized in Asia Minor and in the Balkans south of the Danube River, and its influence was renewed over the southern Italian Peninsula in the west and the Crimea in the northeast. Trade, commerce, and learning flourished to restore the Byzantine Empire as the dominant power in Europe. It was precisely during this golden age that Kievan Rus' came into existence and was drawn into the Byzantine sphere or commonwealth. Having developed within Byzantium's cultural orbit, the religion, literature, architecture, and art of Kievan Rus' were all originally inspired by and often directly based on Greco-Byzantine models.

Acceptance into the Byzantine Commonwealth began with the adoption of the empire's official ideology, Christianity in its Eastern, Greco-Byzantine form. At the beginning of Byzantium's golden age, the empire was able to draw not only the Rus' but also many other Slavic peoples into its Christian fold. Its success was primarily a result of the missionary work between the 860s and 880s of two brothers, Byzantine civil servants, and fervent Christians, Constantine – or Cyril, to use his later monastic name – and Methodius. Not only did they bring the new faith to the Slavs, but Cyril created an alphabet (the Glagolitic) and a written language for them. Although the Cyril-Methodiun missions were initially conducted among the West Slavs, in particular those living in the Great Moravian Empire (the present-day Czech Republic, Slovakia, southern Poland, and northern Hungary), it was among the South and East Slavs that the Byzantine Christian tradition was to have its greatest impact. The original written language created by Cyril and Methodius (called Old Church Slavonic) was derived from Macedonian dialects spoken in the Balkans. It was their disciples, however, who created a new Slav script based on Greek letters that came to be known as the Cyrillic alphabet, which to this day is used by the East Slavic and most South Slavic peoples.

Chapter 5 noted how, in the wake of the Varangian Rus' attack on Constantinople in 866, a Christian mission was established in Kiev and an archbishop

THE BYZANTINE EMPIRE
AND ITS ATTITUDE TOWARD KIEVAN RUS'

The Byzantine Empire comprised roughly the eastern half of the Roman Empire, and after the fall of Rome in ca. 476, it carried on the imperial herit-age for another thousand years, until it fell to the Ottoman Turks in 1453. The terms *Byzantine* and *Byzantium* to describe the empire are of even later origin. The citizens of the empire as well as its rulers always considered and desig-nated themselves first and foremost as Romans (Greek: *romaioi*), even though Byzantium was based along the eastern shores of the Mediterranean Sea and Greek was used as the language of administration and culture.

The Eastern Roman, or Byzantine Empire actually came into being before the fall of Rome, when Emperor Constantine I ("the Great," reigned 306–337) decided to transfer his capital to the east. The site chosen was a small Greek settlement, Byzantion, located on the narrow straits of the Bosporus, which separate Europe from Asia and strategically connect the Black Sea with the Sea of Marmora and eventually the Aegean and Mediterranean Seas. When the new imperial capital was ready in 330, it was renamed Constantinople in honor of the emperor who had had it built, the same Constantine who also made Christianity the official religion of the empire. Hence, the Eastern Roman, or Byzantine, Empire had three basic components: (1) Roman political tradition (with its heritage of written law and authority centralized in a supreme ruler), (2) Hellenic culture (which carried on the tradition of classical Greece), and (3) Christian belief.

During its more than a thousand years of existence, the boundaries of the Byzantine Empire changed often. Its greatest territorial extent was reached in the mid-sixth century under Emperor Justinian I (reigned 527–565), when it encompassed the northern and southern shores of the eastern Mediterranean, including much of the Balkans, Anatolia, the southern Crimea, and the eastern shores of the Black Sea. Byzantium's nadir came during its final days in the mid-fifteenth century, when the empire was reduced to the imperial capital of Constantinople, the Peloponnesos, and a few other scattered urban centers. For nearly a thousand years, however, and in cultural terms even longer than that, the Byzantine Empire continued to influence not only the lands under its direct political control, but also the many civilizations within what the late twentieth-century Russian-British historian Dmitry Obolensky called the Byz-antine Commonwealth. The commonwealth's sphere included many Slavic peoples and Kievan Rus'. The Byzantine impact on Kievan Rus' has perhaps been summed up best by the Ukrainian-American Byzantinist Ihor Ševčenko:

Throughout more than a thousand years of their history, the Byzantines viewed their state as heir to the Roman Empire, which pretended to encompass the whole civilized world. It followed that the Byzantine state, too, was a universal empire, claiming rule over the whole civilized world: that Byzantine emperors were by right world rulers; that the Byzantines were Romans; and that they were the most civilized people in the world. True, they had improved upon their Roman ancestors in that they were Christians; also, by the seventh century the Latin component had all but disappeared from their highbrow culture, which from then on was essentially Greek; but, like ancient Romans, the Byzantines felt entitled to pour scorn on those who did not share in the fruits of civilization, that is, on the barbarians. The best thing these barbarians could do was to abandon their bestial existence, and to enter – in some subordinate capacity of course – into the family of civilized peoples headed by the Byzantine emperor. The way to civilization led through Christianity, the only true ideology, of which the empire held the monopoly. For Christianity – to be more precise, Byzantine Christianity – meant civilization.

Throughout a millennium of propaganda, these simple tenets were driven home by means of court rhetoric – the journalism of the Middle Ages – of court ceremonies, of imperial pronouncements and documents, and of coinage.

By the ninth century, the following truths were held to be self-evident in the field of culture: the world was divided into Byzantines and barbarians, the latter including not only the Slavs – who occupied a low place on the list of barbaric nations – but also the Latins; as a city, the New Rome, that is, Constantinople, was superior to all others in art, culture, and size, and that included the Old Rome on the Tiber. God has chosen the Byzantine people to be a new Israel: the Gospels were written in Greek for the Greeks; in His foresight, God had even singled out the Ancient Greeks to cultivate the Arts and Sciences; and in Letters and Arts, the Byzantines were the Greeks' successors. 'All the arts come from us,' exclaimed a Byzantine diplomat. … The Byzantines maintained these claims for almost as long as their state endured.

SOURCE: Ihor Ševčenko, "Byzantium and the Slavs," *Harvard Ukrainian Studies*, VIII, 3/4 (Cambridge, Mass. 1984), pp. 289–290.

sent to Tmutorokan'. During the next century, not only did Christianity have a limited presence in Kiev, but it was also not entirely clear to which sphere of the Christian world Varangian Rus' converts would give their allegiance. Princess Ol'ha, for instance, was baptized in Constantinople, but later she addressed a request to King Otto I of Germany, who obliged by sending a Latin-rite bishop with jurisdiction over the Rus'. In the end, when her grandson Volodymyr the Great finally decided to accept Christianity, it was to Byzantium that he turned. Therefore, when Volodymyr I made Christianity the state religion at the end of the tenth century, he began a process whereby the extensive Rus' lands were endowed with a unifying ideology based on an imported religion that brought with it the more general influence of Byzantine Greek culture.

As early as during Volodymyr the Great's reign (978–1015), Greek clergy, teachers, and artists came to Kiev, where they firmly established Byzantine models. A debate still continues over the exact ecclesiastical relationship between Byzantium and Kiev during Volodymyr's reign. Was the early Rus' church independent, or did it receive bishops from Byzantium, or Bulgaria, or Rome? Documented evidence indicates that, during the reign of Iaroslav the Wise, the Kievan church was definitively under the jurisdiction of the Byzantine ecumenical patriarch in Constantinople, that its first known head was a Greek (Metropolitan Ioann I), and that many of his successors were Byzantine Greeks.

Byzantine influence was also apparent in the monastic movement. Three types of monastic life were followed in Byzantium: (1) the life of the eremites, one of individual solitude, practiced in part on Mount Athos, along the northern shore of the Aegean Sea; (2) the life of the *lavra*, or hermits, who lived separately and were brought together by an abbot only for Sunday religious services; and (3) the life of the cenobites, in whose monasteries, eventually following the Studite rule, a highly organized and centralized community lived together and practiced identical discipline under the authority of an abbot. The second and especially the third types of Byzantine monasticism were most widespread in Kievan Rus' and took the form of self-administered monasteries headed by an elected head (archimandrite or hegumen), or a smaller number of hermitages (*skyty*) made up of secluded individuals who were ultimately dependent on a larger monastery. The term *lavra* came to mean a large monastery that was self-administered and not under the jurisdiction of a local bishop but rather the highest church authority in the region, in this case the metropolitan of Kiev. Only one such institution existed on Ukrainian lands in Kievan Rus', the Caves Monastery (Pechers'ka Lavra) in Kiev itself.

Of the seventy or so earliest monasteries founded in the Rus' lands before the thirteenth century, almost all were situated in or near cities. Moreover, the importance of monastic establishments was not limited to the religious sphere. They also played a significant role in the economic and cultural life of Kievan Rus'. It was the monasteries that were largely responsible for spreading the Christian faith and therefore the Rus' identity, and it was within monastic walls that chronicle writing and artistic production such as icon painting were undertaken. By far the most influential of the monasteries in Kievan Rus' was the Monastery of the Caves (Pechers'ka Lavra), founded in 1015 just outside of the city of Kiev, along the cliffs on the right bank of the Dnieper River. The Monastery of the Caves played a decisive role in the capital city's economy; it was the primary center of cultural life for all of Kievan Rus'; and it maintained its influence in the realm through the activity of numerous bishops who had been members of its community.

Because of the close relations with Byzantium in the religious and cultural spheres, it is not surprising that the direction of Kievan cultural life was directly affected by events in the great empire to the south. In 1054, soon after the end of Byzantium's golden age, the beginnings of a division occurred between the Eastern and Western branches of the Christian Church, headed respectively by the pope in Rome and the ecumenical patriarch in Constantinople. In that year, the pope accused the ecumenical patriarch of heresy and excommunicated him. To be sure, doctrinal and liturgical differences between the church in the East and West were present ever since the first centuries of Christianity. Much of the recent controversy, however, was related to the question whether any ecclesiastical see had the right to assert the kind of authority claimed by the pope in Rome. The year 1054 marked, therefore, the beginning of a process that was to result in two distinct Christian traditions: the Roman/Latin or Catholic Church in the West, and the Byzantine Greek or Orthodox Church in the East. At first, the divisions between the two Christian worlds were not impenetrable, and clerics, secular rulers, and intellectuals from Kievan Rus' continued to maintain relations with the Latin West. Eventually, however, the differences increased to the point that a substantial chasm was created between the two branches of the same faith. The result was that the East Slavs of Kievan Rus' and its successor states were to remain in the religious and cultural sphere of the Byzantine, Orthodox East.

While it is true that Greek culture reached Kievan Rus' via Byzantium, it was only Greek Christian culture that was of interest to the Rus'. Christian-inspired religious writings as well as Christian models in art and architecture were what dominated the cultural importations from Byzantium, while pagan authors of the Greek classical and Hellenic tradition that were represented in Byzantine humanistic thought remained alien. This is because Hellenism, with its non-Christian inspiration, was from the outset regarded with suspicion and before long was almost totally disapproved of in Kievan cultural circles.

Kievan Rus' architecture

Christian models from Byzantium were sought after, copied, and adapted without restraint. Byzantium's influence is most evident in the architectural style and building techniques (characterized by the use of narrow elongated bricks) of the literally hundreds of churches and monasteries erected in Kievan Rus'. The most outstanding of these was the Church of the Dormition, the so-called Tithe Church (Desiatynna) completed under Volodymyr the Great in 996, and the magnificent Cathedral of the Holy Wisdom, or Cathedral of St Sophia, begun in Kiev by Iaroslav the Wise in 1037. The Cathedral of St Sophia was completed in 1100, and although its exterior has been radically altered over the centuries, the original interior, with its remarkable mosaics and frescoes, is still intact. The Kievan church took as its namesake the ultimate fount of Orthodoxy, the Hagia Sophia in Constantinople.

The monumental Tithe Church and the Cathedral of St Sophia, like all other churches in Kievan Rus', adopted the centralized Greek cross for their basic ground plan. Over the central transept was built a dome, often gilded on the outside, around which were smaller domes. This form was in stark contrast to the basilica plan of western churches, with their long naves, transepts, and towers above their western facades. Kievan Rus' church interiors also followed Byzantine models and were covered with glittering mosaics. The altars were separated from the congregation by a high screen, known as an iconostasis from the images of the saints, or icons, placed on it. The strict rules associated with icon painting were also transmitted from Byzantium and were followed almost slavishly in the monastery workshops of Kievan Rus'.

Kievan Rus' language and literature

In the realm of literature, Kievan Rus' was also inspired by Byzantium, although it soon began to diverge from Greco-Byzantine models. This was first evident in language. The Old Slavonic written language, which evolved from the ninth-century missionary activity of Constantine/Cyril and Methodius in the Balkans, eventually found its way to Kievan Rus'. Old Slavonic writings flourished in the First Bulgarian Empire, which had officially become Christian in 865. When the Byzantines destroyed the First Bulgarian Empire in 1018, several Bulgarian refugees fled to Kiev, where under the solicitous rule of Iaroslav the Wise they continued to propagate the Bulgarian version of what, after taking to itself various local elements, came to be known as Old Slavonic or simply Slavonic. This language served as the linguistic medium of the educated elite, and, most important, it was accepted as a liturgical language by the new church in Kiev, and thereby gained the prestige of a sacred language worthy to be used alongside the other cultured medium, Greek.

Book production first became relatively widespread during the reign of Iaroslav the Wise. He encouraged copyists to translate Greek works, especially historical and hagiographic writings, into Slavonic, and he set up a kind of research and copying center as well as a library at the Cathedral of St Sophia in Kiev. Clearly, the vast majority of the literary production in Kievan Rus' was religion-oriented – whether sermons, monastic statutes, or lives of the saints. Lives of the saints, known as *chetyi minei*, or readings for each month, were particularly popular and appeared in the form of translations from the Greek (*Nicholas the Wonderworker, John Chrysostom, Andrew the Simple*) or of original accounts of Rus' figures. By far the earliest and most popular subjects were Volodymyr the Great's martyred sons, Borys and Hlib, about whom several hagiographical works were written that stressed the need for younger princes to obey their seniors and condemned quarrels between rulers. The didactic and moralistic nature of much of Kievan literature was also evident in the famous *Paterik*, an anthology about the lives of the monks in Kiev's Monastery of the Caves. First begun in the thirteenth century, the *Paterik* remained in manuscript form until it was published in the late seventeenth century.

While religious tracts dominated Kievan literature, there were some works that had a wholly, or at least partially, secular purpose. Among the more important of these are the chronicles, which are still our primary source of knowledge about the period. The best-known chronicle, the *Poviest' vremennykh liet* (Tale of Bygone Years), generally referred to as the *Primary Chronicle*, owes its origin to the desire of Iaroslav the Wise to provide a historical foundation for his policy of unifying and centralizing Kievan Rus'. Begun at the grand prince's court in the mid-eleventh century, it was copied and expanded several times at court and in monasteries during the second half of the eleventh century. A thorough revision was completed in 1113 at Kiev's Monastery of the Caves by the monk Nestor and later twice reworked by his monastic colleagues (ca. 1118 and 1123). It is these last two versions that have come down to us, although only in copies from the late fourteenth

WHAT WAS THE LANGUAGE OF KIEVAN RUS'?

What was the language of Kievan Rus'? is a question frequently asked, although it might be phrased more properly, What were the *languages* of Kievan Rus'? Since the territory covered by Kievan Rus' today encompasses the linguistic spheres of Belarusan, Russian, and Ukrainian, it is often assumed that the answer must be an older form of one or of all three of those languages. Soviet and some western writers even use the term "Old Russian language" (*drevnerusskii iazyk*) to describe the linguistic medium supposedly used in Kievan Rus'. In fact, the language of Kievan Rus' was not Old Russian, nor was it Old Belarusan or Old Ukrainian.

As in most medieval and even some contemporary societies, there were in Kievan Rus' at least two types of language, the spoken and the written. Moreover, within each of these categories there were several variants. The spoken language had different dialects. The written language had various forms, depending on whether it was being used for commercial, administrative, religious, familial, or other purposes.

Of the spoken language, modern scholarship has little direct evidence, since the written sources derive from the tenth century at the earliest and are in a literary medium (Old Slavonic) that was imported into Kievan Rus' and was not based on the local speech. Faced with this source problem, scholars have turned to indirect evidence and have proposed several, often conflicting theories. The controversy concerns two questions: (1) at what time, or during what transitional period, was an existing common Slavic spoken language replaced by the earliest stages of Ukrainian, Belarusan, and Russian? and (2) was the transition direct, or was it preceded by a period during which there existed a common East Slavic or Rus' language, from which, in turn, Ukrainian, Belarusan, and Russian subsequently developed?

Advocates of the second theory – a transition from a common East Slavic or Rus' language to Ukrainian, Belarusan, and Russian – are not in agreement as to the date of the transitional period. Some place it during the tenth and eleventh centuries (A. Kryms'kyi), others in the twelfth (A. Shakhmatov, N. Trubetskoi, N. Durnovo, H. Lunt) or the fourteenth (I. Sreznevskii, T. Lehr-Spławiński) century. Soviet scholarship advanced the view that the supposed Old Russian language (*drevnerusskii iazyk*) spoken by all the East Slavic inhabitants of Kievan Rus' did not begin to be replaced until the rise of the Grand Duchy of Lithuania in the fourteenth century, at the earliest. If that were the case, then the Ukrainian and Belarusan languages could be dated only from the fourteenth century. Some Ukrainian scholars, however (O. Ohonovs'kyi, S. Smal'-Stots'kyi, G. Shevelov), who are advocates of a linguistic continuum directly from a common Slavic language to Ukrainian, place the beginnings of Ukrainian in pre-Kievan times, that is, in the seventh and eighth centuries. Finally, among those who accept the existence of a common East Slavic language, there is debate regarding the number of regional dialects that may have existed. Did these dialects coincide with the early East Slavic tribal divisions, or, alternatively, with the speech areas of what later became Ukrainian, Belarusan, and Russian? Or did they fit some other pattern? In short, apart from the existence of dialectal differentiation, there is nothing definitive that can be maintained about the spoken language of Kievan Rus'.

With regard to written language, the existence of texts allows for less arbitrary opinion, although here, too, there is debate as to how the texts should be classified. One thing is certain: the written language of Kievan Rus' was not based on any of the spoken languages or dialects of the inhabitants. In other words, it had no basis in any of the East Slavic dialects, nor did it stem from some supposed older form of Ukrainian, Belarusan, or Russian. Rather, it was a literary language, known as Old Slavonic, originally based on the Slavic dialects of Macedonia, which were those best known to its creators, Constantine/Cyril and Methodius, in the second half of the ninth century. Old Slavonic subsequently evolved on neighboring Bulgarian lands before being brought in its Bulgarian form to Kiev in the first half of the tenth century.

Following the conversion of Kievan Rus' to Christianity in the 980s, Old Slavonic gradually began to be used in religious and secular writings. Then, in 1037, as part of Iaroslav the Wise's efforts to enhance the cultural prestige of his realm, Old Slavonic was made the official language of the Rus' church. As a sacred language used in church liturgies, Old Slavonic initially retained its Old Bulgarian form in Kievan Rus'. By about 1100, however, several local East Slavic elements had entered this imported literary language. The result was the evolution of a distinct Rus', or East Slavic, variant (recension) of the language, known as Church Slavonic or, simply, Slavonic.

In a manner somewhat analogous to that of Latin in the medieval West, Church Slavonic was also used as a spoken language, especially by the clerical elite of Kievan Rus' society. Whereas by the end of the Kievan period spoken Church Slavonic was limited to clerical circles, as a literary language it was to be used in some form by all the East Slavs – Ukrainians, Belarusans, and Russians – until well into the eighteenth century. Only in modern times, in particular in the nineteenth century, were the spoken languages of the East Slavs, whether Russian, Ukrainian, or Belarusan, gradually raised to a status that made them suitable for use as literary languages capable of replacing the Church Slavonic that had been the language of most writings since Kievan times.

Hence, to the question, What were the languages of Kievan Rus'? several kinds of answer are possible. With regard to the spoken language, informed hypotheses suggest that Slavic linguistic unity among the inhabitants of Kievan Rus' began to break down at perhaps the time of the era of political disintegration during the mid-twelfth century, and that out of this differentiation Ukrainian, Belarusan, and Russian began to take shape in the thirteenth and fourteenth centuries. The written language dates from the tenth century; initially Old Slavonic, an imported linguistic medium based on Old Macedonian and Old Bulgarian, under some local influences evolved into a standard Rus' or East Slavic version known as Church Slavonic.

Finally, the simultaneous existence of at least two distinct languages, literary and spoken, that was characteristic of Kievan Rus' society, set a pattern on Ukrainian lands for many centuries to come. Indeed, much of subsequent Ukrainian cultural development to the twentieth century is the story of the struggle between those leaders who favored the maintenance of a literary "high language" (Church Slavonic, Greek, Latin, Polish, or Russian) and those who preferred to raise the spoken Ukrainian vernacular to a level appropriate for intellectual and literary communication.

century (the Laurentian edition, based on the 1123 version) and the mid-fifteenth century (the Hypatian edition, based on the 1118 version).

Although the *Primary Chronicle* is the most famous, it was only one of many in its genre. Each of the major cities and principalities, including Kiev, Chernihiv, Volhynia, Galicia, and Pereiaslav in Ukraine, had its own chronicle. Some were rather dry compilations of unadorned historical facts, others, like the thirteenth-century *Galician-Volhynian Chronicle,* were interpretive histories (in this case showing the "thievery of the dishonorable boyars") and stylized works of literature. It is interesting to note that the authors of each of the regional chronicles began by reproducing the text of the *Primary Chronicle.* In so doing, the medieval chroniclers, to quote the Soviet Russian literary scholar N.K. Gudzii, consciously revealed "their connection with the interests not only of one given province alone, but of the land of Rus' as a whole."[1]

Undoubtedly, the best literary work associated with Kievan times and an incomparable witness to the high level that Rus' culture had reached in the medieval period is the *Slovo o polku Ihorevi,* or *Lay of Ihor's Campaign.* Its literary qualities are so highly advanced that several scholars since its publication have suspected that it could not possibly have been written at so early a time. The skeptics (A. Mazon, A. Zimin, E. Kennan) have argued that the manuscript (found only in the late eighteenth century and first published in Moscow in 1800) was a forgery by an eighteenth-century East-Slavic patriot, or perhaps by the Czech Slavist Josef Dobrovský, trying to show that ancient Kievan Rus' had attained a level of culture higher than that of contemporary western Europe. Those who have accepted the authenticity of the *Lay of Ihor's Campaign* (R. Jakobson, D. Likhachev, D.Čyževskij) have argued that it was composed soon after the events recounted in the tale took place, and some (O. Pritsak) have suggested that its unknown author was probably a native of Galicia.

The story concerns the real-life exploits of Prince Ihor of Chernihiv, who set out in 1185 from his stronghold of Novhorod-Sivers'kyi, on the Desna River northeast of Kiev, to confront the Polovtsians. Ihor is captured by the Polovtsian khan Končak, who tries to persuade him to be his ally in controlling all of Rus'. But Ihor refuses to accept a political alliance with the heathen Polovtsian enemy, vowing instead to die defending his Christian Rus' homeland. In addition to the obvious attempts of the author to invoke a sense of Rus' patriotism, the work is memorable for its aesthetically impressive poetic descriptions of the steppe and its portrayal of the emotional state of Ihor's wife, who, waiting at home not knowing what has happened to her husband, is psychologically distraught.

The *Lay of Ihor's Campaign* not only shows the high degree to which the civilization of Kievan Rus' had developed, but also – together with other artistic forms, whether architecture, painting, or literature – makes it clear that common goals and cultural aspirations prevailed throughout the medieval Rus' realm. The cultural products, along with the common social structure and economic base of the realm, make it possible to speak of a unified Rus' civilization that began to take shape in the eleventh century and that lasted for another 300 years, whether radiating from its center in Kiev or, as later, evolving within the various principalities of the realm.

THE LAY OF IHOR'S CAMPAIGN

The following excerpt, with the lament of Iaroslavna for her beloved husband Ihor, captures the lyrical beauty of this twelfth-century epic poem.

Iaroslavna weeps at dawn
On the walls of Putivl' city, saying:
   'O Dnepr, son of Renown!
   You cut through the mountains of stone,
   Through the Polovtsian Land!
   You cradled the long boats of Svyatoslav
   Till they reached the army of Kobiak.
   Then cradle, O Lord, my Beloved to me,
   That I may not soon send my tears to him,
   To the Sea.'

Iaroslavna weeps at dawn
On the walls of Putivl' city, saying:
   'O Bright and Thrice-Bright Sun!
   For all you are warm and beautiful!
   Then why, O Lord, did you send
   Your hot rays onto the troops
   Of my Beloved!
   On the waterless plain,
   Why did you warp their bows with thirst
   And close their quivers with sorrow!'

SOURCE: *The Tale of the Campaign of Igor*, translated by Robert C. Howes (New York 1973), p. 48.

8

The Mongols and the Transformation of Rus' Political Life

The year 1240 is traditionally viewed as a crucial turning point in the history of eastern Europe. It is the year in which the Mongols captured and razed the city of Kiev and in which Kievan Rus' is considered to have ceased to exist. In its stead, Mongol rule – described prosaically by latter-day historians as the "Tatar yoke" – had begun. On closer examination, however, it seems that the Mongol presence did not radically change Kievan Rus' society. Rather, it hastened and completed changes in Kievan political and socioeconomic life that had begun nearly a century before the arrival of the Mongols. This process was marked by three trends: (1) the gradual disintegration of Kievan Rus' as a unitary entity; (2) the diffusion of political and economic power away from the center; and (3) the rise of three powerful and independent states from within the former Kievan federation: Galicia-Volhynia, Vladimir-Suzdal', and Novgorod.

The completion of these trends took place during the century following the "fall" of Kiev. During this "Mongol era" of Kievan history, the social and administrative structure of Rus' society remained the same, and local princes, if they recognized the ultimate authority of the Mongols in eastern Europe, were essentially left to rule undisturbed in their local patrimonies as they had done before. This last era of Kievan Rus' history saw a different evolution in each of the three regional successor states. On western Ukrainian territory, the principality, later the Kingdom, of Galicia-Volhynia was to lead an independent existence until 1349. But before examining the specific evolution of Galicia-Volhynia, it is necessary to review the beginnings of the Mongol presence and to examine its general impact on eastern Europe.

The rise of the Mongols

As their name suggests, the Mongols were a nomadic people who originated in Mongolia. In 1206, a local tribal leader named Temujin succeeded in having all the Mongol and Turkic tribes of Mongolia submit to his authority and swear allegiance to him as the new emperor or khan. In his new role, he adopted the name Chinggis (in some English-language writings Genghis, or Chingiz), and he was to become known in history as the Great or Chinggis Khan.

During the next two decades, until his death in 1227, the armies of Chinggis Khan conquered a vast territory stretching from northern China and Manchuria on the Pacific coast in the east, through Mongolia and southern Siberia, to Central Asia and northern Persia as far as the Caspian Sea in the west. The ability to conquer and control this vast expanse of land is attributable to the highly disciplined nature of the Mongol army and administration. In terms of administrative and cultural experience, the Mongols borrowed heavily from the peoples they conquered, in particular the Chinese. Their large armies were led by Mongol generals but composed primarily of soldiers from the lands they subjugated, especially Tatars (originally from the Mongolo-Chinese borderland) and Turkic peoples of Central Asia.

The Mongol armies quickly developed a reputation for invincibility and ferocity. Tales of the massacres of whole cities and regions became widespread in some of the conquered regions, and it became common for western sources to describe Chinggis Khan as the "scourge of humanity."[1] In reality, Chinggis Khan and his successors were not much different from other empire builders in history, and if his Mongol armies carried out brutal destruction, they did so not as an end in itself but as a means of inspiring fear and convincing their enemies that they must submit to Mongol rule or perish. Those rulers who submitted immediately and recognized Mongol rule were usually left to reign over their respective territories, which more often than not even flourished under the new order. The creation of a world empire from China to Europe, therefore, was the goal of Chinggis Khan, not wanton and indiscriminate destruction. Working from the basis of the Mongol power already established, the successors of Chinggis Khan in the mid-thirteenth century were able to expand Mongol rule even farther, southward throughout China and westward toward the Middle East and eastern Europe. Within the vast territory from the Pacific Ocean to Europe, a new era of stability and economic prosperity was created – the Pax Mongolica.

It was not Chinggis Khan but rather his generals and descendants who were to conquer eastern Europe and make large parts of Kievan Rus' subject to the Mongol Empire. Already during the last years of Chinggis's life, a Mongol expeditionary force on its way into northern Persia swung northward across the Caucasus Mountains into the Kuban steppe region. In 1222, the Mongols defeated first the Alans and then the Polovtsians/Kipçaks, continuing their route north of the Sea of Azov into the Crimea, where early in the next year they captured the coastal city of Sudak. In the meantime, the frightened Polovtsians turned to the Rus' princes. Three senior princes (from Kiev, Chernihiv, and Halych) and several junior princes joined the Polovtsians in an offensive attack against the invaders. When, in the spring of 1223, a joint Rus'-Polovtsian army met the Mongol expeditionary force on the Kalka River near the Sea of Azov, after three days of battle it was totally routed.

This disaster on the Kalka for the southern Rus' princes and the Polovtsians had no immediate consequences, however, because the Mongol expeditionary force returned home across the eastern steppe. To contemporary Rus' commentators, the Mongols were just another in the long line of steppe invaders who seemed to vanish as quickly as they appeared. In the words of the chronicles, "We know nei-

MAP 9

THE MONGOL INVASIONS

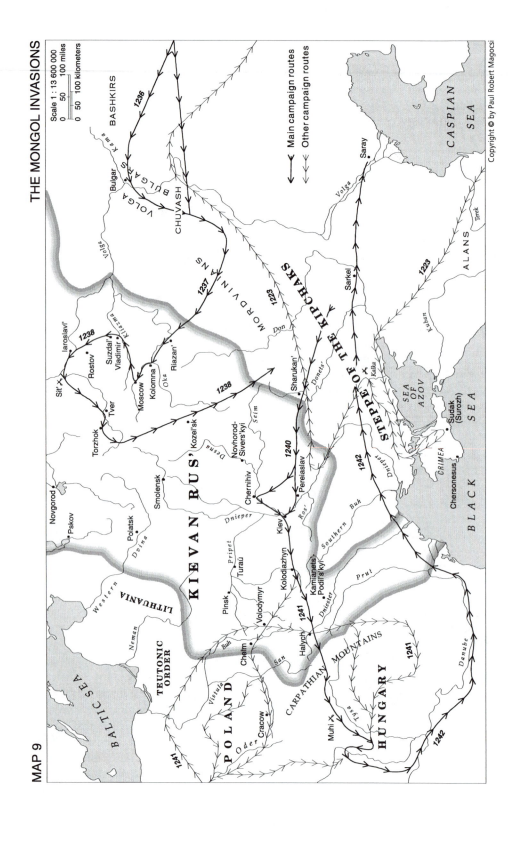

Scale 1 : 13 600 000

0   50   100 miles

0   50   100 kilometers

→ Main campaign routes

↠ Other campaign routes

Copyright © by Paul Robert Magocsi

ther from whence they came nor whither they have gone. Only God knows that, because He brought them upon us for our sins."[2]

The experience on the Kalka River seemed to be an isolated tragedy, and life in Kievan Rus' went on as usual. The unsuspecting Rus' princes even increased their internecine conflict, with the consequence that between 1235 and 1240 alone the city of Kiev changed hands no fewer than seven times. Meanwhile, the Mongols had decided to return, this time with a massive army of between 120,000 and 140,000 troops under the command of Batu, the grandson of Chinggis Khan and ruler of the western part of the Mongol Empire. The first step was to eliminate all possible centers of resistance on the eastern borders of Kievan Rus'. To accomplish this, the Mongols destroyed the Volga Bulgar state in 1236, then sent a force southward to eliminate the Alans in the Kuban Region and the Polovtsians in the Ukrainian steppe. By the end of 1237, the Mongols were ready to turn to the Rus'.

The Mongol invasion of Kievan Rus'

The Mongols began their invasion of Kievan Rus' with a systematic attack on its northern cities. First came Riazan', in December 1237, and it was followed in rapid succession by Kolomna, Moscow, Vladimir, Suzdal', Iaroslavl', and Tver' during the first three months of 1238. Although the way to Novgorod was open, the Mongols decided not to continue westward but instead to turn southward, where they spent nearly the next two and a half years in the steppe region between the Donets' and the Don Rivers. There, in the traditional homeland of the Polovtsians – the Steppe of the Kipçaks – the Mongols prepared for the next stage of their assault on eastern Europe. Of the Polovtsians in their midst, some surrendered and were allowed to become Mongol subjects, some joined the Karakalpaks and other Turkic allies of Kievan Rus' who had settled the frontier district along the Ros' River, and others fled farther westward across the Carpathian Mountains into Hungary, where they were favorably received and Christianized.

Besides eliminating the Polovtsians, during the summer of 1239 the Mongols undertook expeditionary strikes against the southern Rus' principalities of Pereiaslav, Novhorod-Sivers'kyi, and Chernihiv. In October 1239, Chernihiv fell, and during the next year, from their base in the steppes, the Mongols kept close watch over the principality of Kiev and its southern defense system along the Ros' River. Finally, in late 1240, the Mongol army as a whole was ready to resume its march.

After a siege lasting several weeks, Kiev fell on 6 December 1240. The Mongols then moved farther west. Their armies divided: one group proceeded toward Volodymyr, in western Volhynia, and the other southward toward Halych, in Galicia. Both cities fell in 1241 after short sieges. The Mongols then moved farther south and west. The main force in Halych, under Batu, crossed the Carpathian Mountains and entered Hungary. The force in Volodymyr split, moving northward toward the Teutonic Order and westward into Poland. It finally turned southward across Moravia in order to join Batu's main army already in Hungary. The Mongols remained in Hungary until the spring of 1242, when, upon learning of the death of the great khan in Mongolia, Batu decided to return eastward. The Mongol armies started back hurriedly along a route that passed along the southern bank of the Danube, across the Ukrainian steppe north of the Black Sea and Sea of Azov, and, finally, to the lower Volga region. There, Batu established his headquarters near the mouth of the Volga River, in Saray, which before long was to develop into a powerful administrative and commercial center from which the Mongols ruled their eastern European conquests.

The Golden Horde

The political entity created by Batu represented one of four regions or hordes into which the Mongol Empire was divided. The Mongols referred to their farthest western region as the Kipçak/Qipçaq Khanate, a name taken from the Kipçaks, or Polovtsians, some of whom remained after 1238–1239 as subjects of the Mongols. In Slavic and western European sources, the Mongol-led Kipçak Khanate came to be known as the Golden Horde. The Mongols themselves were a small minority, descendants of the 4,000 Mongol troops assigned to the region by Chinggis Khan. Most of the Kipçak Khanate's population consisted of Turkic peoples – descendants of the Polovtsians and, later, the Tatars, who were to form a large portion of the Mongol armies in the west. The original leaders of the Golden Horde, who were Mongol descendants of Chinggis Khan, were eventually replaced by Tatars, who for the next two centuries were able to keep the principalities of Kievan Rus' in direct or indirect subjugation. Each Rus' prince, no matter how strong his principality had become, until 1480 had to submit to the Golden Horde and pay an annual tribute. If a prince rebelled, his lands were likely to be invaded, and his army, at least in the early decades, to be destroyed by the Mongol forces.

If the Rus' princes paid their tribute to the Mongols, however, they were left alone. It is certainly true that during the era of Mongol expansion its generals showed little mercy toward those enemies who resisted and then suffered defeat. But it was not in the Mongols' interest to transform Kievan Rus' into an uninhabited and unproductive wasteland. Even during the Mongol invasions between 1237 and 1241, the actual physical destruction of Rus' towns and cities was probably less than what writers recorded in contemporary and later chronicles. Moreover, when the alarm of imminent attack was sounded, the inhabitants of many towns and cities fled to the countryside, where they remained in safety until returning home after the Mongol armies had passed through on their relatively quick campaigns through the north (December 1237 to March 1238) and south (November 1240 to February 1241).

In essence, life in Kievan Rus' returned to what it had been before the appearance of the Mongols. Those few centers on Ukrainian lands that had been hit directly (Chernihiv, Pereiaslav, Kiev, Kolodiazhyn, Kam'ianets'-Podil's'kyi, Halych, Volodymyr) had to be rebuilt, and the population which had fled to the countryside was temporarily dislocated, but as the English medievalist J.H. Fennell has written: "The same princes ruled the same districts; the same chronicles were kept in the same centers ...; and the same enemies harassed the same segments of the western frontiers."[3]

The fundamental reason for the absence of any profound change was the Mongols' lack of interest in ruling over the lands of Kievan Rus' directly. After all, from their perspective, Kievan Rus' was a peripheral territory not located directly along the lucrative trade routes emanating from Central Asia and terminating along the northern shores of the Black Sea. It seemed best, therefore, simply to hold the Rus' lands in vassalage. The easiest way to do that was to cooperate with the existing ruling elites, who would be expected to render political obeisance and, of course, pay tribute. Initially, the Mongols were particularly successful in co-opting some of the most powerful Rus' princes, such as Aleksander Nevskii of Novgorod and Vladimir-Suzdal' in the north and Danylo of Galicia in the south.

Whereas the Mongols subsequently had mixed success in controlling the Rus' princes (Mykhailo of Chernihiv, the grand prince of Kiev, for instance, was among those who remained recalcitrant in the early days, until his torture and assassination by the Horde in 1245), they seemed to be consistently able to work with the hierarchy of the Orthodox Church. Manifesting their well-known tolerance of foreign religions, the Mongols guaranteed all existing rights held by the church and even extended further privileges. Church lands and individual priests (and eventually their families as well) were exempted from taxes, and church authorities were given the right to judge in civil as well as criminal cases their own clergy and all church people. As a result, the Mongol era in Kievan history witnessed a marked improvement in the status of Orthodoxy. Not only did the church increase its wealth, it also was finally able to complete the process of Christianization, begun "officially" in the late tenth century but made effective in the far-flung countryside only as Orthodoxy expanded its influence under Mongol rule in the late thirteenth century. The new role of Orthodoxy was all the more enhanced, since the Mongols favored the further diffusion of power among the Rus' princes, which left the Orthodox Church as the only real unifying force in an otherwise politically fragmented Kievan realm. It is also interesting to note that in the southern (Ukrainian) as well as in the northern Rus' lands, many peasants and small artisans in the cities willingly subjected themselves to the new Mongol order. After all, the Mongols promised peace and stability in return for an annual payment in grain or other goods. Because at least initially they delivered on their promise, the new order of peaceful stability, the Pax Mongolica, may have seemed for many peasants and artisans, as well as for the Orthodox Church, a welcome change from the interprincely wars and frequent nomadic raids that had marked the previous era of disintegration in Kievan Rus'.

For their part, the Mongols and Tatars of the Golden Horde continued the traditions followed by many of their nomadic predecessors, who had settled on the steppe between the Caspian and Black Seas and had derived their wealth from control of the great international trade routes that passed through the region. The Golden Horde's first capital of Saray, known later as Old Saray (Saray-Batu), and its successor New Saray (Saray-Berke), farther upstream near the bend where the Volga almost meets the Don, served not only as the administrative and cultural center of the Golden Horde, but also as the nexus for trade routes spreading out in all directions. The famous Silk Road from China and passing through Cen-

MAP 10

THE GOLDEN HORDE, circa 1300

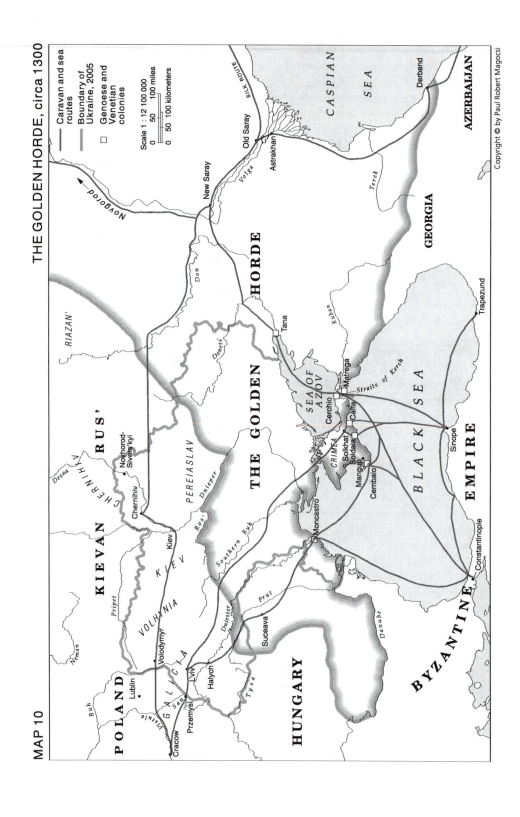

Caravan and sea routes
Boundary of Ukraine, 2005
Genoese and Venetian colonies

Scale 1 : 12 100 000
0   50   100 miles
0 50 100 kilometers

POLAND

Lublin
Cracow
Przemysl
Lviv
Halych
Volodymyr

KIEVAN RUS'

CHERNIHIV
Chernihiv
Novhorod-Sivers'kyi

Kiev

KIEV

VOLHYNIA

GALICIA

HUNGARY

RIAZAN'

PEREIASLAV

THE GOLDEN HORDE

Novgorod

New Saray

Old Saray

Astrakhan

CASPIAN SEA

SILK ROUTE

Volga

Terek

Don

Donets'

Ros'

Dnieper

Southern Buh

Dniester

Prut

Suceava

Moncastro

Danube

Tysa

San

Buh

Vistula

Neman

Pripet

Desna

Derbend

AZERBAIJAN

GEORGIA

Tana

SEA OF AZOV

Kuban'

Matrega
Cerchio
Caffa
Straits of Kerch

CRIMEA

Solkhat
Soldaia
Mangup
Cembalo

BLACK SEA

Sinope

Trapezund

Constantinople

BYZANTINE EMPIRE

Copyright © by Paul Robert Magocsi

tral Asia converged on both Old and New Saray, and from there merchants moved southward along the western Caspian coast to Azerbaijan and Persia; northward up the Volga to the northern Rus' lands of Vladimir-Suzdal' (later Muscovy), Tver,' and Novgorod; and westward to the Crimea, via Tana at the mouth of the Don River and from there across the Sea of Azov to the coastal cities along the Straits of Kerch and Black Sea. Subordinate routes went north from the Crimea across the steppe to Chernihiv, Kiev, and Galicia and from there westward to central Europe.

The Pax Mongolica and Italian merchants

Under the protection of the Pax Mongolica, the old Khazar trade pattern from the Far East to the Byzantine Empire, which had been disrupted for several centuries by Kievan Rus', was now restored. The Crimea was part of the Mongolo-Tatar Golden Horde, and its coastal cities were to be once again revived, this time under the leadership of Italian merchants from Venice and, especially, Genoa. In 1266, the Mongols allowed the Genoese to build some warehouses at the former Bosporan Kingdom port of Theodosia, which soon came to be known as Caffa. Within a few decades, Genoese and, to a lesser degree, Venetian influence spread throughout the region, with the result that among the old centers of the Bosporan Kingdom, Panticapeum/Bospor became Vosporo/Cerchio, Tanais became Tana, Hermonassa became Matrega, and Sugdeia became Soldaia. The Genoese also controlled Cembalo, on the southern coast of the Crimea, and farther west they revived the Rus' port of Bilhorod, at the mouth of the Dniester River, under the name Moncastro. All these cities became not only markets for international trade, but also centers of local manufacturing and crafts.

The main center for the Caspian-Black-Mediterranean Sea trading network was Genoese-controlled Caffa (today Feodosiia). Caffa grew rapidly and by the last decades of Genoese rule in the second half of the fifteenth century it had over 70,000 inhabitants. Like the other cities in the region, Caffa was inhabited by a heterogeneous mix of Armenians, Greeks, Slavs, Vlachs, Karaites, and Tatars, although its administration was in the hands of about a thousand Genoese, whose trading companies (factories) and bankers maintained good relations with the Byzantine Empire and were directly linked to the economy of their homeland city of Genoa. The Genoese domination in Caffa was symbolically enhanced by the establishment of a Roman Catholic bishopric as early as 1311. The main local industry was shipbuilding, but Caffa's greatest wealth came from its control of the international trade in silks and spices from Central Asia and, later, the more local trade in fish, grains, hides, and slaves, which came from the Mongol-controlled lands of eastern Europe and then were brought on Genoese or Venetian ships to the Byzantine Empire and further on across the Mediterranean Sea to the ports of southern Europe.

Whereas the Genoese were able to reconcile their differences with the Mongol rulers of the Golden Horde and were also able to remove their Venetian rivals from the Crimea, Genoese control of the coastal regions and its dominance over

ITALIANATE CRIMEA AND THE BLACK DEATH

Crimea's port city of Caffa was an economic success story. But international trade requires the movement of all kinds of people and products, some of which turn out to be more dangerous than others.

In the Genoese sea-wall at Caffa, there is a tall gateway. … Six hundred years ago, columns of slaves in irons would enter this gate, and gangs of men carrying bales of Chinese silk shipped across the Sea of Azov from Tana. But one day in 1347, an invisible immigrant made its way under the arch and began to explore Caffa.

The Black Death came to Europe through this gate, the pandemic of pneumonic plague which within a few years had reduced the European population by one-third or more. … The disease must have taken hold among the nomad inhabitants of the Pontic Steppe before it infected the 'Latin' cities of the Black Sea coast. And it had traveled a long way across Eurasia from Manchuria or Korea, carried down the Silk Route by traders, porters, and soldiers to the fringes of Europe and the Black Sea.

The Silk Routes brought wealth, but then death. … Between December 1347 and September 1348, the Black Death had killed three-quarters of the European population in Crimea and the other Black Sea colonies. But it also killed half the population of Venice, the slaves and journeymen as well as the grandees, and suddenly there was a labour shortage. All over Europe … there was a famine of manpower.

.....

Good businessmen do not miss an opportunity. The impact on the slave market was enormous. Everywhere on the Mediterranean littoral, from Egypt to Crete and Spain, the price of foreign slaves rose steeply. Most of Venetian slavers at Tana had died horribly in 1348, but the survivors were rewarded by a boom in demand and prices which roared on for half a century. By 1408, no less than 78 per cent of Tana's export earning came from slaves. Out of their misery, and out of the profit born of the Black Death, one palace after another was raised along [Venice's most prestigious thoroughfare], the Rialto.

SOURCE: Neal Ascherson, *Black Sea* (New York, 1995), pp. 95–96.

maritime trade was to be challenged by another force. Already in the late thirteenth century, a Christian principality called Theodoro arose in the mountainous highlands behind the coastal region. It was based in the region that from the fifth to tenth centuries had been controlled by Crimean Goths and that formed the territory of the Orthodox Archeparchy, and later Metropolitanate of Gothia. Hence, Theodoro is also known in some sources as the Principality of Gothia. From the 1360s the principality's capital was Mangup, the largely inaccessible mountain-top town and former Gothic center of Doros located about halfway between Bakhchysarai and the Black Sea coast. At the time the Theodoro principality was inhabited by a heterogeneous mix of peoples, including Crimean Goths, Byzantine Greeks, Hellenized Alans, Tatars, Kipçaks/Polovtsians, and Karaites.

From their fortified center at Mangup, the princes of Theodoro, who were mostly Byzantine Greeks, in the course of the fifteenth century expanded their realm down to the Crimean coast, where in the far southwest they developed the port of Avlita and immediately above it on the cliffs constructed the fortress of Kalamita (today Inkerman). During the reign of Prince Aleksei (ca. 1405–1455), the Theodorites captured several port cities from the Genoese, thereby expanding their rule along the Black Sea coast from Cembalo (today Balaklava, an eastern suburb of Sevastopol') eastward to Alushta. In essence, from the late thirteenth to the late fifteenth centuries, the classic symbiotic relationship between the steppe hinterland and the coastal cities was reestablished, and an era of stability was accordingly brought to eastern and southern Ukraine under the hegemony of the Golden Horde, the Genoese, and the principality of Theodoro-Mangup.

While the Pax Mongolica restored a degree of stability and economic prosperity in large parts of eastern Europe, often with the active or passive assistance of Rus' princes and clergy, the elite of Kievan society could not help but be ideologically opposed to Mongol rule. The ideological gulf between the Christian Rus' and their Mongolo-Tatar overlords further widened after 1313, when the Golden Horde officially adopted Islam. On account of that gulf, contemporary and subsequent chroniclers describe the Mongols in negative terms, with the result that the image of the "Tatar yoke" still prevails in most histories of Ukraine and other countries of eastern Europe. Furthermore, the decline of Kiev, already well under way before 1240, together with the opposition of some to the new Mongol order, encouraged the departure from Kiev and other southern Rus' cities of certain members of the political, economic, and intellectual elite, who moved either northward to Vladimir-Suzdal' or westward to Galicia-Volhynia. This migration northward and westward was undertaken by only a small proportion of Ukraine's inhabitants, however. It was not a large-scale exodus resulting in the depopulation of the middle Dnieper region, as suggested in the nineteenth-century writings of Mikhail Pogodin and subsequent Russian historians (see chapter 2).

It was, nonetheless, during this last era of Kievan Rus' history that under the watchful eye of the Mongol rulers the gradual realignment of political power among the Rus' lands was completed. In the north, Novgorod continued its separate existence, while within Vladimir-Suzdal' the new city of Moscow soon would become the dominant political force. In the south, Galicia-Volhynia was the only Rus' principality on Ukrainian territory to survive as an independent state.

9

Galicia-Volhynia

The last era of Kievan Rus' history on Ukrainian territory coincides with the rise to prominence of the principality, later the kingdom, of Galicia-Volhynia. It was one of the three new power centers established during the era of political transformation within Kievan Rus', which, in Ukrainian history, can be said to have lasted from the Mongol appearance in the 1240s until the demise of Galicia-Volhynia a century later.

In many ways, Galicia and Volhynia were similar to the other lands of Kievan Rus'. Both were ruled by princes descended from Iaroslav the Wise; their economies were integrated with that of the rest of the Kievan lands; and their religious and secular culture as well as legal and social structures belonged to those of Kievan Rus'. In its historical development, Galicia-Volhynia was a kind of microcosm of Kievan Rus'. Both Galicia and Volhynia experienced periods of political and economic stability made possible by powerful and charismatic princes as well as periods of decline and instability marked by conflict over the transfer of power, civil war, and foreign invasion.

But despite the many similarities between Galicia-Volhynia and the rest of Kievan Rus', there were some differences, in particular with regard to foreign relations, demography, and social developments. Located along the western periphery of the Kievan realm, Galicia and Volhynia were less often subjected to the attacks of the nomadic peoples from the east, who had easier access, for instance, to the Kiev, Pereiaslav, and Chernihiv principalities. In contrast, Galicia and Volhynia were open to invasion from their immediate neighbors – Poland, Hungary, and, later, Lithuania. Also, both principalities, but especially Galicia, were more densely populated than any of the other Rus' lands. This demographic fact, combined with the relative freedom from nomadic raids, allowed for the early growth of a prosperous agricultural economy, which in turn contributed to the existence of a wealthy stratum of landowning boyars. The early princes in Galicia also tended to give more power to their retinues and, later, to the boyars than did the princes in other Rus' lands. Consequently, the political power of the boyars was great, and their strength would have disruptive consequences for Galician political life. Finally, although Galicia and Volhynia, like other Rus' lands, had become part of the

Eastern Christian, Orthodox world, they were bordered by Roman Catholic countries in the west (Poland) and south (Hungary). This meant that the influence of Catholicism would be felt more strongly in these principalities than anywhere else in Kievan Rus'.

The history of Galicia-Volhynia during the Kievan period can be divided into three stages. The first stage began in the 980s, the years for which there is first mention of the territory in the chronicles. It lasted until 1199, the beginning of the second stage, when the heretofore separate principalities, now joined together, struggled to create a stable power base that could ensure internal stability and withstand foreign invasion, especially from their western neighbors. The third stage, from 1238 to 1340, marked the apogee of Galician-Volhynian power, beginning with the reign of Danylo and lasting until the united kingdom was again divided and lost its independence to the two new dominant powers in the region, Poland and Lithuania.

Galicia and Volhynia before their unification

The earliest mention of Galicia and Volhynia appears in the *Primary Chronicle*'s entry for the year 981, which records that "Volodymyr went to the Poles and seized their towns, Peremyshl' [Przemyśl], Cherven', and other towns."[1] The incident reflected Volodymyr the Great's policy of expanding the Kievan realm, especially toward the west, where the main object of contention between the Poles and the Rus' was control of the so-called Cherven' cities (Brest, Chełm/Kholm, Cherven,' Belz) and Przemyśl, along the western borders of Galicia. The Rus'-Polish struggle continued, with the result that during the century following Volodymyr's acquisition these cities changed hands at least five times. This conflict subsequently produced a still-unresolved historical debate. Rus' tradition suggests that the original East Slavic Cherven' settlements (located on both sides of today's Polish-Ukrainian border) were "taken back" in 981; Polish historiography asserts that they were originally part of a Polish political patrimony and simply were "taken away."

The immediate goal of Volodymyr and his successors, however, was to secure control over this economically strategic borderland. The Cherven' cities were directly located along the international trade route that connected Kiev with Cracow and on to Bohemia and the rest of central Europe. Apart from the interest of Kiev's early rulers in controlling eastern Europe's international trade routes, Galician territory was valuable in its own right, because near the city of Halych were salt mines. Salt, as a preservative, was one of the most valuable medieval commodities, and the subsequent salt trade transformed Halych into Galicia's leading city. Some scholars have argued that the very name Halych is derived from the Indo-European word for salt, *hal*. On economic and perhaps linguistic grounds, therefore, Galicia (the Latin name derived from the Rus'-Ukrainian form *Halychyna*) could be considered the "land of salt."

Galicia's strategic and economic value encouraged the princes of Kiev and of neighboring Volhynia to try to extend their control over the area. Volhynia had

MAP 11

TEUTONIC ORDER

LITHUANIA

(ca. 1254)

Toruń

Hrodna

POLATSK

(1251-52)

Vistula

Buh

Brest

TURAŬ-PINSK

Pinsk

Pripet

Turaŭ

Dniepr

Liubech

POLAND

VOLHYNIA

(1252-54)

(1280-1302)

Chełm

Volodymyr

Styr

Sandomierz

Cherven'

Luts'k

KIEV

Cracow

San

Belz

(1238-40)

Kiev

Jarosław

Sanok

Przemyśl

L'viv

Zvenyhorod

Ros'

GALICIA

CHORNI KLOBUKY

Kosice

Halych

Terebovlia

Zbruch

Kamianets' Podil's'kyi

Southern

(1280-1320)

C A R P A T H I A N   M O U N T A I N S

Tysa

HUNGARY

Siret

Prut

Dniester

Buh

GOLDEN HORDE

(1160-1240)

Bilhorod

Danube

to Constantinople

Copyright © by Paul Robert Magocsi

Lands temporarily held by Galicia-Volhynia

‡ Orthodox metropolitan seat

‡ Orthodox eparchial seat

Trade routes

Scale 1 : 6 860 000

0   50   100 miles

0   50   100 kilometers

been assigned in Iaroslav the Wise's last testament to his fifth-oldest surviving son, Ihor. But while Iaroslav before his death in 1054 had given Galicia to his grandson, Rostyslav, the bequeathal was not mentioned specifically in his testament. Its omission, therefore, seemed to justify the claims of both Kiev's and Volhynia's rulers to Galicia. Rostyslav himself was driven from the area, and his three sons, who formed the Rostyslav dynasty, were continually under attack from their Rus' neighbors to the east, especially Prince Ihor and his son David of Volhynia.

It was not until the conference of Liubech in 1097 that the rest of the Rus' princes finally recognized Rostyslavych rule over Galicia. Nonetheless, the Volhynian prince David almost immediately violated the Liubech accord by attacking Galicia again and blinding its ruler (described in great detail in the *Primary Chronicle*). This act so incensed the other Rus' princes that they convened another meeting at Liubech (1100), at which they deprived David of his throne in Volhynia. As a result, in the early twelfth century Volhynia passed to the Mstyslav branch of Volodymyr Monomakh's descendants.

Galicia, meanwhile, was able to survive as an independent principality under the able rule of Volodymyrko (reigned 1124–1153) and his son Iaroslav Osmomysl' ("of Eight Minds," reigned 1153–1187), the two most outstanding princes of the Rostyslav dynasty. It was during the reign of Iaroslav Osmomysl' that Galicia first realized its economic potential. He extended the principality's influence down the Dniester River as far as the Black Sea. This made possible the opening of an important international trade route from the Baltic Sea (via the Vistula and Buh Rivers) across Galicia to Bilhorod, at the mouth of the Dniester, and from there across the Black Sea to Constantinople. Moreover, when in the second half of the twelfth century the Polovtsians effectively cut off access to salt from the Crimea, Kiev's new primary source of that valuable commodity became Galicia.

In political terms, this first period in the history of Galicia and Volhynia was marked by (1) efforts on the part of the princes in both principalities to create their own distinct dynasties (the Ihorevyches in Volhynia and the Rostyslavyches in Galicia), and (2) an ongoing struggle between the rulers of the two principalities, set in motion by the Volhynian princes' claim to authority over what they considered a single Galician-Volhynian patrimony. By the twelfth century, the rivalry between Galicia and Volhynia had worsened, since rulers on both sides frequently were calling for assistance from abroad, especially from Hungary, as well as from the boyars living within the territory of their respective antagonists. The result was an increase in the independence of the boyars vis-à-vis princely authority and frequent invasion by the Hungarians, especially in Galicia.

In 1189, during their invasions from the south, the rulers of Hungary proclaimed themselves kings of Galicia and Lodomeria (the Latin name for Volhynia). Although the Hungarian presence did not last long, the addition of the new title to the Hungarian crown would have important consequences in the future. Not only did it provide Hungary with a pretext for continued expansionist efforts north of the Carpathians during the next century and a half, but six centuries later the claim to Galicia and Volhynia as expressed in Hungary's royal title provided the Habsburg emperors (who upon their accession simultaneously became kings of Hungary) with a legal justification for their annexation of Galicia in 1772.

The unification of Galicia and Volhynia

The second period in the history of Galicia and Volhynia began in 1199, when at the death of their own Rostyslavych prince the politically powerful boyars in Galicia decided to invite their dynasty's enemy, Roman (reigned 1197–1205), the ruler of Volhynia, to rule over them. By accepting the invitation, Roman finally achieved Volhynia's long-term goal of gaining control over Galicia. For their part, the Galician boyars had expected an enhancement of their own political role under the rule of an "absentee" Volhynian prince. In fact, the opposite occurred.

Roman, who had experience as a ruler in Volhynia and, previous to that, in Novgorod, not only founded a new dynasty, the Romanovyches, but also reversed the policies of Galicia's Rostyslavyches. During his short, six-year reign, Volhynia and Galicia were united through his person as the ruling prince of the Romanovyches. He also curbed the power of the boyars, expelled those who opposed him, and promoted the interests of the urban and rural population. On the international front, Roman formed an alliance with Poland and held the Hungarians in check.

The activity of Roman and the presence of a strong Galician-Volhynian power base frightened the grand prince in Kiev. As a result, a coalition of Rus' armies was formed and sent against Galicia-Volhynia. Roman not only defeated his adversaries, but in 1200 captured Kiev as well. But since Kiev by the beginning of the thirteenth century had lost its appeal as a power center, Roman (like Andrei Bogoliubskii of Vladimir-Suzdal' before him) decided to appoint subordinates to rule in Kiev and to return to his more prosperous capital of Halych. It was during Roman's absence that in 1203 the former ruler of Kiev, together with the Polovtsians and Rus' allies from Chernihiv, retook the city, after sacking it even more mercilessly than Andrei Bogoliubskii's coalition had done three decades before. Toward the end of his short career, Roman's alliance with the Poles broke down, and in 1205 he was killed in battle against them. He left only his wife and two very young sons, Danylo and Vasyl'ko, who were as yet unable to rule.

The rest of this second period of Galician-Volhynian history, following the death of Roman, was marked by a power vacuum in the region. Nearly four decades of civil strife followed, which paralleled the breakdown of order that was occurring in the Kievan realm as a whole during its era of disintegration before 1240. In Galicia-Volhynia, a complicated series of events unfolded that were dominated by internal rivalry between princes and boyars and by frequent foreign invasion. The period can be explained in terms of the four principles that guided what might be called the political program of the Galician boyars: (1) to oppose the establishment of any kind of hereditary princely dynasty; (2) to block especially Roman's son Danylo, who enjoyed popularity among the masses; (3) to put up various pretenders to the princely throne, thereby weakening the prestige of the position; and (4) to allow the role of the prince to be nominal at best, with real power resting in the hands of the boyars. Attempting to implement these principles, the Galician boyars first drove Roman's widow and two sons from the region. Then they invited other Rus' princes to accept the princely throne; sided at different times with invading armies from Hungary, Poland, Lithuania, and Novgorod; and in 1214 even placed one of their own (a boyar named Volodyslav Kormyl'chych) on the throne. This was the only instance in Kievan Rus' history in which someone not of royal blood, that is, not a descendant of Iaroslav the Wise, ruled one of the Rus' principalities.

Meanwhile, Danylo, who had been five years old at the time of his father's death in 1205, had grown to manhood and had attempted twice to regain his throne (1230–1232 and 1233–1235). He had already become known for his courageous participation in the first battle against the Mongols on the Kalka River in 1222. Finally, in 1238 Danylo returned to Halych. He succeeded in regaining his throne, and for the next quarter century he was to remain ruler of a reunified Galician-Volhynian realm. With this third and final accession of Danylo to princely power in 1238, the last period of Galician-Volhynian history began.

While the Mongols were ravaging the northern Rus' lands, Danylo was left alone to unite his own patrimony. He even expanded eastward, taking control of Kiev on the eve of the Mongol attack in late 1240. As we saw in chapter 8, when the Mongol armies finally began their advance across the southern Rus' lands, they passed rapidly through Galicia-Volhynia in early 1241 on their way to Poland and Hungary. Because Poland and Hungary were weakened by the Mongol incursions, Danylo was able to exclude both these powers as well as Lithuania in the north from further interference in Galician affairs.

In order to restore prosperity in his realm after forty years of interprincely war and foreign invasion, Danylo introduced a policy whereby foreigners, especially Armenians, Germans, Jews, and Poles, were invited to settle in his realm, particularly in the cities, to which they brought their advanced artisanal and commercial skills. The resultant peace and stability also made possible a renewal of Galicia's salt trade and a revival of its role as a commercial emporium located between eastern and central Europe.

Although he never acknowledged it, Danylo was actually helped in his activity by the Mongols. After the Golden Horde's Khan Batu returned from Mongolia to his headquarters at Saray, near the mouth of the Volga River, he turned his attention to establishing Mongol administrative control over eastern Europe in cooperation with those Rus' princes who could be made to see the advantages of the new Pax Mongolica. Danylo was potentially one such leader, and in 1246 Batu demanded that he appear in Saray to make his obeisance. Because the khan knew of Danylo's bravery in battle against the Mongols at the Kalka River and was aware of the Rus' prince's firm control over Galicia and Volhynia, Danylo was treated with great respect even though he had to pledge himself a vassal of the Mongol ruler. Danylo's pride and that of his military entourage was deeply wounded, however. In the words of the *Galician-Volhynian Chronicle*: "Oh, the greatest disgrace is to be thus honored by the Tatars. Danylo Romanovych, the great prince who ruled the land of Rus' – Kiev, Volodymyr, and Halych – and other lands with his brother, is now on his knees and is called a slave!"[2]

For their part, the Mongols approved of Danylo's rule in Galicia-Volhynia. And the Poles and Hungarians in their turn were impressed with Danylo's stature in the eyes of the all-powerful Mongols, who only a few years before had ravaged both Poland and Hungary. Danylo was even given the responsibility of collecting the Mongol tribute, a function that in the early years of Mongol rule was almost always carried out by the khan's personal representatives (*baskaki*). Thus, what Danylo perceived as personal humiliation, others – in particular his western rivals – viewed as a great political victory. In retrospect, his decision to submit to the Mongols played an important role in ensuring Galicia-Volhynia's strength and prosperity.

Nonetheless, Danylo was dissatisfied, and almost immediately he made plans for a crusade against the Golden Horde. His strategy was to neutralize his neighbors and to organize a coalition that would include forces from western Europe. First, he transformed his former enemies – Hungary, Poland, and Lithuania – into allies, mostly through the establishment of marriage ties. Then, in 1245, he began negotiations with the pope, requesting support for his anti-Mongol coalition as well as recognition of royal status. As part of these negotiations, Danylo, the Galician church hierarchs, and some of the boyars indicated a willingness to acknowledge the pope as head of their church. These developments culminated in 1253, when a papal delegation was sent to crown Danylo King of Rus' (*rex Russiae*), whereby he was recognized as a full-fledged monarch in the context of the western European feudal order.

But the Mongols became suspicious of Danylo's ventures in foreign policy and began fomenting discontent both among those Rus' boyars who opposed Danylo's Roman Catholic orientation and among the Turkic *Chorni Klobuky*, who lived along Galicia-Volhynia's southern frontier region. Danylo suppressed this movement in 1254, and two years later he even ousted the Mongol troops from northern Podolia and eastern Volhynia. The khan was not about to accept such insubordination, however, and in 1259 he sent a large Mongol army (under Burunday) to reassert his authority over this recalcitrant Galician Rus' prince. The Mongols raided freely throughout Galicia and Volhynia, and they forced Danylo to join them in a campaign against Lithuania as well as to dismantle the fortifications he had built around several of his cities (Volodymyr, Luts'k, Kam'ianets'-Podil's'kyi, and L'viv).

Disheartened by the lack of support in the West for his anti-Mongol crusade (as a result of which he repudiated any further Roman Catholic influence in his realm) and faced with the bitter fact that he was still a vassal of the Mongol khan, Danylo died in 1264. But it must be reiterated that the policy of submission to the Mongols, a policy he had personally despised, made it possible for his kingdom to prosper for most of his reign and thus to remain, along with Vladimir-Suzdal' and Novgorod in the north, one of the three leading Rus' states to evolve from the Kievan federation during the realignment of political power that culminated after the Mongol invasion.

The long reign of Danylo's son, Lev (1264–1301), was marked by a renewal of the stability in the Galician-Volhynian Kingdom that had begun to break down during the last years of his father's rule. This stability was owing to Lev's conduct as ruler in fulfilling his duties to the Mongol khan and in maintaining the alliance with Hungary formed by Danylo. It was also during Lev's reign that L'viv (founded by Danylo in 1256) was made the capital of the kingdom.

The prestige attained by the kingdom was also reflected in the high level of Galician-Volhynian culture during the thirteenth-century reigns of Danylo and Lev. The founding of new cities and the fortification of several older centers encouraged an extensive program of civil and church architecture. Examples of the latter included several churches (no longer standing) in Danylo's temporary capital of Chełm and the strongly western-influenced Church of St Nicholas in L'viv. From this era also derives the most poetic and stylized of Rus' historical writings, the *Galician-Volhynian Chronicle*, begun at the initiative of Danylo. The literary qualities of this thirteenth-century work seem to continue the tradition of generally high standards set earlier, and some scholars suggest that the *Lay of Ihor's Campaign*, the famous epic poem attributed to the previous century, was likely composed by a native of Galicia.

The metropolitanate of Rus'

Galicia-Volhynia's rulers were deeply concerned with ecclesiastical affairs. In this regard, they followed in the footsteps of Kiev's greatest leaders, Volodymyr the Great and Iaroslav the Wise, who had understood the value of religion as a means of forging ideological unity throughout the vast Rus' realm. Their desire to achieve the conceptual merger of territorial and religious identities was realized as Christianity finally took root in the countryside during the last era of Kievan history, after 1240. More and more it became evident that one was of the Rus' land because one was of the Rus' faith, and vice versa. This convergence of religious and territorial identities, which in modern times was transformed into a national identity, was of particular importance in Galicia-Volhynia, which bordered on Roman Catholic countries.

Because of the degree to which the church contributed to the political and cultural outlook of medieval Kievan Rus', the question of where the head of that church, the metropolitan, would reside was of the greatest importance. His presence lent significant prestige to the local secular ruler. Beginning with the first known Rus' metropolitan, the Greek Ioann I, who was in office during the first decades of the eleventh century, all the heads of the Orthodox Rus' Church resided in Kiev. This tradition continued until the 1240s and the aftermath of the Mongol invasions, at which time the metropolitan of Kiev disappeared during the fall of the city.

Danylo was then ruling in Galicia-Volhynia and, well aware of the political value of the church, he proposed that the new metropolitan be a native of Galicia, specifically Cyril, the bishop of Chełm. With Danylo's support, Cyril (reigned 1243–1281) was elected metropolitan of Kiev in 1243, although it was not until 1251 that he traveled to Constantinople in order to be consecrated in his new post by the ecumenical patriarch, the ultimate authority of the Rus' church. The ecumenical patriarch agreed to Cyril's election, but on the condition that he not reside in Galicia, because Danylo had been negotiating with the pope. Barred from Galicia by his ecclesiastical superior, Cyril was unenthusiastic about returning to Kiev. There, the political situation remained as unstable as it was before the Mongol invasion. In other words, the frequent changes in Kiev's rulers (or their absence) placed in jeopardy the metropolitan's regular income, something that was traditionally guaranteed by the grand prince himself. This consideration prompted Cyril to move to one of the new power centers other than Galicia, namely, the grand duchy of Vladimir-Suzdal' farther north and its capital of Vladimir-na-Kliazma, where he resided for long periods of time and was assured of greater political stability and a steady income. Despite Cyril's absence, Kiev remained the nominal seat of the metropolitan. In contrast to Cyril, his successor Maksym the Greek (reigned 1283–1305), while maintaining the title of Metropolitan of Kiev and All Rus', left the city in 1299 and settled permanently in Vladimir-na-Kliazma the following year. In turn, Maksym's successor moved once again, this time from Vladimir to Moscow, which after 1326 became the permanent residence of the Kievan metropolitanate.

It is therefore the year 1299 which can be seen to mark the final demise of Kiev as the center of the Rus' realm. Its decline had gone through various phases. By the first half of the twelfth century, the city had lost its preeminence as the economic center of Kievan Rus'. Then, political authority had become diffused during the period of disintegration (1132–1240), and it had gradually been reconsolidated in three new power centers – Galicia-Volhynia, Vladimir-Suzdal', and Novgorod – during the hundred years after 1240. Finally, during this last period of realignment of political power (1240–1349), Kiev lost its cultural preeminence as symbolized by the departure (temporarily after the 1240s, permanently after 1299) of Kiev's metropolitans and the permanent transfer of the residence of the Rus' church to the north (1326).

At the same time, the rulers of the other power center in the Rus' lands, Galicia-Volhynia, were reluctant to see the metropolitan's office, with its great symbolic value, slip from their grasp. Consequently, their goal was to create, if possible, a new metropolitanate. From the standpoint of the ecumenical patriarch in Constantinople, a division of the Rus' church was not necessarily advantageous, but that consideration had to be weighed against the threat of Roman Catholicism, which, in the absence of a metropolitan on the southern Rus' or Ukrainian lands, might make new inroads into the Orthodox Rus' realm. The ecumenical patriarch therefore eventually supported the establishment of a Galician metropolitanate, which came into being in 1303. Of the fifteen eparchies at the time in the Kievan metropolitanate, the six within what Constantinople called Little Rus' (Halych, Przemyśl, Volodymyr-Volyns'kyi, Luts'k, Chełm, Turaŭ) were placed under the new metropolitan of Galicia, with his seat at Halych. This meant that by the beginning of the fourteenth century Galicia-Volhynia not only was a politically strong and economically viable state, but also it had the cultural prestige that came with being the seat of an Orthodox metropolitanate.

The demise of Galicia-Volhynia

But at the very moment of its seeming apogee, the Galician-Volhynian kingdom entered a period of decline that proved to usher in its final demise. The last of the Romanovyches – Iurii I (reigned 1301–1315) and Lev II (reigned 1315–1323) – introduced an anti-Mongol policy which prompted increasing attacks by the khan's forces. Finally, in the absence of a male successor, a Roman Catholic prince (Bolesław, of the Romanovyches on the female side) acceded to the throne. In an attempt to assuage his subjects, Bolesław converted to Orthodoxy and took the name Iurii II (reigned 1323–1340).

Iurii II tried to restore the strength of the kingdom by bringing in foreign advisers, especially from the Germanic Teutonic Order along the Baltic Sea, and by introducing the German model of administration in the cities. This model was embodied in the so-called Magdeburg Law, according to which cities were allowed their own legal system and self-government and thus were protected from the interference of the prince or boyars. The establishment of the Magdeburg Law in two Galician cities (Sanok in 1339; L'viv in 1356) set a pattern that was continued during the rest of the fourteenth century and that had a beneficial impact on the region's economy. In Galician tradition, however, the still-influential land-based boyars resented Iurii's urban policies and his dependence on foreign advisers. Moreover, they continued to suspect him of sympathizing with Roman Catholicism. In 1340, several boyars formed a conspiracy and poisoned their ruler.

Galicia-Volhynia was now plunged into several decades of internal anarchy and foreign invasion. The boyars offered the throne to a duke from Lithuania (Liubartas), but he was immediately challenged by Hungary and, in particular, by Poland, which at the time was under its most successful medieval ruler, Casimir III ("the Great," 1333–1370). Casimir's armies led two major military campaigns against Galicia-Volhynia (1340 and 1349), and for the next half century fought with Lithuania and at times with Hungary for control of the former Rus' kingdom. The Lithuanians under Duke Liubartas managed to get a foothold in Volhynia, but it was not until after Casimir's death in 1370 that they managed to secure control over that territory. At the outset of the fifteenth century Volhynia became a distinct principality within the Grand Duchy of Lithuania. As for Galicia, by 1387 Hungary was no longer willing or able to enforce its claims, with the result that it became part of the Kingdom of Poland.

With the fall of the Kingdom of Galicia-Volhynia after 1340, the last independent political entity on the territory of Ukraine to embody the heritage of Kievan Rus' ceased to exist. The other two power centers within the Kievan realm, Vladimir-Suzdal' and Novgorod, would survive, but in a different form. During the fifteenth century, one of the cities of Vladimir-Suzdal', Moscow, became a powerful duchy in its own right. It eventually annexed the other parts of Vladimir-Suzdal', Novgorod, and other northern Rus' principalities to form a Muscovite state. The new duchy and later tsardom of Muscovy had already acquired the seat of the Metropolitanate of Kiev in 1326; by the end of the fifteenth century it was claiming all of Kievan Rus' as part of its inheritance. Muscovy was to use this claim as an ideological justification for its subsequent expansion to the south and west.

Meanwhile, the southern Rus' or Ukrainian lands beyond Galicia-Volhynia remained nominally under the hegemony of the Golden Horde's Pax Mongolica. In the second half of the fourteenth century, however, the power of the Golden Horde in eastern Europe would be effectively challenged for the first time, by a new state, the Grand Duchy of Lithuania. That state's attempt from the 1340s to gain control of Volhynia marked the beginning of a process that after a half century would see the incorporation of most Ukrainian lands into Lithuania. The fall of Galicia-Volhynia, then, marked the beginning of a new era in Ukrainian history, the course of which would be determined by the destinies of the Grand Duchy of Lithuania and, subsequently, the Kingdom of Poland.

PART THREE

The Lithuanian-Polish-Crimean Period

10

Lithuania and the Union with Poland

The disappearance of the Galician-Volhynian Kingdom in the mid-fourteenth century heralded the beginning of a new era in eastern European history and in Ukrainian lands in particular. The Pax Mongolica, which had allowed for a high degree of self-rule in the old lands of Kievan Rus' under the nominal hegemony of the Golden Horde, was to be successfully challenged for the first time by a new power, the Grand Duchy of Lithuania. Before the end of the fourteenth century, most Ukrainian lands that had been part of Kievan Rus' had been incorporated into Lithuania. Unlike the Golden Horde, Lithuania was to undergo a gradual process of internal change that eventually would alter the Rus' lands under its control. Therefore, Kievan Rus' and the Kievan period in Ukrainian history ended not with the invasions of the Mongols in 1237–1241, but with the arrival of the Lithuanians a century later.

The consolidation of the Lithuanian state

The Grand Duchy of Lithuania began its rise to power in the 1230s, at which time a prince named Mindaugas (reigned ca. 1240–1263) succeeded in uniting several Lithuanian tribes and the land called Samogitia (Lithuanian: Žemaitija) into a feudal state. Closely related to though distinct from the Slavs, the Lithuanians had lived since prehistoric times along the eastern coast of the Baltic Sea and in the inaccessible swamps and forests along the valleys of the Western Dvina and Neman Rivers. Although the Lithuanians were in close contact with the neighboring East Slavic tribes, they were outside the orbit of Rus' culture and remained pagans.

Rus' princes, beginning with Volodymyr the Great (983), had fought from time to time against Lithuanian and other Baltic tribes, especially the Jatvingians. The first real threat to the Lithuanians came, however, not from the east, but from the west. In 1226, a Roman Catholic duke of Mazovia, in northern Poland, who felt threatened by a neighboring Baltic tribe, the pagan Prussians, invited German knights and other adventurers returning from the Crusades in the Christian Holy Land to spread their missionary zeal along the shores of the Baltic Sea. The Knights of the Teutonic Order arrived in 1233 along the lower Vistula River,

MAP 12

THE EXPANSION OF LITHUANIA

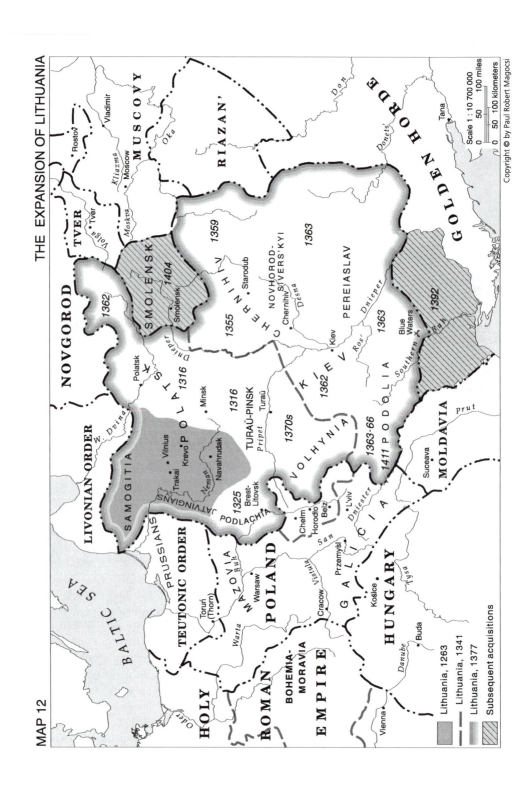

Copyright © by Paul Robert Magocsi

Scale 1 : 10 700 000

0   50   100 miles

0   50   100 kilometers

Lithuania, 1263

Lithuania, 1341

Lithuania, 1377

Subsequent acquisitions

setting up their stronghold at Thorn/Toruń. Filled with the fervor of religious fanatics and still smarting from their expulsion from the Holy Land by the Saracens at the end of the twelfth century, the Teutonic Knights turned their energies toward northern Europe. By the 1270s, they had exterminated most of the Prussian population. The knights were now ready to turn to other Lithuanian and Baltic tribes farther east. In fact, they had the Lithuanians almost surrounded, since in 1202 another Germanic knightly order had come into existence in Livonia, just north of Lithuania. In 1237, this Livonian Order became a branch of the Teutonic Knights.

It was the threat posed by the Teutonic and Livonian Knights in the west and north that prompted the Baltic tribes to unite under Mindaugas in the 1230s and to expand toward the south and east. Their expansion brought them into conflict with the Rus' princes of Polatsk, with the Poles, and then with Danylo of Galicia-Volhynia. Like Danylo, the politically astute Mindaugas also negotiated with the pope, adopting (if only temporarily) Roman Catholicism and receiving a crown in 1254. This politically inspired act brought temporary peace with the Christian Teutonic and Livonian Knights – even if the mass of Lithuanians remained pagan – and it allowed Mindaugas to direct his attention further southward. There, however, he was confronted by Danylo, who through military force, diplomatic alliances, and dynastic marriages kept Mindaugas from achieving at least one of his goals, the acquisition of Volhynia.

The policy of expansion southward was carried on by the successors of Mindaugas, especially Gediminas (reigned 1316–1341), who became founder of the dynasty of Lithuanian rulers known as the Gediminids. Not only did Gediminas add to the rest of his realm the Polatsk principality, the Brest and Podlachia regions of northwest Volhynia, and the Turaŭ-Pinsk principality (that is, most of present-day Belarus), he also was the first Lithuanian ruler to encroach directly upon the Golden Horde's sphere of influence. As early as the 1330s, a Lithuanian prince ruled in Kiev, although his was a kind of joint stewardship with the Golden Horde, in that he ruled under the supervision of a Tatar official. It soon became evident, however, that from his new capital at Vilnius Gediminas was not content with sharing authority over the lands of old Rus'. In anticipation of future territorial acquisition, Gediminas assumed as his title "King of Lithuania and Rus'" (*Lethewinorum et Ruthenorum rex*).

Lithuania, however, was not the only claimant to the territorial heritage of Kievan Rus'. The northern city of Moscow, which had developed from the Rus' principality of Vladimir-Suzdal' into an independent grand duchy, continued the tradition begun by Vladimir's rulers in the twelfth century of claiming Kiev as their "patrimony and ancestral property."[1] Yet while ideologically prepared to claim Kiev, Muscovy had not yet consolidated its authority over its immediate Rus' neighbors (Tver' and Novgorod) and so could hardly hope to challenge powerful Lithuania farther south and west.

Unlike the rulers of Lithuania and Muscovy, each of whom claimed to be the legitimate descendants and heirs of the Kievan patrimony, the Golden Horde simply tried to transform the local Rus' princes into vassals who would recognize the ultimate authority of the Tatars in eastern Europe. They were successful until the second half of the fourteenth century, when Mongolo-Tatar authority witnessed its first crisis. Beginning in 1357, two decades of internal political crises racked the Golden Horde. They were followed by the arrival in the 1390s of a new threat from the east in the person of Timur (Tamerlane). This fierce competitor for leadership throughout the Mongol world destroyed the capital of Saray in 1396 and almost brought to an end the Golden Horde's existence.

This period of weakness in the Golden Horde coincided with the rule in Lithuania of Gediminas's son Algirdas (reigned 1345–1377), who shared the realm with his brother Kestutis (reigned 1345–1382). During their joint rule, they achieved their father's ambitious goal of conquering all the lands of old Rus'. In the words of Algirdas (1358), "All of Rus' simply must belong to the Lithuanians."[2] A struggle for Volhynia began in the early 1340s, but that region was not fully secured until the 1370s. In the interim, however, other principalities in the southern Rus' or Ukrainian lands were annexed by Lithuania: Chernihiv and Novhorod-Sivers'kyi gradually after 1355, Kiev and Pereiaslav in 1362, and Podolia in 1363. Also, for nearly four decades (1340 to 1377) Lithuania challenged Poland and at times controlled the Chełm/Kholm and Belz regions. Hence, by the third quarter of the fourteenth century, all the Rus' principalities on Ukrainian territory with the exception of Galicia had princes of the Gediminid dynasty ruling them. The symbolic moment marking the beginning of the new order in eastern Europe was the decisive victory of the Lithuanian army over the Golden Horde in 1362 at the Battle of Blue Waters. Thus, within a century of the death of Mindaugas, who had first united the Lithuanian tribes of the Baltic region, a vast territory that included the western and southern principalities of Kievan Rus' (much of what are today the republics of Belarus and Ukraine) had come under the political hegemony of the Grand Duchy of Lithuania.

What was the secret of this rapid Lithuanian success? The strength of the Lithuanian armies, which were the first to challenge successfully the previously invincible Golden Horde, certainly made territorial expansion possible. But how were the pagan Lithuanians, with their relatively primitive social and administrative structure, able to control lands that had a much higher level of political and cultural development? The most plausible explanation is that at least initially the Lithuanians changed little in the territories they took over, a policy summed up by one grand duke with the phrase "we are not introducing anything new and we will not disturb what is old" (*my novin ne uvodim, a starin ne rukhaem*).[3]

The territorial integrity of the Rus' principalities was initially maintained, and, most important, the Orthodox faith was left undisturbed and sometimes even promoted. Although the successors of Mindaugas reverted to paganism, which remained the official religion of the realm, many Lithuanians, especially among the sons of Gediminas, became Orthodox Christians. Moreover, throughout the fourteenth and early fifteenth centuries, the grand duchy's pagan rulers lobbied hard in Constantinople in an effort to obtain their own Orthodox metropolitanate (and for brief periods it did come into existence) or to have the seat of the metropolitan of Kiev and All Rus' transferred from Moscow back to Kiev after the city had come under Lithuanian control in the 1360s. Finally, the Lithuanians initially left intact the legal and social structures of Kievan Rus' and even adopted Ruthenian, a Belarusan version of Church Slavonic written in Cyrillic, as the grand duchy's official language. As the enactors of such policies, the Lithuanians were in fact welcomed by most of the Rus' princes, who were content to live in what was effectively a Lithuanian-Rus' state, the official name of which was the Grand Duchy of Lithuania, Rus', and Samogitia.

The Polish-Lithuanian connection

The height of Lithuanian power was reached at the beginning of the fifteenth century, but even before, there occurred a series of events that was to change profoundly the direction of Lithuanian and Ukrainian history. The first was the ending of the joint rule of Algirdas and Kestutis. In 1377, Algirdas died. His son and successor, the ambitious Jogaila, was unable to rule with his uncle Kestutis and in 1382 arranged for his relative to be assassinated. The latter's son, Vytautas, who expected to rule at least part of the realm as had his father, fled to the Teutonic Order. At this time, the Teutonic Knights were at the height of their power and were still intent on converting, or, if necessary, destroying, the pagan Lithuanian state. Vytautas persuaded the Knights to join him in a campaign against his cousin Jogaila. Fearing a Teutonic invasion, Jogaila turned to the only other strong power in the region – Poland. But why should Roman Catholic Poland have been interested in the plight of the heathen Lithuanian Jogaila on its eastern frontier? The answer calls for a review, however brief, of developments in Poland.

By the late eleventh century, the Polish Kingdom under the leadership of rulers from the Piast dynasty had come to control most of the territory that is within the present-day boundaries of Poland. The Piasts were the first dynasty and the creators of Poland. Consequently, the concept of the Polish state and the ruling Piast dynasty was undifferentiated. Piast success in gathering territories under its rule suffered a reverse during the thirteenth century, when Poland lost a significant portion of its territory: in the northwest, to German principalities of the Holy Roman Empire; in the southwest, to the Kingdom of Bohemia-Moravia; and in the north, to the Teutonic Order. Surrounded by such powerful neighbors, Poland's only outlet was in the east, and when the kingdom revived in the fourteenth century, it was precisely toward the east that its foreign policies were directed. Under the leadership of Casimir III ("the Great," reigned 1333–1370), Poland signed accords with Hungary, its only ally in central Europe, and, taking advantage of the decline of the Galician-Volhynian Kingdom after 1340, gradually brought under its control Galicia and from Lithuania annexed the Chełm-Belz region and western Podolia. This territorial expansion in the east was complete by the time of Casimir's death in 1370.

Casimir had no male heir, however, and before his death he chose as a successor his nephew, the king of Hungary, Louis I ("the Great," reigned 1342–1382). Louis was of the Anjou or Angevin dynasty, which had two branches based in France. He headed that Angevin branch which ruled territories in various parts of

Europe: Provence in the south of France, the Kingdom of Naples and Sicily in southern Italy, and (after 1308) Hungary. In 1370 he added Poland to his family's extensive patrimony. Louis was not really interested in Poland, however, so he proposed that the future husband of one of his three daughters should rule there in his stead. To prepare the Polish nobles for his plans, he summoned them to the city of Košice in northern Hungary. In return for the nobles' support, Louis was forced to make several concessions: (1) renunciation of the king's right to impose upon the nobility an extraordinary levy for troops and war money, (2) perpetual exemption of the nobility from having to pay taxes, (3) agreement that official posts in Polish provinces would be held only by nobles who were natives of the province, and (4) agreement that only a person of Polish and of non-royal blood could become a *starosta*, or royal governor of one of the twenty-three most important castles.

These concessions, known as the Statutes of Košice (1374), set the tone for future relationships between the king and the nobles in Poland. Whereas the Piasts had been the founding and, in a sense, a national dynasty whose hereditary right to rule was never seriously contested, after the death of Casimir III the traditional fusion of the identities of state and dynasty was broken. Casimir's successors were considered foreigners; hence, Polish nobles felt they had the right and even the duty to negotiate with their future ruler before pledging allegiance to him. This was the origin of that rather unique system of aristocratic democracy in Poland, whereby the nobility (the magnates and gentry), subsequently represented in a central Diet (*Sejm*), were to play a decisive – and sometimes destructive – role in Polish political life.

Having reached an accommodation with Poland's nobility, Louis turned to the question of which dynastic arrangement would enable him to continue his essentially absentee rule. Since he had only daughters, the husband of one of them would have to be king. His oldest daughter died in 1378, and after Louis's own death four years later his second daughter decided to remain in Hungary. This left his youngest daughter, Jadwiga. The Polish nobles favored a dynastic connection with the offspring of Louis, but they objected to the fact that the five-year-old Princess Jadwiga was betrothed to an Austrian prince. At this point, the Lithuanian Jogaila entered the picture.

It was precisely during Poland's succession crisis in the 1380s that Jogaila's grand duchy was threatened by his cousin Vytautas, who in alliance with the Teutonic Order was preparing to invade Lithuania to regain his patrimony. For his part, Jogaila was in need of allies and was impressed by the strength and prestige of a Poland that in the recent past had been ruled by the powerful Casimir III and Louis I of Hungary. Being themselves in need of a ruler, the Polish nobles accepted Jogaila's overtures. Through Jadwiga's mother, they persuaded the now eleven-year-old girl to break her promise of marriage to the Austrian prince (with whom she had loved to play as a child) and in the interest of the nation marry instead the thirty-seven-year-old Lithuanian pagan grand duke, Jogaila. As his part of the bargain, Jogaila had to agree to certain demands made by the Polish nobles, which were incorporated into a document known as the Union of Krewo/Krevo (1385).

In return for Jadwiga's hand, Jogaila was to accept both Roman Catholicism, not only for himself but for his whole nation, and the permanent union of Lithuania with Poland. This new Christian monarch was then crowned as Władysław II Jagiełło, King of Poland (reigned 1386–1434), and thereby founded a dynasty known as the Jagiellonians.

Jagiełło also had to promise to work for the recovery of all Lithuanian and Rus' lands that supposedly had once belonged to Poland (*terras suas Lithuanae et Russiae coronae Regni Poloniae perpetuo applicare*). It is interesting to note that at the negotiations at Krevo, the Polish nobility claimed as its ancient patrimony not only Galicia but all the other Belarusan and Ukrainian lands of Kievan Rus'. Thus, in 1385 the Polish nobles not only reasserted their power vis-à-vis their future king, but also set the foreign policy he was expected to follow.

After assuming the throne, Jagiełło carried out his side of the bargain. Immediately following his coronation in early 1386, he returned to the Lithuanian capital of Vilnius and, like Volodymyr the Great of Kievan Rus' 400 years before, destroyed pagan statues and promoted mass conversions. While Jagiełło's policy would have favorable results for members of the Lithuanian nobility who converted to Roman Catholicism, it would have negative repercussions for the vast numbers of inhabitants living in the grand duchy – namely, the Orthodox Rus' population (Belarusans and Ukrainians). Almost immediately after taking power, Jagiełło agreed (1387) that all Roman Catholic princes of Lithuanian origin could remain in the Rus' lands they ruled as long as they pledged themselves vassals of the king.

Such a policy was, not surprisingly, met with opposition by Jagiełło's brethren in Lithuania, who were always jealous of their rights and wary of any infringement of them. But even before their discontent could lead to serious consequences, the whole Polish-Lithuanian relationship was altered by the untimely death of Jadwiga (by then only twenty-four) in 1399. The queen's death automatically abrogated the Union of Krewo, and in the absence of any offspring from her marriage to Jagiełło, the union of the two countries based on the crown no longer had validity. As early as 1392, Vytautas had broken for a second and final time his alliance with the Teutonic Knights and, as part of a new arrangement with his cousin Jagiełło, he ruled as vice-regent of Lithuania. Now, in 1401, Vytautas was recognized by Jagiełło as the acting grand duke of Lithuania. Polish lords and Lithuanian boyars met to work out a new political relationship, which was enshrined in a pact signed at Horodło in 1413. At Horodło, Vytautas was confirmed as grand duke for life, and Poles and Lithuanians agreed that the future political relationship between their countries could be determined only as a result of periodic consultation and by mutual agreement. When Vytautas died in 1430, the dynastic link with Poland was restored, since Jagiełło's son by a later marriage, Kazimierz Jagiełłończyk, was chosen by the Lithuanian boyars as their grand duke. Kazimierz retained that title even after he became king of Poland (1447), and the same year he issued a charter that reiterated the rights and privileges of the grand duchy. Thus, Lithuania remained united with Poland through the person of its ruler and at the same time maintained its independence.

Lithuania was nonetheless gradually influenced by Polish models of governing and administration, which were to replace those that the grand duchy had inherited from Kievan Rus'. Already during the period of Jagiełło and Vytautas, the Rus' principality of Kiev was abolished (1394). Other principalities on Ukrainian territory (Volhynia, Chernihiv, Novhorod-Sivers'kyi, Podolia) continued to exist for a while longer, but all were eventually abolished (1430s–1440s) and the Rus' prince in each territory replaced by an official (*voievoda*) appointed by and responsible to the grand duke. The same fate awaited the Kiev principality, which was restored in 1440, only to be permanently abolished in 1471. Under Vytautas ethnic Lithuanian nobles (boyars) of the Catholic faith were favored in appointments throughout the new administrative structure. Some, as a result, developed a sense of superiority to the Orthodox Rus' boyars, whom they called by the pejorative Lithuanian term *gudai*. After the death of Vytautas in 1430, however, the Orthodox Rus' nobles were given full political rights in Lithuania, allowing them to be appointed to the grand duke's governing Council of Lords as well as to official posts as provincial and district governors (*voievodas* and *starostas*).

The situation of the Orthodox Rus' in Galicia was less favorable, especially after 1387 when Hungary and Lithuania gave up their claims and recognized the province to be part of Poland. In Kievan times, the Orthodox boyars had been a potent political force in the former Galician Rus' kingdom, but now several were forced to leave the area. They were replaced by Polish officials and gentry, who, together with the Roman Catholic church, were awarded large tracts of land. Facing a continual decline in status, some Galician Rus' leaders looked south for help from Orthodox Moldavia, which in the late fifteenth century united with Walachia and became a powerful state under the leadership of Prince Stefan ("the Great," reigned 1457–1504). Cooperation between the Galician Rus' and Moldavia took the form of a popular revolt under a local leader, Petro Mukha, who between 1490 and 1492 led nearly 10,000 Moldavian and Rus' peasants (as well as several petty nobles and townspeople) in an unsuccessful attempt to overthrow Polish rule in southern Galicia.

The status of the vast majority of the Orthodox Rus' population who remained under Lithuanian rule varied during the fifteenth century. The end of the old Kievan Rus' political order combined with intermittent discrimination against Orthodox lay and religious leaders gave rise to a new phenomenon: emigration eastward to Muscovite lands. The sixteenth century, in particular, was characterized by the flight of numerous Rus' nobility, clergy, townspeople, and even peasants from Belarus and Ukraine, who moved from what they considered an oppressive Roman Catholic environment in Lithuania to a more hospitable one in lands under the control of Orthodox Muscovy.

Muscovy and the Polish-Lithuanian union

This movement of people to the east, as well as Muscovy's expansion westward, prompted increasingly frequent conflict during the sixteenth century, as a result of which Lithuania lost some of its eastern lands, including the cities of Chernihiv, Novhorod-Sivers'kyi, Starodub, and Smolensk. The situation became especially serious during the 1560s, when the aggressive tsar of Muscovy, Ivan IV ("the Dread," reigned 1547–1584), turned his attention westward and, in 1563, captured Lithuania's stronghold of Polatsk. Faced with this Muscovite threat, the Lithuanians turned to their own grand duke and simultaneously the king of Poland, Zygmunt II Augustus (reigned 1548–1572), who was known to favor closer union between Poland and Lithuania in an effort to mount a definitive response to Muscovy. In any case, the attacks from the east would continue, since they represented part of a larger struggle between Muscovy and Poland, both of whom claimed the lands that had formerly been part of Kievan Rus'.

In order to further their goals in the east, Zygmunt and the leading Polish magnates favored some fusion with or perhaps the incorporation of Lithuania, which until then had been in only personal dynastic union with Poland. Representatives of both sides met in 1569 in the city of Lublin. Some Lithuanian nobles rejected the maximalist position proposed by the Poles, which advocated full incorporation, and negotiations dragged on for several months. The deadlock was finally broken when Zygmunt II unilaterally ordered the incorporation into the Polish Kingdom of the contested borderland region of Podlachia as well as of the Ukrainian-inhabited lands farther south, which were thereupon transformed according to the Polish administrative pattern into the palatinates of Volhynia, Bratslav, and Kiev (including the former Rus' principality of Pereiaslav). A segment of the local Orthodox Rus' nobility in these three palatinates welcomed annexation by Poland, notably the gentry, who acquired thereby all the privileges of their Polish brethren. These included freedom from military service and most forms of taxation, the right to use state lands for life and manage them as personal estates, and the right to elect government officials and to hold political or ecclesiastical office. The new Polish palatinates of Volhynia, Bratslav, and Kiev were also allowed to retain certain rights, including the full legal protection of the Orthodox church, the use of Ruthenian as the administrative language, and Lithuanian law according to the Second Lithuanian Statute of 1566 (popularly known as the "Volhynian Statute").

Although Volhynia, Bratslav, and Kiev entered Poland as distinct territorial entities, in a sense they functioned together as a unit. The nobility in all three palatinates retained a sense of common purpose, which derived from the fact that their allegiance to Poland was not the result of territorial annexation, but rather a voluntary union following a negotiated settlement. That settlement, moreover, assured them of local privileges – including laws embodied in the Second Lithuanian ("Volhynian") Statute – which in large part were based upon and helped to define their distinct Rus' political, religious, and cultural heritage. The estimated number of inhabitants in the Ukrainian territories annexed by Poland in 1569 was approximately 937,000. To this number can be added the approximately 573,000 inhabitants of the western, largely Ukrainian-inhabited palatinates of Rus' (Galicia), Belz, and Podolia, which were already part of Poland and where a Polish legal system was already in place.

Faced with the loss of its southern regions, the Lithuanian nobles agreed to what became known as the Union of Lublin. According to this covenant, signed on 1 July 1569, Poland and Lithuania would henceforth be united in a "common

MAP 13

THE POLISH-LITHUANIAN COMMONWEALTH, circa 1570

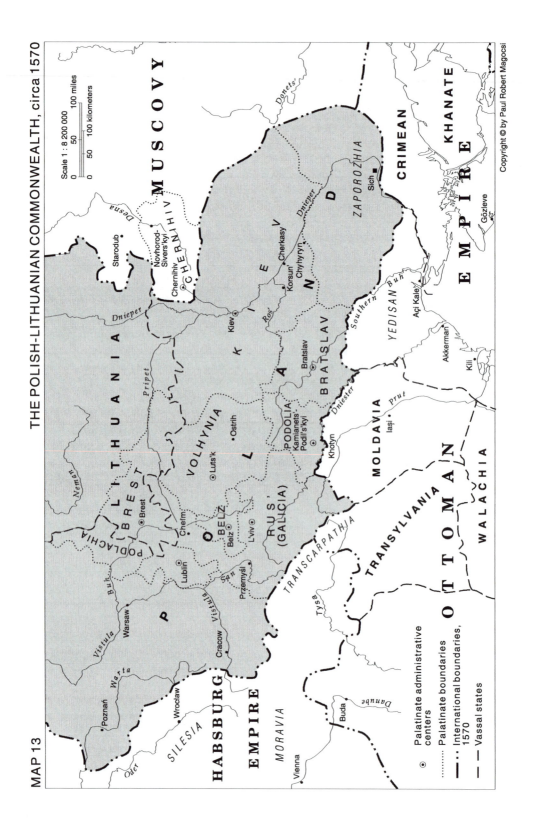

Scale 1 : 8 200 000

MUSCOVY

CRIMEAN

KHANATE

EMPIRE

HABSBURG

EMPIRE

OTTOMAN

Copyright © by Paul Robert Magocsi

Palatinate administrative centers

Palatinate boundaries

International boundaries, 1570

Vassal states

republic" (*Rzeczpospolita*) with a king elected by both regions and represented by one Diet (*Sejm*). While it is true that after Lublin Lithuania retained its own army, treasury, law code, and local administration, in subsequent decades the grand duchy's particularities were brought more and more in line with the character of the rest of Poland. In foreign affairs, the new state acted as a single entity known as the Polish-Lithuanian Commonwealth. In short, the Union of Lublin transformed the relationship between Poland and Lithuania from that of a personal dynastic union into that of a federal union.

Thus, during the nearly two hundred years from the second half of the fourteenth century, when Rus' principalities in Ukraine first came under Lithuanian rule, neighboring Poland succeeded in steadily bringing the Grand Duchy of Lithuania within its political and cultural orbit. This effort culminated in the Union of Lublin in 1569, as a result of which Poland replaced Lithuania as the principal rival of Muscovy for control of the heritage of Kievan Rus'. In the case of Ukrainian lands, the former principality of Galicia (since 1387 the Rus' palatinate, or Red Rus') and the palatinates of Belz and Podolia were joined, after 1569, by Volhynia, Bratslav, and Kiev, all of which became integral parts of the Polish Kingdom. Henceforth, the history of Ukraine would be largely determined by the fate of Poland.

11

Socioeconomic Developments

While Lithuanians still lived within the perimeters of their traditional homeland along the Neman River valley and Baltic Sea coast, and before they were united into a political entity in the thirteenth century, their social structure was relatively simple. Basically, three social strata existed: (1) tribal princes and their families, (2) freepersons organized into tribal units, and (3) slaves, people who originally had been prisoners of war. But during the reign of Grand Duke Gediminas in the early fourteenth century, when Lithuania was rapidly expanding its borders southward into Belarus and Ukraine, it came into contact with the more highly developed social structure on lands that had once been part of Kievan Rus'. The Lithuanian rulers left intact much of what they found in the Rus' lands and only gradually developed a distinct social structure that took into consideration the needs of the new Lithuanian-Rus' state while adopting for their own purposes both the older social system of Kievan Rus' and the newer social relationships that were forming in neighboring Poland. By the sixteenth century, the outlines of the Lithuanian social structure were clear. It consisted of the following strata: the grand duke (Lithuanian: *kunigas*), hereditary princes and non-hereditary boyars (*bajorai*) and gentry, clergy, townspeople, Jews, and peasants.

Lithuania's social structure

While it is true that during the era of territorial expansion the Lithuanian grand dukes left intact much of the administrative and, in particular, Orthodox cultural and religious structure of Kievan Rus', they began to superimpose their control on this vast territory in two ways. First, they recognized the inherited right to the large landed estates of the princes (*kniazi*), both the ducal princes descended from their own Gediminid dynasty and those of the Rus' dynasty of Riuryk. At the same time, they made huge land grants to those Lithuanian and Rus' boyars who fought alongside them in their conquests. Despite the enormous wealth of these boyars, they, unlike the hereditary princes, enjoyed no immunity, either as individuals or as a social estate. Rather, in return for his land, each was bound by feudal obligations to the grand duke. Another group, with even fewer privileges than the boyars,

SOCIAL ESTATES IN LITHUANIA AND POLAND

LITHUANIA	POLAND
1 **Grand Duke**	1 **Crown**
	king
	royal officials
2 **Nobility**	2 **Nobility** *(szliachta)*
hereditary princes *(kniazi)*	magnates
non-hereditary nobles	gentry
boyars	middle
gentry	petty
3 **Clergy**	3 **Clergy**
Roman Catholic	Roman Catholic
Orthodox	Orthodox
	Protestant
4 **Townspeople**	4 **Townspeople**
merchants	merchants
artisans	artisans/tradespeople
unskilled laborers	unskilled laborers
5 **Jews**	5 **Jews**
merchants	merchants/money lenders
artisans/tradespeople	artisans/tradespeople
	leaseholders *(arendars)*
6 **Peasants**	6 **Peasants**
tenant farmers	free homesteaders
proprietary serfs	proprietary serfs

was of mixed origin and eventually came to be known as the gentry. This group consisted of small landholders who received their property as a result of military service performed for the grand duke or, in some cases, for the powerful hereditary princes and dukes.

The vast majority of the inhabitants were peasants, the descendants, from Kievan Rus' times, of independent agriculturalists (*liudi*), cooperative landholders (*siabry*), and state peasants (*smerdy*). The principal trend in the evolution of the peasantry was its members' loss of rights to their land; accordingly, by the end of the fifteenth century most were tenant farmers either on the crown lands of Lithuania's grand duke or on the estates of the nobility.

Among the smallest of Lithuania's social strata was that of the townspeople. They consisted of two subgroups, the merchants and the artisans, each of which had its own guild system. Both subgroups included a significant number of foreigners – Germans, Armenians, Jews – who had been invited by Lithuania's grand dukes to settle in urban areas. In the sixteenth century, most cities in the Belarusan and Ukrainian lands of Lithuania had a Rus' majority, but the Rus' inhabitants were frequently discriminated against in favor of Roman Catholics and foreigners.

Unlike in the Kievan period, the cities of Lithuania declined in economic and political importance. And even though during the fifteenth and sixteenth centuries most cities were granted municipal self-government (the Magdeburg Law), they were excluded from any participation in the central government. The cities did not even have a monopoly on trade, and as we shall see below, they were undercut by the economic activity of the nobility.

Although Lithuania maintained only a tenuous political relationship with Poland in the fifteenth and sixteenth centuries, its social structure was steadily brought closer to that of its neighbor to the west. This became particularly evident in a strengthening of the status of the nobility – both boyars and gentry – and a concomitant weakening of the peasantry. As early as 1387, within a year of Jagiełło's coronation as king, the Lithuanian boyars were granted the rights and privileges of the Polish nobility. Then, according to the agreement at Horodło (1413), the Lithuanian boyars and Polish nobles were merged into a single estate responsible for deciding the relationship between the two countries as well as for electing the grand duke. It was also at this time that the term *boyary* was replaced by the Polish term *pany* (lords) to describe the group. The Lithuanian lords also had the right to maintain their own military regiments, and after 1447 they became exempt from paying taxes. In this way, Lithuania's princes and boyars were gradually being fused into a single estate of hereditary lords. During the reign of Grand Duke Vytautas (1392–1430), such privileges were given only to boyars of the Roman Catholic faith, but after 1434 they were extended to the Orthodox as well.

Lithuania's administrative structure

In the course of the fifteenth century, the former Rus' principalities were gradually replaced by palatinates (*voievodstva*), which in turn were divided into districts (*povity*). Unlike in Poland, where the nobility was the dominant political force at the palatinate level, in Lithuania the central government attempted to reduce the autonomy of the palatinates by replacing the local boyars with officials appointed by and directly responsible to the grand duke. These included (1) the governor of each palatinate, known as the *voievoda*, or palatine, who had administrative, military, and judicial authority; (2) the head of each district, known as the *starosta*; and (3) the castellan, who was responsible for the maintenance of royal castles and other military fortifications as well as for summoning the local nobility to arms in times of danger. Apart from his power of patronage in the appointment of palatines, district heads, and castellans, the political influence of the grand duke was enhanced by economic privileges, including income from the so-called grand ducal lands, revenue from various kinds of taxes, and, in particular, the exclusive right to sell salt and alcohol (the right of *propinatsiia*).

While boyar influence may have been challenged at the local level by the centralizing administrative tendencies of the grand duke, in fact the driving force of Lithuania's government – especially with regard to foreign affairs – was the Council of Lords (*pans'ka rada*). The council consisted of the Roman Catholic bishop of Vilnius and the Lithuanian and Rus' *voievoda* of each palatinate and *starosta* of certain districts. The council's power over the legal structure of the country was institutionalized in 1529 (the First Lithuanian Statute), after which the grand duke pledged to keep intact all former laws and not to make any new ones without the consent of the council. The role of the gentry in Lithuanian sociopolitical life developed more slowly. It was not until the Union of Lublin (1569) that the Lithuanian and Rus' gentry were freed from military and other feudal obligations and merged with the boyars in one noble estate (*szlachta*), as in Poland. Gentry political influence came somewhat earlier, since from the fifteenth century this group in Lithuania had its own district assemblies (*seimyky*).

The grand duchy's legal system was strongly influenced by that of former Kievan Rus'. The Rus' Law (*Ruskaia Pravda*) alongside customary law governed Lithuanian society until 1468, when Lithuania issued its own code (*Sudebnik*). Three new codes followed in the sixteenth century, each known as the Lithuanian Statute. The first edition (1529) emphasized the rights of the state and of the boyars and magnates, and the second (1564–66) and third (1588) editions reflected a gradual increase in privileges for the gentry as well as a decline in the legal status of the peasantry. The continuing influence of Kievan Rus' law was evident not only in the content of the Lithuanian codes, but in their form. The law codes, along with all other state documents, appeared in the grand duchy's official state language, Ruthenian, which was essentially a Belarusan version of Church Slavonic written in the Cyrillic alphabet. It should also be noted that the Rus' (Belarusans and Ukrainians) were considered alongside Lithuanians as the ruling groups in the grand duchy. Hence, the Second Lithuanian Statute (1566) specified that the grand duke could not appoint foreigners to offices of the state administration, but only native Lithuanians and Rus'.

Despite its strong links to the Kievan past, by the second half of the fifteenth century Lithuania was more and more adapting to the societal model of Poland, which since the death of its last Piast ruler in 1370 itself had set out on a path that was to transform the country into an aristocratic democracy headed by an elected king. This process was a long one, lasting two centuries.

Poland's social and administrative structure

Poland's social structure consisted of several estates (Polish: *stany*). These are frequently confused with socioeconomic classes. Unlike classes in the modern sense, the estates in Polish society were defined on the basis not of a relationship to the means of production or any other measure of wealth or economic status, but of an intended function within society as expressed by specific legal rights and privileges. Accordingly, one can speak of six estates in fifteenth- and sixteenth-century Poland: the crown, the nobility, the clergy, the townspeople, the Jews, and the peasants. Membership in these estates was largely hereditary, and social mobility, while not impossible, was deliberately encumbered by complex legal difficulties. Again, wealth was not a determining factor. Hence, there may have been townspeople, Jews, even peasants who were richer than certain nobles, but with rare exceptions they were barred from entering the noble estate.

The crown estate consisted of the king and his officials, whether senators, ministers, territorial officers, or holders of royal monopolies. The role of the crown was to represent the unity of the realm, whether the Polish Kingdom alone or, through the person of the king, Poland in relationship with the Grand Duchy of Lithuania. After 1573, the king was the elected head of the Polish-Lithuanian Commonwealth. The crown's authority was progressively restricted by concessions to the Polish nobility and the grand dukes of Lithuania as outlined in varying agreements reached between the late fourteenth and late sixteenth centuries (Košice, 1374; Krewo, 1385; Horodło, 1413; Lublin, 1569; the Henrican articles, 1573; and thereafter a *pacta conventa* with each newly elected king). Nonetheless, the king remained a significant force in Polish society. His political influence was based on the right to distribute offices – those of senator, palatine, castellan, *starosta*, and military leader (hetman) – and royal lands. Moreover, the king's symbolic importance remained intact, since until the very end of Poland's existence in the second half of the eighteenth century there was never any questioning of the need for a crown estate and for a hereditary or, later, elective king to function at the head of the social structure.

The most influential estate in Poland was the nobility, or *szlachta* (pronounced *shlakhta*). Although there was only one estate of the nobility, all of whose members were equal before the law, in practice there existed great discrepancies with regard to the wealth, social prestige, and political influence of Poland's nobles. Both contemporary and subsequent analyses of Polish society therefore divide the nobility into at least two groups: (1) the magnates, or heads of great families who, because of their extensive wealth, practically ran the affairs of the state; and (2) the gentry, who had limited wealth – in some cases they did not even own land (the *non-possessionati*) – and who often served as clients of the great magnates. Writings on the subject sometimes classify the gentry as either the middle gentry or the petty gentry. The point is that, despite great disparities among the magnates, middle gentry, and petty gentry, all were recognized as part of one legal estate, the nobility or *szlachta*, and all shared equally the legal privileges of that estate. In a sense, the social history of Poland during the fifteenth and sixteenth centuries is the story of how the nobility succeeded in increasing its privileges vis-à-vis not only the crown, but also the church, the townspeople, and the peasants. The justification for the nobility's privileges derived from its role as defenders of the realm against foreign invasion. In fact, the nobility did fill that role at least until the end of the sixteenth century, although thereafter the traditional call to arms in times of danger (*pospolite ruszenie*) was gradually replaced by a small permanent armed force supported by taxation.

Compared to that of other European countries at the time, the Polish nobility represented a relatively large proportion of the country's population. Moreover, their absolute and relative numbers continued to grow. Whereas in 1569 there were about 500,000 nobles, representing 6.6 percent of the population in the Polish-Lithuanian Commonwealth, by 1648 the number had increased to one million, or 9 percent of the population. Of the nobles in 1648, an estimated 5,000 to 10,000 were magnates, and the remaining 900,000 or more were gentry.

The administrative structure of the country also reflected the needs of the influential noble estate. Poland was divided into palatinates (Polish: *wojewódstwa*), headed by the king's representative, the palatine (*wojewoda*) . But politically more important were the noble assemblies, or dietines (*sejmiki*), which formed the basic unit of constitutional life in Poland. There was a long tradition of noble assemblies, which originally were organized by the nobility for military purposes. The concept of permanent dietines was crystallized after 1454, when the king agreed neither to summon the army nor to raise taxes without consulting the nobility beforehand. Each palatinate had its own dietine, and from the dietines developed the idea of a single legislative institution, the central Diet (*Sejm*). Poland's Diet met for the first time at 1493 in Piotrków and, thereafter, once every two years for six-week sessions held mostly in Warsaw and (after 1569) in the Lithuanian town of Hrodna.

The Polish Diet was made up of two houses: (1) the Senate, consisting of Roman Catholic (never Orthodox) bishops, palatines, castellans, and major functionaries of the central government and, later, Lithuanian ministers of state, all appointed by the king mostly from the ranks of the magnates; and (2) the Chamber of Deputies (generally middle gentry), consisting of delegates chosen by the local dietines. Hence, with the development of the permanent diet, Poland acquired a governmental system marked by checks and balances among three interest groups – the king, the magnates, and the gentry. Until 1569, Poland and Lithuania each had its own Diet (*Sejm/Soim*), but after the agreements reached at Lublin, the nobles from both parts of the Commonwealth sat in one body.

In terms of procedure, the diet, like the dietines, was conducted on the principle of unanimity, a medieval practice that was never replaced by the more modern principal of majority vote. As will become evident in later periods, this antiquated principle on occasion degenerated into the infamous practice of the *liberum veto*, whereby the negative vote of a single member could, and sometimes did, bring all business to a standstill. But as long as the system of aristocratic parliamentarism worked, especially in the sixteenth and first half of the seventeenth centuries, Poland had a political structure characterized by a balance of power between three estates: the monarch, the magnates, and the gentry.

Peasants, nobles, and Jews

To ensure the continuance of their dominant role in the Polish socioeconomic structure, the nobility (magnates and gentry) encouraged changes in the legal system. They were particularly eager to regulate to their own advantage the status of the peasantry. The result was the implementation of what has come to be known as

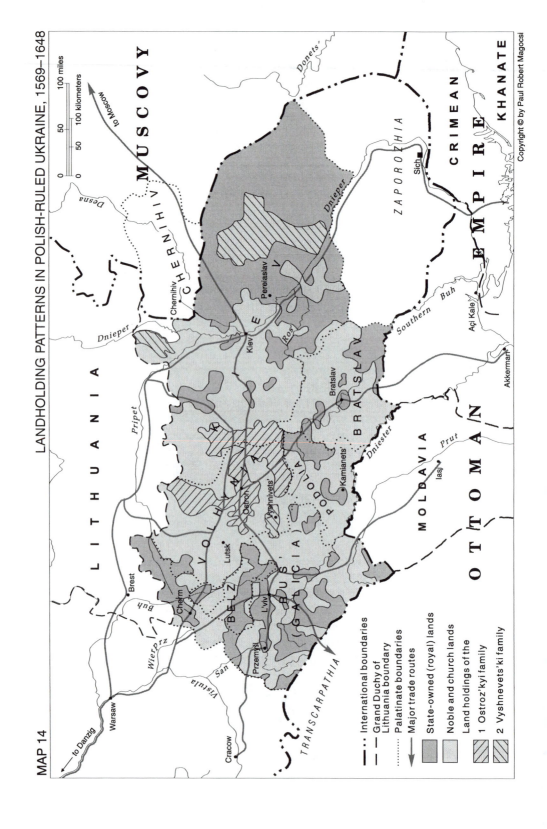

MAP 14

LANDHOLDING PATTERNS IN POLISH-RULED UKRAINE, 1569–1648

Copyright © by Paul Robert Magocsi

International boundaries
Grand Duchy of
Lithuania boundary
Palatinate boundaries
Major trade routes

State-owned (royal) lands

Noble and church lands

Land holdings of the
1 Ostroz'kyi family
2 Vyshnevets'ki family

MUSCOVY
LITHUANIA
CHERNIHIV
ZAPOROZHIA
CRIMEAN EMPIRE KHANATE
MOLDAVIA
OTTOMAN
TRANSCARPATHIA
GALICIA
PODOLIA
BRATSLAV
VOLHYNIA
BELZ

Cracow
Warsaw
to Danzig
Brest
Chełm
Przemyśl
L'viv
Lutsk
Ostroh
Vyshnivets'
Kamianets'
Bratslav
Kiev
Chernihiv
Pereiaslav
Sich
Akkerman
Açı Kale
Iaşı

to Moscow

Vistula
San
Wieprz
Buh
Pripet
Dnieper
Desna
Dnieper
Ros'
Southern Buh
Dniester
Prut
Donets'

0   50   100 miles
0   50   100 kilometers

the second serfdom, or neo-serfdom. The initial stage of neo-serfdom saw a series of edicts approved by the Polish Diet (between 1496 and 1520) which placed an increasing number of legal restrictions on the peasant's ability to leave his or her manorial estate. Particularly advantageous to the nobility was a law passed in 1518, according to which the royal court decided not to accept the complaints of subjects on lands not owned by the crown. Thus, when duty-free periods expired, or when landlords began to introduce unilaterally the *corvée* (labor obligation), or when they simply seized peasant lands, the peasant living on noble- or church-owned lands could no longer turn to the royal courts. He or she could resort to the local courts, but they were all controlled by nobles, who were unlikely to rule in favor of a peasant plaintiff.

The implementation of neo-serfdom in Poland culminated in 1573. After that date, peasants (men and women) were forbidden under any conditions to leave the manorial estates on which they resided. The *corvée*, whereby a serf was obliged to render unpaid labor, came to constitute the principal economic relation between noble landowners and peasants. In the Grand Duchy of Lithuania, which included most Ukrainian territory until 1569, serfdom was similarly introduced during the second half of the sixteenth century. As a result of an agricultural reform implemented in 1557, peasants were deprived of property rights to land. Three decades later the Third Lithuanian Statute of 1588 confirmed full bondage by removing the so-called right of transfer, with the consequence that all peasants who had lived with one landowner for a period of ten years became thenceforth "immovable."

There were some free peasants, rural laborers, and serfs on both church and crown lands, but by the sixteenth century the vast majority of peasants were serfs of the nobility. Serfdom was put into practice in areas that had particular economic significance, such as those adjacent to the Vistula River and its tributaries (including the upper Buh and San Rivers in Ukrainian-inhabited Galicia and western Volhynia), as well as in all densely populated areas, where peasants had smaller and less economically viable holdings and were consequently more likely to become indebted to the local landlord. By the second half of the sixteenth century, there was a density of approximately 36 inhabitants per square mile (14 inhabitants per square kilometer) in the more western regions of Poland, including Ukrainian-inhabited Galicia, Belz, and western Podolia, whereas farther east, in the palatinates of Volhynia, Kiev, and Bratslav, the density was as low as 8 persons per square mile (3 persons per square kilometer). Thus, whereas by the end of the sixteenth century serfdom had become widespread in the more densely inhabited western Ukrainian lands, farther east, where large manorial estates (*latifundia*) were being formed, the peasants had not yet been enserfed, although they were being subjected to an increasing number of duties.

The situation in eastern Ukraine generally evolved in the following manner. Large magnates, whether of Rus' (Ukrainian) or Polish origin, managed to obtain from the king grants of huge tracts of land (on the condition that they be settled) as well as official posts in the sparsely populated eastern Ukrainian territories. For instance, by 1590 the palatine of Kiev, Prince Kostiantyn/Vasyl' K. Ostroz'kyi, owned, in the Kiev, Galician, and, especially, Volhynian palatinates,

THE MANORIAL ESTATE

The evolution of the manorial estate (*latifundium*) was directly related to the rise of neo-serfdom in Poland. On the estates of magnates and gentry, and some-times on royal and church lands, the large manorial farm known in Ukrainian as the *fil'varok* (from the Polish *folwark*) was organized. The goal in setting up the *fil'varok* was to make the most efficient use of serf labor for the maximum production of grain. By the second half of the sixteenth century, the average size of a *fil'varok* was 148 acres (60 hectares), and on it lived the landowner and his family, the landowner's personnel, and between fifteen and twenty serf families.

The *fil'varok* itself was generally divided into three parts: (1) the demesne fields, or the lands belonging to the landlord, consolidated through the acquisi-tion of smaller peasant holdings; (2) the lands belonging to the *soltys*, a village administrator of the landlord; and (3) strip holdings belonging to individual serfs. Generally, the village was in the center of the *fil'varok*, where the land-lord's manor house, the residence of the *soltys*, peasant dwellings, and the tav-ern were located. Near the village center was a common pasture; surrounding it were the demesne fields; and beyond them were the lands belonging to the *soltys* and the serfs' strip holdings.

In return for their labor (*corvée*), serfs and their descendants had the security of possessing some lands or, as it were, of eventually belonging to them. As long as the conditions of serfdom were tolerable, such "attachment" to the land seemed an improvement on a cash economy in which a serf could become bankrupt during bad economic times and be evicted from land and home.

The amount of labor owed by a serf was related to the size of his or her land allotment. Whereas on royal estates there was a uniform system of labor obli-gations, on magnate- and gentry-owned estates (which by the late sixteenth century accounted for 78 percent of holdings in Ukraine) the number of unpaid work days was determined by the landlord or his estate administrators. The amount of *corvée* required of serfs therefore varied greatly. For instance, at the end of the sixteenth century, the number of unpaid labor days for serfs who had a typical allotment of land varied from 3 to 6 days per week for one or more members of a household. On magnate estates in Volhynia during the 1620s, however, the requirement was 4 to 6 days and, in some places, even 7 work days per week for a standard unit of land. In a typical serf household, the hus-band and older sons spent most of their time fulfilling the *corvée* requirement of the landlord, and the wife and younger children worked the small strips allot-ted to them in what was at best subsistence-level agriculture, that is, the raising of just enough food to support the family.

As long as Poland's grain trade was growing, the *fil'varok* manorial estate system played a positive role in increasing the landlord's wealth and providing indirectly for the minimal well-being of peasant serfs. But with the leveling off and eventually the decline of the grain trade in the second half of the seventeenth century, landowners tried to make up their losses by increasing the number of serf work days and by expanding the manorial estate system into Poland's recently acquired Ukrainian lands in the east.

approximately 1,300 villages, 100 towns, 40 castles, and 600 churches. Similarly, by the early seventeenth century the Vyshnevets'kyi family owned nearly the entire Left Bank of the Kiev palatinate (claiming 230,000 subjects), and in Volhynia 13 noble families owned 57 percent of all land. These powerful magnates, as well as hundreds of smaller gentry, encouraged the migration of peasants from the more densely populated western territories of Poland, and the peasants were only too glad to escape the increasingly burdensome restrictions placed upon them by the serf system. To encourage these new immigrants, many of whom had to flee illegally from the manorial estates, the large landowners in the east offered them exemptions from rent and labor obligations (*corvée*) that could last up to 15, 20, or 30 years. Even when these periods ran out, the subsequent labor dues and taxes were less than on estates in the western palatinates of Poland. Consequently, even if by the middle of the seventeenth century serfdom had not yet taken hold in Ukrainian lands east of Galicia, the efforts of landlords to restrict privileges and exact new labor dues brought discontent and the potential for social conflict.

Whereas the nobility made concessions in order to attract settlers to the east, from the beginning they either owned outright or controlled the local mills for processing grain. They also retained the exclusive privilege of distilling and selling alcohol. The Polish and polonized Rus' magnates and gentry were often not willing, however, to run the huge estates over which they had control. Instead, they relied on leaseholders (arendars), mostly Jews, who eventually became the linchpin of Poland's *arenda* (leaseholding) economic system.

Arenda is a Polish term referring to the lease of fixed assets, such as land, mills, inns, breweries, and distilleries, or of special rights, such as the right to collect customs duties and taxes. The Polish landowning nobility was anxious to exploit the rich agricultural resources of the area that formed the basis of a profitable and expanding grain trade with western Europe through Poland's Baltic ports, but they had little interest in administering vast landed estates on their own. They continued, however, to cultivate their luxurious habits and cultural pursuits, even though they lacked the capital or commercial skills necessary to exploit their properties and support their style of life. The landowners therefore turned to the Jews for money and for their expertise in leasing. The Jews obliged, and by the sixteenth and seventeenth centuries they had come to dominate the *arenda* system and to manage a considerable portion of the agricultural economy in Ukrainian lands. Not surprisingly, because they served as middlemen for Polish landlords, Jews became symbols of oppression and exploitation in the eyes of the Ukrainian peasant masses.

THE COMING OF JEWS TO UKRAINE

Jews have had a long tradition of settlement on Ukrainian territory, which can be traced back to the Greek cities of the Bosporan Kingdom in the fifth and fourth centuries BCE and the Khazar Kaganate in the seventh and eighth centuries CE. As entrepreneurs from the Near East, Jews were welcomed by the Bosporan and Khazar rulers, and they settled as traders and merchants in the ports of the Crimea and in the heartland of Khazaria along the lower Volga and Don Rivers. The Jews of Polish-ruled sixteenth-century Ukraine, however, were the descendants not of the refugees of Khazar times (with the exception of a few Turkic-speaking Karaite immigrants), but of migrants originally from the Germanic lands of central and east-central Europe. Anti-Jewish violence and other forms of persecution connected with the Crusades and the popular hatred of Jews in medieval Germanic lands forced them to seek refuge in Poland beginning at the close of the eleventh century.

Following the destruction caused by the Mongol invasions of the mid-thirteenth century, Poland's kings wished to rebuild the country's economy and, therefore, welcomed immigrants, whether Jews or Germans from the west or Armenians from the east. The newcomers settled primarily in urban areas and helped Poland revive its cities. Before the end of the thirteenth century, the Jews had been awarded the first of many privileges (beginning with the 1264 Statute of Kalisz of Prince Bolesław "the Pious") that defended them as a group whose main business was moneylending. The Jews were originally servants of the royal court (*servi camerae*), and as such they collectively paid a separate tax, often higher than that of Christians. They were, however, entitled to administer themselves in a self-governing municipality known as the *kahal* (Yiddish: *kehile*). Jewish self-government in Poland-Lithuania became formalized in the mid-sixteenth century, when the kahals joined to form an umbrella organization known as the Council of Lands. The "lands" were composed of self-governing councils (four in Poland, one in Lithuania), each of which regulated the internal social, economic, ethical, educational, and legal aspects of Jewish life, and which as a unified body represented Jewish interests vis-à-vis the Polish crown and central governmental institutions. Two of the councils were based on Ukrainian territory, one in Galicia (the "Lvov Land"') and the other in Volhynia.

The first Jews came to Poland from Bohemia after 1098 and settled in neighboring Silesia, an initally Polish-ruled land that was later germanized when it became part of Bohemia-Moravia. Subsequent Jewish immigrants came from Moravia itself and from Germanic lands farther west. All were of the Ashkenazi tradition, speaking the medieval German dialect of Yiddish. By the sixteenth century, Poland had also become attractive to Jews of the Sephardic tradition from as far away as Spain, Italy, and the Crimea.

In the Ukrainian lands, small communities of Ashkenazi Jews developed in Galicia and Volhynia in as early as the twelfth century, when these regions were still ruled by their own Rus' princes. The Jewish communities there really began to expand, however, only during the fourteenth and fifteenth centuries, after the regions had become part of Poland and Lithuania. The Jews in Lithuania were even better off and were awarded a wide body of privileges (1388–1389), including tax-free concessions for their places of worship and burial, and the right to trade, hold any craft, and own land.

The further spread of Jews eastward into Ukrainian lands along both the Right and the Left Banks was directly related to Poland's territorial expansion and the colonizing efforts led by Rus' (Ukrainian) and Polish magnates and gentry after the Union of Lublin in 1569. In this process, Jews became servitors on manorial estates owned by the nobility. According to one Jewish historian (Israel Friedlander), as leaseholders they functioned as "sponges to convey the wealth of the country and the toil of its inhabitants into the pockets of the lords." Some Jewish arendars not only held leases, but also obtained contracts to administer entire estates. This meant that they had the authority to set labor requirements for the manor's peasant serfs. With the spread of the Polish manorial estate system into central and eastern Ukraine, the overall number of Jews continued to grow, so that by 1648 there were an estimated 85,000 living in Ukrainian lands. At the same time, the economic status of at least one segment of Jewish society (the arendars and their assistants) vastly improved.

The realignment of international trade patterns

The expansion of Poland's magnates and gentry into Ukrainian lands in the late sixteenth and early seventeenth centuries and their development and exploitation of the region's agricultural resources made them part of the new international economic order that was coming into being in eastern Europe. In the early centuries of Kievan Rus', the highly important international trade routes which crossed eastern Europe transported mainly luxury goods from the Orient via the northern Black Sea ports to Byzantium or to Kiev, and thence northward up the Dnieper to the Baltic Sea ports or westward overland through Galicia to central and western Europe. By the eleventh century, Kiev's dependence on international trade as a source of income had lessened, with the result that agricultural and related production became the mainstay of the economy.

This trend toward a profit-making agriculture-based economy with export to the southern Crimean and Byzantine markets was interrupted in the twelfth century by the nomads' seizure of control of the steppe and by the decline of the Byzantine Empire. Then, with the arrival of the Mongols in the mid-thirteenth century, an economic as well as a political realignment took place in eastern Europe. The Mongols made international trade from the Orient and Central Asia via the Black Sea to a revived Byzantium or to the Mediterranean ports of Venice and Genoa their most important economic concern. By the first half of the fifteenth century, however, the Mongolo-Tatar domination of the Black Sea region had declined, and in 1453 the Byzantine Empire ceased to exist. The rise of the Lithuanian and, later, Polish presence in eastern Europe that culminated in the sixteenth century eventually made agricultural production economically viable once again. But the traditional trade routes to the south were cut off, since the Ottoman Empire, which succeeded Byzantium, was locked in a fierce struggle with Christian powers for control of the Balkans and Black Sea region.

As a result, a new western European-oriented economic order emerged, in which the Polish Kingdom and later the Polish-Lithuanian Commonwealth functioned as a supplier of raw materials to western European countries, for which finished products were received in return. That Poland could find a ready market for its products was a result of changes taking place simultaneously in western and southern Europe. A population explosion during the fifteenth and sixteenth centuries, combined with a phenomenal acquisition of wealth from the New World (especially by Spain and Portugal), produced an ever-increasing need for foodstuffs and building materials in western Europe, which now had the financial means (gold and silver from the Americas) to pay for extensive imports.

Poland's economic and cultural revival

From its ports along the Baltic Sea and by land through Lublin and Poznań, Poland shipped to central and western Europe lumber products (timber, tar, potash), cattle (10,000 were exported annually during the early sixteenth century, and 40,000 annually by the end of the century), and raw hides. The most important export, however, was grain, grown in western Ukraine (Galicia and western Volhynia) and shipped down the Vistula and its tributaries to the Baltic port of Gdańsk (Danzig), which Poland had recovered from the Teutonic Order in 1455. It was from the Vistula grain trade that Poland really acquired its wealth. The growth of the grain trade was indeed remarkable: in 1491–1492, an estimated 13,000 tons (12,000 metric tons) were exported, and that figure rose rapidly to 152,000 tons (138,000 metric tons) in 1563 and to a high figure – never to be repeated – of 272,000 tons (248,000 metric tons) in 1618. In return, Poland imported manufactured goods: cloth from Flanders, England, and France, and wine from Spain, France, and Portugal. The growth of the grain market and its lucrative return only increased the appetite of Poland's nobility for more land and greater control over those who toiled on it.

It is also interesting to note that, unlike in Poland in previous centuries and in much of contemporary western and central Europe, the role of Polish cities and townspeople in the economic expansion was limited and even decreased during the period under consideration. The wealthiest townspeople had fewer rights than the poorest noble, and only the largest cities had self-governing privileges. Of the smaller towns, many were owned outright by nobles. But most important was the fact that the Vistula grain trade bypassed the cities entirely, since international shippers (mostly Dutch) and merchants in the Baltic port of Gdańsk, near the mouth of the Vistula, dealt directly with the nobles.

Poland's increasing economic wealth was matched in the sixteenth century by its cultural achievement. The Italian Renaissance, with its humanist ideas, and the German and Czech religious reformation reached Poland at about the same time. The result was a fertile intellectual and creative environment fostered by various segments of the nobility and symbolized by the creative genius of the writer Jan Kochanowski, the political theorist Andrzej Frycz-Modrzewski, and the renowned astronomer Copernicus. The Polish language was transformed into a literary medium for creative belletristic and scholarly writing, which flowed from the country's new printing presses. Painting, sculpture, and architecture flourished, and Polish universities were among the leading centers of learning in Europe.

Given this atmosphere, it is not surprising that the Lithuanian and Orthodox Rus' nobility in the east were attracted as by a magnet to sixteenth-century Western-oriented Polish culture. Many of them aped Polish customs, adopted the Polish language, and, in the case of the Rus', converted to Roman Catholicism, the official state religion. As for that portion of the Rus' nobility (whether in Lithuania or in Ukraine) who remained Orthodox, Polish political identity became an important element in their outlook. It is precisely from this segment of the Ukrainian nobility that the concept *gente Ruthenus, natione Polonus* (a Pole of Rus' religion) developed. In this regard, it is interesting to note that in 1569, on the eve of the agreement at Lublin to unite Poland and Lithuania, it was the Rus' magnates and gentry who for the most part wanted the remaining Ukrainian lands in Lithuania – Volhynia, Bratslav, eastern Podolia, and Kiev – to become, as Galicia had previously, an integral part of Poland. While there may have been some disagreement in 1569 over the exact political relationship with the Polish Kingdom, the leading strata of the population, whether Orthodox or Catholic, was anxious to become part of the Polish sphere and to obtain the political and economic advantages that would thereby accrue. Accordingly, the leading strata in Ukrainian society welcomed Polish rule in the late sixteenth century.

Still, there remained the vast majority of the population, represented by peasant-serfs and a small number of Rus' townspeople. As long as Poland's agriculture-based economy was thriving as a result of the Vistula grain trade, both groups led a tolerable existence. But when grain prices began to fall in the early seventeenth century, Ukrainian peasants and townspeople – not unlike their Polish and Lithuanian counterparts in other areas of the Commonwealth – began to suffer the negative effect of economic change whereby the nobility attempted to make up for its losses by exploiting the serfs further and by limiting the prerogatives of the townspeople. Added to these general economic developments was the fact that the Rus' (Ukrainians and Belarusans) were differentiated from the rest of society by their Orthodox Rus' religious identity. That identity was to prove an extra liability in a Polish society that was experiencing both economic difficulties and the gradual growth of social and religious intolerance. As will become evident in the next two chapters, the manner in which the Rus' townspeople and peasants reacted to these changes and the degree to which their Orthodox church became involved were to have a profound effect on Ukraine's relationship to the rest of Poland.

12

The Orthodox Cultural Revival

Ever since the Kievan period, literature, art, and architecture in Ukraine had been closely linked to religion. It was from Byzantium that Kievan Rus' received Christianity, and the educated elite and the cultural forms they produced were for the most part inspired by and linked to the Orthodox Church. To be sure, there were some examples of secular cultural phenomena, such as the historical chronicles and the epic *Lay of Ihor's Campaign*, but Rus' culture was cast largely in a religious mold during the Kievan period of Ukrainian history.

This situation remained essentially unchanged during the Lithuanian-Polish era, which lasted from the fourteenth to the mid-seventeenth century in much of Ukrainian territory. Religion and elite culture were inseparable. Moreover, following the Byzantine tradition, church and state were always closely associated. Again, this was the continuation of a trend established in the Kievan period, when another characteristic evolved as well: the fusion of religious and territorial-national identity. One was of the Rus' land because one was of the Orthodox Rus' faith, and vice versa. Political and religious developments therefore were dependent upon each other. Such interdependence was of special significance when, during the two centuries between 1349 and 1569, most Ukrainian lands progressively came under the political, social, and cultural domination of Lithuania and Poland, countries whose governing and dominant social strata were Roman Catholic. In effect, the future of the Ukrainian people depended on the fate of its Orthodox Rus' church within a basically Roman Catholic environment.

The Metropolitanate of Kiev

Educated Ukrainians were well aware of the crucial symbiotic relationship of politics, religion, culture, and the survival of the Rus' as a people. The first two centuries of Lithuanian-Polish rule did not bode well for the Orthodox Rus' Church in Ukraine. The reason was related in large part to the complicated status of the highest dignitary in the Orthodox Church, the metropolitan of Kiev and All Rus'. As one of the aftereffects of the Mongol presence beginning in the 1240s, the metropolitans tended to reside not in their seat of Kiev, but rather in the northern

The Metropolitanate of Kiev and All Rus'

Because of the close relationship between church and state in the Orthodox world, the status and the place of residence of the metropolitan of Kiev, the head of the Orthodox Church of Rus', were to have wide-ranging political and cultural implications in the lands once part of Kievan Rus'. The metropolitan derived his canonical authority from the ecumenical patriarch of Constantinople, and consequently the attitude of that prelate always had to be taken into account.

In principle, the ecumenical patriarch favored a single, unified Kiev metropolitanate (archeparchy). During the fourteenth century, in an effort to counter the political decline of the Byzantine Empire, the mother church in Constantinople drew closer to the South Slav and East Slav Orthodox churches, and crucial to the relationship it hoped to achieve was the maintenance of an undivided Metropolitanate of Kiev and All Rus'. The attempt was complicated by the fact that in the second half of the fourteenth century the ecclesiastical territory of the Kievan metropolitanate was divided politically among four states: Muscovy, Lithuania, Poland, and the Golden Horde. This political reality, coupled with the threat of Roman Catholic influence on the western Rus' lands and the reluctance after 1299 of Kievan metropolitans to reside in their ecclesiastical seat of Kiev, forced the ecumenical patriarch to compromise the principle of jurisdictional unity.

As early as at the beginning of the fourteenth century, Constantinople accepted the distinction between what it designated as the eparchies of Great Rus' (*Megalē Rosiia*) and Little Rus' (*Mikrā Rosiia*). In 1303, the latter jurisdiction became the Metropolitanate of Halych and, at the request of the Rus' rulers of Galicia, was recognized by Constantinople as consisting of six eparchies: Halych, Volodymyr-Volyns'kyi, Chełm, Przemyśl, Luts'k, and Turaŭ. Similarly, in 1317 the powerful Grand Duke Gediminas of Lithuania persuaded Constantinople to give his grand duchy its own metropolitan jurisdiction, with a seat in Navahrudak. Not surprisingly, the metropolitan of Kiev, resident in Moscow, protested against what he considered another division of his ecclesiastical territory. As a result of his protests, both the Galician and the Lithuanian metropolitanates were abolished, restored, and abolished again between 1328 and 1401.

Subsequently, the Lithuanians continued to press not for the establishment of a separate Lithuanian metropolitanate, but for the restoration of the Kievan metropolitanate on their own territory. Accordingly, in 1415 Grand Duke Vytautas initiated the election of Lithuania's own Kievan metropolitan (Hryhorii Tsamblak, reigned 1415–1418), but, again following pressure from the Kievan metropolitan in Moscow, this unilateral Lithuanian move was not recognized by the ecumenical patriarch in Constantinople. Not until the middle of the fifteenth century was the desire of the Lithuanians to have Kievan metropolitans on their own territory fulfilled. This development was the result, however, not of Lithuanian influence on the ecumenical patriarch, but rather of Muscovy's alienation from Constantinople. Just how did such alienation come about?

In 1439, Izydor, the metropolitan of Kiev (reigned 1436–1458) resident in Moscow, along with the ecumenical patriarch in Constantinople accepted an act signed at Florence calling for the union of the Orthodox and Roman Catholic churches. The Florentine act so angered Muscovy's bishops and secular rulers that Izydor was driven from the country. In 1448, Muscovy's bishops elected their own metropolitan of Kiev and All Rus' without the approval of the ecumenical patriarch, a step which eventually led to its complete independence as the Russian Orthodox Church.

As for the rest of the Rus' church on Belarusan and Ukrainian lands within Lithuania and Poland, it too, beginning in 1458, had its own metropolitans of Kiev, who were approved by the ecumenical patriarch in Constantinople and who resided in the Lithuanian town of Navahrudak. The hierarchs held the title Metropolitan of Kiev, Galicia, and All Rus', and included within their jurisdiction, aside from the archeparchy of Kiev, were the eparchies of Volodymyr-Brest, Luts'k-Ostroh, Przemyśl-Sambir, Chełm-Belz, Pinsk-Turaŭ, Polatsk-Vitebsk, Chernihiv-Briansk (until 1500), Smolensk (until 1514), and (from its restoration in 1539) Halych-L'viv.

Rus' cities of Vladimir-na-Kliazma and Moscow. Finally, in 1326 Moscow became the permanent residence of the metropolitan, although during the next century a few resided for certain periods of time in Kiev.

Meanwhile, in the western Rus' (Belarusan and Ukrainian) lands that had come under Lithuanian and Polish rule in the fourteenth century, various efforts were made to create new Orthodox metropolitanates in Galicia and Lithuania or to restore the Kievan metropolitanate so that its seat would be within the borders of Lithuania. In theory, all such moves had to receive the blessing of the highest authority of the Orthodox Church, the ecumenical patriarch in Constantinople. In practice, metropolitans were at times appointed without the approval of Constantinople; and the metropolitan of Kiev, resident in Moscow, remained, like the Muscovite secular authorities, staunchly opposed to any effort that would divide western Rus' lands from what he considered his own unified ecclesiastical jurisdiction. In short, the Kievan metropolitanate became an object of political rivalry between Lithuania and Muscovy. From 1458 it was effectively divided into two metropolitanates: that of Kiev headed by its metropolitan resident in Navahrudak (Lithuania), and that of Moscow and All Rus' (implying an on-going claim to the Kiev jurisdiction) headed by a metropolitan resident in Moscow.

This meant that from the second half of the fifteenth century Ukrainian territories had no metropolitan in residence. As a result, not only was the country deprived of the political and sociocultural prestige that traditionally attended the presence of the metropolitan, but the concomitant lack of effective authority led to an almost total breakdown of ecclesiastical order. Galicia and Volhynia, in par-

MAP 15   RELIGION AND CULTURE, 16th and 17th CENTURIES

Legend		
—•• International boundaries, 1570	‡ Metropolitan see	▲ Important monastery
••••••• Orthodox eparchial boundaries, 1570	‡ Eparchial see	▢ Printshop
▬ Boundary of Ukraine, 2005		Kiev Brotherhood

Scale 1 : 8 150 000
0   50   100 miles
0   50   100 kilometers   Copyright © by Paul Robert Magocsi

ticular, were becoming increasingly susceptible to Roman Catholic pressure fol-
lowing the creation in 1375 of a Roman Catholic archbishopric of Halych and
L'viv, which set up new dioceses to promote the Latin rite in western Ukraine.
The Polish king also exercised his prerogative of designating hierarchs for vacant
Orthodox sees. More often than not, the appointments were used as instruments
of political patronage and, in some cases, went to recently ordained powerful mag-

nates who used their new religious posts for further political and economic self-aggrandizement. Religion seemed the last thing on the minds of these church leaders, who continued to live the style of life of the nobility (even maintaining armed retainers). Orthodox morals and religious life in general suffered accordingly.

Nor could much help be expected from neighboring Orthodox powers. As for the ultimate authority in the Orthodox world, the ecumenical patriarch in Constantinople, his position and influence were directly related to the status of the Byzantine Empire. At the beginning of the fifteenth century, Byzantium itself faced imminent collapse, and by 1453 the Ottoman Turks had captured Constantinople, putting an end to the thousand-year-old Eastern Roman Empire. Now, finding himself in an aggressive Islamic environment, the ecumenical patriarch had all he could do to preserve the existence of the Orthodox Church in former Byzantine lands, let alone be seriously concerned with the fate of the church elsewhere.

Other Orthodox states were similarly powerless or unwilling to help the western Rus' church on Ukrainian lands. Orthodox Moldavia and Walachia, from which Galicia had traditionally received help, were fighting for their own survival in the face of the Ottoman advance into the Balkans, which eventually overtook them by the early sixteenth century. For their part, Muscovy's government and its own Kievan metropolitans were not about to give help to what they considered a rival Orthodox Church on Polish and Lithuanian territory. At best, Muscovy served as a place of refuge for those Rus' gentry, clergy, townspeople, and even peasants from Belarusan and Ukrainian lands who decided to escape eastward, away from the increasing Roman Catholic influence in their homelands. Finally, for those Rus' magnates and gentry who remained at home, many became convinced that it was not worth maintaining Orthodoxy if conversion to Roman Catholicism and acceptance of the Polish language and Polish customs would assure them of a favorable position in the new sociopolitical and economic order.

The monastic movement

Deprived of the support of the state (which it had enjoyed in Kievan times), cut off from the ecumenical patriarch in Constantinople, and more often than not administered by opportunistic bishops of aristocratic origin who were uninterested in religion, the Orthodox Church in Ukraine was left to its own devices. One option was a withdrawal from the temporal world into the realm of spirituality. It is no coincidence, therefore, that between the fifteenth and early seventeenth centuries several monasteries and hermitages (*skyty*) were newly founded or rebuilt, first in Galicia, then in Volhynia and in central and eastern Ukraine. Among the more important that came into being (or were rebuilt) during this period were, in Galicia, the Maniava hermitage; in Volhynia, the Pochaïv, Kremenets', Dubno, and Derman' monasteries; in Kiev, the Epiphany, St Michael's Golden-Dome, St Nicholas (Small), and Vydubychi monasteries; and in other parts of central and eastern Ukraine, the Novhorod-Sivers'kyi, Trinity-St Elijah (in Chernihiv), Mezhyhiria (near Vyshhorod), Hustynia (near Pryluky), Mhar (near Lubny), and Trakhtemyriv monasteries. Other older monasteries continued functioning, including in Hungarian-ruled Transcarpathia on Chernecha Hora near Mukachevo; in Galicia, St Onufrius (L'viv) and Univ; in Volhynia, Zhydychyn; and among the most important of all the Caves Monastery (Pechers'ka Lavra) in Kiev. Icon painting, manuscript and printed book production, and schools flourished in some or all of these monasteries, which thus helped to preserve the spirit of Eastern Christianity.

Monasteries also functioned as places for the physical repose and spiritual refreshment of thousands of faithful who visited annually as pilgrims. Aside from their religious function, the pilgrimages to the monasteries played a role in promoting a sense of community, whereby visitors from different parts of the Orthodox Rus' world came to realize that they were part of a larger group. In that sense, monasteries functioned as pre-modern communication centers that encouraged what later would be called a national consciousness. Nevertheless, the monastic movement and the customary faith of the lower clergy and the masses were insufficient to counteract the prevailing sociopolitical environment of the Polish-Lithuanian Commonwealth. The result was a continual decline in the status of Orthodoxy, which made its future survival in Ukraine questionable. Among the first elements to grasp the seriousness of the religious and cultural crisis were the Rus' townspeople and some magnates and gentry. Each group felt threatened by the decline of Orthodoxy and consequently of its own status in society, and each reacted to the situation in its own way.

The role of townspeople and magnates

The importance in society of townspeople, particularly Rus' townspeople, had declined from what it was in Kievan times. The towns played no role in Polish-Lithuanian political life; they were largely passed over by the growing Vistula grain trade; and those that governed themselves according to the Magdeburg Law thereby reinforced their isolation and laid themselves open to eventual exploitation by the politically and economically influential nobility.

The cities did become centers of intellectual ferment, however, especially during Poland's cultural renaissance after the 1550s. Not only Polish, but also German, Jewish, and Armenian culture flourished in Ukraine's cities. These groups had in fact come to dominate urban life, with the consequence that by the sixteenth century Orthodox Rus' townspeople felt themselves to be on both the economic and the sociocultural defensive.

There was one other people, however, who worked together with the Orthodox Rus' populace in defense of its religious culture. These were the Greeks, who by the sixteenth century had come to play an important role in the economic, cultural, and eventually political (especially diplomatic) life of Ukraine. The Greeks were not only of the same Orthodox faith as the Rus', they also had a close relations – and therefore acted as intermediaries – with the hierarchs of the Eastern patriarchates (Antioch, Alexandria, Jerusalem) and the ecumenical patriarchate of Constantinople, which had ultimate jurisdiction over the Orthodox Church in Poland-Lithuania. It was not uncommon for wealthy Greek merchants, such as

Manopolis Maripeta, Konstantyn Korniakt, and Oleksii Balabanos in L'viv, to make generous donations to Orthodox churches and monasteries. As well, Greek scholars and churchmen, among the best known of whom were Arsenii of Elasson and Cyril Lucaris, played significant roles in the new schools, printshops, and brotherhoods that were established in the second half of the sixteenth century. It was the brotherhoods, in particular, which took it upon themselves to defend and promote Orthodox cultural and religious interests in the Ukrainian and Belarusan lands of the Polish-Lithuanian Commonwealth.

Urban-based brotherhoods (*bratstva*), or confraternities, have a long tradition in the Christian world; their origins in Ukraine, however, remain a source of controversy. Some scholars say they continued the tradition of the religious *bratchiny*, which were secular societies in the service of the church in the Kievan period; others argue that they evolved according to the model of the urban guilds in medieval western Europe, which developed in Ukrainian cities after the introduction of the Magdeburg Law; still others suggest they were influenced by the Greek brotherhood associations (*adelfotes*). Whatever their origin and whatever their degree of organizational cohesion – probably rather loose during the early period – brotherhoods came into existence in western Ukrainian cities, especially L'viv, during the first half of the sixteenth century.

From the very beginning, the urban brotherhoods were associated with individual churches. In a sense, a brotherhood was a kind of business and professional association, whose primary goal apart from the social (they held banquets and fairs) was to support the Orthodox Church. For instance, during the 1530s, L'viv townspeople, with the help of the influential Volhynian Rus' magnate (and general in the Lithuanian army) Prince Kostiantyn I. Ostroz'kyi, succeeded in persuading the Polish government to restore the Orthodox eparchy of Halych (abolished with its metropolitanate in the early fourteenth century) and to guarantee non-interference in Orthodox affairs by the local Roman Catholic bishop. As a result, an Orthodox bishop was appointed in 1539, and the seat of the eparchy was moved from Halych to L'viv.

But it was not until the last decades of the sixteenth century that the brotherhoods came to play a more organized and influential role. Until that time, the magnates played the leading role in the Orthodox cultural revival. Whereas it is true that following the Union of Lublin in 1569 and the incorporation of most Ukrainian lands into the Polish Kingdom many Ukrainian magnates and gentry became polonized, it is also true that a few secular leaders worked hard to promote Orthodoxy and to revive and raise the level of Rus' culture in general. In fact, it is to the Orthodox magnates that credit is due for the establishment of the first printing presses on Ukrainian territory as well as of the first advanced schools of the period.

In 1567, on the estate of Prince Hryhorii Khodkevych at Zabludów, in northeastern Podlachia, the first printing press was set up by a refugee from Muscovy, Ivan Fedorov, who is known in Ukrainian cultural history as Ivan Fedorovych. At Zabłudów, Fedorovych published a didactic Gospel (1569) and a book of psalms (1570). Then, in 1572, he went to L'viv, briefly to Derman', and then to Ostroh in Volhynia, where he set up his printing press on the estate of Prince Kostiantyn/ Vasyl' K. Ostroz'kyi. The Ostroz'kyi estate was at the time the leading center of the Orthodox cultural revival. A school was opened there ca. 1576, which later became known as the Ostroh Academy. The academy became a haven for Ukrainian and foreign (especially Greek) scholars, and it helped to train a whole generation of Ukrainian intellectual leaders. Eager to reverse the deterioration within the Orthodox Church, the Ostroh Academy focused its attention on the Byzantine roots of the Orthodox tradition. Accordingly, Greek was made the language of instruction. Some Latin was also taught, but it is not known whether Church Slavonic was used. Despite the emphasis on Greek and Latin, however, the local Rus' culture was not forgotten. On the printing press, which operated at Ostroh between 1578 and 1612, were published about two dozen books, undoubtedly the most famous of which was the Ostroh Bible of 1581. This was the first complete text of the Bible in Church Slavonic, based on the Greek and translated by a group of scholars at the academy under the editorship of Herasym Smotryts'kyi.

But such ventures remained largely dependent on the good will and religious patriotism of a few individuals. In fact, the tenuousness of their achievements soon became evident when several descendants of these cultural philanthropists and Orthodox patriots became Roman Catholic. The result was that most of the Orthodox intellectual oases had disappeared by the beginning of the seventeenth century. Even the famed Ostroh Academy was transformed in 1620 into a Jesuit College by Prince Kostiantyn Ostroz'kyi's Roman Catholic daughter. In the end, the future of Orthodoxy and Rus' culture was not to be guaranteed by the acts of a few magnates. Instead, it was to depend largely on the evolution of the urban brotherhoods.

L'viv's Stauropegial Brotherhood

The most important of these urban brotherhoods was the one in L'viv associated with the Church of the Holy Dormition (Uspens'kyi Sobor) in that city. At about the time of its formal establishment, the L'viv brotherhood received particular encouragement as a result of its interaction with visiting Orthodox prelates from the former Byzantine Empire. Since 1453, the ecumenical patriarch of Constantinople (who was still the de jure head of Orthodoxy in Ukrainian and Lithuanian lands) and the patriarchs of Antioch, Jerusalem, and Alexandria had found themselves within the Islamic Ottoman Empire. And whereas the Ottomans permitted the community of Orthodox Christians (*Rum milleti*) to practice their faith, the Islamic government often clashed with and in some cases imprisoned church leaders. Moreover, the Orthodox Church was deprived of the enormous sources of wealth (in particular, landholdings) in its possession from the days of the Byzantine Empire. Consequently, the church had to fall back on its own members for support. But a community that was no longer part of the ruling elite had decidedly limited resources. Accordingly, the Orthodox leadership turned to the only other country that might provide some help – the tsardom of Muscovy.

Beginning in the sixteenth century, several Orthodox prelates from the Ottoman Empire traveled north to Moscow, and some of them stopped in Ukraine along the way. Among them was Patriarch Joachim of Antioch (reigned 1581–1592), who stayed for a short while in L'viv in early 1586. There, he was shocked by what he saw in the local Orthodox Church, in particular the moral lapse of some of its bishops and priests (by then it was not uncommon for twice-married clergy to be ordained). He was encouraged, however, by the activity of the L'viv Dormition Church Brotherhood, and he gave it his full support. He accepted the charter of the brotherhood, granting it in 1586 the right of stauropegion, whereby it was placed directly under his control and freed from any interference by the local bishop. This was an exceptional privilege for a lay organization, although one often granted to monasteries. What was unique, however, was that the patriarch also gave the L'viv Dormition Brotherhood the authority to report on abuses within the local Orthodox Church. Not unexpectedly, the granting of such a supervisory role to a lay organization did not please the local hierarchs, who felt, and rightly so, that their own authority was being undermined.

For its part, the L'viv Stauropegial Brotherhood took up the cultural and moral challenge. It quickly amended its charter, with the result that the social aspect of the organization was replaced by a focus on religious and, especially, educational activities. Now known as the Stauropegial Brotherhood, the organization constructed a new building which included a home for the poor and sick. It also bought the Fedorovych press and set up a printing shop. The brotherhood had already established a school in 1585, and soon it became the model for other such institutions throughout Ukrainian and Belarusan lands. Its curriculum included not only Greek but also Church Slavonic, and among its leading scholars was Stefan Zyzanii.

The patriarch had also given the L'viv Stauropegial Brotherhood supervisory responsibility over all brotherhoods in Ukraine. Joining the already-existing ones, several others were soon established: Przemyśl, Rohatyn, and Krasnystaw in 1589, Brest and Horodok in 1591, and Lublin in 1594. At each of these brotherhoods, schools were established according to the Greco-Slavonic model of the L'viv Stauropegial Brotherhood and, in general, education became the primary function of the brotherhoods.

But whereas the brotherhoods were to play an overwhelmingly positive role in promoting education and in preserving Church Slavonic culture within a Polish-oriented Latin environment, their role as self-styled protectors of Orthodoxy would before long bring them into conflict with the hierarchy of the church. This conflict would cause an immense disruption not only in Ukrainian religious life, but in Ukrainian society as a whole. The events in Ukraine did not unfold in isolation, however, but were influenced by the most powerful movements in sixteenth-century Europe – the Reformation and Counter Reformation.

13

Reformation, Counter Reformation, and the Union of Brest

From the time of the acceptance of Christianity by the Roman Empire in the fourth century and through the subsequent spread of this faith throughout the European continent, the interrelatedness of politics and religion had been a fundamental component of the development of western civilization. Beginning in 1054 and culminating in the early thirteenth century, the Christian world became divided into two spheres – the Catholic, with its seat in Rome, and the Orthodox, with its seat in Constantinople. Between the two spheres, there was an important difference in the relationship of church and state. The Eastern Christian, or Orthodox Church was an arm of the state, whether in Byzantium or in other lands, like Kievan Rus' and Bulgaria, where Orthodoxy was established. In the West, the Roman Catholic Church remained comparatively beyond the control of the ruling secular power and itself evolved into an independent political entity known as the Papal States. Based in the center of the Italian Peninsula, the pope administered the Papal States and numerous other ecclesiastical states north of the Alps in what are today Germany and Austria. As a result of the papacy's secular activity, medieval western Europe witnessed an ongoing struggle between church and state for control of the political and economic development of nearly half the continent.

As the Roman Catholic Church's political and economic power increased, so too grew the kind of abuses often associated with temporal power. Consequently, certain committed Roman Catholics came to realize that the religion professed by their church was little other than an ideological facade erected to preserve the solidly entrenched vested interests of the priesthood and of the ecclesiastical and secular governments allied to the church. Moral abuses were particularly disconcerting to pious laypersons, because they seemed to contradict the Christian ideals professed by the church.

The Protestant Reformation

There were several attempts to reform the Roman Catholic Church from within, led especially by certain monastic orders. But when these attempts failed to bring about substantial change, the movement for reform passed beyond the perimeters of the church into a more public arena. Among the earliest reformers was the Czech priest Jan Hus, who at the beginning of the fifteenth century criticized the Roman Catholic Church and preached a return to the true principles of Christianity. His successors, known as Hussites, had come to control much of Bohemia and Moravia by the end of the fifteenth century. Although Hussite ideological influence was felt beyond the borders of those provinces, its long-term impact essentially was limited to those two regions in the heart of central Europe.

More influential was the activity of the German priest and religious reformer Martin Luther, who in 1517 posted on the doors of the cathedral in Wittenberg his famous theses protesting abuses in the Roman Catholic Church. He was followed soon after in France and Switzerland by the theologian John Calvin. Although the followers of these men, subsequently described as Lutherans and Calvinists, were divided over certain theological issues, they all had one common purpose: to protest what they considered the extensive temporal power of the Roman Catholic Church and to reform that organization. If reform was not possible, then they were prepared to establish new organizations that would be responsible only to God and not to the pope in Rome or to any other earthly hierarch. The source of their inspiration was the Bible, and they believed every individual had a duty to study the Bible as a source of inspiration and truth. Because they were opposed to or in protest against Rome, the followers of this movement were called Protestants, and the movement itself, originally inspired by the need for change or reform, came to be known as the Reformation.

The Reformation spread rapidly through central and western Europe, where from the beginning it was inextricably involved in politics. Several princes and other local leaders took up the Protestant cause as a way of rebelling against their Roman Catholic secular superiors. If an individual local ruler converted to Protestantism, his people were made to follow – a reflection of the contemporary principle of *cuius regio, eius religio* (the religion of the ruler is made the religion of the land). In this way, much of Europe north of the Alps became Protestant during the sixteenth century.

The Reformation reached Poland and, notably, Lithuania during the first half of the sixteenth century. Even the Teutonic Order along the Baltic, an order founded for the purpose of promoting Roman Catholicism among the "heathens," voluntarily accepted the Reformation in 1525 and transformed itself into a secular state, becoming a vassal of Poland the following year. Poland's age-old military struggle with the Teutonic state came to an end, although Prussia now became a center of Lutheranism, the influence of which radiated southward and eastward from centers like the University of Königsberg (est. 1544). The Reformation was particularly well received among the magnates of Lithuania, including both Roman Catholic and Orthodox families such as the Radziwiłłs, the Khodkevyches, the Volovyches, the Sapiehas, and the Vyshnevets'kyis, all of whom adopted some form of Protestantism.

Moreover, in Poland-Lithuania there was a great variety of movements from which to choose. Lutheranism, Calvinism, and Unitarianism (or Anti-Trinitarianism) were among the major sects, although all of them, in what became typical of Protestantism, were further divided and subdivided into numerous subgroups.

The success of the Reformation was in large part due to specific contemporary conditions in Poland-Lithuania. King Zygmunt II Augustus (reigned 1548–1572) prided himself on upholding the Renaissance ideals of humanism and tolerance. Moreover, because those groups who embraced Protestantism – the magnates and some gentry – were already independent of the king, the Reformation in Poland-Lithuania did not become an excuse for political action. Accordingly, the strident overtones characteristic of religious developments in western and central Europe were initially avoided, with the result that at least during the first three-quarters of the sixteenth century Poland and Lithuania witnessed the generally peaceful coexistence of Roman Catholicism and Protestantism.

In Ukrainian lands, Protestantism did not have the same kind of impact, in numbers of converts, as in Poland or even Lithuania, although a recent estimate suggests that there were as many as 400 Protestant congregations (the vast majority Unitarian or Socinian) in Ukrainian territory, especially in Volhynia, at various times between the sixteenth and eighteenth centuries. Protestantism did, however, have an important indirect impact in that its existence stimulated and heightened intellectual discourse on religious issues. Its most direct impact was on education.

The great emphasis placed by the Protestants on individual reading and study of the Bible required a literate population and the wide availability of Bibles. Wherever Protestantism spread, therefore, so too did schools and printing presses, and these contributed to a rise in the cultural level of given areas. Principles of Protestant education greatly influenced intellectual centers in Ukraine such as the Ostroh Academy. In fact, many of the members of the Orthodox intellectual circle at Ostroh became either Protestants or Protestant sympathizers. Accordingly, it is no surprise that among the most significant projects undertaken at Ostroh was a translation of the Bible into Church Slavonic. Nevertheless, while there were some attempts to translate parts of the New Testament into contemporary Ukrainian (the Peresopnytsia Gospel, 1556–61), the Protestant thrust toward publication in the vernacular (the reformers Hus and Luther were also primary formulators of literary Czech and German respectively) was not followed in Ukraine. The leading Ukrainian writers of the time, Herasym Smotryts'kyi, Lavrentii Zyzanii, and Ivan Vyshens'kyi, noted primarily for their religious polemics, all used Church Slavonic. Church Slavonic had prestige because it had been the ecclesiastical language since Kievan times. In no way, however, did it reflect the common speech of the contemporary Ukrainian population. But since Orthodoxy, unlike Protestantism, did not rely on intellectually persuasive argumentation, there really was no need to raise vernacular Ukrainian to the level of a literary language.

The Counter Reformation and Orthodox Ukraine

The rapid spread of the Reformation through Europe could not go unchallenged by the Roman Catholic Church, and by the second half of the sixteenth century a reaction had begun which came to be known as the Counter Reformation. One result of the Counter Reformation was the outbreak of religious wars, in which much of Europe was devastated in the name of Roman Catholic or Protestant religious truth. The conflict continued until as late as the seventeenth century. On the intellectual front, the Counter Reformation was spearheaded by the newly founded Jesuit Order, which used Protestant techniques – education and the dissemination of learning – in an effort to reconvert to Roman Catholicism those who had fallen into what was considered Protestant "apostasy." The Jesuits arrived in Poland in 1564 to begin their work on behalf of the Roman Catholic Church.

The Ukrainians in Poland-Lithuania had not converted en masse to Protestantism, but from the Roman Catholic point of view, they too were unacceptable because they were Orthodox. And in their bid to rid Poland of Protestantism and thereby to transform Poland into the eastern bastion of Roman Catholicism, the Jesuits and their supporters in the government decided to address the "Orthodox problem" at the same time. From the Catholic perspective, the problem was the conversion of individual Orthodox adherents; from the Orthodox perspective, it was bringing together once again two separate but equal ecclesial entities, that is, church union.

The period since the division between Roman Catholicism and Orthodoxy had seen efforts, albeit unsuccessful, to reunify the two halves of the Christian realm. Ukraine had always played a key role. For instance, during the heyday of the Galician-Volhynian Kingdom in the mid-thirteenth century, Prince Danylo had initially promised to support church union in return for the pope's support in his crusade against the Mongols. Even more significant had been the activity of Metropolitan Izydor (reigned 1436–1441), the last Kievan hierarch resident in Moscow to be appointed by the ecumenical patriarch of Constantinople. Soon after his appointment in 1436, Izydor left Moscow to take part in negotiations for church union being held in Florence. The ecumenical patriarch himself favored these talks because through them he hoped to gain western help against the Ottoman Turks, who were then at the very gates of Constantinople. Metropolitan Izydor did, in fact, agree to the terms of the Florentine Union, and the act was signed in July 1439. Two years later, however, when Izydor finally arrived back in Moscow, the local authorities, incensed by his action, immediately put him in prison. Izydor eventually escaped, but for all intents and purposes the idea of church union ended with him.

In the atmosphere of the Counter Reformation prevailing in late sixteenth-century Poland, the idea of church union was revived once again. This time its ideological proponents were the Jesuits. Since their arrival in Poland in 1564 and in Lithuania in 1569, the Jesuit ideological thrust had been focused on education and publication. The Jesuit school system, including colleges (the first founded in Jarosław in 1575, and twenty-two more in Ukrainian lands before 1648), quickly became renowned. Moreover, it was not long before the sons of Orthodox and recently converted Protestant nobles who had been sent to Jesuit educational institutions converted to Roman Catholicism. Jesuit brotherhoods and printing presses also turned out much polemical material directed at both Protestants and Orthodox. In their anti-Orthodox polemics, Jesuit writers, the most famous of whom were Piotr Skarga and Antonio Possevino, focused on the theme of church union. In the course of their ideological onslaught, the Jesuits also pushed for the universal adoption of the Gregorian calendar, introduced by Pope Gregory XIII in 1582.

This seemingly technical matter met with strong opposition from the Orthodox. They viewed the Julian calendar as integral to their traditional religious life and something not to be given up easily, if at all, especially if the change was to be implemented by force.

Nonetheless, despite the Jesuit call for church union, the actual initiative came not from the Roman Catholics, but from the Orthodox themselves. Coincidentally, it was at this very time in the 1580s that Orthodox patriarchs from the Ottoman Empire, traveling to Muscovy in search of financial assistance, visited the church in Ukraine, where they decided to grant wide-ranging responsibility to the Stauropegial Brotherhood at the Dormition Church in L'viv. In 1588–1589, Jeremiah II (reigned intermittently 1572–1595) became the first ecumenical patriarch to visit personally the Metropolitanate of Kiev. Before leaving Constantinople, he reiterated the stauropegial status to the L'viv Dormition Church Brotherhood and extended his blessings to its other activities (the school, hospice, and printing press). During his return trip from Moscow, the ecumenical patriarch stopped in Vilnius, where he defrocked twice- and thrice-married clergy, including the metropolitan of Kiev Onysyfor Divochka (reigned 1579–1589). Jeremiah II also recognized the stauropegial status of a second monastery in L'viv, that of St Onufrius.

Jeremiah's actions reflected a general policy of attempting to restore the authority of the ecumenical patriarchate over the Orthodox Church within the Rus' world. As part of the process, Constantinople's long-standing alienation, since 1458, from the Kievan metropolitans resident in Moscow was finally healed in 1589, when it recognized the autocephaly, or independence, of the Russian Orthodox Church, to be headed henceforth by its own patriarch of Moscow. Yet at the same time the ecumenical patriarch issued decrees for the governance of the Orthodox Church in Poland-Lithuania, and his action sent a clear message to Moscow's new patriarch that the Kievan metropolitanate in Belarusan and Ukrainian lands was to remain under the jurisdiction of Constantinople.

Not surprisingly, the seeming high-handedness of Constantinople's ecumenical patriarch vis-à-vis the Orthodox Church in Ukraine and his courting of the L'viv Stauropegial Brotherhood caused great dissatisfaction among certain local hierarchs, especially the bishop of L'viv, Gedeon Balaban (reigned 1569–1607). As a result, Balaban turned to the Polish Roman Catholic archbishop of L'viv, whom he begged in 1589 "to liberate [our] bishops from the slavery of the patriarchs of Constantinople."[1]

The Union of Brest

Dissatisfaction with Constantinople prompted greater interest in Rome, and as early as 1590, at a synod of the Metropolitanate of Kiev in Poland-Lithuania, Balaban joined three fellow Orthodox bishops in signing a letter to the Polish king Zygmunt III (reigned 1587–1632), in which they indicated their readiness to recognize the supremacy of the pope and their intention to unite with the Catholic Church of Rome. The four Orthodox bishops realized that their efforts on behalf of church union would not be successful without the support of the Rus' magnates. In this regard, their own ecclesiastical ranks expanded in 1593, when the magnate Adam Potii, the former secretary to the king of Poland and the holder of several governmental offices, was consecrated under the name Ipatii as Orthodox bishop of Volodymyr.

But it was Potii's patron, the powerful magnate and palatine of Kiev Prince Kostiantyn/Vasyl' K. Ostroz'kyi, whom the bishops needed on their side if the idea of church union was to be a success. As founder of the Ostroh Academy, Prince Ostroz'kyi had already expressed interest in the idea of church union, which he saw as a means of improving the status of the Orthodox Church in what otherwise was becoming an increasingly Roman Catholic–oriented Polish-Lithuanian state. Ostroz'kyi's understanding of union, however, implied the participation of what he considered the "whole Ecumenical Church," that is, the entire Roman Catholic and Orthodox world, including the ecumenical and other eastern patriarchs as well as neighboring Moldavia and Muscovy. He passed on his own plan for union to his protégé, Bishop Potii, for presentation at a regional episcopal council.

It was at this critical juncture that relations between Ostroz'kyi and the pro-union Orthodox bishops broke down. Instead of promoting Ostroz'kyi's all-encompassing approach, Bishop Potii, together with Bishop Kyrylo Terlets'kyi of Luts'k (reigned 1585–1607), acted unilaterally and issued two letters of intent (December 1594 and June 1595) pledging allegiance to Rome. The letters of intent were then approved by the Polish king. In response, Ostroz'kyi condemned what he called "our faithless pastors, the metropolitan and bishops," who "through the evil and cunning work of the ever-malign devil ... [have become] tempted by the glories of this world, and blinded by their desire for pleasures ... have forsaken our holy patriarchs and gone over to the Latin side."[2] Ostroz'kyi's criticism did have an effect, since even Bishop Balaban of L'viv, one of the earliest initiators of the movement, now repudiated the idea of union.

Nevertheless, the pro-union bishops, joined by metropolitan of Kiev Mykhail Rahoza (reigned 1589–1599), pressed forward, and in June 1595, during an episcopal synod at Brest, they approved a document containing thirty-three articles that set forth their understanding of union with Rome. This document later came to be considered the "constitution" of the Kievan metropolitanate "pertaining to union with the Roman church," and it addressed theological, liturgical, ritual, administrative, and interchurch matters. The underlying concern was that the union with Rome would not change Eastern church practices, such as use of the liturgy of St John Chrysostom, the Slavonic rite, the Julian calendar, a married clergy, and administrative autonomy.

In December 1595, Bishops Potii and Terlets'kyi took the two episcopal letters and the Brest articles to Rome. It is important to note that the pope neither approved nor rejected the proposed articles. Instead, on 23 December he issued a papal decree (*Magnus Dominus et laudabilis*) recognizing "all sacred rites and ceremonies which the Ruthenian [Rus'] bishops and clergy use" as long as they were "not opposed to the truth and doctrine of the Catholic faith."[3] Thus, what later members of the Uniate or Greek Catholic Church believed to be their historic rights guaranteed by the Union of Brest were nothing more than their own demands, which could be approved or rejected at the discretion of the pope and

THE VIEWS OF PRINCE KOSTIANTYN OSTROZ'KYI

In June 1595, just after the pro-union Orthodox hierarchs issued their second letter of intent and the thirty-three articles which outlined their understanding of church union with Rome, Prince Ostroz'kyi issued the following appeal to the people of Rus':

> In these days, through the evil and cunning work of the ever-malign devil, the chief leaders of our faith, tempted by the glories of this world and blinded by their desire for pleasures, our faithless pastors, the metropolitan and the bishops, have forsaken our holy patriarchs and gone over to the Latin side. ... Changing into wolves they secretly agreed among themselves like the damned, like Judas the Betrayer of Christ with the Jews, to tear away the Orthodox Christians of this region without their knowledge and to drag them down to ruin. Because the majority of the population of this land, particularly the Orthodox Christians, consider me to a certain extent to be a defender of Orthodoxy and because I have fear before God and before you, dear brethren, to take any part of the blame on my head, I inform you all together and individually that I have determined to stand firmly, in an alliance with you, against these dangerous enemies of our salvation. What can be more shameless, more unjust, than when those six or seven persons, like robbers, plot secretly and forsake our pastors-patriarchs? Without asking us they entangle us in this betrayal, us the Orthodox, like mute curs. Why obey such persons? When the salt has lost its savor it should be cast out and trampled underfoot. ...

SOURCE: Ivan Wlasowsky, *Outline History of the Ukrainian Orthodox Church*, Vol. I (New York and Bound Brook, N.J. 1974), p. 255.

his advisers. It is, in fact, the question of which articles in the 1595 project are "not opposed" to the Catholic faith which has remained a source of conflict between Rome and the Uniate (later, Greek Catholic and then Ukrainian Catholic) Church to the present day.

When Bishops Potii and Terlets'kyi returned from Rome, King Zygmunt III, himself an ardent supporter of church union, called upon Poland-Lithuania's Orthodox hierarchs to convene in the city of Brest, in far southwestern Lithuania, in October 1596. All the hierarchs of the Kievan metropolitanate arrived in Brest in the fall of that year, but they did not meet together. Instead, the pro-union bishops and Kievan Metropolitan Rahoza – joined by three Roman Catholic bishops representing the pope, two Jesuits (including Piotr Skarga), and three senators with armed retinues representing the Polish king – met at the cathedral in Brest. The anti-union forces led by the Orthodox bishops of L'viv (Gedeon Balaban) and Przemyśl (Mykhail Kopystens'kyi) – joined by a representative of the ecumenical patriarch, nine archimandrites, twenty-five lower clergy, and twenty-two Rus' Orthodox and Protestant nobles led by Prince Ostroz'kyi – gathered at the opposite end of Brest in the home of a Protestant nobleman. Each group criticized and excommunicated the other.

THE UNION OF BREST

The Union of Brest was an extended process consisting of several phases. It began with a letter issued by several Orthodox bishops declaring their intention to recognize the supremacy of the pope (1590). Five years later, the letter was followed by two statements signed by several Orthodox bishops expressing their intention to pledge allegiance to the pope (2 December 1594 and 12 June 1595); a list of articles spelling out thirty-three rights, the acceptance of which the Eastern church leaders claimed as a necessary prerequisite to union (11 June 1595); and the acceptance by Pope Clement VIII of the Ruthenian (Rus') bishops and nation into the Roman church (23 December 1595). All this culminated in a declaration signed by the Kievan metropolitan and several bishops at the pro-union synod of Brest (9 October 1596).

The declaration pronounced at Brest reasserted that only the pope, not the ecumenical patriarch, was head of the Rus' Church, whose traditional liturgy and rites, moreover, were not to undergo any changes. The rights and privileges spelled out in the thirty-three articles of 11 June 1595 included the following:

1. Since there is disagreement between the Romans and the Greeks over the procession of the Holy Spirit, which greatly prejudices union for no other reason than that we mutually do not wish to understand each other, we, therefore, request that we be not compelled to any other faith but that testified to by the Gospels and the writings of the Holy Fathers of the Greek faith, that is, that the Holy Spirit does not proceed from two principles nor through a double procession but proceeds from one principle as source, from the Father through the Son.

2. The Divine Liturgy as well as all morning, evening, and nocturnal prayers shall remain unaltered according to ancient custom and tradition accepted in the Eastern Church. Namely, the Sacred Liturgy of which there are three: Basil's, Chrysostom's, and Epiphany's, which is celebrated during Lent with presanctified gifts, as well as all other rites and ceremonies of our church which we have preserved hitherto; that indeed the same be preserved in Rome under the obedience of the Holy Pontiff and all these to be conducted in our language.

3. That the mystery of the most Holy Body and Blood of our Lord Jesus Christ remain for all time unaltered and intact as it has been until now under both species of bread and wine.

6. We accept the new calendar (Gregorian) if the old calendar cannot be used, on the condition, however, that the time and manner of celebrating Easter and other feasts will be preserved and remain whole and intact as it was during the time of unity.

9. The married priesthood shall be preserved intact, except for bigamists.

10. The offices of metropolitan, bishop, and other ecclesiastical ranks shall be conferred only upon those of the Ruthenian or Greek nation and that would be of our

faith. Our ecclesiastical canons state that offices such as that of the metropolitan, the bishops, and other similar ranks be filled by appointments made by ecclesiastical authorities rather than civil authorities.

16. Marriages between Ruthenian Catholics and Roman Catholics shall be a free affair and neither party shall be coerced to accept the rite of the other because they are members of the same church.

19. In keeping with ancient custom, archimandrites, hegumens, monks and their monasteries will be subject to the bishops in whose eparchies they reside ...

21. Archimandrites, hegumens, priests, archdeacons, deacons, and other ecclesiastics of our rite should receive and enjoy the same honor and respect enjoyed by the Roman Catholic clergy and enjoy the ancient freedoms and privileges granted by King Władysław. They shall be free from all taxation as regards both their persons and ecclesiastical properties (not as it has been unjustly until now).

33. Therefore, we the undersigned desire to establish a holy union for the glory of God and peace in the Church. We consider these articles necessary to our Church and require their approval from the highest bishop and His Royal Majesty.*

Twelve of the thirty-three articles were directed to the king of Poland (including 10, 16, 21 and 33, given above); the remaining twenty to the pope (including 1, 2, 3, 6, 9, 19, and 33, given above). While the pope accepted the "Ruthenian bishops and nation" into the Catholic Church, he did not accept the list of thirty-three articles the bishops put forth as a constitution. He merely admitted that he "considered and understood" their "petitions and offers." In fact, only the articles that pertained to liturgical matters (2 and 3, given above) were accepted by Rome, since they were, in the words of the papal decree *Magnus Dominus et laudabilis*, dated 23 December 1595, "not opposed to the truth and doctrine of the Catholic faith."

In essence, the Union of Brest, which the Uniate (later, Greek Catholic and then Ukrainian Catholic) Church claimed as the legal basis for its distinct existence, became a twofold source of future conflict. Those Orthodox Rus' who refused to join the union never acknowledged the legitimacy of the decision at Brest. For its part, the Roman Catholic Church, while acknowledging the Union of Brest, never accepted the 1595 "constitution." The pope, after all, who is responsible only to God, does not enter into contracts with anyone. At most, he had merely "considered and understood" the "petitions and offers" of the Uniates.

*Russel P. Moroziuk, *Politics of a Church Union* (Chicago 1983), pp. 17–21.

The basic polemic was as follows. The Roman Catholic king supported the union and the concept that the bishops, as leaders, must decide religious questions, and the people must follow. The Orthodox side countered that religious questions cannot be decided without the approval of the faithful; since the pro-union bishops apparently did not have that approval, they had acted illegally and therefore had lost their authority as bishops. With the aid of local printing presses, there developed a spirited polemic on both sides, in which the leading thinkers of the time – Piotr Skarga and Bishop Potii for the Catholic-Uniate side, and Stefan Zyzanii, Iurii Rohatynets', and Ivan Vyshens'kyi for the Orthodox side – participated.

Not surprisingly, the king accepted the decisions of the pro-union bishops. Their agreement came to be known as the Union of Brest of 1596. In a sense, the Union of Brest was the equivalent in the cultural sphere of what had been achieved in the political sphere in 1569 with the Union of Lublin. While it is true that the creation of the new Uniate Church may not have been what the Jesuits and other advocates of the Counter Reformation in Poland hoped to achieve, in the circumstances, given that outright conversion seemed an impossible goal, Uniatism appeared an acceptable compromise.

With the Polish government on its side, some Uniate hierarchs, especially Bishop Potii of Volodymyr (who for his efforts on behalf of the union was made metropolitan of Kiev in 1600), confiscated property from the now-illegal Orthodox Church and increased their pressure on the two remaining Orthodox bishops in the region, Balaban in L'viv and Kopystens'kyi in Przemyśl, to join the union. In Volhynia, several dozen prominent Orthodox nobles did join. The Orthodox cause was left in the hands of the brotherhoods and of magnates and gentry led by Prince Ostroz'kyi. The Orthodox nobles carried on their struggle in the local dietines and the Polish Diet, where they worked in alliance with the other beleaguered religious group, the Protestants. Their efforts were partially successful: in 1607 the Polish Diet granted the Orthodox Church legal status once again and agreed not to interfere in the appointment of its hierarchs. But despite such protection, many Orthodox eparchial sees remained vacant, and in general, Orthodoxy was in a much weakened position vis-à-vis the Roman Catholic and Uniate churches, both of which had the full support of the king and certain other sectors of Polish society.

Thus, within less than three decades, the Orthodox cultural revival, which had begun with such promise in the 1570s, found itself in a situation in which the institution it defended seemed on the verge of disappearing. The valiant efforts of Rus' townspeople (through the brotherhoods) and magnates (through schools and printing presses) could not stem the overwhelming power of Polish society to attract, whether by means of its sociopolitical and secular cultural life or through the religious accommodation of the new Uniate Church. In order to survive, Orthodoxy and the Rus' culture it represented needed some more powerful protector. That protector would be found among the lower echelons of society, which by the early seventeenth century had succeeded in creating an increasingly influential military and political force – the Cossacks.

14

The Tatars and the Crimean Khanate

Traditional historiography about Ukraine has considered the mid-fourteenth to mid-seventeenth centuries as the Lithuanian and Polish, or the Polish-Lithuanian era. Certainly, the Grand Duchy of Lithuania and the Kingdom of Poland ruled significant parts of Ukrainian territory and had a profound impact on the political, socioeconomic, and cultural development of Ukraine and its peoples. But there is a third entity, the Crimean Khanate, which during the same period ruled about a quarter of Ukraine (according to its present-day borders), and which also had a long-standing impact on developments in other Ukrainian territories beyond its direct control. It is for that reason we refer in this book to these centuries as the Lithuanian-Polish-Crimean period in the history of Ukraine.

Chapters 8 and 10 discussed developments in the Crimean peninsula and the steppe zone north of the Black Sea in the course of the fourteenth century. By that time the Golden Horde or Kipçak Khanate, of which Crimea was a part, had allowed a large degree of independence to the Genoese merchants, who as a result came to dominate the trade and commerce flowing through Caffa and several other Crimean Black Sea ports. During the second half of the fourteenth century, however, the Golden Horde entered an extended period of internal political crisis and foreign invasions (by Lithuanians from the north and Timur/Tamerlane from the east), with the result that by the fifteenth century the once-powerful Mongolo-Tatar state was disintegrating. In its stead, Tatar tribesmen established three new states, known as khanates. Two of these came into existence during the 1440s in peripheral regions of the Golden Horde: the Kazan' Khanate along the upper Volga River, and the Crimean Khanate in the Crimean Peninsula and areas north of the Sea of Azov. The third state, the Astrakhan' Khanate, took over the remaining territories of the Golden Horde along the lower Volga River in 1502, when that entity finally ceased to exist. Each of the successor khanates continued the Mongol practice and exacted tribute from those states that held lands formerly part of Kievan Rus': the Kazan' and Astrakhan' khanates received payments from Muscovy; the Crimean Khanate from Muscovy and also from Lithuania and Poland. The three Tatar successor states were formidable powers in their own right. Hence, much of the early history of both Lithuania and Muscovy was

MAP 16

THE CRIMEAN KHANATE AND SOUTHERN UKRAINE, circa 1625

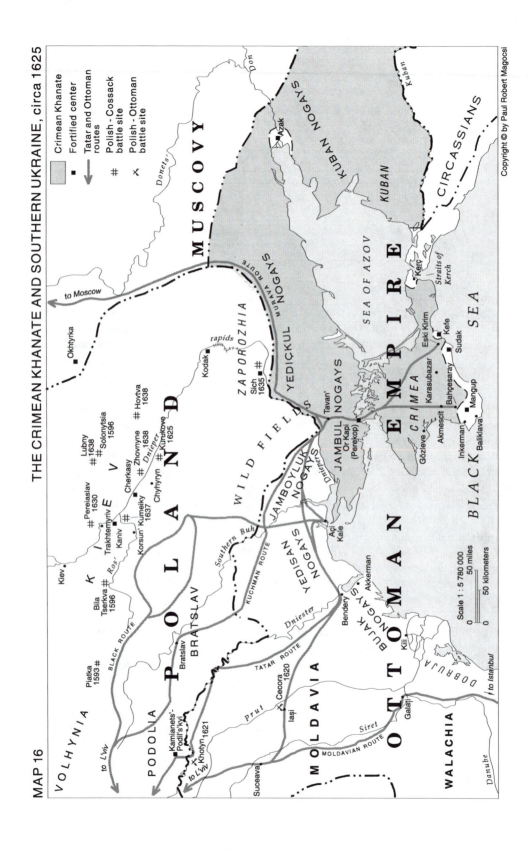

Crimean Khanate
Fortified center
Tatar and Ottoman routes
Polish - Cossack battle site
Polish - Ottoman battle site

MUSCOVY

DONETS

Don

Kuban

KUBAN NOGAYS

CIRCASSIANS

KUBAN

Azak

SEA OF AZOV

Kerc
Straits of Kerch

to Moscow

Okhtyrka

MURAVA ROUTE

ZAPOROZHIA

YEDICKUL NOGAYS

Tavan'
Or Kapi (Perekop)

CRIMEA

Eski Kirim
Kefe
Sudak

BLACK SEA

rapids

Kodak

Sich 1635

WILD FIELDS

Dnieper

JAMBUL NOGAYS

Karasubazar
Bahçesaray
Mangup

Akmescit
Gözleve

Inkerman
Balaklava

Piatka 1593

Bila Tserkva 1596

to L'viv

Kiev

K I E V

Perelaslav 1630

Trakhtemyriv

Kaniv

Korsun'

Cherkasy

Zhovnyne 1638

Chyhyryn 1637

Kumeiky 1637

Lubny 1638
Solonytsia 1596

Hovtva 1638

Kurukove 1625

P O L A N D

Dniester

JAMBOYLUK NOGAYS

Aqi Kale

BLACK ROUTE

Southern Buh

KUCHMAN ROUTE

YEDISAN NOGAYS

Akkerman

Bendery

Kili

BUJAK NOGAYS

to Istanbul

Scale 1 : 5 780 000
50 miles
50 kilometers

PODOLIA

Bratslav

BRATSLAV

Kamianets'-Podil's'kyi

to L'viv

Khotyn 1621

TATAR ROUTE

Cecora 1620

Iasi

Prut

Siret

Suceava

MOLDAVIA

MOLDAVIAN ROUTE

Galati

WALACHIA

Danube

DOBRUJA

VOLHYNIA

O T T O M A N   E M P I R E

Copyright © by Paul Robert Magocsi

marked by efforts to rid themselves of what was considered the odious and humiliating heritage of the Golden Horde's "Tatar yoke" as maintained by the Kazan', Astrakhan', and Crimean khanates.

The Crimean Khanate

It was the Crimean Khanate that had the most direct bearing on Ukrainian lands, and well before the final disintegration of the Golden Horde at the outset of the sixteenth century, it had evolved into a distinct political entity. Ever since 1260s, the Crimean peninsula and steppe lands north of the Sea of Azov formed a part of the Golden Horde. An official from the Horde administered the region from the town of Eski Kirim/Krym/Solkhat (today Staryi Krym), located north of the port of Kefe/Caffa beyond the Crimean mountain crests. The Crimea soon became a refuge for princes of the ruling dynasty of the Golden Horde, some of whom tried but failed to became its supreme leader (khan). One of these exiled leaders was Haci Giray. He was a Chinggisid prince, that is, a descendent of Chinggis Khan, the creator of the Mongol Empire. Haci Giray was invited by local Tatar clan leaders (themselves from the Golden Horde) to rule in the Crimea. He arrived sometime in the late 1430s, proclaimed the independence of the Crimea from the Golden Horde, and after a complicated struggle against various competing political forces in the peninsula, managed to became the first khan of the Crimean Khanate, ruling from ca. 1441 to 1466 and thereby establishing the state's Giray dynasty.

In the course of their rise to power, it was inevitable that the Crimean khans of the Giray family would clash with the rulers of the Golden Horde (who still claimed authority over the Crimea), as well as with other forces in the peninsula itself: the Theodoro-Mangup Principality in the mountainous back country in the southwest; and the Genoese, whose control of trade and the coastal cities posed a particular challenge. In the midst of this three-way struggle for control of the Crimea between Girays, the Theodoro princes, and the Genoese, a new contender entered the field. These were the Ottoman Turks.

Following the fall of Constantinople in 1453, the Ottoman conqueror of the city, Sultan Mehmed II (reigned 1451–1481), was determined to extend his realm north of the Black Sea, which he set out to transform into an "Ottoman lake." In 1475, Ottoman forces arrived in the Crimea and captured Caffa, other Black Sea ports, and the mountain-top fortress of Mangup, thereby destroying the Principality of Theodoro. At the same time, the sultan rejected the Crimean khan's claim for Caffa and other Black Sea coastal towns which were placed directly under Ottoman administration. Place-name changes symbolized the ascendancy of Ottomans, as Italian Moncastro (later captured from Moldavia) became Turkish Aq Kerman/Akkerman (today's Bilhorod-Dnistrovs'kyi), Cerchio became Kerç (today's Kerch), and Tana became Azak (today's Azov). On the Crimean peninsula itself, the ports of Kalamita became Turkish Inkerman, Cembalo became Baliklava (later Balaklava), the fortress of Soldaia became Sudak, and the most important Genoese center, Caffa, became Kefe (today's Feodosiia). Under Ottoman rule, Kefe's port was expanded and its population increased to the point that by the early seventeenth century it was one of the largest cities in all of eastern Europe.

The arrival of the Ottomans prompted a new realignment of political power in the Crimea. The sultan claimed he was a political heir of the Golden Horde, and backed by overwhelming military force he was able to dictate terms to the Giray rulers of the Crimean Khanate. In return for pledging vassalage to the sultan, in 1478 Khan Mengli I Giray (reigned 1468–1473, 1478–1515), with Ottoman military support, was able to regain his throne and to impose his authority vis-à-vis rivals within the region. The Crimean peninsula itself was divided. A narrow strip of non-contiguous territory along the Black Sea littoral from Inkerman to Kerç (Kerch) eventually became part of an Ottoman province (*sancak*), which was named Kefe after its administrative center. Aside from the Crimean littoral, Kefe province included the eastern shore of the Straits of Kerch and the fortress of Azak. The rest of the peninsula was under the authority of the Crimean khan and clan leaders loyal to him.

From the very beginning the Ottomans maintained a special relationship with the Crimean Khanate and its Giray ruling dynasty. The Ottoman sultan claimed authority over all Turkic peoples that inhabited the steppe region stretching far eastward into Central Asia. Since the Girays were direct descendents of Chinggis Khan, the Ottomans used their connection with the Crimean Khanate to legitimize their claims over the Central Asiatic Turkic world. Therefore, in contrast to other Ottoman vassal states which were required to pay tribute and supply troops to the sultan, it was the sultan who provided the Crimean khans with an annual pension and with landholdings in the Turkish provinces of Rumelia and Anatolia. And whenever the Ottomans needed troops from the Crimea, they sent an "invitation" – not an order – to the khan accompanied by campaign expenses.

While it is true that Ottoman interference in Crimean politics progressively increased from the end of the sixteenth century, the Crimean Khanate was nonetheless able to maintain a privileged position within the Ottoman Empire and to follow a basically independent foreign policy vis-à-vis its neighbors. For example, the khanate's first rulers were allied at times with Muscovy, and at other times with Lithuania and Poland, as part of their ongoing efforts to undermine their rivals in the Golden Horde. In fact, it was Haci Giray's son and successor, Mengli I Giray, who in 1502 successfully attacked the Golden Horde's capital of New Saray on the lower Volga River, drove out its ruler, and adopted for himself and his Crimean successors the title, "Great Khan of the Golden Horde and the Kipçak Steppe." Mengli I and those Crimean khans who followed him also proclaimed inheritance to the Golden Horde's right to collect tribute from Poland and Muscovy. Claims such as these brought the Crimean Khanate into conflict with its two neighbors to the north. This was particularly the case with Muscovy, with whom the Crimean Khanate remained in conflict throughout the first half of the sixteenth century for control of former Golden Horde territory, which by then was divided among the Nogay Horde (east of the Volga River) and the Khanates of Kazan' and Astrakhan.

Crimean socioeconomic life

The Crimean Khanate was a state governed by Islamic law, whose rulers and majority Tatar and Turkic population were Sunni Muslims. The head of the state was the khan, always of the Giray dynasty, who derived his preeminent status within the Tatar political leadership because he was a descendent of Chinggis Khan. The Giray khans were not absolute rulers, but instead governed with the active participation of Crimean Tatar clan leaders (*beys*), the most important of which represented the Şirin, Mansur, Barin, and Sicuvut clans, the so-called *karaçi beys*. These four and other Crimean clans (including the Kipçak and Argin) derived their social and economic influence from two sources: ownership of large tracts of land, mostly in the steppe portion of the peninsula north of the mountain crests and foothills; and their ability to supply or deny, at their discretion, troops to the khan. The Crimean clan leaders met periodically in assemblies (the *kurultay*), which formally elected a new khan before submitting his candidacy to the Ottoman sultan for approval. Aside from the *kurultay*, clan leaders together with clerics and elders of the khan's court also sat on the khan's council of the state (*divan*), which effectively determined Crimean governmental policy.

The Tatar inhabitants of the Crimean Khanate, who numbered about 500,000 in the mid-sixteenth century, comprised a heterogeneous population which differed quite radically depending on its origins, linguistic characteristics, and geographic location. In terms of geography, the Crimean Khanate included the territory in the Crimean peninsula as well as an even larger expanse of land beyond the isthmus of Perekop that encompassed the steppes of Ukraine north of the Black Sea and Sea of Azov. The Crimean peninsula itself was geographically diverse; its northern two-thirds consisted of a steppe-like plain that was a continuation of the Ukrainian steppe north of Perekop. The southern third of the peninsula included the foothills and a mountain chain running in an east-west direction parallel to the sea coast. Finally, below the mountain cliffs along the coastal littoral was a narrow strip of land which was the site of several port towns, including the largest of them all, Caffa/Kefe (today Feodosiia).

In the broadest terms, the population living in the Crimean Khanate belonged to two groups: nomadic and sedentary. The nomadic elements lived in the steppe-like plains, which covered the northern two-thirds of the peninsula as well as southern Ukraine. The sedentary population inhabited the peninsula's foothills and mountain valleys as well as the coastal towns and villages.

The Crimean Tatar ruling elite, which included the extended Giray ruling family and the various clan leaders who administered large tracts of land in both the peninsula's steppelands and mountainous regions, were descendants of the Turkic Kipçak nomads and warriors who lived in the heartland of the Mongolo-Tatar Golden Horde. The Crimean elite spoke and developed for administrative purposes a written language that was a mixture of Kipçak Turkic (from the Inner Asian steppe) and Oghuz Turkic (related to the Turkish language of Anatolia, the heart of the Ottoman Empire).

The Crimean peninsula had for millennia become home to numerous other peoples – Scythians, Goths, Alans, Huns, Greeks, Genoese, and Armenians – some of whom were originally nomadic while others were sedentary agriculturalists and town-dwellers. In the course of the fifteenth and sixteenth centuries, most of these groups became linguistically turkicized and they adopted the Islamic faith. This heterogeneous mix of peoples came to be known as Tats, which was initially a derogatory term used by Turkic peoples to describe their neighbors (and converts to Islam), who may have spoken Turkic but were not of "pure" Turkic descent. The Tats referred not only to the peasant farmers of the mountainous foothills and valleys (who spoke the Kipçak-Oghuz Turkic mixed language), but also to the coastal town dwellers who lived under direct Ottoman administration (and who spoke Oghuz Turkic as in Anatolia). It was the Tats who were to become the dominant demographic element in the peninsula, and it was they who provided the Crimean Tatars with characteristics that made them distinct from other Tatars in Central Asia. In other words, the Tats – whether peasant farmers, artisans, tradespeople, or bureaucrats – formed the very core of the Crimean polity.

Crimea's peasant farmers were organized in villages, the land was worked in common, and taxes were assigned by the landlord (usually tribal and clan leaders) to the village as a whole. Peasants were not proprietary serfs, however, and were free to leave the land if they wished. Among the most important and lucrative export products of Crimean agriculture were fruits, tobacco, and honey.

Whereas most of Crimea's diverse peoples assimilated to the peninsula's Turkic-speaking Islamic majority, in that process they left a distinct cultural and linguistic imprint on the Tats, who eventually formed the basis of a Crimean Tatar ethnos. For example, the Turkic language of the coastal Tats contains several loanwords from Italian and Greek, reflecting the former presence of those peoples in the Crimea's ports. There were also a few peoples, who, while adopting Turkic speech, did not become Muslims. These included the Christian Armenians and Greeks (the *urum*, or Greek Tatars) and the Jewish Krymchaks and Karaites. The Krymchaks and Karaites lived primarily in the khanate's largest towns: Akmescid (today Simferopol'), the port of Gözleve (today Ievpatoriia), the Şirin clan "capital" of Karasubazar (today Bilohirs'k), and the khanate's capital Bahçesaray (today Bakhchysarai). The Armenians and Greeks were concentrated in Kefe (today Feodosiia).

The first capital of the Crimean Khanate was the eastern town of Eski Kirim/Solkhat (today Staryi Krym), but already under Khan Haci Giray in the mid-fifteenth century it was moved closer to the center of the peninsula. He chose the mountaintop town of Kirk Yer, located a few kilometers north of Bahçesaray. Kirk Yer functioned as a formidable fortress, while in the valley below at Salaçik (today Starosillia) the khan had his residential palace. It was Haci Giray's son, Mengli I Giray, who expanded the palace complex at Salaçik, which included the Zindcirli *Medrese*, or college (est. 1500) to train Muslim clerics. When Salaçik proved to be too constrained for the growing Crimean state, one of Mengli's sons Khan Sahib I Giray (reigned 1532–1551) moved just a couple kilometers down the valley to Bahçesaray, where in 1532 he founded a new palace that was to become the permanent residence of the Crimean Khans. With its khan's palace, extended gardens, mosques, schools, and other public buildings, Bahçesaray was transformed into an impressive center of Islamic culture as well as the political seat of the Crimean Khanate. It is interesting to note that, while losing its status as the Crimean capital, the mountaintop town of Kerk Yer, later known as Çufut-Kale (which in Crimean Tatar means the Jews' Fortress), retained its importance as the center for the community of Karaites (Hebrew: Karaim), that is Jews who adhere to a form of a non-Talmudic Judaism.

THE KARAITES

The Karaites, also known as Karaim, are a Jewish sect whose origins are unclear and disputed. It is generally assumed that the sect was founded in the eighth century in Baghdad, the capital of the Islamic Abbasid Empire, and that from there it spread throughout the Middle East. In the twelfth century some Karaites settled in the Byzantine Empire (primarily in Constantinople and western Anatolia) and from there migrated to the Crimea beginning in the mid-thirteenth century. It was then that they adopted Turkic speech and eventually developed a distinct literary language (written in Hebrew script) that was rather similar to Crimean Tatar. There are also some scholars (A. Firkovich, S. Szapszal) who argue that the Turkic origin of the Crimean Karaites goes back even earlier to the Khazars who were also present in the peninsula both during and after the existence of their state. Toward the end of the fourteenth century, Lithuania's grand duke resettled several hundred Karaites in his capital of Trakai/Troki, and from there some migrated south to the Rus' towns of Luts'k in Volhynia and Halych in Galicia.

The Karaites in the Crimea were similar in language to the Turkic-speaking Crimean Jews, or Krymchaks (originally centered in Karasubazar, today Bilohirs'k). They differ from the Orthodox Jewish Krymchaks, however, in that they reject the religious commentaries and additions contained in the Talmud and instead believe only in the word of God as expressed in the Old Testament as the sole and direct source of religious law. Much later, and in an entirely different cultural context, some Protestants came to believe that the Karaites, as People of the Scriptures, were precursors of the Christian Reformation. Such beliefs led some Gentiles (especially German Protestants) to assume that the Karaites were different enough from Jews to be exempted from general European anti-Semitism.

The Karaites originally settled in the port of Caffa/Kefe and in Solkhat/Eski Kirim, but after the fall of the Principality of Theodoro-Mangup to the Ottoman Turks in 1475, they became concentrated in the mountaintop towns of Mangup Kale and Çufut Kale. There they lived in isolation from their immediate neighbors, but all the while maintaining contacts with their coreligionists in Lithuania (Trakai) and western Ukraine (Luts'k and Halych). In the eighteenth century Çufut Kale became a major Karaite cultural center, where several books were printed in Hebrew and efforts made to create a Karaite Turkic literary language using the Hebrew and later Russian and Latin (Polish) alphabets. In the second half of the nineteenth century, Çufut Kale was abandoned and the coastal city of Gözleve (by then renamed Ievpatoriia) became a major center of Karaites in the Crimea.

From the outset of Russian rule in the 1780s, the imperial authorities made a legal distinction between Karaites and other Jews, distinctions which the Karaites themselves welcomed, arguing that they were an especially honest and industrious people loyal to the tsar. Consequently, the Karaites became a privileged and often wealthy group (numbering 5,400 in the Crimea in 1897) who were exempt from military service and granted religious autonomy. The most eminent Karaite scholar, writer, and active champion for equal rights was Abraham Firkovich from Luts'k in Volhynia, who from 1832 until his death in 1874 served the community in Çufut Kale and coastal Ievpatoriia.

Karaite distinctiveness took a strange turn during the World War II Holocaust period, when Nazi Germany occupied the Crimea. After extensive study, the Nazi authorities in Berlin declared that from the standpoint of their racial ideology the Karaites were non-Jewish. In contrast to the Jewish Krymchaks, who were virtually all killed by Nazis, the Karaites were left alone. Karaite behavior during the Holocaust ranged from indifference to the fate of the Krymchak Jews to actual collaboration with the Nazi administrators in the Crimea.

The Nogay Tatars and slavery

Whereas the Crimean Khanate quickly took on the characteristics of a stable sedentary society associated with the agricultural, artisan, and commercial pursuits of the majority of the population living in the southern third of the peninsula, there was yet another important element within the khanate's political sphere. These were the Nogay Tatars, that is, Kipçak-speaking nomadic peoples of Turkic origin who pastured their flocks on Ukraine's steppe lands north of the Sea of Azov and the Black Sea stretching from the Kuban River in the east to the Danube River in the west. The Nogay were originally one of the many tribal groupings within the Golden Horde. In 1556, when Muscovy finally subdued the Astrakhan Khanate and the Nogay heartland east of Volga River and north of the Caspian Sea, a portion of the Nogays migrated westward to the steppe zone north of the Sea of Azov and Black Sea. In this region the Nogays themselves were split into several tribal confederations: the Kuban Nogay (east of the Sea of Azov), the Yediçkul Nogay (north of the Sea of Azov), the Camboyluk Nogay (north of the Crimea), the Yedisan Nogay (between the Southern Buh and Dniester Rivers), and the Bujak Nogay (between the Dniester and Danube Rivers).

These Nogay tribes, generally referred to as "Tatars," are the subject of much attention in Ukrainian history. Theoretically, the various Nogay tribes were expected to recognize the authority of the Crimean khan, usually in the form of a representative (*serasker*) sent from Bahçesaray. In practice, however, they usually followed their own whims and often rebelled against the Crimean Khanate. "Yet," as the historian Alan Fisher has remarked, "the Nogays served a useful purpose for the Crimean Khanate: They prevented the establishment of solid Slavic settlements in the steppe and provided the Crimean slave markets with a never ending supply of captives."[1]

By the early sixteenth century, the Crimean economy had come to be based largely on the slave trade. Slavery was legal according to Islamic law, but only persons from outside the Muslim world could be enslaved. Therefore captives taken in wars against non-Muslim powers were prime candidates for slavery. While slaves formed an integral part of the Ottoman Empire's socioeconomic system, that society allowed for various forms of manumission, both for slaves and their offspring, leading in part to a situation in which the empire was in constant need of replenishing this human commodity. Before long the Ottoman's new vassal state, the Crimean Khanate, became the primary source of slaves. From the standpoint of the Crimean authorities, whenever there was a downturn in agricultural productivity, the state could supplement its income with profits earned from selling slaves. Just to the north of the Nogay steppe were the non-Muslim lands of Ukraine and southern Russia, which at the time were nominally under the control of Poland, Lithuania, and Muscovy. It was there that Tatars from the Crimea turned to seek out Christian Slavs to enslave.

The Tatars, whether the khan's armies or Nogay slave-raiders, entered the Ukrainian lands of Poland-Lithuania via several invasion routes that began at Perekop, the site of a major defensive fortress (called in Turkic: Or Kapi or Ferahkerman) that was located on a narrow sliver of land where the Crimean peninsula joins the steppe to the north. The khanate's military forces, almost exclusively cavalry, ranged in size from 10,000 to 30,000 in the sixteenth century. While the Nogay slave-raiding parties were much smaller, their incursions were more frequent, with the result that the number of captives they managed to acquire were quite astonishing. Some scholars have estimated on average 20,000 captives from Poland-Lithuania each year, with total losses from the period 1500–1664 reaching about one million people. A certain number of captives were allotted to the Crimean khan and the remainder to all those who participated in a given campaign. Most, however, went to the Ottoman Empire: perhaps a fifth to the sultan as tribute, and the rest sold to Ottoman buyers at the Crimean Tatar slave markets in Bahçesaray, Karasubazar, the port of Gözleve, but most importantly at the Ottoman-ruled port of Kefe.

And what happened to the captives from Ukraine when they reached the heart of the Ottoman Empire? The slaves functioned at all levels of Ottoman society with the result that their fates differed widely. At the lowest end of the social scale were galley slaves conscripted into the imperial naval fleet and field hands who labored on Ottoman landed estates. House servants fared somewhat better. But there was yet another segment of captives, both male and female, who clearly improved their social and economic status while living in the Ottoman world. These people included converts to Islam, who served in various positions of the Ottoman military administrative system. Females, meanwhile, were conscripted into the harems of the Ottoman elite. The most renowned of these was a captive from Galicia, Nastia Lisovs'ka. Known as Roksolana, or Hurrem (her Turkish name), she became the favorite wife of Sultan Süleyman I ("the Magnificent") and a personage of political influence in her own right during the apogee of Ottoman power in the mid-sixteenth century.

After the mid-sixteenth century, it was the Nogay tribes, especially the Yediçkul, who were increasingly responsible for the slave raids. The Tatars in the Crimean peninsula were more interested in the role of middlemen between their Nogay suppliers in the north and Ottoman purchasers in the south. It is also from this period, the sixteenth and early seventeenth centuries, that the anonymous lyrical epic tales known as *dumy* arose among the Rus' of Ukrainian society. Not surprisingly, the earliest *dumy* stressed only the negative aspect of captivity, as in laments on the fate of young men coerced to serve in the armies of the Ottoman Turkish "infidel" (*Duma about the Lament of the Captives*), or of young women forced to enter harems and serve the personal needs of the Ottoman rulers (*Duma about Marusia from Bohuslav*).

Was Ottoman and Crimean Slavery All That Bad?

The tradition of alleged suffering at the hands of the Ottoman Turks was embedded in the Ukrainian-Rus' psyche through the recitative chanting of epic tales known as *dumy*. The following is an excerpt from the *Duma About the Lament of the Captives*, one of the most famous examples of this genre of oral literature sung for generations until today by minstrels (Ukrainian: *kobzari*) usually playing a hand-plucked string instrument, the *bandura* or *kobza*.

On the holy day of Sunday, it wasn't the grey eagles screaming,
But the poor captives weeping in bitter slavery,
Raising their arms, shaking their chains,
Begging and imploring the merciful Lord:
'Send us, O Lord, a fine rain from the sky
And a wild wind from the Dnieper steppe!
Maybe a swift wave will rise on the Black Sea,
Maybe it will break the Turkish galley loose from its anchor!
Oh, we have had enough of this accursed Turkish slavery;
The iron chains have dug into our legs,
They have cut our white young Cossack flesh to the yellow bone.'

They spilled innocent Christian blood.
The poor captives began to see Christian blood on their bodies,
They began to curse the Turkish land, and the infidel faith:
O Turkish land, O infidel faith,
O separation from fellow Christians,
You have parted many from their fathers and mothers,
Brothers from their sisters,
Husbands from their faithful wives!
Liberate, O Lord, all the poor captives
From bitter Turkish slavery,
From infidel captivity!
Let them reach the quiet waters,
The bright stars
The merry homeland,
The Christian people,
The Christian cities!*

The *dumy* and other laments that have come down to us, whether in written form or in oral folklore, reflect the view of those inhabitants who managed to avoid abduction and remain in their homeland. But what about the views of those who were captured? Clearly, not all felt Ottoman and Crimean slavery was a fate worse than that they would likely endure if they never left home. Documentary evidence about the attitudes of Christian Rus' captives living in the Crimea and Ottoman world is rare, but there is one example by a contemporary chronicler which suggests that for the Rus' people of Ukraine "life in slavery" in a foreign land had its advantages. In the *Tale of the Cossack War Against the Poles* (1720), the author Samiilo Velychko relates what happened during the raid into the Crimea in 1675 by the Zaporozhian leader Ivan Sirko. On his way back to Zaporozhia carrying extensive booty, including 13,000 Muslim and Christian captives in tow, Sirko stopped somewhere in the steppe at a safe distance from the Crimean border.

> Turning to the Christians who numbered 7,000 males and females, Sirko said: 'Whoever wants can come with us to Rus'; for those who do not want to come, then return to Crimea.' When the Christians [originally from Rus'], as well as the Christians who were already born in Crimea and the *tumy* [persons of mixed Turkic-Rus' origin] heard this, a certain number, namely 3,000 of them, preferred to return to the Crimea rather than go live in a Christian land … He [Sirko] allowed those to depart for the Crimea. As they were leaving, he asked why they were so eager [to return] to Crimea? They responded that they already had in Crimea their own houses and property and therefore it was a better life for them there than in Rus' where they have nothing.**

This story does not end on the happy note, however. When the disbelieving Sirko was finally convinced that these (for him ungrateful) Rus' Christians really wanted to return to the Crimea, he ordered the Cossacks to massacre the entire group.

SOURCES:
* *Ukrainian Dumy*, translated by George Tarnawsky and Patricia Kilina (Toronto and Cambridge, Mass. 1979), p. 23.
** Samiilo Velychko, *Litopys*, Vol. II (Kiev 1991), p. 191.

Thus, the Crimean Tatars and their Nogay allies represented the most recent in a long line of nomadic or sedentary civilizations (the Scythian, the Sarmatian, the Khazar, the Golden Horde) that came to dominate the southern steppes of Ukraine and that continued the symbiotic economic relationship between the coastal cities and the hinterland. Because captured slaves represented the most important resource in the Crimean economy, much of the area south of the Bratslav and Kiev palatinates from the Southern Buh to the Dnieper Rivers and beyond became a sparsely settled or entirely uninhabited no-man's-land, known as the Wild Fields. In effect, this part of the country became what the name *Ukraine* suggested: a borderland or frontier, not in the sense of the end of a civilized area, as is often assumed, but rather in the sense of a buffer zone between Poland-Lithuania to the northwest, Muscovy to the northeast, and the Crimean Khanate and Ottoman Empire to the south.

15

The Cossacks and Ukraine

The rise of the Cossacks, whose origins go back to the period of Lithuanian rule in Ukraine, ushered in a new era in Ukrainian history. Because of its importance, the Cossack era has received extensive treatment in Ukrainian historiography. Most Ukrainian historians (M. Kostomarov, M. Hrushevs'kyi, V. Lypyns'kyi, D. Doroshenko), and for that matter nineteenth-century literary figures and nurturers of the national psyche (T. Shevchenko, I. Franko), consider that the phenomenon of Cossackdom embodied the best characteristics of Ukrainians, which are supposedly reflected in the Cossack desire for freedom, independence, and a democratic way of life. Others, while admitting that the Cossacks played an important historical role, criticize their tendencies toward destructive rebellion and the rejection of state formations (P. Kulish) or their inability to create a high standard of civilization and express an all-national purpose (V. Antonovych), so that Ukrainians were unable to create their own state. Whatever judgments have subsequently been passed, all Ukrainian historians agree that the Cossack phenomenon occupies a central position in the Ukrainian historical process.

The steppe

The Cossack phenomenon is part of the history of the steppe. During the period of Kievan Rus', large portions of southern Ukraine, in particular the steppe zone, remained only sparsely settled. This was because that region kept its age-old reputation as a stamping ground for nomadic peoples, the most recent of whom during Kievan times were the Pechenegs and Polovtsians. Following the Mongol invasion of the mid-thirteenth century, the line where towns, villages, and farming communities ended receded even farther north. The result was a marked decrease in the number of inhabitants in the former principalities of Kiev and Pereiaslav, which in the second half of the fourteenth century had been annexed by Lithuania but were still subject to destructive raids from Mongolo-Tatar–held territory farther south. Although the Kiev and Pereiaslav regions were never entirely depopulated, by the fifteenth century they had an average of a mere 8 inhabitants per square mile (3 inhabitants per square kilometer), whereas in western Ukrainian lands such as parts of Galicia, Volhynia, and Podolia the average density at times

THE NAME *UKRAINE*

The name *Ukraine* (Ukrainian: *Ukraïna*) as a designation for a territory is both very old and relatively new. Etymologically, the term is of Slavic origin and is derived from the Indo-European root **krei* "to cut," with the secondary meaning of an edge (*krai*) or borderland (*ukraïna*). Some linguists, among them Jaroslav Rudnyckyj, have surmised that the name Ukraine is connected with the pre-Slavic past, and that the name *Antae* (the group which inhabited Ukrainian lands until about the seventh century CE) is the Iranian translation of the Slavic words for borderland and border people. While such views assist those who support the idea of continuity between the Antae, the Rus', and modern Ukrainians, they remain linguistic hypotheses unsupported by concrete evidence in written sources.

The name *Ukraine* is first attested in written documents which date from a much later period but which describe events in the twelfth and thirteenth centuries. The oldest reference is 1187, the year Prince Volodymyr of Pereiaslav died and at which time, according to the Hypatian text of the *Primary Chronicle* (copied in the fifteenth century): "The *ukraïna* groaned with grief for him."* But neither in this instance of the term nor in others in the *Primary Chronicle* (Hypatian text), describing events in 1189, 1213, 1280, and 1282 in various Ukrainian lands (Halych, the Buh region, etc.), is the term *ukraïna* ever used in reference to a specific territory. Rather, when it is used, *ukraïna* simply means an undefined borderland. The term *ukraïna* appears as well in other Rus' chronicles, describing non-specific borderland areas in the Pskov, the Polatsk, and other northern principalities.

It is not until the sixteenth century that the name *Ukraine* is used for the first time to refer to a clearly defined territory. At that time, Polish sources began to use the name in its Polish form, *Ukrajina*, to describe the large eastern palatinate of Kiev, together with Bratslav (after 1569) and Chernihiv (after 1619). With the rise of the Cossacks as a political force in the seventeenth century, the name *Ukraine* was still used, but once again in a less territorially specific manner. The Cossacks referred to Ukraine as their "fatherland" or their "mother," and western European cartographers (G. Beauplan, J.B. Homman) often drew maps indicating that "Ukraine is the land of the Cossacks." In actual practice, however, the Cossacks used the name *Ukraine* in a poetic sense, to describe their generic homeland, but officially they called their state the Zaporozhian Host, or Lands of the Army of Zaporozhia.

With the demise of Polish rule, the name *Ukraine* fell into disuse as a term for a specific territory, and it was not revived until the early nineteenth century. At that time, writers who promoted the national movement began to speak of *Ukraine* as the appropriate name for all territory in which Ukrainians lived. The term was once again non-specific, however, because in the context of Russian and Austrian imperial rule there was no possibility of a distinct administrative entity called Ukraine.

Not until the revolutionary period beginning in 1917 did the name *Ukraine* come again to specify a specific territory. It was used by the Ukrainian National Republic, by the Hetmanate, and by the Bolshevik party. The Hetmanate was formally called the Ukrainian State (Ukraïns'ka Derzhava). The Bolsheviks called the entity they created the Ukrainian Soviet Socialist Republic, which after 1920 had specific boundaries largely encompassing the lands inhabited by ethnic Ukrainians.

Thus, as a term referring to a non-specific and even ethnically non-Ukrainian territory, the name *Ukraine* dates from the twelfth and thirteenth centuries; as a name for a specific territory, it dates from the late sixteenth century; as a name for lands inhabited by ethnic Ukrainians, it dates from the nineteenth century; and as name referring to a state it dates from the twentieth century.

*Cited in Henryk Paszkiewicz, *The Making of the Russian Nation* (London 1963), p. 305 n.293.

reached 36 inhabitants per square mile (14 inhabitants per square kilometer). Such demographic discrepancy did not begin to change until the second half of the sixteenth century, notably after 1569, when Poland annexed the Ukrainian-inhabited palatinates of Volhynia, Kiev, and Bratslav from Lithuania, and then in 1618, when it annexed Chernihiv from Muscovy.

By the end of the sixteenth century, Poland had become the granary of Europe. Its continuing economic well-being depended on the development of new sources of agricultural exploitation. Ukrainian lands became especially attractive, prompting local Rus' nobles, joined by their Polish counterparts farther west, to stake out claims to large tracts of land and settle them with peasants from the more populated palatinates of Galicia, Belz, and western Volhynia. The settlement eastward was gradual, beginning in eastern Volhynia and Podolia and then continuing into the palatinates of Kiev, Chernihiv, and Bratslav – three regions which in Polish sources came to be referred to collectively as Ukraine (*Ukraina*). Nonetheless, along the southern fringes of these three palatinates, and beyond that along both sides of the lower Dnieper River, lay the open steppe – the Wild Fields (Polish: *Dzikie Pole*) in contemporary writings – which remained untouched by any sedentary agricultural population. Actually, the steppe was a kind of no-man's-land separating the settlements within Poland-Lithuania farther north from another civilization based along the southern fringes of Ukrainian territory, that of the Crimean Tatars.

The seemingly unbounded natural wealth of the Ukrainian steppe land outweighed the danger of living there, so that as early as in the fifteenth century a few individuals from more settled areas in the northwest began to venture down the Dnieper and its tributaries in search of fish, wild buffalo and horses, and the eggs of wildfowl. In 1590, a Polish writer described Ukraine as: "the richest part of the Polish state. Its fields are as blissful as the Elysian ... There are so many cattle, wild animals, and various birds in Ukraine that one could think her the birthplace of Diana and Ceres. In the Ukrainian apiaries so much honey is produced that one forgets the Sicilian Gela and the Attic Hymettus. ... It is hard to count the Ukrainian lakes teeming with fish. In short, Ukraine is like that land which God promised to the Hebrews, flowing with milk and honey."[1]

At first, these expeditions in search of food lasted only a few weeks; soon, however, they lasted whole summers, long enough to plant a crop and harvest it from the rich soil. Among the earliest seekers of wealth were members of the lesser gentry and townspeople, groups whose status in Polish-Lithuanian society was steadily being eroded by the power of the great landowning magnates in Ukraine. Tales of the steppes's natural wealth spread rapidly, and before long the gentry and townspeople were joined by even larger numbers of peasants, some of whom came from as far west as Podolia and Galicia. The landlords in the north were not about to miss an opportunity to increase their own wealth, and they demanded a portion of the foodstuffs and natural wealth their peasants brought back from the Ukrainian wilderness. Not surprisingly, the more daring decided not to return for the winter at all, but to make permanent homes in this no-man's-land.

The rise of the Cossacks

This new mode of existence – traveling to the wilderness in order to fish, hunt, perhaps do some farming, and then returning home in the winter or, eventually, remaining in the wilderness permanently – came to be known as the Cossack way of life. Indeed, the danger from Nogay slave-raiding parties was ever present, and to cope with the threat the Ukrainian peasants- and townspeople-turned-frontier dwellers were forced to protect themselves and become skilled in the art of self-defense. Before long, self-defense was transformed by some into offensive attacks against Nogay slave-raiding parties and Crimean Tatar trade caravans. By the early sixteenth century, the Cossacks had already grouped into small bands of armed men engaged in trade (especially livestock, furs, slaves) and banditry. Their favorite source of booty was the Islamic world, both the rich commercial centers on the Crimean Peninsula and the towns of Walachia and Dobruja, near the mouth of the Danube River, which had come under Ottoman control.

Besides these individuals, drawn to the Ukrainian steppe by its natural wealth and the prospect of booty from raids against Tatar caravans, there was another kind of Cossack. This was the freebooting warrior of various social and ethnic origin who entered the service of Lithuanian and Polish frontier officials or of the powerful magnates, who usually maintained their own armies. In fact, the very first group to be systematically described as Cossacks were Tatar renegades from the Crimean khan's armies who had been hired by Lithuanian and Muscovite rulers. This helps to explain why the very term Cossack – later associated exclusively with anti-Tatar Slavic groups – probably derives from the Turkish term *qazaq*, meaning a freebooting warrior or raider.

By the fifteenth century, it was common practice for Lithuanian frontier officials

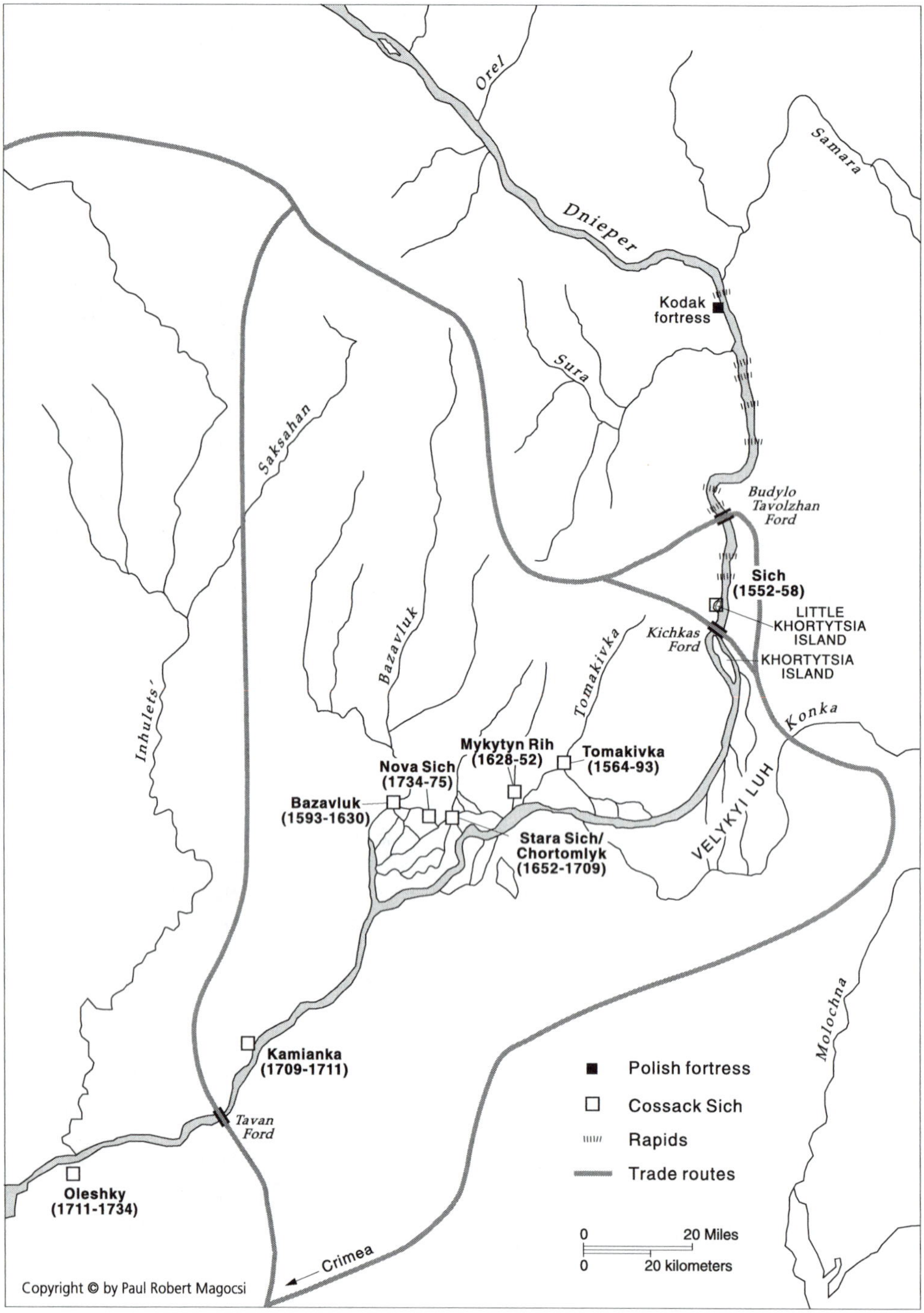

MAP 17   ZAPOROZHIA

Orel

Samara

Dnieper

Kodak
fortress

Sura

Saksahan

Budylo
Tavolzhan
Ford

Sich
(1552-58)

LITTLE
KHORTYTSIA
ISLAND

Kichkas
Ford

KHORTYTSIA
ISLAND

Bazavluk

Tomakivka

Konka

Inhulets'

Mykytyn Rih
(1628-52)

Tomakivka
(1564-93)

Nova Sich
(1734-75)

Bazavluk
(1593-1630)

Stara Sich/
Chortomlyk
(1652-1709)

VELYKYI LUH

Molochna

Kamianka
(1709-1711)

Tavan
Ford

Oleshky
(1711-1734)

Crimea

■   Polish fortress

□   Cossack Sich

〰   Rapids

━   Trade routes

0   20 Miles

0   20 kilometers

Copyright © by Paul Robert Magocsi

(*voievody* and district *starosty*) to hire Cossacks to help defend the grand duchy's frontier fortresses against Tatar raiding parties, especially in the Kiev and Bratslav palatinates. Because of their residence in frontier towns, these military forces were referred to as "town Cossacks" (*horodovi kozaky*), and in some contemporary documents (especially Muscovite), all Cossacks came to be called *cherkasy*, after the name of one of the fortified towns (Cherkasy) where many were concentrated. At least until the end of the sixteenth century, the town Cossacks were led by appointees of the king, usually local district *starosty*, who were called hetmans by their followers. Nor did these Cossacks serve only in a defensive capacity. Beginning in 1489, Cossacks led by crown-appointed hetmans attacked Tatar caravans and Turkish bases not only in the Crimea, but as far south as the Balkans and Anatolia. By the end of the sixteenth century, Cossack attacks against the Tatars and Turks were taking place virtually every year.

The Cossacks living farther south, away from the towns, built their own fortified centers, which, while frequently changing location, generally carried the name *sich*. The first *sich* was built in 1552 on the island of Little Khortytsia (Mala Khortytsia) in the Dnieper River, south of the rapids below the waterway's first major bend. Because the first *sich* and the several subsequent ones were set up beyond the rapids (in Ukrainian: *za porohamy*), the Cossacks living there soon came to be known as the Zaporozhian Cossacks or the Zaporozhian Host. This name was applied in order to distinguish them from other Cossacks who at the same time had begun to develop in similar circumstances farther east along the southern Muscovite frontier and who were known as Don Cossacks. The land on both sides of the Dnieper River where the Zaporozhian Cossacks established their *sich* military fortresses was called Zaporozhia.

It is to Zaporozhia that townspeople and an increasing number of peasants from Ukrainian and Belarusan lands farther north and west (Galicia, Volhynia, western Podolia) came in an attempt to escape the increasing burdens of Poland's manorial system. They were joined by other adventurers of various social backgrounds and origin (Romanians/Moldavians, Tatars, Turks, Jews) who desired to live within the government-less environment of the Cossack steppe. The newcomers settled in the *sich* itself as well as in the nearby wilderness of Zaporozhia on both banks of the Dnieper River. It should be noted that during these early decades, at least until the end of the sixteenth century, the differentiation between town Cossacks farther north and those based in the *sich* in Zaporozhia was not pronounced, since both recognized the same hetman as their leader and often joined together in expeditions against the Tatars.

The *sich* itself was a fortified center surrounded in part by high walls of wood as well as by lowland swamps or tributaries of the Dnieper River. Behind the walls were living quarters for resident Cossacks – only men were permitted inside – whose number in later years sometimes reached as high as 10,000. The central square (*maidan*) contained a church, a school, and the residence of the community's leaders. Beyond the walls was a marketplace (*bazar*) where goods from cities and fortified centers farther north (Kiev, Kaniv, Cherkasy) and from the Crimea and the Ottoman lands in the south were traded.

THE COSSACKS OF ZAPOROZHIA

An excellent insight into the way of life of the Zaporozhian Cossacks comes from the pen of Guillaume le Vasseur de Beauplan, a French military engineer who spent seventeen years (1630–1647) in Poland in the service of its army. He published several detailed maps of Ukraine as well as a descriptive narrative (1651), from which the following excerpt is taken:

The valor of these Cossacks having been mentioned, it will not be out of place to speak [here] of their customs and activities. Among these people are found individuals expert in all the trades necessary for human life: house and ship carpenters, cartwrights, blacksmiths, armorers, tanners, harness makers, shoemakers, coopers, tailors, and so forth. They are very skillful at preparing saltpeter, which is found in abundance in these regions, and make from it excellent gunpowder. The women are employed at spinning flax and wool, from which they make cloth and fabrics for their everyday use. All are well able to till the soil, sow, harvest, make bread, prepare foods of all sorts, brew beer, make mead, braha, spirits, etc. As well, there is not one of them, of any age, sex or rank whatever, who does not try to drink more than his companion, and to outdo him in revelry. What is more, there are not Christians [anywhere else] who are their equals in not caring for the morrow.

It is quite true that in general they are all proficient in the whole range of crafts. … In short, they are all quite clever, but they limit themselves only to useful and necessary matters, and especially to those relating to country living.

The fertile land produces grain in such abundance that often they do not know what to do with it, the more so because they have no navigable rivers that empty into the sea, except the Borysthenes [Dnieper], which is blocked fifty leagues below Kiev by [a series of] thirteen rapids. … That is what prevents them from transporting their grain to Constantinople, and hence engenders their laziness and unwillingness to work, except when pressed by necessity or when they are unable to buy what they need. They prefer to borrow goods that are necessary to their comfort, from their good neighbors the Turks, rather than take the trouble to work for them. They are content if they have enough to eat and drink.

There is nothing about them coarser than their clothing. They are sly, crafty, clever, [and yet] sincerely generous, without ulterior motives or ambitions to become very rich. They greatly value their liberty, and would not want to live without it. That is why the Cossacks, when they consider themselves to be kept under too tight a rein, are so inclined to revolt and rebel against the lords of their country. Thus, seven or eight years rarely pass without a mutiny or uprising.

Beyond that, they are a faithless people, treacherous, perfidious, and to be trusted only with circumspection. They are a very robust people, easily enduring heat and cold, hunger and thirst. They are tireless in war, daring, courageous, or rather reckless, placing no value on their own lives.

SOURCE: Guillaume Le Vasseur, Sieur de Beauplan, *A Description of Ukraine* (1660), translated by Andrew B. Pernal and Dennis F. Essar (Cambridge, Mass. 1993), pp. 11–13.

The Zaporozhian Sich was governed by the principle of equality. Accordingly, all major decisions, especially those pertaining to military policy and foreign alliances, were made during a general meeting called the *rada*. In practice, there were "class" distinctions even within the *sich*, so that by the end of the sixteenth century it was common practice for two separate *rady* to meet: one for the officers (*starshyna*) and one for the rank and file (*chern'*). Neither *rada* dominated the other, and officers always felt that their policy decisions could be overturned – even brutally – by the rank and file. Departing from subsequent romanticized images of the supposedly egalitarian existence in Zaporozhia, one historian, Linda Gordon, has perhaps more aptly suggested that "the system of Cossack self-government was not democracy but dictatorship tempered by mob intervention."[2]

The head of the Zaporozhian Cossacks, elected by all members present at the *rada*, at first was called simply the elder (*starshyi*), and later the *sich otaman* or *koshovyi otaman*. Until the end of the sixteenth century, the Zaporozhians also recognized as their leaders those hetmans appointed by the Polish king, most often from among the ranks of district *starosty*, who commanded registered Cossack troops stationed in the fortress towns. The first of these recorded in contemporary documents is Prince Dmytro Vyshnevets'kyi, the *starosta* of Cherkasy and Kaniv, who as hetman built the first *sich* on Little Khortytsia island as a defensive measure against the Tatars. By the last decade of the sixteenth century, the Zaporozhians meeting at the *rada* would at times elect their own hetmans.

The Cossacks in Polish society

When, as a result of the Union of Lublin in 1569, Zaporozhia and the Ukrainian steppe came under the nominal authority of Poland, the Cossacks – whether at the sich or in the towns farther north – considered themselves subjects of the Polish king. The rugged life on the steppe, however, and their evolution into a valued military force imbued the Cossacks with a sense of independence that inevitably clashed with the efforts of the magnates to extend further their control over what previously had been uninhabited and uncultivated territory. Nor was the struggle simply one between peasants seeking freedom and nobles trying to enserf them. Instead, the Cossacks, whether in the fortress towns or in Zaporozhia, became one of the many rival interest groups in a Ukrainian society that was increasingly coming under the influence of Polish social norms.

For instance, town Cossacks in the service of the large Rus' magnates (the Ostroz'kyis, Vyshnevets'kyis, etc.) tended to increase the influence of that social group in Polish society. In response, Poland's kings would themselves try to entice the Cossacks into the service of the crown by granting them privileges. Also, those gentry who lost lands or became indebted to the magnates found an outlet for their discontent in flight to the *sich*. Even among magnates, there were different views of the Cossacks. While the Orthodox Rus' magnates essentially appreciated the defensive role of the town Cossacks and accommodated their demands, Polish nobles farther removed from the frontier had little tolerance for what they considered the "pro-Cossack policies" of the king and magnates in Ukraine. For their part, the Cossacks not only maneuvred among these various interest groups in Polish-

Lithuanian society, but also increased their own political leverage by entering into agreements – often short-term military alliances – with foreign powers. In effect, by the second half of the sixteenth century, the Zaporozhian Cossacks had become a political as well as a military force in their own right, a player in eastern Europe's complex diplomatic game of chess involving frequent wars and rapidly changing alliances among the Polish-Lithuanian Commonwealth, the Habsburg Empire, Muscovy, the Crimean Khanate, Walachia, Moldavia, and the Ottoman Empire.

With the growth of Cossack military potential, it was inevitable that conflict, whether motivated by personal discontent or by discontent with policy, would arise between the independent-minded steppe frontier dwellers and the local authorities. In fact, beginning in the final decade of the sixteenth century and lasting for nearly the next half century, there occurred no less than seven uprisings, led by Kryshtof Kosyns'kyi (1591–1593), Severyn Nalyvaiko and Hryhorii Loboda (1594–1596), Marko Zhmailo (1625), Taras Fedorovych (1630), Ivan Sulyma (1635), Pavlo Pavliuk-But (1637), and Iakiv Ostrianyn (1638). All these figures were subsequently immortalized as defenders of the traditional Cossack liberties and of Ukraine's struggle for freedom.

Whereas the causes of these uprisings varied, there were a few general trends. Throughout this whole period, the Cossacks never questioned the premise that they were subjects of the Polish king. In fact, what they wanted was to become recognized as a distinct estate with its own "traditional liberties" within Polish-Lithuanian society. While it is true that by the early seventeenth century sharp distinctions had evolved among the Cossacks, some kind of special status within Poland for the group as a whole was still the goal.

The legal distinctions within Cossack society were actually the result of Polish governmental policy, in particular that of the king. In an attempt to impose some kind of control over the ever-growing number of Cossacks and to ensure their military service to the crown instead of to local magnates or foreign powers, Polish kings introduced a policy of registration. The first registration occurred in 1572, and several others took place during the following years, the most ambitious perhaps being that of King Stefan Batory (reigned 1576–1586) in 1578. According to his program, the so-called registered Cossacks were (1) recognized as being in the Polish military service; (2) no longer to be subject to the control of the local gentry, or *szlachta*-dominated administration (at least during their time of service); and (3) to be paid for their services. The registered Cossacks were drawn from the town Cossacks, since the Polish government did not recognize the legal existence of the *sich*. The number of registered Cossacks generally remained small, ranging from 300 in the first register of 1572, to 6,000 under King Stefan Batory in 1578, to 8,000 in 1630. But the crown's effort to maintain control over a manageably sized Cossack force was undermined during periods of international conflict, especially in the first half of the seventeenth century, when kings encouraged large numbers of Cossacks (frequently peasants who had only recently fled to Zaporozhia) to enlist in the crown's service. For instance, by 1620 the Cossack registers had swelled to 20,000.

The existence of the register contributed to sharp distinctions between, on the one hand, the Cossacks in and near the frontier towns and, on the other, the Cossacks in Zaporozhia. Among the "traditional liberties" promised by King

SOCIAL ESTATES IN SIXTEENTH- AND EARLY SEVENTEENTH-CENTURY UKRAINE

1 **Crown**
    the Polish king

5 **Jews**

2 **Nobility**
    magnates
    gentry

6 **Peasants**
    manorial and monastic serfs
    free peasant homesteaders

3 **Clergy**
    Orthodox
    Uniate
    Catholic

7 **Cossacks**
    town (registered)
    Zaporozhian (unregistered)

4 **Townspeople**
    patricians
    merchants
    artisans
    workers

Stefan Batory to those on the register was the right of Cossacks to elect their own leaders and to be judged by their own peers, and perhaps most important of all was the royal confirmation of their right to the lands they held. This meant that the Cossacks of lesser-gentry status might regain lands they had lost to the great magnates or gain new lands. At the same time, the right meant landed-gentry status for registered Cossacks who were of peasant or town origin but had managed to get hold of a piece of land. In effect, it was not long before the registered Cossacks became wealthy property owners in their own right.

Living a more stable existence with their families in the middle regions of the Kiev and Bratslav palatinates, these landowning Cossacks were anxious to obtain even more privileges within the Polish administrative structure. In particular, they hoped to be recognized as on a par with the Polish *szlachta*. For their part, however, the Polish and local Orthodox Rus' magnates could never accept as equals those whom they considered Cossack upstarts and freebooting rabble. Conversely, the vast majority of Cossacks, who lived in Zaporozhia and who, not being on the register, were known as unregistered Cossacks, scorned their registered comrades-in-name who were in Polish service. The Zaporozhians wanted nothing to do with the Polish or any system of governmental control and preferred to live the traditional Cossack way of life: hunting, fishing, trading, farming a little, and raiding the Crimea and the Ottoman Empire in the south.

A MALE-DOMINATED SOCIETY?

The stereotypical image of the Zaporozhian Cossacks passed down through generations of writers is of a brotherhood of brave male warriors whose ideals were to fight hard and drink hard. This image of the Cossacks often became the image of Ukrainian society as a whole. As for women, there seemed to be no place for them. They were forbidden to enter Zaporozhia's military and administrative headquarters (the sich), lest male privacy be violated or "the brothers" be disturbed during their macho rituals and pursuits. In short, women in Cossack lore either were not mentioned or were relegated to a subordinate role. But was this really the case?

The following is another excerpt from the pen of Guillaume le Vasseur de Beauplan, the insightful contemporary observer of seventeenth-century Ukraine.

Fulfilling the promise I made above, let us relate something of the customs they [the Cossacks] observe in some of their marriages, and in what way they sometimes go courting one another. These practices will no doubt seem new and unbelievable to many [readers]. In that country, contrary, to the practice current in every [other] land, it is the girls who are seen courting the young men who please them.

One of their special practices, which is very carefully observed, almost always assures the young ladies success in their efforts. Indeed, they are more certain to succeed than the young men would be, if occasionally they tried to take the initiative. Here is how these girls proceed. An amorous young lady goes to the house of the father of the young man (whom she loves), at a time when she believes that the father, the mother, and her beloved will be together at home. Upon entering the house, she says *Pomahai Bih*, meaning, 'May God bless you,' which is the usual form of greeting when one enters one of their homes. When she has sat down, she pays compliments to the one who has wounded her heart. ... [She continues:] 'I recognize in your face something of an easy-going nature. You will know how to love your wife and govern her well, and your virtues make me hope that you will be a good husband. Your fine qualities lead me to beg you very humbly to accept me as your wife.'

Having spoken thus, she addresses the father and mother in like terms, humbly requesting their consent to the marriage. However, if she receives a refusal or some excuse [or other], [perhaps] that he is too young and not yet ready for marriage, she answers them [saying] that she will not leave until she becomes his wife, as long as they are both yet alive. When these words have been pronounced, and the girl has shown herself tenacious and determined never to leave the room without obtaining what she seeks, the father and mother are obliged, after a number of weeks, not only to give their consent, but also to persuade their son to look favorably on the girl, as one who must be his wife. Similarly the young man, seeing the young lady persevere in wishing him well, begins then to consider her as one who will someday be the mistress of his will. He therefore earnestly begs his father and mother to permit him to direct his affections toward that girl.

In such a manner, amorous young ladies of this country cannot fail to be provided with husbands at a young age, since by their stubbornness they force the father, the mother, and their beloved to accede to their wishes, for fear, as I have said above, of incurring God's wrath, and suffering some dreadful misfortune.

SOURCE: Guillaume Le Vasseur, Sieur de Beauplan, *A Description of Ukraine* (1660), translated by Andrew B. Pernal and Dennis F. Essar (Cambridge, Mass. 1993), pp. 70–71.

The political interaction among the king, the Polish and Rus' magnates and gentry, the gentrified registered Cossacks, and the Cossacks of Zaporozhia began to play itself out with increasing complexity after 1572, when the last Jagiellonian ruler died and the monarch was henceforth elected by the Diet. Polish kings were becoming more and more dependent on the whims of the magnates and gentry. Only those two factions of the nobility could, through the Diet, authorize the necessary funds or supply military forces to sustain Poland's foreign ventures. But most often they were reluctant to do so, especially when it seemed to them that a particular king, whether for dynastic or for economic reasons, was too eager to enter into war with Muscovy, or Sweden, or Moldavia. Faced with such internal political opposition, Poland's elected kings saw in the Cossacks a ready-made force that could be used to further their own foreign policy and military goals without their having to depend on the cooperation of the noble estates. This intent is what gave rise to the policy of registration, whereby Poland's kings would grant or restore Cossack privileges in return for military service. For their part, the Polish and polonized Rus' magnates and gentry opposed these direct relations between king and Cossacks, not to mention the continuing existence of a group that remained outside their control. The Rus' magnates in Ukraine, however, favored the existence of the registered Cossacks as long as they remained in their service and not that of the king.

The international role of the Cossacks

The vast majority of the unregistered Cossacks in Zaporozhia continued their policy of providing short-term service to Poland's kings and seeking alliances with foreign powers. During the last decade of the sixteenth century, they accepted an invitation from the Habsburg emperor of the Holy Roman Empire to join in a crusade against the infidel Ottomans. They took this occasion to raid and loot at will the Ottoman provinces of Walachia and Moldavia. Then, in the second decade of the seventeenth century, they fought on the side of Poland's king Zygmunt III during his frequent invasions of Muscovy. It was also during these decades that they built a large naval fleet, which, under the leadership of their daring hetman, Petro Sahaidachnyi, raided Ottoman cities along the northern as well as southern shores of the Black Sea. In the tradition of the Varangian Rus' almost 800 years before, Sahaidachnyi's Cossacks even plundered the outskirts of the impregnable Ottoman capital of Istanbul.

The Ottomans held the Poles to blame for the exploits of their unruly Cossack subjects, and not surprisingly, Polish-Ottoman relations deteriorated as a result. In the spring of 1620, a combined Turkish-Tatar army defeated a Polish force at the Battle of Ţuţora/Tsetsora Fields, near the Moldavian town of Iaşi. The way to Poland was now open. The Ottomans made further military preparations, and the following spring, in 1621, they advanced with an army of over 100,000. In desperation, the Poles called on the services of Hetman Sahaidachnyi, and it was his force of 40,000 Cossacks (drawn from Zaporozhia as well as from the ranks of the registered) that made possible a Polish victory over the Turks at the Battle of Khotyn in northern Moldavia, near the border with Podolia.

Thus, during the first half of the seventeenth century, a seemingly unbreakable cycle arose within the Crimean-Ottoman-Polish triangle that surrounded Cossack Ukraine. The Zaporozhian Cossacks would raid the Crimea and the Ottoman Empire. In response, the Ottoman Empire would threaten and sometimes carry out military invasions against Poland. The Polish government would demand that the Zaporozhians cease their anti-Ottoman and anti-Crimean raids, and to back up its demands would periodically send punitive expeditions to intervene in Zaporozhian affairs. The Zaporozhians would rebel against this interference, and wars against Poland would result, with sometimes one side, sometimes the other winning. In the end, nothing decisive ever occurred, and the cycle was repeated.

The Polish-Cossack conflicts before 1648, however limited in scope to the border regions near Zaporozhia, witnessed much of the brutality that accompanies any civil conflict. Polish frontier aristocrats like the hetmans Stanisław Żółkiewski, Stanisław Koniecpolski, and Stanisław and Mikołaj Potocki seemed to take special delight in trying to put down what they considered the Cossack rabble, and their victories at the battles of Lubny (1596), Pereiaslav (1630), and Kumeiky (1637) left a heritage of bitter hatred. For their part, the Zaporozhian Cossacks had no illusions about the Polish *szlachta*, and they felt betrayed by their own registered Cossacks, who often sided with the Poles. They felt especially betrayed by the king, who seemed ever ready to call upon their services for campaigns in Moldavia, or Muscovy, or Sweden, or against the Ottomans, but careless of living up to his promises of greater privileges or payments. Because of the Polish system of government, however, even if the kings were desirous of fulfilling their promises, they could almost never effectively do so over the heads of the *szlachta* opposition. Thus, the pre-1648 period left the Zaporozhian Cossacks with a deep-seated hatred and distrust of the Poles, combined with an ingrained historical memory of their own courageous hetmans such as Dmytro Vyshnevets'kyi and Petro Sahaidachnyi, their successful campaigns against the Crimean Tatars and Ottoman Turks, and their ability to circumvent Polish aristocratic control over their lives. It was on this era (the 1630s) that Nikolai Gogol', a nineteenth-century Ukrainian author who wrote in Russian, based his famous novel of Cossack revolt against Polish rule, *Taras Bul'ba* (1835).

The Cossacks and Orthodoxy

The role of the Cossacks in Ukrainian life was not limited, however, to military raids and protection of the frontier. Before long, they combined their desire for freedom and self-rule with a deep commitment to defend the Orthodox faith. The ideological link between the Cossack struggle for self-rule and its defense of Orthodoxy was in large part forged during the first two decades of the seventeenth century by Iezekiïl Kurtsevych, the archimandrite of the Trakhtemyriv Monastery (halfway between Kiev and Cherkasy) and Hetman Petro Sahaidachnyi. A native of Galicia and probably of noble descent, Sahaidachnyi was educated at the Ostroh Academy, where he was imbued with an Orthodox spirit. He then went to the *sich*, where the Zaporozhians elected him hetman. He not only increased the commitment of the Zaporozhian Cossacks to the Orthodox faith, but also led them in numerous victories against the Tatars and the Turks, and – in the service of Poland – against the Muscovites. In return for his loyalty to Poland, so crucial to the king on the eve of the 1621 Battle of Khotyn against the Ottoman Turks, Sahaidachnyi included in his demands the full restoration of the Orthodox Church, most of whose eparchial sees had been left vacant after the Union of Brest in 1596.

Meanwhile, during the first two decades of the seventeenth century Kiev itself was undergoing a revival which was to make it once again the center of Rus'-Ukrainian culture. The Monastery of the Caves (Pechers'ka Lavra), founded under Iaroslav the Wise during the mid-eleventh century, was headed from 1599 to 1624 by another native of Galicia, Ielysei Pletenets'kyi. While Sahaidachnyi was raising the military and political prestige of the Cossacks, Pletenets'kyi was busily engaged in creating a new basis for Orthodox cultural activity in Kiev. In 1615, he brought to the monastery a printing press from Striatyn, in Galicia, and during its first fifteen years of operation (1616–1630) it produced forty titles, more than any other press in the rest of Ukraine or Belarus. Among the titles were works of literature, history, and religious polemic, liturgical books, and texts for the growing number of schools. The last category included Pamvo Berynda's *Leksykon slaveno-rosskii* (Slaveno-Rusyn Lexicon, 1627), the first dictionary in the East Slavic world, which, together with another contemporary work, published elsewhere, Meletii Smotryts'kyi's *Grammatika slavenskaia* (Slavonic Grammar, 1619), established a standard for the Church Slavonic language that was to be used among all East Slavs for the next two centuries.

Pletenets'kyi also brought to Kiev's Monastery of the Caves a group of Galician intellectuals (Iov Borets'kyi, Zakhariia Kopystens'kyi, Lavrentii Zyzanii) who had been trained or taught at L'viv's Stauropegial Brotherhood school. Following the L'viv tradition, Kiev received its own brotherhood and school in 1615, where a Greco-Slavonic curriculum was established according to the L'viv model. Moreover, in the midst of this cultural revival, Hetman Sahaidachnyi moved his administration to Kiev, making it once again the seat of political and military power as well as the cultural center of Ukrainian lands. And to show his further support of the Orthodox revival, the hetman enrolled all his Zaporozhian Cossacks in the recently established Kiev Brotherhood.

Buoyed by the support of the Cossacks and their dynamic leader Sahai-dachnyi, the Orthodox clergy and lay leaders felt that the time had come to restore the organizational framework of their church. By the second decade of the seventeenth century, the metropolitan's office and all the Eastern-rite eparchies on Belarusan and Ukrainian lands in Poland-Lithuania with the exception of L'viv were in the hands of the Uniates. The Cossacks, however, had refused to allow the Uniate metropolitans – Ipatii Potii and his successor, Veliamyn Ruts'kyi (reigned 1614–1637) – to take up their seat of Kiev. Now, in 1620, the Orthodox group took advantage of a visit by the patriarch of Jerusalem, Theophanes, who in October of that year stopped in Kiev on his way to Muscovy. They persuaded the patriarch to ordain an Orthodox metropolitan for Kiev as well as four bishops for the sees of Przemyśl, Polatsk, Volodymyr-Volyns'kyi, and Luts'k. Early the following year, two more Orthodox bishops were ordained, for Chełm and Pinsk. The ordinations were performed in secret and without the approval of the Polish government. When the government found out, it accused Patriarch Theophanes of being a Turkish spy and outlawed the newly appointed metropolitan and bishops.

In response, in 1621 the new Orthodox metropolitan, Iov Borets'kyi (reigned 1620–1631), and the six bishops published their first manifesto. Of particular interest is their characterization of the Cossacks:

We all know about the Cossacks, that these chivalrous men are of our race, are of our kin, and are true Orthodox Christians. ... They are the descendants of the glorious Rus', of the seed of Japheth who fought [Byzantine] Greece on land and on sea. They are the descendants of that warlike race which under Oleh, the Rus' monarch, attacked Constantinople. They are the same as those who with Volodymyr, the sainted king of [Kievan] Rus', conquered Greece, Macedonia, and Illyria. Their ancestors, together with Volodymyr, were baptized and accepted Christianity from the church at Constantinople, and even to this day they are born, are baptized, and live in this faith.[3]

Referring to more recent times, the Orthodox bishops stated: "[The Cossacks'] second purpose is to set the prisoner free. ... It is truly said that no one in the whole world does so much for the benefit of the persecuted and oppressed Christians ... as the Army of Zaporozhia with their daring and their victories. What other peoples achieve by words and discourses, the Cossacks achieve by their actions."[4] The Cossacks were now armed with a historical ideology and viewed by the highest Orthodox authorities as latter-day descendants of the biblical Japheth and the Kievan Rus' princes.

The registered Cossacks, in particular, took advantage of the situation and put forth a new demand in all their negotiations with the Poles: recognition of the already-appointed bishops and thereby the full reconstitution of the Orthodox Church in Poland-Lithuania. During the next decade, the Polish king Zygmunt III often made promises regarding Orthodoxy, but he refused to recognize the consecration of its seven hierarchs. Finally, following the death of the king in 1632, a period of interregnum ensued during which the Polish Diet prepared for the election of a new monarch. Several Orthodox Rus' noblemen seized the opportunity to introduce the Cossack question into the royal electoral debates. For the first time they demanded that the Cossacks be recognized as a noble estate within the Polish social structure, and they renewed their call for the legalization of the Orthodox hierarchy. Not surprisingly, there was great opposition from the Polish *szlachta*. The newly elected king, Władysław IV (reigned 1632–1648), needed troops for a campaign against Muscovy, however, and was therefore predisposed to favoring the Cossack requests. Although the question of noble status was decided against the Cossacks, the new king, through personal persuasion, was able in 1632 to push through a compromise agreement known as the "Pacification of the Greek Faith."

The compromise of 1632 finally regulated Orthodox church life in Poland-Lithuania. The metropolitan and bishops were to be elected by the Orthodox clergy and nobility, confirmed by the Polish king, and blessed by the ecumenical patriarch of Constantinople. The secretly elected Orthodox hierarchy of 1620 was not recognized, however. With regard to Orthodox-Uniate relations, the eparchies of the Metropolitanate of Kiev were divided between the two churches (see map 15). The archeparchy of Kiev, the eparchies of L'viv-Halych, Przemyśl-Sambir, Luts'k-Ostroh, and the newly created eparchy of Mstsislaŭ went to the Orthodox; the eparchies of Polatsk, Chełm, Volodymyr, Pinsk-Turaŭ, and Smolensk (then under Polish rule) went to the Uniates. Moreover, each church was to have its own metropolitan of Kiev. The Orthodox metropolitan was to reside in Kiev itself, the Uniate metropolitan in Vilnius or Navahrudak in Lithuania. As well, Orthodox schools, printing presses, brotherhoods, and new churches were permitted; several churches and monasteries held by the Uniates (including all but one in Kiev) were returned to the Orthodox Church; and Orthodox adherents were once again permitted to hold office in municipal government. Despite protests from the Uniate metropolitan and Polish Catholic bishops, the king upheld the agreement of 1632 and reconfirmed it three years later.

Taking advantage of the favorable political situation, Orthodox nobles in the Polish Diet nominated in November 1632 a fellow deputy, Archimandrite Petro Mohyla (Petru Movilă), as metropolitan of Kiev (reigned 1632–1647). Within days, the nomination was approved by the king and a blessing requested from the ecumenical patriarch. This meant that the recently elected Metropolitan Isaia Kopyns'kyi (reigned 1631–1632) the successor to Metropolitan Borets'kyi who was secretly elected in 1620 – was removed from office.

The new and dynamic Metropolitan Mohyla/Movilă was the son of the Romanian Orthodox ruler of Walachia and Moldavia. In 1627, just two years after his arrival in Kiev, he was made archimandrite of the city's influential Monastery of the Caves. The ambitious and talented Mohyla was convinced that the survival of Orthodoxy depended on the creation of a well-educated group of clerics trained in the best traditions of their religious antagonists, the Jesuits. Accordingly, he sent monks to Poland to be educated, and he opened a new school on the Jesuit Latin model at the Kiev monastery.

Mohyla's policies were by no means universally accepted within Poland-

ORTHODOX VERSUS UNIATE

Despite the compromise of 1632, hailed in Polish governmental circles as the "Pacification of the Greek Faith," the struggle among the Rus' people between adherents of Orthodoxy and of Uniatism continued unabated through the whole first half of the seventeenth century. The struggle took many forms: court cases, debates in the Diet, and the publication of polemical pamphlets in defense either of the Orthodox faith and Ruthenian language or of the rightness of union with Rome.

Meanwhile, Orthodox defections to the Uniates continued among all strata of society, and included that of the once-staunch defender of Orthodoxy, Archbishop Meletii Smotryts'kyi, who in 1628 became a Uniate. Even more pronounced were conversions to Roman Catholicism among members of the powerful Rus' magnate families (the Ostroz'kyis, Vyshnevets'kyis, Sangushkos, Chartoryis'kyis, Zbaraz'kyis, and Zaslavs'kyis) and the further spread eastward of Roman Catholic influence through the establishment of several new Jesuit schools between 1608 and 1646 (in L'viv, Luts'k, Kam'ianets'-Podil's'kyi, Ostroh, Brest, Ovruch and as far east as Novhorod-Sivers'kyi and Kiev). It was the advance of Roman Catholicism that prompted discussion of the possibility of a "new union," including a proposal put forth in 1645 by none other than the Orthodox metropolitan of Kiev, Petro Mohyla/Movilă.

The passions and zeal of the Orthodox-Uniate struggle produced intellectual debates and legal battles as well as physical violence against individuals and the destruction or forcible acquisition of rival churches. Among the more brutal and memorable instances of violence was the assassination of the Uniate archbishop of Polatsk in Belarus, Iosafat Kuntsevych (reigned 1617–1623), by the angered Orthodox citizens of Vitsebsk, where the prelate's residence was located. Following his death in 1623, Kuntsevych was hailed by the Uniates of Poland-Lithuania as a martyr for their faith, and in 1867 he was canonized by the Roman Catholic Church. The intensity of the Orthodox-Uniate antagonism in the early seventeenth century is conveyed in the following contemporary description, from Bishop Iakiv Susha's biography of Kuntsevych (1665):

> The ringing of cathedral bells and the bells of other churches spread. This was the signal and call to insurrection. From all sides of town masses of people – men, women, and children – gathered with stones and attacked the archbishop's residence. The masses attacked and injured the servants and assistants of the archbishop, and broke into the room where he was alone. One hit him on the head with a stick, another split it with an axe, and when Kuntsevych fell, they started beating him. They looted his house, dragged his body to the plaza, cursed him – even women and children. ... They dragged him naked through the streets of the city

all the way to the hill overlooking the river Dvina. Finally, after tying stones to the dead body, they threw him into the Dvina at its deepest.*

*Osyp Zinkewych and Andrew Sorokowski, comps., *A Thousand Years of Christianity in Ukraine* (New York, Baltimore, and Toronto 1988), p. 121.

Lithuania's Orthodox milieu. Actually, the metropolitan's election at the end of 1632 represented a victory for the Orthodox Rus' nobles over the Cossacks, who had supported the deposed and still-smarting Metropolitan Kopyns'kyi and the other hierarchs secretly ordained in 1620. Kopyns'kyi, together with those pro-Muscovite sympathizers, looked to the tsar and hoped for reconciliation with the patriarch in Moscow. Consequently, they worked against what they considered Mohyla's pro-Western (i.e., Roman Catholic) orientation. Hearing the complaints of such traditionalist clerics, the Cossacks even threatened to do away with Mohyla and his "Latin-oriented" intellectual circle, whom they considered infiltrators poisoning the minds of Orthodox youth.

Despite his critics, Mohyla moved ahead in trying to implement his vision for the revival of Orthodoxy within Poland-Lithuania. While he was still archimandrite of Kiev's Monastery of the Caves, the school he founded there in 1631 was merged the following year with the city's brotherhood school into one institution, the Kievan, or Mohyla, Collegium. The collegium maintained the traditions of scholastic education then prevailing in Catholic Jesuit schools, and great emphasis was placed on the study of Latin. Mohyla believed that the future of Orthodoxy in Belarus and Ukraine lay in an accommodation with Poland – albeit on an equal basis – and for this reason he tried to undermine the traditional attitude of the Ukrainian Orthodox clergy, who until then had looked eastward to Muscovy as their only salvation. During the first half of the seventeenth century, discontented Orthodox clergy and monks had continued to seek refuge in Muscovy. Now, under the leadership of the capable and intellectually astute Mohyla, the Orthodox Church and its centers of learning in Ukraine could hold their own as a source of cultural attraction against the Catholic West.

The calm before the storm

By the 1630s, Cossack pressure had succeeded in restoring the legal status of the Orthodox Church in Poland-Lithuania. Its own demands, however, remained unmet. The registered Cossacks were not recognized as a distinct social estate, and the Zaporozhians continued to clash with Poland's governmental authorities, either because of their disagreements with frontier officials in Ukraine or because of their unauthorized attacks on the Crimea and the Ottoman Empire. As a result, the cycle of Polish-Cossack friction continued: Cossack service in Poland's foreign military ventures was followed by their discontent with unfulfilled promises and then by Polish military efforts to subdue them. The latter included the construction in 1635 of a fortress at Kodak to secure the frontier and stop the flight of runaway peasant serfs to Zaporozhia (see map 16).

The reaction of the Cossacks was to raze the fortress at Kodak within a few months of its construction and then to mount two major rebellions – 1637 (led by Pavlo Pavliuk-But) and 1638 (led by Iakiv Ostrianyn and Dmytro Hunia) – in which the registered Cossacks as well as the unregistered Zaporozhians participated. The first ended with the beheading of the Cossack leader by victorious Polish forces following their victory at the Battle of Kumeiky (December 1637). The second ended after the Polish victory at Zhovnyne (June 1638) and the departure of Ostrianyn with 1,000 of his followers to the Muscovite-controlled Sloboda Ukraine. After the 1638 defeat, the number of registered Cossacks, which had continued to fluctuate during the seventeenth century, was reduced to 6,000; they were allowed to live only in the districts of Cherkasy, Chyhyryn, and Korsun'; their election of the hetman and offices above the rank of colonel were abolished; and a large military garrison was stationed at the rebuilt Kodak fortress. Finally, all the unregistered Cossacks farther down the Dnieper in Zaporozhia were declared outlaws.

For the next ten years, the situation remained relatively quiet, and some Poles felt that perhaps the Cossack problem was at last under control. Yet nothing had really changed. The magnate-dominated manorial system continued to increase its hold over the agricultural sector; discontented peasants, townspeople, and lesser gentry continued to flee to Zaporozhia; and the Orthodox Church, while restored to legal status, was forced to compete with the government-favored Uniate church for the control and maintenance of individual parishes. Meanwhile, the Cossacks were drawn into the vagaries of Polish politics, which had traditionally set the king in opposition to the nobility.

The latest instance of Cossack involvement came during the reign of Władysław IV, a king who was particularly fond of foreign ventures, whether against Sweden (as a member of the Vasa dynasty, he had claims to the Swedish crown), against Muscovy (Poland still interfered in the yet-unstable Muscovite state), or against the Ottoman Turks (the traditional enemy). In 1646, Władysław made plans for a crusade against the Turks, but when the Polish Diet refused to grant him funds, he naturally turned to the registered Cossacks. The latter received a secret charter and banner from the king, and an army was assembled, but the Diet got wind of the agreement and before the end of 1646 demanded the demobilization of the army. The following year, Władysław capitulated to the Diet's wishes, and the potential advantages accruable to the Cossacks from the venture were lost.

All these factors – socioeconomic, religious, and political – contributed to an increase in the heritage of hatred between the Cossacks and the Polish nobility, who, because of their political power, came to represent the whole Polish-Lithuanian Commonwealth. Continual tension could erupt into conflagration at any time. In 1647, the spark was finally lit by the personal misfortune experienced by one Cossack official, Bohdan Khmel'nyts'kyi.

PART FOUR

The Cossack State, 1648–1711

16

Khmel'nyts'kyi and the Uprising of 1648

Bohdan Khmel'nyts'kyi is the central figure in Ukrainian history during the seventeenth century. Some have also considered him the most important leader in modern Ukrainian history. First of all, it was during his tenure of less than a decade as hetman (1648–1657) that the Cossacks, and with them half of Ukraine's territory, changed their allegiance from Poland to Muscovy. This proved to be the beginning of a process that was to result in the further acquisition by Muscovy of Ukrainian territory from Poland until the final disappearance of the Commonwealth from the map of Europe at the end of the eighteenth century. Even more important for Ukrainian history was the fact that Khmel'nyts'kyi succeeded in bringing most of central Ukraine under his control and in ruling the territory as if it were an independent state. His Cossack state consequently provided an inexhaustible source of inspiration for future generations of Ukrainians, many of whom strove to restore what they considered to have been an independent Ukraine under Khmel'nyts'kyi.

A pivotal figure in the history of eastern Europe during the seventeenth century, Bohdan Khmel'nyts'kyi has been viewed in radically different ways. Not surprisingly, traditional Polish historiography considered Khmel'nyts'kyi the leader of a destructive uprising that seriously undermined and eventually destroyed the Polish state, while Russian historiography has viewed him as a leader who successfully led the Orthodox "Little Russians" into the fold of a united Russian state. Ukrainian writers see Khmel'nyts'kyi as an outstanding leader who successfully restored the idea of national independence that had lain dormant since Kievan times. Although some Ukrainians may criticize him for his sociopolitical and diplomatic failures, especially his decision to submit to Muscovy, all agree that his rule was a crucial turning point in Ukrainian historical development. Jewish historians view Khmel'nyts'kyi as the instigator of the first genocidal catastrophe in the modern history of the Jews. They point out that not only was the vibrant Jewish community in Ukraine largely decimated, but this early "holocaust" brought about the inner-directed and mystic emphasis which marked the subsequent development of eastern Europe's

Ashkenazi Jews. Finally, Soviet Marxist writers, both Russian and Ukrainian, tended to stress the popular revolutionary aspect of the Khmel'nyts'kyi years. Beginning in the 1930s, they placed the Cossack leader into that small but politically significant pantheon of acceptable pre-Soviet national heroes, especially because he was so instrumental in setting out along a course which led to the "reunification" of the brotherly Ukrainian and Russian peoples. Thus, for some, Bohdan Khmel'nyts'kyi has been a hero, either qualified or of the highest order, while by others he is seen as a villain or even the devil incarnate. Who was this man, whose career is still the subject of historical debate and contemporary political polemics?

Khmel'nyts'kyi's early career

Bohdan Zinovii Khmel'nyts'kyi was born about 1595. His actual birthplace has not been determined with certainty, although many believe it was his father's estate at Subotiv, near Chyhyryn, not far from the Dnieper River and about forty-three miles (seventy kilometers) south of the frontier town and Cossack center at Cherkasy. The boy's father, Mykhailo, was a registered Cossack of gentry origin, probably from Belarus, who had served in Galicia (in the town of Zhovkva just north of L'viv) on the staff of the renowned early seventeenth-century Polish general Hetman Stanisław Żółkiewski. Subsequently, Mykhailo Khmel'nyts'kyi was invited by the district *starosta* at Chyhyryn to serve in that town, where he soon became vice-*starosta* and settled on an estate in nearby Subotiv, where his son Bohdan was later born.

In the absence of an Orthodox school in the relatively nearby city of Kiev (one was not opened there until 1615), Bohdan was sent to a Jesuit school in Galicia (at Jarosław). After completing his education, he served with his father and the Cossacks who fought with Hetman Żółkiewski in the latter's abortive campaign against the Turks in 1620. Both Żółkiewski and Mykhailo Khmel'nyts'kyi were killed at the Battle of Ţuţora/Cecora, near Iaşi in Moldavia, while the young Bohdan was captured and sent to Constantinople. For the next two years, until his mother forwarded enough money to redeem him, Bohdan studied Turkish and learned much about Ottoman and Crimean politics, as well as about the difficulties faced by the Greek Orthodox Church in the sultan's capital. After his return home in 1622, Khmel'nyts'kyi served with the registered Cossacks in his native region of Chyhyryn.

At this time, during the 1620s and 1630s, Khmel'nyts'kyi was known to favor an increase in the number of registered Cossacks and an extension of their privileges. Some Poles suspected that he participated in the Cossack rebellions of 1637 and 1638, although there is no proof that this was the case. He was, therefore, allowed to hold the post of captain (*sotnyk*) of the Chyhyryn Cossacks. During the relatively peaceful years after 1638, Khmel'nyts'kyi turned his attention to the family estate near Chyhyryn, where he seemed destined to spend the rest of his life as a typical registered Cossack whose primary object was to enhance the status of his group so that it might eventually be accepted as on a par with the nobility (gentry) in the rest of Polish-Lithuanian society. But the steppe zone in which Khmel'nyts'kyi, like his father before him, lived was undergoing rapid colonization and change, and without the appropriate documents the Khmel'nyts'kyi family's claims to noble status meant little to aggressive magnates who had a tradition of appropriating lands from the gentry, whether or not they were of proven noble status. Accordingly, Khmel'nyts'kyi's social status remained uncertain, and he was forced to seek a modicum of security by rendering military service to the king or by engaging in economic activity in an effort to increase at least his material wealth.

The uncertainty of his own position was responsible for Khmel'nyts'kyi's favoring changes on behalf of the registered Cossacks, whose status had declined after the abortive revolts of 1637–1638. He was particularly encouraged by King Władysław IV's plans in 1646 to organize a new crusade against the Ottomans. Courted for their military potential, the Cossacks saw the king's plans as offering a way of improving their own situation. In fact, Khmel'nyts'kyi was one of a four-member Cossack delegation summoned to Warsaw in 1646 to negotiate with the king. So much the greater, then, was his disappointment when the Polish nobility succeeded in thwarting Wladysław's effort. Nonetheless, the Cossack delegation supposedly received a secret charter from the king, which promised to restore those privileges the Cossacks had enjoyed before 1638.

The first few months of 1647 witnessed a series of events that was to mark a turning point in Khmel'nyts'kyi's life. Because of his importance as a historical figure, it is not surprising that many legends have grown up around him, in particular about this crucial period. The more colorful of these legends, drawn from several later sources, make up what the historian Mykhailo Hrushevs'kyi has dubbed the "Khmel'nyts'kyi affair." The so-called affair refers to a "struggle over a woman" named Matrona/Helena, in whom Khmel'nyts'kyi – himself married with a family – supposedly had an amorous interest. Eventually, Helena married Khmel'nyts'kyi's local rival, the Polish vice-*starosta* of Chyhyryn, Daniel Czapliński. Just before Czapliński won the hand of Helena, he raided Khmel'nyts'kyi's estate at Subotiv, appropriated its movable property, and at some point flogged the Cossack leader's son, who as a result of his injuries died soon after. The violence and terror undoubtedly contributed to the untimely death of Khmel'nyts'kyi's wife sometime in 1647.

Khmel'nyts'kyi was a business rival of Czapliński's superior, the Chyhyryn *starosta*, Alexander Koniecpolski, who for his part felt that the Cossack leader was encroaching on his liquor monopoly. In response to the raid on his estate, Khmel'nyts'kyi sought justice in the local court, but was unsuccessful. He then journeyed to Warsaw and put his case before the Polish Senate. There, too, he received no satisfaction. While in the capital, he even turned to King Władysław, who, though he sympathized with Khmel'nyts'kyi, admitted that he was powerless to intervene in Poland's *szlachta*-controlled legal and administrative system.

Khmel'nyts'kyi's appeals to the royal court and Senate in Warsaw served to alienate his enemies further, and after returning home in late 1647 he was promptly arrested on Koniecpolski's orders. Helped by friends, Khmel'nyts'kyi managed to escape and, with nowhere else to turn, decided to follow in the footsteps of hundreds of discontented registered Cossacks and lower gentry before him. In January 1648, he fled to the Zaporozhian Sich and its Cossack host, who lived in relative safety beyond the reach of the Polish authorities.

These basic facts were later embellished by several authors in such a way that the long-standing political, social, and economic friction between Poles and Cos-

MAP 18

THE KHMEL'NYTS'KYI ERA

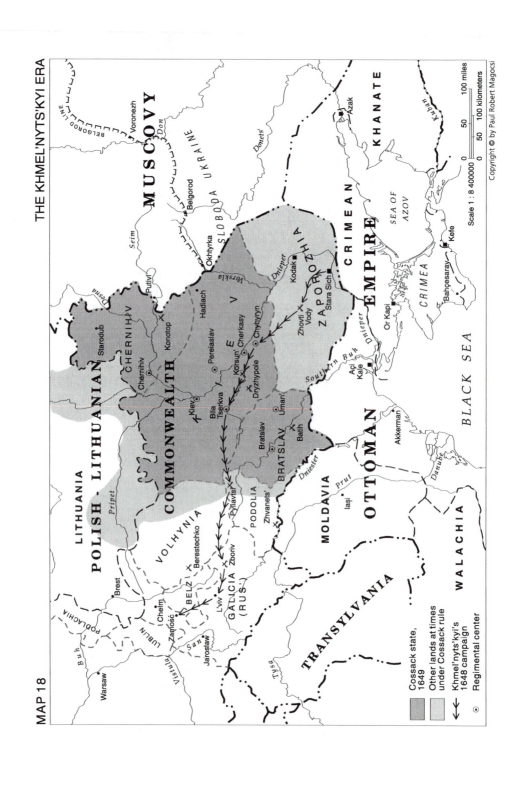

Cossack state, 1649

Other lands at times under Cossack rule

Khmel'nyts'kyi's 1648 campaign

Regimental center

Scale 1 : 8 400 000

0   50   100 miles
0   50   100 kilometers

Copyright © by Paul Robert Magocsi

sacks was made to seem less important as motivating Khmel'nyts'kyi's actions than his supposed rivalry with a minor local Polish official over the love of a woman. In the end, however, it was not a personal quarrel over "Helena of the steppes," but the ever-present social, religious, and national tensions in seventeenth-century Ukraine that set the stage for a series of events which would result in profound changes in both Ukrainian and Polish society.

The uprising of 1648

While the Zaporozhians may have been subdued after the failure of the revolts in 1637 and 1638, they were not eliminated. Now it seemed that the right leader – one who they heard was even trusted by the king – had arrived in Zaporozhia in the person of Bohdan Khmel'nyts'kyi. Khmel'nyts'kyi immediately set out to allay the traditional attitude of suspicion on the part of the Zaporozhians toward the "gentrified" registered Cossacks, and before the end of January 1648 he was elected hetman. The new hetman anticipated conflict with the Poles and, drawing on his experience with the Ottoman world, concluded an alliance with the Crimean Tatars. Crimea's khan, Islam III Giray (reigned 1644–1654), was receptive to an alliance for at least two reasons: he could punish the Poles for attacks on his khanate, and he might be able to placate rising discontent among his own Tatar nobles by giving them the opportunity to plunder Ukrainian lands, where war booty could be obtained with the ostensible approval and protection of the Cossacks themselves. In fulfillment of their side of the alliance, the khan called on Tugay-Bey, the administrator of the powerful Crimean fortress at Perekop/Or Kapi, who together with 4,000 Nogay and other Tatar cavalry joined in common cause with Khmel'nyts'kyi's Cossacks.

Although Poland's governing and military circles were divided on how to handle this new Cossack-Tatar threat, they were convinced of their own superiority in military skills if not number of troops. A Polish land army together with Polish cavalry and registered Cossacks in Polish service – a force about 9,200 under the supreme command of Crown Hetman Mikołaj Potocki and including his son Stefan Potocki – set out toward Zaporozhia, where Khmel'nyts'kyi had from 4,000 to 5,000 Cossacks under his banner together with 3,000 to 4,000 Tatar cavalry under Tugay-Bey. To their surprise, the Polish forces were intercepted en route and defeated by the Zaporozhians and their Crimean allies at the Battle of Zhovti Vody on 5–6 May. In the course of the battle, Stefan Potocki was captured by the Tatars (he later died of his wounds), and the registered Cossacks on the Polish side deserted to Khmel'nyts'kyi. With this expanded Cossack-Tatar force, Khmel'nyts'kyi was able to pursue the Poles and defeat them in a second battle, at Korsun', on 15–16 May, in which both Polish commanders were captured. To make matters worse for the Poles, King Władysław died on the eve (10 May) of the Polish defeat at Korsun'.

Upon hearing the news of the Cossack victories, discontented elements throughout much of the Kiev palatinate were inspired to revolt. Peasants drove out or killed their Polish landlords and Jewish estate managers; Orthodox clergy called for vengeance against Roman Catholic and Uniate priests; and townspeople plotted against the wealthy urban elements. Added to the turmoil was the arrival after the victory at Korsun' of the Crimean khan himself with an enormous army upward of eleven thousand troops. Like the Tatar forces already in Ukraine, all were authorized to plunder and collect booty. Such restrictive "guidelines" were almost immediately forgotten, however, as the Tatar troops began to attack indiscriminately towns and villages and either kill or capture the local inhabitants to send to the Crimean slave markets.

Thus, by the outset of the summer of 1648, two of Poland's leading commanders had been captured, its eastern army had been defeated, its Ukrainian peasant population was in revolt, its Tatar enemies were ravaging the countryside at will, and its king was dead. Moreover, Poland's traditional enemies – the Zaporozhian Cossacks and Crimean Tatars – were flushed with victory and there seemed to be no defense against them. Undoubtedly, the Ukrainian peasant masses and the vast majority of the unregistered Zaporozhian Cossacks were ready to rid themselves of Polish rule once and for all. But was Bohdan Khmel'nyts'kyi ready?

Khmel'nyts'kyi's way of life, like that of other relatively comfortable registered Cossacks, was that of an aspiring country gentryman. While he had been personally wronged by local rivals, his initial goal was simply to obtain justice. If justice could not be obtained through legal channels, then a military victory against the Polish army might force the authorities to act favorably on his behalf. Even after Khmel'nys'kyi had defeated Poland's eastern army twice, it is likely that he would have welcomed the possibility of remaining a subject of the king of Poland if he had been assured of personal legal redress and the restoration to his fellow registered Cossacks of the privileges they had enjoyed before the abortive revolt of 1637–1638. It was too late to go back, however, whether he wanted to do so or not. Khmel'nyts'kyi's actions, motivated by personal resentment, set in motion a sequence of events over which he did not have complete control. He had to ride the waves or be submerged.

At first, Khmel'nyts'kyi tried to resist the Cossack-peasant uprising, which after doing away with the local Polish nobility would, he surmised, probably turn on the Rus' gentry and registered Cossacks as well. He hoped to find support among Poles for his desire to control what he considered the excesses of the revolution. In June 1648, pretending not to know of the king's death, Khmel'nyts'kyi stopped his army at Bila Tserkva, just southwest of Kiev, and sent an emissary to Warsaw demanding that the traditional Cossack privileges be restored; that the number of registered Cossacks be increased to 12,000; that the Cossacks be paid for their services of the last five years; and that the Orthodox be treated justly, in particular by having the churches and monasteries still held by the Uniates restored to it. In return, the hetman pledged his loyalty to the king.

The Polish Diet was overjoyed with Khmel'nyts'kyi's modest demands and agreed to have them considered by the new king, whom they were still in the process of choosing. Khmel'nyts'kyi then returned to his estate near Chyhyryn and in early 1649 even managed to marry Matrona/Helena, after her short-lived marriage to Czapliński was annulled. It seemed that Khmel'nyts'kyi was on the verge of obtaining all he had wanted.

Events were not to leave him in peace, however. Other Cossack leaders, like the popular Maksym Kryvonis and Danylo Nechai, led the peasant masses and

KHMEL'NYTS'KYI AND THE JEWS

Jewish chroniclers of the seventeenth century provide vastly different and invariably inflated figures with respect to the loss of life among the Jewish population of Ukraine during the Khmel'nyts'kyi uprising. The numbers range from 60,000–80,000 (Nathan Hannover) to 100,000 (Sabbatai Cohen) killed and from 300 communities to 670,000 households destroyed. Almost without exception, today's specialists on the period reject what they describe as the grossly exaggerated figures in the chronicles. The Israeli scholars Shmuel Ettinger and Bernard D. Weinryb speak instead of the "annihilation of tens of thousands of Jewish lives," and the Ukrainian-American historian Jaroslaw Pelenski narrows the number of Jewish deaths to between 6,000 and 14,000. The most recent calculations by the Israeli Shaul Stampfer place the figure between 18,000 and 20,000, which represents about half of the Jewish population living in the Ukrainian lands of Poland-Lithuania at the time.

Despite the correctives provided by recent scholarship, the old chronicles manage to retain a strong hold on the modern reader's imagination. Perhaps the best known and most often published chronicle is the *Yeven Metzulah*, by the rabbi of Ostroh, in Volhynia, Nathan Hannover. A Hebrew version was first published in Venice in 1653, and has since then appeared in many translations, including several in English under the title *The Deep Mire* or *The Abyss of Despair*. In the introduction to the 1983 edition of the Hannover chronicle, an American specialist in Judaic studies, William B. Helmreich, still refers to the events of the Khmel'nyts'kyi era as "one of the worst catastrophes ever to befall the Jewish people." In the following excerpts from *The Abyss of Despair*, Hannover tells us why he chose his title and, how the attitudes of the Cossack hetman Khmel'nyts'kyi are supposedly characteristic of all Ukrainians.

I named my book YEVEN METZULAH (THE DEEP MIRE), because the words of the Psalmist [Psalms 69:3] allude to these terrible events, and speak of the oppressors, the Tatars and the Ukrainians [Hannover's actual term is "Greeks," i.e., Orthodox Christians] as well as of the arch-enemy, Chmiel [Khmel'nyts'kyi], may his name be blotted out, may God send a curse upon him. This book may thus be a chronicle to serve future generations.

For while he [Khmel'nyts'kyi] was soft spoken, he had seven abominations in his heart; a man plotting iniquity, in the manner of all the Ukrainians, who at first appear to the Jews as friends, and speak to them pleasant and comforting words, beguiling them with soft and kind speech, while they lie with their tongues and are deceitful and untrustworthy.*

The Khmel'nyts'kyi era is known in Jewish circles as the *gzeyres takh vetat*, an acronym referring to the evil Decrees of 1648–1649. At least until the second half of the twentieth century, a fast day (20th of Sivan in the Jewish calendar) was each year observed by eastern European Jews in memory of the victims of

Khmel'nyts'kyi. Moreover, the account of Hannover, with its vivid and often sensationalist descriptions of brutality, has continued to influence the popular image of Khmel'nyts'kyi's uprising among Jews to this day. Recent Jewish scholarship has pointed out, however, that Hannover's goal was "not to provide an objective history, but to preserve the memory of the holy communities that had been destroyed"; in short, "his descriptions are often inaccurate" and for the most part not those of an eyewitness but those of someone who "used the works of others creatively to build up his narrative."** Of Ukraine's Jews who were not killed during the Khmel'nyts'kyi era (that is, more than half the original population), many survived either by fleeing to protected fortress-cities, or they fled abroad. Within a few years, most of the refugees, unwilling to live abroad, returned to their homes. This explains why before the end of the seventeenth century Jewish communities were once again flourishing in Ukraine.

*Nathan Hanover, *Abyss of Despair: The Famous 17th-Century Chronicle Depicting Jewish Life in Russia and Poland during the Chmielnicki Massacres of 1648–1649*, translated by Abraham J. Mesch, 2nd ed. (New Brunswick, N.J. and London 1983), pp. 25 and 34.

**Shaul Stampfer, "Gzeyres takh vetat," in Gershon David Hundert, ed., *The YIVO Encyclopedia of Jews in Eastern Europe*, Vol. I (New Haven and London, 2008), pp. 646–647.

unregistered Cossacks in new revolts which heaped further destruction on Roman Catholic Poles, Uniate Ukrainians, and Jews throughout the Kiev palatinate. These revolts had a particularly devastating impact, in both the short and the long term, on the Jews (see Chapter 28). The number of Jewish victims during the period from 1648 to 1652 has been estimated from the tens to the hundreds of thousands, although the results of recent more systematic research give the more likely figure of 18,000 to 20,000.[1] Whatever the exact number, or whoever was responsible – the peasants, the Zaporozhian Cossacks and their independent-minded leaders like Kryvonis and Nechai, or the Crimean Tatars, who sold captured Jews in the Ottoman slave markets – it is Khmel'nyts'kyi who is held to blame in Jewish sources to the present day. The widely used *Encyclopedia Judaica* describes him with borrowings from Jewish chroniclers: "'Chmiel the Wicked,' one of the most sinister oppressors of the Jews of all generations, ... and the figure principally responsible for the holocaust of the Polish Jewry in the period." His reputation among Jews remains unchanged, "even though in reality," the same source admits, "his control of events was rather limited."[2] Whatever the validity of Jewish opinion about Khmel'nyts'kyi, the fact remains that in the socioeconomic system of the Polish-Lithuanian Commonwealth the Jews, alongside the Poles, had come to represent the oppressor. In the great social upheaval which began in 1648, the Jews found themselves caught between the proverbial hammer and anvil, and the result was the destruction of many of their communities.

By the end of the summer of 1648, the Cossack-peasant revolts had spread farther westward, engulfing the rest of the Kiev palatinate, as well as the Bratslav, Podolia, and (partially) Volhynia palatinates. At this point, Jeremi Wiśniowiecki,

an influential Polish magnate from the Left Bank and a descendant of the Rus'
Vyshnevets'kyi family who had become a fervent Roman Catholic and patriotic
defender of Poland, decided to take matters into his own hands. Impatient with
the seemingly inconclusive discussions of the Cossack question on the part of
the Polish government in Warsaw, Wiśniowiecki decided to attack the rebels. He
was repulsed, however, by Cossack cavalry forces led by Maksym Kryvonis. This
development prompted Khmel'nyts'kyi to come out of his short-lived seclusion.
He marched westward toward Volhynia, where in September 1648, together with
Kryvonis, he routed a large Polish army of 80,000 soldiers near the village of Pyliav-
tsi. The Cossack forces together with their Crimean Tatar allies then moved on to
L'viv, where after successfully cutting off the city from outside aid, they accepted a
ransom from the urban authorities.

Now the way to Warsaw was open, and Khmel'nyts'kyi was urged by his Cossacks to strike there, at the heart of Poland. He set out in the direction of Warsaw
but in November stopped at Zamość, about a third of the way between L'viv and
Warsaw. Once again, in the hope of gaining greater concessions from the Polish
government, Khmel'nyts'kyi preferred negotiation. The hetman's conditions were
the following: (1) that traditional privileges be restored to the Cossacks; (2) that
free access to the Black Sea, without Polish forts like Kodak to block their way, be
granted them; (3) that the right to be dependent on the king alone, not on local
Polish officials, be given the hetman; (4) that amnesty be extended to all participants in the rebellion; and (5) that the Union of Brest and thus the Uniate Church
be abolished. The new king, Jan Kazimierz (reigned 1648–1668), promised to do
his best to fulfill these conditions. In the meantime he asked Khmel'nyts'kyi to
cease hostilities and to return home.

Considering broken Polish promises in the past – whether because of an
absence of goodwill on the part of the king or, more likely, the interference of
the Polish nobility – one might well wonder how it was possible for Khmel'nyts'kyi
to believe things would be different this time. But whether or not he believed the
Poles, Khmel'nyts'kyi still hoped to function within the Polish-Lithuanian Commonwealth. As a result, he agreed to put a stop to unruly Cossack and peasant
rebellions and to return home.

Khmel'nyts'kyi as a national leader

The hetman's attitude began to change, however, after his arrival in Kiev. At the
head of a victorious Cossack army, which had within the space of less than a year
defeated Poland's leading military forces, Khmel'nyts'kyi entered Kiev on Christmas Day (according to the Julian calendar) in January 1649. There he was greeted by the Orthodox metropolitan of Kiev, Syl'vestr Kosiv, and by the patriarch of
Jerusalem, Paisios, who was in Kiev at the time. As they had done with Hetman
Sahaidachnyi in 1620, the Orthodox hierarchy provided a religious and national
ideological context for Khmel'nyts'kyi's actions. The hetman was called a modern-
day Moses who had succeeded in leading his Rus' people out of Polish bondage.
In the opinion of the Orthodox leadership, the events of the past year had a bearing on the religious and cultural survival of the whole Rus' people (Ukrainians

and Belarusans), and not just the particular interests of a single group, whether Khmel'nyts'kyi himself, or the registered Cossacks, or the Zaporozhian Host as a whole. Patriarch Paisios was particularly concerned with the international implications of the events in Ukraine. With the long-term goal of mobilizing the whole Orthodox world to free the church from the Ottoman yoke, the patriarch urged Khmel'nyts'kyi to work in close harmony with the neighboring Danubian principalities of Moldavia and Walachia and to recognize the authority of the tsar of Muscovy.

Khmel'nyts'kyi was undoubtedly affected by the new role conferred upon him. He is reported to have said to the commissioners of the Polish king: "I have hitherto undertaken tasks which I had not thought through; henceforth, I shall pursue aims which I have considered with care. I shall free the entire people of Rus' from the Poles. At first I fought because of the wrongs done to me personally; now I shall fight for our Orthodox faith. ... I am a small and insignificant man, but by the will of God I have become the independent ruler of Rus'."[3]

Whether or not Khmel'nyts'kyi fully grasped the leadership role in which fate had cast him, in practical terms it was impossible for him to control the peasant uprisings (which by the end of 1648 had spread farther westward to Galicia and almost as far as the Vistula River), or to expect that the masses, having had a taste of freedom, would calmly return home to their duties within the Polish socioeconomic system. Moreover, the hetman must have been impressed by the Orthodox hierarchy's expectations of him, expressed by no less than a patriarch from the Holy Land itself. Khmel'nyts'kyi proceeded to undertake diplomatic negotiations with Moldavia, Walachia, Muscovy, and its allies the Don Cossacks, as well as with Protestant Transylvania and the Lithuanian Prince Radziwiłł, who because of their own anti-Catholic interests might help him in his anti-Polish efforts.

It was the alliance with the Crimean Khanate, however, that remained the centerpiece of the hetman's foreign policy. Since the beginning of the Khmel'nyts'kyi uprising, Crimean forces had fought alongside the Cossacks and celebrated in all their joint victories over the Poles. The Tatar military commander Tughay-Bey even negotiated with the Poles on behalf of the hetman and Zaporozhian interests. Cossack-Tatar ties were enhanced further by Khmel'nyts'kyi's close personal relationship with Tughay-Bey, who the hetman referred to as "my brother, my soul, the only falcon in the world!"[4] Fully confident in the "eternal" Cossack friendship with the Crimean Tatars, Khmel'nyts'kyi now took an entirely different approach to Poland. By the spring of 1649, when the king's negotiator Adam Kysil' – himself an Orthodox Rus' nobleman loyal to Poland – met with Khmel'nyts'kyi again, the change in the Cossack hetman was evident. Khmel'nyts'kyi now styled himself "Autocrat of Rus' by the Grace of God" and talked of liberation for all the Rus' people living in the Polish-Lithuanian Commonwealth.

It seemed inevitable that hostilities would break out again. By the summer of 1649, Khmel'nyts'kyi, together with his Crimean Tatar allies, had surrounded the Polish army led by King Jan Kazimierz at Zboriv. A peace, or, more precisely, a truce, was signed in August whereby (1) the number of registered Cossacks was raised to 40,000; (2) the Kiev, Chernihiv, and Bratslav palatinates (collectively known as Ukraine) were declared Cossack territory, to be rid of the Polish military, Jews, and Jesuits; (3) the Orthodox metropolitan was to be given a seat in the Polish Senate; and (4) an amnesty was declared for nobles who had participated in the uprising. Apart from the 40,000 on the register, those others who called themselves Cossacks as well as the rebellious peasants were expected to return as serfs to their landlords. While the clergy and Cossack officers were satisfied with the Zboriv agreement, the peasants and peasants-turned-Cossacks clearly were not.

Khmel'nyts'kyi once again seemed to be wavering in his role as leader of the whole Rus' (Ukrainian and Belarusan) society. After all, he was imbued with gentry values and concerned with social stability; he was not a revolutionary who favored the overthrow of the social order. In any case, the Zboriv peace gave him a convenient respite in which to begin organizing a structure for the rapidly expanding Cossack state. He made Chyhyryn the hetman's capital and from there conducted extensive diplomatic negotiations in an effort to find allies who would share his vision of eastern Europe.

Khmel'nyts'kyi's vision departed from the traditional approach of the Christian powers, whether that of Catholic Poland and the Habsburgs or that of Orthodox Muscovy backed by the Eastern patriarchs. The traditional alliances had instinctively been directed against the Ottoman "infidels." Khmel'nyts'kyi, however, hoped to form a great coalition of Orthodox, Islamic, and Protestant powers – Moldavia, the Ottoman Empire, the Crimean Tatars, Transylvania, and Lithuania's powerful Protestant figure Prince Radziwiłł – to force Poland's rulers to make structural changes in their society. The Cossack hetman also hoped to entice Poland's rival in the west, Brandenburg, and even Cromwell's Protestant England into helping him force the restructuring of the Polish-Lithuanian Commonwealth into a federation of three equal states – Poland, Lithuania, and Ukraine – to be headed by a new king, György Rákóczi of Transylvania.

The key to this grandiose scheme was initially the Danubian principality of Moldavia, where Khmel'nyts'kyi and the Tatars led a campaign in 1650 to force the Moldavian ruler (Vasile Lupu) to give his daughter in marriage to the hetman's son, Tymish. The marriage finally took place in 1652, but only after further Cossack military intervention, which alarmed neighboring Walachia and Transylvania and led to war with those two states and the death of Tymish in 1653.

Khmel'nyts'kyi's war with the Poles continued while he was being drawn into Danubian politics. The attempted alliance with Lithuania's Prince Radziwiłł failed (the prince instead sided with the Poles and captured Kiev during the Polish-Cossack conflict of 1651); the Cossacks were defeated in June 1651 at the Battle of Berestechko, in Volhynia; and Khmel'nyts'kyi agreed to abide by conditions set in the peace treaty signed at Bila Tserkva (September 1651). The Bila Tserkva agreement reduced the number of registered Cossacks to 20,000 and restricted their residence to the royal lands of the Kiev palatinate. The Bratslav and Chernihiv palatinates were returned to Polish governmental administrators, and nobles were allowed to return to their estates. Although the Bila Tserkva treaty was never ratified by the Polish Diet (it was blocked by the application of one member using the privilege of the *liberum veto*), Khmel'nyts'kyi upheld its provisions, even sending Cossack detachments to put down peasant uprisings against returning Polish noblemen in the Kiev palatinate. Not surprisingly, the hetman's actions caused great discontent among the peasants and unregistered Cossacks, who in desperation moved farther east to lands along the upper Donets' and Don Rivers that were under Muscovite control. There they were allowed to form tax-exempt settlements, known as *slobody*, from which the whole region got its name – the Sloboda lands, or Sloboda Ukraine. Khmel'nyts'kyi was able to defeat Polish armies in 1652 (at Batih, in Bratslav) and in 1653 (at Zhvanets', in Podolia), and in the treaty signed at Zhvanets' (December 1653) the favorable conditions established by the 1649 Zboriv treaty were restored.

It was becoming increasingly clear to Khmel'nyts'kyi, however, that his efforts against the Poles could at best end in a stalemate, with no real improvement for the Cossack lands within the Polish-Lithuanian Commonwealth. Also, with the death of his son, Tymish, in August 1653, it was equally evident that the hetman's diplomatic effort to create a grand coalition against Poland had become entangled in the uncertainties of Danubian politics and in the end had produced nothing positive. Even his military alliances with the Crimean Tatars had proved uncertain at best – the khans having chosen to negotiate independently with the Poles during the battles at Zboriv (1649) and Zhvanets' (1653) and having retreated at a critical moment during the battle at Berestechko (1651). Finally, Khmel'nyts'kyi's intention to submit as a vassal to the Ottomans (his submission was proposed in 1650 and confirmed by Istanbul in 1652) resulted in little more than the sultan's urging the Crimean khans to help the Cossacks. With failure evident in all corners, there seemed only one course of action left whereby Khmel'nyts'kyi might break the military and political stalemate with Poland. That alternative was the tsardom of Muscovy, and it is there that Khmel'nyts'kyi turned next.

Muscovy and the Agreement of Pereiaslav

Khmel'nyts'kyi's efforts to create an international coalition of the Cossacks, the Ottoman Empire, and its vassal states directed against Poland had failed. The ongoing military conflict with Poland moreover, had reached a stalemate. Accordingly, by 1653 the Cossack hetman had been forced to conclude that forming an alliance with Muscovy might be the sole means of helping the Rus'-Ukrainian cause. In fact, at the instigation of the visiting Orthodox patriarch of Jerusalem, the Zaporozhian Cossacks had been negotiating with Muscovy since the very outset of the 1648 revolution, and the discussions became more frequent beginning in early 1652. But what was Muscovy's view of the Cossack problem and, in particular, of the Ukrainian territories? And what did the tsar and his advisers think of Khmel'nyts'kyi's continual requests to form an alliance? Before trying to answer these questions, it is necessary to glance, however briefly, at developments in Muscovy itself.

Muscovy was only one, and initially not the most important, of the several northern Rus' lands which followed a separate historical development after the transformation of Kievan Rus' in the thirteenth century. At that time, Muscovy was a principality within the Grand Duchy of Vladimir-Suzdal', which, alongside Novgorod, was the most powerful center in northern Rus'. From their capital city, Vladimir-na-Kliazma, the rulers of Vladimir-Suzdal' claimed they were the successors of the grand princes of Kievan Rus'. It was also to Vladimir-na-Kliazma that the head of the Orthodox Rus' Church, the metropolitan of Kiev, went after the Mongol invasion, and eventually, in 1299, he transferred his residence there. But any possibility of the northern Rus' lands' being united under the leadership of Vladimir-na-Kliazma or any other city was thwarted by the Mongols of the Golden Horde. The Mongols' military strength enabled them to enforce a policy whereby the northern Rus' principalities, whose rulers were their vassals, remained independent of one another and dependent solely on the khans in their capital at Saray, on the lower Volga.

The rise of Muscovy

It was precisely during the period of greatest Mongol political influence in the late thirteenth and fourteenth centuries that the various principalities within the

Grand Duchy of Vladimir-Suzdal' (Rostov, Suzdal', Tver', and others) increasingly asserted their independence. Among them was Muscovy, which also proved the most deferential to Mongol rule. As a result, Muscovy was granted certain favors by the Golden Horde. In the fifteenth century, at the end of which the Golden Horde had itself broken up into three khanates (the Crimean, the Astrakhan', and the Kazan'), the Grand Duchy of Muscovy, led by a series of talented and able rulers, took the opportunity to begin uniting the northern Rus' lands. This process was largely completed during the reign of Grand Duke Ivan III (reigned 1462–1505) at the beginning of the sixteenth century. It is important to note that Ivan III considered as part of his goal to gather together not only the northern, or ethnic Russian, territories of former Kievan Rus', but also the ethnic Belarusan and Ukrainian territories. Muscovy, however, was not yet completely independent of the Kazan' and Astrakhan' Tatar khanates along its eastern and southeastern borders, which claimed the tribute formerly paid to the Golden Horde. Particularly problematic throughout much of the sixteenth century were the Crimean Tatars, who mounted major attacks against Muscovite lands on an almost annual basis in an effort to extort more tribute as well as take prisoners for their slave trade. Nor was Muscovy a match for the powerful Grand Duchy of Lithuania, which firmly controlled the Rus' (Belarusan and Ukrainian) lands in the west and south.

The Grand Duchy of Muscovy consequently had for the moment to be content with control only over the northern Rus' lands. But ideologists around Ivan III seemed to be preparing for the future. They emphasized Muscovy's supposed right to the so-called Kievan inheritance, implicit in Muscovy's considering itself a "Second Kiev" – the political and cultural successor to Kievan Rus'. Also of symbolic importance was the marriage of Ivan III, a descendant of the Riuryk dynasty, to a Byzantine princess, which linked Muscovy (as similar marriages had linked Kievan Rus' centuries before) with the imperial heritage of Byzantium. Moreover, the head of the Orthodox Rus' Church, who retained the title Metropolitan of Kiev and All Rus', under pressure from Muscovite rulers had transferred his residence from Vladimir-na-Kliazma to Moscow in 1328. Then, in the mid-fifteenth century, on the eve of Ivan III's accession to power, the Muscovite church began its evolution toward autocephaly.

Beginning in 1448, the metropolitans in Moscow were elected without the approval of the ecumenical patriarch in Constantinople. Ecclesiastical circles also made possible the revival of chronicle writing in Muscovy and other northern Rus' lands, in which scribes composed new texts and "improved" the old with the object of having all such accounts support the dynastic claims of the Muscovite princes that they were descended from Riuryk and his Kievan successors Volodymyr the Great and Iaroslav the Wise. Finally, under Ivan III's successor, Vasilii III (reigned 1505–1533), the idea of Moscow as the Second Kiev was enhanced by the use of an even more prestigious epithet whereby Moscow became the "Third Rome." Thus, by the beginning of the sixteenth century, Muscovy had all the ideological symbols necessary for implementing its claim to be the political successor of Kievan Rus', the inheritor of the Orthodox mantle from Byzantium (which had fallen in 1453), and therefore the rightful ruler of all the East Slavs who inhabited the Rus' patrimony – Russians, Belarusans, and Ukrainians.

But much still had to be accomplished in the realm of politics. In large measure, it was accomplished during the second half of the sixteenth century under the Muscovite ruler Ivan IV (reigned 1547–1584), known in history by the epithet "the Terrible," or, more precisely, "the Dread." Ivan IV was the first Muscovite ruler to be crowned as tsar, or absolute ruler in the tradition of Rome's caesars. His realm was thereby transformed into the tsardom of Muscovy, with a nominal claim to universal rule. Under Ivan IV, the domination of the Tatars was finally broken in the 1550s, when both the Kazan' and the Astrakhan' khanates were destroyed. The Crimea, whose khan never gave up his claims to sovereignty over Kazan' and Astrakhan', continued to invade and ravage Muscovite lands for another two decades until they finally stopped after being defeated in 1572 by Ivan's armies.

With his eastern flank secured, the aggressive tsar was able to turn his attention to the west. There the results were mixed. Although in 1558 the Muscovites were finally able to break the power of the Livonian Knights (the last of the Teutonic military orders to survive along the Baltic Sea in what is present-day Latvia and Estonia), that achievement created a power vacuum into which Sweden and Lithuania entered. The consequence was almost a quarter century of costly wars between these two powers as well as against Muscovy for control of Livonia. It was also during these struggles that the borderland between Muscovy and Lithuania – the regions around Smolensk, Starodub, and Chernihiv – changed hands several times. And it was this Muscovite threat to Lithuania's eastern borders that encouraged the grand duchy to draw closer to Poland and to agree to the Union of Lublin in 1569.

Such foreign military campaigns were extremely costly to Muscovy, and at the time of Ivan IV's death in 1584 the tsardom was in a shambles. The limited success of Ivan's foreign ventures was matched by the disastrous results of his domestic policies. These policies were directed at weakening the power of the boyars, the wealthy magnates who had ruled Muscovy during his youth. Despite Ivan's brutal methods, the boyars were not entirely eliminated as a political force. When the tsar died in 1584, he left no suitable successor. This was because he had murdered his eldest son with his own hands in a characteristic fit of rage (1581), while another son and his successor, the retarded Fedor I (reigned 1584–1598), left the government in the hands of his brother-in-law, the powerful boyar, Boris Godunov. Consequently, the tsardom of Muscovy entered a period of boyar rule that was to last almost three decades. Marked by widespread civil war, famine, and foreign invasion, this period came to be known as the *Smutnoe Vremia*, or Time of Troubles. The very existence of the Muscovite state seemed to hang in the balance.

Muscovy, Poland, and Ukraine

It was during Muscovy's Time of Troubles that Poland, strengthened after its unification with Lithuania in the Polish-Lithuanian Commonwealth in 1569, came to play a dominant role in Muscovite politics. Polish-Lithuanian armies invaded Muscovy several times at the beginning of the seventeenth century. The Poles supported a pretender to the Muscovite throne (the so-called False Dmitrii), and after 1608 Poland's king put forth his own son, the future Władysław IV, as a candidate for tsar. With the help of the Zaporozhian Cossacks under Hetman Sahaidachnyi, the Poles occupied Moscow on several occasions. Although Polish forces were finally driven out in 1612, Władysław IV, who was indeed elected king of Poland in 1632, continued for the next few years to claim the Muscovite throne.

In 1613, Muscovy's Time of Troubles came to an end with the election of a new tsar, Mikhail Romanov (reigned 1613–1645). He became the founder of a new dynasty, the Romanovs, who were to rule Muscovy and later the Russian Empire until 1917. Tsar Mikhail and his successor, Aleksei (reigned 1645–1676), succeeded in restoring order within the Muscovite tsardom. It was also during their long reigns that the basis of the modern Russian state evolved. That state was marked by one overriding characteristic – centralized authority. By the last years of Mikhail's reign in the 1640s, the power of the aristocratic boyars (as expressed in their council, the *Zemskii sobor*) had diminished, and a bureaucratic structure had been set up throughout Muscovite territory to act as a conduit for all authority, which rested in the person of the tsar. Special chancelleries were established in Moscow to administer the realm's towns and rural areas. It was through these chancelleries that the central government issued decrees (*gramoty*) instructing the residents of each town and rural district how to run their administrations. Soon nothing could be done in the tsardom without instructions from the chancelleries in Moscow. Complementing this administrative structure was a social structure that became highly stratified as well. Each individual from the tsar down to the peasant had a given place in society, and the primary function of each was service to the state. Such stratification allowed for a stable tax base from which the central authority could draw funds.

Accordingly, by the mid-seventeenth century the two states which had come to control most of eastern Europe – Poland and Muscovy – had completely different political structures. Whereas in Poland the authority of the elected king was circumscribed by the Polish nobility (magnates and gentry) through the central diet (*sejm*) and local dietines (*sejmiki*), and whereas in the countryside the resident magnates and gentry ran their properties as autonomous entities with almost no interference from a central government, in Muscovy the boyars (magnates) had lost their political prerogatives to a hereditary tsar who ruled the country through an increasingly complex bureaucratic system in which, correspondingly, it became more and more difficult to act without the approval of the central government.

In one respect, Poland and Muscovy were similar. Both came to establish socio-economic and judicial systems that transformed their respective peasant populations into serfs. In Muscovy, that process began in the late fifteenth century and was complete by the mid-seventeenth century. In 1649, a new law code (the *Ulozhenie*) outlined fully all aspects of the service state, in which the primary function of each individual was service to the state. The code, which remained the basis of Russian law until as late as 1833, legalized serfdom and bound the peasants to the land. Land was often awarded to the Orthodox Church or to individuals within the military or civil service, and the serfs attached to land that became their property were forbidden to leave it.

It was during the Time of Troubles (1605–1613) that Ukrainians increased their contacts with Muscovy. Registered Cossacks who served in the Polish army participated in Poland's numerous invasions of Muscovite territory, which thus became a source of booty. Before long, however, Muscovy became for Ukrainians not simply a place to raid, but a source of aid. This was particularly the case with regard to religious affairs.

As a result of the Union of Brest in 1595, the Orthodox Church was outlawed in Poland-Lithuania. Although the church managed to survive in that country's Ukrainian- and Belarusan-inhabited lands, thanks to the dedication of a few Rus' magnates, the brotherhood movement, the monasteries, and the political pressure of the Cossacks, its situation remained precarious. This continued to be true even after 1632, when the Orthodox hierarchy was finally permitted to function legally once again. Consequently, during the decades following the Union of Brest the beleaguered Orthodox Church in Poland sought help from other Orthodox states, in particular Muscovy.

By the 1620s, Ukrainian monasteries were making frequent requests to the Orthodox tsar in Moscow for money to build churches or to purchase vestments. Then, beginning in 1623 and each year thereafter, Ukrainian monks arrived in Putivl', Okhtyrka, and other towns along the Polish-Muscovite border begging the tsar to allow them to come to Muscovy in order to practice "the Christian [Orthodox] faith, which the Poles want to suppress."[1] At the same time, Orthodox hierarchs like Metropolitan Iov Borets'kyi of Kiev and Bishop Isaia Kopyns'kyi of Przemyśl, both secretly consecrated in 1620 but not recognized by the Polish government, sent messages or traveled personally to Muscovy, asking the tsar to take their land and its inhabitants under his "mighty hand." Even after the Orthodox Church hierarchy of Poland-Lithuania was legalized in 1632, traditionalist hierarchs continued to express pro-Muscovite attitudes, especially as they were in opposition to the pro-Polish and Latin-oriented policies of the new Orthodox metropolitan of Kiev, Petro Mohyla.

Finally, large numbers of peasants and discontented Cossacks sought refuge by fleeing to Muscovy. Even before the outbreak of the revolution, in the decade between 1638 and 1648, as many as 20,000 people emigrated from the Left Bank to Sloboda Ukraine, the free-settlement frontier just north of what is today Kharkiv and the Russian-Ukrainian border (see map 22). The migrants went east for several reasons. They were fleeing the spread of Poland's expanding manorial system, or they were refugees from the Cossack uprisings, the most recent being the unsuccessful ones in 1637 and 1638. Also, in general they hoped to find greater psychological and physical security under tsarist rule.

Precisely what kind of psychological and physical security? First, the Orthodox Ukrainians and Belarusans of Poland-Lithuania would no longer be discriminated against or persecuted for their religion under tsarist rule. Second, Muscovy offered greater protection against Tatar raids, which, despite the existence of the Zaporozhian Cossacks, still took their annual toll of the Ukrainian population. The Polish response to the Tatar threat was to build fortified centers near the edge of the steppe zone, staffed, usually, with registered Cossacks. The Tatars naturally could and did ride around these centers. In contrast, the Muscovites, beginning in the late sixteenth century, built a series of fortified lines or abatis (*zasechnaia cherta*) consisting of felled tree trunks and palisades of sharply pointed logs interspersed with wooden blockhouses, some of which developed into fortified towns. These lines were built progressively farther southward and eastward until a major defense system known as the Belgorod Line had been constructed, between 1635 and 1651. The Belgorod Line ran for more than 480 miles (770 kilometers) from Okhtyrka, near the Polish border, straight across Sloboda Ukraine through Belgorod and on to Voronezh, farther northeast (see maps 18 and 22). Along this line twenty cities were founded between 1637 and 1647, half of them in Sloboda Ukraine. An extension known as the Ukrainian, or Izium Line was built from the bend in the Donets' River near the fortress town of Izium westward to the Dnieper River. Behind these lines emigrants from Ukraine sought refuge. Thus, Orthodox inclinations and migrational patterns revealed that a pro-Muscovite attitude among Ukrainians had existed long before Bohdan Khmel'nyts'kyi ever came on the scene.

Khmel'nyts'kyi and Pereiaslav

Khmel'nyts'kyi himself had become part of this pro-Muscovite trend. Despite his victories in May 1648 over the Polish armies at Zhovti Vody and Korsun', the Cossack hetman remained concerned that the conflict with Poland was not yet over. Hence, between June 1648 and May 1649 he addressed seven letters to Muscovy asking for military assistance, offering Cossack services to the tsar, and expressing the hope that at the very least the Muscovite army would not attack his Tatar allies. At that very moment, however, the tsar was incapable of action, since Moscow itself was facing a serious revolt that was to last through the summer and early fall of 1648. Moreover, the nineteen-year-old, still politically weak Tsar Aleksei was reluctant to antagonize Poland, which he would certainly do if a Muscovite-Zaporozhian alliance were concluded.

While it is true that at the beginning of the seventeenth century Muscovy had succeeded in reestablishing internal order after the Time of Troubles, in foreign affairs the tsardom remained on the defensive, especially vis-à-vis Polish military might. For instance, as late as 1634, Polish kings still laid claim to the Muscovite throne, and after military campaigns in 1618 and again in 1633–34 Muscovy was forced to give up to its western rival territories around Smolensk and Severia (including Starodub and Chernihiv). Faced with a renewal of Nogay Tatar raids from the south and a potential Swedish invasion of Livonia, along the Baltic Sea, Muscovy did not feel it could afford to alienate Poland. Thus, Tsar Aleksei's refusal of Khmel'nyts'kyi's requests in 1648–49 was understandable.

Khmel'nyts'kyi's victories during the next two years, however, revealed that Poland's armies were not invincible after all. Consequently, when the Cossack leader, having exhausted his Balkan and Ottoman foreign policy ventures, turned to Tsar Aleksei on numerous occasions between 1652 and 1653, much had changed. The Russian Orthodox Church, led by its new and enterprising patriarch Nikon (reigned 1652–1666), was anxious to reform itself by using the intellectual talents of Rus' churchmen trained in Mohyla's Collegium at Kiev. Nikon, who was the tsar's closest adviser on Ukrainian matters, urged the Muscovite government to support the Cossacks' requests. It is not surprising, therefore, that it was the Russian Orthodox patriarch who was serving as the mediator when in April 1653 Khmel'nyts'kyi's envoys asked the tsar to extend his protection over the Cossacks.

Finally, in June of that year, Tsar Aleksei agreed to accept the Zaporozhian hetman and his Cossacks "under the tsarist majesty's high arm."

As a result of this decision, Muscovite ambassadors were dispatched in late December 1653 to meet with Khmel'nyts'kyi. The meeting place chosen was the town of Pereiaslav, along the Dnieper River, halfway between Kiev and the hetman's capital of Chyhyryn. According to Muscovite sources, on the day of the ambassador's arrival the local archpriest led a multitude of Pereiaslav's citizens to greet the Muscovite envoys and to "thank God for having fulfilled the desire of our Orthodox people to bring together Little and Great Rus' under the mighty hand of the all-powerful and pious eastern tsar."[2]

The negotiations at Pereiaslav lasted for several days during the month of January 1654. Disagreements arose because the Cossacks expected that the tsar would swear an oath to them, as was the practice for Polish kings. Moreover, the Orthodox metropolitan of Kiev, Syl'vestr Kosiv (reigned 1647–1657), was opposed to negotiations that he feared would lead to the subordination of his jurisdiction to the patriarch of Muscovy. In the end, Khmel'nyts'kyi and the Cossacks did swear an oath of allegiance to the tsar, after which the Muscovite envoys were sent to several other Ukrainian cities to administer the oath.

The 1654 Agreement of Pereiaslav, which resulted in the union of the Cossack-controlled territory of Ukraine with Muscovy, actually consisted of three elements: (1) the oath sworn by the Cossacks and the people of Pereiaslav and other Ukrainian cities in January 1654; (2) Khmel'nyts'kyi's twenty-three "Articles of Petition," brought to Moscow by his delegates and dated 14 March 1654; and (3) the tsar's response in the form of a patent and what became known as the eleven "March Articles" issued later that same month. Within the next few months Muscovite officials visited over a hundred towns whose inhabitants swore an oath of allegiance to the tsar, which meant the acceptance of the following basic principles. The Zaporozhian army was granted confirmation of its rights and liberties, including the independence of Cossack courts and the inviolability of Cossack landed estates. The Zaporozhian army was to elect its hetmans, who must swear allegiance to the tsars. Chyhyryn was to remain the hetman's capital, from which relations with foreign countries (with the exception of Poland and the Ottoman Empire) could be conducted. The number of registered Cossacks was fixed at 60,000, all of whom were to receive wages from that part of the revenue from Ukraine to which the tsar was entitled. The tsar would provide the Cossacks with military supplies. The traditional rights of the Ukrainian nobility were confirmed. Urban dwellers could elect their own municipal governments. Finally, the Orthodox metropolitan and other clergy throughout Poland-Lithuania were to be "under the blessing" of the patriarch in Moscow, who promised not to interfere in ecclesiastical matters.

When the negotiations between the Cossack envoys and the Muscovite government were finally completed in August 1654, the tsar's title was changed from Tsar of All Rus' (*vseia Rusii*) to Tsar of All Great and Little Rus' (*vseia Velikiia i Malyia Rusii*). Thus, without having made any special effort, Tsar Aleksei had taken a significant further step toward Muscovy's goal, set out in the late fifteenth century by Grand Duke Ivan III, to unite under one Orthodox ruler all the lands formerly within the sphere of medieval Kievan Rus'.

THE AGREEMENT OF PEREIASLAV

The following excerpts are from the Articles of Petition brought to Moscow by Hetman Khmel'nyts'kyi's delegates on 14 March 1654.

Before Your Tsarist Majesty we, Bohdan Khmel'nyts'kyi, the Hetman of the Zaporozhian Army, and the entire Zaporozhian Army as well as the entire Ruthenian Christian world, bow our forehead to the face of the earth.

1. In the beginning, grant that Your Tsarist Majesty will confirm our rights and our military freedoms as they have existed for ages in the Zaporozhian Army, which was governed by its own laws and which possessed its own prerogatives in matters of property and of justice; grant that neither a military commander nor a boyar nor court official shall interfere with the courts of the Army and that its members be judged by their own elders. ...

2. That the Zaporozhian Army to the number of sixty-thousand men always be at full strength.

3. That the gentry that has turned to Russia and taken an oath, in accordance with the immaculate commandment of Christ, to You, Our Great Sovereign, Your Tsarist Majesty, continue to retain the class privileges of their estate. That from among their own elders they continue to select their own judicial officials and to hold possession to their own property and freedoms, as it had been under the Polish kings.

4. That in the cities there be selected from among our own worthy people officials who are to govern or supervise Your Tsarist Majesty's subjects and who are to transmit to Your Tsarist Majesty's treasury the incomes justly belonging to it.

5. That to the office of hetman there be attached the district of Chyhyryn with all of its appurtenances in order that it might continue to provide income to that entire office.

6. That the Zaporozhian Army on its own select from within itself a hetman and make him known to His Tsarist Majesty since this is an ancient custom of the Zaporozhian Army.

7. That no one take away Cossack properties.

8. That to the general secretary of the Zaporozhian Army there be allocated, because of the kindness of His Tsarist Majesty, one thousand gold pieces for the employees of his office and a mill to provide for quartermaster needs.

9. That to each colonel there be assigned a mill because expenditures are great.

10. Additionally, for justices of the Zaporozhian Army three hundred gold pieces to each, as well as a mill, and for each court recorder, one hundred gold pieces.

11. That the chiefs of staff of the Zaporozhian Army and the regimental chiefs of staff that are on permanent military duty be granted a mill.

12. For the manufacture of ordnance equipment and of artillery and for all persons employed with ordnance, we request attention to both the problems of winter and of quarters.

13. That the rights granted through the centuries by princes and kings to both clerical and lay persons not be violated in any way.

14. That envoys from foreign lands coming to the Zaporozhian Army with good intentions be freely received by the Lord Hetman and the Zaporozhian Army.

15. Inasmuch as in other countries tribute is paid in one sum, we also wish to give in the accepted manner to those persons appointed by Your Tsarist Majesty.

16. Our envoys are to seek an agreement to the effect that no visiting commander shall violate our rights. And wherever among local people there are qualified persons, these shall see that justice is done with respect to violations of local laws and traditions.

17. That His Tsarist Majesty write down our privileges in charters stamped by seals, one for Cossack freedoms and a second for the freedoms of the gentry, so that these freedoms might be forever. And when we shall receive this, we ourselves are to maintain order among ourselves. He who is a Cossack shall have Cossack freedoms, and he who is a land-working peasant shall give to His Tsarist Majesty the customary obligation, as before.

18. With respect to the Metropolitan there are to be discussions, and concerning this matter we have given oral instructions to our envoys.

19. That His Tsarist Majesty send troops quickly and directly to Smolensk without delay, so that the [Polish] enemy might not improve his position and consolidate with others.

20. That for any eventuality a contingent of persons, around 3,000 or preferably more, should be stationed here along the border with the Poles.

21. That there be paid 100 *efimki* to each colonel, 200 gold pieces to each regimental chief of staff, 400 gold pieces to each chief of staff on the highest staff level, 100 gold pieces to each centurion, and 30 gold pieces to each Cossack.

22. If the [Crimean Tatar] Horde should become aggressive, then it will be necessary to move against them from Astrakhan' and Kazan'.

23. That His Tsarist Majesty will henceforth order the supplying of rations and powder for artillery for the fortress of Kodak, which was constructed at the frontier with Crimea and in which the Lord Hetman at all times posts 400 men and provides them with all kinds of provisions.

SOURCE: John Basarab, *Pereiaslav 1654: A Historiographical Study* (Edmonton 1982), pp. 230–236.

The Agreement of Pereiaslav subsequently proved an important turning point in eastern European history. It signaled a gradual change whereby Muscovy, not Poland, became the dominant power in the region. As for Ukraine, 1654 ended a six-year period which marked the culmination of more than a half century of Cossack struggle for autonomy within Poland. When the Polish solution no longer seemed feasible, the Cossacks sought autonomy within Muscovy instead.

Historians have debated at length the juridical significance of the agreement – or treaty, as some say – at Pereiaslav. Some consider it to reflect the incorporation of Ukraine into the tsardom of Muscovy with guarantees for autonomy, whether based on a treaty (B.E. Nolde) or on personal union (V. Sergeevich). Others consider Ukraine to have become a kind of semi-independent vassal state or protectorate of Muscovy (N. Korkunov, A. Iakovliv, M. Hrushevs'kyi, L. Okinshevych). Still others see it as no more than a military alliance between the Cossacks and Muscovy (V. Lypyns'kyi, O. Ohloblyn), or an "atypical" personal union between two juridically equal states (R. Lashchenko).

Aside from the debates among legal scholars and historians, Pereiaslav and its instigator, Bohdan Khmel'nyts'kyi, have taken on a symbolic force in the story of Ukraine's relationship with Russia and have become the focus of either praise or blame. For instance, in the nineteenth century the Ukrainian national bard, Taras Shevchenko, designated Khmel'nyts'kyi the person responsible for his people's "enslavement" under Russia (see chapter 29). The government of Tsar Alexander III (reigned 1881–1894), however, erected in the center of historic Kiev a large equestrian statue of Khmel'nyts'kyi, his outstreched arm pointing northward as an indication of Ukraine's supposed desire to be linked with Russia. After World War II, the Pereiaslav myth was resurrected, this time by Soviet ideologists, who, on the occasion of the 300th anniversary of the agreement in 1954, transformed the event into the ultimate symbol of Ukraine's "reunification" with Russia, from whom it had been forcibly separated by foreign occupation since the fall of Kievan Rus'.

Whatever writers subsequently have speculated about Pereiaslav, one thing is certain. After 1654, the tsardom of Muscovy considered Cossack Ukraine, which it henceforth referred to as *Malorossiia*/ Little Russia, its legal patrimony. Since the tsar was an autocrat, whatever rights or liberties he granted the Cossacks at Pereiaslav were "gifts" he could take back whenever he wished. As it turned out, the Agreement of Pereiaslav was understood differently by the Cossacks and Muscovy, with the result that from the very outset misunderstandings arose between the two parties. Matters became even more complicated in 1659, when in connection with the election of new hetman (Khmel'nyts'kyi's son Iurii), the Cossacks were obliged to accept a revised version of the 1654 Articles of Petition together with New Articles (18 points) drawn up in Muscovy. The second Agreement of Pereiaslav from 1659 was the only one referred to by Muscovy in its future negotiations with the Cossacks; that is, each time a new hetman took office.

Despite the disputes about the textual validity of Pereiaslav one (1654) and Pereiaslav two (1659), and despite ongoing military conflict and change of borders in the region, all Ukrainian territory east of the Dnieper River, together with Kiev, was to remain within the Muscovite, later Russian state. At the end of the eighteenth century, further territorial acquisitions were made, whereby most Ukrainian lands (with the exception of Galicia, Bukovina, and Transcarpathia) found themselves within the Russian Empire. It is with Pereiaslav, then, that one can speak of the beginnings of the Muscovite or Russian phase in Ukrainian history.

18

The Period of Ruin

The agreement concluded at Pereiaslav in 1654 resulted in an extension of Muscovy's borders to include the Ukrainian-inhabited former Polish palatinates of Chernihiv, Kiev, and Bratslav, as well as the Zaporozhian steppe farther south on both sides of the bend in the Dnieper River. The agreement, however, did not bring peace to Ukrainian lands. Rather, it ushered in, or, perhaps more precisely, simply continued, a period of conflict marked by foreign invasion, civil war, and peasant revolts which was to last uninterruptedly until 1686, when a so-called eternal peace was concluded between two of the three dominant powers in the region, Poland and Muscovy.

The years 1657 to 1686 at times witnessed an almost complete breakdown of order. All or some of these years have been characterized in Ukrainian history as the Period of Ruin (*Ruïna*), whose very beginning (1655–61) is known in Polish history as the Deluge (*Potop*). These characterizations represented the eastern variant of a series of political and social convulsions that at the time were racking all of Europe, from England and Ireland in the west to Russia in the east, and from Scandinavia in the north to Italy and Spain in the south – collectively referred to by historians as "the crises of the seventeenth century." In a sense, these crises represented the culmination of a struggle which had been taking place for several centuries within many European states between a centralized authority, usually vested in a king, on the one hand, and rival political centers, often noble and urban estates, on the other. The struggle has also been viewed as a phase in European history in which the political power of representative assemblies (the English Parliament, the French États Généraux, the Muscovite Zemskii Sobor, etc.) was either substantially reduced or entirely eliminated and replaced by governing systems in which all power rested in the hands of monarchs who, with their closely controlled administrations, attempted to rule in a more efficient and, so they pretended, enlightened manner.

In this new era of enlightened absolutism, states like the Polish-Lithuanian Commonwealth, which maintained the tradition of diffused power, seemed fated to lose ground against more highly centralized and absolutist neighbors – whether Brandenburg in the west, Sweden in the north, Muscovy in the east, or the Austrian and Ottoman empires in the south. Moreover, the age did not augur well for those elements on the periphery of established states, such as the Cossacks, whose desires for local autonomy and the maintenance of an estates system in which they would have special privileges were out of step with the general trend in European society. After the seventeenth century, that trend favored the development of strongly centralized and bureaucratized state structures. It might therefore be argued that the efforts of the Cossacks to preserve their autonomy in Ukraine represented an anomaly doomed from the start – unless, of course, they could create an independent and centralized state structure of their own.

Indeed, there were some Cossacks, especially from among the registered and officer class (the *starshyna*), who tried to create a distinct and viable state structure. But they were continually opposed by unregistered and other independent-minded peasants-turned-Cossack farther south in Zaporozhia, whose only goal seemed to be to maintain a society free of any kind of control beyond their own traditional and rudimentary democratic local order. Faced with these contradictions within Cossack society, the only reasonable solution for those Cossacks seeking social stability was to attempt to obtain autonomy within some existing state. In the short run, this solution proved feasible, although in the long run loss of autonomy and absorption by the controlling state structure turned out to be inevitable. The process, of course, which now appears inevitable in historical hindsight, was neither apparent nor complete for at least another century. The Period of Ruin can be seen as the first stage in this long process.

The Period of Ruin in Ukrainian history began with the death of Bohdan Khmel'nyts'kyi in 1657, by which time Poland and Muscovy were already engaged in a war as a result of Ukraine's placing itself under the sovereignty of the tsar three years before. The period ended in 1686 with an agreement between Poland and Muscovy to recognize each other's sphere of influence over Ukraine, which they divided roughly along the Dnieper River. Because the Period of Ruin is marked by such complexity, only its basic outline will be presented here.

Changing international alliances

The Agreement of Pereiaslav in 1654 prompted an immediate change in the alliance structure in eastern Europe. The new Muscovite-Cossack alliance forced the Crimean Tatars, who were traditional enemies of Muscovy, to break with the Cossacks and to form an alliance with the Poles instead. Tsar Aleksei, feeling confident in the military potential of his new subject, Hetman Bohdan Khmel'nyts'kyi, decided to launch a preemptive attack on Poland as early as April 1654. His goal was not only to acquire the long-disputed territories along the Muscovite-Lithuanian border, but also to detach the Belarusan lands from the Polish-Lithuanian Commonwealth and to include them in the recently created Muscovite-Ukrainian federation. In fact, the Belarusan peasants rebelled against their Polish and Lithuanian landlords, welcomed the tsar as liberator, and helped make possible Muscovy's conquests in 1656 as far as Vilnius and Kaunas. At that point, Aleksei even changed his title once again, this time from Tsar of All Great and Little Rus' to Tsar of All Great and Little and White Rus' (*vseia Velikiia i Malyia i Belyia Rusii*). Aleksei seemed about to realize the age-old Muscovite dream of uniting all the Orthodox lands that had once been part of Kievan Rus'.

Meanwhile, the Poles together with their new Crimean Tatar allies were ravaging the Bratslav palatinate in Ukraine. This continued until Khmel'nyts'kyi, with Muscovite help, finally fought them to a military stalemate in January 1655 (the Battle of Dryzhypole). The Cossacks and Muscovites cooperated in military matters, including operations in Galicia, but at the same time Khmel'nyts'kyi continued to follow an independent diplomatic policy. For instance, the hetman wanted the newly conquered Belarusan lands incorporated into a Cossack state, and in order to be certain that Poland would be permanently damaged he joined with Poland's enemies to the north, west, and south – namely, Sweden, Brandenburg, and Transylvania. All these states were led by Protestant rulers who hoped to destroy Roman Catholic Poland once and for all. Sweden's armies under King Charles X Gustav (reigned 1654–1660) invaded Poland in 1655 and captured both Warsaw and Cracow. Sweden was joined by Brandenburg, which had its own designs on Polish-controlled Prussia. Eventually, Lithuania (led by the son of the Protestant Janusz Radziwiłł) and the majority of Poland's nobility recognized Sweden's Charles X as their king.

It was precisely at this moment, when Poland was at its nadir, that a wave of patriotism spread through the country, inspired by accounts of the defense of the Catholic monastery of Częstochowa. The otherwise politically contentious and militarily passive nobility was moved by a new-found sense of patriotism and united behind their king. With support from Poland's nobility, assistance from the Crimean Tatars, and the signing of a truce in November 1656 with Muscovy (who now feared the expansion of Swedish influence), King Jan Kazimierz was able to restore his authority.

Khmel'nyts'kyi, meanwhile, was disturbed by Muscovy's truce with Poland. Since he considered himself a free political agent (notwithstanding the Agreement of Pereiaslav), he took the opportunity to renew diplomatic alliances with Moldavia, Walachia, and Transylvania in the south and with Lithuania, Brandenburg, and Sweden in the north. This move reflected a basic change in his diplomatic orientation, from dependence on the Islamic world (the Ottoman Empire and the Crimean Khanate) to alliance with Protestant northern and southern Europe (Sweden, Brandenburg, and Transylvania), which he hoped might bring independence for Cossack Ukraine. According to the negotiations over the future division of Poland, the Cossacks and each of the Protestant allies were to obtain parts of the kingdom.

These plans all hinged on the military success of Sweden. Charles X, however, was for the moment interested in the Brandenburg theater of operations. Moreover, the Swedish king faced political difficulties at home which forced him to withdraw his troops from Poland during the second half of 1656. In the end, the grand alliance was limited to Transylvanian troops under the Hungarian Protestant prince György II Rákóczi (reigned 1648–1660) and Khmel'nyts'kyi's Cossacks. But instead of cooperating, the Zaporozhians and Transylvanians clashed over what each considered their rightful share of territorial spoils in Galicia and

Volhynia. Thus, Khmel'nyts'kyi's grandiose diplomatic plans – this time based primarily on an alliance with Protestant countries – failed once again to result in the destruction of Poland. Moreover, the Cossack hetman's new diplomatic ventures alienated the Muscovites and his recently acquired sovereign, Tsar Aleksei, who in response tried to weaken Khmel'nyts'kyi's authority by sowing discord within the Zaporozhian army. At this critical moment, in August 1657, the hetman died.

The pattern for Ukrainian politics set by Khmel'nyts'kyi was to be followed by his successors. Unable to create an independent state structure of their own, and desirous of acquiring an advantageous position within some existing state, the Zaporozhian leaders decided that their future and the future of Ukraine lay with Orthodox Muscovy. Nonetheless, almost from the outset Khmel'nyts'kyi considered himself independent of the tsar and was not averse to following an independent foreign policy. Also, the long-standing friction between the so-called Cossack *starshyna* (i.e., the hetman, his officers, and the well-to-do registered Cossacks) on the one hand and the mass of more socially undifferentiated Cossacks in Zaporozhia on the other – a friction which was evident under Polish rule during the first half of the seventeenth century and which surfaced on more than one occasion during the 1648 revolution – was now being used by the Muscovite government for its own purposes. Essentially, from their base at the *sich* along the lower Dnieper River, the Zaporozhian Cossacks and their peasant supporters favored the alliance with the tsar. For its part, Muscovy used Zaporozhian loyalty as a counterweight to the independent-minded policy of the hetman and the Cossack *starshyna*. Of course, the Muscovite government knew that their erstwhile and somewhat reluctant allies, the Cossack *starshyna*, were not averse to renewing traditional alliances with the Poles if they felt doing so would bring them greater advantages.

The Cossack turn toward Poland

Khmel'nyts'kyi's successor, Hetman Ivan Vyhovs'kyi, chose the Polish orientation. Vyhovs'kyi was elected hetman in 1657 by the *starshyna*, but he was immediately challenged by Cossacks in the Zaporozhian *sich*. The reason was simple. Even the universally respected Khmel'nyts'kyi had gotten his revolutionary start by going to the *sich* and being chosen hetman by its members. Hence, when Vyhovs'kyi tried to go around the *sich* by dealing directly with the *starshyna*, the Zaporozhians rebelled. The rebellion, led by Iakiv Barabash and joined by Cossacks in the Poltava region under Martin Pushkar, was aided by Muscovy.

In the end, Vyhovs'kyi was able to defeat the Zaporozhian rebels as well as their allies, although he remained disenchanted with Muscovy's interference in Cossack affairs. While not breaking entirely with the tsarist government, he signed a treaty with Sweden in October 1657 (at Korsun'), which promised the creation of an independent Cossack state that would include Galicia and Volhynia as well as eastern Ukrainian lands. When the Swedish alliance failed to produce concrete results, and when it became clear that Muscovy would lend its support to the anti-*starshyna* Cossack rebels, Vyhovs'kyi, with the counsel of his talented advisor Iurii Nemyrych, decided to try once again to reach an accord with the Poles. Nemyrych was a Rus' magnate who before 1648 had converted to Protestantism and become one of Protestantism's intellectual mentors in Poland. He subsequently served with the Polish army against Khmel'nyts'kyi and later favored the election of a Protestant king to the throne of Poland, from either Transylvania or Sweden. Finally, in 1657 Nemyrych entered the service of Hetman Vyhovs'kyi, and soon afterward he returned to the fold of Orthodoxy.

Nemyrych promoted the idea that for Poland to survive it should be transformed into a federation of three states – Poland, Lithuania, and the Grand Duchy of Rus'. Although the Cossack negotiators originally demanded that Galicia and Volhynia be part of the new state, in the end the Grand Duchy of Rus' was to consist of the palatinates of Kiev, Chernihiv, and Bratslav. Rus', together with the two other members of the tripartite federation, Poland and Lithuania, would sign a mutual defense pact which also set as its goal the conquest of the shores of the Black Sea. Muscovy could become part of the confederation should it so desire. As for Rus', it would have its own judicial system, treasury, and mint, and a standing army of 10,000 men under the Cossack hetman, who would automatically become palatine of Kiev and hold a seat in the Polish Senate. The hetman, together with high-ranking Cossack military leaders, were to receive large grants from the king's, or crown lands, and most important, members of the Cossack *starshyna* would be recognized as a social estate equal to the Polish gentry. In that context, each year the hetman would recommend to the king 100 Cossacks from each regiment to receive the hereditary patent of nobility. Moreover, all Cossack and Polish landholdings confiscated after 1648 would be returned to their original owners. Finally, the Uniate Church would be abolished within the Grand Duchy of Rus'; the Orthodox Church would be made fully equal to the Roman Catholic Church throughout Poland-Lithuania; Kiev's Orthodox Collegium would be raised to the status of an academy; and a second Orthodox higher institution of learning would be established. Nemyrych's final version of the treaty was put forward to the Poles in the small town of Hadiach in September 1658. Notwithstanding the opposition of Poland's Roman Catholic nobility to many of the terms, the plan, which became known as the Union of Hadiach, was approved by the Polish Diet in 1659.

The Union of Hadiach could be viewed as an attempt by a far-sighted political thinker to create a framework for federation among eastern Europe's warring Christian powers: Poland, Lithuania, Muscovy, and the Zaporozhian Host. Conversely, it could be viewed as yet another attempt by the Cossack elite, the *starshyna*, to gain legal entry into the Polish nobility and thereby become part of the ruling stratum of the Polish-Lithuanian Commonwealth. After all, the Union of Lublin, which in 1569 had created the Commonwealth, was basically the union or equalization of two dominant social estates, the Polish and the Lithuanian nobility. The proposal at Hadiach was to add a third component, the Rus' nobility of Cossack origin. In this sense, the Union of Hadiach could be considered another attempt by one segment of Orthodox Ukrainian society to assure itself of a legally and socially recognized place within the ruling structure of what was to be known as the Grand Duchy of Rus' within a Polish-Lithuanian-Rus' Commonwealth. In the end, the Hadiach proposal was an ingenious attempt to satisfy the

THE UNION OF HADIACH

The original treaty was signed on 6 September 1658 near Hadiach by two commissioners of the king and commonwealth, and by Ivan Vyhovs'kyi, hetman of the Zaporozhian armies. The text was subsequently emended and ratified by the Polish-Lithuanian Diet in May 1659, although it continued to carry the original date. The following excerpts are based on an unpublished translation by Andrew Pernal of the emended text.

The Zaporozhian Army, being burdened by various oppression, took up its defense not out of its own free will, but out of necessity; since His Majesty [the king of Poland] has forgiven with His Fatherly Heart all that which took place during the turmoil and calls for unity, they [the Zaporozhians] ... take part in this Commission and afterwards in common counsel to achieve a sincere agreement.

That the Old Greek [Orthodox] religion, the same one with which the Old Rus' joined the Crown of Poland, be retained by its own prerogatives and free exercise of church services, as far as the language of the Ruthenian nation extends.

To this Greek religion is granted the authority of freely erecting new churches, chapels, and monasteries as well as maintaining and repairing the old ones. With regard to the churches formerly founded for and properties [formerly donated to] the church of the Old Greek religion, these shall be retained by the Old Greeks, the Orthodox, and restored [to them]. ...

The [Orthodox] metropolitan of Kiev, the present one and his successors in the future, [together] with the four Orthodox bishops [from the Crown], [those] of Luts'k, L'viv, Przemyśl, and Chełm, and the fifth from the Grand Duchy of Lithuania, [that] of Mstsislaŭ, [and their successors in the future] shall sit in the Senate, according to their own order [of seniority], with such privileges and free vote as are enjoyed in the Senate by the Most Reverend Spiritual Lords of the Roman rite. ... In the Palatinate of Kiev, senatorial dignities shall be conferred only upon nobles of the Greek rite; whereas, in the palatinates of Bratslav and Chernihiv, senatorial honors shall be conferred by alteration; thus, after the death of a senator of the Greek rite, he is succeeded by a senator of the Roman rite. ...

Also, in order that mutual affection may spread within the towns of the crown and the Grand Duchy of Lithuania, wherever churches of the Greek rite are to be found, the Roman [Catholic] burghers shall enjoy, equally with those of the Greek religion, common liberties and freedoms. ...

His Majesty and the estates of the crown grant permission for the building of an academy in Kiev, which is granted the same prerogatives and liberties as the academy of Cracow, only ... that there be no professors, masters, [or] students of the Unitarian, Calvinist, [or] Lutheran sects. In order that [in the future] there be no occasion for altercation among the students, His Majesty shall command that all other schools which were [established] hitherto in Kiev be transferred elsewhere.

His Majesty, Our Gracious Lord, and the estates of the crown and the Grand Duchy of Lithuania also consent to [the establishment of] another academy, wherever a suitable place for it shall be found, which shall enjoy the same rights and liberties as the Kievan [academy]. ... Wherever this academy shall be set up, no other schools shall be founded there for all times.

Grammar schools, colleges, [other] schools, and printing houses, as many as will be necessary, shall be permitted to be established without difficulty. ...

Since the honorable Hetman and the Zaporozhian Army, [hitherto] separated from the commonwealth, are returning and renouncing all foreign protection. ... security shall be provided [by an amnesty] to persons of all social positions, from the lowest to the highest [rank] and excluding no one; ... in short, all those who served or are serving in any capacity under the honorable hetmans, both the former one and the one at present. ...

The entire commonwealth of the Polish, grand ducal Lithuanian, and Rus' nations, as well as the provinces belonging to them shall be restored as they existed before the war [of 1648]; that is, these three nations shall retain, as before the war, their own intact boundaries and liberties, and in accordance to the stipulation of the law; [their right to participate] in the councils, the courts, and the free elections of their lords, the kings of Poland and the grand dukes of Lithuania and Rus'. If, as a result of war with foreign states any agreement be reached that is detrimental to the boundaries or liberties of these nations, the above-named nations shall stand by their liberties as a commonwealth one and indivisible, without discord among themselves over the [differences between the two] faiths. ...

The Zaporozhian Army shall number ten thousand [men], or whatever [figure] the honorable Zaporozhian hetman shall enter in the register.

The mercenary army shall number thirty thousand [men], which just as the Zaporozhian [Army] shall remain under the command of this same Hetman. [The funds] appropriated for these troops shall come from the taxes voted at the Diet by the commonwealth [and levied] in the palatinates of Kiev, Bratslav, Chernihiv, and others.

The quarters for the Zaporozhian Army are assigned in the [same] palatinates and estates in which they were stationed before the war [of 1648]. All of the liberties granted to this Army by the charters of the most illustrious kings of Poland are confirmed: they [the Cossacks] shall retain their former liberties and practices. ...

No tenant of the estates of His Majesty or prefect, nor any hereditary or annuitant lord, nor their sub-prefects, officials, or any other servants shall collect, for whatever pretext, any taxes from Cossack farms, villages, towns, or homes. As [befits a] knightly people, [the Cossacks] shall be exempt from the heaviest and the lightest burdens [of taxation], including duties and tolls throughout the crown and the Grand Duchy of Lithuania. Also, they shall be free [from the jurisdiction] of various courts of the prefects, tenants, lords, and [those of] their deputies, and be subject only to the jurisdiction of their own hetman of the Rus' armies. Moreover, the Cossacks shall be permitted to retain [such rights as the making of] all kinds of beverages, hunting on the land, fishing in the rivers, and other benefits according to [their] old customs. ...

The honorable Hetman of the Rus' armies shall recommend to His Majesty as being worthy of [having conferred upon them] the coats of arms of nobility; all without difficulty shall be ennobled and accorded all the liberties [enjoyed] by the nobility [of the commonwealth] … one hundred [persons] shall be ennobled from each regiment.

No one shall lead any Polish, Lithuanian, or foreign armies [without the consent of the hetman] into the palatinates of Kiev, Bratslav, and Chernihiv. …

The three united nations shall endeavour, by all possible means, that there be free navigation on the Black Sea for the commonwealth.

Should His Tsarist Majesty [of Muscovy] refuse to return to the commonwealth the provinces [He occupied], and [should He] invade the commonwealth, then all the forces of the crown and the Grand Duchy of Lithuania, as well as the Rus' Zaporozhian armies under the command of their Hetman, shall unite and wage war [against the tsar].

Real estates, personal properties, crown lands, and sums of money confiscated from the nobles of the Rus' territories, even [from those] who served in the Zaporozhian Army and who at present are rejoining the fatherland, shall be returned [to them]. …

[The hetman] shall not receive any legations from foreign states, and if any should arrive, he shall send them on to His Majesty.

To all property owners from both sides shall be afforded the possibility of safe return to and repossession of [their former holdings], including the [right of the secular] Roman-rite clergy to the bishoprics, parishes, canonries, rectories, and properties belonging to them that are located in the palatinates of Kiev, Bratslav, Chernihiv, and Podolia, as well as in the Grand Duchy of Lithuania, in Belarus, and Severia. …

Since the hetman, the Zaporozhian Army, and the [hitherto] separated palatinates [from the commonwealth] are repudiating all protection of other foreign nations and are returning of their own free will as freemen to freemen, equals to equals, and honorable to honorable; therefore, for better security and for more certainty that this current agreement be adhered to, His Majesty and the commonwealth shall permit the Rus' nation their own chancellors, marshals, and treasurers, with the rank of senator.

Stanisław Kazimierz Bieniewski,	Ivan Vyhovs'kyi,
Castellan of Volhynia, Prefect of	Hetman of the Zaporozhian armies,
Bohuslav, Commissioner	by his own hand, in the name of
	the entire army
Ludwik Kazimierz Jewłaszewski,	
Castellan of Smolensk, Commissioner	

demands of the Cossack *starshyna* as well as to achieve peace among the region's warring states.

Unfortunately for the plan's proponents, the problem of the semi-independent Zaporozhian Cossacks was not resolved, since at best only a few of their elite might have been ennobled. Much more difficult to overcome was the heritage of animosity toward the Poles among broad segments of Ukraine's population, who still remembered the wars of the Khmel'nyts'kyi period. Finally, the disenfranchised

Zaporozhians distrusted Hetman Vyhovs'kyi and continued to look toward Muscovy, which in any case was not about to join the Hadiach confederation. Thus, the Union of Hadiach died a stillborn death.

Despite its failure, Hadiach warrants attention for two reasons. It was the last attempt to resolve the Ukrainian or Rus' problem as a whole within a Polish framework. Moreover, it was used by later apologists for Poland as an example of the supposed tolerant nature of the Polish-Lithuanian Commonwealth. More important, Hadiach revealed how much less interested were the leading social strata in Ukraine, the Cossack *starshyna*, in attaining independence for their homeland than in retaining or expanding their own social and political privileges within an existing state. If their own interests could not be furthered in Poland, then perhaps Muscovy might offer a better chance. In essence, the whole Period of Ruin in Ukrainian history can be viewed as a time when the Cossack *starshyna* continually shifted its allegiance from Poland to Muscovy and sometimes even to the Ottoman Empire in a desperate attempt to find a strong ally that would guarantee its leadership role within Ukrainian society. The *starshyna* was hampered in its efforts, however, by two forces: (1) the governments of Poland and Muscovy, each of which had its own preferences as to how "peripheral" areas within its realm should be governed; and (2) the lower-echelon Cossacks from Zaporozhia and the peasants, who from the outset were opposed to the idea of replacing rule by a Polish or polonized Rus' aristocracy with rule by their "own," but a no less oppressive, Cossack aristocracy.

Anarchy, ruin, and the division of Ukraine

During this era of continual civil war and foreign invasion, the Cossack *starshyna* had little effective control over events. The proposed Union of Hadiach, for instance, was viewed by Muscovy as a declaration of war, and in the spring of 1659 Tsar Aleksei sent an army of 100,000 troops to invade Ukraine. Although the Muscovites were defeated by a combined Polish-Tatar-Cossack force near Konotop (8 July 1659), Hetman Vyhov'kyi's position was not improved. Revolts, especially on the Left Bank and in Zaporozhia, led by Cossacks who were discontent with the *starshyna*'s pro-Polish orientation resulted in the demise of Vyhovs'kyi in September 1659.

Following the Battle of Konotop in 1659, a new stalemate developed between Muscovy and Poland. What evolved was a situation whereby the Cossack state was divided between a Polish sphere of influence on the Right Bank and a Muscovite sphere of influence on the Left Bank (including Kiev and the region west of the city). Within each of these spheres, periods of cooperation were counterbalanced by periods of conflict involving various factions: the governments of Poland or Muscovy; the Cossack *starshyna*; the lower-echelon Cossacks, led by the *sich*; and the peasantry. There were efforts made by a few Cossack hetmans like Khmel'nyts'kyi's second son Iurii Khmel'nyts'kyi (in office 1659–1663) and, especially, Petro Doroshenko (in office 1665–1676) to unify these diverse factions and to restore the prestige of the Cossack state that existed after the 1648 revolution, but none were successful.

MAP 19

UKRAINIAN LANDS AFTER 1667

∘∘∘∘ Ottoman boundary, 1672-1699
──── Boundary of Ukraine, 2005

LITHUANIA

POLISH - LITHUANIAN

M U S C O V Y

Voronezh

Don

Seim

Desna

Starodub

Belgorod

SLOBODA UKRAINE

Chernihiv

Baturyn

Vorskla

COMMONWEALTH

Brest

Nizhyn

HETMANATE

Kiev

Pereiaslav

Bila
Tserkva

Ros

Dnieper

Stara
Sich

ZAPOROZHIA

Dnieper

Buh

Desna

Warsaw

Buh

PODLACHIA

LUBLIN

Chelm

BELZ

Lviv

GALICIA
(RUS')

Przemysl

San

Mukachevo

Tysa

TRANSYLVANIA

Vistula

Luts'k

VOLHYNIA

Zhytomyr

E K

PODOLIA

Kamianets-
Podil's'kyi

Bratslav

BRATSLAV

Southern

Dniester

Dniester

MOLDAVIA

Prut

OTTOMAN

WALACHIA

Danube

BUJAK

YEDISAN

CRIMEAN

Or Kapi

CRIMEA

Bahçesaray

Kefe

SEA OF AZOV

Azov

K H A N A T E

E M P I R E

BLACK

SEA

Kuban

CIRCASSIANS

Scale 1 : 8 650 000
0   50   100 miles
0   50   100 kilometers

The possibility of an independent Ukrainian Cossack state became even more remote after Poland and Muscovy, exhausted by their inconclusive wars, decided to reach a modus vivendi. In 1667, both states signed the Treaty of Andrusovo, which was to last thirteen years and which delineated their de facto spheres of influence in Ukraine. In other words, Ukraine's Right Bank went to Poland, its Left Bank to Muscovy. The city of Kiev was placed under Muscovite suzerainty for two years, although this initially temporary time period was extended. In the end, Ukraine's historic center would remain permanently within Muscovy. As for Zaporozhia, it was placed under the joint protection of Poland and Muscovy.

Within this new political constellation, Ukraine had two hetmans, one for the Polish Right Bank and one for the Muscovite Left Bank. The two hetmans often clashed with their own protectors – Poland and Muscovy – as well as with each other, especially when some dynamic leader tried to reunite both halves of Ukraine. The career of Hetman Petro Doroshenko epitomizes the confusion of the time. In 1665, he began as hetman in Poland's Right Bank, but subsequently he turned against Poland, signed a treaty with the Ottoman Empire and the Crimea, and, in 1668, invaded Muscovy's Left Bank. His pro-Turkish orientation – which revived a policy established two decades before by Bohdan Khmel'nyts'kyi – seemed to be the only policy that might bring some change in Ukraine's status at a time when Muscovy and Poland preferred to remain at peace. Ukraine turned out to be the greatest loser, however, since an Ottoman army arrived and, with its Crimean allies, ravaged the Right Bank. Finally, after defeating Poland in 1672, the Ottomans annexed a huge swath of territory in Right Bank Ukraine (Podolia, Bratslav, and southern Kiev palatinates). Meanwhile, Doroshenko scrambled wildly, changing his allegiance several times among Poland, the Ottoman Empire, and, finally, Muscovy, where he was forced to settle (with honors) after his defeat and abdication from the hetmanate in 1676.

With the Ottomans in control of at least one-third of Ukraine, Muscovy and Poland preferred to maintain peace with each other. Right Bank Ukraine, meanwhile, remained a theater of war. There, Ottoman forces courted the local Cossacks (Hetman Iurii Khmel'nyts'kyi was made Prince of Ukraine, 1677–1681, by the sultan) and together they clashed with the Muscovite army and their allies, the local Cossacks on the Left Bank. In what seemed to be perpetual conflict, the peasants on the Right Bank, who had already begun to emigrate in large numbers while Doroshenko was still hetman, continued to flee eastward across the Dnieper River to the Left Bank and Sloboda Ukraine. Consequently, much of the Right Bank became deserted. Finally, in 1681 Muscovy and the Ottoman Empire signed a peace treaty (the Treaty of Bakhchysarai) whereby both parties agreed to a twenty-year armistice. Although the Ottomans continued to hold Podolia and Bratslav, they agreed that a buffer zone, or no-man's-land without settlers, would be maintained in the heart of Ukrainian territory, that is, in eastern Bratslav and central and southern Kiev between the Southern Buh and Dnieper Rivers.

For its part, Poland could never acquiesce to Ottoman control of Podolia or any other part of what it considered the historical Polish patrimony. Moreover, Poland was now ruled by Jan Sobieski (reigned 1674–1696), famous for his successful defense of Habsburg Vienna and crusade against the Ottoman Turks. Joined by Habsburg Austria, Venice, and the Papacy, Sobieski formed the so-called Holy Alliance against the Ottoman Empire. In order to continue his military ventures, he needed peace along Poland's long eastern boundary. For this reason, in 1686 Poland decided to strike a new agreement with Muscovy. The pact became known as the "eternal peace" which, in effect, simply rendered more permanent the arrangement reached two decades earlier at Andrusovo. Poland renounced all claims to Left Bank Ukraine, as well as to the cities of Kiev, Starodub, and Smolensk, which had been retaken during the seventeenth century by Muscovy. Poland also acknowledged the supremacy of the tsar alone over the Cossacks in Zaporozhia, and it guaranteed all rights to the Orthodox Ukrainian population in its own sphere of influence on the Right Bank. Thus, by 1686 the two principal Christian states in eastern Europe, Poland and Muscovy, had agreed to a partitioning of Ukrainian territory more or less along the Dnieper River. The palatinates of Podolia, Bratslav, and southern Kiev were to stay under Ottoman control until the end of the century, whereas the rest of southern Ukraine and Crimea were to remain even longer within the Ottoman Empire, either under the direct authority of the sultan (Bujak and Yedisan) or under his vassal, the Crimean Khanate.

The Period of Ruin, which for Ukraine started in 1657 and ended three decades later with the signing of the so-called eternal peace in 1686, witnessed great changes in the political status of the country. The period began with Hetman Bohdan Khmel'nyts'kyi and his successors controlling much of Ukrainian territory. In their efforts to maintain autonomy, however, Khmel'nyts'kyi and his successors continually transferred their allegiance among Ukraine's three powerful neighbors. The result, by 1686, was a Ukraine ravaged by civil war and foreign invasion, with little hope of independence or even full autonomy, and with its territory divided among Poland, Muscovy, and the Ottoman Empire.

19

The Structure of the Cossack State

Prior to the revolution of 1648, Cossacks living on Ukrainian lands were nominally under the jurisdiction of the Polish Kingdom. By the second half of the sixteenth century, when they had developed into a well-organized military force, there existed two types of Cossacks: (1) town Cossacks, who lived in or near frontier border towns and who were in the service of the Polish administration; and (2) Zaporozhian Cossacks, who lived farther south in the no-man's-land below the bend of the Dnieper River between the Polish Kingdom and the Crimean Khanate.

Both the town Cossacks and the Zaporozhian Cossacks were charged, or charged themselves, with the defense of the Polish frontier against incursions by the Tatars and Ottoman Turks. Both groups also led offensive campaigns in concert or alone against their traditional Tatar and Ottoman enemies in the south. Especially during the early decades of the seventeenth century, they frequently fought with Poland's armies in its wars against Sweden, the Livonian Knights, and Muscovy. As both groups of Cossacks were drawn more and more into Polish military ventures, they also were affected by Poland's attempts to gain greater control over their activity.

Registered and unregistered Cossacks

One result of Polish interference in Cossack life was a greater differentiation between the two Cossack groups. This differentiation was symbolized most graphically by the policy of registration, whereby registered Cossacks, most often from the border towns, were made an integral part of the Polish frontier military administration. The unregistered Cossacks, mostly in Zaporozhia, in contrast remained beyond the pale of Polish authority, with the consequence that their territory was viewed with suspicion as a place where runaway serfs and others who posed a potential threat to the Polish-Lithuanian social order found refuge.

The registered Cossacks, who by the first half of the seventeenth century ranged in number from about 6,000 to 8,000, resided in or near the Polish administrative centers in the Kiev, Bratslav, and Chernihiv palatinates. They frequently owned their own estates, and some developed a degree of wealth and social prestige which, together with their privileges as registered Cossacks, transformed them into a kind of Ukrainian gentry, even though they were not recognized as members of the noble estate in Poland. It is from this group of the Cossack elite that many of the officers and other officials were drawn to staff the new administration of the Cossack state after 1648. This upper-class Cossack stratum generally came to be known as the *starshyna*.

The unregistered Cossacks consisted of two groups: (1) Cossacks from Zaporozhia and even farther north who may have served with the Polish army in its time of need (in 1620 the register reached 20,000), but who were soon after removed from the register; and (2) a steady stream of peasants and others who, discontent with the increasing burdens of serfdom, fled south to lead the Cossack way of life in landlordless Zaporozhia.

The fortified center of Zaporozhia, the *sich*, moved several times in the course of the seventeenth century, usually progressively southward onto islands or among tributaries of the Dnieper River. By the second half of the century, the *sich* had developed a more organized administrative structure. While the Sich Council (*sichova rada*), made up of all members who had equal votes, remained the highest source of authority in administrative and military matters, it was often unwieldy and gradually gave way to the decisions set by the Council of Elders (*rada starshyn*). The latter council was made up of an elected judge, a chancellor (*pysar*), an aide-de-camp (*osaul*), lieutenants of the varying military units (*kurinni otamany*), and the head or chief of the *sich*, the *koshovyi otaman*. Whereas at various times the *sich* elected its own hetmans (P. Sahaidachnyi, B. Khmel'nyts'kyi), by the second half of the seventeenth century the office of *koshovyi otaman* had replaced that of the hetman as the highest office in Zaporozhia. Elected to a one-year term – though subject to removal by the Sich Council at any time – the *koshovyi otaman* represented the Zaporozhian Sich to the outside world.

Apart from the *sich*, the steppe region immediately on both sides of the Dnieper River was inhabited by married Cossacks and free homesteaders, that is, former serfs and others who had come to Zaporozhia to lead the Cossack way of life. As well as engaging in fishing, hunting, cattle raising, and, later, farming, the married Cossacks and free homesteaders joined the Cossacks from the *sich* in raids against the Tatars and Turks, served in the foreign ventures of the Polish kings, and took part in attacks against Polish military forces and local administrators during times of Polish-Cossack friction. Satisfied with their own situation beyond the reach of Polish royal and local noble governmental authority, the unregistered Cossacks in the *sich* and in the surrounding Zaporozhian countryside were often suspicious of the town Cossacks and, later, *starshyna* farther north. Consequently, during the frequent revolts against Polish rule, the Zaporozhian Cossacks were often pitted against registered Cossacks in Polish service.

Internal administration

As a registered Cossack and aspiring member of the gentry, Bohdan Kmel'nyts'kyi initially hoped to obtain personal justice and to uphold and improve the status of his

WHAT TO CALL THE COSSACK STATE?

The new Cossack state, which came into being in 1649 in the course of the Khmel'nyts'kyi uprising, was officially known as the Army of Zaporozhia (Viis'ko Zaporiz'ke) or the Zaporozhian Host, even though it was not centered in Zaporozhia. Despite its name, it was the creation of the registered Cossacks living in Ukrainian territories farther north and not of the Zaporozhians, who were united with it only through the personal leadership of Khmel'nyts'kyi. Another source of confusion is the number of names given to the Cossack state: the Army of Zaporozhia, the Army of Lower Zaporozhia, the Hetmanate, and Little Russia. Actually, the Army of Lower Zaporozhia referred specifically only to the Zaporozhian lands, while the Hetmanate and Little Russia (especially in Muscovite and Russian sources) referred to those Cossack regiments on the Dnieper's Left Bank that were under the direct authority of the hetman (excluding Zaporozhia and Sloboda Ukraine), which after 1667 had come under Muscovite hegemony.

In this and subsequent chapters, the term *Cossack state* will be used with reference to the period between 1649 and 1711. While it is true that by the second half of the seventeenth century there were already pronounced differences among the various Cossack regions (the Hetmanate, Sloboda Ukraine, Zaporozhia, the Right Bank), the term *Cossack state*, which implies a single entity, is justified by the fact that throughout this period most hetmans from Bohdan Khmel'nyts'kyi to Ivan Mazepa tried to create some kind of autonomous or independent entity consisting of all lands inhabited by Cossacks. After 1711, the individual regional names will be used. In any case, after that date it was only in the Hetmanate that the tradition of Cossack statehood was preserved.

social group within the Polish-Lithuanian Commonwealth. When it became increasingly evident, however, that the revolutionary events he had set in motion in 1648 could not be contained, and that his limited demands on behalf of his estate represented an insufficient response in a rapidly changing military, political, and social situation, the Cossack leader was forced to create a new administrative structure for the territories that had come under his control. The result was the Cossack state.

Technically, the Cossack state came into existence at the peace reached at Zboriv in August 1649 between Khmel'nyts'kyi and the Polish government. By the terms of the Zboriv agreement, the palatinates of Kiev, Bratslav, and Chernihiv – that is, the region within Poland that had come to be known as Ukraine – were cleared of Polish administrative and military authorities, who were then replaced by Cossacks. The boundaries of the Cossack state, which encompassed 78,000 square miles (200,000 square kilometers), were reaffirmed by the Zhvanets' treaty with the Poles in December 1653, and by the Agreement of Pereiaslav with the Muscovite tsar in early 1654. Similar boundaries (minus the Starodub region in

MAP 20

THE COSSACK STATE, 1651

Copyright © by Paul Robert Magocsi

⊙ Regimental center
■ Fortified towns

Scale 1 : 5 850 000

0   50   100 miles
0   50   100 kilometers

northern Chernihiv) were again proposed for the Grand Duchy of Rus' in the tripartite confederation of Poles, Lithuanians, and Ukrainians outlined in the Union
of Hadiach (1658).

The boundaries of the Cossack state were influenced by the changing military
situation during the Khmel'nyts'kyi uprising and the Period of Ruin that followed.
The state reached its greatest territorial extent under Bohdan Khmel'nyts'kyi, and
included the Kiev, Bratslav, and Chernihiv palatinates on both the Left and Right
Banks of the Dnieper River. Moreover, Zaporozhia, along the southern fringes of

the Kiev palatinate, and even some Belarusan lands of Lithuania, in the north, recognized the suzerainty of the hetman (see map 18). This situation changed substantially after Khmel'nyts'kyi's death. Following the Treaty of Andrusovo reached
between Muscovy and Poland in 1667 and later renewed as the so-called eternal
peace of 1686, the Cossack state remained divided more or less along the Dnieper
River between Poland and Muscovy, with both powers having a joint protectorate
over Zaporozhia. In consequence, only Ukrainian territory on the Muscovite eastern bank, or Left Bank, continued to survive as an autonomous Cossack state. This
territory, consisting of the old Polish palatinates of Chernihiv and eastern Kiev (as
well as the city of Kiev on the Right Bank) and measuring about 80,000 square
miles (208,000 square kilometers), has come to be known in historical literature
as the Hetmanate.

As for Sloboda Ukraine, it had a Cossack administrative system, although the
region never became part of either the Cossack state or the Hetmanate. Instead,
from its earliest settlement during the 1630s Sloboda Ukraine was always ruled
directly from Moscow. Zaporozhia, too, enjoyed a distinct status. It also was not part
of the Hetmanate, although after 1686, when Poland gave up its claims to a joint
protectorate, the area was theoretically dependent upon both the Hetmanate's
government and the tsar. To distinguish it from the Hetmanate, which still carried
the official name Army of Zaporozhia (*Viis'ko Zaporiz'ke*), the lands within Zaporozhia proper were called the Army of Lower Zaporozhia (*Viis'ko Zaporiz'ke Nyzove*),
and the region in essence functioned as an autonomous body with little regard for
the hetman and his government. Instead, Zaporozhia maintained a tradition of
loyal respect for the faraway tsar, who, because of his distance, would be less likely
to interfere in its affairs, at least for the time being.

As early as under Bohdan Khmel'nyts'kyi, the Polish palatinates of Kiev, Chernihiv, and Bratslav, each with its own palatine, district officials (*starosta* and vice-
starosta), and administration made up largely of aristocrat-controlled courts and
other governmental offices, were replaced. Under Cossack rule, the new state was
divided into military-administrative units called regimental districts (*polky*), each
named after its regimental town center. The number of districts fluctuated with
the changing boundaries of the Cossack state. In 1649, when the Cossack state
included lands on the Right and Left Banks, there were sixteen regimental districts (a seventeenth was added in 1651), with 272 companies; at the end of the
eighteenth century, the Hetmanate on the Left Bank alone consisted of ten regimental districts, with 174 companies.

Each regimental district was headed by a colonel (*polkovnyk*), who served as both
the supreme military and the supreme civil authority in his territory. Because of his
dual authority and the fact that long periods of political instability precluded effective control by any higher, central governmental structure, the regimental colonels
often became all-powerful and semi-independent figures, miniature hetmans in a
sense. Initially, the colonels were elected by all the Cossacks in the regiment, who
met together in a loose regimental council (*Polkova rada*), but by the eighteenth
century they had come to be appointed by the hetman. The regimental council
also met to decide common problems, but by the eighteenth century that council

THE COSSACK STATE ADMINISTRATION

CENTRAL ADMINISTRATION

HETMAN

General Military Council (*Heneral'na viis'kova rada*)	Cabinet General (*Heneral'na starshyna*)	Council of Officers (*Rada starshyn*)
all Cossacks	1 general quartermaster (*heneral'nyi oboznyi*)	**Smaller Council** 1 hetman 2 general staff
	2 general chancellor (*heneral'nyi pysar*)	**Larger Council** 1 hetman
	3 general treasurer (*heneral'nyi pidskarbnyi*)	2 general staff 3 regimental colonels and officers' staff
	4 general judges – 2 (*heneral'ni suddi*)	
	5 general aides-de-camp – 2 (*heneral'ni osauly*)	
	6 general standard bearer (*heneral'nyi bunchuzhnyi*)	
	7 general flag-bearer (*heneral'nyi khoruzhnyi*)	

General Military Chancellery
(*heneral'na viis'kova kantseliariia*)

1 general military treasury
2 general military court
3 general accounting office

REGIMENTAL ADMINISTRATION

COLONEL (*polkovnyk*)

Regimental Council (*Polkova rada*)	Regimental Staff (*Polkova starshyna*)	Regimental Officer Council (*Rada polkovoï starshyny*)
all Cossacks	1 regimental quartermaster (*polkovyi oboznyi*)	1 colonel 2 regimental staff

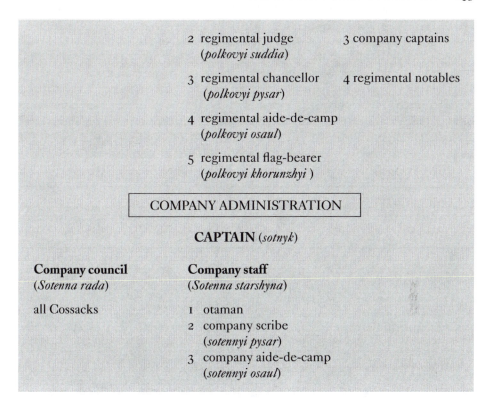

2 regimental judge (*polkovyi suddia*)	3 company captains
3 regimental chancellor (*polkovyi pysar*)	4 regimental notables
4 regimental aide-de-camp (*polkovyi osaul*)	
5 regimental flag-bearer (*polkovyi khorunzhyi*)	

COMPANY ADMINISTRATION

CAPTAIN (*sotnyk*)

Company council (*Sotenna rada*)	**Company staff** (*Sotenna starshyna*)
all Cossacks	1 otaman
	2 company scribe (*sotennyi pysar*)
	3 company aide-de-camp (*sotennyi osaul*)

had disappeared, and regiments were effectively being run by the colonel assisted by his regimental staff (*Polkova starshyna*) and a regimental officer council (*Rada polkovoï starshyny*). The regimental staff consisted of a quartermaster (the regiment's second in command), judge, chancellor, aide-de-camp, and flag-bearer.

Each of the regimental districts in turn was divided into companies (*sotnia*), which ranged in number from eleven to twenty-three according to the size of the regimental territory. Each company was headed by a captain (*sotnyk*), who was assisted by a small staff (*Sotenna starshyna*) that included an otaman (the second in command), a scribe, and an aide-de-camp. At first, captains were elected by all Cossacks in the company, who met in a council (*Sotenna rada*), but by the end of the seventeenth century they had come to be appointed by the hetman or the regimental colonel and effectively held their office for life. In keeping with the trend espoused by Muscovy toward a service state, the office of captain became hereditary and included among its privileges authority over manorial peasants.

At the top of the Cossack administrative structure was the hetman, his Cabinet General, and two councils, the General Military Council and the Council of Officers. The supreme authority rested with the hetman, who was elected by the General Military Council. The hetman ruled without limit of tenure, which in practice meant until he died or was removed by force. In theory, he could be dismissed by the General Military Council for misconduct. The hetman had full executive power over the administration, the judiciary, finances, and the army, and he nominated and later appointed the colonels of the regimental districts. After 1649, the hetman had at his disposal all the income from the former estates of the Polish king located in the Kiev, Chernihiv, and Bratslav palatinates (about 100,000 gold pieces anually). In subsequent years, the Cossack government's income came primarily from duties levied on foreign imports and from taxes on the sale of alcohol. The hetman also had the right to grant lands and mills as a reward for military service, and he often did so as a way of reimbursing supporters when the state treasury was low. Finally, the hetman had the right to conduct foreign policy, although the Muscovite government tried to limit this privilege, especially during the eighteenth century.

The hetman's immediate central administration consisted of the Cabinet General (*Heneral'na starshyna*), or the General Staff, which he appointed. The senior member of the hetman's cabinet was the general quartermaster. He was the officer responsible for the artillery, who also functioned as acting hetman (*nakaznyi hetman*) when the hetman was out of the country or at a time between the death of one hetman and the accession of another. Other cabinet members included a general chancellor, a general treasurer (two after 1728), two general judges, two general aides-de-camp, a general standard bearer, and a general flag-bearer. The hetman's Cabinet General functioned simultaneously as the supreme military command and the cabinet of governmental ministers in the Cossack state. The state was administered by several central institutions (the treasury, the court, and the accounting office) that eventually became subordinate to the General Military Chancellery, headed by the general chancellor. The General Military Chancellery was responsible for the implementation of decrees issued by the tsars and hetmans and for the investigation of all complaints against officials.

The two other elements of the central administration were the General Military Council and the Council of Officers. The General Military Council (*Heneral'na viis'kova rada*) had its origins in the sixteenth-century Zaporozhian Sich. It both elected hetmans and had the right to dismiss them, and in theory all Cossacks had the right to participate in its proceedings. This irregular assembly, which declined in importance in the decades before Bohdan Khmel'nyts'kyi, became influential once again during the unstable Period of Ruin, when it included clergy, townspeople, and peasants as well as Cossacks. The so-called Black Council (*Chorna Rada*) of 1663 was the best known, some would say an infamous, example of this unwieldy body. After the Period of Ruin, the importance of the General Military Council waned again, and it became primarily a ceremonial body, convened only to acclaim the new hetman elected previously by the smaller Council of Officers.

The Council of Officers (*Rada starshyn*) took three different forms. The first, or Smaller Council consisted only of the hetman and his Cabinet General; the second, or Large Council included those two elements as well as the regimental colonels and at times their officers' staff. There were also periods when enlarged sessions of the Council of Officers took place. These included all the elements of the Large Council, to which were added company captains (*sotnyky*) and at times mayors of towns and higher clergy. In contrast to the smaller Council of Officers, which met several times a week, the enlarged sessions of the council met at the hetman's residence twice a year, between Christmas and Epiphany and again at Easter. The main concerns of the various forms of the Council of Officers were the state's financial problems, the status of mercenary military units within the Cossack forces, and at times military campaigns and the codification of laws. There were never any clear-cut lines of function and authority between the hetman and the various forms of the Council Officers, which by the eighteenth century functioned primarily as an advisory body to the hetman who could accept or disregard at his discretion the advice given him.

The seat of the hetman and his government was first at Chyhyryn, near Bohdan Khmel'nyts'kyi's birthplace. Chyhyryn served as the Cossack capital from 1648 to 1663. In subsequent years, when the Cossack state was divided, Chyhyryn served for a time (1665–1676) as the seat of the Right Bank Cossack administration. The Left Bank had its own capitals: Hadiach (1663–1668), Baturyn (1669–1708), and, finally, Hlukhiv, which remained the seat of the Hetmanate until its demise in the 1780s.

International status

The Cossack state and, later, the Hetmanate were never fully independent, but rather were more or less autonomous units within a larger state structure, whether Poland or Muscovy. Between 1649 and 1654, and on the Right Bank between 1658 and 1676, the Polish king was the ultimate sovereign. The relationship between the Cossack state and Poland was based on a kind of personal union between the hetman and the king. The hetman was chosen by the Cossacks, and no Polish administration was permitted on Cossack territory. Between 1654 and 1657, and then on the Left Bank after 1663, the Muscovite tsar was the ultimate sovereign over the Cossack state and the Hetmanate.

The relationship between Muscovy and the Hetmanate was based on the agreements of Pereiaslav (the original 1654 and revised 1659 versions) and on amendments implemented upon the installation of each new hetman (1663, 1669, 1672, 1687). Following Muscovy's practice of centralized authority, the tsar's government was anxious to maintain control over its ever-expanding realm. Within a few years after 1654, therefore, the Muscovite government stationed its own representative on Cossack territory. For example, according to the revised articles of Pereiaslav concluded in 1659, a Muscovite governor (*voevoda*) with a garrison was to be stationed in Kiev, Nizhyn, Pereiaslav, Bratslav, and Uman'. By 1665, not only was Muscovy claiming direct rule over the cities of Kiev, Chernihiv, Pereiaslav, Nizhyn, Poltava, Novhorod-Sivers'kyi, Kremenchuk, Kodak, and Oster, but the tsar's government was sending officials to ensure that all taxes, including revenue on liquor, be returned directly to the tsar's treasury. Although Cossack protests forced Muscovy to repeal these measures in 1669, tsarist governors remained in Kiev and in four other cities on the Left Bank – Chernihiv, Nizhyn, Pereiaslav, and Oster. The Muscovite presence continued to increase, with the result that by the eighteenth century the Hetmanate gradually had lost control of its own governmental affairs. In Moscow itself, matters pertaining to Ukraine's Cossack state were at first handled by the Central Ministry for Foreign Affairs (Posolskii prikaz, 1654–1663), but after the appearance of a separate hetman on the Left Bank in 1663, a special chancellery was created, the Central Ministry for Little Russia (Malorossiiskii prikaz), which continued to function until 1722.

20

Mazepa and the Great Northern War

The Period of Ruin in Ukrainian history, which ended in 1686 after the establishment of the so-called eternal peace between Muscovy and Poland, was followed by another quarter century in which Ukraine was for long periods of time the scene of foreign invasion, civil war, and political upheaval. In a sense, the crises of seventeenth-century Europe were continuing in the eastern half of the continent. In Ukraine, the situation did not really begin to stabilize until after 1711.

The quarter century from 1686 to 1711 was initially characterized by political stability, but then came the first stage of the Great Northern War. Looked at in another way, it was the final phase in the centuries-long struggle between Muscovy and Sweden for control of the Baltic Sea and the continuation of Muscovy's struggle against the Ottoman Empire (and the latter's Crimean allies) for access to the Black Sea. Caught between these monumental conflicts was Ukraine. The intensity of the military and political struggle during eastern Europe's last "seventeenth-century crisis" was heightened by the presence of dynamic, young, and talented leaders who ruled two of the great powers in question, Charles XII of Sweden and Peter I of Muscovy. Their contemporary in Ukraine was Ivan Mazepa, himself an experienced and very capable leader who held the post of hetman from 1687 to 1709, and who, next to Bohdan Khmel'nyts'kyi, was the most influential of Ukraine's Cossack leaders. Because the quarter century before 1711 was a turning point in the history of eastern Europe, and because these three figures – Charles XII, Peter I, and Mazepa – played such a dominant role during these years, an enormous historical literature on each of them exists. Not surprisingly, there is great controversy about their personalities and careers.

The image of Mazepa

Mazepa was traditionally viewed by Russian historians of the imperial era (S. Solov'ev, V. Kliuchevskii) as a "traitor," because he deserted Peter I at a critical moment and allied himself with Sweden's Charles XII. Such a view was based on the assumption that Ukraine was an integral part of the Russian Empire, that is, of a "one and indivisible Russian state," and that Mazepa's turn to an external power was therefore a treasonous act. The Russian public in general was influenced perhaps even more by the words of their nineteenth-century national bard, Aleksandr Pushkin, who, in his well-known poem "Poltava," referred to Mazepa as a "Judas" and a "snake." Subsequently, Russian historians in the West modified such views. In a popular American college textbook of Russian history used in the decades after World War II, the Columbia University professor Michael Florinsky commented: "Mazepa, a traitor and villain according to official Russian historiography, was motivated by the legitimate and honorable desire to safeguard the autonomy of his country and to save it from destruction by siding with the probable winner, although his methods were those of the most unscrupulous politician."[1]

In contrast, Soviet writers, whether Ukrainian or Russian, continued to propagate the traditional Russian imperial conception. In the multivolume *Radians'ka entsyklopediia istorii Ukrainy* (Soviet Encyclopedia of the History of Ukraine, 1971), the entry on Mazepa began with the terse and uncompromising identification "Ivan Stepanovych Mazepa (1644–1709), traitor of the Ukrainian people,"[2] and another multivolume work, *Istoriia Ukrains' koi RSR* (History of the Ukrainian SSR, 1979) referred to "Mazepa, whose name has gone down in history as a synonym of treachery and betrayal."[3] Such views defined the popular image of Mazepa in some Russian émigré circles as well as in Soviet society, whereby the hetman symbolized the treacherous desires of all those "evil forces" who wanted to separate from an "indivisible mother Russia," whether a Soviet or a non-Soviet Russia. The terms *mazepintsi* (Mazepa-ites) and *mazepinstvo* (Mazepa-ism) came to be used in imperial Russian, Soviet Marxist, and even post-Communist Russian discourse as synonyms of treachery toward the state and opportunistic separatism.

Mazepa initially found little favor among Ukrainian historians as well, especially those of the populist school during the second half of the nineteenth century (M. Kostomarov, P. Kulish, O. Lazarevs'kyi, V. Antonovych), who considered him a traitor because he seemed to have acted primarily in the interests of the Cossack elite and not of the nation as a whole. Beginning in the last decade of the nineteenth century, however, other Ukrainian historians (M. Hrushevs'kyi, V. Lypyns'kyi, D. Doroshenko, B. Krupnyts'kyi, O. Ohloblyn) reassessed Mazepa. Although critical of certain policies, they nonetheless regarded him as a national patriot who, in response to harsh Muscovite rule and the overwhelming ravages of war, tried in the classic Cossack fashion to obtain independence for his homeland by concluding alliances with foreign powers other than Muscovy. For Ukrainian political activists in the twentieth century such as Dmytro Dontsov, Mazepa became the subject of uncritical panegyric, with the result that in the end he has been transformed by some historians (such as N. Polons'ka-Vasylenko) into "the symbol of the struggle for the independence of Ukraine."[4]

It is interesting to note that already in the early nineteenth century Mazepa had become a hero for the Romantic movement in western and central Europe. The era's most famous writers – Lord Byron in England, Victor Hugo in France, and Juliusz Słowacki in Poland – all composed poems about Mazepa, usually based on tales of real or imagined episodes in the life of the Ukrainian leader. Musicians were even more attracted to the Mazepa legend. Four operas were written entitled

Mazepa, the most famous by Peter I. Tchaikovsky (1883; the other three by little-known composers in the Russian Empire, Boris Vietinghoff-Scheel, 1859, Adam Minchejmer, 1875, and the Spaniard Felipe Pedrell, 1881); a cantata for chorus, by the Irish composer Michael Balfe (1862); and a piano work by the German Johann Karl Loewe (1830). Perhaps the most famous musical work was the tone poem for orchestra, "Mazepa," by the Hungarian Franz Liszt (1851). Finally, in the twentieth century, the Polish composer Tadeusz Szeligowski wrote a score for a ballet entitled *Mazepa* (1957), which also was the name and subject for two early British (1908) and American (1910) silent films, and more recently, for feature-length French (by Bartabas, 1993) and Ukrainian (by Iurii Illienko, 2005) films and a German film for television (by Brian Lange, 1996). Who, then, was this controversial Ivan Mazepa, and how did his career affect developments in Ukraine?

The rise of Mazepa

Mazepa was born in 1639 in Bila Tserkva, on the Right Bank of the Kiev palatinate. His father, Stepan-Adam, was among those Orthodox Rus' gentry who hoped to improve their precarious status by joining the Khmel'nyts'kyi uprising. After 1654, Stepan Mazepa became commander of the Cossack forces in Bila Tserkva and subsequently remained in the service of Poland. Ivan's mother, Maryna, née Mokiievs'ka, was a descendant of an old Rus' noble family who later in life became a cultural and religious activist in her own right. The young Ivan received a solid education on the Jesuit Latin model at the Mohyla Collegium in Kiev, and in 1649, at the height of the Khmel'nyts'kyi uprising, he was sent to the Jesuit College in Warsaw, where after a time he came to the attention of Poland's new king, Jan Kazimierz. The king was interested in creating a circle of young pro-Polish Orthodox Ukrainians, and Mazepa soon became his page, or gentleman-in-waiting. The king even paid for the young courtier's travel and education in Holland between 1656 and 1659, during which time he visited Germany, Italy, and France. When he returned from western Europe, Mazepa entered the service of the king, who sent him on diplomatic missions to the Cossacks. This stage of his career lasted until 1663, when, in consequence of court intrigue and some amorous misadventures (the latter were particularly developed by the nineteenth-century Romantic writers and librettists), Mazepa returned home to Bila Tserkva.

In 1669, Mazepa entered the service of Petro Doroshenko, the Right Bank hetman who, with the aid of the Ottoman Turks and Crimean Tatars, was trying to reunite the divided Cossack Ukraine. Mazepa rose rapidly through the ranks and became general aide-de-camp (*heneral'nyi osaul*) in Doroshenko's Cabinet General. In 1674, Mazepa was sent on a mission to the Crimea, but he was captured en route by the Zaporozhian Cossacks (who at the time were pro-Muscovite and fiercely anti-Crimean). He was imprisoned by the Zaporozhians and eventually sent to Moscow. His imprisonment did not last long, however, since he managed to find his way into the good graces of the Muscovite government – revealing to them all the pro-Ottoman and pro-Crimean plans of Hetman Doroshenko in the process. Convinced that Mazepa could be of use to them, the Muscovites sent him back to Ukraine, but this time to the Muscovite-controlled Left Bank and in the service of that region's hetman, Ivan Samoilovych. Again, the capable Mazepa rose rapidly and, in 1682, became general aide-de-camp in the hetman's Cabinet General.

The next stage in Mazepa's career was determined by Muscovite foreign policy. Having concluded the "eternal peace" with Poland in 1686, Muscovy decided to eliminate the Crimean menace (the Tatars had participated in Doroshenko's anti-Muscovite ventures) once and for all. An anti-Turkish "Holy Alliance" was struck between Austria, Poland, the Papacy, Venice, and Muscovy. The Muscovite government, led by Sophia (as regent 1682–1689), decided to take action first. In early 1687 Sophia dispatched southward an enormous army of 100,000 men led by Prince Golitsyn. Golitsyn's forces were to be joined by 50,000 Cossacks and were to strike at the heart of the Crimea. Hetman Samoilovych opposed the plan and only reluctantly went along. The hetman's premonitions were on the mark, however, and the ill-planned military venture ended in a fiasco. But to avoid total disgrace Prince Golitsyn, the favorite of regent Sophia, found – probably with the connivance of Mazepa – a scapegoat in Hetman Samoilovych. The very person who had been opposed to the military campaign was now blamed for its failure. As a result, Samoilovych was arrested and sent to Moscow, and in July 1687 the Muscovites managed to have the ever-resourceful Ivan Mazepa elected to the office of hetman in his place.

As part of the new hetman's confirmation, the prerogatives of the Muscovite government and the traditional privileges of the Cossacks were reaffirmed. The governmental prerogatives included Cossack recognition of the supremacy of the tsar, Cossack agreement not to conduct foreign affairs, and a limitation of 30,000 on the number of registered Cossacks. Among the traditional Cossack privileges were exemption from having to pay taxes, reaffirmation of the right to retain existing landholdings, and restrictions on the power of the Muscovite governors (with their garrisons in Kiev, Chernihiv, Pereiaslav, Nizhyn, and Oster) to interfere in local affairs. Also, the hetman's residence was to remain in Baturyn.

Mazepa as hetman: The early phase

The first thirteen years of Mazepa's rule, from 1687 to 1700, were characterized by a marked degree of stabilization in the Hetmanate. It was also a period that witnessed a flowering of culture and an improvement in the economic and legal status of the Orthodox Church (see chapter 21). Mazepa began his career as hetman with no real local power base, however, and was viewed by the established Cossack *starshyna* (officer elite) as an upstart and foreigner from Poland. But he was a master of political intrigue, and before long he was able to create a small coterie of staunch supporters. These consisted mainly of members of the Cossack *starshyna* and of Orthodox church hierarchs, whom he enriched by making them large land grants. Himself a member of the gentry, Mazepa protected the interests of his social estate by suppressing the peasant and rank-and-file Cossack revolts which broke out at the beginning of his rule and by reinforcing laws which fixed the number of days (at two) that manorial peasants were required to work for their landlords, whether hereditary Cossack gentry or Orthodox monasteries.

Mazepa was helped in his struggles for power by Muscovy. While he was in Moscow on an official visit in August 1689, a palace revolution took place in which the regent Sophia was deposed and replaced by her younger half-brother and rival, Peter I (reigned 1682–1725), who came to be known in Russian and Western writings as Peter the Great. Although he had been a supporter of Sophia and her advisers, the adept Mazepa quickly befriended Peter, who developed a strong liking for and trust in the older Cossack hetman. Mazepa continued to enjoy the confidence of the new tsar, with the result that in the years following, when political rivals in the Hetmanate made use of the Cossack privilege (which had become common practice) of sending denunciations against the hetman directly to the tsar, Peter rejected all their attacks outright. For his part, Mazepa served Peter faithfully in his anti-Ottoman wars, and the tsar reciprocated with a steadfast loyalty and friendship as well as with lavish gifts and land grants. With such help from the highest quarters, Mazepa was able to survive all attempts by his Cossack rivals to unseat him. At least until 1700, the relations between Mazepa and Peter I were as good as relations had ever been between a hetman and a tsar.

Aside from having no local power base, Mazepa faced a source of anti-hetman activity in the Zaporozhian Sich. In theory, Zaporozhia was dependent on both the hetman and the tsar, but juridically it was beyond the territorial administration of the Hetmanate, and in practice it followed its own autonomous policy. After the death of Bohdan Khmel'nyts'kyi in 1657, the *sich* was generally opposed to the hetmans, whether those on the Right or those on the Left Bank. As had been the case since at least the beginning of the seventeenth century, the hetman and his registered Cossack entourage were suspected of fostering their own aristocratic ambitions at the expense of the rank-and-file Cossacks in Zaporozhia. Moreover, the *sich* remained an implacable foe of Poland and any notion of renewed Polish rule in Ukraine, an idea favored by some of Khmel'nyts'kyi's successors. Zaporozhia, therefore, nominally remained in the pro-Muscovite camp.

Zaporozhia's pro-Muscovite policy began to fade, however, as a result of Moscow's anti-Crimean campaigns. It may seem paradoxical, but the Zaporozhian Cossacks, who had come into existence because of the need for protection against Crimean Tatar raids, were now beginning to be dissatisfied with Muscovy's concerted efforts to destroy their "enemy" in the Crimea. Looked at another way, the "Tatar threat" was in itself a justification for the Cossacks' existence. If there were no more threat, then Muscovy would have no more need of its Zaporozhian frontier defenders. In this sense, the underdeveloped steppe, with potentially lucrative booty in the Crimea just to the south, was something the Cossacks of Zaporozhia wanted to preserve. For this reason, the Zaporozhians did not take part in Muscovy's abortive campaign against the Crimean Khanate in 1687, or in a similar campaign with similar results led by Prince Golitsyn two years later, in 1689.

The Zaporozhians did not trust Hetman Mazepa. In particular, they opposed his participation in Muscovy's anti-Crimean campaigns and his policy of settling refugees from the Right Bank on Zaporozhian territory (near the Oril' and Samara Rivers). Motivated by their distrust, in 1692 the Zaporozhians revolted. They were led by a Cossack named Petro Ivanenko, or Petryk, a figure otherwise little known to historians. Petryk declared himself the true hetman, signed an alliance with the Crimean Tatars, and proclaimed his intention to liberate the Hetmanate and Sloboda Ukraine by establishing an independent state in alliance with the Tatars. In 1692 and again in 1693, Petryk led a combined Zaporozhian and Crimean Tatar force into Hetmanate territory. Although he was rebuffed by Mazepa, he tried twice more (1694 and 1696), albeit without success, to foment anti-Hetmanate revolts among the populace. The Petryk revolts reveal the degree to which Cossack society in Ukraine remained deeply divided even under Muscovite hegemony.

Muscovy moved next in its effort to subdue the Tatars and to gain access to the Black and Azov Seas in 1695. This time, the Zaporozhians participated with Mazepa and the Muscovites in an attack on the powerful Ottoman fortress of Azaq/Azov, at the mouth of the Don River. After an initial defeat, they took the fortress in 1696. Four more years of war followed, with the Cossacks renewing their sea raids on Ottoman and Crimean towns along the Black Sea until a thirty-year truce was finally signed in Constantinople between Muscovy and the Ottoman Empire in 1700. As a result of this treaty, Muscovy gained access to the Sea of Azov and Black Sea, and each side agreed to dismantle its fortresses along the lower Dnieper River. Tsar Peter was now free to turn to Muscovy's other historical goal, the Baltic Sea.

The dynamic Peter was the first tsar to travel to western Europe, and he was particularly fascinated by what he saw in Holland and England. He was determined to bring Western ways to the antiquated Muscovite governmental and social structure. He also saw Western technology as a means of modernizing the Muscovite army and fulfilling his other dream, military conquest. The Baltic Sea became Peter's symbolic "window to the West," and to make clear his orientation he planned to build a new capital for Muscovy on the marshes of the Neva River near where it flows into the Gulf of Finland, an arm of the Baltic Sea.

First, however, Peter had to wrest control of the eastern coast of the Baltic Sea from Sweden. In order to do so, he forged new diplomatic alliances with Sweden's traditional enemies, Denmark and Poland. (The second alliance was actually with August of Saxony, who recently had been elected king of Poland and who promised to involve Poland on Muscovy's side if that should be necessary.) Accordingly, by 1700 all sides were preparing for the outbreak of what was to be called the Great Northern War.

Mazepa during the Great Northern War

Notwithstanding the impressive diplomatic and military alliance he had forged, Peter soon discovered that he had a formidable foe in the eighteen-year-old King Charles XII of Sweden (reigned 1697–1718). In 1700, the first year of hostilities, Charles defeated the armies of Denmark and Muscovy at the Battle of Narva, near Russia's present-day border with Estonia. Charles then proceeded southwestward toward Poland, and by 1702 he had captured Warsaw and Cracow. Many Polish nobles gave their support to Charles, and Sweden proposed its own candidate, Stanisław Leszczyński, as king of Poland. Poland was thus divided between supporters of King August of Saxony and supporters of Sweden's ally, Leszczyński. It was at this point that Ivan Mazepa was drawn directly into the conflict.

Fearing that his ally, August, would be completely overwhelmed by Swedish forces and Polish Leszczyński supporters, Tsar Peter needed to act quickly. He desperately wanted to preserve the existence of an anti-Swedish Polish kingdom, and to this end in 1704 he ordered Mazepa to cross over into the Right Bank and to give support to the beleaguered King August of Poland. Mazepa promptly complied and led a Cossack army as far west as Poland's Ukrainian-inhabited palatinate of Belz. But Charles XII maintained the upper hand in western Ukrainian lands where the heavily fortified city of L'viv, in Galicia, fell to Swedish forces in September 1704. Mazepa was, however, able to hold on to the Right Bank palatinates of Kiev and Bratslav, where from 1705 a Cossack administrative stucture was set up. In effect, Ukrainian territory much as it had been under Bohdan Khmel'nyts'kyi, was reunited. The local Cossacks in the Right Bank welcomed the fact that Mazepa had driven out the Poles, although Tsar Peter now expected the region to be returned to his Polish ally, King August.

Mazepa had other plans, however. Since the outbreak of the Great Northern War in 1700, Ukraine's dependence on Muscovy had cost Ukraine dearly. More than 40,000 Cossacks had been sent into battle, and the annual casualty rates in some regiments were as high as 60 or 70 percent. Moreover, the Cossacks had had to serve primarily in regions far from their homeland or to engage in building fortifications or in other supportive and, in their eyes, militarily demeaning tasks for the Muscovite army and government. Most deeply resented was their having had to participate in the construction of the new imperial capital of St Petersburg, during which hundreds of Cossacks perished in the swamps and low-lying regions near the Gulf of Finland. The Cossacks were also apprehensive of Peter's plans to reorganize them and to send them to Prussia for training as foot soldiers (dragoons). Finally, the civilian population of Ukraine was deeply discontent. Between 1705 and 1708, both the hetman and the tsar received numerous complaints from peasants and town dwellers about the abusive conduct of Muscovite troops stationed on Ukrainian territory. All these factors contributed to an atmosphere in which Mazepa and some of his closest advisers began to have serious doubts about the advantages of being an ally of Muscovy, especially when so strong a power as Sweden's Charles XII seemed to be the dominant force in eastern Europe.

In 1705, when Mazepa and was setting up a Cossack administration on the Right Bank, the Ukrainian hetman was contacted by supporters of the pro-Swedish candidate for the Polish throne, Stanisław Leszczyński. At first Mazepa rejected the approach, but a year later he was more receptive. Nothing specific was agreed upon, but as time passed it seemed to Mazepa that Ukraine, which had suffered as a result of Tsar Peter's military ventures, might best be served by an alliance with Poland and, in particular, with its Swedish protectors. Mazepa seemed to be following in the footsteps of Bohdan Khmel'nyts'kyi, who during the early 1650s had tried to forge a Cossack alliance with Protestant countries in which Sweden would play a leading role. Again, no firm decisions were reached. Mazepa's negotiations were kept secret, and certainly no plans were made for an uprising against Muscovy. Mazepa remained Peter's faithful servant. External events, however, forced Mazepa to reconsider his position.

Having decisively defeated August of Saxony in 1706, and having installed the pro-Swedish King Stanisław I Leszczyński (reigned 1706–1709) on the Polish throne, Charles XII led a force of 50,000 men eastward toward Moscow in early

1708. At the same time, rumors spread that Charles's Polish ally King Stanisław was about to attack Left Bank Ukraine. Mazepa turned to Peter, requesting Muscovite troops to help in the Cossack defense. Peter refused, however, claiming he had no forces to spare. In the context of other complaints against the Muscovites, this refusal seemed to Mazepa a breach of the Pereiaslav accord. At that moment, in the summer of 1708, Charles XII himself suddenly turned southward toward Ukraine in order to rest and to strengthen his army as the first step in a planned sweep around the right flank of the Muscovite army. In response, Peter dispatched Muscovite troops under Prince Aleksandr Menshikov to intercept the Swedes, and ordered Mazepa to attack the invaders. Mazepa was now faced with a dilemma: obey the tsar's orders as he had done so many times in the past, or join Charles in the hope that a Cossack-Swedish alliance might bring eventual peace and political advantages to Ukraine. After delaying several weeks in a desperate attempt to put off the inevitable, Mazepa finally made his decision in October 1708. With fewer than 4,000 Cossacks, he defected to the Swedes. In return for the hetman's support and a Cossack uprising against Muscovy, Sweden, which Mazepa thought soon to be the undisputed power in eastern as well as northern Europe, would guarantee the independence of a Cossack Ukraine on both banks of the Dnieper River. Both these hopes turned out to be illusions. Mazepa had made no plans for a popular uprising, and none occurred.

When Peter learned of Mazepa's defection, he was shocked, disbelieving that the seventy-year-old hetman to whom he had remained loyal despite frequent denunciations from Ukraine (one had been brought to him from the Hetmanate's general judge, Vasyl' Kochubei, and the colonel of the Poltava regiment, Ivan Iskra, as recently as 1708) would turn on him. But finally the tsar had to believe the truth. His retribution was swift. He ordered the advancing Muscovite army under Prince Menshikov to take the hetman's capital, Baturyn. On 2 November 1708 Baturyn fell to the Muscovite troops, and for the next three days all Cossack government buildings were ransacked and destroyed. The inhabitants fared no better and, as recent archeological excavations have revealed, between 13,000 and 15,000 men and women (including the elderly and children) were massacred. Many bodies were summarily thrown into the Seim River whose waters ran blood red for several days. The object was to erase all memory of Baturyn as the center of Cossackdom.

The Muscovite authorities designated the town of Hlukhiv as the new Cossack capital, and it was there that they arranged for the election of a new hetman, Ivan Skoropads'kyi. Tsar Peter I himself arrived in Hlukhiv, where he participated in ceremonies to show present and future generations what fate awaited "traitors" to the Muscovite state. On 5 November 1708, an effigy of Mazepa was hung in the public square and the hetman's name was thrice declared an anathema in Orthodox Church services held simultaneously in Hlukhiv and Moscow. As for supporters of Mazepa who could be found, a special court was established in Lebedyn, where over 900 Cossack officers were tortured, found guilty, and executed. During this nightmare, several Cossacks turned informer and were richly rewarded for their services.

Meanwhile, Mazepa and his followers in the Swedish camp were joined by an unexpected ally, the Zaporozhian Cossacks led by Kost' Hordiienko. Hordiienko had become disillusioned with Muscovy's anti-Tatar policies and now accepted the

MAZEPA'S DEFECTION

In a sense, the decision taken by Ivan Mazepa in October 1708 to form an alliance with the Swedish king was just another example of Cossack actions following the 1654 agreement of Pereiaslav. Was that agreement, and the subsequent revisions, an indication of permanent Cossack subordination to the rule of the Muscovite tsars? Or was it a political contract that could be broken if either of the parties did not fulfill its contractual obligations? Mazepa justified his action with the following explanation, as subsequently related by his successor and protégé, Pylyp Orlyk.

After returning to Baturyn with the Swedish King, I intended to write a letter to his Tsarist Majesty expressing our gratefulness and listing all our previous and current grievances: the privileges that had been curtailed and the impending destruction that faced the entire population. In conclusion, [I intended] to declare that we, having voluntarily acquiesced to the authority of his Tsarist Majesty for the sake of the unified Eastern Faith, now, being a free people, we wish to withdraw, with expressions of our gratitude for the Tsar's protection and not wishing to raise our hands in the shedding of Christian blood. We will look forward, under the protection of the Swedish King, to our complete liberation.

Commenting on Mazepa's decision, the Ukrainian-Canadian historian Orest Subtelny writes:

Mazepa's line of argument is striking in how often certain phrases and ideas are repeated and stressed: rights and privileges; overlordship freely chosen and open to recall; and protection, always the issue of protection. For anyone with an acquaintance with medieval political theory, these concepts strike a familiar note. They are the components of the contractual principle, European feudalism's most common regulator of the political relations between sovereigns and regional elites. ...

The contractual arrangement was an act of mutual obligation. The vassal promised his lord obedience, service, and loyalty in return for the latter's protection and respect for the vassal's privileges and the traditions of his land. If the vassal had good reason to believe that his lord was breaking his obligations, he had the right – the famous *ius resistendi* – to rise against him to protect his interests. Thus, in theory, the lord as well as the vassal could be guilty of disloyalty. Throughout Europe, the contractual principle rested on the prevailing cornerstone of legal and moral authority – custom. The German *Schwabenspiegel*, one of the primary sources for customary law in East Central Europe, provided a concise summary of the principle: 'We should serve our sovereigns because they protect us, but if they will no longer defend us, then we owe them no more service.' Mazepa's position could not have been stated more succinctly.

SOURCE: Orest Subtelny, "Mazepa, Peter I, and the Question of Treason," *Harvard Ukrainian Studies*, II, 2 (Cambridge, Mass. 1978), pp. 170–171.

idea of the Swedish alliance. In the spring of 1709, about 8,000 Zaporozhian Cossacks agreed to fight alongside the Swedish army. In their absence, however, a Muscovite army attacked their stronghold, the Stara Sich, and destroyed it.

Despite military defeats at the hands of the Muscovite army during the winter of 1708–1709, Charles XII decided to take the initiative and to advance toward Moscow indirectly via Ukraine (see map 21). In May 1709, the Swedish army under Charles XII, with Mazepa and his Zaporozhian Cossack allies (a total force of 22,000 to 28,000), reached the city of Poltava, on the Left Bank. They were met on 8 July by a Muscovite army which with its Cossack allies numbered 40,000. Commanded by Tsar Peter I himself, the Muscovite forces won a resounding victory. Although all the leading Swedish generals and officers were captured, Charles XII and Mazepa managed to escape and make their way to the Ottoman Empire. Even though hostilities were to continue along the Baltic Sea coast, the Battle of Poltava in July 1709 proved an important turning point. Sweden's heretofore dominant role in eastern and central Europe, especially its influence in Poland, was coming to an end. Sweden's place was taken by the tsardom of Muscovy, which under its powerful ruler Peter I would soon be renamed the Russian Empire.

Mazepa and Ukraine after Poltava

The epilogue to Poltava was disastrous for Ukraine. Those Cossack officers who had previously supported Mazepa but had denounced him in an effort to gain favor with the tsar were now stripped of their recently won rewards, tried for high treason, and executed. Cossack autonomy in the Hetmanate was substantially reduced, and the new hetman, Ivan Skoropads'kyi, became a puppet in the hands of Muscovite officials stationed in Hlukhiv to keep watch over him.

Two months after the Battle of Poltava Mazepa died in exile in Bendery, an Ottoman-ruled town along the lower Dniester River. The Cossacks who were with him, however, continued their struggle. Based in Bendery, they formed what might be considered the first Ukrainian political emigration. They chose a successor to Mazepa, Pylyp Orlyk, who formulated a political program as part of a treaty with the Zaporozhian Cossacks. Orlyk's program contained a constitution for a proposed independent Ukrainian state. In 1711, the exiled hetman signed a treaty of alliance with the Crimean Tatars, and he managed to negotiate an agreement with the Ottoman Empire which recognized his authority over Right Bank Ukraine and Zaporozhia. That same year Orlyk led the first of several campaigns against Muscovite forces in the Right Bank, although he failed to obtain the support of the local inhabitants, largely because of the pillaging and enslavement of civilians carried out by his Crimean Tatar allies. After the defeat of Orlyk's last campaign in 1714, he went permanently into exile.

Tsar Peter I was worried by Orlyk's incursions into the Polish-controlled Right Bank and, in particular, by an Ottoman declaration of war against Muscovy, prompted by diplomatic activity in Istanbul on the part of Charles XII. In response, Peter led a Muscovite army in an attack on the Ottoman Empire. Along the way, his troops occupied the Right Bank and scattered what remained of Hetman Orlyk's forces. By July 1711, the Muscovite forces were deep into the Ottoman principality of Moldavia, where they hoped to obtain help from the local Orthodox population. This time Peter went too far, however, and his Muscovite forces were resoundly defeated by the Ottoman Turks along the lower Prut River.

Thus, two years after his triumph at Poltava, Peter experienced a major setback at the hands of the Ottomans. As a result, Muscovy was forced to surrender the fortress at Azov as well as other territory along the northern shore of the Sea of Azov which it had fought so hard to acquire during the last decades of the seventeenth century. Muscovy also had to remove its forces from the Right Bank and to renounce any claim to that region of Ukraine which was to remain part of Poland. In the wake of this reassertion of Ottoman power, the remaining Zaporozhian Cossacks from Orlyk's army accepted protection from the Ottoman Empire and established a new *sich* at Oleshky, near the mouth of the Dnieper River (see map 17).

In a sense, the years between 1687 and 1711, dominated in eastern Europe by the figures of Charles XII of Sweden and Peter I of Muscovy and in Ukraine by that of Hetman Ivan Mazepa, were an extension of the Period of Ruin that had racked the country after the death of Bohdan Khmel'nyts'kyi in 1657. From the very beginning of Mazepa's tenure as hetman, his Cossack armies had been called on to participate in Muscovy's wars against the Ottoman Empire in the south and against Sweden in the north. Only at the very end did Mazepa abandon his alliance with the tsar in return for a vaguely conceived independence under a Swedish protectorate. Mazepa's decision came too late and without preparation. In the end, its only result was to divide Ukrainian society even further, to make it more dependent than ever on Muscovy, and to hasten what turned out to be the dissolution of Cossack autonomy.

21

Socioeconomic and Cultural
Developments in the Cossack State

The momentous events of the revolutionary era that began in 1648 under Bohdan Khmel'nyts'kyi brought changes in the balance of power among the region's
leading states – Poland, Muscovy, and the Ottoman Empire. The era also had a
profound effect on the social structure of Ukrainian society. At first glance, little
change is apparent, since at least six of the social estates that existed in Ukraine
before 1648 were still in existence in the Cossack state: the crown, the nobility,
the Cossacks, the clergy, the townspeople, and the peasants. There were, however,
significant changes in the relative importance of certain social estates as well as in
the status of groups within the individual strata.

For instance, the crown, or royal estate, represented by the Polish king before
1648, was now represented, at least on territory under Muscovite hegemony, by
the tsar of Muscovy. Two groups, the Rus' gentry and the Cossacks, had their status recognized, while others, such as the Roman Catholic and Uniate clergy and
the Jews, were driven out of Cossack-ruled lands and forced to live on Right Bank
Ukrainian territory that remained under Polish rule. Finally, most peasants in the
Cossack state were freed from their labor obligations and the other duties owed to
their estate landlords.

Social structure

The new estate of the nobility resulted from a merger of some older nobles with
members of the Cossack officer elite, or *starshyna*. Whereas the upheaval of 1648
and succeeding years forced the Polish and polonized magnates and gentry to flee
the lands under Cossack rule, many of the lesser gentry of Orthodox Rus' background joined the Cossack cause, first fighting in Khmel'nyts'kyi's armies and then
joining the administration of the fledgling Cossack state that came into existence
in 1649. In fact, many of Khmel'nyts'kyi's successors in the office of hetman (Ivan
Vyhovs'kyi, Pavlo Teteria, Ivan Mazepa) were members of the gentry who joined
the Cossacks. The gentry who served the new state were allowed to retain their
landed estates as well as the services of the peasants living on them. This phenomenon was particularly widespread in the northernmost region of the Cossack state

SOCIAL ESTATES IN THE COSSACK STATE

1 **Crown**
   the Muscovite tsar
2 **Nobility**
   hereditary Rus' magnates and
      gentry
   Cossack gentry – Distinguished
      Military Fellows
3 **Cossacks**
   officers
   rank and file
4 **Clergy** (Orthodox)
   black, or monastic, clergy
   white, or married, clergy

5 **Townspeople**
   patricians
   merchants
   artisans
   workers
6 **Peasants**
   manorial and monastic
      peasants
   communal peasants
   free peasant homesteaders

(the old Chernihiv palatinate, with its region of Starodub), where, with the exception of the Polish and polonized Rus' magnates, who were driven out, the status of the nobility effectively did not change. In other words, service to the Cossack state rather than hereditary status from Polish times was what allowed the former Rus' gentry to retain its position as the elite in Ukrainian society.

The desire for hereditary noble status had been the goal of the upper-echelon, or registered, Cossacks well before 1648. Whereas all Cossack efforts to enter the noble estate had been unsuccessful during Polish rule, entry now became possible in the new Cossack state. The process lasted for several decades during the second half of the seventeenth century and resulted in the creation of a social stratum known as the Distinguished Military Fellows (*Znachni viis'kovi tovaryshi*). For all intents and purposes, this group became the core of the new noble estate.

The Distinguished Military Fellows were drawn from among the most economically prosperous Cossacks and nobles in the service of the Cossack state. The largest proportion were from the *starshyna*, who manned the highest military and administrative posts in the government. Since the state, especially at times of great instability such as the Period of Ruin, was unable to pay for the services of its administrators, it recompensed them by assigning to each official post properties such as landed estates, mills, fishing ponds, or the privilege of distilling alcohol (*propinatsiia*). In a continuation of the previous Polish practice, Cossack officials were initially allowed to keep these properties only on a temporary basis, that is, for as long as the state needed their services. It was not long before the peasants who resided on such lands were expected to carry out the "customary service," although this time to the new landlord, a Cossack governmental official. By the end of the seventeenth century, many of these Cossack "service officials," like their noble counterparts, had gained the right to retain the property assigned to them even after leaving governmental service. This meant they were able to maintain landholdings within their families, who then received a hereditary gentry title to be held by the future descendants of these new members of the Cossack nobility. In this manner, the former Polish and polonized Ukrainian magnates and gentry were replaced by Orthodox Rus' families loyal to the Cossack state, families to which some of the leading figures of the time belonged – Nemyrych, Mazepa, Skoropads'kyi, Apostol, Myklashevs'kyi, Horlenko, Kochubei – each of whom acquired landed estates of enormous size and wealth.

In theory, such privileges were available to all Cossacks on the register, the number of whom was set as high as 60,000 following the agreement of Pereiaslav in 1654 but was later reduced by the Muscovite government to 30,000 in 1669. In practice, however, access to the noble status was limited to the Distinguished Military Fellows. These were primarily officials in the immediate entourage of the hetman's administration (Fellows of the Standard, or *bunchukovi tovaryshi*), military leaders in the central administration (Military Fellows, or *viis'kovi tovaryshi*), and the leading officials of the regimental districts (Fellows of the Banner, or *znachkovi tovaryshi*). As members of the Distinguished Military Fellows, they had their names entered on special rosters (*komputy*), which later served as proof of membership in the highest social stratum in the Cossack state. Having attained such status and privileges, the Cossack nobles were intent on maintaining the exclusiveness of their group and were therefore reluctant to allow newcomers into their ranks.

Below the uppermost echelons of the *starshyna*, who entered the noble estate, the remaining Cossack estate consisted of lower-level officers and rank-and-file members. While in subsesquent years a certain number of these ordinary Cossacks did by various means enter the hereditary noble group of the Distinguished Military Fellows, the vast majority were unable to do so. Not surprisingly, those who were left out, the common Cossacks (*chern'*), resented their upper-class brethren-turned-gentry, and they rebelled against the hetman and his entourage, notably during the Period of Ruin. The stronghold of the rank-and-file Cossacks remained in Zaporozhia, which continued to serve as an asylum for all kinds of discontented people from the Hetmanate and other parts of Ukraine.

Like the noble and Cossack estates, the clerical estate underwent internal rearrangement. The Catholic and Uniate clergy, both of which were dependent upon and associated with Polish rule, were driven out of the Cossack state. In contrast, the Orthodox clergy held an especially privileged position and to an extent were even coopted into the leading Cossack governmental circles. The black, or monastic, clergy in particular was able to raise its status. For instance, at no time during or after the Khmel'nyts'kyi era were peasants legally permitted to abjure their duties on monastic lands. Moreover, the monastic clergy was exempt from taxes, and the monasteries under its control had treasuries and landholdings (worked by manorial peasants) whose value usually far exceeded that of the estates of secular landlords. The Orthodox hierarchy accordingly was on an economic and social par with the most powerful nobles, and bishops and abbots were usually elected from among the nobility.

The so-called white, or married, clergy also had a favorable status in the Cossack social structure. They too were exempt from taxes, and their male offspring generally entered the priesthood or the Cossack civil service. Priests often became

Cossacks – usually members of the *starshyna* – and vice versa. The ease with which the offspring of priests could enter the noble and Cossack strata precluded the development of a closed clerical estate. The interests of the clerical estate per se were most consistently maintained and defended by the black, or monastic, clergy.

The fifth and perhaps the least important of the social estates was that of the townspeople, or burghers. Their status depended on the rights enjoyed by urban areas. Numerous towns in the Cossack state enjoyed the self-governing privileges of Magdeburg Law, whereby the municipal government had control over its own courts, finances, and taxes. Most of these centers had received the privilege from Poland before 1648; a few more received it from Cossack courts (Oster, Kozelets'). The remaining towns, especially new ones which sprang up in the Left Bank and which did not enjoy the privileges of Magdeburg Law, were considered by Cossack leaders as sources of personal profit and income for the state. Cossack leaders often controlled commerce and took over municipal offices themselves, thus limiting the prerogatives of the town dwellers. Such appropriation was made easy by the smallness of the towns, most of them not exceeding 5,000 inhabitants. Even the largest towns (Kiev, Pereiaslav, Korsun', Uman') had no more than 15,000 inhabitants. Within the towns, the rich patricians' wealth enabled them to hold office in the Cossack state, and many bought themselves the title of nobility. Artisans and workers, in contrast, were often indistinguishable from the rank-and-file Cossacks or the peasants. In such a fluid social system, a strong burgher estate, with interests of its own, never developed.

One group in traditional Ukrainian society, the Jews, who lived partly in the towns and partly in the countryside, had its status radically changed after 1648. Previously an integral part of the Polish arenda economic system, the Jews were initially barred from lands under the control of the Cossacks unless they converted to Christianity. Some did convert, thereby giving up their Judaism but remaining as urban-dwelling merchants and in some instances becoming Cossacks. A few Cossacks of Jewish ancestry rose to leading positions in the government (from the Hertsyk, Markovych, and Kryzhanivs'kyi families). Those who did not convert were exiled to the Polish-controlled Right Bank.

The vacancy left by Jewish merchants and their previous role in international trade was soon filled by another group, Orthodox Christian Greeks. As early as 1657, Hetman Khmel'nyts'kyi issued a decree (*universal*) granting Greek merchants special trading and legal privileges, including the right to their own courts. Subsequent hetmans extended further trading privileges to the country's Greek merchants. In particular, it was in Nizhyn where, after 1675, Greeks not only dominated the city's economic and civic life, but also later had their own Greek Orthodox church community, brotherhood, and court system.

The last and largest estate was the peasantry. The status of the peasantry was naturally affected by the patterns of landholding. In a sense, the whole seventeenth century witnessed a struggle among three types of landholding system on Ukrainian territory: (1) the manorial estate (*latifundium*), on which peasants owed certain labor duties; (2) the communally owned peasant land; and (3) the individual peasant homestead. The first type, the manorial estate, was a product of Polish rule and was limited to areas under its control. The second and third categories, communal and individual peasant holdings, were typical of those territories beyond the direct control of Polish governmental authority, that is, the Cossack borderlands of the far eastern Left Bank and, in particular, Zaporozhia. In these two regions, communal ownership seemed to prevail until the early seventeenth century.

The social and political changes resulting from the Khmel'nyts'kyi uprising of 1648 undermined the manorial type of landholding, as Polish landlords were driven from those parts of Ukraine held by the Cossacks, and peasants left their manors to join the rebel armies. Nonetheless, the manorial system was not abolished entirely, because the Ukrainian gentry landowners who fought with Khmel'nyts'kyi as well as the Orthodox monasteries expected their peasants to remain and continue to perform their labor obligations. Thus, the second half of the seventeenth century, especially on the Left Bank, witnessed a struggle between the reimposition or continuation of the manorial system on the part of the Cossack gentry and Orthodox monasteries on the one hand, and the tendency of demobilized rank-and-file Cossacks and recalcitrant peasants to set up individual homesteads on the other hand.

As a result of the uprising of 1648, all manors (*latifundia*) belonging to the Polish crown were declared free military villages. They included (1) lands given to Cossack officers as remuneration for their services; and (2) lands within self-governing villages inhabited by peasants, who retained their personal freedom although they had to pay taxes. These two types of free military village represented approximately 50 percent of all landed property in the Cossack state. The other half consisted of lands owned outright by Cossack and Ukrainian gentry (33 percent) and lands under the jurisdiction of the Orthodox Church (17 percent).

The last decades of the seventeenth century and especially the eighteenth century witnessed the transformation of free military villages held by Cossack officers into de facto hereditary landholdings as well as an increase in the size of already-existing hereditary manorial estates, whether owned by the Cossack gentry or by Orthodox monasteries. Both these trends tended to reduce the number of free peasant homesteads. At the same time, the labor obligations and other duties of peasants living on the hereditary manors continued to increase, with the result that by the end of the seventeenth century it was common practice for peasants to have to work two days a week for their landlords. Nonetheless, the peasants in the Cossack state and, later, the Hetmanate never became fully enserfed. They retained their freedom of movement and personal rights as long as the Hetmanate existed.

Thus, while the Khmel'nyts'kyi uprising of 1648 and the Period of Ruin which followed (1654–1686) witnessed great political and military changes, including the incorporation of the Left Bank and Zaporozhia into the tsardom of Muscovy, the basic social structure in those regions, with its nobility, Cossacks, clergy, and peasants, and the noticeable absence of a strong urban estate, remained unaltered and essentially the same as under Polish rule.

Economic developments

Given the almost unending military conflict that took place throughout much of Ukrainian territory during the Khmel'nyts'kyi era and Period of Ruin, it is not surprising that the economy generally suffered a decline during the years 1648 to 1686. Before 1648, Ukraine's economic wealth had been increasingly based on agriculture, especially the growing of grain such as wheat, which was shipped north from the Right Bank and exported through the Polish port of Danzig/Gdańsk on the Baltic. The Khmel'nyts'kyi uprising and subsequent military conflicts had a devastating effect on this trade, which can be graphically illustrated by the following figures. In 1648, Polish grain exports through Danzig reached 32 million hundredweight units (1.5 million metric tons); by 1715, they had decreased to less than 1 million hundredweight units (45.5 thousand metric tons), a mere three percent of the pre-revolutionary figure.

The figures reveal not simply a loss of production, but also a change in the type of produce grown in Ukraine and a change in trade patterns. With respect to the type of produce, there was less emphasis on wheat and more on barley, hops, buckwheat, oats, millet, hemp, and flax. Mulberry trees for silk production were grown in certain areas, especially near Kiev. Added to these agricultural products were alcohol, tar, wood, and, especially, potash. As for trade patterns, commerce with Poland decreased during the Period of Ruin, while trade with the Cossacks' new sovereign, Muscovy, increased. Even more important, however, was Cossack trade with the Islamic world, especially the Ottoman Empire and the Crimean Khanate. This trade actually dominated the Cossack state and Hetmanate until the first quarter of the eighteenth century. To the Ottoman Empire were sent meat, furs, and grain in return for silk, Oriental rugs, velvet, Persian textiles, cotton material, and fruits. With the Crimea Ukraine exchanged grain for horses, cattle, and sheep. Most of this trade was carried out by Turkish, Armenian, Jewish, and Greek merchants, especially from the multinational urban areas along the Crimean coast. Some of these traders moved north, where they settled permanently and came to play an important role in the towns and cities of Ukrainian lands within Poland and Muscovy.

Beginning with Bohdan Khmel'nyts'kyi, most Cossack hetmans passed decrees to stimulate foreign trade. The reason for their encouragement of trade was simple: in a period of war and the breakdown of the traditional economic relationship with the Polish lands in the west, the Cossack leadership needed a constant source of income, and one of the most reliable sources was the duties and tariffs levied on foreign trade.

The Cossacks also promoted industry, although not until after 1686 was substantial growth in this sector possible. Until 1648, the most important industry was iron mining and processing. On the eve of the uprising, there were about 100 ore pits and iron works in the Ukrainian lands, owned by either the nobility or the monasteries. Both the nobles and the monasteries used manorial peasants to work in these industries as part of their labor duties. When the uprising drove out the Polish magnates, the peasants refused to work. Only the monastery-owned industrial enterprises continued to function and even to flourish because of the increased need for iron for armaments and the decline in the total number of operational plants. By the 1750s, there were only twenty-eight iron plants left, mostly in the Polish-ruled Right Bank.

Church and state

Religion remained an important part of life in Ukraine under the Cossack state. The Cossacks had been defenders of Orthodoxy since the early seventeenth century; accordingly, the Orthodox Church gained from the changes that took place after 1648. In fact, the Orthodox Church was made the beneficiary by Khmel'nyts'kyi and his successors of properties confiscated from the Uniate and Roman Catholic churches located in Cossack-held territory. The increasing social and economic prestige of the Orthodox Church also prompted its leaders to expect to play a more decisive role in governmental affairs. The result was at times misunderstanding and conflict of interest between church hierarchs and Cossack hetmans.

Even more problematic was the Cossack state's foreign policy and its implications for the Orthodox Church in Ukraine. Although many hierarchs in Ukraine had looked to Muscovy for support, especially during the first half of the seventeenth century, the attitude of some began to change after the church's position was legalized in Poland in 1632 and when the dynamic Petro Mohyla became metropolitan. Mohyla's successors, Syl'vestr Kosiv (reigned 1647–1657) and Dionysii Balaban (reigned 1657–1663) were openly opposed to Muscovy, in particular because they feared that the Orthodox Church in Ukraine, still under the jurisdiction of the ecumenical patriarch in Constantinople, might be subordinated to the patriarch in Moscow. It was with this concern in mind that Metropolitan Kosiv remained unenthusiastic during the Pereiaslav negotiations of 1654. In response to the tsar's demands that the Orthodox Metropolitanate of Kiev be placed under the jurisdiction of the Patriarchate of Moscow, Kosiv reiterated that his church's "first freedom" was obedience to the ecumenical patriarch of Constantinople. Such dichotomous views on the question of jurisdiction for the Orthodox Metropolitanate of Kiev remained unresolved during the years of uncertainty that marked the Period of Ruin.

It was not long, however, before the fears of Metropolitan Kosiv and his successor, Balaban, proved justified. In the decades after 1654, the Orthodox eparchies of the Kievan metropolitanate located in Belarus and Muscovy (Mstsistlaŭ and Chernihiv) were gradually placed under the jurisdiction of the patriarch of Moscow. Whenever bishops in these eparchies died, the Moscow patriarch simply appointed new ones, who were considered the "guardians" for Muscovy of the Metropolitanate of Kiev. In Kiev itself, the last metropolitan to recognize the authority of Constantinople died in 1675; thenceforth, the see was administered by Moscow-appointed "guardians." Eventually, the tsar's government directed the Cossack hetman Ivan Samoilovych to organize a synod (church council) to elect a metropolitan for Kiev who would be expected to recognize the patriarch of Moscow as his superior. In 1685, Bishop Gedeon Chetvertyns'kyi of Luts'k was elected Orthodox metropolitan of Kiev (reigned 1685–1690), and before the end of the year he traveled to Moscow to be consecrated by the patriarch. In 1686, the ecumenical patriarch of Constantinople, otherwise suspicious of Muscovy's intentions, approved the appointment. The decisive factor was pressure on the ecumenical patriarch by the Ottoman government, which in the political circumstances of the moment was concerned not to alienate Muscovy.

This meant that after 1686, the Orthodox faithful living in Muscovite territory (including the Cossack state) came under the ecclesiastical jurisdiction of the autocephalous Russian Orthodox Church headed by its patriarch in Moscow. In Ukrainian lands within Muscovy, the Orthodox jurisdiction included the Eparchy of Chernihiv and the Metropolitan-Archeparchy of Kiev (from which the Eparchy of Pereiaslav was created in 1701), while the Sloboda Ukraine was incorporated into the Eparchy of Belgorod. The Uniate Metropolitan of Kiev also continued to exist, although its metropolitans (elected by church councils and approved by the pope) were never able to reside in Cossack- and Muscovite-controlled Kiev. Instead, they were forced to move from residence to residence in Polish-Lithuanian territory that had not yet come under Muscovite or Russian rule. Thus, the year 1686 marks another important step in Muscovy's efforts to implement its long-standing claim to the political, religious, and cultural heritage of lands once belonging to Kievan Rus'.

Cultural developments

Cultural life in the Cossack state also reflected greater rapprochement between Ukrainian lands and Muscovy. Despite the military and social disruptions during the Period of Ruin, which had weakened the traditional centers of learning such as the Kievan Collegium and the brotherhood schools, a degree of intellectual activity continued. Older printing presses in L'viv (Galicia), Pochaïv (Volhynia), and Kiev continued to publish books, and at various times printing shops operated in Novhorod-Sivers'kyi and Chernihiv. Most of the book production from this period consisted of sermon literature by churchmen like the Bishop of Chernihiv, Lazar Baranovych (reigned 1657–1694), Antonii Radyvylovs'kyi, and Ioanikii Galiatovs'kyi, the rector of the Kievan Collegium and the author of the most famous work in the sermon genre, *Kliuch razuminnia* (The Key to Understanding, 1659). But perhaps the most outstanding religious work to date from the period was the collection of episodes in the lives of monks in Kiev's Monastery of the Caves. The tales had been gathered together as early as the thirteenth century but were not published until the seventeenth century. They first appeared in Polish (1635) and finally in Church Slavonic (1661) under the title *Paterik (Kievo-Pecherskii Paterik)*, compiled by the monastery's influential archimandrite, Inokentii Gizel'.

The Cossack state also provided an appropriate environment for another kind of literary endeavor – the recounting and writing of history. At the level of the broad populace, the oral folk tradition expressed in epic songs (*dumy*) from the early seventeenth century was continued and enriched by songs about Bohdan Khmel'nyts'kyi, his successors, and other Cossack exploits. Perhaps even more ideologically significant was the copying of medieval chronicles from the Kievan period, with new chronological supplements that traced the exploits of the Cossacks. Several works of this nature were compiled during the 1670s and 1680s, including the *Kroinika z litopistsov starodavnikh* (Chronicle from Ancient Chroniclers) by Teodosii Safonovych and the *Obshirnyi sinopsis ruskii* (Comprehensive Rus' Chronicle) by Panteleimon Kokhanovs'kyi.

Clearly the most important and subsequently the most influential historical work to date from this period was the *Sinopsis ili kratkoe sobranie* (Synopsis, or A Short Collection) attributed to Inokentii Gizel'. First published in Kiev in 1674, it was republished twice (1678 and 1680), and then in several subsequent editions in Muscovy up until the beginning of the nineteenth century. The *Sinopsis* quickly became the most popular and widely used textbook in Ukraine and Muscovy. Its real significance lies in the fact that it is the first attempt at providing a historical continuum for the history of the East Slavs from earliest times to the seventeenth century – and one, moreover, which justified Muscovy's self-perception as the successor to the Kievan inheritance.

According to the *Sinopsis*, the autocracy of the Muscovite tsars derived from the Kievan grand princes. Thus, Moscow, the capital of all Rus' (as indicated in the tsar's title), was the natural successor to Kiev. From such a perspective, the union of Cossack Ukraine with Muscovy in 1654 was viewed as simply the logical conclusion of history – a renewal of the unity of the Rus' lands. Gizel' even added an ethnic element, speaking of a so-called Slaveno-Rus' nation. And in what was to become the classic pattern of the "foundation myth" (dear to the hearts of all ideologists of nation-building), Moscow was described as having been founded by Mosokh, the sixth son of Japheth and a grandson of Noah. Hence, with biblical sanction, the city's ostensible founder was now transformed into the forefather of all the Rus' peoples. In the end, whether or not it was actually Gizel' who composed the *Sinopsis*, and if so, whether subsequent editions may have changed the emphasis of the original text, the fact remains that this influential book originated in an Orthodox cultural environment in Kiev. Moreover, it was that environment which formulated the first comprehensive historical framework for what later would become the Russian imperial view of eastern European history – namely, the displacement or transfer of power centers from Kiev, to Vladimir-na-Kliazma, to Moscow, and eventually to St Petersburg (see chapter 2).

Such a state of affairs, whereby intellectual leaders from peripheral areas were willing to provide an ideological underpinning for the new political order, was of course nothing new in Muscovy. After all, it had been the monk Filofei from provincial Pskov in the far northwest (at the time a satellite of Muscovy's enemy Novgorod) who provided Muscovy with its epithet "the Third Rome" soon after his native city fell to its eastern neighbor at the beginning of the sixteenth century. Now, in the second half of the seventeenth century, intellectuals from Kiev and Left Bank Ukraine were in the vanguard in promoting and justifying Muscovite rule in their homeland.

The apogee in the close relations between local Cossack rulers and the Orthodox Church, and correspondingly in the influence of churchmen from Ukraine in Muscovy, was reached during the reign of Hetman Ivan Mazepa. In his own desperate search to build a local power base, the "newcomer" Mazepa quickly befriended the Orthodox Church, further enriching it with gifts of money, land, and even whole villages. Together with the new Orthodox metropolitan of Kiev, Varlaam Iasyns'kyi (reigned 1690–1707), Mazepa helped to maintain the Kievan church's traditional autonomy in the face of the patriarch of Muscovy, under whose jurisdiction the Orthodox Church in Ukraine found itself after 1686.

Mazepa also had a strong personal commitment to education and the arts, and the Orthodox Church benefited directly from his cultural patronage. The Kievan Collegium, which had declined during the devastations of the Period of Ruin, was revived under Mazepa. Finally, at the hetman's instigation, a tsarist decree was issued in 1694 transforming the collegium into an academy, which meant that it gained administrative autonomy and could expand the range of subjects taught. In 1700, another collegium was established in Chernihiv, and higher education in Ukrainian lands was thereby strengthened further. These schools, especially the Kievan Academy, attracted and produced some of the leading Orthodox teachers and writers found anywhere in eastern Europe at the time, including Syluan Ozers'kyi, Ioasaf Krokovs'kyi, Stefan Iavors'kyi, and Teofan Prokopovych.

Perhaps the most monumental and lasting cultural achievement came in church architecture, marked by the initiation of several major projects during the first decade of Mazepa's rule, that is, before the Great Northern War began to take its financial and military toll. In fact, it is mainly on the basis of its architectural monuments that the whole era of Mazepa has been remembered as the flowering of the Ukrainian Cossack baroque. Although Baturyn remained the administrative capital of the Cossack state, it was to Kiev that Mazepa turned his attention. During the 1690s, the hetman initiated the construction of the Church of the Epiphany (Bohoiavlennia) and the Collegiate Church of St Nicholas, also known as the Great Nicholas (Velykyi Mykola), with its monumental wooden iconostasis, completed in 1696. Mazepa's tenure was also characterized by the restoration of several earlier structures, to which undulating baroque facades and cupolas were added. Among the restored and in some cases completely transformed structures in Kiev were the Collegiate Church of the Assumption in the Monastery of the Caves, the Monastery Church of St Michael of the Golden Domes, the St George Cathedral at the Vydubets'kyi Monastery (built 1696–1701), and, finally, the monumental eleventh-century Byzantine-style Cathedral of the Holy Wisdom, or Cathedral of St Sophia. By the mid-seventeenth century, the St Sophia had deteriorated to a virtual ruin. Restoration was begun under Metropolitan Petro Mohyla and continued by Mazepa between 1691 and 1705, and externally the cathedral was transformed into the baroque structure familiar to observers today. Beyond Kiev, Mazepa also underwrote the cost of constructing anew or restoring churches in Chernihiv, Baturyn, Hlukhiv, Pereiaslav, and Mhar.

In the realm of culture and its integral relationship with Orthodoxy, the era of Mazepa was thus characterized by an increasingly pronounced tendency among Ukrainian intellectuals to welcome their homeland's new relationship with Muscovy. Mazepa's patronage both raised the level of culture in Ukraine and increased the influence of Ukrainian culture and thought in Muscovy itself. The second half of the seventeenth century witnessed the beginnings of an exodus of Ukrainian intellectuals from the Kievan Collegium and, later, Academy to Moscow that would increase during the first decades of the eighteenth century. For their part, Muscovite tsars and patriarchs were more than anxious to tap the talent of those trained in the Kievan Academy, and a steady stream of figures like Epifanii Slavynets'kyi, Symeon Polots'kyi, Dmytro Tuptalo, and, eventually, Stefan Iavors'kyi and Teofan

Prokopovych were brought to Moscow, where they almost single-handedly transformed the educational, religious, and cultural life of the newest leading power in eastern Europe, Muscovy.

The transformation of Ukraine after 1648

The era that began with Khmel'nyts'kyi's uprising against Polish rule in 1648 ended more than a half century later with Ukrainian lands still under the rule of eastern Europe's three leading powers – Poland, Muscovy, and the Ottoman Empire. The relationship among these three powers with regard to Ukraine had changed, however. Muscovy was clearly the dominant force by the beginning of the eighteenth century.

In the midst of the international struggle for control of Ukrainian lands, the indigenous Cossacks also strove to carve out their own political destiny either by forming a semi-independent state or, in the case of Zaporozhia, by rejecting all formalized structures in favor of a traditional frontier society with little or no governmental presence. Neither the proponents of statehood nor those of an underdeveloped frontier were able to achieve their goals without outside aid. Both groups, therefore, turned at various times to Poland, Muscovy, the Ottoman Empire, and powers even farther afield, such as Sweden. In the end, the orientation toward Muscovy proved the most lasting, with the result that the Hetmanate and Zaporozhia became, as Sloboda Ukraine had previously become, fully a part of the Muscovite sphere. Certain Cossack leaders at times may have questioned the Muscovite orientation, but they were unable to stop the extension of that state's sphere of influence over Ukrainian lands.

During these same decades, which witnessed efforts in the direction of Cossack statehood, Ukrainian lands also experienced important socioeconomic and cultural transformations. Whereas the basic social structure remained intact, the composition and interrelation of the different strata were altered. The most important change was the replacement of the Polish nobility with a fledgling Cossack nobility and Orthodox clerical estate as the new elite in Ukrainian society. As for Ukraine's economy, its primary dependence on Poland came to an end, being replaced by greater interaction with the Crimean and Ottoman world to the south as well as a slow but steady trend toward interaction with Muscovy in the north. In terms of culture, the Orthodox Church, which included virtually all of Ukraine's intellectual leaders, was steadily being drawn into the orbit and service of Muscovy. The reorientation toward Muscovy in various quarters of Ukrainian society can therefore be seen as largely voluntary. It began among Orthodox sympathizers in the 1620s and 1630s, reached an important milestone with Khmel'nyts'kyi's momentous decision of 1654, and continued to develop during the rest of the seventeenth century, culminating during the era of Mazepa. The process was to go on throughout the eighteenth century.

PART FIVE

Ukrainian Lands in the Eighteenth Century

Ukraine's Autonomy and the Russian Empire

With the end of Mazepa's hetmanship and the failure of his successor, Pylyp Orlyk, to provoke a revolt on the Right Bank in 1711, Ukrainian territories remained divided between three states: Muscovy, Poland, and the Ottoman Empire. The most important of these Ukrainian territories were (1) the Hetmanate, Sloboda Ukraine, and Zaporozhia (from 1734) within Muscovy; (2) most of the Right Bank, Volhynia, Podolia, and Galicia within Poland; and (3) southern Ukraine within the Ottoman Empire or its vassal state, the Crimean Khanate. Two smaller regions in the far southwest were Bukovina in another Ottoman vassal state, Moldavia, and Transcarpathia in the Austrian-ruled Kingdom of Hungary. Of interest in this chapter are Ukraine's territories within Muscovy (Sloboda Ukraine, Zaporozhia, and the Hetmanate) and within the Ottoman Empire (in particular, the Crimean Khanate).

Muscovy becomes the Russian Empire

Peter I's military ventures at the beginning of the eighteenth century were both extensive and very costly. They did, however, set the stage for the transformation of the tsardom of Muscovy into the Russian Empire. This transformation actually occurred in 1721, when Peter adopted the title emperor, thereby renaming the tsardom of Muscovy (with its recently acquired territories) the Russian Empire. The change in name was more than symbolic since, during the reign of Peter, Muscovy (now Russia) became the leading state in eastern Europe. By the second decade of the eighteenth century, the formerly powerful Polish-Lithuanian Commonwealth was becoming a dependency of the Russian Empire, and Sweden's presence was on the decline. When, in 1721, the second stage of the Great Northern War came to an end, Russia was firmly established on the Baltic Sea, having acquired northern Latvia, Estonia, and the eastern shores of the Gulf of Finland. Symbolic of the Russian presence were the spires of St Petersburg, Peter's proverbial "window to the West" at the eastern end of the Gulf of Finland. Begun in 1703, the new capital of the Russian Empire was inaugurated in 1712.

While Sweden effectively had been checked in the north, Peter's military thrusts

MAP 21

UKRAINE, early 18th CENTURY

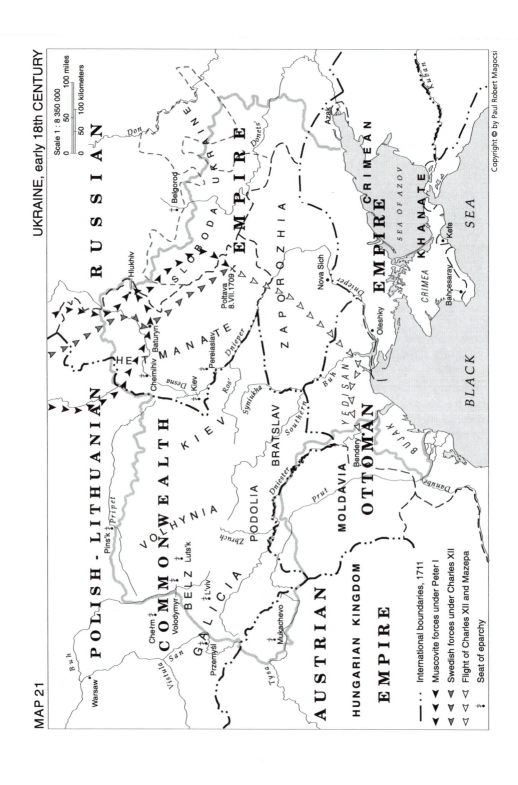

Scale 1 : 8 350 000

0   50   100 miles
0   50   100 kilometers

POLISH - LITHUANIAN
COMMONWEALTH

RUSSIAN EMPIRE

SLOBODA UKRAINE

HETMANATE

ZAPOROZHIA

CRIMEAN KHANATE

OTTOMAN EMPIRE

AUSTRIAN EMPIRE

HUNGARIAN KINGDOM

MOLDAVIA

PODOLIA

BRATSLAV

KIEV

GALICIA

BELZ

VOLHYNIA

YEDISAN

BUJAK

CRIMEA

BLACK SEA

SEA OF AZOV

Warsaw

Pins'k

Chełm
Volodymyr
Luts'k
Przemyśl
L'viv
Mukachevo

Chernihiv
Baturyn
Hlukhiv
Belgorod

Kiev
Pereiaslav
Poltava 8.VII.1709 ×

Nova Sich

Oleshky

Bendery

Bançesaray
Kefe
Azak

Don
Donets'
Desna
Dnieper
Ros'
Syniukha
Southern Buh
Dniester
Zbruch
Prut
Tysa
San
Vistula
Buh
Pripet
Kuban
Danube

Copyright © by Paul Robert Magocsi

· · ·   International boundaries, 1711
▼   Muscovite forces under Peter I
▽   Swedish forces under Charles XII
▽   Flight of Charles XII and Mazepa
‡   Seat of eparchy

against the Ottoman Empire were less decisive, and it was not until the second half of the eighteenth century that the Russian Empire was finally able to acquire control of the Crimea and the northern shores of the Black Sea. A truce with the Ottoman Empire and peace with Sweden and Poland after 1721, however, provided the Russian imperial government with the respite necessary for it to increase its control over its far-flung domains. Peter I and his successors – among them Anna (reigned 1730–1740) and most especially Catherine II (1762–1796) – set out to create an expanded bureaucracy and administration for a centralized state that was more and more anxious to remove any peculiarities of autonomy or even semi-independence that might have existed within lands under the tsar's sceptre. Ukrainian territories were a particular object of attention, and the last vestiges of autonomy in Ukraine were to disappear by the second half of the eighteenth century. The process occurred in stages and within three decades. The first territory to be fully incorporated into the Russian imperial governmental structure was Sloboda Ukraine in the 1760s; then followed Zaporozhia in the 1770s; and finally the Hetmanate and the Crimean Khanate in the 1780s.

Sloboda Ukraine

Sloboda Ukraine (*Slobids'ka Ukraïna*) was the first Ukrainian territory to become part of Muscovy. In Kievan times, it was a sparsely settled frontier region, and from the time of the Mongol invasion in the mid-thirteenth century it had remained largely uninhabited. Then, during the Cossack revolts against Polish rule in the seventeenth century, many people from both the Right Bank and the Left Bank who had hoped to find peace and refuge by going eastward to Muscovy were allowed to establish free settlements, or *slobody*, along the tsar's southern frontier, and from these the region derived its name. Muscovy encouraged such settlements, which together with its own fortified defensive system (the Belgorod Line) helped to protect central Russia from Tatar incursions. Beginning in 1638 and following each subsequent military and political upheaval in Cossack Ukraine, people fled eastward to what by then was known as Sloboda Ukraine. The last major influx of immigrants arrived in the 1730s, following the revolts in the Right Bank. In the late seventeenth century, the population of Sloboda Ukraine was approximately 120,000; a century later, in 1773, that number had increased more than fivefold to 660,000.

The newcomers brought with them the Cossack system of joint military and civil administrative organization which they had established on the Left and Right Banks. Already by 1650, four regiments had been formed in parts of Sloboda Ukraine, and in 1685 a fifth was added. They were, from west to east, the Sumy, Okhtyrka, Kharkiv, Izium, and Ostrogozhsk regiments, located on both sides of the present-day northeastern boundary of Ukraine. The Sloboda Ukraine was not only preoccupied with military affairs and the defense of the Russian Empire's southern frontier. Agriculture developed in the free (*sloboda*) villages and a few towns evolved from the forts that functioned as regimental settlements. The largest of these was Kharkiv (over 8,000 inhabitants in 1732), which eventually became the

MAP 22   SLOBODA UKRAINE

⊙ **Regimental center**   ▨▨ **Boundary of Ukraine, 2005**

▢ **Sloboda Ukraine**   ••••• **Regimental boundaries**
   ca.1700

ᴗᴗᴗ **Fortified lines**

Scale 1 : 4 800 000

0   50 miles

0   50 kilometers

Copyright © by Paul Robert Magocsi

most important economic, educational, and cultural center for the entire Sloboda Ukraine.

As in the Hetmanate, each regiment had its own colonel and staff of officers, the *starshyna,* who constituted the region's elite. Also as in the Hetmanate, the regiments in Sloboda Ukraine fulfilled both military and civil administrative functions. Unlike in other Cossack territories, the Sloboda regimental colonels were elected for life, and the Muscovite government did not allow them to be united under a higher office, such as that of hetman. In military matters, each Sloboda regiment was responsible to the government-appointed *voevoda* in Belgorod, while civil matters were regulated by charters (*gramoty*) issued by the authorities in Moscow, first by the Section for Social Ranks, and then after 1688 by the All-Russian Section of the Central Ministry for Foreign Affairs (Posolskii Prikaz). Thus, while Sloboda Ukraine enjoyed a high degree of local autonomy, its component regimental parts were forbidden to unite or to become part of the neighboring Hetmanate.

In 1732, the number of registered Cossacks was set at 23,000 in four of the Sloboda regiments, although as many as 85,000 troops could be mobilized at any one time to fight along with the Russian armies. The Sloboda Cossacks were employed by Muscovy in the seventeenth century to fight against recalcitrant hetmans (Vyhovs'kyi, Doroshenko, Briukhovets'kyi) and in the eighteenth century to serve in the Russian Empire's foreign campaigns (against Persia in 1722–1723 and Ottoman Turkey in 1736–1739). They were also used to build fortifications and canals in various parts of the empire.

The local autonomy of Sloboda Ukraine was left undisturbed until 1732. In that year, the imperial government under Empress Anna made the first attempt to dispense with Sloboda Ukraine's autonomous status. A census was taken; the number of registered Cossacks was fixed at 23,000, with all others being liable to taxes; certain privileges were removed; and all regiments were placed under the responsibility of a Russian official. Protests from Sloboda Ukraine won a temporary cancellation of these reforms, but the Russian government's long-term intentions were clear. Until the reforms were reinstated, imperial troops were stationed in the area. Finally, according to an imperial manifesto issued in July 1765, the traditional Cossack regiments were abolished and in each was formed a new light calvary (hussar) or lancer (uhlan) regiment. With this manifesto Empress Catherine II effectively abolished the autonomous status of the Sloboda Ukraine.

In its stead was created a unified Russian province called Sloboda Ukraine (*Slobodsko-ukrainskaia guberniia*), which was ruled by a governor-general resident in Kharkiv. Like other provincial governors in the empire, he was responsible directly to St Petersburg. The Cossacks were stripped of their traditional privileges and given the status of military residents: those who were not in actual military service had to pay taxes. As for the Cossack *starshyna* (officer elite), it was given a status equal to that of the Russian nobility. Despite some protests, Sloboda Ukraine after 1765 became an integral part of the Russian Empire.

Zaporozhia

The second of Ukraine's autonomous regions was Zaporozhia. It had a more turbulent history than Sloboda Ukraine, but its ultimate fate was the same: full incorporation into the Russian imperial governmental structure. From the time of the death of Bohdan Khmel'nyts'kyi in 1657, the Army of Lower Zaporozhia – as the region in question was officially known – followed a course that was independent of, and most often antagonistic toward, the hetmans and registered Cossack elite who ruled the Cossack state on both sides of the Dnieper River and, later, the Left Bank Hetmanate. As part of their anti-hetman policy, the Zaporozhians traditionally favored alliances with Muscovy. In the late seventeenth century, however, they began to be displeased with the tsar's anti-Crimean wars. The Zaporozhians rightly suspected that these wars would lead to an increase in the authority of the central government over all of southern Ukraine and eventually the Crimea, which would mean an end to the source of the Cossack's freebooting livelihood. Therefore, under their dynamic leader Kost' Hordiienko, the Zaporozhians broke with Peter I in 1709 and allied themselves instead with Ivan Mazepa and his Swedish protector, King Charles XII. The Muscovites responded by destroying the Zaporozhian Sich. This forced the Zaporozhians to establish new headquarters in Crimean territory at Oleshky, on the lower Dnieper, where between 1711 and 1734 they were under the protection of the Crimean khan.

MAP 23

ZAPOROZHIA AND NEW RUSSIA

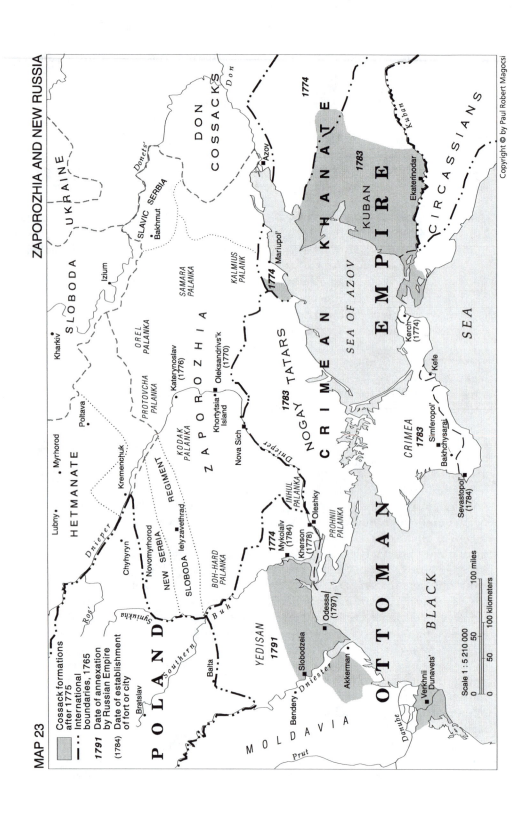

Cossack formations after 1775

—·—·— International boundaries, 1765

1791 Date of annexation by Russian Empire

(1784) Date of establishment of fort or city

Scale 1 : 5 210 000

0   50   100 miles

0   50   100 kilometers

POLAND

HETMANATE

Lubny •   • Myrhorod

Kharkiv ■

SLOBODA

Izium ■

Poltava •

Kremenchuk ■

Chyhyryn •

Novomyrhorod •

NEW SERBIA

SLOBODA REGIMENT

Ielyzavethrad ■

BOH-HARD PALANKA

Bratslav

Balta ■

YEDISAN
1791

Slobodzeia ■

Akkerman ■

Bendery •

MOLDAVIA

OTTOMAN

Verkhnii Dunavets' ■

Prut

Danube

BLACK

Odessa (1797) ■

Kherson (1778) ■

Mykolaiv (1784) ■
1774

Oleshky ■

PROHNII PALANKA

INHUL PALANKA

Nova Sich

Khortytsia Island

Oleksandriv'sk (1770) ■

ZAPOROZHIA

KODAK PALANKA

Katerynoslav (1776) ■

PROTOVCHA PALANKA

OREL PALANKA

SAMARA PALANKA

KALMIUS PALANK

Mariupol' ■
1774

Azov ■

DON COSSACKS

SLAVIC SERBIA

Bakhmut ■

UKRAINE

Donets

Don

NOGAY TATARS
1783

CRIMEAN KHANATE
1783

KUBAN
1783

Ekaterinodar ■

CIRCASSIANS

Kuban

SEA OF AZOV

Kerch (1774) ■

Kefe •

CRIMEA
1783

Simferopol' •

Bakhchysarai ■

Sevastopol' (1784) ■

EMPIRE

BLACK SEA

Dnieper

Buh

Southern Buh

Syniukha

Ros'

Dniester

1774

Copyright © by Paul Robert Magocsi

Not surprisingly, the independent-minded Zaporozhians soon became dissatis-fied with their new protectors, especially since as subjects of the khan they were cut off from trade with the Hetmanate and were unable to raid their traditional source of booty, the Crimean Khanate. Almost immediately after 1711, individual Zaporozhians began to ask Muscovy to allow them to return home under the tsar's protection. Their leader, Hordiienko, stood firm in his anti-Muscovite views, how-ever, and nothing changed for the Zaporozhians as a whole until his death in 1733. By that time, Russia was making preparations for a new campaign against the Ottoman Empire and was receptive to negotiating with the Zaporozhians. The result was the Agreement of Lubny, signed in 1734. The Zaporozhian Cossacks regained all their former lands, which came to be known as the Free Lands of the Zaporozhian Host (*Vol'nosti Viis'ka Zaporiz'koho Nyzovoho*), and they were permitted to retain their traditional laws and customs. During wartime, they were to serve under the command of the Russian army stationed in the Hetmanate, and they were to receive for their services an annual payment of 20,000 rubles. A new sich, the Nova Sich, was established on the Dnieper River, a little downstream from their old headquarters, which had been destroyed earlier in the century by Peter I. The Nova Sich was under the direct control of the imperial Russian governor-general in Kiev and, for a time after 1750, the hetman in the Hetmanate.

The number of Cossacks who returned from the Ottoman Empire was no more than 20,000. This meant that at least initially they had a vast territory in Zaporo-zhia at their disposal. In an attempt to maintain a measure of control over this territory, they introduced a more formal administrative structure. Eight districts (*palanky*) were formed in Zaporozhia and near Oleshky. Each district was headed by a colonel appointed by the chief (*koshovyi otaman*) of the Nova Sich, although these colonels never had the degree of power or number of administrative support staff that their counterparts in the Hetmanate had. In addition to building a state administration, the Zaporozhians, who remained concerned with the demograph-ic and political vacuum in their extensive territory and the potential for inter-ference with their status by the Russian imperial government, began to colonize their lands with peasants. Many of these peasants were refugees from the Polish-controlled Right Bank and the Left Bank Hetmanate who resented the increasing burdens of serfdom. By 1762, there were approximately 33,700 Cossacks and over 150,000 peasants in Zaporozhia.

But incursions from the north proved to be inevitable, since the Russian Empire was determined further to integrate the border regions of its increasingly far-flung realm. St Petersburg's initial steps toward integration were to build fortifications and settle colonists. In 1735, the government built a fortress near the Nova Sich, and in the 1750s it set up a line of fortifications along Zaporozhia's western border with the Ottoman Empire (the Southern Buh and Syniukha Rivers). Also dur-ing the 1750s, the imperial government initiated its own colonization program to encourage an influx of new settlers who would be directly dependent on the central authorities. In 1751, St Petersburg invited over 200 Serbian colonists from southern Hungary, who were joined a year later by Bulgarians, Greeks, Romanians, and more Serbs from the Balkans. The settlers were given the northwest region of

Zaporozhia between the Dnieper River in the east and the Syniukha River in the west. Organized into a frontier military region, this area became known as New Serbia (*Nova Serbiia*), with its center at Novomyrhorod (then on the Russian-Polish border).

In 1754, the Russian government coopted more Zaporozhian land all along the southern border of New Serbia to create a Cossack frontier military region made up of over 6,000 Cossacks from Sloboda Ukraine and the Hetmanate. This became known as the Sloboda regiment (*Slobids'kyi polk*) with its military and administrative headquarters at a fortress that in 1775 became the city of Ielysavethrad (today Kirovohrad). Finally, beyond the far northeastern corner of Zaporozhia, more Serbs, who were living as refugees in southern Hungary, as well as Bulgarians, Romanians, and Greeks from the Balkans were settled after 1753 by the Russian government. As in New Serbia, the colonists were organized as a frontier military regiment, and the whole region, with its center in Bakhmut (today Artemivs'k), came to be known as Slavic Serbia (*Slaviano-Serbiia*).

The Zaporozhians resented the imperial Russian colonization of their northern frontier, and they often clashed with the Serb colonists. Nonetheless, the Zaporozhians continued to serve faithfully with the imperial army in its wars against the Ottoman Empire between 1735 and 1739, and again between 1768 and 1774. In the context of tsarist Russian policy as a whole, however, the eventual demise of Zaporozhian autonomy was inevitable. That demise was to take place in two stages. In preparation for its war with the Ottomans, the tsarist government in 1764 abolished the Serbian and the Sloboda frontier regions and joined them with fifteen southern companies from the Hetmanate to form an imperial province called New Russia (*Novorosiiskaia guberniia*), with an administrative center at Kremenchuk.

These administrative changes seem not to have disenchanted the Cossacks, who continued to fight loyally and valiantly with tsarist forces in their campaigns against the Ottomans between 1768 and 1774. At the very same time, Russia's borderlands to the east of Ukraine were rocked by a series of revolts which seriously threatened tsarist rule. Sporadic uprisings occurred in Zaporozhia as well, but it was among the Don and Iaik Cossacks just to the east that large-scale revolts took place, culminating in the greatest uprising in eighteenth-century Russia – the Pugachev rebellion of 1773–1775.

Once the Pugachev rebellion was finally put down, Empress Catherine was determined to reorganize all the borderlands so as to impose greater control over their inhabitants. Zaporozhia in particular became an area of concern because it was part of the southern borderland facing the Ottoman Empire. Ironically, although the Zaporozhians had remained staunchly loyal during the Russo-Turkish war (1768–1774), they were among the hardest hit by the new, more stringent tsarist policy. Moreover, the very fact that Russia was successful against its Ottoman adversary (from whom it obtained a very favorable peace settlement at Küçük Kaynarca in 1774) made the protection afforded by the Zaporozhian Cossacks seem superfluous.

Accordingly, on 4 June 1775, victorious Russian troops returning from their Ottoman campaigns suddenly attacked and destroyed the Zaporozhian Sich.

Some Cossacks were immediately pressed into Russian military service; some were left as free farmers; others sought protection in the Ottoman Empire, where they were allowed to settle near the mouths of the Danube River. That same year, 1775, most of Zaporozhia was annexed to the imperial province of New Russia, which together with two neighboring provinces was from the following year governed by Empress Catherine's favorite, Prince Grigorii Potemkin.

Potemkin was eager to impress his sovereign. To do so, he began a dynamic colonizing program that brought new settlers from various parts of Europe, including especially large numbers of Romanians from nearby Ottoman-ruled Moldavia and smaller groups of Armenians and Greeks from the Crimea, along with Bulgarians, Turks, and Albanians from the Ottoman Empire. From farther afield came Italians, Corsicans, Danzigers, Swedes, and especially Germans. The colonists were attracted to New Russia by the free land and tax-exempt privileges (at least for the first two or three decades of their settlement) they were offered. Germans were especially favored. Besides the aforementioned privileges, they were exempted from military service, granted unlimited duty-free trade across the border, and allowed free sale of salt and spirits. Racked by the Seven Years' War (1756–1763) in central Europe, Catholic and, especially, Protestant Germans, including Mennonites, took advantage of several Russian imperial decrees (issued in 1763, 1789, and 1790) and immigrated to the Ukrainian steppe. There, in the center of New Russia, they settled on and near Khortytsia Island, a historic center of the Zaporozhian Cossacks. These Germans, and others who followed in even greater numbers during the early part of the nineteenth century, founded numerous colonies along the Black Sea littoral between the Southern Buh and Danube Rivers and later became known as Black Sea Germans (*Schwarzmeerdeutsche*).

With Empress Catherine's backing and encouragement, Potemkin also succeeded in establishing the basis for several new towns throughout New Russia and the Crimea that grew up around existing or reconstructed fortresses. Among these were Ielyzavethrad (today Kirovohrad) and Katerynoslav (today Dnipropetrovs'k) in Zaporozhia; and, from lands acquired from the Ottoman Empire, Sevastopol' in the Crimea, Mariupol' on the northern shore of the Sea of Azov, and Mykolaïv and Kherson, both river ports with direct access to the Black Sea. It was after the death of Potemkin, however, that the empire's most important Black Sea port was established. In 1794, Catherine provided substantial funds to a Neapolitan-born soldier in the imperial Russian service, Admiral Giuseppe de Ribas, to create a harbor and settlement for a new city to be called Odessa. De Ribas was assisted by several of his own family members and by other Italian merchants and entrepreneurs who provided the otherwise ethnically diverse city with a distinctly Italianate flavor.

Potemkin's undertakings were often costly and unproductive. His excesses were such that, during Catherine's trip in 1787 to the recently acquired Crimea, his urge to impress her caused him hastily to set up settlements all along her route through southern Ukraine (i.e., New Russia), many of which were simply facades with nothing behind them. This episode gave rise to the proverbial phrase, "Potemkin village," meaning an illusory facade designed to cover an undesirable fact or condition. In contrast to Potemkin's empty facades, Catherine's policies of administrative integration were quite real. In 1775, her government abolished the autonomy of Zaporozhia, just as it had abolished that of Sloboda Ukraine ten years before. Having transformed territory to its east and south into integral parts of the Russian Empire, Catherine was now ready to turn to the last semi-autonomous Cossack region on Ukrainian territory.

The Hetmanate

The Hetmanate had the most highly developed form of autonomous self-government in Russian-ruled Ukraine. It was the direct successor to Khmel'nyts'kyi's Cossack state, and, at least until the end of Mazepa's reign, it maintained control over its own internal affairs, even if it was subject to Muscovy with respect to foreign policy and military ventures. The Hetmanate was hardly helped by Mazepa's defection to the Swedes. The antagonistic tone was set by Peter I, who in 1723 issued a decree declaring that "from the first hetman Bohdan Khmel'nyts'kyi, and even Skoropads'kyi, all hetmans were traitors."[1] Peter's ultimate purpose was to end all forms of Cossack autonomy in the Hetmanate; the only question was how best to achieve that goal. The decades from Mazepa's defection in 1708 until the 1780s witnessed several changes in policy on the part of the tsarist government toward the autonomous status of the Hetmanate, changes which reflected in part the requirements of foreign policy and in part the different attitudes of the Russian Empire's administrators and internal policy makers.

In November 1708, immediately after learning of Mazepa's defection, Peter arranged for the election of a new hetman, Ivan Skoropads'kyi. As a personality, Skoropads'kyi was easy to manipulate, and he proved to be no real hindrance to Peter's plans. The tsar did not reassert the articles of the Agreement of Pereiaslav or negotiate any other agreement with the Cossacks as had previously been done whenever a new hetman was elected. Rather, he chose to confirm a more limited number of traditional rights by tsarist decree. At the same time, he transferred the capital of the Hetmanate from Baturyn farther north to Hlukhiv, near the Muscovite border, and a representative of the tsar was assigned there to oversee the hetman's activity. Peter also began to appoint colonels directly to the Cossack regiments, and he and his successors made large land grants in Hetmanate territory to imperial administrators, most of whom were former generals of German background (B.C. Weissbach, J.B. Münnich). As loyal tsarist subjects with no local roots, these men had little concern for Cossack autonomy. The Cossack forces were more frequently than before used by the imperial government for non-military purposes: to build canals in Russia (at Tsaritsyn in 1716 and at Lake Ladoga in 1721), and to construct fortifications, as in the Caucasus (along the Terek River, in 1718) and along the southeastern border of the Hetmanate (1731–1735).

With the close of the Great Northern War in 1721, Peter had an even greater opportunity to address Ukrainian affairs. The following year, as part of a general restructuring of the Russian imperial government, responsibility for the Hetmanate was changed in 1722 from the College of Foreign Affairs to the Senate, which was concerned with the empire's internal affairs. That same year, the Little Russian Collegium was established. The Russian government justified these actions on three grounds: that the Cossack system of administration and justice had broken down in the Hetmanate; that the central government had received numerous complaints of illegal Cossack enserfment of the peasantry; and that the tsar's treasury had received an inadequate share of taxes and revenue from the Hetmanate.

It was to expedite further complaints, which since the Agreement of Pereiaslav all Cossacks had a right to make directly to the tsar, that in 1722 the imperial Russian government established the Little Russian Collegium, composed of six Russian military officers stationed in the Hetmanate. As a body, the officers were commissioned with the following tasks: (1) to hear complaints lodged against local Cossack courts and, if necessary, decide controversial cases; (2) to control financial affairs; and (3) to intervene against *starshyna* oppression of the rank-and-file Cossacks and peasantry. The Little Russian Collegium became, in effect, a parallel government in the Hetmanate. Even the malleable Hetman Skoropads'kyi protested this incursion against Cossack autonomy.

But Skoropads'kyi's complaints had no impact and, in any case, he died two months after the Collegium was established, in July 1722. As his successor, the Cossacks chose Pavlo Polubotok, a more dynamic leader who from the outset protested against the activity of the Little Russian Collegium. The tsar never confirmed Polubotok's election, however. Instead, he was arrested in St Petersburg, where he died in prison in 1724.

The Hetmanate continued to be ruled exclusively by the Little Russian Collegium, although in 1726, under the new ruler Empress Catherine I (reigned 1725–1727), plans were made to restore the office of hetman. The change in attitude reflected the government's desire to avoid any difficulties in its southern regions during preparations for a new war with the Ottoman Empire and, in part, the influence of Catherine's political ally Aleksandr Menshikov, who had large landholdings in the Hetmanate and was opposed to the Collegium's introduction of direct taxation. Accordingly, in 1727 the Little Russian Collegium was abolished, and with Menshikov's intervention the Russian government arranged to have a new hetman, Danylo Apostol, elected. Soon after, a code consisting of twenty-eight articles was drawn up to regulate Russia's relationship with the Hetmanate. This was, in effect, the first single document to cover all aspects of the Hetmanate, and it remained in force until the demise of the region's autonomy.

The document, which was issued in 1728, came to be known as the 28 Confirmed Articles. According to its provisions, the Hetmanate could not conduct any foreign relations, although it could deal with Poland, the Crimean Khanate, and the Ottoman Empire about purely border problems, provided that any agreements with these countries received the prior approval of the Russian imperial government. While the Hetmanate continued to maintain ten regiments, it was allowed only three regiments of mercenary troops. Moreover, in time of war the Cossacks were required to serve under the resident imperial Russian commander. With regard to judicial and administrative matters, a general court was established to consist of three Cossacks and three governmental appointees; a commission was set in place to create a new law code; duties on foreign goods were to revert to the imperial treasury; and Russian and other non-local landlords were permitted to retain their landholdings, although no new peasants from the north could be brought in.

From the standpoint of the imperial government, the 28 Confirmed Articles were a step backward in what seemed to have been Russia's determined effort since Peter I to abolish the Hetmanate's autonomous status. It was not long, however, before St Petersburg returned to more restrictive policies. Hetman Apostol died in 1734, and in his stead a Governing Council of the Hetman's Office was created that consisted of three governmental appointees and three Cossacks. Together, the six members were to rule the Hetmanate and to work on codifying a body of law for the region. In practice, the head of the Governing Council, or "Second Little Russian Collegium" as some historians (D. Doroshenko, N. Polons'ka-Vasylenko) call it, administered the country single-handedly, especially during the costly wars against the Ottomans, in which the Cossacks participated between 1735 and 1739. The only concrete result of these conflicts was that the Ottoman Empire agreed to renounce its protectorate over the Zaporozhian Cossacks, who in any case had already returned to Russian control, in 1734.

In the 1740s, the imperial Russian government once more backed away from its anti-Hetmanate policy. Again, this development was largely owing to the role played by certain individuals. The court favorite – and eventually the husband – of the new empress Elizabeth (reigned 1741–1762) was Oleksii Rozumovs'kyi, the son of a registered Cossack, who because of his musical talent (he was a singer in the imperial choir) and good looks came to her attention. Rozumovs'kyi managed to interest Elizabeth in his homeland. In 1743, he succeeded in winning the restoration of the office of the metropolitan of Kiev, which had been downgraded by Peter I in 1721 to an ordinary archbishopric. Then, in 1747, he pushed through plans for the election of a new hetman. The choice fell on his younger brother, Kyrylo Rozumovs'kyi, a remarkably well educated youth who, as a result of his brother's connections, had been made president of the Imperial Academy of Sciences in St Petersburg at the age of eighteen. In 1750, Kyrylo was elected hetman in Hlukhiv.

Kyrylo Rozumovs'kyi was an eighteenth-century intellectual dilettante par excellence. Educated in France, Italy, and Germany, he displayed the typical imperial Russian aristocratic predilection for western culture, and he tried to impose this outlook on the Hetmanate's capital in Hlukhiv. In that otherwise small provincial town, he established an Italian opera, opened coffeehouses, introduced French-language schools and Parisian fashions, and erected a Versailles-like hetman's palace. He even had elaborate plans to return to Mazepa's old capital at Baturyn, which had became his personal property in 1760, and to build there an even more elegant cultural complex.

But despite these "improvements," Rozumovs'kyi preferred the imperial capital of St Petersburg to provincial Hlukhiv. During his long absences, the Cossack *starshyna* ran the Hetmanate and held periodic congresses somewhat like noble diets. They succeeded in limiting the rights of the peasants even further (1760), and they introduced a new system of justice whereby local judges could be chosen only from the *starshyna*. It seemed that the Cossack elite, left to its own devices, was on the verge of introducing a Polish-style administrative system in which all social and legal power rested in the hands of the nobility.

The Cossack *starshyna* was helped in its efforts by the imperial Russian government. Beginning in the 1730s and especially during the rule of Empress Anna (reigned 1730–1740) and Tsar Peter III (reigned 1761–1762), the nobility was granted several privileges, including permanent exemption from state service. The hope was that, following such improvements in their status, the nobles would pay more attention to the economic well-being of their landed estates. In the end, members of the Hetmanate's Cossack *starshyna* proved themselves quite willing to go along with a system that guaranteed them so many privileges.

Having laid the groundwork to attract the Hetmanate's elite into Russia's social structure, the imperial government could once again return to its policy of centralization. Centralization became the dominant goal of Catherine II. Influenced in part by the ideas of the European Enlightenment, which argued that a single territory with a rational system of unified central government could be run more efficiently and manageably than could a variety of regions with antiquated social systems and specific forms of self-government or autonomy, Catherine turned her attention primarily to the Baltic provinces and Finland in the north (a portion of which had been obtained by Russia in 1743) and to the Ukrainian lands in the south. Her attitude toward these regions was summed up in 1764 in instructions to the empire's new prosecutor-general: "To call [these lands] foreign and to treat them on that basis is more than a mistake; it would be sheer stupidity. These provinces … should be russified in the easiest way possible, so that they should cease looking like wolves to the forest. The approach is easy if wise men are chosen as governors of the provinces."[2] Catherine had already done away with the autonomous features of Sloboda Ukraine in 1765 and of Zaporozhia in 1775. Now she was ready to turn to the Hetmanate.

First came the office of the hetman. It was permanently abolished in 1764, after Rozumovs'kyi unsuccessfully tried to have it become the hereditary property of his family. Rozumovs'kyi, who never much cared for ruling in the Hetmanate, was easily placated with a new imperial title and the equivalent of a lavish pension, including large estates in Baturyn, where he finally settled in 1775 and lived comfortably until his death in 1803. In his stead, a new Little Russian Collegium was created, this time composed of four imperial appointees and four Cossacks and headed by a president, Count Petr Rumiantsev. Rumiantsev proceeded cautiously but firmly. While he curbed the excesses of the Cossack gentry in accumulating more land, he also legalized the landlords' control over their peasants, and thus contributed further to the eventual enserfment of the peasantry in the Hetmanate.

Rumiantsev's reforms were interrupted for a while in 1769, when Russia renewed its war with the Ottoman Empire. The war lasted five years, but this time the Russians finally won lasting success. According to the provisions of the Treaty of Küçük Kaynarca, signed in 1774, Russia received from the Ottoman Empire an enormous financial indemnity (4,500,000 rubles). It also acquired a slice of territory between the Dnieper and Southern Buh Rivers; parts of the Crimean Khanate around Mariupol' and Kerch, the former neutral zone south of Azov; and Istanbul's recognition of independence for the Crimean Khanate under Russian protection. This increase in the Russian presence along the Black Sea after 1774 was followed by the destruction of the *sich* and an end to Zaporozhian autonomy a year later.

Once the southern fringe of Ukrainian lands had been secured, the further integration of the Hetmanate into the Russian Empire could proceed. In 1781, the Cossack regimental system of administration was dismantled. At the same time, the Little Russian Collegium was once again – and for the last time – abolished and the Hetmanate divided into three imperial provinces (*namestnichestva*): Novhorod-Sivers'kyi, Chernihiv, and Kiev, which were no different from other provinces in the empire. Next, in 1783, the peasantry's freedom of movement was restricted, and the process of their enserfment thereby completed. That same year, the Cossack military system of regiments was abolished and replaced by ten cavalry units of the imperial army.

The Crimean Khanate

In contrast to Sloboda Ukraine, Zaporozhia, and the Hetmanate, which were part of the Muscovite/Russian state since at least the mid-seventeenth century, the Crimean Khanate was a sovereign political entity in vassalage to the Ottoman Empire. Therefore, any Russian advance on the Crimea would first have to address the reality of Ottoman rule over much of the steppe lands north of the Black Sea and the Sea of Azov.

Even before Russia gained the upper hand in this region, the status of the Crimean Khanate had changed. By the outset of the seventeenth century, the Ottomans were playing an increasingly influential role in Crimean politics, including the selection and deposition of the state's ruling khans. No longer was the Crimea able to refuse what now became Ottoman orders to supply the sultan with military forces. Even more problematic, however, was the recompense, or lack of it, that the Crimean Khanate got from its increasing outlay of troops. As the fortunes of the Ottoman Empire itself declined, so too did income for the Crimea in the form of war booty, which at best declined or dried up entirely. Finally, Muscovy stopped its annual tribute payments to the khans by 1700, and subsequent Russian military victories and international treaties put an effective end to the export of captives from its lands, thereby undermining the slave trade which had been the mainstay of the Crimea's economy.

By the 1730s, the balance of military power had permanently shifted. Russian armies were able to invade at will Crimean territory, even capturing the capital of Bahçesaray and destroying the khan's palace in 1736. But it was the Russian-Ottoman war of 1768–1774 that really changed everything. Early in the conflict the Russians managed to gain the allegiance of the Nogay Tatars, and that meant the effective loss to the khanate of lands beyond the Crimean peninsula. In 1770 the khan himself and the Crimea's most powerful clan, the Şirin, decided to abandon their association with the Ottomans and instead to pledge their loyalty to the sovereign of Russia. This resulted in the Treaty of Karasubazar, signed in 1772, which created an independent Crimean state. The Crimea was still headed by the Giray dynasty, but it was now under the protection of the Russian Empire. The Ottomans finally accepted the loss of the Crimean Khanate (including their own Kefe province along the peninsula's Black Sea littoral) as part of the provisions of the Treaty of Küçük Kaynarca (1774).

The first years of independent Crimea were characterized by an internal struggle among Tatar supporters of Russia versus those who hoped for the return of Ottoman overlordship. Tsarist military intervention ended those controversies, however, and allowed for the installation in 1776 of the pro-Russian Şahin Giray as khan. The new khan set out to reform the governing structure of the Crimea, but his efforts at centralization alienated most clan leaders who were reluctant to give up their traditionally dominant role in Crimean political and socioeconomic life. When it became clear that Khan Şahin was unable to contain the revolts against his regime, and when the Russian government got tired of supporting an unpopular ruler, Empress Catherine II issued a manifesto in 1783 that unilaterally put an end to the short-lived independent Crimean state and annexed it to the Russian Empire. The khanate's lands in the peninsula and north of the Sea of Azov (i.e., the Nogay but not Kuban steppe) were made part of a Russian administrative entity (*guberniia*) called Taurida.

The transformation of the Crimean Khanate from an Ottoman to a Russian territory took place during the reign of Empress Catherine II. She was, therefore, credited with the annexation of 1783, which made an enormously positive impression on the Russian public and the empire's allies abroad. After all, it was Catherine II who finally fulfilled the age-old dream of the Muscovite and Russian rulers, and it was she who achieved something which even the dynamic Peter I had failed to realize: the acquisition of the Crimean Peninsula and most of the coastal region north of the Black Sea and the Sea of Azov.

Transformation under Russian rule

The efforts of Russia's rulers to entice the political and social elite of the empire's various lands – both older and recently acquired ones – was a long process that reached its apogee under Catherine II. In 1785 she issued a Charter of Nobility reconfirming all previous rights and, most importantly, recognizing all land already held by nobles as their legal property. The result was indeed what the imperial authorities had hoped: that many landlords serving the government in St Petersburg or in other urban centers would go back to their landholdings. While it is true that Russia's nobles may have had few political rights, they did have many social and economic privileges.

Catherine's 1785 Charter of Nobility was also applied to the formerly autonomous lands in Ukraine. Responding to a request made to Catherine II a decade earlier by the uppermost echelon of the Cossack elite, the imperial government agreed to recognize most of the Distinguished Military Fellows (there was still some question about the regimental-level Fellows of the Banner) as members of the Russian nobility (*dvorianstvo*). This recognition assured the Distinguished Military Fellows of full rights to their hereditary estates and exemption from compulsory state service. With this act, the leading stratum of the Hetmanate and Sloboda Ukraine was coopted fully and, for its part, enthusiastically into the Russian imperial social structure. In contrast, the corporate strength of the other leading social estate, the Orthodox clergy, was reduced when, in 1786, as had been the practice in the rest of the Russian Empire, most of the church's monastic landholdings were secularized and eventually distributed among gentry landlords. In effect, although the Orthodox hierarchs continued to retain extensive privileges and access to funds, they did so as functionaries of the state who were dependent on the imperial treasury and not on income from their own landed wealth.

In the Crimea, the hereditary Tatar nobles (*mirza*) were considered the equivalent of the Russian nobility (*dvorianstvo*) and therefore they were offered all the privileges of Catherine's 1785 Charter. To encourage them to function within the Russian imperial order, they were made members of a newly established Crimean Assembly of the Nobility. Crimea's Muslim clergy, many of whom held high positions in the religious hierarchy of the former khanate, also fared well in the new order and were actually given more privileges than their Orthodox Christian clerical counterparts. Aside from a state salary, Muslim clergy were allowed to keep their vast landholdings (representing an estimated 30 percent of Crimea's productive land), they could own serfs, and they were exempt from taxation.

While the process of abolishing autonomy and self-rule may have taken somewhat longer in the Hetmanate and in the Crimean Khanate than in Sloboda Ukraine and in Zaporozhia, the result was the same. One decade after another, Sloboda Ukraine (1760s), Zaporozhia (1770s), and finally the Hetmanate and the Crimea (1780s) were transformed with the result that autonomy on Ukrainian territory located within the Russian Empire was eliminated. A system of administrative division into imperial provinces, each directly responsible to St Petersburg, was put in place instead. By the end of the eighteenth century, the government of Empress Catherine II had succeeded in making all Ukrainian lands under her rule an integral part of the Russian Empire.

23

Socioeconomic Developments

Just as tsarist Russia between the 1760s and 1780s eliminated the governmental and administrative peculiarities of territories on the fringes of its realm, which included Sloboda Ukraine, Zaporozhia, the Hetmanate, and the Crimean Khanate, so too did it succeed in integrating the social structure and economic life of these lands with those of the rest of the empire. The process of socioeconomic change was gradual, with the eighteenth century witnessing essentially a continuation of trends begun during the previous century.

While the decades following the 1648 Khmel'nyts'kyi uprising witnessed the disappearance of the Polish nobility and the liberation of many peasants from serf status, the eighteenth century saw the rise of a new Cossack gentry, which improved its socioeconomic status by increasing the labor obligations of the peasants on its lands and by reducing the rights and privileges of the poorer Cossacks. Nonetheless, whereas peasants made up the vast majority of the population in the rest of Russia and Poland, as late as the 1760s they made up only half (50.6 percent) of the population of the Hetmanate. In effect, the social estates in eighteenth-century Ukraine remained the same as in the previous century (see page 265) – nobility, Cossacks, clergy, townspeople, and peasants – although their internal composition was altered.

The changing social structure

The eighteenth century witnessed increasing differentiation among the Cossacks, who in the 1760s represented 45 percent of the Hetmanate's and 25 percent of the Sloboda Ukraine's population. In the second half of the seventeenth century, the highest level of officers from among the Cossack elite (Distinguished Military Fellows) had begun moving up the social scale, and later, joining with those hereditary Orthodox Rus' nobles who had supported the Khmel'nyts'kyi uprising, they came to form the newer noble estate which replaced the Polish and polonized Rus'-Ukrainian nobility who had been forced to flee. By the 1760s, there were about 300 members of the oldest Orthodox aristocracy and 2,100 members of the new Cossack gentry. Together, they represented no more than 0.2 percent of the Hetmanate's population. The new Cossack gentry in particular was anxious to improve its status and even began to call itself by the name given to the hated Polish nobility – the *szlachta*. Despite this self-designation, the tsarist government was not yet ready to recognize the Cossack gentry as part of the noble estate.

The economic status of the majority of Cossacks – divided into the military rank and file, helpers, and laborers – continually worsened. For instance, the rank and file were expected to serve as soldiers, but in practice they were neither paid nor allowed to obtain booty. They were, however, like the nobility, not liable for taxes. That privilege was not extended to the Cossack helpers. Both the Cossack rank and file and the Cossack helpers were soldier-farmers, and during their long absences in military service they often neglected their lands. The Cossack laborers were worse off still, since they did not even own land. By the second half of the eighteenth century, the members of all three Cossack groups had, with few exceptions, been reduced to an economic level that was about the same as that of the peasants.

As for the peasants, whether free or proprietary, their status too gradually worsened during the eighteenth century. In the previous century, as a result of the Khmel'nyts'kyi uprising, the majority of the villages formerly owned by Polish landlords had come under the authority of the new Cossack state. These so-called free military villages did not stay free for long, however; they were distributed to the Cossack officers and officials as so-called rank estates, in payment for their services to the state. Initially these "rank estates" were not hereditary, but before long they became the possession of the family of the recipient, and the formulaic "customary service" was expected of the peasants toward their new Cossack "landlord" administrators. Aside from peasants living in free military villages, proprietary peasants on church-owned lands and on manorial estates of the hereditary nobility loyal to the Cossack state (especially in the Chernihiv region) were freed from their duties.

The eighteenth century saw an absolute increase in the number of proprietary peasants on secular and church-owned landed estates as well as a quantitative and qualitative increase in the number and kind of duties they were expected to perform. Two days a week of service to the landlord had become the minimum. At the same time, the tsarist government was granting large tracts of land as rewards to Russian nobles (in particular to generals) for their service to the state. The land grants often included mills and peasants over which – according to a tsarist decree of 1687 – the Cossack government had no control or jurisdiction. Statistics available from specific parts of the Hetmanate confirm these general trends. With regard to land tenure, in seven regiments of the Hetmanate, by the 1730s more than half the estates (56 percent) were owned by the church and hereditary nobles; one-third (33 percent) were free peasant villages; and a mere 10 percent were rank estates held by Cossack officers for the duration of their term of office. The number of free homesteads, however, was rapidly declining. For example, in nine regiments of the Hetmanate there were 27,500 free homesteads in 1729, but that number had decreased to only 2,800 by 1752. Thus, by the 1760s, of the 515,000 male peasants living in the Hetmanate, 90 percent resided on private estates held by the hereditary nobility or the church. A similar process was occurring in the Sloboda Ukraine, where 51 percent of male peasants lived on private estates where they remained impoverished and saddled with an increasing number of labor dues and other obligations.

The status of the other two social estates, the Orthodox Christian clergy and townspeople, continued to differ radically. The clergy was able to increase its wealth and social prestige. As members of a state church, the Orthodox hierarchy and monastic orders were eager and willing to cooperate with the secular authorities in order to preserve their social and economic status. By the mid-eighteenth century, for instance, the monasteries alone owned 10,000 estates, or 17 percent of the land in the Hetmanate. All clergy were exempt from taxes, and because they could marry, much of their amassed wealth was passed on to their children. Nonetheless, despite certain efforts to protect itself from an influx of newcomers, the clergy did not become a closed social estate. Cossacks and peasants could become priests, and sometimes priests became Cossacks or peasants. Many priest's children also entered or married into the Hetmanate's civil service.

The status of the townspeople was in great contrast to that of the clergy. The vast majority (artisans and workers) remained in the same dependent situation during the eighteenth century as during the second half of the seventeenth century. This was because the Cossack administration continued to extract as much profit from urban areas as possible. The number of towns enjoying self-government (Magdeburg Law) increased, yet most of these had fewer than 5,000 inhabitants. Since townspeople, like peasants, had to pay taxes, there was nothing to attract new settlers to urban areas. Artisans continued to operate within the framework of their guilds. The rich patricians of the towns, however, who because of their wealth and status could hold administrative offices in the Hetmanate, became indistinguishable from the privileged Cossack *starshyna* – neither group being liable for taxes. Within urban areas, a special category of inhabitants was the foreign merchants, especially Greeks and Russians, who also enjoyed tax-free status and who came to dominate commerce, especially international trade. In Nizhyn, for instance, the Greeks had their own brotherhood in the 1680s, whose wealthy merchants by the eighteenth century were sponsoring the largest trade fairs on Ukrainian territory.

The leading positions in Ukrainian towns within the Russian Empire were thus in the hands of a group of urban patricians, Cossacks, and foreign merchants. The generally dismissive view of the townspeople as a social estate was reflected in the Cossack censuses, which did not even have a rubric for them. According to estimates from the 1760s, townspeople comprised only 3.3 percent of the population of the Hetmanate. In neighboring Sloboda Ukraine (1773), they represented a mere 2.5 percent of the population.

The population also included Russian peasants, Jews, and settlers who had been invited from abroad. The Russian peasants generally accompanied former imperial military officers, who as nobles were allowed to bring with them peasant-serfs to serve on their new estates in the Hetmanate. The number of Jews in the Hetmanate remained minuscule – about 600 in the eighteenth century – as a result of decrees (1717, 1731, 1740, 1742, 1744) issued by the imperial government, usually over the protests of Cossack leaders, banning Jewish settlement on the Left

Bank. The majority of the Jews had fled or been exiled westward to the Polish-ruled Right Bank, but a few who remained converted to Orthodoxy. From that small group, there were some (from the Hertsyk, Markovych, and Kryzhanivs'kyi families) who attained high-ranking positions in the Cossack administrative structure. Of the settlers invited from abroad by the imperial government, most were settled in Zaporozhia, which after 1775 was incorporated into the province of New Russia. They included Serbs, Bulgarians, and Romanians, who, because of their peasant social status and Orthodox faith integrated easily – and in some cases assimilated – with their ethnic Ukrainian and Russian neighbors. Other newcomers like the Germans, who began to arrive in the last decades of the eighteenth century, maintained their distinct language and religion and remained isolated in their farming communities from the rest of the population. A similar tendency to hold themselves in isolation and look to their own group was characteristic of certain urban dwellers like the rich Greek merchants, who maintained with their "families" a close hold over certain trading enterprises.

Economic developments

Agriculture continued to be the main economic activity on Ukrainian territories throughout the eighteenth century. These same decades also witnessed, at least in Ukrainian lands within the Russian Empire, the growth of a small but vibrant domestic industry as well as the continuation of the pattern whereby Ukrainian trade with Poland and the Ottoman Empire decreased and was replaced by greater integration into the Russian Empire's economic framework.

In agriculture, wheat continued to be the predominant product. Barley, buckwheat, oats, millet, hemp, flax, and hops were also cultivated. After the mid-eighteenth century, with the arrival of Bulgarian and Romanian colonists as part of the settlement of New Serbia and Slavic Serbia, corn was introduced; and after 1783 and the incorporation of the Crimean lands, clover and tobacco became widespread. The potato, which later became the staple of the Ukrainian domestic agricultural economy as it did in many other agricultural economies in Europe, was not introduced until the late eighteenth century and was not produced in quantity until the nineteenth century.

Hunting, fishing, and livestock continued to have economic importance. Horses and cattle were a particularly important commodity in frontier areas, especially in Zaporozhia. Besides meeting the needs of local consumption, the fishing industry expanded to the point that nobles and rich Cossacks operated fish ponds, especially in the Hetmanate and Sloboda Ukraine.

Industrial development took the form of small enterprises, usually of a domestic cottage-industry type, which grew steadily in number especially during the rule of Hetman Mazepa. Also under Mazepa, the Hetmanate was able to revive its iron mines and iron processing industry, which had been largely destroyed during the Khme nyts'kyi era. By the eighteenth century, several establishments, some owned by religious orders (in Kiev, Chernihiv, Novhorod-Sivers'kyi, Nizhyn, Hadiach) and some by secular entrepreneurs (in Sheptakiv, Pochep), were in operation.

The iron industry flourished because of a growing demand for military hardware, church bells, tools, farm implements, and household goods.

Among other industries in the first half of the eighteenth century were distilling and brewing, tobacco pressing, potash and tar production, glass and ceramic making, and textile production and leather working. The textile industry became particularly well developed. In 1726, a linen factory was founded at Pochep, which soon employed 221 workers at 63 benches. In 1756, Hetman Rozumovs'kyi erected a textile factory at Baturyn that initially had 12 machines. By 1800, that number had grown to 76 machines and 100 workers.

Rozumovs'kyi's venture in Baturyn reflects the degree to which he and other hetmans were under the influence of mercantilist economic theory. This theory, which prevailed in western Europe at the time, argued that the state should take the lead in developing its own economy by promoting agriculture and manufacturing. The goal was to obtain a favorable balance of trade. Whereas in older, feudal and manorial-based economic systems development was left at the whim of individual landlords or petty princes, each of whom imposed his own tariff system and taxes, the mercantilist theorists called for the unification and standardization of economic life within a given territory. Cossack hetmans beginning with Mazepa believed in the feasibility of mercantilist economic theory for the Hetmanate. It was in this context that Mazepa passed a whole series of decrees (*universaly*) during his tenure which regularized the duties of the peasants and townspeople, thus protecting both these groups from the whims of the increasingly gentrified Cossack landlords. Hetmans Skoropads'kyi, Apostol, and Rozumovs'kyi continued Mazepa's mercantilist initiatives, since all realized that a regularized economic structure would bring prosperity to the realm and, especially, an increase in tax and tariff revenues.

International trade and commerce

It was the desire of the Hetmanate to increase its income from tariffs that prompted it to encourage trade and commerce. Until 1648, parts of the Right Bank functioned primarily as a source of grain for Poland's lucrative trade from its Baltic Sea ports. After the Khmel'nyts'kyi uprising, the Polish orientation in Cossack Ukrainian trade was weakened, and although it was to be revived by the beginning of the eighteenth century, it never again reached its pre-1648 strength. Instead, trade between Cossack Ukraine and Muscovy, the Ottoman Empire, and the Crimean Khanate increased after 1648. Ukraine's Cossack lands exported cattle, horses, hemp, flax, tobacco, alcohol, wax, saltpeter, textiles, and potash to Muscovy in exchange for furs of varying kinds and some linen, textiles, and leather. Meat, grain, and wax were sold to the Ottomans in exchange for luxury items like silk, rugs, velvet, belts, Persian textiles, citrus fruits, rice, and tobacco. With the Crimea, Cossack traders exchanged grain for horses, cattle, and sheep. In the late seventeenth century, the grain trade with Poland was renewed. The efforts at expanding international trade brought in badly needed revenue in the form of tariffs for the Hetmanate and contributed to the development of a distinct Cossack economy

within the framework of eastern Europe. The mercantilist practices of the hetmans clashed, however, with the similar practices of the Russian government.

Russia, especially under the dynamic Peter I, was anxious to strengthen the
empire by integrating its economy under the direction of the central government
in St Petersburg. From the Russian imperial standpoint, all Cossack territories
– whether the Hetmanate, Sloboda Ukraine, or Zaporozhia – were part of one
imperial realm. Consequently, they should be economically as well as politically
integrated within the imperial system. Starting from this premise, as early as 1701
Peter I issued a decree forbidding Ukrainian merchants to ship certain products
(hemp, flax, potash, leather, wax, salt pork) along the traditional westward routes
to Poland and, via Danzig (today, Gdańsk), Königsberg (today Kaliningrad), or
Breslau (today Wrocław), to western Europe. Instead, Ukrainian products were
required to pass through Russia, to that country's cold water port of Arkhangel'sk,
on the White Sea. This decree effectively cut off Cossack trade with western Europe,
because the Arkhangel'sk-White Sea route – generally frozen and therefore accessible only a few months of the year – would make Ukrainian products prohibitively
expensive. Both Ukraine's merchants and Hetman Mazepa protested this decree,
and it was temporarily rescinded in 1711. It was issued again in 1714, however,
and new products were placed on the list, with the result that the Hetmanate's
international trade became an adjunct of Russia's. Finally, in 1755 the tariff border
between Ukrainian lands and the rest of the empire was permanently abolished.
Thus, in the course of the eighteenth century the economy of Left Bank Ukraine,
like its political and social structure, became progressively isolated from that of the
rest of Europe and integrated into the framework of that of the Russian Empire.

24

Religious and Cultural Developments

While it is true that in the eighteenth century political and socioeconomic life in Cossack Ukraine was characterized by its increasing integration with that of the Russian Empire and isolation from that of the rest of Europe, in the realm of culture, Ukraine remained a distinct and fertile ground where contemporary ideas in education, art, architecture, and literature from western and, in particular, central Europe were able to flourish. The new intellectual currents eventually made their way northward to Moscow. The trend whereby Ukraine served as a conduit for Western culture (often through a Polish prism) had begun in the seventeenth century, and it was continued and accelerated until the end of the eighteenth century.

Much of the cultural development in eighteenth-century Ukraine was expressed in a religious context, as in earlier eras. The Western-oriented Uniate Church, with its own hierarchy headed by a titular metropolitan of Kiev, functioned primarily on lands in Poland-Lithuania. Analogously, the Orthodox Church remained the dominant religious body in Russian-ruled Ukraine. Like other institutions, however, the Orthodox Church became more and more integrated into the Russian Empire.

The integration of the Orthodox Church

The process of integration had begun in 1686, when the Orthodox Metropolitan-ate of Kiev became jurisdictionally subordinate to the patriarch of the Russian Orthodox Church in Moscow instead of to the ecumenical patriarch in Constantinople. Initially, the Orthodox Church in Ukraine retained many of its traditional privileges, and during the reign of Hetman Mazepa (1687–1709) it even expanded and increased its wealth and prestige. But with the fall of Mazepa and the decline of political autonomy in Cossack Ukraine, the distinct status of the local Orthodox Church was undermined.

Under Tsar Peter I, the Russian Orthodox Church itself underwent a profound structural transformation, and this was to have an impact on Ukraine. In 1721, the tsar abolished the office of the Moscow patriarch and replaced it with a council of bishops, the Holy Synod, that henceforth functioned as the highest governing body of the Russian Orthodox Church. At the same time, the tsar issued a new constitution for the church, which omitted any mention of the Metropolitanate of Kiev. In effect, the Kiev metropolitanate ceased to exist. What remained in Russian-ruled Ukrainian lands was an ordinary Archeparchy of Kiev (from which a new Eparchy of Pereiaslav was carved out in 1701) and the Eparchy of Chernihiv, whose eastern region (Sloboda Ukraine) was previously detached and made part of the Eparchy of Belgorod. All three eparchies – Kiev, Pereiaslav, and Chernihiv – were under the Holy Synod of the Russian Orthodox Church.

Considering the symbolic value that the Russian Empire placed on linking itself with medieval Kievan Rus', it is not surprising that in 1743 the title *Metropolitan of Kiev, Galicia, and Little Russia* was restored. Although a few decades later the term *Little Russia* was dropped, the designation *Galicia* was retained since it helped provide ideological justification for Russia's claim to western Ukrainian territories (Galicia, Volhynia, and Podolia), which at the time were still within Poland. Regardless of what he may have been called, in practice the episcopal incumbent in Kiev was little more than the holder of an honorific title, since he had jurisdiction only over the Eparchy of Kiev within the Russian Orthodox Church.

After the abolition of the Hetmanate in the 1770s and 1780s, the integration of the Orthodox Church continued. The Holy Synod took over the right of appointing archimandrites (abbots) to monasteries, a right that had been exercised by the Kievan metropolitan; all monastic property was secularized; and forty-two of the existing sixty-one monasteries and convents were closed. In terms of administrative structure, eparchial boundaries were redrawn to coincide with Russia's new provincial boundaries: by the end of the eighteenth century, the Chernihiv and Poltava eparchies were formed from the Hetmanate, and the Kharkiv eparchy from Sloboda Ukraine. The process of making secular provincial and eparchial boundaries coincide was continued throughout Russian-ruled Ukrainian lands in the nineteenth century.

The Uniates in the Russian Empire fared even worse, especially during the reign of Empress Catherine II. In the 1770s, over 1,200 Uniate churches were given to the Orthodox in the Kiev region's Left Bank, and after 1793–1795, when the Russian Empire acquired the Right Bank, Volhynia, and Podolia during the Second and Third Partitions of Poland, another 2,300 Uniate churches and over 100 clergy were forced to become Orthodox. Finally, in 1796 the Uniate Metropolitanate of Kiev, whose eparchies on former Polish-Lithuanian territory were still functioning, was formally abolished.

The Uniates could do little to reverse the policy of a government intent on destroying their church. In contrast, the Orthodox in Ukrainian lands were recognized and even supported, although only to the degree that they could be made to fit into the framework of the Russian Orthodox Church. The changes in the status of the Orthodox Church in Ukraine were opposed by some Ukrainian hierarchs, but welcomed by others. Those who opposed the changes were either arrested by the tsarist government (Metropolitan Ioasaf Krokovs'kyi in 1718 and Archbishop Varlaam Vonatovych in 1730) or transferred (Metropolitan Tymofii Shcherbats'kyi in 1757). Many others not only welcomed but actually implemented the changes. Among them were the highest officials in the Russian Orthodox Holy Synod: its first president, Stefan Iavors'kyi (at the time metropolitan of Riazan'), and its first two vice-presidents, Teodosii Ianov'kyi (archbishop of Novgorod) and Teofan Prokopovych (archbishop of Pskov). All were Ukrainians who had previously played dominant roles in the religious and cultural life of the Metropolitanate of Kiev. In the end, the tsarist government and Russian Orthodox Church authorities provided enough incentives to Ukrainian hierarchs to make them actively participate in implementing policies which by the close of the eighteenth century had fully transformed the Orthodox Church in Ukraine into an integral part of the Russian Orthodox Church.

Education

As in previous centuries, the church continued to play a leading role in Ukraine's educational system. The vast majority of elementary schools were located next to village churches and were run by the parish sexton (*diak*). By the eighteenth century, the level of education in Ukrainian territories within the Russian Empire was relatively high, and foreign visitors frequently commented on the degree of literacy among the population at large. For instance, there were more elementary schools per number of inhabitants on Ukrainian territory than in neighboring Muscovy and Poland. In the Hetmanate during the 1740s, of 1,099 settlements within seven regiments, as many as 866 had primary schools. An earlier survey, from 1732, lists 129 such schools in the less densely populated Sloboda Ukraine.

At the secondary level, the most important institution remained the Kievan Collegium, established by Metropolitan Petro Mohyla during the 1630s and transformed into an academy in 1701. In the eighteenth century, the Kievan Academy provided a twelve-year program in philosophy and theology. Latin remained the most important language of instruction, followed by Church Slavonic and Greek. As part of the general process of integration throughout the empire, however, Russian became the language of instruction in all subjects after 1765. By the second half of the century, besides courses designed to prepare young men for the priesthood, engineering, modern languages (German and French), music, and painting were being taught. The secular subjects notwithstanding, an increasing emphasis was placed on the training of clerics. Thus, before the 1780s, of the some 1,150 students studying each year, 75 percent planned secular pursuits, whereas three decades later, of over 1,100 students, more than 95 percent were preparing for the priesthood.

The importance of the Kievan Academy was felt far beyond Ukraine. It was the oldest and most influential center of higher learning within the borders of the Russian Empire. Most of the leading hierarchs and intellectuals of the period in both Ukraine and the Russian Empire as a whole (Iasyns'kyi, Iavors'kyi, Prokopovych, Konys'kyi, Tuptalo), as well as many noteworthy political figures (Hetmans Mazepa and Orlyk and Catherine II's chancellor Aleksander Bezborod'ko) and the secular philosopher Hryhorii Skovoroda, were graduates of and/or teachers at the Kievan Academy. It is largely owing to graduates of the academy who moved north that the late seventeenth and first half of the eighteenth centuries have come to be known as the "Ukrainian Era" in Russian intellectual history.

Besides the Kievan Academy, there were secondary schools and/or theological seminaries in Chernihiv (est. 1689, theological seminary 1776), Pereiaslav (est. 1738), Poltava (est. 1779, later transferred to Katerynoslav), and Novhorod-Sivers'kyi (est. 1785). Particularly important was the Kharkiv Collegium, which began in 1726 as a seminary for the Orthodox Eparchy of Belgorod but in 1734 was renamed a college and soon expanded its curriculum to include science and mathematics in order to train students for secular careers. The Kharkiv Collegium was second only to the Kievan Mohyla Academy in the quality of its educational programs.

Because in Orthodox Christianity musical instruments were banned, the human voice took on special importance and was an essential part of religious services. In order to ensure a steady supply of vocal musicians, the Kievan Academy and various seminaries provided extensive programs in choral singing, and a special school to train singers for the imperial court was established in 1738 in the Hetmanate's capital of Hlukhiv. Such a musical environment did indeed have an impact, so that three of the Russian Empire's greatest choral composers in the eighteenth century were from Ukraine – Maksym Berezovs'kyi, Dmytro Bortnians'kyi, and Artem Vedel' – the last two of whom studied at the Kievan Mohyla Academy before moving to St Petersburg to continue their careers.

Finally, as part of Russia's territorial expansion beyond the Hetmanate into southern Ukraine and the opening of the province of New Russia, during the second half of the eighteenth century the imperial government established professional schools in the new cities of Ielyzavethrad (a medical-surgical academy), Mykolaïv (an agricultural school), and Katerynoslav (a music school). Thus, at the elementary as well as the secondary and professional levels, Ukrainian territories in the Russian Empire had a relatively well developed educational system during the eighteenth century.

Architecture and painting

The eighteenth century witnessed the flourishing of Ukrainian architecture and painting. The almost uninterrupted sequence of revolts, civil war, and foreign invasions that had marked the Khmel'nyts'kyi uprising, the Period of Ruin, and the last years of the Mazepa era finally came to a close. This meant that in most Ukrainian lands – Galicia and the Right Bank under Polish rule and Transcarpathia under Austrian rule, as well as the Russian-ruled Hetmanate and Sloboda Ukraine – a period of peace and stability had arrived. Not surprisingly, this era coincided with what has been described as the golden age of Ukrainian art.

In architecture, the flurry of reconstruction and new building in the Ukrainian or Cossack baroque style that characterized at least the first half of Mazepa's rule was continued during the era of stability following the hetman's downfall. The baroque churches, modeled especially on churches in Poland, became ever larger in size. Often topped with several gilded or azure domes, these structures also had elaborate facades marked by the typical baroque half-columns and incomplete pediments, and heavily decorated interiors ingeniously illuminated by the illusionary use of light. Despite the fact that these buildings were for Eastern-rite Christians and were located within the borders of the Orthodox Russian Empire, they clearly looked Catholic in spirit, prompting critics to deride them as products of the "Ukrainian Jesuit baroque."

Among the more important native architects of this era was Ivan Hryhorovych-Bars'kyi. He was best known for his Kiev structures, such as the Trinity Church of the St Cyril Monastery (1750s), the Church of the Holy Protectress in Podil (1766), and the pavilion-like municipal water fountain known as the *Felitsiial* (Samson's Fountain, 1748–49), as well as for his contribution (together with that of Andrii Kvasov) in the completion of the Church of the Nativity of the Mother of God (1752–63) in Kozelets'.

Other architectural trends prevalent in western Europe at the time – neoclassicism and the rococo – were brought to Ukrainian lands by foreign architects. The restraint and simplicity of neoclassicism were visible in the main belfry of the Monastery of the Caves (1731–45) and especially in the reconstruction of the Kievan Academy (1736–40), both by the German architect Johann-Gottfried Schaedel, and in the palace for Kyrylo Razumovs'kyi at Baturyn (1799–1803), by the Italian architect A. Rinaldi. In contrast, the rococo, which evolved from the baroque, carried on the baroque's interest in elaborate decorative elements but used much finer lines that created a sense of lightness and delicacy. Although the technique was employed in some of the structures designed by Hryhorovych-Bars'kyi, it is in the work of the Italian architect Bartolomeo-Francesco Rastrelli that the most outstanding examples are found. Most famous for his impressive structures in imperial St Petersburg, Rastrelli also brought the rococo to Kiev in commissions for Empress Elizabeth I, which he carried out in the stately Mariins'kyi Palace (1747–55), and in the exquisite splash of gold and azure in the Church of St Andrew (1747–53).

Not surprisingly, the baroque was even more prevalent in western Ukrainian lands, which were within the sphere of the Roman Catholic cultural influences of Poland and Hungary. It is from this period that derive the proportionally massive baroque St George Cathedral in L'viv (1745–60) and Town Hall in Buchach (1751), both by Bernard Merderer-Meretini, the Pochaïv Monastery Church (1771–83) by Gottfried Hoffman, and the very Italianate Dominican Church in L'viv (1745–49) by Martin Urbanik.

Wooden architecture was known throughout Ukraine, but it was particularly extensive in the Carpathian Mountain region, where lumber was abundant. Churches entirely in wood were constructed in great numbers, especially in mountain villages during the eighteenth century. These structures, small in scale, still dot the landscapes of southern Galicia as well as Transcarpathia and the Rusyn/Ukrainian area of present-day northeastern Slovakia – the latter areas with their rustic settings providing especially elegant and subtle renditions of Gothic and baroque styles in wood.

Painting also flourished in eighteenth-century Ukraine. Since Ukraine functioned as a conduit for Western cultural influence, it is not surprising that it was there that the heretofore restrictive rules of Byzantine iconography first broke down among the Orthodox East Slavs. Not only was post-Renaissance naturalism introduced into Ukrainian paintings and murals of religious inspiration, but secular portraiture also became popular as a result of the demands of the Polish noble estate and upwardly mobile Cossack *starshyna*. But notwithstanding latter-day art historians who speak in glowing terms of a Ukrainian school of painting under Flemish influence, the portraits from this period are rather awkward, unrefined in style, and hardly comparable to those of even second-rate artists in Flanders. As for religious paintings, most of them reflect Polish baroque models, whose sentimentality, imbued with the Catholic enthusiasm of the Counter Reformation, is often of dubious aesthetic value.

Literature and history writing

In its literary production, eighteenth-century Ukraine was typical of the baroque era, with its wide variety of themes and stylistic complexities. Style often became an end in itself, with the result that, as in the scholastic milieu of the Kievan Academy, form became more important than content. The language used in literature and other writings was a highly stylized form of Church Slavonic (and sometimes Latin or Russian). The opacity of Church Slavonic and its divorce from the spoken Ukrainian vernacular contributed to the formalistic and not particularly vibrant qualities of most literary works of the period, which were in sharp contrast to the spirited religious polemics that characterized the seventeenth century.

Perhaps the most popular branch of literary activity was drama. This genre developed during the seventeenth century under the influence of Polish and Latin plays staged in the brotherhood schools and at the Kievan Collegium. By the eighteenth century, Ukrainian drama had evolved into a distinct form in the works of writers like Dmytro Tuptalo, Teofan Prokopovych, and Hryhorii Konys'kyi. In a cultural environment where religion continued to play a dominant role, it is not surprising that the three authors mentioned above were churchmen and that the most widely produced plays were Christmas and Easter dramas, enactments of the lives of saints, and morality plays. There were also a few works of a largely or exclusively secular nature, the best known being the historical play by Teofan Prokopovych, about the Kievan prince Volodymyr the Great (*Vladymyr*, 1705) and a drama by an unknown author about the Cossack hetman Bodhan Khmel'nyts'kyi (*Mylost' Bozhyia*, or The Mercy of God, 1728). Other secular genres, albeit of smaller proportions, were the *intermediia*, or interlude, and, later, the *vertep*, or puppet play; these were often performed during the entr'actes of morality plays and were distinctive for their comical nature, occasional political satire, and use of the Ukrainian vernacular.

Several genres of poetry were produced during the eighteenth century, including spiritual verses, love and erotic poetry, epigrams, parodies, and patriotic verses glorifying contemporary leaders. The best-known creators in these genres were Ivan Velychkovs'kyi, Klymentii Zynov'iev, Dmytro Tuptalo, and Stefan Iavors'kyi.

There is one writer who stands out among all others from the eighteenth century, Hryhorii Skovoroda. Although he wrote numerous lyrical poems (*Sad bozhest-vennykh pesen'*, or Orchard of Divine Songs, 1735–85), he is best remembered in Ukraine and Russia for his philosophical writings. As the "Ukrainian Socrates," Skovoroda looked to the classical past and in particular followed the admonition of Socrates, Know Thyself. Most of his philosophical writings (in Russian or russianized Church Slavonic) and his teachings as a "wandering scholar" from 1769 until his death a quarter century later had to do with the search for happiness – not happiness derived from material wealth, but happiness attained through self-knowledge. Self-knowledge, he argued, would allow the individual to live life according to the natural order and therefore in accordance with God's will. Despite his use of philosophical models from ancient Greece, Skovoroda typified the other-worldly religious spirit that continued to dominate the culture of eighteenth-century Ukraine.

Among the few writers to depart from the purely religious motivation characteristic of eighteenth-century literature in Ukraine was a group of what might be called "Cossack intellectuals." As the intellectual exodus from Ukraine to Muscovy that began in the late seventeenth century continued and even intensified during the eighteenth century (for instance, it is estimated that between 1700 and 1762 as many as 70 percent of the upper Russian Orthodox Church hierarchy alone were natives of either Ukraine or Belarus), the places of some of these clerical intellectuals were taken by Cossacks serving in the Hetmanate administration. These intellectual chancellerists were most interested in the historical exploits of the social stratum they claimed to represent – the Cossacks. Accordingly, the tradition of Cossack chronicles, begun in the previous century, was continued in works like the *Litopys Samovydtsia*, or *Samovydets' Chronicle*, probably by Roman Rakushka; *Events of the Most Bitter … War … between the Zaporozhian Hetman Bohdan Khmel'nyts'kyi and the Poles*, by Hryhorii Hrabianka; and the four-volume *Tale of the Cossack War against the Poles*, by Samiilo Velychko, all compiled during the first two decades of the eighteenth century. The works of Hrabianka and Velychko, in particular, presented the Khmel'nyts'kyi revolt as a Ukrainian national uprising, and it was this interpretation that deeply influenced the subsequent Ukrainian national movement when these chronicles were published for the first time between the 1790s and the 1840s. The Cossack chroniclers continued a tradition established by their medieval forebears, whose aim was simply to record the events of a given epoch without concern for historical perspective. Beginning in the 1730s, however, a new kind of work began to appear, one which traced historical events in Ukraine from the days of Kievan Rus' and connected them with the Cossack period. Such an approach implied a sense of historical continuity which, in the minds of certain readers, might provide an ideological justification for the maintainance of Cossack autonomy. The first work of this kind was the popular and readable *Kratkoe opisanie Malorossii* (A Short Description of Little Russia), written in the 1730s but not published until four decades later. Several similar historical treatises were written during the last decades of the Hetmanate's autonomous existence, and their authors (Hryhorii Pokas, Petro Symonovs'kyi, Stepan Lukoms'kyi) all argued from historical and political precedent for the idea of Cossack distinctiveness. Although the attempts to sustain autonomy for the Hetmanate after the 1780s eventually proved futile, the work of these Cossack chroniclers set the stage for a fundamental change from a cultural environment in which religious concerns were foremost to one in which secular ideas and a concern for the rights of the individual and the nation would be pervasive.

For this change in Ukraine's intellectual evolution to be effected fully, a new mind-set and ideology had to be introduced. That ideology would come in the form of nationalism, the precepts of which, as we shall see, would dominate Ukrainian thinking throughout the nineteenth and most of the twentieth centuries. But before turning to that new era in the history of Ukraine, however, it is necessary to review events in the eighteenth-century Right Bank and Galicia.

25

The Right Bank and Western Ukraine

While the Hetmanate, Sloboda Ukraine, and Zaporozhia were gradually becoming integrated in the Russian Empire during the course of the eighteenth century, the Right Bank, Volhynia, Podolia, Belz, and Galicia continued to be ruled by Poland. Polish rule in the Right Bank had been seriously undermined by the Khmel'nyts'kyi uprising of 1648. It was only after Poland and Muscovy agreed to divide their spheres of influence more or less along the Dnieper River (in 1667 and 1686) that the Poles were able to restore their authority over most of Ukraine's Right Bank. The restoration, however, did not proceed without difficulty.

First of all, a large part of the Right Bank (the palatinates of Bratslav and southern Kiev) and Podolia were under Ottoman rule between 1672 and 1699 (see map 20). Even after Poland reacquired these territories through a treaty with the Ottoman Empire (1699), the full restoration of Polish rule, at least in the Right Bank, was delayed for more than a decade owing to several factors: (1) a Cossack revolt led by Semen Palii between 1702 and 1704; (2) the control of the region by Hetman Mazepa's forces (from 1704 to 1708) during the Great Northern War; and (3) invasions by Mazepa's successor-in-exile, Pylyp Orlyk, and his Muscovite antagonist, Tsar Peter I (between 1711 and 1714). Only after 1714, which ushered in a period of peace among Poland, Muscovy, and the Ottoman Empire, was it possible for the Polish government to restore a measure of control over the Right Bank.

The return of Polish rule in the Right Bank

With its return to power, the Polish government reinstituted its system of administration based on the palatinate. These included the Right Bank palatinates of Kiev (now only west of the Dnieper River) and Bratslav, as well as, farther west, the palatinates of Podolia, Volhynia, Rus' (Galicia), and Belz, where Polish rule had never been seriously threatened. Each palatinate was ruled by a palatine (Polish: *wojewoda*) appointed by the Polish king, although this royal official's authority was reduced from what it had been in the period before 1648. His responsibilities were essentially to lead the local militia and to chair the local dietine (*sejmik*)

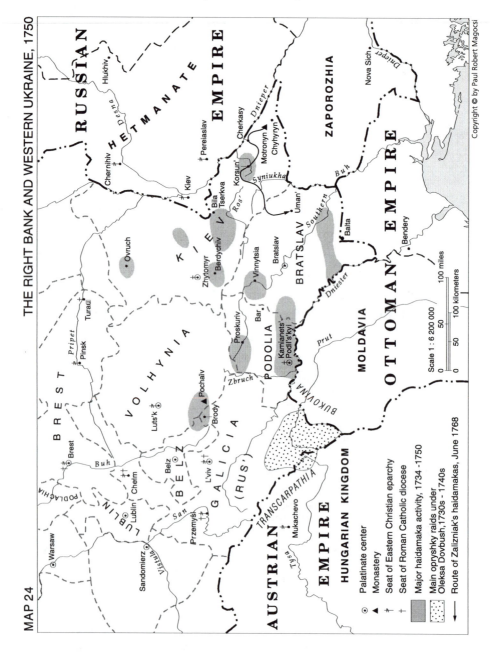

MAP 24

THE RIGHT BANK AND WESTERN UKRAINE, 1750

Legend:

- ⊙ Palatine center
- ▲ Monastery
- ✝ Seat of Eastern Christian eparchy
- ✝ Seat of Roman Catholic diocese
- ▨ Major haidamaka activity, 1734–1750
- ⦂⦂ Main opryshky raids under Oleksa Dovbush, 1730s–1740s
- → Route of Zalizniak's haidamakas, June 1768

Scale 1 : 6 200 000

0   50   100 miles
0   50   100 kilometers

located in the palatine center. In effect, it was not the palatine but the dietines of each palatinate which held real political and administrative power, and they were completely in the hands of the powerful magnates and their gentry vassals. The dietines regulated taxes, controlled the draft, and chose deputies to the central Diet (*Sejm*) in Warsaw.

The decades after 1714 were marked by a return to the Right Bank of old as well as new Polish magnates from the Lubomirski, Seniawski, Rzewuski, Jablonowski, Sanguszko, Branicki, Potocki, Czartoryski, Tyszkiewicz, and other families. Without exception, these families prided themselves on being the initiators of a resettlement plan that ostensibly brought cultivation and civilization once again to the "wild Ukrainian steppe." As a result of the upheavals of the previous century, Poland's kings also once again became holders of huge estates, especially in the Bratslav and the southern regions of the Kiev palatinates.

The manner in which the Polish socioeconomic system was reestablished also followed past models with the reintroduction and/or expansion of manorial estates (*latifundia*). In more heavily populated areas, the arenda system was put in place, and more often than not the leaseholders who ran the Polish estates and mills were Jews. In fact, the eighteenth century witnessed a steady increase in the number of Jews in the Right Bank. Despite the destruction of the Khmel'nyts'kyi era, a century later, in the 1760s, there were over 250,000 Jews in more than eighty communities. Aside from their service as arendars on rural estates, Jews also congregated in large numbers in towns and cities, where they dominated trade and the small handicrafts industries.

In the barren and more underpopulated territories, especially in the eastern Bratslav and southern Kiev palatinates, Polish magnates took the initiative by inviting peasants from the more densely populated Ukrainian-inhabited areas of Galicia, Belz, western Volhynia, and even the Polish-inhabited palatinates farther to the west. Peasants from these regions, whose duties to landlords continually increased, were easily attracted to Poland's southeastern "frontier," where at least initially they were allowed to settle for so-called free periods. This meant they did not have to pay taxes or perform labor duties for their manorial landlords during the period specified.

The eventual fate of the peasantry was to be influenced by the changes in Poland's political life. The eighteenth century was a time when central authority had almost entirely broken down. Poland's kings – August II of Saxony (reigned 1697–1706 and 1709–1733), the beleaguered sovereign who returned to his throne after Muscovy's victory over Sweden in 1709; August III (reigned 1733–1763); and Stanisław Poniatowski (reigned 1764–1795) – became for the most part figureheads. More often than not they were elected because (1) they represented the most acceptable compromise between candidates of the Polish Diet's increasingly contentious Senate and House of Deputies; and (2) they were acceptable to Russia, which by then was playing an increasingly dominant role in Polish politics.

By the eighteenth century, the traditional balance of power within Poland among the crown, the magnates (represented by the Senate), and the gentry (represented by the House of Deputies) had broken down, essentially leaving the field open to the economically and socially powerful magnates. The large magnates fully controlled the countryside, where their huge manorial estates became what have been called little kingdoms, or kinglets. Each magnate maintained his own private army, and, not surprisingly, in the Right Bank, Podolia, and eastern Volhynia the Polish landlords were responsible for reactivating Cossack-like military formations to serve their own interests. This was also the period in which the Polish nobility built hundreds of manorial residences throughout Ukrainian lands west of the Dnieper River, with those of the magnates being virtual palaces. Usually built in the neo-classical style, the most impressive in terms of size and wealth (because of the collections of art they housed) were the palatial residences of the Potockis in Tul'chyn, the Ksawerys at Voronevytsia (near Vinnytsia), the Ilińskis at Romaniv (in Volhynia), the Sanguszkos at Slavuta (near Ostroh), and the Radziwiłłs at Olyka (near Luts'k). Among the most aesthetically moving of these projects was the monumental, yet exquisite Romantic park built on the Potocki estate in Uman' and named Sofiïvka (Polish: *Zofiówka*) in honor of the woman for whom it was built, the second wife of Count Stanisław Szczęsny Potocki.

In such circumstances, the plight of the Ukrainian peasantry varied. In the western palatinates – Rus' (Galicia), Belz, western Volhynia, and western Podolia – the peasants bore the greatest burdens of serfdom. Farther east, especially in those palatinates only recently resettled – eastern Volhynia, eastern Podolia, Kiev, and Bratslav – serfdom had not yet been implemented. Peasants did serve there on manorial estates, but their duties were less or, in instances of duty-free residence, virtually non-existent. The duty-free periods sooner or later ran out, however, and when they did, peasant discontent increased and the potential for revolt became real.

Added to the socioeconomic problem was a cultural one. The restoration of Polish rule in the Right Bank was accompanied by the return of the Roman Catholic and Uniate Churches and the concomitant decline of the Orthodox Church. All this, moreover, was occurring in an era marked by increasing religious intolerance in Poland. The religious intolerance of the late seventeenth and the eighteenth centuries was accompanied by a secular ideology called Sarmatianism (*Sarmatyzm*). According to this belief, Poland's nobles were descendants of the ancient Sarmatians; they accordingly made up the ruling and only core stratum of the Polish nation and had a historic duty to defend Christianity. For Sarmatians, the only acceptable form of Christianity was that represented by the Polish Roman Catholic Church. As an ideology, Sarmatianism was characterized by an extreme intolerance of cultural, political, and religious beliefs other than those of the Polish nobility, which was convinced of its superiority not only to other social estates in Poland but to other nationalities as well. Such self-centered, even xenophobic views on the part of the Polish nobility were bound to have an effect on the Orthodox Ukrainian population living in the eastern borderlands.

From the standpoint of Polish law, the charter of 1632, which had legalized the existence of the Orthodox as well as the Uniate Church, was still in force. The subsequent fate of each of these churches varied greatly, however, according to political circumstances. During the Khmel'nyts'kyi uprising and the rule of his successors in the Cossack state (at least through the hetmanship of Petro Doroshenko until 1676), Roman Catholics and Uniates were barred from the Right Bank. Orthodoxy had full control over religious affairs within the Cossack state, and the church was enriched with large land grants to the point that it became an economic power in its own right. By the late seventeenth century, however, the situation had changed substantially. Several factors – a decrease in the influence of the Cossacks, a reduction in the number of Orthodox adherents because of large-scale flight to Muscovite-controlled territory on the Left Bank, the subordination of the Kievan metropolitan see to Muscovy, the arrival of Polish landlords – contributed to the decline of Orthodoxy in the Right Bank. The decline took place, even though according to the provisions of the Polish-Muscovite "eternal peace" of 1686 Muscovy retained the right to intervene on behalf of the Orthodox Ukrainians living on the Right Bank. In terms of ecclesiastical jurisdiction, the Orthodox population in the Polish-ruled Right Bank and neighboring palatinates was under the authority of the bishop of Pereiaslav, who resided in the Muscovite-controlled Hetmanate. The bishop could not, however, stem the decline of Orthodoxy beyond Muscovy's borders.

Even in the center of the Orthodox cultural revival during the late sixteenth century, Galicia and western Volhynia, the Orthodox Church was virtually eliminated. One after another, the Orthodox eparchies of Przemyśl (1692), L'viv (1700), and Luts'k (1702) became Uniate, as did the Pochaïv Monastery (1713) in Volhynia and the very stronghold of the Orthodox cultural revival, the Stauropegial Brotherhood in L'viv (1708). With the acceptance by Luts'k of the Union, there was no longer any Orthodox eparchy within the boundaries of the Polish-Lithuanian Commonwealth.

Social protest and the haidamak revolts

Faced with the socioeconomic decline of the peasantry, the virtual elimination of the Cossacks, and the dissolution of the Orthodox Church structure and subsequent pressure on the population by Poland's Roman Catholic and Uniate Churches, large segments of the Ukrainian population continued to believe that farther east, beyond the Dnieper River in Russian territory, things were somehow better. Certainly in relation to Polish-controlled Ukrainian territory, tsarist Russia seemed more promising. In the mid-eighteenth century, the Hetmanate, Zaporozhia, and even Sloboda Ukraine still had varying degrees of political autonomy. Moreover, serfdom had not yet been fully imposed in any of those territories, and Zaporozhia still served as a haven for those who wanted to live in a landlord-less society. Finally, Russia was an Orthodox country where Roman Catholics and Uniates were not favored. Thus, socioeconomic and religious discontent mixed with vague hopes for salvation in Russia made a potent recipe for disturbances, large or small, within Polish-controlled Ukrainian territory.

Disturbances did take place throughout the eighteenth century, in different forms ranging from small-scale bandit-like raids on manorial estates to large-scale military campaigns and peasant revolts. Social protests of the oldest and most contained kind took place in the westernmost Ukrainian lands, especially along Poland's border with Hungary, in the Carpathian foothills and valleys of southern Galicia and Transcarpathia. There, small groups of discontented peasants, sheep herders, and, occasionally, demobilized soldiers banded together, attacked property owned by landlords, and sometimes distributed their spoils to the poor peasantry. These Robin Hood–like groups who lived in the Carpathians were known as *opryshky*. Although the *opryshky* had no general religious or ideological motivation, they became the subject of praise in local folklore and literature. The *opryshky* phenomenon began in the sixteenth century and in some places lasted until the twentieth century. The movement was most widespread in the 1730s and 1740s, during which its most famous leader, Oleksa Dovbush, was active.

More widespread was the haidamak movement on the Right Bank (*haidamak* was originally a Turkish word meaning robber or pillager). The haidamak movement consisted of virtually continuous spontaneous revolts by Orthodox peasants and Cossacks against Polish Catholic landlords and their Jewish arendars as well as against the Roman Catholic and Uniate clergy. Besides sporadic revolts limited to specific regions or manorial estates, major uprisings occurred in the years 1734, 1750, and 1768.

The haidamak phenomenon has been distorted in the historical memory of eastern Europeans even more than has the Khmel'nyts'kyi era. Polish historians traditionally have argued that the haidamak movement was "unleashed" by Russia to destroy Poland (T. Morawski) or else that it reflected the fundamentally degenerate character of the Ukrainian people (F. Rawita-Gawroński). Jewish historians have considered the haidamak revolt a "catastrophe" during which their people were "murdered in beastlike fashion" (S. Dubnow). Russian and Ukrainian historians, too, have been critical of the movement's uncontrolled excesses (A. Skal'kovs'kyi, D.L. Mordovets'). But the popular Ukrainian view was created by the influential nineteenth-century "national bard," Taras Shevchenko, who in his poem *Haidamaky* (The Haidamaks) presented them as heroes struggling against national oppression.

The haidamak movement consisted of a kind of ongoing guerrilla warfare conducted by small groups of discontented peasants, servants, or artisans who attacked the manors of the great landowners on the Polish-controlled Right Bank. When necessary, they would seek refuge across the Dnieper River in the Hetmanate or Zaporozhia. The Russian government, however, was generally opposed to what it considered bandits, and haidamaks caught on Russian territory would be arrested and turned over to the Polish authorities. Although their guerrilla-like raids were a nuisance, they could be contained by local Polish authorities and by landlords, with their private armies. Particularly dangerous, however, were situations in which the haidamaks, together with peasants from the Right Bank, were joined and, sometimes, led by Cossacks. The latter could include those in the service of Polish magnates as well as impoverished and politically radical Cossacks and other socially marginal elements (*siroma*) from Zaporozhia and the Left Bank. Such combinations were formed during the first (1734) and last (1768) of the three major haidamak revolts.

The first revolt broke out in 1734, when Russia sent a large army into the Right Bank after the death of Poland's King August II in 1733. That year, the Polish Diet elected the exiled Stanisław Leszczyński, the former pro-Swedish king of Poland (reigned 1706–1709), who planned a return to the Polish throne with the help of France and several Polish nobles. Russia, which opposed such an eventuality, sent an army to drive out Leszczyński and had August II's son, August III, elected instead. The Russian military presence in the Right Bank, however, raised false hopes in the Ukrainian peasantry that their liberation from Polish rule was imminent. A rebellion broke out among peasants in the southern Kiev palatinate and spread quickly to eastern Volhynia and Podolia, where it was led by a Cossack captain known simply as Verlan, previously in the service of a local Polish magnate. But the Russians came quickly to the aid of the new Polish king and put down the revolt.

In 1750, another peasant revolt broke out, when haidamak rebels who had been organized on Zaporozhian territory (perhaps with clandestine Cossack consent and participation) crossed into the Right Bank, where they were joined by peasants unhappy that their settlers' free period had ended in 1750. This revolt, which began in the southern regions of the Kiev palatinate, spread to Bratslav but was put down by the Poles.

The last major haidamak revolt occurred in 1768. It was the largest and it was the only one which seemed to have specific political and social goals. It was inspired also by the characteristic blend of peasant socioeconomic and religious discontent with hopes for salvation in Russia. This last major uprising, which once again began in the southern part of the Kiev palatinate, became known as the *Koliivshchyna* rebellion, a name probably derived from the pikes or lances (*kola*) with which the rebels, called *kolii*, were armed.

During the 1760s, the duty-free periods allowed the recent settlers were coming to an end in the southern Kiev palatinate. But the peasants were reluctant to accept the landlords' demands for labor services and dues. At the same time, an Orthodox revival was under way at the Motronyn Monastery near Chyhyryn. The monastery was headed by the archimandrite Melkhysedek Znachko-Iavors'kyi, who in 1761 was made assistant to the bishop of Pereiaslav. The bishop of Pereiaslav, in the Russian-controlled Hetmanate, who had jurisdiction over the Orthodox population in neighboring Poland, encouraged Znachko-Iavors'kyi's opposition to the Uniate Church. The archimandrite also received support from the Zaporozhian Cossacks. As a result of this activity, Znachko-Iavors'kyi was arrested by the Poles, but he escaped and fled to Russia, where Empress Catherine II received him and apparently promised to intervene on his behalf through diplomatic channels. Buoyed by such news, the archimandrite returned to his monastery, where he renewed his contact with the Zaporozhian Cossacks.

Meanwhile, the Polish nobility was becoming increasingly dissatisfied with Russia's interference in the political affairs of their country. Since the beginning of the eighteenth century, a significant proportion of Poland's nobles had favored either pro-Swedish or pro-French candidates for their country's throne, but their efforts were consistently blocked by St Petersburg, which succeeded in having pro-Russian candidates (August II of Saxony and his son, August III) elected instead. Moreover, Poland's newest king, Stanisław Poniatowski, who came to the throne in 1764, seemed to many nobles little more than a Russian puppet. Accordingly, in early 1768 several Polish nobles organized the so-called Confederation of Bar, based in the eastern Podolia and Bratslav palatinates. The result was a noble-led insurrection whose intent was to rid the country of its pro-Russian ruler. In response, a tsarist army already in Poland was dispatched southward to crush the rebellion.

At the same time the Confederation of Bar was beginning its insurrection, farther east a Zaporozhian Cossack named Maksym Zalizniak, who had been living at Znachko-Iavors'kyi's Motronyn Monastery for over a year, organized a rebel group of Zaporozhian Cossacks against the Polish noble Confederation of Bar. This group believed the Confederation was intent on destroying all Orthodox adherents. In the early spring of 1768, Zalizniak and his forces formed in the traditional haidamak gathering place of Kholodnyi Iar, near the Motronyn Monastery.

UMAN' AS A SYMBOL FOR UKRAINIANS, POLES, AND JEWS

Ever since the haidamak rebellion of 1768 and Gonta's capture of Uman', that town on the Right Bank halfway between Kiev and the shores of the Black Sea has been an important symbol in the historical mythologies of Ukrainians, Poles, and Jews, yet one profoundly different for all three.

Among Ukrainians, Uman' is best remembered from its depiction in *Haidamaky* (The Haidamaks, 1841), the longest of the poems of the most widely read Ukrainian writer, Taras Shevchenko. Based loosely on events during the 1768 haidamak rebellion, Shevchenko's work expresses the wild and often merciless character of peasant revolts against social oppression. While he does not condone the murderous exploits of Zalizniak and Gonta, he sees the past, even with all its evils, as a source of inspiration for Ukrainians in the future.

> Along the entire way
> From Kiev to Uman' the dead
> In heaping piles were laid.
>
> The Haidamaky on Uman'
> Like heavy clouds converge
> At midnight. Ere the night is done
> The whole town is submerged.
> The Haidamaky take the town
> With shouts: 'The Poles should pay!'
> Dragoons are downed, their bodies roll
> Around the marketplace;
> The ill, the cripples, children too,
> All die, no one is spared.
> Wild cries and screams. 'Mid streams of blood
> Stands Gonta on the square
> With Zalizniak together, they
> Urge on the rebel band:
> 'Good work, stout lads! There, that's the way
> To punish them, the damned!'
> And then the rebels brought to him
> A Jesuit, a monk,
> With two young boys. 'Look, Gonta, look!
> These youngsters are your sons!
> They're Catholics: since you kill all,
> Can you leave them alone?
> Why are you waiting? Kill them now ...'

And the two lads were slain.
They fell to earth, still bubbling words:
'O dad! We are not Poles!
We ... we ...' And then they spoke no more,
Their bodies growing cold.
'Perhaps they should be buried, what?'
'No need! They're Catholic.'

Much time has gone by, since a child, a poor orphan,
In sacking and coatless, without any bread,
I roamed that Ukraine where Zalizniak and Gonta
With sanctified sabres had wreaked vengeance dread.
Much time has gone by since, along those same highways
Where rode Haidamaky, exhausted and sore
I tramped through the country, its high roads and by-ways,

And weeping, sought people to teach me good lore.
As now I recall them, my youthful misfortunes,
I grieve that they're past! I would trade present fortune

If only those days could be brought back again. ...*

The popular Polish image of Uman' was, like the Ukrainian, forged by early nineteenth-century Romantic writers and publicists. Some saw the event as one of the worst examples of Cossack barbarism against Polish civilization. Others saw it as a lesson from which Polish society should learn. Among the most widely read and debated works was Seweryn Goszczyński's epic poem *Zamek kaniowski* (The Castle of Kaniv, 1828), based on oral and memoiristic accounts of what the author later called the "Uman' massacre." Goszcyzński suggested that while the Poles may have suffered at Uman', that experience should be used to point the way to reconciliation with Ukrainians and to the creation with them of a common platform in the search for freedom from tsarist oppression for both peoples. Such a message formed the ideological basis of the Uman' Society (Gromada Humań), a Polish revolutionary group founded in exile following the abortive 1831 uprising against tsarist Russia. For that group, Uman' (in Polish: Humań) became the very symbol of Polish regeneration:

The memory of the errors of our fathers, for which our country and we now suffer severe punishment from heaven, commanded us to put our finger to the most painful of wounds. It was fitting for us, children of Humań and noblemen, to take on the name of that theater of horror so as to make humble expiation before heaven, our fatherland and mankind for the guilt of our fathers. It was fitting for us to assume the name of Humań so that with the people of Ukraine, the people of Greek faith, we could make a truce of renewal, a union of the future; so that in the terrible memory we could expunge the mutual suffering; so that with this name we could wash off the mutual hate and remove the bloody memory that came from the persecution of the people of Ukraine and the most terrible reaction that provoked. ...

It is on the hands of the tsars that you should look for the blackened stain of innocent blood. But do not blame the people. They are unfortunate; the victims of ignorance; the plaything of intrigues; the tool of their own and of others' pain. For not only he who dies but also he who kills is worthy of pity. Human is a lesson both for the Polish and the Ukrainian people.[†]

As for the Jewish perspective, the distinguished twentieth-century historian of East European Jewry, Simon Dubnow, called Uman' "the second Ukrainian catastrophe." It was a Yiddish folk song from the late eighteenth century, however, which perhaps best summed up Jewish attitudes:

Our Father in Heaven, how can you stand the sights,
That Ukrainian Jews should suffer such horrible troubles!
Where in the world are such persecutions heard of?
Gonta has even killed small children and taken their money.
The most evil of the haidamaks should come before you,
Lord of the world,
And you should help all who have protected us![‡]

Uman' also became the burial place of Rabbi Nachman of Bratslav, the great-grandson of the founder of Hasidism, Baal Shem Tov. Nachman, himself the founder of an important Hasidic rabbinical dynasty, believed that for some reason a number of the Jews killed in Uman' in 1768 were unable to rise to heaven. Accordingly, he chose to spend his last years in Uman', in a house overlooking the Jewish cemetery, where he too was eventually buried. Since the early nineteenth century, Uman' has been an important site for Hasidic Jewish pilgrimages; they were banned by the Soviets but permitted again in 1989, during the Gorbachev era.

[*]Taras Shevchenko, *Selected Works*, translated by John Weir (Moscow 1964), pp. 97–99, 104.
[†]George G. Grabowicz, "The History and Myth of the Cossack Ukraine in Polish and Russian Romantic Literature" (unpublished PhD dissertation, Harvard University 1975), p. 127.
[‡]Mendel Osherowitsch, *Shtet un shtetlekh in Ukrayne un in andere tayln fun Rusland*, Vol. II (New York 1948), p. 172. Translation by Henry Abramson.

They soon captured several towns in the southern Kiev palatinate (Cherkasy, Smila, Korsun', and others), while disparate haidamak groups raided other parts of the Kiev palatinate and farther afield into Bratslav, Podolia, and southern Volhynia. En route, Zalizniak's forces attracted more peasant supporters and, following the haidamak tradition, killed, often in brutal fashion, all the Polish landlords and Roman Catholic and Uniate clergy they could find. The rebel's most spectacular triumph came at the end of June at Uman,' where a local Cossack captain in the Polish service, Ivan Gonta, who was entrusted with defending the town, suddenly joined the haidamaks. The combined forces of Zalizniak and Gonta then turned on Uman,' captured the town, and massacred as many as 2,000 Poles and Jews living there. It seems that Zalizniak, who in the interim was proclaimed Zaporozhian hetman, wanted to drive all Polish nobles from the Right Bank, including the rebellious Bar confederates. He hoped to return, under the protection of the Polish king, to the supposed ideal conditions before the enserfment of the peasantry and to set up a Cossack-like political entity without landlords or their ideological allies, the Roman Catholics and Uniates.

The Russian Empire's role in the 1768 *Koliivshchyna* revolt of haidamaks was ambiguous. While on the one hand encouragement was given to the Orthodox clergy on the Right Bank, on the other the rebellion of Zalizniak and Gonta seemed to have gone too far. Neither the haidamaks' plans for social liberation and Cossack autonomy, nor the resultant weakening of Poland, nor the possibility of friction along the Ottoman border (the Turks had lodged a strong protest when their border town of Balta was captured by the haidamaks) made the *Koliivshchyna* uprising particularly attractive to tsarist Russia. Consequently, Catherine II ordered her army in Podolia, which had just put down the rebellious Polish nobles of the Confederation of Bar, to crush the haidamaks. This action was accompanied by a Polish pacification in which 5,000 to 7,000 peasants were killed. Gonta and Zalizniak were captured, and to show its good will toward Poland and toward the Ottomans, Russia turned over 900 insurgents to the Poles and then held a show trial near the Ottoman border at which 250 haidamaks (including Zalizniak) were condemned to death (their sentences later were commuted to hard labor in Siberia). As for Gonta, he was considered a traitor because of his actions at Uman.' He was brought to Warsaw and tortured, and his dismembered body put on public display. The blood spilled on both sides during and after the uprising only deepened the enmity between Poles and Ukrainians, with the result that the hadiamak rebellion of 1768, the *Koliivshchyna*, became a lasting symbol – fed by subsequent literary and historical distortion – of Polish-Ukrainian and, to a lesser degree, Jewish-Ukrainian hatred.

The Partitions of Poland

In 1768, Poland had once again been saved by Russia, but this was to be the last time. As a country, Poland had become a political anomaly by the eighteenth century. Its political structure, with a weak elected king and diffusion of authority throughout the country among an independent-minded and often selfishly pacifistic nobility, created a state of internal anarchy which made the country vulnerable to the expansionist tendencies of its neighbors to the west, south, and east. Not only had each of those neighboring countries created increasingly centralized political and military structures, even more ominous for Poland was the fact that all three were headed at the time by highly talented and dynamic rulers: Frederick II ("the Great," reigned 1740–1786) in Prussia, Maria Theresa (reigned 1740–1780) and Joseph II (reigned 1780–1790) in Austria, and Catherine II ("the Great," reigned 1762–1796) in Russia. Poland would have to change, and change quickly, or succumb to its more powerful neighbors. The Poles did attempt to make basic structural changes in their political system, but these came much too late.

In 1772, in order to satisfy their territorial ambitions, Prussia and Russia planned to annex simultaneously portions of Poland's territory. From the time of the haidamak revolt and the uprising of Polish nobles at Bar in 1768, the Russian Empire had maintained a standing army on Polish territory in the Right Bank. In the following year, 1769, it even placed a garrison in the far western city of L'viv, the capital of the Rus' (Galicia) palatinate. This was not particularly surprising, since from the perspective of St Petersburg these so-called Little Russian territories were part of the historical patrimony of the Russian Empire, which was the self-proclaimed descendant of Kievan Rus'.

For its part, Prussia did not want to see Russia's political and military inter-ference in Poland become the basis for unilateral territorial aggrandizement. To prevent such an eventuality, therefore, and to maintain a balance of power in the region as a whole, Prussia urged Austria to join with it and Russia in the territorial partitioning of Poland. Austria had become wary of Russia's victories in its current war (since 1768) against the Ottoman Turks, which made possible the expansion of tsarist influence near Austria's southern borders in the Balkans as well as near its eastern borders in Polish-ruled Ukrainian territories (i.e., Galicia). Hence, with feigned reluctance, Austria went along with the international partitioning scheme.

The result was the First Partition of Poland, whereby Prussia acquired Polish ter-ritory along the Baltic Sea, Russia a swath of territory along Poland's northeastern boundary, and Austria the Ukrainian- and Polish-inhabited palatinates of Galicia-Rus' and Belz. Ironically, of the three partitioning powers, Austria, which had had to be "persuaded" by the others to go along with the scheme, received the largest number of inhabitants (2,650,000) and territory (32,000 square miles [82,000 square kilometers]). Habsburg Austria justified its acquisition by reviving the medieval Hungarian claim to sovereignty over the old Kievan Rus' principalities of Galicia and Volhynia. Since the Habsburgs were simultaneously kings of Hungary, they could argue that they had historic rights over this new territory, which they named the Kingdom of Galicia-Lodomeria (*Königreich Galizien und Lodomerien*), or Galicia (*Galizien*) for short. Two years later, in 1774, the Habsburgs acquired from the Ottoman vassal state of Moldavia the mountainous region of Bukovina, which was thereupon united with Galicia. As a result of these border changes, the Rus-sian Empire withdrew its army, however reluctantly, from Galicia's capital of L'viv.

Thus, the First Partition of Poland in 1772 took place through diplomatic means, without a shot being fired. This was not the case two decades later, when Prussia, Russia, and Austria were once again ready to cooperate in acquiring more territory from Poland. Sensing the new threat, the Poles tried to restructure their political system (adopting the Constitution of 3 May 1791), and in a rare display of national unity they fought against the Prussian and Russian armies invading the country. But it was too late. Poland was partitioned in 1793 and 1795. The last partition removed Poland entirely from the map of Europe.

MAP 25

THE PARTITIONS OF POLAND

BALTIC
SEA

1795

1772

Polatsk

Kaunas

Vitsebsk

Kaliningrad
(Königsberg)

Vilnius

Smolensk

Gdańsk
(Danzig)
1772

PRUSSIA

LITHUANIA

Mahilioŭ

1795

1793

1795

1793   Warsaw

Brest

Pripet

1772

Warta

BREST

Chernihiv

Desna

LUBLIN

Buh

VOLHYNIA

1795

1795   Luts'k

1793

RUSSIA

Cracow

San

BELZ

1772   L'viv

GALICIA

Zhytomyr

Kiev

KIEV

Ros'

TRANSCARPATHIA

Dniester

Southern

PODOLIA

Kamianets'

Buh

1774   BUKOVINA

MOLDAVIA

BRATSLAV

AUSTRIA

Copyright © by Paul Robert Magocsi

OTTOMAN EMPIRE

0   50   100 miles
0   50   100 kilometers
Scale 1 : 9 000 000

—·· International boundaries, 1770
– – – Boundary of Lithuania, 1770
—— Boundary of Ukraine, 2005
1772 Date of acquisition of area

Acquisitions by 1795
  Austrian Empire
  Russian Empire
  Prussian Empire

Of the Polish-ruled Ukrainian territories, Russia acquired the palatinates of Kiev, Bratslav, Podolia, and eastern Volhynia during the Second Partition in 1793, and western Volhynia and Chełm (east of the Buh River) during the Third Partition in 1795. As in other parts of the Russian Empire, these newly acquired areas were divided into provinces (*gubernii*), each with its own governor directly responsible to St Petersburg. The former Polish palatinate of Kiev (together with the city of Kiev, which had belonged to Russia since the late seventeenth century) became the province of Kiev; Volhynia together with eastern Chełm became the province of Volhynia; and the Podolia and Bratslav palatinates became the province of Podolia.

Thus, Polish rule over Ukrainian territories, which had begun to take hold as long before as the fourteenth century (Galicia and Belz) and which had expanded considerably in the late sixteenth century (Volhynia, Podolia, the Right and Left Banks), slowly withered in the seventeenth century until it finally came to an end in 1795. The last decades of the eighteenth century also witnessed the end of Ottoman and Crimean rule over lands north of the Black Sea and the Sea of Azov (see chapter 22). All Ukraine's territories were now under the control of only two states, both of which were major European powers: the Russian Empire, which held the vast majority; and the Austrian Empire, which held the western lands of Galicia, Belz, Bukovina, and Transcarpathia.

PART SIX

Ukraine in the Russian Empire

26

Administrative and Political Developments in Dnieper Ukraine

With the elimination of Poland from the map of Europe following the Third Partition in 1795, all Ukrainians came to live under the rule of two multinational states: the Russian Empire and the Austrian, later the Austro-Hungarian, Empire. This political situation prevailed until the twentieth century and the outbreak of World War I in 1914. The vast majority of ethnic Ukrainians – close to 85 percent – lived within the boundaries of what will be referred to as Dnieper Ukraine in the Russian Empire. This and the next four chapters will discuss developments to 1914 in Dnieper Ukraine. Another six chapters will concentrate on Ukrainian-inhabited lands in the Austro-Hungarian Empire to 1914.

Territorial divisions

The tone of administrative and political life in Dnieper Ukraine was set by Empress Catherine II during the 1780s, when the last vestiges of autonomy as embodied in the Hetmanate and the Crimean Khanate were abolished. All of Dnieper Ukraine was henceforth to be administered in the same manner as other parts of the Russian Empire. Despite several changes during the course of the nineteenth century, the administrative system retained five basic levels: (1) the village and city, (2) the county, (3) the province, (4) the region, and (5) the empire, headed by the tsar and his central administration in St Petersburg.

Administrative restructuring began in 1775, when Catherine II issued the Fundamental Law for the reorganization of the empire. The object of this law was to create a standard administrative pattern throughout the realm. The basic unit was the imperial province (*namestnichestvo*). Each imperial province was to have a roughly equal number of up to 700,000 inhabitants, and its territory was subdivided into counties or districts (Russian: *uezdy*; Ukrainian: *povity*), each of about 70,000 inhabitants. The imperial province was headed by a governor appointed by the tsar and responsible directly to St Petersburg. This administrative system was applied to Ukrainian territories as well, although after 1797 the old imperial provinces (Russian: *namestnichestva*) were replaced by a greater number of smaller provinces (Russian: *gubernii*).

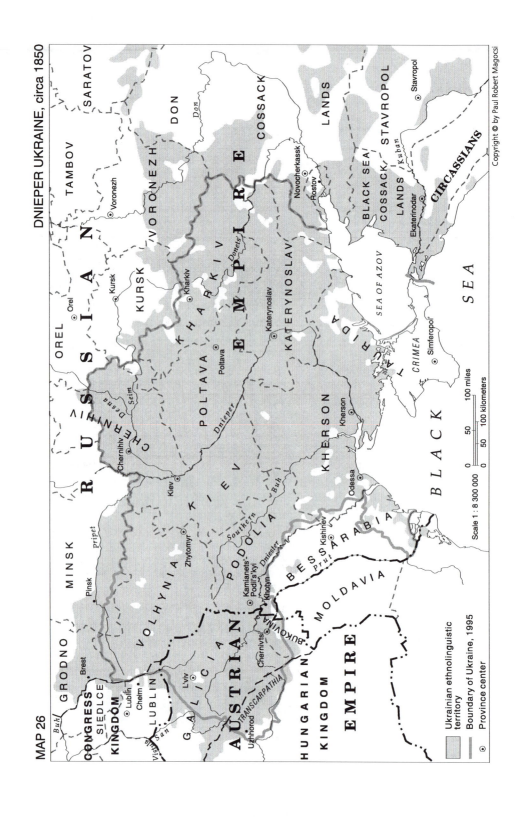

MAP 26

DNIEPER UKRAINE, circa 1850

Copyright © by Paul Robert Magocsi

Ukrainian ethnolinguistic
territory

Boundary of Ukraine, 1995

Province center

Scale 1 : 8 300 000

0   50   100 miles

0   50   100 kilometers

The largest concentration of ethnic Ukrainian inhabitants lived in nine provinces. These included, on the territory of the former Hetmanate, the provinces of Chernihiv and Poltava. In former Sloboda Ukraine, an imperial province of the same name was established (although without certain territory in the north and northeast), and in 1835 it was renamed the province of Kharkiv. From former Zaporozhia, which initially had become part of New Russia in 1775, the provinces of Katerynoslav and Kherson (including lands between the lower Dnieper and Dniester Rivers acquired between 1774 and 1791 from the Ottoman Empire) were created. Of the old Crimean Khanate, both the peninsula and the steppe/coastal region between the lower Dnieper River and Sea of Azov became the province of Taurida. The lands acquired from Poland in 1793 and 1795 became the provinces of Kiev (including the city and surrounding area formerly within the Hetmanate), Volhynia, and Podolia. The Kiev, Volhynia, and Podolia provinces were together referred to as the Russian Empire's Southwestern Land (*Iugo-zapadnyi krai*); here they will be referred to as the Right Bank.

Besides the nine "Ukrainian" provinces, ethnic Ukrainians also inhabited areas in immediately adjacent provinces or regions of the Russian Empire. These included, in the east, parts of the Don Cossack and Black Sea Cossack Lands; in the southwest, parts of the province of Bessarabia (both the coastal region and an area around Khotyn in the north); and in the northwest, the regions around Brest and Chełm. These last two borderland regions had a complicated history. In 1795, the areas near Brest and Chełm west of the Buh River were annexed by Austria, but in 1809, Russia acquired this as well. From 1815 to 1864 these lands were incorporated into the Russian-ruled autonomous Congress Kingdom of Poland; thereafter, they were divided between the provinces of Grodno, Siedlce, and Lublin.

Administrative structure

Like the old imperial provinces, the smaller provinces (*gubernii*) that formed the basis of the imperial Russian administrative structure during the nineteenth century were each headed by a governor (Russian: *gubernator*) appointed by the tsar. The governor was assisted by a board of administration (*gubernskoe prisutstvie*) and various bureaus or committees responsible for specific problems – taxes, public welfare, agriculture, and so on.

Below the province level was the county or district (Russian: *uezd*; Ukrainian: *povit*), for which the most important officials were the police commandant (*ispravnik*) and gentry marshal (*predvoditel' dvorianstva*). The county administration also had a ruling board (*nizhnii zemskii sud*) and various bureaus or committees.

Whether in Dnieper Ukraine or in the Russian Empire as a whole, it was the nobility who directed local government. Each county had its own gentry assembly (*sobranie dvorianstva*) consisting of all nobles over twenty-five years of age whose lands in the county produced an annual income of at least 100 rubles. The gentry assembly elected the gentry marshal and police commandant, who were, as mentioned above, the two leading officials at the county level of administration.

ADMINISTRATIVE STRUCTURE
IN DNIEPER UKRAINE BEFORE THE 1860s

Tsar
Councils, committees, Senate
Central ministries

Governor-general of Kiev	Governor-general of Little Russia	Governor-general of New Russia	Cities under Magdeburg Law
Right Bank (1832–1914) Kiev, Volhynia, Podolia	Left Bank (1802–1856) Chernihiv, Poltava, Kharkiv (from 1835)	New Russia (1797–1874) Katerynoslav, Kherson, Taurida, Bessarabia	(to 1831) Kiev (to 1835)

Province (*guberniia*)				
Governor (*gubernator*)				
Board of administration (*gubernskoe prisutstvie*)	Judicial bodies	Various bureaus	Gentry marshal	Gentry assembly
		Treasury Public welfare Agriculture Statistics Excise		

County or district (*uezd / povit*)			
Police commandant (*ispravnik*) and gentry marshal (*predvoditel' dvorianstva*)			
Board of administration (*nizhnii zemskii sud*)	Judicial bodies	Various bureaus	General assembly (*sobranie dvorianstva*)
Police commandant, chairman 2 gentry 2 non-gentry	Gentry court Non-gentry court	Treasury Excise Education	

Village			City		
Council	Elder (*starosta*)	Police	Council (*duma*)	Executive board	Police

The gentry assembly also chose officials to head the various county bureaus as well as delegates to the provincial gentry assembly. The assembly at the provincial level functioned in the same manner as that at the county level, that is, it elected officials to head various provincial bureaus and nominated candidates for the post of provincial gentry marshal.

The lowest level of administration included the village and township/city. Cities experienced a particular development. Those that historically enjoyed self-rule remained outside the provincial structure until 1831 (Kiev until 1835), when Magdeburg Law was abolished. Thereafter, cities and towns, each with its own council (*duma*) and executive board, were made subordinate to the county or provincial administration of the area in which they were located. The only exception was the port of Odessa, which with a small hinterland formed a territory dependent directly on the central government.

As part of the reform of the 1860s, the so-called zemstvo institutions were introduced in certain parts of the empire. These were established in an effort to democratize governmental administration at the local level and at the same time to resolve pressing social problems by encouraging local initiative and activity. It should be kept in mind that the zemstvos, which existed at both the county and the provincial level, did not replace any existing institution. Rather, they were responsible for a limited number of local matters. Because the zemstvos were administrative entities parallel to the provincial and county gentry assemblies and boards of administration, they often clashed with these bodies over matters of

ADMINISTRATIVE STRUCTURE IN DNIEPER UKRAINE AFTER THE 1860s

Tsar
Councils, committees, Senate
Central ministries

Region	
Governor-general of Kiev	Odessa
Governor-general of New Russia	City governor

Province (*guberniia*)				
Governor (*gubernator*)				
Board of administration	Judicial bodies	Various bureaus	Gentry assembly	Zemstvo assembly

Governor, chairman
Gentry marshal
Chairman of zemstvo
  executive
Member of provincial
  court
Prosecutor (*prokuror*)
Administrators
		Treasury
		Public welfare
		Agriculture
		Statistics
		Excise
			Gentry marshal
			Members
				Chairman
				Executive
				  board
				Members

County or district (*uezd*)					
Police commandant (*ispravnik*)/ gentry marshal (*predvoditel' dvorianstva*)/zemstvo chairman					
Board of administration (*uezdnoe prisutsvie*)	Judicial bodies	Various bureaus	Gentry assembly	Zemstvo executive (*uprava*)	Zemstvo assembly (*sobranie*)

Gentry marshall
Police inspector
		Treasury
		Excise
			Gentry
			  marshal
			Chairman
				Chairman
				School board
				Public health
				  board
				Transportation
				Fire
					Landowners
					Wealthy towns-
					  people
					Village communes

City (*gorod*)			
Council	Executive board	Mayor	Police

Rural district (*volost'*)			
Land captain (*zemskii nachal'nik*) and police captain			
Board of administration (*volostnoe pravlenie*)	Assembly (*volostnoi skhod*)	Court	Tax office
Elder, chairman Village elders Tax collectors	Elder (*starshina*) 4 members		
Village commune (*sel'skoe obshchestvo*)			
Elder (*starosta*)	Assembly (*skhod/hromada*)	Tax collector	Police

jurisdiction. The main functions of the zemstvos at both the provincial and the county level were to levy taxes, assign funds to finance their own operations, and elect their own officers. They were also charged by the central government with responsibility for operating the courts and for matters such as road maintenance, education, fire prevention, and hygiene.

In theory, the zemstvos were to be made up of delegates elected every three years to assemblies (*sobranii*) from three groups in the population: private land-owners, peasants living in communes, and certain categories of urban dwellers. In practice, the peasants took very little interest in the zemstvos, which remained almost entirely in the hands of the gentry. For instance, in 1903, at the district level throughout the Ukrainian provinces, 83 percent of the zemstvo delegates were nobles, while only 9.3 percent came from peasant communes, and 7.7 percent from urban areas. Thus, for most of their existence the zemstvos represented and were concerned with gentry interests, which meant distributing the tax burden as much as possible to the peasantry. Only after the 1905 Revolution did several zemstvo assemblies show an active interest in peasant society, chiefly by establishing primary schools, hospitals, and agricultural stations.

The peasants' concerns were addressed in their own bodies of self-government, which came into being in 1861 with the creation of the rural district (*volost'*). The rural district was, in turn, made up of village communes (*sel'skie obshchestva*). The village commune had its own assembly (Russian: *skhod*; Ukrainian: *hromada*), which elected a village elder (*starosta*) as well as delegates to the rural district assembly (*volostnoi skhod*). Each rural district also had its own board of administration and was headed by a land captain (*zemskii nachal'nik*) and police captain appointed by the central government.

Above the province, the basic administrative division was the office of governor-general (*general-gubernator*). This post was never established throughout the Russian Empire as a whole, although it was often found in the borderland regions. The Ukrainian provinces fell into this category, and by the 1830s had as many as three governors-general: the Governor-General of Kiev for the Right Bank (Kiev, Volhynia, and Podolia, 1832–1914); the Governor-General of Little Russia for the Left Bank (Chernihiv, Poltava, and Kharkiv, 1802–1856); and the Governor-General of New Russia and Bessarabia for the steppe Ukraine and Crimea (Kherson, Katerynoslav, and Taurida, 1797–1874). The governors-general had supervisory capacity over the provincial governors within their respective jurisdictions, and they were responsible for setting general policy for the region as a whole.

Finally, at the very top of the imperial administrative structure was the tsar in St Petersburg. By the nineteenth century, the Russian Empire had become an absolute hereditary monarchy, and with the adoption of the Law of Succession to the Throne in 1797, the Romanov family – specifically the eldest son of each tsar – was given exclusive title to the imperial throne. Thus, unlike in previous centuries, in the nineteenth century the royal mantle could be passed without difficulty from one tsar to the next. During that time, the empire had five rulers: Alexander I (reigned 1801–1825), Nicholas I (reigned 1825–1855), Alexander II (1855–1881), Alexander III (reigned 1881–1894), and Nicholas II (reigned 1894–1917). Until the very end of the Russian Empire's existence in 1917, the tsar, in contrast to rulers or governments in most other parts of Europe, had absolute control over his subjects. Not even the revolutionary events and constitutional experiments during the first decade of the twentieth century limited in any serious way the tsar's authority.

At the imperial level, the Russian Empire was administered by several ministries, each headed by a single minister appointed by the tsar. The ministerial system, adopted in 1802 (instituted in 1811), replaced the old system of colleges, or *collegia* (i.e., state departments headed by boards of twelve members) set up a century earlier by Peter I. By the end of the nineteenth century, there were ten ministries and several other administrative agencies. From the standpoint of the empire's administrative structure, the most important of these was the Ministry of Internal Affairs, which headed a chain of command that went down from the imperial level through the provincial governors to the county police commandant, rural district police captain, and, finally, village commune police.

The imperial administration also consisted of various bodies, such as the Committee of Ministers, the Council of Ministers (est. 1857), the State Council (est. 1801), the Senate, and the tsar's Chancery. Some of these, in cooperation with the tsar, were responsible for legislative and judicial as well as administrative matters. The result of such a system was often jurisdictional overlap. Finally, in 1906, in an attempt to alleviate the problem of overlapping jurisdictions, a new governmental structure was adopted. Henceforth, there were to be clear divisions between legislative (State Council and State Duma), executive (Council of Ministries), and judicial (Senate) responsibilities. All these branches at the imperial level of government were under the supreme authority of the tsar.

In essence, the administrative structure of the Russian Empire was designed so that despite certain areas of administrative autonomy (provincial and county gentry assemblies and zemstvos, and rural district and village commune assemblies) there was a chain of command represented by certain officials (especially in the police) whose ultimate authority rested in the unchallenged authority of the tsar. Within such a centralized and autocratic structure, Ukraine had no real distinct administrative life. The Dnieper-Ukrainian lands formed an integral part of the Russian Empire, which throughout the nineteenth century managed to follow a relatively stable existence.

The evolution of the Russian Empire, 1814–1914

After the end of the Napoleonic Wars and the defeat of France in 1814, the Russian Empire emerged as Europe's greatest land power. Of Russia's traditional enemies, Poland had ceased to exist; Ottoman Turkey was growing weaker and on its way to becoming the proverbial "sick man of Europe"; and France was in the throes of its post-Napoleonic defeat. Immediately to the west, the tsarist government was, at least during the first half of the nineteenth century, closely allied with both the Austrian Empire and Prussia, who together with Russia saw themselves as part of a Holy Alliance "destined" to protect and preserve stability in Europe. Russia's prestige was therefore at its height in the decades after 1815. Even when revolution spread throughout most of Europe in 1848, the Russian Empire was virtually unique in not experiencing political disturbance. As the strongest and most stable force of the day, the tsar was even called upon by Habsburg Austria to intervene in its struggle with the Hungarians. Hence, it was the army of Tsar Nicholas I that put down the Hungarian revolution in 1849 and that saved the Austrian Empire from disintegration.

The first half of the nineteenth century also marked the continual territorial growth of the Russian Empire. Territorial annexations followed in a virtually uninterrupted sequence. Along its western borders the empire acquired Finland (1809), Bessarabia (1812), and, by reacquisition, Poland's Congress Kingdom (1815). To its south and east it added the Transcaucasian kingdoms (1801–1828), Transcaspian and Central Asian territories (1822–1895), and the Amur and maritime provinces (1858–1860) near Chinese Manchuria and along the Pacific coast in the Far East. Before the end of the nineteenth century, the Russian Empire had come to control one-sixth of the surface of the globe.

All this does not mean that the empire was without problems. For instance, in 1853, when St Petersburg pressed for greater influence over Ottoman-ruled lands in the Balkans and for free access through the Bosporan straits near Constantinople, western Europe's Great Powers felt obliged to respond. Anxious to protect their own commercial interests in the Near East, Britain, France, and Sardinia-

Piedmont came to the defense of the Ottoman Empire. In response to Russia's invasion of the Balkans, a joint British and French fleet crossed the Black Sea, disembarked along the coast of the western Crimea, and laid siege to the strategic port and fortresses (Inkerman and Balaklava) surrounding Sevastopol'. With the fall of Sevastopol' in 1854, Russia had been defeated in what became known as the Crimean War. Aside from disrupting the economy of the peninsula and provoking uprisings among a portion of the Crimean Tatar population which supported the Western invaders allied to the Ottomans, the Crimean War revealed several weaknesses of tsarist rule and the need for reform. The war also left an indelible imprint on the Western mind, since among the heroes of the Crimean campaign were the nurse Florence Nightingale and a British unit immortalized by Alfred, Lord Tennyson in his poem "The Charge of the Light Brigade" (1854).

Aside from foreign invasion, the restless Poles revolted twice against Russian rule, in 1830–1831 and in 1863. Then, at the beginning of the twentieth century, tactless Russian expansion in the Far East was checked by the Japanese, who unexpectedly won the Russo-Japanese War of 1904–1905. This was followed by a revolution in the streets of St Petersburg which forced the tsar to make certain political concessions, however nominal, to his increasingly restless subjects. The Revolution of 1905 was only the symbolic capstone of several decades of increasingly widespread revolutionary activity by a host of Russian and non-Russian political activists who hoped to overthrow the existing order. Finally, Russia's greatest problem was its economic backwardness vis-à-vis the rest of Europe, only partially alleviated by the abolition of serfdom in 1861 and the beginnings of industrialization in the very last decade of the nineteenth century.

Nevertheless, none of these external and internal problems seriously shook the structure of the Russian Empire. On the contrary, the imperial system, despite its backward social structure and increasingly discontented national minorities, especially in the European parts of Russia, continued to survive and even flourish until 1914 and the outbreak of World War I.

Given the situation of Dnieper Ukraine, it is not surprising that political activity directed to improving the status of Ukrainians as a distinct national entity was for the longest time virtually non-existent. At best only a few individuals and movements appeared on Ukrainian territory with the goal of changing the existing order. As early as the 1790s, a Ukrainian nobleman, Vasyl' Kapnist, published tracts critical of Russia's centralizing policies and traveled to Berlin to conduct secret negotiations for Prussian assistance in case of a Cossack rebellion against tsarist rule. Somewhat later, during Napoleon's invasion of Russia in 1812, when the latter's Austrian allies were stationed for several months in western Volhynia, some French diplomats put forth vague ideas about a separate Ukrainian entity. The 1820s also brought political activity to Ukrainian territory in the form of the Masonic movement and activity by military officers' societies which led to the abortive Decembrist revolt in St Petersburg in 1825. The regiment stationed in Chernihiv began to advance toward Kiev at this time but was speedily repulsed. By the 1830s, the Right Bank had become transformed into a fertile seedbed for Polish revolutionary activity. None of these movements, however, ever considered the idea of a separate Ukrainian cultural or political entity.

It is not until the very end of the nineteenth century and the beginning of the twentieth century, a time when the first Ukrainian political parties came into being, that it is possible to speak in terms of a specifically Ukrainian political life. At that time, several parties were formed, and while some supported the existing regime and others cooperated with Russian socialist revolutionaries, there were still others who considered Ukraine a distinct entity worthy at least of some kind of cultural and even political autonomy. Yet despite the fact that these parties were represented in Russia's first and second parliament, the Dumas of 1906 and 1907, each of which had a Ukrainian bloc of deputies, the embryonic Ukrainian political movement remained stillborn within an autocratic and highly centralized imperial structure that since the 1860s had actively suppressed any manifestation of national separatism within its borders.

For all these reasons, Ukrainian history in the Russian Empire during the nineteenth century is basically the history of a region whose economic life and social structure were integrated with, subordinate to, and dependent upon developments in the rest of the empire. Yet despite the seemingly complete integration of the Dnieper-Ukrainian lands in the Russian Empire, the region had a long and distinct historical and cultural tradition, whose memory was kept alive in the writings of a small group of intellectual leaders. This group, known as the nationalist intelligentsia, succeeded in creating a national movement that eventually was to win the hearts and minds of ethnic Ukrainians as it tried to prepare them to accept the idea of independent statehood when, after the collapse of the Russian Empire in 1917, an opportune political moment finally arrived. Before turning to the Ukrainian national awakening and the subsequent national movement in the Russian Empire, it is first necessary to look at socioeconomic developments in Dnieper Ukraine.

27

Socioeconomic Developments in Dnieper Ukraine

The structure of Ukrainian society within the Russian Empire during the nineteenth century was essentially the same as it had been during the eighteenth century. The composition of the various social estates and their relative size were to change, however, in some cases substantially. The status and evolution of the social estates also varied according to the four regions of Dnieper Ukraine. This variation was due to the fact that each of the four historical regions – the old Hetmanate (Chernihiv and Poltava provinces); Sloboda Ukraine (Kharkiv province); Zaporozhia and the Crimea (Kherson, Katerynoslav, Taurida provinces); and the Right Bank and western lands (Kiev, Podolia, and Volhynia provinces) – had been acquired at a different time by the Russian Empire, and each had its own distinct social structure. The social strata in question were the nobility, the Cossacks, the peasantry (state peasants and serfs), the townspeople, and the clergy.

Social estates before the 1860s

The noble estate in Dnieper Ukraine consisted of Russian hereditary nobles (Russian: *dvoriane*; Polish: *szlachta*), whether Russians, Poles, or russified or polonized Ukrainians, as well as members of the Cossack gentry (*starshyna*) and Crimean Tatars who were granted noble status. The process whereby noble status was granted to the Cossack gentry in the Hetmanate was especially complex. Initially, as part of Catherine II's Charter of the Nobility (1785), the Cossack elite was itself allowed to determine who was qualified to belong to the Russian nobility (*dvorianstvo*). Locally elected functionaries made recommendations to the governor-general of Little Russia, Petr Rumiantsev, who happened to be very accommodating with respect to the claims put before him. As a result, by the early 1790s the number of recognized nobles (*dvoriane*) in the Hetmanate had reached more than 30,000. Most of these new nobles had been members of the Cossack officer class (*starshyna*) in the former Hetmanate. After 1790, however, Little Russia's new governor-general, Mikhail Krechetnikov, became suspicious of the large number of claimants to the nobility and removed 22,702 of them (the so-called taxed nobles) from the rolls. This left only 12,597 who could be considered "nobles without any doubt." Not surprisingly, Krechetnikov's action prompted numerous litigations and petitions, with the result that in 1803 the imperial government issued a decree allowing a certain number back into the noble estate. By the beginning of the nineteenth century, there were approximately 24,000 nobles in Left Bank Ukraine.

In Right Bank Ukraine and Volhynia, access to the Russian imperial nobility (*dvoriane*) depended on one's previous status. Members of the Polish *szlachta*, who numbered over 260,000 in those regions in 1795, were immediately given the status of Russian nobility. More problematic were those individuals, mostly ethnic Ukrainians, who based their claims on having belonged to the Cossack elite. Since the Cossack social structure in the Right Bank Ukraine and Volhynia was dismantled much earlier, that is, in the second half of the seventeenth century, it was very difficult to determine who among them over a century later might qualify for acceptance into Russian nobility. Although as many as 104,000 Ukrainians in the Right Bank claimed they were nobles, the Russian imperial authorities dismissed over 87,000 claims outright and put another 22,000 claims under consideration. Things were a bit more straightforward in the Sloboda Ukraine, where the Cossack officer stratum (*starshyna*) in each of the region's five regiments was given noble status. Also, in the former Crimean Khanate, a good portion of the Tatar elite (clan leaders and lower nobility – *mirza*) accepted induction into the ranks of the Russian nobility.

Those individuals from Ukrainian lands who were accepted into the noble estate eventually were to enjoy all the privileges outlined in Catherine's 1785 Charter of the Nobility. These included inviolability of person and property; the right to trial by one's peers; exemption from state service, from taxes, and from the quartering of troops; and legal ownership of the serfs on one's estates. Such privileges were undoubtedly attractive to Dnieper Ukraine's elite, and those individuals who obtained them became fully integrated into the imperial social structure. The vast majority of nobles from Dnieper Ukraine staffed the region's new administrative structure and took part in imperial political life. A few came to play leading roles in the Russian Empire as a whole. For instance, Prince Aleksander Bezborod'ko became imperial chancellor under Catherine II and Paul I, and the princes Viktor Kochubei, Petr Zavadovskii, and Dmitrii Troshchinskii and the sons of Hetman Kyrylo Rozumovs'kyi – Aleksei Razumovskii and Andrei Razumovskii – all served as ministers under Alexander I. These individuals were the latest examples of a strong tradition begun during the second half of the seventeenth century whereby natives of Ukraine, while continuing to be Little Russians, made excellent careers in the imperial Russian world.

By 1835, the long and complicated process of deciding who was and who was not a noble in Dnieper Ukraine finally came to an end. In the Hetmanate, all holders of former Cossack military and civil officer rank (except the lowest) were recognized as hereditary nobility. This meant that the rank-and-file Cossacks (176,886 in 1764) and Cossack helpers (198,295 in 1764) were excluded. While some of the rank and file, who by 1803 numbered about 200,000, were to remain part of a distinct Cossack social estate, others, together with the former Cossack helpers

SOCIAL ESTATES IN DNIEPER UKRAINE

Eighteenth century	*Nineteenth century*
1 Nobility	**1 Nobility**
Russian *dvoriane*	
Polish *szlachta*	
Tatar *mirza*	
2 Cossacks	**2 Military residents (1866)**
officers	
rank and file	
helpers	
3 Peasants	**3 Peasants**
state peasants	state peasants
proprietary serfs	serfs (to 1861)
	proprietary peasants (after 1861)
4 Townspeople	**4 Townspeople**
5 Clergy	**5 Civil servants**
	government functionaries
	clergy
	6 Cossacks
	Kuban
	Black Sea
	Azov

became state peasants. The Cossack rank and file who did not become state peasants emigrated to towns and cities to become merchants and artisans, or to frontier areas like the Kuban River valley. Between 1805 and 1850, about 57,000 chose emigration. Eventually, the government tried to close off entry into the Cossack estate, whose members by the 1860s had become indistinguishable from state peasants.

In Sloboda Ukraine, rank-and-file Cossacks became military residents (*viis'kovi obyvateli*), a group which continued to exist until 1866 and was similar to the state peasants. Their duty to the state was to provide soldiers for the five imperial regiments in the area (four hussars and one ulan). The fate of the Cossacks in Zaporozhia was quite different.

Following the destruction of the *sich* in 1775, traditional Cossack military social structures ceased to exist. Some Cossacks were drafted into the imperial army; others were left in Zaporozhia as free homestead farmers. Still others were allowed to function as Cossacks with their own military formations in the service of the Russian Empire (see map 23). Among the latter were: (1) the Katerynoslav Cossack army (together with regiments of the Buh Cossack Army) settled in 1787 just north of Mykolaïv along the Russia's borders with what was still Ottoman-held Yedisan; and (2) the Black Sea Cossacks formed in 1788 and settled in the southern Yedisan with their center in Slobodzeia. These formations were, however, short-lived. In 1796 the Katerynoslav Cossacks were disbanded and they followed the Black Sea Cossacks who even earlier (1792) had been resettled to the Kuban' region east of the Sea of Azov.

Those Cossacks who opposed Russia's destruction of Zaporozhia and its *sich* fled southward to the Ottoman Empire, which in 1775 allowed them to settle in the delta of the Danube River, with their center (Zadunais'ka Sich) at Verkhnii Dunavets'. It was not long, however, before some elements within this Danube Cossack Host became displeased with Ottoman hegemony and sought a possibly better existence, whether in the Austrian Empire (in the Banat Region along the lower Tisza River, 1785–1812), or back once again in the Russian Empire. When some did indeed return in 1828, the Ottomans responded to what they considered betrayal by destroying the Danubian Host's *sich* at Verkhnii Dunavets'. The sometimes dramatic, but more often prosaic, plight of the Danube Cossacks under Ottoman protection was later immortalized in the nineteenth-century Ukrainian opera by Semen Hulak-Artemovs'kyi, *Zaporozhets' za Dunaiem* (The Zaporozhian Cossack Beyond the Danube, 1863).

In the Kuban region the tsarist government allowed the Black Sea Cossacks a degree of autonomy, and during the first half of the nineteenth century their units were steadily replenished by rank-and-file Cossacks migrating from the central Ukrainian lands of the former Hetmanate. The Black Sea Cossacks were joined by the neighboring Frontier, or Border Army, based along the upper Kuban and Terek Rivers and made up primarily of Russian Don Cossacks, and from 1860 on these units became known as the Kuban Cossack Army (*Kubans'ke Kozache Viis'ko*). In the early 1860s, the Azov Army, that is, Cossacks from beyond the Danube who returned from the Ottoman Empire in 1832 and who were settled north of the Sea of Azov, also joined the Kuban Cossacks. Thus, the Kuban Cossacks were an amalgam of various Cossack groups that had served the Russian Empire in its struggle against the Ottoman Empire. From their center at Ekaterinodar (today Krasnodar), they were able to maintain a degree of autonomy until the demise of the Russian Empire in 1917.

The next major social stratum, and by far the largest in nineteenth-century Dnieper Ukraine, was the peasantry. As late as 1897, peasants still accounted for 93 percent of all Ukrainians. Until the reforms of the 1860s, this stratum consisted of two distinct and legally differentiated groups – the state peasants and the serfs. The state peasants derived from a variety of disparate groups (including lower-echelon Cossacks), although most had lived on land that originally belonged to the state, including former properties of the Polish crown. In return for the use of state land, they were obliged to pay various taxes and perform duties such as building and maintaining roads. At the beginning of the nineteenth century in the Right Bank, certain state-owned lands were leased to the local gentry, and the state peasants attached to them were required to perform labor duties for the gentry. The imperial government, however, made several attempts to improve the status of state peasants: from 1801, they could buy land from the state with full property rights; in 1837, work duties to the gentry were abolished; and after 1839, those who were leased to the gentry were gradually returned to the jurisdiction of the state, to whom they paid taxes.

The serfs, on the other hand, were proprietary peasants who had lived on lands owned by landlords (whether nobles, Cossacks, or the church) and who were required to perform various kinds of duties for their landlords. Although the number of the duties increased over the course of the eighteenth century, the proprietary peasants still enjoyed freedom of movement. With the abolition of the Hetmanate by Catherine II during the 1780s, however, the local Russian nobility together with the Cossack gentry asked for complete control over their peasants. Their request was granted in a decree issued by Empress Catherine II on 3 May 1783, which introduced the poll tax and gave the nobility the responsibility for seeing that it was paid by the peasants. To ensure that the tax would be paid, the peasants were forbidden all freedom of movement.

It is interesting to note that nowhere in Catherine's decree did the words serf or serfdom appear. The text simply stated that "to ensure the regular receipt of the assessed taxes ... and to prevent any flight and further difficulties for landlords and other rural inhabitants, every peasant is required to remain in his/her place of residence and work."[1] A little over a decade later, in 1796, Tsar Paul I (reigned 1796–1801) extended serfdom to New Russia, or the Steppe Ukraine, and to the Caucasus region, arguing that the exemption from serfdom in those areas was a menace to the welfare of serf owners in neighboring provinces. As for the Right Bank, the serfdom that had already existed was simply continued when the Russian Empire acquired these territories from Poland in 1793 and 1795. Thus, by the beginning of the nineteenth century, all peasants in Dnieper Ukraine who were not living on state lands became fully enserfed.

Within the peasant social stratum, there was a marked variation from region to region in the proportion of state peasants to serfs. Serfdom was most strongly entrenched in the former Polish palatinates west of the Dnieper, where in 1858, serfs made up three-quarters of the peasantry. In contrast, state peasants outnumbered serfs two to one in the former Hetmanate, and three to one in Sloboda Ukraine. The proportion of serfs was lowest in Taurida, the southernmost province of the Steppe Ukraine, where in 1858 they formed only 5.8 percent of the population.

It is also interesting to note that while the total number of serfs increased between 1803 and 1858, it did so by only 273,000. This figure by no means reflects a natural demographic increase, which would have seen at least a doubling in the number of serfs during this fifty-five-year period. In fact, their numbers remained stable, especially during the last twenty years of the period (1838–1858), despite continuing demographic increases and the influx of serfs from elsewhere in the empire onto estates in Dnieper Ukraine owned by Russian landlords. The main reason for the stable number of serfs in Dnieper Ukraine is the mass flight to the Don and Kuban regions, where instead of direct control of the imperial government or local landlords there was a degree of Cossack autonomy. It is as a result of this migration that the Kuban and parts of the Don region became ethnically Ukrainian.

What did serfdom mean for the peasants in the Russian Empire upon whom it was imposed? Aside from the right to own their own tools, serfs really had no rights. A serf was little more than human chattel and often was worth even less than an animal. A male or female serf could be and was bought and sold as property. During the first half of the nineteenth century, the imperial government attempted to improve the lot of the serfs by prohibiting their sale without land (1808) or without their immediate families (1833). In the end, however, the serfs remained the property of their landlords, who had judicial authority over them, often determined how and if they could marry, and in practice set the amount of their obligation.

The duties of serfs usually took two forms: labor dues (Russian: *barshchina*; Ukrainian: *panshchyna*) and monetary rents (*obrok*). In Russia, the relative unproductivity of serf-based agriculture led nobles to encourage their serfs to provide monetary rents (with the money often earned as a result of their hiring themselves out as wage laborers in industry or as artisans and petty traders). In Dnieper Ukraine, however, the opposite occurred. The high fertility of Ukraine's black soil and closer access to revenue-earning foreign markets through the Black Sea ports made it profitable for the nobility to exploit serf labor on their manorial domains. It is not surprising, therefore, that before the 1860s, 83 percent of serfs in the former Hetmanate and Sloboda Ukraine and 99 percent in the Right Bank and Volhynia fulfilled their obligations in the form of labor dues. The amount of dues varied from landlord to landlord, but could be anywhere from three to six days per week. Some serfs were also assigned by their landlords to work in plants and factories, with the result that there evolved a social stratum of landless peasant serfs, who in some areas made up as much as 25 percent (in the Left Bank in the 1840s) of the total population.

The remaining two social strata were the townspeople and the civil servants, including clergy. By Catherine II's charter on cities issued in 1785, townspeople were subdivided into six groups: (1) property owners, (2) merchants, (3) artisans, (4) non-residents and foreign merchants, (5) distinguished citizens (bankers, former officials, intellectuals), and (6) unskilled workers and small tradespeople. In all categories, particularly the first five, the urban dwellers were made up almost exclusively of Russians and Jews, along with Poles in the Right Bank and Greeks in the Black Sea coastal cities. The proportion of ethnic Ukrainians among townspeople was small, and those who lived in cities for any length of time usually became russified or polonized. Russian served as the lingua franca for all townspeople, with the result that the cities in Dnieper Ukraine became islands ethnically and culturally divorced from the surrounding countryside.

The civil servant group included governmental officials at all levels and the clergy. The clergy began to lose its separate social status between 1786 and 1788, when the Russian imperial government secularized the church estates in the Hetmanate, where its holdings were particularly extensive in land, mines, and small factories. The clergy consequently became dependent exclusively upon the state. As an integral part of the imperial civil service, the Orthodox Church also became an instrument of russification in the former Hetmanate, Sloboda Ukraine, and Zaporozhia.

The reforms of the 1860s

The most important change in the socioeconomic development of Dnieper Ukraine came as a result of the reforms implemented throughout most of the Russian Empire during the 1860s. By the middle of the century, it had become obvious to the leading circles in St Petersburg that the country was economically backward and that the institution of serfdom was a liability with respect to social progress. Russia's loss to Britain and France in the Crimean War of 1853–1855 seemed to underline the message that the empire was backward vis-à-vis Europe. The pressure of public opinion, stifled under the repressive regime of Tsar Nicholas I, was released after his death in 1855, and demands were put forth for some kind of change. The new tsar, Alexander II, was convinced that revolution would occur unless there were reforms, and in 1856 he called on the nobility to take the initiative. When the nobility procrastinated, the central government itself took the lead. On 19 February 1861, Alexander II, who came to be known as the reforming tsar, issued a manifesto abolishing serfdom. As a result of the "great emancipation," as this act came to be known, the serf was liberated from his or her personal and legal subjection to the landlord. The former serf could engage in trade, buy and sell property, and marry at his or her own volition.

The economic status of the former serfs, now proprietary peasants, was not necessarily improved by emancipation. On the one hand, each peasant was allowed to keep the land he or she had used as a serf; in Dnieper Ukraine in 1863, that meant an average of between 7 and 16 acres (between 2.8 and 6.6 hectares) per household. On the other hand, the proprietary peasant had to pay for the land. According to the regulations, the government reimbursed the landlord outright 80 percent and the peasant was to pay the remaining 20 percent. The proprietary peasant was expected to make so-called redemption payments to the government for its 80 percent over a period of forty-nine years.

The government knew it would be difficult, if not virtually impossible, for the former serfs to make the redemption payments. It decided, therefore, to give a significant portion of the land not to individual proprietary peasants but rather to the village commune (*obshchina*). This meant that the land became the property of the commune, which in turn would divide it among or redistribute it to individual households for their temporary use. The basis of division was the number of persons in a family. Any changes in a household's size would be compensated for in periodic redistribution or by reassignment of land from other households. The communal system also allowed for implementation of the principle of communal liability, or collective responsibility. In other words, the government and former landlords would be more easily assured of taxes and repayments once these became the responsibility of the entire community.

The idea of the commune was attractive to Russian thinkers of various political persuasions. Among these were the Slavophiles, conservative mid-nineteenth century Russian thinkers who believed in the superiority of Russian civilization to European. They argued that the commune, prosaically described as the *mir*, was the original social unit in medieval Rus', that it was one of the superior features of Russian civilization, and that it was therefore best suited for revival throughout the countryside. The leftist populists (*narodniki*) also welcomed the commune, believing that collective land ownership would in any case be the general pattern in a future socialist society.

In Ukraine, communal property existed before the reform era, but was limited to pastures and forests. On the other hand, while the commune (*obshchina*) as applied to arable land may have been the norm in Russia, it was completely foreign to Ukraine. Nevertheless, in the early 1860s the imperial Russian government introduced communal landholding patterns among the former serfs. Of the 2.8 million households in eight Ukrainian provinces that received land, 58 percent of the allotments were given with individual property rights and 42 percent with communal rights. The commune pattern was especially widespread in certain regions, representing over 90 percent of households in Kharkiv, Katerynoslav, and Kherson provinces. The central government believed, therefore, that over two-fifths of all households in Dnieper Ukraine were functioning as communes.

Reality was much different, however, because over 80 percent of the communes did not comply with the rules of repartition. Land initially allotted to individual households on a temporary basis in practice was used as if it were the property of the family. Nonetheless, while it is true that rules were violated in this respect, two-fifths of Dnieper Ukraine's rural households were still legally within communes, and this was to have a negative impact on agriculture and on the status of those who worked the land. Aside from encouraging inefficient agricultural practices (irrational land distribution, involuntary crop rotation), the formal existence of the communes made it impossible for individuals to prove that they owned the land assigned to them.

The situation was somewhat better for the state peasants. In 1863, those living in the Right Bank were reclassified as proprietary peasants and were therefore liable for forty-nine-year redemption payments. Legislation passed in 1866 allowed state peasants in other parts of Dnieper Ukraine, however, to purchase their allotments with full legal rights of ownership or to pay rent to the government. Most chose individual ownership, and aside from purchasing former state lands many were able to expand their holdings with new acquisitions. This opportunity came about because many landlords were unable to adjust to the new socioeconomic system and began to sell their lands, especially during the 1870s. In Dnieper Ukraine alone between 1861 and 1914, nobles sold 25 million acres (10.1 million hectares) of land, 17 million acres (6.9 million hectares) of which were purchased by state peasants, and the remainder by merchants. In effect, the social system put in place by Catherine II at the end of the eighteenth century, whereby the agriculture-based economy of the country was in the hands of landlords with their enserfed peasants, was now being reversed. The nobles were again leaving the land and entering state service and the administration.

Tsar Alexander's abolition of serfdom was followed by other reforms, among the more important of which was the establishment of the zemstvos (see chapter 26), which provided a limited form of local self-government and local control over education and social services. The zemstvos were introduced in the Left Bank and the Steppe Ukraine between 1864 and 1870, but it was not until 1911 that they were set up in the Right Bank. The nearly half-century delay before their introduction in the Right Bank reflected the government's concern that even a small increase in local self-government might enhance the position of the Polish nobility, who still dominated the socioeconomic life of the region and who only recently (1863–1864) had revolted against Russian imperial rule. Another significant reform was in the law courts. After 1864, all male citizens, regardless of social origin, became equal before the law; trials were made public; the jury system was introduced; courts were made independent of the administration; and judges became irremovable and were properly compensated. As a result, the Russian judicial system compared favorably with the systems of other European countries governed by the rule of law.

The post-reform era also witnessed a profound demographic change in Dnieper Ukraine as a result of the rapid growth of towns and cities. Between 1863 and 1897, the urban population more than doubled, reaching over 3 million inhabitants living in 130 towns and cities. Most of these urban centers remained small in size, so that in 1897, only twelve of them, each with more than 50,000 inhabitants, could properly be classified as cities. The five largest cities – Odessa, Kiev, Kharkiv, Katerynoslav (Dnipropetrovs'k), Mykolaïv – each at least tripled or quadrupled in size between 1863 and 1897, and then doubled again during the next decade and a half before the outbreak of World War I (see table 27.1). Yet the marked urban growth in

TABLE 27.1
Population of Dnieper Ukraine's largest cities, 1860–1914

	ca. 1860	1897	1914
Odessa	113,000	404,000	669,000
Kiev	65,000	248,000	626,000
Kharkiv	50,000	174,000	245,000
Katerynoslav/Dnipropetrovs'k	19,000	121,000	220,000
Mykolaïv	32,000	92,000	104,000

Dnieper Ukraine largely passed by the ethnic Ukrainian population. By 1897, only in the smallest towns (under 15,000 inhabitants) that were linked to the agrarian economy of the nearby countryside did ethnic Ukrainians make up a slight majority (50 percent). In the rapidly growing eight largest cities, which dominated the urban economy and accounted for more than three-quarters of Dnieper Ukraine's industrial production and work force, ethnic Ukrainians made up only 18 percent of the population.

Commentators have frequently explained this phenomenon by attributing to Ukrainian peasants a profound and almost mystic attachment to the land that somehow provided a psychological barrier to residence in urban areas. Others, like the Ukrainian-Canadian political economist Bohdan Krawchenko, have suggested more prosaic reasons. Because agriculture proved profitable to landlords in Dnieper Ukraine, peasants were required to pay their dues in labor rather than in monetary rents. Consequently, they did not migrate to the cities as peasants were encouraged to do in Russia. Thus, as more and more Russians became members of a skilled or semiskilled labor force, as many as 93 percent (ca. 1900) of Ukrainian migrant laborers remained unskilled manual workers. When industrial development finally began in eastern Ukraine during the last decades of the nineteenth century, factory owners found it more efficient to "import" already-skilled Russian workers than to depend on local, unskilled Ukrainian labor.

Despite the administrative and judicial reforms of the 1860s and the subsequent growth of cities, the basic problem of the Russian Empire – its backward economy and the poverty of the vast majority of its inhabitants, the peasantry – went unresolved. The peasant's livelihood depended on land, and for many access to that commodity had become more difficult. Some state peasants did improve their status following the reforms of the 1860s, but many state and, in particular, proprietary peasants still had huge redemption payments to make as part of the emancipation settlement, while others, who had been serfs employed in factories or mines, received no land at all. As a result, more and more peasants became indebted and/or propertyless.

Moreover, for those who initially held land, the traditional practice of dividing plots among male offspring, a practice that was intensified by population growth, tended to increase the number of the landless. As for those who continued to hold land, their plots became smaller and smaller. For instance, in eight Ukrainian provinces the average size of peasant landholdings decreased by 55 percent between 1863 and 1900 (see table 27.2) To place these figures in a more

TABLE 27.2
Average size of peasant landholdings in Dnieper Ukraine, 1863–1900 (in acres [hectares])[2]

Province	1863	1900	Percentage of decrease
Volhynia	11.4 (4.6)	4.7 (1.9)	51.5
Podolia	7.2 (2.9)	3.2 (1.3)	53.8
Kiev	7.9 (3.2)	3.2 (1.3)	58.5
Chernihiv	9.1 (3.7)	5.4 (2.2)	41.2
Poltava	6.9 (2.8)	4.2 (1.7)	40.0
Kharkiv	12.3 (5.0)	5.2 (2.1)	57.6
Katerynoslav	17.2 (7.0)	6.2 (2.5)	61.6
Kherson	16.6 (6.7)	5.9 (2.4)	63.9

meaningful context, it should be noted that on the basis of a comprehensive statistical analysis of peasant landholdings in the Russian Empire (by Iurii Ianson), it was estimated that in Dnieper Ukraine 13.6 acres (5.5 hectares) of land at the

very least were needed to support a peasant household. Such a plot was significantly larger than the average holding in 1900. Another way to look at the land
squeeze is to compare the number of people living on arable land in Dnieper
Ukraine with the number in other European countries. At the beginning of the
twentieth century, for every 250 acres (100 hectares) of arable land there were 79
rural inhabitants in England, 84 in France, and 107 in Germany. In six of the nine
Ukrainian provinces in the Russian Empire, however, there was an average of 150
rural inhabitants for every 250 acres (100 hectares) of arable land.

These conditions in the Ukrainian countryside had two simultaneous results:
(1) the growth of a large class of agricultural day-laborers who, because of their
lack of skills, were not absorbed by the growing industrial sector; and (2) a significant emigration to the east, where land was more plentiful. During the second half of the nineteenth century, large numbers of Ukrainians emigrated not
only to the Don and Kuban River valleys, but to Central Asia, Siberia, and the Far
East along the Chinese border and Pacific coast. During the less than two decades
between 1896 and 1914, as many as 1.6 million Ukrainian peasants (especially
from Poltava, Chernihiv, Kiev, and Kharkiv provinces) sought to improve their lot
by going east.

In an attempt to ameliorate the condition of the peasantry, a new era of reform
was begun in the Russian Empire after the Revolution of 1905. The minister of the
interior at the time, Petr A. Stolypin, felt that new reforms were needed to avert
revolutionary disturbances in the countryside in the future. He was convinced that
the root of Russia's economic backwardness lay in the communal system of land
ownership. Accordingly, he instituted two laws, in 1906 and 1910, aimed at replacing the village commune system with a stratum of prosperous peasants. In Dnieper
Ukraine, more than 226,000 peasants withdrew from the communes landholdings
that amounted to 4.7 million acres (1.9 million hectares). Again, the percentages
varied from region to region. In the Right Bank and Volhynia, 48 percent of the
peasants left the communes; in the Steppe Ukraine, 42 percent; in the former
Hetmanate and Sloboda Ukraine, only 16.5 percent. As a result, the landholdings
in most of Dnieper Ukraine on the eve of World War I were in the form of what was
known as either the *khutir* or the *otrub*.

The *khutir* was like an individual North American farmstead surrounded by land
received in an allotment from the commune as private property to farm, expand,
or sell. Successful homesteaders who increased their holdings by purchasing other
khutory eventually became known as kulaks. The *otrub* consisted of a household in
the village and the strips of land (*otruby*) beyond the village center that were given
to it. At least three-quarters of the land reorganized in all the Dnieper-Ukrainian
provinces except Kiev and Chernihiv was in the form of *otruby*; in Kiev and Chernihiv, an average of 55 percent of the land had *khutory*.

Economic developments

The Ukrainian lands in the Russian Empire continued to function as a supplier of
agricultural products or industrial raw materials. In agriculture, grain production

continued to expand, especially after the opening up of vast tracts of arable land in the steppe region – some 2 million acres (800,000 hectares) in the early nineteenth century and another 15 million acres (6 million hectares) by the 1860s. This expansion helped transform Dnieper Ukraine into the most important agricultural land in the Russian Empire. A few statistics will confirm its significance. Wheat was the empire's major crop, and Dnieper Ukraine accounted for more than 75 percent of all wheat exports from Russia every year except two between 1812 and 1859. By the second decade of the twentieth century (1909 to 1913), Dnieper Ukraine's agricultural production had increased further, to account for 98 percent of Russia's wheat exports, 84 percent of its corn, 75 percent of its rye, and 73 percent of its barley. Even more impressive was the region's ranking vis-à-vis other countries: between 1909 and 1913, Dnieper Ukraine produced 43 percent of the world's barley, 21 percent of its rye, 20 percent of its wheat, and 10 percent of its corn. The nineteenth century also saw the growth of the sugar beet crop, especially on the Right Bank.

Most of the grain exports left via the Black Sea ports, in particular Odessa. Founded in 1794 on the site of a small Turkish fortress, Odessa in 1817 was given duty-free status by the imperial government. Commerce flourished, with the result that by 1847 Odessa accounted for more than half of all exports from the Russian Empire. Almost all the exporting firms in Odessa were in the hands of Greek, Italian, and Jewish merchants who had settled in what became an international trading emporium.

The phenomenal growth of agricultural production and its role in Russia's international trade also increased the need for a better transportational infrastructure. Until the 1860s, all grains as well as salt and fish were transported from the Ukrainian hinterland to Odessa by river barges and overland by the so-called *chumaky* – groups of wagon drivers who banded together in caravans to transport goods across the steppe. By the second half of the nineteenth century, the *chumaky* and river barges had begun to be replaced, although by no means entirely, by railroads. Given the value of agricultural products, it is not surprising that the first railroad in Dnieper Ukraine was constructed in 1865 to cover the distance of 137 miles (222 kilometers) between Odessa and Balta, a town on the southern border of the province of Podolia within the grain-producing area of the steppe. Between 1868 and 1870, this first line was extended in two directions to connect Balta with Kiev (via Zhmerynka and Kremenchuk). The 1870s witnessed the construction of several new lines, connecting Dnieper Ukraine with Moscow, St Petersburg, and ports along the Baltic Sea from which grain was exported. This same period also saw the opening of the first railroads in the Dnieper-Donbas region (the Donets' and lower Dnieper River basins), which was to become the center of Dnieper Ukraine's industry. Thus, before 1914 Dnieper Ukraine had a railroad network that covered 10,500 miles (16,000 kilometers).

Less developed was the road system and river transport. Some concrete roads were constructed in the late eighteenth century, but this means of transportation received less attention after railroad construction began. Consequently, by 1914 there was only 0.5 mile of road for every 40 square miles (0.8 kilometer of

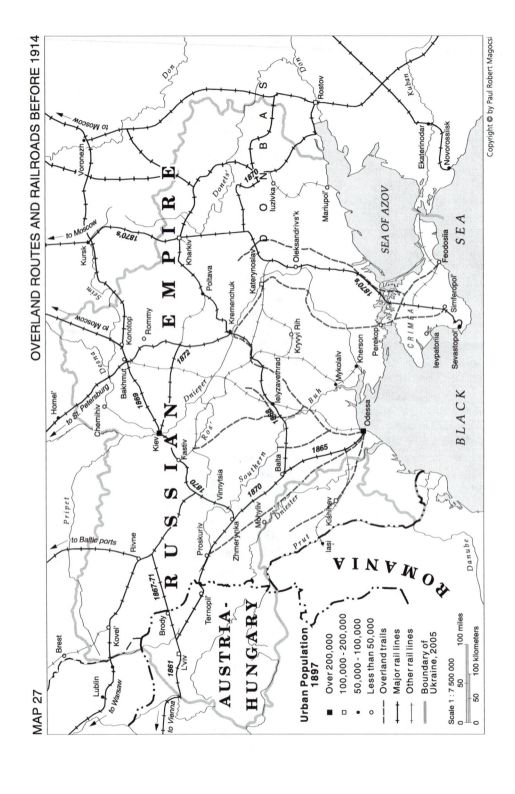

MAP 27

OVERLAND ROUTES AND RAILROADS BEFORE 1914

Urban Population 1897

- ■ Over 200,000
- □ 100,000 - 200,000
- ● 50,000 - 100,000
- ○ Less than 50,000

— — — Overland trails
—┼┼┼— Major rail lines
—†††— Other rail lines
———— Boundary of Ukraine, 2005

Scale 1 : 7 500 000

0 50 100 miles
0 50 100 kilometers

Copyright © by Paul Robert Magocsi

road for every loo square kilometers) of Ukrainian territory. River transport fared somewhat better, especially after the introduction of the steamship in 1823. The Dnieper River remained the busiest river. Its value was enhanced by the construction of canals, which together with various tributaries made possible connections with the Neman River in the north (as early as 1765–1775) and, via the Pripet River, with the Buh and Vistula Rivers in the west (1846–1848). The total freight traffic on the Dnieper and Southern Buh Rivers (primarily lumber and grain) more than doubled during the late nineteenth century – from 1.7 million tons (1.6 million metric tons) in 1884 to 2.6 million tons (2.4 million metric tons) in 1914.

Although agriculture played the dominant role, Dnieper Ukraine had its own industrial enterprises as well. The kinds of industry changed during the first half of the nineteenth century, however, largely as a result of the mercantilist policy of the Russian Empire, in which Ukrainian performance was made to serve imperial economic interests. During the eighteenth century, the government in St Petersburg began to limit the traditional Dnieper-Ukrainian exports of saltpeter, potassium, and tar, since these competed with similar products from Russian lands. For instance, the Hetmanate's large linen factory at Pochep, founded in 1726, was dismantled and rebuilt in Russia, and the important porcelain works in Hlukhiv were closed. The textile industry survived in Dnieper Ukraine, but its growth was limited owing to unfavorable tariffs. In the Kiev region alone, sales decreased by 44 percent between 1842 and 1847.

Factories which produced distilled alcohol, soap, and metallic and leather wares and which processed sugar and tobacco, however, continued to flourish. Moreover, the number of industrial enterprises continued to grow steadily during the nineteenth century, both before and after the 1860s era of reforms. If in 1793 there were 200 industrial plants in Dnieper Ukraine, by 1832 that number had risen to 779, and by 1860 to 2,329.[3] Also, contrary to the practice in the previous century, most of the new factories were established not by noble landowners, but by enterprising capitalists. These new entrepreneurs reintroduced into Dnieper Ukraine glass, paper, and, especially, textile factories which before long were competing with factories in Russia. Of the factory proprietors, in 1832, 47 percent were Russian, 29 percent were Ukrainian, 17 percent were Jewish, and 4 percent were foreigners.[4]

The organizational structure of industry also changed. In general, between 1800 and 1861 the number of factories owned by landowning nobles and employing serfs decreased, whereas the number of factories owned by capitalist entrepreneurs and employing hired laborers increased. For instance, in 1828, 54 percent of all factories were owned by landowners, and as much as 74 percent of the work force in all factories were serfs. Certain industries, especially distilling and sugar processing, with plants located in the countryside, employed serf laborers almost exclusively. This state of affairs changed, however, with the growth in the number of factories and the willingness, especially during the 1850s, of landowners to allow industrial enterprises in the cities to hire serfs from the countryside. Accordingly, by 1861 the figures were the reverse of those three decades earlier.

Now, 94 percent of the factories were owned by capitalist entrepreneurs, and 74 percent of the work force were hired laborers.[5] Throughout the period before the era of reforms, the size of the factories remained modest. The largest were the sugar refineries, which averaged between 150 (in 1848) and 305 (in 1857) workers per plant. Textile factories averaged 100 workers per plant. The total number of workers in all industries increased substantially, however, from 15,000 in 1825 to 81,800 in 1860.[6]

Industry in Dnieper Ukraine expanded at an even faster rate after the era of reforms and the rapid growth of the urban population during the last decades of the nineteenth century. If in 1860, there were 2,300 industrial enterprises, by 1895 that number had risen to over 30,000. The size of the work force followed suit, increasing from 82,000 employees in 1860 to over 6.3 million in 1914. In terms of production, the most important industries were sugar refining, coal mining, iron and steel production, and metallurgy and machine building.

The sugar industry was particularly well developed in the provinces of Kiev and Podolia, where the largest proportion of the sugar beet crop was grown. Until mid-century, production was carried out on the estates of Polish magnates (the Bobrzyńskis, Branickis, Potockis); thereafter, the industry was dominated by a few large-scale firms owned by family dynasties like the Brodskiis, Iakhnenkos, Symerenkos, and most especially, the Tereshchenkos, who were able to take advantage of new technical developments and thereby to improve output. For example, between 1863 and 1890 a smaller number of refineries (152 instead 188) produced twelve times as much sugar. By 1914 Dnieper Ukraine accounted for 85 percent of the Russian Empire's crystal sugar and 75 percent of its refined sugar.

Coal mining was centered in the Donbas region. By 1880, Dnieper Ukraine had over 250 mines and was the leading coal producer in the Russian Empire, accounting for 43 percent of its total production. Hand in hand with coal mining arose the metallurgical industry. From its beginnings in the 1870s until 1902, twenty-three blast furnaces producing pig iron came into operation in the Dnieper-Donbas region, as well as several metallurgical and locomotive factories in the provinces of Kharkiv and Katerynoslav.

Despite the expansion in sugar refining, coal mining, metallurgy, and machine building, as well as in other industries such as alcohol distilling and textile and glass manufacturing, agriculture continued to be the dominant element in Dnieper Ukraine's economy before 1914. Because the entire economic structure of Dnieper Ukraine remained subordinate to the needs of the Russian Empire as a whole, it should come as no surprise that despite its abundance of agricultural products the majority of Ukraine's rural population enjoyed a subsistence-level existence at best. This is because Dnieper Ukraine's agricultural produce, in particular its grain, was used to supply the large export trade which helped Russia meet its international payments. In effect, grain exports became the basic source of foreign currency that the Russian Empire needed to purchase machinery abroad and to accumulate capital for further industrial investment at home.

In other words, it was the imperial treasury, the foreign merchants in Odessa, and western European investors (French, Belgian, English) in the Dnieper-Donbas region who gained the most from the economic structure of nineteenth-century Dnieper Ukraine. As for the largely ethnic Ukrainian peasantry, the steady increase in their numbers could not be absorbed by the agricultural sector – or, for that matter, by the industrial sector, because Dnieper Ukraine's new factories were filled with immigrant workers from Russia brought in by foreign entrepreneurs anxious to have immediate access to a skilled industrial work force. Accordingly, to improve their economic status ethnic Ukrainians had to leave their homeland. The Russian Empire did, of course, have seemingly unlimited expanses of land farther east, and it is to these territories – especially the relatively closer Don and Kuban valleys, as well as to Central Asia, southern Siberia, and the Pacific maritime provinces – that ethnic Ukrainian peasants moved in the hope of improving their economic lot.

The Peoples of Dnieper Ukraine

Like most parts of Europe, Dnieper Ukraine was inhabited by peoples of various national and religious background. Ethnic Ukrainians, who represented nearly three-quarters of the total population, were by far the numerically largest group living in eight of the nine provinces that made up Dnieper Ukraine. But there were also significant numbers of Russians, Poles, Jews, Germans, Crimean Tatars, and others (see table 28.1).

TABLE 28.1
Nationality composition of Dnieper Ukraine, 1897[1]

Nationality	Number	Percentage
Ukrainians	17,040,000	71.5
Russians	2,970,000	12.4
Jews	2,030,000	8.5
Germans	502,000	2.1
Poles	406,000	1.7
Belarusans	222,000	0.9
Crimean Tatars	220,000	0.9
Romanians/Moldavians	187,000	0.8
Greeks	80,000	0.3
Bulgarians	68,000	0.3
Czechs	37,000	0.2
Others	71,000	0.3
TOTAL	23,833,000	99.9

Peoples other than ethnic Ukrainians were not geographically distributed evenly. Some lived primarily in certain regions, others were concentrated for the most part in cities. In general, the rapidly growing cities in nineteenth-century Dnieper Ukraine were islets of non-Ukrainian culture (see table 28.2).

Irrespective of their numbers and geographic location, some of these other peoples maintained distinct ways of life, with their own laws, schools, customs, and cultural forms, in some instances completely divorced from and even alien to

TABLE 28.2
Nationality composition of Dnieper Ukraine's urban
population, 1897[2]

Nationality	Number	Percentage
Russians	1,050,000	34.0
Ukrainians	937,000	30.3
Jews	830,000	27.0
Others	268,000	8.6
TOTAL	3,085,000	99.9

that of their ethnic Ukrainian neighbors, whether in the countryside, the towns, or the cities. Nonetheless, these peoples had in some cases for centuries inhabited Dnieper Ukraine, and together with ethnic Ukrainians they were part of what had become in the course of the nineteenth century a rich multicultural civilization.

The Russians

Russians first began to enter Ukrainian territories in substantial numbers during the second half of the seventeenth century. This first wave was composed primarily of military officers and soldiers (as many as 11,600, according to an agreement signed in 1663), who were stationed in the Hetmanate and Sloboda Ukraine after the incorporation of these territories into the tsardom of Muscovy. After 1709, when the gradual elimination of Cossack autonomy began, numerous Russian nobles (such as Rumiantsev, Golitsyn, Dolgorukii, Menshikov, and Iusupov) were granted large estates, to which they often brought enserfed Russian peasants.

It was not uncommon to find that after a generation or two the Russian peasants would become assimilated to the local ethnic Ukrainian population. This did not happen to the nobility, however. They maintained a social and cultural distance from ethnic Ukrainians and from all others who were not of their rank, through their aristocratic way of life and use of the imperial language, Russian, or, even more often, foreign languages like French and German. Nevertheless, as landowners, several nobles developed a sense of local patriotism toward "Little Russia," whose particular rights and privileges they at times defended against the encroachment of the central government, especially when the latter wanted to introduce new taxes. Such "economic patriotism" was particularly marked during the eighteenth century.

There was still another group of Russian settlers in Ukrainian territories who maintained a distinct identity from the rest of population. These were the Old Believers, or Old Ritualists (*starovery/staroobriadtsy*), religious traditionalists who opposed the reforms introduced into the Russian Orthodox Church in the mid-seventeenth century. To escape persecution in Muscovy for their beliefs, Old Believers fled to the tsardom's borderlands, including the Hetmanate in Ukraine, where from the 1660s they were allowed to settle in "schismatic free settlements," especially in what later became the northern districts (especially Starodub) of

MAP 28

THE PEOPLES OF UKRAINE, circa 1900

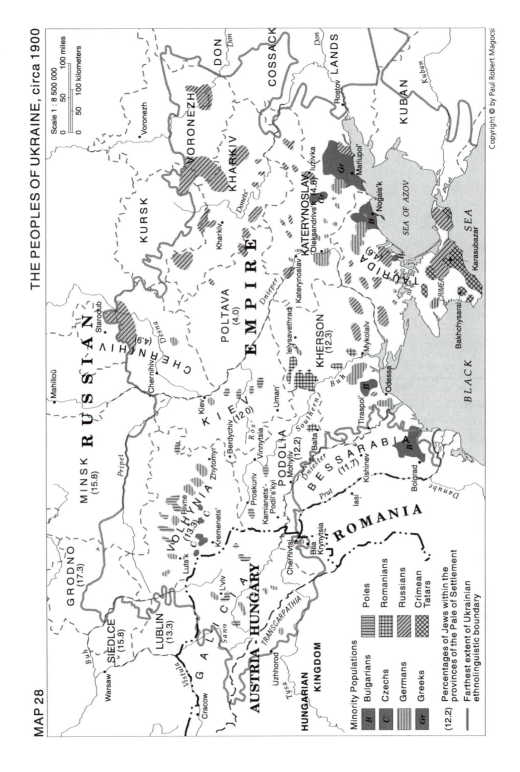

Scale 1 : 8 500 000

Copyright © by Paul Robert Magocsi

Minority Populations

B	Bulgarians
C	Czechs
	Germans
Gr	Greeks
	Poles
	Romanians
	Russians
	Crimean Tatars

(12.2) Percentages of Jews within the provinces of the Pale of Settlement

Farthest extent of Ukrainian ethnolinguistic boundary

Chernihiv province. It was not long, however, before the newcomers clashed with the Hetmanate's authorities, who tried unsuccessfully to reduce their economic privileges. As a result, in the second half of the eighteenth century many Old Believers moved farther south into the steppeland of what later became the Kherson and Taurida provinces.

By the mid-nineteenth century, 10 percent of all Old Believers in the Russian Empire lived in the nine "Ukrainian" provinces, and by 1904 their number had reached 167,000. Old Believers also settled in the southern part of Bessarabia province and in neighboring Moldavia and Walachia, where they were known as Lipovany. In the 1760s and 1780s some Lipovany moved to the Austrian province of Bukovina, where their major settlement at Bila Krynytsia became the metropolitan see for local Old Believers as well as for those in the Russian Empire (until 1905). In keeping with their religious convictions, the Old Believers, wherever they lived, considered outsiders unclean and did not mix with "fellow" Russians, ethnic Ukrainians, or any of the other peoples among whom they lived. As part of their lifestyle, Old Believers refused to serve in the military, wore traditional dress, and used only Russian in their daily lives and church services.

It was during the nineteenth century that large-scale immigration of Russians to Dnieper Ukraine took place. Initially, rural areas in the southern provinces of Kherson and Taurida were the primary goals of settlement, but with the industrialization of the Dnieper-Donbas region after the 1880s it was to industrial cities of the Donets' and lower Dnieper River valleys that Russians flocked. By 1897, Dnieper Ukraine had 2.9 million Russian inhabitants, making up 12.4 percent of the total population. The Russians were particularly well represented in Ukraine's urban areas. In the first half of the century (1832), they comprised a disproportionately high percentage of factory owners (44.6 percent), merchants (52.6 percent), and city dwellers (35.5 percent). The proportion of Russians in cities continued to increase, with the result that by the end of the century (1897) they made up more than half the population of Mykolaïv (66.3 percent), Kharkiv (63 percent), and Kiev (54.4 percent), and a substantial percentage of that of Odessa (49.1 percent) and Katerynoslav (41.8 percent). In all urban areas in Dnieper Ukraine considered as a whole, Russians accounted for 34 percent of the inhabitants.

As a result, most cities in Dnieper Ukraine were Russian in flavor, not simply because they were part of the Russian imperial framework, but because they were in fact inhabited to such a substantial degree by ethnic Russians and russified Ukrainians. The holders of the highest administrative and governmental posts, the owners of factories and other enterprises, and the workers in mines and factories (68 percent in Katerynoslav in 1897) in Dnieper Ukraine were Russians. Several Russians, russified Ukrainians, and russified Jews who had been born or who worked in Dnieper Ukraine played an outstanding role in the region's intellectual and scholarly life as university professors in the humanities and social sciences (Izmail Sreznevskii, Timofei Florinskii, Vladimir Ikonnikov, Stepan Golubev, Ivan Vernadskii, Vladimir Peretts, Mikhail Rostovtsev), and in the natural sciences and engineering (Sergei Reformatskii, Iosef Kosonogov, Aleksander Fomin, Vladimir Vernadskii, Igor Sikorskii). The empire's cultural life was enriched by several creative artists who were either born or who worked in Ukraine, and who, regardless of their origins (perhaps ethnic Ukrainians, or of nationally mixed parentage, or not Russian at all) were – and continue to be – associated with some of the greatest achievements of Russian culture in the nineteenth and early twentieth centuries. Among the best known were the writers Nikolai Gogol', Kondratii Ryleev, Aleksei Tolstoi, Vladimir Korolenko, and Nikolai Leskov; the philosopher Nikolai Berdiaiev; the naturalistic painters Ilia Repin and Ivan Aivazovskii; the radical modernist painter Kazimir Malevich; the Symbolist painter and designer Mikhail Vrubel'; the sculptor Aleksandr Archipenko; the composers Reinhold Glière, Igor Stravinsky, and Sergei Prokofiev; and the ballet dancers and choreographers Serge Lifar and Vaslav Nijinsky. Kiev was also the home of the conservative political activists Vitalii Shul'gin and Vasilii Shul'gin, who on the pages of their newspaper *Kievlianin* (1864–1919) tried to protect what they considered the best interests of the Russian Empire. Many of these scholars, writers, artists, and political activists expressed a deep love for their Little Russian homeland. With few exceptions, however, they were unsympathetic to the Ukrainian national movement if not openly opposed to the idea that a distinct Ukrainian nationality even existed.

The Poles

While Russians played a dominant role in the Left Bank and steppe regions of Dnieper Ukraine during the nineteenth century, Poles continued to be the most important group in the Right Bank, or so-called Southwestern Land (Volhynia, Kiev, and Podolia provinces). The total number of Poles in the Right Bank increased from approximately 240,000 in 1795 to 322,000 in 1897. Their relative numerical strength declined, however, slipping from 10 percent of the population in 1795 to 3.5 percent in 1897.

Despite the relative smallness of their group, the Poles played a particularly influential role in the Right Bank, because when the area was incorporated into the Russian Empire, the Polish and polonized Ukrainian *szlachta* was immediately granted the status of nobility (*dvorianstvo*). Initially, in 1795, this meant that as many as 260,000 persons – as much as 7.7 percent of the area's population – were nobles. Despite their legal status, the vast majority of Polish nobles held no land and, in many cases, were economically at the same level as or worse off than townspeople and state peasants. In effect, only 30,000 could actually be considered part of the Right Bank's elite, that is, nobles who had both hereditary status and a sufficient amount of land to allow them voting rights in noble assemblies. This smaller elite, however, enjoyed numerous privileges. They retained title to their estates and control over the serfs living on them, and they came to dominate the administration, courts, and schools in the Right Bank, all of which remained Polish.

It was the Roman Catholic Church, however, that was most successful in maintaining a sense of Polishness among the broadest segment of the population, even after the group's intellectual and social elite had been weakened or driven into exile following the periodic failure of its conspiratorial and revolutionary activities. At the hierarchical level, the church suffered losses following the Partitions of Poland (1772–1795). Over the course of nearly a century, Roman Catholic dioceses were abolished, restored, transferred, and abolished again by the Russian government. Beginning in 1798, all Roman Catholics east of the Congress Kingdom came under a single Latin-rite archdiocese with its seat in the Belarusan town of Mahilioŭ. In Dnieper Ukraine, several Roman Catholic dioceses (Kiev, Kam'ianets'-Podil's'kyi, Volodymyr, and Chernihiv) were abolished, with the result that by 1866 only the dioceses of Luts'k-Zhytomyr (with its seat at Zhytomyr) remained to serve primarily the Poles in the Right Bank. In the interim, a new Roman Catholic diocese was established at Tiraspol (1847) with jurisdiction over southern Ukraine and Bessarabia, where most of its faithful were recent German colonists. Although its hierarchy was weakened, in local Roman Catholic parishes the Polish language continued to be used and functioned as an important means of preserving Polish identity in the Right Bank.

In effect, the Right Bank, together with the Russian Empire's other "Polish" provinces, located farther north than Dnieper Ukraine – Vilna, Grodno, Vitebsk, Mogilev, and Minsk – became a stronghold of Polish national feeling. This character was due largely to the educational system, which from 1803 to 1823 was under the direction of Prince Adam Czartoryski. As curator of schools in the empire's "Polish" provinces, Czartoryski had a free hand in managing education. As a result, Polish culture among younger generations was preserved by the Polish university at Vilnius (in Polish, Wilno) and by the lyceum in a town which Poles dubbed their "Volhynian Athens" – Kremenets' (in Polish, Krzemieniec). Consequently, the Polish nobility was not russified, and the whole area was filled with Polish patriots who became involved in several underground societies, such as the Kiev branch of the Society of the United Slavs (Towarzystwo Zjednoczonych Słowian, est. 1823) and the Southern Society (est. 1821), a republican group which called for the emancipation of the serfs. More conspiratorial in nature were the branches in Kiev of the Association of the Polish People (Stowarzyszenie Ludu Polskiego), founded by Polish students at the University of St Vladimir in the wake of the abortive 1830–1831 revolt, and the Provincial Committee in Rus' (est. 1862), which was responsible for planning an uprising in the Right Bank as part of the 1863 Polish revolt against tsarist rule.

In the economic sphere, the Polish nobility was active in Dnieper Ukraine's textile, porcelain, glass, metallurgy, and, especially, sugar processing industries. In agriculture, there were negative repercussions following the abortive Polish revolts of 1831–1832 and again 1863 (which led to the confiscation of many Polish estates). Polish-owned industries also felt the loss of serf labor in factories both before and after the era of reforms. Nevertheless, the Polish nobility continued to be one of the most influential social estates in the Right Bank until the outbreak of World War I. Indicative of this influence was the landholding pattern: in 1909, 46 percent of private landholdings (representing 15 percent of all land in the Right Bank) was still owned by Poles.

The socioeconomic changes during the second half of the nineteenth century also contributed to an increase in the number of Poles in Right Bank cities, especially Kiev, whose population by 1874 was 8.2 percent Polish. As a result,

WHAT UKRAINE MEANS FOR POLAND

As well as an inspiration for literary works, Ukraine became for many Poles the very place where the spiritual regeneration of Poland was to take place. For that reason, the Ukrainian people were worthy of respect and even emulation, although the lands they inhabited – in particular the Right Bank – could not be imagined in any other way than as an integral part of Polish territory. This point of view was summed up best in 1842 by Seweryn Goszczyński, a member of the "Ukrainian school" of Polish literature, in a critique of the poetry of another member, Józef Bogdan Zaleski.

> The part of Poland called Ukraine received a calling which within the general [Polish] national calling has not yet been fully understood or explained; it has, along with its history, unique spiritual features which distinguish it and elevate it above the other parts [of Poland]; in short, it is there that the spirit of freedom of the Polish people abided and showed itself most energetically in battle with oppression, and immortalized with bloody features both its wrongs and its protestation against them. If we look at the entire life of the Polish people we will not find this phenomenon existing anywhere else with such force, tenacity and consequences so decisive and terrible for the Fatherland. ...
>
> This feeling of freedom among the Ukrainian people showed itself in a guise that is perhaps too wild for the present age; it led to fratricidal crimes ... we do not justify this. ... Nevertheless, despite all the charges that Poland can make against Ukraine, it is certain that its Cossack life afforded beautiful deeds for the nation's glory, and even in its horrors, it was a historical, palpable warning for the nation of the sources of its downfall. It also foretold in its bright, Polish aspect the future which our regeneration will develop, and which we are already entering in spirit. It is for this reason that we have such poetry about Ukrainian history and its land, and it is for this reason that the heart of the [Polish] nation has such love and admiration for it. Yes, the spirit of the Polish people sensed the truth in the idea of Ukraine; in the sufferings [of the Ukrainian people] it saw the apotheosis of its own martyrdom, and in the spectre of its past it saw its foe to whom it now pays its respect through its love. In this homage the [Ukrainian] people and the [Polish] gentry are united.

SOURCE: George G. Grabowicz, "The History and Myth of the Cossack Ukraine in Polish and Russian Romantic Literature" (unpublished PhD dissertation, Harvard University 1975), pp. 107–108.

Polish culture continued to flourish throughout the region. Kiev (Polish: Kijów) in particular had its Polish schools, theater, newspapers, publishing house, cultural organizations, sports clubs, and legal and illegal political societies. On the eve of and during World War I the city proved to be a formative influence on the outstanding twentieth-century Polish poet Jarosław Iwaszkiewicz and the world renowned "Russian" painter of Polish origin Kazimir Malevich.

But Polish culture was not limited to urban areas. Throughout much of the nineteenth century the rural areas of the Right Bank were not only the home but also the source of literary inspiration for the leading Polish Romantic poet and dramatist Juliusz Słowacki and for members of the so-called Ukrainian school of Polish literature (Michał Czajkowski, Józef Bogdan Zaleski, Seweryn Goszczyński, and others). Within the Right Bank's tranquil environment of rural manorial estates owned by a privileged landed gentry, several other leading Polish creative artists of that era began their lives. Among them were the musicians and composers Juliusz Zarębski, Ignacy Jan Paderewski, and Karol Szymanowski; the historical novelist Józef Kraszewski, who spent over three decades as a landowner and tenant farmer in Volhynia; and the architect Leszek Dezider Gorodecki/Vladyslav Horodets'kyi, whose buildings still grace the streets of Kiev. It was also on one such manorial estate in Podolia, owned by Polish poet and playwright Apollo Korzeniowski, where his son, Józef Teodor Konrad Korzeniowski, spent the first five years of his life before moving on and eventually becoming one of the greatest English-language novelists of the nineteenth century – Joseph Conrad.

It was another Polish author, however, the Nobel Prize laureate Henryk Sienkiewicz, who, although not a native of the Right Bank, was to have the greatest impact on the mind-set of Poles in the Russian Empire and elsewhere. In 1884, Sienkiewicz published the initial volume of what became his enormously popular trilogy on seventeenth-century Poland. Entitled *Ogniem i mieczem* (With Fire and Sword), this first novel of the trilogy was a panegyric to Polish civilization, which was depicted as threatened in the "wild steppes of Ukraine," where the defender of the Commonwealth and "magnate of steel" on his white stallion, Prince Jeremi Wiśniowiecki, was pitted against the "cunning" and often "drunkenly enraged" Cossack hetman Bohdan Khmel'nyts'kyi. Because the trilogy subsequently became required reading for Polish schoolchildren (and remains so to the present day), Sienkiewicz's powerful if distorted stereotypes are what generations of Poles most readily remember when they think about Ukraine and Ukrainians.

The Jews

Although Russians and Poles represented a numerical minority in Dnieper Ukraine, members of these groups occupied the leading strata in the political and socioeconomic life of both the Left and the Right Banks. There were, however, other peoples who enjoyed neither numerical nor political strength in nineteenth-century Dnieper Ukraine. Historically, the Jews were the most important in this category.

Since the late sixteenth century, the Jews had enjoyed municipal self-government within a framework known as the Council of Lands, and in the countryside they became an integral part of the arenda economic system that was established throughout Ukrainian territory under Polish rule (see chapter 11). As middlemen in the arenda system between the Polish landlords and the Ukrainian peasants, the Jews before long were perceived by Ukrainians as their oppressors. The result was that during periods of social upheaval such as those in the mid-seventeenth century (the Khmel'nyts'kyi revolution) and the second half of the eighteenth century (the haidamak revolts), Jews often suffered material and physical destruction at the hands of the rebellious peasants. With the slow disintegration of the Polish state in the eighteenth century, the self-governing Council of Lands ceased to exist; then, in 1844, the tsarist government abolished the *kahal* (Yiddish: *kehile*), or Jewish self-government at the local level.

Despite the decline of their self-governing status and their loss of life and property during the haidamak revolts, the Jews remained an integral part of Poland's economy on the Right Bank. Their numbers, moreover, grew steadily in Dnieper Ukraine, from over 300,000 at the end of the eighteenth century and over 900,000 in the middle of the nineteenth century to over 2 million in 1897. The last figure represented 8.5 percent of the total population in the nine provinces (including the Crimea) of Dnieper Ukraine.

Although Jews were found in all parts of Dnieper Ukraine, nearly three-fifths (1.2 million) lived in the Right Bank. Their continued high concentration in the Right Bank was due to the Russian imperial government's restriction on their movement farther eastward. The tsars generally preferred that Jews living under their rule remain on territories that had been acquired from the partitioned Polish-Lithuanian Commonwealth. These territories, which came to be known as the Pale of Settlement, included the tsarist provinces in what is today Poland, Lithuania, and Belarus as well as all provinces of Dnieper Ukraine with the exception of Kharkiv.

Within this so-called Pale of Settlement, the vast majority of Jews lived in small towns and cities. According to the 1897 census, 27 percent of the urban population throughout Dnieper Ukraine consisted of Jews. In the Right Bank alone, 72 percent of the Jews lived in towns with over 1,000 persons; in three-fifths of those towns they represented at least 40 percent of the population. In the Left Bank, 65 percent of the Jews lived in towns with over 1,000 persons, and in the Steppe Ukraine the figure was 76 percent. In Dnieper Ukraine as a whole, 26 percent of all Jews lived in twenty cities, each of which had over 10,000 Jews.

Being an urban population, the Jews engaged primarily in trade, banking, industry, and in operating small shops and businesses. By 1832, they comprised 17 percent of the factory owners and 21 percent of the merchants in Dnieper Ukraine, although in the Right Bank, where Jews were concentrated, the percentages were significantly higher (93 percent of factory owners and 96 percent of merchants in Volhynia).[3] Jews were especially well represented in certain industries, and by 1872 they owned 90 percent of the distilleries, 57 percent of the sawmills, and 49 percent of the tobacco industry. A few Jewish-owned companies based in Ukraine came to play a dominant role in the empire as a whole. Among them was the Aleksander Sugar Refinery, founded in 1876 in Kiev by Izrail Brodskii. Before the end of the century, Kiev became the base for numerous other Brodskii refineries that accounted for about one-quarter of the entire sugar production in the Russian Empire. Following in the industrial and philanthropic interests of his father, Brodskii's son Lazar expanded the company and made donations to several Jewish and non-Jewish cultural and welfare institutions. In his will, Lazar left funds for the construction

MEMORIES OF THE *SHTETL*

The *shtetl* was the epitome of Jewish life not only in Dnieper Ukraine but also in the western Ukrainian lands under Austro-Hungarian rule – Galicia, Bukovina, and Transcarpathia. The following description by Joachim Schoenfeld, who grew up before World War I in the Ukrainian town of Sniatyn in far southeastern Galicia, reveals the hold the *shtetl* continued to have on the imagination of those who grew up in it.

> I was born and raised in the *shtetl* of Sniatyn. Since the life of the Jews in all the *shtetls* of Galicia, and indeed throughout eastern Europe, was, with slight deviations, more or less the same, my picture of life in Sniatyn reflects that in hundreds of other *shtetls* as well and can be taken as an approximate description of all of them.
>
> Although I never returned to my *shtetl* after the First World War, all my love and my most fervent feelings go back to that era. Even today, although thousands of miles away from it, after having fought in many trenches on different battlefields during the First World War, after having survived Hitler's concentration camps, and after having traveled through many countries, happiness overcomes me when I think back to those days and manage to recapture some of the tableaus of former years.
>
> This happiness, however, is soon overshadowed by sadness and sorrow that this, our past, doesn't exist anymore. With affliction and grief I mourn the desolation of the Yiddish *shtetl*. ... Actually it may be wrong to call the place a *shtetl*, and not a city as it really was. However, having in mind the core of the city, where the Jews lived on a kind of isle, surrounded by a sea of Gentiles, I call it the *shtetl*.[*]

The degree to which the *shtetl*, while economically and physically inseparable from its surroundings, still functioned in a spiritual world of its own, is summed up in the following description of a young Jewish child growing up in the late nineteenth-century Russian Empire.

> He could not tell you a thing about Russia, about Poland, about Lithuania and its people, laws, kings, politicians. ... But you just ask him about Og, King of Bashan, and Sihon, King of the Emorites, and Nebuchadnezzer, King of Babylon! Ask him about the Euphrates and the Jordan. He knew about the people who lived in tents and spoke Hebrew or Arabic. ... He knew nothing concerning the fields about him, nothing about rye, wheat, potatoes, and where he got his bread from. ... But he knew about vineyards, date palms, pomegranates, locust-trees ... he lived in another world.[†]

[*]Joachim Schoenfeld, *Shtetl Memoirs: Jewish Life in Galicia under the Austro-Hungarian Empire and in the Reborn Poland, 1898–1939* (Hoboken, N.J. 1985), p. 1.

[†]Meyer W. Weisgal and Joel Carmichael, eds., *Chaim Weizman: A Biography by Several Hands* (London 1962), p. 68.

in Kiev of the still-functioning Bessarabian Covered Market (the Bessarabka, 1910–12), the income from which was originally intended for Jewish charities.

Despite the achievements of individual Jews in the uppermost echelons of Dnieper Ukraine's economy, the vast majority lived a modest existence that often bordered on poverty. They were spread throughout villages and small towns, each of which had its own sub-community, known in Yiddish as the *shtetl* or *shtetele*. The *shtetl* had an atmosphere of its own that was governed by two basic values: (1) humaneness (Yiddish: *menshlikhkeyt*), which made it an environment in which economic and psychological support could be found in times of crisis as well as on an everyday basis; and (2) Jewishness (Yiddish: *yidishkeyt*), a religious environment, both at home and on the streets, that provided daily spiritual sustenance in the midst of an otherwise alien Christian world. Daily life in the *shtetl* revolved around the synagogue, the home, and the market, which was also the place where Jews interacted with their non-Jewish neighbors (*goyim*). The attractiveness of small-town life in the nineteenth- and early twentieth-century *shtetl* has been immortalized by numerous writers and artists, among the most famous of whom was the Ukrainian-born Sholem Aleichem (Shalom Rabinovitz), whose stories were later used as the basis for the popular American musical *Fiddler on the Roof*. In fact, it was the psychological comfort afforded by *shtetl* life that made many Jews reluctant to leave their centuries-old homes in Dnieper Ukraine and other parts of eastern Europe even in times of economic hardship and physical danger.

Dnieper Ukraine, especially the Right Bank, also became a fertile ground for Jewish culture. It was there that some of the most important cultural and political movements in all of modern Jewish history arose. These movements may have begun as the direct result of catastrophe in the community. Thus, after suffering the destruction of the Khmel'nyts'kyi era, Jews throughout Ukraine – and, for that matter, in other parts of Europe – began to believe that their only hope lay in the imminent arrival of the Messiah. This belief produced a cultural environment that allowed for the widespread acceptance of Sabbatianism, that is, the belief that the Messiah had actually come in the person of Shabetai Tsevi.

Sabbatianism reached Ukraine and other eastern parts of Poland-Lithuania during the late seventeenth and early eighteenth centuries, and there it became part of the largest messianic movement in Jewish history since the second century CE. The eighteenth century, with its haidamak and peasant disturbances in the Right Bank, produced a social and psychological instability within Jewish communities that in turn set the stage for the birth of Hasidism in Podolia. Founded by Yisra'el ben Eli'ezer, the Baal Shem Tov (usually referred to by the initials BeShT), Hasidism was a mystical movement which stressed the mercifulness of God and encouraged joyous religious expression in music and dance. While following Jewish law, the movement represented a reaction to the academic formalism and rigidity of the rabbinical Talmudists, who placed a much greater emphasis on intensive study of the Talmud (the authoritative book of Jewish law and tradition) than on other, less intellectual forms of religious expression. Because of its popular appeal, Hasidism spread rapidly, and it would remain the dominant variety of Judaism among Ukrainian and other central and eastern European Jews until the twentieth century. At about the same time that Hasidism appeared in Podolia, this region also witnessed the appearance of Jacub Leib, known as Jacub Frank, who, following in the tradition of Shabetai Tsevi, proclaimed himself the Messiah. Later, however, he converted to Roman Catholicism, and his followers, known as Frankists, eventually rejected Judaism entirely, and some became leading members of the Roman Catholic Church.

The nineteenth century produced new movements which had emigration as their goal. The desire to emigrate was a direct result of the upheaval in Jewish communities in the wake of pogroms in 1881–1883 and 1903–1906. The first pogroms were prompted by a rumor that the Jews had assassinated the "reforming" tsar Alexander II in March 1881, and that as a result the government supposedly had authorized attacks on Jews. The pogroms at first received the support of some Russian revolutionary circles, including the People's Will (Narodnaia Volia) organization. It was this organization that actually had carried out the assassination of the tsar, in the hope that its action would awaken the masses to revolt, destabilize society, and eventually bring down the tsarist regime. For their part, the Russian governmental authorities, at least during the initial pogroms of April and August 1881, did not interfere, but permitted the violence and robbery to take place. The "Russian pogroms" of 1881–1883 were concentrated in Dnieper Ukraine, first in Ielysavethrad (today Kirovohrad) in Kherson province, and then in all provinces of Dnieper Ukraine except Volhynia and Kharkiv. The perpetrators primarily confined their actions to beatings and the looting of property, although some reports suggest several dozen killed. When the imperial government finally got around to the matter, it blamed the pogroms of the early 1880s on the inept reaction of provincial governors, who subsequently intervened with force to stop further pogroms.

Two decades later, at the beginning of the twentieth century, a more serious wave of pogroms began, in 1903, at Chişinău (in Russian, Kishinev), in the empire's far southwestern province of Bessarabia. These outbreaks were much more violent, and in addition to the widespread material damage an estimated 800 Jews were killed in pogroms reported to have occurred in over 600 towns and villages throughout Dnieper Ukraine and Bessarabia. Among the most violent were those of 1905 in Zhytomyr (May), Odessa (October), and Katerynoslav (October). This latest wave of pogroms, between 1903 and 1906, was directly related to the tsarist government's struggle against the growing revolutionary movement. The right-wing press blamed the revolutionary activity on the Jews, and the authorities stood aside as monarchist organizations, popularly known as the Black Hundreds, moved throughout the countryside instigating disturbances and inflaming the passions of the local population against the Jews.

Although not part of a pogrom, the most infamous manifestation of anti-Semitism occurred in 1911, when Black Hundred pressure led to the arrest in Kiev of a Jew named Mendel Beilis. Many Christians believed the myth that Jews needed human blood for ritual purposes, and Beilis was therefore accused of having carried out the ritual murder of a twelve-year-old Christian boy. When Beilis's trial finally took place, in October 1913, it attracted attention around the world.

POGROMS

In the most general sense, the term *pogrom* refers to an attack on the persons or property of the members of any religious or ethnic minority group by the members of the presumed or actual dominant group in a society. The attacks may include some or all of the following: looting, the destruction of personal, religious, and business-related property, beating, rape, and murder. Although pogroms have been – and still are – committed against minority populations in various parts of the world, the term is associated primarily with attacks against Jews living in the western regions of the Russian Empire (the so-called Pale of Settlement, including Dnieper Ukraine), especially between 1881 and 1921.

Historians still debate several questions concerning the pogroms, including (1) how much physical and material damage was done; (2) whether the pogroms occurred primarily in urban areas or in the countryside; and (3) whether they broke out spontaneously, reflecting pent-up anti-Semitic attitudes on the part of the local population, or were the result of organized efforts on the part of local officials, national governments, or specific political groups who often used outsiders (such as migrant Russian workers) to carry out their destructive work. Regardless of the ongoing debate about motivation and damage, for the potential and actual Jewish victim the very term *pogrom* awakened an instant fear and sense of helplessness at the prospect of danger to life and limb. The following passage provides an insight into what a pogrom meant for an ordinary Jew in early twentieth-century Dnieper Ukraine:

The pogrom began with us Tuesday night. The first looting took place then. On the next morning we learned that six were slain. The whole day of Wednesday robberies continued in the town. On Thursday again five or six people were killed, but the most terrible day for our town [Slovechno] was Friday, when the most fiendish murders and atrocities took place. On Friday morning we came out of our house and fled wherever our legs took us. Wherever we went we were met with shots. The peasants encompassed the town with firing and drove the fleeing Jews into one place. Several hundred of us found ourselves in the house of Avrum-Ber Portny, and there we were all piled and heaped up on one another. It was close in the house, and terror and anguish reigned among us. When a certain peasant (Kosenko, from Slovechno) appeared and declared that he was the head of the insurgent forces, we began to entreat him and offered him money. He answered that since we had disobeyed his orders to leave the town he had decided to kill us all. Immediately the firing began through the windows of the place where we were gathered. Then the peasants began to beat us up; they beat us with whatever came handy, trampled on us with their feet, and threw bombs. How many killed, it is hard to be sure at present, but very many.

Many corpses remained at home and in the streets. The summer heat caused a stench of putrefaction from the bodies. Everywhere were pools of human blood. At evening we hid again, since looting and killing were still going on. All the Jews hid, and cowering each in his hole in a cellar or garret or in the bushes, expected death.

SOURCE: Elias Heifetz, *The Slaughter of the Jews in the Ukraine in 1919* (New York 1921), pp. 382–383.

After a month of deliberation, the jury found the defendant not guilty.

Both waves of pogroms had a profound effect on Jewish life, in forcing secular leaders in particular to reassess the future of their people in the Russian Empire. Was there a future for Jews in Russia? Or was emigration the only sensible option? Following the pogroms of the early 1880s, Dnieper Ukraine saw the rise of some of the earliest movements to propagate the idea of emigration (*aliyah*) for Jews to Palestine (Eretz Israel). Two of these movements that predated the worldwide Zionist movement – and which also had as its goal emigration to Palestine – were the Hibbat Zion (Love of Zion) and the BILU organization. BILU, an acronym for the biblical phrase "House of Jacob, come, let us go," was founded in 1882 by Jewish students in Kharkiv and was the first Zionist pioneering movement. Its goals were undermined, however, by opposition from the Ottoman government, which controlled Palestine at the time. Another movement which began in Dnieper Ukraine was Am Olam (Eternal People), which urged Jews to become agricultural-ists in preparation for their return to Israel. However, Am Olam succeeded only in establishing a few Jewish farming colonies in the United States (New Odessa, Oregon, 1883, and two settlements in South Dakota, 1882). After the 1880s, the opposition of the Ottoman government, combined with the uncertain hardships of becoming pioneer farmers in Palestine, prompted those Jews who decided to leave Dnieper Ukraine to go instead to the rapidly expanding industrial regions of the northeastern United States. By the end of the nineteenth century, Jews were emigrating to the United States in large numbers. For instance, during the two decades between 1894 and 1914, which marked the height of the immigrant flow from eastern Europe to the United States, Jews made up as much as 59 percent of all immigrants from the Russian Empire.

Most Jews, however, did not leave their centuries-old homes in Dnieper Ukraine, but remained and continued to play an important role in the economic, the cultural, and, eventually, the political life of the country. In many ways, educated Jews faced the problem of multiple identities, as did educated ethnic Ukrainians (see chapter 29). Attracted by the possibilities for social and economic mobility, many Jews assimilated into Russian culture and in certain cases even rejected entirely their Jewish heritage. Such rejection was quite common among those who joined the socialist movement, such as the Ukrainian-born Marxist Pavel Aksel'rod and two activists destined to play leading roles in the Russian Revolution and civil war: Evgeniia Bosh, a Bolshevik official in the first Soviet government in Ukraine, and Lev Bronshtein, the political ally but longtime ideological opponent of Lenin (and then Stalin) and the theoretician of the idea of "permanent revolution" who is better known to the world as Leon Trotskii.

Many others remained loyal to their ancestral heritage and worked to promote Jewish culture in Dnieper Ukraine. It was not long, however, before a debate arose over the form in which, and the language in which, Jewish culture should be propagated. The native spoken language of virtually all Jews in Dnieper Ukraine and elsewhere throughout the Russian Empire was Yiddish. Since it was not yet a standard literary language, this Germanic form of speech (heavily mixed with Slavic elements) was often subjected to denigration and scorn by intellectuals, who felt that Hebrew or Russian would be the appropriate medium for Jewish secular as well as religious culture. It was often the Zionists who favored Hebrew, and in Dnieper Ukraine the most active figures were the essayist Ahad Ha-Am (Asher Hirsh Ginsberg) and the outstanding Hebrew poets Hayim Nachman Bialik and Sha'ul Tshernichowsky. While not necessarily, eschewing Hebrew, other Jewish activists were concerned to ensure that the rich Yiddish culture and language be preserved for future generations. Important work on behalf of Yiddish in Dnieper Ukraine was carried out before World War I by the ethnographer S. An-ski (Shloyme Zaynvl Rapaport) and the writers Sholem Yankev Abramovitsh (Mendele Moykher-Sforim) and Sholem Aleichem. The debate as to whether Hebrew or Yiddish was the more appropriate language for secular Jewish culture was to continue into the 1920s.

The Germans and Mennonites

German colonization in Dnieper Ukraine began when Empress Catherine II (herself of German origin) issued the first of several imperial manifestos (1763) inviting Germans to settle in underdeveloped and sparsely inhabited lands in the European part of the Russian Empire. They included the recently acquired southern Ukrainian steppe lands known at the time as New Russia. To encourage immigration, the Russian government offered the German newcomers several incentives: land gratis or at a nominal fee, guarantees for freedom of religion (including the right to proselytize among the Muslim population), the right to local self-government in agricultural communities, exemption "in perpetuity" from military and civil service, and exemption from taxes for a period of up to thirty years. Initially, only a few Germans took advantage of Catherine's decrees to settle in Dnieper Ukraine. They included about 1,100 Mennonites, who settled in 1789–1790 near Khortytsia Island, the former Zaporozhian Cossack stronghold in the lower Dnieper River opposite the new town of Oleksandrivs'k (today Zaporizhzhia). Most of the early German colonists instead went farther east to the steppe land along the middle Volga River.

It was as a result of a new decree, issued by Tsar Alexander I in 1804, that the largest number of Germans began to settle in Dnieper Ukraine. These immigrants came primarily from the German states of Baden, Württemberg, and the Palatinate, and from the Germanic province of Alsace in France – that is, those areas near the Rhine River which had suffered most during the Napoleonic Wars – as well as from the area around Danzig in West Prussia. Most settled in the steppelands north of the Black Sea and Sea of Azov, which had only recently been acquired from the Ottoman Empire, that is, the southern Kherson and Bessarabia provinces between the Dnieper and Danube Rivers, the areas along the Dnieper

River south of Katerynoslav, the territory north of the Sea of Azov (especially along the Molochna River, where 1,200 Mennonite families settled), and the Crimea. These German colonists in the Steppe Ukraine came to be known as Black Sea Germans (*Schwarzmeerdeutsche*). According to the 1897 census, they numbered 283,000, representing 4.6 percent of the population of the provinces of Kherson, Taurida, and Katerynoslav. By 1911, German sources put their number at 489,000, of whom 43 percent were Protestants (Lutherans), 37 percent Roman Catholics, and 20 percent Mennonites.

Other concentrations of Germans were found in Volhynia, where they arrived in large numbers between the 1860s and the 1880s. Local Polish landowners were deprived of part of their serf work force after the emancipation act of 1861, and they were economically undermined following anti-Russian revolt of 1863. Consequently, they invited German colonists to run their estates or sold them their land outright. If in 1860 there were at most 5,000 Germans in Volhynia, by 1897 their number had risen to 171,000. Almost all the Volhynian Germans were Evangelical Lutherans.

By the outbreak of World War I, there were close to three-quarters of a million Germans living in Dnieper Ukraine, concentrated primarily in the steppe area near the Black Sea and in Volhynia. They lived in compact rural colonies that in 1914 numbered 966. They were engaged almost exclusively in agriculture, and their villages were regarded as models of farming and husbandry techniques. Although the well-to-do farmers hired household servants and farmhands from among the local inhabitants, in general the Germans kept a certain distance from the Slavic (ethnic Ukrainian and Russian) inhabitants that surrounded them. For that matter, Germans maintained little contact with co-ethnics of different religious backgrounds. In other words, Catholics, Protestant Lutherans, and Mennonites lived in separate communities. Each community had its own local self-governing body and even regional assemblies, and its own German-language schools and churches (often built in the Gothic style). Many also had their own newspapers and journals, the most important of which was the Odessa daily *Odessauer Zeitung*, which appeared uninterruptedly for over half a century (1863–1914). These privileges stemmed from the tsarist decrees of 1763 and 1804 that were originally intended to attract new colonists to settle in the empire. During the reform era, however, which attempted to respond to public criticism against the special status of certain sectors of tsarist society, many of the privileges given to the original colonists were rescinded. The new decrees passed between 1871 and 1884 were related to land administration, the tax system, education, and military service. All Germans were now required to pay new taxes, to study Russian in their previously all-German-language school system, and to perform military service. The abolition of what had been "perpetual" privileges was resented by many Germans, who in the 1870s began emigrating to the United States and Canada.

The Mennonites, in particular, were troubled by the imposition of the military service requirement, since they viewed the previous exemption not as a privilege but as a right corresponding to their religious commitment to pacifism and nonviolence. Driven by what they considered a violation of their religious beliefs, nearly one-third of Dnieper Ukraine's Mennonites (18,000) emigrated abroad in the 1870s. Those who stayed behind eventually worked out an accommodation with the tsarist government, whereby their young men would perform four years' service in special forestry camps.

The Mennonites were distinguished from other German-speaking peoples in Dnieper Ukraine on the basis not only of their religious beliefs but also of their origins. Almost all had come from territory known as West Prussia near the Baltic city-state of Danzig, to which their ancestors had immigrated from the Netherlands in the mid-sixteenth century. They spoke a distinct language known as Low German or Mennonite Platt (*Plaut-Dietsch*), which was used in writing and taught in their schools along with standard literary German (*Hochdeutsch*). After West Prussia was annexed by Prussia following the First Partition of Poland in 1772, the Prussian government placed certain restrictions on the Mennonites. It is not surprising, therefore, that they were attracted by the privileges offered by Catherine II and her successors to settle in the Russian Empire.

In their new homes, which in New Russia (southern Ukraine) were centered in the "Old Colony" around Khortytsia Island and along the Molochna River north of the Sea of Azov, the Mennonites established a series of flourishing agricultural communities which, thanks to the creative ideas of Johann Cornies, achieved a well-deserved reputation throughout the Russian Empire for innovations in soil cultivation, stock raising, afforestation, and related trades such as wagon building, tool making, and, especially, the milling of flour. To sustain their agricultural prosperity, they operated their own banks and mutual credit associations. Taking advantage of the right of self-government, the Mennonites established an extensive system of compulsory education for boys and girls (an exception at the time in the Russian Empire). These included German-language private secondary schools, although by the late 1880s government regulations required that all courses be taught in Russian, with the exception of religion for which German continued to be used.

Mennonites believed that their successes were due to the favorable policies of the Russian imperial government and to their own ability to avoid interacting – except in the most formal sense – with ethnic Ukrainians and other peoples, including the German Catholics and Lutherans who lived in their midst. By practicing what they called *Absonderung* (avoiding associating with people not of their faith), the Mennonites were able to preserve an exclusive group identity. Tsarist governmental practices before and, to a degree, even after the reform era contributed favorably to Mennonite self-maintenance, with the result that the community in Dnieper Ukraine, despite the emigration of the 1870s, had grown to nearly 70,000 strong by World War I. Not surprisingly, later Mennonite historians have looked back with great fondness on life in tsarist Russia, which enabled this distinct religious community to build "a state within a state" – a virtual "Mennonite Commonwealth."[4]

The Crimean Tatars

In contrast to other peoples in Dnieper Ukraine, the Crimean Tatars had a unique

The Peopled of Dnieper Ukraine 367

history with their own state structures on Ukrainian territory. The rise of Crimean Tatar statehood was related to the disintegration of the Golden Horde. In the mid-fifteenth century, the Tatars created their own state, or khanate, which after 1475 was closely allied with and eventually became a vassal state of the Ottoman Empire (see chapter 14). When Ottoman influence north of the Black Sea progressively waned in the eighteenth century, the Crimean state became subject to tsarist rule and was fully incorporated into the Russian Empire in 1783 (see chapter 22). For many centuries before that, however, Muscovy and Ukraine were at the mercy of nomadic Tatar raiding parties, with the result that a long heritage of friction developed between the Muslim Tatars and the Christian Slavs (ethnic Ukrainians and Russians). Not surprisingly, when the Russian Empire finally acquired the Crimean Khanate, it was anxious to liquidate the Crimean Muslim heritage as an unwanted reminder of the former "Tatar yoke."

Fearing the impending consequences of tsarist rule and desiring to live in an Islamic state, Crimean Tatars began to emigrate en masse to the Ottoman Empire, with the result that by the end of the eighteenth century an estimated 100,000 had left the lands of the former khanate. It seems that the majority of these early emigrants were not from the Crimean peninsula itself, but rather Nogay Tatars from the southern Ukrainian steppe. Despite this initial wave of emigration, it should be stressed that at least initially the Russian imperial government attempted to reach an accommodation with its new subjects. Catherine II considered Crimea "the pearl in the tsarist crown" and was herself known to be sympathetic to the last khan, Şahin Giray, and to the Muslim faith. In her 1783 decree proclaiming annexation, Catherine pledged on behalf of herself and her successors "to preserve and defend the ... property, temples, and ancestral faith" of the Crimea's inhabitants.[5] Indeed, the khanate's clan leaders (*beys*) and scores of lower nobles (*mirzas*) were granted the status of Russian nobility (*dvorianstvo*) and allotted large swaths of land (with their peasant inhabitants) that had previously belonged to the khan. At the same time, towns like Bahçesaray and Karasubazar were to remain Tatar enclaves and the peasantry was not transformed into serfs but remained legally free. Catherine's tolerant policies toward the Crimean Tatars and their cultural heritage were continued by Prince Mikhail Vorontsov when he served as governor-general of New Russia (1828–1854), which included the Crimea.

By the mid-nineteenth century, however, Russian policy toward the Crimea and its Tatar inhabitants changed markedly. The small Crimean Tatar town of Akmescit was greatly expanded and transformed into the imperial administrative center of Simferopol', where Russian administrators from the north gradually directed the transfer of Tatar landholdings in the peninsula to Russian nobles. It was, however, the Crimean War, which began in late 1853, that proved to be the crucial turning point in Russian-Tatar relations. The otherwise liberal tsar-reformer, Aleksander II, who ascended the throne in early 1855 just as the Crimean conflict ended, adopted a policy intended to rid the peninsula of its Crimean Tatar inhabitants. Reacting to the new attitude of the Russian imperial authorities, during the next decade, no less than 200,000 Crimean Tatars emigrated to the Ottoman Empire. They were replaced by an ever increasing number of Slavic (Ukrainian and especially Russian) in-migrants whose new permanent presence changed the face of Crimea's human and cultural landscape. Whereas at the outset of Russian rule in 1783, Tatars made up 90 percent of the Crimea's population, by 1854 their percentage dropped to 60 percent, and by 1897 to only 34 percent. Tatar culture also suffered. Many monuments constructed under the Crimean Khanate were destroyed or left in ruins. Mosques, in particular, were demolished or remade into Orthodox churches.

In part as a reaction to such developments, the Crimea became the birthplace of a Tatar national revival that began in the 1880s under the leadership of Ismail Gaspirali/Gasprinskii. Under his direction, the nationalist movement rejected the traditional clerical aspects of Crimean Tatar society and sought to introduce reforms into the antiquated Muslim-controlled educational system and social structure, including the emancipation of women. He also tried to stem the tide of Crimean Tatar emigration to the Ottoman Empire. The historic Crimean capital of Bahçesaray was the center of activity for Gaspirali, and it was there that he founded the newspaper *Tercüman* (The Interpreter, 1883–1914), which he hoped would serve not only the Crimean Tatars but other Tatars and Turkic peoples in the Russian Empire as well. With this goal in mind, his newspaper and other publications were written in Ottoman Turkish, although in a simpler form in which florid Arabic and Persian vocabulary and phrases were omitted and vernacular Crimean Tatar added.

Despite Gaspirali's innovative and extensive cultural achievements, he was criticized by conservative religious leaders (*mullahs*) who opposed his secular orientation and New Method schools, while his views on national identity were challenged by some who otherwise supported the Crimean Tatar revival. Debates centered on a few key issues. Did the Crimean Tatars form a distinct nationality that should have its own literary language? Or, did the adoption of Turkish imply that they were only a branch of a single pan-Turkic entity?

By the beginning of the twentieth century, a new generation of intellectuals known as the Young Tatars (Genç Tatarlar), centered in Karasubazar (today Bilohirs'k) instead of Bahçesaray/Bakhchysarai, moved beyond Gaspirali's primarily cultural interests to more social and political concerns. They also made Crimea and its Tatars, instead of all Turkic peoples of the Russian Empire, their primary focus, although the language of their publications, including the newspaper *Vatan Hâdimi* (Servant of Fatherland, 1906–), favored the idea of Turkish linguistic unity through the medium of Ottoman Turkish. One of their leaders, Abdüreşid Mehdi, was elected to the Second Duma (1906) on a program committed to regaining lands lost by Crimean Tatars over the past century. The question of Crimean Tatar particularism versus pan-Turkic unity and the related issues of an appropriate literary language and national identity remained unresolved until the 1920s.

The Romanians

The Romanian presence in southwestern Ukraine dates back long before the nineteenth century. In addition to the province of Bessarabia, the region between the

Prut and Dniester Rivers where Romanians traditionally formed the vast majority of the population, they inhabited lands east of the Dniester (in Romanian, Nistru) River, which they called Transnistria. Ninety-three percent of the 187,000 Romanians/Moldavians recorded in Dnieper Ukraine (1897) lived in the provinces of Kherson and Podolia, primarily along the eastern bank of the Southern Buh River.

Traditionally, the Romanians were known either as Moldavians or as Vlachs, names which derived from their homeland territories, the Danubian principalities of Moldavia and Walachia. By the nineteenth century, the term *Romanian* had replaced *Vlach*, while the term *Moldavian* in both Romanian and East Slavic sources continued to be used in the sense of a Romanian from Moldavia.

Relations between Ukraine and the two Romanian principalities were traditionally very close, both when Moldavia and Walachia were independent entities and after the early sixteenth century, by which time they had become vassal states of the Ottoman Empire. One important reason for the good relations was the fact that Romanians and Ukrainians were Orthodox, and that although the Romanians spoke a Romance language, it had many Slavic borrowings and was written in the Cyrillic alphabet until the mid-nineteenth century. Romanians from Transnistria were among the many peoples who joined the Zaporozhian Cossacks, some of whose otamans and hetmans – Ioan Nicoară Potcoavă (Ivan Pidkova), Ioan Grigore Lobodă (Hryhorii Loboda), Ioan Sîrcu (Ivan Sirko), Dumitru Hunu (Dmytro Hunia), and Dănilă Apostol (Danylo Apostol) – were of Romanian origin.

Moldavian-Ukrainian relations were particularly close during the seventeenth century, the time when Petru Movilă (Petro Mohyla), the son of Moldavia's ruler, in 1632, became metropolitan of the Orthodox Church in Kiev and when the Zaporozhian hetman Bohdan Khmel'nyts'kyi and his son Tymish during the 1640s and 1650s tried to forge an alliance with their neighbor to the southwest. It was also during the last three decades of the seventeenth century that large numbers of Romanians began to migrate from Moldavia to Transnistria. The movement of people began when the Ottoman Empire controlled Podolia and the southern Right Bank (see map 19), and was initiated during the short-lived rule (1681–1685) of Gheorghe Ducu, the *voevoda* of Moldavia whom the Ottomans designated as their "Hospodar of Ukraine."

Romanian migration to Transnistria continued during the eighteenth century and was directly related to the many wars between the Russian and Ottoman empires. For example, in the wake of the war of 1735–1739, tsarist troops returning from their invasion of Ottoman Moldavia brought with them nearly 100,000 Romanians. At the end of the century, when Russia acquired Yedisan (Ottoman territory between the Dniester and Southern Buh Rivers), a new wave of Romanians settled that area, this time as peasant-serfs on the large landed estates awarded by the Russian government to several Moldavian boyars (nobles) of the Cantacuzino, Sturdza, Catargiu, and Rosetti families.

Initially, Romanians were allowed to use their own language in public affairs, in the few schools that existed, and in their Orthodox churches, which until 1828 were under the jurisdiction of a Romanian metropolitanate at Iași. That same year, however, the Romanian parishes in Dnieper Ukraine were placed under the authority of local bishops of the Russian Orthodox Church, and the Romanian language was replaced by Russian. Effectively, for the rest of the nineteenth century there was no organized Romanian cultural life in Dnieper Ukraine. Nevertheless, most Romanians did not lose their national identity, largely because they remained illiterate and therefore "protected" from assimilation to a foreign language (Russian) they could not understand.

It was not until the first decade of the twentieth century that Romanians in Dnieper Ukraine became interested in the cultural survival of their people. The early stages of a national revival took the form of discussions among university student groups and more popular efforts to have Romanian reintroduced into parishes of the Orthodox Church where they predominated. This was the so-called Movement from Balta, led by a monk from that town in southern Podolia, Ieromonah Inochentie. Despite these efforts, the status of Romanians and their language in Dnieper Ukraine had not changed by the time World War I broke out in 1914.

Other peoples

There were also several other peoples living in Dnieper Ukraine. Numerically, the most prominent were the Belarusans, followed by Bulgarians, Greeks, and Czechs. Somewhat exceptional among these groups were the Belarusans. Nearly 70 percent lived in northern Chernihiv province near Belarus; and the remainder were spread throughout the new industrial cities in the eastern and southeastern provinces of Kharkiv and Katerynoslav. Despite their relatively large numbers (222,000 in 1897), Belarusans did not develop a distinct cultural life in Dnieper Ukraine. This is because for the most part they had a low, or non-existent, sense of their national distinctiveness; moreover, being of the Orthodox faith, they tended to blend easily with the linguistically related ethnic Ukrainians and Russians among whom they lived.

The number of Bulgarians was actually larger than the 68,000 indicated in table 28.1, since Bessarabia is not one of nine provinces considered as part of Dnieper Ukraine. It was, however, precisely in the southern part of Bessarabia, which today is within Ukraine, where a significant number of Bulgarians lived (38,000 in 1897). Together with the Bulgarian settlements in Kherson province (north of Odessa) and in Taurida province (both in Crimea and along the northern shore of the Sea of Azov), the total number of Bulgarians in Ukraine at the end of the nineteenth century was 116,000.

Most Bulgarians arrived in the Bessarabia and Kherson provinces between the 1780s and 1830s. For the most part they were fleeing the disruptions in their homeland (still part of the Ottoman Empire) that resulted from the periodic Russian-Ottoman wars during those decades. In the 1860s, after southern Bessarabia was for two decades lost by Russia to Romanian-ruled Moldovia, large numbers of Bulgarians left the region in order to live again under Russian rule, this time resettling in Taurida province along the northern shores of the Sea of Azov in the town of Nogais'k (today Prymors'k) and in several nearby villages. The Bulgarians were especially attracted by favorable tsarist decrees that provided them with free land and exemptions for an initial period of time from military service and taxes. Most settled in the rural countryside, where they were engaged primarily in animal husbandry (especially sheep raising) and agriculture (grains, vegetables, fruits, grapes for wine, and tobacco). In the absence of their own Bulgarian Orthodox Church (a distinct jurisdiction did not come into being in their ancestral homeland until 1870), Bulgarians went to Dnieper Ukraine's Russian and Greek Orthodox parishes. For this reason many Bulgarians, such as those who were part of the merchant community in Nizhyn, were known as "Greeks." Efforts were taken, however, to preserve Bulgarian identity in Dnieper Ukraine through education. By the second half of the nineteenth century, Bulgarian was taught in at least fifty elementary schools and at a *gymnasium* in Bolgrad (est. 1859) in southern Bessarabia, and training was provided at a Bulgarian teacher's college at Preslav near Nogais'k. Odessa was of particular importance to Dnieper Ukraine's Bulgarians, because it was there that many cultural activists received their training at the Orthodox Theological Seminary and at the city's *gymnasium,* among whom was the influential journalist, teacher, and leader in the Bulgarian liberation movement, Hristo Botev.

The presence of Greeks on Ukrainian territory goes back to the sixth century BCE, when colonists created Greek city-states along the northern shores of the Black Sea and the Sea of Azov, and in the Crimea (see chapter 3). Greeks continued to play an important role in the economy of urban Ukraine and in particular its Orthodox religious and cultural life during the medieval period of Kievan Rus' and during the sixteenth and seventeenth centuries (see chapters 12 and 13). It was the Greeks of Crimea who had the longest continuous existence as a distinct community, and by the end of the eighteenth century they had evolved into two distinct groups: the so-called Tatar Greeks (*urumi*) and the Hellene Greeks (*rumei*). The first group consisted of Greeks who, in the course of two millennia had integrated with the various Turkic peoples and Goths of the Crimea and who spoke a Turkic language similar to Crimean Tatar. The Hellenes were the descendants of colonists from the Byzantine Empire and the Ottoman-ruled Balkans (Rumelia), who continued to speak modern Greek. Both these groups continued to be represented in the Crimea as well as in a region north of the Sea of Azov. It was there, during the period of the independent Crimean Khanate (1774–1783), that over 18,000 Tatar Greeks (*urumi*) were forcibly resettled and where they founded the port city of Mariupol' and nearly two dozen villages in the nearby hinterland.

From the mid-1770s to 1812, there was a steady flow of Greeks eastward. This was a time when the Russian Empire prided itself as a safe haven for fellow Orthodox believers fleeing conflict with their Ottoman rulers in the Balkans. Aside from the Crimea and the Azov region around Mariupol', this latest wave of Greeks settled in imperial Russia's several new Black Sea ports: Mykolaïv, Kherson, and most especially Odessa. The settlers came from all social strata including farmers, merchants, and artisans, as well as aristocratic landowners and displaced governmental officials, such as Ypsilantes, Cantacuzino, and Caragea families who had been part of the Phanariote Greek ruling stratum in the Ottoman vassal states of Moldovia and Walachia. There were also older Greek communities in many urban areas of central Ukraine, including Katerynoslav, Pereiaslav, and Kiev. By 1897, about 80,000 Greeks lived throughout Dnieper Ukraine, although the vast majority were concentrated in Azov region around Mariupol'.

Dnieper Ukraine's Greeks maintained their cultural and inner-directed community life through the creation of brotherhoods, which in turn supported their Greek Orthodox churches, Greek-language elementary schools, cultural institutions, and printshops. It was the community in Odessa, however, that had the greatest impact on Greek life, not only in the Russian Empire but on the Greek homeland as well. Odessa's Greeks were especially influential in international trade, and certain family-owned commercial dynasties (the Serafino, Iannopulo, Marazli, Paleologos, and Raili) operated throughout most of the nineteenth century some of the wealthiest firms of their kind in the entire Russian Empire. The city also became an important center in the early stages of the Greek national independence movement. In 1814, the Philike Hetaira (Society of Friends) was founded in Odessa, and six years later the city's wealthy Greek merchants arranged for a visit by the national patriot Alexander Ypsilantes, whose anti-Ottoman activities were encouraged by the tsarist Russian government.

Among the numerically smallest groups in Dnieper Ukraine were the Czechs (37,000 in 1897), almost all of whom were concentrated in rural areas in central and western Volhynia near Rivne and Luts'k. They arrived in the late 1860s and early 1870s at the invitation of the post-reform tsarist government, which offered them exemptions from taxes and military service as well as administrative self-government at the village level. The Czechs fulfilled the expectations of the Russian authorities by operating efficient farms and local plants (especially breweries). There were also several thousand Czechs living in Kiev, where they worked in (or in some aces owned) some of the city's industrial enterprises and where they set up Czech cultural organizations (Comenius Society), sport's clubs (Sokol), and newspaparers (*Ruský Čech, Čechoslovan*). It was the Kiev community which made the city an important center of the Czechoslovak liberation movement during World War I (see chapter 39).

The cultural diversity of the cities in Dnieper Ukraine was increased as a result of industrialization during the second half of the nineteenth century. The new industrialists and some of their managers in places like Kharkiv, Ielysavethrad (today Kirovohrad), Katerynoslav (today Dnipropetrovs'k), and Iuzivka (today Donets'k) came from England, Wales, France, Belgium, and Germany. For example, the new city of Iuzivka, founded in 1869, was named for its primary benefactor, the Welshman John Hughes. The business practices and cultural attitudes of these well-to-do newcomers may have influenced a small segment of the indigenous economic and social elite. Most, however, did not establish long-lasting roots in Dnieper Ukraine and therefore did not have a cultural impact on their imperial Russian surroundings.

Odessa was the exception. There, even some of the smallest groups made their cultural presence felt. French culture, for instance, flourished in the uppermost echelons of Odessa society, not because of the presence of a few thousand French residents in the city, but because of the generally positive attitude of imperial Russian society toward French culture and specifically because of institutions like the Richelieu lycée (secondary school), founded in 1817 and named after the former governor-general of New Russia who was later prime minister of France, Armand-Emmanuel de Richelieu. The Italians, who by mid-century numbered around 30,000, left an even greater mark on Odessa: Italian opera, a Roman Catholic Church, and popular cafés where Italian had once been spoken remained long after the Italians themselves, who numbered less than a thousand in 1897, had left the city.

Thus, Dnieper Ukraine was the homeland not only of ethnic Ukrainians who made up the vast majority of the population, but also of several other peoples. They included the Russians and Poles, who played a disproportionately influential role in the political, social, and economic life of the country, as well as Jews, Germans, Crimean Tatars, and other smaller groups, who for the most part followed rather distinct paths of economic and cultural development largely oblivious to the mass of ethnic Ukrainians among whom they lived.

29

The Ukrainian National Awakening in Dnieper Ukraine before the 1860s

There was no distinct Ukrainian territorial entity and no effective political activity specifically on behalf of ethnic Ukrainians in Dnieper Ukraine during most of the nineteenth century. Territorial autonomy had ended the previous century with the elimination of the Sloboda Ukraine (1760s), Zaporozhia (1770s), and the Hetmanate (1780s). While memories of this past autonomy persisted in the minds of the Cossacks, most of them were to be coopted into the Russian imperial social structure, as part of either its elite or its intermediate social strata. In the absence of a politically concerned social stratum, therefore, autonomy of the kind previously enjoyed in Ukrainian lands was no longer feasible at the beginning of the nineteenth century. For the idea of Ukrainian specificity to take hold, something new had to be found, even if it came from abroad. That new something was found, and it did come from beyond Dnieper Ukraine – it was nationalism.

The idea of nationalism

Stated most simply, nationalism is an ideology which divides humanity into nationalities and which argues that the optimal social system is one in which nationalities enjoy cultural and political autonomy or, preferably, complete independence. As a political ideology, nationalism arose in Europe during the late eighteenth and early nineteenth centuries. It was in many ways a product of the French Revolution, in which the people and not the state or its leading representative, whether king or nobility, were held to be the supreme source of political legitimization. Nationalism also evolved as a reaction to the French Revolution, or, more precisely, a reaction to the spread of French dominance throughout Europe, whether in culture or in politics. This was particularly the case in the German lands, where at the beginning of the nineteenth century several writers, reacting to the presence of Napoleon's soldiers and to the widespread use of the French language and French cultural models by the German elite, began to argue that the German language and culture was at least the equal of the French and so should be accorded respect, if no where else than in its own homeland. Some German authors, like Johann Gottlieb Fichte and Friedrich Wilhelm Joseph

WHAT IS A NATIONALITY?

In English, the terms *nationality* and *nation* are often used interchangeably. This usage results in great confusion whenever an effort is made to define what the terms mean. In particular, confusion arises with regard to the relationship between a given people and the state structure in which they live. One must remember that most states both today and in the past have included within their borders peoples of different cultural and linguistic backgrounds.

In this book, the terms *nation* and *nationality* are distinguished. *Nation* (Ukrainian: *natsiia*) is used to refer to the legal citizens of a given state. Thus, the *French nation* or the *Ukrainian nation* refers to all the inhabitants of France or Ukraine who are citizens of those countries regardless of their linguistic or ethnocultural background.

The term nationality (Ukrainian: *natsional'nist'*) is used to refer to a group of people (Ukrainian: *narod*) who may have one or more of the following observable characteristics in common: a distinct territory (possibly but not necessarily statehood), language, historical tradition, religion, cultural values, and ethnographic features. Taken together, these characteristics distinguish members of one nationality from their neighbors. It should be noted that ethnic or ethnographic groups (Ukrainian: *etnohrafichni hrupy*) also may have all or many of these same characteristics in common.

What, then, distinguishes a nationality from an ethnic group? The primary distinguishing feature is not the presence or absence of all or some of the characteristics listed above, but rather an awareness among members of a given group of people that they have such common characteristics and that it is these characteristics which distinguish them from neighboring peoples or nationalities. In other words, a nationality must have (1) certain objective elements, such as those listed above, in common; and (2) certain subjective elements – a self-perception of belonging and the will to belong to a distinct group.

The number of objective elements in common varies from nationality to nationality. Language, for instance, was thought for a long time to be an essential, even the defining, characteristic of a nationality. This is obviously not the case, since the Brazilians, the Americans, and the Irish are all distinct peoples or nationalities even though they have never had or have lost a distinct language. Accordingly, it is possible to identify oneself as of Ukrainian nationality without knowing the Ukrainian language. As for the subjective factor, the awareness that one belongs to a nationality is a learned process passed on through the family and especially through the school system.

Finally, because of the multinational reality of most states in the world, there has arisen the legal concept of the national minority (Ukrainian: *natsional'na menshyna*). In a real sense, there are no national minorities, only nationalities living in one or more states. Most states, however, have had as their goal to become a nation-state; that is, they have operated on the premise that all the inhabitants within their boundaries belong, or should be made to belong, to a single "state" nationality. Some states have recognized that they rule over several different peoples or nationalities. For legal and constitutional purposes, the non-state nationalities are classified as national minorities.

von Schelling, stressed German cultural uniqueness, but another influential German, Johann Gottfried Herder, argued that every culture in the world has its own particular worth and value.

According to Herder, a people's unique cultural values were best expressed in its language. In his *Letters Addressed to Humanity*, published in 1783, Herder posed what was to become for national enthusiasts an oft-repeated rhetorical question: "Has a people ... anything dearer than the speech of its ancestors? Therein resides its whole intellectual wealth, tradition, history, religion, and principle of life – its very heart and soul. To deprive a people of its speech is to deprive it of its one eternal good."[1] Herder's influence was enormous throughout central and eastern Europe, because he seemed to provide a universally applicable justification for pride in one's own culture, which in turn was of great importance for stateless peoples living in multinational empires in which their languages and cultures were unrecognized, scorned, or both. The Slavic peoples, especially the Ukrainians, held a particular attraction for Herder. In his widely read travel diary, published in 1769, Herder wrote: "Ukraine will become one day a new Greece; the beautiful climate of this country, the gay disposition of the people, their musical inclination, and the fertile soil will all awaken. ... There will rise a great and cultured nation whose boundaries will extend to the Black Sea and thence into the far-flung world."[2] Despite their quaintness to modern ears, such descriptions were remarkably successful in instilling pride in downtrodden peoples during the era of Romanticism in the early nineteenth century.

As nationalism spread throughout Europe after the French Revolution, its implementation and goals varied from place to place according to political circumstances. There were, in effect, two types of nationalism: (1) state-imposed nationalism, and (2) intelligentsia-inspired nationalism. State-imposed nationalism emanated from above, that is, from governments in already-existing independent states who hoped to gain the loyalty of their citizens by convincing them that they were united because they apparently belonged to a certain nationality. Intelligentsia-inspired nationalism emanated from groups who lived in multinational states where a language, culture, and identity other than their own was dominant, and whose leaders – the nationalist intelligentsia – worked to convince their self-defined constituencies that they formed a distinct national group. As a distinct national group, they deserved cultural and political autonomy if not independent statehood.

Often it is assumed that the first type, state-imposed nationalism, existed in western Europe, whereas the second, intelligentsia-inspired nationalism, was a phenomenon of eastern, or, more precisely, central and eastern Europe. But the distinction is false: even in the first half of the nineteenth century there were peoples in central and eastern Europe – like the Greeks and Serbs – who had independent states simultaneously with or before their intelligentsias were able to work out a common national identity, and there were also states – like the Russian Empire and Austrian Empire – which attempted to create a "state nationality," that is, an imperial Russian or Austrian nationality, and to impose it on its several peoples.

Western Europe also had intelligentsia-inspired nationalism, as among the Irish, or the Frisians, or the Catalans, or, for that matter, the Germans and Italians, all of whom during the first half of the nineteenth century were without their own states but fostered national movements led by intelligentsias whose ultimate goal was cultural autonomy and political independence. Conversely, western Europe had states like Norway, or Belgium, or Luxembourg, where political independence preceded the existence of a Norwegian, Belgian, or Luxembourgian nationality, which had to be created; and it had multinational states like France, Britain, and Spain, which tried to impose – as did Russia and Austria – an imperial French, British, or Spanish identity on its nationally diverse inhabitants. The point is that in classifying national movements, it is not possible to assume that western Europe experienced only one type of nationalism and central or eastern Europe only the other.

Ukrainian nationalism, in both the Russian and the Austrian Empire, belongs to the intelligentsia-inspired variety. But before reviewing the manner in which Ukrainian nationalism evolved in the Russian Empire, two more principles need to be kept in mind. One is that people are not born with a national identity; they must learn that they belong to a particular nationality. Before the nineteenth century, most people in Europe spoke a dialect of a particular language and more often than not would identify themselves by religious affiliation, or, sometimes, by geographic or regional affiliation. The task undertaken by small groups of intellectual leaders known as the intelligentsia was to convince the members of a particular group that they belonged to a larger nationality. They did so by spreading their ideas via newspapers, journals, reading circles, cultural organizations, and theater and, where the government was favorably inclined, through the educational system. The diffusion of a sense of national identity depended, of course, on the existence of a literate population and a network of communication facilities, which in turn was determined by the degree of urbanization, industrialization, and general modernization of a given society.

If the diffusion of a sense of national identity was in itself difficult enough, an added problem for the intellectual leadership had to do with which social strata should constitute a given nationality, the ruling elite (usually the nobility) or all groups (including the peasant masses). Even if a consensus was reached as to social strata, there might still remain the question of which national identity was most appropriate. More often than not among stateless peoples, including Ukrainians, the intelligentsia was divided among factions identifying themselves with different nationalities. This was particularly the case in areas like Ukraine, where many nationalities lived side by side. In a sense, nationalist movements came to resemble ideological marketplaces where rival factions propagated their wares. Since no one was born with a fully formed national consciousness, it was possible for persons to be swayed by one or more of the competing factions. Accordingly, it is not surprising to find in Ukrainian lands members of the same indigenous population opting to identify themselves as Poles, or Russians, or Ukrainians.

Another concept to keep in mind is that of multiple loyalties or identities as opposed to that of mutually exclusive identities. Very often in multinational states individuals can feel perfectly comfortable with more than one national identity. Hence, for many residents in Dnieper Ukraine it was perfectly normal to be both a Little Russian and Russian, or a Russian from Little Russia speaking "Little Russian," that is, Ukrainian. Many nobles of Cossack origin, whom we perhaps too simplistically describe as russified, fall into this category, as does the great Russian-language writer from Dnieper Ukraine, Nikolai Gogol'.

As Ukrainian nationalism evolved, however, its leaders became convinced that for their movement to survive, the otherwise "natural" hierarchy of multiple loyalties or identities had to be replaced by a framework of mutually exclusive identities. In other words, one could not be a Russian from Little Russia or a Pole from Ukraine; one had to be either a Pole or a Ukrainian, or a Russian or a Ukrainian. Those who believed in mutually exclusive identities favored the term *Ukrainian* over *Little Russian* precisely in order to heighten a perceptual difference. In a real sense, the evolution of the nineteenth-century Ukrainian national revival can be seen as the story of the conflict between a framework of multiple loyalties on the one hand and one of mutually exclusive identities on the other, and of how this conflict sometimes had a traumatic effect on the individuals involved.

Finally, intelligentsia-inspired national movements can be viewed as going through at least three basic stages: (1) the heritage-gathering stage, (2) the organizational stage, and (3) the political stage. The first stage consists of efforts by individuals to collect the linguistic, folkloric, literary, and historical artifacts of a given people. The second stage is one in which organizations, schools, and publications are formed to propagate knowledge about the cultural heritage that has been collected. The third stage witnesses efforts at participation in political life, often with the intention of obtaining autonomy or independence. The Ukrainian national movement of the nineteenth century can be seen in terms of this three-stage model.

The phenomenon of multiple loyalties

The original motivation of those who contributed to the first, heritage-gathering stage of the national movement in Dnieper Ukraine was not a desire for social innovation. Rather, it was the desire to revive something from the past, or, more precisely, to use the past to acquire something in the present. Such use of the past was of particular concern to the Cossack elite (*starshyna*) in the Left Bank. After Catherine II issued her Charter of the Nobility in 1785, the Cossack *starshyna* was less concerned with protesting the dissolution of the Hetmanate's autonomy than with struggling to gain entry into the Russian nobility (*dvorianstvo*) with all its social and economic privileges.

Between 1785 and 1835, the imperial authorities first recognized Cossack noble status en masse, then rescinded it, then granted it again, but selectively (see chapter 27). This inconsistency prompted numerous Cossacks to submit petitions to the newly established Imperial Heraldry Office, set up in 1797. In order to prove their general premise that the whole Cossack *starshyna* was the equivalent of the Russian nobility (*dvorianstvo*), or to justify the merits of specific requests that certain individual Cossacks were indeed of noble status according to local "Little Russian" conditions, the supplicants were forced to examine a host of treaties between Ukrainian hetmans and Muscovite tsars, charters with Polish kings and Lithuanian princes, and other documents, including chronicles, historical and familial memoirs, genealogies, and descriptions of local traditions. One by-product of this practical search for legal justification was a new interest in the past, which soon resulted in several publications about the history of Ukraine. It is no coincidence that many of the earliest histories of Ukraine date precisely from the period when the Cossack elite was desperately trying to enter the Russian nobility.

Each of these early histories expressed a deep local patriotism and love for the Ukrainian past. Nonetheless, all were written in Russian, and all were imbued with the notion that Ukraine, or Little Russia as it was known at the time, was a natural and integral part of the Russian imperial world. Thus, the early histories of Ukraine implicitly accepted the principle of a hierarchy of multiple loyalties or identities.

Folklore also proved to be fertile ground for cultivation by the intelligentsia during the heritage-gathering stage of the national revival. At the same time that the first published histories of Little Russia were appearing, Hryhorii Kalynovs'kyi published his *Opisanie svadebnykh ukrainskikh prostonarodnykh obriadov v Maloi Rossii i slobodskoi ukrainskoi gubernii* (Description of Ukrainian Folk Marriage Customs in Little Russia and the Sloboda Ukrainian Provinces, 1777). This was followed by Prince Nikolai Tsertelev's *Opyt sobraniia starinnykh malorossiiskikh piesnei* (Attempt at a Collection of Ancient Little Russian Songs, 1819). A russified Georgian born in Dnieper Ukraine, Tsertelev was a staunch local patriot who felt the urge to collect folk songs from the old bards in whose midst he lived. Commenting on the texts, he argued that Ukrainian folk songs exhibit a moral quality which sets them apart from the songs of their greedier and more aggressive neighbors.

The first systematic assemblage of Ukrainian folk songs was undertaken by Mykhailo Maksymovych, who published three collections: *Malorossiiskiia piesni* (Little Russian Songs, 1827), *Ukrainskiia narodnyia piesni* (Ukrainian Folk Songs, 1834), and *Sbornik ukrainskikh piesen* (A Collection of Ukrainian Folksongs, 1849). Developing further Tsertelev's approach, Maksymovych stressed the differences between Russians and Ukrainians on the basis of their folk songs. His collections had an enormous impact on Ukrainian intellectuals who sought to discover the riches of their people's indigenous culture. Following Maksymovych's, several other folk-song collections were published, among the more important at the time being six volumes (which included many contrived texts) entitled *Zaporozhskaia starina* (Zaporozhian Antiquity, 1833–38), edited by the Russian Slavist Izmail Sreznevskii.

THE EARLY HISTORIES OF UKRAINE

Before the noble status of the Cossacks became an issue, there was only one published general history of Ukraine, *Kratkaia lietopis' Malyia Rossii* (A Short Chronicle of Little Russia, 1777), which was an updated version of a chronicle written in the 1730s. Hryhorii Hrabianka's earlier *Dieistviia preziel'noi ... brani Bogdana Khmel'nitskogo, getmana Zaporozhskogo s poliaky* (Events of the Most Bitter ... War ... between the Zaporozhian Hetman Bohdan Khmel'nyts'kyi and the Poles, 1710) was published in an abridged form in 1793, and another general work by Aleksandr Rigel'man, *Lietopisnoe poviestvovanie o Maloi Rossii i eia narodie i kozakakh voobshche* (Chronicle Account about Little Russia, Its People, and Cossacks in General), was completed in 1787, but not published until 1847.

The controversy over the Cossacks' status and the practical historical research it stimulated soon gave rise to a flurry of publication. Some of the new works were polemics defending the rights of Ukraine's Cossacks to noble status (Roman Markovych, ca. 1800; Tymofii Kalyns'kyi, ca. 1800 and 1808; Vasyl' Poletyka, 1809; Adriian Chepa, 1809; Fedir Tumans'kyi, 1809); others were more extensive general histories. Among the latter were an amateurish description of Ukraine by Iakiv Markovych, *Zapiski o Malorossii, eia zhiteliakh i proizvedeniiakh* (Notes on Little Russia, Its Inhabitants and Its Works, 1798), and the more serious five-volume compilation of Mykola Markevych, *Istoriia Malorosii* (History of Little Russia, 1842–43). One work, however, eclipsed all the other early histories – the four-volume *Istoriia Maloi Rossii* (History of Little Russia, 1822) by Dmitrii Bantysh-Kamenskii, a member of Dnieper Ukraine's nobility. Bantysh-Kamenskii's work was based on a wide body of archival sources and imbued with a sense of deep loyalty to the Russian Empire. His history was so popular that it went through three more editions (1830, 1842, 1903), and it remained the basic source for Ukraine's history until the very end of the nineteenth century.

The other important element in the heritage-gathering stage of intelligentsia-inspired national movements – language – did not fare as well as history and folklore in Dnieper Ukraine. In other Slavic national revivals undertaken about the same time, linguists played a prominent role, and dictionaries and grammars were prepared as the essential building blocks for national cultures. The stature of figures like Josef Dobrovský and Josef Jungman among the Czechs, Pavel Josef Šafárik and L'udovít Štúr among the Slovaks, Ljudevit Gaj among the Croats, and Vuk Karadžić among the Serbs attests to the significance of linguists in the national movements of other Slavic peoples. But Ukrainians, at least in Dnieper Ukraine, seemed to lag behind. During the whole first half of the nineteenth century, only one grammar, by Oleksii Pavlovs'kyi (*Grammatika malorossiiskago nariechiia*, 1818), and one small dictionary, by Ivan Voitsekhovych (*Sobranie slov malorossiiskago na-*

riechiia, 1823), appeared. Moreover, both these authors did not consider Ukrainian a distinct language; for them, what they called "Little Russian" was a dialect of Russian.

Literary works also began to appear, but even they were unable to provide the basis for a vibrant Ukrainian literary movement. The first work written in modern Ukrainian, the publication of which was begun in 1798 by the so-called father of Ukrainian literature, Ivan Kotliarevs'kyi, was entitled *Eneïda*. It was a travesty using Ukrainian themes of Virgil's classic Latin epic poem, the *Aeneid*. While the language of Kotliarevs'kyi's *Eneïda* as well as of his operetta *Natalka Poltavka* (1819) and vaudeville show *Moskal' charivnyk* (The Muscovite-Sorcerer, 1819) were definitely Ukrainian, their subject matter seemed to suggest that Ukrainian was appropriate only for jocular or slapstick themes. This attitude to the language barely changed even after the appearance in Ukrainian of works by writers like Petro Hulak-Artemovs'kyi, Hryhorii Kvitka-Osnovianenko, and Ievhen Hrebinka, who wrote burlesques, feuilletons, short stories, and fables. In short, for those who wanted to compose works in more serious genres, it was necessary to use Russian. This, of course, is precisely what one of the greatest Ukrainian writers of the period, Nikolai Gogol', did. The lack of confidence in Ukrainian language and culture was summed up in 1840 by the otherwise patriotic folklorist Mykhailo Maksymovych: "Everything written here in Little Russian is in some sense artificial and has only a regional character like a German writing in the Alemannic dialect. We cannot have a literature in the South Russian language, there can only be individual works in this language ..."[3]

Despite its limited achievements in language and literature, the national revival in Dnieper Ukraine during the heritage-gathering stage of the late eighteenth and first decades of the nineteenth century made some important gains, especially in the realm of history and folklore. It is interesting, if somewhat unexpected, to note that the Russian imperial government generally supported these developments. The result was the beginning of the organizational stage in Dnieper Ukraine's national awakening. Of great importance in this regard was the establishment of the first two modern universities on Ukrainian territory, at Kharkiv in 1805 and Kiev in 1834. Kharkiv University was begun at the initiative of a local Ukrainian philanthropist and gentryman, Vasyl' Karazyn. The university was created for a very practical purpose: to train imperial bureaucrats. Classes, therefore, were not conducted in Ukrainian, or, for that matter, in Russian; instead, Latin, French, and German were used, for several decades. Owing to its largely foreign-born faculty, the latest intellectual currents in western Europe, especially those associated with Romanticism and nationalism, reached the otherwise provincial town of Kharkiv.

It was not long before individuals in the university's intellectual environment developed an interest in the area in which it was located. As a result, by the 1820s Kharkiv had become the first center of the Ukrainian cultural revival. Among the activists in the Kharkiv circle were the Russian folklorist and philologist Izmail Sreznevskii and the Ukrainian writers Petro Hulak-Artemovs'kyi, Hryhorii Kvitka-Osnovianenko, Amvrosii Metlyns'kyi, and Mykola Kostomarov. Kharkiv became the place where the first anthologies of Ukrainian literature (*Ukrainskii al'manakh*, 1831; *Ukrainskii sbornik*, 1838–41) and the first periodicals partly devoted to Ukrainian themes (*Ukrainskii viestnik*, 1816–19; *Ukrainskii zhurnal*, 1823–25) were published. Although these periodicals appeared for the most part in Russian and had as their primary goal to expose their readers to western European literature, they also became a forum for publications in Ukrainian by the Kharkiv circle of belletrists and scholars. It was also at Kharkiv that the term *Ukrainian*, instead of *Little Russian* or the older *Rus'/ Rusyn*, was used to designate the majority population of Dnieper Ukraine.

The University of St Vladimir in Kiev was established in 1834 not, like Kharkiv University, at the initiative of local philanthropists, but rather by the Russian government. Moreover, while Kharkiv University had a somewhat mundane purpose – to train functionaries for imperial service – Kiev University had from the outset a clear political purpose – to transform the Polish-dominated Right Bank into an ideologically integrated part of the Russian Empire. In fact, the establishment of the university was a direct result of the abortive Polish revolt of 1830–1831, in which thousands of Polish nobles from the Right Bank had participated. While the Polish revolt did not present any serious military threat to the empire, it did convince Tsar Nicholas I that four decades after their incorporation into Russia, the Polish nobility in the strategically located western provinces was still politically unreliable.

To rectify this problem, Nicholas entrusted his newly appointed minister of education and the head of the Imperial Academy of Sciences Sergei S. Uvarov with the task of transforming the polonophile school system of the western provinces, including Dnieper Ukraine's Right Bank, into an instrument of Russian imperial ideology. In the pursuit of this goal, Polish secondary schools were russified, the excellent Polish lycee at Kremenets', in Volhynia, was closed, as was the Polish university at Vilnius on the basis of which a new Russian-language university named for St Vladimir was opened in 1834 in Kiev. Uvarov himself chose Kiev as the site of the new institution because, as he said, it was the "mother of Russian cities" and therefore an appropriate starting point for imperial Russia's cultural expansion westward.

Kiev's University of St Vladimir and its initially small professorial staff were to be concerned primarily with research into the history of Russia's western provinces in Ukraine and Belarus. These territories had once belonged to Kievan Rus', and from the imperial perspective they should now be ideologically as well as politically integrated into the empire of the tsars. In the process of cultural reclamation, in which Polish youth would be trained in a Russian imperial spirit, the local Little Russian movement would have a special role to play. It was to be used as a weapon to de-polonize Kiev and the Right Bank. It is not surprising, therefore, that one of the leading Ukrainian intellectuals of the day, Mykhailo Maksymovych, was made rector of the new university.

To promote further research in Slavic studies, in particular research concerned with Dnieper Ukraine, or Little Russia, in 1838 Uvarov provided generous government-funded research and travel fellowships for the empire's leading scholars. Two of them, Osyp Bodians'kyi of Moscow University and Izmail

Sreznevskii of Kharkiv University, were already actively engaged in scholarship about Ukraine. In Kiev itself, three volumes of a literary and scholarly journal, *Kievlianin* (1840, 1841, 1850), appeared, and in 1843 the Imperial Archeographic Commission was set up to collect and publish historical documents. Meanwhile, the Ukrainian folklorist and historian Bodians'kyi, after returning from his research trip abroad, became secretary of the Imperial Society for the Study of Russian History and Antiquities in Moscow, where he began a series of publications entitled *Chteniia* (1846–1918). Under his editorship during its first three years, *Chteniia* consisted of twenty-three volumes containing a wealth of historical material about Ukraine.

Thus, it was the Russian imperial government which provided a solid organizational basis for research into Ukrainian matters. After all, such action was in keeping with tsarist Russia's official ideology, propounded by the education minister Uvarov in 1833, that the ideological pillars of the empire should be Orthodoxy, autocracy, and nationality. With respect to the last concept, a Little Russian local identity was considered an acceptable and even a desirable complement to a Russian imperial national identity. It was, or so it seemed at the time, just a lower stage in a sociocultural framework that recognized a hierarchy of multiple and complementary loyalties and identities.

The belief in mutually exclusive identities

At the very same time, another approach began to appear among Dnieper Ukraine's budding intelligentsia, the approach reflected in the principle of mutually exclusive identities. This approach was evident in a limited way in the published commentary appended to the collections of folklorists like Tsertelev and Maksymovych, in which they pointed out differences between Russian and Ukrainian folk songs. Differentiation, however, most poignantly shaped a work entitled *Istoriia Rusov ili Maloi Rossii* (History of the Rus' or Little Russia, 1846). To this day, scholars are uncertain who wrote the *Istoriia Rusov*, although they agree the text was composed sometime in the first decade of the nineteenth century, was circulated in several copies during the 1820s and 1830s, and, finally, was published in 1846 by Bodians'kyi as the very first title in the *Chteniia* series of the Imperial Society for the Study of Russian History and Antiquities.

Like the other histories of Little Russia from this period, the *Istoriia Rusov* put great emphasis on the Cossacks, particularly, their independent and semi-independent political life during the seventeenth and eighteenth centuries. Unlike the other works, however, the *Istoriia Rusov* treated Little Russia not as a province of a larger Russian world, but as an independent country that only recently had come under Russian hegemony. Thus, the *Istoriia Rusov* proposed the idea of historical continuity and statehood in Ukraine from the era of Kievan Rus', through the Lithuanian period, and on to the time of the Cossacks. In order to inspire patriotism and arouse national passion, the *Istoriia Rusov* adopted a tone more like that of a moral tract than that of a straightforward historical narrative. It set up a clear dichotomy between the world of the Muscovites and that of the Ukrainians. In a philosophical framework of truth and justice and good versus evil, it was inevitable that the Muscovites should be depicted in a negative light. In the words of the *Istoriia Rusov*: "Serfdom and slavery in the highest degree reign among the Muscovite people and ... with the exception of what God created and the tsar donated they have nothing of their own and can have nothing. It is as if the people were created only that they might become serfs."[4]

This picture was in stark contrast to the image of the freedom-loving and democratic way of life – albeit romanticized and historically distorted – which supposedly prevailed in Cossack Ukraine. The reader was obviously prompted to wonder whether the contemporary Rus', that is, ethnic Ukrainians, should continue to suffer under the Muscovite yoke. The answer given by the *Istoriia Rusov* is reminiscent of the ideologies of the American and French revolutions: "Whenever any form of government becomes destructive of these ends [i.e., tries to deprive people of their inalienable rights], it is the right of the people to alter or abolish it and to institute a new government, laying its foundation on such principles and organizing its powers in such form as to them shall seem most likely to effect their safety and happiness."[5] This was a clarion call, in the language of the Enlightenment principle of universal liberty, for the rebirth of statehood in Ukraine.

While the *Istoriia Rusov* may not have been a serious piece of historical scholarship, it succeeded in using history to inspire a whole generation of Ukrainian patriots, who first became active during the 1840s and 1850s. Adopting the spirit of the *Istoriia Rusov*, Mykola Markevych composed his five-volume *Istoria Malorossii* (History of Little Russia, 1842–43), which argued that Ukrainians, not Russians, were the true descendants of Kievan Rus'. Even greater was the *Istoriia Rusov*'s impact on three figures who were to become the leading symbols of the Ukrainian national awakening: Mykola Kostomarov, Panteleimon Kulish, and Taras Shevchenko.

Mykola Kostomarov was born in far eastern Sloboda Ukraine near Voronezh as the son of a Russian military officer of noble origins and his Ukrainian serf wife. He attended Kharkiv University, where he became enamored of history as well as of Herder's philosophy concerning the intrinsic value of individual national cultures and languages. He published Ukrainian poetry in the organs of the Kharkiv circle, and in an early study he argued the need for a distinct Ukrainian literature. A secondary-school teacher by profession, Kostomarov moved to a position in Kiev in 1845.

Panteleimon Kulish was the son of a Cossack from Chernihiv province who was unsuccessful in obtaining entry into the Russian nobility. The young Kulish studied for a while at the University of St Vladimir in Kiev and then from 1840 taught in a secondary school in Luts'k. He published his first novel in 1843 in Russian. Two years later, his greatest historical novel, *Chorna Rada* (The Black Council), began to appear, also in Russian. Initially, Kulish was a national patriot of the Little Russian variety, and he generally felt comfortable with the idea of multiple identities. In November 1845, Kulish went to St Petersburg for a little over a year, but during his time there he maintained close contact with Kiev.

The third member of the intellectual trio, and the one who in the end would have the greatest influence on the Ukrainian national movement, was Taras Shevchenko. Of the three, Shevchenko had the most humble origins. He was born into a serf family on an estate in Kiev province. Quite exceptional, given the era and his station in life, was the fact that the young Taras was taught to read and write. He also revealed a talent for painting. After a stormy adolescence, which included flight from his father and stepmother and wanderings through the countryside, Shevchenko eventually returned to the estate of his master (Vasilii Engel'gardt), whose son brought him to St Petersburg in 1830. Shevchenko was sent to study at the Imperial Academy of Art, and before long became the darling of St Petersburg's high society. In 1838, the famed Russian artist Karl Briullov painted a portrait, and he used the income from its sale to purchase Shevchenko's freedom. Shevchenko remained in St Petersburg, where he continued to paint, to study – especially Ukrainian history – and to write poetry.

Within two years, he published his first major work of poetry, *Kobzar* (The Minstrel, 1840). In the words of George Luckyj, "The appearance of the *Kobzar* is the single most important event in Ukrainian literature. It heralded a new and bold beginning, an attempt to express what was still thought by many to be impossible – a wide range of feelings and ideas in Ukrainian of the highest artistic form."[6] Gone are the hesitations about using "Little Russian" for other than minor literary genres. The appearance of *Kobzar* began a process of perceptual change whereby Shevchenko's contemporaries came to believe that the Little Russian dialect could perhaps become a full-fledged language. In other writings, Shevchenko took Kotliarevs'kyi, Kvitka-Osnovianenko, and Gogol' to task for believing otherwise.

Shevchenko's *Kobzar* and his next major work, *Haidamaky* (The Haidamaks, 1841), were also radical in content. The subjects of both epic poems were the historical exploits of the Ukrainian people, who were depicted as representatives of an independent nation until its brutal subjugation by Muscovite Russian and Polish oppressors. Shevchenko created not only the medium – the language – but also the message – national pride, expressed in heartrending and memorable literary passages. In complete contrast to his Little Russian contemporaries, who still believed in multiple loyalties, Shevchenko thought in terms of mutually exclusive Russian and Ukrainian identities. His most uncompromising castigation of Muscovite Russian rule appeared in two poems, "The Caucasus" (1845), which is an indictment of Russia's conquest of the Caucasus peoples, and "The Dream" (1844), in which the poet mocks the imperial family and its ancestors. Shevchenko's depiction of Tsar Peter I was strikingly different from the already well-known poem on the same historical personality by the leading Russian poet of the day, Aleksander Pushkin. Shevchenko has the "free hetman" Pavlo Polubotok address Peter:

Accursed tsar, insatiate,
Perfidious serpent, what
Have you done, then, with the Cossacks?

You have filled the swamps
With their noble bones! And then
Built the capital
On their tortured corpses, and
In a dark dungeon cell
You slew me too, a free Hetman,
In chains, with hunger martyred![7]

Himself not a member of the noble estate, Shevchenko had little sympathy with its view of Ukrainian history. His revolutionary message was that Ukrainians formed a nationality made up of all social strata. According to him, all Ukrainians were politically and culturally deprived, and the vast majority of peasants and serfs were socially oppressed as well. Accordingly, whereas the seventeenth-century hetman Bohdan Khmel'nyts'kyi was a hero for the nineteenth-century Ukrainian nobility because he had begun a political process ending in their own present-day wealth and social status, for Shevchenko it would have been better if the Cossack leader had never been born.

... Oh, Bohdan
Oh, my foolish son!
Look you well, now, on your mother
On Ukraine, your own,
Who, as she rocked you, sang about
Her unhappy fortune,
And singing, wept a mother's tear
Looking out for freedom! ...
Bohdan, O my little Bohdan!
Had I known, in the cradle
I'd have choked you, in my sleep
I'd have overlain you.
Now my steppes have all been sold, ...
My brother, Dnieper, now runs dry
And is deserting me.
And my dear graves the Muscovite
Is plundering utterly.[8]

Shevchenko spent the early 1840s in St Petersburg and on several gentry estates in Dnieper Ukraine. He had gone to Ukraine as a member of St Petersburg's elite, who were continually courted by the culturally starved provincial landed gentry. Then, in June 1845, Shevchenko returned home, not as a star from the St Petersburg cultural elite, but rather to take up a post in Kiev as researcher in the recently created Imperial Archeographic Commission. It was in Kiev, in 1845, that Shevchenko had an opportunity to become acquainted with the other two members of Dnieper Ukraine's intellectual triad, Kostomarov and Kulish.

By the mid-1840s, Kiev had become the center of a small group of Ukrainian enthusiasts who, under the leadership of Mykola Hulak and Vasyl' Bilozers'kyi, founded, probably early the following year, a secret society called the Saints Cyril and Methodius Brotherhood (Bratstvo Sviatoho Kyryla i Metodiia). While there is some doubt whether Shevchenko (who was traveling in the Ukrainian countryside as part of his job with the Archeographic Commission) and Kulish (who left Kiev for Rivne and then St Petersburg in November 1845) ever belonged to the brotherhood, they, together with Kostomarov – an active member – were nonetheless to be implicated in its activity.

And what was that activity? It consisted mainly of discussions and the formulation of a program, the goal of which was the propagation of social equality, Slavic brotherhood, and, indirectly, Ukrainian patriotism. With the Cyril and Methodius Brotherhood, the national movement, emphasizing an exclusive Ukrainian identity, entered what could be considered its second, organizational stage. The brotherhood drew up a document entitled *Knyha bytiia ukraïns'koho narodu* (Books of Genesis of the Ukrainian People), probably authored by Kostomarov, which in a messianic spirit traced the history of the world and the place of Ukraine in it. Particular emphasis was given to the growth of the Cossack movement and to how the "landlords saw that all the people would become Cossacks, that is, free."[9] This ideal state of affairs lasted until "the German tsarina, Catherine [II], a universal whore, atheist, and murderer of her own husband, ended the Cossack Host. ... And Ukraine was destroyed."[10] Ukraine's destruction, however, was more apparent than real, because at whatever future time one of the brotherhood's goals – the federation of all the Slavs – was realized, "then all the peoples, pointing to that place on the map where Ukraine is delineated, will say: behold, the stone which the builders rejected has become the cornerstone."[11]

The program of the Cyril and Methodius Brotherhood in Dnieper Ukraine included the abolition of serfdom and the establishment of schools to educate the masses. The idealistic organization remained stillborn, however, because a fellow Ukrainian infiltrator reported the group to the tsarist police. Ten of its members, including Shevchenko and Kulish, were arrested in the spring of 1847. Put on trial, all were found guilty. Hulak was imprisoned for three years; Kostomarov for one year and a period of exile; Bilozers'kyi and Kulish for four months and a period of exile. Shevchenko, because of his fiery poetry and its anti-Russian impact on Little Russians, was exiled to the Ural Mountains for an indefinite period as a private soldier and, in accordance with the personal, handwritten instructions of Tsar Nicholas I, was "under the strictest supervision, forbidden to write or to sketch."[12] All the accused were forbidden to live in Ukraine after their terms were served.

With the trial and sentencing of the Cyril and Methodius Brotherhood's members, the first hesitant effort at Ukrainian organizational life was completely aborted. The trial also revealed that the Russian imperial government – which not only had tolerated but also actively had supported Little Russian cultural activity – from now on would suspect provincial patriotism of a relationship with national separatism. The publication of Shevchenko's writings in the early 1840s, however, had provided the Ukrainian movement with a new *raison d'être*. He had succeeded in giving the movement an alternative to the provincial Little Russian mentality that had dominated Ukrainian intellectual circles until the 1840s. Even if organizations were expunged by a hostile regime, the linguistic and literary potential of Ukrainian culture as realized by Shevchenko could be revived as the instrument of a viable national movement whenever the political environment was opportune.

The Ukrainian National Movement in Dnieper Ukraine after the Era of Reforms

The demise of the Cyril and Methodius Brotherhood and the dispersal of its members seemed a serious blow, yet it did not mean the end of the Ukrainian national movement. By the late 1850s, another Ukrainian revival was under way both within and beyond Dnieper Ukraine.

The Right Bank and the khlopomany movement

Within Dnieper Ukraine itself, the new revival was the result of specific conditions in the Right Bank. Chapter 28 showed how the Polish gentry continued to dominate the socioeconomic and cultural life of Russia's so-called Southwestern Land (Kiev, Volhynia, and Podolia provinces), how the area became a stronghold of Polish nationalism and supporter of the Polish rebellion of 1830–1831, and how the tsarist government reacted by abolishing or replacing Polish schools in the area with Russian ones and by using the Little Russian cultural revival as a force with which to counteract Polish nationalism. In 1838, to ensure the implementation of its new policy, the imperial government appointed General Dmitrii G. Bibikov as governor-general for the three Right Bank provinces. Bibikov was an outstanding example of the stern bureaucrat who helped to enforce the repressive rule of Tsar Nicholas I (reigned 1825–1855). Bibikov was determined to reduce the heretofore dominant role of the Polish gentry in the Right Bank. In order to achieve this goal, he implemented several governmental decrees which regulated the duties of the serfs and which, to a certain degree, improved their status. He also took up the chairmanship of a regulatory commission to revise the privileges of the gentry. The result was that between 1840 and 1845 more than 64,000 persons had their noble status revoked. According to the imperial authorities, these persons could not prove with a sufficient amount of acceptable documentation a legal right to belong to the noble estate. Accordingly, a large group of Polish and polonized Ukrainian gentry now became state peasants or townspeople, and were thereby brought closer to the mass of the Ukrainian peasantry among whom they lived.

Actually, Polish concern with the specific culture of the Right Bank was already well advanced in the 1830s. The Polish national revival and the Romantic movement in Polish literature had produced several writers who were avidly interested in the history of the Right Bank. They included a group of local patriots known as the "Ukrainian school" of Polish literature: the poets Antoni Małczewski, Józef Bogdan Zaleski, and Seweryn Goszczyński, the prose writer Michał Czajkowski, and the critic Michał Grabowski. For a while, the group also included the greatest Polish Romantic writer of the day, Juliusz Słowacki, a native of Volhynia who wrote several plays based on Ukrainian historical themes.

Apart from these Polish Romantic writers of the Ukrainian school, there evolved a kind of populist movement among the existing and now-demoted Polish gentry who were disillusioned by the failure of their November Insurrection of 1830–1831 and who considered that the future of the Polish cause would depend upon the support of the local peasantry. The result was an attempt to understand the Ukrainian peasantry, including its language and culture. This attempt was carried a stage further by the so-called *khlopomany*, or peasant lovers.

The *khlopomany* were sons of the Polish gentry who were studying in Kiev and who called for the emancipation of the peasantry and the democratization of society. As Poles or polonized Ukrainians of the noble estate, they felt guilty for the centuries of oppression levied upon the Ukrainian peasantry. Hence, when talk of a new Polish revolt began in the late 1850s, the *khlopomany* rejected such an option. Some members of the group went even further: they rejected their Polish identity and returned to what they considered themselves, or their forefathers, originally to have been – Ukrainians. As in the Left Bank, the framework of multiple identities – being a Pole from Ukraine or a Polish Ukrainophile – was now replaced by a framework of mutually exclusive identities: one had to be either a Pole or a Ukrainian, not both. Among the sons of Polish gentry who became conscious Ukrainians were the linguist Kostiantyn Mykhal'chuk, the ethnographer Borys Poznans'kyi, the economist Tadei Ryl's'kyi, and, the most famous activist of them all to "return to Ukrainianism," Volodymyr Antonovych. Antonovych was to become professor at the University of St Vladimir in Kiev and the first professional historian of Ukraine.

Ukrainianism in St Petersburg and the renewal of the organizational stage

While the *khlopomany*, or peasant lovers, were adding new strength to the Ukrainian national movement on the Right Bank, the imperial capital of St Petersburg was serving as another kind of setting for the cultural revival. The accession to the throne in 1855 of the "reformer" tsar Alexander II brought a certain relaxation in the police-state environment that had been created by his predecessor, Nicholas I. In these new conditions, St Petersburg soon became the home of the leading members of the Cyril and Methodius Brotherhood. Kulish, who was already in the city, was allowed to publish after 1855. Four years later, Kostomarov arrived to take up the influential post of head of the department (*katedra*) of Russian history of St Petersburg University. Even the "dangerous" Shevchenko was released from exile and allowed to settle in the imperial capital, where he was made a member of the

Imperial Academy of Art and was again permitted to paint and to publish until his early death in 1861.

Kostomarov and Kulish produced major monographs on Ukrainian history in the 1850s. They included Kostomarov's biography of the Cossack hetman Bohdan Khmel'nyts'kyi (1857; 2nd ed., 1859; 3rd ed., 1876) and Kulish's two-volume *Zapiski o Iuzhnoi Rusi* (Notes on Southern Rus', 1856–57). In accord with the tradition established during the first half of the nineteenth century, these works appeared in Russian, although Kulish republished his historical novel *Chorna Rada* (1857) in Ukrainian and compiled two editions of a Ukrainian-language primer (*Hramatka*, 1857, 1861) for use in Sunday language schools for adults. Owing to subsequent restrictions by the tsarist government, Kulish's primer did not enjoy widespread pedagogical use; nonetheless, it provided the model from which modern Ukrainian orthography derives.

Besides publishing their own creative writings, Kostomarov, Kulish, and Shevchenko joined other Ukrainians in St Petersburg in starting a cultural circle known as the Hromada with the support of two philanthropic Ukrainian land-owners, Vasyl' Tarnovs'kyi and Hryhorii Galagan. The St Petersburg Hromada published several works by Ukrainian writers, as well as the journal *Osnova* (1861-62), which during the two years of its existence became the platform of the Ukrainian national movement. It was on the pages of *Osnova*, for instance, that Kostomarov published his influential article "Dvie russkii narodnosti" ("Two Rus' Nationalities"), in which he decisively put forth the thesis that on historical, cultural, and linguistic grounds Russians and Ukrainians formed two distinct nationalities (see chapter 2).

Ukrainian hromadas also arose in Kiev in 1861 under the leadership of the *khlopomany* (Antonovych, Ryl's'kyi, and Mykhal'chuk) and Left Bank Ukrainian populists (Chubyns'kyi and Stoianov), as well as in Kharkiv, Poltava, and Cherni-hiv, where under Leonid Hlibov the journal *Chernyhovs' kyi lystok* (1861–63) was published. The aim of the hromada movement in Dnieper Ukraine was to pre-pare the peasantry for their national as well as economic liberation by teaching them about Ukrainian language and culture in the so-called Sunday schools and by publishing books and staging plays in Ukrainian. The first Sunday school was founded in 1859 in Kiev. By 1862, there were sixty-seven spread throughout sev-eral Dnieper-Ukrainian towns and villages. It was for those schools that Kulish and even Shevchenko (*Bukvar' iuzhnorusskii*, 1861) published elementary primers.

These developments marked the height of the populist era, during which it became the vogue for the intelligentsia to don traditional Ukrainian dress (at least colorfully embroidered shirts – *vyshyvani sorochky*) and to go out into the coun-tryside. They hoped that by doing this they might learn by osmosis about peasant ways and gain the peasants' trust and confidence. In the face of an ever-skeptical peasantry, such expectations were rarely fulfilled. Nonetheless, on the eve of the era of reforms and the emancipation of the serfs, it seemed that with the hromadas the Ukrainian intelligentsia was well on its way to providing an organizational basis for the national movement. The apparent tolerance of the Russian government was short-lived, however.

Russian reaction to the Ukrainian movement

The mood was already changing in Russian intellectual circles. During the first half of the century, for instance, Ukrainianism or Little Russianism had been favored. In the words of Orest Pelech, a perceptive observer of that period, "The Ukrainian language and works using it occupied a peculiar position in the *Zeitgeist* of the Empire's educated public: it was considered quaint, humorous, beautiful, and therefore, chic."[1] It is not surprising, then, that those public intellectuals who represented the main currents of Russian thought at the time – the "liberal" Westernizers and "conservative" Slavophiles – initially welcomed the Little Russian cultural movement and even published works in Ukrainian on the pages of their periodical press. In the 1860s, however, the mood changed, and writers in several patriotic Russian organs (*Viestnik Iugo-zapadnoi Rossii, Kievlianin, Moskovskie viedomosti, Russkii viestnik*) began to argue that Ukrainian, or Little Russian, was only a dialect of the Russian language. Their approach seemed to provide an answer to the rhetorical question posed a few decades earlier by Aleksander Pushkin, Russia's foremost Romantic poet: "Will not all the Slavic streams merge into the Russian sea?"[2]

Pushkin's formulation encapsulated the widespread interest at the time in the ideology of Pan-Slavism; namely, the view that all the Slavic peoples somehow formed a unified body (based on linguistic and cultural criteria) and that they should cooperate in order to promote their cultural and political interests regardless of the country, or empire, in which they lived. In Ukraine, Pan-Slavic ideas clearly inspired Kostomarov and all those in sympathy with the Cyril and Methodius Brotherhood. Shevchenko himself wrote a moving poem, "Ieretyk" (The Heretic, 1845), in homage to the fifteenth-century Czech religious reformer, Jan Hus, a hero for the West Slavs (Slovaks and Czechs), who in the 1830s were the originators of the ideology of Pan-Slavism. The West Slavs placed great emphasis on the specific value and worth of each of the Slavic peoples, regardless of their numerical size or political influence. By the second half of the nineteenth century, however, Russian publicists adopted – and transformed – the ideology of Pan-Slavism. Convinced of their own political superiority and armed with self-confidence in their self-professed role as protector against the threat from German and Ottoman Turkish enemies, Russian publicists argued that all Slavs, for their own best interests, might as well merge with the "Great Russians." At the very same time, Polish publicists were claiming that Ukrainianism, or Little Russianism, was being used as a weapon – as indeed it was – to de-polonize the Right Bank. Ukrainian writers like Kostomarov and Kulish filled the pages of the journal *Osnova* with responses to both the Russian and the Polish charges.

These intellectual debates soon entered the world of real politics, and by 1862, provincial governors in Little Russia were receiving more and more reports of a supposed desire on the part of Ukrainian leaders "to separate Ukraine from Russia." Such information was passed on to the central government in St Petersburg. Indeed, the landowners, who had just been deprived of their serfs, were always suspicious of the populist intellectuals and their cultural work among the peasantry. The peasants, in turn, were not especially pleased with the terms of the emancipation. By asso-

THE VALUEV DECREE

In March 1862, Pylyp Morachevs'kyi submitted a Ukrainian translation of parts of the New Testament to the Imperial Academy of Sciences. The academy approved the text, but it was rejected by the Holy Synod of the Russian Orthodox Church, partly on the ground that a translation into a legally nonexistent language would be politically dangerous. In connection with this matter, the minister of the interior, Count Petr Valuev, issued a circular to the office of censorship on 18 July 1863. This circular has came to be known as the Valuev Decree.

For some time there have been debates in the press about whether a distinct Little Russian literature can exist. Those debates were prompted by the appearance of works by a few writers noted for their more or less outstanding talent or originality. More recently, the question of a Little Russian literature has taken on another aspect that, as a result of purely political circumstances, has nothing to do with strictly literary interests. Previous works written in the Little Russian language were intended solely for the educated classes of South Russia; now, however, the supporters of a Little Russian nationality have turned their attention to the un-educated masses. Those supporters, who hope to have their political ideas implemented, have undertaken the publication of books for basic reading, primers, grammars, geography texts, etc. under the pretext of spreading literacy and enlightenment. The criminal actions of many of these individuals have been the subject of an investigation by a special commission.

In St Petersburg, there is even a fund to publish inexpensive books in the South Russian dialect. Several of these books have already been reviewed by the board of censorship in St Petersburg. A certain number will also be presented to the board of censorship in Kiev. The Kiev board has had some difficulty reviewing these publications because of the following circumstances: (1) teaching in all schools is without exception conducted in the common Russian [*obshchesusskii*] language and nowhere is use of the Little Russian language permitted; (2) the very question of using this dialect in schools is not resolved, and the very mention of the question is greeted on the part of most Little Russians with consternation such as we have seen in the press.

They [the press commentators] argue convincingly that a Little Russian language has not, does not, and cannot exist, and that its dialects as spoken by the masses are the same as the Russian language, with the exception of some corruptions from Poland. In other words, the common Russian language is fully understandable to Little Russians as to Great Russians, and is even more understandable than the so-called Ukrainian language that has been created for them by a few Little Russians and especially by Poles. Those people attempting to prove the opposite are reproached by the majority of Little Russians themselves for separatist intentions that are dangerous for Russia and detrimental to Little Russia. This phenomenon is even more deplorable and deserving of attention, since it coincides with the political intrigues of Poles and virtually owes it origins to them. This is evident from the fact that the majority of Little Russian works received by the board of censorship are actually submitted by Poles. Finally, the governor-general of Kiev has concluded that the proposed publication of a Little Russian translation of the New Testament now being examined by the board of ecclesiastical censors is dangerous and harmful.

Taking into consideration the alarming situation in our society that certain political events have brought about, and knowing that the question of teaching in local dialects has not yet been sufficiently resolved in the legal code, the minister of the interior, pending agreement with the minister of education, the chief procurator of the Holy Synod, and the chief of police, has deemed it necessary to issue an order on censorship concerning the publication of books in the Little Russian language. Only those works which are in the category of belles-lettres are permitted; the approval of books in the Little Russian language that have religious content as well as those of a pedagogical nature or that are intended for mass consumption is to cease. These instructions were brought to the attention of His Majesty the Emperor, and His Majesty was pleased to grant them his royal favor.

SOURCE: I.O. Hurzhii, ed., *Khrestomatiia z istoriï Ukraïns'koï RSR* (Kiev 1970), pp. 168–169.

ciating populist cultural work and peasant discontent with political separatism, the economic and social elite of Dnieper Ukraine now had, so they felt, a sure way of turning the imperial government against the Ukrainian movement. Finally, in 1863 the Poles revolted against tsarist rule once again. After the January Insurrection of 1863 was suppressed, the imperial government was more determined than ever to end all manifestations, real or apparent, of separatism. The well-known conservative Russian journalist Mikhail Katkov conceived the idea on the pages of his influential journal *Russkii viestnik* that the Ukrainian movement was little more than a "Polish intrigue."

In the resultant atmosphere of suspicion and mutual recrimination, several Ukrainian populists were arrested, the hromada societies and Sunday schools were closed, and their publication activity ceased. As if that were not enough, the tsarist minister of the interior, Count Petr Valuev, issued an internal circular on 18 July 1863 banning the publication of religious and educational books in Ukrainian. Aside from the supposedly politically provocative content of such books, their very form was found questionable. This is because the ministerial decree accepted the view of the contemporary Russian press that: "the Little Russian language has not, does not, and cannot exist." In short, the Valuev decree ended the Russian-Little Russian debate by administrative fiat and with a message that was unequivocal: There is no Little Russian or Ukrainian language, and those who believe there is represent a minority and most likely an anti-imperial, separatist minority.

Despite the restrictions imposed on publishing in Ukrainian (belles-lettres were still permitted), the closing of the Sunday schools, and the limitations placed on the activity of the hromadas, Ukrainians in Kiev were active once again in the early 1870s. This time, however, their activity was of a purely scholarly nature, essentially confined to debates in the Kiev Hromada and to work connected with the Southwestern Branch of the Imperial Russian Geographic Society, established in Kiev in 1873. Ukrainian scholarship, albeit written in Russian, was indeed coming into its own. Some extremely important works, especially in ethnography, date from this period, sponsored by the Geographic Society. They include a collection of Ukrainian historical songs (1874–75) by Volodymyr Antonovych and Mykhailo Drahomanov, Ukrainian tales (1876) by Drahomanov, *chumak* songs (1874) by Ivan Rudchenko, and the monumental seven-volume ethnographic and encyclopedic statistical compendium dealing with the Right Bank (1872–78) by Pavlo Chubyns'kyi. In 1874, the Geographic Society also sponsored an impressive Archaeological Congress, and the same year the Russian-language newspaper *Kievskii telegraf* (1859–76) became the unofficial organ of the Kiev Hromada.

Yet even these limited cultural activities seemed too much for the Russian imperial government. Actually, it was a founding member of the Kiev branch of the Imperial Russian Geographic Society, a landowner from Poltava and imperial Russian administrator, Mikhail Iuzefovich, who sounded the alarm. In 1875, he sent two memoranda to St Petersburg claiming that Kiev had once again become a center of Ukrainian separatism. That same year, Tsar Alexander II appointed a commission to report on the "ukrainophile propaganda in the southern provinces of Russia."[3]

The commission concluded that the "activity of the Ukrainophiles" presented a danger to the state. It proposed extending the 1863 Valuev Decree to forbid the publication of all Ukrainian books and to prohibit their importation from abroad, especially from Galicia. Plays, lectures, even lyrics to musical compositions should be banned; suspect organizations and newspapers closed; and "dangerous" pro-Ukrainian teachers removed from the classrooms. In short, Russian officialdom was now prepared to back up fully its belief that the Ukrainian language and Ukrainian nationality did not exist.

All the recommendations of the commission were accepted by Tsar Alexander II in May 1876, while he was "taking the cure" at a spa in Ems, Germany. For that reason, the prohibitory measures against the Ukrainian movement came to be known as the Ems Ukase (decree) of 1876. Also at about the same time, the Ukrainian activists Mykhailo Drahomanov and Mykola Ziber were removed from their professorial posts at Kiev's St Vladimir University. In 1881, the new tsar, Alexander III, allowed some modification of the Ems Ukase, whereby dictionaries and musical lyrics could be published in Ukrainian if they used Russian orthography, and Ukrainian plays could be staged if local authorities approved each performance in advance. Permanent Ukrainian theaters or troupes performing only in the "Little Russian dialect" were expressly forbidden, however. It is true that during the last decades of the nineteenth century and until World War I, Dnieper Ukrainian writers, actors, and musicians sometimes managed through ingenious ploys or monetary bribes to avoid tsarist restrictions on publication and performance. Nonetheless, the restrictions of the Ems Ukase remained in effect, and for all intents and purposes stifled the Ukrainian movement. Indeed, schools and churches continued to exist, but they gave no help to the Ukrainian national orientation.

THE EMS UKASE

In the interests of the state and in order to suppress the dangerous activity of Ukrainophiles, it would be necessary to take into consideration these measures:

A. For the Ministry of the Interior

(1) Not to allow, without special permission from the administration of the Department of Printing, the importation into the [Russian] Empire of any kind of book published abroad in the Little Russian dialect.

(2) To prohibit the publication in the [Russian] Empire of all original works or translations in the [Little Russian] dialect, with the exception of historical sources provided that they, if pertaining to oral folklore (songs, tales, proverbs), appear in the common-Russian [*obshcherusskaia*] orthography (that is, not in the so-called *kulishivka* [Ukrainian alphabet]).

(3) To prohibit all stage performances in the [Little Russian] dialect, as well as lyrics to musical scores and public lectures (such as those which today are little more than ukrainophile manifestations).

(4) To support the newspaper *Slovo*, which is published in Galicia and is oriented against hostile ukrainophilism, and to provide it with a limited but steady subsidy [the archival document indicates 1,000 rubles – written by hand in the margin], without which it could not survive and would have to cease publication.

(5) To ban the newspaper *Kievskii telegraf* for the following reasons: that its nominal editor, Snezhko-Blotskii, is completely blind and is unable to function in any way as editor, and that as a result the newspaper is directed arbitrarily by individuals ... who are politically very unreliable.

B. For the Ministry of Education

(6) To increase supervision on the part of the local school authorities so that in lower-level schools no teaching in any subject is permitted in the Little Russian dialect [which does not exist – written by hand in the margin].

(7) To remove from all lower- and middle-level school libraries in the Little Russian provinces books and brochures prohibited in the second paragraph of this proposal.

(8) To pay careful attention to the teaching personnel in the school districts of the Kharkiv, Kiev, and Odessa provinces, and to request from the inspectors in those districts a list of names of teachers with notes on each about his or her loyalty and relationship to the ukrainophile orientation. With regard to disloyal or questionable teachers, they should be transferred to provinces in Great Russia and replaced by new teachers from Great Russia.

(9) To appoint in the future for the aforementioned districts teaching personnel who are trustworthy and completely reliable. Such reliability should be based not only on words but on deeds.

(10) To close for an indefinite period the Kiev Branch of the Imperial Geographic Society and to allow its eventual reopening only if the local governor-general is given control, which should occur following the permanent dismissal of all those persons who in any way could be suspected of not being of a pure Russian orientation.

C. For the Third Section [secret police] of His Majesty's Supreme Chancellery

(11) To exile immediately from the [Little Russian] land [Mykhailo] Drahomanov and [Pavlo] Chubyns'kyi as incorrigible agitators who are dangerous for the region.

Imperial Commission on Ukrainophile Propaganda in the Southern Provinces of Russia, 1875.

SOURCE: Fedir Savchenko, *Zaborona ukraïnstva 1876 r.*, 2nd ed. (Munich 1970), p. 381.

Schools in Dnieper Ukraine

The number of schools in Dnieper Ukraine actually declined from the eighteenth to the first half of the nineteenth century. In 1856, the nine provinces in Dnieper Ukraine had only 1,320 elementary, secondary, and higher schools, with 67,000 students. This figure represented a mere 0.5 percent of the potential student body. The reforms of the 1860s, however, did provide for the establishment of a greater number of schools, and it was in anticipation of this development that in the late 1850s the populist movement and hromada societies began their cultural work. This included the publication of Ukrainian elementary-school primers and grammars by Shevchenko and Kulish. Within a few decades the numbers did increase, to 3,100 schools in 1898, and then to 4,700 schools with 460,000 students in 1909. These figures need to be placed in context, however.

There was, for instance, no compulsory education in the Russian Empire, whose per capita investment in education was at the time one of the lowest in the world. Although the zemstvos were permitted to organize village schools in 1874, those schools combined with the church- and state-run schools were insufficient in number for the population of Dnieper Ukraine. The result was that at the beginning of the twentieth century, an estimated two-thirds of school-aged children never entered a classroom. At best, 18 percent of Dnieper Ukraine's entire population could read, although in the predominantly Ukrainian-inhabited villages there was as much as 91 to 96 percent illiteracy (1897).

Even for those few ethnic Ukrainian children who attended school, exposure to the Ukrainian language or culture was out of the question. A law of 1804 permitted non-Russian languages to be used as a medium of instruction, and this law was what allowed Polish schools to flourish on the Right Bank at least until the restrictions following the abortive Polish insurrection of 1830–1831. Ukrainian, however, was classified as a dialect of Russian and therefore could not be considered as a medium of instruction.

Nationalist ideologists of all persuasions of course knew quite well that schools were the most effective breeding grounds for creating in young people an awareness of national identity and a sense of common national purpose. Nonetheless, the Russian Empire, with its poor record on investment in education, never took full advantage of the potential that schools had for promoting a state-imposed national identity. The resultant high rates of illiteracy in Dnieper Ukraine paradoxically helped to protect ethnic Ukrainians against russification. Consequently, by World War I the vast majority of Dnieper Ukrainians, unaffected by Russian or other nationalist ideology, were ready to be molded into whatever a government in control of the educational system might wish.

The church in Dnieper Ukraine

The Orthodox Church had more access to the peasant masses than the schools. By the nineteenth century, however, the church had changed radically from what it previously had been. Historically, the Orthodox Rus' Church in Ukraine had played a part in fostering the cultural well-being and sense of identity of the people. During the Kievan period, and later, during the late sixteenth century, it had become the stronghold of Ukrainian Rus' culture in the face of Polish political, social, and cultural pressure. It had also been closely allied to the Cossack movement and to the Hetmanate state. Through the centuries, the Orthodox Church in Ukraine had tried to maintain jurisdictional autonomy, in relation first to the Byzantine Empire, then to Poland, and finally to Muscovite Russia. In the course of the eighteenth century, however, Russia's civil authorities beginning with Tsar Peter I reduced the jurisdictional autonomy of the Orthodox Church in Ukrainian lands (see chapter 24). The office of the metropolitan of Kiev was abolished and all eparchies in Dnieper Ukraine were made fully subordinate to the Holy Synod of the Russian Orthodox Church based in St Petersburg.

The situation was much more complicated and more difficult for Dnieper Ukraine's non-Orthodox Christians, most of whom were living in the Right Bank. Soon after 1793, when the Russian Empire acquired these lands from the Polish-Lithuanian Commonwealth, Catherine II guaranteed freedom of religion both to Roman Catholics (mostly Poles) and to Uniates, or Greek Catholics (mostly Ukrainians and Belarusans). Despite such an "enlightened" measure, both Catholic churches were generally considered by Russian society to be intruders on historic Orthodox Rus' lands. Consequently, it was not long before the status of Roman and Uniate (Greek) Catholics declined.

Between 1778 and 1847, several Roman Catholic dioceses in Belarusan and Ukrainian territories were alternately abolished, restored, and reorganized. In the end, only two Roman Catholic dioceses remained in Dnieper Ukraine – Zhytomyr, in the Right Bank (mostly for Poles), and Tiraspol, in southern Ukraine (mostly for recent German settlers).

The Uniate Church eventually fared much worse. On the eve of Catherine II's death in 1796, the Uniate Metropolitanate of Kiev (excluding the Eparchy of Chełm/Kholm in the Russian-ruled Kingdom of Poland) was abolished; many monasteries of the Basilian order were closed; and several thousand Uniates were forced to become Orthodox. Two years later the eparchies of Luts'k and Volodymyr-Brest were restored (1806), and within a decade the church was fully reconstituted as the Uniate Metropolitanate of Russia, with its seat in Polatsk. This development proved to be temporary, however, especially after Emperor Nicholas I came to the throne. In response to the emperor's desire to create a society governed by the principles of "Orthodoxy, autocracy, and nationality," the Ukrainian-born Uniate bishop of Lithuania, Iosyf Semashko (reigned 1832–1839), became enamored of Orthodoxy and in 1827 began to draw up plans for the abolition of the Uniate Church. His efforts bore fruit in 1839, when the entire church was abolished once again – this time permanently. Semashko went on to become the Orthodox bishop of Vilnius and Lithuania, while the Belarusan and Ukrainian Uniate faithful were "voluntarily" converted to Orthodoxy. Those clergy who refused (593 of a total of 1,898) were exiled to Siberia or to the interior of Russia. Only in the region of Chełm, which was part of the empire's jurisdictionally distinct Congress Kingdom, did a Uniate (Greek Catholic) eparchy survive, although it too was dismantled by the Russian imperial government in 1875.

Consequently, by the middle of the nineteenth century, Ukrainians in Dnieper Ukraine were all part of the Russian Orthodox Church administered by the Holy Synod in St Petersburg. Church jurisdictions were reconfigured so that there were nine eparchies: Kiev, Chernihiv, Poltava, Kharkiv, Katerynoslav, Kherson, Taurida (created in 1859), Podolia, and Volhynia; as well as Kishinev/Chişinaŭ and Kholm/Chełm (created in 1907) covering lands in part inhabited by ethnic Ukrainians. Some of these eparchies had more than one bishop, so that by 1917 there were a total of twenty-six in Dnieper Ukraine. Each eparchy had its own seminary, preparatory schools for the seminary, and schools for daughters of the clergy, as well as official journals, some of which contained important scholarly studies in addition to official church material. All the schools and publications used Russian exclusively.

Russian was also used in sermons. Even the traditional Church Slavonic liturgy was rendered with Russian pronunciation. While parts of the Bible were translated into Ukrainian during the second half of the nineteenth century, the translations were never used in Dnieper Ukraine. In fact, in was the request to publish Pylyp Morachevs'kyi's translation of the four gospels and the Book of Acts that prompted a debate in governmental circles which led eventually to the restrictions of the 1863 Valuev decree. Other books of the Bible in translations by Panteleimon Kulish and the Galician-Ukrainian Ivan Puliui were published in the Austro-Hungarian Empire (1869 and 1871), but it was not until 1904 that the full text of both testaments in a Ukrainian translation by Kulish, Puliui, and Ivan Nechui-Levyts'kyi was published in Vienna by the British Bible Society. In Dnieper Ukraine, only a Church Slavonic text (with pronunciation in Russian) was permitted.

Devotion to Holy Russia headed by a God-anointed tsar were attitudes that were particularly entrenched among Orthodox bishops in Dnieper Ukraine. Whether or not they were natives of Ukraine, virtually all the hierarchs felt themselves Russian, and often they became the most active opponents of a distinct Ukrainian national identity. In essence, the Orthodox Church in Dnieper Ukraine became an instrument of russification and a foremost representative of the official imperial ideology, with its glorification of the tsar, Orthodoxy, and Russian nationality.

The return to the heritage-gathering stage

With the outlawing of publications in Ukrainian in 1863 and 1876, the absence of cultural organizations, and a school system and church structure opposed to the Ukrainian idea, the national movement in Dnieper Ukraine was basically forced to lie dormant during the last decades of the nineteenth century. Its only manifestations were scholarship, some theatrical and musical performances, and the activity of the émigrés.

In the field of Ukrainian scholarship there were important results, especially the studies in Ukrainian history by Volodymyr Antonovych of Kiev's University of St Vladimir. Antonovych founded what became known as the Kiev school of Ukrainian history, the most famous graduate being Mykhailo Hrushevs'kyi. Scholars at Kharkiv University also contributed to advances in Ukrainian scholarship, among them the social historian Dmytro Bahalii, the linguist Oleksander Potebnia, and the folklorist Mykola Sumtsov. The studies of these and other scholars were, of course, published in Russian, as were the two most important journals of Ukrainian scholarship at the time, *Sbornik Khar'kovskago Istoriko-filologicheskago obshchestva* (1886–1914) and *Kievskaia starina* (1882–1907).

Whereas the establishment of a permanent Ukrainian theater was forbidden, the 1881 modification of the Ems Ukase did permit performances in Ukrainian if local authorities approved and if a play in Russian was given as well. The subject matter of Ukrainian plays, moreover, was restricted to folkloric themes and comedies. Serious drama, including translations of classical works from other countries, could be performed only in Russian. Despite such limitations, several Ukrainian theatrical troupes were founded during the 1880s. Under the capable leadership of playwrights like Marko Kropyvnyts'kyi, Mykhailo Staryts'kyi, and Ivan Tobilevych (pseudonym: Karpenko-Karyi) and performers like Mykola Tobilevych (pseudonym: Mykola Sadovs'kyi), Panas Tobilevych (pseudonym: Panas Saksahans'kyi), and Mariia Sadovs'ka-Barliotti, Ukrainian plays were presented with great success throughout Dnieper Ukraine and even in St Petersburg.

Many of these figures also contributed to Dnieper Ukraine's musical culture by appearing in performances of the first Ukrainian operas and operettas. The late nineteenth century was, after all, the era of nationalism in music throughout the European Continent, where composers like Verdi, Sibelius, Smetana, Erkel, and Moniuszko aroused patriotic fervor in, respectively, their Italian, Finnish, Czech, Hungarian, and Polish countrymen. Ukrainians, too, were part of these general European trends. In 1863, Semen Hulak-Artemovs'kyi wrote an opera, *Zaporozhets' za Dunaiem* (The Zaporozhian Cossack beyond the Danube), which because of its accessible storyline and engaging melodies inspired a deep sense of Ukrainian patriotism in generations of theater-goers, whether in urban opera houses or in numerous small towns and even village settings where it was – and still is – performed. It is also from this period that Ukraine's national anthem, "Shche ne vmerla Ukraïna" (Ukraine Has Not Yet Died), derives, with words first published by Pavlo Chubyns'kyi in 1863 and set to musc the same year by Mykhailo Verbyts'kyi. The most influential of all composers, however, was Mykola Lysenko. His life's goal was to create a Ukrainian national school of music, and with that aim he compiled transcriptions of hundreds of folk songs and promoted Ukrainian music at numerous choral recitals throughout Dnieper Ukraine for nearly two decades beginning in the 1890s. Nothing had greater influence on audiences than his operas based on Ukrainian themes – *Natalka from Poltava* (1889) and *Taras Bul'ba* (1890) – which were filled with heart-rending melodies that both epitomized and uplifted the Ukrainian national spirit among generations of listeners.

Ukrainian literature fared worse than theater and music. The reason was not because there were no Ukrainian belletrists; in fact, a new generation arose that included talented authors like Oleksander Konys'kyi, Lesia Ukraïnka, Mykhailo Kotsiubyns'kyi, Borys Hrinchenko, and Ivan Nechui-Levyts'kyi. These and other Ukrainian-language authors even managed to publish in Russian-ruled Dnieper Ukraine. Whether because of the benign content of the material or the inefficiency and lax attitude on the part of tsarist government officials, by the 1890s publishing houses in Chernihiv and Kiev managed to avoid the censors and publish Ukrainian-language books. In the imperial capital itself, St Petersburg, the seemingly innocuous Charitable Society for the Publication of Inexpensive Books for General Use produced several titles after 1898 in the Ukrainian language, especially for the peasantry. Moreover, Ukrainian-language journals from Austrian Galicia still managed to reach subscribers in Dnieper Ukraine.

Nevertheless, the restrictions of the 1876 Ems Ukase remained formally the law of the land in one form or another until 1917. Consequently, the impact of Ukrainian literary, dramatic, and musical works on the public-at-large was limited because of small print runs, the lack of serious or sustained literary criticism, and the absence of permanent Ukrainian-language theaters. Even musical works suffered, so that Lysenko's opera *Taras Bul'ba* was not performed in public until after World War I. Marginalized in their own homeland, many of the Russian Empire's Ukrainian-language writers and composers were forced to publish or have their works performed abroad, particularly in Austria's province of Galicia.

Since the national movement in Dnieper Ukraine had been stopped by the Russian government at the organizational stage and forced to revert to the heritage-gathering stage, the only possibility for evolution toward the third, political stage existed among émigrés living abroad. The most important of these were Mykola Ziber, Serhii Podolyns'kyi, and, especially, Mykhailo Drahomanov, all of whom were forced to leave the country after the promulgation of the Ems Ukase in 1876. Drahomanov was actually delegated by the Kiev Hromada to keep the Ukrainian movement alive in the emigration. He did so by publishing a journal, *Hromada* (1876–82), in Geneva, Switzerland, and by informing western European circles of the Russian Empire's treatment of Ukrainians. Drahomanov developed the view that the Ukrainian problem was essentially a social one, and that only after grass-roots cultural work and the economic liberation of the peasantry was achieved could serious development in the political realm be expected. Drahomanov was also a supporter of democratic federalism. At the local level, he advocated the introduction of self-governing and independent peasant communes (*hromady*) that in theory would cooperate whenever the need arose. At the national level, he envisioned the transformation of the Russian Empire into a republic of twenty states, four of which would be on Ukrainian territory.

The beginnings of the political stage

At the very end of the nineteenth century, there was a revival of organizational activity, which soon developed political and not simply cultural goals. The tsarist state was becoming increasingly suspicious of any kind of political activity, so Ukrainian leaders had to proceed cautiously. In fact, most of the older intelligentsia, grouped around the Old Hromada society and the scholarly journal *Kievskaia starina* in Kiev, promoted cultural rather than political activity as what the Ukrainian movement most needed. In 1897, about twenty of the loosely affiliated hromada societies scattered throughout Dnieper-Ukrainian cities united at the initiative of the historian Volodymyr Antonovych and the writer Oleksander Konys'kyi to form the General Ukrainian Non-Party Democratic Organization (Zahal'na Ukraïns'ka Bezpartiina Demokratychna Orhanizatsiia). As its name suggested, this group concentrated on publication and cultural work in village clubs and reading rooms.

But these same apolitical hromada societies, especially the ones in cities that had university students as members, became breeding grounds for political organizations. Among the earliest of these was the Taras Brotherhood (Bratstvo Tarasivtsiv), a secret group of young enthusiasts founded in 1891. Before its liquidation two years later by the tsarist police, the Taras Brotherhood formulated a program calling for liberation from tsarist despotism and the need for the further development of a Ukrainian national consciousness.

University students, this time in Kharkiv, were also responsible for the establishment of the first Ukrainian political party in the Russian Empire, the Revolutionary Ukrainian party, founded in 1900. The problems faced by this first party were similar to those encountered by later Ukrainian political groups. The imperial government, at least until 1905, generally forbade the existence of "Ukrainian" organizations. Consequently, Ukrainian political groups initially had to remain underground, and this limited the number of adherents they could attract. In fact, none of the pre-World War I Ukrainian parties ever had more than a few thousand members.

With the growth of cities in Dnieper Ukraine and worsening conditions among industrial workers, it is not surprising that socialism, as formulated by the German political philosophers Karl Marx and Friedrich Engels, became attractive to political activists in the 1890s. Neither Marx nor Engels took the nationality question seriously, however, so they left little guidance in this area for their social-democratic followers. Engels was scornful of most Slavic peoples in particular, whom he considered at best "remnants of peoples (*Völkertrümmer*), still found here and there, that are no longer capable of leading a national existence and must be incorporated into the larger nations."[4] It was not until 1899 – and in the Austro-Hungarian Empire – that social democrats began to give serious attention to the nationality question. Austrian socialists like Otto Bauer and Karl Renner argued that individual nationalities will remain even after the social transformation of society.

In essence, social democrats throughout Europe were faced with the question of how to organize their political parties, whether on the territorial or national principle. In other words, should there be social democratic parties that represent supporters throughout an entire state, or, following Bauer and Renner in Austria-Hungary, should there be parties for individual nationalities which, in turn, would be loosely associated in a federation of social-democratic parties? Of the two leading socialist parties in the Russian Empire, the Socialist Revolutionary party (est. 1902) favored federalism and national-cultural autonomy, whereas the Social-Democratic Labor party (est. 1898), with its Menshevik and Bolshevik wings, supported one party for the empire as a whole. The argument of the latter was that federalism and national-cultural autonomy were reactionary phenomena that would assist the bourgeoisie in continuing to dominate the masses at the expense of social change. The differing positions on the nationality question are what posed a dilemma for Ukrainians and political activists from other national minorities in the Russian Empire. Should ethnic Ukrainians join with all-Russian parties operating on Ukrainian lands, or should they form their own parties on either a territorial or an ethnolinguistic basis? Should Ukrainians seek some form of autonomy, even independence, or should Ukrainian lands remain an integral part of a future restructured Russian Empire? Debates on these issues are what led to splits, mergers, and the creation of several new parties during the first two decades of the twentieth century.

Dnieper Ukraine's first party, the Revolutionary Ukrainian party, for instance, came into existence in 1900 because young enthusiasts from Kharkiv – some Marxists and some nationalists – did not want to join any of the all-Russian revolutionary parties. They were at a loss, however, to draw up a program on their own and so turned to a recently graduated lawyer, Mykola Mikhnovs'kyi, who provided them with the text of patriotic speech, printed as a pamphlet in Austrian Galicia under the title, *Samostiina Ukraïna* (Independent Ukraine). Initially, the Revolutionary Ukrainian party found inspiration in the pamphlet, which, as its title implies, called for the creation of an independent Ukrainian state. Mikhnovs'kyi's basic premise was that national independence must be obtained for Ukrainians before social liberation could be achieved.

Not all Revolutionary Ukrainian party members agreed, however, and arguments regarding national versus social priorities (*Samostiina Ukraïna* never even mentioned the word socialism) led to a falling-out with Mikhnovs'kyi, who in 1902 established his own Ukrainian People's party. National independence was the primary goal of the People's party. Those remaining in the Revolutionary Ukrainian party in contrast emphasized their commitment to social change before national independence, and in 1903 they even accepted a merger with the small Ukrainian Socialist party (est. 1900). The emphasis on socialism, however, soon gave rise to controversy over Marxist ideology and the issue of relations with the burgeoning all-Russian socialist movement.

Influenced by Lenin's views on the nationality question, several figures (M. Melenevs'kyi-Basok, Dmytro Antonovych, Oleksander Skoropys'-Ioltukhovs'kyi) left the Revolutionary Ukrainian party in early 1905 to form the Ukrainian Social-Democratic Union, better known by its Ukrainian acronym, Spilka. The Spilka was little more than a regional unit of the Marxist Russian Social-Democratic Labor party, and it accepted the latter's view that nationalism was a bourgeois ideology invented to confuse and divide the working proletariat.

With the departure of the left-wing socialists who formed the Spilka, the Revolutionary Ukrainian party preserved its ideological commitment to socialist principles and continued to stress the idea of Ukrainian national distinctiveness within a future federated Russian republic. To emphasize its goals, the party changed its name in 1905 to the Ukrainian Social-Democratic Labor party. Notwithstanding its relative weakness during the early years, the party had several members (Symon Petliura, Volodymyr Vynnychenko, Mykola Porsh) who later were to play leading roles in Ukrainian political life.

Besides the national socialist, anational socialist, and nationalist political orientations – represented respectively by the Ukrainian Social-Democratic Labor party, the Spilka, and the Ukrainian People's party – Dnieper Ukrainian politics had a more moderate orientation, represented by the Ukrainian Democratic, later Ukrainian Democratic Radical party. Founded in 1905, this party was headed by such leaders from the General Ukrainian Non-Party Democratic Organization as Ievhen Chykalenko, Serhii Iefremov, and Borys Hrinchenko, who had become convinced that it was necessary to move from the purely cultural to the political sphere. This group called for the introduction of a parliamentary government, civil liberties, the use of the Ukrainian language, and a local Ukrainian parliament, all within a federated democratic Russian Empire. To promote its program, the Ukrainian Democratic Radical party published the first Ukrainian-language daily newspapers in Kiev, *Hromads'ka dumka* (1905–06) and *Rada* (1906–14), and generally cooperated with the Russian Constitutional Democratic party (the Kadets).

After 1905, the new Ukrainian political parties, which had until then led a semi-legal existence, were given a chance to function openly. In fact, the whole Ukrainian movement was given a new lease of life. This change was related to Russia's defeat in the Russo-Japanese War of 1904–1905 and the subsequent domestic disturbances that came to be known as the Revolution of 1905. As a result of these events, Tsar Nicholas II was compelled in October to issue a manifesto that called for elections to Russia's first parliament, known as the Duma. In this new atmosphere, which also gave rise to the Stolypin agrarian reforms and a decline in the influence of the zemstvos (see chapter 26), the enforcement of censorship laws was relaxed. In February 1905, in response to a tsarist request about censorship, the Russian Academy of Sciences declared that "Little Russian" (i.e., Ukrainian) is a language distinct from "Great Russian" and recommended that the restrictions of the 1876 Ems Ukase and of the revised version of 1881 be lifted.

Although the Ems Ukase was never repealed, its provisions were not enforced, with the result that in December 1905 the first Ukrainian-language newspapers in the Russian Empire began to appear – *Khliborob* in Lubny, *Ridnyi krai* in Poltava, and *Hromads' ka dumka* in Kiev. By 1908 there were nine newspapers with a circulation of 20,000 copies as well as the first Ukrainian-language scholarly publications (*Ukraïna,* 1907, and *Zapysky Ukraïns'koho naukovoho tovarystva,* 1908–18). Language standardization was enhanced following the appearance of several grammars (including scholarly ones by Ievhen Tymchenko and Ahatanhel Kryms'kyi) and the monumental four-volume dictionary of the Ukrainian language (1909) under the editorial direction of Borys Hrinchenko. Public access to these materials was made possible through new publishing houses, bookstores (by 1908 nine in Kiev and several other cities specialized in Ukrainian publications), and the opening of forty Prosvita popular-education societies on the model used in Austrian Galicia.

While the tsarist ministry of education did not lift its ban on Ukrainian-language instruction in schools, beginning in 1906 one Orthodox bishop (Parfenii Levyts'kyi) encouraged Ukrainian to be used in sermons and church schools in the Podolia eparchy; and a few university professors (Mykola Sumtsov at Kharkiv and Oleksander Hrushevs'kyi at Odessa) lectured in Ukrainian. Finally, in the fall of 1905, the L'viv University historian and president of the Shevchenko Scientific Society in Austrian Galicia, Mykhailo S. Hrushevs'kyi, began to return for extended periods of time to the Russian Empire, where he worked closely with the Ukrainian parliamentary club in St Petersburg. In 1907, he moved the influential Ukrainian-language civic and literary journal, *Literaturno-naukovyi vistnky,* from Austrian Galicia to Kiev, and the following year he became head of the first openly pro-Ukrainian learned society in the Russian Empire, the Ukrainian Scientific Society.

When elections were held in 1906 to the Duma, the Russian Empire's first parliament, sixty-two members were returned from the Ukrainian provinces, and forty-four of these declared themselves as ethnic Ukrainians. The participation of the new political parties was limited, however, as the socialists boycotted the election, and the Ukrainian Democratic Radicals, fearing the prospect of being able to exert little influence, joined the ticket of the moderately liberal Russian Constitutional Democratic party, the Kadets. Notwithstanding their cooperation with the Kadets, who were sympathetic to non-Russian nationalities but opposed to federalism or political autonomy for such groups, the Democratic Radicals, led by Illia Shrah, set up a Ukrainian parliamentary caucus to press for Ukrainian language rights. At the same time, they beagn publishing in St Petersburg a Russian-language organ, *Ukrainskii viestnik* (1906), to inform the empire's politically conscious public about Ukrainian issues.

Despite optimistic expectations, Russia's first attempt at parliamentary democracy was short-lived, and just over two months following its convocation (10 May 1906) the First Duma was dissolved. Elections were held the following year to the Second Duma, which lasted not much longer than the first (5 March to 15

June 1907). Two-fifths of the deputies were socialists, and among them were four-teen from the Ukrainian Social-Democratic (Spilka) party, who joined with other nationally-conscious deputies to form a forty-seven member caucus called the Ukrainian Labor Club (Ukraïns'ka Trudova Hromada) with its own Ukrainian-language organ, *Ridna sprava – Visti z Dumy* (St Petersburg, 1907). The caucus demanded the introduction of the Ukrainian language into schools, the establish-ment of a university department of Ukrainian studies, and local autonomy.

Yet as soon as Tsar Nicholas II felt secure, Russia's tentative experiment with parliamentarism was decisively curtailed. Even though the Third and Fourth Dumas met, in 1907–1912 and 1912–1917 respectively, in the interim the elector-al laws had been changed. This meant that the Duma was even less representative than before (50 percent of the seats were now in the hands of the landed gentry) and was politically ineffective. Moreover, there were very few nationally conscious Ukrainian representatives in the Third and Fourth Dumas, and no Ukrainian par-liamentary club.

Accordingly, the few political advances made by the Ukrainian movement since 1905 were quickly reversed. By 1908, several members of the Ukrainian Social-Democratic Labor party and the Spilka had been arrested, and the weakened organizations forced underground or into exile and eventual dissolution. Mikh-novs'kyi's small Ukrainian People's party as well as the relatively influential and politically moderate Ukrainian Democratic Radical party ceased to exist. In 1908, members of the latter group, headed by Chykalenko, Iefremov, and Hrushevs'kyi, formed the non-party Society of Ukrainian Progressivists (TUP), but this group was forced to revert to the apolitical cultural approach to the Ukrainian problem. Despite their restricted activity, the Ukrainian Progressivists continued to exist in the hope that the political situation would eventually improve and that Ukrain-ian cultural life might be encouraged to function within a future constitutional and parliamentary Russian Empire. Meanwhile, its members tried to publicize and defend the Ukrainian cause in the face of growing Russian chauvinist opinion.

Such chauvinism was evident in both the policies of the imperial government and the writings of Russian publicists. In 1910, Petr A. Stolypin, the tsarist min-ister of the interior concerned with containing potential revolutionary activity by a combination of police repression and gradual socioeconomic reform in the countryside, issued an order closing the Prosvita societies, prohibiting universi-ty lectures in Ukrainian, and enforcing once again the 1876 ban on Ukrainian-language publications. These official acts were complemented by a campaign in the Russian-language press in Dnieper Ukraine (*Kievlianin*, Kiev) to castigate what was described as the blasphemy of Ukrainian separatism. There was also outspo-ken criticism by Russian nationalist intellectuals like Vasilii Shul'gin and Timofei Florinskii and even by more moderate Kadet leaders like Pavel Miliukov and Petr Struve, who at best might tolerate some Ukrainian cultural activity but who con-sidered any talk of political autonomy a dangerous threat to the "natural" unity of Russia. Consequently, the revival of organizations representing ethnic Ukrainians and the first attempts at Ukrainian political activity during the first decade of the twentieth century were brought to an untimely end by the reinstitution of imperial bureaucratic repression and a backlash of Russian public opinion.

By the outbreak of World War I in 1914 the Ukrainian national movement in Dnieper Ukraine at most had gone through the first, heritage-gathering stage of intelligentsia-inspired nationalism. Political circumstances in the Russian Empire either precluded its further evolution outright or allowed the early organizational and political stirrings insuffient time in which to develop. The result was that the Ukrainian-oriented intelligentsia, with its conceptual framework of mutually exclusive identities, was effectively cut off from working with and educating the population at large in a Ukrainian national spirit. Meanwhile, that same population was subjected to a state-imposed national movement and was continually exposed to the Russian imperial ideology, whether in schools, churches, or the army. And if an ethnic Ukrainian peasant ever left the village, he or she entered "Russian" towns and cities, albeit on Ukrainian territory, where all official transactions – in factory workplaces, in governmental offices, on the railroads, and so on – were conducted in Russian.

Given this environment, it is not surprising that the conceptual framework of a hierarchy of multiple loyalties continued to prevail in Dnieper Ukraine until World War I. Ukrainianness as something distinct from Russianness had no prestige, and being a Ukrainian brought no tangible social, economic, or cultural advantages in the nineteenth-century Russian Empire. Those ethnic Ukrainians who were socially mobile could improve their status only by becoming completely russified or, at the very least, by being Russians from Little Russia. As for the idea of an exclusive Ukrainian ethnic identity, it prevailed only among the intellectual and political fringes of Dnieper-Ukrainian society. Accordingly, before 1914 it was not in the Russian Empire but rather in the Austro-Hungarian Empire, particularly in Galicia, that Ukrainian nationalism survived and even prospered.

Part Seven

Ukraine in the Austrian Empire

The Administrative and Social Structure of Ukrainian Lands in the Austrian Empire before 1848

Austria acquires Ukrainian lands

Ukrainian lands north of the Carpathian Mountains became part of the Habsburg Empire as a result of an international power struggle in central and eastern Europe that led to the First Partition of Poland in 1772. In that year, without firing a shot, Habsburg Austria received what came to be known as Galicia. This included the former Polish palatinates of Rus'-Galicia (minus the Chełm region), Belz, Podolia west of the Zbruch River, and Cracow and Sandomierz south of the Vistula River.

After the diplomatic fait accompli of 1772, the Habsburg rulers of Austria justified their new territorial acquisition by reviving medieval Hungary's late twelfth-century claim to the Galician-Volhynian Kingdom (see chapter 9). In the interim, the Habsburgs had become the hereditary kings of Hungary, and this ostensibly gave them historical rights to the 1772 "reacquisition" of Hungarian territory, which they officially named the Kingdom of Galicia and Lodomeria (the Latin name for Volhynia), or Galicia (German: Galizien) for short. Two years later, at the close of the Russo-Turkish war in 1774, Austria took advantage of the Ottoman Empire's weakened position and seized the mountainous region of northern Moldavia known as Bukovina. After an initial twelve years of Austrian military administration, Bukovina was joined to neighboring Galicia, of which it was to remain a part until 1849.

One other territory had been part of Austria's Habsburg Empire even before 1772. This was Transcarpathia, or historical Subcarpathian Rus', which since the eleventh century had been an integral part of the Kingdom of Hungary. The local East Slavic population, known as Rusyns or Rusnaks, lived in the mountainous northern regions of seven Hungarian counties, an area that today is located in Ukraine's Transcarpathian oblast and the so-called Prešov Region of northeastern Slovakia.

As a result of the Third Partition of Poland, the final one, in 1795, Austria nearly doubled the size of Galicia by adding an extensive territory that stretched from the Pilica River in the west to the Buh River in the north and east and that included the entire upper valley of the Vistula River almost as far north as Warsaw. This new,

MAP 29   UKRAINIAN LANDS IN THE AUSTRIAN EMPIRE, 1772–1815

International boundaries, 1815

West Galicia, 1795-1809

Boundary of Russian Empire,
1809-1815

Ukrainian ethnolinguistic territory

Boundary of former
Polish palatinate

RUS'   Name of palatinate other
than administrative center

Administrative center of
former Polish palatinate

0   50 miles
0   50 kilometers
Scale 1 : 4 750 000

primarily Polish-inhabited territory was named West Galicia, although it was not
to remain in Habsburg hands for long. Following Austria's defeat by Napoleon,
West Galicia together with the Polish-Ukrainian ethnographic borderland region
around Zamość was ceded to the French dependency known as the Duchy of War-

saw. Then, following the defeat of Napoleon, Europe's boundaries were redrawn in 1815 at the Congress of Vienna. Austria's northern boundaries were fixed and were to remain unchanged for nearly a century, until the outbreak of World War I in 1914. Austria's province of Galicia was restored according to the boundaries it had had in 1772, excluding the region around Zamość. At its far western end, the city of Cracow and its environs north of the Vistula River were detached from Galicia and made into a free republic, although under Austria's protection.

The structure of the Austrian Empire

What was this Austrian Empire in which large numbers of Ukrainians found themselves during the last quarter of the eighteenth century? In a sense, the empire was a relic from the Middle Ages, a time when royal families acquired territories as part of their personal patrimony. The family in question were the Habsburgs, who, beginning in the thirteenth century with the Germanic territories of Austria, Tyrol, Carniola, and Styria and a capital at Vienna along the middle Danube River, steadily expanded their realm. By the late eighteenth century, Habsburg possessions were, in Europe, second only to the Russian Empire in territorial size. To provide some idea of its extent, Habsburg territory at the end of the eighteenth century consisted of what are today the entire countries of Austria, the Czech Republic, Slovakia, Hungary, Slovenia, and Croatia and substantial parts of Italy, Romania (Transylvania), Serbia (Vojvodina), Poland, and Ukraine.

The inhabitants of the Habsburg domains were as diverse as the territories under its rule. The major languages spoken were German, Hungarian, Czech, Slovak, Polish, Ukrainian, Slovenian, Serbo-Croatian, Romanian, and Italian. These were only the ten major languages, however, all of which appeared on the empire's paper money by the late nineteenth century. There were also numerous others, including Yiddish, Romany, and Armenian.

The administrative structure of the Austrian Empire was initially quite complex, since each new territory acquired over the centuries – whether a kingdom, or a grand duchy, or a duchy, or simply a city – often retained its own traditional customs and administration. The largest of these entities, and because of its self-governing status the most distinct, was the Hungarian Kingdom. For centuries that powerful kingdom had ruled large parts of central Europe, but in the early sixteenth century Hungary was overrun by the Ottoman Turks. It was also at that time that the Habsburgs laid their first claim to the Hungarian throne. When the Ottomans were finally driven out of the Danubian Basin at very end of the seventeenth century, the Habsburgs ruled Hungary as the country's titular kings, although they were obliged to permit a degree of self-rule, the extent of which was to vary according to political circumstances. It was not until 1867 that the Hungarian Kingdom finally acquired virtual self-governing status, and it is only from this date that the term Austro-Hungarian Empire can properly be used.

Galicia and its inhabitants belonged to the non-Hungarian part of the Austrian Empire. The non-Hungarian part did not really even have a name; it was simply a conglomerate of historical territories or provinces. They included Bohemia, Moravia, Silesia, Galicia, Upper and Lower Austria, Vorarlberg, Tyrol, Salzburg, Styria, Carniola, Gorizia-Gradisca, Trieste, Istria, and Dalmatia, and, for more than half of the nineteenth century, the Italian provinces of Lombardy and Venetia. For want of another name, the historical literature often refers to all these provinces either as Austria, that is, the Austrian half of the Habsburg Empire, or as Cis-Leithenia, that is, "lands on this [the Vienna] side of the Leitha River," which formed the border with Hungary.

Many of the provinces had their own assemblies, made up of representatives from three estates – the clergy, the magnates, and the gentry landowners – which together often struggled to preserve a degree of provincial autonomy in the face of an ever-growing bureaucracy and a central administration in the imperial capital of Vienna. At the head of that administration was the monarch, a member of the family of Habsburg, who was assisted by several imperial governing boards known as chancelleries. All appointees to the imperial chancelleries were made by the emperor, who in effect was the state's ultimate authority. The Hungarian Kingdom had its own parliament elected by the Hungarian nobility, although its authority over the kingdom's affairs varied according to the political fortunes of that country vis-à-vis the Habsburg central administration in Vienna.

Despite its diversity, the Habsburg Empire was not simply a motley conglomerate of territories and peoples held together by military force or political inertia. There were, indeed, several factors which contributed to a sense of unity within the empire. Moreover, the number and reach of the integrating factors increased in the course of the nineteenth century. Some of them obtained until – and even after – the demise of the empire in 1918. Among them was the bureaucracy, which became an efficient and fair, if sometimes overbearing, instrument of Austrian rule. Others were the legal system, the army (in which every male had to serve), and the schools, which provided universal and compulsory education at the elementary level. All these institutions promoted a sense of imperial Habsburg patriotism among the empire's inhabitants. German was the official language of the administration and upper levels of education, and it functioned as the common language, the lingua franca, of those elements of the population – administrators, intellectuals, tradespeople, even some peasants – who needed a means of communicating with fellow citizens of the empire.

Perhaps more pervasive were the tangible symbols of Habsburg imperial culture, which became entrenched in the psyches of the empire's inhabitants. Architecture was one such symbol. Even today there are sections in cities as widely scattered as Milan, Prague, Budapest, Sarajevo, L'viv, and Chernivtsi that resemble each other as well as the squares and buildings in the imperial capital Vienna of which they are copies. At the more popular level, the coffeehouse culture and Sunday strolls along the corso past parks with bandstands allowed for the waltzes of Johann Strauss, Jr, and songs from operettas by Strauss and the Hungarian-born Franz Lehár and Emerich Kálmán to become a kind of "national" music for the empire as a whole, their melodies probably as well known as was the local folk music to each of the respective nationalities. Finally, the Habsburg rulers themselves became symbols of unity and, in some cases, national heroes for several of the empire's peoples.

This was certainly true of the eighteenth-century rulers Maria Theresa and Joseph II. Even Franz Joseph, whose nearly seven decades of rule from 1848 to 1916 coincided with the height of nationalist passion among the empire's peoples, became for many of them a unifying imperial Austrian symbol. He was respected, even revered as a "father figure" who stood above the national and social conflicts of the late nineteenth century. The point is that despite its enormous heterogeneity, the Habsburgs succeeded in creating a sufficient number of unifying and integrative elements so that the Austrian Empire became an acceptable social and political framework for most if its inhabitants up to and even after the outbreak of World War I in 1914.

The demographic and administrative status of Galicia and Bukovina

Galicia and Bukovina with their Ukrainian inhabitants entered the Austrian Empire at a favorable time in its history. In 1699, the Habsburgs had finally driven the Ottomans out of territory that formerly had been under either Hungary or Austria. The threat from the "infidels" (the Turks had besieged Vienna as recently as 1683) had at last ended, and the Habsburgs could now turn to consolidating authority within their lands. To accomplish this, however, they needed to reform the antiquated social and administrative structure of the empire into a more functional structure. Reforms were carried out by two of Austria's most dynamic and talented rulers, the Empress Maria Theresa (reigned 1780–1790) and her son Joseph II (reigned 1780–1790). Since Joseph became co-regent in 1765, many of the Theresian reforms were actually implemented by him. For this reason, the whole reform period is often known simply as the Josephine era.

Both mother and son were enlightened rulers convinced that the good of society as a whole depended on the proper functioning of the state. A successful state in turn depended on the ability of each inhabitant to serve. Thus, each person had a role to play in the system, and it is in this context that Emperor Joseph II described his own role as that of the first servant of the state. Since Galicia became part of the Habsburg Empire during the last years of Maria Theresa's reign, the enlightened Austrian theory of government was applied to this new territory.

In 1772, the Austrian province of Galicia comprised 31,700 square miles (82,000 square kilometers). According to the census of 1786, the province had 2.7 million inhabitants, divided more or less evenly along the San River between Poles in the western half of the province (the former Cracow and Sandomierz palatinates) and Ukrainians in the eastern half (the former Rus' and Belz palatinates). By 1849, the population had more than doubled, to 4.9 million inhabitants, with a slightly higher number of Ukrainians than Poles (see table 31.1). The vast majority of Ukrainians lived in eastern Galicia, where of a population of 3.1 million they made up 71 percent of the inhabitants. The number of inhabitants increased in Bukovina dramatically, from 75,000 in 1775 to 380,000 in 1846. Bukovina's population was more or less evenly divided between Ukrainians in the northern half of the province and Romanians in the southern half.

TABLE 31.1
Nationality composition of Galicia, 1849[1]

	Number	Percentage
Ukrainians	2,303,000	46.8
Poles	2,258,000	45.9
Jews	328,000	6.7
Germans	27,000	0.6
Others	3,000	0.0
TOTAL	4,919,000	100.0

In terms of religious identity, the Poles were Roman Catholic and the Ukrainians Uniate, or Greek Catholic, although there was also a small minority known as *Latynnyky*, who were either Ukrainian converts to Roman Catholicism or ukrainianized Poles who retained their Roman Catholic faith. In Bukovina, the Ukrainians were for the most part Orthodox, although there was a small minority of Greek Catholics. The social structure of Galicia in the 1770s was overwhelmingly agrarian: 87.2 percent of the population lived in 6,300 rural villages. Nearly three-quarters (72 percent) of the population were serfs, of whom 78 percent were owned by the Polish *szlachta* and 22 percent worked on former Polish crown lands. The Polish *szlachta* numbered 95,000, or 3.4 percent of the total population.

Since Galicia was acquired during an era of reform in the Habsburg Empire, the former Polish administrative system was entirely dismantled. After 1786, Austrian laws replaced Polish ones. The local dietines (*sejmiki*) in Poland's former palatinates were abolished; and while elected town councils survived for a while, they too were later replaced by administrators and bureaucrats appointed from Vienna. Following the pattern in other provinces of the Austrian half of the empire, a body called the Assembly of Estates was set up in L'viv (in German, Lemberg), the province's administrative capital. The Assembly was composed of clergy, magnates, and gentry, and though it could send petitions to the emperor, it had no real power of its own.

All political power was effectively in the hands of the emperor's appointee, a governor (German: *gubernator*; Polish: *naczelnik*) who ruled with his administration from L'viv. Within a decade of the Austrian acquisition of Galicia, the whole province was divided into nineteen regions (German: *Kreise*), one of which after 1787 became Bukovina. The free city-state of Cracow remained outside this structure from its inception in 1815 until 1846, when it too was made an integral part of the province of Galicia.

The reforms initiated by the Habsburg rulers were intended to apply throughout the empire and to affect all areas of life. Their objective was to transform the Austrian Empire into a rationally organized modern bureaucratized state. In 1775, most of the internal tariffs left over from medieval times were abolished (although the customs boundary with Hungary continued until 1851); between 1766 and 1788, criminal procedures were regulated and standardized, and torture was abolished; in 1781, an edict of toleration applicable to all religions was implemented, following the earlier governmental declaration that the three Catholic rites in Galicia (Roman, Greek, and Armenian) were of equal standing; in 1782, the entire imperial administration was centralized in Vienna for the Austrian lands and in Buda for Hungary; also in 1782, "unnecessary" monastic estates were secularized; in 1783, a church fund was established making parish priests state employees; and in 1784, German was made the sole official language of the empire. Other reforms had a particularly favorable effect on Galicia. In 1777, Maria Theresa restructured the educational system with the intention of producing worthy and responsible citizen-servants of the state. To ensure that this goal was achieved, Joseph II made elementary education compulsory, with instruction in the vernacular language of the local regions.

Galicia's nobility and peasantry were also deeply affected by the Josephine reforms. The former dominant position of the Polish *szlachta* came to an end. Whereas the magnates and gentry who made up the *szlachta* had always been economically and thus politically differentiated, in legal practice both groups had been equal under the old Polish system. The Austrian government destroyed the "egalitarian" character of the *szlachta* by splitting it into two estates, the magnates and the gentry. Moreover, the tax-exempt status of both groups was removed, and they were made subject to Austrian law. No longer did the nobility have the kind of personal and property guarantees they enjoyed in the old Polish-Lithuanian Commonwealth, where they often were able to circumvent the law.

The peasant-serfs in particular were affected by the Austrian reforms. Serf obligations became strictly defined under Maria Theresa, with the result that their dependence on the arbitrary will of the noble landlord was lessened. Joseph II went even further, and in 1781 he abolished many of the more restrictive aspects of serfdom. The peasant was now free to marry without the lord's permission, to change his or her occupation, and to leave the land provided a replacement could be found. Moreover, he or she had the right to justice in courts which were no longer in the hands of the Polish landlords. The land was divided into dominical, or *demesne*, estates, owned by the lord, and rustical lands, held by the peasant. In theory, Austrian law prevented landlords from adding rustical lands to their estates, except through an otherwise complicated administrative process. In practice, however, the landlords could and did add such land easily enough during the periodic land surveys. That the transfers did not take place to any significant degree was owing to economic self-interest. In the absence of wage labor, it was more profitable for landlords that the peasantry hold land. By 1844, 70 percent of the arable land, 69 percent of the meadows, and 64 percent of the pastures were classified as rustical lands, although 98 percent of the forests belonged to landlords' dominical estates.

At the same time, these otherwise positive reforms subjected the peasants to heavier taxes and to long-term compulsory military service. Because the landlords were expected to make provision for collecting taxes and for supplying military recruits, the peasants soon viewed them as an evil force juxtaposed to the good and understanding emperor in Vienna. Joseph II was particularly lionized after his death. Consequently, when the new emperor, the otherwise competent Leopold II (reigned 1790–1792), was forced to reinstate certain aspects of serfdom (although according to the lord-peasant regulations introduced by Maria Theresa), Joseph II became for Galician-Ukrainian peasants the symbolic prototype of the good emperor, whose efforts on behalf of the downtrodden were to be remembered in prayers and folklore for decades to come. Although the abolition of serfdom was reversed, most of the Theresian and Josephine reforms, especially in the realms of the legal system, education, religious tolerance, and equality among the various Catholic rites, remained in force. They were to have an especially positive effect on Ukrainian life in the Austrian Empire.

The economic status of Galicia before 1848

Owing to the general policies of the empire, the economic situation in Galicia did not improve significantly during the first seventy-five years of Austrian rule. Like other European powers of the time, Austria favored the policy of mercantilism, in which the state takes an active role in directing the economy. The Austrian Empire adopted a particular brand of mercantilism, however, based on the concept of autarchy. This meant that Austria was less interested in achieving a favorable balance of trade than in creating an internally self-sufficient economic system based on regional specialization and complementarity. Essentially, the empire's eastern lands were to supply agricultural products and, wherever possible, raw materials for its western lands, especially the highly industrialized provinces of Bohemia, Moravia, and Lower Austria. Since Galicia and Hungary were in the eastern, agricultural zone, industrialization in these regions was not encouraged. This was because manufactured goods produced there might compete with those from the western portion of the empire, which needed to distribute its goods in the Hungarian and Galician markets in order to survive. Although in theory the system was reasonable, in practice Galicia, like Hungary, became an internal colony of Austria's western provinces. Moreover, the maintenance of serfdom and, once again, the control of the agricultural sector by tradition-minded Polish landlords worked against any modernization or increase in productivity. At the same time, the average size of peasant land allotments continued to decline, and the number of peasants holding the smallest plots of land increased dramatically. For instance, between 1818 and circa 1853, the number of peasants holding less than 2.7 acres (1.1 hectares) of land increased by 114 percent, and the number of those holding 2.7 to 6.9 acres (1.1 to 2.8 hectares) increased by 62 percent. These two smallest land units represented 35 percent of all holdings in 1819 and 44 percent in 1847–1859.

In short, the economy of Galicia did not improve and the peasant masses remained at a mere subsistence level. The industrial sector remained small and was actively discouraged from expanding. For example, at the end of the eighteenth century there were only 40 iron works, 26 textile mills, 26 glass works, 8 sugar refineries, and 18 printing shops throughout all of Galicia, and most of these were in the western, or Polish, half of the province. The eastern, or Ukrainian, half had only a few paper mills and several breweries and distilleries. Looked at in another way, while Galicia (together with Bukovina) had 20 percent of the empire's population, only 5.5 percent of its inhabitants were engaged in some kind of industrial activity.

Other peoples in eastern Galicia

In Galicia east of the San River, the Ukrainians comprised a 71 percent majority of the population. The second-largest nationality were the Poles, who in 1849 numbered 635,000, or 20.4 percent of the inhabitants in eastern Galicia. It was not their number, however, but rather their political and social influence that distinguished the Poles wherever they lived in Galicia. The province's leading social strata, the noble magnates and gentry, were exclusively Poles or descendants of Rus' gentry who had been polonized centuries ago. Although during the Josephine reform era the Austrian government tried to limit the political and administrative influence of the Polish nobles, their economic and social influence remained all-pervasive as long as serfdom existed. Then, with the return to a conservative trend in Austrian politics after 1815, Vienna more and more depended upon the Polish gentry, especially the magnates, to run the affairs of the province. Besides the magnates and gentry, there were a large number of Polish peasants who had been settled in eastern Galicia during the previous several centuries by their landlords, and a small group of Roman Catholic clergy, who served the religious needs of the Polish nobles and peasants.

Despite their status as a numerical "minority" in eastern Galicia, it is inappropriate to refer to the Poles as a minority. Although their situation initially changed during the reform era that coincided with the early decades of Austrian rule in Galicia, it was not long before the Polish magnates and gentry were restored to the same leading roles as when the province was still part of the Polish-Lithuanian Commonwealth. By the same token, the magnates and gentry equated their social status with the very meaning of Polish nationality. Accordingly, only a noble could be a Pole, and it was irrelevant for them whether the peasant masses among whom they lived were ethnically Polish or Ukrainian. As for the territory of Galicia, it was the land that Polish nobles and their ancestors had inhabited for centuries and, as such, an inalienable part of the Polish cultural patrimony, regardless of what state ruled it.

As in Dnieper Ukraine, the Jews were an important element in Galicia. They are known to have inhabited the cities of L'viv and Halych as early as during the thirteenth-century Kingdom of Galicia-Volhynia. It was with the beginning of Polish rule in the second half of the fourteenth century, however, that Jews came in larger numbers as part of the arenda economic system that prevailed in all parts of Polish-controlled Ukraine. By the mid-1770s, just after Galicia had become part of the Austrian Empire, Jews comprised 3.1 percent of the province's entire population, but 8.7 percent of the inhabitants in the eastern half of the province. Under Austrian rule, their numbers continued to increase: from 144,000 in 1776 to 328,000 in 1849. Three-quarters of Galicia's Jews lived in the eastern half of the province, and about 60 percent in small towns and cities.

Seven towns – Brody, Belz, Buchach, Rohatyn, Peremyshliany, Deliatyn, and Sokal' – were almost entirely Jewish. In several cities – L'viv, Zhovkva, Drohobych, Stanyslaviv, Ternopil', and Kolomyia – Jews accounted for one-third or more of the inhabitants. The following percentages, which are from 1900, reflect Jewish occupational patterns throughout the nineteenth century: 63 percent engaged in industry and commerce, 14 percent in agriculture, and 5 percent in civil service and the liberal professions.

Like the other peoples of Galicia, the Jews were deeply affected by the Josephine reforms. Their traditional system of local self-government, known in Poland as the Council of Lands, was abolished by the Austrian government, which viewed it as a relic of the medieval past. Initially, the Austrians set up their own form of internal Jewish autonomy (a system of congregational districts presided over by a general directorate headed by the community's chief rabbi), but even this seemed to clash with Joseph II's goals of administrative standardization. Consequently, in 1785 it was abolished together with rabbinical civil law, which had previously governed the community. From Vienna's point of view, Jews were to be given full equality according to the edict of religious toleration. This also meant that while they would not be singled out for discrimination, they would also have the same responsibilities as other citizens. They would have to pay the same taxes, serve in the army, and use German, not Yiddish, as a medium of secular culture. After Joseph's death, when many of his reforms were undone, some new restrictions were placed on Jews which affected their freedom of movement and ability to serve in certain offices and professions. In short, the status of the Jews in Galicia fluctuated with the internal political fortunes of the Habsburg Empire.

Joseph's reforms also had a profound impact on Jewish culture in Galicia. The previous dominance of the rabbis and the traditionalist way of life as set down in the Talmud and rabbinical law came to an end. Although traditional rabbinic talmudism continued to exist, Galician Jewish culture now came to be dominated by two other trends – the Haskalah and Hasidism.

The Haskalah, or enlightenment movement, originated in Germany in the 1760s and soon afterward entered Galicia. Its goals were to abolish the inward-looking attitudes of the Jewish communities, traditional dress, talmudic education, and the "bastardized dialect" Yiddish. In a sense, the Haskalah was a complement to the Josephine efforts at assimilation. When Vienna's policies in that direction finally ended in 1806 (the year in which the 104 German-language schools set up specifically for Jews in 1787 were closed), the Haskalah carried on the enlightenment by establishing its own modern secular educational system and its own reformed Jewish synagogues, called temples. The models in education were created by Josef Perl in his German-language Jewish secondary schools (*gymnasia*) in Brody and Ternopil'.

Despite the advances made by the Haskalah, it was the Hasidic movement that was to have the greatest impact on nineteenth-century Galician Jewry. Hasidism had originated in Dnieper Ukraine, in the neighboring province of Podolia, during the second half of the eighteenth century. The Hasidim were noted for their emphasis, in opposition to that of the learned rabbinical tradition, on the emotional aspect of religious experience. This was expressed through mass enthusiasm, group cohesion, and leadership under a charismatic *tsadik* (righteous one) or *rebbe* (rabbi, head of the community). The *tsadik/rebbe* attracted around his person devoted followers and created a dynastic court whose authoritative mantle was passed on and maintained by his sons or close relatives. Galicia, together with Bukovina, was home to several influential Hasidic dynasties – the Rokeahs of the Belz dynasty, the Halberstams of the Sandz (Nowy Sącz) dynasty, the Ruzhin dynasty based in Sadagora, and the Mendels of the Kosov-Vizhnits (Kosiv-Vyzhnytsia) dynasty – all of which flourished in the nineteenth and twentieth centuries and whose followers are still found in Israel, western Europe, and North America. Because of its mystical and "superstitious" nature, Hasidism was castigated both by traditionalist rabbis (*misnagdim*, or opponents) and by Austria's enlightened reformist Jews and supporters of the Haskalah. Nonetheless, Hasidism enjoyed popular appeal among the Jewish masses, and by the 1830s it had become the dominant way of Jewish life in Galicia.

Among the numerically smaller groups were the Germans. They began to immigrate to Galicia in the late thirteenth and the fourteenth centuries as priests, soldiers, artisans, and traders. By the sixteenth century, most of these settlers from late medieval times had assimilated into Polish culture. A second wave of German colonists arrived in Galicia after it became part of the Austrian Empire. Anxious to improve the economic status of its new province and to secure Germanic influence, the Habsburg government issued two decrees (1774 and 1781) according to which the new colonists would receive land allotments, exemption from military service, and tax-free status for a period of six years. Between 1781 and 1785, 13,000 Germans, mostly from the Palatinate and other southwestern German states, took advantage of the Austrian offer and settled in Galicia. They were followed by 2,000 more Germans from the Sudetenland, that is, Austria's northwestern Bohemia, who came during the first half of the nineteenth century.

The Germans in Galicia were split between Evangelical Lutherans and Catholics. Their numbers rose steadily, from an estimated 27,000 in 1849 to 65,000 in 1910. About two-thirds resided in eastern Galicia, in a belt of small villages stretching from Zhovkva in the north, on past L'viv, to Drohobych and Stryi in the south. The Galician Germans kept to their agricultural pursuits without much interaction with the surrounding Slavs, whether Ukrainians or Poles. Isolated for the most part in rural areas, Galicia's Germans produced only a few individuals who engaged in cultural pursuits. They included the L'viv-born writers Thaddäus Rittner and the better-known Leopold von Sacher-Masoch. The latter's numerous short stories, with their titillating descriptions of sexual perversion drawn from the author's observations in the Galician countryside, became very popular in the rest of Europe through French translations, and they provided the "new science" of psychoanalysis with vivid examples of human behavior that subsequently gave rise to the term *masochism*.

Finally, there was a small Armenian community. Since the Middle Ages, the Armenians had played an important role as artisans and tradespeople, especially in L'viv. The community reached its height during the seventeenth century and then declined in size. By the first half of the nineteenth century, there were only 3,000 Armenians left. In the late seventeenth century, the Christian Armenians of Austria-Hungary entered into union with Rome, and L'viv became the seat of an Armenian-rite Catholic archbishopric with jurisdiction throughout the Habsburg Empire. While the Armenian-rite Catholic Church continued to function in L'viv with its own bishop and cathedral church, by the nineteenth century the clergy and its small flock had become completely polonized.

The Ukrainian National Awakening in the Austrian Empire before 1848

The years between 1772, when Austria first acquired Galicia, and 1848, the outbreak of revolution, were marked by a national awakening among Ukrainians in the Habsburg Empire. During these seventy-five-odd years, the Ukrainians essentially went through the first, heritage-gathering stage of an intelligentsia-inspired national movement. They also embarked upon some aspects of the second, organizational stage, in particular because of help and encouragement offered by the Austrian imperial government.

As a result of reports sent back by the very first Habsburg officials who entered the new province in 1772, it became clear to Vienna that the East Slavic population living in the eastern half of Galicia was distinct in religion and language from the Poles as well as from the Russians. The imperial government eventually was convinced of the distinctiveness of Galicia's East Slavs, even though they, like the Russians, used Church Slavonic publications in their religious and cultural affairs, and in their own language called themselves *rusyny* (Rusyns), or *rus'kyi* (Rusyn), which to outsiders sounded very much like Russian. The Austrian government therefore did not designate them as *Russen*, the German equivalent of Russian, but as *Ruthenen* (English: Ruthenian). In fact, *Ruthenen* was the only official designation given to Ukrainians living in the Habsburg Empire until its demise in 1918. (The Polish term was *Rusini*, which derived from the Ukrainian *rusyny*.) Determining who the Ruthenians *were not* did little, however, to answer who they *were*. It was the search for a positive identity and the need to express this identity through a literary language that would preoccupy the local intelligentsia during the national awakening before 1848. At the risk of being anachronistic, we will nonetheless use throughout the rest of this discussion the more modern ethnonym *Ukrainian* when referring to people who at the time were designated Ruthenian.

The Austrian government and the Ukrainian national awakening

The Ukrainian movement in Galicia received its first stimulus largely as a result of the Theresian and Josephine reforms in religion and education. Since Ukrainians were almost all members of the Uniate, or Greek Catholic, Church, any change in that organization's status would directly affect the group as a whole. Joseph II, who was still co-regent when Galicia was acquired, felt that all the rites within the Catholic Church, which in Galicia meant the Latin, Greek, and Armenian rites, should be equal, or, as he said, be as "three daughters of one mother" (*drei Töchter einer Mutter*). This attitude represented a marked improvement for the Uniate Church. Although under the Polish-Lithuanian Commonwealth that church had been de jure equal to the Roman Catholic Church, in practice it was regarded as a poor cousin offering limited financial and social possibilities. Under Habsburg rule, the economic disparity between the Uniates and Roman Catholics was somewhat reduced, since the government secularized much of the church's property and made all religions equally dependent upon the state. In 1774, as a mark of its new status, the Eastern-rite hierarchy requested that the term *Uniate* be replaced, since they felt it was derogatory. From that year, the church in the Austrian Empire was officially designated as Greek Catholic.

The Greek Catholic eparchies that Austria acquired between 1772 and 1795 (L'viv, Przemyśl, and part of Chełm) were under the authority of the Uniate metropolitan of Kiev. The Uniate metropolitan had not resided in his titular city, however, since it had become part of Muscovy in the late seventeenth century. This meant that his jurisdiction was effectively limited to territories within the Polish-Lithuanian Commonwealth. After 1793–1795, when the Russian Empire acquired from Poland-Lithuania all Greek Catholic eparchies not in Habsburg territory, relations between the two "halves" of the church, now split between Austria and Russia, became difficult. While struggling for his own survival (the Russian government abolished the Uniate Church between 1796 and 1806), the metropolitan of Kiev viewed as a threat to his authority Austria's plans to restore an independent Greek Catholic metropolitanate of Galicia, the Metropolitanate of Halych and Rus', which had ceased to exist in the early fifteenth century. In the end, the Vatican approved Austria's request, and in 1808 the Greek Catholics of Galicia received their own metropolitan province, with a seat in L'viv and division into two eparchies, based in L'viv and Przemyśl.

Austrian policy was particularly important for education. The several educational reforms not only improved the status of the Greek Catholic clergy, but also had a effect on the peasant masses. Maria Theresa's decree of 1777 provided for the establishment of three types of schools at the elementary level. In Galicia these included (1) a normal school in L'viv for teachers' training; (2) district schools in larger cities; and (3) triviums, or basic elementary schools, in towns and villages. Then, in 1781, Joseph II supplemented the reform by making elementary education compulsory. While German was used in the district schools, Ruthenian, or, more precisely, Slaveno-Rusyn, was used in the more widespread village schools. At this time, the first elementary textbooks were published in Slaveno-Rusyn, which in essence was the liturgical language Church Slavonic mixed with the local Ukrainian vernacular.

At the more advanced level, special provisions were made to train prospective Greek Catholic clergy. In 1775, the Austrian government opened a Greek Catholic seminary in Vienna attached to the parish church of St Barbara and hence known by its Latin name, the Barbareum. Forty-six places were made available for Greek Catholic seminarians from both Galicia and Hungary. The Barbareum was important not only for the theological training it provided, but also because it exposed young Ukrainians to the secular intellectual world of Vienna and to other more culturally advanced Slavic peoples like the Czechs, Slovenes, and Serbs, who came to the imperial capital to study and teach. Although the Barbareum was closed nine years later, in 1784, to be replaced by a general seminary in L'viv, it had a great impact in promoting an awareness of Slavic culture among its students, many of whom were subsequently to become leading members of the Greek Catholic hierarchy in Galicia and in Hungary. In 1803, some years after the Barbareum was closed, a *konvikt*, or student dormitory, was opened in its place to house Greek Catholic seminarians studying in Vienna. For the next ninety years, until 1893, the *konvikt* served the same sociocultural function as had the Barbareum – namely, that of a meeting place for Greek Catholic intellectuals from Galicia and Hungary and for other Slavs throughout the empire.

Another innovation instituted by the Austrians was the Studium Ruthenum, opened in 1787 in L'viv and attached to the newly founded university there. The Studium Ruthenum was intended to train Greek Catholic seminarians who did not know Latin. In a sense, the Studium Ruthenum became the first Ukrainian school at the university level. All courses were taught in Slaveno-Rusyn, and several texts were translated into that language. Nevertheless, after two decades, the Studium Ruthenum was gradually phased out, and in 1809 it was closed. As with the Barbareum, its functions were taken over by the Greek Catholic branch of the general seminary in L'viv.

The closing of the Barbareum in Vienna and the Studium Ruthenum in L'viv also reflected a change in Austrian policy. The fervor of the Josephine reform era had really ended with his death in 1790. His successors, Leopold II (reigned 1790–1792) and, especially, Franz I (reigned 1793–1835), were less inclined to train from scratch a new stratum of imperial functionaries than to cooperate with the existing elite in Galicia, which continued to be the Polish magnates and gentry and the Polish-controlled Roman Catholic Church. As an expression of the new attitude on the part of the Austrian government, compulsory elementary education was abolished in 1812. Those schools that remained came under the control of the Roman Catholic Church, which by 1817 had succeeded in having Polish taught in all village elementary schools (triviums) throughout Galicia. This measure gave rise to protests on the part of the Greek Catholic hierarchy, which prompted the imperial government to issue a decree in 1818 that made Ruthenian (Slaveno-Rusyn) the language of instruction in Greek Catholic schools. By 1843, there were 2,132 lower-level schools in eastern Galicia, 938 of which used Ruthenian, Polish, and German – 921 solely Ruthenian, 190 Polish, and 81 German. In the five secondary schools (*gymnasia*), German and Latin, and later German and Polish, were used; at L'viv University, only German was used.

The point to remember about the educational system in Galicia during the first half of the nineteenth century is that Ukrainian, or the antiquated book language called Slaveno-Rusyn, was taught at the elementary level in schools under Greek

Catholic supervision, while at the secondary level the only language used besides the official and thereby somewhat neutral German was Polish. Moreover, in the absence of the Studium Ruthenum and in the context of the actual social superiority of the Polish nobility and Roman Catholic Church, the Polish language continued to have greater prestige. The practical result was that many young Greek Catholic seminarians, the only potential Ukrainian leaders, fell increasingly under the sway of Polish culture.

There were some attempts to reverse this polonophile trend, but they no longer came from the Austrian government. Instead, the initiative came from a small number of intellectual leaders, mostly clergy. It is with their activities that the heritage-gathering stage of the intelligentsia-inspired variety of nationalism was to begin among Ukrainians in eastern Galicia.

The heritage-gathering stage in Galicia

The first center of the heritage-gathering stage of the Ukrainian national movement was Przemyśl (in Ukrainian, Peremyshl'), in particular among members of the consistory of the local Greek Catholic eparchy led by Bishops Mykhailo Levyts'kyi (reigned 1816–1858) and Ivan Snihurs'kyi (reigned 1817–1847) and including the priests Ivan Mohyl'nyts'kyi, Iosyf Levyts'kyi, Iosyf Lozyns'kyi, and Antin Dobrians'kyi. As early as 1816, this group of clerics attempted to establish in Przemyśl a society for organizing and promoting Ukrainian schools, but the effort never got off the ground. That same year, however, the Greek Catholic consistory did establish an institute for the publication of elementary textbooks, and a series of these were published in Slaveno-Rusyn.

Works devoted to local history also began to appear. It is interesting to note that the earliest of these came from the pen not of a Galician Ukrainian, but of an Austrian official, Johann Christian von Engel, who at the end of the eighteenth century published in German a two-volume history of the Galician-Volhynian Kingdom (1792–93). It was later republished (1796) as part of a multivolume history of the world undertaken in the spirit of the Enlightenment and universalism as propounded in Germany at the time. Engel presented Galicia as a part of the Hungarian patrimony, which, he argued, had been occupied for several centuries by Poland before being rightfully returned to Hungary (this, of course, was the official Habsburg imperial view). Despite its ideological bent, Engel's history had a positive effect in raising pride on the part of the Ukrainians in Galicia with respect to their own past.

The first serious studies by a Galician-Ukrainian historian were by Denys Zubryts'kyi, one of a few non-clerical intellectual leaders. He published several works on local history, including a general survey of the Rus' people (1836) and a history of the city of L'viv (1844). All his works appeared in either Polish or German, with some later ones in Russian as well. This was because Zubryts'kyi looked down on the speech of Galicia's Ukrainians, which he considered the "language of cowherds." Such views were partly the result of his correspondence with Russian scholars, especially Mikhail D. Pogodin, who was a proponent of the idea that there existed one Russian people with three branches – the Great Russian, the Belorussian, and the Little Russian. Zubryts'kyi's pro-Russian, or russophile, views were also encouraged by his contact with Dnieper-Ukrainian scholars. It was in a letter to Zubryts'kyi that in 1840 the renowned Dnieper-Ukrainian ethnographer and first rector of Kiev's St Vladimir University, Mykhailo Maksymovych, made the statement that while there could be individual Little Russian dialectal writers, a Little Russian literature would never really come into being (see chapter 29).

Interaction with other Slavic leaders, whether in the Russian Empire or in the Austrian Empire, was an important feature of the Galician-Ukrainian national awakening. For instance, it was Polish scholars like Wacław Zaleski (Wacław z Oleska) and Żegota Pauli who published some of the first collections of Galician-Ukrainian folk songs. The impact of Czech and Slovak authors – Josef Dobrovský, Karel Zap, Jan Kollár, Pavel Šafárik – as well as the Slovenian Jernej Kopitar was no less important. The Czechs in general provided an inspiring model for a Slavic cultural revival, and it was their leading linguist and the spiritual father of Pan-Slavism, Josef Dobrovský, together with the Slovenian Kopitar (both of whom taught and worked in Vienna), who had a particularly strong influence on how Galician Ukrainians viewed the problem of language.

It was language more than history, ethnography, or literature that preoccupied activists in the Galician-Ukrainian national movement before 1848. In a sense, the language question had been with the Galician Ukrainians from the very outset, having arisen as one of the practical implications of the Theresian and Josephine reforms. These reforms called for compulsory education at the elementary level in the vernacular, and they described the Galician-Ukrainian vernacular as *ruthenisch*, or Ruthenian. The problem immediately arose as to what Ruthenian was. According to the local intelligentsia, Ruthenian was the Galician-Ukrainian variant of Church Slavonic, known at the time as Slaveno-Rusyn. Because it was the language used in the Greek Catholic Church and in old books and manuscripts, it had dignity and was therefore acceptable. Accordingly, it was used as the language of instruction in the Barbareum, in the Studium Ruthenum, and in elementary schools.

Then came Romanticism, with its interest in national cultures and local languages. With the publication of Galician-Ukrainian folk songs, the writings of Dobrovský and Kopitar, and the example of other Slavic peoples, it became clear (if it had not been so before) that the Slaveno-Rusyn book language was far from any spoken Galician-Ukrainian vernacular. Moreover, Slaveno-Rusyn proved ill suited to and in most cases incapable of expressing modern concepts and secular ideas. These seemingly innocuous linguistic concerns gave rise to questions of national identity, with the result that before long the language question took on important political ramifications.

One part of the debate centered on whether the Galician-Ukrainian vernacular was at all suitable for publications. Some leaders felt that the vernacular lacked the necessary dignity and prestige, qualities that were the strengths of Slaveno-Rusyn. But if the antiquated Church Slavonic-based Slaveno-Rusyn language proved insufficient for modern discourse, then perhaps some other book language, Russian or even Polish, should be adopted instead. Among those who supported use of a ver-nacular-based language there was yet another matter for debate. The vernacular-ists were displeased with Slaveno-Rusyn not only because it was essentially Church Slavonic, that is, a non-living liturgical language, but also because it was written in the Church Slavonic alphabet (*kyrylytsia*). More appropriate would be the modern Cyrillic civil script, the so-called *grazhdanka*. There were even some vernacular-ists who proposed abandoning the Cyrillic alphabet altogether and instead adopt-ing the Roman, or Latin, alphabet based on Polish orthography. Not surprisingly, proponents of the latter option were accused of favoring national assimilation to the Poles, although such accusations were not entirely fair. Each of the linguistic camps, whether proponents of Slaveno-Rusyn, vernacular in the Latin alphabet, or vernacular in the Cyrillic civil script, composed their own grammars.

It was during the course of the alphabet controversy that the best-known Gali-cian-Ukrainian leader from this period, Markiian Shashkevych, first came to public attention. In a polemical tract published in 1836 (*Azbuka i abecadło*), Shashkevych rejected the use of the Latin alphabet, arguing that it was unsuited to the language of Galician Ukrainians. Efforts continued to be undertaken to introduce Latin let-ters, but all were ultimately unsuccessful.

Shashkevych was a student in the 1830s at the Greek Catholic branch of the general seminary in L'viv, and he and two of his colleagues, Iakiv Holovats'kyi and Ivan Vahylevych, formed a circle which came to be known as the Ruthenian Triad (*Rus'ka triitsia*). Imbued with a romantic love of their people and inspired by the example of other Slavs in the Habsburg Empire, the Triad collected folk songs and composed poetry in the Galician-Ukrainian vernacular.

The activity of the Ruthenian Triad was looked upon with suspicion, however, by both the local Greek Catholic hierarchy and the Austrian authorities, which were reacting to new conditions on the European continent. During the late eight-eenth century, Vienna had given support to its various nationalities, including the Ukrainians, but by the second decade of the nineteenth century its policies had begun to change. Europe's dominant powers – Russia, Prussia, and Austria – in the wake of the Napoleonic Wars had become greatly concerned with containing France and with maintaining the political status quo established by the Congress of Vienna in 1815. These three autocratic states, known as the Holy Alliance, were intent on controlling and eradicating wherever possible all revolutionary ideas, most of which were associated with democratic liberalism from France and roman-tic nationalism from Germany.

The leading representative of this conservative, even reactionary, trend was Aus-tria's influential foreign minister, Prince Clemens von Metternich. At his urging, censorship was made stricter, and the police were allowed to establish a widely spread spy network. The ruling elite in Vienna became suspicious of anything new, and it was especially anxious about Galicia, where Polish revolutionary activity, which had supported the abortive uprising against Russia in 1830–1831, was still ongoing. Consequently, by proposing linguistic change, in itself relatively harm-less, the Ruthenian Triad found themselves doing the wrong thing in the wrong place at the wrong time.

As a result, the Triad's most famous publication, *Rusalka dnistrovaia* (Nymph of the Dniester, 1837), could not be published in Galicia but only in the "other half" of the Austrian Empire, in Hungary's capital of Buda, where the censorship laws were more relaxed. Since the book was banned in Galicia, only a few copies reached Ukrainian readers there. To the present-day reader, there is certainly nothing startling in *Rusalka*, from either a literary or a political point of view. It contained local Ukrainian folk songs, some original literary works, and a few translations of Serbian and Czech songs. It was "revolutionary," however, in that it was the first publication to use vernacular Galician Ukrainian written in the modern civil script. This became the orthographic model subsequently adopted for the Ukrainian national movement in Galicia.

The products of Galician-Ukrainian cultural life in the decade following the appearance of *Rusalka dnistrovaia* were limited to individual publications. They included historical works by Denys Zubryts'kyi; several grammars, each proposing a different linguistic and orthographic orientation (Ivan Vahylevych, 1845; Iosyf Lozyns'kyi, 1846); and a two-volume anthology of new literature in the vernacular (*Vinok rusynam*, 1846–47). Also during the 1840s, the Ukrainian problem, both in its historical context and from a contemporary perspective, for the first time was brought to the attention of other Slavic peoples, by Vahylevych, Holovats'kyi, Zubryts'kyi, and Levyts'kyi, whose writings appeared in St Petersburg, Moscow, Warsaw, Prague, and Leipzig.

Bukovina and Transcarpathia before 1848

Ukrainians living in what was the southernmost part of Galicia, the formerly Ottoman-ruled area of Moldavia known as Bukovina, did not experience the first, or, for that matter, any, stage of the national awakening in the decades before 1848. Elementary education was under the supervision of the Roman Catholic diocese of L'viv, and the few dozen lower-level schools used German and/or Romanian as the language of instruction. The three upper-level schools – a gymnasium, a teachers' college (normal school), and a theological institute in the administrative center of Chernivtsi – provided instruction in German or Latin. Even after 1818, when as a result of pressure from the Greek Catholic bishop of L'viv some vernacular was to be used in elementary schools, the only texts acceptable for Austria's Orthodox Slavic population were written in Serbian.

The only unusual activity among Bukovina's Ukrainians was a peasant revolt led by the Hutsul mountaineer Lukiian Kobylytsia. The revolt of 1843, directed largely against Romanian landowners, spread to such a degree that Austrian troops were called in the following year to put down the disturbances.

Transcarpathia, the region south of Galicia on the other side of the Carpathian Mountains, unlike Bukovina saw the beginnings of a national awakening. The East Slavic inhabitants of Transcarpathia and what is today far northeastern Slovakia for centuries maintained a subsistence-level existence as shepherds and peasant-serfs in the mountain valleys of northeastern Hungary. Like the East Slavs in neighboring Galicia and Bukovina, they called themselves Rusyns or used the local name,

Rusnaks. By 1843, Transcarpathia's Rusyns numbered 470,000 and were distinct from other inhabitants of Hungary in their use of East Slavic dialects and their membership in the Greek Catholic Church.

It was a series of problems associated with the Greek Catholic Church that prompted the national awakening in Transcarpathia. Although the Uniate/Greek Catholic Church had been established in the region in 1646, its bishops remained jurisdictionally subordinate to the Hungarian Roman Catholic bishop of Eger. In the mid-eighteenth century, an active struggle for jurisdictional independence from the bishop of Eger was led by Transcarpathian hierarchs, especially Bishop Mykhailo Ol'shavs'kyi (reigned 1743–1767). The hierarchs were aided in their efforts by amateur historians, mostly priests, who sought in old chronicles and charters legal justification for the reestablishment of an independent eparchy based in Mukachevo. Their search resulted in the first published histories of Transcarpathia, all written in Latin, including a three-volume work (1799–1805) by Ioanykii Bazylovych.

As with the Galician awakening, Vienna had a decisive impact on Transcarpathian national developments. At the initiative of Empress Maria Theresa, a Greek Catholic eparchy was established in Mukachevo in 1771 (its seat was transferred to Uzhhorod in 1780), and elementary schools as well as a seminary were opened where instruction was given in Slaveno-Rusyn, that is, in more or less the same variety of Church Slavonic as the one used in Galicia at the time. Particularly instrumental in raising the cultural standards of the Transcarpathian clergy was Bishop Andrei Bachyns'kyi (reigned 1773–1809). Young seminarians were sent to the Barbareum in Vienna, and several other Transcarpathians (Mykhailo Shchavnyts'kyi, Petro Lodii) taught at the Studium Ruthenum in L'viv. In 1807, Bishop Bachyns'kyi tried to make his Transcarpathian eparchy part of Galicia's Greek Catholic Metropolitanate of Halych and Rus', which was restored the following year. His efforts were blocked, however, by the Hungarian government.

The Transcarpathian awakening was limited to the achievements of its Greek Catholic Church in the areas of jurisdictional independence and the education of some priests. In general, northeastern Hungary was a backward provincial area. For instance, Transcarpathia's largest "city," Uzhhorod, at the beginning of the nineteenth century had a mere 3,000 inhabitants. The limitations of an underdeveloped social and cultural environment, therefore, and not any pressure from the Hungarian government in the form of national assimilation (a policy known as magyarization, which was not to become a serious concern until the second half of the nineteenth century), prompted whatever local intellectual talent there was to seek careers abroad. Their primary goal was the Russian Empire, where in Dnieper Ukraine and Russia proper new universities and lycées were being established in the first decades of the nineteenth century. Before long, some of the leading positions in the Russian Empire's new educational institutions were held by Transcarpathians. Ivan S. Orlai headed the *gymnasium* in Nizhyn and, later, the Richelieu lycée in Odessa; Petro Lodii was a dean of L'viv University and, later, of St Petersburg University's faculty of law; and, perhaps the most distinguished of all Transcarpathian ex-patriots, Mykhailo Baludians'kyi, was appointed first rec-

tor of St Petersburg University and a leading adviser on legal reform to the tsarist government. In terms of the national movement, all these Transcarpathians
accepted the concept of the hierarchy of multiple loyalties; in other words, they
considered themselves Russians from Little Russia. Some, like Orlai, expressed
their russophile views in publications. These subsequently had an impact on their
Transcarpathian homeland, where the idea that the local East Slavic population
ostensibly belonged to a "common-Russian" nationality was implanted in the first
half of the nineteenth century.

Leaving aside the intellectual emigration, in Transcarpathia itself a few writers, among them the historian and grammarian Mykhailo I. Luchkai and the
philosopher and poet Vasyl' Dovhovych, continued to maintain an awareness of
the region's East Slavic cultural inheritance through their writings (only some of
which were published in their lifetimes) and through contact with Slavic leaders
abroad. Transcarpathia had no cultural organizations before 1848, however, and
its leaders had not yet developed a clear sense of their national identity.

While the Galician-Ukrainian and, to a certain extent, Transcarpathian national
movements got off to a promising start after 1772 with help from the Austrian government in the areas of education and church organization, by the first decades
of the nineteenth century these achievements had largely been undermined. In
Galicia, the new conservative political and social environment allowed the Polish
nobility to regain its former dominant position and encouraged a trend toward
assimilation to Polish culture and language among all educated individuals,
regardless of their national background. In Hungary, the provincial environment
of Transcarpathia hampered all kinds of cultural activity, whether or not they were
East Slavic in orientation, and prompted the region's intellectual elite to emigrate
abroad. In the absence of any real organizational framework, it was left to the
heritage-gathering intelligentsia to carry out its activity in the areas of historical
writing, ethnography, and language. In order for the national movement firmly to
get under way, however, it was necessary to await some more profound change in
the political and social environment. That change did come, with the revolution
of 1848.

33

The Revolution of 1848

The year 1848 has become enshrined as a landmark in modern European history. The reason is that simultaneously throughout much of the Continent revolutions broke out which were to have a profound effect on the future of the societies involved in the events. The year 1848 was particularly significant for central Europe, both for the Germanic lands and for the Slavic and Hungarian lands in the Prussian and Austrian empires. The causes of the 1848 revolutions – whether political, socioeconomic, or national – varied from place to place. In some places, like the Austrian Empire, all three kinds of cause were present, although the national question was to give rise to the greatest number of immediate and subsequent changes. For this reason, the 1848 revolution has come to be known, at least in central Europe, as the "Springtime of Nations."

Referring to the year 1848 as the Springtime of Nations has become a cliché, but clichés sometimes reflect truths, and in the case of Ukrainians in the Austrian Empire the cliché could not be truer. The year indeed witnessed the rebirth of all aspects of Ukrainian life in lands under the Habsburg sceptre. In that year alone, Ukrainians established their first political organization, their first newspaper, their first cultural organization, and their first military units in modern times. They also took part in their first elections. This is to say nothing of the fact that the vast majority of the group – over 95 percent of whom were peasants – were liberated from serfdom. In a sense, a social stratum which virtually coincided with the nationality as a whole was reborn. For the first time since the introduction of serfdom centuries before, peasants were treated as human beings. As such, they now had to be reckoned with in political, cultural, social, and economic life. Given all these factors, 1848 was indeed a springtime for Austria's Ukrainians.

The revolution in Austria

What had happened in the Austrian Empire to make it ripe for revolutionary activity? After 1815, Austria became a virtual police state concerned with maintaining the status quo both within its own borders and within Europe as a whole. The leading proponent of these objectives, Prince Metternich, had a powerful influence over Emperor Franz I (reigned 1792–1835) and, especially, his successor, the inept Emperor Ferdinand (reigned 1835–1848).

Ironically, Galicia proved a major trouble spot for the Austrian Empire in the first half of the nineteenth century. The western, Polish-inhabited regions, especially the autonomous republic of Cracow, continued to be a seedbed for Polish revolutionary activity aimed at reconstituting Polish statehood. In fact, the Cracow republic was seen by Polish patriots as a kind of Piedmont, that is, the territorial basis from which a restored independent Poland would eventually develop. Cracow, therefore, remained a center of revolutionary agitation even after the abortive 1830–1831 uprising against Russia.

By the 1830s, however, certain Polish leaders in Galicia as well as farther east in the Right Bank and other Russian-controlled areas felt that any future success on behalf of a restored Poland must depend upon the support of the peasantry. For its part, the Polish peasantry continued to view the Polish nobility with suspicion and was not about to join in revolution those whom they considered their exploiters. In fact, when several Polish gentry activists in Galicia proclaimed a national and social revolution in 1846, the Polish peasantry, not without the acquiescence of the Austrian government, turned on the gentry estate owners and massacred them. Austrian garrisons eventually put down the uprising, but not before the peasants had done the government's work and effectively eliminated this latest attempt at a Polish revolt. In retaliation, Vienna rescinded the autonomous status of Cracow, which henceforth became an integral part of the rest of Galicia. Thus, in 1846 the Polish peasantry unwittingly helped to preserve the social and political status quo in Austrian Galicia.

Two years later, in 1848, the disturbances proved too widespread for the Austrian government to control. The causes of the 1848 revolution, which began in Vienna in March, were many. They included news of the February revolution in Paris, which galvanized public opinion in Vienna; unrest in Austria's northern Italian provinces of Lombardy and Venetia; radical agitation in the Hungarian diet; preparations for elections to an all-German National Assembly in Frankfurt; and a prolonged economic crisis in Austria's cities. All these factors provided the background for the events leading to the week of 6 to 12 March, when in Vienna several members of the urban educated professional classes (lawyers, doctors, professors) and students began circulating petitions calling for the immediate introduction of civil liberties (freedom of the press, trial by jury, civil rights, academic freedom), emancipation of the peasants, and a constitutional representative government. The climax came on 13 March, when students and the liberal urban elite clashed with troops in front of the building of the diet of Lower Austria. Afraid of widespread urban revolution, the imperial government forced the resignation of Metternich, who had become the symbol of the bureaucratic police state. That same day, the government announced the end to press censorship and allowed for the formation of a national guard. Then, in April, it permitted the convocation of a constitutional assembly (*Reichstag*), although it limited the vote to property owners and thereby eliminated participation of the urban working class. Finally, in May the government announced the abolition of serfdom. Thus, within less than two months from 13 March, the Austrian imperial government initiated a series of reforms from above in the hope of counteracting revolution from below. The Habsburgs, however, did too little too late.

Not surprisingly, their greatest problem was with Hungary. The Hungarians had been whipped into a patriotic and anti-Austrian frenzy during the 1840s by their diet's fiery orator, Lajos Kossuth. Within three days after the 13 March events in Vienna, the Hungarians demanded the creation of a national diet to govern their kingdom's own affairs as well as a national army (*honvéd*) to provide its own defense. When Vienna refused to allow a separate army, the newly elected Hungarian diet formed one anyway, as well as a separate budget and currency. In response, Vienna dispatched a military force into Hungary, whose newly created national army, now under the leadership of Kossuth, authorized that the imperial "invaders" be resisted with force.

In October, with civil war in Hungary imminent, workers and troops in Vienna rebelled. Emperor Ferdinand had fled from the capital in May, and although the city was finally restored to order after the October rebellion, the weak Habsburg sovereign was convinced by his closest advisers to abdicate in favor of his eighteen-year-old nephew, Archduke Franz. The transfer of power took place on 2 December 1848. In deference to the liberal spirit of the times, the new sovereign added the name Joseph as a symbolic gesture to the enlightened liberalism of his eighteenth-century predecessor. It was as Franz Joseph that the young emperor was to rule Austria for the next sixty-eight years, until 1916, just two years before the complete demise of the Habsburg Empire.

The accession of a new monarch gave the Hungarians under Kossuth a legal excuse to continue on their independentist political course. According to tradition, each new Habsburg sovereign, after coronation in Vienna as emperor, had to travel to Hungary to be crowned king of that country. Since Franz Joseph was not crowned in Hungary – the coronation was not possible in the prevailing revolutionary circumstances – the Hungarians refused to recognize him as their sovereign. In the face of renewed Austrian military attacks, Kossuth retreated to the eastern city of Debrecen, where in April 1849 he declared Hungary an independent republic. Fierce fighting with the imperial army continued until the summer. Only after Franz Joseph called upon Tsar Nicholas I of Russia to help him, and after an imperial Russian army crossed the Carpathian Mountains to join in the Austrian campaign, were the Hungarian revolutionaries defeated, in August 1849. With the defeat of the Hungarians by the combined forces of Russia and Austria, the only major threat to the existence of the Austrian Empire was put to rest.

The revolution in Galicia and the Ukrainians

The revolution of 1848 had a lasting impact on the political, socioeconomic, and, especially, cultural life of Ukrainians in the Austrian Empire. The achievements by Ukrainians in these three areas were played out not only in Galicia, but also in the imperial capital of Vienna and in the provincial city of Prague. Throughout 1848, the Austrian government gave its support to the Ukrainians, both to their efforts to obtain recognition as a nationality and to their attempts to achieve political and cultural rights. In return, the Ukrainian leadership turned a blind eye to the political reaction and repressive measures that at the same time were being carried out by Habsburg authorities against certain other peoples in the empire. The inclination of the Austrian government to support Ukrainian demands was actually a heritage from 1846, when, following the abortive Polish revolution in Galicia, Vienna appointed the energetic and innovative Count Franz Stadion as governor of the province. In Vienna's view, the Polish gentry and intelligentsia were untrustworthy. Consequently, Governor Stadion was prepared and expected to use any element, whether the Polish peasants or the Ukrainian peasants – or, as will become evident, the Ukrainian intelligentsia – to counteract the Polish gentry. Some commentators consider this an application of the classic policy of divide and rule (*divide et impera*), a view which presumes – and incorrectly so – that the Polish gentry was united with the Polish or Ukrainian peasantry or with the Ukrainian intelligentsia. In fact, Stadion's policy was simply to form an alliance with whatever force would strengthen the interests of the Austrian state. In this sense, Austrian and Ukrainian interests coincided in 1848.

Accordingly, when news of the revolutionary events in Vienna reached Galicia in March 1848, and when in response the Poles immediately established the Polish National Council demanding extensive autonomy for what they considered a purely Polish land, Stadion urged Ukrainian leaders to formulate their own demands. The result was a Ukrainian petition addressed to the Austrian emperor dated 19 April, calling for recognition of their nationality and for the division of Galicia into Polish and Ukrainian parts, a proposal that had actually been put forward by Governor Stadion as early as 1847. Then, on 2 May 1848, under the leadership of L'viv's Greek Catholic auxiliary bishop, Hryhorii Iakhymovych (reigned 1841–1863), the first Ukrainian political organization was established, the Supreme Ruthenian Council (Holovna Rus'ka Rada). One week later, on 10 May, the Supreme Ruthenian Council issued a manifesto declaring that Ukrainians were a people distinct from both Poles and Russians, and that they were "part of a great Ruthenian people that speaks the same language and numbers 15 million, of whom 2.5 million live in Galicia."[1] The Supreme Council soon had thirty-four branches throughout eastern Galicia, and on 15 May it began publishing (with financial help from Governor Stadion) the first Ukrainian newspaper to appear anywhere, *Zoria halytska* (L'viv, 1848–57).

Polish leaders in Galicia were displeased with these developments, and almost immediately several polemical pamphlets appeared which argued (1) that the Ruthenians of Galicia were not a distinct nationality but rather Poles of the Greek Catholic faith, and (2) that Ukrainian was no more than a dialect of Polish. Also, to counteract the Supreme Ruthenian Council, another body known as the Ruthenian Council (Rus'kii Sobor) was set up on 23 May by polonized nobles of Ukrainian origin, who argued that they were the true representatives of Galicia's Ukrainian population. The Ruthenian Council issued its own newspaper, *Dnewnyk ruskij* (L'viv, 1848), written in Ukrainian (with issues in both a Cyrillic and a Polish-based Latin alphabet) and edited by Ivan Vahylevych, formerly one of the Ruthenian Triad, who by 1848 had become a

THE SUPREME RUTHENIAN COUNCIL

The first Ukrainian political organization, the Supreme Ruthenian Council (Holovna Rus'ka Rada), issued in L'viv on 10 May 1848 a manifesto addressed to the Ruthenian people (*rusyny*) that outlined its ideological beliefs and political goals.

Brothers!

You know that our Most Illustrious Austrian Emperor and King issued to all the peoples of his realm, including us Ruthenians in Galicia, a decree dated 25 March 1848 that contained a constitution. This means a fundamental legal statute that allows all of our people, through their duly elected representatives, to participate in the law-making process and thereby ensure guarantees for our freedom and well-being.

Among the freedoms given to us is the right of assembly in order to discuss the common social good and to inform our Most Illustrious Ruler of the needs of the people and our province. ...

We Galician Ruthenians are part of a great Ruthenian people [*narod*] that speaks the same language and numbers 15 million, of whom 2.5 million live in Galicia. At one time our people were independent and the equal of the most powerful peoples in Europe; we had our own literary language, our own laws, and our own rulers. ... As a result of an unfortunate turn of fate and various political misfortunes, our great people gradually declined, lost its independence, its rulers, and fell under foreign rule.

As a result of these misfortunes, many of our leading figures gradually gave up the Ruthenian rite of their fathers, and at the same time lost their Ruthenian language and left their people, even though the change of rite could not transform their nationality, since Ruthenian blood still flowed in their veins. ...

But since everything in life changes, and as spring replaces harsh winter, so too, brothers, has our unfortunate status been transformed because of the constitution. ...

Our first task will be to preserve our faith and to put our rite and the status of our church and priests on the same level as that of other rites.

[We must also] develop and enhance all aspects of our nationality by perfecting our language and introducing it into lower- and secondary-level schools; by publishing a periodical press; by maintaining contacts with our own writers and those of other Slavic peoples; by distributing good-quality and practical books in Ruthenian; and by emphasizing through whatever means that our language is equal to and should be introduced alongside others in public and governmental affairs.

We will protect our constitutional rights, determine the needs of our people, seek to improve our people's welfare through constitutional means, and continually defend our rights against any attacks or defamation. ...

And so, brothers, believe in us Ruthenians and know that only through such [constitutional] means can we become what we should become – an honorable, enlightened, and free people!!!

SOURCE: *Zoria halytska*, 15 May 1848, cited in Kost' Levyts'kyi, *Istoriia politychnoï dumky halyts'kykh ukraintsiv, 1848–1914*, Vol. I (L'viv 1926), pp. 21–24.

firm believer in the need for Polish-Ukrainian cooperation. Galicia's Governor Stadion was particularly disliked by Polish spokespersons, who argued that there would have been no problems if Stadion had not "invented the Ruthenians."

In the end, such Polish protestation was in vain. Because of the rapidly changing situation, Ukrainian leaders, albeit mostly clergy, were coopted into the political process. Moreover, the new circumstances forced them to justify their existence as a group somehow distinct from the previously dominant one – the Poles. In this way, the 1848 Springtime of Nations brought Ukrainians firmly into the political and national arena of Galicia and, as we shall see, into the Habsburg Empire as a whole.

Governor Stadion was also instrumental in arranging for an early announcement in Galicia of the imperial decision to end all labor obligations connected with serfdom. Although the imperial decree was not issued throughout the empire until 15 May, in an effort to undermine those Poles who hoped to make the abolition of serfdom their own political issue, Stadion announced the provisions of emancipation in Galicia on 22 April. All serf duties were abrogated, but the peasants were still expected to pay an indemnity to their landlords. Not surprisingly, this requirement was to provoke bitter resentment on their part. Nonetheless, by far the largest stratum of the Ukrainian population, the peasantry, had suddenly as a result of emancipation become a factor to be considered in political life. Indeed, the recently liberated Ukrainian peasants began to exercise their new role as early as June 1848, during elections to the first Austrian parliament.

The preliminary constitution decreed by the emperor on 25 April provided for a bicameral parliament (*Reichstag*) composed of a House of Lords appointed by the emperor and a House of Deputies elected by property owners. The Austrian parliament was to share legislative powers with the emperor and prepare a proposal for a new constitution. The elected chamber had 383 deputies, and although urban workers were excluded from the vote, the peasants, as landholders, were not. In fact, more than one-quarter of all deputies were peasants. Galicia (excluding Bukovina) was allotted 100 deputies, 25 of whom were Ukrainians, and of these, 15 were peasants, 8 were Greek Catholic clergy, and 2 were members of the so-called secular intelligentsia (including Governor Stadion). The Ukrainian parliamentary delegation from Galicia was therefore more or less representative of the actual social structure in the eastern half of the province.

Despite their limited or non-existent knowledge of German, the Ukrainian peasants participated in the debates. Not surprisingly, their primary concern was the question of indemnification for lands acquired as a result of the emancipation from serf duties. One of the most memorable of all speeches in Austria's first parliament was delivered on this very topic by the Galician-Ukrainian peasant deputy Ivan Kapushchak. In passionate if broken German, Kapushchak drew a clear distinction between the "good emperor," who had brought about the emancipation and the wicked designs of the policy makers surrounding him, who had willfully distorted his good intentions. After outlining how the peasants literally had been paying dues for the previous several centuries, Kapushchak argued that if anybody owed anything, it was the lords who owed indemnity to the peasants.

The other important issue before parliament was the question of a constitutional and administrative framework for the Austrian Empire. Some of the leading intellectuals of the time took an active part in drawing up the final proposal, including the Czechs František Palacký and František Rieger, the Pole Franciszek Smolka, and the Austro-Germans Franz Schuselka and Kajetan Mayer. Eventually, a compromise was reached between those who favored centralism (mostly Germans) and those who favored federalism (mostly Slavs).

In a sense, however, all the work of the parliament was in vain. After the urban uprising in October 1848, the legislative body moved from Vienna to the small Moravian town of Kroměříž. Because the German name of the town was Kremsier, the body is known in Austrian history as the Kremsier parliament. Regardless of its name, its fate was sealed following the reestablishment of imperial authority, at least outside Hungary, in early 1849. On 7 March, the Kremsier parliament was dissolved, its constitutional proposal scrapped, and in its stead a new constitution (written by Galicia's Governor Stadion) was decreed from above by the imperial government – the so-called octroy constitution of 4 March 1849. As for the problem of peasant indemnification to their landlords, some compensation could be expected, but the actual amount and terms would have to await the passage of future laws. In any case, the peasant delegates seemed satisfied that they had received land and freedom from duties to their former landlords as a result of the emperor's declaration of 15 May 1848.

While it is true that the constitutional proposals of Austria's first elected body were never adopted and that the question of indemnification was left in abeyance, the significance of the Kremsier parliament should not be underestimated. During its few months of existence, Ukrainians from Galicia (including peasants who less than half a year before had been serfs) participated for the first time in a modern political process. The lessons they learned were important and would not be forgotten.

Aside from the parliamentary deliberations at Vienna and Kremsier, Galician Ukrainians participated in the Slav Congress in Prague. This congress came about as a reaction to the all-German National Assembly convened in Frankfurt in May 1848 to discuss the problem of the German lands. When the Czech leaders Palacký and Rieger were invited to Frankfurt (since from the German point of view Bohemia and Moravia, their homeland, constituted German territory), the Czechs adamantly refused the invitation. Instead, they invited Slavic leaders from within and beyond Austria to meet in June 1848 at their own congress in Prague. The goal of what came to be known as the Slav Congress was to discuss ways to restructure the Austrian Empire so that it would reflect the Slavic majority living there. The Slav Congress was by no means radical in orientation. On the contrary, while it may have reflected a sense of Pan-Slavic unity, it also was undeniably loyal to the Habsburg Empire. A reflection of the latter sentiment was the now-famous letter of rejection sent by Palacký to the meeting of Germans in Frankfurt: "Truly," wrote the Slav leader, "if it were not that Austria had long existed, it would be necessary, in the interest of Europe, in the interest of humanity itself, to create her."[2]

Galician Ukrainians also came to Prague. Actually, both the Supreme Ruthenian Council and the pro-Polish Ruthenian Council sent delegates, three and five in number, respectively. In this first public manifestation of Slavic solidarity, the presence of the Ukrainians confirmed that they were a nationality in their own right. In fact, one of the three sections of the congress was devoted specifically to Polish-Ukrainian relations, in particular to the problem of Galicia. Initially, the Polish delegates wanted all of Galicia to become an integral part of a restored Poland, while the Ukrainians wanted to be recognized as a distinct nationality and to have Galicia remain in Austria, although administratively divided into Polish and Ukrainian provinces. The resulting compromise (7 June) called for the use of Polish in schools where Poles predominated and Ukrainian where Ukrainians predominated. While the Ukrainians may not have obtained the division of Galicia, they did gain recognition as a distinct nationality in the eyes of their fellow Slavs. This achievement had important psychological as well as political consequences, felt beyond the confines of the congress itself. The Slav Congress was dissolved on 12 June, less than two weeks after it was convened following the imperial army's bombardment and capture of Prague.

The Galician-Ukrainian national movement: The organizational stage

Ukrainian achievements in the cultural realm proved to be more enduring than was Ukrainian political activity. The first Ukrainian newspaper, *Zoria halytska,* which began to appear in May 1848, continued to be published until 1857. Other journals also began publication in L'viv in 1849 (*Halycho-ruskii vîstnyk, Novynŷ, Pchola*) and in Vienna in 1850 (*Vîstnyk dlia Rusynov avstriiskoi derzhavŷ*). The overall increase in the number of Ukrainian publications was remarkable. In 1848 alone, 156 titles appeared, almost five times as many as the largest number to appear in any previous year in Galicia (32 in 1847) – not to mention Dnieper Ukraine in the Russian Empire, where in that same year a total of only one book and a few pages in two other books appeared in Ukrainian. The 1848 figure takes on even greater significance when it is understood that not until 1879 did more publications in Ukrainian appear in any one year. Moreover, most of the serial publications and many of the books and pamphlets appeared in the Galician-Ukrainian vernacular, not in the Slaveno-Rusyn book language. The Church Slavonic alphabet (*kyrylytsia*) was still used, however.

The year 1848 also witnessed the convocation of the first Galician-Ukrainian cultural society, the Congress of Ruthenian Scholars (Sobor Uchenykh Rus'kykh), which met in L'viv in October. Its ninety-nine participants discussed problems of education, scholarship, and linguistic usage, although nothing significant resulted. More lasting was the Galician-Rus' Matytsia (Halyts'ko-Rus'ka Matytsia), a society established in L'viv to promote education and popular culture. In the 1860s, the Matytsia began to publish an important scholarly and literary journal. Aside from engaging in political activity, the Supreme Ruthenian Council founded a cultural organization, the so-called National Home (Narodnyi Dom). The organization was first housed, in 1849, in a building donated by the Austrian government, but between 1851 and 1864 a fund drive was undertaken which resulted in the construction of a new center that included a museum, a printing shop, and a library. Besides having symbolic and practical value as a venue for Ukrainian cultural events in L'viv, the National Home published books and provided student scholarships.

Another important cultural achievement came as a result of the imperial government's decision in December 1848 to establish the Department (*katedra*) of Ruthenian Language and Literature in the faculty of philosophy at L'viv University. This department became not only the oldest but also the most enduring of all university departments in Ukrainian subjects, existing until the outbreak of World War II in 1939. The first head of the department was a former member of the Ruthenian Triad, Iakiv Holovats'kyi. He immediately proceeded to demonstrate in his lectures (some of which were published) that Ruthenian, or Ukrainian, was a distinct Slavic language with a long literary history.

Finally, the Galician Ukrainians had their own military units. Responding to the emperor's call for the creation of provincial national guards (a call first made in March and then repeated in the fall of 1848), the Ukrainians formed two units: a peasant frontier defense (November 1848) and the Ruthenian Sharpshooters (Ruthenische Bergschützen, January 1849). Both units were voluntarily constituted as an indication of loyalty to the Habsburg emperor. The more important of the two, the Ruthenian Sharpshooters, had as its specially stated goal the defeat of the "conceited" and "arrogant" revolutionary Magyars. The Sharpshooters accompanied Austrian regular army units into Hungary to defend the fatherland, but they arrived after the Hungarian revolutionary army was forced to surrender in August 1849 and thus too late to shed their blood for the emperor.

The revolution of 1848 in Bukovina and Transcarpathia

As Bukovina was territorially part of Galicia, the Bukovinians participated in the June 1848 elections to the first Austrian parliament. Of the eight deputies from the region, five were Ukrainians, including the peasant leader Lukiian Kobylytsia, only recently released from prison. Kobylytsia soon became dissatisfied with the proceedings in Vienna, returned home, and organized two peasant meetings in late 1848. He was arrested, however, for revolutionary agitation among the peasantry.

The discontent of Kobylytsia and his Ukrainian followers was owing to the unresolved problem of peasant indemnification for their recently acquired land (Bukovina's peasants were officially emancipated in August 1848, four months after those in other parts of Galicia), and to their opposition to the attempt by local

Romanian leaders to separate Bukovina from Galicia. According to the imperial constitution decreed on 4 March 1849, Bukovina was made into a separate crown-land province of Austria. This development had no effect on the national movement, however, and with the exception of a handful of publications, no Ukrainian cultural advances were made in Bukovina as a result of the upheavals of 1848.

In Transcarpathia, however, the situation proved very different. In late March 1848, when news of the revolutionary activity in Budapest reached Transcarpathia's cultural and religious center of Uzhhorod, the local Greek Catholic hierarchy gave its blessing to those young seminarians who rushed to join the Hungarian national guard. But a very small group led by the Transcarpathian mining engineer Adol'f Dobrians'kyi had other goals in mind. In January 1849, after Hungary's struggle against the Habsburgs turned into a serious military conflict, Dobrians'kyi traveled to Vienna and presented a memorandum to Emperor Franz Joseph calling for unity with Galicia's Ruthenians. Dobrians'kyi then went on to L'viv, where he was received favorably by the Supreme Ruthenian Council, which consequently added the goal of unity with Transcarpathia to its own platform.

In effect, from the very outset the Transcarpathian political and national revival as formulated by Dobrians'kyi was associated with Vienna and therefore directed against Hungary's revolutionary efforts. The association with Vienna was reinforced when the imperial government appointed Dobrians'kyi as Austrian liaison with the tsarist Russian army that arrived in the summer of 1849 to crush the Hungarians. Thus, the Transcarpathian leader was to play an important role in helping those forces that were to destroy the Hungarian revolution.

Another aspect of Dobrians'kyi as well as of his contemporary, the popular writer Aleksander Dukhnovych, was their russophilism. Following in the tradition of those Transcarpathians who in the earlier part of the century had gone to the Russian Empire, Dobrians'kyi and Dukhnovych came to believe that they and their people were part of the Russian nationality. Certain Transcarpathian leaders were, therefore, profoundly moved by the presence of tsarist troops as they crossed through the Carpathian Mountains on their way to crush the Hungarian revolutionaries.

Russophilism was at this time acceptable in Austria. Hence, after Habsburg imperial forces defeated the Hungarian revolution and Vienna administratively reorganized Hungary, the northeastern sector of the kingdom, inhabited primarily by Carpatho-Rusyns/Ukrainians, became the Uzhhorod District, and Dobrians'kyi its deputy head and actual administrator. During the Uzhhorod District's brief existence between November 1849 and March 1850, Dobrians'kyi hoped to transform what he considered a Ruthenian administrative entity into a semi-autonomous national unit within the empire.

In the realm of culture, the period between 1847 and 1850 saw the appearance of the first schoolbooks and literary almanacs in the Transcarpathia's East Slavic vernacular as well as the establishment of the first cultural society and the publication of the text that later became the Carpatho-Rusyn national hymn. All these cultural developments were almost exclusively the work of the dynamic Greek Catholic priest Aleksander Dukhnovych.

Thus, 1848 marked the real beginnings of a Transcarpathian national awakening, with cultural and even some political achievements. The first real contacts with Galicia began, although the Transcarpathian movement had from its outset two particularities: (1) dependence on Vienna in the face of a hostile Hungarian environment; and (2) the spread of the idea that the local Slavic inhabitants, who called themselves Carpatho-Rusyns or Rusnaks, formed part of the Russian nationality.

The significance of the revolutionary year 1848 for Ukrainians living within the Austrian Empire cannot be overstated. At a time when in Dnieper Ukraine the first efforts at creating a Ukrainian organization, the Cyril and Methodius Brotherhood, were being liquidated and the leading members of the Ukrainian intelligentsia (Shevchenko, Kostomarov, and Kulish) were being exiled from their homeland, Ukrainians in Austrian Galicia and, to a lesser degree, in Hungarian Transcarpathia were making remarkable advances in their national life. In Galicia, Ukrainians had their own political and cultural organizations, their own newspapers and publications, and their own deputies to a national parliament. Their largest social group, the peasantry, was emancipated from serfdom, and its members began to participate in political life. Ukrainians also interacted with other Slavs in the Austrian Empire, and those in Galicia even had their own military formations. Moreover, all these developments took place with the blessing, the encouragement, and at times at the initiative, of the imperial government and its representatives.

The Administrative and Socioeconomic Structure of Ukrainian Lands in the Austrian Empire, 1849–1914

Following the revolutionary era that began in March 1848 and ended decisively in August 1849 with the defeat of the Hungarians, Austria entered a period of neo-absolutism during which the imperial administration in Vienna attempted to undo the achievements of the 1848 revolution and to restore the absolute power of the emperor. During the next two decades, from 1849 to 1868, there were several attempts at restructuring the Austrian Empire. Each new attempt was a direct result of the interplay of external and internal forces, namely, international developments and pressure from the empire's many nationalities, in particular the Magyars. The process unfolded in three distinct phases: the first, 1849 to 1859, marked a neo-absolutist phase, with government exclusively under the control of Vienna; the second, 1860 to 1866, was a time of constitutional experiment; finally, the third, 1867 to 1868, witnessed the creation of the Austro-Hungarian dual monarchy, the structure which prevailed until the very demise of the Habsburg Empire in 1918. Each phase had a direct effect on the administrative structure of Galicia, Bukovina, and Transcarpathia, and therefore on the Ukrainians living there.

Administrative structure

Already during the revolutionary era, the Kremsier parliament was disbanded (March 1849) and its constitutional proposals scrapped. Even the more centralized constitution decreed the same month by the emperor was never put into effect, and it was eventually annulled, on 31 December 1851. Hence began a period of neo-absolutism, in which there was no thought of an Austrian parliament. Instead, the Habsburgs ruled the empire directly from the imperial court in Vienna and, in some areas, including Galicia and Hungary, through martial law administered by the imperial army. Martial law in Galicia lasted until 1854, after which an imperial civil administration was set up, headed by a viceroy (German: *Statthalter*; Polish: *namiestnik*; Ukrainian: *namistnyk*) who was appointed by and responsible only to the emperor. The whole province was also administratively reorganized. In 1867, the nineteen regions (*Kreise*) were replaced by seventy-four and, later, eighty-three districts (*Bezirke/powiaty/povity*), each with its own sheriff (*starosta*) in charge of the

MAP 30

UKRAINIAN LANDS IN AUSTRIA-HUNGARY, circa 1875

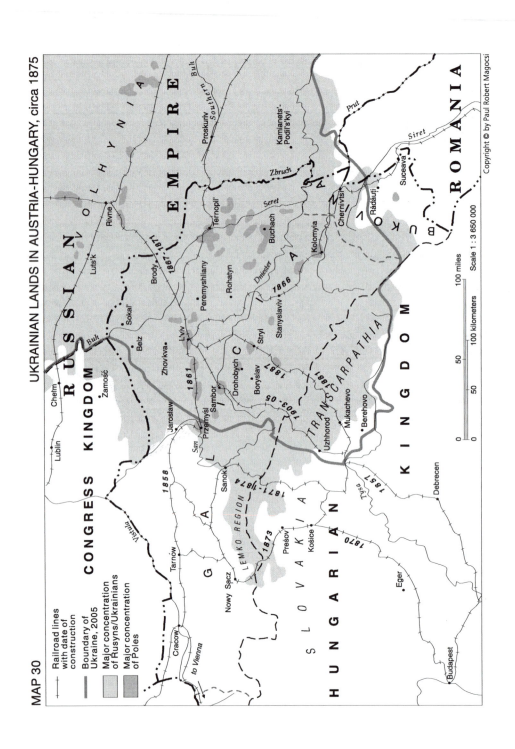

Railroad lines
with date of
construction

Boundary of
Ukraine, 2005

Major concentration
of Rusyns/Ukrainians

Major concentration
of Poles

Scale 1 : 3 650 000

Copyright © by Paul Robert Magocsi

district administration. Besides the districts, there were also two self-governing cities, L'viv and Cracow.

The status of Bukovina remained uncertain. While the imperial constitution of 4 March 1849 proposed that Bukovina be a separate province, that constitution never went into effect. As a result, it was not until 1854 that Bukovina's full administrative separation from Galicia occurred. In 1860, however, that move was rescinded and Bukovina once more became part of Galicia. As for Transcarpathia, it, like the rest of Hungary, was under martial law, although one of the military districts was centered in Uzhhorod, and part of the Transcarpathian population thus effectively united under the nominal rule of its local leader, Adol'f Dobrians'kyi. The Uzhhorod, or "Ruthenian," District lasted only five months, however, and after its dissolution in March 1850 the Transcarpathians had no separate administrative status. Their homeland continued to be divided into several Hungarian counties (Hungarian: *megye;* Ukrainian: *komitaty* or *zhupy*), each headed by a Magyar official.

In Galicia, the first viceroy to function under the new centralized system of Austrian rule was the Polish count Agenor Gołuchowski. Gołuchowski was a wealthy landowning magnate from Galicia and a confidant of Emperor Franz Joseph and his immediate entourage. Gołuchowski also represented what initially was a small group of Polish leaders who felt that the future of the Polish cause did not lie in revolutionary activity, but rather in organic cultural and economic work with the broader mass of the Polish population and in cooperation with the three imperial states that ruled Polish territory. Gołuchowski was convinced that Austria offered the best political future for Poles. Accordingly, he was more than willing to cooperate with the Habsburgs, provided that Vienna recognized all of Galicia as a Polish land and that it granted complete cultural if not political autonomy to the Poles living there.

A dominant figure throughout this whole period, Gołuchowski served as Galician viceroy three times between 1849 and 1875 and as Austrian imperial minister of internal affairs between 1859 and 1861. The emperor needed a reliable administrator, and he trusted Gołuchowski. Gołuchowski knew this, and, taking advantage of Vienna's weakness at certain times, he was able to advance the Polish cause and transform Galicia into an area in which Poles monopolized the upper echelons of the administration, the educational system, and economic life – a state of affairs that was to last at least until the outbreak of World War I in 1914. During the period of imperial administrative rule before 1859, Gołuchowski successfully foiled Vienna's inclination to divide Galicia into two provinces, a division which would effectively have meant a Polish and a Ukrainian province. He also succeeded in having many German officials removed, in having Polish replace German in secondary schools (*gymnasia*), and in restricting the further spread of Ukrainian schools. He even tried to introduce the Latin alphabet for Ukrainian publications in 1859, although this effort failed after strenuous protests by Ukrainian leaders.

International developments and Austria's internal politics

The year 1859 was a crucial turning point for Austria, since it lost a war with

France and its ally, the expanding Italian nation-state of Sardinia-Piedmont. This loss underlined Austria's internal weaknesses, and plans were made to restructure the empire. It was evident that centralized rule from Vienna had failed. Influenced by Count Gołuchowski, who was now imperial minister of internal affairs, the Austrian government proposed a new solution in February 1861. This marked the dawn of the era of constitutionalism and representative government in Austrian history. Each of the Austrian provinces received its own diet (German: *Landtag*; Polish: *sejm*; Ukrainian: *soim*), and a central parliament (*Reichsrat*) with representatives from all the provinces was established in the imperial capital of Vienna. The year 1861 also saw the reinstatement of Bukovina as a separate province, a status it retained until the demise of the empire. Thus, with the dawn of Austrian constitutionalism, the Ukrainians of Galicia and Bukovina became active members in the political process at both the provincial and the imperial level.

The next important turning point in Austrian history came in 1866. In that year, neighboring Prussia, under the dynamic leadership of Chancellor Otto von Bismarck, defeated Austria in a war that lasted no more than six weeks. With this victory, Prussia eliminated Habsburg influence over the Germanic lands in central Europe. Five years later, in 1871, Bismarck united the smaller German states under the leadership of Prussia to form the German Empire. Austria's defeat by Prussia in 1866 was attributed to the failure of the Hungarians to cooperate in the war effort. Consequently, Vienna was once again forced by external events to try to resolve the Hungarian problem as well as to respond to the continuing demands of the empire's other nationalities.

The result was a compromise reached with the Hungarians in May 1867 and known as the *Ausgleich*. According to the *Ausgleich*, the Hungarian Kingdom was left to govern itself except in foreign affairs, some economic matters (currency, tariffs), and the military, all of which were to be the common concern of the whole empire. As for the other "kingdoms and lands represented in the parliament" – the official if rather awkward name for the Austrian, or non-Hungarian, territories – a revised constitution was promulgated in December 1867. This document guaranteed individual citizens equality before the law; freedom of the press, speech, and assembly; and protection of the interests of the various nationalities, including equal rights for all languages in local use in schools, administration, and public life. With the implementation of the *Ausgleich* in 1868, the Austrian Empire was transformed into the so-called Habsburg Dual Monarchy, or Austria-Hungary.

Meanwhile, Count Gołuchowski was back in office as viceroy in Galicia following Austria's defeat by Prussia in 1866. Again, Vienna wanted his support, and again he was willing to give it so long as Polish interests in Galicia were served. While the *Ausgleich* may have resolved one problem in the empire, it inevitably prompted demands from other nationalities. After all, if Hungary could gain self-rule, why should not the "Polish" Kingdom of Galicia and Lodomeria or, for that matter, the "Czech" Kingdom of Bohemia-Moravia gain it too? The Poles put forth their program in the so-called Galician Resolution of 1868, which demanded wide-ranging political autonomy for the province, including legislative power for

AUSTRIA'S PARLIAMENTARY STRUCTURE

When Galicia's diet was established in 1861, it had 150 seats. After 1901, that number was raised to 161, and after 1911, to 228. The Bukovinian diet had 31 seats for most of the period until 1911, and thereafter it had 63. Deputies to the provincial diets were elected according to the curia system, which allotted to four social strata a specific number of deputies. Among the deputies in Galicia in 1861 were 44 elected by the great landowners, 3 elected by the chambers of commerce, 23 elected by the cities, and 80 elected by small towns and rural communes. Provincial diets also included several ex officio members. In Galicia after 1875, they included seven bishops (3 Roman Catholic, 3 Greek Catholic, 1 Armenian); 2 university rectors and, after 1900, the president of the Polish Academy of Sciences; and the rector of the polytechnical school in L'viv. Finally, each diet was presided over by a marshal and vice-marshal appointed by the emperor. The diets had limited authority and were basically concerned with local agricultural and, later, industrial development, hygiene, and elementary and secondary schools. Until 1873, the diets also elected deputies to the newly established central parliament (*Reichsrat*) in Vienna.

Austria's central parliament also came into being in 1861. It consisted of two houses: a House of Lords (*Herrenhaus*), made up of members appointed by the emperor; and the more important House of Deputies (*Abgeordnetenhaus*). Until 1873, the members of the House of Deputies were elected by the provincial diets; then, by voters according to the curia system; and finally, after 1907, by universal male suffrage. The number of deputies in the Austrian parliament steadily increased, from 203 in 1861 to 516 in 1907.

The heritage of Viceroy Gołuchowski's rule in Galicia was strongly felt in the new administrative structure. Although Ukrainians made up close to half the province's population, by the demise of the empire in 1918 they had never elected more than one-third of the deputies in the Galician diet. (Their largest representations were 66 of 228 deputies in 1914, and 49 of 150 deputies in 1861.) In Bukovina, where Ukrainians also made up close to half the province's population, they had no deputies at all in the provincial diet until 1890. Thereafter, their largest number was 17 of 63 deputies in 1911.

In the Austrian parliament's House of Deputies, Ukrainians had at most only one-quarter of the seats allotted to Galicia (their largest representation was 27 of 106 seats in 1907). Moreover, from Gołuchowski's third term in 1871–1875 until the outbreak of World War I in 1914, all subsequent Galician viceroys were Poles, all the marshals in the Galician diet were Poles, and all the district sheriffs were Poles.

the local diet, a separate supreme court, and responsibility on the part of the vice-roy to the diet. Vienna was not prepared to go so far, fearing – and rightly so – that meeting these demands would encourage similar demands by other nationalities and lead to the disintegration of the empire. If Gołuchowski was to continue to support Vienna, however, he needed something to appease the supporters of the Galician Resolution. Accordingly, the Austrian government agreed to permit several administrative changes in the province. Polish became the language of internal administration, secondary schools, and L'viv University; and the Provincial School Board, which theoretically was subordinate to the Galician diet, became an independent body and instrument of further polonization within the educational system. Also, in 1871 the Ministry of Galician Affairs was created in Vienna to represent the interests of the province directly with the imperial government. From the ministry's establishment in 1871 until the empire's demise in 1918, all ministers of Galician affairs were Poles.

Hence, while it is true that Ukrainians participated in the political system and were guaranteed certain legal rights with respect to the promotion of their national culture, the realities of Austrian political life, on both the domestic and the international front, forced the central government in Vienna to depend on the leading stratum in Galicia, which was made up almost exclusively of Poles. In effect, the Ukrainians became a minority in Galicia, forced to struggle for any advance in their national life, more often than not in the face of intransigent Polish opposition. This state of affairs, which lasted until 1918, is perhaps best summed up by the Ukrainian-Canadian scholar Ivan L. Rudnytsky:

The dominant position of the Poles was bolstered by the social privileges of the landed nobility and the upper middle class. Conversely, for the Ukrainians the struggle for national and social emancipation was one and the same. In addition to the clash between the social interest of the two nationalities there was an invidious conflict on the psychological plane. The outlook of the Polish intelligentsia and middle class was largely derived from the gentry tradition. The origins of the Ukrainian intelligentsia were plebeian; every educated Ukrainian was only one or two generations removed from either a parsonage or a peasant hut. Thus even those Polish and Ukrainian groups whose formal education and living conditions were similar displayed divergent social mentalities. Both communities viewed the present conflict as if it were similar to the great seventeenth-century wars between the Polish aristocracy and the Ukrainian Cossacks.[1]

Social structure and economic developments

In the first half of the nineteenth century, Galicia was an underdeveloped agrarian region whose raw materials were exploited by the more industrialized provinces in the western part of the Habsburg Empire. This characterization is true also for the second half of the nineteenth century. Some industrialization took place during the very last decades of the century, however, and changed Galicia's economy somewhat from one dependent exclusively on agriculture.

The size of Galicia's population increased substantially during the second half

THE PROBLEM OF STATISTICS

During the second half of the nineteenth century, several European countries began to undertake censuses every ten years. These censuses produced a wide variety of statistical data. Among the most controversial questions, in particular in multinational Austria-Hungary and the Russian Empire, were those concerning national identity. Actually, the question asked by both Austria-Hungary and Russia concerned native language ("mother tongue," "language of daily use"), but the answers to the question were generally used by contemporary political activists – and are still used by scholars today – to describe the national composition of these states. Not surprisingly, spokespersons for each nationality were interested in arriving at the highest figure possible for their group in order to justify demands for greater political representation, more schools, and social and cultural services that might otherwise go to another national group.

The census question about language was useful if one wanted to know about languages spoken. Difficulties arose, however, when language data was used as a basis for arriving at national affiliation. For instance, the Austrian statistics on language for Galicia in 1910 were the following:

Polish	4,672,000	58.3%
Ukrainian	3,208,000	40.2%
German	90,000	1.1%
Other	10,000	0.1%

When these figures are used to describe the number of Poles or Ukrainians in Galicia – as they frequently have been used – serious discrepancies present themselves. For instance, there turn out to be no Jews, even though we know from the statistics on religion that there were 856,000 Jews recorded in Galicia in 1910. The same statistics tell us that the vast majority of Jews (808,000) gave Polish as their language, thereby inflating the number of "Poles," and that a smaller number of Jews gave German (26,000) or Ukrainian (22,000) as their language, thereby increasing the number of these nationalities, if only slightly. Similarly, 235,000 Greek Catholics recorded their spoken language as Polish, even though a significant portion were probably of Ukrainian ethnicity. Table 34.1 attempts to correct these discrepancies by using statistics on both language and religion to gauge the approximate numerical size of Galicia's nationalities.

The operative word is approximate. This is because all statistics, especially those relating to national identity in multinational states, must be treated with great caution. One should never assume that numbers are wholly accurate; at best, what they provide is an estimate.

TABLE 34.1
Nationality composition of Galicia, 1910[2]

	Number	Percentage
Poles	3,629,000	45.5
Ukrainians	3,421,000	43.0
Jews	856,000	10.7
Germans	64,000	0.8
Czechs	9,000	0.0
Others	1,000	0.0
TOTAL	7,980,000	100.0

of the nineteenth century, from 4.9 million inhabitants in 1849 to 7.9 million in 1910. The numerical relationship between the province's two leading groups – Poles and Ukrainians – also changed, although not to the degree suggested by Austrian governmental statistics, which used spoken daily language as the criterion for national identity. Table 34.1 provides a more realistic estimate, based on a combination of statistics on language and on religion. These revised statistics suggest that between 1849 and 1910 the percentage of Poles in Galicia remained the same (just under 46 percent), while that of Ukrainians declined slightly, from 47 to 43 percent. The decline in the percentage of Ukrainians was even greater in eastern Galicia, from 71 to 62 percent. The reasons for this proportional change were (1) an increase in Polish colonization from western to eastern Galicia, and (2) the large-scale emigration of Ukrainians abroad beginning in the 1880s.

Despite the enormous overall increase in Galicia's population, its socioeconomic status did not change substantially. Although the population of the provincial capital, L'viv, quadrupled in size during the second half of the nineteenth century, in 1910 it was still a relatively small city of only 207,000 inhabitants, over 80 percent of whom were Poles or Jews. The next-largest cities in eastern Galicia were Przemyśl and Kolomyia, with fewer than 40,000 inhabitants each, and Ternopil' and Stanyslaviv (today Ivano-Frankivs'k) with fewer than 30,000. As is clear from these figures, the vast majority of Galicia's population remained rural.

In fact, more than three-fifths of the province's inhabitants were engaged in agricultural pursuits. Although the serfs were legally freed from bondage in 1848, in a sense they remained economic serfs. There were several reasons for this. The right of the peasants to use the gentry-owned woods and pastures (the traditional servitude) was revoked with the emancipation, and now the peasants had to pay for the privilege. Their only source of income was their plots of land, but these were too small to provide a sufficient income. The peasants were forced to borrow and before long experienced chronic indebtedness. This state of affairs was only made worse as landholdings were repeatedly subdivided among offspring. In 1859, 66 percent of those who made up Galicia's agricultural sector fell into the category of small-sized landowners (owning less than 14 acres [5.7 hectares]), and another 25 percent were middle-sized landowners (owning up to 28 acres [11.5 hectares]). In subsequent years, the average size of a peasant holding steadily decreased, from 12 acres (5 hectares) in 1859, to 7 acres (3 hectares) in 1880, and finally to 6 acres

(2.5 hectares) in 1900. There was a slight increase in the total amount of arable land available, but it proved insufficient to offset the increasing demographic growth. There were some areas of Galicia, such as the former Podolia in the province's far southeastern corner, where the economic status of the peasantry stabilized and improved during the last decades of the nineteenth century. Throughout most of the province, however, the peasants seemed to be caught in an inescapable cycle of indebtedness, land subdivision, and rapid demographic growth.

The difficult economic situation gave rise to frequent peasant strikes, especially at the beginning of the twentieth century. Many peasants also sought relief by emigrating abroad. Beginning in the 1880s, Galician peasants sought their fortunes in the New World, where they settled in the alien industrialized environment of the northeastern United States. By the turn of the century, emigrants were also departing for Canada and Brazil, although in these countries they settled primarily in agricultural regions that provided for a way of life more similar to the one they had had at home. Between 1881 and 1912, an estimated 430,000 Ukrainians left Galicia and Bukovina, and another 170,000 left Transcarpathia. Emigration grew to such proportions that both the Austrian and the Hungarian authorities, fearing the complete depopulation of certain areas, tried – although with little success – to control the exodus.

The only real way to stop emigration was to improve the Galician economy. Although the general Austrian principle of treating Galicia as a source of raw materials for the empire's western provinces as well as a market for the latter's industrial goods had not changed, the beginnings of industrialization were embarked upon. In the 1880s in particular, industrial development was encouraged by the dynamic marshal of the Galician Diet, Mikołaj Zyblikiewicz. Railroad construction had already begun in the 1860s, and by 1914 Galicia, together with Bukovina and Transcarpathia, had a rather well developed network totaling 2,294 miles (3,700 kilometers). As in other parts of central and eastern Europe, however, the coming of the railroad at least initially had a negative effect on local economies. Hence, in 1861, when L'viv was connected via Cracow to Vienna, a larger supply of goods from the western industrialized regions than before was dumped on the Galician market. Provincial administrators tried to overcome such economic imbalances, and among other measures they encouraged the development of a credit and banking system for Galicia. Investors were solicited not only from Vienna, but from abroad, especially from France, England, the United States, and Canada. Emigrants also began to send money home, which helped to increase the amount of investment capital in the province. By 1900, foreign investments in Galicia amounted to 1.3 billion crowns, at a time when the province's entire budget was only 20.5 million crowns.

As a result of these developments, modest industrial growth took place in Galicia. By 1902, there were 335 plants (with at least twenty workers each), employing 26,000 workers; by 1910, these figures had increased to 448 plants, with 36,000 workers. The workers were employed in food processing (34 percent), lumber and wood processing (20 percent), clothes manufacturing (16 percent), mineral – mainly oil – extraction (15 percent), and machine building and metal-

THE UKRAINIAN DIASPORA

Migration is nothing new to the peoples of Ukraine. In the sixteenth century, ethnic Ukrainians discontented with Poland's economic and cultural policies emigrated eastward to Muscovy. In the early eighteenth century, the first political emigration, associated with the Cossack hetman Pylyp Orlyk, fled westward from Muscovite rule. At the beginning of the nineteenth century, individuals from Transcarpathia who sought better careers than they could pursue at home emigrated to the Russian Empire. A few decades later, Ukrainian cultural activists led by Mykhailo Drahomanov were forced by political persecution to emigrate from the Russian Empire to western Europe.

There was also extensive out-migration from Ukraine to other parts of the tsarist realm. The imperial capital of St Petersburg became in the course of the nineteenth century the place where for various reasons the nationalist intelligentsia settled and concentrated its energies on behalf of Ukrainian culture. This group was somewhat of an exception, however, since numerically the largest ethnic Ukrainian diaspora, which emigrated eastward to central Asia and southern Siberia, established no specifically Ukrainian institutions to preserve and promote their native heritage.

This is in stark contrast to the massive emigration of ethnic Ukrainians, virtually all from Ukrainian-inhabited lands in the Austro-Hungarian Empire, who beginning in the 1890s went across the ocean to North America. They differed from all previous emigrations both quantitatively and qualitatively. Those who left Ukrainian lands in this newest emigration, which was to number about 600,000 by 1914, established distinct community structures in the United States and then Canada. These structures still exist over a century later.

The American and Canadian experience also served another important function with regard to national development. Most East Slavic emigrants from Galicia and Bukovina had little or no sense of a national identity when they left home. It was only in the United States and Canada, where they were surrounded by peoples from all over Europe and the world, that they embarked on their own nationality-building process, learning about their Ukrainian identity and passing it on to their children and grandchildren.

The Ukrainian nationality-building process in North America was initially carried out by secular organizations, the oldest and still the largest of which is the Ukrainian National Association (Ukraïns'kyi Narodnyi Soiuz), established in 1894 in Jersey City, New Jersey, across the river from New York City. This and similar organizations not only functioned as insurance companies to protect immigrant workers who might be struck by illness or injury, but also promoted Ukrainian culture and national awareness through the organization of cultural events and the publication of Ukrainian-language newspapers, annual almanacs (*kalendari*), and books.

Among the most important Ukrainian institutions in North America were the churches. Although concerned with saving souls, it was not long before the churches in North America began to serve the same function as in the western Ukrainian homeland, particularly Galicia. That is, the churches and their parish priests became as interested in preserving the Ukrainian language and fostering a Ukrainian identity as they were in sustaining purely religious activity. The earliest Ukrainian churches were almost all Greek Catholic. This is because as many as 80 percent of the pre-World War I immigrants came from Galicia and Transcarpathia, where Greek Catholicism was the predominant religion until 1918.

Quite apart from the Orthodoxy brought by the few Bukovinian immigrants, the 1890s witnessed the beginning of an Orthodox movement in the United States, which over the next three decades attracted tens of thousands of Greek Catholics. These Orthodox converts initially joined the Russian Orthodox Church in North America, as members of which they gave up or never developed a Ukrainian identity. Ukrainian Orthodoxy per se did not really take hold until the 1920s, when Ukrainians already in North America together with new immigrants joined parishes associated with the Ukrainian Autocephalous Orthodox Church (only recently established in Soviet Ukraine), or with a new body, the Ukrainian Orthodox Church in America, under the jurisdiction of the ecumenical patriarchate in Constantinople. The Ukrainian diaspora, particularly in North America, was to function for most of the twentieth century as the only environment in which certain Ukrainian churches could survive, especially after the Soviet Union's ban against the Autocephalous Orthodox Church in 1930 and against the Greek Catholic Church in 1946.

An integral part of the Ukrainian nationality-building process in North America was an ongoing interest in the European homeland. That interest, moreover, was not simply a passive, informational one. Ukrainian immigrants and their descendants hoped to influence economic and, in particular, political developments in Ukraine. Ukrainian immigrants were especially active in lobbying the United States and Canadian governments and in supplying economic assistance to various pro-independence political factions in the course of the Ukrainian revolution and of the diplomatic negotiations that led to the realignment of borders following World War I. During the interwar years, the immigrants turned their attention to the shortcomings of Polish rule in Galicia, and they tried to bring the world's attention to the 1921 and 1933 famines in Soviet Ukraine. On the eve of and during World War II, they protested against the Hungarian occupation of Carpatho-Ukraine and the Soviet annexation of eastern Galicia. When the Soviet Union and the United States became wartime allies, the anti-Soviet views of most Ukrainian immigrants were no longer appreciated by the American and Canadian governments. But, with the coming of the Cold War era, the immigrants were successful in bringing thousands of displaced persons (DPs) – many of whom had fought the Soviets – to North America. Among the DPs were ethnic Ukrainians from "eastern" or Soviet Ukraine, which was a relatively new phenomenon for the diaspora in North America, which until then had been dominated by "western" Ukrainians from Galicia and Bukovina. For nearly four decades, until the demise of the Soviet Union in 1991, this larger and more territorially representative east-west Ukrainian diaspora undertook a virtual unending public relations campaign against the "Soviet occupation of Ukraine." Finally, with the beginning of the Gorbachev reform era in 1985, the Ukrainian diaspora was mobilized to help victims of the Chornobyl' nuclear disaster, to assist pro-independence movements like Rukh, and to provide support for the various churches which were again allowed to function legally in the homeland.

The large-scale emigration of ethnic Ukrainians to North America that had characterized the decades before World War I was not to be repeated. There were several reasons for this: United States government restrictions against southern and eastern European immigration implemented in 1924; the negative impact of the world economic depression of the 1930s; and the strict controls against emigration imposed by Soviet authorities on territories under their control.

Aside from the masses of emigrants who left their homeland primarily for economic reasons, the twentieth century also saw a steady stream of Ukrainian political and religious leaders who sought refuge abroad, either in North America or, more often, nearer home, in central and western Europe. Among the numerous exiles were refugees from tsarist, Soviet, and Polish rule, including Viacheslav Lypyns'kyi and Dmytro Dontsov before World War I; Mykhailo Hrushevs'kyi, Symon Petliura, Volodymyr Vynnychenko, Pavlo Skoropads'kyi, Dmytro Doroshenko, Nestor Makhno, Ievhen Petrushevych, and Ievhen Konovalets' during the interwar years; Andrii Mel'nyk, Stepan Bandera, Mstyslav Skrypnyk, Ivan Kedryn-Rudnyts'kyi, George Shevelov, and Volodymyr Kubiiovych during World War II; and Iosyf Slipyi, Valentyn Moroz, Leonid Pliushch, and Iosyp Terelia during the last decades of Soviet rule.

Particularly because of the high profile of these and numerous other political, religious, and cultural figures, the Soviet government maintained continual surveillance of the Ukrainian emigration wherever it was located, whether from listening posts at home or through the widely spread Soviet espionage networks abroad. The reason was simple: at a time when the Soviet regime was denying the validity of certain aspects of Ukrainian culture, outlawing Ukrainian churches and religious orders, suppressing information about certain historical events, and banning movements that promoted the idea of independent Ukrainian statehood, these very same elements were being kept alive and well among Ukrainian immigrants and their descendants in the diaspora.

The diaspora fulfilled its role as a preserver of Ukrainian culture and national consciousness through the creation in western Europe and North America of several educational and scholarly institutions, such as the interwar Ukrainian Free University, begun in Vienna and later continued in Prague and Munich, and, from the post–World War II years, the Shevchenko

Scientific Society and Ukrainian Academy of Sciences in New York City; the St Clement Ukrainian Catholic University in Rome; the Ukrainian encyclopedia project in Sarcelles, outside Paris; the Ukrainian Studies Program at Harvard University in Cambridge, Massachusetts; the Canadian Institute of Ukrainian Studies at the University of Alberta in Edmonton, Canada; and the Chair of Ukrainian Studies and English-language *Encyclopedia of Ukraine* project at the University of Toronto, Canada. In short, the Ukrainian diaspora, despite numerous internal conflicts, maintained for posterity all those elements of the Ukrainian cultural patrimony that in Soviet times were being suppressed in the Ukrainian homeland.

It was not until independence came to Ukraine in 1991 that the diaspora was able to establish relatively unhindered relations with its ancestral land. Those relations have taken several forms: economic investments; financial support for cultural projects and political activity; and even the return of individuals, some of whom have taken up posts in independent Ukraine's government and church institutions.

working (10 percent). The most remarkable growth was in the oil industry, following the discovery in the 1870s of fields in eastern Galicia near Drohobych and Boryslav. Financed and operated by Austrian, French, and English companies, oil production increased eightyfold between 1875 and 1910. In fact, by the outbreak of World War I in 1914, eastern Galicia accounted for almost 4 percent of the world's oil production. Conversely, Galicia's small iron ore and coal production decreased by almost 50 percent between 1858 and 1889.

In the end, despite some industrial development, Galicia remained an economically underdeveloped agrarian society under Austrian rule. To an even greater degree, so did the other Ukrainian-inhabited regions of the Austro-Hungarian Empire, Bukovina and Transcarpathia: in those regions, there were virtually no industries prior to World War I.

Other peoples in eastern Galicia and Bukovina

Most of the administrative, commercial, and industrial development in late nineteenth-century Galicia was directed not by Ukrainians, but rather by Poles and Jews. The Poles' numbers continued to increase, not only west of the San River but also in the province's eastern, "Ukrainian" half. The reason for the rather dramatic increase was a steady migration of Poles from western to eastern Galicia. They settled in agricultural communities in the midst of Ukrainians as well as in towns and cities, especially L'viv. By 1890, one-third of all Poles living in eastern Galicia had immigrated from west of the San. By 1910, there was a total of 890,000 Poles in eastern Galicia. In terms of socioeconomic composition, 68 percent were peasants; 16 percent were engaged in industry; 8.5 percent were engaged in trade and transport; and 7.5 percent were engaged in administration, the professions, and service jobs.

Not only did the Poles dominate the administration and economic life of Galicia as a whole, they also transformed much of eastern Galicia, especially its cities, into oases of Polish culture. Accordingly, in relatively liberal Austria, L'viv (or Lwów, as it was known among Poles) became one of the leading centers of the Polish national revival among the lands carved out of the pre-partition Polish-Lithuanian Commonwealth. Besides a host of Polish newspapers, publishing houses, theaters, cultural societies, and schools, L'viv boasted its own Polish-language university, the Polish Historical Society, and a distinguished library and research center known as the Ossolineum. The city also became home to some of Poland's leading historians (Oswald Balzer, Michał Bobrzyński), philologists (Alexander Brückner), ethnographers (Wacław Zaleski, Pauli Żegota), and writers (Jan Lam, Jan Zachariasiewicz), and from eastern Galicia came the leading author of Polish theatrical comedies, Count Aleksander Fredro (the maternal grandfather of the future Greek Catholic metropolitan, Andrei Sheptyts'kyi).

Galicia was also a crucially important center for Polish political life in general during the late nineteenth century. Whereas Cracow was the stronghold of conservative politicians (the Stańczyks) loyal to the Habsburg Monarchy, eastern Galicia and L'viv became the center for more socially oriented and nationalistic movements, including the Polish Social Democratic party (est. 1892), the Peasant party (Stronnictwo Ludowe, est. 1895), and the Galician branch of National Democratic party – the Endecja (est. 1905). It was in eastern Galicia that the movement for Polish independence headed by Józef Pilsudski found a home during the decade before the outbreak of World War I in 1914, and where the para-military Union of Active Struggle (Związek Walki Czynnej) and the Riflemen Association (Związek Strzelecki) were set up to train young Poles for a future armed struggle Russia.

It is not surprising, therefore, that Poles in nineteenth-century Austria quite naturally considered L'viv – and, for that matter, all of Galicia – an integral part of the Polish patrimony. The idea that "things should remain as they always have been" (*naj bude, jak buwało*) was most adamantly promoted by a group of Polish landowners from eastern Galicia known as the Podolians. These self-styled representatives of Galician autonomy were convinced that the future of the province would best be guaranteed if political as well as economic power – based on land, not on any experiments with industrialization – remained in the hands of the Polish nobility.

The other influential people in Galicia, the Jews, also continued to expand in size and economic influence during the second half of the nineteenth century. Whereas in 1849 there were 328,000 Jews, by 1910 their numbers had more than doubled, to 872,000, a figure that represented 11 percent of the total population of the province. Three-quarters of Galicia's Jews (660,000) lived in the eastern half of the province, in both cities and small towns (76.2 percent) and in the surrounding Ukrainian countryside. The number of Jews grew as a result of a high birthrate and in-migration of refugees from pogroms in the neighboring western provinces of the Russian Empire.

The Jews remained an important factor in the Galician economy. By 1910, 77 percent of the group were engaged in commerce, industry, and small handicrafts. With the beginnings of industrial development during the last decades of the nine-

UKRAINE'S OTHER DIASPORAS

The formulation *Ukrainian diaspora* almost always refers to communities of ethnic Ukrainians and their descendants living in various places outside Ukraine. But since Ukraine was – and is – home to many different peoples, it has generated several Ukrainian diasporas or, more precisely, diasporas from Ukraine. Among the most important of these other Ukrainian diasporas are those represented by Crimean Tatars, Jews, Russians, Carpatho-Rusyns, Poles, Germans, and Mennonites, each of which has maintained in various ways and in differing intensity relations with their ancestral homelands in Ukraine.

The first group to experience large-scale emigration from Ukrainian lands were the Crimean Tatars. Some scholars have suggested that between 1783 and 1922 no less than 1.8 million emigrated to the various lands of the Ottoman Empire. Their exodus began in 1780s in connection with the collapse of the independent Crimean Khanate and was to continue for nearly a century, reaching a high point in the 1860s when, of the 784 villages from which emigrants left, 330 were completely abandoned. As Muslims, the Crimean Tatar emigrants sought refuge in the relatively nearby sacred "land of the Caliph," that is, the Ottoman Empire. However, as the Ottoman Empire itself was in the course of the nineteenth century steadily being reduced in size, the Crimean diaspora was before long to find itself in new countries. Hence, the Crimean Tatars who first went to Circassia and the Bujak, eventually found themselves in the Russian Empire, while those who settled in the Black Sea coastal region of Dobruja were by the late 1870s living in Romania and Bulgaria. Such political changes prompted in 1877–1878 a second emigration from Dobruja, when between 80,000 and 100,000 Crimean Tatars moved to the Ottoman heartland of Anatolia, which itself was transformed into the secular Republic of Turkey in 1924.

Wherever they went, the Tatar emigrants from the former Crimean Khanate maintained distinctions between their two subgroups: the nomadic Nogays from the steppe, who continued to practice herding and livestock raising; and the sedentary Tats from the southern and coastal Crimea, who in the diaspora as at home were farmers or urban artisans, traders, and workers. In general, the Crimean Tatars who settled in Ottoman Anatolia tended to assimilate with the surrounding Turkish population, while those who settled and remained in Dobrudja retained a distinct identity in contrast to the dominant Christian inhabitants of Romania and Bulgaria. Still today Tatars/Nogays are an officially recognized national minority in Romania (25,000) and Bulgaria (5,000).

Despite strong assimilationist tendencies, the Crimean diaspora has at certain times generated political and cultural movements directed at the group's former homeland. An early example of this was evident among the 8,000 strong Crimean diaspora, including part of the Giray dynasty, which fled southeastward and settled in the Circassian lands in the Caucasus Mountains. In the late eighteenth and early nineteenth century, the Girays and their supporters in Circassia promoted efforts (all in vain) to unseat Russian rule in the Crimea and to return to their homeland. Giray princes also served in the Balkan provinces of the Ottoman Empire, where military regiments were formed among Crimean Tatar émigrés who fought in conflicts against the Russian Empire. This included participation in the Allied (British and French) landings on the peninsula during the early stages of the Crimean War (1854).

Even more important as a Crimean diaspora center was the Ottoman capital of Istanbul. There, under the leadership of Noman Çelebi Cihan and Cefer Seydahmet, the Crimean Students Association (Kirim Talebe Cemiyeti, est. 1908) and the Vatan/Fatherland Society (Vatan Cemiyeti, est. 1909) were set up to support the Crimean Tatar national revival in the homeland. The underground Vatan Society was the first to call for Crimean independence. Until that goal was achieved, and for nearly a decade beginning in 1908, several enthusiasts returned from the Ottoman Empire to Russian-ruled Crimea, bringing with them books and other nationalist literature which they distributed as teachers in Ismail Gaspirali's New Method school system. The most famous of these cultural enlighteners was the renowned Crimean Tatar patriotic poet Şevki Bektöre. Exile political activity increased during World War I, when activists in Istanbul lobbied the Ottoman government and tried to galvanize support from the Tatar diaspora to create an independent Crimean state allied to the Ottoman Empire. Despite the subsequent opposition of Atatürk's Republic of Turkey toward the political aspirations of Crimean exiles, this did not deter individuals like the anti-Communist Cafer Seydahmet, who until his death in 1960 continued to lobby international organizations and foreign states in an effort to dislodge Soviet rule from the Crimea.

Nonetheless, the Crimean diaspora (estimated at anywhere between two million to five million persons) was never able to change Turkey's basic acceptance of Soviet rule in their homeland, nor to generate any serious protests on the part of the Turkish government against the wholesale deportations of Tatars from the Crimea to Soviet Central Asia in 1944. During the post-World War II decades, one Crimean Tatar exile writing in Turkish, Cengiz Dağci, did manage to keep the memory of the Crimea alive in the minds of his increasingly turkified Crimean Tatar countrymen. Dağci's quite popular writings did seem to have some impact in helping to raise cultural awareness among Turkey's Crimean Tatar diaspora and to prepare it for the unexpected changes that were to occur in their homeland following the collapse of the Soviet Union in 1991.

The next numerically significant "other diaspora" from Ukraine are the Jews. Hundreds of thousands of Jews from Ukrainian lands in Austria-Hungary and the Russian Empire began emigrating to North America, in particular to the northeastern cities of the United States, between the 1880s and 1914. During those early decades, the Jews founded numerous organizations (*landsmanschaftn*) that brought together immigrants from specific communities. For instance, in the 1940s there were in the United States as many as 31 separate organizations of Jews from the city of Odessa alone, which were among the nearly 800 groups that formed an umbrella body known as the National Conference of Ukrainian Jewish Organizations. The National Conference was particularly active in trying to help the relatives of its members in Soviet Ukraine during World War II through the Jewish Council for Russian War Relief.

A few prominent Jews from Ukraine have been able to maintain contact with the non-Jewish culture of their geographic birthplace, which they invariably identify as "Russia." This has been particularly the case with musicians, such as Nathan Milstein, the world-renowned violinist from Odessa, and Vladimir Horowitz, the Kiev-trained piano virtuoso, who after six decades of living abroad was finally able to fulfill his dream during the late 1980s by returning home to perform in what he called "my Russia." Others had professions which enabled them to have ongoing direct relations with Ukraine, even during the years of Stalinist rule, when contacts with the West were severely restricted. Sol Hurok, for instance, was a New York impresario who for several decades after World War II brought to the West numerous performing ensembles from the former Soviet Union (including from Ukraine). Even more prominent was Armand Hammer, an American-born member of a family of successful entrepreneurs in pre–World War I southern Ukraine and himself a wealthy businessman who invested in industrial development in the Soviet Union in the 1920s and again after World War II.

Another type of Jewish emigrant from Ukraine consisted of those who remained in Europe. Some, like the French novelist from Kiev, Irène Némirovsky, the French painter and fashion designer born near Kremenchuk, Sonia Delaunay (Sarah Shtern-Terk), or the British publishing magnate and Labor party member of parliament, Robert Maxwell (Ludwig Koch), a native of Transcarpathia, functioned exclusively in the society of the countries to which they immigrated. Others remained linked to their homeland. Of the latter category, some retained that link through their writings, such as the German-language writers Manes Sperber (from eastern Galicia) and Paul Celan (from northern Bukovina), who since the 1930s enriched Austrian literature with works containing themes inspired by their birthplaces – small Jewish *shtetlakh* in Ukraine. Others, like Simon Wiesenthal, a native of eastern Galicia, set up in Vienna after World War II a Documentation Center devoted to research on the Holocaust and the worldwide pursuit of Nazi war criminals.

These musicians, businesspeople, writers, and civic activists were the exception, however, with regard to their views of their ancestral homeland, whatever they may have called it. Before 1914, most Jews emigrated from Ukraine because they were seeking to improve their economic situation, but their diaspora-born descendants have tended to remember the pogroms and other forms of persecution as the primary cause forcing their own ancestors, and by association all Jews, to seek refuge abroad. The view in the Jewish diaspora of the ancestral homeland in Ukraine and other parts of central and eastern Europe became clouded further by the massive destruction of entire families and communities during the World War II Holocaust. As a result, today the popular image of Ukraine among people of Jewish heritage living in North America and other countries tends to be negative. Such an attitude has at times contributed to friction between Jewish and Ukrainian organizations and spokespersons on the rare occasions when the two diaspora communities have been brought together by political issues, such as emigration policy from the former Soviet Union or the prosecution of alleged war criminals, which in the 1970s and 1980s were of concern to the United States, Canadian, and Israeli governments.

There is, of course, a Jewish diaspora from Ukraine in Israel. Among the earliest immigrants were small groups, often Zionists, who arrived in Palestine during the interwar years of the twentieth century. The most prominent of these individuals was a native of Kiev, Golda (Mabovitch) Meir, later prime minister of Israel, and Vladimir Jabotinsky, the Odessa-born Zionist leader who was exceptional in that he supported the idea of an independent Ukraine. Much larger numbers of Jews from Ukraine, this time mostly survivors of the Holocaust, arrived in Palestine and the newly created state of Israel in the years just after World War II. These people have maintained links with their homeland through numerous community organizations (*landsmanschaftn*) based in various Israeli cities and towns that try to keep alive the memory of their pre-Holocaust communities in Ukraine. There are also the followers of several Hasidic dynasties. While the Hasidim focus their lives around religion and may show little interest in the "old country" from which they were forced to flee, their lifestyle – including year-long winter dress in the tropical Israeli climate – is a constant reminder of traditional life in the *shtetlakh* of Ukraine.

An entirely new group comprise Jews who were allowed to leave the Soviet Union after political pressure was put on that country by Western powers, in particular the United States. In the 1970s alone, over 46,000 Jews from Soviet Ukraine emigrated to Israel. After a lull because of Soviet restrictions in the early 1980s, the numbers increased dramatically during the last years of Soviet rule and especially the first decade of independent Ukraine. Between 1989 and 2001 no less than three million Jews from Ukraine arrived in Israel. For the most part, these former Soviet citizens are Jews in name only. They speak Russian, associate with Russian culture, have little knowledge of the rich Jewish heritage of the world they left behind, and certainly have no affinity with the idea that Ukraine may be something distinct from Russia and worthy of interest in itself. As always, there are exceptions, and in this case two exceptional ones in Israel are: Iakov Suslensky from Odessa, an author and civic activist best known for his promoting the cause of ethnic Ukrainians who helped Jews during the Holocaust; and Moisei Fishbein, a distinguished Ukrainian-language poet and self-styled Ukrainian nationalist.

Another significant diaspora from Ukraine is represented by people of East Slavic heritage – in many cases individuals born into Ukrainian-speaking families – who consider themselves Russian. Wherever these people have lived, they have retained the hierarchy of multiple loyalties that was commonly held throughout Ukraine during the nineteenth century. In other words, they are Russians, or Little Russians, from Ukraine.

Most of these Little Russians were part of the massive emigration from the Russian Empire that occurred after the Bolshevik Revolution and Russian Civil War (1917–1920). They created no specifically Little Russian organizations, but instead integrated fully with the rest of the Russian immigrant community, whether in central and western Europe or in North America. Several adapted easily and made distinguished careers in their new homelands, such as the aviation designer Igor Sikorsky, the biologist Theodosius Dobzhansky, the chemist George Kistiakowsky, and the historian Michael T. Florinsky in the United States, and the diplomat George Ignatieff in Canada. Others, like the Yale University historian George Vernadsky (the son of the first head of the Ukrainian Academy of Sciences) and the Orthodox priest and theologian Georges Florovsky, who taught for many years in Paris and at Harvard and Princeton Universities, devoted much of their scholarship to developments in Ukraine. They invariably described it, however, as "West Russia" and therefore as an integral part of a single Russian civilization.

Often the Little Russian immigrants regarded and wrote nostalgically about Ukraine as their "Russian" homeland, which might be occupied by the Bolsheviks but one day would be brought back into the fold of a "one and indivisible" democratic Russia. There were also Little Russians less tolerant of and indeed openly hostile to the notion that Ukraine could ever become a sovereign state, denying even that Ukrainians existed as a distinct nationality. Such views were propagated in a spate of books and pamphlets that were popular in certain circles of the Russian immigration, with self-explanatory titles such as *The Ukrainian Question: The Historic Truth Versus the Separatist Propaganda* (1920), by Prince Aleksandr Volkonskii; *Le plus grand mensonge du XX siècle: l'Ukraine* (The Greatest Lie of the Twentieth Century: Ukraine, 1939), by Vasilii Shul'gin; and *Ukraine, a Russian Land* (1940), co-authored by Sergei Obolenskii. During the Cold War, a time when Russian patriots abroad felt their entire heritage was being unjustly associated with Communism and the Soviet enemy, some reacted by criticizing American political leaders who, as they saw it, accepted the "propaganda of Ukrainian émigré specialists" and recognized Ukraine as a legitimate if occupied national entity and as a full-fledged member of organizations like the Munich-based Anti-Bolshevik Bloc of Nations.

Little Russians have been particularly active in the various jurisdictions of the Russian Orthodox Church that have flourished in western Europe and North America both before and after the Bolshevik Revolution. During the interwar years, many Russian émigré clergy either were from Ukraine or had functioned there as hierarchs before the civil war forced them to leave. Among the latter group were Metropolitan Antonii (Aleksei Khrapovitskii, reigned 1920–1927), the head of the Synod Abroad, based at the time in Sremski Kar-

lovci, Yugoslavia, and Metropolitan Evlogii (Vasilii Georgievskii, reigned 1921–
1946), the head of the Exarchate for Western Europe, based in Paris, which
was first under the Patriarchate of Moscow and later under the Ecumenical
Patriarchate of Constantinople. Metropolitans Antonii and Evlogii were typical
of other clerics from "Little Russia" who denied that Ukrainians exist as a distinct people and who condemned as superfluous and uncanonical all efforts to
create an autocephalous Ukrainian Orthodox church. To this day, the Orthodox
Church in America (formerly the Russian Orthodox Church in North America)
and the Russian Orthodox Church Abroad (the Synod, based in New York City)
are made up largely of clergy and faithful who themselves or whose parents
came from Ukraine but who identify themselves as Russians.

Another East Slavic diaspora are the Carpatho-Rusyns. They derive from the
Transcarpathian oblast (historic Subcarpathian Rus') of Ukraine and the immediately neighboring areas of Slovakia (the Prešov Region) and southeastern
Poland (the Lemko Region). Whereas some sought work in western European countries (France, Belgium), the vast majority went to North America, in
particular to the United States, where an estimated 225,000 arrived between
the 1880s and 1914. Thereafter the numbers were much smaller, about 25,000
to the United States and at most 20,000 to Canada. When Carpatho-Rusyns
first arrived and from the 1880s settled in large concentrations in the industrial
regions of the northeastern United States they interacted closely with other
Rusyns (Ukrainians) from eastern Galicia through their Greek Catholic faith.

Already before 1900, however, different attitudes toward national and religious identity resulted in the evolution of a distinct Carpatho-Rusyn community with its own secular organizations and church jurisdictions, both Greek
Catholic and Orthodox. At this time a large number of Carpatho-Rusyns
together with some Galician Rusyns converted to Orthodoxy; as part of that
process they also adopted a Russian national identity and, together with "Little Russians" from Ukraine, they formed the backbone of the Russian diaspora
in North America for much of the first half of the twentieth century. Among
such "Russians" were two Carpatho-Rusyns from the Prešov Region in Slovakia who were particularly predominant in church life: St Aleksei (Alexis Toth),
hailed "the father of Orthodoxy in America" for his proselytizing efforts before
World War I; and Metropolitan Laurus (Vasyl' Shkurla), the primate of the Russian Orthodox Church Abroad (the Synod), who was instrumental in healing
the breach with the Russian Orthodox Church – Moscow Patriarchate at the
outset of the twenty-first century.

Those Carpatho-Rusyns who maintained a distinct identity and community structures have at times played an important role in developments in their
ancestral homeland. This was particularly so after World War I, when organizations like the Greek Catholic Union and the American National Council of
Uhro-Rusyns lobbied successfully for the incorporation of Subcarpathian Rus'
(present-day Transcarpathia) into Czechoslovakia (see chapter 41), and more

recently in the years since the Revolutions of 1889 and the collapse of the Soviet Union, when American-based organizations like the Carpatho-Rusyn Research Center and the Carpatho-Rusyn Society have assisted the revival of a Carpatho-Rusyn identity in Ukraine and neighboring countries.

A relatively newer diaspora from Ukraine comprises Poles from the *Zieme zabrane*, or "territories taken from Poland" after World War II. Among these were Poles from eastern Galicia and western Volhynia who were forced into exile between 1939 and 1946 after their "Polish" homeland was forcibly annexed to the Soviet Union. Most of the nearly half-million Poles remaining at the close of World War II in what by then was Soviet Ukrainian territory were, according to an agreement with the Soviet Union, resettled in postwar Poland, especially in Silesia and other territories annexed from defeated Germany.

The former Germanic city of Breslau in Silesia, ruled for centuries by Czechs and later Prussians and then renamed Wrocław in 1945, became a major destination for Poles from Ukraine. In many ways, postwar Polish Wrocław became a "new Lwów," where some of the most important Polish institutions formerly in L'viv were reestablished, including the Ossolineum Library and the monumental panoramic painting of the 1794 Battle of Racławice, created in 1894 as the symbol of the Polish peasantry's contribution to the heroic but ultimately unsuccessful struggle to maintain Poland's independence in the late eighteenth century. So pervasive has the "easterner's" presence become that there are today guidebooks and phrasebooks which point out the ongoing impact of the "Lwów dialect and pronunciation" on the Polish spoken language of Wrocław.

World War II also displaced thousands of Poles from Galicia and Volhynia to various parts of Europe and North America, where they were to remain permanently. For example, immediately after the war, a contingent of the Polish diaspora from Ukraine, specifically from the city of L'viv, established in London, England, the L'viv Circle (Koło Lwowian) to perpetuate through lectures and publications the memory of Polish Lwów. Almost without exception, the Poles from L'viv and other eastern territories (*kresy*) resented the Ukrainians, who, they believed, usurped their Polish homeland with the aid of Soviet power. Such attitudes have from time to time caused friction between Poles and Ukrainians in the diaspora, especially when the subject of the UPA (Ukrainian Insurgent Army) is discussed in the Polish press and other publications abroad.

The Poles from Ukraine who found themselves in postwar Poland were for decades forbidden by the pro-Soviet Polish authorities to discuss publicly the fate of their homeland. Privately, however, the "easterners" shared with other Poles their resentment against the Soviets and, by default, against Ukrainians, who, from their perspective, had taken possession of their Polish patrimony. The suppression of public memory about Galicia and Volhynia came to an end with the political changes brought about by Gorbachev in the mid-1980s. Since that time, Poland has experienced an outburst of interest in its former eastern lands. Numerous books, pamphlets, reprintings, and journals devoted to "Polish" western Ukraine have appeared. L'viv, in particular, has been the focus of attention through publications, media reports, and the activity of over a dozen Friends of Lwów societies founded throughout Poland since 1989.

It seems that members of the Polish diaspora from Ukraine, as well as their descendants and sympathizers, are finally resigned to the reality that the international boundaries established in 1945 are not going to change. They hope, however, that by supporting independent Ukraine and bringing it closer to the European Union that they will be able to contribute to the restoration of Polish monuments there and to encourage a positive reappraisal of the Polish contribution to the history and culture of western Ukraine.

Finally, there are many Germans who have emigrated from Ukraine and whose descendants still live in the mid-western agricultural states and provinces of the United States and Canada where their forebears first settled. A descendant of one of these settlers, Edward Schreyer, reached the highest government office, serving as Governor-General of Canada in the early 1980s. In general, the late-nineteenth-century immigrants and their descendants have been absorbed into the large German-American and German-Canadian communities, or they have identified themselves and their organizations as "Germans from Russia."

The Mennonites, too, have generally referred to the place they emigrated from as Russia (technically the Russian Empire), even though the vast majority left lands within what is present-day Ukraine. The numerous scholarly centers for Mennonite studies, among them the Chair of Mennonite Studies and Menno Simons College at the University of Winnipeg and Conrad Grebel College at the University of Waterloo in Ontario, invariably focus their work on communities who trace their origins to Ukraine. Although the Mennonite diaspora continues to emphasize its origins as being "from Russia," and although there are virtually no Mennonites left in the farmlands of southern Ukraine, several diasporan groups began after independence in the 1990s to visit their ancestral villages in Ukraine and to send humanitarian aid there, knowing full well that the recipients were local ethnic Ukrainians (or in some cases Russians), but not Mennonites.

teenth century, a few Jews were able to amass substantial wealth in Galician banking, oil, trade, industry, and even large-scale landowning. These achievements were exceptional, however. The vast majority, in part because of rapid demographic growth and the province's relatively limited economic opportunities, remained poor. For these reasons, Galicia's Jews, like its Ukrainians, began to emigrate en masse, first to neighboring Hungary (Transcarpathia and eastern Slovakia), then to the imperial capital of Vienna, and finally to the northeastern United States, where between 1881 and 1910, 237,000 Jewish *Galitsiyaner* (173,000 from eastern Galicia alone), as they were known, sought to improve their economic status.

Despite emigration, Galicia in the second half of the nineteenth century remained the center of a vibrant Jewish political and cultural life. Jews had their own political parties which cooperated with Polish parties, and they had members in both the Galician diet and the imperial parliament in Vienna. They were particularly well represented on regional and urban councils. Although they initially cooperated with the Poles, by the beginning of the twentieth century many Jewish candidates were cooperating with the Ukrainians in order to counteract Polish political dominance.

While the vast majority of Galicia's Jews remained Hasidic traditionalists who eschewed contact with the gentile world, the cultural elite favored assimilation. In a sense, the members of the Jewish elite were similar to those Ukrainians who accepted the principle of multiple loyalties. For them, dual identity meant being a German or a Pole of Jewish religious background. The Ukrainian option was less desirable, although in 1910 over 22,000 Jews declared that their native language was Ukrainian and therefore were classified as Ukrainian. Ukrainophile Jews were in the minority, however. As for the Germanophiles and Polonophiles, the latter group prevailed after the 1870s. Jewish Polonophiles attended Polish schools and adopted a Polish national identity.

In politics, some Jewish Polonophiles wholeheartedly embraced the Polish national cause (Wilhelm Feldman), while others allied themselves with Polish and Ukrainian socialists whose primary interest was the transformation of Galicia's socioeconomic system. Still another faction rejected any expectation that real improvement for Jews could ever be achieved in Galicia, or, for that matter, anywhere else in central and eastern Europe. These were the Zionists, who, from the time their first Galician organization was established in Przemyśl in 1874, looked to only one avenue to Jewish salvation – emigration to Palestine. Given the reality of Ottoman rule, emigration to Palestine was not immediately possible, and before long some Galician Zionists had formulated the concept of self-emancipation through participation in local politics in order to improve the status of Jews while they still remained in Europe.

One of the aspects of self-emancipation was a new attitude toward the indigenous Yiddish culture of Jews in the Austro-Hungarian Empire as well as elsewhere in central and eastern Europe. Neighboring Bukovina, in particular Chernivtsi, was the home of the founder of Yiddish theater, Avrom Goldfadn, and the site of the first world congress of Yiddish language and culture. Organized by Nathan Birnbaum and other Zionist leaders, the Chernivtsi language congress, notwithstanding fierce opposition on the part of the supporters of Hebrew, set in motion a process whereby Yiddish was finally codified as a distinct literary language.

Late-nineteenth century Galicia and Bukovina also produced several accomplished writers who, while living most of their lives well beyond the world into which they were born and to which they had initially been acculturated, continued to find artistic inspiration in their native Jewish heritage. The writer and editor Karl-Emil Franzos, who spent most of his life in Vienna and Berlin, depicted Jewish life in Galicia and Bukovina in several of his German-language novels and short stories. Two other Galician-born Jews were to make their literary careers after World War I, by which time Austria-Hungary had ceased to exist: the German-language

Austrian novelist Joseph Roth, whose writings are imbued with themes from life during the last years of the Habsburg Empire; and the Yiddish- and Hebrew-language Israeli writer and Nobel laureate, Shemu'el Yosef Agnon, several of whose novels are set in eastern Galicia. Thus, the Jews of Galicia, most of whom lived in the eastern part of the province, during the last seventy-five years of Austrian rule engaged in a broad spectrum of political, socioeconomic, and cultural activity, sometimes in cooperation and at other times in competition with the Ukrainians and Poles among whom they lived.

Chernivtsi was also the main center for Bukovina's Romanians. Although in 1900 they constituted only 14.3 percent of the city's population, Chernivtsi (in Romanian, Cernăuţi) had by that time become the home of several Romanian schools, cultural organizations, newspapers, and political groups. Among the articulate portion of the Romanian population, the large landowners, led by the Austrian officials Eudoxiu Hurmuzaki and Alexandru Petrino, were quite content with centralized Habsburg rule. They were challenged, however, during the last two decades of the nineteenth century by a movement of intellectuals who in 1892 founded the Romanian National party. The party urged the implementation of greater autonomy for Bukovina and an improvement in the economic status of the province's Romanian peasantry.

The oldest and most important cultural organization was the Society for Romanian Literature and Culture in Bukovina (Societate pentru Literatura si Cultura Română in Bucovina), founded in Chernivtsi in 1863. Over the next half century, it published literary journals (*Foaia,* 1865–69; *Aurora Română,* 1881–84), provided scholarships for Romanian *gymnasium* students, encouraged the creation of a Department of Romanian Language and Literature at the newly established University of Chernivtsi (1875), and, in 1897, opened a printing shop for a wide variety of Romanian-language books, school texts, and newspapers. As well, the society continually pressed the Austrian government to extend Romanian-language education in Bukovina, with the result that by 1900, classes were taught in Romanian in 115 elementary schools, that is, in 37 percent of all elementary schools in the province.

During the last three decades of Habsburg rule, Romanian leaders were concerned primarily with two issues. The first was the growth of the local Ukrainian movement, which they feared was displacing them in their "own province." The other issue was Romanian irredentism from neighboring Romania. Moldavia and Walachia had united in 1858 and then, two decades later, as the Kingdom of Romania, had become independent of the Ottoman Empire. Irredentists saw that achievement as only the first step toward the eventual reunification of all "Romanian" lands, which meant adding to the Romanian Kingdom three territories: Transylvania from Hungary, Bessarabia from Russia, and Bukovina from Austria. Nonetheless, despite such irredentist calls from the south, the Romanians in Bukovina remained for the most part satisfied with the increasing cultural and administrative autonomy they enjoyed under Habsburg rule.

The Ukrainian National Movement in Austria-Hungary, 1849–1914

The remarkable achievements in Ukrainian cultural, organizational, and political life during the revolutionary period of 1848–1849 came rather suddenly. They were, moreover, in large part initiated from above, by the Austrian imperial government in Vienna. For its part, the mass of the Ukrainian population was not yet ready to enter the world of modern politics. Much work still had to be done in the areas of education and economic development, and much experience gained in the realm of politics. This is precisely what was achieved during the second half of the nineteenth and first two decades of the twentieth centuries, that is, between 1849 and the outbreak of World War I in 1914.

During this period, the Ukrainian national movement, especially in Galicia, went through both the second, organizational stage and the third, political stage of intelligentsia-inspired nationalist movements. Before the movement could pass successfully through these stages, however, it had to have ideological unity, that is, a clear idea of who the East Slavic population living in eastern Galicia, northern Bukovina, and Transcarpathia actually was. It was this struggle to obtain a consensus on national identity that marked much of the national movement among the Ukrainians in the Austrian Empire during the second half of the nineteenth century. As long as the movement remained small, the issue of national identity was germane for only a limited number of intellectuals, who in the decades before 1848 confined themselves to arguing about language. But after 1848, when Ukrainians entered political, educational, and organizational life, the stakes rose and the need for a clearer understanding of national self-identity became more pressing than ever before.

In search of a national identity

Most discussions about late nineteenth-century eastern Galicia and, to a lesser degree, Bukovina and Transcarpathia treat the Ukrainian problem as one in which the question of national identity was fought by two opposing factions or orientations – the so-called Russophiles and Ukrainophiles. Such an approach is an oversimplification. Before 1848, there were basically two orientations among the

Galician-Ukrainian educated elite with respect to the question of national identity: the Polonophiles and the Rus' patriots.

The Polonophiles accepted the notion that the East Slavs of Galicia were *gente Rutheni, natione Poloni,* that is, Ruthenians of the Polish nation. This meant that even though the East Slavic population of Galicia – and, by extension, Ukraine in general – spoke distinct dialects and followed the Eastern Christian rite, their cultural and national loyalties were directed toward Poland. According to such a premise, they were similar in essentials to the Mazovians, for example, or to any other regional branch of the Polish nationality. In other words, they were Poles (of the Greco-Byzantine instead of the Latin rite) who spoke Ruthenian/Rusyn (Ukrainian) dialects of the Polish language and used literary Polish for intellectual discourse. In stark contrast, the Rus' patriots believed that the spoken language and culture of the East Slavic population were not Polish, but rather integrally related to those of the larger East Slavic world within the Russian Empire. Following the revolution of 1848, the Polonophile orientation lost its attractiveness among the Galician-Ukrainian educated elite, but the Rus' orientation continued to gather adherents among the ever-growing secular as well as the religious elite. Still unclear, however, was how these Rus' patriots would define their relationship to the larger East Slavic world.

Out of the effort to define that relationship more precisely, three orientations developed during the second half of the nineteenth century: (1) the Old Ruthenian, (2) the Ukrainophile, and (3) the Russophile. In a sense, at the beginning of this period all Rus' patriots were Old Ruthenians (*starorusyny*). And while it may be true that Ukrainophile tendencies among certain leaders were evident as early as the 1830s and Russophile tendencies in the 1850s, greater clarification among the three orientations did not begin to take place until the late 1860s.

How did these three orientations differ from each other, and in what ways, if any, were they similar? Basically, their differences stemmed from conflicting interpretations of the historical past and views about the national language. As for their similarities, all three orientations shared the belief that the origin of Austria's East Slavs must be traced back to medieval Kievan Rus'. All three also used the same term to describe themselves and their culture: they were the people of Rus', who called themselves *rusyny* (Rusyns or Ruthenians) and who spoke the *rus'kyi* (Rusyn or Ruthenian) language.

Although all three orientations started from a similar terminological premise, their understanding of terms differed. The Ukrainophiles argued that the terms *rusyny* and *rus'kyi* were antiquated forms of the preferable and more modern terms *ukraïntsi* (Ukrainians) and *ukraïns'kyi* (Ukrainian). The language and the group therefore should be called Ukrainian. The Russophiles argued that the terms *rusyny* and *rus'kyi* were local variants of the forms *russkie* (Russians) and *russkii* (Russian). Accordingly, the people in question were really Russian and the language they spoke was Russian, or, more precisely, the "Little Russian dialect" of Russian. In the end, only the Old Ruthenians continued to use the original terms, *rusyny* and *rus'kyi*, which also implied that the concept of Ruthenianism was limited to East Slavs within the Austro-Hungarian Empire. While Galicia's Old

OLD RUTHENIANS, RUSSOPHILES, AND UKRAINOPHILES

Behind what may seem little more than a semantic sleight of hand or a play with words, there were profound perceptual differences among the three factions of Austria-Hungary's Ukrainian intelligentsia, especially between the Russophiles and the Ukrainophiles. The Old Ruthenians and the Russophiles agreed that the three branches of the East Slavs – Great Russians (*velikorossy*), Belorussians (*belorossy*), and Little Russians (*malorossy*) – comprised one Russian, or a common-Russian (*obshcherusskii*), nationality. While the Old Ruthenian and Russophile ideologists admitted that there were recognizable cultural and linguistic differences among the three component parts of this "common-Russian people," the Russophiles went a step further. They argued that members of all three East Slav components should identify themselves as Russian and use one literary language, Russian, for intellectual discourse. In this sense, the Russophiles in the Austrian Empire resembled those Ukrainians, or Little Russians, in Dnieper Ukraine who held to a hierarchy of multiple loyalties. In other words, they considered themselves "Little Russian" Russians from Galicia.

In contrast, the Ukrainophiles considered the idea of a single common-Russian nationality an ideological fantasy. They regarded the East Slavs of Austria-Hungary as belonging to a distinct Ukrainian nationality living on compact ethnographic territory that stretched from the Carpathian Mountains in the west to the Caucasus Mountains in the southeast. This last, geographic formulation was put forth to counteract the Russophile formulation that a single Russian people lived on lands that stretched from the Carpathians to the Pacific Ocean.

The ideological underpinnings of the three national orientations in Galicia were differing interpretations of the history of the East Slavs. All three orientations began with the premise that Kievan Rus' was the starting point of the history of the East Slavs and that one important component of that medieval state was the principality, later the Kingdom, of Galicia-Volhynia. As for what happened after the disintegration of Kievan Rus' in the thirteenth century and of the Galician-Volhynian Kingdom in the fourteenth century, each orientation presented a different understanding. The Old Ruthenians essentially limited their discussion to eastern Galicia, as if it were a kind of distinct territorial and even ethnocultural unit. For the Old Ruthenians, the era of Polish domination between 1340 and 1772 was a negative and Austrian rule a positive phenomenon.

Both the Russophiles and the Ukrainophiles viewed Galicia as part of a larger unit, but not the same unit. The Russophiles adopted the notion accepted in the Russian Empire of the unity of East Slavic historical development under the hegemony of the northern Rus' princes and, later, Muscovy as expressed in the linear theory of the displacement of political centers: from Kiev to Vladimir-na-Kliazma to Moscow to St Petersburg (see chapter 2). Within this framework, they considered Galicia a "Russian" land, whose unity with medieval "Kievan Russia" had been interrupted temporarily by Polish and Austrian occupation along the way to its eventual "reunification" with "mother Russia," to take place at some future time.

The Ukrainophiles rejected the theory of the transfer of political centers, which, by implication, treated Ukraine (South Russia or Little Russia) as a province. Instead, they argued that Kievan Rus' formed the basis of a distinct civilization centered on Ukrainian territory and subsequently maintained in the Galician-Volhynian Kingdom and then the Cossack state. Rus'-Ukrainian historical continuity was still being sustained during the nineteenth century in the language and folklore, that is, in the collective psyche of the Ukrainian people. Eastern Galicia, as well as northern Bukovina and Transcarpathia, was part of this larger Ukrainian whole. It is no coincidence that it was precisely in Galicia's administrative center of L'viv that the Ukrainian viewpoint was given its most elaborate presentation during the late nineteenth and early twentieth centuries, in the historical writings of Professor Mykhailo S. Hrushevs'kyi.

Ruthenians never went so far as to argue that they formed a separate nationality, their perceptual horizons nonetheless remained limited to the realm of the Habsburgs.

Language as the symbol of identity

The schematization outlined above is most clearly borne out in the evolution of the language question. On one point, all three factions were in agreement: that the written language used by Galicia's Ukrainians should not employ the Roman (Latin) alphabet. Efforts in the direction of the Roman had been made in 1848 by the former Ruthenian Triad member Ivan Vahylevych in the pro-Polish Ruthenian Council's short-lived newspaper, *Dnewnyk ruskij*, and again in 1859 by the Polish viceroy of Galicia, Agenor Gołuchowski, who tried to introduce a Czech-based Roman alphabet. Both attempts failed, however, with the result that the vast majority of Ukrainian publications in Galicia appeared in the Cyrillic alphabet, first in the Church Slavonic (*kyrylytsia*) script and then, beginning in the late 1850s, in the modern civil (*grazhdanka*) script.

With respect to the language itself, the old controversy opposing a book language with prestige to one based on the spoken vernacular (which was associated with peasant vulgarisms) continued. In 1848, the Supreme Ruthenian Council called for the introduction in schools and publications of "that language which our people speak,"[1] and initially the vernacular was used. After the conservatives in the clerical leadership came to dominate the national movement, however, there was a return to the Slaveno-Rusyn book language. This meant essentially Church Slavonic, but now with fewer local vernacular elements and an increasing number of borrowings from Russian. Some leaders, like Ivan Naumovych, even argued that the "Great Russian" literary language as used by the Muscovites was really the creation of Little Russians. If that were the case, the Galician Ruthenians, as Little Russians, were simply taking back what rightfully belonged to them in the first place. In the end, it was a Galician "Russian" recension of Church Slavonic that was used by the Old Ruthenians in their publications, the best known of which was the newspaper *Slovo* (L'viv, 1861–87). The language was called *ruskyi* (later *russkyi*) by its practitioners, but it was never codified, lacked systematic rules, and it was described by its detractors – both Ukrainophiles and Russophiles – as the *iazychie*, or macaronic jargon.

In the 1860s, some leaders active since 1848 were joined by younger Galicians who favored use of the local vernacular. They were inspired especially by the writings of the Dnieper Ukrainian Taras Shevchenko, who was just becoming known in Galicia. Because of their interest in the peasants and the spoken language, these Galicians became known as the *narodovtsi*, or populists. Their first attempts to publish journals in the Galician vernacular (*Vechernytsi*, 1862–63; *Meta*, 1863–66; *Nyva*, 1865; *Rusalka*, 1866) during the 1860s were short-lived. Following the 1863 and 1876 restrictions on publishing in Ukrainian that were imposed in the Russian Empire, however, a few Dnieper Ukrainians, led by Panteleimon Kulish and Oleksander Konys'kyi, gave their support to the Galician populists and founded two organs, *Pravda* (1867–96) and *Zoria* (1880–97), and, after their demise, the journal *Literaturno-naukovyi vistnyk* (1898–1932). Although published in L'viv, these publications served both Galician and Dnieper Ukrainians, and they became the leading Ukrainian organs for literary works and for political, social, and cultural commentary. The Galician Ukrainophiles also established their own vernacular newspaper, *Dilo* (1880–1939), which appeared daily after 1888.

Despite their belief in ethnolinguistic unity with Ukrainians in the Russian Empire, until the very end of the century, Galicia's populist Ukrainophiles referred to their nationality and the vernacular language they were using as Rusyn/Ruthenian (*rus'ka narodnist,' rus'ka mova*). It was not until the late 1890s and, more notably, the first decades of the twentieth century that the populist intelligentsia adopted the term *Ukrainian* instead of *Rusyn/Ruthenian* to describe their nationality and language.

This same period also witnessed serious attempts to codify the Galician vernacular through the publication of grammars (Mykhailo Osadtsa, 1863; Omelian Ohonovs'kyi, 1880, 1889; Stepan Smal'-Stots'kyi and Fedir Gartner, 1893, 1907, 1914) and the first large-scale dictionaries of the Ukrainian, or, as it was officially called, the Ruthenian, language (Omelian Partyts'kyi, 1867; Ievhen Zhelekhivs'kyi, 1886). The populist Ukrainophiles received a particular boost when in 1892 the Austrian school administration in both Galicia and Bukovina accepted the vernacular (according to the model of the Zhelekhivs'kyi dictionary) for use in schools and for official purposes. No less important for the Ukrainophile success in language was the fact that the movement had a number of outstanding writers. Not only did Dnieper Ukraine's leading authors (O. Konys'kyi, M. Kotsiubyns'kyi, I. Nechui-Levyts'kyi, L. Ukraïnka, B. Hrinchenko) publish in the pages of Galicia's journals, the region also produced its own literary genius in the person of Ivan

Franko. Although Franko started out as an Old Ruthenian writing in what he later called the *iazychie*, quite early in his career he switched to a vernacular-based medium, in which he wrote an astonishingly large body of prose, poetry, plays, translations, essays, and scholarly works. Because of his multifarious talent, Franko showed that the Galician variant of Ukrainian was a viable instrument of expression for all kinds of intellectual endeavor.

Faced with the success of the populist Ukrainophiles on the question of language, a few members of the Old Ruthenian camp (Pylyp Svystun, Osyp A. Markov, Osyp Monchalovs'kyi, Iuliian Iavors'kyi, Semen Bendasiuk) rejected the uncodified Slaveno-Rusyn book language (the *iazychie*) and adopted instead standard literary Russian. During the 1890s, they started several newspapers and journals (*Besieda*, 1887–97; *Prikarpatskaia Rus'*, 1909–15), and at the beginning of the twentieth century they took over the Old Ruthenian cultural organizations (the National Home, the Galician-Rus' Matytsia), whose publications they russified. Their activity marked the emergence of a distinct Russophile movement in Galicia. Whether in the area of language or – as will become evident – in that of organizational and political life, the Russophiles arrived on the Galician scene too late.

There are no hard and fast chronological markers of when Galicia's Old Ruthenian, Ukrainophile, and Russophile factions arose or when they ceased to exist. Moreover, it was not uncommon to find supporters of one orientation joining one or both of the ideological rivals at different times in their careers. Generally, however, it is safe to assume that most Galician leaders had an Old Ruthenian provincial national outlook until the 1860s. Then, during that decade and especially during the 1870s, the populists, later known as the Ukrainophiles, split off. While there were committed individual Russophiles active in the 1850s, it was not until the 1890s that their distinctness from the Old Ruthenians became clear. But notwithstanding the chronological framework proposed here, it is possible, when looking at the first half of the nineteenth century, to consider individuals like the historian Denys Zubryts'kyi as a Russophile and the Ruthenian Triad (M. Shashkevych, Ia. Holovats'kyi, and I. Vahylevych) as Ukrainophile in orientation, and, when looking at the second half of the century, to recognize that the former Triad member Holovats'kyi as well as a few leading Old Ruthenians (Ivan Naumovych, Venedikt Ploshchans'kyi) became Russophiles well before the advent of a full-blown Russophile movement in the 1890s. Put another way, the nationality movement in late nineteenth-century Galicia was characterized by a marked degree of ideological fluidity.

The national movement in Galicia: The organizational stage

The Ukrainian national movement in Galicia underwent a vibrant development during the second half of the nineteenth century. The oldest organizations, the Stauropegial Institute, the National Home, and the Galician-Rus' Matytsia, continued to remain in the hands of the Old Ruthenians. Each of these organizations maintained a library, museum, archive, and printing shop as part of its operations in L'viv, and each was responsible for publishing newspapers, journals, scholarly works, and school texts. By and large, however, they had little direct contact with the peasant masses in rural areas.

The young populists of the 1860s hoped to correct this situation, and when they were unable to obtain positions of leadership in the Old Ruthenian organizations, they created their own. Among the first of these was the Ruthenian Club (Rus'ka Besida), established in L'viv in 1861 as a kind of social society. Three years later, the Ruthenian Club established the first permanent Ukrainian theater anywhere, and with cadres from both Galicia and Dnieper Ukraine successfully propagated the vernacular through plays staged in both L'viv and the surrounding country-side.

In terms of impact on broader segments of the Ukrainian population, the Prosvita Society, founded in L'viv in 1868, was among the region's most influential organizations. Prosvita, which means enlightenment, had as its original goal the promotion of culture and education at both the popular and the scholarly level. From the 1870s, however, it concentrated almost exclusively on popular culture and on work among the people. It did so through the offering of adult education classes, the establishment of village reading rooms, and the publication of textbooks and works in Ukrainian literature and history. In the 1890s, Prosvita entered the economic field, organizing stores, community warehouses, savings and loan banks, and agricultural and commercial cooperatives. By 1906, the Prosvita Society had, besides its main building in L'viv, a broad network throughout eastern Galicia, including thirty-nine affiliates or branches, 1,700 reading rooms, and 10,000 members. In its publication program, Prosvita issued eighty-two titles between 1869 and 1914, which totaled 655,000 copies. All were in vernacular Ukrainian.

Prosvita's efforts in the important field of economic activity were not in isolation. The cooperative movement became widespread during the 1890s, with the result that on the eve of World War I there were more than 500 Ukrainian cooperatives and mutual credit associations. Among the more prominent were the National Trade Association (Narodna Torhivlia, est. 1883), the Dniester Fire Insurance Association (est. 1892), the Village Farmer Association (Sil's'kyi Hospodar, est. 1898), the Provincial Credit Union (Tsentrobank, est. 1898), the Provincial Audit Union (Kraiovyi Soiuz Reviziinyi, est. 1904), and the Provincial Dairy Union (Maslosoiuz, est. 1907). The cooperatives, all operated by Ukrainians, helped peasants and tradespeople to obtain credit and therefore the financial means to produce and sell their products. Thus, the cooperative movement made possible a process of organic social growth in which an improvement in economic standards developed hand in hand with an increase in Ukrainian national consciousness.

After the Prosvita Society redirected its energies to focus on education for the masses, the populist Ukrainophiles founded a new organization to promote literature and literary scholarship. In 1873, the Shevchenko Society was established in L'viv at the initiative of and with financial support from leaders in Dnieper Ukraine, where at that very time Ukrainian scholarship was being hampered by new restrictions imposed by the tsarist government. The initial, literary orientation of the Shevchenko Society changed in 1892, again at the initiative of Dnieper Ukrainians such as Volodymyr Antonovych and Oleksander Konys'kyi. The organization was renamed the Shevchenko Scientific Society (Naukove Tovarystvo imeny Shevchenka). Five years later, in 1897, the society received a new president, the dynamic Dnieper-Ukrainian historian Mykhailo S. Hrushevs'kyi, who at the time was head of the department of Ukrainian history at L'viv University.

Under Hrushevs'kyi's leadership, which lasted until 1913, the Shevchenko Scientific Society became an unofficial Ukrainian academy of sciences, with permanent and corresponding members from all Ukrainian lands. Patterned on the Austrian Imperial Academy of Sciences in Vienna, it was divided into three sections: the historical-philosophical, the philological, and the mathematical-natural sciences-medical. Each of the sections published at least one scholarly periodical and/or series of scholarly monographs, including the historical-philosophical section's prestigious *Zapysky* (L'viv, 1892–1939). With the exception, perhaps, of the scholarly achievements during the brief period of Ukrainianization in Soviet Ukraine during the 1920s, the work sponsored by the Shevchenko Scientific Society in pre-World War I Austrian Galicia represented the apogee of Ukrainian scholarly endeavor.

The Old Ruthenians and Russophiles simply could not keep up with the organizational talent of the populist Ukrainophiles. The Old Ruthenian National Home and Galician-Rus' Matytsia had some scholarly pretensions, but by the 1880s their journals had become no more than outlets for the dry and rather antiquated historical compilations of a few authors (Bohdan Didyts'kyi and, especially, Antin Petrushevych). At the beginning of the twentieth century, the younger Russophiles (Pylyp Svystun, Osyp Monchalovs'kyi) took over these organizations and tried to revive scholarship in a "Galician-Russian" ideological and linguistic mode, but its reach was largely restricted to a small circle of supporters.

At the popular level, the Old Ruthenians followed the lead of the Prosvita Society, establishing the Kachkovs'kyi Society (Obshchestvo imeny Mykhaila Kachkovs'koho) in Kolomyia in 1874. Two years later, its headquarters were moved to L'viv, and at the initiative of the priest Ivan Naumovych, an Old Ruthenian with strong Russophile inclinations, the Kachkovs'kyi Society published in the vernacular what became a very popular journal, *Nauka* (1871–1914). It contained cultural and economic information in a language and style quite accessible to the peasant masses. Aside from its main building in L'viv, by 1906 the Kachkovs'kyi Society had 26 affiliates, 1,261 reading rooms, and over 9,000 members. Between 1875 and 1914, it published 400 booklets in print runs ranging from 5,000 to 10,000 copies. Although these figures were more or less comparable to the Prosvita Society's, the Old Ruthenians and later Russophiles had nothing to compare with the populist-Ukrainian theater and the wide range of Ukrainian cooperatives and mutual credit associations.

In the realm of education, the Ukrainians in Galicia were unequal to the Poles, notwithstanding their roughly equal numerical size. In relative terms, however, and considering the fact that there were no Ukrainian schools at all in the Russian Empire, Galicia's Ukrainians made remarkable progress during the second half of the nineteenth century. By 1914, there were approximately 3,600 elementary schools in eastern Galicia (including the Lemko region), 71 percent of which (2,500) were Ukrainian. At the secondary level, the Ukrainians had 6 state *gymnasia* (two in L'viv and one each in Przemyśl, Kolomyia, Ternopil', and Stanyslaviv), separate classes for Ukrainian students at 2 Polish *gymnasia* (Berezhany and Stryi), and 15 private *gymnasia*. There were also 10 teachers' colleges in eastern Galicia, each of which offered bilingual instruction, in Polish and Ukrainian. Most important from the standpoint of the debate as to the proper national orientation was the Austrian government's decision in 1892 to recognize the vernacular Ukrainian (Rusyn) language as the standard for instructional purposes. As a result of this decision, the Old Ruthenian and Russophile orientations were effectively eliminated from the all-important educational system.

Although Ukrainians did not have their own university, there were departments (*katedry*) at L'viv University, which offered Ukrainian-language instruction in subjects related to Ukrainian culture as well as in some general subjects (law and theology). To the Department of Ruthenian Language and Literature, established in 1848, several new Ukrainian departments were added, bringing the total to ten by 1914. The most influential was the department devoted to Ukrainian history. Officially, it was called the Second Department of World History with Particular Emphasis on the History of Eastern Europe. It was established in 1894, and because the first head was the Dnieper-Ukrainian scholar Mykhailo Hrushevs'kyi, the emphasis was on teaching and research in the history of Ukraine.

The Greek Catholic Church had a special relationship to the national movement. Ever since the first half of the nineteenth century, seminarians and village priests had been among the earliest national awakeners. In fact, until 1848 the national movement consisted almost exclusively of clerics. Even in subsequent decades, as the nationalist movement grew and as its leadership was taken over by secular figures, priests continued to play a crucial role as conduits for national sentiment among rural folk. It was the priests who often taught young people in the village schools and who reached parishioners of all ages through the medium of Church Slavonic or the local vernacular. Hence, by their very speech they reminded the faithful that they belonged culturally to the eastern, Rus' world. And unlike their celibate Roman Catholic counterparts, married Greek Catholic priests were able to share their patriotic fervor with their wives and together pass it on to their children. It is not surprising that well into the twentieth century many of the leading activists in the national movement – whether of the Old Ruthenian, the Ukrainophile, or the Russophile orientation – were the wives, sons, or daughters of village priests.

The relationship of the Greek Catholic Church hierarchy to the national movement was more complex. For much of the second half of the nineteenth century, many bishops and their priestly consultors in the episcopal sees of L'viv and Przemyśl adopted a rather cautious and, at times, distanced attitude. This should come as no surprise. Nationalism, like religion, is an ideology, and it was one that in eastern Galicia was becoming increasingly attractive to an ever-greater number of people who otherwise might have directed their psychic energy – and financial support – exclusively to the church. Then there was the question of the various orientations within the national movement and its potential divisiveness among priests. Until the late 1860s, this was not a problem, since the national movement was still dominated by Greek Catholic priests, many of whom were members of the metropolitan consistory at the St George Cathedral in L'viv. Known as the St George Circle (*sviatoiurtsi*), this group became the bulwark of the Old Ruthenian orientation, which emphasized the use of the Slaveno-Rusyn (Church Slavonic) language and Old Slavonic alphabet, as well as the belief that in order for individuals to preserve a Rus' identity in Galicia they first had to be faithful Greek Catholics. Because of its traditionalist approach, the Greek Catholic Church was initially suspicious of, and even antagonistic toward, the secular populist Ukrainophiles, especially the outspoken socialist activists like Ivan Franko and Mykhailo Pavlyk.

It was not, in fact, until the beginning of the twentieth century that the Greek Catholic Church hierarchy began to change its stance. The change was in large measure related to the appointment in 1900 of Andrei Sheptyts'kyi as metropolitan (reigned 1900–1944). Sheptyts'kyi was a towering figure (in both physical stature and sociocultural influence) from a polonized Ukrainian family, who rediscovered his Rus' roots and eventually embraced wholeheartedly the Ukrainian national cause. Because of his aristocratic status, moreover, he was welcomed among both the Polish and the Austrian social and ruling elites. While remaining tolerant of the Old Ruthenians and individual Russophile priests, Sheptyts'kyi firmly rejected the Russophile position on national identity. After some initial skepticism, the Ukrainophiles eventually embraced Sheptyts'kyi since they saw in him a leader able to restore the historic bond between religion and nationality. In effect, under Sheptyts'kyi's leadership the Greek Catholic Church in Galicia gradually changed its outlook, with the result that by the beginning of the twentieth century it was becoming a bulwark of Ukrainianism.

The national movement in Galicia: The political stage

The national movement in the second half of the nineteenth century was influenced by political developments in various contexts: the provincial Galician, the imperial Austrian, and the international. In the Galician context, Ukrainian political life was characterized by a struggle to achieve the following goals: (1) the division of the province into two parts, each with its own diet, administration, and board of education; (2) equality for the Ukrainian language in schools and public life; (3) the establishment of a Ukrainian university; and (4) the implementation of universal suffrage. With the exception of universal suffrage, Galicia's Ukrainians failed to achieve fully any of these political goals. They did, however, make some important progress in all four areas.

In Galician provincial politics, the Ukrainians were invariably opposed by the Poles, whose own political interests were in most cases diametrically opposed to Ukrainian interests. Polish-Ukrainian relations varied from almost total alienation to attempts at compromise and cooperation. At first, Ukrainian political desires were expressed through umbrella-like organizations in the tradition of the 1848 Supreme Ruthenian Council. As a result of the post-revolutionary return of Austrian absolutism, the Supreme Ruthenian Council was obliged to abolish itself in 1853. Old Ruthenian leaders attempted to revive the body by founding the Ruthenian Council (Rus'ka Rada) in 1870. When the populists proved unable to work with this group, they established their own National Council (Narodna Rada) in 1885. Finally, in 1900 the Russophiles established yet another National Council (Narodnyi Soviet). All three councils survived until 1914, but none had any long-term impact on political developments.

More influential were political parties, which first came into being during the 1890s. This was a decade of growing international tension in which the threat of war with the neighboring Russian Empire loomed large on the horizon. In such an atmosphere, Vienna urged the Poles to attempt to reach an accord with the Ukrainians. Because the Old Ruthenians were adamantly anti-Polish, the Poles, led by the viceroy of Galicia, Kazimierz Badeni, turned instead to the Ukrainophiles. The Ukrainophiles, who of the two were the stronger faction, were led by the Austrian parliamentary deputy Iuliian Romanchuk of the National Council. Urged by some Dnieper-Ukrainian leaders, Romanchuk agreed to cooperate with the Poles in an attempt to bring about internal harmony within the province. This cooperation marked the dawn of the so-called New Era, in which Galician Ukrainians gained a few advantages in the realm of education (including the department of Ukrainian history, the "Second Department of World History," at L'viv University). But the results were far below general expectations, and this brief period of Polish-Ukrainian rapprochement ended before the close of the century.

There was one group of Ukrainophiles who had from the very outset opposed any cooperation with the Polish-dominated provincial administration and its supporters. These were the socialists Ivan Franko and Mykhailo Pavlyk, who in 1890 founded the Ukrainian Radical party. The new party called for the complete transformation of Galician society according to socialist principles, and by 1895 it had proclaimed as essential the unification of Ukrainians on both sides of the Austro-Russian border and the creation of an independent Ukrainian state. Ukrainian independence was first proposed by Viacheslav Budzynovs'kyi at the founding congress of the Radical party, and then by another party activist, Iuliian Bachyns'kyi, in a book entitled *Ukraïna irredenta* (1895). This was the first time the goal of an independent Ukraine had been expressed anywhere, and it preceded by nearly a decade the similar formulation of the goal formulated by Mykhailo Mikhnovs'kyi and its adoption by the Revolutionary Ukrainian party in Dnieper Ukraine.

As a result of the failure of the New Era and its attempt at Polish-Ukrainian compromise, the political spectrum in Galicia was reorganized at the very end of the century. Romanchuk and the democratic populists, now joined by a few former radical socialists (among them Ivan Franko), in 1899 formed the National Democratic party. This party intended to work through existing political channels

INDEPENDENCE FOR UKRAINE

Iuliian Bachyns'kyi's *Ukraïna irredenta*, which called for an independent Ukraine, was ready for publication in 1893. It did not appear in print, however, until the very end of 1895, when Galicia's Ukrainian Radical party finally adopted independence as part of its platform. In the words of Bachyns'kyi:

I wish to make as the primary order of the day the future of the Ukrainian nation [*natsiia*], not only in Austria but also in Russia. ...

With regard to Dnieper Ukraine, the primary issue is the struggle for a constitution in Russia. ... But aside from its struggle against absolutism, the small group of already-conscious Ukrainians must also now begin to promote to whatever degree possible among Ukrainian society in Russia the idea of political independence for Ukraine. ...

This matter depends to a large degree on the position of Ukraine with regard to the constitutional struggle in Russia, that is, with regard to what is now the primary order of the day – the question of the internal *reorganization* of Russia. The position that Ukrainians take on this issue and the results of their work on its behalf will determine how easy or difficult will be the further struggle for the political independence of Ukraine. ...

As for Galicia ... everything depends on two things: the struggle against Austrian centralism; and the [need for] changes in the electoral system of the provincial diet and imperial parliament. ...

Considering the political transformation of Ukrainian society in Galicia, what is the situation with regard to the struggle on behalf of the idea of the *political independence of the Ukrainian people* [italic in original]?

The Radical party was the first party to make one of its primary goals the idea of political independence for the Ukrainian people. ... The party's economic principles and cultural ideals cannot be achieved, however, without a politically independent Ukraine. ... The idea of political independence for the Ukrainian people has, in fact, attracted new cadres of supporters among the Galician-Ukrainian "intelligentsia" and the Galician-Ukrainian proletariat.

SOURCE: Taras Hunczak and Roman Sol'chanyk, eds., *Ukraïns'ka suspil' no-politychna dumka v. 20 stolitti: dokumenty i materiialy*, Vol. I (New York 1983), pp. 27–33ff.

in order to achieve the division of Galicia into two provinces. The division was to be only a first step, after which eastern Galicia would be unified with Dnieper Ukraine to form an independent state. In contrast, the Radical party and the newer Ukrainian Social-Democratic party (est. 1900) were less concerned with national unity than with the complete socioeconomic transformation of Galician society. Finally, the Russophiles joined together with some Old Ruthenians to establish the Russian National party (est. 1900). Old Ruthenian-Russophile political cooperation did not last long, however, because the Russophiles became increasingly anti-Austrian and were not averse to cooperating with the Poles. Both attitudes were anathema to the Old Ruthenians, but potentially attractive to the Poles, who were concerned about the ever-increasing strength of the Ukrainophile movement. Consequently, the Polish viceroy of Galicia, Andrzej Potocki, and some prominent Polish political leaders threw their support behind the local Russophiles. Thus, by the beginning of the twentieth century, Ukrainian political life was divided between moderate and more left-wing Ukrainophiles on the one hand, and a decreasing number of Old Ruthenians along with younger, more assertive Russophiles on the other.

With the breakdown of political compromise that characterized the New Era, relations between Galicia's Poles and Ukrainians grew increasingly strained. This was particularly the case after universal suffrage was introduced throughout the Austrian half of the empire in 1907. That same year, the Ukrainophiles received twenty-two seats and the Russophiles five seats in the elections to the imperial parliament. In Galicia, however, the old curia system was maintained for elections to the diet, so the Poles were able to continue their control of that body. Ukrainian discontent was further exacerbated by corrupt electoral practices during the 1907 dietary elections, which were accompanied by the deaths of several Ukrainian peasants. These factors, combined with the Polish decision to support the Russophiles, created a tension that culminated in April 1908 in the assassination of the Galician viceroy, Andrzej Potocki, by a Ukrainian university student, Myroslav Sichyns'kyi. Sichyns'kyi's trial became a cause célèbre for the Ukrainophile movement, and his imprisonment only provoked further friction between Polish and Ukrainian university students for the next several years.

The national movement in eastern Galicia also had serious international implications. The tsarist Russian government had long ago accepted the Russophile view that Galicia as well as northern Bukovina and Transcarpathia was part of the patrimony of Kievan Rus' and, as such, should one day be reunited with "mother Russia." St Petersburg, therefore, was willing to give support to any elements in Galicia that were in agreement with this goal. It was in this context that the Ems Ukase of 1876, which outlawed the Ukrainian language in the Russian Empire, contained a specific clause calling for support for Galicia's Old Ruthenian newspaper, *Slovo*. Subsidies and expressions of moral support were indeed sent to Galicia through Mikhail F. Raevskii, the Orthodox chaplain attached to the Russian embassy in Vienna, and, via correspondence and other channels, between Pan-Slavist publicists in the Russian Empire and their sympathizers in Galicia. In consequence of such contact, in 1867 the first head of the Department of Ruthenian Language and Literature at L'viv University, Iakiv Holovats'kyi, was stripped of his professorial post and forbidden to return to the Austrian Empire after particpating in a scholarly conference in Russia.

Holovats'kyi had, of course, been a well-known early populist Ukrainophile who later in life became a Russophile. One important reason for his change of heart and that of several Old Ruthenians was their disillusionment with Habsburg Austria and its seemingly declining international status during the 1860s. Vienna, moreover, had withdrawn its support of the Ukrainian national movement in the

1850s, and by the 1860s it was backing the Poles and their influential viceroy, Agenor Gołuchowski. Furthermore, Austria had just lost wars against Sardinia-Piedmont and France in 1859 and Prussia in 1866. All this suggested to some Old Ruthenian leaders that the Austrian Empire was on the decline and that the day was imminent when tsarist Russia would take over Galicia.

Such Russophile inclinations among the Old Ruthenian leadership (including sympathy for Orthodoxy) were brought to light in 1882, when the Austrian government held a trial in L'viv at which several Old Ruthenian leaders and the Transcarpathian Russophile activist Adol'f Dobrians'kyi were accused of promoting Orthodoxy and seeking to detach Ukrainian-inhabited lands from Austria. Although they were acquitted of the charges, the damage was done. The Old Ruthenian orientation became tainted in the eyes of much of Galician and official Austrian opinion; some of its leaders were removed from office (including the Greek Catholic metropolitan Iosyf Sembratovych); others were forced by subsequent circumstances to emigrate to Russia (including the head of the Kachkovs'kyi Society, Father Ivan Naumovych, and the *Slovo* editor Venedykt Ploshchans'kyi).

After the demise of the Old Ruthenians, St Petersburg eventually found new supporters among a younger group of Galician Russophiles. Many of them openly declared their hope of becoming part of Russia; others silently shared the same aspiration. As part of its stepped-up campaign against Austria-Hungary, the tsarist government provided large sums of money to spread Orthodoxy among Greek Catholics in Galicia and Transcarpathia and particularly among immigrants from these regions in the United States. In fact, the rapid growth of Russian Orthodoxy in the United States was encouraged by tsarist policy during the two decades before the outbreak of World War I, and Orthodox immigrants helped to spread that religion in their native villages when they returned home. The Carpathian region, whence many immigrants had come, was particularly susceptible. Bukovina had, of course, always been Orthodox. Now Orthodoxy began to reach as well the mountainous areas of southwestern Galicia (the Lemko region) and Transcarpathia, where it was equated with faith in the tsar and with the Russian nationality. To encourage its spread, the Galician-Russian Benevolent Society was established in St Petersburg in 1908 and the Carpatho-Russian Liberation Committee in Kiev in 1913. Russophilism in the form of Orthodoxy was thus given a new lease of life in the Austro-Hungarian Empire on the eve of World War I.

The populist Ukrainophiles were also influenced by developments beyond the borders of Galicia, primarily as a result of interaction between Dnieper-Ukrainian national leaders and their counterparts in Austria-Hungary. The first important figure in this relationship was Mykhailo Drahomanov, a professor at Kiev's St Vladimir University, who was forced to leave Dnieper Ukraine in the wake of the Ems Ukase of 1876. Drahomanov traveled through Galicia and Transcarpathia, and from exile in Switzerland and, later, Bulgaria he continued to maintain close contact with his Galician disciples. The most devoted of these disciples were Ivan Franko, Mykhailo Pavlyk, and Ostap Terlets'kyi, who under Drahomanov's influence became convinced that Ukrainian political independ-

ence would not be possible before economic self-sufficiency and cultural awareness were achieved. First, however, Galician society had to be restructured on a
socialist basis.

More conservative in approach but no less influential was Panteleimon Kulish,
who during the 1880s urged the Galician Ukrainians to reach an accord with the
Poles. A similar goal was propounded during the following decade by the Dnieper-
Ukrainian writer Oleksander Konys'kyi and the historian Volodymyr Antonovych,
whose influence resulted in the Galician-Ukrainian attempt at compromise with
the Poles known as the New Era.

The last important figure among the Dnieper Ukrainians was Mykhailo S.
Hrushevs'kyi, who, unlike his countrymen from the east, actually lived and worked
for a substantial period of time in Galicia. His scholarship and organizational work
as professor at L'viv University and president of the Shevchenko Scientific Society
left an indelible imprint on Galician, and, for that matter, all, Ukrainian cultural
life. Hrushevs'kyi was less sympathetic to the idea of cooperation with the Poles.
He felt that in the relatively liberal environment of Austria, Galician Ukrainians
should build a solid national and cultural social fabric which could serve as a kind
of Piedmont for a future independent Ukrainian state. When the winds of political change finally struck the Russian Empire following the revolution of 1905,
Hrushevs'kyi and others turned their attention to the Ukrainian revival in Kiev.
But hopes placed in Dnieper Ukraine proved to be short-lived. After a few years,
Russia's post-revolutionary liberal period was followed by a return to tsarist absolutism and restrictions on Ukrainian culture. Given this state of affairs, Austrian Galicia seemed to be the only place where Ukrainian national life could flourish. In
this sense, even the Dnieper-Ukrainian political leader Ievhen Chykalenko could
later recall, "Galicia was for us a model in the struggle for our nation's rebirth; it
strengthened our faith and hope for a better future. Galicia was a true 'Piedmont'
of Ukraine, because prior to 1906 a Ukrainian press, scholarship, and national life
could develop only there."[2]

The belief in Galicia as a Piedmont notwithstanding, during the first decades
of the twentieth century an independent Ukrainian state seemed only a distant
future possibility. This was because the Austro-Hungarian Empire, despite all its
difficulties, was still a viable political entity. And Galician Ukrainians seemed fully
aware of the reality of its vilability. Consequently, by and large they remained loyal
subjects of Emperor Franz Joseph who were committed to the perpetuation of
Habsburg Austria. Even Galician-Ukrainian political leaders, whose rhetoric in the
parliamentary and dietary forums often sounded harsh and aimed at the destruction of the existing order, were beginning to reassess what seemed in the context
of all the Ukrainian lands the relatively positive aspects of Habsburg rule. In that
regard, it is not surprising that representatives of all Ukrainian political parties in
Galicia could declare at a meeting in December 1912, "With a view to the welfare
and future of the Ukrainian people on both sides of the border, in case of war
between Austria and Russia the entire Ukrainian community will unanimously and
resolutely stand on the side of Austria against the Russian Empire, as the greatest
enemy of Ukraine."[3]

AT THE BOTTOM OF THE PECKING ORDER

In both relative and absolute terms, Ukrainians in Habsburg Austria (Galicia and Bukovina) by the end of the nineteenth century had enjoyed more legal and national rights than Ukrainians anywhere else. This explains, in part, why even decades after Austria-Hungary ceased to exist, former Ukrainian subjects of the Habsburgs continued to remember with great fondness the "good old days" under Emperor Franz Joseph.

As with most nostalgic memories, however, the more unpleasant realities were frequently forgotten. Some were brought to light in an award-winning German-language film by the Hungarian director István Szabó. The film, *Colonel Redl* (1984), is based loosely on a real-life figure of the same name. Colonel Alfred Redl was a career officer in the Austro-Hungarian Army who on the eve of World War I was demoted from the high post of imperial chief of military intelligence, roughly equivalent to the present-day director of the CIA in the United States. Early in the film, it is made clear that Redl was born in L'viv, or Lemberg as it was called in German, and that he is of Ruthenian (*ruthenisch*) nationality, although his father's family had immigrated to Galicia from Hungary sometime in the early nineteenth century.

In the film, Redl and his superiors – none other than the heir apparent to the throne, Franz Ferdinand, best remembered for his assassination in 1914 at Sarajevo – are concerned about corruption and lax discipline among the Habsburg army's officer corps. They are determined to set an example by holding a public trial that will uncover treasonous activity and thereby send a strong message to the officers that they had better mend their ways. Redl diligently sifts through the intelligence files and comes up with what he considers five ideal dossiers from which a suitable show trial can be fabricated.

"Excellent idea, Redl," says the heir apparent, Franz Ferdinand. "But it all depends on the particular person."

Redl suggests either a Captain Max von Dornheim or a Lieutenant-Colonel György von Komjáthy from Budapest.

Franz Ferdinand responds: "Look, Colonel Redl, this trial must prove to the army and the officer corps that the enemy is within our ranks and that we'll strike down mercilessly those who neglect their duty. We must also show to the monarchy's peoples and to the whole world a united, strong Austro-Hungarian Army. This is, above all, a political matter.

"Therefore, the accused cannot be an Austrian, especially not an Austrian aristocrat, since that would weaken the trust in our supreme command.

"Nor can he be a Hungarian. After all, we live in a dual monarchy. It's not advisable to irritate the enemy from within.

"He certainly can't be a Czech. They always have demonstrations and too many parliamentary scandals and independence movements. They'd consider such a trial a direct provocation.

"It definitely can't be a Jew. The Dreyfus case [in which an officer of Jewish background in the French Army was falsely accused of treason and eventually acquitted] tore Europe apart. We'd stir up international indignation, not to mention how it would strain our emperor's contacts with the Rothschild Bank, contacts that are vital to the monarchy.

"And, finally, it can't be a Serb or Croat. That region is just too dangerous.

"We must look elsewhere."

"Do you have Hungarian blood in you?" continues Franz Ferdinand. "Ruthenian," answers Redl.

"You see," says the heir apparent, "that's what we need," a Ruthenian.

"Look for an exact double of yourself, Redl."

"I'd have to look in Galicia," Redl replies.

"Then look there," says Franz Ferdinand. "Find someone with a similar background, career, and connections. Then you'll have your man!"

The scriptwriter, who throughout the film emphasizes the conflicts and tensions among officers of different national backgrounds, poignantly captures the real spirit of the Habsburg Empire. When the chips were down, it was clear to the highest rulers who were at the bottom of Austria-Hungary's nationality pecking order and were therefore dispensable – the Ruthenians, or Ukrainians.

In the last months before the outbreak of World War I, the ever-present friction with the Poles also seemed something that could be overcome. Negotiations between representatives in the Galician diet resulted in the approval in early 1914 of a new provincial statute. The electoral law was changed so that there would be separate Polish and Ukrainian chambers in the diet. Moreover, the provincial board of education was to be divided into Polish and Ukrainian sections, and the imperial government in Vienna agreed to resolve the issue of a Ukrainian university favorably within four years. These reforms seemed finally to satisfy both national groups, and the immediate future for Galicia's Ukrainians seemed to augur well. It was 1914, however. And in August of that year Europe was to be torn apart by a war that would spread to other parts of the world and that at its end would bring about the complete transformation of Ukrainian society.

The national movement in Bukovina

The population of Bukovina, which became a distinct province in 1861, almost doubled during the last seventy-five years of Austrian rule, increasing from 447,000 in 1851 to 795,000 in 1910. During this period, the proportion of Ukrainians in the population as a whole declined slightly, from 42 percent to 38 percent. The other numerically important group were the Romanians (34 percent in 1910), followed by a sizable Jewish (12 percent) and smaller German (8 percent) and Polish (4 percent) minorities. In the northern half of the province (if it is divided more or less by the present Ukrainian-Romanian boundary), the Ukrainians traditionally constituted the majority (58 percent in 1910), followed by the Romanians (17 percent), Jews (15 percent), Germans (6 percent), and Poles (5 percent). Ukrainians primarily inhabited rural farming areas and the mountainous valleys of northern and western Bukovina; the few towns and one city – Chernivtsi (85,000 inhabitants in 1910) – were inhabited for the most part by Jews, Romanians, Poles, Germans, and, in some cases, the so-called Lipovany, Russian Old Believers who immigrated to the region in the eighteenth century.

Of all the Ukrainian-inhabited territories of the Austro-Hungarian Empire, Bukovina was the last to experience a national revival. This is largely because the Orthodox Church, of which the Bukovinian Ukrainians were members, had for the longest time been controlled by Romanian hierarchs who had no interest in fostering the Rus' culture of the inhabitants living in the northern half of the province.

It was not until the late 1860s that the first national organizations were founded. They included the Ruthenian Society (Ruskaia Besida), established in 1869 in Chernivtsi to promote popular culture, and the Ruthenian Council (Ruskaia Rada), founded one year later as a political group to defend national interests and to prepare Ukrainians for participation in elections to the Bukovinian diet and Austrian parliament. Initially, both organizations were in the hands of Old Ruthenians or of Russophiles (the priests Vasyl' Prodan and Sydir Vorobkevych, and Ivan Hlibovyts'kyi), and not surprisingly, the first publications and journals (*Bukovinskaia zoria*, 1870–71) they issued used the traditional Slaveno-Rusyn book language.

By the 1880s, the activity of the populist Ukrainophiles in neighboring Galicia was serving as an inspiration for the Bukovinians, and consequently both the Ruthenian Society and the Ruthenian Council came under the control of the populists. After 1884, the Ruthenian Society became for Bukovina what the Prosvita Society was for Galicia. It established a network of cultural organizations throughout the province which by 1914, in addition to the main center in Chernivtsi, numbered 9 branches and 150 reading rooms, with about 13,000 registered members. Also at this time, Bukovina's first major writer to use the vernacular, Osyp Fed'kovych, began to edit the populist literary journal *Bukovyna* (Chernivtsi, 1885–1918). The Ruthenian Society published *Bukovyna*, as well as several other periodicals, some original works, and some translations, all in the Ukrainian vernacular. The Ruthenian Society also made possible the organization of several other cultural groups, and it was largely responsible for having the Department (*katedra*) of Ruthenian Language and Literature established during the very first year of the newly founded Franz Josef I University in Chernivtsi in 1875. A second Ukrainian department (in pastoral theology) was established at the same university in 1899.

At the all-important elementary school level, the Ukrainians in Bukovina were relatively well off. They had their own inspector (Omelian Popovych) on the Provincial Board of Education, whose activity helped to ensure a steady rise in the number of Ukrainian elementary schools, from 165 in 1896 (131 Ukrainian and 34 Ukrainian-German or Ukrainian-Romanian) to 216 in 1910 (compared with

177 Romanian, 82 German, 12 Polish, and 5 Hungarian). There were also three Ukrainian *gymnasia* (Chernivtsi, 1896; Kitsman, 1904; Vashkivtsi, 1908) as well as public (1871) and private (1907) teachers' colleges in Chernivtsi.

In political life, the Ruthenian Council was taken over in the mid-1880s by the populist Ukrainophiles (Iustyn and Ierotei Pihuliak, Ivan Tymins'kyi, Omelian Popovych). Consequently, the Old Ruthenians and Russophiles (Vasyl' Prodan, Ivan Hlibovyts'kyi, Hryhorii Kupchanko) established their own National Council (Obshchestvo Narodnaia Rada) and continued to publish several newspapers in Slaveno-Rusyn and Russian (*Pravoslavnaia Bukovina*, 1893–1901; *Pravoslavnaia Rus'*, 1909–10; *Russkaia pravda*, 1910–14). Nonetheless, the Old Ruthenian and Russophile factions remained in the decided minority, even after St Petersburg increased its aid to the Orthodox movement during the first decade of the twentieth century and found sympathizers among local younger Russophile leaders (especially the Gerovskii brothers).

The political field was consequently left open to the Ukrainophiles, among whom the leading figures were the Galician-born Stepan Smal'-Stots'kyi, who since 1885 had headed the Department of Ruthenian Language and Literature at Chernivtsi University, and his rival, the local landowner Baron Mykola Vasyl'ko. In 1890, the Ukrainians obtained their first political representation: three deputies in the Bukovinian diet in Chernivtsi and one deputy in the Austrian parliament in Vienna. Finally, in 1911 Bukovina underwent a political reorganization whereby the old curia electoral system was replaced by one based on nationalities and professions. This meant that despite their actual electoral strength, the Ukrainians were guaranteed 17 of 63 seats in the diet, compared with 22 for the Romanians, 10 for the Jews, 6 for the Austro-Germans, 6 for the Poles, and 2 others. Such administratively imposed efforts at equality reflected Austria-Hungary's determination to resolve the nationality problem within its borders. Bukovina was held up as a kind of model for other Habsburg provinces, and for a while the term *homo Bukovinensis* was used in Austro-German literature to describe a person of tolerance and of a high and varied culture. It was in such a positive atmosphere that the Ukrainian national movement was able to flourish in Bukovina during the quarter century before World War I.

The national movement in Transcarpathia

A marked decline in the national movement in Transcarpathia during the second half of the nineteenth century stood in sharp contrast to its rise in Galicia and Bukovina. Following the revolution of 1848 and its immediate aftermath, when some political and cultural progress was made under the dynamic leadership of Adol'f Dobrians'kyi and Aleksander Dukhnovych, the Transcarpathian national movement began to wane. This was especially evident after 1868, when as a result of the Ausgleich the Hungarian Kingdom had finally succeeded in obtaining the right to control its own internal affairs without interference from Vienna. Dukhnovych died in 1865, and four years later Dobrians'kyi, who had aided the tsarist Russian army in its invasion of Hungary in 1848, was forced to leave the country. The Russophile orientation which both these leaders had supported was carried on by a small minority of Greek Catholic priests and writers (Anatolii Kralyts'kyi, Ivan Sil'vai, Aleksander Mytrak, Iulii Stavrovs'kyi-Popradov, and Ievhen Fentsyk). This group even managed to publish a few newspapers (*Svît*, 1867–71; *Novŷi svit* 1871–73; *Karpat*, 1873–86; *Listok*, 1885–1903), either in the traditional Slaveno-Rusyn language or a local version of Russian. The 1860s also witnessed the establishment of a few organizations concerned with assisting students and raising the cultural standards of the population (the Society of St John the Baptist in Prešov, est. 1862; the Society of St Basil the Great in Uzhhorod, est. 1866), the first printing shop with Cyrillic letters in Uzhhorod (est. 1863), and some teaching in Slaveno-Rusyn at the elementary level.

The political compromise between the Austrian and Hungarian halves of the Habsburg Empire was to have a decidedly negative effect on the national movement in Transcarpathia. In 1868, the Hungarian government passed a law entitled "On the Equality of the Rights of the Nationalities." Equality, according to this law, meant that since "all citizens of Hungary constitute a single nation, the indivisible, unitary Magyar nation ... every citizen, to whatever nationality he belongs, is an equal member."[4] For a long time, the Magyars had been a minority in the Hungarian Kingdom, and their own nationalist leadership was now determined to reverse what they perceived as a dangerous state of affairs. In one sense, Hungary adopted a liberal policy since, according to its understanding of equality, no person, whether Slovak, Romanian, German, Serbian, or Carpatho-Rusyn, was discriminated against. Each had equal access to whatever Hungarian society had to offer, just as long as he or she became a Magyar. In fact, many educated members of Hungary's various nationalities, including Carpatho-Rusyns/Ukrainians, did adopt fully a Magyar identity. Known derogatorily by their fellow Carpatho-Rusyns as magyarones, they frequently worked in the administration and schools within their native region, where they became the fiercest proponents of the favoring magyarization of the non-Magyar inhabitants.

Since a Slavic-oriented national intelligentsia had always been a minority among the Transcarpathians, it was not really difficult or out of character for the majority of educated Carpatho-Rusyns/Ukrainians to become magyarized. These magyarones reached the uppermost echelons of the local Greek Catholic Church, in both the eparchy of Mukachevo (with its seat in Uzhhorod) and the eparchy of Prešov (in present-day Slovakia), which was established in 1818. In the words of Mukachevo's Greek Catholic bishop Stefan Pankovych (reigned 1867–1874), "If now we live under the rule of the Magyars, then we should become Magyars."[5]

Despite the pervasively Magyar environment, Transcarpathia did experience a kind of populist movement during the last decade of the nineteenth century. A few younger leaders (Evmenii Sabov, Iurii Zhatkovych, Avhustyn Voloshyn, Mykhailo Vrabel') tried to turn the assimilatory tide by replacing the antiquated Slaveno-Rusyn and the foreign Russian languages with the local vernacular in local publications. In fact, several grammars and popular journals (*Nauka*, 1897–1914; *Nedîlia*, 1898–1918) were published at the turn of the century in the Transcarpathian vernacular. This trend also gave rise to the view that the Transcarpathians were neither Russians nor Ukrainians, but rather a distinct Carpatho-Rusyn nationality. The Transcarpathian national leadership, which had always maintained contacts with Galicia (especially with the Old Ruthenians), began to be displeased with the rise of Ukrainianism there. Even Avhustyn Voloshyn, who later became one of the leading Transcarpathian Ukrainophiles, in 1910 referred to "those terrible diseases of Ukrainianism and radicalism that have recently spread in Galicia [and that] have brought about continual strife and have alienated the Rusyn from his church, his language, and even from his name Rusyn."[6] Whether or not such an assessment was correct, some Transcarpathian leaders believed it.

Despite such efforts at preserving a Carpatho-Rusyn identity, the nationalist intelligentsia in Transcarpathia, whether Russophiles or independent-minded Rusynophiles, were in a decided minority. Hungarian governmental pressure to encourage assimilation increased, as was graphically revealed in the school system. Following a new school law passed in 1907, the number of Transcarpathian schools using Slaveno-Rusyn or the vernacular declined precipitously. For instance, whereas in 1874 there were 479 such schools, after 1907 there were none. All that were left were Magyar-Rusyn bilingual schools, but even these declined, from 255 in 1896 to 34 in 1913. The vast majority of the clerical and secular intelligentsia were more than willing to assimilate to Hungarian culture and to be considered Magyars of the Greek Catholic faith.

Nevertheless, with regard to the Ukrainian national movement, Transcarpathia was the notable exception in the Austro-Hungarian Empire. During the years 1848 to 1914, developments in Galicia and to a certain extent in Bukovina made possible the preservation of the Ukrainian national idea. The Galicians as well as their counterparts in Dnieper Ukraine felt this to be the case.

While Ukrainianism was being suppressed in the Russian Empire, all the fundamentals that make possible a viable national life – historical ideology, language, literature, cultural organizations, education, religion, and politics – were being firmly established in Austrian Galicia. The Habsburg rulers and their imperial administration may have used German as a functional medium of communication, but they did not associate themselves with any one of the empire's nationalities. Ukrainians, therefore, could exist within the socially and politically acceptable framework of a hierarchy of multiple loyalties without having to give up their national identity. In other words, a Galician or a Bukovinian could be both a Ukrainian national patriot and a loyal Austrian Habsburg subject. The two identities were compatible. The Austro-Hungarian Empire thus stood in marked contrast to the Russian Empire, where accepting the idea of a hierarchy of multiple loyalties meant that an East Slav in Ukraine (or Little Russia) could be only a Russian from Little Russia, or simply a Russian. Being a Ukrainian in the Russian Empire in the sense of being something distinct meant rejecting the dominant social and political values of tsarist society and thereby placing oneself, even in the best of circumstances, on the fringes of society.

Despite its numerous problems – economic deficiencies, national friction between Poles and Ukrainians, internal controversy among different factions of the nationalist intelligentsia – late-nineteenth-century Austrian Galicia provided a setting in which it was proved beyond a doubt that a Ukrainian nationality existed and could adapt to and flourish in a modern social environment. Yet the long era of the Austrian Order – the *Pax Austriae,* which had made such a social and national transformation possible for Ukrainians – was to come to an end. For all its positive aspects, in 1914 Austria-Hungary was about to stumble into war, a conflict that within four years would destroy the Habsburg Empire and change the face of Europe.

Part Eight

World War I and the Struggle for Independence

36

World War I and Western Ukraine

August 1914 is a landmark in modern history. Although people did not realize it at the time, that fateful month witnessed a series of events that were to lead to the outbreak of war – the first world war. That war was to change the face of Europe and set the stage for another conflict that two decades later would change the face of the world. Ironically, by 1914 most Europeans anticipated, and some even hoped, that war would break out. Few, if any, could have foreseen its consequences. During the next four years, most European countries, as well as the United States, Canada, Japan, and the Middle East, were drawn into a conflict that in the end mobilized an incredible 65 million men, of whom 8.4 million were killed and 21 million were wounded. The statistics boggle the mind. No war until that time had cost so much in human lives.

The outbreak of World War I

In the narrowest sense, the war began in Austria-Hungary after the heir to the throne, Franz Ferdinand, was assassinated in June 1914 by a Serbian nationalist. In a larger sense, the war was a result of power politics, a game that European states had played throughout history. By the end of the nineteenth century, Europe's great powers included Great Britain, France, Germany, Italy, Russia, and Austria-Hungary. Another power was the Ottoman Empire, but despite its territorial extent it was weak vis-à-vis Europe's other, more modern states. Each of the great powers was afraid that its rivals would take advantage of the weakened Ottoman state, and therefore all were willing to come to the aid, at least diplomatically, of the proverbial "sick man of Europe."

At the beginning of the twentieth century, the existing international alliances saw the Triple Entente (Great Britain, France, and Russia) pitted against the Triple Alliance (Germany, Austria-Hungary, and Italy). As in previous decades, each side was anxious to block any attempted advance by the rival side with regard to the Ottoman Empire. There was, of course, nothing sacred in the composition of the two great power alliances and, given sufficient reason, any member could easily have realigned itself.

The goals of each member within these alliances were different. Great Britain hoped to contain the growing military strength of Germany, while Germany saw Britain as a rival to be equaled or overtaken, especially on the sea. France's chief object was territorial: to recover the provinces of Alsace and Lorraine on its eastern borders that had been lost to Germany in the Franco-Prussian war of 1870–1871. Italy had for much of the nineteenth century striven to achieve unity and independence and had been opposed to the Habsburgs. Now it hoped to acquire southern Tyrol and lands along the northern Adriatic Sea still ruled by Austria-Hungary. For the moment, however, Italy's attention was turned toward establishing colonies in northern and eastern Africa. Since Italian interests in Africa clashed with French interests, France's rivals, Germany and Austria-Hungary, became Italy's allies.

Russia's primary hope was to weaken the Ottoman Empire further and thereby achieve its centuries-old foreign policy goals. As a complement to the warm water ports on the Black Sea, which it had acquired in the late eighteenth century, Russia felt it needed unhindered access to if not outright control of the narrow straits held by the Ottomans between the Black and Aegean Seas (the Bosporus and the Dardanelles). Such access or control would allow Russia an easy passage to the trade routes of the Mediterranean. But because Russia was deterred by its own allies, especially Great Britain, from any direct assault on the Ottoman Empire, it directed its attention instead to stirring up national and irredentist feelings in the Balkans, among the Slavs and Romanians who were either still struggling to gain independence from the Ottoman Empire or had gained independence but still had further territorial claims to Ottoman-held lands. Russia's activity in the Balkans reflected, in part, the spirit of the Pan-Slavism that had become integral to Russian intellectual and political thought during the nineteenth century. In fact, it was as a result of direct and indirect aid from St Petersburg that Serbia (1817), Greece (1829–1830), Romania (1858–1862), Montenegro (1878), and Bulgaria (1878) became autonomous and, later, independent states. Russia and its smaller Balkan allies also had their sights set on liberating the supposedly oppressed Slavs in the Austro-Hungarian Empire. Not surprisingly, Austria-Hungary was wary of the increasing Russian influence in the Balkans as well as of the effects of that influence on the Slavic peoples living within its own borders.

The Balkans became the area of greatest political tension, because alongside the great power rivalries in the region were conflicts among the Balkan states themselves. Two wars, in 1912 and 1913, reflected the bitter local rivalries among Bulgaria, Serbia, and Greece for territorial expansion, especially over Ottoman-controlled Macedonia. These tensions and conflicts prompted commentators to refer to the Balkans as the "powder keg of Europe." In 1914, the powder keg's fuse was lit.

In June 1914, Austria-Hungary's heir to the Habsburg throne, Franz Ferdinand, was on a state visit to Bosnia-Herzegovina. This formerly Ottoman-ruled Balkan land had been occupied by the Habsburg Empire in 1878 and finally annexed and placed under the joint authority of Austria and Hungary in 1908. While riding in an open car along the streets of Sarajevo, Bosnia's administrative center, Franz Ferdinand and his wife were assassinated by a young terrorist who was a member of a nationalist organization based in neighboring independent Serbia.

Certain ruling circles in Habsburg Vienna, especially among the military, were convinced that now was the time to teach "little Serbia" a lesson once and for all. Like their counterparts in many other European countries, the Austro-Hungarian military believed in the idea of a so-called preventive war; that is, strike at one's enemy as soon as possible in order to weaken him before he develops into a greater threat. Convinced of the feasibility of a short preventive war, the Habsburg government received assurances of support from its German ally and then issued an ultimatum to Serbia. In response, Serbia's "Slavic brother" in the east, tsarist Russia, pledged to support its threatened Balkan ally. All last-minute attempts at reconciliation (including Serbia's acceptance of most of Austria's demands) failed, and on 28 July 1914 Austria-Hungary declared war on Serbia. Russia mobilized along its borders with Germany and Austria-Hungary. Then Germany responded by declaring war on Russia on 1 August. By 12 August, each of the great powers had declared war on one of the others, and the two prewar coalitions evolved into the Allied Powers (Great Britain, France, and Russia) and the Central Powers (Germany and Austria-Hungary). Subsequently, the Ottoman Empire and Bulgaria joined the Central Powers, and Italy, which initially had decided to remain neutral, joined the Allies in 1915. Finally, in 1917 the United States entered the war on the side of the Allied Powers.

The results of the war are well known. When an armistice was finally signed on "the eleventh hour of the eleventh day of the eleventh month" (November) in 1918, the Central Powers had surrendered. At the time of the armistice, all the great monarchies of the Central Powers were disintegrating, and the government of the third leading member of the original Allied Powers – the Russian Empire – had been overthrown by revolutions in March and November 1917. The second of these, the Bolshevik Revolution, resulted in Russia's dropping out of the war. But how did Europe's first great civil war of the twentieth century – to quote the former West German chancellor Willy Brandt – affect Ukrainians?

The Russians in Galicia and Bukovina

The Ukrainians in Austria-Hungary, not those in Dnieper Ukraine, were the first to be affected by the war. On 1 August 1914, several leaders of Ukrainian parties in Galicia (7 National Democrats, 4 Radicals, 4 Social-Democrats) joined together to form a non-partisan organization called the Supreme Ukrainian Council (Holovna Ukraïns'ka Rada). This council, headed by the Austrian parliamentarian Kost' Levyts'kyi and the political activist Mykhailo Pavlyk, declared its loyalty to Austria and issued an appeal for a united stand against the Russian Empire. Within a week after its founding, the Supreme Ukrainian Council called for volunteers to serve in the Austrian Army. Although some 28,000 initially responded, in the end only 2,500 were selected to serve in a military formation known as the Ukrainian Sich Riflemen (Ukraïns'ki Sichovi Stril'tsi). This unit was to fight within Austrian ranks against the tsarist army on the eastern front.

MAP 31   WESTERN UKRAINE DURING WORLD WAR I

■ Major fortress   ⊔⊔⊔ Russian advances
✕ Major battle   ▨ Major concentration
                         of Rusyns/Ukrainians

Scale 1 : 4 600 000

0   50 miles
0   50 kilometers

The war's eastern front soon encompassed Galicia and Bukovina. Because those provinces bordered on the Russian Empire, and because in recent years the local russophile movement had expressed a sense of kinship with Russia, in early 1914 both the Hungarian and the Austrian governments held treason trials of suspected russophile and Orthodox subversives in Transcarpathia (at Sighet Marmaţiei/Syhit Marmaros'kyi, December 1913 to February 1914) and Galicia (L'viv, March 1914). Then, with the outbreak of war in August, the Polish viceroy in Galicia ordered the arrest of several Russophiles whom he suspected – and in some cases rightly so – of being subversives within Austria.

During the first few days of August, the Austro-Hungarian Army (under Field Marshal Conrad von Hötzendorff) ventured into Russian territory, but beginning on 5 August a series of swift Russian counterattacks not only pushed back the Habsburg troops but enabled the Russians to enter Austria-Hungary. The Russian advance was rapid: by 3 September, tsarist armies had captured L'viv, and two days later they reached the San River. This meant that all of Ukrainian-inhabited Galicia as well as Bukovina came under tsarist Russian control. During their rapid and ignominious retreat, the Habsburg troops, especially units of the Hungarian national army (*honvéds*), took revenge upon many inhabitants whom they considered Russian spies. Peasants in eastern Galicia quite naturally identified themselves, if asked, as *rus'kyi,* in the sense of Rusyn, but to untutored Austrian and

Hungarian ears this sounded like "Russian." Consequently, several thousand people – Russophiles, Ukrainophiles, and unsuspecting Greek Catholic or Orthodox peasants – were summarily shot, hanged, or herded off to internment camps in the western "Austrian" half of the empire, the most infamous being at Talerhof, near Graz, in Styria. It is from this period that the deep hatred between Ukrainophiles and Russophiles in Galicia derives, each side having accused the other of aiding and abetting the local Poles and Austrians in their anti-"Russian" fervor.

The tsarist army pushed into Galicia as far west as the Dunajec River during September 1914, and following some reverses in Bukovina it regained that province in November. Russian troops even penetrated several Carpathian passes and reached a few Rusyn-inhabited mountainous areas in northeastern Hungary (present-day eastern Slovakia and Transcarpathia). It was the capture of eastern Galicia and northern Bukovina, however, which the Russians considered a great political as well as military achievement. These territories were regarded in tsarist society as "Russian" lands, "temporarily separated" from the homeland but now, after centuries finally "reunited" with "mother Russia." To underscore this conception, Tsar Nicholas II himself paid a triumphant visit to L'viv in the spring of 1915.

In its newly acquired territory of Galicia, the tsarist Russian government installed a civilian administration headed by Count Georgii Bobrinskoi, a cousin of the head of the Galician-Russian Benevolent Society, founded in St Petersburg before the war. The tsarist officials turned for support to the local Russophiles (Semen Bendasiuk, Volodymyr Dudykevych, Iuliian Iavors'kyi) who had remained in Galicia or had just returned from the Russian Empire, where they had emigrated before the war or fled after the outbreak of hostilities. Even some local Polish leaders (Professor Stanisław Grabski and the former viceroy Leon Piniński), who had expected Russia to create a Polish state, worked with the tsarist forces. In Bukovina, the tsarist army was welcomed by local Russophiles (especially the Gerovskii brothers, Aleksei and Georgii), as well as by the Orthodox hierarchy in Chernivtsi, which asked its priests "to pray for the tsar and for the victory of the Russian army, which did not come as enemies, but as saviors from Austrian oppression."[1]

The Ukrainophiles, meanwhile, were considered the enemy by tsarist officials. Ukrainian cultural institutions and cooperatives were closed, Russian replaced Ukrainian in schools, and in Galicia plans were made to dismantle the Greek Catholic Church. Those Ukrainophile leaders who had not already fled westward before the tsarist army's advance were arrested and deported to the Russian Empire, including the Greek Catholic metropolitan of L'viv, Andrei Sheptyts'kyi, and until recently the president of the now-closed Shevchenko Scientific Society, Professor Mykhailo Hrushevs'kyi, apprehended in Kiev soon after his return there at the end of 1914. Russia's efforts to liquidate the Ukrainian movement in eastern Galicia ended in the spring of 1915. Beginning with the battle of Gorlice (2–5 May 1915), the Austro-Hungarian Army, with German help, drove the tsarist forces out of most of Galicia and Bukovina. During the rapid Russian retreat in June, local Russophile leaders persuaded more than 25,000 Galicians to flee eastward. The tsarist government settled this group around Rostov, near the mouth of the Don River, where they remained until the end of the war. The tsarist army was, however, able to hold on to the region of Galicia between the Seret and Zbruch Rivers (including Ternopil') for most of the war.

With the return of Austrian rule to most of Galicia and Bukovina in the summer of 1915, many persons suspected of having cooperated with the Russians were arrested and deported to the Talerhof internment camp. Two new treason trials were held in Vienna (1915 and 1916), at which twenty-four Russophiles from Galicia and Bukovina, including two parliamentary deputies (Dmytro Markov and Volodymyr Kurylovych), were found guilty and sentenced to death. The sentences were commuted to life imprisonment, but all were released from prison in 1917. At these trials, several Ukrainophiles gave testimony, thereby further embittering relations between the two national orientations.

Ukrainian institutions functioned once again following the return of Austrian rule. Again there was an interruption in the summer of 1916, when a successful Russian offensive (led by General Aleksei Brusilov) brought much of Bukovina and about one-third of eastern Galicia under tsarist control. Within a few months, however, the tsarist forces were driven back, although they continued to hold Galicia's Ternopil' region, between the Seret and Zbruch Rivers, and virtually all of Bukovina. In both these areas, the Russians again set up a civil administration. This time, the local Ukrainophile movement suffered less, especially after the February 1917 revolution in Russia, when several Dnieper Ukrainians were appointed as administrators, including the historian Dmytro Doroshenko, who became governor-general of Russian-controlled Bukovina and far eastern Galicia. Russian rule in these regions lasted until late 1917, which meant that for most of the war Galicia and Bukovina were military zones along the eastern front.

Ukrainian political activity in Vienna

Because Galicia and Bukovina were in the war zone, the center of Ukrainian political life in the Austro-Hungarian Empire was transferred to the imperial capital of Vienna. In general, as the war progressed and as Austria-Hungary's military fortunes waned, Ukrainian political demands increased. Nonetheless, it should be remembered that most Ukrainian leaders remained loyal to the idea of a Habsburg Empire until the very last months of the war.

Vienna was also a center for refugees from Dnieper Ukraine and the new headquarters of the Union for the Liberation of Ukraine (Soiuz Vyzvolennia Ukraïny), established in L'viv in August 1914. Since the Union was beholden to Austria for its hospitality and even for some financial aid from the Habsburg government, the liberated Ukraine it projected could not include Galicia, Bukovina, or Transcarpathia. In practice, the organization engaged in educational work to raise the national consciousness of Dnieper-Ukrainian prisoners of war held in Austria.

In contrast, Ukrainians from Galicia and Bukovina were politically engaged. On 5 May 1915, they founded in Vienna the General Ukrainian Council (Zahal'na Ukraïns'ka Rada). Headed by the parliamentary deputy Kost' Levyts'kyi, this group called for an independent Ukrainian state based on territories in the Russian Empire, but only for autonomy in Galicia and Bukovina. With this goal in mind, the council pressed the old demand for the division of Galicia into separate Polish and Ukrainian provinces.

While the Austro-Hungarian government welcomed calls for the creation of an independent state in Dnieper Ukraine, the creation of which would weaken its Russian enemy, it was not about to sanction a division of Galicia. Tampering with Galicia would clearly alienate Poles both within and beyond the province, and the Habsburgs wanted to cultivate their support. Indeed, in November 1916 Austria and Germany announced their intention to create a Polish kingdom from lands they had captured from the Russian Empire. Although Vienna would not go as far as to include Galicia in the new Polish kingdom, it promised the province greater autonomy. Given this larger scenario, the Ukrainian demand for a separate province in eastern Galicia was simply out of the question. Galician-Ukrainian political leaders protested vigorously, and within a few weeks after the death of Emperor Franz Joseph on 21 November 1916, the new emperor, Karl I (reigned 1916–1918), promised that the Ukrainian demands would be settled favorably. This could not happen, however, until the war was over. Once again Vienna adopted what had become its standard response to political problems – procrastination.

Austria's nationalities, however, were no longer in the mood to wait or to be satisfied with promises. This became evident in 1917, when the Austrian parliament, closed by imperial decree since the beginning of the war, was allowed to reconvene. Deputies from each of the empire's nationalities converged on Vienna and immediately put forth demands for greater autonomy. The Ukrainian Parliamentary Representation, led by Ievhen Petrushevych, declared unequivocally that his people's continued subordination to the Poles within the boundaries of one province would be a violation of their national rights as well as of the principle of the self-determination of nations. The Habsburg government tried to appease Petrushevych and his colleagues by appointing the first Ukrainian ever to the imperial cabinet, Ivan Horbachevs'kyi, as minister of health.

Yet by 1917 Austria's half-hearted efforts at compromise held less interest, because momentous events were taking place elsewhere that would alter the future of Europe as well as profoundly affect the fate of Ukrainians within and beyond the boundaries of the Austro-Hungarian Empire. Among the various war aims of the Allied Powers one was quite clear: to liberate the Slavic and Romanian peoples from foreign domination, that is, from Habsburg rule. In April 1917, the United States joined the Allies, and American support in supplies and soldiers gave an enormous boost to the struggling forces of Britain and France on the Western Front. Of even greater immediate significance were the events of 1917 in the Russian Empire. There, in March, a revolution broke out that toppled the centuries-old tsarist regime. It was followed by other developments that overshadowed events in the Habsburg Empire and had a profound and lasting impact on Ukrainians everywhere.

37

Revolutions in the Russian Empire

The seemingly unending carnage of World War I placed an enormous burden on the societies and economies of those European countries directly involved in the conflict. The strain was felt particularly by states that had weak socioeconomic structures prior to 1914. Among the weakest of these was the Russian Empire, and it is not surprising that the realm of the tsar became the first major casualty of the war.

By 1917, the Russian Empire had sustained the greatest losses of all the combatants. Of the 15 million men tsarist Russia mobilized, more than half became casualties – 1.6 million killed, 3.8 million wounded, 2.4 million made prisoner. Nor do these staggering figures take into account the equally great or even greater losses among the civilian population, or the losses of property, transportational facilities, and livestock, especially in the western provinces of the empire. Added to the war losses was the fact that the fragile Russian economic structure had virtually broken down, with severe food shortages, especially in the cities, the result.

Russia's first revolution of 1917

By the beginning of 1917, the economic situation had worsened considerably. In the imperial capital of Petrograd (the former name, St Petersburg, had been changed in 1914, because in an era of mounting hysteria it sounded too Germanic), food riots, strikes, and other demonstrations became a common occurrence. Criticism of the government by politicians was unrelenting, especially among the leftist opposition in Russia's parliament, the Duma. The crisis came to a head on 8 March 1917, with a massive protest led by women against food shortages in Petrograd. The imperial troops were called out, but they refused to fire on the crowds. Instead, they joined the workers, and on 12 March they established together a council, the Soviet of Workers' and Soldiers' Deputies. The example of the Petrograd Soviet was soon copied in towns and cities throughout the empire. The soviets demanded an immediate end to the war, the breakup of the imperial army, and the replacement of the monarchy with a governmental structure based on elected councils (soviets). With the establishment of the workers' and soldiers' councils, the first revolution of 1917 in Russia had begun. (Although the events began in March, the literature frequently speaks of the "February Revolution," since it occurred in February according to the Julian calendar – two weeks "behind" the Western Gregorian calendar – at the time in use in tsarist Russia.)

Despite their precipitous formation and rapid proliferation in the major towns and cities of the empire, the soviets (workers' and soldiers' councils) did not take the initial lead in the February Revolution. Instead, they deferred to several deputies in the Duma, who, under the leadership of Prince Georgii L'vov, took it upon themselves to negotiate with the emperor about the increasingly critical political and social situation. Together with the Russian Army's high command, the Duma representatives convinced Tsar Nicholas II that he should abdicate. After some discussion, the tsar agreed, and on 15 March 1917, without a single shot having been fired, the Russian monarchy came to an end.

With the monarchy defunct, liberal-minded deputies in the Duma hoped that Russia would be transformed into a parliamentary democracy of the western European variety. A final decision as to the actual form of a new government would have to wait, however, until the convocation of an elected constituent assembly. In the meantime, the Duma representatives, led by Prince L'vov, formed the self-appointed Provisional Government to direct the affairs of state. This transitional government, which had no electoral mandate, derived its authority from the now-defunct Duma, the Army High Command, and informal agreements with civic organizations like the Zemstvo League and the War Industries Committee.

The Provisional Government was immediately recognized by the Allies, and it used the old tsarist bureaucracy to carry out its directives. During this transitional period, the Provisional Government's primary goal was to prepare for elections to a constituent assembly which would decide on Russia's governmental future. Most immediately, it lifted tsarist censorship and other restrictions on civil liberties; it democratized local government; and it instituted a broad political amnesty.

Nonetheless, the two main problems that had faced the tsarist regime remained – the war and food shortages. Moreover, the Provisional Government had great difficulty in imposing its authority throughout the vast Russian Empire. One major stumbling block was the problem of "dual power." In effect, at least two centers of authority claimed to rule the entire post-tsarist Russian Empire: (1) the Provisional Government, and (2) the soviets (or councils) of workers' and soldiers' deputies. Aside from these two bodies, there were also several nationalist governments that sprang up in individual borderland regions. Initially, the relationship among these various entities was characterized by cautious tolerance. Some individuals even served in more than one body; for instance, the Petrograd Soviet's vice-chairman, Aleksander Kerenskii, became a member and, later, the head of the Provisional Government. But by the summer of 1917 the cautious tolerance between the soviets and the Provisional Government had been replaced by suspicion and opposition. And when the actual authority in most cities, including the capital of Petrograd, fell to the local soviets of workers' and soldiers' deputies, as it did before long, they more often than not blocked whatever directives were issued by the Provisional Government. The most contentious issue between the two bodies was the Provisional Government's decision to remain a loyal ally of the Allies and to continue its war effort against Germany and Austria-Hungary. This policy from the outset was opposed and subsequently undermined by the soviets.

Despite its precarious situation, the Provisional Government, led after 21 July by its minister of war, Aleksander Kerenskii, continued in power for most of 1917. Throughout its brief existence, it managed to survive a left-wing Bolshevik (July) and a right-wing military (September) attempt to overthrow it. But the Provisional Government was never able to overcome the problems that had toppled the monarchy – the economy and the war. Nor did it succeed in convening a constituent assembly, which it had proclaimed as its primary goal. As the year 1917 wore on, the masses, faced by what seemed like government inertia, became ever more impatient, and their political mood more radical. They intensified their demands – the peasants for land, the workers for food and control of the factories, the soldiers for an end to the war, and the national minorities for autonomy or independence.

Revolution in Dnieper Ukraine

In a sense, it is more accurate to refer to revolutions in the plural when talking about the Russian Empire in 1917. Not only were there two Russian revolutions – in March and again in November – there were also several revolutions on territories inhabited by members of the empire's many nationalities. Thus, in the wake of the first Russian revolution, the Ukrainian revolutionary era began as well.

The Ukrainian revolution began in March 1917, when the first political changes took place in the Russian Empire. It was to last until October 1920, when the international situation in eastern Europe finally stabilized. By that time, Ukrainians found themselves living within the boundaries of four states – Soviet Ukraine, Poland, Czechoslovakia, and Romania. The revolutionary era of March 1917 to October 1920 proved a decisive period in modern Ukrainian history. The era witnessed several attempts to establish an independent Ukrainian state. Although these efforts were ultimately unsuccessful, the goal was not forgotten, and further attempts would be made during subsequent decades.

The revolutionary era also saw the creation of the Soviet Ukrainian state, which, in close alliance with Soviet Russia, was to survive the revolutionary era and, by the second half of the twentieth century, unite most Ukrainian lands under its rule. Finally, all developments during the Ukrainian revolutionary era of 1917 to 1920 unfolded in an extremely complex environment marked by struggles between competing Ukrainian governments, peasant uprisings, foreign invasion, and civil war. Because of the importance of the Ukrainian revolutionary era, it will be treated at some length. So that its complexity can be explained in an understandable manner, the era will be divided into three phases: (1) the Central Rada – March 1917 to April 1918; (2) the Hetmanate – April to December 1918; and (3) the Directory, Civil War, and the Bolsheviks – January 1919 to October 1920.

The Central Rada

Phase one of the Ukrainian revolutionary era began on 13 March 1917, when news of the events in the imperial capital of Petrograd reached Kiev. Local leaders immediately reacted by setting up new organizations, in order to be prepared for anticipated governmental changes or to maintain order in the absence of other authority. Three such organizations came into existence, representing the Provisional Government, the local soviets, and the Ukrainian nationalists.

Civic and political activists in Kiev first took the initiative by forming the Executive Committee of the Council of United Civic Organizations (Ispolnitel'nyi Komitet Soveta Ob'edinennykh Obshchestvennykh Organizatsii, or IKSOOO). Besides former tsarist functionaries, IKSOOO included some political parties and national associations, each of which was concerned with maintaining public order. All the elements in IKSOOO supported the Provisional Government. The second organization included the various soviets of workers' and soldiers' deputies, which, as in Petrograd and the rest of the empire, were set up in several Dnieper-Ukrainian cities. The first soviets were formed in Kharkiv on 15 March and in Kiev the following day. The third organization represented Ukrainian nationalist leaders, who, on 17 March, established in Kiev their own council, the Central Rada. The Central Rada was made up of Ukrainian leaders from the prewar Society of Ukrainian Progressivists (TUP) as well as representatives of Ukrainian-oriented professional groups, civic organizations, and political parties, especially the revived Ukrainian Social-Democratic Labor party and the newly founded Ukrainian Socialist-Revolutionary party. On 20 March, the Rada elected in absentia Mykhailo S. Hrushevs'kyi, the former professor at L'viv University in Austrian Galicia, as its president. Owing to the lifting of restrictions following the February Revolution, Hrushevs'kyi was permitted to leave Moscow, where he had spent the war years under tsarist police surveillance after his arrest in 1914.

If in Petrograd and other Russian cities two centers of authority vied for power, in Dnieper Ukraine the lines of authority were blurred among three forces: the Provisional Government (IKSOOO); the Kiev Soviet of Workers' and Solders' Deputies; and the Central Rada. For instance, the Kiev Soviet cooperated with IKSOOO and together they negotiated possible cooperation with the Central Rada. Moreover, the membership of the Kiev Soviet and the Central Rada often overlapped, since many people believed both organizations were councils of workers and peasants. Also, all three bodies – IKSOOO, the Soviet, and the Rada – initially recognized the authority of the Provisional Government in Petrograd. The Central Rada even congratulated the Provisional Government on its formation, only expressing the hope that it would allow local autonomy for Ukraine.

For its part, the Provisional Government was so absorbed by problems in Petrograd that it initially ignored the Rada and Dnieper Ukraine in general. Consequently, the Central Rada and the various soviets took steps to establish their own authority not only in Kiev but throughout the Ukrainian countryside. It was not long before three bodies each claimed to represent Ukrainian (in the territorial sense) interests: (1) the Provisional Government, consisting of the former imperial bureaucracy and armed forces and supported at the local level by IKSOOO; (2) the soviets of workers, soldiers, and peasants' deputies throughout both urban areas (representing for the most part the Russian and russified industrial proletariat) and rural areas (including ethnic Ukrainians and other peoples); and (3) the Central Rada, supported by nationally conscious Ukrainian leaders and organizations. In theory, the Rada was recognized as an organ of the Provisional Government whose authority was also accepted by the soviets. In practice, especially as 1917 wore on, the Rada, the soviets, and the Provisional Government drew farther apart and began competing with one another for the allegiance of the masses and control of Dnieper-Ukrainian territory.

Left alone by the Provisional Government, the Central Rada under Hrushevs'kyi's urging strove to become the supreme representative body for Ukrainian lands. It was rapidly transformed from a kind of clearinghouse for the diverse activity of Ukrainian national organizations into a political body that aimed to represent all inhabitants of Dnieper-Ukrainian territory regardless of their nationality. The Rada's goals were in theory achievable, since the revolutionary environment encouraged a rebirth of Ukrainian political life, which had basically lain dormant since 1908. Because it wished to reflect the regional, social, and national diversity of Dnieper Ukraine, the Central Rada became an exceptionally large general assembly with at times upwards of 900 members. The Central Rada met only infrequently, and to make the body more operative, a Little (Mala) Rada of about sixty members was created to function as a kind of executive committee which would meet more often and decide on legislative and policy matters. In June 1917, the Central Rada chose the General Secretariat, which functioned as a governmental cabinet with a membership of between eight and fourteen ministers.

The membership of the Central Rada was dominated by leftist political groupings. The largest bloc of members were representatives from the soviets of workers, soldiers, and peasants (57 percent); they were followed by representatives of socialist political parties (13 percent), whether of Russian, Jewish, Polish, or Ukrainian national orientation. The leading Ukrainian parties were the revived Ukrainian Social-Democratic Labor party (headed by Volodymyr Vynnychenko, Mykola Porsh, and Symon Petliura); the newly formed Ukrainian Socialist Revolutionary party (headed by Mykhailo Hrushevs'kyi, Pavlo Khrystiuk, and Mykola Kovalevs'kyi); and the Ukrainian Socialist-Federalist party (headed by Serhii Iefremov, Dmytro Doroshenko, and Oleksander Shul'hyn), which evolved from the Society of Ukrainian Progressivists (TUP), the group most instrumental in establishing the Central Rada. The general aim of these leading parties and therefore the Central Rada as a whole was to implement far-reaching social reforms and to raise the prestige of Ukrainian culture and language.

Among the first steps taken by the Central Rada in its efforts to represent Ukrainian interests was to convene, on 19–21 April 1917, the All-Ukrainian National Congress, made up of 900 delegates from all parts of Dnieper Ukraine as well as 600 other participants. The Rada also reorganized itself to be more representative of the country as a whole, and it passed resolutions calling for autonomy for Ukraine within Russia. Specifically, this meant the separation of nine "Ukrainian" provinces into a special administrative area, the ukrainianization of the

First Universal of the Ukrainian Central Rada to All Ukrainian People Whether Residing in Ukraine or Beyond its Borders

Ukrainian people! A People of peasants, workers, toilers!

By your will you have entrusted us, the *Ukrainian Central Rada,* to guard the rights and freedoms of the Ukrainian land.

Your finest sons, who represent villages, factories, military barracks, Ukrainian communities, and associations, have elected us, the Ukrainian Central Rada, and ordered us to stand firm and defend these rights and freedoms.

Your elected representatives have, therefore, expressed their will.

Let Ukraine be free! Without separating from Russia, without breaking with the Russian state, let the Ukrainian people have the right to manage its own life on *its* own soil. Let a National Ukrainian Assembly [*Soim*], elected by universal, equal, direct, and secret balloting, establish order and harmony in Ukraine. Only our Ukrainian Assembly has the right to establish laws to provide order here in Ukraine.

Those laws which would govern the entire Russian state should be promulgated in an All-Russian Parliament.

No one can know better than we what we need and which laws are best for us.

No one can know better than our peasants how to manage their own land. Therefore, we wish that after all the lands throughout Russia held by the nobility, the state, the monasteries, and the tsar have been confiscated and have become the property of the people, and after a law concerning this has been enacted by the All-Russian Constituent Assembly, the right to administer Ukrainian lands shall belong to us, to our Ukrainian Assembly [*Soim*]. ...

They elected us, the Ukrainian Central Rada, from among their midst and directed us ... to create a new order in a free autonomous Ukraine. ...

We thought the Central Russian Government would support us in this task, and that in cooperation with it, we, the Ukrainian Central Rada, would be able to provide order in our land.

But the Provisional Russian Government rejected all our demands and pushed aside the outstretched hand of the Ukrainian people. We have sent our delegates (envoys) to Petrograd so that they might present the following demands to the Russian Provisional Government:

That the Russian government by a special act publicly declare that it does not oppose the national will of Ukraine, the right of our people to autonomy.

That the Central Russian Government accredit our Commissar on Ukrainian Affairs for all matters concerning Ukraine.

That local power in Ukraine be united under one representative from the Central Russian Government, that is, by a Commissar in Ukraine chosen by us. That a definite portion of funds collected from our people, for the Central

Treasury be turned over to us, the representatives of this people, for its own national-cultural needs.

The Central Russian Government *rejected* all of these demands.

It was not willing to say whether or not it recognizes the right of our people to autonomy and the right to manage its own life. It avoided giving an answer, and referred us to a future All-Russian Constituent Assembly.

The Russian Central Government did not wish to accredit our Commissar and *did not want to join us in the establishment of a new order.* Likewise, *it did not wish to recognize a Commissar for all Ukraine* with whom we might bring our land to order and accord.

It also refused to return funds collected from our own land for the needs of our schools, education, and organizations.

Hence, the Ukrainian people is forced to *determine its own destiny.* We cannot permit our land to fall into lawlessness and decline. Since the Russian Provisional Government cannot provide order for us, since it does not want to join us in this great task, then we must do it ourselves. This is our duty. ...

That is why we, the Ukrainian Central Rada, issue this Universal to our entire people and proclaim: from this day forth we shall build our life.

Let every member of our nation, each citizen of a village or city know that the time has come for a great undertaking.

Hereafter, each village, rural district, city, or zemstvo governing board which upholds the interests of the Ukrainian people should have *the closest of organizational ties with the Central Rada.*

In places where for some reason administrative authority remains in the hands of people hostile to the Ukrainian cause, we propose that our citizens carry out a broad, vigorous organizational effort to enlighten the people and then *elect an administration.*

In cities and areas where the Ukrainian population is intermixed with other nationalities, we propose that our citizens immediately come to an *agreement and understanding with the democratic elements of these nationalities*, and jointly begin preparations for a new order.

The *Central Rada* hopes that non-Ukrainian peoples living on our territory will also be concerned to maintain order and peace, and that in this difficult time of disorder in the entire state, they will join us in a united and friendly fashion to work for the organization of an autonomous Ukraine.

When we complete this preparatory organizational work, we will call together representatives of all the peoples of Ukraine and will establish laws for the country. The All-Russian Constituent Assembly must ratify all the laws and the new order we will prepare. ...

Strong and courageous hands are needed [for this task]. The people's hard work is needed. But above all, for the success of this work, extensive funds are needed. Until now, the Ukrainian people turned over all funds to the All-Russian Treasury, but in turn it has not, nor does it now receive that which is its due.

Consequently, we, the Ukrainian Central Rada, order all the organized citizenry of our villages and towns and all Ukrainian community executive boards and organizations to institute a special tax on the population for the national cause, effective the first day of the month of July, to be transmitted accurately, immediately, and regularly to the treasury of the Ukrainian Central Rada.

Ukrainian people! Your fate lies in your own hands. In this difficult time of universal anarchy and ruin, prove by your unity and your statesmanship that you, a nation of workers and tillers of the soil, can proudly take your place beside any organized nation-state, as an equal among equals.

Kiev
10/23 June 1917

SOURCE: Taras Hunczak and Roman Sol'chanyk, eds., *Ukraïns'ka suspil'no-politychna dumka v 20 stolitti: dokumenty i materiialy*, Vol. I (New York 1983), pp. 295–298. Italics in original.

school system, and the creation of a Ukrainian army. When in early June the Rada sent a delegation to inform the Provisional Government of its actions, it received an evasive reply. Ostensibly, Petrograd could not recognize the Rada because such matters fell under the jurisdiction of the future all-Russian constituent assembly. The Rada was not deterred. It simply continued its efforts to extend its influence throughout Dnieper Ukraine.

At the same time, nationalist enthusiasm began to spread among Ukrainian soldiers in the Russian Army. Some units employed Ukrainian as a language of command and looked to the Central Rada in Kiev, not to the Provisional Government in Petrograd, for leadership. Finally, in mid-May the First Ukrainian Military Congress recognized the Rada as the legitimate representative body of Dnieper Ukraine and welcomed the continued formation of Ukrainian national units in the former Imperial Russian Army.

Encouraged by the deliberations at the First Ukrainian Military Congress, at the end of May the Central Rada sent a delegation to Petrograd to urge the Provisional Government to approve the idea of Ukrainian autonomy within a federated Russian state. The Provisional Government once again replied that no decisions could be made until after the establishment of an all-Russian constituent assembly. At the same time, the Provisional Government refused to grant permission for the convening of a second Ukrainian military congress.

The Ukrainians were dismayed by the Provisional Government's seeming lack of concern. A second military congress met anyway, and when it concluded on 23 June the Central Rada issued its First Universal. Reminiscent of the historic proclamations of past Cossack hetmans (the term *universaly* had been used by Khmel'nyts'kyi and Mazepa for their official decrees), the Central Rada's First Universal proclaimed Ukraine an autonomous land within a federated Russia and called on the population to pay a special tax to aid the national cause. The decla-

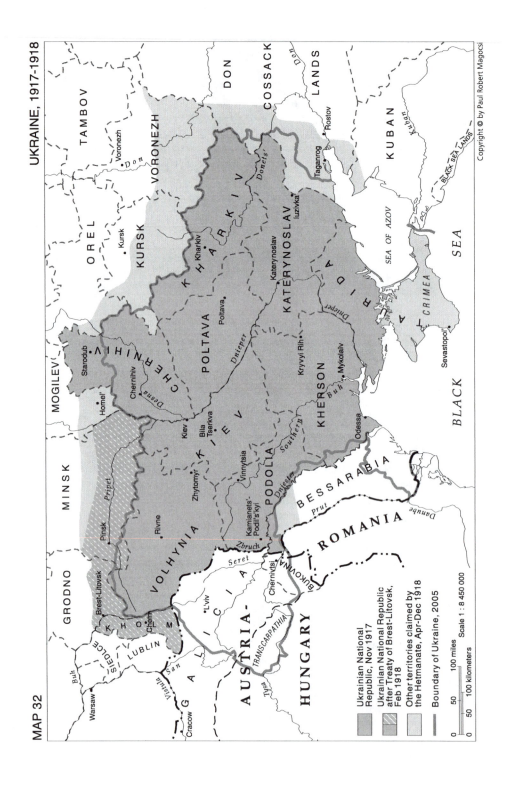

MAP 32

UKRAINE, 1917-1918

Copyright © by Paul Robert Magocsi

Ukrainian National
Republic, Nov 1917

Ukrainian National
Republic after Treaty of Brest-Litovsk,
Feb 1918

Other territories claimed by
the Hetmanate, Apr-Dec 1918

Boundary of Ukraine, 2005

Scale 1 : 8 450 000

0   50   100 miles

0   50   100 kilometers

ration of autonomy was enthusiastically supported by the First All-Ukrainian Peasant Congress, which began its meeting in Kiev the same day (23–29 June). In an effort to direct the destiny of the country, on 28 June the Central Rada created a governing council, the General Secretariat, made up of nine members under the direction of the writer and socialist politician Volodymyr Vynnychenko.

Russians in both Kiev and Petrograd were stunned by the Rada's declaration of autonomy and its creation of the governing General Secretariat. Almost *immediately,* the Russian press characterized the Rada's action as a "betrayal" and a "stab in the back of the revolution."[1] In an attempt to avoid further tension, in mid-July the Provisional Government sent a delegation to Kiev headed by its soon-to-be chairman, Aleksandr Kerenskii. A compromise was reached whereby the Rada would make no further demands for autonomy until the convocation of an all-Russian constituent assembly. In the interim, however, the Rada's newly formed General Secretariat could rule in Dnieper Ukraine, although according to "Instructions" to be received from the Provisional Government. The compromise with the Provisional Government was outlined in the Second Universal, issued by the Central Rada on 16 July. The Rada's authority was limited, however, to only five provinces: Volhynia, Podolia, Kiev, Poltava, and Chernihiv south of the present-day Russian-Ukrainian border.

In reality, the agreement had little practical effect on relations between Petrograd and Kiev, as friction continued to mount between the Provisional Government and the Central Rada's General Secretariat. But the Provisional Government's public recognition of the Rada and General Secretariat enhanced their image in the eyes of other peoples in Dnieper Ukraine who had previously been invited to join the Central Rada, but only now did so. At the end of July 1917, when the Rada numbered 822 members, 15 percent of the places were allotted to Russians, Jews, and Poles, who also had 18 out of 54 members in the Little Rada. To enhance its image further, in late September the Rada convened in Kiev the Congress of Minority Peoples, at which the presence of delegates of nationalities from many parts of the former empire created the semblance of a united front. The congress hoped to persuade the Provisional Government to give in to its demands for more minority rights. By the early autumn, however, the Provisional Government was facing problems more serious than the problem of minorities.

The Bolshevik Revolution

The greatest challenge to the Provisional Government remained the war. In June 1917, Aleksandr Kerenskii, the minister of war, ordered a new military offensive. The Russian Army was successful at first, but by July the Germans had counterattacked. The Russian Army was routed, discipline broke down, and desertions mounted. The final disintegration of Russia's military had begun.

Another threat to the Provisional Government came from left-wing socialist parties. One of these was the Russian Social-Democratic Workers' party, which was divided between two factions: the Mensheviks, who represented the majority (despite their Russian name, which means minority), and the Bolsheviks. Both the Mensheviks and the Bolsheviks were committed to the overthrow of tsarist society and the establishment of an industrialized socialist state, one in which the means of production and the land would be in the hands of the working proletariat (whether industrial or agrarian) led by a government controlled by the proletariat's leaders, the party. The two factions differed, however, on tactics. The Bolsheviks argued that a dominant role should be given to "professional revolutionaries" who would use the party to lead the proletarian masses to victory. In contrast, the Mensheviks adopted a gradualist approach, anticipating that revolutionary change in the Russian Empire was not likely to come at least for another decade. In the end, neither group seemed destined to put its vision of social change into practice, since during the decade before World War I repressive tsarist policy had sent most of the leading revolutionaries into internal exile or prison or had forced them into exile abroad. With the fall of the monarchy, however, the Russian revolutionaries were released, and they streamed back to Petrograd and Moscow from Siberia and from abroad.

The leader of the Bolshevik faction of the Social-Democratic Workers' party, Vladimir Ulianov, known as Lenin, had been in exile in Switzerland and therefore was blocked by the Eastern front from returning to Russia. Lenin's disruptive potential as an opponent of the new Provisional Government was recognized by the Germans. Accordingly, they gave him passage across their territory in a "sealed train" (actually a passenger car that was locked and guarded), ostensibly to prevent the Bolshevik "contamination" of Germany. Upon his arrival on 16 April 1917 at the Finland Station in Petrograd, Lenin immediately called for the overthrow of the Provisional Government. He was soon joined by several of his former Menshevik rivals, including the talented Ukrainian-born Jew Leon Trotskii.

The Bolsheviks' basic tactic was to increase the party's ranks and to place as many of its members as possible in the Petrograd Soviet and in every other soviet of workers' and soldiers' council throughout the empire. Through the soviets, each of which had its own armed workers' militias eventually known as the Red Guards, the Bolsheviks hoped to gain control of the country. Their tactic proved successful, and by early autumn the Petrograd and Moscow soviets had a Bolshevik majority. A symbol and a reflection of the Bolsheviks' success was their manipulative use of what became the two most popular slogans of 1917: "Peace, Land, and Bread" attracted supporters to the extent that between February and October alone the Bolshevik party grew from 24,000 to 350,000 members; and "All Power to the Soviets" encapsulated the party's goal of attaining political dominance.

In contrast, the Bolsheviks in Dnieper Ukraine remained relatively small in number, with only about 22,000 members by August 1917. Moreover, the party was divided into three separate and, often, competing groups: the Kharkiv-Katerynoslav group, the Kiev group, and the tiny Odessa group.

In Russia, meanwhile, Bolshevik tactics seemed to be working, and flushed with success they attempted to overthrow the Provisional Government in July. They were defeated, however, and Lenin was forced into exile again. This time he retreated only to nearby Finland, whose autonomous status was restored in March by the Provisional Government.

Despite Lenin's departure, the Provisional Government was challenged once again, in early September, this time by an attempted right-wing military coup, led by General Lavr Kornilov. The Provisional Government survived this threat too, but clearly its days were numbered. The army was disintegrating further, the food situation had worsened, and the nationalities were increasing their demands. Simply put, the country was on the verge of chaos.

Chaos was exactly what the Bolsheviks wanted, and on 20 October Lenin secretly returned to Petrograd. Again, he called for a general insurrection and decided to use the second All-Russian Congress of Soviets, then meeting in Petrograd, as the means to achieve his goals. On 7 November 1917 the Bolsheviks, through the Congress of Soviets, proclaimed themselves the rulers of Russia. Later that night and into the early hours of the next morning the Bolsheviks, with the help of Red Guards from the Petrograd Soviet, drove out the Provisional Government. From that moment the course of Russian and European history was to change. The new order proclaimed by the Bolsheviks was to be headed by the Council of People's Commissars, whose leading members were Lenin as chairman and Trotskii as commissar for foreign affairs. The third figure, the commissar for nationalities, Iosif Stalin (the pseudonym of the Georgian-born Iosif Dzhugashvili), was only subsequently to become a figure of importance in the Bolshevik hierarchy.

The Bolshevik coup in Petrograd immediately influenced developments in Dnieper Ukraine. A serious power struggle developed among supporters of the three local factions: the Provisional Government; the Kiev Soviet of Workers' and Soldiers' Deputies; and the Central Rada. The Bolshevik tactic was to gain control of the soviets and through them legitimize their party's authority. The immediate serious challenge to Bolshevik plans seemed to be the lingering presence of local representatives of the Provisional Government. Not yet ready to act on their own, the Bolsheviks decided to cooperate with and even join the Central Rada, which on 12 November was able easily to take over power from the departing military and local administration of the Provisional Government. In other towns and cities throughout Dnieper Ukraine, power was already in the hands of local soviets of workers,' soldiers,' and peasants' deputies, many of which included both Ukrainian nationalist and Bolshevik groups.

The seemingly cooperative relations between nationalist and Bolshevik supporters could not last long, however, because the Central Rada had already, on 8 November, condemned the coup in Petrograd and announced its intention to resist any similar attempts in Dnieper Ukraine. In this momentary political power vacuum, on 20 November 1917 the Central Rada issued its Third Universal. The document proclaimed for the first time the existence of the Ukrainian National Republic (Ukraïns'ka Narodnia Respublyka), although instead of independence it favored federation with Russia. The territory of the new Ukrainian National Republic was to consist of nine former imperial provinces: Kiev, Podolia, Volhynia, Chernihiv, Poltava, Kharkiv, Katerynoslav, Kherson, and Taurida (excluding the Crimea). While not opting for complete independence, the Rada was nonetheless sensitive to the heady revolutionary fervor of the moment. The Third Universal therefore called for (1) the seizure of noble- and church-owned large landholdings and their distribution among the peasants, (2) the introduction of an eight-hour work day for the urban proletariat, (3) the nationalization of industries, (4)

THIRD UNIVERSAL OF THE UKRAINIAN CENTRAL RADA (PREAMBLE)

Ukrainian people and all peoples of Ukraine!

A heavy and difficult hour has fallen upon the land of the Russian Republic. In the capitals to the north a bloody civil struggle is raging. The Central Government has collapsed, and anarchy, lawlessness, and ruin are spreading throughout the state.

Our land is also in danger. Without a single, strong national authority, Ukraine may also fall into the abyss of civil war, destruction, and ruin.

Ukrainian people! You, together with the other fraternal peoples of Ukraine, have entrusted to us to guard the rights acquired through your struggles, and to create order and build a new life on our land. Therefore, we, the Ukrainian Central Rada, by your will and in the name of establishing order in our country and of saving all of Russia proclaim:

From this day forth, Ukraine becomes the Ukrainian National Republic.

Although not separating from the Russian Republic and therefore maintaining its unity, we nonetheless shall stand firmly on our own land, so that our strength may help all of Russia, and so that the entire Russian Republic will become a federation of equal and free peoples.

Until [the convocation of] a Constituent Assembly of Ukraine, all power to establish order in our country, to promulgate laws, and to govern belongs to us, the Ukrainian Central Rada, and to our government – the General Secretariat of Ukraine.

We shall use our power and authority to stand guard over freedom and revolution not only in our land, but also throughout all of Russia.

Kiev
7/20 November 1917

SOURCE: Taras Hunczak and Roman Sol'chanyk, eds., *Ukraïns'ka suspil'no-politychna dumka v 20 stoliini: dokumeny i materiialy*, Vol. I (New York 1983), pp. 340–341.

the granting of constitutional (non-territorial) autonomy to national minorities, (5) the abolition of the death penalty, (6) the strengthening of local self-government, and (7) the adoption of concrete measures to end the war. Finally, the Third Universal set 9 January 1918 as the date for elections to a Ukrainian constituent assembly, which would meet on 22 January. During the rest of November and December 1917, the Central Rada tried to consolidate its authority. It received support from the soviets in Kiev and from soviets in several of the country's largest cities, including Katerynoslav, Odessa, and Mykolaïv. Only the

Kharkiv Soviet refused to recognize the Rada, pledging itself directly to Petrograd instead.

The Ukrainian National Republic

The tenuous cooperation between Dnieper Ukraine's Central Rada and local Bolsheviks loyal to the Soviet Council of People's Commissars in Petrograd was not destined to last long. The Rada antagonized Petrograd when it ordered Ukrainian units in the Russian Army not to obey the orders of the Bolsheviks and when it questioned the claims of the Bolsheviks to act as an all-Russian government. Accordingly, Petrograd issued an ultimatum (received in Kiev on 17 December) stating that unless the Central Rada suspended its activity within forty-eight hours, the "Council of People's Commissars [would] consider the Central Rada in a state of open war against the Soviet government in Russia and Ukraine."[2] Dnieper Ukraine's Bolsheviks planned to convene the All-Ukrainian Congress of Workers,' Soldiers,' and Peasants' Deputies on 17 December, which they expected to dominate and through which they hoped to take power throughout the countryside. Aware of this projected Bolshevik tactic, which was the one previously used so effectively in Petrograd, the Central Rada initially opposed the idea of a congress of soviets. Eventually, however, the Rada decided to prepare for a congress, and it called on its supporters throughout Dnieper Ukraine to join in its efforts.

When the Congress of Soviets met in Kiev as planned, on 17 December 1917, the Bolsheviks, who had at most 100 of 2,500 delegates, quickly discovered that they were far outnumbered by supporters of the Rada. Then, when the congress rejected the ultimatum of the Soviet government in Petrograd, the Bolsheviks, joined by a few other delegates, demonstrably walked out of the meeting and departed for Kharkiv. In Kharkiv, delegates from local soviets in the industrialized regions of the Donbas and Kryvyi Rih were already holding their own congress, and together with the representatives from Kiev they renamed it the First All-Ukrainian Congress of Soviets of Workers,' Soldiers,' and Peasants' Deputies. Despite some friction between the "Kievans" and other delegations, on 25 December 1917 the central executive committee of the Kharkiv congress was able to form the first Soviet government in Dnieper Ukraine (Respublyka Rad Ukraïny). The new government was headed by the People's Secretariat (Narodnyi Sekretariat), consisting of twelve ministers. With one exception, all the ministers were Bolsheviks, the most influential being Mykola Skrypnyk, who later served as the chairman. Hence, by the end of 1917 the almost year-long struggle for political power in Dnieper Ukraine had come down to two competing forces: (1) the Ukrainian National Republic, called into being by the Central Rada, which came to dominate the Kiev Soviet; and (2) the Soviet Ukrainian government, called into being by the All-Ukrainian Congress of Soviets of Workers,' Soldiers,' and Peasants' Deputies, which was based in Kharkiv and made up mainly of Bolshevik-led workers from eastern Ukraine.

The Soviet Ukrainian government in Kharkiv was subordinate to the Bolsheviks in Petrograd, and with their help it began a campaign to undermine politically and then to remove from Kiev by military force the Central Rada and its Ukrainian National Republic. The Ukrainian entities in Kiev were described by the Bolsheviks as the "enemies of the people." Particularly helpful to the Kharkiv Soviet government was the arrival, on 25 December, of a Soviet Russian army led by Vladimir Antonov-Ovseenko. Together with the local Red Guards in Kharkiv and other eastern Ukrainian cities, Antonov-Ovseenko marched on Kiev. For its part, the Central Rada depended for defense on a motley array of forces: some Free Cossack units, workers' battalions, and other groups such as the Haidamak Kish (under Symon Petliura) and the Galician-Bukovinian Battalion of Sich Riflemen (under Ievhen Konovalets'), made up of former Austrian prisoners of war. The Bolshevik invasion led by Antonov-Ovseenko at the beginning of 1918 marked the beginning of the military struggle for control of Dnieper Ukraine.

Faced with the loss of most of the Left Bank and the Donbas to Antonov-Ovseenko's Red Army and the impossibility of further negotiation with the Bolshevik government in Russia, the Rada met in Kiev on 22 January 1918 – the day on which the Third Universal had called for the convening of a Ukrainian constituent assembly. The Rada's response to the continued Bolshevik invasion was to issue, on 25 January, its Fourth Universal, which proclaimed the existence of an independent Ukrainian National Republic. (The document was actually dated 22 January, so that date was subsequently celebrated as independence day by Ukrainians in interwar Galicia and, until 1991, by Ukrainians living abroad). The Fourth Universal meant nothing to the Bolsheviks, who continued their drive toward Kiev. In the city itself, Bolshevik elements staged a coup on 29 January, but it was another ten days before Antonov-Ovseenko's Red Army took the city. In the interim, the Rada of the recently proclaimed independent Ukrainian National Republic was forced to flee and take up residence farther west, in Zhytomyr. On 9 February, the Bolsheviks ruled in Kiev.

Meanwhile, the Bolshevik government in Petrograd made good its promise to end Russia's participation in the war. In December 1918, it entered into peace negotiations with Germany and Austria-Hungary, as delegates from both sides met in the town of Brest-Litovsk. The Bolsheviks desperately needed peace in order to consolidate their authority over the country. The Central Powers also wanted to eliminate the eastern front so that Germany could concentrate its forces against France and Italy in western Europe. Moreover, Germany and, especially, Austria-Hungary were in desperate need of foodstuffs and raw materials, which they hoped to obtain from Dnieper Ukraine. For these reasons, the Central Powers welcomed the presence of delegates from the Ukrainian National Republic's Central Rada as well as from Finland, Poland, and the Baltic states, each of which had recently declared or was about to declare its independence from Russia. German, Austro-Hungarian, and Ukrainian interests thus coincided, and on 9 February 1918 the Central Powers signed with the Ukrainian National Republic a treaty at Brest-Litovsk.

Soviet Russia's representative at Brest-Litovsk, Leon Trotskii, bitterly opposed the idea of any dismembering of the former tsarist empire, as did the Ukrainian

THE TREATY OF BREST-LITOVSK

Whereas the Ukrainian people has, in the course of the present world war, declared its independence, and has expressed the desire to establish peace between the Ukrainian People's Republic and the powers at present at war with Russia, the Governments of Germany, Austria-Hungary, Bulgaria, and Turkey have resolved to conclude a Treaty of Peace with the Government of the Ukrainian People's Republic; they wish in this way to take the first step towards a lasting world peace, honorable for all parties, which shall not only put an end to the horrors of the war, but shall also contribute to the restoration of friendly relations between the peoples in the political, legal, economic, and intellectual spheres. ...

Article I.

Germany, Austria-Hungary, Bulgaria, and Turkey on the one hand, and the Ukrainian People's Republic on the other hand, declare that the state of war between them is at an end. The contracting parties are resolved henceforth to live in peace and amity with one another.

Article II.

1. As between Austria-Hungary on the one hand, and the Ukrainian People's Republic on the other hand, in so far as these two powers border upon one another, the frontiers which existed between the Austro-Hungarian monarchy and Russia prior to the outbreak of the present war will be preserved.

2. Further north, the frontier of the Ukrainian People's Republic ... will be delimited in detail by a mixed commission, according to the ethnographical conditions and after taking the wishes of the inhabitants into consideration. ...

Article III.

The evacuation of the occupied territories shall begin immediately after the ratification of the present Treaty of Peace. ...

Article IV.

Diplomatic and consular relations between the contracting parties shall commence immediately after the ratification of the Treaty of Peace.

With respect to the admission of consuls on the widest scale possible on both sides special agreements are reserved.

Article V.

The contracting parties mutually renounce repayment of their war costs, that is to say, their state expenditure for the prosecution of the war, as well as payment for war damages, in other words, damages sustained by them and their nationals in the war areas through military measures, including all requisitions made in enemy territory.

Article VI.

Prisoners of war of both parties shall be released to their homeland in so far as they do not desire, with the approval of the state in whose territory they shall be, to remain within its territories or to proceed to another country. ...

Article VII.

The contracting parties mutually undertake to enter into economic relations without delay and to organise the exchange of goods on the basis of the following stipulations:

Until 31 July of the current year a reciprocal exchange of the surplus of their more important agricultural and industrial products, for the purpose of meeting current requirements, is to be effected according to provisions settled on both sides by a commission composed of an equal number of representatives of both parties, which shall sit immediately after the Treaty of Peace has been signed. ...

The exchange of such products as are not determined by the above-mentioned commissions shall be effected on a basis of free trading. ...

In regard to the economic relations between Bulgaria and the Ukrainian People's Republic, these shall, until such time as a definitive commercial Treaty shall have been concluded, be regulated on the basis of most-favored-nation treatment. ...

In regard to the economic relations between the Ottoman Empire and the Ukrainian People's Republic, these shall, until such time as a definite commercial treaty shall have been concluded, be regulated on the basis of most-favored-nation treatment. ...

The Ukrainian People's Republic shall make no claim to the preferential treatment which Germany grants to Austria-Hungary or to any other country bound to her by a customs union and directly bordering on Germany, or bordering indirectly through another country bound to her or to Austria-Hungary by a customs union, or to the preferential treatment which Germany grants to her own colonies, foreign possessions, and protectorates, or to countries bound to her by a customs union.

Germany shall make no claim to the preferential treatment which the Ukrainian People's Republic grants to any other country. ...

Article VIII.

The establishment of public and private legal relations, the exchange of prisoners of war and interned civilians, the amnesty question, as well as the question of the treatment of merchant shipping in the enemy's hands shall be settled by means of separate treaties with the Ukrainian People's Republic, which shall form an essential part of the present Treaty of Peace, and, as far as [is] practicable, come into force simultaneously therewith. ...

Final Provision.

The present Treaty of Peace shall be ratified. The ratifications shall be exchanged in Vienna at the earliest possible moment.

The Treaty of Peace shall come into force on its ratification, in so far as no stipulation to the contrary is contained therein.

Brest-Litovsk
February 9, 1918

Alleged Secret Clauses
United States Department of State Report,
June 20, 1918

A report from Stockholm states that the following secret clauses were included in the treaty which the Central Powers signed with the Rada of the Ukraine on 9 February, 1918. The object was stated to be the simplification of future relations along racial lines.

(a) All claims to districts to the west of the Dniester River are given up by Ukraine as well as all Ukrainian territory in eastern Galicia.

(b) An adjustment is to be made in Austria in regard to her frontier to the east of Galicia and the district of Lemberg [L'viv] is to be made the western limit of eastern Galicia, the division to be made on language lines.

Alleged Secret Agreement
as Published in the Vienna Newspaper,
Neue Freie Presse, July 7, 1918

In view of the fact that the Ukrainians have granted to the minorities living in Ukraine, and among the Poles, a far-reaching autonomy and the possibility of cultural development, therefore, we [the Austro-Hungarian government] also declare, in order to insure the national-cultural development of that part of the Ukrainian people who live within Austrian territory, and for the purpose of a closer connection between our states, that at the latest by 31 July, a bill will be introduced into Parliament dealing with the creation of a special crown-land from the Bukovina and that part of eastern Galicia which is preponderatingly [*sic*] inhabited by Ukrainians. The Austrian government will use all constitutional means at its disposal to the end that this bill may be given legal force through parliamentary action.

SOURCE: *Texts of the Ukraine "Peace"* (Washington, D.C. 1918), pp. 9–25, 141.

Bolsheviks, who, against Petrograd's orders, continued to wage a guerilla campaign against the Germans. Ultimately, it was Lenin who had the last word. Desperately in need of peace, on 3 March 1918 Soviet Russia signed with the Central Powers a separate treaty of Brest-Litovsk, whereby the Bolsheviks agreed "to conclude a peace at once with the Ukrainian National Republic" and to clear that territory of pro-Soviet troops. Negotiations between the Soviet Russian government and the Ukrainian National Republic dragged on for the next five months with no conclusive results. On the other hand, the Central Powers recognized Ukraine as a sovereign state and between February and September 1918 concluded with it several agreements to supplement the original 8 February Brest-Litovsk text. Among these was an agreement by the Central Powers to return Ukrainian prisoners of war (especially numerous in German and Austrian camps) and to equip them for self-defense and for any struggle which might take place with the Bolsheviks.

The territory of the Ukrainian state recognized at Brest-Litovsk included not only the nine former imperial provinces previously claimed by the Central Rada (Volhynia, Podolia, Kiev, Chernihiv, Poltava, Kharkiv, Kherson, Katerynoslav, and northern Taurida), but also the former province of Kholm and the southern third of Minsk and Grodno provinces, including the city of Brest-Litovsk itself. The Ukrainian delegates at Brest-Litovsk also laid claim to the Ukrainian-inhabited territories in Austria-Hungary, but the best they could obtain was a secret protocol according to which the Austrian government reluctantly agreed to introduce, by 20 July 1918, a parliamentary bill proposing the creation of a separate crown land consisting of "Bukovina and that part of eastern Galicia which is preponderatingly [sic] inhabited by Ukrainians."[3] The implementation of this protocol depended, however, on Ukraine's ability to fulfil its treaty obligations, which included supplying 1 million tons (63,000,000 pounds) of grain to the Central Powers by 31 July 1918.

The initial signing of the Treaty of Brest-Litovsk took place the very day (9 February) the Central Rada was driven out of Kiev by the Bolsheviks. By that time, all major centers in eastern Ukraine (Kharkiv, Chernihiv, Poltava, Katerynoslav) were also in the hands of the Soviet Red Guards. Faced with this situation, the Central Rada called for aid from the Central Powers. On 18 February German troops entered Ukrainian territory and, backed by their support, the forces of the Ukrainian National Republic were able to drive the Bolsheviks out of Kiev on 2 March. Thus, the first Bolshevik occupation of Kiev had lasted a mere twenty days. In the face of the German advance, the Soviet Ukrainian government, still bitterly divided into a Kiev faction and a Kharkiv faction (the latter having established in February its own Donets'-Kryvyi Rih Soviet Republic), fled to Soviet Russia. It is interesting to note that Germany's ally, Austria-Hungary, had initially refused to send any of its troops into Ukraine. When it finally did so at the outset of March, the question arose as to spheres of interest between the Central Powers. German forces dispersed throughout most of Ukraine's provinces, while Austro-Hungarian troops were assigned to southern Volhynia, Podolia, Kherson, and Katerynoslav. Despite such territorial demarcation, the Germans frequently crossed into the Austro-Hungarian sphere, and this caused friction, sometimes quite serious, between the two Central Powers.

As for the authorities of the fledgling Ukrainian National Republic, they were now faced with a dilemma. With its very existence threatened by the Bolsheviks (the fighting continued in eastern Ukraine until late April), the Central Rada could survive only with German and Austro-Hungarian assistance. In return, Ukraine was expected to supply huge quantities of grain and other foodstuffs, which would be difficult to obtain from a reluctant Ukrainian peasantry. After living more than a year in a revolutionary environment with little effective governmental authority anywhere, the peasantry was not about to give up its grain simply in response to a request by a far-off government in Kiev that claimed to represent Ukrainian national interests.

The result was tension between the peasant countryside and the government of the Ukrainian National Republic, and especially between the Central Rada and the German military authorities. It was not long before the Germans were convinced that the existing Ukrainian government would be ineffective in any effort to acquire raw materials and foodstuffs. Accordingly, the Germans laid plans to install their "own" Ukrainian government. On 28 April 1918, the German Army deposed the Central Rada of the Ukrainian National Republic.

Thus, fourteen months after the first revolution in the Russian Empire had begun in February 1917, the first phase of the Ukrainian revolutionary era came to a close. During these fourteen months, and in the midst of competing political and, later, military factions on Ukrainian territory, the Central Rada, led by Mykhailo Hrushevs'kyi, emerged in Kiev as a force demanding first autonomy and then independence for a Ukrainain National Republic. After the second Russian, or Bolshevik, Revolution in November 1917, the Central Rada initially cooperated with the local Bolsheviks. Their relationship soon dissolved, however, and the Rada was forced to abandon Kiev in the face of a Bolshevik attack that ostensibly represented a Soviet Ukrainian government based in Kharkiv. Like the Soviet Ukrainian government, which depended on the military support of Soviet Russia, the Central Rada of the Ukrainian National Republic was able to sustain itself only with the help of outside military support from the Central Powers. And when, in particular, the German military leadership became displeased with the policies of the Central Rada, it was overthrown.

38

The Period of the Hetmanate

The second phase of the Ukrainian revolution was shorter than the first. It lasted less than eight months, from late April to mid-December 1918. This phase has come to be known as the period of the Hetmanate, because the government which replaced the Central Rada was headed by a chief of state who carried the title of hetman. The accession to power of Dnieper Ukraine's new government was directly related to the needs of the Central Powers.

The establishment of the Hetmanate

When Germany and Austria-Hungary could tolerate no longer what they considered the Central Rada's lack of enthusiasm in supplying them with foodstuffs, on 24 April 1918, the chief of staff of the German Army stationed in Dnieper Ukraine (General Wilhelm Groener) decided to act. He met with Pavlo Skoropads'kyi, a lieutenant-general in the former tsarist army, to propose that he become ruler of Ukraine. The conditions put forth by the German military amounted to a virtual surrender of Ukraine's sovereignty to the occupying powers. The Germans had already begun to requisition grain themselves from the peasants; given a choice, however, they preferred to have a "Ukrainian" government do this and more. Skoropads'kyi was given several conditions, among which were (1) acceptance of the Treaty of Brest-Litovsk, (2) abolition of the Central Rada's constituent assembly, (3) German control over the size and disposition of the Ukrainian army, (4) German approval of all cabinet ministers, (5) abolition of all limitations on the export of raw materials or manufactured goods, (6) recognition of the rights of the large landowners, and (7) payment for land when and if holdings should be divided. Skoropads'kyi accepted.

Skoropads'kyi's acquiescence to German demands represented a swing to the right in the political spectrum of the Ukrainian revolution. Aside from limiting Ukraine's sovereignty, the Hetmanate also reversed the generally leftist orientation of the Central Rada on social issues and land tenure as outlined in the Third Universal of 20 November 1917. In a sense, Skoropads'kyi was responding to the needs of the traditional elite in Dnieper Ukraine, who had been overshadowed by the revolutionary events but were still a force to be reckoned with. This elite included the large landowners, the commercial and industrial interests, and former tsarist administrators, most of whom were Russians or russified Ukrainians ("Little Russian" Russians) initially bemused by and then fiercely opposed to the Ukrainian nationalist and radical socialist positions of the Central Rada. In fact, it was a group of over 6,400 delegates from seven "Ukrainian" provinces (Kiev, Poltava, Chernihiv, Podolia, Volhynia, Kherson, and Kharkiv) meeting in Kiev at the Congress of the Landowners' Alliance who, on 29 April 1918, greeted Skoropads'kyi and conferred upon him the title of hetman.

Skoropads'kyi was a descendant of the early eighteenth-century hetman Ivan Skoropads'kyi, Tsar Peter I's candidate to hold the highest Cossack office after Mazepa's defection. Pavlo Skoropads'kyi, therefore, had a long and distinguished Cossack gentry *(starshyna)* lineage and was from that social stratum which had entered voluntarily into the Russian imperial nobility and which became entrenched as part of the leading group in nineteenth-century Dnieper Ukraine. It was this Cossack gentry which most easily had adopted the hierarchy of multiple loyalties. In other words, its members were simultaneously Little Russians, Russians, and loyal subjects of the tsar. Notwithstanding his sociocultural background, Pavlo Skoropads'kyi, in the wake of the first revolution in the Russian Empire, began to ukrainianize the 34th Corps during the summer of 1917. And it was the First Ukrainian Corps, as the 34th later came to be known, which protected the Central Rada in Kiev from demobilized Bolshevik sympathizers returning home after the disintegration of the imperial army. The ukrainianization of his corps did not necessarily mean that Skoropads'kyi was sympathetic to either the national or the social goals of the Rada, many of whose members continued to view him simply as a "Russian general of Little Russian extraction."[1] Essentially, Skoropads'kyi remained opposed to revolution of any kind, nationalist or socialist, throughout his career. For this reason, he seemed the ideal leader for the financial and social elite represented in the Congress of Landowners.

On 29 April, following a meeting of the congress, Skoropads'kyi proclaimed himself Hetman of All Ukraine. He was also welcomed by that other element in Dnieper Ukraine which desired political and social stability – the Orthodox Church hierarchy. Like the Congress of Landowners, the church had hardly been enamored of the Central Rada, whose Third Universal of November 1917 had, among other things, confiscated church landholdings. Anticipating a return of stability and order, the Orthodox bishop of Kiev (Nikodim) blessed the new hetman in a special service *(moleben')* held in the historic Cathedral of the Holy Wisdom, the St Sophia. Skoropads'kyi thus received the imprimatur of the church as well as of the established economic and social strata of Dnieper-Ukrainian society. Supported thus by the local establishment and backed by the German military, Skoropads'kyi proceeded to dissolve the Central Rada (actually meeting at the same time in Kiev in another building). He also immediately restored the right of private ownership according to the terms that existed before the revolution. In theory, Skoropads'kyi was supposed to be heading a provisional government which later would be replaced by an elected Ukrainian parliament. In practice, elections were never held, and Skoropads'kyi ruled as a dictator. All power – legislative, exec-utive, and control of the military – was vested in him. The country referred to here as the Hetmanate (which some scholars prefer to call the "Second Hetmanate," in order to stress continuity with the eighteenth-century Cossack entity) was formally called the Ukrainian State (Ukraïns'ka Derzhava).

Not surprisingly, the Hetmanate-Ukrainian State under Skoropads'kyi was opposed by all left-of-center political parties, whether or not they were sympa-thetic to Ukrainian nationalist demands. Therefore, any attempts to include in the hetman's cabinet the Social Democrats, the Socialist-Revolutionaries, or even the moderate Socialist-Federalists – parties which had dominated the Central Rada – failed. With no alternative, Skoropads'kyi was forced to create a govern-ment described by one of its members and later apologists (Dmytro Doroshenko) as "made up of individuals who were Ukrainian by blood but Muscovite in spirit."[2] In other words, most of its members were Little Russians of the pre-revolutionary imperial variety. Nonetheless, five of Skoropads'kyi's original cabinet members were conscious Ukrainians, albeit right of center in the political spectrum. The most important of this group was Dmytro Doroshenko, a prewar Ukrainian politi-cal activist and historian who served as Skoropads'kyi's minister of foreign affairs.

The German military, who had made Skoropads'kyi's accession to power possible, were now given a free hand in obtaining the grain that the Central Powers, espe-cially Austria-Hungary, needed so badly. With the tacit approval (and sometimes active cooperation) of Dnieper Ukraine's large landowners, German and Austro-Hungarian army units led punitive expeditions against an uncooperative peasantry. By the summer of 1918, the forced collection of fines and the shooting of hos-tages had become commonplace. Faced with this violence, the Ukrainian Peasant Congress meeting in Kiev (8–10 May) lodged protests against the Skoropads'kyi government, and the secretly held Second All-Ukrainian Workers' Congress (13–14 May) and the fifth congress of the Ukrainian Social-Democratic Labor party (13–14 May) called for the overthrow of the Hetmanate and the establishment of a constitutional Ukrainian National Republic. The opposition forces crystallized into a new organization, eventually called the Ukrainian National Union, which included representatives of most political parties; of postal, telegraph, and railroad workers; and of the All-Ukrainian Alliance of Zemstvos, headed by Symon Petliura, which represented rural areas. Skoropads'kyi attempted to cooperate with these groups, but his initiatives failed, especially following an increase in peasant attacks on German soldiers and the assassination of their commander in Ukraine, Field Marshal Hermann von Eichhorn, on 30 July 1918.

Authoritarian in form, Ukrainian in content

While it is true that Skoropads'kyi's rule was based externally on the German mil-itary presence and internally on the support of the traditional elite in Dnieper-Ukrainian society, the period of the Hetmanate had some positive impact on Ukrainian national development. First of all, the very fact that Skoropads'kyi's government accepted – albeit at the insistence of the Central Powers – the Treaty of Brest-Litovsk meant that it represented an internationally recognized state called Ukraine.

Nor was it a Ukrainian state in name only. The educational reforms initiated by the Central Rada in 1917, which had begun to ukrainianize elementary schools and *gymnasia*, organize Ukrainian courses for teachers, and publish Ukrainian textbooks, were all continued under the Hetmanate. The years 1917–1918 in fact witnessed a true renaissance of the Ukrainian word. During those two years alone, over 1,800 Ukrainian-language titles were published in 16.2 million copies, a level of publication not to be attained again until 1930. Just as impressive were gains at the highest educational levels. In October 1918, new Ukrainian-language universities were opened in Kiev and in Kam'ianets'-Podil's'kyi, and a historical-philological faculty in Poltava. Each of these institutions had departments (*katedry*) in Ukrainian subjects, and departments in Ukrainian language, history, art, and law were opened as well at the older universities in Kiev (St Vladimir), Kharkiv, and Odessa. In the fall of 1918, Kiev became the seat of the National State Library, the National State Archives, and, on 14 November, the Ukrainian Academy of Sciences. Thus, the Hetmanate deserves credit for significant advances in creating an intellectual and educational infrastructure for a Ukrainian state.

The specifically Ukrainian aspect of developments in religious affairs was more ambiguous during the period of the Hetmanate. Developments in Ukraine were inevitably dependent on those within the Russian Orthodox Church. The revolutionary events of 1917 prompted changes in the Russian Orthodox Church. The church reestablished as its supreme head the office of patriarch of Moscow, and early in 1918 the Holy Synod, which had governed the church since the days of Tsar Peter I, was abolished by the Soviet government. In Dnieper Ukraine, certain Orthodox clergy wanted to reassert the Ukrainian nature of their church. Some priests hoped to obtain autonomy within the Russian Orthodox Church; others went a step further and called for complete jurisdictional independence – autocephaly – from the renewed Moscow Patriarchate.

The "autonomists" and the "autocephalists" met at the First All-Ukrainian Church Congress, which opened in Kiev in January 1918, but nothing was achieved because the meeting was abruptly ended owing to the Bolshevik invasion from the east. When the church congress reconvened seven months later, in July, the supporters of autocephaly were barred from the meeting, and the remaining delegates reiterated their jurisdictional subordination to the patriarch of Moscow, Tikhon. Kiev's metropolitan, Antonii Khrapovitskii (reigned 1918–1919), maintained close relations with Hetman Skoropads'kyi, who welcomed the creation on 22 July of an autonomous Orthodox Exarchate for Ukraine. This meant (1) that Ukrainian could be used in sermons and some parts of the liturgy; (2) that the metropolitan of Kiev and Halych would henceforth be elected by a council of bishops (*sobor*) from Ukraine; and (3) that the Ukrainian Exarchate would make its own appointments, all subject, however, to the blessing of the body's supreme authority, the patriarch of Moscow. Not all Orthodox clergy or lay supporters were pleased with autonomy within the Russian Orthodox Church – the Moscow Patriarchate, and in November the Hetmanate's minister of religion, Oleksander

Lotots'kyi, openly called for jurisdictional independence (autocephaly) for the Ukrainian Orthodox. The autocephalous movement was not to make serious headway, however, until after the fall of the Hetmanate.

The fall of the Hetmanate

By the autumn of 1918, the Hetmanate's days were numbered. Because it was dependent exclusively on Germany, as the war efforts of the Central Powers declined so too did the status of the Skoropads'kyi German client state. Faced with such bleak prospects, the Hetmanate's minister of foreign affairs, Dmytro Doroshenko, attempted negotiations with the Allied Powers, who were opposed to the Bolsheviks but in favor of retaining the territorial integrity of the former Russian Empire. This meant, of course, that they were opposed to an independent Ukrainian state. The Hetmanate also began to negotiate with its internal opponents, the Ukrainian National Union, headed by Volodymyr Vynnychenko. This time, negotiations were successful, and in late October a new cabinet was formed in which members of the National Union received five portfolios. Plans were even begun to introduce a land reform and to convoke a parliament.

Within a couple of weeks, however, relations between the government and the opposition deteriorated to such a degree that the National Union decided to organize an uprising against Skoropads'kyi. Moreover, the Ukrainian Bolsheviks, who had undertaken an abortive revolt against Skoropads'kyi in August, were still capitalizing on Ukrainian peasant discontent against his regime and also spreading revolutionary propaganda among the war-weary German soldiers. Finally, it became clear to all that the end of the war was in sight and that it was only a matter of time before the German Army would return home, leaving Skoropads'kyi to fend for himself. With an unenviable fate looming, the Hetmanate's representatives actively looked for support among the Allied Powers (through the French in Odessa). Then, in an attempt to save the rapidly deteriorating situation, Skoropads'kyi carried out his own coup. He appointed a new cabinet and, apparently in an effort to curry favor with the Allies and at the same time obtain military aid from anti-Bolshevik White Russian forces, he abandoned the idea of Ukrainian statehood. On 14 November he proclaimed the federative union of Ukraine with a future non-Bolshevik Russia.

Skoropads'kyi's turn to a Russian alliance convinced the opposition that the time had come to act. The Ukrainian National Union formed its own revolutionary body, called the Directory, headed by Volodymyr Vynnychenko and Symon Petliura to restore the Ukrainian National Republic. Vynnychenko obtained a guarantee of neutrality from the Central Powers, and he also reached an agreement with representatives of the Soviet Russian government (Khristiian Rakovskii and Dmytro Manuïl's'kyi), who had been in Kiev since the spring, ostensibly negotiating a peace treaty with Skoropads'kyi. Vynnychenko received assurances from the Soviet representatives that Moscow would recognize the Directory of the Ukrainian National Republic after it came to power in return for his own assurances that the Bolshevik party would be allowed to operate on Ukrainian territory.

Thus, the Directory was doing as the Rada had done a year before – cooperating with the Bolsheviks against a new common enemy, this time Skoropads'kyi.

The Directory's uprising began on 14–15 November 1918, when its spokespersons demanded the surrender of Skoropads'kyi and his supporters. In order to obtain military support, Vynnychenko and Petliura left Kiev for Bila Tserkva, farther to the west, where they attracted to their cause discontented peasants and, more important, the well-organized volunteer Sich Riflemen, the battalion of former Galician and Bukovinian prisoners of war on the eastern front headed by Colonel Ievhen Konovalets' and Andrii Mel'nyk. The Directory leaders and the army of the restored Ukrainian National Republic reached Kiev on 21 November, but they were unable to take the city, which was being defended by some units still loyal to Skoropads'kyi, by the Germans, and by Russian volunteers. The next three weeks saw a stalemate between the Directory and the Hetmanate.

Meanwhile, on 11 November 1918 Germany signed an armistice with the Allied Powers, thus ending World War I. German troops in Dnieper Ukraine finally could begin their long-awaited return home. On 14 December they abandoned Kiev. The Directory allowed the Germans safe passage and, in turn, entered the city. Skoropads'kyi abdicated and fled to Germany, and on 19 December the Directory reinstalled in Kiev the Ukrainian National Republic.

Despite its authoritarian nature and its dependence on Dnieper Ukraine's russified elite, the Hetmanate had managed for most of its eight-month existence to remain Ukrainian both in form and, at least in education and cultural institutions, in content. Skoropads'kyi never resolved the problem of peasant discontent with the German requisitions, however, nor could he arrive at a lasting modus vivendi with the political opposition. His government initiated a vain attempt to obtain support from the Allied Powers, and then in October made a last-minute effort to create an alliance with an anti-Bolshevik Russia. But all this had failed to save him, and by the end of 1918 his German protectors were gone as well. In place of the Hetmanate, a restored Ukrainian National Republic under the leadership of the Directory was now left to deal by itself not only with the anti-Bolshevik Russians, the so-called Whites, but also with an even greater threat to its existence, the Bolshevik Reds.

39

The Directory, Civil War, and the Bolsheviks

With the fall of Skoropads'kyi's Hetmanate government and the reestablishment of the Ukrainian National Republic under the leadership of the Directory, Dnieper Ukraine entered the third and final phase of its revolutionary era. It was to last from the very beginning of 1919 until October 1920, when the Soviet government finally established itself throughout the country. The events of this period were highly complex and have probably been summarized best by the American historian of Russia, Richard Pipes.

The year 1919 in Ukraine was a period of complete anarchy. The entire territory fell apart into innumerable regions isolated from each other and the rest of the world, dominated by armed bands of peasants or freebooters who looted and murdered with utter impunity. In Kiev itself governments came and went, edicts were issued, cabinet crises were resolved, diplomatic talks were carried on – but the rest of the country lived its own existence where the only effective regime was that of the gun. None of the authorities which claimed Ukraine during the year following the deposition of Skoropads'kyi ever exercised actual sovereignty. The Communists, who all along anxiously watched the developments there and did everything in their power to seize control for themselves, fared no better than their Ukrainian nationalist and White Russian competitors.[1]

This description of 1919 also can be applied to most of 1920, although that year the internal anarchy was made even worse by external invasions by Soviet Russian, White Russian, and Polish forces. Because of the complexity of this third and last phase of the revolutionary era in Dnieper Ukraine, it would be difficult to provide a straightforward chronological survey of events. A thematic approach therefore seems preferable. Although the following themes or factors unfolding during this period are interrelated and impinge upon one other, for purposes of discussion each will be treated separately and in isolation from what is an extremely complex historical mosaic. Among the factors to be considered are (1) the Directory of the Ukrainian National Republic; (2) the Bolshevik, or Communist, party in Russia and in Dnieper Ukraine; (3) the peasant revolution; (4) the anti-Bolshevik White Russians; (5) the Allied Powers; (6) the West Ukrainian National Republic; and

(7) Poland. Their consideration will be followed by a discussion of how peoples other than Ukrainians fared during the revolutionary era in Dnieper Ukraine.

The Directory of the Ukrainian National Republic

The Directory of the Ukrainian National Republic, which came to power in Kiev in mid-December 1918, had few concrete plans for governing the country. The five-member Directory was headed by Volodymyr Vynnychenko, who in practice shared power with the head of the republic's armed forces, Symon Petliura. Relations between the two men were strained from the very beginning, however, and this only contributed to the overwhelming difficulties faced by the Directory in its attempt to establish authority over territories that it claimed as belonging to the Ukrainian National Republic.

The political program initially proclaimed by the Directory reflected the preferences of Vynnychenko, a left-wing socialist who spoke vaguely about the need to create a state based on workers' councils (soviets). For many it sounded like Bolshevism, and while Vynnychenko was indeed sympathetic to many Bolshevik goals, he was opposed to their authoritarian methods. Vynnychenko was also a Ukrainian patriot and therefore a supporter of the Directory's call for Ukrainian as the state's official language and autocephaly (jurisdictional independence) for the Orthodox Church in Ukraine.

Clearly, the political spectrum proposed by the Directory in late 1918 reflected a sociopolitical disposition that had swung away from Skoropads'kyi's Hetmanate and back to the left. Therefore, the Directory restored much of the legislation adopted by the Central Rada before April 1918, including the redistribution of lands that had been returned by the Hetmanate government to the large landowners and the church. On the one hand, the Directory acted as a successor to the Central Rada, but it did not welcome back to its ranks the first president of the Ukrainian National Republic, Mykhailo Hrushevs'kyi. On the other hand, the proclamations about land redistribution initially attracted mass support on the part of the peasantry and among soldiers loyal to the idea of Ukrainian statehood. The Directory of the Ukrainian National Republic found its legitimization in the Labor Congress (Trudovyi konhres) that was convened in Kiev on 22 January 1919 and which began its deliberations the following day. The question, of course, remained whether the Directory could deliver on any of the promises outlined in its fine-sounding proclamations with wording that was of particular concern to Vynnychenko, a figure whose real talent was that of belletrist, not politician.

The first discrepancy between proclamations and reality had to do with the very territory that allegedly comprised the state. The Directory-led Ukrainian National Republic claimed even more territory than had Skoropads'kyi's Hetmanate (compare maps 32 and 33), although in fact it had effective control over very little – and much of the time none – of that territory. From the standpoint of Ukrainian nationalism, the Directory's most important act was the declaration of union with the West Ukrainian National Republic. Chapter 41 will elaborate on the fate of the independent West Ukrainian National Republic, which came into being in

November 1918 in Austrian Galicia. Of significance here is that the Galicians and Dnieper Ukrainians proclaimed the unity *(sobornist')* of all Ukrainian lands in a solemn ceremony held in Kiev on 22 January 1919, exactly one year after the original declaration of Ukrainian independence in the Dnieper-Ukrainian lands. This act was confirmed by the Labor Congress meeting at the time in Kiev. With its nearly 400 delegates (including 36 from the West Ukrainian Republic) the congress took on the character of a Ukrainian legislative assembly.

While the 22 January 1919 declaration of Ukrainian unity may have been solemn, it was little more than that. The Galician and Dnieper Ukrainians were to follow distinct and, often, conflicting political and military policies. Even more ominous was the fact that the Directory was surrounded on all sides by enemies, and within two weeks it was to be driven out of Kiev. On 5 February the Directory set up the first of its numerous and short-lived headquarters in Vinnytsia. Then for the rest of 1919 and 1920, it moved from place to place throughout the Right Bank, always under imminent threat of capture by its various enemies. The most serious of those enemies were the Bolsheviks.

The Bolsheviks

Chapter 38 showed how the Bolsheviks initially cooperated with the Central Rada in November 1917. Soon after, they formed a Soviet Ukrainian government and, with Bolshevik Russian help, drove the Central Rada out of Kiev. Bolshevik control of the city lasted for only three weeks in February 1918, until the German Army forced them out of Kiev and, shortly after, out of Dnieper Ukraine entirely. Now the scenario was to be repeated. This time it was the Directory that in November 1918 cooperated with the Bolsheviks in driving out Skoropads'kyi. As soon as that was accomplished, the Ukrainian Bolsheviks and their Russian Bolshevik supporters prepared to invade Dnieper Ukraine a second time and to unseat their short-lived Directory ally.

Since their first efforts at ruling Dnieper Ukraine back in February 1918, Ukraine's Bolsheviks had had time to reassess the situation. No consensus ever developed, however, and the party remained divided into several conflicting factions. The basic division concerned the relationship of Ukraine's Bolsheviks to the all-Russian Bolshevik party. One Ukrainian faction favored an independent party policy, the other preferred subordination to the all-Russian leadership, which itself in March 1918 had moved the capital to Moscow and had renamed the party the All-Russian Communist (Bolshevik) party.

Internal factionalism came to a head soon after Ukraine's Bolsheviks were pushed entirely out of the country by the German Army and its ally, Hetman Skoropads'kyi. They regrouped in Taganrog, on the far eastern shores of the Sea of Azov, where on 18 April they dissolved their own Soviet Ukrainian government and replaced it with a coordinating committee that was to direct the struggle against the German occupier. The varying factions now clashed over long-term policy as well as short-term tactics. The left-wing "independentists," mostly from Kiev (Georgii Piatakov, Mykola Skrypnyk, Volodymyr Zatons'kyi), called for the creation of a separate

Ukrainian Bolshevik party, while the right-wing "internationalists," mostly from Kharkiv and Katerynoslav (Emmanuïl Kviring and Iakiv Epshtein), opposed any idea of a separate Ukrainian party. In the end, the two groups compromised. On 19–20 April 1918, the distinct Communist party (Bolshevik) of Ukraine – (CP(b) U) was established, although after July it became subordinate to the All-Russian Communist party. The factions still remained divided over tactics: the left-wing "independentists" favored an alliance with the peasantry and an immediate uprising against Skoropads'kyi and the Germans; the right-wing "internationalists" preferred to depend on the leadership of the industrial proletariat and to wait for the supposedly imminent world revolution while in the meantime following the directives of the All-Russian Communist party.

In addition to the two factions within the Communist party (Bolshevik) of Ukraine, there were other, non-Bolshevik Communists in Ukraine. These were former Ukrainian Socialist-Revolutionaries, who in May 1918 formed the non-Bolshevik Ukrainian Socialist-Revolutionary party of Communist Fighters, or the Borotbists for short, who rejected the idea of the monolithic party governmental system demanded by the Bolsheviks. The Borotbists remained in Dnieper Ukraine throughout 1919 and even formed a separate government with support from the peasant army of Otaman Matvii Hryhoriïv.

During the period of the Hetmanate the Communist party (Bolshevik) of Ukraine virtually ceased to exist on Ukrainian territory: it had only 4,300 members by mid-1918. The leadership moved its place of exile from Taganrog to Moscow. There, in the Soviet capital, Lenin put pressure on the various factions until the CP(b)U, for all practical purposes, became subordinate to the All-Russian Communist party. Internal dissension nonetheless continued between the left- and right-wing Ukrainian Bolsheviks, and it became especially critical after the fall of Skoropads'kyi in mid-December 1918. The left-wing Ukrainian Bolsheviks were ever anxious to act, independently of instructions from Moscow if necessary. They were, in fact, already close to the Ukrainian border at Kursk, where on 28 November 1918 they secretly formed a "provisional" Soviet Ukrainian government (Tymchasovyi Robitnychno-Selians'kyi Uriad Ukraïny) with the intention of marching into Dnieper Ukraine. These plans were unfolding at the very time Soviet representatives from Moscow (Khristiian Rakovskii and Dmytro Manuïl's'kyi) were assuring Vynnychenko that they would cooperate with the Directory and recognize a restored Ukrainian National Republic in a post-Skoropads'kyi Ukraine.

In the end, the Ukrainian Soviet government in Kursk launched an attack on the Directory. The invasion began in mid-December and proceeded rapidly, with the result that by February 1919, less than two months after it had come to power, the Directory and forces of the Ukrainian National Republic were driven out of Kiev. In their stead, the Bolsheviks installed a "provisional" government, which was soon renamed the Ukrainian Soviet Socialist Republic (Ukraïns'ka Radians'ka Sotsialistychna Respublyka). This second Bolshevik presence in Kiev proved to be longer than the first, lasting from February to August 1919, and it was more successful than its predecessor in establishing its authority.

The Ukrainian Soviet Republic was Ukrainian in the territorial, not the nation-

MAP 33

UKRAINE, 1919–1920

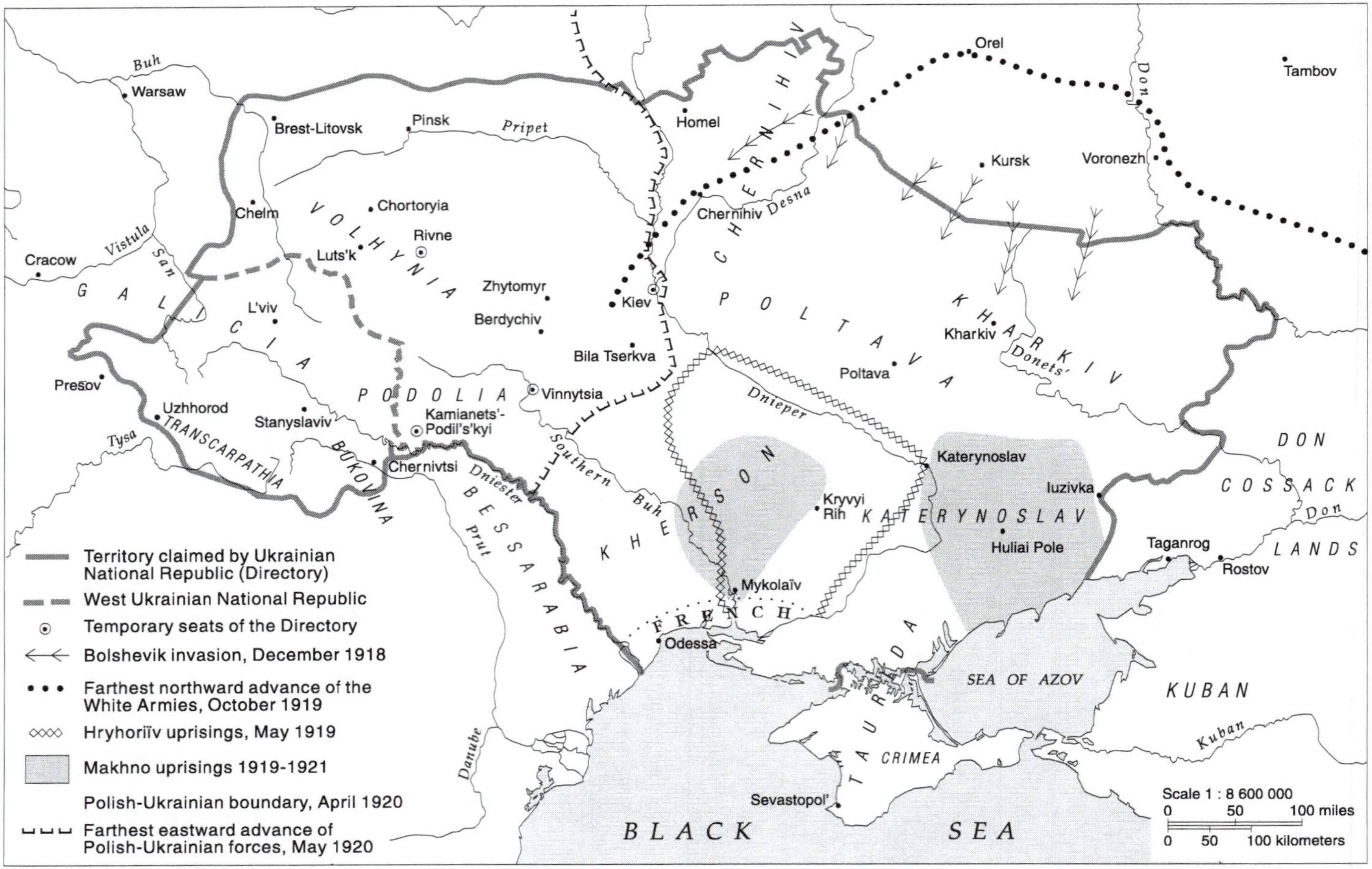

Tambov

DON

COSSACK

LANDS

Don

Voronezh

Rostov

Orel

Taganrog

KUBAN

Kursk

K H A R K I V

Kuban

Donets'

Kharkiv

KATERYNOSLAV

Iuzivka

SEA OF AZOV

P O L T A V A

Katerynoslav

Huliai Pole

Poltava

Dnieper

CRIMEA

CHERNIHIV

Chernihiv

Desna

Kryvyi
Rih

Mykolaiv

TAURIDA

Sevastopol'

Homel

Kiev

KHERSON

Odessa

BLACK

Bila Tserkva

Southern

Buh

FRENCH

SEA

Vinnytsia

Zhytomyr

PODOLIA

BESSARABIA

Berdychiv

Dniester

Prut

Pripet

V O L H Y N I A

Kamianets'-
Podil'skyi

Pinsk

Chortoryia

Rivne

Chernivtsi

Danube

Tysa

Brest-Litovsk

Luts'k

G A L I C I A

BUKOVINA

TRANSCARPATHIA

Chelm

L'viv

Stanyslaviv

Buh

Warsaw

Uzhhorod

San

Vistula

Presov

Cracow

Don

Don

Territory claimed by Ukrainian
National Republic (Directory)

West Ukrainian National Republic

⊙   Temporary seats of the Directory

↓   Bolshevik invasion, December 1918

••• Farthest northward advance of the
     White Armies, October 1919

◇◇◇ Hryhoriiv uprisings, May 1919

     Makhno uprisings 1919–1921

⌐⌐⌐ Polish-Ukrainian boundary, April 1920

     Farthest eastward advance of
     Polish-Ukrainian forces, May 1920

Scale 1 : 8 600 000

0   50   100 miles
0   50   100 kilometers

Copyright © by Paul Robert Magocsi

al, sense. It was headed by Khristiian Rakovskii, a Russophile of Bulgarian-Romanian origin, whose administrative apparatus was dominated for the most part by Russian or russified Ukrainian Bolsheviks with little or no sympathy for Ukrainian cultural aspirations. Even more problematic was the crude approach the Ukrainian Soviet government took to the volatile land question. Instead of distributing land to the peasants, a project which had been enshrined in a Bolshevik slogan from the time of Lenin's return to Russia in April 1917, the Ukrainian Soviet government confiscated all landed estates and then undertook to transform them into communally held state farms. This policy provoked deep displeasure and resulted in uprisings on the part of the peasantry, which grew into what has been called the "green revolution" or Ukrainian peasant jacquerie.

The peasant revolution

Despite all the political concerns of the numerous social and national factions, the land question remained the major issue in Dnieper Ukraine as well as throughout much of the former Russian Empire. During Ukraine's revolutionary era, each of the governments in power – the Ukrainian National Republic of the Central Rada and later Directory, the Hetmanate, and the Bolsheviks – attempted to resolve the land question. But in an era of revolutionary change and the general breakdown of authority, the peasants were not about to wait long for their land hunger to be satisfied. When, in April 1918, the socialist-oriented government of the Central Rada was replaced by the more conservative Hetmanate, the peasants reacted immediately to what they saw as an attempt to turn back the social clock in favor of the large landowners.

Between April and June 1918 alone, numerous peasant uprisings, especially against the forces of the occupying Central Powers, broke out and were responsible for an estimated 15,000 deaths among the German military. The peasants were committed to removing Skoropads'kyi and his German protectors, and they joined en masse the 100,000-strong army that nominally represented the Ukrainian National Republic and that backed the Directory in its coup against the Hetmanate. This army, while clearly the largest of any in Dnieper Ukraine at the time, was hardly a united force responsible to orders from the Directory's military chief, Symon Petliura. Rather, it was a motley assortment of peasants and some village elders and schoolteachers, led by self-proclaimed partisan commanders (*otamany*) and their followers, whose only real common bond was opposition to Skoropads'kyi's rule. Subsequently, when the peasants thought the Directory incapable of fulfilling their needs, they deserted it and joined the advancing Bolsheviks in the early months of 1919.

It was in fact Ukrainian peasants, under the partisan commanders Matvii Hryhoriïv and Nestor Makhno, who made up the vast majority of the so-called Red Army that was led by the Bolshevik commander Antonov-Ovseenko and launched against Kiev in late 1918 by the Bolshevik government, then based in Kursk. Despite their cooperation with the "Reds," the partisan commanders (*otamany*), let alone the masses of recruits, had little sense of what Bolshevism really was.

Instead, the commanders perceived themselves as descendants of the Zaporozhian Cossacks and haidamaks who had a duty to liberate the people from all those they considered their oppressors, whether they be representatives of the former Russian imperial regime, Ukrainian nationalists, Jews and other suspect groups (especially Black Sea Germans and Mennonites), or even Bolsheviks. More often than not, local commanders were little more than marauders who, taking advantage of the power vacuum in Dnieper Ukraine, pillaged and robbed at will wealthy landowners, merchants and artisans, and well-to-do and even poor peasants whose villages happened to be along their ever-changing "military" paths.

If the peasants were displeased with the Central Rada and, in particular, with Skoropads'kyi's Hetmanate, it was not long before they came to scorn the Bolsheviks as well. The Ukrainian Soviet Republic's policy of rule by Bolshevik-controlled councils (soviets), the creation of communal farms, and the forced confiscations of grain for Soviet Russia's Red Army quickly alienated the peasantry. By April 1919, peasant uprisings were again common, and the following month both Hryhoriïv and Makhno, who had fought along with the Bolsheviks, now turned against them. Murders of Bolshevik officials, pogroms against Jews, Germans, and other well-to-do elements (1,236 pogroms were recorded in 1918–1919), and attacks on towns became the order of the day. Anarchy pure and simple reigned throughout the Ukrainian countryside.

In a real sense, it was the peasantry, or, more precisely, the various peasant armies, who by the summer of 1919 controlled most of Dnieper Ukraine. At best, Bolshevik rule was limited to the cities, but even there it was to be challenged. In August, the Bolsheviks were driven a second time out of Kiev and once again entirely out of Dnieper Ukraine. Unlike in early 1918, when the German Army pushed out the Bolsheviks, it was White Russians from the east and forces loyal to the Ukrainian National Republic from the west who did the job this time.

The White Russians

Who were the White Russians, and what relationship did they have with Dnieper Ukraine? Despite the conditions in Petrograd that gave rise to the February/March 1917 revolution and the abdication of the tsar, large segments of the empire's population were oblivious to political changes or actively opposed to the liberal-democratic orientation of the Provisional Government and, in particular, to radical socialism as proposed by the Bolsheviks. Among the most conservative forces (many of whom favored a return of the tsar) were generals in the former imperial army, which by December 1917 had ceased hostilities against the Germans.

During 1917, the size of the army was significantly reduced as recruits anxious to go home left its ranks, but by the spring of 1918 the numbers had grown once again. This time the army attracted an assortment of diverse elements who had one thing at most in common: opposition to the Bolsheviks. Because of their antagonism to the Bolsheviks, or Reds, they came to be known as the White Russians, or Whites. (This is a political term that should not mistakenly be associated with the ethnic Belarusans, who are also sometimes designated in English as White Russians.) In May 1918, White generals took control of most of the peripheral areas of the former Russian Empire and clashed immediately with the Bolsheviks' newly organized Red Army under the direction of Lenin's revolutionary collaborator, Leon Trotskii. The Russian Civil War had begun.

The strength of the Whites was based primarily in the Baltic region (General Nikolai Iudenich), in Siberia (General Aleksander Kolchak), and in the Don Cossack Lands (General Anton Denikin). Wherever they were in power, the Whites established governments which claimed to be the legal representation for all Russia according to its former imperial boundaries. White influence reached its peak in the summer of 1919, when the movement almost succeeded in driving the Soviet government out of Moscow.

In Dnieper Ukraine, the most important White Russian movement was that led by General Anton Denikin, whose Volunteer Army, as it was known, was based in the neighboring Don Cossack Lands. The Don Cossacks themselves had enjoyed a favored position as a military caste with a high degree of self-rule during tsarist times. Their essentially autonomous status was abolished, however, by the Bolsheviks. The Don Cossacks responded by proclaiming an independent republic (16 May 1918) and by joining the White forces of General Denikin en masse. Moving north and west from his base in the Don Cossack Lands, Denikin's Volunteer Army by September 1919 had driven the Red Army out of Dnieper Ukraine and was well on the way to Moscow.

The Allied Powers

The growing success of the Whites in 1919 was related to another phenomenon – intervention in Russia and Ukraine by the Allied Powers. While World War I was still in progress, the Allies landed troops in Russia (in at least one instance with the agreement of the Soviet government) in order to keep munitions from falling into the hands of the Germans. After the outbreak of civil war, however, the Allies decided to intervene. They clearly intended to give support to the Whites, whose generals had fought on the side of the Allies during the war and who were now fighting to rid themselves of what was already regarded in the West as the "plague of Bolshevism and world revolution." Accordingly, Britain, France, and the United States landed troops in northern Russia, and Japan and the United States did the same along the Pacific coast of far eastern Siberia. In December 1918, an expeditionary force from France (together with units of soldiers of another ally, Greece) landed in Odessa, and, in cooperation with the local Whites proceeded to control Dnieper Ukraine's Black Sea coast between the mouths of the Dniester and Dnieper Rivers.

Meanwhile, the Directory of the Ukrainian National Republic, which had retreated from Kiev before the Bolshevik-led assault in February 1919, reconstituted itself in various cities – depending on the military situation – notably in Podolia (Vinnytsia, Kam'ianets'-Podil's'kyi) and Volhynia (Rivne). Vynnychenko resigned and was replaced by Symon Petliura, who became simultaneously head of the Directory and commander of the Ukrainian National Republic's armed forces. Petliura had three goals: (1) to continue the struggle against the Bolsheviks, (2) to reach an accord with the victorious Allies, and (3) to cooperate with the Galicians from the West Ukrainian National Republic. In all three areas, he failed. In fact, in only one area was the Petliura government successful: it reached an accord with the new government of Poland.

In his negotiations with the Allied Powers, the Petliura government soon learned that certain western European powers, especially France, with its troops along the Black Sea near Odessa, remained committed to the idea of a unified Russia. The Allies were opposed, therefore, to an independent Ukrainian state and urged Ukrainians to cooperate with the anti-Bolshevik White Russians. This proved unacceptable, however, since General Denikin, like other White Russian generals, defended the idea of a unified Russia and was completely opposed to the aspirations of the nationalities. By August 1919, Denikin had gained control of most of Dnieper Ukraine's Left Bank and had driven the Soviet Ukrainian government out of Kiev. During the next two months, White Russian political convictions were underlined by their actions: the arrest of Ukrainian nationalist and Bolshevik sympathizers, the return of property to large landowners, and pogroms against Jews. These policies hardly endeared the Whites to the local population or made them potential allies for Petliura's struggling Ukrainian nationalist government.

The West Ukrainian National Republic and Dnieper Ukraine

Relations between Petliura and the West Ukrainian National Republic, with which the Ukrainian National Republic had united on 22 January 1919, proved no better than relations with the Whites. The West Ukrainian National Republic, based in former Austrian Galicia and led by Ievhen Petrushevych, had its hands full. Since November 1918, the West Ukrainians had been engaged in a bitter war with the Poles for control of Galicia (see chapter 41). Finally, in July 1919 the Galician-Ukrainian forces and government were driven from the province. With his well-trained Ukrainian Galician Army, Petrushevych joined forces with Petliura in Podolia. But the personalities and goals of the two leaders turned out to be diametrically opposed. The Galicians, who had expected to receive aid from the Allied Powers, not unexpectedly favored cooperation with General Denikin, the White Russian ally of the West. Petliura, on the other hand, who anticipated no help from the Allies, favored cooperation with Poland – the mortal enemy of the West Ukrainian National Republic.

Petliura went ahead anyway in his negotiations with Poland. Within the space of a year, he signed an armistice (June 1919), agreed on boundaries (December 1919), and approved a treaty of mutual cooperation signed in Warsaw (April 1920). For its part, the Ukrainian Galician Army, although without any authorization from Petrushevych, signed its own agreement in November 1919 with General Denikin. As a result, the Galician-Ukrainian forces became part of Denikin's "Armed Forces of the South of Russia." Thus, the solemn declaration of union between the Galician and Dnieper Ukrainians reached at the beginning of 1919 proved meaningless once the two groups actually tried to work together. Internal controversies arising from policy differences and personality clashes, combined with an unfavorable constellation of international forces, brought about a complete breakdown in cooperation between the Petliura-led Ukrainian National Republic and the Petrushevych-led West Ukrainian National Republic.

Nonetheless, by the end of 1919 the tragic discord between the two Ukrainian nationalist bodies had become a moot issue. General Denikin's administration had aroused the ire of Dnieper Ukraine's population; peasant armies led by Nestor Makhno and Danylo Zelenyi, among others, were once again on the move; and by December 1919, the Red Army had returned and was rapidly taking over most of Dnieper Ukraine. Before the end of the year, General Denikin had retreated to the Crimea and the Black Sea coast; Petliura's remaining Ukrainian National Republic forces had fled to the northwest corner of Volhynia; and in January 1920, whatever was left in Podolia of the Ukrainian Galician Army, which had only recently fought on the side of the Whites, joined the Bolsheviks as the Red Ukrainian Galician Army. This chaos resulted in a political vacuum, which by February 1920 allowed most of Dnieper Ukraine to come under the control of the Red Army. Protected by the Red Army, the Ukrainian Soviet Socialist Republic under the direction of the Communist party (Bolshevik) of Ukraine was restored. This marked the final Bolshevik advance, because with the exception of some territory briefly ceded in a war with Poland, Dnieper Ukraine was from February 1920 to be ruled by a Ukrainian Soviet Socialist Republic in the closest alliance with Soviet Russia.

Poland and Dnieper Ukraine

On 9 November 1918, an independent republic of Poland was proclaimed, and it was immediately considered one of the victorious Allied and Associated Powers. The new country's eastern boundaries were not yet fixed, however. Poland's leaders had different views on how to resolve the border problem. Many, including the country's first head of state, Marshall Józef Piłsudski, hoped to incorporate lands at least as far east as the Dnieper River, which had been part of Poland before the partitions that obliterated the old Commonwealth in the late eighteenth century.

By July 1919, the Poles had secured all of Galicia following a bloody war with the West Ukrainian National Republic (see chapter 41). Much more problematic for Poland were the other lands of the former Commonwealth (present-day Lithuania, Belarus, and most of Ukraine), since they were also claimed by the Soviet government in Moscow. As early as February 1919, Polish forces clashed with Red Army units in western Belarus. Skirmishes alternating with political negotiations continued throughout the rest of the year as part of a drawn-out struggle between Poland and Soviet Russia for control of a broad swath of territory, extending virtually from the Baltic Sea in the north to the Black Sea in the south. All efforts to reach an armistice between the two states proved unsuccessful, including an Allied proposal for a temporary boundary (December 1919).

The proposal was later presented to the Soviet government over the signature of the British Foreign Secretary Lord Curzon (July 1920), and henceforth came to be known as the Curzon Line (see map 35).

In the course of the Polish-Soviet war, the Poles sought to engage the support of Ukrainians, in particular during its large-scale eastward offensive that began in the spring of 1920. For its part, the beleaguered Ukrainian National Republic, which by then was faced by a Polish advance from the west and a Bolshevik (later, a White Russian) advance from the north and east, decided to negotiate with the Poles. In April 1920, a treaty was concluded in Warsaw between the Petliura-led Ukrainian National Republic and Poland. Among other points, the Treaty of Warsaw recognized Poland's control of all of Galicia as well as western Volhynia. Not surprisingly, this agreement completely alienated the West Ukrainian leaders from Petliura.

Soon after the Treaty of Warsaw was signed, Petliura's troops joined the Poles in an invasion of Dnieper Ukraine. Their rapid advance brought them within a month (May) as far as Kiev. The joint Polish-Ukrainian advance proved to be short-lived, however, because the Soviet Red Army, supported especially by its cavalry under Semen Budennyi, mounted a successful counteroffensive. On 11 June, the Red Army drove the Poles out of Kiev and began a rapid advance westward. It was in the course of that advance that, on orders from Moscow, the Galician Socialist Soviet Republic was formed on 15 July. With its seat in Ternopil', the Revolutionary Council of the new Soviet republic controlled for about seven weeks most of Galicia east of L'viv.

Confident of its success, the Soviet government rejected the armistice and the Curzon Line proposed by the Allied Powers (11 July) and ordered its Red Army to move on farther westward. By mid-August the Red Army had reached the outskirts of Warsaw and threatened to take Poland's new capital. Under the direction of Marshall Piłsudski, the Polish forces managed to regroup and to push back the Soviets. Within a month peace talks began in the Latvian town of Riga that resulted in an armistice (18 October 1920) and a temporary border – significantly farther east of the Curzon Line – that became finalized when a formal Polish-Soviet treaty was signed a few months later. According to the armistice and the Treaty of Riga of March 1921, Poland agreed to recognize the "independence" of Soviet Ukraine.

It was during the spring and summer of 1920 that the civilian population of central and western Ukraine, whether ethnic Ukrainians, Poles, Jews, Czechs etc., suffered extensive loss of life and property. As the warring armies moved back and forth, rural and urban residents could never be certain which week, day, or even hour they might be subject to attack by forces loyal either to Poland, the Soviets, the Ukrainian National Republic, or to marauding troops loyal only to themselves. The chaotic nature of these months in Ukraine were captured in dispatches compiled by a Red Army correspondent, Isaak Babel, which were later published in Russian in what became the well-known book, *The Red Cavalry* (*Konarmiia*, 1926).

As the Polish-Soviet war entered its last phase, the Soviet Ukrainian government re-established itself and by late November 1920 Soviet troops succeeded in driving out the last remaining forces loyal Ukrainian National Republic, together with its government headed by Petliura across the Riga armistice line into eastern Galicia. Petliura still hoped to dislodge the Bolsheviks, and small units loyal to the Ukrainian National Republic conducted raids from Poland in the northwestern borderland regions of Soviet Ukraine until November 1921. But these never posed any serious threat to Soviet rule. As for Petliura, he continued to head the Ukrainian National Republic's government-in-exile from various places in Poland until 1923, after which he left that country and eventually ended up in Paris.

Thus, by October 1920 the third and last phase of the Ukrainian revolution came to an end. It was marked by military invasions at various times by the Bolsheviks, the White Russians, the Allies, and Poland. Throughout the period, peasant uprisings and marauding anarchist forces dominated the countryside, while isolated in various cities or in mobile railway cars the government of the Ukrainian National Republic tried in vain to reach accords with their Galician counterparts and, at times, with one or more of the foreign invaders. In the end, the country was exhausted, and only the Ukrainian Bolsheviks, backed by Soviet Russia, were able to establish a lasting government. The non-Bolshevik Ukrainians – whether supporters of the Central Rada, the Hetmanate, or the Directory-led Ukrainian National Republic – were forced into exile, where from countries in central and western Europe they continued to maintain the trappings of government (with cabinets, hetmans or presidents, and diplomatic missions) in the hope that some day they might return home to rule.

40

The Revolutionary Era and Dnieper Ukraine's Other Peoples

How did the revolutionary era affect other peoples in Dnieper Ukraine, and what, if any, views did they have toward Ukrainian national aspirations? Like the ethnic Ukrainians, none of the Ukraine's other peoples formed a united political front. Each group was divided into diverse political factions, some of which, like the leftists, even denied the value of identification with their "own" nationality. In general, however, it is reasonable to conclude that with few exceptions most of the other peoples – whether Jews, Russians, or Poles – were opposed to Ukrainian independence and to separation from Russia.

Despite such negative attitudes toward Ukrainian separatist aspirations, in 1917 the Central Rada of the Ukrainian National Republic set out to attract support from Dnieper Ukraine's "other" peoples. Already in July 1917 the Central Rada made provision for 30 percent of its membership to be comprised of members representing Russians, Poles, and Jews. The Rada's executive body, the General Secretariat, also created a General Secretariat for Nationality Affairs with sub-departments (vice-secretariats) responsible for each of the above-mentioned groups. Adopting the nationality theories advocated by the Austrian socialists Otto Bauer and Karl Renner, the Central Rada enacted a law in January 1918 that provided for national-personal autonomy. National-personal, or national-cultural autonomy meant that an individual was guaranteed certain rights with a view to the protection of his or her language and culture regardless of place of residence. This autonomy was different in kind from territorial autonomy, in which a specifically defined geographic area was granted autonomous status. Among the rights guaranteed by national-personal autonomy were schools, cultural institutions, and religious societies. All would receive financial support from the central government, which in turn would establish tax revenues according to a fiscal plan devised by the nationalities themselves. Interestingly, only Jews, Russians, and Poles were singled out as eligible for national-personal autonomy; seven other groups (Belarusans, Czechs, Romanians, Germans, Tatars, Greeks, and Bulgarians) would first have to petition for and receive governmental approval in order to obtain autonomous status.

The Jews

The Jews had fifty deputies in the Central Rada (equally divided among five Jewish political parties) and five deputies in the Little Rada. Jews also received posts in the General Secretariat and, later, in the Council of Ministers of the Ukrainian National Republic, in which the Ministry of Jewish Affairs was created (headed at various times by Moyshe Zilberfarb, Ya'akov Latzky-Bertholdi, Avrom Revutsky, and Pinkhes Krasny). Yiddish was made an official language (it even appeared on some of the Ukrainian National Republic's paper money); Jewish schools and a department of Jewish history and literature at the university in Kam'ianets'-Podil's'kyi were established; and plans were made to revive the historic Jewish self-governing communities (the kahals/*kehilat*) that had been abolished by the tsarist government in 1844. Of Jewish political parties, the socialists were the first to cooperate with the Central Rada, and others, including the Zionists, eventually followed. All Jewish parties, however, strongly opposed the idea of an independent Ukraine and either abstained from voting on or voted against the Fourth Universal.

The promising atmosphere in Jewish-Ukrainian relations created by the Central Rada during the first phase of Dnieper Ukraine's revolutionary era changed during the Hetmanate of the second phase and then dissolved completely during the anarchy and civil war of the third phase (1919–1920). Hetman Skoropads'kyi's government effectively ended the experiment in Jewish autonomy, but it at least maintained social stability in the cities and part of the countryside. During the third phase of the revolutionary era, maintaining such stability proved well beyond the powers of the Directory of the Ukrainian National Republic, faced as it was with foreign invasion, civil war, and peasant uprisings. Even though the Ministry of Jewish Affairs was revived and Jewish autonomy theoretically restored, this meant little to Dnieper Ukraine's Jews who faced a wave of pogroms and so-called excesses (less violent attacks in which there was usually no loss of life) that intensified after May 1919. Of the 1,236 pogroms and excesses in 524 localities recorded between 1917 and early 1921 in Dnieper Ukraine, three-quarters of them occurred in the year 1919 alone (especially between May and September). Estimates of the number of persons killed in the pogroms during the entire period range from 30,000 to 60,000. Another result of the pogroms was a change in Jewish settlement patterns. Fearful of their lives, tens of thousands of Jews fled small towns in the countryside for the relative security of larger cities. Since their homes and businesses were looted or destroyed, most Jews decided to remain in the larger cities where their percentage among the inhabitants increased dramatically. For instance, if in Kiev the percentage of Jews was 19 percent in 1917, by 1920 it had risen to 32 percent.

Regardless of whether the pogroms and excesses were carried out by White Russian armies, by forces loyal to the Bolsheviks, by troops under the banner of the Ukrainian National Republic, or by uncontrolled marauding bands nominally under military chieftains (like Hryhoriïv and Makhno), the Directory of the Ukrainian National Republic and particularly its leader, Symon Petliura, have been

PETLIURA AND THE POGROMS

... Officers and Cossacks! It is time to know that the Jews have, like the greater part of our Ukrainian population, suffered from the horrors of the Bolshevist-communist invasion and now know where the truth lies. The best Jewish groups such as the Bund, the Fareynikte [United Jewish Socialist Workers' party], the Poale Tsiyon [Workers of Zion], and the Folkspartey [Folks party] have come out decidedly in favor of an independent Ukrainian state and cooperate together with us.

The time has come to realize that the peaceable Jewish population – their women and children – like ours have been imprisoned and deprived of their national liberty. They [the Jews] are not going anywhere but are remaining with us, as they have for centuries, sharing in both our happiness and our grief.

The chivalrous troops who bring equality and liberty to all the nationalities of Ukraine must not listen to those invaders and provocators who hunger for human blood. Yet at the same time they cannot remain indifferent in the face of the tragic fate of the Jews. He who becomes an accomplice to such crimes is a traitor and an enemy of our country and must be placed beyond the pale of human society. ...

... I expressly order you to drive away with your forces all who incite you to pogroms and to bring the perpetrators before the courts as enemies of the fatherland. Let the courts judge them for their acts and not excuse those found guilty from the most severe penalties of the law.*

The excerpt above is from an order by Petliura issued on 26 August 1919 to the troops of the Ukrainian National Republic. Despite this and other actions taken by him earlier in the year to assist the Jewish population, the relationship of Petliura to the pogroms of 1919 has remained a controversial issue. Subsequent literature on the subject differs greatly, according to whether the authors are of Jewish or Ukrainian background. The following are examples of the often extreme difference of opinion about Petliura.

In 1976, the Jewish writer Saul S. Friedman published a book about the assassination of Petliura with the provocative title *Pogromchik*, which concludes with ten reasons why Petliura was "responsible for the pogroms." Among them are the following:

1. Simon Petlura was Chief of State, Ataman-in-Chief, with real power to act when he so desired. No Ukrainian leader enjoyed comparable respect, allegiance or authority.

2. Units of the Ukrainian Army directly under his supervision (the Clans of Death) committed numerous atrocities. Instead of being punished, the leaders of these units (Oudovichenko, Palienko, Angel, Patrov, Shandruk) received promotions.

3. Insurgents dependent upon Petlura for financial support and war material committed pogroms in his name. Petlura maintained a special office to coordinate the activities of these partisans. Rather than punishing them, he received their leaders with honors in his capital.

6. There is good reason to believe that Petlura may have ordered pogroms in Proskurov

and Zhitomir in the early months of 1919, and that the Holovni Ataman [Petliura] was in the immediate vicinity of these towns when pogroms were raging. Yet he did nothing to intervene personally; nor did he command the expeditious punishment of the major pogromchiks.

7. Petlura's famous orders of August 26 and 27, 1919, forbidding pogroms, were issued eight months too late, at a time when the Holovni Ataman had no real power. They were designed specifically for foreign consumption.

8. What funds were authorized for the relief of pogrom victims were a trifle compared with how much was needed and how much had been stolen from the Jews. Like Petlura's famed orders, they were too little and too late.[†]

In 1969–1970, the American scholarly journal *Jewish Social Studies* published a debate about Petliura and the Jews during the revolutionary years. The Ukrainian-American historian Taras Hunczak came to the following conclusions:

The frequently repeated charge that Petliura was antisemitic is absurd. Vladimir Jabotinsky, perhaps one of the greatest Jews of the twentieth century – a man well-versed in the problems of East European Jewry – categorically rejected the idea of Petliura's animosity towards the Jews.… .

Equally absurd is the attempt on the part of some to establish Petliura's complicity in the pogroms against Ukrainian Jewry. Particularly disturbing is the recent attempt by Hannah Arendt to draw a parallel between the case of Petliura and Adolf Eichmann, Hitler's notorious henchman.

…

In view of the evidence presented, to convict Petliura for the tragedy that befell Ukrainian Jewry is to condemn an innocent man and to distort the record of Ukrainian-Jewish relations.[‡]

[*]Pavlo Khrystiuk, *Zamitky i materiialy do istorii ukraïns'koï revolutsiï, 1917–1920 rr.*, Vol. IV (Vienna 1922), pp. 167–168.

[†]Saul S. Friedman, *Pogromchik* (New York 1976), pp. 372–373

[‡]Taras Hunczak, "A Reappraisal of Symon Petliura and Jewish-Ukrainian Relations, 1917–1921," *Jewish Social Studies*, XXXI (New York 1969), pp. 182–183.

blamed in most subsequent Jewish writings. The pogroms have so clouded the historical record that authoritative sources like the *Encyclopedia Judaica* have concluded that no Ukrainian government, neither the Central Rada, nor the Hetmanate, nor the Directory, was ever sincere about Jewish autonomy or about "really developing a new positive attitude toward the Jews."[1] Whoever or whatever is responsible for the pogroms of 1919–1920 in Dnieper Ukraine, there is no question that their occurrence poisoned Jewish-Ukrainian relations for decades to come both in the homeland and in the diaspora.

The Russians

The Russian minority in Dnieper Ukraine invariably opposed the idea of separation from Russia. This applied across the political spectrum, from the left-wing Bolsheviks, who actually made up the majority of the members in the Communist party (Bolshevik) of Ukraine, to the right-wing monarchists, known as the Bloc of Unaffiliated Russian Electors and represented by the ukrainophobic Russian-language daily newspaper *Kievlianin* (Kiev, 1864–1919), edited by Vasilii Shul'gin. When, in July 1917, the Central Rada was opened to national minorities, the Russians had fifty-four deputies. There were also eight Russians in the Little Rada and a few who at various times held ministerial portfolios in the Ukrainian National Republic's General Secretariat and its Secretariat for Nationality affairs, which included an undersecretarial/ministerial post for Russian affairs (held by Dmitrii Odinets). As the Central Rada moved increasingly toward autonomy and then independence for Ukraine, however, the Russian deputies began leaving the assembly until only four Socialist-Revolutionaries and Minister Odinets remained. With the establishment of the Hetmanate in April 1918, the majority of Russians, especially from the center and right side of the political spectrum, supported the new government of the Ukrainian State. These same groups also welcomed the efforts of General Denikin's Volunteer Army to restore Russian control over Ukraine in 1919.

The Russians' attitude toward Ukrainian aspirations is not surprising. From their perspective, they lived in Little Russia, which for them was an inalienable part of the Russian homeland. As for Ukrainianism, most Russians considered it little more than a political idea concocted by a few misguided intellectuals or a byproduct of the anti-Russian designs of foreign powers, especially Austria-Hungary and Germany. According to such a scenario, the peasant masses were not Ukrainians, they were Little Russians. It was simply inconceivable to Russians (or, for that matter, russified Ukrainians) imbued with such attitudes that their beloved Little Russian homeland could ever be torn from mother Russia and transformed into an "artificial" independent Ukrainian state.

The Poles

Poles living in Dnieper Ukraine exhibited mixed reactions to the events that engulfed them during the revolutionary era. It was actually owing to World War I that the number of Poles in Dnieper Ukraine increased. This was the result of large numbers having fled eastward from the Congress Kingdom, the Russian Empire's far-western Polish-inhabited entity, which for extensive periods of time was held by the invading armies of the Central Powers. Cities on the Right Bank received many Poles during this influx; for instance, in 1917 their number in Kiev alone reached 43,000, or 9.5 percent of the inhabitants.

Following the February Revolution in the Russian Empire, the Poles in Dnieper Ukraine organized themselves essentially into two groups. The Polish Executive Committee in Rus' (Polski Komitet Wykonawczy na Rusi), led by Joachim Bartoszewicz, primarily represented the landowning class and conservative National

Democrats (Endecja), who were sympathetic to the Polish liberation movement. The Polish Democratic Center, an umbrella organization of several parties that included political activists like Mieczysław Mickiewicz, Roman Knoll, and Stanisław Stempowski, represented more liberal political trends, although it too supported the interests of Polish landowners and shared their inclination for an independent Polish state. Leaders of the Polish Democratic Center party took advantage of the Central Rada's invitation to participate in its administration, and it obtained places for twenty deputies in the Central Rada and two in the Little Rada. Then, following the Fourth Universal in January 1918, the ministerial portfolio for Polish affairs (headed by Mickiewicz) was created as part of the Council of Ministers of the Ukrainian National Republic.

The Polish ministerial portfolio ceased to exist following the fall of the Central Rada in April 1918. The Skoropads'kyi-led Hetmanate cooperated instead with the Polish Executive Committee, which welcomed the conservative intention of the government to restore the large landed estates. The days of the Polish landlords and their hold over the Right Bank countryside were numbered, however. In response to the peasant revolts and anarchic conditions which dominated the 1919–1920 period, and following the establishment of Soviet rule in Dnieper Ukraine, large numbers of Poles fled westward to the new Polish state. Consequently, the number of Poles remaining in Dnieper Ukraine decreased by at least one-third, from 685,000 in 1909 to 410,000 in 1926.

The Germans and Mennonites

The only numerically sizable national minority able entirely to avoid dealings with the Central Rada or with other non-Bolshevik governments in Dnieper Ukraine were the Germans. Maintaining the aloofness that had characterized them since tsarist times, the Germans remained in their rural communities and tried to keep as uninvolved as possible with both the Ukrainians and the Russians in their midst and in the urban centers. Because of the all-encompassing changes and cataclysmic events of the revolutionary era, however, the Germans were unable to remain unaffected for long. In relative terms, perhaps they suffered the most of all Dnieper Ukraine's peoples.

Already during World War I, the Germans living in Volhynia and in the Chełm region, that is, in areas closest to the front, had been deported in 1915 by the tsarist Russian government, primarily to Siberia. They were suspect in the eyes of Russian officialdom, who feared (and in some cases with justification) their possible collaboration with the advancing German Army. Then, during 1919 and the height of the peasant leader Makhno's military ravages, many German villages, especially in Katerynoslav province, were attacked in destructive pogroms. Their inhabitants either were killed or, if they managed to escape, eventually reached Germany, the United States, or Canada. The pacifist Mennonites and their prosperous rural farms proved especially easy targets for Makhno's anarchist bands. As a result of the World War I deportations and emigration abroad, brought about by the destruction of farmsteads during the revolutionary era, the number of Germans in Dnieper Ukraine decreased by almost two-fifths, from 750,000 in 1914 to 514,000 in 1926.

MENNONITES CAUGHT IN THE REVOLUTION

The reaction of Ukraine's indigenous German, in particular Mennonite, inhabitants to the revolution and civil war is summed up by Dietrich Neufeld in a diary-like memoir from 1919–1920 later published under the title *A Russian Dance of Death* (1977). Of particular interest in the book are the Mennonites' perceptions of their own place in the former Russian Empire, of the anarchist leader Makhno, of their Ukrainian neighbors, whom they refer to as Russians, and finally – because they are pacifists – of the difficult decision to take up arms in self-defense.

Even these peaceful Mennonite settlers who up till now have remained aloof from all history-making events are caught up in the general upheaval. They no longer enjoy the peace which dominated their steppe for so long. They are no longer permitted to live in seclusion from the world.

...

Makhno. Who doesn't quake at that name? It is a name that will be remembered for generations as that of an inhuman monster. ... His professed aim is to put all 'capitalists' to the sword. Even the Bolsheviks – dedicated to the same cause but more sparing of human life on principle – are too tame for him. His path is literally drenched with blood.

...

Presumably, the Makhnovites despoiled our people because of their alleged sympathy for Denikin. It can't be denied that our colonists, though professing neutrality, do not show much sympathy for the peasants. While the peasants opposed the re-establishment of the old regime, the [Mennonite] colonists remained loyal to that cause. They even allowed themselves to be enlisted in Denikin's army. Actually, they were tricked into doing so by being assured that they would be organized into local Self Defence units only.

Many of our young men, who as a consequence of the German occupation had developed distinctly anti-Russian attitudes, were eager to avenge the looting and suffering inflicted on our people [in 1918, before the German troops arrived]. ... They supported the German army of occupation and, in some cases, had been foolish enough to inform against certain of the revolutionary leaders.

...

One can criticize the Zagradovka [Zahradivka] Mennonites for taking up arms instead of holding fast to the principle of non-resistance. As good Christians they had no right to show hatred toward their neighbor. Their duty was to love him even when he wronged them. Instead, they made common cause with a soldiery which plundered and murdered – even though we have no reason to suspect any young Mennonites of a similar lack of restraint.... .

The Zagradovka Mennonites took up arms without hesitation. They are to be doubly blamed for that. First, it was politically unwise. Then again it was in glaring contradiction to their hitherto professed concept of non-resistance. The Russian peasants pointed out this contradiction and called them hypocrites. A bitter truth was held up to the [Mennonite] colonists: 'When our Russia, our women and children, were threatened with attack in 1914, then you refused to take up arms for defensive purposes. But now that it's a question of your own property you are arming yourselves.' Certainly it was a crying shame that the [Mennonite] colonists' actions were inspired neither by a desire to protect the state nor by a true Christian spirit.

...

We Mennonites are aliens in this land. If we didn't realize that fact before the war we have had it forced upon us during and after the War. Our Russian neighbors look on us as the damned Nyemtsy [Germans] who have risen to great prosperity in their land. They completely ignore the fact that our forefathers were invited here [one hundred and thirty] years ago in order to cultivate the vast steppes which lay idle at the time. They refuse to admit that our farmers were able to achieve more than Russian farmers by dint of industry and perseverence, as well as through better organization and management, rather than through political means. ...

This is no longer our homeland. We want to leave! The magic word 'emigration' travels like a *buran* [winter wind] from place to place. Whenever two or three colonists get together the conversation is sure to be about emigrating. It is the one idea that keeps us going, our one hope.

SOURCE: Dietrich Neufeld, *A Russian Dance of Death: Revolution and Civil War in the Ukraine*, translated by Al Riemer (Winnipeg 1977), pp. 11, 18–19, 26–27, 63–64, 73, 79.

The Czechs

The smaller Czech community (ca. 30,000) based primarily in Volhynia maintained good relations with the tsarist regime and with the Ukrainian nationalist governments which followed. It also took an active part in the political and military movement that was to result in the establishment of an independent Czechoslovakia in late 1918. Kiev in particular became the center of Czech activity for the entire Russian Empire. It was home to the Charitable Society (Dobročinný), the Comenius Educational Society, the newspaper *Čechoslovan,* and it was the site where in August 1914 a volunteer unit of Czech soldiers (Česká družina) was formed to fight within the ranks of the Russian Army against what was considered the "common enemy of the Slavs," Germany and Austria-Hungary.

In the course of the war, Czechs from various parts of the Russian Empire as well as exiles from Austria-Hungary gravitated to Kiev. The most famous of these was the writer Jaroslav Hašek, who from 1916 lived in Kiev where he published the first installments of what was to become the extremely popular novel, *The Good Soldier Švejk.* In the wake of the Bolshevik Revolution and Russia's departure from the war in December 1917, the Czech military unit Česká družina formed by Czech and Slovak prisoners-of-war, was transformed into what became known as the Czechoslovak Legion. The Legion's purpose was to continue fighting against the Central Powers on behalf of independence for a future Czechoslovakia. Also in 1917, Ukraine's Czechs formed a branch of the Czechoslovak National Council based in Paris and they greeted its leader and future president of Czechoslovakia, Tomaš G. Masaryk, who arrived in Kiev in late 1917. Masaryk maintained favorable relations with the Ukrainian National Republic and he secured safe passage for Czechoslovak Legionnaires who left Ukrainian territory in February 1918. Among the Czechs who remained in their homes in Volhynia, plans were made to participate actively as a minority community in the Ukrainian National Republic, but the collapse of the Directory and the onset of Bolshevik rule precluded the fulfillment of such goals.

The Crimean Tatars

The Crimean Tatars were different from other peoples in Dnieper Ukraine in that they were concentrated in one area, the Crimea, a territory claimed by the Hetmanate, but in which no Ukrainian government had any authority during the revolutionary era. Under tsarist rule, hundreds of thousands of Tatars had, in the course of the nineteenth century, fled from the lands of the former Crimean Khanate and settled in the Ottoman Empire. It was among these exiles, especially in the Ottoman capital of Istanbul, that the Crimean Tatar nationalist movement arose during the first decade of the twentieth century. The most important Istanbul-based nationalist organization was the Vatan/Fatherland Society, whose goal was independence for the Crimea. The slow but steady return to the Crimea of nationally conscious Tatar activists from Ottoman exile, which began in 1908, was to continue even after the outbreak of World War I in 1914. Among the most prominent of these returnees were the founders of the Vatan Society, Noman Çelebi Cihan and Cafer Seydahmet, who in the first years of the war were drafted into the tsarist Russian Army. Both served in the army's Crimean Cavalry Regiment, where they helped to transform many of its soldiers into patriots who one day might fight on behalf of the Crimean Tatar cause.

Developments in the Crimea were in many ways analogous to the three phases of the revolutionary era in Dnieper Ukraine. In the first phase, immediately following the Russian Revolution of February 1917, the representatives of the Provisional Government in St Petersburg tried to establish its authority in the region by working with former tsarist officials and the established conservative elements (landowners and clerics) among the Crimean Tatars. Meanwhile, younger Crimean Tatar national activists with ties to the Istanbul-based émigré Vatan Society convoked in Simferopol' in March the All-Crimean Muslim Congress. The congress formed a Crimean Muslim Central Executive Committee and elected (in absentia) as its leaders Noman Çelebi Cihan and Cafer Seydahmet, both of whom were still serving in the tsarist army. Still other activists created in the summer of 1917 a nationalist political party Milli Firka, whose program was socialist in orientation, calling for the break-up of the large estates held by private landowners and the church. The nationalist leaders were determined to replace the Muslim clergy as the leading force in Crimean Tatar society. This was not an easy task, since the conservative clerical leaders (*mullahs*) together with Crimea's Russian and Tatar large landowners (*pomeshchiks*) continued to be recognized by the Provisional Government in St Petersburg.

Unable to find a common ground with the Provisional Government, the Crimean Muslim Central Executive Committee and the Milli Firka party made plans to convene a "national parliament" which they called the Kurultay, the historic name for the gathering of tribal leaders that chose Crimea's khans. On 24 November 1917, the Crimean Tatar Kurultay was held on the grounds of the former palace of the khans in Bahçesaray/Bakhchysarai. The Kurultay elected a Crimean Tatar government, or National Directorate, to be based in Simferopol' and headed by Çelebi Cihan and Seydamet. Before the end of 1917 a constitution was adopted which declared the formation of an independent Crimean Democratic Republic. The new government gained control of the Crimean Cavalry Regiment demobilized from the tsarist army, and it began to negotiate with the Ottoman Empire to support Crimea's political demands.

Throughout 1917, Crimean Tatar leaders had maintained cordial relations with the Central Rada of the Ukrainian National Republic in Kiev, which was sympathetic to their demands for cultural and territorial autonomy. The reaction of the local Russian and Ukrainian inhabitants who made up no less than a half of the Crimea's population was quite different, however. Particularly problematic were the armed forces of the imperial Black Sea Fleet based in the Crimean port of Sevastopol', which after the Revolution of November 1917 supported the Bolsheviks. In January 1918, the Bolshevik-led sailors and marines from the Black Sea Fleet attacked the Crimean Republic's headquarters in Simferopol', dispersed the Crimean Tatar nationalist leadership, and two months later (19 March 1918) called into being the Taurida Soviet Socialist Republic. While in power for a few months, the Soviet regime ravaged the Crimean countryside, with the express goal of eliminating Tatar "bourgeois nationalists," Muslim clergy, and wealthy landowners. To drive their point home, the Bolshevik forces captured and killed the president of the Kurultay, Noman Çelebi Cihan, thereby unwittingly transforming him into a national martyr. From then on he has been remembered as the ultimate patriot whose love for his country is embodied in the words he wrote that became the Crimean Tatar national anthem, "Ant Etkemen" (I Pledge).

In the spring of 1918, the second phase of Crimea's revolutionary era began, and it too was quite analogous to the Hetmanate period unfolding at the same time in Dnieper Ukraine. The German Army, already in Ukraine, moved toward the Crimea and brought with them a Muslim cavalry unit comprised of Crimean Tatar exiles from Dobruja in Romania and commanded by a Tatar from Lithuania, the former tsarist General Matwiej Sulejman Sulkiewicz. In the second half of April 1918, the German forces took over all of Crimea and brought to an end the Taurida Soviet Republic. The Crimean Tatar leadership welcomed the arrival of the Germans and, in return, they were allowed to restore the Kurultay in the hope that some form of Tatar self-rule could be achieved, this time under the protection of the German Army and General Sulkiewicz, who from June headed the government of the Crimean People's Republic. Sulkiewicz favored a future independent Crimean Tatar state, but those hopes were never realized, because the Germans returned home soon after the armistice that ended World War I was signed in November 1918.

The third phase of the revolutionary era in Crimea encompassed the years 1919 and most of 1920. This was an incredibly complex period when, as in Dnieper Ukraine, attempts to continue nationalist rule (in this case Crimean Tatar) were challenged by pro-Russian liberal forces, the anti-Bolshevik Whites, and the Bolshevik Reds in alliance with Soviet Russia. The least effective of these was the administration that succeeded General Sulkiewicz, and that from November 1918 to April 1919 was headed by Solomon Krym, a Karaite Jew and wealthy Crimean landowner. In contrast to the independentist orientation of his predecessor, the Crimean Regional Government under Krym supported a unified Russia along the lines of western European liberal democratic states.

For a few months (April–June 1919), Bolshevik rule was restored in the form of the Crimean Soviet Socialist Republic based in Simferopol', but by early July this entity collapsed following the arrival of White Russian armies (and thousands of anti-Bolshevik refugees) headed by General Anton Denikin. As the cause of the Whites throughout Russia gradually faded, Denikin and his successor General Petr Vrangel' hoped to transform the Crimea into an "island bastion" of anti-Communism. It was to be a purely "Russian bastion," however, and with that in mind the White forces showed no tolerance for the Crimean Tatars or for any of their political demands. Therefore, for nearly a year Denikin's troops actively repressed Crimean Tatar activists until the Whites themselves were entirely driven from the peninsula. In the face of widespread repression, many Crimean Tatars in the Milli Firka nationalist party joined guerilla units known as "green bands" to fight against the Whites. Whereas some Milli Firkists (Cafer Seydahmet) remained adamantly opposed to Russian rule, whether White or Red, the leftists in the party (Veli Ibrahimov) favored an alliance with the Bolsheviks in common cause against the Whites. The alliance did not last long, however.

In October 1920, the Red Army succeeded in driving the last White Russian forces and refugees out of the Crimea, allowing the Bolsheviks to establish again Soviet rule throughout the peninsula. Almost immediately the Soviet regime outlawed the Milli Firka nationalist party, and under the direction of Béla Kun, the exiled Hungarian Communist leader in Soviet service, an estimated 60,000 real or suspected opponents of Soviet rule (including "Tatar nationalists") were killed. Whereas local Bolsheviks had little appreciation for the Crimean Tatars and their national interests, the Soviet leadership in Moscow, especially Vladimir Lenin, was more sympathetic. Acting on a report about the devastated conditions in the peninsula, in October 1921 the Communist authorities in Moscow created a distinct Crimean Autonomous Socialist Soviet Republic, although not within the jurisdiction of Soviet Ukraine but rather within the Russian Federated Soviet Socialist Republic. To what degree, if any, the Crimean Soviet Republic would be Tatar in nature is a topic discussed below in chapter 45.

41

The West Ukrainian National Republic

From the very beginning of World War I in August 1914, the western Ukrainian lands, in particular Galicia and Bukovina, were in the center of military activity along the eastern front. As a result, Galician and Bukovinian political life was restricted largely to the activity of its leaders, who spent most of the war years in the imperial Habsburg capital of Vienna. When the Austrian parliament was reconvened in May 1917, the Ukrainian Parliamentary Representation led by Iuliian Romanchuk refused flatly any future political status that would place the Ukrainians of Galicia in the same province with the Poles. Hence, the old call for the division of Galicia was reiterated once again, although now it was the minimal demand of the Ukrainian leaders. The Austrian response was the same as before – procrastination. The Habsburg government continued to argue that no internal structural changes to the empire could be made until the end of the war. In February 1918, at the negotiations which led to the Treaty of Brest-Litovsk, the Austrian government did promise that a law outlining the division of Galicia would be drawn up by July of that year. Nothing came of the promise, however. Nevertheless, many Galician Ukrainians continued to hope that their political needs could be met within the context of the Habsburg Empire.

Austria's Ukrainians prepare for their postwar future

By the fall of 1918, when it became obvious that the Central Powers had lost the war, certain Galician and Bukovinian Ukrainians began to prepare for the inevitable change in the status of the Austro-Hungarian Empire. By late 1918, the international situation had altered radically. The Allied Powers had already adopted as their war aim the so-called Fourteen-Point Peace Program issued in January 1918 by the United States president Woodrow Wilson, with its proclamation that a future peace should be governed by the principle of national self-determination. One of Wilson's Fourteen Points proposed independence for a restored Poland. Another called for autonomy for all the peoples of Austria-Hungary, although many in the empire understood "autonomy" to mean national self-determination or independence. The Ukrainians, like other Habsburg peoples, took the Allies' proclamations seriously. The first to respond to the new political environment were Ukrainian officers in the Austro-Hungarian Army, who in September 1918 organized in L'viv the Central Military Committee to coordinate plans with the Ukrainian Sich Riflemen (then stationed in Bukovina) for the eventual seizure of power.

Realizing that the old order was doomed, on 16 October 1918 Emperor Charles (reigned 1916–1918) issued a manifesto proposing that the Austro-Hungarian Empire be transformed into a federal state and calling upon the nationalities to organize themselves for that transformation. Once again, Vienna was responding to a pressing political crisis with a solution that was too little too late. Federalism was hardly an acceptable proposal for national movements that already had embarked on separate paths toward independence and were acting as if the empire already had ceased to exist. The Ukrainians, however, ever hopeful of a Habsburg solution, responded.

A week before the 16 October manifesto, Galicia's best-known Ukrainian leaders – Ievhen Petrushevych, Iuliian Romanchuk, and Metropolitan Andrei Sheptyts'kyi (back home after his release from detention in a Russian monastery) – had met to make plans to convoke a Ukrainian constituent assembly. The emperor's manifesto now seemed to confirm the legality of such an assembly. With the cooperation of other political and religious leaders from Galicia and Bukovina, the Ukrainian National Council (Ukraïns'ka Narodna Rada) was constituted in L'viv on 18 October. The new council chose Ievhen Petrushevych as its president and, invoking the principle of national self-determination, proclaimed the existence of a state on all Ukrainian lands within Austria-Hungary. Transcarpathia was also included in the proposed Ukrainian state, even though no representatives from that region were present at the L'viv national council. Despite the proclamation of Ukrainian statehood, there was no mention of secession from Austria-Hungary. This meant that the Ukrainians left open the possibility of belonging to a federation within the Habsburg Empire and, therefore, acted within the "legal" guidelines of the 16 October imperial manifesto.

West Ukrainian independence and war

The Ukrainian National Council did, however, claim the right to rule over the territories it considered its own, and on 1 November 1918 it demanded that the viceroy in Galicia (Karl Huyn) surrender his authority. Faced with pressure by Ukrainian units of the imperial army, the last Habsburg viceroy turned over his governmental offices to the Ukrainians. That same day, the National Council proclaimed that the state, which had first been called into being on 19 October, was henceforth an independent country. Thus, 1 November 1918 became the "second" Ukrainian independence day. A week later, the new state was given the name West Ukrainian National Republic (Zakhidn'o-Ukraïns'ka Narodna Respublika).

Blossoming out of a dying empire, western Ukrainian independence seems to have been achieved with ease. But appearances are frequently deceiving. The

MAP 34   THE WEST UKRAINIAN NATIONAL REPUBLIC, 1918–1919

—▪▪— Boundary of Austria-Hungary, Russia, and Romania to 1918	Boundary of Ukraine, 2005
— — Boundary of Hungarian Kingdom to 1918	Lands claimed by Western Ukrainian National Republic
∘∘∘∘ Ruthenian Land, Dec 1918 - Apr 1919	

0   50 miles
0   50 kilometers
Scale 1 : 4 230 000

Copyright © by Paul Robert Magocsi

Poles were not about to let the Ukrainians take over what they considered their own national patrimony, Galicia – both the heavily Ukrainian-populated eastern half and the Polish western half. Several Polish organizations in L'viv armed themselves, and on 1 November, the same day the Austrians surrendered the reins of government, the Ukrainians found themselves engaged in a war with the local Poles. Initially, the Ukrainians held L'viv and other cities in eastern Galicia, but by 21 November they had been driven from their new capital, and they were forced to move their government, first to Ternopil' and in early January to Stanyslaviv.

In the midst of war with the Poles, the Ukrainian National Council passed a law on 13 November 1918 that formally created an independent West Ukrainian National Republic with a regular force called the Ukrainian Galician Army. The new state was to include the Ukrainian-inhabited lands of Galicia (primarily east of the San River), of Bukovina, and of Transcarpathia (parts of seven counties in northeastern Hungary). It was only in eastern Galicia, however, that the Ukrainians were able, at least for a while, to set up an administration, because Bukovina had already been occupied by Romanian troops on 11 November, and with the exception of the short-term presence of a few troops Transcarpathia never came under West Ukrainian control.

Until the convocation of a parliament *(Soim),* to which elections were planned for June 1919, the supreme authority of the West Ukrainian National Republic rested in the National Council headed by Petrushevych. To administer the lands under its control, the National Council set up the Provisional State Secretariat on 9 November 1918, which was headed first by Kost' Levyts'kyi and then, beginning with the new year, by Sydir Holubovych. The proposed parliament, which never came into existence, was to have 226 members, 66 of whom were to be from national minorities (33 Poles, 27 Jews, and 6 Germans). Also, as early as 10 November 1918 the Galicians made plans to unite with their fellow Ukrainians in Dnieper Ukraine. These plans were formalized on 3 January 1919, when the National Council, meeting by then in Stanyslaviv, passed a law approving the unification of the West Ukrainian National Republic with the Ukrainian National Republic in Dnieper Ukraine. The Galicians sent a delegation to Kiev, where, on 22 January 1919 (the "third" Ukrainian independence day), a great national manifestation before the Cathedral of St Sophia proclaimed, "From this day the two parts of a single Ukraine – the West Ukrainian National Republic (Galicia, Bukovina, and Hungarian Rus' [Transcarpathia]) – that have been separated from each other are merging together."[1] In theory, the West Ukrainian National Republic became the Western Province *(Zakhidnia Oblast')* of the Ukrainian National Republic. In fact, the western Ukrainians led a rather separate political, military, and diplomatic existence.

By the spring of 1919, that existence was becoming more and more threatened. The Ukrainian Galician Army, at the time under Brigadier-General Mykhailo Omelianovych-Pavlenko, had proved itself an effective fighting force that by February 1919 managed to push back the Poles and surround L'viv. Their efforts, however, were soon to be undermined by the military and diplomatic superiority of their enemy.

In the world of international politics, Ukraine had a serious problem. Both Dnieper Ukraine and eastern Galicia were relatively unknown in the West. Poland, in contrast, had strong support among the Allied Powers, which by early 1918 had made Poland's independence one of its war aims. As in the old Austrian Galician days, in crucial moments, the Habsburg government had favored Polish over Ukrainian interests, so in 1919 the victorious Allies allowed Polish interests to prevail over those of the relatively unknown and therefore unimportant Galician Ukrainians.

Not that the Galician Ukrainians were completely unknown. The leading Allied Powers, already meeting at the Paris Peace Conference in early 1919, all had "Eastern experts." Some were not only aware of but even sympathetic to Ukrainian demands. The Ukrainians, for their part, sent delegations which prepared memoranda in Paris, while immigrants in the United States and Canada lobbied their respective governments to recognize the cause of Ukrainian independence, whether in Galicia or in Dnieper Ukraine. After all, President Wilson's inspiring principle of self-determination for nations could certainly be applied to the Ukrainians in eastern Galicia.

But whereas the Ukrainians (who had no diplomatic status) were limited to issuing memoranda and proclamations, the Poles had official representation at the Paris Peace Conference and could make their case known directly, especially through their popular (in western circles) spokesperson, the concert pianist and at the time Poland's premier and minister of foreign affairs, Ignacy Jan Paderewski. Since the beginning of 1919, Paderewski had been suggesting in a rather demagogic fashion that any ideas of Ukrainian statehood only reflected the bankrupt political aims of the German and Austrian enemy, who had hoped to divide and rule the western regions of the former Russian Empire. Those areas, he argued, should rightfully become the eastern regions of a restored Polish state. As for the Ukrainians, according to Paderewski (himself a native of Right Bank Ukraine), they were all Bolsheviks, an epithet implying they were a great danger to the Allies and to European stability in general. Not all the peacemakers in Paris were taken in by Paderewski's flowery rhetoric, however, and on several occasions during the spring of 1919 there were attempts to establish an armistice between Ukrainian and Polish armed forces, which would have left at least some of eastern Galicia in Ukrainian hands. But such intervention was of no avail.

Finally, in April 1919 the well-trained and well-equipped Polish Army, consisting of 100,000 men under General Józef Haller, arrived in Poland. Haller's army had experience fighting alongside the Allies in France, and among its ranks as advisors were several French officers who came to serve in Poland. The Allied Powers expected the Polish Army from France to be deployed against any westward advance by Soviet Russia. Stopping the Bolsheviks was certainly something the Allies would welcome. Instead, the Polish government sent Haller and his troops to Galicia together with French military advisors, among whom was a young captain named Charles de Gaulle. Despite stiff resistance on the part of the Ukrainian Galician Army (especially during the Chortkiv offensive in June), by 16–18 July 1919 the Poles had succeeded in driving the Ukrainians and their government out of Galicia.

And as for Wilson's principle of the right of nations to self-determination? It was sacrificed in the face of what at the time was considered an even greater danger – Bolshevism. That danger was outlined in a cable, dated 25 June, from the Allied Powers in Paris to the government of Poland in Warsaw:

With a view to protecting the persons and property of the peaceful population of eastern Galicia against the dangers to which they are exposed by the Bolshevik bands [sic], the Supreme Council of the Allied and Associated Powers have decided to authorize the forces of the Polish Republic to pursue their operations as far as the river Zbruch. ... This authorization does not in any way affect the decisions to be taken later by the Supreme Council for the settlement and political status of Galicia.[2]

Despite the cable's qualifications, Poland was in effect given an imprimatur from the victorious Allies to occupy all of Galicia.

The West Ukrainian government-in-exile

In the midst of the deteriorating military situation, the National Council of the West Ukrainian National Republic invested its president, Ievhen Petrushevych, with the title of dictator. This gave him full authority to determine the political and military policies of the West Ukrainian National Republic. After the defeat at the hands of the Poles, Petrushevych left Galicia, going eastward across the Zbruch River to nearby Kam'ianets'-Podil's'kyi, where the Ukrainian National Republic under Petliura's leadership was itself trying desperately to survive a Bolshevik offensive that was rapidly bringing under its control most of Dnieper Ukraine.

In theory, according to the January 1919 declaration of Ukrainian unity, Petrushevych and his government were a part of Petliura's Ukrainian National Republic. In Kam'ianets'-Podil's'kyi, the Galician and Dnieper Ukrainians had a chance to test their proclaimed unity. Their failure to cooperate could not have been greater. Chapter 39 outlined how, given the situation, Petliura favored an alliance with Poland as a means of repelling the Bolshevik and White Russian advances from the east. Fresh from a brutal military defeat, Petrushevych would have nothing to do with the Poles, and some of his supporters (especially the military) favored an alliance with one of Petliura's archenemies – the White Russian general, Anton Denikin.

Besides these tactical differences, there were other reasons why the Galician Ukrainians were reluctant to cooperate with the Dnieper Ukrainians. Petrushevych and his entourage felt that Galicia was the most developed region of Ukraine in terms of national culture and, most important at the moment, in terms of effective military strength. The old Piedmont theory was still uppermost in their minds. In other words, Galicia should first be made into a strong, independent Ukrainian state, and then other Ukrainian lands would follow its lead. Finally, the Galicians continued to have great faith in the Allies and in the Paris Peace Conference, from which they expected a confirmation of their national rights. Little did they realize that the political maneuvering which had brought some successes in pre-1914 Austria meant nothing in 1918–1919, when only military strength and diplomatic leverage with the Allied Powers carried any weight. On both counts, the Galicians, and, for that matter, all Ukrainians, were sorely wanting.

These are some of the reasons for the complete failure of cooperation between Galicia's West Ukrainian National Republic and the Ukrainian National Republic. By the end of 1919, both republics were in disarray. Petliura fled to Poland to prepare, with Polish help, for one last confrontation with the Bolsheviks; Petrushevych fled to Vienna to carry on what proved to be a vain diplomatic struggle in western and central European capitals on behalf of his Polish-occupied homeland.

Bukovina and Transcarpathia

Although since its establishment in late 1918, the West Ukrainian National Republic had claimed sovereignty not only over eastern Galicia but also over Bukovina and Transcarpathia, these two territories followed decidedly other paths in the immediate postwar era. Bukovina's Ukrainian political leadership had worked together closely with the Galicians in Vienna during the war years and then participated with them in the Ukrainian National Council in L'viv, which proclaimed independence (1 November) for all Ukrainian lands within the disintegrating Austro-Hungarian Empire. Parallel with developments in Galicia, the Ukrainian Committee was set up in Bukovina's administrative center of Chernivtsi on 25 October 1918, under the leadership of a Ukrainian deputy to the Austrian imperial parliament, Omelian Popovych. Two days later, Romanian deputies from the Austrian parliament and the Bukovinian diet established their own Romanian National Council. It was also at this time that Austrian army units of Ukrainian Sich Riflemen stationed in Bukovina and commanded by Archduke Wilhelm Habsburg (Vasyl' Vyshsyvanyi) were called by the Ukrainian National Council to L'viv on 1 November, leaving Bukovina's Ukrainians without any serious defense force.

Members of Bukovina's Ukrainian Committee headed by Popovych tried to negotiate with their Romanian counterparts but only succeeded in reaching an agreement with the parliamentary deputy, Aurel Onciul. As it turned out, he had only limited influence among Bukovina's Romanians. On 6 November, Austrian officials surrendered their authority to Popovych and Onciul, who were respectively acting in the name of the Ukrainian Committee (now National Council) and the Romanian National Council, each of which was to administer that part of Bukovina where its nationality was in the majority. These developments, however, proved to have no real impact over subsequent events, because most of Bukovina's Romanian leaders had other plans.

The Romanian National Council was actually led by Iancu Flondor, and he opposed any ideas of power-sharing with Ukrainians. This is because the council's leaders expected that all of Bukovina would soon be "reunited" with Romania. Therefore, when the Austrians surrendered on 6 November 1918, Flondor's response was to call on Romania to send troops. Five days later, a Romanian force entered Chernivtsi. The Ukrainians who had no serious armed force to back them, did not resist and all of Bukovina was annexed to Romania.

In Transcarpathia, the situation was much more complex. Following the example of other groups within the disintegrating Habsburg Empire, the Transcarpathian Rusyns/Ukrainians set up several national councils in late 1918 to discuss the fate of their homeland. The Hungarians, too, were not idle. On 31 October politicians led by Count Mihály Károlyi formed a revolutionary government in Budapest, which two weeks later (12 November) was transformed into the independent republic of Hungary. The new republic laid claim to all territories under the former jurisdiction of the Hungarian Kingdom, including Transcarpathia.

Hungary's national minorities were displeased with this turn of events and made plans to dissociate themselves from their former rulers. Among the several national councils that met in Transcarpathia in November and December 1918, three political orientations evolved. One council (Uzhhorod) favored remaining with Hungary; the other two councils looked elsewhere – the Prešov council favored joining the new state of Czechoslovakia, the Sighet council an independent Ukraine. In an attempt to head off moves in either of the latter two directions, the new Hungarian Republic passed a law on 21 December 1918 creating an autonomous province called the Ruthenian Land (Rus'ka Kraina). As an autonomous part of Hungary, the Ruthenian Land was endowed in February 1919 with its own governmental minister (Oreszt Szabó) and local governor (Agoston Stefan), and in March it held elections to a Ruthenian diet based in the town of Mukachevo.

While the Hungarian Republic was trying to assert its control over Transcarpathia, two local leaders from that region traveled to Galicia, where on 3 January 1919 they asked for help from the West Ukrainian National Republic. Then, on 21 January more than 1,200 Rusyns/Ukrainians met in the small town of Khust to proclaim their desire to join a united Ukraine (Soborna Ukraïna). One part of Transcarpathia, the far-eastern Hutsul region, even declared an independent Hutsul Republic in early January and accepted aid from the West Ukrainian National Republic. The Hutsul Republic managed to survive for the next six months until its government was driven out by Romanian troops.

Neither the Hungarian nor the Ukrainian orientation, however, was to prevail in Transcarpathia. An unexpected source was to make a crucial difference in the political future of the region. This source was the United States, in particular immigrants from Transcarpathia. Known at the time as Uhro-Rusyns (i.e., Rusyns from Hungary), in July 1918 the group chose a young Pittsburgh lawyer, Gregory Zhatkovych, to represent them in finding a solution for the fate of their homeland. Zhatkovych first favored the idea of an independent Rusyn state (Rusinia), but after meeting with President Woodrow Wilson and the Czech leader Tomáš G. Masaryk (who was in the United States working on behalf of a future independent Czechoslovakia), the Rusyn-American leader came to favor the Czechoslovak solution. He arranged a plebiscite among immigrants in the United States, who in December voted overwhelmingly (66 percent) to join the Czechoslovak republic.

Armed with the Rusyn-American decision, the new government in Prague, by then headed by President Masaryk, dispatched troops in late December 1918 to occupy Transcarpathia. By January, the Czechoslovak forces had gotten only as far as Uzhhorod (on the present-day Ukrainian border with Slovakia), because the rest of the region was being administered by the pro-Hungarian government of the autonomous Ruthenian Land. Then, in March, when Hungary became a Soviet state (under Béla Kun), the autonomous region was taken over by a Bolshevik regime. This Communist threat to the Danubian Basin prompted war between a Hungarian Soviet army on the one hand and Czechoslovak and Romanian forces on the other. The Hungarian Communists were eventually defeated, and by the summer of 1919 Czechoslovak and Romanian forces were occupying all of Transcarpathia. On 8 May 1919, Uzhhorod became the site of the convocation of the Central Ruthenian National Council, which accepted the decision of the Rusyn immigrants in the United States and declared its voluntary union with Czechoslovakia, although with the understanding that all Rusyn-inhabited territories south of the Carpathians would be granted political as well as cultural autonomy.

The Ukrainian revolution: Success or failure?

By the summer of 1919, each of the three Ukrainian territories in the former Austro-Hungarian Empire had found itself in a new country. Eastern Galicia was held by Poland, northern Bukovina by Romania, and Transcarpathia by Czechoslovakia. Only in the case of Transcarpathia was the new political situation supported by the local population. None of these territorial arrangements, however, was internationally recognized as yet. That recognition had to await the decisions of the Peace Conference in Paris, where leaders of the victorious Allied Powers had been sitting since early 1919 in an effort to redraw the map of Europe.

With the de facto incorporation of western Ukrainian lands into Poland, Romania, and Czechoslovakia by mid-1919, and with the establishment of Bolshevik rule in Dnieper Ukraine in early 1920, the efforts to create a sovereign state that incorporated all territory inhabited by ethnic Ukrainians and that would be independent of the surrounding powers effectively came to an end. Faced with this result, most non-Marxist writers have subsequently considered the Ukrainian revolutionary era a failure. Their reasoning? Ukrainians were unable to achieve the supposedly ultimate goal of national movements – independent statehood. Accordingly, the record of those revolutionary years, 1917–1920, has been searched in detail for what went wrong.

Many reasons are given for the failure of the revolution: (1) political inexperience that resulted in destructive in-fighting and a lack of firm leadership; (2) the total breakdown of cooperation between Galician and Dnieper Ukrainians; (3) submission to foreign powers, especially Germany; (4) invasions by the White Russians and the Bolsheviks; (5) the refusal of any of the Allied Powers to aid the Ukrainian cause; (6) the failure to resolve the land question and the reluctance of the peasant masses to support their "own Ukrainian" governments, and their tendency to join destructive marauding bands instead; and (7) the opposition of the many minorities on Ukrainian territory to the idea of Ukrainian independence. Finally, the most important reason given for the perceived failure is that Ukrainians as a people were not sufficiently conscious of their national identity in 1917–1920 to want to struggle and sacrifice themselves for Ukrainian statehood.

Looked at in another way, however, the Ukrainian revolutionary era was a success. One might well wonder why so many ethnic Ukrainians did in fact struggle and sacrifice their lives for the idea of independence. This was particularly remarkable in the formerly Russian-ruled Dnieper Ukraine, where the Ukrainian national movement was virtually non-existent or, at best, limited to a handful of individuals. Then suddenly, after 1917, energy and sacrifice on behalf of the national cause burst forth, in the political, social, cultural, and military spheres. And even if these efforts did not bring about the hoped-for independence, the revolutionary experience itself instilled in ethnic Ukrainians a firm sense of national purpose – achieved, moreover, not after several generations of peacetime cultural work, but in less than half a decade. From such a perspective, the Ukrainian revolution was a remarkable success.

On the other hand, this period was never viewed as a failure by apologists for the Ukrainian Soviet Socialist Republic. After all, it was the revolutionary era that gave birth to the Soviet Ukrainian government, which, after three attempts, finally established its authority over a large portion of Ukrainian-inhabited territory. In Soviet Ukrainian terms, therefore, independence was indeed achieved for most of Dnieper Ukraine between 1917 and 1920. All that remained was for subsequent generations to bring that achievement to all Ukrainian lands. The next six chapters will explore the impact of Soviet and non-Soviet rule on all Ukrainian-inhabited territories, where the differing heritages and goals of the revolutionary era would be kept alive.

PART NINE

The Interwar Years

42

The Postwar Treaties and the Reconfiguration of Ukrainian Lands

The autumn of 1918 witnessed the end of World War I, as one by one the Central Powers – Bulgaria (29 September), Ottoman Turkey (30 October), Austria-Hungary (3 November), and finally Germany (11 November) – accepted armistices to end hostilities. For their part, the victors, known officially as the Allied and Associated Powers – Great Britain, France, Italy, the United States, and Japan – agreed to meet in Paris in order to draw up formal peace treaties. In January 1919, the heads of state of the four Allied Powers concerned with the European theater of war – Prime Minister Lloyd George of Great Britain, Premier Georges Clemenceau of France, President Woodrow Wilson of the United States, and Premier Vittorio Emanuele Orlando of Italy – arrived in Paris in order to participate in the work of the peace conference.

Although World War I had ended by late 1918 and peace negotiations were under way by the beginning of 1919, hostilities had not yet ceased in eastern Europe. On Ukrainian lands, they were to last at least another two years, until late 1920. Although some of the decisions reached by the peacemakers in Paris had a direct impact on Ukrainian territories, especially on those within the former Austro-Hungarian Empire, the diplomatic proposals that came out of Paris generally followed military faits accomplis over which the peacemakers had little or no control. For instance, because the Allied Powers claimed supreme authority over lands formerly part of the Austro-Hungarian Empire, they felt obliged to intervene in the Polish-Ukrainian war that raged in eastern Galicia between November 1918 and July 1919. Their efforts to impose an armistice, however, were ignored by both the Poles and the Ukrainians. Thus, the June 1919 decision of the Allied Powers to allow Polish troops to occupy Galicia as far as its eastern boundary along the Zbruch River was little more than recognition of what in fact had already taken place. In other words, neither the goodwill of some Allied leaders in Paris, who were legitimately concerned and even appalled by the Polish seizure of eastern Galicia, nor the protestations of the diplomatic mission of the West Ukrainian National Republic directed at the peacemakers really had any impact on events in Ukraine. When its work was finally over, the Paris Peace Conference merely confirmed on paper what had already been decided in the field – namely, the division of western Ukrainian (former Austro-Hungarian) territories among the new states of Poland and Czechoslovakia and the expanded Kingdom of Romania.

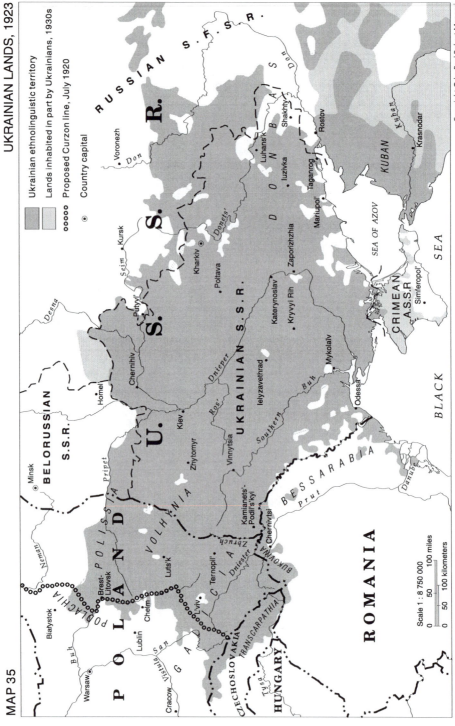

MAP 35

UKRAINIAN LANDS, 1923

Ukrainian ethnolinguistic territory

Lands inhabited in part by Ukrainians, 1930s

ooooo Proposed Curzon line, July 1920

⊙ Country capital

Copyright © by Paul Robert Magocsi

The Paris Peace Conference

The instruments through which the new political realities were recognized consisted of a series of peace treaties, signed at various palaces just outside the French capital, between the victorious Allies and Associated Powers and the defeated Central Powers, is known as the Paris Peace Conference. The first and ultimately the most controversial of these treaties was signed with Germany on 28 June 1919 at Louis XIV's former palace of Versailles. The Versailles treaty had no direct bearing on Ukrainian lands except that it noted – but postponed – a decision on the eastern frontiers of Poland, which would be "subsequently determined by the principal Allied and Associated Powers."[1] Poland was obliged, however, to accept at Versailles a treaty which guaranteed full rights and numerous religious, educational, linguistic, and other privileges to minorities living within its borders.

The next treaty was signed with Austria on 10 September 1919 at the palace of St Germain-en-Laye. The St Germain treaty did have a direct bearing on northern Bukovina and Transcarpathia. All of Bukovina, including Chernivtsi and the northern Ukrainian-inhabited portion of the old Austrian province, was recognized as part of the Kingdom of Romania. Similarly, all the "Ruthene territory south of the Carpathians" was recognized as part of the new republic of Czechoslovakia, and it was to be endowed with the "fullest degree of self-government compatible with the unity of the Czecho-Slovak state."[2] The St Germain decision on Transcarpathia was later reconfirmed in a separate treaty signed with Hungary at Trianon on 4 June 1920.

As for eastern Galicia, the Treaty of St Germain did not award this territory to Poland, as is frequently but incorrectly assumed. Rather, article 91 of the treaty stated that with regard to Galicia as a whole, Poland was merely its military occupant and that the region's actual sovereign remained the Allied and Associated Powers. Because of Galicia's unsettled international status, which was related to the whole question of Poland's eastern boundary, the Paris mission of the West Ukrainian National Republic (headed by Vasy Paneiko and, later, Stepan Vytvyts'kyi) lobbied hard for a favorable resolution regarding the eastern half of the former Habsburg province. The Peace Conference's Commission for Polish Affairs on the Council of Ambassadors even submitted a proposal, in September 1919, for an autonomous province of eastern Galicia, but three months later this idea was rejected by the Poles.

In 1921 and 1922, the Galician question was discussed at the newly established League of Nations in Geneva and at several international conferences in western Europe (Genoa, Prague, London). By 1923, the Council of Ambassadors, overwhelmed with more pressing international problems in western Europe, had grown tired of the Galician question. In March of that year, it simply relinquished its theoretical authority over the region and awarded to Poland all of Galicia from Cracow to the Zbruch River. Only then did it become clear that the almost unwavering faith placed in the Allied Powers by the leaders of the West Ukrainian National Republic had been entirely unwarranted. After 1923, Galicia was internationally recognized as Polish territory.

Soviet Ukraine and the Soviet Union

If the authority of the peacemakers in Paris was at best tenuous in western Ukrainian lands, in Dnieper Ukraine it was non-existent. One example was a proposal of the Allies (signed by then British foreign minister, Lord Curzon) submitted in July 1920 at the height of the Polish-Soviet war as an armistice line and potential boundary between the warring powers. Although of great importance later, the Curzon Line, as it came to be known, was at the time of its formulation completely ignored. Instead, decisions on boundaries were to be determined by the outcome of the war between Poland and Soviet Russia (in which the latter's ally, Soviet Ukraine, was also involved). As a result of an armistice reached in October 1920 and a final treaty signed at Riga on 18 March 1921, Poland agreed to recognize both Soviet Russia and Soviet Ukraine; however, the final Polish-Ukrainian boundary was much farther east of the Curzon Line, leaving Ukrainian-inhabited eastern Galicia, southern Podlachia, western Volhynia, and western Polissia all within Poland.

As for Soviet Ukraine, in theory it was independent and linked with Soviet Russia (officially the Russian Soviet Federated Socialist Republic) only by a treaty of alliance concluded on 28 December 1920. It is significant to note, however, that this treaty of alliance between two ostensibly independent states actually made both the Ukrainian military and the Ukrainian economy (including domestic and foreign trade) subject to decisions made in Moscow by the All-Russian Communist (Bolshevik) party. Initially, this left only foreign affairs, agriculture, justice, and education under Soviet Ukrainian jurisdiction. In spite of its technical status as an independent state, Soviet Ukrainian diplomatic activity ceased almost immediately. Then, in February 1922, the diplomatic prerogatives of Soviet Ukraine were, like those of other "sovereign" Soviet republics, delegated to Soviet Russia. In essence, Soviet Ukraine and its governmental apparatus, led by the Communist party (Bolshevik) of Ukraine – which owed its own existence to the presence of the Red Army – became completely subordinate to the All-Russian Communist (Bolshevik) party and the Soviet government in Moscow. The relationship of Ukraine and other Soviet republics to Soviet Russia was clarified in the months following the formation of the Union of Soviet Socialist Republics in December 1922. The new Soviet Union was nominally a federal state made up of four Soviet socialist republics: the Russian Soviet Federated Socialist Republic, the Ukrainian S.S.R., the Belorussian S.S.R., and the Transcaucasian S.F.S.R. Subsequently, three new republics were carved out of the Russian S.F.S.R. – the Turkmen S.S.R. (1925), the Uzbek S.S.R. (1925), the Tadzhik S.S.R. (1929) – and the Transcaucasian S.F.S.R. was divided into the three separate republics of Azerbaijan, Armenia, and Georgia. This meant that by 1929 the Soviet Union consisted of nine republics.

According to the Soviet Union's first constitution, promulgated on 31 January 1924, governmental authority was nominally divided between the federal level in Moscow and the constituent republics, including Soviet Ukraine. The authority left to the republics, however, was steadily reduced. The December 1920 treaty of alliance between Soviet Russia and Soviet Ukraine, for instance, had already

Treaty of Union between the Russian Soviet Federated Socialist Republic and the Ukrainian Soviet Socialist Republic

The governments of the Russian Socialist Federated Soviet Republic (S.F.S.R.) and the Ukrainian Socialist Soviet Republic (S.S.R.), proceeding from the declaration on the rights of peoples to self-determination as declared by the Great Proletarian Revolution, and recognizing the independence and sovereignty of each other as well as the need to consolidate their power for purposes of self-defense and of economic reconstruction, have decided to conclude the present workers' and peasants' treaty of union for which they have nominated the following representatives:

For the Soviet Russian government – the chairman of the Council of People's Commissars, Vladimir Il'ich Lenin, and the People's Commissar for Foreign Affairs, Georgii Vasilevich Chicherin; for the Soviet Ukrainian government – the chairman of the Council of People's Commissars and the People's Commissars for Foreign Affairs, Khristiian Georgievich Rakovskii.

The aforementioned representatives, with the powers invested in them, have agreed to the following:

1. The Russian S.F.S.R. and the Ukrainian S.S.R. agree to a military and economic union.

2. Both states consider it necessary to declare that the obligations which they are taking upon themselves in relationship to each other can only serve the general interests of the workers and peasants, inclusive of the present union treaty between the two republics, although the fact that the territory of the Ukrainian S.S.R. previously belonged to the former Russian Empire does not imply any obligations on the part of the Ukrainian S.S.R. toward that former entity, whatever such obligations might be.

3. For the better realization of the goals set out in paragraph 1, both governments declare the formation of the following joint commissariats: (1) defense; (2) national economy; (3) foreign trade; (4) finances; (5) employment; (6) transportation; (7) postal and telegraph services.

4. The unified people's commissariats of both republics are part of the Council of People's Commissars of the Russian S.F.S.R. and they have in the Council of People's Commissars of the Ukrainian S.S.R. their own authorized representatives who have been approved and are responsible to the All-Ukrainian Central Executive Committee and Congress of Soviets.

5. The procedure and form of internal administration for the joint commissariats will be decided upon by mutual agreement between the two governments.

6. The leadership and control of the united commissariats will be determined by the All-Russian Congress of Soviets of Workers,' Peasants,' and Soldiers'

Deputies as well as by the All-Russian Central Executive Committee, to which the Ukrainian S.S.R. will send its representatives on the basis of a decision of the All-Russian Congress of Soviets.

7. The present treaty is subject to ratification in compliance with the highest legal authorities of both republics.

The original text is presented for signature on two copies in the Russian and Ukrainian languages in the city of Moscow, 28 December 1920.

SOURCE: *Radians'ke budivnytstvo na Ukraïni v roky hromadians'koï viiny,1919–1920: zbirnyk dokumentiv i materialiv* (Kiev 1957), pp. 182–183.

placed military and economic affairs entirely in the hands of Moscow. The 1924 Soviet constitution reduced further Soviet Ukraine's powers, giving to the central government (1) authority to lay down general principles controlling education, justice, and health; (2) control over the exploitation of natural resources, including the use of surface land; (3) power to annul decisions of the union republics; and (4) authority to handle the foreign affairs of each republic. Thus, by the beginning of 1924, Soviet Ukraine and the other Soviet republics had become little more than regional entities within the Moscow-dominated Union of Soviet Socialist Republics. Still, at least during the first few years of the Soviet Union's existence Soviet Ukraine managed to maintain a degree of control over its own economic, political, and, especially cultural destiny. It is these aspects of Ukrainian development that will be addressed next.

43

Soviet Ukraine: The Struggle for Autonomy

By the fall of 1920, the Soviet Ukrainian government, backed by the Red Army, was in control of most of the nine "Ukrainian" provinces that had formerly been part of the Russian Empire. In the "revolutionary" Soviet society coming into being, Ukraine had to have a new governing structure. It also had to have a new capital. Already in early 1920, the choice fell on Kharkiv, the center of the leftist Bolshevik movement during the revolutionary era (as opposed to "counter-revolutionary" Kiev, the seat of the "bourgeois-nationalist" Ukrainian National Republic). As such, Kharkiv was transformed through a massive urban construction program in order that it could house governmental, Communist party, cultural, and educational institutions befitting the center of a Soviet republic.

It remained unclear, however, to what degree the new Soviet Ukrainian government was to be similar to, separate from, or subordinate to the all-Russian Soviet government based in Moscow. The answer to these questions was worked out during the next two decades, that is, from about 1920 until the outbreak of World War II in 1939. During this period, two trends evolved in Soviet Ukraine. One was a struggle for political, economic, and cultural autonomy; the other was an effort to integrate all aspects of Ukrainian life in the larger Soviet society.

Although it is true that these two fundamentally conflictual processes often occurred simultaneously, it is possible to make chronological distinctions based on the relative strength of the efforts to achieve autonomy as opposed to integration. In this regard, the years 1920 to 1927 might be considered the high point of the trend toward Ukrainian autonomy. They were followed by a transitional period, from 1928 to 1932, when the central Soviet government and Soviet Ukraine began to redefine their policies and priorities. Subsequently, the years 1933 to 1939 witnessed a series of developments that definitively set Soviet Ukraine on a course of full integration with the rest of Soviet society.

The government of Soviet Ukraine

The administrative framework of Soviet Ukrainian society derived from the revolutionary era and was founded on the Bolshevik-controlled councils (soviets) of workers,' peasants,' and soldiers' deputies – later, simply the councils (soviets) of workers' deputies. From the smallest to the largest, each administrative unit – village, town, city, district (*raion*), and region (*oblast'*) – had its own council (soviet) of workers' deputies. The country's highest legislative unit was a unicameral parliament known first as the All-Ukrainian Congress of Soviets, comprised of workers,' peasants,' and soldiers' deputies, which after 1937 became the Supreme Soviet (Verkhovna Rada) of Soviet Ukraine. When the Congress of Soviets was not in session (it met only twice a year for a few days), its legislative and executive functions were carried out by a fifteen-member executive committee. There were also people's commissariats, or ministries, to administer the various branches of state operation. Finally, there was the Council of People's Commissars, later the Council of Ministers. The council was headed by a chairman, who was roughly the equivalent of a premier in European parliamentary democracies. The council's role was to formulate legislation introduced in the Supreme Soviet and to carry out policy decisions made by the all-Soviet government in Moscow.

Soviet Ukraine's relationship to Moscow was of crucial importance, and following a period of initial vagueness it became clear only in 1922. When Soviet Ukraine's first constitution was promulgated in March 1919, it was at the same time decided that close economic and administrative ties should be established with Soviet Russia. In practice, this meant that the Soviet Ukrainian commissariats (ministries) of defense, communication, and economy were to be subordinate to the central ministries in Moscow. This arrangement was confirmed by a treaty signed on 28 December 1920 (see text insert in chapter 42) that established an economic and military union between Soviet Russia and Soviet Ukraine. Soviet Ukraine remained a "sovereign state," however, and conducted diplomatic relations with other states. Not surprisingly, the lines of authority between Soviet Russia and Soviet Ukraine were often blurred. They were not clarified until the period between December 1922, when the Union of Soviet Socialist Republics (for short, the Soviet Union) was formed, and January 1924, when a constitution for the new state was promulgated.

Within the new union, Soviet Ukraine became one of four republics, along with those established in Russia, Belarus, and Transcaucasia. The supreme legislative organ of the state was the Congress of Soviets (later, the Supreme Soviet), composed of two chambers: (1) the Soviet of the Union, whose members were elected (one deputy for every 300,000 people) regardless of national or republic origin; and (2) the Soviet of Nationalities, which represented sixty nationalities, with a fixed number of deputies from union republics, autonomous republics, autonomous regions, and national districts. The Congress of Soviets, later the Supreme Soviet, elected the thirty-seven-member Presidium, which effectively was the highest permanently functioning organ of state power. The Presidium was headed by a chairman (analogous to a president in other countries), and its role was to direct the state's major domestic and all foreign affairs. The legislative decisions of the Supreme Soviet were carried out by the Council of People's Commissars, later the Council of Ministers, the highest organ of state power. The actual functioning of the state administration was carried out by specific commissariats or ministries, which, depending on the portfolio, were all-union ministries or joint union-republic ministries. Within this new governmental structure, deputies and officials from Soviet Ukraine could and did serve in various levels of the republic and all-union governments. In theory, the Soviet Union was a voluntary federal entity whose component republics had the right to secede. In practice, since any changes in the union would have to be brought about by the federal government, legal secession was impossible.

The Communist party (Bolshevik) of Ukraine

Notwithstanding the existence of a Soviet Ukrainian government with various levels of authority, decisions about the relationship between Soviet Ukraine and Soviet Russia were determined not by the governments of these countries, but rather by the All-Russian Communist (Bolshevik) party in Moscow. From the very beginning, the source of political legitimization in Soviet Ukraine was the Communist party (Bolshevik) of Ukraine, the CP(b)U. There were elections to the various Councils of Workers and to the Supreme Soviet, but voters were always given a single slate of candidates, most if not all of whom were Communists. Certainly, all members of the Supreme Soviet's Presidium and of the Council of Ministers and the heads of the various ministries had to be Communists. Therefore, while the Soviet Ukrainian government may have been a structurally distinct entity, its personnel was drawn from CP(b)U ranks. Since according to Bolshevik practice as determined by Lenin the party was to be a tightly knit body of dedicated professionals following clear lines of command and military discipline, all members were required to carry out party directives. Put another way, government leaders and functionaries were simply carrying out policies determined in Moscow.

CP(b)U policies were not always clear-cut, however, especially during the early 1920s. The party itself seemed foreign to Ukraine. From a low point of fewer than 5,000 members in mid-1918, CP(b)U ranks began to grow again in 1919. The vast majority of new members were drawn not from Dnieper Ukraine, but rather from among the demobilized Russian soldiers who had fought in the Red Army during the revolution. As late as 1922, non-ethnic Ukrainians comprised 77 percent of what then was the 56,000-member CP(b)U. With few exceptions, the non-ethnic Ukrainian leadership and rank-and-file were ill disposed to the idea of a distinct Ukrainian political or cultural entity, even if it were Communist.

Regardless of the views of its membership, the CP(b)U was not an independent party, like other Communist parties in Europe, but rather a branch of the All-Russian, later All-Union Communist (Bolshevik) party in Moscow, whose directives it was required to follow. Yet despite the Bolshevik principles of party discipline and subordination to the Moscow leadership, the CP(b)U did include leaders and rank-and-file members who strove to create a party and a Soviet Ukrainian government that would be independent of Moscow. Nor was the drive for political autonomy limited to certain elements within the CP(b)U. Post-revolutionary Soviet Ukrainian life was still marked by flux and even by a degree of pluralism. And while political parties other than the Communists were banned, Soviet Ukraine had two other Communist parties besides the CP(b)U that for a time functioned openly.

The second Communist party had its beginnings in May 1918, when left-wing members of the Ukrainian Socialist-Revolutionary party formed the non-Bolshevik Ukrainian Socialist-Revolutionary party of Communist Fighters. Associated with the journal *Borot'ba* (The Struggle) and popularly known as the Borotbists (Borot'bisty), they were a peasant-based party that favored independence from the Russian-dominated Bolshevik leadership. After a failed attempt at accommodation with the CP(b)U, the Borotbists and other left-wing elements formed the Ukrainian Communist party of Borotbists. This new party numbered 15,000 members – nearly as large as the CP(b)U, which at the time had about 16,500 members. The Borotbists continued their call for greater autonomy for Ukraine, and in early 1920 they tried to enter the Comintern, or Communist International, the self-proclaimed Moscow-based Communist leadership of the world socialist movement, as a distinct party. The Borotbist request for entry into the Comintern was turned down by Lenin, and in March 1920 the party disbanded. More than 4,000 of its members were admitted to the CP(b)U. Among the Borotbists to join the former rival party were Vasyl' Blakytnyi, Oleksander Shums'kyi, and Hryhorii Hryn'ko. These and other former Borotbists were to pursue from within the CP(b)U the goals of federalization and, later, cultural autonomy for Soviet Ukraine.

The third party was known as the Ukrainian Communist party, or the Ukapists for short, a name derived from its Ukrainian initials (UKP). Formed in January 1920, the Ukapists were made up of varied elements: independentists from the Ukrainian Social-Democratic Workers' party, former Borotbists who did not join the Bolsheviks, and some members of the federalist opposition (Iurii Lapchyns'kyi) who had left the CP(b)U. With never more than a few hundred members, the Ukapists were a Marxist party that adopted the ideology of national Communism. As an opposition group (represented by the newspaper *Chervonyi prapor*), they criticized the policies of the CP(b)U-dominated Soviet Ukrainian government and applied unsuccessfully on two occasions to enter the Comintern. After a second rejection, the Comintern ordered the Ukapist party to dissolve itself, which it did in early 1925. The party's members were admitted into the CP(b)U.

In such an environment, the only possible way to struggle for autonomy was from within the ranks of the country's dominant party, the CP(b)U. At the time, opposition to centralism was dubbed "nationalist deviation," even though such deviation was promoted in Soviet Ukraine by Bolsheviks from the pre-revolutionary era such as Khristiian Rakovskii and Mykola Skrypnyk who had been and remained opposed to Ukrainian nationalism. Those who favored federalism believed that Communism would be enhanced in Soviet Ukraine if the country were allowed to function independently of the new Soviet Russian government and party bureaucracy in Moscow. From his post as head of the government, the former internationalist Rakovskii began in late 1921 to push the limits of federalism by encouraging Soviet Ukrainian diplomatic activity. For instance, between 1920 and 1923 Soviet Ukraine concluded forty-eight international treaties, and it was recognized de jure as a sovereign state by nine countries (including Germany, Poland, Italy, and Turkey) and de facto by three others (including Great Britain) and the League of Nations. While it is true that no treaty was signed by the Soviet Ukrainian government which was not approved in advance by Moscow, the very fact that foreign relations were carried on at all gave support to those Ukrainian Communists who favored some form of political autonomy or equality in any federal relationship with Russia.

Rakovskii and Skrypnyk also took an active part in discussions within the All-Russian Communist (Bolshevik) party in Moscow regarding relations between the various Soviet republics. Discussion on that subject intensified in 1922, when the new general secretary of the all-Russian party, Iosif Stalin, began pressing for the unification of the various Soviet republics. He openly criticized the "right of nations to self-determination," and he proposed that Ukraine and all other Soviet republics enter the Russian S.F.S.R., albeit with a degree of autonomy. Stalin's view, known at the time as "autonomization," was opposed by Bolshevik leaders in the various republics. Even more important was the criticism of Lenin, who considered the approach of Stalin and his supporters tantamount to Great Russian chauvinism and a revival of the idea of a "one and indivisible" *(edinaia i nedelimaia)* Russia.

In response to Lenin's criticism, Stalin backed away from autonomization and pretended to side with republic leaders who were calling for the creation of a new state formation. The new state came into being in December 1922 as the Union of Soviet Socialist Republics – the Soviet Union. Although the republics maintained their distinct identities as theoretically equal members of the new union, the crucial question was the relationship between the all-union center in Moscow and the union republics. The dilemma was to be resolved in the course of 1923 during the debates about a constitution for the new state. By this time, Lenin was physically incapacitated (he lost the power of speech in March 1923 and died in January 1924), and Stalin was thereby encouraged to renew his drive to transform the Soviet Union into as centralized a state as possible. In the absence of Lenin, the "federalist" opposition was left largely to republic leaders, among whom the most outspoken were Bolsheviks from Georgia and Soviet Ukraine's Rakovskii and Skrypnyk.

In the end, Stalin and the centralists won the day. Among other matters, the union government in Moscow was given responsibility for all international relations; internal as well as external trade; the armed forces; economic development (including use of all surface and subsurface natural resources); the judiciary; the monetary and banking system; and taxes at the union, republic, and local levels. With the creation of the Soviet Union and the final passage of its constitution in January 1924, it became clear that any subsequent efforts to obtain serious political autonomy for Soviet Ukraine would be in vain. The supporters of autonomy therefore turned their attention in another direction – toward culture. The result was the phenomenon known as Ukrainianization.

The policy of Ukrainianization

Ukrainianization was part of an all-Soviet policy known as "indigenization" *(korenizatsiia)*. It was implemented over the course of a decade beginning in 1923, whereby the CP(b)U hoped to legitimize its rule in Soviet Ukraine by attracting to its ranks a broader spectrum of the local population. Particular emphasis was given to promoting the Ukrainian language and culture. From the standpoint of the All-Russian Communist party and the CP(b)U, indigenization made logical sense, because if successful it would assure centralized control of the countryside through local, "homegrown" cadres. But in a so-called revolutionary society in which social and economic transformation needed to be carried out in the most

COMMUNISM AND THE NATIONALITY QUESTION

Soviet Ukraine, following the lead of Soviet Russia, was ruled by a Communist party which traced its ideological roots to the nineteenth-century German political philosopher and founder of scientific socialism Karl Marx, and his disciple Friedrich Engels. Marxist philosophy had an enormous impact on socialists in the former Russian Empire, among whom was the Bolshevik leader, Vladimir Lenin. Lenin adapted Marxism to conditions in tsarist Russia by creating his own ideology or "practical guide" to political action, which came to be known as Marxism-Leninism.

Marx and Engels constructed a philosophical system which analyzed human historical development and postulated a universally applicable body of social observations which ostensibly could both describe humanity's past evolution and predict or determine its future. Among the more important principles of Marxist philosophy was that of dialectical materialism. Materialism is a theory asserting that only matter exists and that all material phenomena can be observed and scientifically explained. With respect to human society, Marx believed that the most important factor was the economic one – that is, that every individual's action was determined by his or her economic status and interests. In economic terms, every society consisted of only two categories of people, who were differentiated by their relationship to the means of production. Some owned the land, capital, factories, and shops; others did not. All societies, therefore, were reducible to two classes of people: the owners or exploiters, and the workers or exploited.

The dialectical aspect of materialism provided the dynamic element in Marx's philosophy. Everything in life changes all the time, and these changes follow the laws of the dialectic – from thesis, to antithesis, and finally to synthesis. Moreover, these "social" laws follow a rigorous and scientifically established pattern. With regard to historical and socioeconomic evolution, there are several stages through which every society must pass: the slave-owning stage, feudalism, capitalism, socialism, and communism. The final and qualitatively highest stage, communism, promised a social setting in which there would be equality among all people and therefore no exploitation by one class of another.

It was this philosophical system of Marx and Engels that Lenin adapted to conditions in Russia. Since the Russian Empire lagged behind more developed societies in western Europe and in terms of social evolution it was somewhere between the stages of feudalism and bourgeois capitalism, Lenin argued that revolution would speed up the unfolding of the inevitable dialectical march of history. Lenin's ideas on revolution were developed after 1903, following discord within the Russian Social-Democratic Workers' party, which split into the Lenin-led Bolsheviks and the Mensheviks. To carry out the revolution that would hasten the evolutionary process and bring about a socialist and eventually a communist society, Lenin created a tightly knit group of dedicated revolutionaries, the so-called vanguard of the proletariat. This vanguard would lead the working exploited classes into a new historical era.

When, in November 1917, Lenin's Bolsheviks somewhat unexpectedly took over the reins of power in the Russian Empire, they emphasized the role of the Bolshevik party as the undisputed leader during a period known as the dictatorship of the proletariat. This period was supposed to be temporary, to last only until the achievement of a classless, communist society. Among the implications of the dictatorship of the proletariat for Lenin was ruthless party-imposed discipline. The imposition of discipline was justified by ideology and achieved by the creation of an extensive secret police force. As for ideology, Marxism provided a philosophical framework based on scientific "laws." Since Marxism-Leninism was a science, anyone who opposed it could be proven absolutely and demonstrably wrong. Opponents, whoever they were, either were lacking in knowledge or philosophically misguided (a shortcoming that could be corrected by "re-education" in prisons and forced labor camps), or they were irredeemable class enemies of the new order. And since this new order reflected the inevitable march of history, class enemies could justifiably be eliminated, whenever and in whatever way necessary, as obstacles to scientifically predetermined social progress. The elimination of real or suspected class enemies was carried out by a virtual army of secret police, established by the Bolshevik regime as early as 7 January 1918. From that time until the dissolution of the Soviet Union in 1991, the secret police had several different names: the Cheka (1918), GPU (1922), OGPU (1923), NKVD (1934) NKGB (1941), MGB (1946), and KGB (1954).

Since Marxism-Leninism purported to be an all-inclusive philosophical system, it is not surprising that, in the context of Russian and eastern European society, it offered ideological guidelines regarding the nationality question. Both Lenin and his Bolshevik colleague Stalin, who most often wrote on this subject, believed from the very outset that the "rights of nations are not an isolated self-contained question, but part of the general question of the proletarian revolution, a part which must be dealt with from the point of view of the whole."* Moreover, for the Bolsheviks it was only among the proletariat that nationalities were represented. The bourgeoisie, the feudal aristocracy, and the industrialists, in their view, did not legitimately belong to any nationality.

Since true nationalities consisted exclusively of the proletariat, it followed that the Bolsheviks were opposed to the oppression of nationalities or national minorities living in multinational states or empires. The argument against national oppression was taken up in 1913 by Stalin in a brochure entitled *Marxism and the National Question*, in which he accepted what he called the principle of the "right of self-determination." "The right to self-determination," Stalin wrote, "means that a nation can arrange its life according to its own will. It has the right to arrange its life on the basis of autonomy. It has the right to enter into federal relations with other nations. It has the right to complete secession. Nations are sovereign and all nations are equal."* It might seem from this statement that national interests were more important than class interests. Support, however, would not be given to every national demand. "On the contrary," continued Stalin, "it is the duty of Social-Democrats [as the Bolsheviks were officially known before the war] to conduct agitation and to endeavor to influence the will of nations so that they may arrange their affairs in the way that will best suit the interests of the proletariat."*

The seeming contradiction between Bolshevik proclamations on behalf of the right to self-determination of nations and their continued support for the primacy of proletarian class interests can easily be explained in the context of the Marxist dialectical view of history. As Lenin asserted, nationalism and the nationalities it spawned represented just one phase in history, which eventually would "wither away." In their place would arise a nationless international society of workers, whose common proletarian class interests would unite them and override any linguistic or national differences.

Actually, Lenin identified two types of nationalism: (1) the nationalism of an oppressing country, which was a manifestation of the rivalry induced by the race for colonial markets; and (2) the nationalism of the subjected peoples who were exploited by colonial regimes. When the Leninist equation was applied to eastern Europe, tsarist Russian nationalism represented the oppressive type, Ukrainian nationalism the subjected type. In the end, both forms of nationalism were considered by Marxist-Leninists simply transitory social phenomena of the capitalist era of history. Accordingly, both were to be fought against because they had no intrinsic merit and were reactionary and harmful to the unity of the revolutionary class movement.

Nevertheless, as long as the capitalist (and in some cases imperialist) stage of society's development had not yet completely vanished, and as long as the new socialist stage was still struggling to replace them, there might be occasion to cooperate with and even foster the subjected type of nationalism, especially if such cooperation would help the cause of socialism. In his writings on imperialism, Lenin even speculated that revolutions were likely to occur in areas inhabited by nationally subjected peoples, which he referred to as the "weakest links" in the capitalist-imperialist system.

It was the potential political value of the subjected type of nationalism that prompted the Russian Bolsheviks and their Ukrainian counterparts to cooperate on occasion with Ukrainian National Republic, both in its Central Rada and Directory phases. Moreover, when the second attempt by the Soviet Ukrainian government to rule, between February and July 1919, failed in part because of its inability to appreciate the presumed national interests of the population, Lenin himself, at the Eighth Congress of the Russian Communist (Bolshevik) party in December 1919, submitted a resolution that obligated all party members "to facilitate in every way the removal of obstacles to the free development of the Ukrainian language and culture."† The Borotbist opposition had been calling for such a policy all along. Now Lenin, although not without opposition from internationalist elements in the CP(b)U, pushed for use of the Ukrainian language so that it could serve as "a weapon of communist education of the working masses." Marxist-Leninist ideological arguments finally won out, with the result that on 27 February 1920 the CP(b)U passed a decree guaranteeing the Ukrainian language equal status with Russian in all areas of life.

*J.V.Stalin, *Marxism and the Nationality Question* [1913] (New York 1935), pp. 1–3, 18–19, and 53.
†*Vos'maia konferentsii RKP(b) dekabr' 1919 goda* (Moscow 1961), p. 189.

rational and efficient manner – including the practical use of a single mode of communication, the Russian language – why should the Soviet state have been concerned with promoting non-Russian languages and cultures? Would it not have been simpler, and in the long run less problematic, to continue the already well advanced policy of russification begun under the tsars, a policy which could be implemented even more efficiently through the system of universal education promised by the new socialist state?

Some might argue, as certain contemporary Bolshevik leaders did, that as a result of World War I and the Ukrainian revolutionary era (during which millions of Ukrainian peasant recruits interacted with and discovered their differences from other nationalities) a substantial proportion of the rural population became nationally conscious and was therefore beyond assimilation. Notwithstanding this practical reality, the Soviet government's actions were determined first and foremost by ideological strictures that were the product of its understanding of Communism and the nationality question.

This did not mean that the CP(b)U suddenly had a change of heart from its traditional internationalism and indifference to Ukrainian and other non-Russian cultures and languages. The party, in fact, continued to be dominated by a non-ethnic Ukrainian majority whose leaders were opposed especially to the cultural and linguistic aspects of Ukrainianization. This group was led by the CP(b)U first secretary, the russified Volga German Emmanuïl Kviring, and by its second secretary, the Ukrainian-born opponent of Ukrainian distinctiveness, Dmitrii Lebed' (Dmytro Lebed'). Lebid' espoused the theory of "the struggle of two cultures," according to which he argued that the "higher" Russian culture of the urban proletariat should remain dominant in society and in no way be replaced by the "lower" Ukrainian culture of the backward countryside. As a way of pushing their point of view, the internationalists accused their opponents, in particular the former Borotbists and nationally conscious Ukrainians Shums'kyi and Blakytnyi, of "nationalist deviation" and tarred them and their supporters with accusations of "Shums'ky-ism."

Meanwhile, Moscow and particularly Stalin favored Ukrainianism, that aspect of indigenization (*korenizatsiia*), which, they hoped, would strengthen the CP(b)U's otherwise weak roots in the countryside. The result was that despite the opposition of Kviring and Lebed', in the summer of 1923 the CP(b)U adopted a program for Ukrainianization of the party apparatus, schools, and cultural-educational organizations. From that moment, the CP(b)U itself helped to transform the Soviet republic it headed into a country that was becoming Ukrainian in fact as well as in name.

The spread of Ukrainianization is reflected in and was fostered by several developments: (1) changes in the governmental leadership and in the administrative and demographic structure of the country, (2) the return of outstanding cultural leaders from the emigration, and (3) remarkable achievements in education and all areas of modern Ukrainian culture.

Ukrainianization, the governing elite, and demographic change

Although Kviring and Lebed' continued to head the CP(b)U, in July 1923 Vlas Chubar was appointed head of the Soviet Ukrainian government. Chubar was the first ethnic Ukrainian to hold this post, and he was essentially sympathetic to the Ukrainianization program. It was under his leadership that the first public decree on Ukrainianization was promulgated (1 August 1923), which aimed to "guarantee for the Ukrainian language a position to which it is entitled because of the numerical and other specific importance of the Ukrainian people on the territory of Soviet Ukraine."[1]

But despite such support from the highest levels of the government, Ukrainianization got off to a slow start. In order to speed up implementation of the new policy, in April 1925 the internationalist Kviring was replaced as first secretary of the CP(b)U by Lazar Kaganovich, a Ukrainian-born Jew and trusted associate of Stalin. Kaganovich was sent from Moscow to ukrainianize in a more vigorous manner the party and state apparatus. During the three years of his tenure as first secretary he pursued the task with energy and even pressed for the Ukrainianization of Red Army units stationed in Soviet Ukraine. Former nationalist-minded Borotbists purged from the CP(b)U in 1922 for "nationalist deviation" were brought back into political favor, among them Oleksander Shums'kyi, who was appointed to the influential post of commissar of education, and Hryhorii Hryn'ko, who was made commissar of state planning.

The implementation of Ukrainianization by a party that from its beginnings had been internationalist in orientation was made possible not only as a result of the placement of certain pro-Ukrainian leaders in key positions, but also because of a change in the composition of the rank and file. The indigenization program, after all, meant "rooting" the party in the local region, and this is exactly what happened. For instance, whereas in 1924 only 33 percent of the CP(b)U members were ethnic Ukrainian, by 1933 that figure had nearly doubled, to 60 percent. Simultaneously, the number of ethnic Ukrainians in the Communist Youth League (Komsomol) increased from 59 percent in 1925 to 72 percent in 1933.

A change in the administrative structure of Soviet Ukraine was also, in part, related to the general move in the direction of Ukrainianization. During the early years of Soviet rule, the former tsarist provinces (gubernii) were retained, and a few others added. Moreover, as in tsarist times, the central Soviet government in Moscow often dealt directly with the provinces, thereby bypassing the Ukrainian

UKRAINIANIZATION

The implementation of Ukrainianization followed the promulgation of several internal and public decrees. In June 1923, the Central Committee of the CP(b)U adopted a set of resolutions regarding Ukrainianization in party work, and in July it published a decree that dealt with schools and educational institutions. These guidelines were incorporated into a resolution, dated 1 August 1923, that was adopted by the Council of People's Commissars and the Ukrainian Executive Committee of the Soviet Ukrainian government. The resolution's preamble was followed by twenty-six paragraphs outlining the principles of and the means by which Ukrainianization was to be implemented. With regard to language, all government employees who within one year of the decree's publication still did not know Ukrainian would lose their jobs and be unable to hold any governmental past until they had "a knowledge of Ukrainian" (paragraphs 21 and 22). An excerpt from the preamble of the 1 August resolution follows.

The peaceful conditions that have resulted from the victory over the counterrevolution and [1921] famine have made it possible for the Soviet government to extend further the liberating nationality policy which the October [Bolshevik] Revolution began following the removal of rule by landlords and capitalists who, together with the tsarist bureaucracy in Ukraine, functioned not only as exploiters of the workers and peasants but also as russifiers who persecuted and oppressed the Ukrainian nationality.

Despite a certain lack of commitment on the part of activists on the cultural front, the Soviet government in Ukraine had during its brief existence achieved much for the development of Ukrainian culture, schools, and publications. Nevertheless, those efforts have not been enough to remove the inequality between the [Russian and Ukrainian] cultures that is the result of centuries of repression.

For that reason, the most pressing task of the government is to remove the inequalities in the realm of national cultures. ... And to achieve that goal it is necessary to increase the Ukrainianization of the entire government apparatus. ...

The workers' and peasants' government of Ukraine considers it necessary that the state will concentrate its efforts as soon as possible on the spreading of knowledge of the Ukrainian language. The formal distinction that until now has existed between the two most widely used languages in Ukraine – Ukrainian and Russian – is inadequate. The relatively slow development of Ukrainian schools and Ukrainian culture in general, the lack of suitable textbooks, and the lack of sufficiently trained personnel have caused a situation whereby the Russian language for all practical purposes is dominant.

In order to remove such inequality, the workers' and peasants' government will initiate a series of practical measures which, while respecting the equal rights of the languages of all nationalities in Ukraine, will guarantee for the Ukrainian language

> a position to which it is entitled because of the numerical and other specific impor-
> tance of the Ukrainian people on the territory of Soviet Ukraine.
>
> SOURCE: Taras Hunczak and Roman Sol'chanyk, eds., *Ukraïns'ka suspil'no-polïtychna dumka v 20 stolitti: dokumenty i materiialy*, Vol. II (New York 1983), pp. 77–78.

republic governmental level. In 1923, Soviet Ukraine was redivided into fifty-three *okruhy* (regions), which in turn were subdivided into *raiony* (districts) that replaced the former tsarist *volosti*. Finally, in 1925 the provinces (*gubernii*) were abolished, and the status of Soviet Ukraine was thereby raised. The all-union government in Moscow now had to deal directly with the Soviet Ukrainian government, since there was no possibility of recourse to another administrative entity.

Of even greater long-term importance than administrative changes was what might be called the demographic revolution that had been set in motion, in particular the migration from the countryside to the cities. Since the nineteenth century, nationalist leaders had been well aware that for their movements to survive they would have to take control of urban areas. In other words, the national culture and language they promoted would have to become the natural vehicle of expression in cities and towns, where the decisions about a country's administrative, economic, cultural, and educational orientation were made. Control of cities, therefore, was of crucial significance to emerging nationalities. In this regard, the Ukrainian movement was helped by the general Soviet policy of industrialization (see chapter 44) and by Soviet Ukraine's policy of Ukrainianization.

The wartime and revolutionary era, with its attacks on towns and cities and the loss of food produce as a result of the destruction of agricultural exchange relationships, saw a marked decline in Dnieper Ukraine's overall urban population: from 5.6 million in 1914 to only 4.2 million in 1920. The reconstruction of the 1920s, however, allowed for a rapid growth in the urban population, with the result that by 1928 Soviet Ukraine's cities had reached their prewar level. This process was to continue: whereas in 1920 only 15 percent of Soviet Ukraine's population lived in cities, by 1939 the figure had more than doubled, to 36.2 percent.

The influx of ethnic Ukrainians from the countryside, coupled with a return on the part of russified urban dwellers to the identity of their rural forefathers, not only increased the size but also changed significantly the national composition of cities. Whereas in 1920 ethnic Ukrainians represented only 32 percent of the country's urban population, that figure rose steadily (47 in 1926), to over 58 percent by 1939. The percentage of ethnic Ukrainians increased dramatically not only in Kiev (42 percent in 1926) and other Right Bank cities, but also in the industrial east, where Russians had traditionally dominated. Accordingly, by 1933, in three of the five largest industrial centers (Kharkiv, Luhans'k, and Zaporizhzhia) ethnic Ukrainians accounted for over half the population, while in a fourth, Katerynoslav/ Dnipropetrovs'k, the figure was 48 percent.

The face of Soviet Ukraine's cities was altered as well. As the CP(b)U Politburo member Volodymyr Zatons'kyi said in summarizing the government's attitude during the 1920s: "We will ensure that a Ukrainian ... when he goes to the city will not be russified. ... And yes, we will repaint [i.e., remove Russian from] the signs in towns."[2] Laws passed in 1925 hastened the process whereby the Ukrainian language came to be used in governmental business and on public signs, posters, and other official forms. The effort to create a new urban environment was symbolized by the replacement of many names associated with pre-revolutionary tsarist times: Katerynoslav became Dnipropetrovs'k; Oleksandrivs'k, Zaporizhzhia; Iuzivka, Stalino; Luhans'k, Voroshylovhrad; Bakhmut, Artemivs'k; and Ielyzavethrad, Zinovivs'k, then Kirovohrad.

The rise in Ukrainian-language publications was a graphic example of how Ukrainianization spread not only in the cities but also in the towns and villages. In the early 1920s, book production fell far below what it had been during the revolutionary years. In 1918, for instance, Ukrainian-language titles accounted for 70 percent of all books, but it was not until 1925 that Ukrainianization reached the book publishing industry, and not until 1930 that Ukrainian-language production surpassed what had been achieved during the revolutionary era. Ukrainian-language newspapers followed a similar pattern, falling precipitously from 127 titles during the revolutionary era to 30 (in a total circulation of only 9,700 copies) in 1922. The situation gradually began to change so that by 1926, there were 81 Ukrainian-language newspapers, representing 30 percent of total circulation. It was not until 1930 that the language of the press reflected more or less proportionally Soviet Ukraine's national composition. In that year, there were 552 Ukrainian-language newspapers, which accounted for 77 percent of total circulation. The high point was reached in 1932, when 92 percent of the country's newspaper circulation was in Ukrainian (1,278 titles with a 950,000 circulation).[3]

Ukrainianization and the return of the émigrés

The return of prominent Ukrainian-oriented politicians and scholars from the emigration in other parts of Europe and from Polish-ruled Galicia is a second sign that Ukrainianization was taking hold, and those who returned contributed to the implementation of the policy. As early as 1920, the former head of the Ukrainian National Republic's Directory, Volodymyr Vynnychenko, was invited to return home and offered the post of deputy premier and commissar of foreign affairs in the Soviet Ukrainian government. Although he quickly became disillusioned and, after a brief visit, returned to exile in the West, the very fact of the invitation seemed to suggest a more tolerant attitude on the part of the Soviet Ukrainian government, and prompted much discussion within émigré circles in western and central Europe as well as in Galicia. Many exiles began to consider seriously the possibility of returning to the Ukrainian homeland, even if it were a Soviet one. The policy of Ukrainianization in particular made Soviet rule seem tolerable and even attractive. Among those who returned were former political activists in the Ukrainian National Republic (Pavlo Khrystiuk, Mykola Chechel', Iurii Tiutiunnyk) and the West Ukrainian National Republic (Mykhailo Lozyns'kyi, Stepan

Rudnyts'kyi), many of them also distinguished scholars who took up leading positions in Soviet Ukraine's cultural establishment.

By far the most important of those who returned was the renowned historian, former president of the Shevchenko Scientific Society in L'viv, and first president of the Ukrainian National Republic's Central Rada Mykhailo S. Hrushevs'kyi. Hrushevs'kyi's arrival in Kiev in 1924 heralded the beginning of achievements in education and culture that are a third manifestation of the spread of Ukrainianization and that acted to stimulate it further. Hrushevs'kyi's presence was particularly significant for the All-Ukrainian Academy of Sciences. Within the academy, he revived the old historical section of the prewar Ukrainian Scientific Society, and himself headed it as well as the Archeographic Commission. He also revived or founded several new scholarly journals in which he and his disciples published the results of their research.

The academy as a whole, which had been founded in 1918 during the Hetmanate, managed to survive a period of retrenchment between 1920 and 1922. In the new environment of Ukrainianization, the number of its full-time researchers rose to 160 in 1924. During the presidency of the distinguished botanist Volodymyr Lyps'kyi, who was in office from 1922 to 1928, and the tenure of the renowned linguist and Orientalist Ahatanhel Kryms'kyi, who held the post of permanent secretary from 1918 to 1929, the number of scholarly works published by the academy rose steadily from 22 in 1923 to 136 in 1929. The activity of the academy also promoted work on standardization of the Ukrainian language, in consequence of which in some fields, especially in the natural sciences, Ukrainian was used as a medium in publications for the first time. Moreover, the Ukrainian academy devoted itself to the universal aspects of humanistic learning. It maintained contacts with other scholarly institutes throughout the world, and it supported research programs, for instance, in Arabic, Iranian, Hebrew, and Byzantine culture. In strictly Ukrainian subjects, the most marked advances were made in Ukrainian linguistics (numerous dictionaries were either published or begun) and in history, the field dominated by Hrushevs'kyi and his school. Besides the All-Ukrainian Academy of Sciences, each of the universities (renamed in 1920 institutes of people's education) had departments in Ukrainian subjects held by leading prewar scholars, such as the historians Dmytro Bahalii at Kharkiv, Mykhailo Slabchenko at Odessa, and Oleksander Ohloblyn at Kiev. Thus, the period of Ukrainianization after 1923 made possible the growth of Ukrainian scholarship to its most advanced level so far. Scholars in Soviet Ukraine were able to carry on the traditions established in Austrian Galicia before World War I and were permitted, at least until 1928, to operate in a relatively free intellectual atmosphere.

Ukrainianization in education

The future of scholarship, to say nothing of the Ukrainian nationality in general, depended on the younger generations, whose attitudes would be determined largely by the formal education they received. Here, too, under the direction of the

Soviet Ukrainian government, significant progress was made. It was a result of (1) the general Soviet emphasis on education, with its goal of eliminating illiteracy by 1927; and (2) the specific policies of Soviet Ukraine's Ministry of Education, which after 1923 was given a free hand in carrying out the government's Ukrainianization policy. That very year, the first of several education laws was passed decreeing that wherever ethnic Ukrainians predominated, instruction for all children must be in Ukrainian, and that in places where other peoples of Ukraine ("national minorities") formed compact groups, education in their respective native languages was guaranteed. Regardless of the main language of instruction, Ukrainian and Russian were required subjects in all schools throughout Soviet Ukraine.

The results were impressive. By 1933, the total number of students and teachers had increased threefold over prewar levels. Nor were adults forgotten. A wide network of literacy schools *(likpunkty)* was set up throughout the country. The result was a remarkable rise in the level of literacy, which in 1897 had stood at only 28 percent. By 1926, 64 percent of Soviet Ukraine's total population and 42 percent of its ethnic Ukrainian inhabitants were literate.

As the regime mounted its offensive against illiteracy, there inevitably arose the question of which language to use in the expanding educational establishment. Until 1923, the CP(b)U's theory of the "struggle of two cultures" favored Russian in the adult schools. With the implementation of Ukrainianization, however, there was a change of policy regarding language, with the result that by 1925, 81 percent of all adult literacy schools reportedly were using Ukrainian. From the standpoint of Ukrainian-language instruction, elementary schools fared even better. By the 1927–1928 school year, 82 percent of all schools at the elementary level were using Ukrainian, and 76 percent of the total school population was attending Ukrainian-language schools. Looked at in another way, by 1929 over 97 percent of all elementary students in Soviet Ukraine were enrolled in Ukrainian-language schools. The Ukrainianization of secondary schools *(profshkoly)* was as dramatic. Whereas in 1922 less than 1 percent of the secondary schools used Ukrainian as the language of instruction, by 1929 that figure had risen to 66 percent, with another 16 percent using both Ukrainian and Russian.

At the top of the Soviet Ukrainian educational system was the category, higher educational institution (*Vyshchyi Uchbovyi Zaklad*), the so-called VUZ, of which there were three types: (1) institutes of people's education (former universities), (2) technical colleges, and (3) workers' preparatory schools. The last were designed to prepare underqualified students for full entrance into the institutes (universities). By 1928, over 35,000 students, or nearly 57 percent of the total number enrolled in all three types of VUZy, were ethnic Ukrainians. In part because of the reluctance of the teaching staff to give up using Russian, the percentage of students in the VUZy who received instruction in the Ukrainian language increased only gradually, standing at only 42 percent in 1928. But all students were required to study Ukrainian history, language, literature, and economic geography, and well before the end of the decade knowledge of Ukrainian became a requirement for admission to and graduation from all institutions of higher learning. Indeed, by

the end of the 1920s a significantly large Ukrainian intelligentsia was being created for the first time in Dnieper Ukraine. This was a group educated in Ukrainian
and now able to pursue careers in urban settings that were becoming increasingly
Ukrainian in content as well as form.

Ukrainianization in the arts and literature

The period of Ukrainianization brought profound changes in other areas of culture. All the most modern currents in literature, painting, sculpture, the theater,
music, and the cinema made their way into Soviet Ukraine, where artists, whatever
their craft, strove to create new forms often based on a combination of traditional
motifs and highly avant-garde movements. The 1920s was, after all, perceived as
a period of great promise during which an egalitarian sociopolitical system could
be created. Such a hope was held in many echelons of Soviet society, and artists in
particular were caught up in the spirit of optimism.

The new creative environment was most evident in the experimental Berezil'
Theater (est. 1922) of the director Les' Kurbas; the modernistic canvases of painters like Mykhailo Boichuk and Anatolii Petryts'kyi; and the musical compositions
of Lev Revuts'kyi and Borys Liatoshyns'kyi as well as the writings of the musicolo-
gist Mykola Hrinchenko, who called on Ukrainian composers to create a body
of work that would be clearly distinguishable from the all-pervading influence of
Russian compositions. An entirely new art form, the cinema, also made its appearance during the 1920s. The cinema was especially welcomed by Soviet authorities
because of its ability to convey political and social messages through the visual
medium, accessible to large numbers of illiterate or semi-literate people. One of
the world's foremost directors during this period was the Ukrainian Oleksander
Dovzhenko, who not only worked in his homeland but used Ukrainian themes in
his most famous films – *Zvenyhora* (1927), *Arsenal* (1929), and the internationally
acclaimed classic *Zemlia* (1930).

A particular problem faced by the creative and analytical intelligentsia in Soviet
Ukraine was the degree to which new forms of Ukrainian art and literature should
diverge from the traditional formal dependence on Russian models. The Central
Committee of the CP(b)U itself sounded the clarion call in June 1926 for a distinct Ukrainian mode or form of cultural expression. While supporting the idea of
cooperation with the cultures of other peoples, the party nonetheless made it clear
that it stood for "the independent development of Ukrainian culture [and] for an
expression of all the creative forces of the Ukrainian people. The party stands for
the wide utilization by the Ukrainian socialist culture now under construction of
all the heritages of world culture, for a decisive break with the traditions of provincial narrowness, and for the creation of new cultural values adequate for the crea-
tiveness of a great class."[4]

Several writers made a conscious effort to break out of the mold of Romanticism and Realism that dominated Ukrainian literary life in the nineteenth century
and, instead, to imbue their work with currents and styles prevalent in avant-garde

western Europe. Among them were three poets whose best works coincided with the creatively free decade of the 1920s: the symbolist Pavlo Tychyna, the neo-classicist Maksym Ryl's'kyi, and the futurist Mykhail (Mykhailo) Semenko.

Other Ukrainian-language writers, in their search for new cultural values that would fashion a socialist culture reflective of the needs of the peasantry and proletariat, established literary groups. The best known of the groups were the Association of Revolutionary Peasant Writers (Pluh, 1922–1932), founded by Serhii Pylypenko; the Association of Proletarian Writers (Hart, 1923–1925), founded by Vasyl' Blakytnyi (pseudonym of Vasyl' Ellans'kyi); and the Free Academy of Proletarian Literature (VAPLITE, 1925–1928), founded by Mykola Khvyl'ovyi. VAPLITE and Khvyl'ovyi in particular carried the cultural implications of the Ukrainianization policy to their farthest. In April 1925, he called for the complete spiritual independence of Ukraine. By this he meant a turn "away from Moscow" toward western Europe, where Ukrainian culture should seek its true inspiration. The stance of Khvyl'ovyi and other writers associated with VAPLITE seemed so radical that they came to the attention of the Russian Communist (Bolshevik) party in Moscow. In 1926, Stalin himself condemned Khvyl'ovyi in a letter to the Ukrainian party first secretary Kaganovich.

Religion

There was at least one element in Soviet Ukraine that would not be used by the government in its program of social transformation – the church. The Bolsheviks had all along adopted Marx's view that religion was the "opium of the people," that is, an "ideological" drug fed to the masses by the feudal and capitalist classes to prevent them from resisting their exploitation. In the Soviet Union, the world's first egalitarian socialist society, "exploitative ideologies" such as religion were to have no place. Atheism, instead, became the offical mode of thought and source of spiritual sustenance. Religion per se was not outlawed, but the activity of all the churches was severely restricted, and some were entirely banned.

Leaving aside the inhospitable environment, the status of Orthodoxy in Soviet Ukraine was complicated by defections from the Russian Orthodox Church – Moscow Patriarchate and the creation of alternative churches. One of the grounds of dissatisfaction had to do with the question of autocephaly or independence for the Orthodox in Ukraine. During the revolutionary era, the Russian Orthodox Church under Patriarch Tikhon in July 1918 had created an Exarchate of Ukraine, headed by its own metropolitan, which had a degree of autonomy but nonetheless remained jurisdictionally subordinate to the Patriarchate of Moscow. This was not acceptable to the "autocephalist" clergy, who favored an entirely independent church. Although in January 1919 autocephaly had been supported in principle by the Directory of the Ukrainian National Republic, it could not be implemented because of the disruptions of the civil war and anarchy that prevailed throughout 1919 and 1920.

Now the autocephalous movement was able to take advantage of the relative stability brought about by Bolshevik rule and to renew its activity. The All-Ukrainian Orthodox Church Council (*Rada*) in Kiev, which had come into being already in 1917, proclaimed in May 1920 autocephaly (jurisdictional independence) for the Orthodox Church in Ukraine. The new body consisted of parishes formed by groups of laypersons (at least twenty were needed to form a parish) who often proceeded to take over existing church buildings, including the Cathedral of St Sophia in Kiev, from the Ukrainian Exarchate of the Russian Orthodox Church – Moscow Patriarchate. These expropriations were recognized by the Soviet authorities, who had previously removed church structures from under the control of the bishops. In fact, as part of its own effort to weaken the Russian Orthodox Church, whose patriarch, Tikhon, refused to reach an accommodation with the new rulers, the Soviet government supported the Ukrainian autocephalists in their effort to institute reform "from below."

The Ukrainian Autocephalous Orthodox Church formally came into being with the convocation in October 1921 of a council (*sobor*) in Kiev, which created a hierarchy headed by the church's first metropolitan, Vasyl' Lypkivs'kyi. His appointment was made in extraordinary circumstances. When no existing canonical Orthodox bishop agreed to consecrate Lypkivs'kyi, the laypersons and clergy who met at the October 1921 council consecrated him using the allegedly early Christian practice of "laying on of hands." This act of consecration in the absence of a canonical bishop was a radical departure from Orthodox practice, and it alienated certain Ukrainian supporters of autocephaly. Consequently, the Ukrainian Autocephalous Orthodox Church was isolated from the rest of the Orthodox world, which considered the manner in which it came into being, and therefore its very existence, uncanonical (against church law).

Such details meant little to the Soviet authorities, who initially allowed the Ukrainian Autocephalous Orthodox Church to grow. At its height in early 1924, the church, which was based in the capital of Kharkiv, claimed to have between 3 and 6 million followers in 1,000 parishes led by thirty bishops, along with 1,500 priests and deacons. The church attracted particular support among nationally minded intellectuals and other patriots, who believed in its value as a Ukrainian institution. In fact, its defenders believed the Autocephalous Orthodox Church represented the vanguard of a free Ukraine. In other words, it complemented those forces within the new regime that wished to create a distinct Ukrainian entity within a loose Soviet federation.

The Bolsheviks were even more interested in undermining the Russian Orthodox Church–Moscow Patriarchate by supporting the so-called Renovationist Church, formed in 1922 by a group of disparate Orthodox factions opposed to Patriarch Tikhon. The Renovationists were fully supported throughout the Soviet Union by the Communist authorities, which gave them church buildings formerly held by the Russian Orthodox Patriarchal Church. The Renovationist movement found support also in Soviet Ukraine, and in 1923 it formed there its own independent body, the Ukrainian Orthodox (Synodal) Church, popularly known as the Living Church (Zhyva tserkva). Thus, by the early 1920s, Orthodoxy in Soviet Ukraine was divided into three factions: those remaining in the Ukrainian Exarchate of the Russian Orthodox Church – Moscow Patriarchate (the Tikhonites); those in the Ukrainian Autocephalous Orthodox Church (the Lypkivtsi); and those in the Orthodox Autocephalous (Synodal) Church (the Renovationists). The relations among the three were marked by recrimination and conflicts over the control of church property.

The Soviet Ukrainian government would have preferred to see Metropolitan Lypkivs'kyi's Autocephalous Church merged with the more politically pliable Renovationists. When this did not occur, the authorities forced the dissolution of the All-Ukrainian Orthodox Church Council and pressured the church to remove Metropolitan Lypkivs'kyi, who was indeed replaced in 1927. This was but the preliminary to an increasing exertion of pressure against the Autocephalous Church that would lead to its eventual abolition.

Ukrainianization in the era of transition

The removal of Metropolitan Lypkivs'kyi from the leadership of a nationalist-oriented religious body was symbolic of the Soviet regime's increasing concern with the direction of Ukrainianization. The policy itself was not yet being questioned, rather the manner of its implementation, which depended in part on what it was expected to achieve. Policy makers in the CP(b)U never reached a consensus as to what precisely was the ultimate goal of Ukrainianization.

For some, Ukrainianization was a means of giving legitimization to the Communist regime without threatening the unified and centralized nature of the Soviet Union. Adherents of this view strongly supported the indigenization aspects of Ukrainianization. Others saw Ukrainianization as a means of transforming the country and its inhabitants into a nationally conscious Ukrainian entity that would further justify the creation of a Soviet Ukrainian republic that was largely autonomous with respect to, if not independent of, Soviet Russia. Adherents of this view supported in particular the cultural, educational, and ideological activity of individuals and institutions working to raise the level of a distinct Ukrainian cultural life.

The dilemma of finding the "right track" for Ukrainianization was addressed by the CP(b)U as early as the summer of 1926, when Kaganovich presented a report to the party's Central Committee entitled "On the Results of Ukrainianization." Although the report gave unqualified praise for the achievements in education, governmental administration, and the building of the party, it nonetheless criticized writers like Khvyl'ovyi and Mykola Zerov for their efforts to free Ukrainian literature from Russian influence, efforts which it stated were somehow linked to the "growth of capitalism" that was occurring as a result of the New Economic Policy (see chapter 44). The first casualty of the party's ideological redirection was the commissar of education and active ukrainianizer Oleksander Shums'kyi, who was removed from his post in early 1927. This measure was followed by the condemnation for "nationalist deviation" of the entire leadership of the Communist party of Western Ukraine and its expulsion from the Comintern in early 1928 (see chapter 46).

In fact, the year 1928 heralded a transitional period for Soviet Ukraine. While the policy of Ukrainianization was still in force, and many achievements in Ukrainian culture and in the greater extension of Ukrainian language use were still to come, it also was becoming clear that the CP(b)U had begun to back away from the "radical" ukrainianizing policies of the mid-1920s. The next five years, from 1928 to 1932, would determine whether Soviet Ukraine would be allowed to continue to set for itself policies that would sustain a distinct Ukrainian life, or whether the country would lose control of its destiny and become further integrated into the Soviet Union.

Soviet Ukraine: Economic, Political, and Cultural Integration

The period of transition in Soviet Ukrainian society that began in 1928 reflected a general shift in policy throughout the Soviet Union commonly referred to as Stalinism or as the "Stalinist revolution." The policy changes were inspired by Iosif Stalin, who, as general secretary of the All-Union Communist (Bolshevik) party, continued to consolidate and increase his power. In the 1930s, he became a virtual dictator, in a sense the new tsar of a Soviet empire. The changes introduced after 1928 were directed primarily at the Soviet economy, although they inevitably had profound implications in the political, national, and cultural spheres as well.

War communism and the New Economic Policy – NEP

The emphasis placed on the economy was not surprising, since it was through economic transformation that Marxist-Leninist ideologists promised to create an egalitarian society. In the new society, the means of production would be in the hands of the working proletariat represented by a state ostensibly of their own making and led by a revolutionary elite whose legitimacy derived from the principle of the "dictatorship of the proletariat." The workers' state would create a rational structure of economic production and distribution to fulfill the individual needs of all workers. As early as June 1918, a little more than half a year after the Bolsheviks came to power, an attempt was made to transform Russian society, or at least those areas of the old tsarist empire controlled by the Bolsheviks, into an ideal, classless, communist state. All industries were nationalized, that is, taken over by the state and run by paid technical experts responding to the central government's directives from Moscow. Nationalization applied to small-scale as well as to large-scale industries, to transportation and communication facilities, and to rural areas, where the large landed estates were not broken up but preserved in the form of state-owned farms and collectives. The use of money was prohibited and, instead, barter relations were established among industries and between industry and the agricultural sector. This radical approach to the economy was known as "war communism."

The results of war communism were catastrophic. It brought about almost complete paralysis in the industrial sector, a dramatic increase in inflation, and peasant resistance to forced grain requisitioning and state expropriation of the land. It was not long before the Bolshevik leadership realized that the war communism approach had failed. Consequently, in March 1921, at the 10th Congress of the Communist party of the Soviet Union, Lenin decided to make what he called a "strategic retreat" in the revolution. This did not mean that nationalization of industry or communalization of land was abandoned as the ultimate goal, but that that goal was put off until the new Soviet society was ready. Lenin's famous dictum, One Step Backward to Make Two Steps Forward, was thus to be implemented. The symbolic step backward was the return to a market economy that came to be known as the New Economic Policy, or NEP for short.

NEP was introduced in 1921, following an end to forced grain requisitioning and the introduction instead of a tax in kind. Soon other measures followed that permitted the peasants to dispose of their surplus produce freely, allowing thereby for the development of a thriving local agricultural market and trade. Also, small-scale industries were denationalized, resulting in the rise of a new class of small businessmen, the so-called Nepmen. The New Economic Policy, which was to function from 1921 to 1928, was dubbed by its opponents "state capitalism." Whatever it was called, NEP placed the Soviet economy on the road to recovery, with the consequence that by the mid-1920s production levels that had existed in the Russian Empire on the eve of World War I had been reached once again.

NEP in Soviet Ukraine

In Soviet Ukraine, economic policy followed a pattern similar to that in other lands under Bolshevik control. A variation of war communism was introduced during the second period of Bolshevik rule in 1919 (February–August) and then restored after the third and final Soviet advance in early 1920. The land question was the most problematic. Whereas in 1919 the land confiscated from the large estates was not given to the peasants but rather redistributed as agricultural communes and state farms, the Soviet Ukrainian government that returned to Kiev in February 1920 adopted a new policy. The government immediately passed a law embodying the principle that all land should belong to those who work it. In practice, this meant that peasants had the right to hold land from former estates for a period of up to nine years.

The government also encouraged the poorer peasants and landless agricultural day-laborers to compete with the more prosperous peasants for the acquisition of land under the new system. At times, the result was one that Bolshevik ideologists hoped for: friction and, eventually, clashes reflecting a "class struggle" between rich and poor peasants. Subsequently, the Soviet Ukrainian government felt obliged to intervene and restore order. The authorities did so and then eliminated the "anti-revolutionary" peasants by issuing a law in October 1920 that authorized the seizure of land owned by so-called kulaks (Ukrainian: *kurkuli*). At the time, kulaks were defined as those who owned in excess of 80 acres (32.5 hectares). Although the peasants received about 30 million acres (12 million hectares) of redistributed land, they were displeased with the corrupt manner in which the process took place. Their anger, however, was aroused particularly by the continued war-communism policy of requisitioning. According to this policy, peasants were expected to turn over most of their grain to the state (beyond 30 pounds [14 kilograms] per month) without compensation. And to ensure delivery, armed detachments (usually consisting of Bolshevik Russian or russified industrial workers) were sent from the cities to carry out the requisitioning.

The introduction of NEP in 1921, with its encouragement of local markets and putting an end to requisitioning, did not initially produce the hoped-for positive results in the Ukrainian countryside. This is because requisitioning was replaced by a complex tax in kind (*prodnalog*), whereby peasants had to pay the government in foodstuffs that frequently totaled half their harvest. "Revolutionary courts" were set up throughout the countryside to punish those who did not pay the tax. The tax burden and the government-instigated class warfare against the kulaks resulted in a new "peasant war" against the Soviet authorities that broke out spontaneously or was led by "armies" like those of Nestor Makhno which had continued to be active since the period of civil war. As late as April 1921, as many as 102 armed bands roamed the Ukrainian and Crimean countryside. Added to the onerous taxes, class warfare, and armed uprisings was a severe drought that struck in 1921 and destroyed half the harvest. The result was a famine that lasted nearly two years, claiming between 800,000 (official reports) and an estimated 1.5 to 2 million lives. As for Bolshevik promises of a rational and egalitarian workers' state, a popular jingle summed up the real view of the Ukrainian masses: "In tsarist times there was bread and oatcakes [*khlib i palanytsi*] / Now with the Communists there is nothing to eat [*nema shcho ïsty*]."

It was not until 1923, when the tax in kind was abolished, that conditions in the Soviet Ukrainian countryside began to stabilize. NEP, with its agrarian markets and the reintroduction of capitalism in the small-scale industrial sector (resulting in competition, free trade, and fluctuating prices, as well as unemployment), made possible the recovery of the Ukrainian economy. By 1927, the gross national product of Soviet Ukraine had finally reached its prewar level.

The end of NEP

Despite its successes, the New Economic Policy was never meant to be more than a temporary measure to get the economy – disrupted since 1914 by World War I, civil war, and the misguided extremes of war communism – back on its feet. NEP, the proverbial one step backward, had yielded positive results. Now, it seemed the time had come to take the first of the proverbial two steps forward. Lenin, who died in 1924, was no longer around to lead in taking them. That task was left to his successor, Iosif Stalin.

Stalin's economic revolution was in large measure related to his struggle to attain uncontested political power. Accordingly, calls for change in economic policy were often issued as a means to discredit Stalin's political opposition. The methods used in eliminating those he considered rivals or a threat to his power were often brutal, and the process of elimination was to continue at least until the

MAP 36

SOVIET UKRAINE, 1932

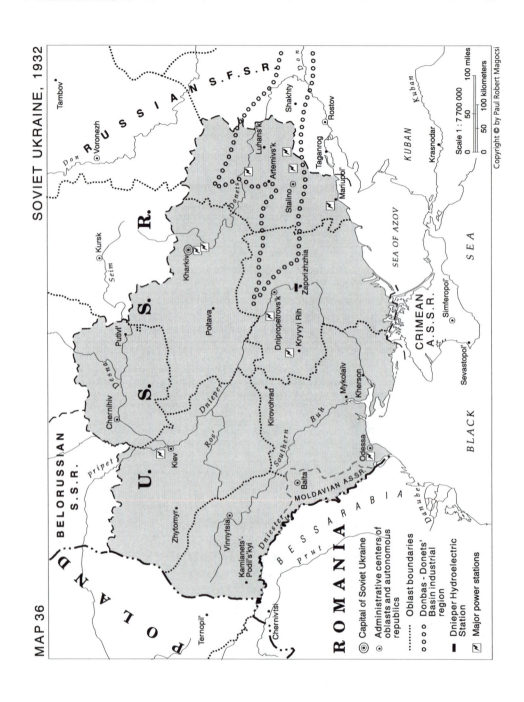

Copyright © by Paul Robert Magocsi

◎ Capital of Soviet Ukraine
⊙ Administrative centers/of oblasts and autonomous republics
······· Oblast boundaries
ooooo Donbas - Donets' Basin industrial region
▬ Dnieper Hydroelectric Station
⚑ Major power stations

Scale 1 : 7 700 000

0   50   100 miles
0 50 100 kilometers

outbreak of World War II. It began in 1926, when all the Old Bolshevik leaders, starting with Lenin's close colleagues Trotskii and Grigorii Zinov'ev, were removed from office, put on trial, exiled, or executed.

In the economic sphere, in 1928 Stalin introduced the concept of a planned command economy. All decisions were to be made at the center in Moscow and implemented throughout the Soviet Union, which was treated as a single economic unit. This comprehensive, supposedly more rational approach to economic development meant the immediate end to NEP. In its stead, the first so-called Five-Year Plan was introduced, setting for all aspects of Soviet agriculture and, especially, industry, production schedules and goals which were to be met by the end of five years. The new approach spelled the end not only of NEP, but also of any individual prerogatives the constituent republics still had over their economies according to the 1924 Soviet constitution.

In 1927, the State Planning Commission (*Gosplan*) was established to oversee the economy. To ensure coordination, between 1927 and 1932 certain structural changes were introduced in the relationship between the republics and the central government. Title to all land was assumed by the central government (1928); republic commissariats for agriculture were made subordinate to the central commissariat for agriculture (1929); all heavy industry, forest, and forest produce industries were separated from republic control and put under central commissariats (1932); technical and scientific schools and public health facilities, including hospitals and sanatoriums, were put under central commissariats; and finally, throughout the country, new economic regions (or oblasts) were established over which Moscow had direct control, without being required to go through the individual Soviet republics in which they were located. In Soviet Ukraine, this administrative reorganization coincided with the abolition in 1932 of the smaller *okruhy* and their replacement with seven larger oblasts – Kiev, Kharkiv, Vinnytsia, Dnipropetrovs'k, Odessa, Chernihiv, and Stalino. By taking direct control of these oblasts, the central Soviet government in Moscow effectively revived the administrative practice that had prevailed during tsarist times and during the early years of Soviet rule (until 1925).

The overall goal of the First Five-Year Plan (1928–1932) was rapid industrialization. In order to find the monetary resources (capital) to pay for industrialization, the central government decided to end NEP by nationalizing all remaining sectors of the economy and to collectivize the agricultural sector, income from which would accrue to the state. Through this otherwise simplistic or primitive accumulation of capital, the government would have the means to invest in industrialization. Abolishing NEP was relatively easy; collectivizing agriculture would be the real challenge. Given the generally backward state of the Soviet economy and the ingrained traditional habits of the country's rural inhabitants, the implementation of full collectivization would require a leadership of unbending purpose, one willing to carry out the task whatever the cost. And even if Stalin could not live up to the meaning of his self-chosen revolutionary name as a leader of steel will, he could legitimize his actions by using political argumentation based, if ever so tangentially, on the "iron laws" of Marxist-Leninist ideology.

Central planning and industrialization

With regard specifically to Soviet Ukraine, the First Five-Year Plan put greatest emphasis on the development of heavy industry. The goal was to transform the country into the Soviet Union's leading industrial center for coal extraction and metallurgy as well as its primary source of grain, sugar, and fats. The Second Five-Year Plan (1933–1937) was designed to complete the technological reconstruction of industry, transportation, and agriculture by perfecting collective farming and centralized control over industry. The Third Five-Year Plan (1938–1941, cut short by World War II) was devoted in large measure to developing Soviet Ukraine's chemical and machine building industries.

Centralized planning did transform Soviet Ukraine, in part, into an industrialized society. The transformation was concentrated, however, in certain areas, in particular the lower Dnieper urban triangle (Dnipropetrovs'k–Kryvyi Rih–Zaporizhzhia) and the Donets' Basin (Donbas), whose industrial base had already been established during the last years of tsarist rule. While the Soviets expanded upon that base, most of the rest of the country remained what it had always been – an agriculture-based society.

Even after the decision to initiate the First Five-Year Plan was agreed to in 1927 and its final text approved in April 1929, controversy within the highest ranks of the All-Union Communist party continued. At first, a fierce political struggle developed between Stalin and Trotskii's supporters over the plan's general contents. Even after the Trotskyists were defeated, there was still debate over what Soviet territories would be favored for heavy industrial investment. Finally, in May 1930 the All-Union Communist party Central Committee decided on Soviet Ukraine as one of the two areas in which to concentrate investment.

Assured of investment from Moscow, Soviet Ukraine proceeded to create the necessary infrastructure for heavy industry. Several power stations were completed, primarily in the eastern and southern parts of the country, including the massive Dnieper Hydroelectric Station just north of Zaporizhzhia (begun in 1927), several in the Donbas-Donets' Basin, and others near the industrial centers of Kharkiv, Kiev, Dnipropetrovs'k, Kryvyi Rih, Mariupol', and Odessa. These stations accounted for a nearly tenfold increase in electric power production in Soviet Ukraine between 1928 and 1940. Nearly 400 large-scale tractor, combine, and mining-machinery plants were constructed, although most of the machines had to be imported from abroad.

The transportation system was also expanded, with nearly 2,480 miles (4,000 kilometers) of new railroad track being laid during the interwar years, especially in the Donbas-Donets' Basin and the lower Dnieper industrial triangle. Although paved highway construction lagged behind during the 1920s, it more than tripled in extent after the introduction of central planning, from 2,400 miles (3,900 kilometers) in 1928 to 8,500 miles (13,700 kilometers) in 1940. The number of motor vehicles rose even more dramatically, from 11,400 in 1932 to 84,300 in 1937 (three-fourths of which were trucks used in collectivized agriculture).

What were the results of centralized planning in Soviet Ukraine? Whether one accepts Soviet statistical data or revised, non-Soviet data, the results are still impressive. At the end of the first two five-year plans, in 1937, Soviet Ukrainian industrial output was either 5.5 times (Soviet data) or 3.4 times greater than it had been at the beginning, in 1928. As for the pattern of industrial production, it remained the same. There was an increasing emphasis on the areas of heavy industrial producer goods (iron, steel, coal, building products), particularly machine building, at the expense of consumer products and food for human consumption.

For instance, between 1928 and 1937 the output in machine building and metalworking increased by 6.1 times, and in industrial producer goods by 3.1 times, while that in food processing increased by only 1.4 times. The greatest increases were in the production of mineral fertilizers (17.7 times), electric power (9.8 times), and industrial lumber (5.2 times). In food processing, there was only one significant increase: the production of raw spirits nearly quadrupled during the first two Five-Year Plans.

In the context of the Soviet Union as a whole, Ukraine's industrial output between 1928 and 1940 decreased in most areas of heavy industrial producer goods, with the exception of machine building and metalworking, in which Soviet Ukraine's share of production actually increased, from 17.5 percent to 19.6 percent. Yet even for several products which experienced a relative decrease, Ukraine's percentage of production still remained nearly half or more the output of the entire Soviet Union (see table 44.1).

TABLE 44.1
Ukrainian industrial output in selected
categories, 1928–1940 (percentage of total
Soviet output)[1]

Product	1928	1940
Coke	95.7	74.5
Soda ash	81.6	81.0
Iron ore	77.0	67.6
Pig iron	71.9	64.7
Coal	69.9	50.5
Rolled steel	58.1	49.7
Steel ingots	56.7	48.8

The collectivization of agriculture

Stalin's "revolution from above" and the introduction of the First Five-Year Plan in 1928 meant an end to the relatively free-market system that prevailed in the Ukrainian countryside during the period of the New Economic Policy. The step backward represented by NEP was to be compensated for by two steps forward – industrialization and collectivization. The theoretical justification for collectivization was that it would correct the shortcomings of NEP. According to Soviet ideologists, these shortcomings were that NEP (1) sustained a pattern of low productivity and capital formation on small farms; (2) made impossible the application of new technological inventions; (3) stood in the way of integration into a planned economy; and, perhaps of most concern, (4) promoted a capitalist market economy that inherently constituted a major threat to the building of socialism and communism. Aside from theory, the government needed food at low cost and right away to feed the rapidly growing urban work force, as well as an excess in grain production that could be sold for export to pay for the machinery being bought abroad and installed in the country's new industrial enterprises. To solve these concerns and meet these needs, Soviet central planners decided that agricultural lands should be collectivized as quickly as possible and by whatever means necessary.

Although collectivization had never been abandoned as an ideal goal, during the NEP period it had depended solely on voluntary action. Consequently, by October 1928 only 3.4 percent of farms (representing 3.8 percent of arable land) had been collectivized in Soviet Ukraine. Faced with this stark reality and in serious doubt that a significant number of other peasants would voluntarily give up their land, the economic planners added to the First Five-Year Plan the goal of 12 percent, later revised to 25 percent, of arable land to be collectivized by 1932. But even these ambitious goals seemed too restrained for Moscow. Accordingly, in February 1929 the Central Committee of the All-Union Communist party called for the implementation of forced collectivization. By March 1930, 65 percent of farms and 70 percent of livestock in Soviet Ukraine had been forcibly collectivized. In many cases, even household wares and the family cow and chickens were expropriated for the collective. There was a brief respite in 1930, when peasants were allowed to leave the collectives if they wished (and a majority did so), but before the end of the year the pace was accelerated even further, with the result that by the close of the First Five-Year Plan (1932), 70 percent of farms had been collectivized. Despite claims about success back in early 1930, it was not until October 1935 that 91.3 percent of farms in Soviet Ukraine (representing 98 percent of arable land) were collectivized.

Essentially two entities came into existence on arable lands: state farms and collective farms. State farms (Ukrainian: *radhosp;* Russian: *sovkhoz*) were managed by the government with the help of hired labor and were hailed by Soviet leaders as the ideal in agricultural establishments. They were usually large in size (over 5,000 acres [2,000 hectares]) and well endowed with farm machinery. Collective farms (Ukrainian: *kolhosp;* Russian: *kolkhoz*), in contrast, were ostensibly voluntary cooperatives in which the peasants worked on property with machinery owned by the collective. Collective farm workers fulfilled quotas on crop production set by the state and received whatever was left over. The manner of distributing the remaining foodstuffs was calculated on the basis of the number of (labor) days an individual worked.

To equip the state and collective farms with machinery, beginning in 1929 the so-called Machine and Tractor Stations (MTS) were established throughout the countryside. Each MTS was supplied with between thirty and sixty tractors and other farm machines produced by Soviet Ukraine's rapidly growing machine building industry. Between 1930 and 1940, the number of MTS in Soviet Ukraine rose from a mere 47 to over 1,000 (with 85,000 tractors, 50,000 trucks, and 31,000 combines). By 1938, the MTS supposedly serviced 99 percent of all land under cultivation. Aside from their intended purpose, the MTS also became centers of Communist party authority and propaganda in the midst of an often hostile rural environment.

Despite the regime's preference for state farms, it was collective farms that actually made up the vast majority in Soviet Ukraine. According to data from 1938, 79 percent of the land was in collective farms, while only 9.7 percent was in state farms (including experimental stations). As for the remainder, 8.3 percent comprised state forests, and only 0.4 percent individual households.

What were the results of the rapid collectivization of the early 1930s in terms of agricultural production? Using data before and after the period in question, that is, for 1928 and 1940, what effect, if any, did collectivization have in comparison to NEP? We might look at data from 1940, the end of the period, and from 1913, the last normal year of tsarist rule. These figures reveal that between 1913 and 1940 there was actually a decrease in the area of land producing food grains (wheat, rye, corn, barley, oats, millet, buckwheat, vegetables), from 61 to 53 million acres (24.7 to 21.4 million hectares). The most dramatic drop was an 85 percent decrease in the production of spring wheat, which was only partially offset by twofold increases in winter wheat, millet, and legumes. The overall decrease in food grains was matched, however, by a more than two-and-one-half times increase in industrial and livestock crops (sugar beets, flax, hemp, sunflower, cotton, castor beans, winter rape, tobacco), from 2.2 to 6.7 million acres (0.9 to 2.7 million hectares) between 1913 and 1940. So the collectivization of Ukrainian agriculture was accompanied by gains in productivity, especially in industrial crops. But at what cost?

Aside from statistics, there was the human element. Ukrainian peasants – and, for that matter, Russian and other peasants in the Soviet Union – did not look with favor on the prospect of having to give up what was almost a mystical part of themselves, the land. Nor did the peasants give up their land without a fight. Their protests took different forms: the slaughter of livestock, the burning of fields, the driving out of the new collective farm officials (acts often led by women – the so-called *babs'ki bunty*, "women's revolts"), and, finally, armed insurrection. When all these measures failed, peasants fled to what rapidly became overcrowded cities. The flight became so serious that in December 1932 the authorities implemented a system of internal passports. The new document was available only at one's original place of residence and had to be shown in order for one to reside elsewhere. The internal passport system not only helped stem the tide of internal migration, but also allowed the secret police to track people's movements more easily.

Yet despite the various forms of protest, collectivization continued. After all, collectivization, like industrialization, was part of "The Plan" being made in Moscow allegedly for the greater good of a socialist or communist society. If, to implement The Plan, the bond between the peasant and his or her land had to be broken, it would be. And if the tie could not be broken "voluntarily," then in the interests of the "greater good" – fulfillment of The Plan – recalcitrant peasants could be eliminated. At this point, theory became practice.

Dekulakization and the Great Famine

Marxism-Leninism had always preached class war as an expression of the historical dialectic leading inevitably to world socialist revolution. Class war was now to become part of the Soviet drive toward collectivization. In Soviet Ukraine as elsewhere in the Soviet Union (especially the rich agricultural regions of the Don, lower Volga, and Kuban River valleys, and the lowlands north of the Caucasus Mountains), the relatively well-to-do peasants who had expanded their landholdings after the pre-revolutionary tsarist reforms of 1906 were called kulaks (*kurkuli*). Now, because they were opposed to collectivization, they were branded by the Soviet regime "enemies of the people" and presented throughout the 1920s in government propaganda as wealthy land-grabbing exploiters of their fellow villagers. In lieu of such inflammatory but vague rhetoric, the Soviets attempted to provide a concrete definition of who qualified as a kulak. Accordingly, a decree in May 1929 defined a kulak as someone who had a minimum income of 300 rubles (or 1,500 rubles per household) and who used hired laborers and owned any kind of motorized farm machinery. According to these criteria, at the time of the decree there were 71,500 kulaks, representing a mere 1.4 percent of all households, in Soviet Ukraine. With respect to the so-called wealth of the kulaks, it should be kept in mind that the average income of an urban worker was the same as or greater than (300 to 500 rubles) the kulak minimum and included social security benefits not available to rural agriculturalists. Moreover, most of the farmsteads that used hired labor were headed by war invalids or widows, not well-to-do peasant entrepreneurs. In short, the term kulak and the even vaguer category of kulak henchmen (*pidkurkul'nyky*) had less to do with actual wealth than with the need of the Soviet authorities to have an all-purpose term with which to brand whomever they considered their enemy in the countryside.

The authorities set out to eliminate the kulaks. Beginning in 1927, they were made to pay heavy taxes. The following year, they were deprived of their franchise, as priests, former policemen, and other declared anti-Soviet elements had been deprived previously. The kulaks were also increasingly harassed by members of the local youth organization (Komsomol) and the so-called Committees of Poor Peasants, a state of affairs contributing to the "historically inevitable" class warfare. Finally, in January 1930 the Central Committee of the All-Union Communist party in Moscow ordered "the liquidation of the kulaks as a class." They were physically rounded up – men first, women and children later – and shipped off to Central Asia, Siberia, and the Soviet Far East. During the forced transport and as a result of exposure to the elements at their place of exile where they had no shelter, thousands died. This did not seem to matter to the Soviet authorities, since the elimination of a despised "class" was achieved. By March 1930, nearly 62,000 kulak households, or an estimated quarter million people, had been eliminated from Soviet Ukraine during the period known as dekulakization.

The kulaks were gone, but there remained the mass of the peasants. They proved especially problematic in the course of 1931 and 1932. These were years marked by resistance to collectivization in the form of refusals to deliver grain to the collectives and state farms. In the end, the collective farms themselves became centers of opposition, as their administrators argued that it was impossible to fulfill The Plan's unreasonable crop quotas. This meant little, however, to Stalin and the central authorities, who were concerned only with the industrialization of the country. Neither he nor the All-Union Communist party hierarchy would tolerate either the ineffectiveness of local officials or the stubbornness of the peasantry, whose only value, as they perceived it, was to provide food for urban industrial workers – the true vanguard of the revolution. Accordingly, the party in Moscow called on urban workers to go into the countryside to implement the government's decisions. These were the so-called 25,000 "best sons of the fatherland," 7,000 of whom came from Soviet Ukraine itself. Between 1929 and 1931, there were as many as 10,000 of these "twenty-five thousanders" at work in the Ukrainian countryside, where they played a leading role in expropriating kulak property, organizing collectives, and supervising grain shipments. Backed by soldiers and the secret police, these party functionaries simply ordered that grain be seized. Anyone who protested was declared a kulak or kulak henchman and therefore an enemy of the revolution. Many such "new" kulaks were exiled to Siberia and other remote parts of the Soviet Union. Others were imprisoned or killed, or fled to the cities to hide. The actions of the twenty-five-thousanders accounted for the removal of approximately one million men, women, and children from the rural areas in 1931 and 1932.

The forced removal of the kulaks and a return to the policy of forced collectivization during the second half of 1930 had a negative effect on the harvest. The 1930 grain harvest of 21.1 millions tons (18.4 million metric tons) dipped in 1931 to 18.3 million tons (16.7 million metric tons), of which 30 to 40 percent was lost in the harvesting process because the new collective farms were poorly administered and were staffed by peasant laborers reluctant to work on land not their own. At the same time, the central government's quota for grain deliveries remained the same in both 1930 and 1931 – 7.7 million tons (7 million metric tons), over twice the figure demanded in the mid-1920s, when sociopolitical conditions in the countryside were relatively stable.

Government policy had indeed produced the "class war" the Bolsheviks had always predicted. This was a war in which poor peasants led by party officials and backed by the army were pitted against opponents of collectivization and requisitioning, who now were all lumped together under the opprobrious term *kulak*. The result was that by 1932, Ukrainian villages were in dire straits. Famine broke out in the spring, the grain harvest dropped to only about 15 million tons (13.7 million metric tons), and there was little seed to be planted for the next season. The situation continued to worsen, with the result that in the winter and spring of 1933 starvation in the countryside became the norm.

For their part, officials in Moscow argued that the peasants were simply hiding grain. Accordingly, a law on the inviolability of socialist property was passed in

Ukraine's Holodomor:
Death by Famine

Not only did the Soviet authorities deny there was a famine in Ukraine at the time it was happening, they continued for decades thereafter to claim that any talk of famine in 1933 was part of an international conspiracy, aided by Ukrainian émigrés in the "imperialist West," to besmirch the good name of the Soviet Union. On the eve of the fiftieth anniversary of the famine in 1983, scholars and publicists in North America (Robert Conquest, James Mace, Marco Carynnyk) began to uncover the reality of the human catastrophe. Subsequently, the United States Congress created a Special Commission on the Ukraine Famine, which in 1990 published its findings in a multivolume work. Following the Gorbachev revolution in the mid-1980s, Soviet Ukrainian scholars (Stanislav Kul'chyts'kyi, Volodymyr Maniak, among others) were also able to assert openly for the first time that indeed there had been a famine in the early 1930s. The new research conducted during the late 1980s uncovered a wealth of often gruesome data, including estimates that ranged from 4.5 to 5 million deaths in 1933 alone to 10 million deaths during the rest of the 1930s attributable to the famine.

We will probably never know how many people died directly or indirectly as a result of the Great Famine (Ukrainian: *Holodomor*). In any case, numbers themselves fail to convey the real meaning of the tragedy, particularly to citizens of the twentieth century, who have been virtually numbed by the knowledge of humankind's ability to inflict death and destruction upon itself. In lieu of further statistics, the view of one eyewitness might help us comprehend more fully how the famine affected the lives of the ordinary man, woman, and child. The following description is included in a posthumous novel, *Forever Flowing* (1970), by a Ukrainian-born Russian writer of Jewish descent, Vasilii Grossman. It is an account, given later, by a Russian woman and Communist party activist who was sent to Soviet Ukraine in 1928 to help implement collectivization.

As a Party activist, I was sent to Ukraine in order to strengthen a collective farm. In Ukraine, we were told, they had an instinct for private property that was stronger than in the Russian Republic. And truly, truly, the whole business was much worse in Ukraine than it was with us. I was not sent very far – we were, after all, on the very edge of Ukraine, not more than three hours' journey from the village to which I was sent. The place was beautiful. And so I arrived there, and the people there were like everyone else. And I became the bookkeeper in the administrative office. ...

How was it? After the liquidation of the *kulaks*, the amount of land under cultivation dropped very sharply and so did the crop yield. But meanwhile people continued to report that without the *kulaks* our whole life was flourishing. The village soviet lied to the district, and the district lied to the province, and the province lied to Moscow. ... Our village was given a quota that it couldn't have fulfilled in ten years! In the village soviet even those who weren't drinkers took to drink out of fear. It was clear that Moscow was basing its hopes on Ukraine. And the upshot of it was that most of the subsequent anger was directed against Ukraine. What they said was simple: you have failed to fulfill the plan, and that means that you yourself are an unliquidated *kulak*.

Of course, the grain deliveries could not be fulfilled. Smaller areas had been sown, and the crop yield on those smaller areas had shrunk. So where could it come from, that promised ocean of grain from the collective farms? The conclusion reached up top was that the grain had all been concealed, hidden away. By *kulaks* who had not been liquidated yet, by loafers! The *kulaks* had been removed, but the *kulak* spirit remained. Private property was master over the mind of the Ukrainian peasant.

Who signed the act that imposed mass murder? I often wonder whether it was really Stalin. ... Not the tsars certainly, not the Tatars, nor even the German occupation forces ever promulgated such a terrible decree. For the decree required that the peasants of Ukraine, the Don, and the Kuban be put to death by starvation, put to death along with their tiny children. The instructions were to take away the entire seed fund. Grain was searched for as if it were not grain, but bombs and machine guns. The whole earth was stabbed with bayonets and ramrods. Cellars were dug up, floors were broken through, and vegetable gardens were turned over. From some they confiscated even the grain in their houses – in pots or troughs. They even took baked bread away from one woman, loaded it onto the cart, and hauled it off to the district. Day and night the carts creaked along, laden with the confiscated grain, and dust hung over the earth. There were no grain elevators to accommodate it, and they simply dumped it out on the earth and set guards around it. By winter the grain had been soaked by the rains and began to ferment – the Soviet government didn't even have enough canvas to cover it up!

... So then I understood: the most important thing for the Soviet government was the plan! Fulfill the plan! Pay up your assessment, make your assigned deliveries! The state comes first, and people are a big zero.

Fathers and mothers wanted to save their children and tried to hide at least a tiny bit of grain, but they were told: 'You hate the country of socialism. You are trying to make the plan fail, you parasites, you subkulaks, you rats.'

Incidentally, when the grain was taken away, the party activists were told that the peasants would be fed from the state grain fund. But it was not true. Not one single kernel of grain was given to the starving.

Who confiscated the grain? For the most part, local people: the district executive committee, the district party committee, the Komsomol, local boys, and, of course, the militia and the NKVD. In certain localities army units were used as well. I saw one man from Moscow who had been mobilized by the party and sent out to assist collectivization, but he didn't try very hard. Instead, he kept trying to get away and go home. And again, as in the campaign to liquidate the *kulaks*, people became dazed, stunned, beastlike. ...

Well, then came an autumn without any rain, and the winter was snowy. There was no grain to eat. ... No bread. ... They had taken every last kernel of grain from the village. There was no seed to be sown for spring wheat or other spring grains. The entire seed fund had been confiscated. The only hope was in the winter grains, but they were still under the snow. Spring was far away, and the villagers were already starving. They had eaten their meat and whatever millet they had left; they were eating the last of their potatoes, and in the case of the larger families the potatoes were already gone.

Everyone was in terror. Mothers looked at their children and began to scream in fear. ... The children would cry from morning on, asking for bread. What could their mothers give them – snow? There was no help. The party officials had one answer to all entreaties: 'You should have worked harder; you shouldn't have loafed.' And then they would also say: 'Look about your villages. You've got enough buried there to last three years.'

... It was when the snow began to melt that the village was up to its neck in real starvation. The children kept crying and crying. They did not sleep. And they began to ask for bread at night, too. People's faces looked like clay. Their eyes were dull and drunken. They went about as though asleep. They inched forward, feeling their way one foot at a time, and they supported themselves by keeping one hand against the wall. They began to move around less. Starvation made them totter. They moved less and less, and they spent more time lying down. ...

No dogs and cats were left. They had been slaughtered. And it was hard to catch them, too. The animals had become afraid of people, and their eyes were wild. People boiled them. All there was were tough veins and muscles. From their heads they made a meat jelly.

The snow melted, and people began to swell up. The edema of starvation had begun. Faces were swollen, legs swollen like pillows; water bloated their stomachs. ... And the peasant children! Have you ever seen newspaper photographs of children in the German camps? They were just like that: their heads like heavy balls on thin little necks, like storks, and one could see each bone of their arms and legs protruding from beneath the skin, how bones joined, and the entire skeleton was stretched over with skin that was like yellow gauze. And the children's faces were aged, tormented, just as if they were seventy years old. ... And the eyes. Oh, Lord!

Now they ate anything at all. They caught mice, rats, snakes, sparrows, ants, and earthworms. They ground up bones into flour and cut up leather, shoe soles, and smelly old hides to make noodles of a kind, and they boiled down glue. When the grass came up, they dug out the roots and ate the leaves and buds. They used everything there was: dandelions, burdocks, bluebells, willowroot, sedums, nettles, and every other kind of edible grass and root and herb they could find. ...
And no help came!

SOURCE: Wasyl Hryshko, *The Ukrainian Holocaust of 1933*, translated by Marco Carynnyk (Toronto 1983), pp. 92–96.

MAP 37

THE GREAT FAMINE

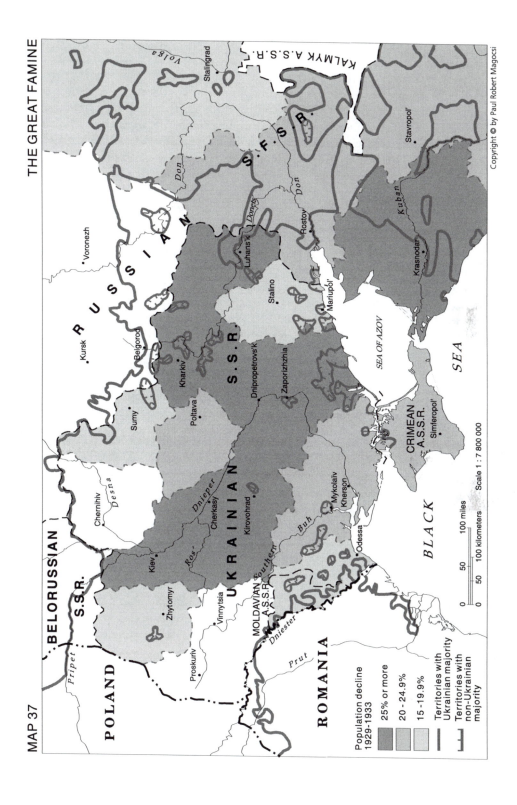

Population decline
1929-1933

25% or more

20 - 24.9%

15 -19.9%

Territories with
Ukrainian majority

Territories with
non-Ukrainian
majority

Scale 1 : 7 800 000

100 miles

100 kilometers

POLAND

BELORUSSIAN

S.S.R.

RUSSIAN

S.F.S.R.

KALMYK A.S.S.R.

UKRAINIAN S.S.R.

ROMANIA

MOLDAVIAN A.S.S.R.

CRIMEAN A.S.S.R.

BLACK SEA

SEA OF AZOV

Pripet

Desna

Dnieper

Ros'

Southern Buh

Dniester

Prut

Don

Donets

Don

Kuban

Volga

Chernihiv

Kiev

Zhytomyr

Proskuriv

Vinnytsia

Cherkasy

Kirovohrad

Mykolaiv

Kherson

Odessa

Sumy

Poltava

Kharkiv

Belgorod

Kursk

Voronezh

Dnipropetrovs'k

Zaporizhzhia

Stalino

Mariupol'

Luhans'k

Rostov

Stalingrad

Stavropol'

Krasnodar

Simferopol'

August 1932, whereby the act of taking anything from the collectives – even an ear of wheat or the broken root of a sugar beet – could and often did result in confiscation of property, a ten-year prison term, and even execution. Yet at the same time that famine was raging throughout the country's agricultural heart-land – Dnieper Ukraine as well as the neighboring Kuban and northern Caucasus regions – the Soviet Union was exporting grain abroad. Put another way, officially a famine never occurred. This makes it impossible to know with even relative accuracy the exact cost in human lives. There is, moreover, great disagreement as to the cause of the famine. Was it the result of bureaucratic bungling during the collectivization campaign? Was it part of an explicit policy against recalcitrant peasants, regardless of nationality? Was it an attempt to eliminate nationalist opposition in all areas deemed critical to the Soviet Union (the famine occurred in the Kuban, in the Don Cossack-inhabited northern Caucasus, and in the German-inhabited middle Volga regions as well as in Soviet Ukraine)? Or was it an act of genocide directed specifically against ethnic Ukrainians?

Although conclusive answers regarding causation continue to elude researchers of the period, there is agreement that several million deaths did occur in Soviet Ukraine during the Great Famine of 1933. The most conservative estimate of the number of famine victims, either from starvation or from disease related to malnutrition, is 4.8 million people. This figure represents 15 percent of Soviet Ukraine's population at the time. Even according to such a conservative figure, this meant that during the spring and summer of that fateful year of 1933, 25,000 people died every day, or 1,000 people every hour, or 17 people every minute.

The apogee and the decline of Ukrainianization

The enormous changes brought about by the Stalinist revolution of 1928 culminated in 1933 with the introduction of the Second Five-Year Plan and the virtual elimination of private landholdings in the agricultural sector. The transitional years 1928 to 1932 also provided an answer to the dilemma of whether Soviet Ukraine would become a truly distinct republic or just another subordinate entity within the Soviet Union. In an era of ideological absolutes, there seemed to be no middle ground. By 1933, it was clear that total integration in the Soviet Union was to be Ukraine's fate.

Nonetheless, the period 1928 to 1932 was a transitional one. This meant that two conflicting developments were taking place simultaneously. The Ukrainianization of cultural life, a process begun in earnest in the mid-1920s, was by the early 1930s witnessing some of its greatest successes. At the same time, the non-Communist and, later, Communist intellectual cadres who had made Ukrainianization possible were systematically being removed from power and, eventually, imprisoned and/or killed.

The transitional period began with personnel changes in the Soviet Ukrainian government and the CP(b)U. Kaganovich was replaced by the Polish-born Stanislav Kosior (or Kossior) as head of the party. The real power and influence in both the party and the government, however, was Mykola Skrypnyk, the Old Bolshevik originally sent to Dnieper Ukraine by Lenin himself during the revolutionary period. Formally, Skrypnyk took the demoted Shums'kyi's post as commissar of education. In fact, Skrypnyk became what one writer has called a "sort of commissar of the nationality question"[2] and the ultimate authority on Ukrainianization, Ukrainian culture, and Ukrainian political life in general. The years 1928 to 1933 can be characterized, then, as the Skrypnyk era in Soviet Ukrainian history.

Skrypnyk's goal was simple. He was never a Ukrainian nationalist. Rather, as a proletarian internationalist and a firm believer in Bolshevik ideology, he held that a distinct Soviet Ukrainian state should be created as an equal to Soviet Russia, to be joined after the "world revolution" by other future soviet states like Germany and France. It was in preparation for such an eventuality that Skrypnyk continued to promote Ukrainianization and, therefore, Ukrainian "national" interests.

With Skrypnyk given free reign to promote his views, Ukrainianization during the Skrypnyk era continued to attain new successes. The program of adult education continued to reduce illiteracy, with the result that by 1938, 98 percent of the population of Soviet Ukraine had been declared literate. Whether that figure is accepted or, what is likely to be more reliable (80 to 85 percent) is less material than the fact that instruction in the adult literacy schools was almost entirely in Ukrainian. The Ukrainianization of the regular school system also reached its height in 1932–1933, by which time 88 percent of all students in Soviet Ukraine were receiving their instruction in Ukrainian. Publishing in the Ukrainian language also attained its highest level at this time: by 1930, nearly 80 percent of all books published were in Ukrainian, and by 1932 nearly 92 percent of all newspaper circulation was in Ukrainian.[3]

Yet at the very same time that Ukrainianization was flourishing, Ukrainian cultural institutions and individual activists were being undermined. The year 1928 was a harbinger of things to come. In February, the Marxist economist Mikhail Volobuev, who argued that Soviet Ukraine could prosper only if the republic had control over its own economic development and national budget, was denounced in public for his "heretical" views until forced to recant. In March, the Soviet Union's first major show trial was held in Shakhty, a mining town in Russia's part of the Donbas which until 1925 was within Soviet Ukraine. Over fifty engineers and technicians were denounced as "bourgeois specialists," accused of cooperating with foreign interests in order to "wreck" industrial production, and in general held up as symbols of the "internal opposition" – real or imagined – that the regime was determined to uncover and prosecute. Also suspected of anti-Soviet opposition was the Ukrainian intelligentsia. It is not surprising, then, that before the end of 1928 the head of the Ukrainian Institute of Marxism-Leninism, the historian Matvii Iavors'kyi, was denounced. The cause given was his description of the coming into being of the CP(b)U as owing to indigenous conditions, along with the inference that the Ukrainian party was itself worthy of continuing to lead the country along a distinct path toward socialism. Such a view was a "deviation" from the accepted Soviet wisdom of the time.

Volobuev and Iavors'kyi were Marxists by conviction. Both had by 1930 been denounced for "nationalist deviation," soon after arrested, and sent to labor camps in Siberia (where they eventually died). Now it was time to turn to the non-Marxist intellectual elite, especially those centered in the All-Ukrainian Academy of Sciences. The technique was for the secret police to proclaim the existence of counterrevolutionary organizations and then to find their agents. In November 1929, the fictitious Union for the Liberation of Ukraine (Spilka Vyzvolennia Ukraïny, or SVU) was "uncovered," and the following month the Ukrainian Autocephalous Orthodox Church was linked to the alleged conspiracy. As a result of its "involvement," the Autocephalous Church was forced to dissolve itself in January 1930.

As for the All-Ukrainian Academy of Sciences, its ranks were decimated during the trial held in the spring of 1930 against the SVU. Half of the forty-five defendants were associated the Academy of Sciences, including established scholars like the historians Osyp Hermaize and Mykhailo Slabchenko; the linguists Vsevolod Hantsov, Hryhorii Holoskevych, and Hryhorii Kholodnyi; and the supposed head of the SVU conspiracy, the vice-president of the academy since 1923, Serhii Iefremov. All the defendants were convicted, and although (in Soviet terms) they were given relatively lenient sentences, within the next few years almost all were rearrested and never returned from their incarceration. As for the Autocephalous Orthodox Church, any efforts by its clergy to continue functioning after its "self-liquidation" on the eve of the SVU trial were suppressed by Soviet security forces. During the next eight years, 2 metropolitans, 26 bishops, and 1,150 priests were arrested and/or disappeared in labor camps. Even the 300 parishes allowed to reconstitute themselves as a new organization called simply the Ukrainian Orthodox Church were progressively eliminated until the last was suppressed in 1936.

Leaving aside all consideration of the personal tragedies of the SVU defendants, this first political "show" trial, held ostentatiously and lasting for over a month in the Kharkiv Opera House, proved a convenient means of warning others that contact with Ukrainians in Poland and with émigrés elsewhere, as well as criticism of the government's policies of industrialization and collectivization, must cease. The SVU trial also served to equate Ukrainian national aspirations with treason, an equation reiterated over the next few years, during which an estimated fifteen other counterrevolutionary organizations were "uncovered." Some of these uncoverings also ended in trials that allowed the authorities to drive home their message to the public: "bourgeois nationalism" was one of the greatest dangers to Soviet society. Just as a peasant became a "counterrevolutionary kulak" if he or she did not agree with collectivization and the forced requisitioning of grain, so too did an intellectual become a "counterrevolutionary bourgeois nationalist" if he or she did not favor the party's ever-changing approach to the nationality question.

Arguing that "bourgeois nationalists" were the enemies of the people, between 1931 and 1934 the Soviet authorities removed from their positions the leading lights of the Ukrainian intelligentsia, whether or not they were Communists. Their subsequent fate was often imprisonment, exile, even execution. There was no question that non-Communists had to be replaced, beginning with Mykhailo Hrushevs'kyi. In 1931, he was removed from his post in the All-Ukrainian Academy of Sciences and exiled to Russia, where he died in 1934. Hrushevs'kyi at least was not imprisoned. Many of his colleagues were not so lucky. Several prominent linguists (O. Kurylo, Ie. Tymchenko, O. Syniavs'kyi, M. Sulyma), historians

(V. Bazylevych, F. Ernst, O. Hrushevs'kyi, V. Miiakovs'kyi, F. Savchenko), writers (S. Pylypenko, V. Pidmohyl'nyi, V. Pluzhnyk, M. Semenko, B. Antonenko-Davy-dovych), and non-Bolshevik politicians, including all the old Borotbists and Uka-pists who later joined the CP(b)U (O. Shums'kyi, A. Richyts'kyi) as well as non-Communists who returned from exile (M. Chechel', M. Shrah, P. Khrystiuk), were arrested and, whether executed or sent to Siberia, were never heard from again. At the organizational level, the Institute of Marxism-Leninism was abolished (1931); all the independent writers' associations were liquidated, with only one, the Asso-ciation of Soviet Writers of Ukraine, being permitted to continue (1934); and the All-Ukrainian Academy of Sciences was completely reorganized, its humanistic branches thenceforth required to work exclusively on proletarian themes.

Skrypnyk was not particularly disturbed by the "ideological cleansing" and purg-es of the non-Communist intelligentsia. He even spoke publicly during the SVU trial, attacking those individuals accused of "nationalist deviation" in Ukrainian language matters, although carefully avoiding comment on the substance of what they were doing. What they were doing was, after all, supported by Skrypnyk him-self, who remained committed to expanding Ukrainianization in the belief that this expansion would preserve the achievements of the Bolshevik Revolution.

Although the policy of Ukrainianization was still officially supported by the CP(b)U, the "internationalist" elements in the party now made the protection of national minorities their primary issue. They argued that Russians should remain the dominant demographic force in urban and industrial areas (their position assisted, if necessary, by the russification of incoming ethnic Ukrainians from the countryside) and that limitations should be placed on the Ukrainianization pro-gram. The justification given by the internationalists in the party was that Ukrain-ian nationalism was associated with kulaks and the peasant question. It therefore posed an even greater threat than Great Russian chauvinism. Skrypnyk respond-ed to the internationalists' arguments by calling for more investment in Soviet Ukraine from the all-union budget and for an intensification of Ukrainianization in the areas of education, publication, and governmental administration. His ide-ological justification remained straightforward: socialism could be achieved in Ukraine only after the creation of a firm national-cultural base, and any attempt at the russification of ethnic Ukrainian urban dwellers would only exacerbate the national issue. Throughout these debates, Stalin pretended to remain aloof, even reiterating at the 16th Congress of the All-Union Communist party in June 1930 the party's commitment to the existence of the national republics and its contin-ued concern over the danger of Great Russian chauvinism.

The end of Ukrainianization

By 1933, however, the social and political instability in Soviet Ukraine warranted increased attention. In January 1933, in response to the complaints of the CP(b)U leadership that the grain quotas and forced collectivization were having a disastrous effect on the country, Stalin dispatched to Soviet Ukraine Pavel Postyshev, a Russian-born Bolshevik who had served for a while as head of the CP(b)U in Kharkiv before being recalled to Moscow. Although designated second secretary of the CP(b)U and theoretically subordinate to Kosior, Postyshev was in fact given free reign to root out from the party all persons suspected of "nationalist deviation." The object was to crush whatever opposition to Stalin still existed within the Ukrainian party.

The scapegoat for all the CP(b)U's difficulties was found in Skrypnyk. Within one month of his arrival in Soviet Ukraine, Postyshev had Skrypnyk removed as commissar of education, and in June he attacked him by name at the party plenum for having filled his commissariat with "wrecking, counterrevolutionary nationalist elements."[4] Since language was traditionally equated with the survival of national distinctiveness, it is not surprising that among Skrypnyk's greatest sins was his promotion of Ukrainian language reforms, including linguistic purism and a new orthography (popularly known as the *skrypnykivka*) approved in 1928. Seemingly esoteric academic issues took on profound political significance: the revised Ukrainian alphabet and the search for a "pure" Ukrainian vocabulary offered clear evidence, in the words of one critic, that "Comrade Skrypnyk ... had taken the path of alienating the Ukrainian language from Russian and bringing it closer to Polish."[5]

Unlike many other Ukrainian Marxists accused of "nationalist deviation," Skrypnyk refused to recant. Instead, he committed suicide in July 1933, just one month after another "national deviationist," the writer Mykola Khvyl'ovyi, shot himself. With the death of Skrypnyk, the process of Ukrainianization and any possibility of creating a Soviet Ukraine distinct from the rest of the Soviet Union came to an end. By the very beginning of 1933, the transitional period that had begun in 1928 was over, and it was clear that in the coming years all efforts would be made to transform Soviet Ukraine into a land economically, politically, and culturally an integral part of the Soviet Union.

Purges and integration

The large-scale purges of the CP(b)U and governmental institutions in Soviet Ukraine initiated in 1933 under Postyshev were in one sense a prelude to what would take place throughout the rest of the Soviet Union. Stalin had become obsessed with the need for total control, which he felt could be achieved only by the elimination of all whom he perceived as disloyal. In 1934, the so-called Great Purge began, which brought the arrest, exile, or death of millions of persons – mainly Communists and officials in Soviet government and industry. Almost all the Old Bolshevik leaders were forced to confess in bizarre show trials between 1936 and 1938, and on the eve of World War II the Red Army's leading generals were shot. Fear and suspicion became the norm in these years of Stalin's Soviet Union, characterized by one western specialist (Robert Conquest) as the era of the Great Terror. No one could be sure that a neighbor, a co-worker, even a family member was not a secret police informer ready to accuse him or her of being a counterrevolutionary, because of some offhand comment or joke about daily life, or – absurd as it may sound – such things as favoring use of the letter *g* (the Ukrainian Cyrillic letter г that does not appear in Russian) in the "Skrypnyk alphabet." During the first year of Postyshev's presence in Soviet Ukraine, nearly 100,000 persons were purged from the CP(b)U. The process continued,

THE PURGES

In March 1938, the last of the major show trials against Stalin's presumed or actual political enemies took place in Moscow. Its defendants were twenty-one members of the so-called Right Opposition, who had opposed Stalin's policies of rapid industrialization through central planning and forced collectivization. Aside from their views on the direction of Soviet society, the accused were charged as well with espionage on behalf of Germany and Japan, attempted dismemberment of the Soviet Union, and conspiracy to eliminate the entire Soviet leadership. The best-known defendant, Nikolai Bukharin, was also accused of conspiracy to kill Lenin and Stalin as early as 1918.

Among the defendants were two who had played leading roles in Soviet Ukraine during the 1920s, the former head of government before Ukrainianization, Khristiian Rakovskii, and the former commissar for state planning during the early years of Ukrainianization, Hryhorii Hryn'ko. Both subsequently held high posts in the central Soviet government and party hierarchy in Moscow. In his last statement before being sentenced to death, Hryn'ko told the court what the Soviet authorities wanted their public to know about the supposedly "nefarious" period of Ukrainianization. Stalin and his remaining supporters were so pleased with the information that "came out" at the trial that its entire proceedings were translated into and published in English so that the world would know to what degree the Soviet Union was threatened internally as well as externally. In his last public confession, Hryn'ko provided Soviet propagandists with a useful script about the so-called dangers of Ukrainian nationalism.

In order that the path may be clear by which I arrived at committing the enormous chain of crimes against the Soviet power and the country, and at treason against the country, I must recall that I joined the Communist party as one of the Borotbists – the Ukrainian nationalist organization. A large group of the leaders of the Borotbists: Shums'kyi, Poloz, Blakytnyi, I – Hryn'ko, Liubchenko, and others who merged with the Communist party of Ukraine, continued to adhere to and later intensified our bourgeois-nationalist position.

I can enumerate the main stages in the development of the nationalist, conspiratorial, counter-revolutionary work of this Borotbist nucleus.

The first stage was the period approximately of 1925–26. This is what is called the period of Shums'ky-ism. Already at that time Shums'ky-ism was in all essentials a program of severing Ukraine from the U.S.S.R., a program of bourgeois-nationalist restoration in Ukraine. Already at that time it was a sort of large-scale political reconnoitring by the nationalists, a trial of strength, the demand to discredit Russian towns in Ukraine, to discredit Russian cadres, etc.

Shums'ky-ism was crushed politically and undermined organizationally. ... When this nationalist organization [the Borotbists] was smashed, only fragments of it remained. But about 1929, a nationalist organization revived again in Moscow, consisting of Shums'kyi, myself, Poloz, Maksymovych, Solodub and a number of others. This organization approached its program and its tactics differently from the way it did in the first period. ...

In this period the nationalist organization gave its members instructions to collect forces and wage an active struggle, mainly against collectivization, and even to go so far as to organize insurrection. In this struggle we already had connections with certain circles in a certain state which is hostile to the Soviet Union. These allies of ours helped us. To assist the partisan struggle they intensified the smuggling of diversionists and Petliura emissaries, and arms, etc., into Ukraine. ...

This period came to an end at the beginning of 1933 owing to the arrest of nearly the whole of this group. I was the only one not arrested. But I did not lay down my nationalist arms in my fight against Soviet power. ...

At the beginning of 1935 I heard from Liubchenko about the creation in Ukraine of a national-fascist organization, the object of which was to sever Ukraine from the U.S.S.R. ... When I learned about this organization I agreed to join it. ...

In 1935 and the beginning of 1936, I had, in the main, carried out the tasks entrusted to me by the Ukrainian organization. I had established connections with the Right and Trotskyite centre. ...

...

I am making my last plea not in order to defend myself before the Supreme Court. I have nothing to say in my defence. Nor shall I make use of this plea in order to ask for a mitigation of the sentence. I have no right to a mitigation of the sentence. I am wholly and completely in agreement with the description and political evaluation, both of our crimes in general and of my crimes in particular, as given in the speech of the Prosecutor of the U.S.S.R. ...

I face the court as a Ukrainian bourgeois nationalist and at the same time as a participant of the 'bloc of Rightists and Trotskyites.' This is no chance combination. The hunting after bourgeois nationalists and the political corruption of unstable political elements in the national republics are the old-established and stubbornly conducted tactics of the Trotskyites and the Right Oppositionists. ...

As one of the organizers of the Ukrainian national-fascist organization, I operated particularly in Ukraine, that is to say, at the main gates through which German fascism is preparing its blow against the U.S.S.R. ...

This Ukrainian national-fascist organization – including Liubchenko, Poraiko and others – completes the last link in the long chain of criminal deeds committed against the Ukrainian people by various factions of Ukrainian bourgeois-nationalism from the very beginning of the revolution.

The Prosecutor of the U.S.S.R. was right when he said that under the leadership of the Bolshevik party and the Soviet government the Ukrainian people, advancing along the road of the national policy of Lenin and Stalin, have been raised to such a high level as never before in all its previous history. The Bolshevik party and Soviet power have created the Ukrainian state, they have made Ukraine a very rich industrial and collective farming country, they have raised Ukrainian national culture to an unprecedented high level. And this Ukrainian national fascist organization, which it is my sad lot to represent before the court, was, by resorting to bogus slogans of national 'independence,' leading the Ukrainian people to the yoke of German fascists and Polish gentry. ...

The party raised me from the petty-bourgeois mire, it placed me in a high post in the government, a high station, entrusted me with state secrets and with control over the state finances of the U.S.S.R. ...

And to all of this I replied by betrayal, by darkest betrayal, of the party, the fatherland, and Stalin.

And it is in conditions like these, members of the Supreme Court, that I must tell you of my remorse. I very well understand with what scorn and contempt every Soviet person will meet these words of repentance coming as they do from me. Nevertheless, I must say this because it corresponds to the truth, because there is no one else to whom I can address these words. ...

I will accept the most severe verdict – the supreme penalty – as deserved. I have only one wish: I wish to live through my last days or hours, no matter how few they may be, I wish to live through and die not as an enemy taken prisoner by the Soviet government, but as a citizen of the U.S.S.R. who has committed the gravest treachery to the fatherland, whom the fatherland has severely punished for this, but who repented.

SOURCE: *Report of Court Proceedings in the Case of the Anti-Soviet "Bloc of Rightists and Trotskyites" Heard Before the Military Collegiun of the Supreme Court of the U.S.S.R., Moscow, March 2–13, 1938: Verbatim Report* (Moscow 1938), pp. 67–71 and 718–721.

and between 1934 and 1938 the party lost another 168,000 members, or another 37 percent of its total membership. Many higher-level party positions were filled by Stalinist faithful from other parts of the Soviet Union, while new and often younger-generation party functionaries were drawn from Soviet Ukraine itself, where the party had become rooted as a result of indigenization. Once set in motion, the purges seemed to take on a life of their own, confirming the general observation that revolutions often devour their own children. Postyshev himself was removed from his post in early 1937 (he was later shot), and within a year the entire hierarchy (politburo and secretariat) of the CP(b)U was purged. In order to rebuild the party, Stalin dispatched to Soviet Ukraine Nikita S. Khrushchev, but he had to be appointed to the position as Ukraine's first secretary by the all-Union Communist leadership in Moscow because there was no one left in the CP(b)U Central Committee to elect him.

With regard to cultural life, a new policy was adopted throughout the Soviet Union. The era of experimentation and the generally permissive atmosphere that had characterized artistic creativity in the 1920s (including avant-garde and abstract works) was replaced by Stalinist-inspired guidelines known as "socialist realism." The Communist party was now called on to be more vigilant and to exercise increasing control over all creative endeavors in order to insure that cultural works became instruments of education and political propaganda with the goal of depicting the positive achievements of Soviet life. Whether in literature, the visual arts, or cinema, the party-approved style was expected to be simple, direct, and accessibly "realistic," in order to make the socialist message intelligible to the broad masses.

Aside from socialist realism in the cultural sphere, there was socialist competition in the workplace. Soviet policy makers became increasingly preoccupied with the need to refashion popular attitudes toward labor, which in traditional imperial Russian society had generally been considered a burden imposed on workers by feudal landowners and capitalist factory and mine owners. But as industrialization took on increasing importance in Soviet society, so too did the need to imbue the citizenry with a proper work ethic that, in effect, functioned as a corollary to Soviet patriotism. In this regard, Soviet Ukraine became the site for the exploits of modern-day heroes that were to serve as the prototype for the new Soviet man – and woman. This was all part of a movement broadly defined as socialist competition whose goal was to increase worker productivity.

In the early 1930s, one Nikifor Izotov, a miner at Horlivka in the heart of Ukraine's Donets' Basin, became the focus of attention throughout the Soviet Union. He and those who wanted to follow his example, dubbed Izotovites, made it their goal to go beyond the production quotas set by the Five-Year Plans and at the same time to assist fellow workers who could not keep up with their expected daily quota in the mines and factories. In other words, it was not enough to fulfil The Plan, one should over-fullfill it. Even more remarkable than Izotov were the achievements of a native of Russia, Aleksei Stakhanov, who from 1927 worked in another coal mining town in Ukraine's Donets' Basin, Kadiïvka (today Stakhanov). Stakhanov set his first production record in 1935 (extracting 102 tons of coal in a single six-hour work shift), thereby over-fulfiling his quota by a factor of 14.5. It was not long before Stakhanov became a poster boy for Soviet propagandists, who transformed him into a living legend whose labor exploits were lovingly depicted in countless newspaper articles, children's books, and movies. His alleged (and often staged) feats served as the ideal for what became known as the Stakhanovite movement in which individual workers and workers' brigades in mines and factories throughout the Soviet Union set over-fulfillment as their primary goal, that is, production results which were higher than those outlined in the state's Plan. The movement also spread to the agricultural sector and included female Stakhanovites, like Mariia Demchenko from the Cherkasy region, who made her mark in harvesting sugar beets.

It is also somewhat ironic to note that at the very same time the intelligentsia who formed the backbone of the Ukrainianization program was being silenced and persecuted by the Soviet authorities, a self-taught plant breeder from a peasant household in central Ukraine was rapidly on his way to becoming a leading figure in the all-Soviet scientific establishment. This was the case of Trokhym Lysenko, renowned for his theories about inducting hereditary changes in plants (vernalization; Ukrainian: *iarovizatsiia*) by modifying their environment. Stalin became enamored with Lysenko whose agrobiological convictions influenced for decades – often with disastrous consequences – Soviet agricultural policy in its state-owned and cooperative farms and in its forests.

While promoting socialist competition in the workplace, from 1933 the Communist party's goal in Soviet Ukraine's cultural sphere was to reverse the policy of the previous years, in which Shums'kyi's and Skrypnyk's "nefarious" policies had brought about "forced Ukrainianization." More and more emphasis was to be given to Russian culture and the Russian language, considered the medium through which the world's "first socialist state" had been created. In 1933, the alphabet and language reforms instituted in 1928 and associated with Skrypnyk's name were abolished, and decrees were passed requiring that in its alphabet, vocabulary, and grammar the Ukrainian language be brought steadily closer to Russian. By 1937, Soviet ideologists were proposing the intimate union of the two languages, and the following year a law was passed providing for a rigid system of language training designed to ensure that all Ukrainians, whether in the cities or the countryside, would have a fluent command of Russian.

For the new directives to be followed, the educational system could no longer be subjected to "forced Ukrainianization." While it is true that the percentage of students studying in Ukrainian in general schools was even higher in the late 1930s than in the late 1920s, a new educational environment was inaugurated in March 1938, when the study of Russian was made obligatory in all non-Russian schools throughout the Soviet Union. In other areas too, Russian supplanted Ukrainian. Between 1932 and 1939, the circulation of Ukrainian-language newspapers published in Soviet Ukraine declined from 92 to 67 percent, while in half that time the number of Russian-language theaters increased from nine to thirty.[6]

The justification for this new approach was summarized in June 1938 in an address by First Secretary Khrushchev to the 14th Congress of the CP(b)U:

Comrades, now all the people study the Russian language because the Russian workers ... helped to forward the flag of revolution. The Russian workers have set an example to the workers and peasants of the whole world. ...

People of all areas are studying and will study the Russian language in order to study Leninism and Stalinism and to be taught to destroy their enemies. ... The bourgeois nationalists, the Polish and German spies, as they made their way into certain sections of the cultural front, understood remarkably well the force and influence of the teachings of Lenin and Stalin on the minds of the Ukrainian people. Because of this they drove the Russian language from schools. But the Ukrainian people, who in the course of many centuries have battled against their enemies alongside the Russian workers and peasants, are completely dedicated to the general aspirations of the workers' class of the Soviet world. They are tied by vital bonds to the Great Russian people and will fight together with them under the banner of Lenin and Stalin for the complete victory of Communism.[7]

Henceforth, the Russian language was associated with survival in the only world which the future promised – a communist society according to the dictates of Marx, Lenin, and Stalin.

Thus, in just two decades the Communists had come full circle in Dnieper Ukraine. They had begun in 1919 with an attempt to create a socialist society without national distinctions and expressed only in Russian. Two decades later, they were back where they started. In one sense, this is not surprising, because Ukrainianization, like the economic experiment of NEP, was for the Bolsheviks never more than a temporary solution. The proverbial one step backward had been made; two giant steps forward now seemed possible. The year was 1939, however. New clouds hovered over Europe. And before long war was to engulf most parts of the world. In response, Soviet leaders would have to take more steps backward than even the ultimate pragmatist himself, Lenin, would ever have dreamed necessary.

Other Peoples in Soviet Ukraine

With the establishment of Soviet (Bolshevik) rule in Dnieper Ukraine, ethnic Ukrainians were recognized as a distinct nationality. This change in status was a product of Lenin's attempt to resolve the nationality problem in the former Russian Empire by providing its numerous peoples with various kinds of territorial and administrative entities. The relatively complex and hierarchical administrative system actually adopted was developed after the creation of the Soviet Union in December 1922. Initially, the Soviet Union consisted of four constituent republics (one of which was Soviet Ukraine), whose number rose to nine by 1929. The name of each was intended to reflect the state, or titular, nationality living within a given republic. In addition to the national republics, there were other administrative subdivisions, also based in principle on criteria of nationality; namely, autonomous republics, autonomous oblasts, autonomous regions, nationality districts, and nationality village/town soviets.

Whereas ethnic Ukrainians were the numerically dominant element in Soviet Ukraine, 20 percent of the country's inhabitants comprised several other peoples, who after 1924 were formally designated as national minorities (Ukrainian: *natsional'ni menshyny*).

TABLE 45.1
Nationality composition of Soviet Ukraine, 1926[1]

Nationality	Number	Percentage
Ukrainians	23,219,000	80.0
Russians	2,674,000	9.2
Jews	1,574,000	5.4
Poles	476,000	1.6
Germans	394,000	1.4
Moldovans	258,000	0.9
Greeks	105,000	0.4
Bulgarians	92,000	0.3
Belarusans	76,000	0.3
Tatars	22,000	0.1
Czechs	16,000	0.0
Others	109,000	0.4
TOTAL	29,018,000	100.0

The Moldavian A.S.S.R. and the Moldovans

Soviet Ukraine created for its various national minorities some of the above-mentioned administrative subdivisions. The highest category among them was the Moldavian Autonomous Soviet Socialist Republic (Moldavian A.S.S.R.), created in 1924 on a strip of territory along the eastern bank of the Dniester River, which at the time formed the Soviet border with Romania. The creation of the Moldavian A.S.S.R. was part of the Soviet Union's larger strategic goal to acquire the former tsarist province of Bessarabia, located just to the west between the Dniester and Prut Rivers, which at the time was part of anti-Soviet "bourgeois" Romania. The Soviet claim to Bessarabia was based not only on historic grounds (tsarist Russia had held the region for a century before World War I), but also on the claim that Romanian speakers on both sides of the Dniester River, in historic Moldavia, formed a distinct Romance people called Moldovans. Therefore, the Romanian speakers in Soviet Ukraine's Moldavian A.S.S.R. were proclaimed to be a distinct Moldovan nationality, which one day would be "re-united" with their co-nationals when the Soviet Union would extend its borders westward.

Despite being a titular nationality, the Moldovans were, in fact, a statistical minority, numbering only 172,000, or 30 percent of their "own" republic's population. The rest of Soviet Ukraine's Romanians – now reclassified as Moldovans (89,000) – lived farther east, mostly in the rural steppe region near the banks of the lower Southern Buh River. As part of its longer-term "Bessarabian" strategy, the Soviet authorities supported a policy of Moldovanization. Moldovan national village soviets were created within the Moldavian A.S.S.R. (63 by 1931) and just to the east in steppe Ukraine (17), as were Moldovan-language elementary schools. By the 1930–1931 school year, there were 121 of these schools, in which nearly two-thirds of all children in the Moldavian A.S.S.R. were enrolled.

If the Moldovans were a distinct nationality, Soviet policy dictated that they should have their own language. Therefore, the autonomous republic's capital of Balta became the seat of the Moldovan Scientific Committee, headed by Pavel Chior, who together with the linguist Leonid Madan created a grammar book (published in 1929) for a Moldovan standard literary language. Books and newspapers were published in this new standard using the Cyrillic alphabet. Historically, Cyrillic was not uncommon for Romanian-language publications in Bessarabia, although for a short period (1932–1938), when the Moldovanization program was under attack for ideological deviation, the autonomous republic's authorities adopted the Roman/Latin alphabet and language norms that were not very different from literary Romanian. By 1937, the experiment in creating a distinct nationality and culture seemed to run its course, so that most of Moldovan high culture was little more than Romanian in disguise.

Nationality administration in Soviet Ukraine

While Soviet Ukraine had within its borders only one autonomous republic, more widespread were other nationality administrative subdivisions that began to be set

TABLE 45.2
Nationality subdivisions in Soviet Ukraine, 1931[2]

Nationality	Districts	Village/Town soviets
Russian	8	388
German	7	252
Jewish	3	158
Polish	1	157
Bulgarian	3	46
Greek	3	30
Moldovan (outside Moldavian A.S.S.R.)	–	17
Czech	–	12
Belarusan	–	4
Albanian	–	3
Swedish	–	1
TOTAL	25	1,068

up in 1924. These included nationality districts (*raiony*), town soviets (*selyshchni rady*), and village soviets (*sil's'ki rady*), all designed to serve the interests of those peoples who formed the majority of the population in a given locale. The number of nationality districts and village/town soviets continually fluctuated throughout the 1920s and 1930s, although at their height they numbered between 1,000 and 1,200.

Within each of these administrative entities the national minority was allowed to use its own language in education (generally in elementary schools), in government-funded cultural institutions and publications, and in local courts and state administrative offices. Some village and town soviets were located within a given group's nationality district, but most were isolated entities spread throughout the country (see map 38).

Not surprisingly, the status of the various minority peoples during the interwar years was directly influenced by the policies adopted by the Soviet Ukrainian government and the CP(b)U toward the state's titular nationality, the ethnic Ukrainians. Hence, when Ukrainianization was implemented, policies with similar goals were introduced among some of the minorities – Moldovanization, Yiddishization, Polonization, Tatarization, Hellenization. The evolution and fate of those policies also largely paralleled the evolution and fate of Ukrainianization.

The Russians

Of all the national minorities in Soviet Ukraine, the Russians continued to maintain a special status. Their number alone – nearly 2.7 million in 1926 – guaranteed that they would play an important role in Soviet Ukrainian society. This was particularly the case in those geographic areas where they were most densely concentrated, specifically the northeastern industrial and southern steppe regions. In 1930, Russians had eight nationality districts and as many as 388 village and town soviets in which schools, courts, and other administrative bodies operated only in Russian. It is nonetheless interesting to note that although Russians had the high-

MAP 38   NATIONALITY DISTRICTS IN SOVIET UKRAINE, 1931

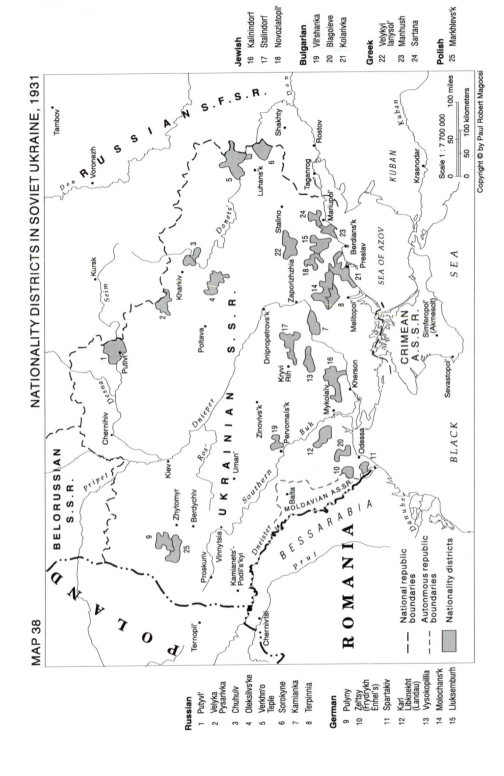

Russian
1 Putyvl'
2 Velyka
   Pysarivka
3 Chuhuïv
4 Oleksiïvs'ke
5 Verkhn'o
   Teple
6 Sorokyne
7 Kamianka
8 Terpinnia

German
9 Pulyny
10 Zel'tsy
   (Frydrykh
   Enhel's)
11 Spartakiv
12 Karl
   Libknekht
   (Landau)
13 Vysokopillia
14 Molochans'k
15 Liuksemburh

Jewish
16 Kalinindorf
17 Stalindorf
18 Novozlatopil'

Bulgarian
19 Vil'shanka
20 Blagoieve
21 Kolarivka

Greek
22 Velykyi
   Ianysol'
23 Manhush
24 Sartana

Polish
25 Markhlevs'k

National republic boundaries
Autonomous republic boundaries
Nationality districts

Scale 1 : 7 700 000

Copyright © by Paul Robert Magocsi

est number of national minority schools (1,539 in 1929–1930), nearly one-fifth of the students from this group had no access to Russian-language schools and attended Ukrainian ones instead.

Regardless of numbers and administrative status, Russians never regarded themselves as a minority. They continued to perceive themselves as representatives of the dominant culture and language in what remained their "Little Russian" homeland. If the Russian language and culture was already dominant during tsarist days, under the Bolsheviks its status was raised to an even higher level as the medium in which the worldwide socialist revolution was unfolding. The revolution was to be led by an industrial proletariat, and this forecast seemed to fit well with the social status of Russians in Soviet Ukraine, 37 percent of whom were urban dwellers. Aside from the Russian industrial workforce, a high percentage of governmental bureaucrats and intellectual elite, especially in the universities, were Russians or russified Ukrainians and Jews who continued to function in terms of language and cultural preferences as if the Bolshevik Revolution had never taken place.

It is not surprising that, furnished with such attitudes, many Russians found the linguistic aspects of Ukrainianization bothersome at the very least. Moreover, many felt confident that the decrees could be ignored until the Ukrainian "social experiment" had run its course. When, by the second half of the 1930s, the course had indeed been run and the Soviet Ukrainian government and CP(b)U were repudiating the policy of "forced Ukrainianization," Russians seemed to regain in Soviet Ukraine the privileged position they had held in tsarist times. There were, however, some Russians who actively supported the idea of greater recognition for Ukraine and its culture. Among the best known was the economic theoretician Mikhail Volobuev, who in the 1920s argued that Soviet Ukraine should control its own economic development, and Nikolai Fitilev, better known as Mykola Khvyl'ovyi, the prominent Ukrainian-language writer who argued that modern Ukrainian culture must break "away from Moscow" and re-orient itself toward "progressive" Europe.

The Jews

Numerically, the second-largest minority living in Soviet Ukraine during the interwar period were the Jews. The Soviet theory on nationalities, as formulated by Lenin and Stalin, recognized the need to protect national minorities, but on theoretical grounds, the Jews did not qualify for such treatment. This is because Jews lacked their own territory, one of the four essential characteristics (alongside language, economic life, and community of culture) which, according to Stalin, determined the existence of nationalities. Before the Bolshevik Revolution, for instance, Lenin had argued: "The Jews in Galicia and in Russia are no longer a nation; unfortunately, they remain a caste."[3] Castes such as the Jews, argued Lenin, should become assimilated.

While in theory assimilation seemed the ideal solution, when the Bolsheviks took over the reigns of government, they were faced with the reality that several million Jews spoke a distinct language (Yiddish), lived a unique mode of life, possessed their own culture, and even lived in compact masses on certain territories, especially along the western frontiers of the former Russian Empire. Therefore, as early as 1918, the Soviet state recognized Jews as a nationality. By 1926, Jews numbered nearly 1.6 million inhabitants, or 5.4 percent of the population of Soviet Ukraine. Although they were most densely settled on the Right Bank and the Black Sea littoral (especially around Odessa), they were also found in large numbers in all parts of the republic. Almost three-fourths lived in urban areas, with especially high percentages in Odessa (36.5 percent of the urban population), Kiev (27.3 percent), Dnipropetrovs'k (26.7 percent), and Kharkiv (19.5 percent).

When, during the early years of Soviet rule, private enterprise, even on a small scale, was abolished, Jews experienced widespread unemployment and poverty. In 1924, in an attempt to alleviate the conditions created by Soviet policy, the All-Union government established special organizations (KOMZET and OZET) whose purpose was to encourage Jews to move to rural areas. Between 1924 and 1930 alone, 162 new Jewish agricultural colonies were established in Soviet Ukraine's countryside, which together with previous ones brought the total to 210. There were also another 40 Jewish agricultural colonies in the Crimea. This movement from towns and cities to the land, which by 1931 accounted for 172,000 Ukrainian Jews engaged in agriculture, was the result of both Soviet governmental policy and private initiative assisted by organizations in the West such as the American Jewish Joint Distribution Committee. Some Soviet enthusiasts even thought a Jewish national homeland could be created on the steppes of southern Ukraine.

The status of the Jews under Soviet rule varied greatly during the interwar years and was directly related to the government's and party's changing attitudes toward the nationality question. Initially, during the period of "war communism" (1918-1921), the Bolsheviks were convinced they could create immediately an internationalist or nationality-less society. Armed with such ideological self-confidence, they adopted a negative attitude toward traditional close-knit Jewish communities (Yiddish: *shtetlakh*) under rabbinic leadership. Hence, most community organizations were abolished, synagogues were closed, Hebrew-language religious education was banned, and the popular grass-roots Yiddish organizations known as Kultur-lige (Culture Leagues) were taken over by the Communist party. Large numbers of Jews, in particular shop owners and small-scale entrepreneurs, also suffered economic hardship during these early years when free-market commerce was outlawed and private businesses nationalized.

As individuals, however, Jews were given full equality alongside all other peoples under Soviet law. For those who continued or chose to adapt to the new social and political conditions, there were, indeed, certain advantages. Many joined the CP(b)U, which, like other republic Communist parties, set up a special Jewish Section (Ukrainian: *Ievsektsiia*) whose task was to attract new party members and to struggle against traditional religious-oriented Jewish life. As part of this rejection, the head of Soviet Ukraine's *Ievsektsiia* at the time, Moyshe Altshuler, argued against promoting Yiddish (other than in primary grades) and that instead higher-level Jewish schools should teach only in Russian. Although the proportion of Jews in the CP(b)U (13.6 percent in 1922) was higher than their proportion in Soviet Ukraine's population (5.4 percent in 1926), the percentage of Jews who became Bolsheviks remained minuscule – less than 1 percent of the group as a whole. It is also true, however, that Jews (or more properly atheists of Jewish background – "non-Jewish Jews") were very prominent in the highest levels of the Bolshevik party. For instance, in 1917, Jews comprised 20 percent of the delegates at the Bolshevik party congress and 6 of 21 members of the party's Central Committee. Their continuing presence in the early years of the Soviet regime gave rise to the popular image of the *zhydokomuna,* or "Jewish-Communist conspiracy," that allegedly made it possible for the Bolsheviks to rule Ukraine. The stereotypical belief in "Jewish Bolshevism" (*zhydo-bolshevyzm*) continued for decades to dominate attitudes among the ever increasing number of people in Ukraine who became opposed to Soviet rule.

Some of the more traditionalist forms of Jewish life experienced a rebirth when the internationalist and war-communist phase of the revolution ended. For instance, with the introduction of NEP in 1921, Jewish business activity was revived. By 1926, 13 percent of all Jews were involved in some form of business, which included ownership of 78 percent of all private factories. Nevertheless, while NEP proved advantageous to some Jews, it did not alleviate the unemployment problem among thousands of Ukraine's Jews.

As a national (not religious) minority, however, Jews were entitled to self-government. By 1930, they had in Soviet Ukraine three nationality districts (Kalinindorf, Novyi Zlatopil', and Stalinodorf) located in the steppe region that were founded in conjunction with the movement of Jews to the land. Subsequently, two more Jewish nationality districts were established in the neighboring Crimean A.S.S.R. (Freidorf, 1931, and Larindorf, 1935). By the early 1930s, within as well as beyond the nationality districts, Jews had 158 nationality village and town soviets and forty-six Jewish divisions of Soviet courts throughout Soviet Ukraine. In the Kalinindorf district (the only one where Jews actually formed a majority of the population) as well as in the village and town soviets, Yiddish was the principal language of the local administration, schools, newspapers, and rural theaters.

Yiddish, in particular, was to experience a renaissance after 1923, when the policy of indigenization was implemented in Soviet Ukraine. In keeping with the Communist party's new emphasis on promoting local languages, yet continuing to reject Hebrew because of its intimate association with the Jewish religion, Bolshevik ideologues promoted the Yiddish language (in 1926 the self-declared mother tongue of 76 percent of Soviet Ukraine's Jews) as the instrument through which a new Jewish proletarian culture could be created. To create new "Soviet" Jews, a Yiddish-language school system was established with four pedagogical institutes and an Institute of People's Education in Odessa; by 1931, the high point was reached with 1,096 schools at all levels, serving nearly 95,000 students. This last figure represented approximately one-third of all Jewish students in Soviet Ukraine's schools. At the more advanced level, scholarship about the Jews of Ukraine was encouraged within the All-Ukrainian Academy of Sciences in Kiev. Already in 1919 a Jewish Historic and Archeographic Commission was set up; it lasted for a decade until encouraged to disband by a rival body, also in the academy. This was the Department (which became the Institute in 1929) of Jewish Proletarian Culture, whose main task was to conduct a struggle against "bourgeois Jewish nationalist ideology and science."

Other institutions were founded that not only preserved Jewish culture, but also made its achievements available to the larger public. Among these were the All-Ukrainian Museum of Jewish Culture in Odessa and the Central Jewish Library in Kiev. Particular attention was given to the theatrical world in Soviet Ukraine, which was the site of several components of the Soviet State Yiddish Theater system, including the Ukrainian division of the Central State Yiddish Theater in Kharkiv (after 1935 in Kiev), regional Yiddish theaters in Odessa, Vinnytsia, and Zhytomyr, and the Central State Yiddish Children's Theater in Kiev. Yiddish poetry and prose flourished, especially during the 1920s with the appearance of works by Leyb Kvitko, Itsik Fefer, Pinkhes Kahanovitsh (pseud. Der Nister), and others. Several Jewish authors from Ukraine made their mark in Russian literary circles, the most outstanding of whom was the prose writer Isaak Babel, whose short stories about his native Odessa and popular novel *The Red Calvary* (1926) were both set in Ukraine. Jewish intellectuals also took an active part in the Ukrainian cultural renaissance, including the writers Illia Hurevych (pseud. Leonid Pervomais'kyi) and Abram Katsnel'son; the literary historian Iarema Aizenshtok; the historian Osyp Hermaize; and the linguist Olena Kurylo. Finally, there was a vibrant Yiddish-language Jewish press with numerous journals and, by 1935, ten newspapers, the largest of which was *Der Shtern* (1925–41), the Kharkiv daily organ of the Central Committee of the CP(b)U.

Following the Stalinist revolution of 1928 and the transition to a more centralized and integrated Soviet Union, Jewish cultural achievements like those of the Ukrainians began to be dismantled. Jews who owned small businesses and factories were deprived of their livelihood with the end of NEP. At the same time, forced collectivization and the liquidation of the kulaks put an abrupt halt to the movement into rural areas. Of the Jewish agriculturalists who survived collectivization and the famine, many returned to live in the cities. Although the nationality districts and village/town soviets continued to exist until 1941, the number of Jews residing in them declined, in most cases below the 50 percent minimum of the population which in theory they were required to have.

In political and cultural life, Jewish activists were persecuted at the same time and in the same way as other intellectuals in Soviet Ukraine who were suspected of "nationalist deviation." In 1930, the Jewish Section (*Ievsektsiia*) of the CP(b)U was dissolved, and most of its leaders were purged from the party. The following years witnessed the closing or curtailment of many Jewish institutions, with the result that by the late 1930s there were only five Yiddish newspapers, only four theaters, and a decrease by nearly half in the number of students in Yiddish schools. Thus, the favorable environment for Jewish culture in Soviet Ukraine that prevailed in the 1920s – albeit in a secular, anti-religious, Yiddish form – had been largely undermined by the end of the following decade.

The Poles

During the Soviet period, the Poles of Dnieper Ukraine not only decreased in number, but experienced as well a sharp decline in socioeconomic and cultural influence. The revolution, civil war, and Polish-Soviet war of 1920 prompted a large-scale exodus of Poles from their traditional stronghold, the Right Bank and the city of Kiev. Wealthy landowners and urban intellectuals in particular fled westward to the new Polish state. For instance, whereas in 1919 there were 685,000 Poles, by 1926 their number had declined to only 476,000, in Soviet Ukraine. As before, as many as 86 percent lived in the Right Bank.

The traditional Polish political, cultural, and social organizations as well as the newer ones created during the revolutionary years were abolished by the Soviet authorities, who were intent on creating a new proletarian framework for the Polish minority. The Poles were given their own sections (bureaus) in the Central Committee of the CP(b)U, as well as in party organizations at the regional and village levels where Poles predominated. By 1931, there existed 1 Polish nationality district (the Markhlevs'k/Marchlewski district, just west of Zhytomyr in Volhynia), 157 Polish village soviets, and 6 Polish-language courts.

The greatest challenge for the Soviet authorities was to undermine the traditionally strong adherence of the Polish minority to the Roman Catholic Church. Such inbred attitudes, Communist policy makers thought, might best be changed through educational and cultural institutions. Hence, a network of 381 Polish-language elementary schools was set up, which by 1929–1930 encompassed 42 percent of eligible students of Polish nationality. Kiev, in particular, became a center of the group's institutional life and home to the Central Polish Library, the Polish Theater, and a short-lived Institute of Polish Proletarian Culture within the framework of the All-Ukrainian Academy of Sciences. Soviet ideology was propagated through these institutions and through seventeen Polish-language newspapers published at various times, including the daily *Sierp* (The Sickle), later *Głos Radziecki* (The Soviet Voice), which appeared between 1922 and 1941.

By 1933, the Poles, like the Ukrainians and most other peoples in Soviet Ukraine, were feeling the negative effects of Stalin's drive toward greater centralization and conformity. Leading Polish Communists in the CP(b)U were purged, their nationality district and village soviets were abolished in 1935, and much cultural activity ceased – among other things, the number of Polish schools had dropped to 134 by 1936. There was even a show trial against purged CP(b)U party members accused of belonging to the so-called Polish Military Organization, which supposedly was plotting to overthrow Soviet rule in Ukraine in favor of the "reactionary" Polish state. Numerous Polish peasants on the Right Bank also fell victim to the collectivization of agriculture in 1929, and the recalcitrant Polish kulaks, like their Ukrainian counterparts, were deported. The most widespread suppression, however, took place in 1937–1938, during so-called Polish Operation directed by Soviet security services (NKVD) against alleged supporters of what was dubbed the fictitious Polish Military Organization. By mid-1938, nearly 135,000 Poles (over half from Ukraine and Belarus) were arrested; of these, 67,000 were executed and the remainder sent to the Gulag or into exile in Kazakhstan.[4]

The Germans

As with the Poles, the number of Germans living in Dnieper Ukraine decreased as a result of World War I, the revolution, civil war, and emigration. Whereas in 1911 they numbered 489,000, by 1926 only 394,000 lived within the borders of Soviet Ukraine. The greatest decreases occurred in Volhynia. Consequently, more than half the group (206,000) lived in the steppe region, with as many as 91.3 percent residing in rural farming areas. Yet even in the steppe region there was a decrease in their number, especially among the Mennonites, who during the 1920s organized associations to help more than 20,000 of their co-religionists to emigrate, mainly to Canada.

Because of their concentration in rural areas, the Germans had a higher number of nationality districts (7) and village soviets (252) than the numerically larger Jewish and Polish minorities. Although efforts were made to find local leaders, most of the nationality districts were headed by Germans from Germany or Austria-Hungary who had found themselves in the Russian Empire during World War I and had joined the Bolshevik ranks. The Germans were also permitted to create their own socialist cooperatives and cultural organizations. A German press, albeit Communist in spirit, continued to appear, and at least during the 1920s the churches – Protestant, Roman Catholic, and Mennonite – were permitted to function and even experienced a certain revival. German-language education, the traditional preserve of the churches, was placed in governmental hands, however. Training for teachers was provided at the state-run German Pedagogical Institute in Odessa. Although in general the Germans remained distanced from the Ukrainian revival of the 1920s, one author, Oswald Burghardt, writing under the pseudonym Iurii Klen, became an important Ukrainian-langauage poet, translator, and literary scholar.

After the revolution, a modus vivendi developed between the Soviet government and the Germans living in rural areas which allowed them an existence that was not substantially different from that of tsarist times. The situation was radically altered, however, as a result of the socioeconomic changes that began with collectivization in 1929. Since the Germans were for the most part well-to-do agriculturalists, especially in comparison with their Slav neighbors, a proportionately larger number of Germans were labeled kulaks. About 10 percent of the Black Sea Germans were deported during dekulakization, and thousands more died during the famine of 1932–1933.

The second half of the 1930s witnessed the almost complete destruction of German religious life in Soviet Ukraine. Protestant and Roman Catholic ministers and bishops were arrested, and many of the Gothic-style churches on the steppe were made into warehouses or used for other non-religious purposes. At the same time, German intellectuals – teachers, clerics, writers – were arrested, and in the uncertain atmosphere many agriculturalists fled to the cities. Nor did the cities prove to be safe havens for ethnic Germans. From 1934 onward, in many industrial areas of the Donbas, "fascist German spy rings" were uncovered among workers and eliminated by the secret police. Thus, even before the end of the interwar period, the distinct German life in Soviet Ukraine had been substantially undermined.

The Crimean Tatars

Among the numerically larger national minorities living on Ukrainian territory during the interwar years, the Crimean Tatars held a unique position. Most of them lived in the Crimean peninsula, which at the time was not even part of Soviet Ukraine. In October 1921, when the post-revolutionary political situation in the Crimea was finally clarified (see chapter 40), the peninsula became the Crimean Autonomous Soviet Socialist Republic (Crimean A.S.S.R.) within the Russian S.F.S.R. The Crimean A.S.S.R. was administered by the Republican Council (Soviet) of Workers, Peasants, and the Black Sea Fleet, which in turn elected an executive organ, the Crimean Central Executive Committee. The government was directed by a twelve-member Council of People's Commissars chosen by the Central Executive Committee.

Despite the Crimea's centuries-long association with the Tatars, by the 1920s they actually made up only one-quarter of the region's population (see table 45.3). Although a numerical minority, the Tatars at least for a while were the dominant political and socioeconomic force in the Crimean A.S.S.R. Not unexpectedly, the leadership role of the Crimean Tatars in many facets of public life caused resentment and friction with the East Slavic inhabitants (especially Russians), who comprised over half of the population of the autonomous republic. Crimea's government even attempted to stop the continued influx of Russian, Ukrainian, Jewish, and other settlers from other parts of the Soviet Union as part of an effort to make possible the "re-Tatarization" of the peninsula's steppeland. In a further effort to reverse what was from the Crimean Tatar perspective a demographic imbalance,

TABLE 45.3
Nationality composition of the Crimean A.S.S.R., 1926[5]

Nationality	Number	Percentage
Russians	301,000	42.2
Crimean Tatars	179,000	25.1
Ukrainians	77,000	10.8
Germans	44,000	6.1
Jews (Ashkenazi)	40,000	5.6
Greeks	16,000	2.3
Bulgarians	11,000	1.6
Armenians	11,000	1.5
Karaites	8,000	1.1
Jews (Krymchaks)	6,000	0.8
Others	20,000	2.8
TOTAL	714,000	100.0

Tatars who had fled mostly to Turkey during Russia's Civil War and the initial Soviet period of war communism (1919–1921) were granted amnesty and encouraged to return home. It is therefore not surprising that for subsequent generations of Crimean Tatars, the period 1923 to 1928 was to be remembered as the "golden age" of the Soviet Crimea.

The "golden age" was in large part due to the activity of Veli Ibrahimov, a former member of the Crimean Tatar National party (Milli Firka), who by 1920 had become a committed Bolshevik and nationalist Communist. Moscow entrusted Ibrahimov with the political and social reconstruction of the Crimea, which during the period of war communism and an accompanying famine (1921–1922) had suffered a 21 percent loss in its population. As chairman of both the Crimean Communist party Central Committee and the government's Council of People's Commissars, Ibrahimov oversaw the introduction of NEP throughout the peninsula and, on the political and cultural front, the local version of indigenization (*korenizatsiia*), known as Tatarization.

Ibrahimov achieved his goals in several ways. As part of the policy of indigenization, he brought Tatars into all levels of the Crimean A.S.S.R. Within a few years the Crimean Tatars (who comprised only 25 percent of the population) made up from 30 to 60 percent of the members in governmental and party organs. Most of the new officials were, like Ibrahimov himself, former members of Milli Firka, the non-Communist Crimean Tatar nationalist party outlawed in 1921. In the economic sphere, he facilitated the return of land to its former owners, whether large landowners or peasant villagers, and the return of industrial enterprises to whatever former management was still around. Finally, in the cultural sphere, he promoted the policy of Tatarization.

Tatarization took different forms. Elementary schools were established in which the Crimean Tatar language (still using the Arabic alphabet) was made the language of instruction. The very question of what the Crimean Tatar literary language is – or should be – was finally resolved. Soviet linguists, together with the Crimean Tatar writer Bekir Çobanzade, created a common Crimean Tatar grammar based on the peninsula's central mountain dialect, which had evolved during the era of the Crimean Khanate. It was considered the *Orta Yolak*, or Middle Road; that is, a common Crimean Tatar language based on the hybrid of Kipçak Turkic and Oghuz (the core of modern Turkish), which became the spoken language of the Tats. Four teacher's colleges were set up (in Feodosiia, Bakhchysarai, Yalta, and Simferopol') to train instructors in the new literary language.

In the autonomous republic's capital city, Simferopol' (now also called by its historic Tatar name Aqmescit), Taurida University was opened in 1918. Of particular importance for Crimean Tatar nationality-building was the university's Oriental Institute. Beginning in 1925, the institute trained a large number of anthropologists and linguists who systematically recorded the Crimean Tatar cultural heritage (language, folklore, music) and, with the support of the central Soviet government, carried out extensive archaeological research at pre-historic and medieval sites throughout the peninsula. The Crimean State Publishing House was set up to make available scholarly studies and literary works in the Crimean Tatar language.

The wide range of published scholarship contributed to a revised understanding of the ethnogenesis of the Crimean Tatar people. No longer were they associated solely with the Mongolo-Tatar nomadic invaders and Turkic Kipçak steppe peoples; rather, they were presented as an amalgam descended from the Scythians, Sarmatians, Alans, and coastal Greeks, who together with the Kipçak nomads formed a unique Crimean Tatar ethnos. Not only were the Crimean Tatars different from other Turkic-speaking peoples, even more importantly they were considered the indigenous inhabitants who, therefore, had a historic right to the Crimean peninsula.

The Tatarization of the Soviet Crimea changed with the coming of the Stalinist revolution in 1928. In January of that year, Ibrahimov was arrested, ostensibly for disagreeing with Moscow's decision to settle a few thousand Jews from Belarus in the Crimea. Four months later, he was executed on charges of "bourgeois nationalism," and his policies and programs were totally discredited. The regimentation of Stalinism thus started even earlier in the Crimean A.S.S.R. than in neighboring Soviet Ukraine. The results, however, were the same. In 1928–1929, dekulakization brought the removal from the Crimea of between 35,000 and 40,000 peasants. The forced collectivization and grain requisitioning which followed led to scattered armed resistance and refusals to sow crops. The drastic reduction in agricultural production combined with governmental confiscations of grain resulted in a prolonged famine between 1931 and 1933 and the loss by starvation of an estimated 100,000 lives – about 60 percent were Crimean Tatars, the rest Russians, Ukrainians, and other inhabitants of the peninsula. As in Soviet Ukraine, the authorities refused to acknowledge the famine or provide the starving with any relief.

Ibrahimov's downfall was also followed by a wide-scale purge from government, schools, and other institutions of all Crimean Tatars suspected of being "tinged with Veli Ibrahimovism." Upward of 3,500 Crimean Tatar government and party officials and intellectuals (including Bekir Çobanzade and Şevki Bektöre) were either exiled or executed. Between 1931 and 1935 the religious facet of Crimean Tatar identity was virtually eliminated with the closure of hundreds of mosques and the exile to Siberia of most of the peninsula's Islamic clergy (*mullahs*).

In an effort to distance the Crimean Tatars even further from their traditional heritage and to bring them more in line with "modern socialist" currents, the face of their language was changed; from 1929 the Arabic alphabet was replaced in all Crimean Tatar publications and public signage with the Roman/Latin alphabet, then from 1938 with the Cyrillic. While it is true that the number of Crimean Tatar-language books and the size of their print runs continued to rise (153 titles in a total of 830,000 copies in 1939 alone), the number of newspapers and journals in Crimean Tatar dropped precipitously (from a high of 23 in 1935 to only 9 in 1938). The new linguistic trends even saw Russian words and grammatical rules introduced into the Crimean Tatar language. The result of such radical linguistic change over such a short period of time was pedagogical confusion and the eventual isolation of a new generation of Crimean Tatars from the wealth of pre-revolutionary and early post-revolutionary literature in the traditional Arabic script. Finally, the efforts to improve the demographic status of the Crimean Tatars were never realized, since Soviet policy continued to promote the "slavicization" of the Crimea. If, by 1938, the absolute numbers of Crimean Tatars increased to 218,000, at the same time their proportion to the rest of the peninsula's inhabitants decreased further, to 19.3 percent. In short, by the end of the 1930s all the achievements of the era of Tatarization led by Veli Ibrahimov until 1928 had been effectively dismantled.

The Greeks

Nearly 90 percent of the 108,000 Greeks recorded in 1926 lived in the far southeast corner of Soviet Ukraine. Most were farmers who lived in compact settlements in the rural steppe just to the west of the industrial city of Stalino (today Donets'k) and in the area surrounding the port city of Mariupol'. There were another 16,000 Greeks who lived in the Crimean A.S.S.R. The Greeks had 30 village soviets, some of which were on the territory of, the others scattered in between, the three Greek nationality districts. The village soviets were divided according to the two historic waves of Greek colonists in Ukraine: sixteen were comprised of Hellene Greeks originally from Walachia (present-day Romania), who initially migrated to the area around Odessa; fourteen others were made of mostly "Tatar Greeks," that is migrants from Crimea who settled around Mariupol'. In contrast to the last century of tsarist rule, when a high percentage of Greeks became russified, the Soviet regime during the interwar years encouraged individuals to identify their ancestral heritage through a program known as Hellenization.

The Hellenization program in Soviet Ukraine witnessed the establishment of sixteen Greek-language elementary schools by 1929, although only a small percentage of ethnic Greek students were enrolled in them. Teachers were trained in a pedagogical college in the city of Mariupol', which from 1930 was also the home to several Greek-language newpapers (*Kolektovistos, Bolsevikos, Kokinaskapnas/Komunistis*), a publishing house (Kolehtivistis), and a theater. These institutions published and performed the works of a small group of Greek writers in Ukraine, led by Georgii Kostoprav, who in 1931, after having written in Russian, returned to the language of his ancestors.

Despite the concerted efforts at a Greek cultural revival in Ukraine, the results, at least in terms of language retention, were minimal. Three-quarters of all Greek children continued to attend Russian-language schools, and even graduates of the Greek pedagogical college reportedly did not have a mastery of their "own" language. Yet even the minimal progress under Hellenization came to an end during the Stalinist political repression of the 1930s. The short-lived nationality districts were abolished, all Greek schools were closed, and leading members of the newly emerging Greek intelligentsia, including Kostoprav, were arrested and sentenced to long prison terms for "nationalist subversion" of Soviet society. The Greek agricultural colonies in the Mariupol' region were, like many other agricultural areas of Soviet Ukraine, hard hit by dekulakization, forced collectivization, and famine.

The Bulgarians

The Bulgarians, numbering 92,000 in 1926, were primarily agriculturalists who specialized in cultivating vegetables, fruits, and grapes for wine. Ninety percent of the group resided in forty-five village soviets, most of which were within three nationality districts: along the Sea of Azov between Melitopol' and Berdians'k; in the area just north of Odessa; and near the town of Pervomais'k along the valley of the Southern Buh River. Bulgarians were allowed schools in their language already under tsarist Russian rule, and this policy was continued by the Soviet regime which increased their number. By the 1930–1931 school year there were seventy-three Bulgarian-language schools where 85 percent of all students of Bulgarian background studied.

The Soviet state created several institutions to train functionaries that could serve in Bulgarian nationality districts and village soviets. These included a Bulgarian Communist party school in Dnipropetrovs'k and later Odessa, a Bulgarian teacher's college at Preslav, and a medical college in Odessa. Language and culture were also promoted through the Dmitrov Bulgarian Theater which operated for seven seasons in Odessa (1934–1941) and a Bulgarian-language press, the most important organ of which was *S'rp i chuk* (The Sickle and Hammer), first renamed *S'vetsko selo* (The Soviet Village) and finally *Kolektivist* (The Collective Farmer). Bulgarian nationality districts, village soviets, cultural institutions, and publications were permitted to last somewhat longer than those of other nationalities, but by 1937 most ceased to exist, except for elementary school classes in the Bulgarian language and the theater in Odessa, which still were allowed to function for a few more years.

Thus, with the partial exception of the Russians, all the national minorities in Soviet Ukraine as well as the Tatars of the Crimean A.S.S.R. experienced a similar fate during the interwar period. From 1924, the Soviet regime permitted a rather high degree of unhindered cultural and small-scale economic development that encouraged the national development of all the peoples of Soviet Ukraine and the Crimean A.S.S.R. But when the Stalinist revolution began after 1928, with its emphasis on central planning, the collectivization of agriculture, and the general administrative regimentation of all aspects of Soviet life, the national minorities were required to fulfill the demands of the Communist party's directives from Moscow or suffer the consequences. Change came at different times for different peoples, earlier for the Crimean Tatars and Jews, somewhat later for the Greeks and Bulgarians. In the end, however, the consequences were more or less the same for all (with the possible exception of the Russians) – the destruction of the groups' secular and religious leadership and the deportation of large numbers of their rural agriculturalists.

Ukrainian Lands in Interwar Poland

As a result of the settlements reached by the Paris Peace Conference and the Treaty of Riga, the restored state of Poland between July 1919 and March 1921 was able to obtain territories inhabited by as many as 4 to 5 million Ukrainians. By 1931, according to official statistics, Ukrainians numbered 4.4 million persons, or 14 percent of Poland's population. Unofficial estimates placed their number at between 5 and 6 million. As a national minority, Ukrainians were guaranteed equality before the law, the right to maintain their own schools, and the right to use Ukrainian in public life and in elementary schools. These rights were outlined in the treaties of Versailles (28 June 1919) and Riga (18 March 1921) as well as in the Polish constitution (Articles 108 and 109) promulgated on 17 March 1921.

The administrative status of Ukrainian-inhabited lands

Ukrainian territories within Poland consisted of (1) the eastern half of the old Austrian province of Galicia, including the Lemko region along the crests of the Carpathian Mountains in "western" Galicia; and (2) the so-called northern Ukrainian-inhabited regions, of western Volhynia, southern Podlachia, Polissia, and the Chełm/Kholm region, all of which had been part of the Russian Empire before 1914. Because the eastern half of former Austrian Galicia became the West Ukrainian National Republic in late 1918, and because according to international law that territory was not considered part of Poland until 1923, eastern Galicia continued throughout the interwar period to undergo a development that was in many ways distinct from that of Poland's "northern" Ukrainian lands.

The reconstituted state of Poland was a republic governed by an elected bicameral legislature consisting of a House of Deputies (*Sejm*) and Senate, which together chose the president for a term of seven years. Poland was a centralized state, administratively divided into palatinates (Polish: *województwa*), which were subdivided into districts (*powiaty*) made up in turn of communes (*gminy*). The palatinates had no relationship to any historical units, and none, with the exception of Silesia, had any autonomous status.

Even before eastern Galicia was internationally recognized as a part of Poland,

MAP 39 UKRAINIAN LANDS IN POLAND, circa1930

its territory was divided into three palatinates: Lwów/L'viv, Stanisławów/Stanyslaviv, and Tarnopol/Ternopil'. Initially, the Polish government considered Ukrainian-inhabited eastern Galicia a distinct territorial entity, and from March 1920 it was referred to by the Polish name *Małopolska Wschodnia,* or Eastern Little Poland. Eventually, in September 1922, the Polish *Sejm* approved a law that proposed self-government for each of the three Ukrainian-inhabited palatinates. This law, however, was never ratified by the Polish government. The other Ukrainian-inhabited lands – historic western Volhynia, western Polissia, southern Podlachia, and Kholm – were divided among the Polish palatinates of Łuck/Luts'k, Brześć/Brest, and Lublin.

The economic status of Ukrainian-inhabited lands

The socioeconomic development of Ukrainian lands within interwar Poland evolved in a manner that was in stark contrast to the situation in neighboring Soviet Ukraine. Eastern Galicia and the other Ukrainian territories in Poland essentially remained what they had been before 1914 under Austrian and Russian rule. In other words, they continued to be treated as territories from which raw materials could be obtained and in which products from the more industrial western and central parts of Poland could find a market. In general, however, the entire Polish economy was agrarian in nature; it remained weak and unstable throughout the interwar period; and it was especially hard hit by the world economic crisis of the 1930s. In these circumstances, there was little hope that the Polish government could make any substantial improvement in the economy of its "peripheral" eastern regions (*kresy*) inhabited by Ukrainians.

Thus, by 1939 eastern Galicia, with over 5 million inhabitants, had a mere 44,000 workers, employed in 534 industrial enterprises. This small industrial sector consisted primarily of woodworking mills (35.2 percent), food processing plants (20.9 percent), building-material factories (14 percent), and metalworking shops (12.5 percent). The oil-producing regions in eastern Galicia (around Boryslav and Drohobych), which had made remarkable progress on the eve of World War I (producing almost 4 percent of world production), never again reached their prewar levels. The highest output under Polish rule (737,000 tons [670 thousand metric tons] in 1923) was only one-third the highest prewar level. Then came the world economic depression and a decline in the traditional foreign investments, which, together with the gradual exhaustion of the oil deposits, reduced the output. By 1938, the eastern Galician fields were producing less than half what they did in 1923. Even less industrial development took place in the northern territories of Volhynia, Podlachia, and Polissia, where there were at most 8,000 industrial workers with steady employment and another 11,000 seasonal workers in basalt and granite factories and in the lumber industry.

Since agriculture was the dominant element in the economy of Poland's Ukrainian lands, the agrarian question was most pressing. The peasants in Poland, notwithstanding their nationality, all expected to benefit from the new political situation and to obtain land. In July 1919, the provisional Polish parliament (*Sejm*) called for agrarian reform. Within a year, the parliament considered a law providing for compulsory partition of the large landed estates, which at the time accounted for 47 percent of the country's arable land. The proposed law was blocked by its opponents, however, and it was not until December 1925 that the Polish parliament succeeded in passing a law that indeed called for the partition of the large estates, but only on a voluntary basis.

Despite the voluntary nature of the reform, the land was partitioned, and by 1938 nearly two million acres (some 800,000 hectares) had been redistributed within Ukrainian-inhabited areas. The redistribution did not necessarily help the local Ukrainian population, however. For instance, as early as 1920, 39 percent of the newly allotted land in Volhynia and Polissia (771,000 acres [312,000 hectares]) had been awarded as political patronage to veterans of Poland's "war for

TABLE 46.1
Landholdings in interwar eastern Galicia, 1931[1]

Size of farms	Percentage
Under 5 acres (2 hectares)	45
5–12 acres (2–5 hectares)	34
12–25 acres (5–10 hectares)	8
Over 25 acres (10 hectares)	2
No data given	11
TOTAL	100

independence," and in eastern Galicia much land (494,000 acres [200,000 hectares]) had been given to land-hungry Polish peasants from the western provinces of the country. This meant that by the 1930s the number of Poles living within contiguous Ukrainian ethnographic territory had increased by about 300,000. Looked at in another way, ethnic Poles comprised 40 percent of the urban population and 21 percent of the rural population in eastern Galicia, and 29 percent of the urban population and 20 percent of the rural population in the "northern" Ukrainian lands. These increases were owing not only to the influx of Poles into the area, but also to a decrease in the number of Ukrainians due to emigration abroad. During the interwar period, approximately 150,000 Ukrainians left Poland, the vast majority – in consequence of United States immigration restrictions after 1924 – going to Canada, Argentina, and France.

The size of individual Ukrainian landholdings in both eastern Galicia and the northern territories remained small (see table 46.1). Size, moreover, was crucial to the welfare of the individual farmer. Contemporary observers concluded that properties less than twelve acres (five hectares) in size were generally inadequate to sustain a single family. Not only were such farms incapable of producing a sufficient amount of food to support the family, but sales in a local market from the surplus of any one crop would not produce enough cash to buy foodstuffs that were not produced at home. Nor could animals belonging to the small landholder make up the shortfall. This meant that farmers who owned less than twelve acres (five hectares) of land – and they made up 79 percent of landholders in eastern Galicia – were forced for at least part of the year to seek supplemental employment elsewhere just to survive.

Leaving aside the problem of small landholdings, Ukrainian farmers in Poland also suffered, at least initially, as a result of the damage caused during World War I. For instance, 20 percent of the rural population lost their homes and farm buildings during the war, and 38 percent of the horses, 36 percent of the cattle, and 77 percent of the hogs were destroyed.

Poland's initial policies and Ukrainian reactions

At the close of World War I, Poland signed international treaties respecting equality for its national minorities and entered guarantees for them into its 1921 constitution. Such agreements might have been acceptable to a group that had developed a perception that they were a national minority. Ukrainians in eastern Galicia, however, had virtually reached a stage of equality with Poles under Austrian rule during the first decades of the twentieth century. Then, when the Habsburg Empire fell, they had created and fought for an independent western Ukrainian state (1918–1919). Even the victorious Allied Powers themselves initially (at least officially, until 1923) held to the possibility of some kind of self-rule for the Ukrainians in eastern Galicia. In this environment, the Ukrainians of Poland, most especially those of Galicia, were not about to accept the status of a national minority in what they considered their own homeland. That would be tantamount to turning back the historical clock. And that is exactly what Poland tried to do.

It is true that some Polish leaders, including the country's legendary national liberator Marshal Józef Piłsudski, at times considered the possibility of recreating a tripartite federated Polish state as a variant of the pre-partition Polish-Lithuanian Commonwealth, which until the eighteenth century had united under one sceptre Poles, Lithuanians, and Ukrainians. Visions based on past models would, of course, require that Poland's boundaries reach at least as far as Kiev and take in Belarus and Lithuania as well. But the inconclusive results of the Polish-Soviet war in 1919–1920 and the creation of the Belorussian and Ukrainian Soviet republics shattered any prospect of a revival of the old Commonwealth on a tripartite federative basis. Moreover, Poland was restricted to smaller frontiers and Piłsudski's expansive federative approach with its tolerance toward national minorities was discredited. It turned out that the most influential political force in the new postwar state was the National Democratic movement, or the Endeks (Polish: Endecja), headed by the increasingly extremist nationalist leader Roman Dmowski. He and the interwar political parties that the Endeks supported promoted the idea of a unitary nation-state in which peoples other than Poles – including Lithuanians, Belarusans, and Ukrainians in the country's eastern borderlands (kresy) – should be assimilated into the Polish nationality.

Not surprisingly, many Ukrainian leaders, especially from Galicia, reacted to the new situation as if a state of war still existed. In fact, the Polish forces which took over the province in mid-July 1919 interned, during the first months, several thousand Ukrainians who had fought (or were suspected of having fought) against them. Ukrainian charges of brutality and executions were countered by Polish accusations of Ukrainian sabotage and allegations of Ukrainian terror in Galicia. Indeed, Ukrainians initiated an underground war, especially after the brief return to eastern Galicia in 1921 of Ievhen Konovalets'. Konovalets' had been the leader of the Galician-Bukovinian Battalion of Sich Riflemen, which until its dissolution in early 1920 had fought with the forces of the Ukrainian National Republic in Dnieper Ukraine. In "occupied" eastern Galicia, Konovalets' established the Ukrainian Military Organization (UVO), which during 1921 and 1922 undertook a campaign that included the burning of Polish estates; the destruction of Polish governmental buildings, railroads, and telegraph lines; and political assassinations. Among these was an unsuccessful attempt to shoot Marshal Piłsudski during the chief of state's visit to L'viv in September 1921, and the successful assassination in October 1922 of a Ukrainian political leader (Sydir Tverdokhlib) who favored cooperation with the Poles and participation in elections to the new Polish parliament.

Because of the tense situation on the international front, most Galician-Ukrainian political leaders followed the instructions of the West Ukrainian government-in-exile, headed by Ievhen Petrushevych in Vienna. The result was a boycott of the first elections to the Polish parliament, held in November 1922. In the northern, non-Galician lands, however, Ukrainians did go to the polls and elected twenty representatives to the House of Deputies (*Sejm*) and five to the Senate. Although these first Ukrainian deputies and senators to the Polish parliament affirmed that their ultimate goal was an independent Ukrainian state, they declared that in the interim, until such a goal became a reality, they were willing to cooperate with the Poles in return for Warsaw's non-interference in their own national life.

The early years of Polish rule also had a negative impact on Ukrainian cultural life in Galicia. The Polish administration closed many of the popular Prosvita Society reading rooms, an action which, combined with the devastation brought about during the war years, produced a marked decline in the number of reading rooms, from 2,879 in 1914 to only 843 in 1923.

As for the educational system, the provincial school administration from the Austrian era, which was based in L'viv and had separate Ukrainian representation, was abolished in January 1921. All decisions were subsequently to be made by Poland's central government in Warsaw and to be implemented by administrators in local school districts. Ukrainians now found themselves within six different Polish school districts (L'viv, Volhynia, Polissia, Cracow, Lublin, and Białystok), although at least initially the Ukrainian school system itself, especially at the elementary level, was left undisturbed.

At the higher levels, Ukrainian education fared much worse. Under prewar Austrian rule the Ukrainians may have expressed dissatisfaction, but their demands for Ukrainian-language university departments (*katedry*) were at least fulfilled. Their constitutional demands for a separate Ukrainian university were also finally met with a promise by the Habsburg authorities that one would be created by 1916. Now, under Polish rule, a parliamentary recommendation for a Ukrainian university was disregarded, and in 1919 all the Ukrainian departments at L'viv University save one were abolished. The one remaining was the old 1848 Department of Ruthenian (Ukrainian) Language and Literature, but even its chair was left vacant until 1927, when it was filled by a Pole, the respected linguist Jan Janów. Faced with this situation, Ukrainians founded an illegal university known as the Ukrainian Underground University, which, with three faculties and at its height 1,500 students, functioned from 1921 until 1925, when it was pressured by Polish authorities to cease operations. Many of its students, as well as other young Galician Ukrainians who had been denied admission to L'viv's Polish university because they had not fought for Poland during the Polish-Ukrainian war, went abroad instead. Neighboring Czechoslovakia was the most popular destination, where they attended either the Ukrainian Free University or the renowned Charles University in Prague.

By 1923, it was clear that the diplomatic activity of the West Ukrainian government-in-exile and the underground sabotage work of the Ukrainian Military Organization had failed to dislodge Polish rule in eastern Galicia. As a result, Ukrainian leaders were forced to adapt to the new political realities. During the fifteen-year period until the outbreak of World War II in 1939, the different responses to their situation on the part of Ukrainians in Poland found expression in essentially three approaches: (1) the cooperative movement, which acquiesced to Polish rule and worked within it to create a solid economic and cultural foundation for the Ukrainian minority; (2) active participation in Polish civic life by political parties, which lobbied through legal means on behalf of Ukrainian cooperatives, schools, and churches; and (3) armed resistance by paramilitary groups, which from the outset rejected Polish rule and strove in whatever way they could to destabilize society.

The cooperative movement

The rather dismal state of agriculture in the Ukrainian lands within Poland was made tolerable only by the remarkable advances of the cooperatives and credit unions. On the eve of World War I, the Ukrainians in Galicia had a total of 609 cooperatives. Although the number of these declined because of World War I (579 in 1921), the following years witnessed a revival, with the result that by 1939 there were 3,455 cooperatives spread throughout the whole region and united by an umbrella organization known as the Audit Union of Ukrainian Cooperatives. Initially, the Audit Union also founded cooperatives in Volhynia and Polissia, but in 1934 the Polish government passed a law requiring Ukrainian cooperatives outside eastern Galicia (the Łwów, Stanisławów, and Tarnopol palatinates) to unite with local Polish cooperatives.

The cooperatives in eastern Galicia, which by 1923 had a total of 600,000 members, promoted the use of modern techniques and machinery in farming. Most important, they provided financing and marketing services. The most influential of all Ukrainian cooperatives was the Maslosoiuz, or Dairy Union, set up already before World War I. The Maslosoiuz expanded steadily during the interwar years, and by 1938 it included 136 district dairies supplied by over 200,000 farms producing enough butter to dominate the Galician market as well as to export to neighboring Czechoslovakia and Austria. Also of importance were the Sil's'kyi Hospodar, or Village Farmer Association – with sixty branches, over 2,000 local units, and 160,000 members (1939) – whose primary concern was to provide farmers with practical and theoretical training in agriculture; and the Tsentrosoiuz, or Union of Cooperative Unions, whose goal was to coordinate the activity of the various cooperatives. By 1938, the Tsentrosoiuz represented 173 central, regional, and individual cooperatives, to whom it sold consumer goods, agricultural machinery, and building materials at wholesale prices, and for whom it marketed Ukrainian agricultural products throughout Poland and abroad.

Ukrainian women in eastern Galicia had their own Ukrainian Folk Art Cooperative, which functioned as part of the Soiuz Ukraïnok (Union of Ukrainian Women). Founded in 1921, the Soiuz Ukraïnok grew rapidly and by 1936 included 45,000 members, in nearly 1,200 urban and village branches. Aside from courses for women on how to operate cooperatives and nursery schools, the group established its own cooperative with the express purpose of popularizing and selling folk art items produced at home.

Each of the cooperatives also had its own Ukrainian-language publications, and

Women and the Ukrainian National Ethos

For stateless peoples like the Ukrainians, whose culture and language for much of the nineteenth and twentieth centuries was suppressed or, at best, tolerated, and who for the most part lacked access to a formal educational system that could preserve and promote their national distinctiveness, the role of the family as a carrier of the national ethos took on special importance. It was in the family that the Ukrainian language and legends about the national past were passed on to younger generations. Since women were at the center of domestic life, it was mothers and grandmothers who for much of the nineteenth and early twentieth centuries became the primary carriers of the Ukrainian national ethos.

It is not surprising, then, that many of the literary images associated with the survival of the Ukrainian language and, by implication, a Ukrainian national identity invoke the relationship of mothers to their children. So many poets have repeated, like a refrain, that as children they "sucked in the Ukrainian language with milk from their mother's breast."

Grandmothers, too, have taken on almost mythical proportions as carriers of the national soul. They seem to have been particularly important for grandsons who went off to school and then remained in the towns or cities. For those grandsons who retained a Ukrainian identity and who may even have taken part in the national revival, grandmothers became larger-than-life symbols. They became, at least in the minds of patriots living in a nationally alien urban environment, repositories of the Ukrainian language and culture who were preserving them for future generations in an allegedly pristine rural environment. The urbanized – and sometimes urbane – nationalist intellectual could periodically recharge his or her patriotic batteries by returning for a weekend or summer holiday to mothers and grandmothers who still presided over the family homestead in the rural village. It is therefore not surprising that among the most common images used to describe the country is *Ukraina-maty*, or Mother Ukraine.

Aside from exercising this all-important role within the family, Ukrainian women assisted in the national movement through the creation of formal structures and organizations. For instance, in late-nineteenth-century eastern Galicia, when Ukrainian national organizations first took on massive proportions, women became active members in the popular Prosvita and Kachkovs'kyi societies. Beginning in the late 1870s, the first specifically women's organizations, both informal groups in Dnieper Ukraine and legally registered organizations in Austrian Galicia, came into being. Among the latter were the Society of Ruthenian Ladies (est. 1878), the Club of Ruthenian Women (est. 1893), and the Women's Hromada (est. 1909), all based in L'viv with branches throughout eastern Galicia. Galicia was also the home of Nataliia Kobryns'ka, a late-nineteenth- and early-twentieth-century short-story writer who today is generally considered Ukraine's pioneering feminist.

Kobryns'ka's views did not, however, have much popular appeal. In part, this is because in contrast to women's movements in other parts of Europe and North America, which at the time were concerned primarily with the liberation of women, the right to vote, philanthropy, or the struggle against prostitution, the movement among Ukrainian women activists had more general goals. They directed their energy to the needs of the existing nationalist movement and, both within male-dominated organizations and in separate women's organizations, worked to raise the status of all Ukrainians by trying to eliminate social ills caused by alcoholism, illiteracy, and economic disparities. Instead of philanthropy, Ukrainian women's organizations actively participated in the self-help or cooperative movement.

The Ukrainian women's movement did not really come into its own until after World War I. The largest and most successful of the women's organizations was the Union of Ukrainian Women (Soiuz Ukraïnok), which functioned in eastern Galicia from 1921 until its abolition by the Polish authorities in 1938. Two of the union's leading activists were Milena Rudnyts'ka, who was elected twice to Poland's House of Deputies, and Olena Kysilevs'ka, who was elected twice to the Polish Senate. From their elected posts, both women were able to initiate programs that helped to improve the status of all Ukrainians in interwar Poland.

At the same time, the women's movement in Soviet Ukraine was following a different path. With the establishment of Bolshevik rule, all previously existing informal and formal women's organizations were abolished. In their stead, the Women's Section (Zhinochyi viddil, or Zhinvid) of the Communist party (Bolshevik) of Ukraine was created in 1920 and headed for its first four years by Lenin's close associate and expert on women's issues throughout the Soviet Union, Aleksandra Kollontai. Activists in the party's Women's Section worked to eliminate illiteracy and to educate women in the countryside about the advantages of socialism. Members of the Women's Section, which was an arm of the Communist party – CP(b)U – also acted as informers against peasants who did not readily accept Soviet socioeconomic policy. The informers did not discriminate on the basis of gender, so that women equally with men accordingly suffered the often fatal consequences of dekulakization, forced collectivization, and famine.

By 1930, the Soviet Union had declared that there was no women's question and that consequently there was no need for the Women's Section of the CP(b)U. After all, according to Soviet law, women were equal to men and therefore had equal access to educational facilities, social services, employment, and participation in the Communist party. Such equality turned out to be a double-edged sword, however, especially with regard to the workplace.

In rural Ukrainian society, women had always worked the fields and tended farm animals alongside men. In rapidly industrializing Soviet Ukraine, women were not only given equal access to employment, but were expected to work full time, just like the men. There seemed, moreover, to be no distinction between the kinds of jobs available to and expected of men and women. Accordingly, it was common in Soviet Ukraine to find women employed as construction workers doing heavy manual labor such as hoisting concrete or laying railroad tracks. In the last years of Soviet rule women made up 52 percent of Ukraine's entire work force (at the time the highest percentage among all developed countries worldwide), and they made up 80 percent of all workers engaged in heavy physical and often low-paying and dangerous labor.

Not much has changed in post-Communist independent Ukraine. Granted, at the outset of the twenty-first century some women have been catapulted to fame throughout the country and abroad, among them the popular singer Ruslana, and, in particular, the successful businesswoman and highly influential political leader Iuliia Tymoshenko. Modern social realities have not, however, changed traditional attitudes in the relationship between men and women. Women are still expected to raise children, cook, wash, and in general maintain the household. This means, effectively, that women are saddled with the double burden of working outside the home in order to contribute to the family budget and working inside the home in order to address the daily needs of the family.

there is no doubt that the movement as a whole was inspired by national patriotism. In approaching the nationality question, however, the cooperative movement and its leaders were aware that political and military action, as undertaken during the immediate post–World War I period, had been unsuccessful. Accordingly, they argued that a period of organic growth and a strengthening of the economic base of Ukrainian society was necessary. There were others in Galician-Ukrainian society, however, who felt that political or even military action would be a more appropriate response to their situation under Polish rule.

Ukrainian political parties, schools, and churches

By the mid-1920s, several Ukrainian political parties had come into existence. The most important was the Ukrainian National Democratic Alliance (Ukraïns'ke Natsional'ne Demokratychne Ob'iednannia), best known by its Ukrainian acronym, UNDO. Founded in 1925, UNDO included some of the leading figures in prewar Galician-Ukrainian life, whose political experience had been formed under the Habsburg Empire (Kost' Levyts'kyi, Volodymyr Bachyns'kyi, Volodymyr Zahaikevych), as well as younger activists who began their political work under Polish rule (Dmytro Levyts'kyi, Ivan Kedryn-Rudnyts'kyi, Vasyl' Mudryi). In a sense, UNDO was a continuation of the prewar Ukrainian National Democratic party, and, like its ideological predecessor, it looked forward to a future independent Ukrainian state. In the interim, however, UNDO hoped to obtain positive changes for Poland's Ukrainians through legal means. Aside from its own party organ *Svoboda* (Freedom, 1897–1939), UNDO was supported by several other newspapers, including the influential Galician-Ukrainian daily newspaper *Dilo* (The Deed, 1880–1939).

More to the left in the political spectrum was the Ukrainian Socialist-Radical party (led by Lev Bachyns'kyi and Ivan Makukh), a continuation of the prewar

Ukrainian Radical party. The Socialist-Radicals favored the secularization of Galician-Ukrainian life and the introduction of socialism, although not of the Marxist variety. On the far left was the Communist party of Western Ukraine (KPZU). Formed in 1921 as the Communist party of Eastern Galicia, it was ordered by the Comintern to join the Communist party of Poland, of which it became an autonomous branch. When, in 1924, the party was declared illegal by the Polish government, the Communists went underground. Subsequently, the KPZU was racked by internal controversy over the direction of events in Soviet Ukraine. One faction, led by Osyp Vasyl'kiv and the theoretician Roman Rozdol's'kyi, favored the policy of "national communism" as carried out by Oleksander Shums'kyi in Soviet Ukraine before his demotion in early 1927. Another faction accepted the idea of internationalist party loyalty and acceptance of guidelines set in Moscow. The matter came to a head with a purge of the Galician "Shums'ky-ites" in 1928. Internal dissension nevertheless continued within the KPZU, largely because of friction with the Polish Communist party apparatus and displeasure among some members with the ever-changing Soviet policy regarding Ukrainianization. Moscow retorted that the Galicians were guilty of "bourgeois-nationalist deviation," until finally, in 1938, the Comintern decided to dissolve the KPZU.

The problem of Soviet Ukraine affected many more Ukrainian leaders in Poland than just the Communists. During the height of the Ukrainianization policy of the mid-1920s, a special West Ukrainian Institute was set up in Kharkiv, and it attracted several left-wing émigrés from Galicia. Even the head of the West Ukrainian government-in-exile, Ievhen Petrushevych, thought cooperation with the Soviets might help the Galician-Ukrainian cause against Poland. Several other Galician intellectuals, including Mykhailo Lozyns'kyi, Antin Khrushel'nyts'kyi, Iuliian Bachyns'kyi, Stepan Rudnyts'kyi, and Oleksander Badan-Iavorenko emigrated to Soviet Ukraine, although subsequently they were swept up in the purges of the 1930s and perished.

The Russophiles, at least in eastern Galicia, remained a political force during the interwar years, although on the national-cultural front they were completely outdistanced by the Ukrainians. Their parties, the Russian Peasant party (Russkaia Selianskaia Partiia) and Russian Agrarian party (Russkaia Agrarnaia Partiia), which merged in 1931, drew their support from the Old Ruthenian and Russophile cultural institutions like the Stauropegial Institute and the National Home, as well as from those villages, especially in the westernmost Lemko region, where the Kachkovs'kyi Society and the Orthodox movement were the strongest. There was also a group of Galician Russophiles who joined the Volhynian and Chełm-based Peasant Union (Selsoiuz), which was Communist in orientation. After splits within this group, some Russophiles (Kyrylo Val'nyts'kyi and Kuzma Pelekhatyi) joined the KPZU, and even though the latter was Ukrainian in orientation they continued to promote their Russophile views on national identity.

These and other non-Communist Ukrainian political parties participated in some or all of the elections to the Polish parliament held in 1928, 1930, 1935, and 1938. The strongest Ukrainian party in both the *Sejm* and the Senate was UNDO, which opposed the settlement of Poles in traditional Ukrainian-inhabited territo-

TABLE 46.2
Ukrainian-language and bilingual schools in interwar Poland,
1922–1938[2]

	Ukrainian schools		Polish-Ukrainian schools	
	1922	1938	1928	1938
Galicia	2,426	352	1,635	2,485
Volhynia	443	8	652	520
Polissia	22	0	–	–

ries and made demands concerning the status of Ukrainian schools, the Ukrainian language, the Greek Catholic and Orthodox churches, and the reaction of the Polish government to Ukrainian terrorist activity.

During the 1920s, the Polish government increased the total number of schools in Ukrainian areas, especially in the formerly Russian-ruled northern territories of Volhynia and Polissia, where the number of elementary schools rose over three-fold, from 1,000 in tsarist times (1912) to 3,100 during the last full year of Polish rule (1938). In eastern Galicia, the number of elementary schools rose from 4,030 to 4,998 during the same period. The Polish administration could also take credit for a decline in illiteracy among people over ten years of age, from 50 percent in 1921 to 35 percent in 1931.

Polish educational policy, however, had a negative impact on Ukrainian language use. In 1924, the government of Prime Minister Władysław Grabski passed a law (known as the *lex Grabski*), over the objections of Ukrainian parliamentary representatives, which set up bilingual Ukrainian and Polish schools. The result was a rapid decline in the number of unilingual Ukrainian schools together with a sharp increase in Polish-Ukrainian bilingual schools in Galicia and Polish schools in Volhynia (1,459 in 1938) (see table 46.2).

Ukrainians viewed bilingual schools as a first step toward the national assimilation of their children. Their concerns were not unjustified, since Polish soon became the primary language in bilingual schools. The response of the Ukrainians was to establish private schools, especially at the secondary level. This effort was undertaken in large measure by the prewar Ukrainian Pedagogical Society (est. 1881), renamed the Native School Society (Ridna Shkola) in 1926. By the 1937–1938 school year, 59 percent of all Ukrainian *gymnasia*, teachers' colleges, and technical schools, with approximately 40 percent of Ukrainian students at those levels, were privately operated.

Since Ukrainians in Poland had only limited control over the formal education of their children, the Plast scouting movement took up the challenge of inculcating youth with a Ukrainian national identity. Plast scouts came into being on the eve of World War I on Ukrainian lands in both the Russian and the Austro-Hungarian Empires, but it was during the interwar years in western Ukraine (in particular Galicia and Transcarpathia) that they had their greatest success. By 1930, the organization had over 6,000 male and female members in branches affiliated with secondary schools in Galicia and with Prosvita societies in western Volhynia. Concerned by Plast's general popularity and the fact that many of its "graduates" after age eighteen joined clandestine Ukrainian nationalist organizations, Poland's authorities increased restrictions on the movement until banning it entirely after 1930. It nonetheless continued to operate underground or through other organizations for the rest of the decade.

The status of Ukrainians was also affected negatively by another law passed in 1924, which excluded Ukrainian language use in governmental agencies. Moreover, the Polish government never referred to the Ukrainians and their language by the modern name *Ukrainian;* instead, it used the historical name *Rusyn* (Polish: *Rusin*), thereby inadvertently contributing to a disliking on the part of many Ukrainians, especially Galician Ukrainians, for their original national designation. Finally, in the 1930s, the Polish government adopted a policy of tribalization, which gave support to the idea that various ethnographic groups (Lemkos, Boikos, Hutsuls) as well as the Old Ruthenians and Russophiles were somehow distinct from the Ukrainian nationality as a whole. This policy was implemented especially in the westernmost Lemko Region, where state schools offered instruction in the Lemko vernacular and where in 1934 a jurisdictionally separate Greek Catholic Lemko Apostolic Administration was established.

The Ukrainian nationality question in Poland was involved with developments in the church as well as in politics and education. These developments were complicated by the fact that Ukrainians belonged to two churches. In eastern Galicia, they were primarily Greek Catholic; in the northern areas formerly part of the Russian Empire, they were Orthodox.

According to an agreement (concordat) between Poland and the Vatican signed in February 1925, the jurisdiction of the Greek Catholic Metropolitanate of Halych, with its seat in L'viv, was reaffirmed, although its activity was restricted to its three eparchies (L'viv, Przemyśl, and Stanyslaviv) in eastern Galicia. With regard to internal developments, the interwar years witnessed a sharpening in the debate within the Greek Catholic Church between those elements (Bishops Hryhorii Khomyshyn of Stanyslaviv and Iosafat Kotsylovs'kyi of Przemyśl, and the Basilian Order), who favored the adoption of a more Western religious model, including celibacy, and those (Metropolitan Sheptyts'kyi, Bishop Nykolai Charnets'kyi, and the Studite Order), who preferred the preservation of the Eastern rite and spirituality. Quite often in the course of the debates, the "Easterners" would present themselves as patriots defending Ukrainian national traditions in opposition to the Western-oriented (critics would say pro-Polish) "Latinizers."

In more general terms, the intellectual life of the Greek Catholic Church was allowed to flourish in interwar Poland. A wide variety of theological and scholarly journals were published, and the Greek Catholic Theological Academy was established in L'viv in 1928. The Academy, headed by the Reverend Iosyf Slipyi, was the only Ukrainian institution of higher learning in Poland. Finally, the Greek Catholic Church's status was upheld throughout the interwar years because it remained under the leadership of Metropolitan Sheptyts'kyi, the "patriarch" of the Ukrainian movement who was respected by the highest Polish ruling and social circles.

In contrast, the Orthodox Church, with over two million Ukrainian adherents in the northern territories (Volhynia, Polissia, and Chełm), was in a less favorable position than the Greek Catholic Church in Galicia. Although historically associated with the tsarist government and its policy of russification, the Orthodox Church in Poland attempted to break with the past, obtaining independence (autocephaly) in 1924 and its own metropolitan see (headed by Metropolitan Dionizy) in Warsaw. The Russophile character of the church also changed as the Orthodox seminary at Kremenets', in Volhynia, and the Orthodox theological department at Warsaw University (after 1924) began to teach in Ukrainian, and liturgical materials were published in Ukrainian. Nonetheless, the Polish authorities especially at the local level remained ill disposed to what was considered a "schismatic" church with roots in Russia. Such attitudes resulted in the so-called revindication campaigns in 1929–1930 and again in 1938, whose goal was to deprive the Orthodox of those churches that had once been Greek Catholic (that is, before Orthodoxy was imposed by the prewar tsarist Russian government). This policy was particularly detrimental to Orthodoxy in the Chełm and Podlachia regions, where in 1929 and 1930 alone, 111 Orthodox church buildings were closed, 59 were destroyed, and 150 were converted into Roman (not Greek) Catholic churches. Physical destruction was particularly rampant in 1938, when within a few months almost 150 church buildings were destroyed in the Chełm and Podlachia regions, prompting protests by Ukrainian deputies in the Polish parliament against what was described as wanton cultural discrimination.

Armed resistance and pacification

Given the generally unfavorable attitude of the Polish government toward its Ukrainian minority, especially evident in educational policy, in the restrictions on the official use of Ukrainian, and in anti-Orthodox discrimination, and given what seemed an inability on the part of the Ukrainian cooperative movement and legal political parties to counteract Polish policy, it is not surprising that for some people armed resistance presented itself as the only viable course of action. Throughout the 1920s, the Ukrainian Military Organization (UVO) continued its policy of political assassination, bomb attacks on governmental buildings, and sabotage against railroad and telegraph installations.

Such activity on the part of the UVO was sporadic, and in any case it was increasingly unpopular among the Galician-Ukrainian public after 1923. To improve the reputation and effectiveness of the underground, a more strictly disciplined and ideologically determined organization seemed necessary. Such a movement arose among Ukrainian émigré youth and student groups in central and western Europe, where the UVO leader Konovalets' had been functioning in exile since 1922. At a meeting held in Vienna in 1929, representatives of several émigré groups founded the Organization of Ukrainian Nationalists (OUN). The UVO leader Konovalets' was made head of the new organization, which before long had branches throughout Ukrainian émigré centers as well as in the western Ukrainian lands of Galicia, Bukovina, and Transcarpathia. Initially there was conflict over the respective roles to be played by the OUN and the older UVO, but by 1932 the latter had been merged with the Galician branch of the OUN and thus had ceased to exist as an independent organization.

The OUN was a highly disciplined underground revolutionary movement dedicated to the overthrow of Polish, Romanian, and, eventually, Soviet rule in Ukrainian territories. The movement drew its ideological inspiration from Dmytro Dontsov, a native of Dnieper Ukraine who in 1908 had fled to Galicia and then gone to Vienna to study. After the war, he settled in L'viv, where he edited the leading Galician-Ukrainian journal of public affairs, the *Literaturno-naukovyi vistnyk* (Literary-Scholarly Herald, 1922–32), and its successor, *Vistnyk* (The Herald, 1933–39). Despite his influence among many OUN members, Dontsov never became a member of the organization and, in fact, remained openly critical of some of its policies.

Dontsov espoused integral nationalism, the theory that the nation, as embodied in an independent state, was the supreme ideal. To achieve this ideal, an aggressive will and the ability to take action, preferably under the direction of a strong leader, were necessary. Such views were common at the time in many parts of Europe, in particular in Italy, Germany, and Spain. By the 1930s, if not before, those countries were being led by all-powerful leaders (Mussolini, Hitler, Franco) who allegedly embodied the will of the nation-states they represented. The OUN translated Dontsov's version of integral nationalism into terroristic activity aimed at overthrowing Polish and Soviet rule and eventually creating an independent Ukraine. By the 1930s, especially after news of the 1933 famine reached eastern Galicia, Soviet Ukraine had lost most of its sympathizers among Poland's Ukrainians. This news, combined with Polish repression and the increasingly worsening economic situation caused by the world depression, made the OUN an attractive alternative for a large number of Ukrainian students and peasant youth whose futures did not look promising.

The OUN's purpose was simple: to destabilize the situation in Poland until the government finally collapsed. Not surprisingly, the OUN opposed UNDO and other political parties which worked through legal channels, and it had little sympathy with the constructive work of the cooperative movement, which, according to OUN leaders, implicitly if not explicitly accepted Polish rule. Throughout the 1930s, the OUN in Galicia (led by figures like Bohdan Kravtsiv, Bohdan Hnatevych, Bohdan Kordiuk, Stepan Bandera, and Lev Rebet) engaged repeatedly in acts of sabotage. These included the well-publicized assassination of a Soviet consular official in L'viv (1933) in protest against the famine in Soviet Ukraine and the assassination of the Polish minister of internal affairs Bronisław Pieracki in June 1934. Despite its popularity among certain segments of the population, most legal Ukrainian political parties and other groups, as well as the still-prestigious Greek Catholic metropolitan Andrei Sheptyts'kyi, publicly denounced the terrorist activities of the OUN.

The Polish government tried to curb the OUN's activity. Its first extensive effort in this direction was the so-called pacification program carried out between 16 September and 30 November 1930. Imagining potential terrorists at every corner, detachments of Polish soldiers and police went through Ukrainian villages interning known activists and indiscriminately beating men and women in the process. While the pacification program did not result in much loss of life – and therefore is in no way comparable to collectivization in Soviet Ukraine, which began in earnest at the same time – it nonetheless deepened the hatred between Ukrainians and Poles. It also became a cause célèbre for many liberals in the West, especially in Great Britain, where Poles were depicted by some members of the House of Commons as brutal oppressors. The Polish policy of pacification in 1930 and the subsequent arrests of Ukrainian activists (a detention camp was set up at Bereza Kartuzka in 1934) only helped to increase sympathy for the OUN and further to alienate Polish and Ukrainian societies.

There were some Poles, however, both inside and outside the government, who favored some kind of compromise with the country's Ukrainian community. Polish socialist deputies, for instance, tried in March 1931 to have the issue of autonomy for Ukrainians discussed in the parliament. More serious was the government's attempt at compromise with the UNDO, in an agreement reached in July 1935. Known popularly as "normalization," this agreement assured Ukrainians of a total of nineteen seats in both houses of parliament, the election of the UNDO activist Vasyl' Mudryi as vice-marshal of the parliament, an amnesty for imprisoned nationalists, and credits to Ukrainian economic organizations. One result of normalization was a split in the UNDO between those who favored and those who opposed cooperation with the government. Owing to the split, the UNDO was never to regain the influence it once had among Poland's Ukrainians. Moreover, the whole policy of normalization failed within a few years. The failure was the result of continued dissatisfaction among most Ukrainians with Polish rule that included ongoing efforts to create an internally strong Polish nation-state and increasing intolerance of the demands of all national minorities.

Thus, political compromise between the Polish authorities and the country's Ukrainians was doomed. And this was exactly what OUN leaders wanted: to discredit the Polish government and especially those Ukrainians who favored an evolutionary political or an economic (cooperative) solution to the problem of their existence in Poland. In the end, the OUN got what it wanted – not only destabilization, but also the destruction of Poland. This destruction came about, however, not as a result of the OUN's efforts, but because of the outbreak of World War II on 1 September 1939.

Ukrainian Lands in Interwar Romania and Czechoslovakia

Ukrainians in Romania

The Ukrainians in interwar Romania, who in 1930 numbered anywhere between 582,000 (official statistics) and one million (unofficial estimates), lived in three geographically separate regions: Bukovina, Bessarabia, and Maramureş. The largest number (461,000) inhabited southern Bessarabia, which until World War I had been part of the Russian Empire. Another 302,000 Ukrainians lived for the most part in the northern half of the former Austrian province of Bukovina. The remaining 17,000 Ukrainians were found in the southern portion of the old Hungarian county of Máramaros (Romanian: Maramureş). They were separated from their brethren north of the Tysa River in Subcarpathian Rus' (Transcarpathia), which in 1919 became part of Czechoslovakia.

Interwar Romania was a parliamentary kingdom ruled by the same Hohenzollern dynasty that had come to power in 1866. During the 1920s, Romanian political life was dominated by the Liberal party, whose goal was to create a centralized state. The result was that newly acquired regions which before World War I had enjoyed various degrees of autonomy (Bukovina, Transylvania) now found themselves in a state determined to do away with all vestiges of self-rule. During the 1930s, Romania's new king, Carol II (reigned 1930–1940), succeeded in weakening the role of parliament until, in 1938, the country was transformed into a royal dictatorship.

Bessarabia's Ukrainians were the first to come under Romanian rule. Tucked in between the Prut and Dniester Rivers and touching the shores of the Black Sea, Bessarabia was the eastern region of the Ottoman vassal state of Moldavia. In 1812, it was annexed and made a province of the Russian Empire. After the March 1917 revolution, the Central Rada in Kiev laid claim to Bessarabia, and local Ukrainians set up schools and cultural societies (notably Prosvita). In response, the Romanians/Moldovans, together with other peoples of Bessarabia, convened in Chişinău in November 1917 a National Council (Sfatul Ţării), which the following month declared the creation of an autonomous republic in federation with non-Bolshevik Russia. Troops from Romania arrived with the purpose of driving out Bolshevik

MAP 40
UKRAINIAN/RUSYN LANDS IN ROMANIA AND CZECHOSLOVAKIA, ca. 1930

Major concentration of
Rusyns / Ukrainians

Boundary of Ukraine, 2005

| 0 | 50 | 100 miles |
| 0 | 50 | 100 kilometers |

Scale 1 : 6 520 000

Copyright © by Paul Robert Magocsi

raids from the east, and under their protection the region's National Council proclaimed on 24 January 1918 an independent Moldavian Democratic Republic of Bessarabia. Despite the skepticism of some Moldavian and non-Moldavian members, the National Council voted on 27 March 1918 for the unification of Bessarabia with the Kingdom of Romania. Caught unprepared by this fait accompli, France, Great Britain, Germany, Italy, and Japan – but not the Soviet Union – on 28 October 1920 signed the so-called Bessarabian Protocol, which recognized Romanian rule. During the interwar years, the Ukrainians in southern Bessarabia were permitted to have their own elementary schools (120), a few cooperatives, and representatives in the Romanian parliament.

Whereas Ukrainians in southern Bessarabia enjoyed minimal cultural and national rights, the situation in northern Bukovina was virtually the opposite. Old Austrian Bukovina had enjoyed more cultural and political autonomy than any other Ukrainian-inhabited land within the Habsburg Empire. This was in large part due to the representational balance between Ukrainians, Romanians, Jews,

Austro-Germans, and Poles that was set up before the war by the Habsburg government. All this was to change after the beginning of Romanian rule in November 1918 (see chapter 41).

What had previously been the multinational administrative and cultural center of Chernivtsi was transformed, at least outwardly, into a Romanian city. Alongside the prewar Society for Romanian Literature and Culture in Bukovina, a whole host of new Romanian schools, civic organizations, and newspapers were founded. The linguistically "neutral" German-language university that the Habsburgs had founded in 1875 was transformed into a fully Romanian-language institution. It was renamed the King Carol I University of Chernivtsi, and one of its most prominent rectors, the nationalist historian Ioan Nistor, was determined to imbue its students with the conviction that they were being educated in a land that had finally been returned to its rightful place within "Greater Romania." The Orthodox Church, with its metropolitan seat in Chernivtsi, also became Romanian in character. The language of internal administration became solely Romanian, and parishes in Ukrainian villages were expected to conduct the traditional Church Slavonic liturgy partly in Romanian (an instruction that, in practice, was rarely followed). Finally, the church's jurisdictional status was altered. In 1921, its name was changed from the Greek-Oriental to the Orthodox Romanian (*ortodox-română*) Church, and in 1925 it became the Metropolitanate of Bukovina and Khotyn within the framework of the autocephalous Romanian Orthodox Church. Its first prelate was the Ukrainian-born Bukovinian Romanophile and avid promoter of all things Romanian, Metropolitan Nectari Kotlearciuc (reigned 1925–1935).

Not surprisingly, the fortunes of Bukovina's Ukrainians were profoundly affected by the new postwar order, so that during what Soviet Ukrainian authors used to call "the years of Romanian boyar occupation," they quickly became worse off than their fellows in Czechoslovakia's Transcarpathia or even Poland's Galicia. Bukovina's diet, provincial administration, school board, and district self-government from the Austrian era were all abolished. On paper, Bukovina survived for a while as an administrative unit, but in 1932 it was eliminated and divided into five Romanian counties.

One aspect of Bukovinian life that did not change much was the economic status of the Ukrainian population. As under Austrian rule, the vast majority continued to work as small-scale subsistence farmers, some of whom supplemented their income by raising livestock, in particular sheep. Like Poland and other countries in central Europe, Romania introduced a land reform program during the 1920s whose goal was to reduce the size of large landholdings. Although 186,000 acres (75,500 hectares) of land from landed estates in northern Bukovina were offered for sale, most did not go to the indigenous population, but rather to Romanian in-migrants from other parts of the country. Moreover, while the newcomers received 10 acres (4 hectares) of land and 2.5 acres (1 hectare) of pasture on average, individual Ukrainian farmers increased their holdings by only half a hectare on average.

Land was paramount, because Ukrainians in Romania had no economic alternatives. In both northern Bukovina and southern Bessarabia industry remained underdeveloped. By 1930, for instance, northern Bukovina had only 15,000 factory workers. This meant that throughout the interwar years of Romanian rule the two regions remained economically backward, with their Ukrainian population engaged almost exclusively in small-scale subsistence agriculture or livestock raising.

Although the economic status of Ukrainians did not change, Ukrainian political and cultural life, which had thrived in Bukovina under prewar Austrian Habsburg rule, came to an end. During the first decade of Romanian rule (1918–1928), Bukovina was under martial law. All Ukrainian cultural societies were closed, the use of Ukrainian was discontinued in the court system, and all Ukrainian newspapers were banned. The educational system was subjected to romanianization. The Romanian language began to be introduced as the language of instruction in schools at the very outset of Romanian rule. Nonetheless, by the 1922–1923 school year, there were still 255 Ukrainian schools. In July 1924, however, a law was passed which classified Ukrainians, to quote the Chernivtsi University rector Ioan Nistor, as "Romanians who had lost the native tongue of their ancestors."[1] Such "Romanians" were not permitted to "send their children to any school, public or private, other than a school in which instruction is given exclusively in Romanian."[2] For all intents and purposes, Ukrainians lost their status as a national minority, and the romanianization of schools was intensified. By 1927, the process was complete: there were no more Ukrainian elementary schools in Bukovina. Only a few hours a week of Ukrainian instruction was offered, and in 1931 two Ukrainian school superintendents were appointed to supervise this minimal program. At the secondary level, all Ukrainian *gymnasia* and technical schools were closed in 1920, and the departments of Ukrainian subjects set up during Austrian rule were abolished at Chernivtsi University.

The status of Ukrainians improved somewhat in 1928, when for a few years the National Peasant party dominated Romanian politics. Ukrainian candidates, who previously had been elected on Romanian tickets (Kost' Krakaliia, Antin Lukasevych, Iurii Lysan), now represented the new Ukrainian National party, established in 1927 and headed by the national leader and art historian Volodymyr Zalozets'kyi-Sas. Ukrainian-language daily (*Chas*, 1928–40) and weekly (*Ridnyi krai*, 1926–30) newspapers were also permitted.

This brief revival of Ukrainian political and cultural activity soon waned, however, with the return of the Liberal party in 1933. Moreover, by the end of the decade, Romania's parliamentary democracy had become meaningless. The state was transformed into an authoritarian dictatorship under King Carol II (reigned 1930–1940), whose government had little sympathy with the country's national minorities.

The Carpatho-Rusyns/Ukrainians of Czechoslovakia

Unlike in interwar Poland and Romania, where the political, cultural, and socioeconomic situation of Ukrainians worsened in comparison with what it had been during the pre-1914 era of Austrian rule, in Czechoslovakia the situation of

Carpatho-Rusyns/Ukrainians improved. Their rather unique status was owing to several factors. Officially known by their historic name, the Carpatho-Rusyns or Subcarpathian Rusyns (*podkarpats'ki rusyny*) voluntarily joined the newly created Czechoslovak republic in May 1919. Moreover, they inhabited the only Ukrainian land to receive specific guarantees for self-government according to international law as outlined in the postwar peace settlements (the Treaty of St Germain). Finally, the republic of Czechoslovakia, headed by the renowned scholar and publicist Tomáš G. Masaryk, considered itself a Slavic state and was favorably disposed to Carpatho-Rusyns/Ukrainians in Transcarpathia as well as to Ukrainian émigrés from Galicia and Dnieper Ukraine who settled in the province and elsewhere in the country. Czechoslovakia's capital, Prague, became the leading intellectual center of Ukrainian émigrés in Europe during the interwar period. Accordingly, the Carpatho-Rusyns/Ukrainians of Transcarpathia found themselves in a favorable political environment.

The new Czechoslovak state was formed as a republic. It had a bicameral central parliament in Prague, consisting of the elected House of Deputies (*Poslanecká Sněmovna*) and the Senate (*Senát*), and a government headed by an elected president who held office for seven years. Only two presidents held office in Czechoslovakia throughout the interwar period: the founder of the republic, Masaryk, until 1935, and after that his longtime minister of foreign affairs, Edvard Beneš. It is useful to note that throughout central Europe most of the small so-called successor states (that is, those new countries which had been carved out of the old prewar empires) began as parliamentary democracies. All with one exception, however, had by the 1930s become authoritarian dictatorships. The exception was Czechoslovakia, which until the very end of the interwar period maintained a liberal democratic system characterized by a representative government and the rule of law. This state of affairs was to have a very positive effect on Transcarpathian developments.

There were, nonetheless, certain political problems. Although a distinct province, known officially as Subcarpathian Rus' (Czech: *Podkarpatská Rus*), was established in 1920 with its own governor, it did not include all "Ruthenes (Rusyns) living south of the Carpathians," as called for in the Treaty of St Germain. Of the 458,000 Rusyns recorded in eastern Czechoslovakia in 1921, nearly 86,000 were placed under a Slovak administration in an area popularly known as the Prešov Region. Although autonomy was promised to Subcarpathian Rus', its specific form was not spelled out.

It is not surprising, therefore, that the very first governor appointed by President Masaryk to administer Subcarpathian Rus', the Rusyn-American lawyer Gregory Zhatkovych, made the questions of autonomy and the unity of all Carpatho-Rusyns into one province his primary concerns. He hoped that autonomy would be implemented (with rights similar to those held by American states) and that the Rusyns under Slovak administration would be united with Subcarpathian Rus'. Failure to obtain these goals prompted Governor Zhatkovych's resignation in protest as early as 1921.

The Czechoslovak approach was similar to the former Habsburg approach in politics – procrastination. Prague argued that autonomy could not be implemented in Subcarpathian Rus' because the local inhabitants were not yet mature enough to participate in a modern democratic political process and because many of the local leaders, especially the traditionally influential Greek Catholic clergy, favored or anticipated a return to Hungarian rule. Until a transitional or educative period was completed, Prague would have to rule the region directly. It was not clear, however, how long this transitional period was to last. In 1928, Czechoslovakia was divided into four provinces, one of which was Subcarpathian Rus' (formally renamed the Subcarpathian Rusyn Land – *Země podkarpatoruská*). Each of Czechoslovakia's provinces was endowed with a provincial diet, and although there were governors appointed from among the local population to head the province of Subcarpathian Rus' (Antonin Beskyd, 1923–1933, and Konstantyn Hrabar, 1935–1938), the administration was de facto in the hands of a Czech vice-governor. Thus, Subcarpathia' political demands – autonomy and the unity of all Carpatho-Rusyns/Ukrainians – were never fulfilled during the era that came to be known as that of the first Czechoslovak republic.

One reason for the Czechoslovak government's reluctance to grant autonomy to Subcarpathian Rus' was the presence of a large Magyar (Hungarian) population, which was considered a potential threat to the political stability of the region. The Magyars were the second-largest nationality in Subcarpathian Rus', with 192,000 inhabitants, or 17 percent of the population, in 1921. They lived in a compact territory running along the border with Hungary, and they made up a significant portion of the population in the area's two largest cities, Uzhhorod (18 percent) and Mukachevo (23 percent). In fact, the Magyars lived on lands that were simply an extension of the Hungarian plain, now separated by an international border from what remained of postwar Hungary. In the new Slavic state of Czechoslovakia, the Magyars found themselves in a situation they had never encountered before: they were a minority in their own homeland.

As a national minority, the Magyars continued to have access to education in their native language at all levels through high school (*gymnasium*), and they enjoyed all the rights granted citizens of democratic Czechoslovakia, including a Magyar-language press free from government control and elected representatives to local legislative bodies as well as the national parliament in Prague, where their deputies and senators addressed the assembly in Hungarian. Nevertheless, many Magyars in Subcarpathian Rus', especially their spokespersons in the National Christian Socialist party and the Magyar National party, assumed that Czechoslovak rule was only temporary and that sooner or later the region would be returned to Hungary. The local Greek Catholic Church, in particular during the early 1920s, included many pro-Hungarian priests and hierarchs, and by the 1930s Magyar politicians in Czechoslovakia led by Count János Esterházy were becoming increasingly susceptible to propaganda from neighboring Hungary that was agitating for the reacquisition of that country's former Highlands (Félvidek) to the north – Slovakia and Subcarpathian Rus'.

Although the political demands put forth by Carpatho-Rusyns/Ukrainians were not fulfilled, the inhabitants of Subcarpathian Rus' acquired concrete experience with democracy. For the first time, the masses participated in fair elections held at the village, county, provincial, and national levels. Regardless of national background, Subcarpathians were elected to both houses of the Czechoslovak parliament (in 1924, 1928, and 1935), where they took an active part in the legislative process. Political parties also came into being, both local Carpatho-Rusyn/Ukrainian parties and branches of all-Czechoslovak parties. Finally, there were even the trappings of a provincial, state-like identity. According to Czechoslovak law, Carpatho-Rusyns were the "state nationality" in Subcarpathian Rus'. They even had their own national anthem (based on a poem attributed to the nineteenth-century national leader Aleksander Dukhnovych: "Subcarpathian Rusyns / Arise from Your Deep Slumber"), sung on all public occasions, as well as an official Subcarpathian Rusyn coat of arms, which appeared on publications and governmental documents.

Subcarpathian Rus' had especially important geopolitical significance for Czechoslovakia. The interwar period found Czechoslovakia surrounded on almost all sides by enemies – Poland, Hungary, and eventually, Germany. The earliest significant threat was that posed by Hungary, which felt that a profound injustice had been done to it by the 1920 Treaty of Trianon. Border revisionism became the dominant slogan of interwar Hungarian foreign policy, and Subcarpathian Rus' as well as Slovakia and Romania's Transylvania were primary objects of Budapest's territorial designs. To protect itself against the Hungarian threat, Czechoslovakia formed the so-called Little Entente with Romania and Yugoslavia. Its only geographic link with these allies was through Subcarpathian Rus'. Thus, the province, which Czech and Slovak leaders had never expected to obtain during the postwar repartitioning of Europe, now became an important geopolitical cornerstone of its foreign policy.

In its economic life, Subcarpathian Rus' did not fare well. Agriculture remained the mainstay of the region's economy, and local industrial development was effectively stifled. This was because it proved economically more beneficial to export products from the highly industrialized western provinces of Bohemia and Moravia-Silesia to Subcarpathian Rus' than to build new factories there. As for products derived from the region's own natural resources, particularly lumber from the Carpathian forests, businesses in Bohemia and Moravia-Silesia found it cheaper and easier to import forest products from neighboring Slovakia.

The result was that the vast majority of the Carpatho-Rusyn/Ukrainian population – 82 percent in 1930 – was engaged in agricultural or forest-related work. Whatever trade or small-scale industry existed was in the hands of the local Magyar and Jewish inhabitants (who made up respectively 15.4 percent and 12.8 percent of the Subcarpathian population in 1930), or of Czechs, who began to arrive in steadily increasing numbers (by 1930 they comprised 2.9 percent of the area's population).

The Czechoslovak government did attempt to improve the economic status of Subcarpathian Rus'. In effect, Prague invested more than it extracted in order to construct a hydroelectric system and a network of modern roads and bridges. Governmental agencies also promoted new methods of cultivation, introduced better strains of existing crops, and provided educational assistance to farmers and livestock breeders. Moreover, a land reform was introduced in the 1920s, which in part broke up the largest estates once owned by the Hungarian nobility. The practical results of the land reform were limited, however. Only 57,000 acres (23,000 hectares) were permanently redistributed, to 9,100 farmers; 20 percent of the land in Subcarpathian Rus' (590,000 acres [239,000 hectares]) remained in the hands of large landowners. Also, the authorities were unsuccessful in their effort to move Carpatho-Rusyn/Ukrainian farmers from their mountain villages to the more fertile lowlands in the southern part of the province. Hence, by the late 1930s as many as 70 percent of the farmers in Subcarpathian Rus' still had less than 5 acres (2 hectares) of land, and another 18 percent had between 5 and 12 acres (between 2 and 5 hectares). Such plots were well below the minimum required to support a single family.

This meant that the need to find supplementary work was as acute as ever. But now there was another problem, one brought about by the geopolitical realignment of postwar central and eastern Europe. The new international boundaries closed off Carpatho-Rusyn/Ukrainian agriculturalists from the nearby Hungarian plain, where they had traditionally added to their income with seasonal work. Czechoslovakia's wealthier provinces of Bohemia and Moravia-Silesia, however, were too far away to make it economically feasible to sell surplus agricultural products from Subcarpathian Rus' there. These new realities were only made worse during the world economic depression of the 1930s, when mortgage foreclosures, strikes, grain shortages, and starvation became common phenomena. Economic discontent was translated into support for the Subcarpathian Communists, whose party was one of the strongest throughout the interwar period. Despite the well-meaning efforts of the Czechoslovak government, the province was simply too far away and too underdeveloped for Prague to have been able to make any substantial economic improvements.

It was in the cultural sphere that the Czechoslovak regime made the most marked progress in Subcarpathian Rus'. The contrast could not have been greater between, on the one hand, the prewar Hungarian government, which had ruled an underdeveloped agrarian society and had limited interest in the peripheral areas of the old kingdom other than concern to magyarize inhabitants of non-Magyar nationality, and, on the other, the democratic Czechoslovak government, which hoped to improve what it considered the backward cultural level of its fellow Slavs at the eastern end of the postwar republic.

Perhaps the longest-lasting changes occurred in the school system. During Czechoslovak rule, there was a dramatic increase in the number of schools (see table 47.1). The expansion of the physical plant was accompanied by an increase in the student body, whose number doubled between 1920 and 1938. This development, combined with programs in adult education, reduced the level of illiteracy from 78 percent in 1910 (near the end of Hungarian rule) to 40 percent in 1930.

The changes in the language of instruction were even more dramatic. During the last years of Hungarian rule before World War I, there were only 34 bilingual elementary schools, which provided a few hours of instruction in the local Rusyn vernacular. The Czechoslovak regime, however, made a concerted effort to offer instruction in some East Slavic medium, whether Ukrainian, Russian, or the local Rusyn vernacular, with the result that in 1920 there were over 300 such "Rusyn" schools in all categories, a number which had risen to over 500 by 1938 (see table

TABLE 47.1
Schools in interwar Subcarpathian Rus'[3]

	Number		Number with instruction in an East Slavic language	
Type	1920	1938	1920	1938
Elementary	475	809	321	469
Municipal	10	52	7	23
Gymnasia	4	8	3	5
Teachers' colleges	3	5	3	4
Professional/technical	3	5	3	5
TOTAL	495	879	337	506

47.1). The actual language of instruction in "Rusyn" schools varied (sometimes from class to class) among Ukrainian, Russian, and Rusyn, with the choice dependent on the preference of the teacher. In large part, the linguistic variety in schools was a reflection of the unresolved problem of Subcarpathian Rusyn national identity. By 1938, there were also elementary and municipal schools which offered instruction in Czech (206), Hungarian (127), German (25), Yiddish (7), and Romanian (4); a Czech-language teachers' college; and *gymnasia* and vocational schools with divisions in Czech, Hungarian, and Yiddish. Finally, Subcarpathian Rus' boasted the only school in the world with Romany (Gypsy) as the language of instruction.

The first long-lasting cultural organizations came into being under interwar Czechoslovak rule. The most important were the Prosvita Society, established in 1920 on the model of the same society in Galicia, and the Dukhnovych Society, established in 1923 and reflecting the models and national ideology of Russophile organizations in Galicia. Each of these societies constructed its own national home in Uzhhorod, the administrative capital, and set up branches and reading rooms throughout the province. By 1929, the Prosvita Society had 96 reading rooms and the Dukhnovych Society 192. Both societies also published numerous books and other works, the most scholarly being the Prosvita Society's journal *Naukovyi zbornyk* (Uzhhorod, 1921–38). These two leading cultural societies were supported in part by the Czechoslovak government, which in 1931 also established the Subcarpathian Rusyn National Theater. The remarkable improvements in education and growth in cultural organizations were accompanied by a rise in literary activity (Vasyl' Grendzha-Dons'kyi, Andrii Karabelesh, Iulii Borshosh-Kum'iats'kyi, and Aleksander Markush being the leading writers), with the result that the interwar era of Czechoslovak rule witnessed a true cultural and national renaissance for Subcarpathian Rus'.

The cultural sphere was not without its problems, however. One concerned religion and a struggle between competing churches. In the new democratic environment, the traditional predominance of the Greek Catholic Church was challenged by the Orthodox, and the consequence was a religious war, notably during the 1920s, and a rise in the number of conversions to Orthodoxy, whose adherents increased from fewer than 1,000 at the outset of Czechoslovak rule to 90,000 in 1930. In part, the rivalry between the churches was related to the nationality question. Those who joined the Orthodox Church often turned to a Russian national identity in reaction to the Greek Catholic Church, which initially was dominated by pro-Hungarian (magyarone) elements, until the 1930s, when it became a bastion of the Carpatho-Rusyn national orientation.

It was, in essence, the issue of national identity and the closely related language question which were the most problematic aspects of Subcarpathia's civic life. Although these problems had existed during the nineteenth century as well, they had been overshadowed by state-imposed magyarization and national assimilation. Now, under the Czechoslovak republic, the local Slavic population and its leaders had the freedom to determine themselves who they were. During the resulting debate, the Subcarpathians were influenced by émigrés, both Ukrainophiles (Ivan Pan'kevych, Volodymyr Birchak, Vasyl' Pachovs'kyi) and Russophiles (Ilarion Tsurkanovich, Andrei Gagatko, and the Gerovskii brothers) from Galicia and Bukovina. Thus, as in neighboring eastern Galicia and northern Bukovina during the late nineteenth century, now in Transcarpathia during the interwar period there arose a struggle between Ukrainophile and Russophile intellectuals for the allegiance of the population. An important difference was the presence of a third orientation, the Rusynophiles, who argued that the East Slavic population of Transcarpathia was neither Russian nor Ukrainian, but rather a distinct Carpatho-Rusyn nationality.

All aspects of interwar Transcarpathian life were affected by the presence of these three orientations – the political parties, the schools, the cultural organizations, and, to some degree, the churches. Although the Czechoslovak administration for the most part remained neutral in the linguistic and nationality controversies, by the 1930s it clearly favored the Rusynophile orientation, that is, the idea of a distinct and, it hoped, pro-Czechoslovak Carpatho-Rusyn nationality. The first and last governors of the province, Gregory Zhatkovych and Konstantyn Hrabar, also favored the Rusynophile view.

Although Russophilism and Rusynophilism had existed in Subcarpathia's cultural life during the nineteenth century, the Ukrainian orientation did not really make its appearance until the 1920s. Led by capable political and cultural leaders (Avhustyn Voloshyn, Iuliian Revai, Vasyl' Grendzha-Dons'kyi), the Ukrainian orientation before long came to be the most dynamic. Nevertheless, by the end of the interwar period, all three national orientations in Transcarpathia were exerting more or less equal political influence.

During the interwar years, the Transcarpathian Ukrainians, or Carpatho-Rusyns as they were known, made remarkable achievements, especially in political and cultural life, under the administration of the democratic first Czechoslovak republic. As a result, of all Ukraine's territories, Transcarpathia, while among the smallest, was the only one to have some control over its political and national destiny during the interwar years. And because it was at the westernmost edge of Ukrainian territory, it was the first to experience change with the coming of a new crisis in Europe in 1938.

PART TEN

World War II to Independent Ukraine

The Coming of World War II

From the very outset of the European crisis in 1938, Ukrainian territories were involved in developments that led to the eruption of the continent's second great conflict in the twentieth century – World War II. Transcarpathia was the first region to be affected. This was because it was part of Czechoslovakia, a country upon which Nazi Germany had territorial designs.

Germany and the "new order" in Europe

The outbreak of World War II did not come as a surprise. Europeans who had lived through World War I and experienced the implications of the peace treaties signed between 1919 and 1920 soon realized that they had at best arranged a truce, and that sooner or later war would break out once again. The treaties associated with the Paris Peace Conference in one sense had been punitive measures directed against those empires on the losing side of the conflict – Germany, Austria-Hungary, and Ottoman Turkey. Postwar Ottoman Turkey was deprived of its non-Turkish inhabited areas, Austria-Hungary ceased to exist entirely, while Germany and the Hungarian state left over from the old Habsburg Empire both felt that their respective national territory and ability to function as viable states had been seriously impaired by the peace treaties. Two-thirds of Hungarian territory was assigned by the peacemakers to neighboring states, with large Magyar minorities left in Czechoslovakia, Romania, Yugoslavia, and Austria (the Treaty of Trianon). Germany lost the industrialized provinces of Alsace and Lorraine to France and certain territories to Poland. Most detrimental, from Germany's viewpoint, was the fact that it was saddled with huge war reparations and the occupation of its own rich industrial Ruhr area by French troops (the Treaty of Versailles).

During the 1920s, Europe's old and new states tried to make the best of the postwar political order through bilateral agreements as well as through multilateral negotiations at the recently established international body known as the League of Nations. By the 1930s, however, the hardships caused by the world economic depression led to the eventual breakdown of serious efforts at peaceful solutions to

Europe's problems. Instead, the revision of the post–World War I treaties became the primary goal of Germany, Hungary, and, to a lesser degree, Italy, with the result that before long the nineteenth-century system of alliances based on power politics had been reactivated. Under Adolf Hitler, who came to power in 1933, Germany became the leader among those states in Europe (Italy, Hungary, Bulgaria) which favored a revision of the existing territorial order.

Hitler attained power not through any revolution, but rather was invited by the elected president to head a coalition government made up of nationalist and other parties, whose leaders thought they could manipulate him for their own ends. But Hitler, as the leader, or *Führer*, of the popular National Socialist German Workers' party – Nazi party for short – had his own agenda for Germany. In January 1933, he accepted the appointment as chancellor of Germany and then proposed new elections, which two months later garnered his Nazi party a slight majority in the parliament (*Reichstag*). Almost immediately (27 March), Hitler claimed dictatorial powers for himself and set Germany on a new course. Taking advantage of modern totalitarian political techniques and a masterful use of demagoguery, Hitler and his Nazi supporters proceeded to eliminate all political opposition through intimidation and, often, brutality. Traditional elements of local German autonomous federalism were abolished, the press and the arts were placed under strict controls, and the already well-developed Nazi theory of racial superiority was implemented, its primary target being the Jews, who were stripped of their citizenship in 1935 and placed under increasingly severe legal and socioeconomic restrictions. Thus, within a few years of his coming to power, Germany's new leader, the Führer Adolf Hitler, had become the undisputed dictator of the country.

Hitler promised to build a new German empire, this time a third empire, or Third Reich, a successor to the Holy Roman and Hohenzollern empires which was to last a thousand years. Nazi Germany began to rearm, and with a new self-confidence Hitler directed his attention to France. He denounced the clauses of the Treaty of Versailles on disarmament (1935) and marched into the Rhineland (1936), which was supposed to remain a demilitarized zone between Germany and France. Hitler also sought new allies, especially Italy's fascist leader, Benito Mussolini, with whom he established the so-called Rome-Berlin Axis (1936), and Spain's fascist leader, General Francisco Franco, whom he aided in that country's civil war (1936–1939). Outside Europe, Germany signed an alliance with Japan that was directed against the Soviet Union (1936).

Central to Hitler's plans for a new Germany was territorial expansion to ensure that the German people had enough *Lebensraum*, or "living space." Eastern Europe and Ukrainian lands in particular were earmarked as the area for the future German *Lebensraum*. The first step, however, was to deal with Germany's immediate eastern neighbors, and by 1938 Hitler was ready to move. The drive for German expansion was expressed in the slogan *Heim ins Reich* (Home in the German State), which in effect called for the unification of all ethnic Germans (*Volksdeutsche*) into one fatherland.

Hitler first turned to German-speaking Austria, which he annexed in March 1938. This act was in clear violation of the Treaty of Versailles, although it did not take place without the cooperation of pro-Nazi elements in Austria itself. Hitler's next move was directed against Czechoslovakia, which, in the German dictator's colorful phrase, was poised like a dagger (reflecting the shape of that country's western borders) at the heart of Germany. All along the edges of this so-called dagger lived a German minority, which, according to the Czechoslovak census of 1930, numbered over 3.2 million persons. These were known as the Sudeten Germans (from the Sudeten Mountains, which covered part of the territory inhabited by Czechoslovakia's ethnic German minority), and their unification with the German fatherland became Hitler's new goal. As in Austria, the call for unification was supported from within by most of the Sudeten Germans, but unlike Austria, the government of democratic Czechoslovakia – officially a Slavic state – was opposed to any designs on its territory. Czechoslovakia had allies in Great Britain and France, who since 1919 had considered this new state a buffer against German expansion in the east. The Soviet Union was also allied with Czechoslovakia as part of its own mutual defense pact with France. Knowing this, Hitler prevailed on British and French leaders to join him and his ally, the Italian fascist leader Benito Mussolini, to discuss the Czechoslovak crisis at Munich, on 28–29 September 1938.

The result was the Munich Pact of 30 September 1938, whereby France and Britain agreed to Hitler's demand for acquisition of the German-inhabited Sudetenland of Czechoslovakia's western provinces, Bohemia and Moravia-Silesia. What was left became the so-called rump state of Czechoslovakia, in which the central government in Prague was forced during the first week of October 1938 to grant both Slovakia and Subcarpathian Rus' (Transcarpathia) their long-awaited autonomy.

Hitler's remarkable success during the 1930s in consolidating his authority within Germany and in obtaining his initial foreign policy goals against France, Austria, and Czechoslovakia – without firing a shot – convinced many people, especially in central and eastern Europe, that the Nazi German model, with its authoritarian fascist system led by one leader (*Führer*), represented the political wave of the future. It is not surprising, therefore, that by the end of the decade most central as well as western European countries, whether or not they were allies of Germany, became one-party national dictatorships led by a Hitler-like leader. In the "new order" in international relations, Nazi Germany was allied with Italy and Spain and was becoming increasingly attractive to Hungary, Bulgaria, Romania, and Turkey, each of which favored territorial revision. On the other hand, Germany was opposed by France, Britain, and their allies in central Europe and the Balkans – Poland, Czechoslovakia, and Yugoslavia – all of which hoped to maintain as long as possible the territorial status quo. The Soviet Union had a reciprocal defense treaty with France, but it was intimidated by Germany's success in foreign affairs and therefore hoped to reach some kind of accommodation with the Nazi leader.

Among Nazi Germany's newest European allies, Hungary was to reap the first rewards. Less than six weeks after the Munich Pact, a conference was held in Vienna (2 November 1938) which resulted in the further dismemberment of Czechoslovakia. This time territory was detached from Czechoslovakia's eastern provinces – Slovakia and Subcarpathian Rus' (Transcarpathia). Although the Hungarians wanted much of Slovakia and all of Subcarpathian Rus', they had to be content with only the Magyar-inhabited southern regions of these two provinces, which included Transcarpathia's two major administrative and cultural centers, Uzhhorod and Mukachevo.

Autonomy for Carpatho-Ukraine

Although reduced in size, Subcarpathian Rus', like Slovakia, functioned as an autonomous unit within the restructured Czechoslovak republic. Transcarpathia's first cabinet (six members) was appointed by Prague on 11 October 1938, on the basis of recommendations made by local leaders. The cabinet was dominated by Transcarpathian Rusynophiles and Russophiles (under Premier Andrii Brodii), but dissolution came abruptly two weeks later (26 October) when the Czecho-Slovak government accused its leading members of being Hungarian and Polish agents (respectively, Brodii and Stepan Fentsyk). In consequence, Prague turned to the Ukrainophiles, and a new cabinet was formed, headed by the respected Greek Catholic priest and educator Avhustyn Voloshyn and the popular interwar parliamentary deputy Iuliian Revai.

After the capital (Uzhhorod) and other Magyar-inhabited regions in the south west of Transcarpathia were "returned" to Hungary as a result of the Vienna Award (2 November), Voloshyn established an autonomous government based in the eastern town of Khust. The autonomous Czechoslovak province now began to be called Carpatho-Ukraine; Ukrainian was made the official language in government and education; and plans were laid to hold elections to an autonomous diet. To protect itself from the continuing guerrilla attacks by Hungarian irregular troops from the south and their Polish allies from the north, in November the Carpatho-Ukrainian government authorized the creation of the Carpathian Sich, a military force led by local Transcarpathians (Dmytro Klympush, Ivan Rohach, Stepan Rosokha) but manned in large numbers by Ukrainians from Galicia, who crossed the mountains to help the small autonomous territory.

In fact, during its few months of autonomous existence in late 1938 and early 1939, Ukrainians in eastern Galicia as well as in émigré circles in central Europe (Prague, Vienna) and North America thought the minuscule Carpatho-Ukraine would become the Piedmont from which an independent and united Ukrainian state would evolve. Such ideas were given weight even in certain governmental circles of Nazi Germany, especially since Hitler hoped to use the Ukrainian issue to undermine its Soviet enemy in the east. To that end, the Nazi German government maintained a consulate in Khust and signed economic agreements with the Carpatho-Ukrainian government.

Hitler had more grandiose plans for eastern Europe, however, and Carpatho-Ukraine was simply too uninfluential to be a part of them. Hence, in March 1939, when the Nazi leader decided to liquidate what remained of rump Czechoslovakia, Carpatho-Ukraine's brief experiment with autonomy was sacrificed to larger German interests. The previous month, in February, the Carpatho-Ukrainians had elected an autonomous diet (on a one-party Ukrainian slate), but the region's

MAP 41   CARPATHO-UKRAINE, 1938–1939

— — Boundary between Slovakia and   ▢ Rusyn/Ukrainian lands
         Subcarpathian Rus', 1928-1938   south of the Carpathians
○ ○ ○ Annexation by Hungary,   ━━━ Boundary of Ukraine, 2005
         2 November 1938

0   25 miles
0   25 kilometers
Scale 1 : 2 125 000

days were numbered. On 15 March 1939, German troops marched into Prague, and Czechoslovakia ceased to exist. Hitler gave the Slovaks a choice: annexation to Hungary or an independent Slovak state under German protection. Not surprisingly, the Slovaks chose statehood. Voloshyn's government, on the other hand, was offered no choice. Instead, Hitler gave his ally Hungary the green light to attack Carpatho-Ukraine. The Czechoslovak Army, still stationed in the region, retreated westward, and in the face of the advancing Hungarian Army the Carpatho-Ukrainian diet proclaimed its independence on 15 March 1939. That same day, Hungarian forces reached Khust, and within a few days, after encountering stiff resistance on the part of the Carpathian Sich army, they managed to take over all of Carpatho-Ukraine. Voloshyn's Carpatho-Ukrainian government was forced to flee abroad, eventually spending the war years in Slovakia or in the former Czecholsovak capital of Prague, now the administrative center of the protectorate of Bohemia-Moravia within Nazi Germany's Third Reich. Several Ukrainophile leaders or suspected sympathizers who remained at home in Transcarpathia were arrested, and Carpathian Sich military personnel were interned by the Hungarian authorities, although after a few months they were all released. All of Transcarpathia, was for the next five and a half years, again to be ruled by Hungary, and although proposals for regional autonomy were discussed in government circles, none was ever granted. In the new political environment, the Ukrainophile national orientation and all its cultural organizations (Prosvita) and publications were banned. Although in theory the Hungarian government favored the idea that the East Slavic inhabitants of Transcarpathia comprised a distinct and pro-Hungarian Uhro-Rusyn nationality, its real goal was to revive the pre–World War I policy of assimilation to Hungarian culture and national identity.

Thus, the first territorial change since World War I to provoke armed conflict in Europe occurred in Transcarpathia (Subcarpathian Rus'/Carpatho-Ukraine) in March 1939. This military clash was contained within the region itself. Hitler's next move, six months later in September 1939, was against Poland. This time the outcome was different – the outbreak of World War II.

The fall of Poland

Having finished with Czechoslovakia in March 1939, Hitler turned his attention to Poland. This time Great Britain and France, who now realized how they had been duped at Munich over Czechoslovakia (the negotiations have been a symbol of capitulation in the face of external threats ever since), vowed that they would stand by their other central European ally, Poland.

Hitler's justification for Nazi Germany's increasingly anti-Polish policy had to do with the 1919 Treaty of Versailles. That accord had separated East Prussia from the rest of Germany by a strip of territory known as the Polish corridor. At the northern end of this corridor was the Baltic port and free city-state of Danzig (Polish: Gdańsk). Hitler considered both the Polish corridor and the Danzig city-state German territories.

Poland's situation was even more precarious because it was bordered in the east by the Soviet Union, which itself was becoming increasingly anxious about Nazi Germany's moves in central Europe. Stalin seemed ready to welcome any kind of agreement with Germany. For his part, Hitler considered Bolshevism an anathema; during the 1930s, the Nazis systematically annihilated the formerly strong German Communist movement. But a solution to the Polish question seemed to have more importance at the moment. Hence, both Stalin and Hitler put ideology aside, did a diplomatic about-face, and approved the signing, between 19 and 23 August 1939, of a non-aggression treaty. Known as the Ribbentrop-Molotov Pact (after the foreign ministers of each country), this German-Soviet treaty provided for (1) a trade agreement, including a two-year German credit to the Soviets for 180 million marks; (2) a ten-year non-aggression pact; and (3) a secret clause establishing a demarcation line between the new allies (along the San, Vistula, and Narev Rivers) should war break out with Poland.

Even before the German-Soviet pact was signed, Hitler had formulated plans for an attack on Poland. Assured of Soviet neutrality, on 1 September 1939 the German Army confidently launched against Poland its first full-scale military operation – a lightning attack (*Blitzkrieg*) consisting of aerial bombing, massive tank movements, infantry, and naval landings. This time Great Britain and France honored their pledges to their ally Poland, and both countries declared war on Germany on 3 September. World War II had begun, although the declarations of war had no effect on Hitler's military operations. In the end, the British and French promise to intervene militarily within two weeks never came about, because despite heroic efforts at defense, the Polish armed forces were sorely outnumbered in troops and outdated in equipment, and within three weeks Poland was brought to its knees. Once again, as in the late eighteenth century, the Polish state ceased to exist.

The German successes from the west made possible a Soviet advance from the east. Beginning on 17 September and meeting little or no Polish resistance, the Red Army was able to take over most Belarusan and Ukrainian-inhabited lands and thereby "reunite" them with their respective Soviet Belorussian and Soviet Ukrainian motherlands. According to a new agreement on German-Soviet spheres of influence, Ukrainian-inhabited lands east of the San and Buh Rivers (i.e., eastern Galicia, western Polissia, and western Volhynia) became part of Soviet Ukraine, and Ukrainian-inhabited lands west of those rivers (i.e., Podlachia, the Chełm region, and the Lemko region) became part of the so-called Generalgouvernement Polen, that is, former Polish lands incorporated into Germany's Third Reich.

The "reunification" of western Ukraine

In those territories held by Soviet troops, elections for a national assembly of western Ukraine were held on 22 October 1939. The people were encouraged to vote for a single slate of candidates who favored annexation to the Soviet Union. Four days later, under the protection of the Red Army, the assembly requested that western Ukraine be annexed to the Soviet Union. On 1 November 1939, the request was approved by the all-union Soviet government in Moscow, which assigned western Ukraine to Soviet Ukraine. The same day, Belarusan territory formerly within Poland (including part of Ukrainian-inhabited Polissia and the city of Brest-Litovsk) was assigned to Soviet Belorussia.

During the following summer of 1940, while Hitler was preoccupied with the war in western Europe, Stalin consolidated his control over the Soviet sphere of influence in central and eastern Europe as provided for in secret clauses of the Ribbentrop-Molotov Pact of August 1939. Thus, in June 1940 the Soviet Union annexed the three Baltic states and created three new Soviet republics – the Estonian S.S.R., the Latvian S.S.R., and the Lithuanian S.S.R. In the very same month, Soviet troops marched into Romanian-ruled northern Bukovina and Bessarabia. Northern Bukovina and the southern Ukrainian-inhabited portions of Bessarabia were annexed to Soviet Ukraine. The Romanian-inhabited areas of Bessarabia were joined with the Moldavian A.S.S.R., which was detached from Soviet Ukraine and raised to republic status as the Moldavian S.S.R.

Within the new territories annexed to Soviet Ukraine, the Soviet system of government and socioeconomic organization was quickly implemented. Six new oblasts were created, industry and trade were nationalized, and within a week of

MAP 42   WESTERN UKRAINE, 1939–1941

oooo International boundary, 1938   ⊙ Oblast center
—·· International boundary, 1940

Copyright © by Paul Robert Magocsi

Scale 1 : 6 600 000

0   50   100 miles
0   50   100 kilometers

its election the national assembly of western Ukraine called for confiscation of the large landed estates. Before the end of 1939, about 6.7 million acres (2.7 million hectares) of land were expropriated from large landowners (mostly Poles), from former Polish state officials, and from the churches and their monasteries. Less than half this land (2.7 million acres [1.1 million hectares]) was redistributed among landless rural dwellers and owners of farms of less than twelve acres (five hectares). The bulk of the confiscated land was given instead to the new Soviet-style state farms (28 by the summer of 1940) and, especially, to collective farms, of which there were nearly 3,000 by June 1941. Although neither of the traditional Ukrainian churches was destroyed, their influence was increasingly undermined by the new Soviet authorities.

With regard to the Greek Catholic Church in Galicia, the authorities tried through various administrative means to weaken the role of the institution and of its very popular leader, Metropolitan Sheptyts'kyi. The government put an end to all church publications; terminated church control of all schools, even seizing its seminaries; banned religion and religious symbols from all schools; cut off income formerly obtained from the church's vast holdings in land and other real estate; and imposed discriminatory taxes. The Orthodox Church in western Volhynia faced similar restrictions and was further weakened by jurisdictional disputes. Certain parishes and hierarchs came under the authority of the Patriarchate of Moscow; others became part of a reconstituted Ukrainian Autocephalous Orthodox Church initially based in the German-controlled Generalgouvernement.

The churches at least survived. Other Ukrainian institutions from interwar Poland fared much worse. All political parties, cultural organizations (including the Prosvita Society and the Shevchenko Scientific Society), cooperatives, and newspapers were closed. Accompanying the destruction of the traditional Ukrainian organizational infrastructure was the arrest and deportation of so-called enemies of the people to labor camps in the far eastern regions of the Soviet Union. The first to be deported in late 1939 were the social elite (professionals, industrialists, bureaucrats) who had not fled westward beyond the San River to Germany's Generalgouvernement. They were followed by two other waves of deportations (April 1940 and, especially, June 1941), which included anyone suspected of actual or potential disloyalty to the Soviet regime. Quite frequently in rural villages, individuals suspected of harboring anti-Soviet attitudes were denounced to the authorities by their neighbors. The denouncers may have been members of the interwar Communist underground or simply opportunists hoping to ingratiate themselves with the new regime. That some of these pro-Soviet elements were Jews helped to reinforce the popular Ukrainian stereotype of the Soviet Union as largely the creation of a "Bolshevik Jewish conspiracy" (*Zhydokomuna*), whose goal was to destroy everything Ukrainian. Whether such a stereotype had any validity, the fact is that in less than two years an estimated half a million ethnic Ukrainians were deported from Galicia and western Volhynia to slave labor camps in Siberia and Kazakhstan.

The Soviet authorities wished to be viewed as the liberators of western Ukraine from bourgeois Polish colonial rule, however, and in an attempt to "win the hearts and minds" of the people they initiated a policy of Ukrainianization. The bilingual schools set up in Ukrainian villages during interwar Polish rule were Ukrainianized, as were the *gymnasia* in the larger towns and cities. The Polish university in L'viv, renamed the Ivan Franko University, was Ukrainianized, and a branch of the Ukrainian Academy of Sciences was established, both institutions being staffed by some leading non-Communist scholars from the interwar period (Ivan Kryp'iakevych,

Mykhailo Vozniak, Ilarion Svientsits'kyi). From the Soviet standpoint, Ukrainianization also meant de-polonization. Consequently, all Polish cultural institutions in L'viv and other eastern Galician towns and cities were abolished as symbols of the feudal and bourgeois past. Aside from these institutional developments, there were also enormous demographic changes. As eastern Poland was being occupied by the Red Army in late September 1939, the initial power vacuum and calls for revenge against all symbols of Polish rule gave rise to renewed civil conflict and bloodshed between Ukrainian and Polish villagers. After order was established, the Soviet government initiated a policy of arrests and forced deportations of all potentially unreliable elements in the population.

The deportations took place in three waves during the first half of 1940. Among the deportees were several categories of people: the interwar socioeconomic elite (mostly Poles); persons suspected of real or alleged anti-Soviet attitudes (mostly Poles and Ukrainians); government officials, police, and civil servants in former Poland (mostly Poles); villagers living along the German-Soviet demarcation line (mostly Poles and Ukrainians); small-scale tradespeople (mostly Jews); and Polish citizens who fled into the Soviet zone during the German invasion in September 1939 (mostly Jews). Of the estimated 550,000 persons in those categories deported from western Volhynia and eastern Galicia to Siberia and other parts of Soviet Central Asia, about four-fifths were ethnic Poles. As a result of such demographic engineering, the urban centers and many rural areas in eastern Galicia lost their Polish character.

The Generalgouvernement

West of the San and Buh Rivers, the Rusyn/Ukrainian population living in the Lemko, Chełm, and Podlachia regions was incorporated into an administrative unit, the Generalgouvernement, which was an integral part of the Third Reich, or Greater Germany (Grossdeutschland). The Lemko and Chełm regions in particular became home to more than 20,000 Ukrainian refugees who had fled Soviet rule east of the San and Buh Rivers. In contrast to the Soviets, the Germans allowed existing Ukrainian institutions to function and the establishment of new Ukrainian-language schools and a relief organization known as the Ukrainian Central Committee. Headed by Volodymyr Kubiiovych, the Central Committee was based in the Polish city of Cracow, which became the center of Ukrainian life in the Generalgouvernement.

Ukrainian church life also flourished under Nazi German rule. The Ukrainian Central Committee succeeded in having forty Orthodox church buildings that had been seized by the Polish government during the interwar years returned to the Orthodox faithful in the Chełm and Podlachia regions. In September 1940, the Ukrainian Autocephalous Orthodox Church (banned by the Soviet regime in 1930) was reestablished, with two eparchies on Ukrainian-inhabited territory. The eparchy based in Chełm was headed by the newly consecrated bishop Ilarion, otherwise the well-known linguist Ivan Ohiienko. Under Ilarion's leadership, the number of Orthodox parishes in the Chełm region and Podlachia increased threefold to 140. The Greek Catholic Church, that is, the Lemko Administration west of the San River, received a Ukrainian apostolic administrator (Oleksander Malynovs'kyi), who tried to reverse the traditional Old Ruthenian and Russophile cultural orientation in the region.

The Organization of Ukrainian Nationalists (OUN), whose Galician branch had conducted a guerrilla campaign against the Poles during the 1930s, was also permitted to exist in the German-controlled Generalgouvernement. The effectiveness of the OUN was lessened considerably, however, by internal factionalism motivated by generational and ideological factors. The older leadership, based in exile in various centers throughout Europe, tended to be conservative, condemning Nazism and stressing the less authoritarian features of Italian fascism. Younger members, who had remained in Galicia and who led the underground struggle during the 1930s, expected in return for their sacrifices at home to be awarded leadership positions in the organization. They believed, moreover, that the models for the OUN should be found in fascist ideas and methods such as those practiced by the Nazis.

These differences came to the fore following the assassination in 1938 by a Soviet secret agent of the OUN leader, Konovalets'. During the succession struggle that followed, at a meeting in Rome in August 1939 the conservative leadership in exile, in an effort to neutralize the younger Galician home cadres, elected Andrii Mel'nyk as the new leader (*vozhd'*) of the OUN. Although nearly fifty years old at the time of his election, Mel'nyk was a reputable activist who had remained in Poland as head of the Ukrainian Military Organization (UVO) during the 1920s. His election did not, however, appease a group of OUN members recently released from internment camps following the fall of Poland. They gave their support instead to the so-called revolutionary leadership headed by Stepan Bandera. All attempts to heal the rift between the two leaders failed, and by the spring of 1941 the OUN was formally split between two factions that came to be known as the Banderites (OUN-B) and Melnykites (OUN-M). The factions struggled for influence over the rank and file, and it was not long before armed conflict broke out among them. But the factional strife in the ranks of the OUN and in other areas of Ukrainian life, both in the German Generalgouvernement and in Soviet Ukraine, was soon to pale in comparison with a profoundly new development – Nazi Germany's invasion of the Soviet Union.

World War II and Nazi German Rule

The Ribbentrop-Molotov Pact of August 1939 was intended to fulfill the immediate needs of Nazi Germany and the Soviet Union. For Hitler, the pact served to neutralize the Soviets while his armies annihilated Poland; for Stalin, it provided a necessary breathing space in which to expand control over a buffer zone along his country's western borders and to reinforce his military forces for what was expected to be the inevitable conflict with the West. In the interim, during the brief era of German-Soviet "friendship" that lasted for just under two years between the summers of 1939 and 1941, each power carved out its respective sphere of influence over various parts of central and eastern Europe and the Near East. It was not long, however, before the interests of both powers clashed. In 1940, when the Soviets took over parts of Romania (northern Bukovina and Bessarabia), the Germans objected, since their own plans included control of Romania's rich oil fields (at Ploeşti). In the end, the disagreement over Romania proved a moot issue, because in the spring of 1941 Hitler abandoned the facade of cooperation with the Bolsheviks. In May, Germany completed plans for a military campaign known as Operation Barbarossa, the invasion of the Soviet Union.

The German and Romanian invasions of Ukraine

On 22 June 1941, Nazi Germany launched an all-out attack on Soviet territory. Operation Barbarossa – as the invasion was known – had three short-term objectives: (1) the destruction of the Soviet armed forces; (2) the capture of the political and industrial centers of Russia (Leningrad and Moscow); and (3) the occupation of Ukraine and the sub-Caucasus region, with its mineral and agricultural wealth. The technique was the same as that used against Poland, a Blitzkrieg of combined ground and air attacks along a front running from the Baltic to the Black Sea. Of the three goals set by the German military planners, only the third was achieved. Although the German forces did come close, they failed to capture either Leningrad or Moscow; and although the Soviet forces suffered extensive defeats, they were not destroyed. The German Army, however, pushed as far as Lake Onega in the north (thus encircling Leningrad); they took Novgorod and reached the outskirts of Moscow in the center; and they overran Ukraine and beyond as far as the outskirts of Stalingrad, at the bend of the Volga River, and the foothills of the Caucasus in the south. This farthest German advance was attained in the summer of 1942.

So rapid was the German Army's advance that by November 1941, just four months after the start of the invasion, virtually all Soviet Ukraine was under German control. In response to Germany's offensive, Stalin and the Soviet government called on the people of Ukraine (14 July 1941) to defend the fatherland. Whether or not they heeded the call – and many, remembering the forced collectivization, famine, and purges of the 1930s, did not – seemed irrelevant. Because the German military advance was so successful and quick, large numbers of Soviet forces were captured in battle or surrendered voluntarily. In desperation, Stalin adressed the Soviet people on radio as early as 3 July 1941, calling on the remaining forces to "make life in the rear of the enemy unbearable." His "strategic plan" was to "destroy all that cannot be evacuated"[1] – a scorched-earth policy which saw the retreating Soviet authorities demolish industrial plants, railroads, food supplies, water resources, cultivated fields, and other resources. Most of the mines in the Donbas were flooded, and the Dnieper Hydroelectric Works, with its dam and generators, was blown up. In their hasty and often panic-stricken retreat, the Soviet authorities were not about to evacuate the thousands of prisoners they had arrested, mostly during their last months of rule in western Ukraine. Their solution, implemented at the end of June and in early July 1941, was to kill all inmates regardless of whether they had committed minor or major crimes or were being held for political reasons. According to estimates, from 15,000 to 40,000 prisoners were killed during the Soviet retreat from eastern Galicia and western Volhynia.

The brutal scorched-earth policy would have been even more destructive had the Soviets not been forced to retreat so rapidly. Despite the haste, some planned evacuation was possible, especially in eastern Ukraine. It included the removal of 3.8 million people and about 850 large industrial plants to the Soviet East. Among the inhabitants who participated in the eastward exodus were about 200,000 Germans living in the Left Bank and the Crimea. According to a Soviet decree of 28 August 1941, they were forcibly deported because of their potential threat as "diversionists and spies" against the Soviet war effort. At the same time, Germans from the neighboring Volga German A.S.S.R. were also deported and their autonomous republic was abolished. In Ukraine's Right Bank and the Black Sea littoral west of the Southern Buh River, however, the local German inhabitants were untouched by the Soviet retreat.

Not all Soviet Ukrainian territory came under German rule. Romania, which joined Nazi Germany's invasion of the Soviet Union, immediately reacquired northern Bukovina and all of Bessarabia, which the country had ruled during the interwar years but lost to the Soviets in 1940. By an agreement signed with Germany at Tighina on 30 August 1941, Romania also acquired the region known as Transnistria, located between the Dniester and Southern Buh Rivers. This included the large Black Sea port of Odessa, which fell to Romanian forces in mid-October, but only after a military operation in which the invaders suffered losses of up to 70,000

MAP 43

UKRAINE, 1941–1944

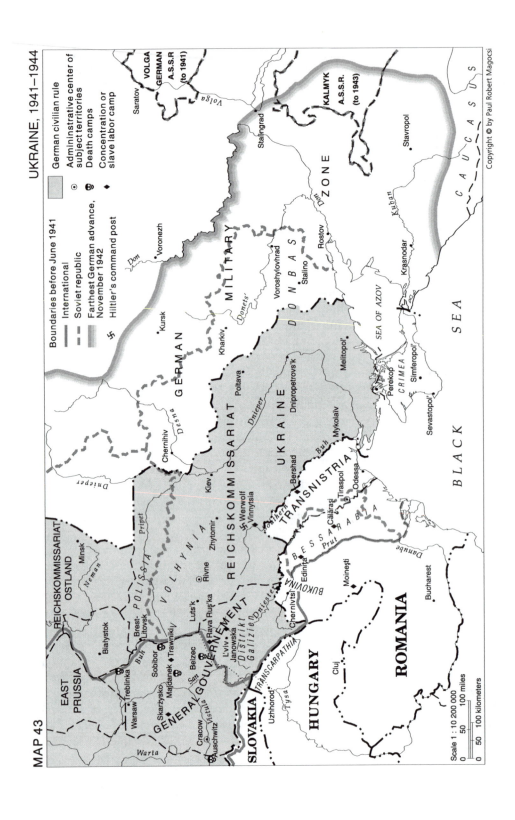

dead and wounded. Transnistria was not formally annexed to Romania, but functioned as a self-governing province under the authority of the country's wartime head of state, Marshal Ion Antonescu. Transnistria's administration was headed by a civil governor, Gheorghe Alexianu, whose headquarters were in the town of Tiraspol.

The new administration viewed the local Romanian inhabitants, who represented only about 10 percent of the 2.3 million inhabitants of Transnistria, as the vanguard of a Greater Romania that would extend eastward beyond the Dniester River. In an effort to enhance the Romanian character of the region, new Romanian-language elementary and secondary schools were opened, a Romanian Scientific Institute was created to coordinate all forms of cultural activity, and a Romanian Orthodox Mission was established to coordinate the work of 250 missionary priests from other parts of Romania, who together with a nearly equal number of local priests tried to serve the 700 churches and chapels that used Romanian in their liturgies. These romanianization efforts continued throughout the war, until the arrival of the Red Army in 1944.

Nazi rule in Ukraine

The vast majority of Ukrainian territory came under the rule of Nazi Germany. And this did not bode well for Ukraine and its inhabitants. In the perceptive words of one scholar describing the mid-twentieth century: "If Europe was ... a dark continent, Ukraine and Belarus were the heart of darkness."[2]

The Nazi regime divided its conquests into three distinct administrative regions: (1) the Generalgouvernement Polen, (2) the Reichskommissariat Ukraine, and (3) the military zone. Galicia east of the San River, only recently incorporated into Soviet Ukraine in the fall of 1939, was made part of the Generalgouvernement on 1 August 1941. Most remaining Ukrainian territory was reorganized into the so-called Reichskommissariat Ukraine (formed 20 August 1941), essentially run as a German foreign colony ruled by a German civil administrator (*Reichskommissar*) resident in the Volhynian town of Rivne. Beyond the Reichskommissariat was the military zone, which stretched as far east as the German Army advanced.

The Crimea, although technically a part of the Reichskommissariat Ukraine, remained de facto in the German military zone. This is because of the difficulty the German Army encountered after it broke through the narrow isthmus of Perekop on 21 October 1941. The Soviet armed forces retreated to the port city of Sevastopol', where they held out for eight months until surrendering in July 1942. During the military struggle for control of the peninsula, an estimated 20,000 Crimean Tatars fought in Soviet ranks. Many were captured or surrendered to the Germans.

The Crimea was of particular interest to Nazi Germany. Not only did it have strategic military value (the southern flank guaranteed control of Ukraine), it was also an important component of Nazi ideology. Hitler decided that the Crimea, after resettlement by ethnic Germans from southern Tyrol and Romania, would be transformed into a pure German colony called Gotenland (the Land of Goths), whose main cities, Simferopol' and Sevastopol', would henceforth be known respectively as Gotenberg and Theodorichhafen. As part of these plans, the Crimean Tatars, who like the Slavs were considered subhumans (*Untermenschen*) in the Nazi racial hierarchy, would have to be removed from the peninsula.

In practice, however, Nazi rule in the Crimea, which was to last a little over two years, followed a different pattern. The German military, in particular, was sympathetic to some kind of accommodation with the Crimean Tatars, who they expected would be more reliable than the local Russian and Ukrainian inhabitants. In fact, many Crimean Tatars greeted the arrival of the Germans as "liberators" from Soviet rule. Putting aside Nazi racial ideology, the German military in the Crimea, in cooperation with Crimean Tatar leaders from the exile community in Turkey (Cafer Seydahmet and Edige Kirimal) and in Romania (Mustecip Ülküsal), organized among captured Soviet soldiers several self-defense battalions. These included nearly 20,000 Crimean Tatars who assisted Germans in hunting down Soviet partisans and other real or suspected anti-Nazi elements.

The German civil authority, through the representative of the Reichskommissariat in the Crimea (Alfred Frauenfeld), already permitted in November 1941 the formation of Muslim Committees in various towns and cities, whose function was to promote Crimean Tatar religious and cultural activity. The former exile from Turkey, Edige Kirimal, who was recognized by the German authorities as the leading spokesperson for Crimean Tatar interests, even expected that some form of autonomy would be accorded his people. It would be incorrect, however, to assume that the German regime favored only Crimea's Tatars. The official languages in use were actually German and Russian, and several Russians held posts in local town and city administrations. As elsewhere in the Nazi German realm, a much worse fate awaited the Jews. Within a year beginning in November 1941, all the remaining Jews in the Crimea (the indigenous Krymchaks as well as the Ashkenazi) – an estimated 30,000 to 40,000 – were killed by German SS units.

Certainly not all Crimean Tatars supported the German presence in their homeland. Aside from the nearly 20,000 fighting on various fronts in the Soviet Army, by 1944 Crimean Tatars made up nearly 17 percent (roughly their proportion of the population) of the Soviet partisans fighting against the German military in the Crimea. Nevertheless, a large percentage of Crimean Tatars did cooperate actively or passively with the occupying regime. Such cooperation provoked antagonism and deep hatred on the part of the local Slavic inhabitants (Russians and Ukrainians) toward whom they considered to be their "collaborationist" Crimean Tatar neighbors. The collaborationist label was to remain and have dire consequences once the Soviet regime returned to power.

The situation in the greater part of German-ruled Ukraine was even more complex than in Crimea. Initially, some Ukrainians welcomed the German invasion, because they hoped that with the end of Soviet rule their country would enjoy a better life and perhaps some form of national sovereignty. The attitude of the Organization of Ukrainian Nationalists (OUN) to the Germans was more complex and, depending on circumstances as they evolved, differed between that body's two factions, the Banderites and the Melnykites. In their turn, Ukrainian nationalist aspirations found different responses among Germany's Nazi leadership and its military. The military felt that some kind of cooperation with the OUN would be useful on territories that were about to be invaded by the German Army. The Nazi leadership, on the other hand, invariably rejected on racially motivated ideological grounds (see below) any serious cooperation with the local ethnic Ukrainian population, which it believed should be conquered and remain totally subordinate within Nazi Germany's new world order. Such views resulted in what seemed contradictory policies toward ethnic Ukrainians, especially during the early weeks of Germany's invasion of the Soviet Union.

As early as 1940, at various camps in Austria and Silesia, the German Army was training instructors for the future recruitment of Ukrainians into police units in the Eastern Territories *(Ostpolizei)*. At first Melnykite but later Banderite activists were prominent in this program. On the eve of the invasion, in April 1941 the German Army allowed the formation under the direction of the Bandera faction of the OUN two military units of about 600 men, known by their code names, Nachtigall and Roland. These units consisted of former members of the Carpathian Sich, who after their release by Hungary had been in Austria and, later, Silesia, hoping to see military action that would allow them to participate in the liberation of their homeland from Soviet rule. At the time, these various military groups were popularly known as the Legions of Ukrainian Nationalists (Legiony/ Druzhyny Ukraïns'kykh Natsionalistiv). During the June 1941 invasion of the Soviet Union, Nachtigall marched with the German Army into Galicia and eventually reached Podolia; Roland was sent southwest into Bessarabia.

In addition to the Nachtigall military unit, other OUN-Banderite activists led by Iaroslav Stets'ko returned to Galicia. Acting independently of the German military, the Banderites brought together a group of sympathizers who on 30 June 1941 proclaimed in L'viv the existence of a sovereign Ukrainian state. Stets'ko managed to obtain support for the "new state" from a Council of Seniors that included the most respected figures in Galician-Ukrainian society, Metropolitan Andrei Sheptyts'kyi and the former Austrian parliamentarian Kost' Levyts'kyi (recently released from prison in Moscow, where he had been held since 1939). The Banderites also organized in the Generalgouvernement a large number of propagandists, the so-called expeditionary groups *(pokhidni krupy)*. Traveling clandestinely by horse-drawn wagons and bicycles, about 1,500 young men (and some women) activists, organized in three expeditionary groups, followed the German military advance into eastern Ukraine, where they hoped to extend their vision for independent statehood.

The *Akt* of 30 June 1941, as the proclamation of the Ukrainian state came to be known, did not sit well with the German military, who knew quite well that Nazi policy makers were on principle opposed to any but the most superficial concessions to the Ukrainians. Consequently, the leading Banderites were arrested and sent to Berlin, including Stepan Bandera (who had never returned to Galicia himself) and Stets'ko, both of whom spent most of the war years (July 1941 to September 1944) in German prisons and concentration camps. The Banderite faction of the OUN was thus eliminated from Galicia, and the Nachtigall and Roland military units, which by then were serving in eastern and southern Ukraine, were demobilized in August 1941 and sent back to bases in Austria and Silesia. Both units were eventually fused into the Guard Battalion 201 and in March 1942 sent to fight against Soviet partisans in Belarus. Before the end of the year, however, the Guard Battalion was permanently disbanded and its officers sent to German prisons.

Following the rather quick alienation between the OUN-Banderites and the Germans, the Melnykite faction of the OUN thought it might be able to fare somewhat better with Ukraine's new rulers. The faction's leader, Andrii Mel'nyk, was joined by former officers from the army of the Ukrainian National Republic who on 6 July 1941 appealed to Hitler to allow them to take part in the "crusade against Bolshevik barbarism."[3] The appeal fell on deaf ears, however. At best, during the invasion the Melnykites were able to send interpreters and other advisers into eastern Ukraine with the German Army, as well as – without any authorization – expeditionary groups similar to those sent by the Bandera faction of the OUN. The center of Melnykite activity during the summer of 1941 was Zhytomyr.

Aside from attempting to raise Ukrainian national and political consciousness among the citizens of German-occupied Soviet Ukraine, the two factions of the OUN fought bitterly against each other. The internecine struggle led to assassinations and mutual accusations of responsibility for these acts and of complicity with the Germans. Following the assassination of two prominent Melnykite leaders (Omelian Senyk and Mykola Stsibors'kyi), the German security forces cracked down on the Banderites (who were blamed for the attacks), executing many of their activists and forcing all their expeditionary groups to disband. Any hopes for future reconciliation between the two factions of the OUN ended after the decimation of the Banderite organization in German-controlled Ukraine.

Having eliminated the more radical nationalist elements in Ukrainian society, the German civilian authorities seemed willing to work with relatively moderate leaders. In western Ukraine, the recently established Council of Seniors in L'viv on 30 July 1941 was transformed into the Ukrainian National Council, headed by Metropolitan Sheptyts'kyi and Kost' Levyts'kyi. The new council, expanded to include members of the prewar UNDO political party and several Greek Catholic prelates, expected to represent the interests of Ukrainians in former Poland (Galicia, Volhynia, the Chełm region) before the German authorities. In practice, it was responsible only for Ukrainians in the Distrikt Galizien, whose annexation to the Generalgouvernement it opposed. Finally, in March 1942, following Metropolitan Sheptyts'kyi's protest to the German government against genocide, the Ukrainian National Council was forced to disband. Henceforth, Ukrainian interests in the entire Generalgouvernement were represented only by the previously established Ukrainian Central Committee, headed by Volodymyr Kubiiovych in Cracow.

Under the auspices of the Cracow-based Central Committee, several Ukrainian cooperatives dismantled in eastern Galicia by the short-lived Soviet regime were revived; elementary, technical, and secondary schools were allowed to function; and Prosvita cultural societies were reopened. Ukrainians were also permitted to enter the lower ranks of the civil and judicial administrative apparatus of the Generalgouvernement. Finally, in April 1943 a volunteer Ukrainian military unit known as the SS Galicia Division (German: *Waffen SS Division Galizien*) was formed. The *Dyviziia*, as it was known in Ukrainian, was one of the many non-German units within the military branch (*Waffen*) of the Nazi elite SS paramilitary organization. It proved attractive to large segments of nationally minded Galician-Ukrainian youth, who were committed to the Galicia Division's declared object of fighting alongside the German Army against the Soviets on the eastern front.

In many ways, the Ukrainian Central Committee and the Galicia Division were a facade for German rule, upholding the pretense that Ukrainians had control of their community life. In reality, the Generalgouvernement was a protectorate within Greater Germany and was subject to the exigencies of direct Nazi rule. All decisions and ultimate power rested in the hands of a German governor-general resident in Cracow, Hans Frank, who in turn was responsible directly to the Führer in Berlin. But the extremes of the wartime Nazi regime, at least in the Generalgouvernement's district of Galicia, were mitigated by the attitude of the local district governor, Otto Wächter. Although a committed Nazi, Wächter was from an Austrian Habsburg aristocratic family and realized the value of counteracting Polish interests by cultivating Galicia's Ukrainians. Throughout the war, the district governor Wächter maintained cordial relations with a fellow Habsburg aristocrat, Metropolitan Sheptyts'kyi. The result was that Ukrainians and their traditional organizational structures in Galicia were allowed to function with less interference from the Nazi authorities than was the case in other German- and Romanian-ruled Ukrainian territories.

The situation within the German Reichskommissariat, carved out of former Soviet Ukrainian territory, was quite different. As part of his declaration of war against the Soviet Union, on 22 June 1941 Hitler proclaimed the liberation of peoples from Bolshevik rule and the recognition of freedom of religion and labor. Under these rather vague proclamations, there occurred a rebirth of Ukrainian national life during the first months of Nazi German rule. During the first few months of the German occupation, over 100 non-Communist newspapers began to appear, new publishing companies and theaters were formed, a society of Ukrainian writers was established, and teachers began to formulate a revised school curriculum that stressed a Ukrainian national message for classes in language, history, and culture. In the countryside, some peasants began to divide among their families land that had belonged to the Soviet collective farms, and others joined to establish voluntary agricultural cooperatives and rural financial institutions.

The churches were able to renew their pastoral work, not to mention their jurisdictional rivalries. The autocephalous Orthodox movement, which had been banned since the early 1930s in Soviet Ukraine, reestablished its organizational structure. The Ukrainian Autocephalous Orthodox Church, recently revived in the German-ruled Generalgouvernement (see chapter 48), was extended to the Reichskommissariat Ukraine under the leadership of Metropolitan Polikarp Sikors'kyi (reigned 1942–1944). In the first half of 1942, six new autocephalous bishops were consecrated, including Mstyslav Skrypnyk of Pereiaslav (reigned 1942–1944). The Autocephalous Orthodox Church was not alone, however;

it had a rival in what came to be known as the Ukrainian Autonomous Ortho-dox Church. Founded at the Pochaïv Monastery in Volhynia in August 1941, the autonomists had their own hierarchy under Metropolitan Oleksii Hromads'kyi (reigned 1941–1943). The autonomists were able to attract to their ranks clergy from the Russian Orthodox Church, because they accepted jurisdictional subor-dination to the Moscow patriarch, even though they considered themselves free to act independently as long as the patriarchate was under Soviet control. Aside from the Autocephalous and Autonomous Orthodox jurisdictions, the Galician-based Greek Catholic Church also set up for the first time a hierarchical struc-ture in central and eastern (former Soviet) Ukraine. This was part of Metropoli-tan Sheptyts'kyi's larger plan of realizing Christian unity through the mediation of the Greek Catholic Church. It was the possibility of missionary activity in "the East" and the overthrow of Bolshevism that prompted Sheptyts'kyi initially to look with favor on the German presence in Ukraine.

Finally, on the political front, in early October 1941 the Melnykite faction of the OUN initiated the creation of the Ukrainian National Council in Kiev (head-ed by Professor Mykola Velychkivs'kyi), which was intended to become the basis for a future Ukrainian government. All these developments during the summer and fall of 1941 led many Ukrainians to believe that the Germans had come as true liberators who would help them reestablish a non-Soviet national life. As it turned out, however, the Nazis, like the Soviet Communists before them, were prisoners of their own ideology. In short, the Nazis had their own plans for Ukraine.

Nazi racial policies and the Holocaust

It was during World War II that Ukraine came to considered one of the most impor-tant components of Germany's *Lebensraum* – a territory where racially pure German citizens could find solace from an "unhealthy urban society" and build instead a predominantly agricultural – and supposedly pristine – environment. For such a racially pure setting to be achieved, local populations would have to be integrated into the new German society. If that were not possible, they would have to be deport-ed elsewhere or, simply, killed. Because Nazi Germany was engaged in war, the building of its *Lebensraum* depended on the fate of its military campaigns. Accord-ingly, after the destruction of Poland in 1939, the Generalgouvernement was first intended to be a dumping ground for Poles and Jews from other parts of what had been Poland. Two years later, when Germany's territorial advances catapulted east-ward and nearly reached the Caucasus, the Generalgouvernement was reclassified as a German-settled territory known as the *Vandalengau* (the province of the Van-dals), and the territory just to the east annexed from Soviet Ukraine was also slated to become a German-inhabited land known as the *Gothengau* (the province of the Goths).

The ideological justification for such a profound demographic reconstruction of eastern Europe is found in the writings of Hitler and other Nazis during the interwar years. At that time, they developed an elaborate theoretical framework that classified all peoples and civilizations worldwide. Their theories were based on racial distinctions. Certain "master" races, the so-called *Herrenvölker*, whose foremost representatives were the Germanic Aryans, were to be served by "inferior" races, the so-called *Untermenschen* (subhumans). Like all Slavs, the Ukrainians were classified among the inferior races, whose sole use was, at best, to serve the master races. The lowest elements in the Nazi racial hierarchy were the Jews and the Gypsies. Both groups were persecuted during the 1930s in Germany, but their ultimate fate was not decided until early 1942, when Hitler approved implementation of a policy known as the Final Solution. As it turned out, the Final Solution meant physical extermination. Since the Reichskommissariat Ukraine was treated as a German foreign colony, Nazi theories about superior and inferior races were put into practice there. This was especially the case after the appointment in the fall of 1941 of the notorious administrator from East Prussia, Erich Koch, as Reichskommissar of Ukraine.

According to Nazi racial theory, there was really only one people living on Ukrainian territory who could be considered superior – the Germans. Even before Nazi Germany's invasion of the Soviet Union, tens of thousands of ethnic Germans living in Ukraine had taken advantage of the clauses on population transfers in the Ribbentrop-Molotov Pact and had begun moving westward at the encouragement of Berlin. Hitler had dreamed of creating in central Europe a Greater Germany to which all the scattered Germans of the Continent could be "repatriated" and in which the whole "master race," living together, could build the "glorious thousand-year Third Reich." To make room for the new repatriates, German boundaries were moved eastward, especially into former Polish territory. It was actually in a region in western Poland along the Warta River known as the Wartheland (German: *Warthegau*) that Germans from the east were settled. The first to arrive, between 1939 and 1940, were Germans from the newly occupied Soviet territories of western Volhynia (60,000), southern Bessarabia (93,000), northern Bukovina (42,000), and eastern Galicia (60,000)

After the German Army invaded the Soviet Union in June 1941 and set up administrations like the Reichskommissariat Ukraine, ethnic Germans in the Right Bank, as well as the Black Sea Germans farther south who had not been deported during the Soviet evacuation, were given a privileged position in Hitler's "new order." Ukraine's Germans were in a sense in the vanguard, since they already lived on territory that was considered part of the future German *Lebensraum*. But now that many were serving a Nazi regime that generally treated non-Germans harshly, a serious hatred developed for the first time between ethnic Ukrainians and their German neighbors, whose families had lived in their midst for well over a century. It is not surprising, then, that in 1943, when the German Army was forced to retreat before the rapidly advancing Soviet troops, close to 350,000 ethnic Germans fled westward, settling first in the Wartheland and then in Germany proper. (Perhaps as many as 250,000 of these Ukrainian Germans were repatriated once again after 1945, this time by the Soviet forces in the eastern zone of Germany, who sent them for resettlement to the Komi A.S.S.R. and Siberia.) Thus, as a result of World War II, the German settlements on Ukrainian territory, some going back to the late eighteenth century, ceased to exist. But notwithstanding their ultimate fate, the German minority in Ukraine had a favored position at least for a few years.

At the other end of the Nazi racial spectrum were the Jews. During the German invasion of the Soviet Union, many Jews, especially in the eastern part of Soviet Ukraine, succeeded in fleeing eastward as part of the Soviet evacuation program of civilians, among them many Communist party functionaries, governmental employees, institutional functionaries, and factory workers. In western Ukrainian territories, however, Jews were prevented from fleeing eastward either because of the rapid advance of the German troops or because of the refusal of Soviet security forces to let them cross the pre-1939 borders of the Soviet Union. Those left behind found themselves under Nazi German rule and were subjected to that regime's genocidal policies known as the Holocaust (Hebrew: *sho'ah*, "catastrophe"; Yiddish: *Khurbn*, "destruction"). The Holocaust reached its highest stage after 1941 with the implementation of a program of systematic mass killings – the Final Solution.

To achieve the Final Solution, the Nazis created special extermination task forces (*Einsatzgruppen*) recruited from the SS and the German secret police (the Gestapo). These units were assigned the task of following the German Army and ridding the occupied areas of all undesirable groups, which in Ukrainian lands meant Communists, the Polish intelligentsia, eventually Ukrainian nationalists, and, especially, Jews. During the very first days of the German invasion, the methods of killing were often random, reflecting the anarchic conditions that raged during the initial weeks of the invasion. The Germans helped to circulate rumors that "Jewish Bolsheviks" had been involved in the murders of thousands of Ukrainian political prisoners killed by the Soviet authorities before their hasty retreat. In L'viv, for instance, after the prisons were opened, about 4,000 Jews were massacred between 2 and 7 July 1941 by German extermination task forces with the assistance of what some sources describe as "Ukrainian auxiliary police" (Ukrainische Hilfspolizei). Among the victims that week was L'viv's respected rabbi, Ezekiel Lewin, whose two sons were among the first of 165 Jews (mostly children) whom Metropolitan Andrei Sheptyts'kyi managed to hide in a network of safe places in several of Galicia's Greek Catholic monasteries and convents. These lives saved were the exception, however; more typical was the fate of an estimated 24,000 Jews, who perished in pogroms perpetrated in other towns and villages throughout eastern Galicia and western Volhynia during July and August.

As soon as the days of invasion were over and a German administration was established, a more systematic approach was adopted for the elimination of the so-called undesirable elements. Jews were first rounded up in specified areas or ghettos, then either (1) shipped off in cattle cars to death camps (Auschwitz, Belżec, Majdanek, Sobibor, Treblinka) in order to be gassed and burned, the method of extermination favored in western Ukrainian lands; or (2) herded to the outskirts of the city, often near a pit, and shot, the method used in central and eastern Ukraine. Mass deportations of Jews from western Ukraine began in March 1942 and were essentially completed within the next year. The most infamous example of the second method of extermination took place in Kiev. In the valley of Babyn Iar (Babi Yar), on 29–30 September 1941, just one week after the Germans

THOU SHALT NOT KILL

The respected metropolitan of the Greek Catholic Church in Galicia, Andrei Sheptyts'kyi, was outraged by the "diabolical" immorality of the German authorities and some of his own Ukrainian people in their murderous activity against Jews. As well as hiding, at great risk, individual Jews, in early 1942 he wrote to the head of the Nazi SS, Heinrich Himmler, protesting the fact that "Ukrainian auxiliary police are being forced to shoot Jews." Then, when the mass deportations of Jews began in the summer of 1942, the metropolitan decried the situation in a letter to the pope, dated 29–31 August 1942:

> Liberated by the German army from the Bolshevik yoke, we felt a certain relief. ... Gradually, the [German] government instituted a regime of truly unbelievable terror and corruption... [so that] now everybody agrees that the German regime is perhaps even more evil and diabolic than the Bolshevik [regime]. For more than a year not a day has passed without the most horrible crimes being committed. ... Jews are the primary victims. The number of Jews killed in our region has certainly surpassed 200,000. ... Almost 130,000 men, women, and children were executed in Kiev within a few days.

Finally, on 21 November 1942 Sheptyts'kyi issued a pastoral letter under the title of the fifth commandment, "Thou shalt not kill," which was read in all churches and published in the official publication of the L'viv Greek Catholic archeparchy. Although referring to political murder, the entire text makes it clear that Sheptyts'kyi condemned all kinds of murder, including that of Jews.

> Those who do not look upon political murder as a sin entertain a peculiar kind of self-delusion – as if politics freed men from the obligation to observe divine law and justified a crime that is contrary to human nature. This is not the case. ... A person who sheds the innocent blood of his enemy, of his political opponent, is just as much a murderer as one who does it for robbery and is just as deserving of God's punishment and the condemnation of the church.

SOURCE: Paul Robert Magocsi, ed., *Morality and Reality: The Life and Times of Andrei Sheptys'kyi* (Edmonton 1989), pp. 154–155 and 135.

took the city, an estimated 34,000 Jews who had not managed to flee the city were shot.

The Nazi extermination task forces often strove to employ local ethnic Ukrainians, Russians, Poles, Germans, and even Jews (through the so-called Jewish Councils: Judenräte) in the organization and implementation of their murderous missions. Some of the local population participated, either willingly or under various forms of coercion. It is interesting to note that in contrast to the solicitous actions toward Jews undertaken by the Greek Catholic Metropolitan Sheptyts'kyi in western Ukraine, the metropolitans of both Orthodox jurisdictions (Autocephalous and Autonomous) helped to incite anti-Semitic attitudes in the local population. They did this through public remarks that associated Communist rule with Jews, thereby implying that as a group they should expect to be punished for their previous "collaboration" with the Soviet regime.

According to an agreement between Germany and Romania, 147,000 Jews were deported between 1941 and 1943 from Bukovina and Bessarabia to Transnistria, where they were held in concentration camps for use as forced labor. An estimated 90,000 died as a result of the deplorable conditions in the camps or other scattered atrocities. As for the Jews native to Transnistria itself, an estimated 130,000 to 170,000 were murdered or died from disease during the first two years of the Romanian occupation (September 1941 to November 1943). A particularly horrible incident took place in October 1941, when the Romanian forces executed 15,000 to 20,000 Jews in Odessa in reprisal for blowing up the Romanian army headquarters in the city.

During the Holocaust, the Nazis were able to kill an estimated 850,000 to 900,000 Ukrainian Jews. This meant the virtual elimination of the Jewish population in western Ukraine and an end to the centuries-old Yiddish and Hebrew culture that had flourished throughout the country. The Holocaust also had another detrimental effect. Even though the murders were systematically carried out under the direction of Nazi special extermination units, Jewish survivors of that time have stressed in memoirs and other testimonies that Ukrainian auxiliary police and militia, or simply "Ukrainians" (a generic term that in fact included persons of non-Ukrainian as well as Ukrainian national background), participated in the overall process as policemen and camp guards and in other supporting jobs. The result is that recollections of the Holocaust, a phenomenon which has dominated Israeli and worldwide Jewish civic culture since World War II, often portray Ukrainians as anti-Semitic by nature. This stereotype has been perpetuated in the popular media and even in scholarly studies, particularly in Israel and North America.

Nazi policies toward ethnic Ukrainians

For the ethnic Ukrainian inhabitants in the Reichskommissariat Ukraine, the promising developments for their national life proved to be short-lived. In September 1941, the expeditionary groups sent by the Banderite faction of the OUN as well as their local supporters were being arrested or executed by the special extermination task forces at the same time that the Jews were being exterminated. The process of destroying Ukrainian nationalists and their organizational life was stepped up after the arrival in November 1941 of Erich Koch as head of the Reichskommissariat Ukraine. Before the end of the year, the recently founded Ukrainian National Council had been banned, and thousands of its OUN-Melnykite supporters had been arrested or killed. The Prosvita societies and cooperatives were abolished, and beginning in January 1942 all schools above the fourth grade were closed. None of these acts is surprising, since according to Nazi racial theory

Ukrainians were an inferior race. As *Untermenschen* (subhumans), Ukrainians did not need their own organizations, they needed only to work for the master German race. Reichskommissar Koch best summed up the Nazi attitude when he quipped, "If I find a Ukrainian who is worthy of sitting at the same table with me, I must have him shot."[4]

The brutal policies of the Nazis provoked various forms of resistance. The Germans generally responded by assigning collective responsibility and annihilating entire villages, notably in the Chernihiv region, Volhynia, and the area immediately north of Kiev. Symbolically, the ravine at Babyn Iar, first used in September 1941 to annihilate those Jews who were still in Kiev, was for two more years used as a site for executions and mass burials, which were to claim an estimated 100,000 to 150,000 more lives (Soviet prisoners of war, partisans, Ukrainian nationalists, and Gypsies as well as Jews). The total number of non-Jews in Ukraine who were victims of Nazi extermination policies reached an estimated 3,000,000 people.

Besides the arrests and systematic killings, there were several other German policies which alienated most inhabitants of Nazi-ruled Soviet territory, even those who initially may have welcomed Germany's armies as liberators from Bolshevism. These policies concerned (1) prisoners of war, (2) the collective farms, and (3) the forced deportation of civilians. Since the Soviet Union had not signed and did not recognize previous international conventions on warfare, the Germans had a convenient excuse to hold Soviet prisoners of war (POWs) under conditions that were effectively designed to bring about their death. Of the 5.8 million Soviet POWs who fell into German hands between 1941 and 1944, 1.9 million died and another 1.3 million disappeared.

As for the peasants, all hopes of getting back land following the fall of Soviet rule were quickly dashed. At first, some German policy makers argued that from the standpoint of supplying foodstuffs to the Third Reich it would be more efficient to allot land to individual peasants. These suggestions were effectively blocked, however, by Reichskommissar Koch, who simply renamed the former Soviet collectives "communal farms." The "new" farms functioned as before, and were expected to fulfill German-imposed grain quotas that in many regions were double the last Soviet norm.

Finally, the so-called *Ostarbeiter* (Eastern workers) program was initiated in the Reichskommissariat Ukraine and other former Soviet territories. This program consisted of the forced deportation between 1942 and 1945 of 2.8 million civilians to work in Germany. The vast majority – nearly 2.3 million – were from Ukraine. In addition to being forced into their work, the *Ostarbeiter* were subjected to draconian labor discipline. Moreover, unlike other foreign workers in Germany, including Ukrainians from Galicia, the *Ostarbeiter* from the Reichskommissariat Ukraine were forced to wear badges at all times indicating that they were workers from the east.

Resistance to Nazi rule

The population of Ukraine began to resist Nazi rule as early as in the summer of 1941. That resistance took three different forms: (1) spontaneous efforts at self-

MAP 44

THE ADVANCE OF THE RED ARMY

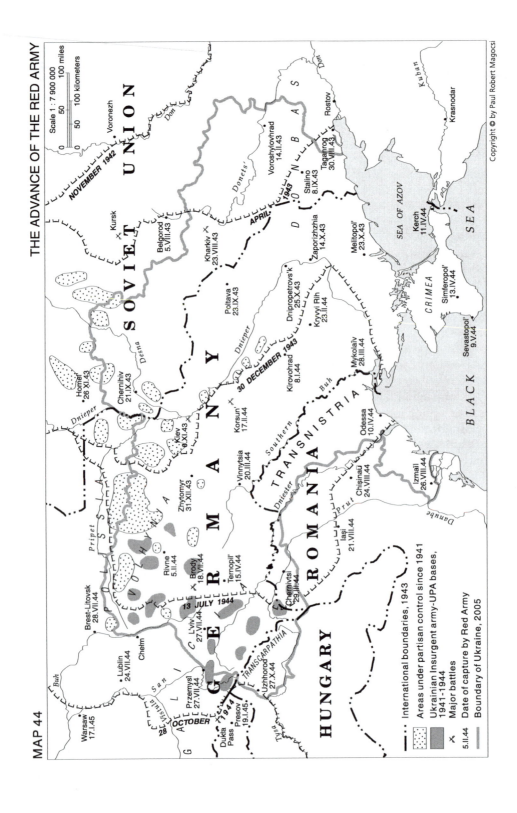

Copyright © by Paul Robert Magocsi

Scale 1 : 7 900 000

International boundaries, 1943

Areas under partisan control since 1941

Ukrainian Insurgent army-UPA bases, 1941-1944

✕ Major battles

5.II.44 Date of capture by Red Army

Boundary of Ukraine, 2005

defense, (2) the organized nationalist (and anti-Soviet) movement, and (3) the Soviet partisan movement. The spontaneous efforts were undertaken in reaction to the more brutal aspects of Nazi rule, especially the practice of imposing collective responsibility, as a result of which entire villages and their inhabitants were destroyed. Local inhabitants who had no particular political orientation formed guerrilla units that often attacked German supply lines. In the course of 1942 and 1943, several such units were formed in eastern Ukraine (the Chernihiv region and the Donbas) and around Vinnytsia in Podolia.

Organized resistance by Ukrainian nationalists was initiated in Volhynia and Polissia, where a guerrilla force led by Taras Bul'ba-Borovets' operated beginning in the summer of 1941 under the aegis of the Ukrainian National Republic in exile. First directed at the retreating Red Army, in March 1942 the unit redirected its attention against the German forces and was renamed the Ukrainian Insurgent Army (Ukraïns'ka Povstans'ka Armiia – UPA). Within the next year, first the Banderite faction and then the Melnykite faction of the OUN formed their own units of the UPA. The various units drew their members from among OUN activists who had escaped arrest by the Germans and from among former Red Army soldiers who had served as German auxiliary police and guards. The latter group included not only ethnic Ukrainians, but also Azerbaijanis, Uzbeks, Georgians, and Tatars, who eventually had their own national units in the UPA. In November 1943, the diverse units of the UPA came under the direction of a supreme command directed by the Banderite faction of the OUN. Throughout 1943, the UPA, whose total forces were approaching 40,000 soldiers, fought in skirmishes against the German Army as well as against Soviet partisans. Initially, Volhynia was the center of operations, but by the summer of 1944 the focus had turned to eastern Galicia, where for nearly a year the UPA – whose numbers by then may have been close to 100,000 – fought several pitched battles against both the retreating Germans and the advancing Soviets for control of the Carpathian mountain passes.

Another aspect of UPA activity was its relationship to Poles. That relationship concerned the civilian population, that is, Poles living in scattered villages throughout the territories of western Volhynia, the Chełm region, and eastern Galicia, as well as the armed Polish resistance movement, in particular the Home Army (Armia Krajowa). The political tensions between ethnic Poles and Ukrainians that stemmed from the interwar years had never gone away. The Nazi German occupation and the military struggle connected with the war only made the situation worse by creating unstable conditions that could and did lead to a renewal of open conflict between the two peoples. This took the form of attacks by the UPA on Polish villages and reprisals by Polish self-defense units and later the Home Army on Ukrainian villages. The underground movement on both sides was concerned with the postwar status of these territories which, each side argued, should belong to either a restored Poland or to an independent Ukraine. Hence, the attacks on innocent civilians were designed to eliminate the presence of Poles and Ukrainians to the advantage of the future state that would rule these territories.

The question of who started this cycle of violence and retribution remains a subject of often emotional debate among historians and eye-witness survivors, but it is certain that several hundreds of thousands were driven from their homes (especially Poles from Volhynia) and that there was considerable loss of life on both sides (50,000 Poles and 20,000 Ukrainians killed are among the more reasonable estimates). In 1942, Ukrainians in the Chełm region were attacked by the Polish underground, allegedly in retaliation for Ukrainian support of the Nazi German regime. By the fall of that that year and continuing until the end of 1943, UPA units were attacking an increasing number of Polish villages in Volhynia. As the Soviet front moved steadily westward, forcing the German Army to retreat, Ukrainian and the Polish underground forces continued to fight against the advancing Soviets as well as against each other, resulting in further loss of life among the Polish and Ukrainian civilian populations in the Chełm region and Galicia throughout much of 1944.

The third form of resistance to Nazi rule was the Soviet partisan movement, which formally began on orders from the Central Committee of the All-Union Communist party within the first week of the German invasion at the end of June 1941. In actual fact, however, Soviet partisans in Ukraine did not attain any significant activity until mid-1943. In order to encourage the movement, the Central Committee of the CP(b)U, following instructions from Moscow, set up on 20 June 1942 the Ukrainian Staff of the Partisan Movement, with headquarters in Voroshylovhrad (Luhans'k), in far eastern Ukraine. By the end of 1943, there were reportedly over 43,000 Soviet partisans active in Ukraine, whose attacks were directed against the German Army and, later, the UPA. Among the more prominent of the Soviet partisan leaders were Sydir Kovpak, best known for his May 1943 raid deep behind German lines as far as the Carpathians, and Petro Vershyhora, who headed the First Ukrainian Partisan Division, which carried out raids deep into western Ukraine during the first half of 1944.

It was the Red Army, however, not the various partisan movements, that determined the future of Ukraine. By the end of 1941 the Soviet Union had reached a rapprochement with Great Britain and the United States which resulted in the Allied wartime alliance and the receipt of desperately needed military supplies, especially from the United States. Armed with such support and a fierce determination to drive out the Nazi invader, the Soviets began an offensive in November 1942. The decisive turning point came at Stalingrad, near the last bend in the Volga River, about 185 miles (300 kilometers) east of Ukraine. After nearly three months of fierce fighting in frigid temperatures, the Red Army defeated the heretofore invincible Germans and forced the surrender of the German Sixth Army after the incredibly costly Battle of Stalingrad. When the battle finally ended on 30 January 1943, more Soviet lives had been lost at Stalingrad alone than by the United States Army on all fronts throughout the entire war.

From Stalingrad, the Red Army pushed westward against fierce resistance from the Germans and their allies. During the early spring of 1943, the German forces were driven out of much of the Donbas, with Voroshylovhrad the first city in Ukraine to be recaptured (14 February). The rest of 1943 was dominated by the Battle for the Dnieper between August and December, during which the Red Army took the entire Left Bank as well as parts of the Right Bank, culminating in the capture of Kiev on 6 November.

The year 1944 began with a Soviet victory at a major battle around Korsun' (24 January to 17 February). This was followed by the rapid retreat of German forces from the entire Right Bank. Farther south during April, the Germans and their Romanian allies were driven out of Transnistria, and all of the Crimea was retaken by the Red Army after Sevastopol' fell to them on 9 May. The capture of Sevastopol', with its militarily invaluable port took on especially evocative connotations for the Crimea's local Russian inhabitants as well as for the Soviet Union as a whole. As the City of Glory (Russian: Gorod Slavye), Sevastopol' – alongside Moscow and Leningrad – became the ultimate symbol of the defense of the Russian/Soviet homeland (*rodina*) against foreign invaders.

By mid-July, the Red Army was poised to enter western Ukraine, with L'viv and all of eastern Galicia falling before the end of the month. It was during the campaign for Galicia that the German unit, the Galicia Division, was virtually decimated by the Red Army – 8,000 out of 11,000 were killed or taken prisoner – at the Battle of Brody (18 July 1944). Finally, in September–October 1944 the Red Army crossed the Carpathian Mountains and took Transcarpathia as part of its operations against German and Hungarian forces defending the road to Budapest. When this campaign was completed in the fall of 1944, virtually all Ukrainian ethnographic territory for the first time had come under Soviet control.

Postwar Soviet Ukraine under Stalin

Although World War II did not end in Europe until the capitulation of the German Army in May 1945, the Germans and their allies were driven out of Ukrainian territory between February 1943 and October 1944. The first task of the Soviet authorities in the areas they recaptured was to reestablish their governmental and administrative authority. The challenge was enormous, since the war had wrought widespread human and material devastation.

Wartime destruction and territorial expansion

World War II, which lasted close to six years, from September 1939 to May 1945, dwarfed even World War I in terms of its geographic scope and human and material destruction. Estimates of human loss range anywhere from 35 to 60 million lives. In this catalog of gruesome statistics, the Soviet Union led all countries, having lost an estimated 11 million combatants and 7 million civilians. Because Ukraine was one of the major war zones of the Soviet Union, it alone accounted for an estimated 4.1 million civilian deaths and 1.4 million military personnel killed in action or taken as prisoners of war. Aside from war-related losses, an estimated 3.9 million Ukrainians were evacuated eastward by the Soviet government during the rapid German advance in 1941–1942, and another 2.2 million were deported to Germany as forced laborers (*Ostarbeiter*).

Material losses were no less devastating as the front moved back and forth across Ukraine. The Soviet scorched-earth policy during its retreat of 1941 was followed by Hitler's orders of 1943 to retreating German troops to create a "zone of destruction" in an attempt to delay the advancing Red Army. Consequently, those cities (Dnipropetrovs'k, Poltava, Kremenchuk) and villages that had not been severely damaged by previous attacks were deliberately destroyed in 1943 and 1944. The results of planned and combat-related destruction meant 28,000 villages and 714 cities and towns in Ukraine were left in total or partial ruin. The center of Kiev, for instance, was 85 percent demolished, and the second-largest city, Kharkiv, was 70 percent in ruins. More than 19 million people were left homeless.

The country's industrial base, which in human terms had cost so much to build, was shattered. Initially, between July and November 1941, the Soviets had dismantled and evacuated 544 complete industrial enterprises. But the rapid German advance combined with subsequent scorched-earth policies implemented by the Soviets and, later, the Germans resulted in 16,150 enterprises being damaged or completely destroyed, 833 coal mines being blown up, and the destruction of electric power stations, dams, railroad lines, bridges, and roads. In the agricultural sector, 872 state farms, 1,300 Machine Tractor Stations, and 27,910 collective farms were destroyed.

But although World War II brought enormous physical destruction to Soviet Ukraine, it also resulted in the territorial expansion of the country. This expansion was a direct result of the enhanced international status of the Soviet Union, which together with China, France, Great Britain, and the United States made up the victorious Allied Powers. It was the Americans, British, and Soviets, however, who inflicted the decisive defeat upon Germany and Japan. Consequently, it was the leaders of these countries, the so-called Big Three – President Franklin D. Roosevelt, Prime Minister Winston Churchill, and General Secretary Iosif Stalin – who were to play the most decisive role in postwar European politics. In fact, even before the war had ended, the Big Three began discussions about their respective spheres of interest in Europe.

Stalin was adamant that Soviet borders should at the very least be extended westward to include those territories taken during the German-Soviet invasion of Poland in September 1939 as well as other lands acquired later. These included, from north to south, the Karelian region of Finland; the former independent states of Estonia, Latvia, and Lithuania; the Belarusan and Ukrainian lands that had been part of interwar Poland; and northern Bukovina and Bessarabia, which had been in Romania. At their first joint wartime meeting held at Teheran in November 1943, Churchill and Roosevelt agreed in principle to Stalin's demands. An immediate problem was Poland. Since Poland had fought on the side of the Allies, its territorial losses in the east had to be compensated. The solution was to detach from Germany territories east of the Oder and Neisse Rivers (Pomerania, Silesia, and the southern half of East Prussia) and to award them to the revived Polish state.

As for Ukraine, the new Soviet-Polish border agreed to by Churchill, Roosevelt, and Stalin at their second conference in Yalta (February 1945) followed quite closely the Curzon Line, which in 1920 Great Britain had proposed as an armistice line and temporary boundary between warring Poland and Soviet Russia (see map 35). This meant that Ukrainian-inhabited eastern Galicia almost as far as the San River, and Volhynia and Polissa as far west as the Buh River, became part of Soviet Ukraine. Farther south, Soviet Ukraine's border with Romania was restored to what it had been from the summer of 1940 until the German invasion of the Soviet Union one year later. Namely, the historic province of Bessarabia located between the Dniester and Prut Rivers was reapportioned: a small chunk of the southern coastal area near Izmaïl was given to Soviet Ukraine; the large central portion of the province, together with a strip of land east of the Dniester River, was reconstituted as the Moldavian Soviet Socialist Republic.

MAP 45

SOVIET UKRAINE, 1945

Copyright © by Paul Robert Magocsi

POLAND

RUSSIAN

BELORUSSIAN S.S.R.

S. F. S. R.

S. S. R.

UKRAINIAN

KUBAN

DONBAS

CRIMEA

SEA OF AZOV

BLACK

SEA

ROMANIA

MOLDAVIAN S.S.R.

BESSARABIA

BUKOVINA

HUNGARY

CZECHO-
SLOVAKIA

TRANSCARPATHIA

GALICIA

VOLHYNIA

POLISSIA

LEMKO
REGION

Warsaw
Białystok
Brest
Chełm
Przemyśl
Prešov
Hajdúdorog
Uzhhorod
Ivano-
Frankivs'k
Drohobych
L'viv
Luts'k
Rivne
Ternopil'
Khmel'nyts'kyi
Chernivtsi
Khotyn
Vinnytsia
Zhytomyr
Kiev
Izmail
Odessa
Mykolaïv
Kherson
Kirovohrad
Cherkasy
Kryvyi Rih
Dnipropetrovs'k
Zaporizhzhia
Poltava
Sumy
Chernihiv
Homel'
Pinsk
Kharkiv
Belgorod
Kursk
Orel
Lipetsk
Voronezh
Rostov
Krasnodar
Stalino
Voroshylovhrad
Zhdanov
Simferopol'
Yalta

Vistula
Buh
San
Pripet
Dniester
Prut
Danube
Southern Buh
Ros'
Dnieper
Vorskla
Donets'
Desna
Seim
Don
Kuban

Scale 1 : 8 100 000

0   50   100 miles
0   50   100 kilometers

◎ Oblast center

Boundaries of Poland,
Czechoslovakia, and
Romania before 1939

Ukrainian ethnolinguistic
territory

Lands inhabited in part by
Ukrainians, 1930s

VOLUNTARY REUNIFICATION, SOVIET STYLE

On 25–26 November 1944, 663 delegates from people's committees representing about 80 percent of the towns and villages in Transcarpathia gathered in the city of Mukachevo at the first National Congress of People's Committees to determine the fate of their homeland. The manifesto unanimously approved by the delegates, which called for "the reunification of Transcarpathian Ukraine with its great motherland, Soviet Ukraine," has been described by one historian and participant (Vasyl Markus) as "a kind of [interim] constitutional act for Transcarpathian Ukraine until its reunification with Ukraine."[*] Ever since that time, the Soviet and the post-1991 Ukrainian governments have argued that the November 1944 manifesto was an expression of the will of the people that justified annexation of the province from Czechoslovakia. It is interesting to view the events through the eyes of two other eyewitnesses, who co-signed the following recollection.

At the time we were students at the Commerce Academy in Mukachevo. That fall we went back to school late. The city had to be put back in order [after the front had passed through], courtyards and sidewalks had to be cleaned, and the airport restored. At the same time Stalin's KGB was already preparing for political work among the masses. They brought us in long lines to the Victory movie house (it was called Scala at the time) to look at films.

We arrived. The hall was quite full, because they had brought in people from other organizations. First the mayor of Mukachevo, comrade Dragula, greeted us. He opened the so-called meeting with the words: 'Comrades, we have gathered here together for a very important purpose; we want to break away from bourgeois Czechoslovakia and unite Subcarpathian Rus' in the framework of a great country, the Soviet Union, with its peaceloving capital Moscow. Whoever is for this, raise your hand.'

The hall was stunned. And since it was so quiet, the mayor said: 'Comrades, silence means approval. We have unanimously adopted the manifesto for the union of Transcarpachia with the Soviet Union. We will address a telegram to that effect to comrade Stalin.'[†]

[*]Vasyl Markus, *L'incorporation de l'Ukraine subcarpathique à l'Ukraine soviétique, 1944–1945* (Louvain 1956), p. 47.
[†]*Podkarpats'ka Rus'* (Uzhhorod), June 29, 1993.

An entirely new acquisition for the Soviet Union was the province of Transcarpathia. Following the Munich Pact of September 1938, Hungary reannexed the region from Czechoslovakia in two stages (November 1938 and March 1939). The Hungarians ruled the area for over five years until driven out by the Red Army in the early fall of 1944. For its part, the Czechoslovak government-in-exile, which had become a member of the Allied coalition, pushed for the restoration of

Czechoslovakia according to its 1938, pre-Munich boundaries. This meant that all of Transcarpathia (Subcarpathian Rus') would once again become Czechoslovak territory. The Allies, including the Soviets, agreed in principle, and when the Red Army entered the region in October 1944, it permitted a Czechoslovak governmental delegation to function there for a few weeks. Before long, however, the Czechoslovak delegation was severely restricted in its activity. Local Communists under the protection of the Red Army – and with the encouragement of Soviet political officers – organized peoples' councils, which by 25–26 November 1944 had called for union of the region with its "Soviet Ukrainian motherland." As for the rest of Czechoslovakia, it was restored as a sovereign state, and although it was influenced but not yet fully controlled by the Communists, it nonetheless felt a sense of loyalty to its Soviet ally and "liberator." In such circumstances, the restored government in Prague was certainly not going to jeopardize Czechoslovak-Soviet relations. Hence, on 29 June 1945, Czechoslovakia's provisional parliament formally ceded Subcarpathian Rus' (Transcarpathia) to Soviet Ukraine.

Owing to postwar Soviet military and political prestige, Soviet Ukraine increased its territory by one-quarter (64,500 square miles [165,300 square kilometers]) and its population by an estimated 11 million. As elsewhere in the country, the new territorial acquisitions were divided into oblasts, which for the most part had no relationship to historical regions. By 1946, Soviet Ukraine had a total of twenty-four oblasts. The new territories also included a significant number of inhabitants other than ethnic Ukrainians, the largest group being the Poles, who numbered about 1.5 million.

The minority question

National minorities were of particular concern to the leaders of many post-1945 European countries, who were convinced that the very existence of minority populations had been one of the main causes of World War II. If future conflicts over national minorities were to be avoided, it seemed, more decisive action was needed. As a result, many countries embarked on a policy of population transfers. These were either voluntary or, more often, involuntary – forced deportations. The largest and most publicized deportation in Europe during this period was the expulsion of 6.3 million Germans from Poland and Czechoslovakia.

The Soviet government also participated in population transfers following agreements with Poland (1 October 1944) and Czechoslovakia (10 July 1946) on the exchange of populations. Between 1945 and 1948, several exchanges – some voluntary, others involuntary – took place. The largest departure from Ukraine was that of nearly 1.3 million Poles from Volhynia and eastern Galicia. There were also 35,000 Czechs who left Volhynia and Transcarpathia. Conversely, nearly 500,000 Ukrainians arrived from Poland (including two-thirds of the Lemko population), and another 12,000 from Czechoslovakia. Finally, there was the question of the *Ostarbeiter* (Eastern workers), POWs, and survivors of concentration camps who at the close of the war found themselves as refugees on German and Austrian territory controlled by four of the Allied Powers (the United States, the Soviet Union, Great Britain, and France). The Allies agreed on the principle of repatriation,

TABLE 50.1
Nationality composition of Soviet Ukraine, 1959[1]

	Population	Percentage
Ukrainians	32,158,000	76.8
Russians	7,091,000	16.9
Jews	840,000	2.0
Poles	363,000	0.9
Belarusans	291,000	0.7
Moldovans	242,000	0.6
Bulgarians	219,000	0.5
Magyars	149,000	0.4
Greeks	104,000	0.2
Romanians	101,000	0.2
Tatars	62,000	0.1
Czechs and Slovaks	28,000	0.1
Armenians	28,000	0.1
Germans	23,000	0.1
Gagauz	23,000	0.1
Roma/Gypsies	22,000	0.0
Others	123,000	0.3
TOTAL	41,869,000	100.0

TABLE 50.2
Ukrainians beyond Soviet Ukraine
(on contiguous ethnolinguistic territory),
1959

Russian S.F.S.R.	900,000
Moldavian S.S.R.	421,000
Poland	250,000
Belorussian S.S.R.	133,000
Czechoslovakia	90,000
Romania	62,000
TOTAL	1,856,000

and by mid-1945 nearly 2 million Ukrainians had been returned, in many cases forcibly.

The worst fears of the repatriates were often realized. Upon their return, tens of thousands were summarily executed, and an estimated 350,000, considered politically unreliable, were sent to labor camps in the Soviet Far East or resettled in Central Asia. In late 1947, when the other Allied Powers learned of and were sufficiently embarrassed by what the Soviets were doing to the repatriates, the process was stopped. By that time, however, only about 250,000 Ukrainian refugees were left in Germany, Austria, and other western European countries. Most emigrated as displaced persons (DPs) to Canada and the United States within a few years.

Yet one other "national" minority experienced a variant of repatriation. These were the Jews who survived the Holocaust. Tens of thousands returned to their homes in various parts of postwar Soviet Ukraine, whether from the Ural region of the Soviet Union (to where they were evacuated with other Soviet citizens as

Nazi Germany was invading the country), or from various parts of Europe, including survivors from German concentration and death camps. Those who returned to western Ukraine did not stay long, but were part of the nearly 200,000 Jews who, between 1944 and 1948, were allowed to leave the Soviet Union for postwar Poland and Czechoslovakia, and who from there continued on to Israel and North America. Those who returned to central and eastern Ukraine were primarily wartime evacuees from the Soviet east, who remained in the country and formed the bulk of the 840,000 Jews recorded in Soviet Ukraine's census of 1959.

Special circumstances prevailed in the Crimea. At the close of World War II it was returned to the Russian S.F.S.R., although administratively demoted from an autonomous republic to an oblast (region). Within one week of having driven the Germans out of the Crimea, on 18 May 1944 Soviet security forces (NKVD) carried out Stalin's order to deport the entire Crimean Tatar population. The Tatars were accused en masse of having "betrayed the [Soviet] Motherland during the Great Patriotic War" and of having "actively collaborated with the German occupying powers"; as collective punishment they were "to be exiled from the territory of the Crimea and settled permanently ... in the Uzbek S.S.R."[2] Deportation began on what Crimean Tatars still remember as the *Qara Kün* (The Black Day) – May 18 – when the inhabitants were given one hour to leave their homes at gunpoint. Remarkably, the process was completed in less than three days, by which time 183,000 Crimean Tatars were deported. In a fashion brutally characteristic of the Soviet regime under Stalin, the deportees were forced onto railway box cars for a trek of several weeks with little food or water. Hundreds died along the way, while tens of thousands more perished within a few months of arriving at their destinations, where in many cases they were simply dumped without any shelter against the blistering summer heat of the Central Asian desert. By far the majority of deported Crimean Tatars (151,000) were resettled in the Uzbek S.S.R., while most of the rest were sent to the Udmurt and Mari oblasts of the Russian S.F.S.R.

Soviet Communist party authorities in Moscow made clear their goal "to create a new Crimea according to Russian order."[3] All Crimean Tatar towns and villages were given new Russian names, Muslim cemeteries and religious buildings were destroyed or transformed for secular use. Then, within a few weeks of the massive 18 May 1944 Crimean Tatar deportation, several of the peninsula's smaller ethnic groups (Armenians, Bulgarians, Greeks) were also forcibly resettled to the depth of the Soviet East. In effect, the Crimea was ethnically cleansed, so that by 1959, most of the peninsula's entire population of 1.2 million was comprised of Russians (71 percent), Ukrainians (22 percent), and smaller numbers of Belarusans and Jews.

Despite all the efforts – often made at great human cost – to have political boundaries coincide with ethnolinguistic boundaries through the exchange and repatriation of populations, Soviet Ukraine was far from an ethnically homogeneous country. According to the first postwar census, conducted in 1959, over 9.7 million people, or nearly one-quarter of the country's inhabitants, were non-Ukrainian (see table 50.1). In comparison with the interwar years (see table 45.1), two peoples were added to the mix, both of which lived in the newly acquired

ETHNIC CLEANSING SOVIET STYLE

Well before the end of the twentieth century, when the term *ethnic cleansing* began to be used to describe the forced resettlement or annihilation of specific peoples, the Soviet Union already had much experience in such policies. It was Stalin himself who once quipped, *net naroda, net problemy* – if there's no people, there's no problem. At the close of World War II, Stalin's convictions were once again put into practice as Volga Germans, Meskhetian Turks, Crimean Tatars, and many smaller minorities were forcibly removed from their historic homelands.

The Soviet State Defense Committee Decree No. 5859ss, dated 11 May 1944 regarding the Crimean Tatars, listed various procedures related to the deportation and resettlement process. The government was to provide compensation for the immovable property taken from deportees. This never happened. Each family could bring 500 kilograms (1,000 pounds) of personal property. Considering the speed of the deportation, this happened in only rare cases. Doctors, nurses, food, and water were assigned to each transport, but they were woefully inadequate. One Russian eyewitness reported what he remembers of the deportation:

> It was a journey of lingering death in cattle trucks, crammed with people, like mobile gas chambers. The journey lasted three to four weeks and took them across the scorching summer steppes of Kazakhstan. They took the Red partisans of the Crimea, the fighters of the Bolshevik underground, and Soviet and [Communist] party activists. Also invalids and old men. The remaining men were fighting at the front, but deportation awaited them at the end of the war. And in the meantime they crammed their women and children into trucks, where they constituted the vast majority. Death mowed down the old, the young, and the weak. They died of thirst, suffocation, and the stench.
>
> On the long stages the corpses decomposed in the huddle of the trucks, and at the short halts, where water and food were handed out, the people were not allowed to bury their dead and had to leave them beside the railway track.*

After the trains stopped, the Crimean Tatar ordeal only got only worse as the deportees were transported by truck to their special settlements in the Uzbek desert. As a result of unhygienic conditions, lack of clean water, and overcrowding, a massive outbreak of typhus broke out. Consequently, between May 1944 and January 1946, nearly 27,000 Crimean Tatars (15 percent of the total) died on the way to, or after they were in, the special settlements to which they were assigned.

*Cited in Ann Sheehy, *The Crimean Tatars and Volga Germans: Soviet Treatment of Two National Minorities*, Minority Rights Group Report, No. 6 (London 1971), p. 10–11.

western Ukrainian lands. In the southwestern lowland area of the Transcarpathian oblast lived a compact community of Magyars/Hungarians (149,000), who were geographically contiguous with the same people living on the other side of the border in Hungary. The other "new" addition were the Romanians, who were linguistically and culturally the same as the Moldovans who had already been living within the boundaries of the Soviet Ukraine (in Transnistria and the Moldavian A.S.S.R.) before World War II. As a result of the Soviet classification system, which considered Moldovans and Romanians to be distinct nationalities, Soviet Ukraine now had both national minorities within its borders. In the Transcarpathian oblast there was a small Romanian minority, while in the neighboring Chernivtsi oblast there were both Romanians (in territory belonging to former Bukovina) and Moldovans (in territory belonging to former Bessarabia). Finally, not all ethnic Ukrainians living on contiguous ethnolinguistic territory were within the boundaries of Soviet Ukraine. An estimated 1.8 million lived just beyond Ukraine's borders, in six surrounding neighboring states and Soviet republics (see table 50.2)

Industrial and agricultural reconstruction

Because of the extent of the destruction inflicted by the war, Ukrainian industry and agriculture had in many ways to be built up again from scratch. In 1945, industrial production was only 26 percent of its 1940 prewar level. Similarly, agricultural productivity was only 40 percent of its 1940 level, even though the new territorial acquisitions had increased the amount of arable land. The first challenge for Ukraine was reconstruction, and this time, unlike in the years following the revolution and World War I, the Soviet planners had a model – their experience after 1928. Stalin remained convinced that since centralized planning under a command economy had worked before, it would work again. As a result, in 1946 the Fourth Five-Year Plan was inaugurated, and in a real sense the recovery plan was remarkably successful. General histories of the post–World War II era often speak of the wonders of West German and Japanese reconstruction, both of which were made possible by western capital (mostly American) and a relatively free-enterprise system. No less impressive during these same years – and without western aid – was the recovery in Soviet industry, including that of Soviet Ukraine. Soviet Ukraine's industrial base was reconstructed, and by 1950 its gross output had already exceeded that of 1940, the last full year of peace before World War II struck the country.

As before the war, the greatest emphasis was placed on heavy industry, and although the areas of consumer goods manufacturing, light industry, and the food industry increased over prewar levels, their expansion was on average only one-quarter the growth in the heavy industrial sector. The Ukrainian industrial recovery was also helped by capital investment and the expansion of the labor force. During the Fourth Five-Year Plan (1946–1950), 19.3 percent of the total Soviet budget was invested in Soviet Ukraine, a percentage which compares favorably with that invested during the last prewar plans (15.9 percent in 1929–1941). Moreover, the work force almost tripled, from 1.2 million in 1945 to 2.9 million in 1955. The latter figure reflects a 33.2 percent increase over the 1940 level. The result was that by the end of the Fifth Five-Year Plan in 1955, Soviet Ukrainian industry was producing 2.2 times more than it had produced in 1940, and the country was already one of the leaders in Europe in the output of certain key commodities. To measure its performance against that of the United Kingdom, France, West Germany, and Italy, for instance, Soviet Ukraine had the highest per capita production of pig iron and sugar, was second per capita in the smelting of steel and the mining of iron ore, and was third per capita in the mining of coal.

Whereas heavy industry continued to make significant advances after 1945, agriculture remained the Achilles' heel of the Soviet Ukrainian economy. There was never any question in the minds of Soviet central planners that, despite the enormous human cost of the 1930s, collectivized farming was still the ideal approach to agricultural organization. Accordingly, the collective and state farms, as well as the supporting Machine Tractor Stations that had been destroyed during World War II, were rebuilt, and collectivization in general was introduced fully between 1947 and 1950 in the recently acquired western Ukrainian territories. Thus, the total number of collective farms in Soviet Ukraine increased from 28,000 in 1940 to 33,000 in 1949. The number of state farms remained practically unchanged, however, standing at 935 in 1950. This meant that collective farms, with their nearly 11.1 million acres (45 million hectares) of land in 1955, continued to exceed by far the amount of land in state farms (12.1 million acres [4.9 million hectares]). Actually, the state farms were more specialized concerns, with the vast majority producing dairy products, poultry, or truck produce. Beginning in 1950, collective farms began to be amalgamated in an effort to make better use of farm machinery and other resources. Hence, while the total amount of land owned by the collectives continued to increase, by 1955 the number of farms had decreased to fewer than half (15,400) their number five years before.

Notwithstanding the best efforts of the central planners, agriculture remained subject to climatic conditions. In 1946, a drought resulted in very low crop yields and subsequent hunger, especially in eastern Ukraine. For the next twenty years, a bad harvest occurred on average every three years. The inefficiency of centralized planning and the generally low productivity of farmers who did not own their own land only made a bad situation worse. Consequently, by the end of the Fourth and Fifth Five-Year Plans (1950 and 1955), the total harvests from Soviet Ukrainian agriculture were still far below their 1940 prewar level.

In addition to problems of productivity was the question of crop selection. As during the interwar years, the land under cultivation for industrial crops (including sugar beets) and fodder continued to increase, while both the cultivation and the output of grains for human consumption decreased. For instance, the human food grain harvest (wheat and rye) in 1950 was only 16.7 million tons compared to 18.1 million tons in 1940. The decrease in food grain harvests came, moreover, at a time when Soviet Ukraine's population was increasing, from 31.7 million inhabitants in 1939 to 41.8 million in 1959. The result of these demographic and agricultural trends was frequently severe food shortages during the first decade after World War II.

The nationality question

The experience of the war years and the expansion of Ukrainian territory contributed to a revival of the nationality question in Soviet Ukraine. Although by
1938 the last vestiges of the Ukrainianization program had been eliminated, with
the end of World War II, it seemed that the various national cultures of the Soviet
Union would be allowed somewhat freer control over their own development.
There was a new spirit of optimism, related to events that had taken place during
the war. Faced with the German occupation of large parts of the country, Stalin
and his governing entourage had decided to make certain symbolic concessions
to the nationalities in the hope that such actions would help to mobilize patriotic
feelings that could in turn be directed toward the overall war effort. In October
1943, the Soviet government decided to pay tribute to a prerevolutionary national
hero by using his name in the newly instituted Order of Bohdan Khmel'nyts'kyi
decoration for valor in military action. This use of pre-Soviet national heroes actually had begun in the very first years of the war, when a series of Russian defenders of the homeland, beginning with the thirteenth-century prince Aleksander
Nevskii (and including Dmitrii Donskoi, Dmitrii Pozharskii, Aleksander Suvorov,
and Mikhail Kutuzov), were invoked as examples of patriotism and sacrifice to the
Soviet homeland. The Soviet government had even begun to court the Russian
Orthodox Church, which after 1941 was spared extreme atheistic propaganda
and, in September 1943, was allowed to elect a new patriarch, Sergei (Ivan Staro-
gorodskii, reigned 1943–1944).

As for Ukrainian sensitivities, the Soviets initiated some cosmetic changes. The
national name, *Ukrainian,* was used to designate four Red Army fronts in the counteroffensive against the Germans. In a sense, this was to have negative results, since
"Ukrainian" armies subsequently were responsible for the sectors that covered
most central European countries, with the result that the name *Ukrainian* became
associated in minds of central Europeans with Soviet-style "liberation." Another
cosmetic change was introduced in February 1944, when the constituent Soviet
republics were given back the old pre-1923 right to enter into direct relations
with foreign states. Soviet Belorussia and Soviet Ukraine were permitted to form
foreign ministries, and in early 1945 Roosevelt and Churchill agreed to Stalin's
request that the two "sovereign" Soviet countries be admitted as full members of
the soon-to-be-created United Nations. As a result, Soviet Ukraine became, in April
1945, one of the original forty-seven founding members of the United Nations.

Soviet Ukraine also received separate missions of the United Nations Relief
and Rehabilitation Administration (UNRRA), which assisted in overcoming the
country's food shortages in 1946, and it obtained some industrial investment from
international sources. No foreign state, however – Great Britain tried in 1947 –
was ever permitted to establish direct relations with Kiev. After all, Stalin had only
"enhanced" Soviet Ukraine's international status in an attempt to gain more votes
for the Soviet bloc in the new international body. Nonetheless, despite the fact
that in foreign affairs it remained entirely subordinate to the Soviet central gov-

ernment, as a founding member of the United Nations and a participant in that body's other international organizations (UNICEF, etc.), Ukraine became a recognizable entity, at least in name, in the world community.

On the home front, any hopes for a lessening of the Soviet Russian chauvinism that characterized the end of the interwar period proved illusory. If anything, russification increased. Stalin himself set the tone as early as 24 May 1945 with a well-publicized toast to the health of the Russian people, that "most outstanding nation," whose "clear minds, firm character, and patience" made them the "leading force in the Soviet Union."[4] In the words of one perceptive observer of this period, Yaroslav Bilinsky, "Soviet nationality policy from 1944 until Stalin's death [in 1953] can be described as a continued and outspoken effort to impress the notion of Russian predominance upon the minds of the non-Russian peoples of the Soviet Union."[5]

These same years also came to be known as the period of the "cult of personality" during which Stalin was glorified as the savior of the Soviet Union. Despite or perhaps because of the Soviet Union's recognized position as the world's second leading power, after the United States, Stalin became increasingly paranoid and instilled in Soviet society a sense of fear and suspicion. Purges of some (and plans for purges of many more) high-ranking party leaders indeed took place. But the bizarre show trials and sweeping attacks against Ukrainian intellectuals of the 1930s were for the most part not repeated between the end of the war and Stalin's death in 1953. Nevertheless, while the methods may have been different, the ultimate aim was the same: to foster the elimination of national distinctions within Soviet society and to create a new Soviet man *(homo Sovieticus)*, whose primary concern would be loyalty to the world's first communist society, loyalty expressed through the medium of the world's only "true revolutionary" language, Russian.

The achievement of this goal required the mobilization of the educational system and of historical ideology. As part of the postwar reconstruction, Soviet Ukraine witnessed the construction of nearly 3,400 new schools between 1945 and 1950. Children were taught that they were first and foremost part of a Soviet homeland. To encourage unity among the country's many peoples, the trend toward more instruction in the Russian language that began in the 1930s was continued. As a result, the total number of students in Soviet Ukraine enrolled in Russian schools rose from 14 percent in 1938–1939, to 17.6 percent in 1950–1951, and to approximately 25 percent in 1955–1956.

With regard to historical ideology, Ukrainians were expected to accept the proposition that the past achievements in their country's development were in large measure due to Ukraine's relationship with Russia. To this end, the Soviet version of Marxist history took on the characteristics of religious dogma. All Soviet Ukrainian historians as well as writers and publicists in general were required to present works that were in conformity with the following four basic theses elaborated in 1954 and approved by the Central Committee of the Communist party of Ukraine in conjunction with the 300th anniversary of "the reunification of Ukraine and Russia."

1 The Russian, Ukrainian, and Belarusan peoples trace their origin to a single root – the ancient Russian people (*drevnerusskii narod*) who founded the early Russian state – Kievan Rus';

2 Throughout its history, the Ukrainian people – and, for that matter, the Belarusan people as well – desired reunification with the Russian people;

3 Reunification was a progressive act;

4 Throughout its entire history, the Russian people was the senior brother in the family of East Slavic peoples. Russia's main virtue consisted in its giving rise to a strong working class, which in turn produced its vanguard, the Communist party.[6]

Western Ukraine

The western Ukrainian lands, especially Galicia, posed a special problem for the Soviet government in its attempt to impose socioeconomic and ideological uniformity. With the exception of wartime occupation during the Napoleonic era and World War I, and the less than two years of Soviet rule in eastern Galicia and northern Bukovina before the German invasion of 1941, western Ukrainian lands had never been part of the Russian or the Soviet empire. The result was that the Galicians, the Bukovinians, and especially the Transcarpathians had acquired a central European mentality forged by decades of Austro-Hungarian, Polish, or Czechoslovak rule. Quite simply, their worldview or political culture was European-oriented and often at odds with that of eastern Ukrainians, who had lived for centuries under tsarist Russian rule and then for nearly three decades under the Soviets. What did link western Ukrainians, especially the Galicians, to the East was their understanding of Ukrainian nationalism. Hence, at the close of World War II, the Soviet government was faced with two serious challenges: (1) to rebuild the economy of western Ukraine according to the centralized command model, and (2) to integrate the nationally fervent Galicians with the rest of the Ukrainian population. All this had to be done, moreover, while there still existed a military movement fighting openly against Soviet troops.

The military movement had begun during the German occupation with the establishment in 1942 of the Ukrainian Insurgent Army (UPA). By 1944, the UPA had between 25,000 and 40,000 soldiers, under the command of General Taras Chuprynka (pseudonym of Roman Shukhevych). Aside from engaging in battles against German and Soviet troops in Volhynia, Podolia, and Galicia, the UPA, in July 1944, initiated the establishment of a provisional government that was embodied in the Ukrainian Supreme Liberation Council. With the departure of the Germans in the fall of 1944, troops of the Soviet secret police (NKVD) focused their attention on the UPA. The result was that during the winter of 1944–1945 Soviet security forces (NKVD) conducted a major offensive against the UPA. Although the insurgents were able to hold their own, their ranks were being depleted by combat losses and, especially, by defections among those who accepted amnesties offered by the Soviet authorities. Nonetheless, a small core of an estimated 6,000 dedicated fighters remained, who against overwhelming odds continued an armed struggle in the hope of creating a non-Soviet independent Ukrainian state.

From late 1945 to 1947, the UPA's main field of operation was along the new Polish-Soviet border. It was particularly anxious to halt the population exchanges whereby Ukrainians west of the border were being "voluntarily" resettled in Soviet Ukraine. In its attempt to block the exodus, the UPA clashed with the army of the newly restored and by then Communist-dominated government of Poland. The fighting continued throughout 1946 and culminated in a UPA ambush in May 1947 that resulted in the death of the Polish vice-minister of defense (General Karol Świerczewski). This event persuaded the Polish authorities, in cooperation with Soviet and, later, Czechoslovak armed forces, to step up their campaign against the UPA and to deal with the remaining Ukrainian population that had not already gone eastward.

In the spring and summer of 1947, the so-called Vistula Operation (*Akcja Wisła*) was carried out, whereby 140,000 Ukrainians, including Lemkos living in the Carpathian region, were forcibly deported to the western (Silesia) and northern (Baltic seacoast) regions of Poland that had only recently been acquired from Germany. The surviving units of the UPA either crossed into Soviet territory or fled across Czechoslovak territory to the American zone of Germany. The UPA members who remained behind kept up guerrilla-type activity in the westernmost regions of Soviet Ukraine, including assassinations of pro-Soviet activists (among them the writer Iaroslav Halan) and sabotage of collectivization efforts, until the early 1950s. Nevertheless, by 1948 the UPA threat to Soviet rule in western Ukraine was effectively spent. Veterans who made it to the West, however, helped to create and sustain in the Ukrainian diaspora tales of the sorely outnumbered UPA freedom fighters who had resisted both the German and the Soviet armies in an ultimately futile attempt to liberate their homeland from foreign rule.

While Poland was doing battle with the UPA, the Soviets were engaged in a struggle on the ideological front. For them to be successful, all the old pre-Soviet institutions in western Ukraine had to be abolished, including the non-Soviet cooperatives, cultural societies, and schools, which only a few years before had been reestablished under the German-ruled Generalgouvernement. Their very existence during the war years made it easy for all of them to be depicted as having been in the "service of the fascists."

The foremost institution associated with the western Ukrainian past was the Greek Catholic Church. At first, when the Soviet forces arrived in the summer of 1944, nothing changed substantially. But in November, the grand old man of the Greek Catholic Church and of Galician-Ukrainian national life in general, Metropolitan Andrei Sheptyts'kyi, died. Sheptyts'kyi's death conveniently opened the way for the Soviets' final struggle against what they considered the ultimate symbol of "reactionary feudalism" and "Ukrainian bourgeois nationalism," the Greek Catholic Church. During the early nineteenth century, Tsar Nicholas I had abolished Greek Catholicism in the Russian Empire, arguing that it was an artificial, Vatican-inspired, anti-Russian creation of Poland set up to undermine the "true"

Orthodox faith of the Rus' people. The Soviets simply upheld the tsarist and Russian attitude that Orthodoxy was the only acceptable religious orientation for all East Slavs.

Nor was the question simply one of Orthodoxy. At issue was the expectation that all believers would belong to the government-recognized Russian Orthodox Church under the jurisdiction of the patriarch of Moscow. Any other Ukrainian Orthodox church was therefore unacceptable. During the course of 1944, the two Ukrainian Orthodox churches that had existed under wartime German rule ceased to exist. The entire Ukrainian Autocephalous Church hierarchy and many of its priests fled to the West, where the church was to survive for the next forty-five years in the United States under Metropolitan, later Patriarch, Mstyslav (Stepan Skrypnyk, reigned 1969–1994). As for the Ukrainian Autonomous Church, most of its hierarchs also fled to the West; those clergy who remained at home came under the jurisdiction of the Patriarchate of Moscow, which in theory they had always recognized. Thus, for the second time in the twentieth century, specifically Ukrainian Orthodox churches were abolished and outlawed in Ukraine, and also in those neighboring countries (Poland, Czechoslovakia) that came under Soviet domination after World War II.

In their struggle against Ukrainian churches, the Soviets did not always have to act alone, since the Russian Orthodox Church had its own agenda for rival Eastern Christian churches that were within what the Moscow patriarchate considered its own sphere of influence. By early March 1945, Stalin had agreed to the abolition of the Greek Catholic Church and to the Russian Orthodox Church's being expected to play a supportive role in the process. During April, the entire Greek Catholic hierarchy headed by Metropolitan Slipyi was arrested, and a message over the signature of the newly elected Russian Orthodox patriarch of Moscow, Aleksei (Sergei Simanskii, reigned 1945–1970), was circulated to the Greek Catholic clergy and faithful of western Ukraine. The message accused the Vatican and the late Metropolitan Sheptyts'kyi of having called upon Greek Catholics "to accept Hitler's yoke" during the war years, and maintained that the only reasonable course now would be to "hasten to return to the embraces of our own mother – the Russian Orthodox Church."[7]

None of the arrested hierarchs, however, accepted the offer to abjure the Catholic faith and join the Orthodox Church. Therefore, to carry out Soviet government plans, the Initiative Group for the Reunification of the Greek (Eastern-rite) Catholic Church was established under the leadership of an Eastern-oriented priest and former close confidant of Metropolitan Sheptyts'kyi, Havriïl Kostel'nyk. In March 1946, the Initiative Committee convened in L'viv a "synod" (although with no Greek Catholic bishop present), which voided the 1596 Union of Brest and subordinated the Greek Catholic Church to the Russian Orthodox Church – Moscow Patriarchate. Of the approximately 3,000 Greek Catholic priests, over 1,100 submitted to the Russian Orthodox Church; about 1,600 were imprisoned; and the rest went underground. In neighboring Transcarpathia, Soviet plans took longer to succeed, because the efforts to organize a synod to end the 1646 Union of Uzhhorod failed. Instead, the assassination of the local bishop (Teodor Romzha) was carried out in late 1947, and in August 1949 a few local Greek Catholic priests simply declared the Union of Uzhhorod void and proclaimed their eparchy's "reunification" with the Russian Orthodox Church.

The Soviet pattern was more or less followed in neighboring countries within the Soviet sphere that still contained Greek Catholic minorities. A politically staged church union was held in Czechoslovakia (Prešov, 28 April 1950), whereas in Romania the Greek Catholic Church was simply abolished by governmental decree (December 1948). In Poland, the Ukrainian population was dispersed, and the hierarchy of the Greek Catholic eparchy of Przemyśl was arrested and turned over to the Soviets. Greek Catholic church property fell into the hands of the Polish Roman Catholic Church. Ironically, among the Soviet bloc countries, only Hungary, with its largely magyarized Greek Catholic eparchy of Hajdúdorog (until 1913 part of Transcarpathia's Mukachevo eparchy), allowed the Greek Catholic Church to function legally.

With the Greek Catholic Church and the Ukrainian Insurgent Army out of the way, the Soviet government was able to proceed more easily with other changes in western Ukraine. These included forced collectivization of the agricultural sector between 1948 and 1951 (during which time 95.2 percent of the land was collectivized) and the introduction of heavy industry and the exploitation of natural resources in a region that until then had been primarily agricultural. By 1955, industrial output in the area was four times greater than it had been during the interwar period. Among the new industries were automobile manufacturing, natural gas extraction, and coal mining.

Along with socioeconomic change came demographic change. In particular, there was a marked increase in the size of the Russian population in western Ukraine. Since the western Ukrainian lands had never been part of the Russian Empire, the number of Russians in the area before World War II had gone from negligible to non-existent. By 1959, however, Russians made up 5.2 percent of the population. Their increase was a result of (1) the influx of over 327,000 Russians (247,000 in Galicia, 51,000 in northern Bukovina, and 29,000 in Transcarpathia) to urban areas, where they took up positions in the party apparatus and new industries (both as managers and workers); and (2) the exodus of Ukrainians. There were three categories of departing Ukrainians: exiles to the West who fled the advance of the Red Army in 1944; nearly half a million persons deported to Siberia and Central Asia because they were politically suspect or because they had relatives who had served in the German Generalgouvernement or with the UPA; and peasants sent to eastern Ukraine and the Donbas area.

By the time of Stalin's death in 1953, Soviet Ukraine had undergone several changes. Its economic infrastructure had been rebuilt to the point where its output, especially in the heavy industrial sector, far exceeded prewar levels, and its newly acquired western Ukrainian lands had been more or less integrated with the rest of the country. The nationality question and the question of Ukrainian identity had been subjected to the same policies adopted by the central Soviet authorities elsewhere in governing their vast multinational empire. Individual national expression was permitted but under certain conditions: only if it recognized Marxist-Leninist theory (as interpreted by Stalin) as the basis for a Communist socioeconomic system, and only if it took place within the framework of a political mind-set that explicitly accepted the superiority of Russian culture and language as a model for and means of expression. How did Stalin's legacy of centralized control over all aspects of Soviet life survive in Ukraine after his death?

Post-Stalinist Soviet Ukraine

On 5 March 1953, Iosif Stalin, the general secretary of the Communist party of the Soviet Union (CPSU) and self-proclaimed generalissimo of the Red Army during World War II, died. Beginning in the 1920s, Stalin had systematically removed his political rivals, with the result that by the time of his death he was absolute ruler over the Soviet empire. The departure of such an all-powerful figure from the governing scene was bound to have an impact not only on the Soviet Union itself but also on those territories, especially in central Europe and the Balkans (East Germany, Poland, Czechoslovakia, Hungary, Romania, Bulgaria, and Albania), which since World War II had come under Soviet domination.

No sooner had his funeral ended than the top Soviet leaders began to criticize Stalin and struggle among themselves for control of the party and governing apparatus. In an effort to avoid the excesses of Stalin's one-man dictatorship, the Politburo decided to try to govern with a collective leadership. Four figures came to the forefront – Georgii Malenkov, Viacheslav Molotov, Lavrentii Beria, and Nikita S. Khrushchev. But despite the lip service paid to collective leadership, it became increasingly clear that Khrushchev, Stalin's former trusted lieutenant who from 1938 to 1949 had headed the Communist party (Bolshevik) of Ukraine, was consolidating his own power base. In September 1953, Khrushchev became first secretary of the Central Committee of the CPSU; by 1958, he had succeeded in removing all his rivals to become the undisputed leader of the country.

Beginning with Khrushchev and continuing for three more decades, Stalin's successors were concerned primarily with the further consolidation of the CPSU's control of the country, so that it would be able to achieve the ultimate goal – the transformation of the Soviet Union from the stage of socialism to that of full communism. As part of the transformation, there were experiments in both economic and political affairs. For instance, in the economic sector there was an attempt to redress the imbalance that favored heavy industrial production over the production of consumer goods and agricultural products for human consumption. Especially under Khrushchev, who remained in office until 1964, there was a pronounced decrease in what had been the excessive party control over cultural life that had characterized the Stalinist era.

Change came as early as 1953, when party spokespersons were allowed to criticize openly the policy of russification that had been imposed on the Soviet Union's nationalities beginning in the 1930s under Stalin. Such criticism was part of a process of de-Stalinization and a general attack on Stalinist rule, which culminated in February 1956 with Khrushchev's "secret" speech before the 20th Congress of the CPSU. Discontent with the nationality question had already been expressed at the June 1953 meeting of the Central Committee of the Communist party of Ukraine, or CPU (the name *Bolshevik* had been dropped the year before), and concern with this issue was to remain on the agenda of Ukrainian party leaders for the next several decades. The year 1953 also witnessed the designation, as head of the CPU, of Oleksii Kyrychenko.

The appointment of Kyrychenko marked a new development in Soviet Ukrainian political life. Not only was he an ethnic Ukrainian (the first to hold the post since the early 1920s), but so were all subsequent CPU party chairmen: Mykola Pidhirnyi/Nikolai Podgornyi (in office 1957–1963), Petro Shelest (in office 1963–1972), and Volodymyr Shcherbyts'kyi (in office 1972–1989). Furthermore, Ukrainian leaders were invariably to play prominent roles at the highest levels of the Soviet regime during the post-Stalinist era. Khrushchev himself had previously been chairman of the Communist party of Ukraine; Kyrychenko, and especially Pidhirnyi/Podgornyi became influential all-Soviet policy makers; and Leonid Brezhnev (an ethnic Russian from Ukraine) rose from being a regional party boss in Dnipropetrovs'k to becoming the dominant leader in Soviet politics during the 1970s and early 1980s. As for their careers while active in Soviet Ukraine, these figures varied in their policies, with some at times defending the republic's economic and specifically Ukrainian cultural interests against interference from the central authorities in Moscow, while others, also at various times, favoring all-Soviet trends toward union-wide economic integration and cultural conformity, including linguistic russification.

Ukraine under Khrushchev

Following the death of Stalin in 1953, Soviet Ukraine, like the rest of the Soviet Union, exhibited seemingly contradictory tendencies. On the one hand, there were efforts to integrate Ukraine more fully into the Soviet system, and, on the other, there was some loosening of control by the Communist party, which under Stalin had tried increasingly to direct all aspects of society. De-Stalinization, or the "thaw," was especially pronounced after 1958, when Khrushchev became the dominant figure in both the Soviet government and the All-Union Communist party (CPSU). The dual approach of integration and a relative loosening of political control from the center was epitomized in Ukraine by two events that took place in 1954.

In February, the Crimea was ceded to Soviet Ukraine as "yet another affirmation of the great fraternal love and trust of the Russian people for Ukraine."[1] This newest territorial acquisition added close to 17,160 square miles (44,000 square kilometers) and 268,000 inhabitants to Soviet Ukraine (1959). Since the entire

Crimean Tatar population was forcibly deported in May 1944, the vast majority of the inhabitants who remained were Russians (71 percent) and ethnic Ukrainians (22 percent). Therefore, when the Soviet authorities, in the name of the Russian people, decided in 1954 to present the Crimea as a gift, it was turning over to Ukraine a "Slavic" land.

The year 1954 also witnessed massive state-organized celebrations throughout Soviet Ukraine commemorating the 300th anniversary of the Agreement of Pereiaslav. Pereiaslav became the symbol, and was so treated in several scholarly and popular historical works, of the "reunification of Ukraine with Russia." What had happened at Pereiaslav three centuries before ostensibly both proved the age-old brotherly love of Ukrainians for Russians and exemplified the general Marxist-Leninist proletarian principle of "friendship among peoples." The "friendship" doctrine, elaborated by means of a projection of present-day concerns upon the past, stressed that historically the various peoples of the former Russian Empire had welcomed the Russians as brothers in the centuries-long struggle that eventually, in the twentieth century, gave birth to the Soviet Union as a "family of nations."

The political thaw under Khrushchev was characterized by at least four developments: (1) amnesties for prioners accused of "anti-state crimes" connected with the war and immediate postwar years, whether they were political, cultural, or religious in nature; (2) the rehabilitation of nearly one-third of the 961,000 residents of Ukraine arrested on political charges during the Stalinist era (1929–1953); (3) the establishment in 1958 of the first permanent Soviet Ukrainian mission to the United Nations in New York City; and (4) a steady increase in the percentage of ethnic Ukrainians in the ranks of the Communist party of Ukraine (CPU). With regard to the last development, not only were most CPU Central Committee and Politburo members ethnic Ukrainians, but also three-quarters of the highest ranking party and state posts throughout the republic were held by ethnic Ukrainians. Finally, the Soviet central government in Moscow began to relax its strict regimentation of culture. The result was a wave of scholarly and literary production that no longer had to conform rigidly to the accepted interpretations of the Stalinist era or to socialist-realist artistic dogma. The new opportunities to publish brought prominence both within and beyond the borders of the Soviet Union to writers like Boris Pasternak, Evgenii Evtushenko, and Aleksander Solzhenitsyn.

The sixties phenomenon

The stepped-up campaign of de-Stalinization, marked by Khrushchev's "secret" speech in 1956 and the subsequent removal of Stalin's body in 1961 from the revered place next to Lenin in the mausoleum on Red Square, also signaled a relaxation of cultural restraints on the non-Russian nationalities. The result was the appearance in Soviet Ukraine of works by several younger writers. Among the more important were the poets Vasyl' Symonenko, Lina Kostenko, Mykola Vinhranovs'kyi, Vitalii Korotych, and Ivan Drach; the prose writers Hryhorii Tiutiunnyk, Ievhen Hutsalo, Volodymyr Drozd, and Valerii Shevchuk; and the literary and social critics Ivan Dziuba, Ivan Svitlychnyi, and Ievhen Sverstiuk.

Although not part of a deliberately organized movement, these writers, together with a few theatrical directors, film directors, composers, and artists, came to be known as the Sixties Group *(Shestydesiatnyky)*. They were joined by a few older writers like Borys Antonenko-Davydovych and Andrii Malyshko, and they were initially encouraged and supported by establishment literary figures like Maksym Ryl's'kyi and Oles' Honchar. Writers associated with the Sixties Group were unified in their rejection of socialist realism as the guiding ideology of literary production. Instead, they reaffirmed the principle that literature, especially poetry, was essentially an expression of the individual. Their writings both implicitly and explicitly sought to renew traditional Ukrainian cultural values and to restore the Ukrainian language, which had suffered increasing sovietization and russification during the Stalinist era. Aside from publishing their own writings, several members of the Sixties Group were active in the movement to rehabilitate Ukrainian authors whose works had been banned in the 1930s (among them Hryhorii Kosynka, Ievhen Pluzhnyk, Oleksa Slisarenko, and Mykola Zerov), and as a group they drew renewed inspiration from the writings of Taras Shevchenko.

In a cultural atmosphere that stressed the reclamation of the Ukrainian past for the spiritual regeneration of the present, it is not surprising that historians played an active role. They began to complain openly about the manner in which Ukrainian history was being treated in official accounts, and by 1957 they were able to obtain their own historical journal *(Ukraïns'kyi istorychnyi zhurnal)*, published in Ukrainian by the Historical Institute of the Ukrainian Academy of Sciences in Kiev under the editorship of the specialist on the Cossack period Fedir P. Shevchenko. Several other historical journals and monographs soon followed. Many presented revisionist views of Ukrainian history that questioned the Soviet theory of the common origin of the East Slavs, stressed the positive achievements of the Zaporozhian Cossacks during the seventeenth century, and reassessed the role of Ukraine during the revolutionary period and civil war (1917–1920). In these reappraisals, the problem of Russian-Ukrainian relations received special attention, and there was open speculation as to whether the "unification" (specifically not "reunification") brought about by the Agreement of Pereiaslav in 1654 had represented a realization of Ukraine's highest ideals.

Other areas of Ukrainian scholarship were also affected by the new environment. The need for a general encyclopedia that classified all knowledge in the Ukrainian language had long been felt. Such a project had been under way during the early 1930s, but its editorial board fell victim to the purges in 1934, and nothing ever appeared. When émigré scholars in the West began in 1949 to publish thematic and alphabetic Ukrainian encyclopedias, it seemed that a concerted effort needed to be undertaken in order to counteract the "distortions of the bourgeois nationalists." Consequently, between 1959 and 1965, a Ukrainian encyclopedia under Soviet auspices *(Ukraïns'ka radians'ka entsyklopediia)* was published in seventeen volumes. It was followed soon afterward by a smaller, three-volume general encyclopedia (1966–68), a four-volume historical encyclopedia of Ukraine (1969–72), and a twenty-six-volume detailed description of each oblast in Soviet Ukraine (1967–74). Other important synthetic compilations included a deluxe six-volume history of Ukrainian art (1966–70) and an eight-volume history of Ukrainian literature (1967–71).

The preparation of general reference and synthetic works in the Ukrainian language on all aspects of Ukrainian culture also emphasized the pressing need for a standard multivolume dictionary of the Ukrainian language. Such a project had begun already during the era of Ukrainianization, but it too had come to an abrupt halt as a result of the purges of the 1930s. By the late 1950s, the dictionary project was revived, and this time it resulted in the eventual appearance of an eleven-volume, 136,000-word dictionary of the Ukrainian language (1970–80). The Soviet Ukrainian scholarly establishment also embraced the newer disciplines, with the creation of the Computer Center in 1957 and the Institute of Cybernetics in 1962. Through their research and publications, including a Ukrainian-language two-volume encyclopedia of cybernetics (1973), these institutes made Ukraine one of the leading centers for the computer sciences in the Soviet Union.

The cultural thaw of the early 1960s also had an impact on painting, decorative design, music, and the cinema. Among the best-known artistic achievements was the internationally acclaimed film produced by the Dovzhenko Studio in Kiev, Serhii Paradzhanov's *Tiny zabutykh predkiv* (Shadows of Forgotten Ancestors, 1964; based on Mykhailo Kotsiubyns'kyi's 1913 novel of the same name). The film idealized traditional Ukrainian culture and language in a form whose artistic and technical quality were remarkably comparable to those of contemporary films in the West.

Economic developments

After an impressive postwar economic recovery, which by 1955 had witnessed a doubling of industrial productivity over the prewar level (1940), the Ukrainian economy began to level off. Actually, during the next six Five-Year Plans, between 1956 and 1985, there was a steady decline in the growth rate of Ukrainian industry, from a high of 13.5 percent during the Fifth Five-Year Plan (1951–1955) to a low of only 3.5 percent during the Eleventh Five-Year Plan (1981–1985). Significant decline, however, did not set in until the 1970s. Until that time, Ukrainian industrial development followed a pattern already well in place during the postwar decade of reconstruction. This pattern included (1) a continual imbalance in favor of heavy industry and an eventual decline of output in all branches of industry, (2) further expansion of the industrial base in western Ukraine, and (3) an initial rise but then leveling off in the growth of the work force.

Some statistical data will illustrate these trends. Whereas between 1950 and 1965 many branches of Ukrainian industry recorded double-digit growth, between 1966 and 1985 all branches recorded half or less the rate of growth of the previous period. With regard to geographic location, the lower Dnieper region and Donbas continued to remain the heartland of Soviet Ukraine's industry. Between 1965 and 1978, however, that region's level of industrial development in comparison to the country as a whole declined from 142 to 129 percent, whereas during the same period the Right Bank and western Ukraine (especially Ivano-Frankivs'k,

Transcarpathia, L'viv, and Ternopil' oblasts) increased their relative industrial output from 62 to 78 percent. The work force stood at 14.1 million in 1980, three times its size in 1940. But whereas Ukraine's annual rate of growth in employment was 4.8 percent throughout most of the postwar war period (1950–1985), the rate was only 1.9 percent during the period's last two decades (1965–1985).

The slower but steady growth of Soviet Ukrainian industry coupled with a dramatic increase in the country's urban population required newer sources of energy. Between 1956 and 1972, a series of five reservoirs (Kiev, Kaniv, Kremenchuk, Dniprodzerzhyns'k, and Kakhovka) were built along the Dnieper River, transforming that waterway into an almost uninterrupted series of lakes stretching from Ukraine's border with the Belorussian S.S.R. virtually to the mouth of the river as it empties into the Black Sea (see map 46). Aside from improving water transport and regulating spring floods, the dams that created the Dnieper reservoirs also became sites for new power stations which brought about a dramatic increase in hydroelectric energy. At the same time, greater growth was occurring in the natural gas industry. The first postwar commercial production of natural gas was in western Ukraine, at fields centered around Dashava, south of L'viv. More important, however, was the development of the Shebelynka field southeast of Kharkiv in the Donbas region. By the late 1960s, this field was producing 68 percent of Soviet Ukraine's and 30 percent of the Soviet Union's natural gas.

But such advances in the hydroelectric and natural gas industries were not enough to fulfill Soviet Ukraine's ever-increasing energy needs. Chronic drought limited hydroelectric output, and rising costs caused a decrease in natural gas production. Consequently, by 1985, hydroelectricity accounted for only 17 percent of the country's energy output, and natural gas for only 18 percent. The lion's share of 70 percent remained energy produced by coal- and oil-based thermal power stations; however, the output of the Donets'k coalfield in the Donbas, which had been exploited steadily since the late nineteenth century, was declining.

In an attempt to counteract these trends and to stabilize future energy resources, the Soviet Union launched an intensive nuclear power program in the 1970s. This resulted in the construction in Soviet Ukraine of four nuclear power plants – near Chornobyl' (1979), at Kuznetsovs'k north of Rivne (1979), at Konstantynivka north of Mykolaïv (1982), and at Enerhodar on the Kakhovka Reservoir (1984) – and in plans for four more plants by the end of the decade. As a result of these efforts, Soviet Ukraine had clearly developed diverse sources of energy for its expanded industrial infrastructure during the six Five-Year Plans that were carried out between 1955 and 1985.

While Soviet Ukrainian industrial production continued to increase, if unevenly, during these three decades, the country's agricultural sector initially remained problematic. It is true that there was a phenomenal increase in the production of industrial and fodder crops (sugar beets and silage corn) between 1950 and 1960, but at the same time there was only a slight increase or even a decrease in crops for human consumption. The result was a continuation of the food crisis in Soviet Ukraine as well as in the Soviet Union as a whole.

The causes of the agricultural crisis were many: planning decisions to invest in industrial and fodder crops, erratic weather conditions, and the basic inefficiency of a command economy with a market system based on one purchaser – the state – from a large body of decreasingly motivated producers on collectives and state farms. Finally, the lack of an efficient transportational infrastructure made it difficult for agricultural products to reach their destinations. It was not uncommon for harvests to remain piled up and unprotected in open fields, rotting before they were picked up for delivery. No Soviet leader ever questioned the inherent shortcomings in the system; instead, they all tried to institute reforms to improve agricultural productivity within the framework of collectivized agriculture.

Khrushchev was among the more aggressive reformers. His attention first turned to industry and the problem of management. Under his leadership, in 1957 the central economic ministries responsible for specific branches of the economy throughout the entire Soviet Union were abolished. Instead, the country was divided into economic regions, each with its own council (Ukrainian: *radnarhosp;* Russian: *sovnarkhoz).* Soviet Ukraine initially was subdivided into fourteen, and later into seven economic regions. The object was to allow local bodies to implement plans developed by the all-Union and Ukrainian state planning committees. The councils of each economic region were responsible for all branches of economic development within their geographic area. In order to coordinate planning between the local enterprises in the individual regions and the all-Union and republican Ukrainian planning ministries, a Ukrainian Council for the National Economy was established in 1960. As a result of the reform, 97 percent of Soviet Ukraine's gross industrial production was now under the control of republican authorities, a situation in marked contrast to that in 1953, when Kiev controlled only 36 percent of the country's enterprises.

The introduction of the economic regions with their councils also had political implications. On the one hand, the decentralization of authority from Moscow to the republics before long allowed regional party secretaries to become virtual economic dictators able to create through patronage their own local power bases. On the other hand, the dismantling of the central ministries in Moscow created an influx of ministerial officials to Soviet Ukraine and other republics which was resented by the local authorities. In effect, the Soviet Ukrainian party hierarchy and managerial elite grew more protective of what became its own vested interests, whether those were understood to be at the regional or republican level vis-à-vis Moscow. A good example of this phenomenon in Soviet Ukraine was the military-industrial complex centered at Dnipropetrovs'k in the Dnieper industrial region, which served as a launchpad for the careers of the long-time Soviet leader Leonid Brezhnev, the CPU first secretary Voldymyr Shcherbyts'kyi, and the future president of independent Ukraine, Leonid Kuchma.

Khrushchev the reformer also turned his attention to agriculture. In 1958, as part of an attempt to increase efficiency, the Machine Tractor Stations were abolished, and their equipment sold to the collective farms. The expectation was that the collectives would somehow show more responsibility in maintaining the farm machinery. An even more grandiose experiment was to increase the amount of land planted with corn. After returning from a visit to the United States (the first by a Soviet leader), Khrushchev was convinced that corn was the crop that would save Soviet agriculture. During the late 1950s, in Soviet Ukraine alone the amount of land planted with corn grew by 600 percent. At the height of the "corn fever," between 1960 and 1963, nearly one-third of all Soviet Ukraine's arable land was planted with this crop.

The increase in corn cultivation was coupled, however, with a decrease by more than half in the amount of land planted with wheat and rye. These undertakings were part of an all-Union agricultural plan of Khrushchev's whereby the "virgin lands" farther east, beyond the Ural Mountains in Siberia and Central Asia, were opened up to grain production. Overall, the experiment failed. The so-called virgin lands at best yielded only low-quality and low per-capita harvests. In Soviet Ukraine, the corn sown was mostly used for fodder, so the already-severe food shortages only got worse. The situation became so critical that in 1963 the Soviet Union was forced to take an unprecedented step. The government violated its long-standing policy of peacetime self-sufficiency by importing grain from abroad, especially from Canada. It was not until the late 1960s and 1970s that Soviet Ukrainian productivity in food grains as well as livestock increased (in some cases it had more than doubled by 1980), but this was after Khrushchev was gone from the political scene.

The Brezhnev era – stability and stagnation

The failure of Khrushchev's agricultural experiments, combined with his contribution to the Soviet-Chinese rift in the area of foreign affairs, resulted in his sudden removal in October 1964 as head of the CPSU and the government of the Soviet Union. In keeping with the principle of collective leadership that had ushered in the post-Stalin era, Khrushchev was replaced by two of his former protégés, Leonid Brezhnev as first (later, general) secretary of the CPSU, and Aleksei Kosygin as premier of the Soviet government.

Although the facade of collective leadership was maintained, by 1971 Brezhnev had become the most important political figure in the Soviet Union. He removed or isolated his leading rivals in the CPSU hierarchy, and to his position as general secretary of the party he added the title of chairman of the Presidium of the Supreme Soviet in 1977. Although ceremonial in nature, the office of chairman of the Presidium made him head of state, a position necessary to the Soviet leader for reasons of international protocol. Born in far eastern Ukraine (of Russian parentage), Brezhnev built a political machine consisting of former engineers, factory directors, and officials from his home region within the lower Dnieper industrial complex. It was from there that the "Dnipropetrovs'k clan," or Mafia as it was popularly known, had helped Brezhnev rise through the party's ranks and to reach the highest positions in the Soviet government and the CPSU.

The Brezhnev era, which lasted until his death in 1982, was marked by an insistence on order and stability in sharp contrast to the spirit of social experimentation and the almost frenetic administrative changes that had characterized Khrushchev's rule. For example, the regional economic councils in Soviet Ukraine and elsewhere were abolished in 1965 and authority for economic development was returned to central ministries in Moscow. The only innovations were in foreign affairs, where Brezhnev was a strong advocate of accommodation with the Soviet Union's superpower rival, the United States. In essence, the Brezhnev era coincided with what came to be known as the period of détente with the West. At the same time, the desire for – and achievement of – domestic stability was to bring a return to Stalinist-like bureaucratic rule (albeit without the excesses) that by the end of the 1970s had resulted in widespread economic and social stagnation throughout Soviet society.

A reimposition of stricter party control over all aspects of Soviet life also had a direct impact on the titular nationalities and national minorities within each republic. Greater limitations on national and cultural activity that was not in strict accord with general Soviet policy were imposed. This policy, as it pertained to the multinational composition of Soviet society, was based on three concepts: *rastsvet* (flowering), *sblizhenie* (drawing together), and *sliianie* (merging or fusing).

These concepts, formulated earlier by Lenin and Stalin, expressed the three stages through which multinational Soviet society was expected to progress. *Rastsvet* referred to the flowering of national cultures, each of which was encouraged to develop fully in a Soviet system that recognized the equality of all nationalities. Having "flowered," the individual national components would naturally experience *sblizhenie* – that is, each culture would be influenced by the others during a process of "drawing together." The best having been taken from all cultures during their drawing together, the final result would be *sliianie,* or the merging of all national cultures into one new, revolutionary Soviet culture. While in theory *sliianie* meant the extraction and then fusion of the best elements from all cultures in a new Soviet amalgam, in practice the process meant assimilation to or at least acceptance of Russian linguistic and cultural forms. Such russification was threatening to the closely related Slavic cultures, the Belarusan and Ukrainian, which were vulnerable to russification particularly on the linguistic front.

Aside from theory was practice, or the question of the time frame. Just when would *sliianie,* or merging, take place? According to Lenin, merging could not occur until the stage of communism had been attained in the socioeconomic sphere. Since Khrushchev had assured the public (at the 22nd Congress of the CPSU in 1961) that the stage of communism would be achieved in Soviet society by 1980, it seemed reasonable to prepare for the alleged inevitable merging of the Soviet Union's nationalities. Accordingly, from the late 1960s there were intense debates about the merging of nationalities among Soviet theoreticians and policy makers. During the course of the debates, some Communists even called for the abolition of what seemed the superfluous and "pseudosovereign" Soviet republics, which by the 1970s, it was argued, had outlived their "historical usefulness."

In the end, the idea of a merging which would eliminate national distinctions and give birth to one Soviet nation *(sovetskaia natsiia)* was replaced by the seemingly more pluralistic but utterly ambiguous notion of "a new historical community of people – the Soviet people" *(sovetskii narod).* When this revised concept was put forth by Brezhnev at the 24th Congress of the CPSU (1971) and then incorporated into the new constitution of the Soviet Union (1977), it was suggested that as part of the dialectical process of history the "flowering" *(rastsvet)* and "drawing together" *(sblizhenie)* of the nationalities would continue. The resultant ambiguity made it possible for proponents of both assimilation and cultural pluralism to justify their actions. Hence, while the 1977 Soviet constitution preserved the existence of the national republics, two years later a second all-Union conference was held in Tashkent on the Russian language – "the language of friendship and cooperation of the peoples of the Soviet Union." The Tashkent conference called for the mandatory teaching of Russian in every non-Russian pre-kindergarten and kindergarten.

National repression and accommodation in Soviet Ukraine

During the last years of Khrushchev's and the early years of Brezhnev's rule, when a "merging" was still the ideal, the increasing activity of the nationalities in the direction of greater cultural distinctiveness was perceived as a danger. Thus, the same Khrushchev – whose policies introduced a period of "thaw" or "liberalization" and the beginning of the sixties-era cultural renaissance in Soviet Ukraine – also revived the merging *(sliianie)* theory with respect to the nationality question. The result was new restrictions on national cultures.

Beginning already in 1963, the Sixties Group of writers were being accused by party ideologists of flirting with "decadent Western artistic notions" and, even worse, with Ukrainian "bourgeois nationalism." Although some members of the group changed their writing in response to warnings from the party, others continued to publish in the so-called *samvydav,* or publishing underground, in which self-published works were illegally produced and distributed. Particularly active were the literary critics and publicists Ivan Svitlychnyi, Ievhen Sverstiuk, Ivan Dziuba, and Valentyn Moroz, and, after 1975, intellectuals associated with the Ukrainian Public Group to Promote the Implementation of the Helsinki Accords on Human Rights, the so-called Helsinki group – Mykola Rudenko, Leonid Pliushch, General Petro Hryhorenko/Petr Grigorenko, and Iurii Badz'o. Unlike the essentially literary innovators of the Sixties Group, the dissidents spoke out boldly and in political terms. By the 1970s, they were issuing petitions to the Soviet government and the United Nations for the restructuring of society so that Ukrainian cultural and political aspirations could be realized. They proposed solutions that ranged from federation to independence, and they reflected a spectrum of political ideologies from national communism (Dziuba) and integral nationalism (Moroz) to pluralist democracy (the Helsinki Group). Regardless of their approach, most activists started from the premise that political change in Ukraine should and could be brought about within the framework of rights guaranteed by the Soviet constitution.

The increasing activity of the Ukrainian dissidents and the publication of their writings in neighboring Czechoslovakia (until the Soviet intervention of 1968) and in the West caused embarrassment for Brezhnev, who at the very same time was trying to lessen international tensions and present the Soviet Union as a responsible member of the world community. Any concern about negative opinion in the West or among the world Communist movement was outweighed, however, by what Soviet authorities felt was the need to combat the dangers of Ukrainian "bourgeois nationalism" within their own borders. The result was a series of arrests and the spectre once again – a little more than a decade after Stalin's death – of political trials.

The first wave of arrests and trials in Soviet Ukraine took place in 1965–1966. The accused were dissident intellectuals whose only crime was their outspoken criticism of the Soviet system. Since their guilt was in effect established before their trials, it was a foregone conclusion that figures like the literary critics Ivan Dziuba, Ievhen Sverstiuk, Ivan Svitlychnyi, and Valentyn Moroz, the writer Mykhailo Osadchyi, and the journalist Viacheslav Chornovil (who had been sent to report on the earliest trials, which he then proceeded to describe as being conducted in violation of the Soviet legal code) would be sentenced to terms in prison.

In 1971–1972, more arrests and trials took place. These affected not only dissidents active in the *samvydav* movement, but also scholars and cultural activists who during the 1960s had been in the forefront of the Ukrainian cultural revival. This last major governmental crackdown in Soviet Ukraine coincided with the removal, in May 1972, of Petro Shelest as first secretary of the CPU. Shelest had risen through the CPU hierarchy during the Khrushchev era, a time when Kiev's party bosses were able to increase Soviet Ukraine's influence and their own personal power base through the regional economic councils. As head of the CPU's Bureau for Industry and Construction, Shelest had contributed to Soviet Ukraine's being granted greater economic self-management, a policy he had continued to promote after becoming first secretary of the CPU in 1963. He had also encouraged Ukrainian cultural development, in particular the use of the Ukrainian language (dropped in 1954 as a compulsory entrance requirement) in higher education. But the trend toward decentralization which allowed Shelest to further Soviet Ukraine's interests was reversed under Brezhnev and Kosygin, who in 1965 abolished the regional economic councils. Shelest's opposition to Moscow's return to economic centralization, his support of Ukrainian cultural interests, and his seeming tolerance of Ukrainian dissidents brought him into increasing conflict with Brezhnev and his supporters.

Moscow argued that the crackdown on Ukrainian dissidents in 1971–1972 was a necessary reaction to the instability in Soviet Ukraine. Shelest, therefore, had to go. The public excuse for his demotion was the fact that in 1970 he had allowed the publication under his name of a popular book entitled *Ukraïno, nasha Radians'ka* (Oh Ukraine, Our Soviet Country). Within a year after his removal as first secretary in May 1972, Shelest was accused of "local nationalism," since the book carrying his name supposedly idealized the Zaporozhian Cossacks, minimalized the "epochal importance" of the "reunification" with Russia in 1654, failed to criticize the "nationalist deviations" in the CPU during the 1920s, and in general promoted the idea of "economic autarchism."

The belated public attack against Shelest, almost a year after his demotion, was part of a campaign against the remnants of "bourgeois nationalism" directed by his successor as first secretary of the CPU, the Brezhnev protégé from the

Dnipropetrovs'k clan, Volodymyr Shcherbyts'kyi. Since the correct party line on Ukraine's historical and cultural past and its place in Soviet society had to be maintained, Shelest's demise was a convenient excuse at the same time to remove many revisionist academicians from their posts and to end publication of most of the recently founded historical journals. There was even a crackdown on traditional folk music groups (Homin in 1971) and singers of Christmas carols *(koliadnyky)*, whose activity was banned. Thus, Shelest's removal sent a clear signal. Under Brezhnev and Shcherbyts'kyi, the authorities were determined to eliminate any suggestion of Ukraine's cultural and administrative distinctness from the rest of Soviet society, regardless of whether the suggestion came from the pens of belletrists, dissidents, scholars, or the first secretary of the republic's Communist party.

The arrests and trials of Ukrainian dissidents and the police surveillance of other cultural activists revealed the continuing dilemma that the nationality question posed for the Soviet leadership. During the Brezhnev era, Ukrainian dissidents were imprisoned on more than one occasion, and some (V. Moroz, L. Pliushch, P. Grigorenko) were forcibly exiled to the West. Unlike in the Stalin years, however, they were not silenced. Moreover, the arrests and other forms of harassment only encouraged further dissident activity. In a sense, the dissidents seemed to welcome their role as martyrs in the struggle to do what they considered their patriotic duty on behalf of Ukraine's cultural and national heritage. Among the "patriot martyrs" were activists in the Greek Catholic Church, which despite its abolition in the late 1940s continued to function underground, conducting secret services and ordaining clergy, in western Ukraine. Those believers who were discovered were arrested and, usually, sentenced to labor camps as punishment for anti-state activity.

Although the persecution of Greek Catholic religious and secular activists (Iosyp Terelia, Vasyl' Kobryn) continued during the 1980s, at the same time there developed a kind of "cultural détente" between the Soviet authorities and those writers and intellectuals (Volodymyr Brovchenko, Borys Oliinyk, Dmytro Pavlychko) who were willing to work on behalf of Ukrainian culture within Soviet guidelines. Some of the directors of academic and cultural institutes who carried out the post-Shelest cultural purges of the 1970s were replaced, and several writers who had been harassed for their unorthodox work (among them Lina Kostenko and Ivan Drach of the Sixties Group) were allowed to publish once again and even be recipients of state awards.

In a sense, the last decade of the Brezhnev era, which began with the removal of Shelest in 1972, resembled the era of tsarist Dnieper Ukraine. Like their nineteenth-century counterparts who accepted Shevchenko's belief in exclusive national identities, the dissidents of the 1970s and 1980s were only a tiny minority of Soviet Ukraine's population. One estimate identified at most only 975 dissidents (between 1960 and 1972) in a country with a population of over forty-eight million. Meanwhile, the vast majority of Soviet Ukraine's inhabitants, better off economically than ever before and spared from foreign invasion for more than a third of a century because of the protective shield of Soviet military might, seemed resigned to or even satisfied with functioning within a system that reflected the principle of a hierarchy of multiple loyalties. In effect, it seemed possible to be simultaneously an ethnic Ukrainian and a Soviet citizen. Of course, such complementary loyalties could realistically be maintained only on the understanding that while a Ukrainian identity and cultural framework was possible in many circumstances, higher forms of cultural and educational endeavor were to be carried out in the "universal Soviet" medium, Russian.

Notwithstanding this analogy, there was at least one crucial difference between the nineteenth century and the last decades of Soviet rule. Whereas in tsarist times being a "Little Russian" Russian often led one to complete national assimilation, Soviet Ukrainianism was a form of political accommodation without assimilation. Despite the increasing dominance of Russian forms in Soviet Ukrainian political, social, and cultural life (including an increase in the number of Russian-language schools and publications and the encouragement of bilingualism in elementary schools), the Soviet system at the same time produced a highly educated and nationally conscious Ukrainian stratum of the population. Also, because of socio-demographic changes, it was cities and not rural villages, especially in central Ukraine, that became the carriers of the Ukrainian ethos.

Urbanization and the new Ukraine

Urbanization was increasing by leaps and bounds. Whereas in 1959 there were 25 cities in Soviet Ukraine with over 100,000 inhabitants, by 1979 there were 46. During the same period, the number of cities with over a million inhabitants increased from one to five. Kiev alone nearly doubled its population (from 1.1 to 2.1 million inhabitants); it was followed in size by Kharkiv, Dnipropetrovs'k, Odessa, and Donets'k, which by 1979 had topped the million mark.

The phenomenal extent of the migration to cities made the 1970s an epochal turning point for Ukrainian society. For the first time in history, the majority of ethnic Ukrainians lived in urban areas (53 percent in 1979), and only a minority were employed in agricultural pursuits (37 percent in 1970, as opposed to 63 percent industrial workers and white-collar staff) (see table 51.1).

Urbanization, moreover, did not lead, as many Soviet and western social scientists predicted, to national assimilation. It turned out that the multicultural urban environment was more likely to produce a sharpening than a lessening of ethno-

TABLE 51.1
Selected characteristics of ethnic Ukrainians in Soviet Ukraine, 1959–1989[2]

	1959	1970	1989
Number of ethnic Ukrainians (in millions)	32.1	35.2	37.4
Percentage of total population	77	75	73
Number giving Ukrainian as mother tongue (in millions)	30.0	32.2	37.4
Percentage giving Ukrainian as mother tongue	94	91	88
Percentage living in urban areas	37	46	60
Percentage employed as industrial workers	34	47	–
Percentage employed as white-collar staff	13	16	–
Percentage employed as collective farmers	53	37	–

cultural awareness. Thus, in the same period when Soviet Ukraine's population grew more urban, the number of persons claiming Ukrainian as their mother tongue continued to increase, from 30 million in 1959 to 37.4 million in 1989. It is also true that there was a slight decrease in the percentage who claimed Ukrainian as their mother tongue (from 94 to 88 percent between 1959 and 1989). But such trends did not necessarily mean that either the Ukrainian language or the Ukrainian identity was seriously threatened, as the dire predictions of dissident writers and Ukrainian commentators in the West were suggesting. A closer look at the 1970 census, for instance, reveals that 96 percent of all Ukrainians knew their native language.

Finally, Ukrainian national identity – like many national identities – does not depend exclusively on an active or even a passive knowledge of the Ukrainian language. This was revealed in studies during the 1970s and 1980s of the supposedly "russified" inhabitants of eastern Ukraine. It turned out that association with a geographic territory (Ukraine) and its material culture, not necessarily its language, was what determined a Ukrainian identity for many otherwise unilingual Russian speakers.

Thus, the Soviet Union, whose Marxist-Leninist ideological imperative called for the "withering away" of nationalities, adopted policies which in the course of the twentieth century created in Soviet Ukraine a highly educated, bilingual, nationally conscious, and largely urban population whose very existence ensured the survival of Ukrainians and their evolution into a distinct and viable nationality. Such a reality was what the Ukrainian-Canadian political scientist Bohdan Krawchenko had in mind when, describing Soviet Ukraine in the mid-1980s, he concluded, "Ukrainian national identity is stronger today than ever in the past."[3]

From Devolution to Independence

When the Soviet president and CPSU general secretary Leonid Brezhnev died in 1982, few if anyone could have predicted that before another decade had passed the Soviet Union would no longer exist. Yet by 1 January 1992 not only had the Soviet Union been formally dissolved, but Ukraine had become an independent state. All this took place, moreover, in the absence of any military or civil conflict.

The last years of Brezhnev's rule were characterized by stagnation in economic and social life. Little changed after his death, since the CPSU chose as his successors first a man incapacitated by ill health (Iurii Andropov) and then an octogenarian (Konstantin Chernenko) who died after only thirteen months in power. The CPSU then did the unexpected. On 10 March 1985, the Politburo elected its youngest member, the fifty-four-year-old Mikhail Gorbachev, to become the party's new general secretary. As a result of that choice, the Soviet Union and political relations throughout the world within a few years would change beyond recognition.

The Gorbachev revolution

Mikhail Gorbachev was a party functionary who in the 1950s began a typical progression through the Communist ranks. He was, however, quite different from all his Soviet predecessors, perhaps with the exception of Lenin. Gorbachev was well educated, articulate, and personable. Moreover, he exuded a sense of self-confidence and optimism that inspired both faith on the part of his supporters and respect from his adversaries. In the first year of his rule, he began to replace older officials with younger, more reform-minded types. This was the first step toward his primary goal, the resuscitation of the Soviet economy.

During the last years of Brezhnev's rule, it had been clear to many Soviet leaders that their country had entered an economic decline which, if unchecked, before long would undermine its status as a world power. Changes in the centralized command economy were essential if the downward spiraling was to be reversed. Gorbachev sounded the clarion call for change with two words that subsequently entered the world's vocabulary: *perestroika* and *glasnost'* – restructuring and openness.

Restructuring belonged primarily to the socioeconomic sphere. Although Gorbachev was never strong on specifics, he and his reform-minded advisers seemed intent on doing away with centralized control over the economy and even, if necessary, implementing some form of free-market system. Gorbachev knew that a slogan like *perestroika* might be proclaimed, as other Communist slogans had so often been proclaimed in the past, but that in order for it to succeed the population as a whole – from the collective farmer, to the factory worker, to the plant manager, to the party functionary – had to be drawn into the process and made to feel that he or she had a stake in its success. To achieve such a radical transformation in people's minds and hearts, Gorbachev argued, Soviet society must henceforth be guided by the principle of *glasnost'*, or openness, and its corollary, democratization. In effect, Soviet citizens were being encouraged to criticize their society. Before long, when people realized that Gorbachev was indeed standing by his promise and promoting *glasnost'* without any resort to police repression, all segments of the population, almost without restraint, began to criticize virtually every aspect of their country.

Gorbachev's efforts at domestic reform were complemented by the complete restructuring of the Soviet Union's relations with the outside world. Gorbachev the economic reformer now became Gorbachev the political visionary. Soviet troops were brought home from Afghanistan (where Brezhnev had sent them in 1979); relations with the United States improved dramatically as a result of Soviet willingness to reduce its military forces and nuclear arsenal; and, most remarkable of all, the Kremlin effectively gave up its interest in dominating what since World War II had been the Soviet bloc in central Europe and the Balkans. This last decision led to what became one of the most important events in twentieth-century history – the Revolution of 1989. In that year alone, the iron curtain was raised; the Berlin Wall came crumbling down; Communist rule disintegrated in Poland, Hungary, East Germany, Czechoslovakia, Romania, and Bulgaria; and the Soviet Army began to withdraw its forces from its former central European satellite countries.

All these monumental events were owing in large part to the actions – whether their consequences had been intended or not – of Mikhail Gorbachev. Comparably profound changes would take place within the Soviet Union as well. With regard to the country's internal political structure, Gorbachev consolidated his power in 1988 by being elected president and then ousting most of his opponents from the CPSU's Politburo. Then, in 1989, elections were held to the Supreme Soviet, which for the first time in Soviet history began to act as an independent-minded legislative body, not surprisingly under the chairmanship of Gorbachev. But Gorbachev's ultimate political masterstroke came in early 1990. Sensing that his efforts to push through *perestroika* would be blocked by conservative-minded Communists, he arranged for the party to give up its monopoly on power and to invest even greater authority in the office of the president, to which he was duly elected.

These remarkable changes in political life inevitably were to have a profound impact on the various peoples (titular nationalities and national minorities) throughout the Soviet Union. The self-imposed limiting of Moscow's authority allowed interethnic squabbling to break out that for decades had been held in check by Stalin, Khrushchev, and Brezhnev. Conflict initially erupted in the Caucasus and Central Asian regions, where Armenians and Azerbaijanis began to fight openly over disputed territory (Nagorno-Karabakh), where Georgians clashed with Abkhazians, and where Uzbeks attacked Meshketian Turks living in their midst. The eruption of interethnic passions such as these, which resulted in bloodshed and the reluctant intervention of the Soviet Army, was to be followed by an even more politically problematic development: the demand on the part of certain Soviet republics for the implementation of their constitutionally guaranteed right to secede from the union. This most serious challenge came from the Baltic republics and reached a crisis in March 1990, when Lithuania unilaterally declared its independence.

Even in those republics where political demands were limited to calls for decentralization and greater autonomy, local leaders, especially from among the Communist- and non-Communist-affiliated intelligentsia, were inspired by Gorbachev's call for *glasnost'*. Their criticisms were largely demands for the conferring of official status on local languages within the republics, for the full use of those languages at all levels of education and cultural life, and for the rewriting of history so as to fill in the so-called blank spots, or deliberate omissions, in the official Soviet version of the countries' pasts. More often than not, these "blank spots" left out events or personages who had struggled for independence from tsarist Russian or from Soviet rule. Filling in the blank spots, that is, rehabilitating national histories, helped to justify new demands on the part of the republics and titular nationalities for autonomy or even independence from Moscow.

The Soviet heritage in Ukraine

Unlike in other Soviet republics, it took a few years before *perestroika* and *glasnost'* (in Ukrainian: *perebudova* and *hlasnist'*) reached Soviet Ukraine. This was largely because the CPU was still led by Volodymyr Shcherbyts'kyi, the Brezhnev appointee and an opponent of Gorbachev, who denied there was any need for fundamental changes in his republic. There were, however, numerous reasons for discontent in Ukrainian society related to the economy, the environment, and culture.

It was the need to revive a stagnating Soviet economy that initially motivated the Gorbachev revolution. And in an officially sanctioned environment that encouraged debate and criticism there seemed to be no shortage of proposals for reform. There was, however, little that actually changed in the Moscow-directed command economy, which as late as 1990 still controlled over 95 percent of industry and agriculture in Soviet Ukraine. Talk of reform without any real reform only caused confusion among and increased the passivity of managers of factories and farm collectives. To make matters worse, the partial ending of state price controls caused inflation, which added to the economic and psychological uncertainty faced by the ordinary Soviet citizen. Aside from rhetoric, it seemed Moscow had nothing to offer, neither technological know-how nor investment capital to modernize Soviet Ukraine's aging industrial infrastructure and to improve its productive capacity. It did not take long for both managers and workers to realize Moscow's inability to bring about real change. Disillusioned with the deteriorating economic situation, these people increasingly supported the more outspoken critics who wished to see Soviet Ukraine liberated from the Soviet centralized bureaucratic system.

Environmental issues were another source of discontent. In fact, it was the explosion on 26 April 1986 at the nuclear power facility at Chornobyl', to the north of Kiev, that made the world aware of Ukraine, and Ukrainians aware of the profound degree to which they lacked control over their lives. The initial reluctance of the Gorbachev government to provide information about life-threatening radioactive fallout perhaps more than anything else alienated the ordinary citizen from the Soviet system. "Chornobyl'," in the words of one Ukrainian political activist, "helped us understand that we are a colony."[1] In addition to its political and cultural imperialism with respect to Soviet Ukraine, Moscow was now accused of environmental imperialism. Nor was the Chornobyl' disaster an isolated incident. Decades of uncontrolled industrial growth with little or no thought given to pollution control had resulted in the widespread contamination of rivers, water supplies, and agricultural lands. Such irresponsible practices had by the 1980s resulted in shockingly poor health in Soviet Ukraine: chronic illness among 46 percent of secondary-school children; miscarriages among 40 percent of pregnant women; and the lowest birthrate (13.3 per 1,000 of the population) among all the Soviet republics.

Finally, there was deep concern about the future of the Ukrainian nationality. Despite the fact that in the 1980s a sense of Ukrainian national identity in broad segments of the population may have been as strong as it ever had been, the Soviet Ukrainian status quo still discriminated against ethnic Ukrainians in numerous ways. Visitors to Kiev or other cities were immediately struck by something ordinary citizens experienced on a daily basis: scorn and derision if the Ukrainian language was used on the streets or in public offices. The low prestige of the Ukrainian language and therefore of Ukrainian culture was a consequence of governmental policies that had changed little since the end of Ukrainianization in the 1930s.

For instance, ever since World War II there had been a steady decline in the publication of Ukrainian books. Whereas in 1958 Ukrainian-language titles had made up 60 percent of book production in Soviet Ukraine, by 1978 that figure had dropped to only 27 percent – the lowest since 1923. Soviet Ukraine's educational system, in particular, seemed not to be responding to the needs of the republic's titular and numerically largest nationality. Whereas during the 1950–1951 school year 81 percent of elementary school students had been enrolled in Ukrainian-language schools, by 1988–1989 the figure was only 47.5 percent. At the higher levels, access was a problem. Whereas in 1939 Ukraine had ranked fourth among the sixteen Soviet republics with respect to the percentage of the population that had completed secondary or higher education, by 1970 it ranked eleventh.

The proportion of ethnic Ukrainians with higher education had suffered a relative decline for several reasons: (1) admissions policies favored children of parents with white-collar occupations; (2) Russian-language entrance requirements favored native Russian speakers; and (3) budgetary and admissions control rested in the hands of central ministries in Moscow (in 1965, only 50 of Soviet Ukraine's 132 VUZy [university-level institutions] were under the jurisdiction of Kiev). Since during these same years Soviet Ukrainian society was becoming increasingly urbanized and better educated, there was a concomitant rise in social expectations, and for many Ukrainians their republic's educational system was simply unable to fulfill these expectations.

Glasnost' in Ukraine

Among the first group of Ukrainians to respond to Gorbachev's call for openness and constructive criticism was the creative intelligentsia, represented in large part by the Ukrainian Writers' Union. This organization had traditionally followed Communist party directives, but in 1986, at a conference of nearly 1,100 members, the policy of the union's executive was changed radically. From that time, the Writers' Union actively promoted the rebirth of Ukrainian culture and language, by encouraging the creation of native-language societies; by rehabilitating, with public fanfare, writers who had been suppressed during the Stalin and Brezhnev eras; and by publishing new works that spoke openly about historical events which for decades had been banned from public discussion. It was not long before writers and critics like Ivan Drach, Ivan Dziuba, Dmytro Pavlychko, and Mykola Zhulyns'kyi would be playing leading roles in Ukraine's civic and political transformation.

Taking up the call sounded by the Ukrainian Writers' Union, writers and other activists established several new organizations and publications to address political, economic, environmental, and cultural issues. Among the first of these was the Ukrainian ecological association, Green World (Zelenyi Svit), founded in late 1987 to lobby the government for stricter controls over the environment and, in particular, for a nuclear-free Ukraine that would be spared any future Chornobyl'-like disasters. Two years later, the Taras Shevchenko Ukrainian Language Society, headed by the writer Dmytro Pavlychko, was created to improve the status of Ukrainian and make it the official language of the country. This goal was partly achieved in October 1989, when Ukrainian was declared the state language.

The largest and most influential of the new organizations was the Popular Movement of Ukraine for Restructuring, better known by its Ukrainian acronym, Rukh (The Movement). Led by the writers Ivan Drach and Volodymyr Iavorivs'kyi and the dissident Mykhailo Horyn', Rukh published its program in February 1989, which called for the "rebirth and comprehensive development of the Ukrainian nation."[2] The program stressed the need for political, economic, environmental, and cultural reforms as well as institutionalized guarantees for human rights. Despite its emphasis on the ethnically Ukrainian character of the country and particular concern for protection of the Ukrainian language, Rukh defended the rights of national and religious minorities. In this regard, Rukh made a special effort to counteract the negative stereotypes associated with traditional Ukrainian-Jewish relations by condemning all forms of anti-Semitism as inimical to the liberal-democratic society it wished to see created in Ukraine. While political concerns and the relationship to Moscow were high on Rukh's agenda, the organization did not call for independence, but rather for the transformation of the Soviet Union into a union of truly sovereign states with assurances that Ukraine could determine its own political, economic, and cultural affairs without interference from Moscow.

Even before the establishment of Rukh and other organizations, there was movement on another very sensitive front, religion. For decades, the Greek, or Ukrainian, Catholic Church, which had been outlawed in the late 1940s, had continued to function in secret in western Ukraine, that is, in former Galicia and Transcarpathia. In addition to the underground Greek Catholic Church, western Ukraine had the greatest number of parishes and monasteries belonging to the Russian Orthodox Church of any area of Ukraine, and many of that church's clergy and faithful remained clandestine Greek Catholics.

With the new atmosphere in the Soviet Union, in 1987 the clandestine Greek Catholic hierarchy decided to "come up from the underground." Their action prompted the Vatican and Ukrainians living in the diaspora to increase their lobbying of the United States and western governments, who in turn exerted diplomatic pressure on the Soviet Union. These efforts bore fruit when in December 1989 Gorbachev's government granted permission to the Greek Catholic Church to register its parishes. Similarly, in the summer of 1989 the Ukrainian Autocephalous Orthodox Church, banned by the Soviets since the early 1930s, began its reconstitution, a process that culminated a year later in a church council (*sobor*) which formally restored the church's hierarchy.

The events in Soviet Ukraine during the Gorbachev era had a profound impact on Ukrainians throughout the diaspora. After having been cut off for decades from their homeland by a hostile Soviet government, non-Communist Ukrainian organizations from the West (especially the United States and Canada) were for the first time allowed to provide the national rebirth in the homeland with advice and financial support. Renewed contacts with the diaspora were most evident in church affairs. Even though the hierarchs of both the Ukrainian (Greek) Catholic and Ukrainian Autocephalous Orthodox churches had resided "temporarily" (since World War II) in the West, they were able to reestablish their authority in the Ukrainian homeland. Local bishops in each church recognized as their superior either the Ukrainian (Greek) Catholic metropolitan (some would say patriarch) Myroslav Cardinal Liubachivs'kyi, in Rome, or the Autocephalous patriarch Mstyslav Skrypnyk, in New Jersey, both of whom were expected to – and eventually did – return home to lead their flocks.

The rebirth of the Ukrainian (Greek) Catholic and Autocephalous Orthodox churches in Soviet Ukraine posed a direct threat to the Russian Orthodox Church under the patriarch of Moscow, which until the Gorbachev revolution had been the only Eastern Christian body permitted to function legally. Faced with the challenge of two renewed Ukrainian churches, in 1989 the Russian Orthodox Church renamed its Ukrainian exarchate the Ukrainian Orthodox Church. At the parish level, the result was a three-way struggle among the various churches for the allegiance of the faithful and – more problematic – for control of church property and the use of church buildings. In general, the Ukrainian (Greek) Catholic Church was the most successful in attracting clergy and parishes in western Ukraine (especially in Galicia), and the Autocephalous Orthodox Church was strongest in the Right Bank and central Ukraine.

Besides the activity of the non-state-run secular and religious organizations, there was a phenomenal rise in new publications. Gorbachev's *glasnost'* effectively ended state censorship and thus allowed for the almost spontaneous appearance of a host of newspapers, journals, bulletins, and flyers ranging in subject matter from politics, religion, and scholarship to sex and how best to emigrate from the Soviet Union. Publicists and historians in particular took advantage of *glasnost'* in order to fill in the "blank spots" in Ukrainian history. Past cultural figures were "rehabilitated," such as the nineteenth-century national activists Panteleimon Kulish and Mykhailo Drahomanov, and the early twentieth-century cultural and political leaders Mykhailo Hrushevs'kyi and Volodymyr Vynnychenko, who, if they had been mentioned previously, had been described as anti-progressivist and anti-Soviet. Researchers also worked diligently to make public documentary evidence concerning recent Ukrainian national tragedies, such as the Great Famine of 1933, which, until the late 1980s, according to Soviet sources had never occurred, and the numerous massacres of Ukrainians by Soviet security forces on the eve of and during World War II (at Vinnytsia and L'viv, among other places), which had been unjustly attributed to the German invaders.

Finally, *glasnost* had an impact on the various national minorities who lived in Soviet Ukraine. Some, like the Poles and Jews, were concerned primarily with improving the cultural, linguistic, and religious status of their respective communities. Beginning in 1988, the taboo against formal relations between Poland and ethnic Poles living in the *kresy* (the Polish term for the western part of the Soviet Union) was effectively ended. This meant that now there could be serious discussion about the national survival of Poles under Soviet rule. In Soviet Ukraine, the first Congress of Poles took place in 1990, and it provided a stimulus for the creation during the following several months of new Polish cultural organizations and of Polish-language newspapers, magazines, and radio programming emanating mostly from L'viv. The status of the Roman Catholic Church was of particular importance in a social environment still characterized by the view that a "Catholic equals a Pole." In 1991, the Vatican reestablished the Polish Roman Catholic hierarchy in Ukraine, and the number of churches that were reopened and that used Polish in their services rose within a few years to some 450.

Jews focused their attention on reviving their religious life and the Yiddish language. With the financial assistance of Jewish organizations abroad, new synagogues were built and educational facilities – including Sunday schools, *yeshivas* (religious schools for men), and *ulpans* (Judaic study centers) – were opened to teach the principles of Judaism as well as the Yiddish and Hebrew languages. A wide range of Jewish organizations concerned with charity, publications, community projects, cultural activity, and property restitution also came into being. Whereas the revival of Jewish life started under *glasnost'* during the last years of Soviet rule, its expansion and most significant achievements were to occur in post-Communist independent Ukraine.

Other peoples were concerned as much with their political as their cultural status. Ever since the 1960s, Crimean Tatar activists were calling for the right to return from "exile" (*sürgün*) in Central Asia to their Crimean homeland, and their campaign had become well known in Soviet dissident circles. In 1967, the people as a whole were exonerated of the accusations of betrayal during World War II and, finally in 1988, the Soviet government gave them the right to return to the Crimea, where their numbers increased dramatically from about 38,000 in 1989 to 120,000 in 1990. The returnees from various parts of Soviet Central Asia were especially concerned with the Crimea's Russian-dominated political leadership, which was calling for union with the Russia should the structure of the Soviet Union ever change. To assert their voice, the Crimean Tatars met in a convention (*kurultay*), which in June 1991 declared national sovereignty for the Crimean Tatar people and its intention to reestablish a sovereign Tatar state. That same convention created a legislative body (*mejlis*) to advocate Crimean Tatar political demands.

Along the far western edge of Soviet Ukraine, the year 1990 marked a somewhat unexpected revival of the so-called Rusyn movement in Transcarpathia. Its leaders demanded recognition of Carpatho-Rusyns as a distinct East Slavic nationality (claiming that a Ukrainian identity had been forced upon the population by the Soviet authorities after World War II), while the regional council (Oblasna rada) established a commission calling for the renewal of an autonomous status for Transcarpathia that harked back to the experience of that region as Subcarpathian Rus' within Czechoslovakia during the interwar years (see chapter 47).

The road to sovereignty and independence

In the midst of the intellectual and civic-minded ferment that reverberated through many segments of Soviet Ukrainian society, an important turning point came in September 1989, when one of the last of the Brezhnevite opponents of Gorbachev, Volodymyr Shcherbyts'kyi, was removed from the Central Committee of the All-Union Communist party (CPSU) and from his post as first secretary of the Communist party of Ukraine. With the fall of Shcherbyts'kyi, the pace of political change quickened in Soviet Ukraine. That same month, Rukh held its first national congress in Kiev, and backed by its nearly 300,000 members it began preparing for elections to Soviet Ukraine's Supreme Soviet (Verkhovna Rada) scheduled for March 1990. In these elections, pro-Rukh candidates were part of the Democratic Bloc, which won just over 100 of the 450 seats contested. In the new parliament – as the Supreme Soviet was popularly called – the Democratic Bloc joined forces with the "democratic" wing of the Communists. Together, they were instrumental in having the parliament declare Ukraine a sovereign state, on 16 July 1990.

By 1991, the formerly Communist-dominated and Moscow-loyalist Ukrainian parliament was in the forefront of the process of creating a legal and administrative infrastructure for a sovereign state. The parliament's work was made easier after the Communists ceased to function as a unified voting bloc, with some joining the opposition in support of specific issues. The change in direction of the parliament was also due in large measure to its new chairman, Leonid Kravchuk, a Communist who quickly adapted to the more nationalist-minded mood of the people. Soviet Ukraine established diplomatic relations with several neighboring

Declaration of Independence

Resolution of the Supreme Soviet of the Ukrainian S.S.R. on the Declaration of Independence of Ukraine

The Supreme Soviet of the Ukrainian Soviet Socialist Republic rules:

To declare Ukraine an independent democratic state on September 24, 1991.

From the moment of declaration of independence only the Constitution of Ukraine, its laws, resolutions of the government, and other legislative acts of the republic are active on its territory.

To hold on December 1, 1991 a republican referendum on the confirmation of the declaration of independence.

L. Kravchuk, Chairman of the Supreme Soviet of the Ukrainian S.S.R.
Kiev, August 24, 1991

Act of Ukraine's Independence Declaration

Proceeding from the mortal danger that threatened Ukraine as a result of the coup d'état in the U.S.S.R. on August 19, 1991:

– developing the centuries-old tradition of the Ukrainian state formation;
– proceeding from the right to self-determination, envisioned by the United Nation-Charter and other international legal documents;
– acting in compliance with the Declaration of State Sovereignty of Ukraine, the Supreme Soviet of the Ukrainian Soviet Socialist Republic declares:

The independence of Ukraine, and the formation of a sovereign Ukrainian state – Ukraine.

The territory of Ukraine is integral and inviolable.

From now on only the constitution and laws of Ukraine are applicable on its territory.

This act comes into force from the moment of its approval.

The Supreme Soviet of Ukraine
August 24, 1991

SOURCE: *News from Ukraine* (Kiev), September 1991, p. 1.

countries before the end of the year, and Kravchuk embarked on several visits to western Europe and North America, acting as if he were the head of an independent state.

The question of Ukraine's relationship with the Soviet Union was finally decided in August 1991, when conservative political forces in Moscow staged an unsuccessful coup (*putsch*) to overthrow Gorbachev. After some initial hesitation in condemning the leaders of the failed *putsch*, Kravchuk acted decisively. On 24

August 1991, he spearheaded a resolution that declared Ukraine an independent state. The declaration also called for a referendum on independence to be held throughout the new republic on 1 December 1991. That same day, presidential elections were scheduled as well.

In the months leading up to the referendum and elections, Kravchuk enhanced his reputation as a defender of Ukrainian interests by opposing Gorbachev's proposals for a new union treaty that would limit the political and economic sovereignty of its members. When the 1 December referendum was finally held, the results were a surprise to even the most ardent believers in independence. No less than 92 percent of the country's inhabitants voted for independence. Over 80 percent of the voters in each of the supposedly russified eastern industrial oblasts (Donets'k, Dnipropetrovs'k, Zaporizhzhia, Kharkiv) voted for Ukraine's independence. Even the Crimea, which as of September 1991 had had its own "state sovereignty within Ukraine," returned a 54 percent majority in favor of independence. Kravchuk won the presidency with a comfortable majority of 62 percent of the vote.

24 August 1991 marked the sixth time in the course of the twentieth century that independence had been declared for all or part of Ukrainian territory. The conditions surrounding the declaration of independence in 1991 differed significantly, however, from those surrounding the earlier declarations, whether those of the immediate post–World War I period (Kiev, 1918; L'viv, 1918; Kiev, 1919) or those on the eve of and during the course of World War II (Khust, 1939; L'viv, 1941). All the previous attempts at independence, whether they had applied to Ukraine as a whole or to one of its parts (western Ukraine, Carpatho-Ukraine), had come at a time of civil war and/or invasion by foreign powers. Furthermore, on previous occasions Ukraine's inhabitants had been consulted only in part or not at all as to their views on independence.

All was different in 1991. Ukraine may have been part of an empire in devolution or dissolution, but that process was esssentially a peaceful one, in which, ironically, the ruling Communist elite participated along with significant segments of the population. And because of the power of the modern media, all this took place under the watchful and sometimes approving eye of the world. Moreover, the declaration of independence by parliamentary representatives was legitimized through a referendum in which 80 percent of eligible voters participated, and which outside and inside observers agreed was conducted in accord with generally accepted democratic practices. The results were almost immediately welcomed by the international community. Independent Ukraine retained its status as a full-fledged member of the United Nations, and within a few weeks it was recognized by most of the leading countries in the world community. The fact that nine out of every ten inhabitants approved independence confirmed that Ukrainian statehood was the wish not only of Ukrainian nationalists. In effect, an independent Ukraine seemed to promise the most attractive alternative for all those who wanted change, whether in politics, the economy, the environment, or cultural life. And for the first time Ukrainians had the opportunity to resolve their problems on their own.

53

Independent Ukraine

In January 1992 Ukraine embarked on an entirely new stage in its long history. For the first time it was able to function as an independent state accepted enthusiastically or grudgingly by all its neighbors, and therefore without any threat to its sovereignty. Ukraine was one of several states that were able to begin a new life following the Revolution of 1989 and the collapse of the Soviet Union two years later, resulting in the end of Communist rule throughout entire Soviet realm that had stretched from central Europe though central Asia to the shores of the Pacific Ocean. Almost all the countries within this vast geographic space proclaimed as their goal freedom and democracy for their citizens and the desirability of replacing centralized command economies with ones based on free-market forces.

Declarations of goals was one thing, their actual implementation was quite another. Ukraine, like all other countries in the former Soviet sphere, entered into what came to be known as a period of post-Communist transition. For several central European countries the transition period could be said to have ended on the eve of their entry to the European Union between 2004 and 2007. Other countries, including Ukraine, have made substantial changes in their political and economic life but they are still in a transitional phase.

Political restructuring

For Ukraine, the most significant break with the past coincided with the end of the domination by a single-party "dictatorship of proletariat" and the creation of a multi-party political system in which the president and parliament would be elected through freely contested elections. In fact, the confirmation and ultimate imprimatur for Ukraine's independence came from the citizens themselves during the December 1991 referendum which coincided with an election for president of the new country. The 1991 election, considered to be free and fair according to international observers, brought the former Communist party ideologue-turned-national Communist, Leonid Kravchuk, to the post of president by a margin of 62 percent of the vote.

In pre-term elections held in 1994, Kravchuk ran again but was defeated in another freely contested election by Leonid Kuchma, who was reelected to a second term in 1999. After two-terms in office – the maximum allowed according to the constitution – a fourth presidential election was held in late 2004. This time the electoral process was accompanied by widespread fraud and corruption, to such a degree that the results were declared invalid by the country's supreme court. The 2004 election became a crucial test of Ukraine's commitment to free elections, a test that it passed in large part due to extensive nation-wide citizen protests that came to be known as the Orange Revolution. As a result of a repeat election, the "orange" choice was victorious in person of Viktor Iushchenko, who was inaugurated as the country's third president in January 2005.

During the early stage of the transitional period, Ukraine set as its goal the creation of a state structure that was similar to those found in Europe – the proverbial West. This meant a balance of responsibility between three branches of government: the executive, as represented by the office of president; the legislative, as represented by the national parliament; and the judicial, as represented by the court system. Of course, existing democratic European states offer a wide variety of models from which to choose. Some are highly unitary (centrist), like France; others are federal in structure, like Germany; still others combine both unitary and federal principles. Moreover, the relationship between the executive, legislative, and judicial branches varies from country to country. Ukraine's state builders were faced with the challenge of which European model, or variant thereof, would best suit their country.

Ukraine's legislative branch inherited the structure that existed in Communist times, that is the Supreme Soviet, or Council (Verkhovna Rada). There was some debate about creating a second legislative chamber, but in the end the national parliament comprises one chamber that is still called the Supreme Council. The council has 450 deputies elected to a four-year term. Initially, the deputies were chosen according to a two-tier system; that is, half from party lists and the other half from each of the 225 electoral districts into which Ukraine was divided. Beginning with the 2006 parliamentary elections, only the party list, or proportional system is in effect. This means that the electorate votes for a particular party, not an individual. Each party prepares in advance of an election a list of its deputy candidates in order of preference (with the party leader in the first position). The number of candidates who become deputies (following the order of preference set by the party) depends on the percentage of votes a given party receives in a parliamentary election.

Considering their experience in previous governmental structures, it is perhaps not surprising that it was the Communists who initially held the highest number of seats in Ukraine's "post-Communist" national parliament: 86 seats at the outset of the 1994–1998 session and 121 seats in the 1998–2002 session. Since the beginning of the twenty-first century the strength of the Communists has progressively waned, however, so that in the most recent parliament session (2006–2010) that party has only 21 deputies.

Actually, the transitional stage in Ukraine has made parliamentary politics quite complex and unstable. During the past decade, there have existed at any time over one hundred registered political parties. The vast majority of parties have been unable to obtain the minimal percentage of votes (four percent until 2002, three percent thereafter) required to qualify for at least one seat in parliament. Therefore, most "parties" who make it into parliament do so as part of a bloc usually consisting of one relatively large party together with several smaller ones. At the outset of the twenty-first century the most important parties and blocs were Our Ukraine, headed by Viktor Iushchenko, the Party of Regions headed by Viktor Ianukovych, and the Tymoshenko Bloc (BIUT) headed by Iuliia Tymoshenko. These parties and blocs have alternatively cooperated or opposed each other depending on particular political circumstances. While all favor the existence of a sovereign Ukrainian state, each has different views on issues of political structure (a stronger presidential office or a stronger parliament), economic reform (its pace and extent), and foreign relations (joining the Western institutions like NATO and the European Union or closer relations with Russia).

The greatest political challenge facing Ukraine after independence was to adopt a constitution. Despite discussions about the possibility of a federal state along the lines of Germany, this option was rejected. The constitution that was finally adopted in 1996 provided for a unitary state in which the president (elected for a five-year term) has extensive powers, including the possibility to form and dismiss the government, as well as the control of foreign and defensive policy, the security service, and the prosecutor general's office.

The one exception to Ukraine as a unitary state was the Crimea. Already during the waning months of Soviet rule, the local Communist leadership arranged for a referendum (January 1991) in which an overwhelming majority of the peninsula's voters (93 percent) approved the reestablishment of the Crimea as an autonomous republic, a status it had had within Soviet Russia before 1945. The Crimean A.S.S.R was formally reconstituted one month later, although this time within the framework of Soviet Ukraine. After Ukraine itself became independent, its relationship to the Crimea remained unclear as long as leaders in Kiev did not adopt a constitution for the country. What followed was a struggle between Simferopol' (Crimea's capital) and Kiev over the status of the Crimea. The region's parliament in Simferopol' acted more quickly and adopted its own constitution in May 1992, which declared Crimea's "state independence." A few months later a revised constitution was adopted (September 1992) describing the Republic of Crimea as a state within Ukraine. The peak of estrangement between Kiev and Simferopol' came in January 1994, when Crimean voters elected as their president Iurii Meshkov. Together with his Russian bloc political allies in the republic's parliament, he called for the "reunification" of the Crimea with Russia.

This clear threat to Ukraine's territorial integrity was dealt with decisively by president Leonid Kuchma soon after coming to office. Under his instigation, in March 1995 the Crimean presidency was abolished and its constitution cancelled. It took three years before a reformulated Crimean constitution was accepted by Ukraine. It provides for only a limited amount of self-government for the Crimean Autonomous Republic which remains firmly within Ukraine. Not even all the peninsula's territory is included within the Crimean republic, since the city of Sev-

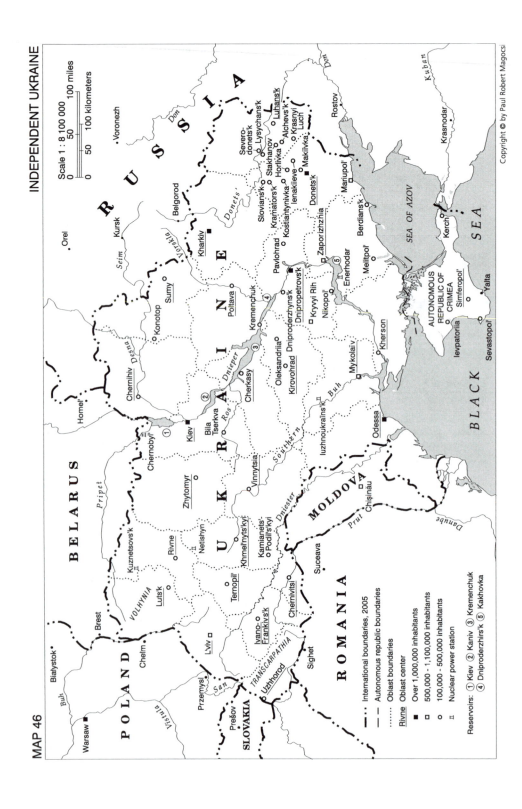

MAP 46

INDEPENDENT UKRAINE

Scale 1 : 8 100 000

0   50   100 kilometers

0   50   100 miles

Reservoirs: ① Kiev ② Kaniv ③ Kremenchuk
④ Dniprodzerzhirs'k ⑤ Kakhovka

- · - · - International boundaries, 2005
- - - - Autonomous republic boundaries
- · · · · · Oblast boundaries

<u>Rivne</u> Oblast center

■ Over 1,000,000 inhabitants
□ 500,000 - 1,100,000 inhabitants
○ 100,000 - 500,000 inhabitants
Ⅱ Nuclear power station

Copyright © by Paul Robert Magocsi

astopol' (home of the Black Sea Fleet) and neighboring suburbs are administered directly by Ukraine's central authorities in Kiev.

Two other regions of Ukraine have also expressed desires for autonomy. In the far western Transcarpathian oblast located along the borders of Slovakia, Hungary, and Romania, the inhabitants approved (by a 71 percent margin) a referendum in December 1991, calling for territorial self-rule (*samouprava*). Although the question was formulated by future President Leonid Kravchuk himself, self-rule has never been implemented by any of the governments in power in Kiev. Farther east, civic activists meeting in the city of Sieverodonets'k called for autonomy for eastern and southern Ukraine, although nothing ever came of this "separatist" movement.

The only significant change in Ukraine's governing structure came as a result of constitutional reform (adopted in December 2004 and implemented in early 2006), whereby the power of the presidency was reduced. In this new parliamentary-presidential system, the Supreme Council selects the prime minister who, in turn, chooses all other governmental ministers that form the cabinet. As head of the government, the prime minister has the primary policy-making role, while the president's powers are mainly in the area of foreign and military policy. While the president can veto legislation adopted by the Supreme Council, the latter, by a two-thirds vote, can override the presidential veto as well as amend the constitution. In effect, the functioning of Ukraine's government is determined by the party or coalition that forms the majority in the Supreme Council (parliament). Such power-sharing between the parliament and president may sound reasonable, but in practice it can and does lead to friction between the president and prime minister, resulting in governmental paralysis. Moreover, Ukraine functions neither as a centrist nor federal state but, to quote one political commentator, as a "decentralized unitary state."[1] The ideal here is, on the one hand, national integration based on shared values and common institutions while on the other, acceptance of the reality of a state comprised of several distinct regions.

Foreign relations

Since Ukraine was until 1991 part of the Soviet Union, it is not surprising that relations with that country's proclaimed successor, Russia, would be the most complex. Russia's governing and civic elite, not mention its public-at-large, have found it difficult to accept the fact that "their" vast Soviet space no longer includes the fifteen "fraternal" republics, all of which by 1991 had become independent states. Ukraine, in particular, had – and still has – a special place in the Russian cultural and geo-political mindset. For many Russians it is simply inconceivable that Little Russia – Ukraine – is no longer a part of the Russian body.

Aside from such powerful, if somewhat intangible beliefs, there remained a whole host of concrete social, economic, and familial ties that had developed between Russia and Ukraine over the centuries and that were deepened even further by seventy-five years of highly centralized Soviet rule directed from Russia's capital in Moscow. The command economy had fully integrated Ukraine with the rest of the Soviet Union, and the political and managerial elites of both countries were closely interwoven. After all, the Soviet Union was for long periods of time headed by Communist party leaders that were from, or closely connected with, Ukraine (Nikita Khrushchev, Leonid Brezhnev, Konstantin Chernenko, among others). In an attempt to maintain these complex interrelations after independence, the leaders of Russia, Belarus, and Ukraine – already in December 1991 on the eve of the formal passing of the Soviet Union – agreed to form the Commonwealth of Independent states (CIS). Most Central Asian and Caucasian republics also joined the CIS; the three Baltic states (Estonia, Latvia, Lithuania) demonstratively refused to do so.

Ukraine's relationship to the CIS was to remain ambiguous. For example, during his second term in office President Kuchma seemed to reorient Ukraine closer to Russia. In 2001, he became the head of the CIS Council of Heads of State and agreed that Ukraine should become part of a single economic space to be created in three stages together with Russia, Belarus, and Kazakhstan. Whereas Ukraine agreed to the first stage, a free-trade zone among the four countries, Kuchma made clear his opposition to being part of the next two stages, which were to result in a currency union and customs union. In effect, not even stage one has been implemented, so that the CIS has never fulfilled the cooperative federative function intended by its Soviet-minded creators back in 1991.

The trend toward separation rather than integration has characterized relations with Russia since Ukraine's independence. Of particular concern was Russia's recognition of Ukraine's borders, which did not occur fully until 1999. The question of the Soviet Black Sea Fleet based in the Crimean port of Sevastopol' proved to be a particularly sensitive issue. The very existence of the fleet symbolized Russia's naval power and its access to the Black Sea and the Mediterranean. Now independent Ukraine was a territorial hindrance to such access. Aside from symbolic and strategic considerations, the Black Sea Fleet was part of the larger question of property assets. In other words, who was to inherit the assets – and debts – of the defunct Soviet state? In general, it is the successor state on whose territory the assets are located. Consequently, Ukraine inherited – among other things – a large amount of conventional military hardware and approximately 5,000 nuclear weapons, making it the world's third power after the United States and Russia. As for the Black Sea Fleet based in the Crimea, which is part of Ukraine, long negotiations finally led in 1997 to an agreement with Russia, whereby the two countries divided the fleet (Ukraine receiving about 18 percent of the ships) and the Russian navy was given a twenty-year lease on Sevastopol's port. By the year 2017, what remains of the Russian fleet is to withdraw from Ukraine.

The other ongoing area of disagreement with Russia has been energy resources. As part of Soviet policy, Ukraine's industries – and domestic sector – had become virtually dependent on gas piped from fields beyond the Ural Mountains in western Siberia. By the same token the Soviet Union gained valuable western currency by supplying "capitalist" western Europe with natural gas that flowed through pipelines across Ukrainian territory. Ukraine is still dependent on energy resources from Russia but would prefer to receive them for much less than what countries in the European Union pay. Quite logically, Russia's argument is that if Ukraine is not part of Russia or willing to be part of a fully functioning Commonwealth of Independent States, then it should pay the same price as any other independent state. On the other hand, Ukraine has the right to expect appropriate transit fees, since it controls the pipelines through which 80 percent of Russia's energy exports reach western and central Europe. Disputes over natural gas prices and over what mechanism this commodity reaches world markets are topics that have continued to dominate Russian-Ukrainian relations throughout the entire post-Soviet transition era. In an effort to free itself from excessive dependency on Russian energy resources, in 1997 Ukraine entered into an agreement with neighbors to its south and southeast. The resultant consortium, named GUAM after the first letters of the participating member states (Georgia, Ukraine, Azerbaijan, Moldova), has as its goal the creation of new transport facilities for Azerbaijani oil crossing through the Caucasus region and the Black Sea to Odessa, and from there across Ukraine to the European Union.

Ukraine's relationship with Russia has also influenced the attitude and policies of its neighbors in Europe and the United States. Ironically, among the first countries to recognize Ukraine's independence was its historic "enemy" Poland. Since the early 1990s, post-Communist Poland has consistently promoted the idea of Ukraine's further integration into Euro-Atlantic structures and would hope that it become a candidate for membership in NATO and the European Union. Such an eventuality is not likely in the short-term, although the European Union does recognize the importance of Ukraine and has singled it out as a key component of its European Neighborhood Policy.

The United States, on the other had, has adopted an entirely new attitude toward Ukraine. Traditionally, American foreign policy makers have throughout the twentieth century ignored or dismissed the idea of Ukrainian independence. As late as 1991, U.S. President George H. W. Bush, on a visit to what was still Soviet Ukraine, warned in his so-called chicken-Kiev speech against nationalist extremists and the danger of their fantasy-like dreams of separating from the Soviet Union. But with the collapse of the Soviet Union, Ukraine for the first time was taken seriously by American's foreign policy-makers. As the largest and economically most powerful former Soviet republic after Russia, Ukraine was now seen as a strategic partner of the United States. After all, without Ukraine it would be difficult if not impossible for Russia to attain the status of its Soviet predecessor as the world's second superpower.

American-Ukrainian relations were particularly favorable during the first term (1994–1999) of President Leonid Kuchma, which coincided with the second term of U.S. President Bill Clinton. As part of its share in Soviet property assets, independent Ukraine became a major nuclear military power. But at the urging of Washington, Ukraine signed in 1994 a tri-lateral nuclear disarmament agreement with the United States and Russia. According to its provisions, within the next two years the last nuclear warheads were removed from Ukrainian territory. The United States, in turn, provided Ukraine with security assurances, paid for the de-nuclearization process, and started pouring in funds to assist the country in its transition to democracy and a market-driven economy. During the presidency of Bill Clinton in the 1990s, Ukraine, after Israel and Egypt, was the third largest recipient of U.S. foreign aid.

As a strategic partner of the United States, Ukraine was considered a buffer between Russia and Europe. And to enhance Ukraine's security, the United States helped it to become part of NATO's partnership for peace program in early 1994. Since that time Ukraine has participated with its troops in America-led military campaigns (Iraq) and in numerous NATO and United Nations peacekeeping missions in the former Yugoslav republics, Lebanon, and several African states. The United States remains a strong supporter of future NATO membership for Ukraine, whose candidacy to this day is still opposed by certain influential western European members of the alliance.

Ukrainian-American relations began to cool during President Kuchma's second term (1999–2004). There were several reasons for the change. From the American perspective, Kuchma's efforts at economic reform were half-hearted and ineffective, and his administration was tainted with charges of corruption, human rights violations, and restrictions on the media (including suspected collusion in the murder of a journalist critical of the government). Moreover, in the wake of the Al-Qaeda attacks against the United States on 11 September 2001, President George Bush, Jr. was keen on seeking accommodation with Russia's president, Vladimir Putin, both of whom had common interests in the "war on terrorism."

Whereas during the closing years of the twentieth century Ukraine's foreign minister Borys Tarasiuk was calling for the country's "return to Europe," by the outset of the twenty-first century President Kuchma was strengthening relations with the CIS and cooperating fully with Ukraine's business leaders (oligarchs) who favored greater integration with Russia. Ukraine's policies, which at different times or simultaneously could be both pro-Western (Europe and the United States) and pro-Eastern (Russia) were referred to by its defenders as "multi-vectorism." For some, the multi-vector approach was the most natural policy for a "buffer state" like Ukraine; for others, including Western policy makers, it seemed like a mark of the country's instability and the confused or opportunistic attitudes of its leaders. The pro-Western (liberal, democratic) and pro-Eastern (authoritarian) conundrum was transformed into a stark choice for citizens to decide during what came to be known as the Orange Revolution.

The Orange Revolution

In retrospect it is now clear that the stage was set for the Orange Revolution two years earlier, when, in the 2002 parliamentary elections, Viktor Iushchenko's Our Ukraine bloc, campaigning on a platform of reform, won a plurality of votes. The victory proved to be short-lived, since political manipulation by deputies loyal to President Kuchma reduced the Our Ukraine bloc (in alliance with the Tymoshenko bloc and the Socialist party) to the role of parliamentary opposition. Iushchenko was determined, however, to be the candidate of reform in the 2004 presidential elections. He was opposed by then Prime Minister Viktor Ianukovych, the chosen favorite of Kuchma and the business interests represented by powerful

oligarchs from the industrial region of eastern Ukraine. Not wanting their business privileges and their often corruptly earned income to be threatened by the
reform-minded Iushchenko, the oligarchs joined with President Kuchma (himself
fearful of possible prosecution for the various scandals associated with his second
term in office) in an attempt to assure that their candidate Viktor Ianukovych
would be next president.

Not surprisingly, Iushchenko and Ianukovych were the two leading candidates
in the first round of the elections (after which the other contenders were eliminated). Iushchenko actually polled the most votes in the first round, but he allegedly lost to Ianukovych in the second round. Despite widespread accusations of
electoral fraud, President Kuchma recognized Ianukovych as his successor. More
ominous was the fact that soon after the second round, President Putin of Russia
was the first foreign leader to congratulate as winner Viktor Ianukovych. It seemed
that the "multi-vector" foreign policy of Ukraine, which of late was leading more in
the direction of Russia, would now be the course the country would adopt under a
Ianukovych presidency. After all, while still governor of his native Donets'k region,
Ianukovych had unabashedly called for making Russian the second state language
of Ukraine, for allowing the populace to hold Russian and Ukrainian dual citizenship, and for making positive relations with Russia a national priority. Throughout the electoral campaign, the Ianukovych forces branded their rival Iushchenko
(who, incidentally, was nearly fatally poisoned under suspicious circumstances) as
an anti-Russian extremist and a puppet of America. The Iushchenko camp was not
about to concede defeat, however, and together with an even more radical reformer, Iuliia Tymoshenko, launched what came to be called the Orange coalition.

The Orange forces led by Iushchenko presented themselves as the vanguard
of revolutionary change that would allegedly cleanse Ukraine of corruption, government inefficiency, and dependence on Russia, and would adopt wide-ranging
economic reforms, implement a Ukrainian cultural revival, and seek the country's early entry into NATO and the European Union. The Orange leaders called
on their supporters to take to the streets and conduct massive protests until the
fraudulent second-round election results were overturned. No one, least of all the
Orange coalition leadership, anticipated the response. Whereas previous political
rallies had attracted at most 150,000 people, in December 2004 no less than 20
percent of the entire population of Ukraine – an estimated 7 million people – took
to the streets and squares of countless towns and cities throughout the country.
Kiev and its large central Independence Square (Ukrainian: *Maidan Nezalezhnosti*,
popularly known as simply the Maidan), became the focal point of the nation-wide
protests, where for seventeen consecutive days in the midst of freezing temperatures and snowfall approximately 2.3 million people (over a half of whom arrived
in the capital from all parts of the country) held vigil until their demand to annul
the second-round presidential elections was fulfilled.

The enormity of the lengthy protests required concerted logistical support,
which came from government and non-governmental agencies in the United
States and the European Union, from the office of the sympathetic mayor of Kiev,
and from thousands of the capital's ordinary citizens who provided free food for

WAS THERE ANYTHING REVOLUTIONARY ABOUT THE ORANGE REVOLUTION?

In the euphoric years immediately following the collapse in 1989 of Communist rule in central Europe, the region's most respected leader worldwide, the former dissident and subsequently president of Czechoslovakia, Václav Havel, warned that the greatest challenge facing his countrymen and women was not the former political system but the "enemy within." In other words, citizens in the post-Communist sphere must learn to overcome their internal fears and the civic mistrust that had been embedded in their souls by decades of totalitarian rule. Perhaps only an outside observer – in this case, a professor from St Louis in the mid-western heartland of the United States and an eyewitness to the Orange Revolution – would be able to decipher the profound transformation that took place in the national psyche of Ukraine's citizens as a result of the events of late 2004.

A million Ukrainians flocked to Kyiv's Independence Square [the Maidan] to demand that a new and fair election be held to overturn the results of an earlier one, which a corrupt and thuggish government had fixed. Although facing constant danger, tens of thousands of peaceful protesters camped out on the freezing Maidan for weeks at a time, until, after a new vote on December 26, justice was finally done. Once a man for whom they voted was finally installed in office they went home, leaving neither gum wrapper nor cigarette butt behind. Ordinary people had accomplished an extraordinary thing. It is called the Orange Revolution.

A year later, corruption in Ukraine was as bad as ever, the economy had taken a nosedive, political murders and assassinations ... remained unsolved and, worst of all, the coalition swept into office by the event on the Maidan had collapsed amidst bitterness, recrimination, and accusations. An upset public complained that the Orange Revolution had changed nothing.

Many Ukrainians have sadly, though understandably, misunderstood the meaning of the Maiden: a fantastic event at a precious moment in history, it must not be forgotten.

The Maidan is, of course, a place, but [it is] also a living entity: a symbol, a message to the world, a source of hope, a warning, and the birth act of a modern democracy.

The events of the Maidan put on the map a corner of Europe the rest of the world would prefer to forget. It is, after all, the ground zero of human suffering in the twentieth century – the scenes of the greatest battles in both world wars, the killing grounds of the Bolshevik Revolution, the bone fields of the Holodomor [the 1933 Great Famine], and the bone heaps of the Holocaust. Ukraine has also been divided, oppressed, disrupted, and systematically stripped of identity. ...

The quiet dignity of those on the Maidan – men and women prepared to die for political principles too often taken for granted elsewhere – opened a window of light into a nation whose history is one of darkness. Their example shames those who would turn their backs to Ukraine, which now has for the first time in its history a lifeline to the rest of the world. A path has opened into a realm of light. The Maiden is therefore a source of hope in a land which has known little of it. ...

The example of the Maidan, in other words, delivers the universal message that even in a quasi-dictatorship, sovereign power resides in the people. It is a statement of honor and dignity, for which the West should be grateful.

The Maidan is also, as put eloquently by Tatiana Korobova, 'about a people, who have discovered humanity in themselves'. ... The extraordinary event on Independence Square ... can also mark the birth of a new modern democracy. Its memory and legacies must be defended. That is the ultimate meaning of the Maidan ... and the Orange Revolution.

SOURCE: John Gillingham, "The Meaning of Maidan," *Harvard Ukrainian Research Institute News*, Spring Issue (Cambridge, Mass. 2006), pp. 1 and 7.

the millions of unexpected guests. Eventually, Ianukovych supporters from eastern Ukraine also arrived in Kiev, but they made up only about 5 percent of the total. In the end, the overwhelming majority of the protestors, who were pro-Orange supporters primarily (77 percent) from central and western (Galicia) Ukraine, achieved their goal. Ukraine's Supreme Court declared invalid the election that had given Ianukovych a majority and called for another run-off election to take place. Its results brought a 52 percent victory for Viktor Iushchenko, who was inaugurated the third president of Ukraine in January 2005. Most important for the functioning of a democratic society was the peaceful transition of political power, in which President Kuchma stepped down and his hand-picked successor Ianukovych remained active in the parliamentary opposition.

The hopes and expectations of the Orange Revolution were not, however, to be realized. Not only were the electoral campaign promises overly optimist, but the coalition's main leaders – Iushchenko and the increasingly popular Tymoshenko – proved themselves unable to work together. While it is true that the populace soon became disillusioned with the political process, it is equally true that a profound and longer-lasting change had occurred among Ukraine's citizenry. For the first time in human memory it was possible for Ukraine's people to take a stand and, through their collective but spontaneous actions in the form of peaceful protests, to reverse the political path that in 2004 the country's authoritarian leaders had tried to impose on them. In the end, Ukraine experienced no radical change as a result of the Orange Revolution, and its future political course is likely to vary between three approaches to governing the state as symbolized by the moderate reformer Viktor Iushchenko, the radical reformer Iuliia Tymoshenko, and the conservative Viktor Ianukovych. Hence, it might be best to remember the year 2004 not as one that witnessed a *revolution*, but rather another – albeit dramatic – phase in Ukraine's ongoing *evolution* from Soviet-style authoritarian rule to a parliamentary and free-market European-style democracy that with regard to political practice reminds one more of Italy than of post-Communist Russia.

Economic developments

The biggest challenge facing Ukraine, like all countries in the post- Communist world, was how to adopt its economy from the centralized command system to market-driven capitalism. An integral aspect of that change was to adopt and integrate Ukraine's economy with rules and patterns of the global economy, still determined largely by the policies of the European Union and the United States. Since independence, Ukraine's economic development has gone through two basic phases. For nearly a decade, until the end of 1999, the country was on the verge of economic collapse; by contrast, since the year 2000, the Ukrainian economy has not only recovered but has made some remarkable advances.

The decade of decline, which coincided with the presidencies of Leonid Kravchuk and the first term of Leonid Kuchma, was most dramatically revealed in Ukraine's Gross National Product (GNP), which between 1990 and 1997 recorded a decrease of 12.6 percent, placing Ukraine nearly at the bottom (158 out of 162) of all countries worldwide. As for Ukraine's Gross Domestic Product (GDP), in 1999 it stood at only half of what it was in 1989, the last relatively stable year during Soviet times. Small businesses in particular faced stagnation because of excessive taxes that at times reached 90 percent. The decline in productivity was accompanied by hyper-inflation which was on average over 2,600 percent between the years 1991 and 1995, reaching a staggering 10,156 percent in 1993.[2]

Inflation had a devastating impact on persons with fixed income and retirees, whose monthly salaries or pensions in the post-Communist transitional period were hardly enough to survive for one week. Even a week's survival assumed, at very the least, that the government would pay its employees and pensioners. In fact, it was quite common in the 1990s for teachers and other government sector employees not to receive any salary at all for several months until the authorities found enough funds to pay them. Desperate to survive, pensioners in particular were reduced to a form of begging by taking to the streets to sell their possessions or whatever other goods they could find in an effort to make some money. Middle-aged and younger people sought another solution – seasonal or permanent emigration. By the outset of the twenty-first century, an estimated 4.5 million Ukrainians had sought survival by going abroad to work for several months of each year or even longer. Nearly 2 million work at various jobs (mostly physical labor) in Russia, with the remainder in Italy, the United States, Poland, Spain, and other countries of the European Union.

In 1994, Leonid Kuchma came to the presidency on a platform promising reform. In the economic sphere this meant dismantling government-owned factories and cooperative farms and turning them over to private ownership. In theory, privatization could have improved the economic lot of large segments of the population; in practice, it turned out to be *prykhvatyzatsiia*, that is, privatization by seizure, which enriched only a few. Former Communist factory managers and other officials were quick to take advantage of the privatization laws and to acquire control over much of the large-scale industrial sector based in south-central and eastern Ukraine. The country's most wealthy capitalists came to be known as oligarchs, many of whom amassed incredible wealth based especially on metallurgy, energy resources, and finance. By 2008, Ukraine had no less than twenty-three billionaires, ten of whom were billionaires several times over. In many ways, post-Communist Ukraine at the end of the twentieth century came to resemble the United States a century before, when laissez-faire capitalism allowed "robber barons" to dominate the American economy.

Whereas Kuchma himself may not have directly benefited from privatization, others around him certainly did; these included his friends, some family members, and in particular his former Soviet managerial colleagues interconnected with oligarchic "clans" based in Kiev, Dnipropetrovs'k, and Donets'k. Ukraine's capitalists depended on a president like Kuchma, who would provide a favorable political environment for their economic ventures. In turn, the president depended on financial and electoral support from the oligarchs in order to be reelected and stay in power. This cozy relationship between Kuchma and the oligarchs created a situation which one North American analyst has dubbed the "blackmail state."[3] In other words, should any oligarch waver in his or her loyalty to the president, the likehood of charges and arrest for economic crimes would follow.

Actually, "oligarchic capitalism" under Kuchma and his successors did pay off. Since the year 2000 Ukraine's economy has grown at a very fast rate. Inflation has dropped remarkably and, while high, is relatively stable, between 10 and 16 percent annually. By way of comparison, between 2000 and 2004 Ukraine's Gross Domestic Product (GDP) rose on average 8.4 percent, while the GDP of the United States rose only 2.7 percent and those of the four largest economies in the European Union (France, Germany, Italy, the United Kingdom) only 1.7 percent.[4] The costs of Ukraine's economic growth have been high, however. In effect, the economic status of the vast majority of the populace has improved only marginally, while the continuing close ties between the government and oligarchs has fostered widespread corruption. Moreover, such conditions, together with the reality of complicated government regulations and problems with property law have tended to discourage foreign investment. It was discontent with "oligarchic capitalism" and political corruption that galvanized supporters of the Orange Revolution in late 2004. Nevertheless, despite the promises of the reformers, the positive and negative aspects of Ukraine's socioeconomic life had not yet changed very much.

Civic and cultural developments

A sovereign independent state has traditionally been the goal of most, if not all, national movements. With the achievement of Ukrainian independence in 1991, the question inevitably arose as to whether this new political entity should encompass a population whose common national identity is based on civic or on ethnic principles. A civic national identity is one based on association with the state, which is understood to represent a community of people who are linked by common citizenship, who live in a specific territory, and who are aware of being subject to a common body of laws and political institutions. An ethnic national identity is one in which the state is assumed to be characterized primarily by its association with a particular ethnicity or nationality defined by its language, historical traditions, and cultural values. What therefore, is a Ukrainian: someone who is of that particular ethnicity; or someone who is a citizen of Ukraine regardless of ethnic background or nationality?

It was during the first-term presidency of Leonid Kuchma that these questions were addressed. The constitution adopted in 1996 basically supports the concept of a civic national identity, since it defines "the Ukrainian people" as "citizens of Ukraine of all nationalities."[5] In this sense the titular and numerically dominant nationality, ethnic Ukrainians, are not given any special privileges with regard to their legal status among Ukraine's citizenry. On the other hand, in a multinational state, in which in 2001 ethnic Ukrainians formed 78 percent of the population – followed by Russians at 17 percent, with the remaining 5 percent divided among nearly 100 nationalities – some decision had to be made about issues such as the language of the state and its cultural values and aspirations. Here, the constitution clearly came out on the side of the titular and numerically dominant nationality. Ukrainian was declared the state's sole official language, whose "comprehensive development" was to be promoted "in all spheres of social life"; meanwhile, "the languages of national minorities," the most important of which was Russian (the mother tongue of 38 percent of Ukraine's inhabitants in 2001), were to be guaranteed "free development."[6] The classification of Russian as a minority language and the enhanced status given to Ukrainian was not accepted easily by Russian speakers, whether of Russian or Ukrainian ethnicity, and there have been and continue to be calls by political forces in eastern and southern Ukraine (in particular the Party of Regions) to make Russian the country's second state language.

Aside from language, the constitution calls on "the state to promote the consolidation and development of the Ukrainian nation, and of its historical consciousness, traditions, and culture."[7] The constitutional phrase, "Ukrainian nation" (*ukraïns'kyi narod*), effectively refers to ethnic Ukrainians. For example, the educational curriculum for teaching history continues, as in the Soviet Union, to be standardized throughout Ukraine. Now, however, the Soviet-Marxist version has been replaced by the Ukrainian national schema formulated by Mykhailo Hrushevs'kyi at the very beginning of the twentieth century (see chapter 2). Kievan Rus' is presented as a medieval proto-Ukrainian state and great emphasis is given to the Cossack state from Khmel'nyts'kyi to Mazepa, which is understood to have struggled for independence from – and not unification with – Muscovy/Russia. As for the Soviet era, it is no longer depicted as a period of unending progress and socioeconomic success, but rather as one of widespread human suffering, artificial famine, and repression of the ethnic Ukrainian national idea.

In order to underscore the Ukrainian national historiographic viewpoint among the public-at-large, the government has introduced several measures of long-lasting impact. In 1996, it adopted the *hryvnia* (the name used in Kievan Rus' and the post-World War I Ukrainian National Republic) as the state's currency on which it placed the portraits of the most famous ethnic Ukrainian national cultural figures (I. Franko, M. Hrushevs'kyi, B. Khmel'nyts'kyi, I. Mazepa, T. Shevchenko, Lesia Ukraïnka, H. Skovoroda) as well as grand princes of Kievan Rus' (Volodymyr "the Great," Iaroslav "the Wise"). In 2003, the government adopted as the national anthem the lyrics, in slightly modified form, of the nineteenth-century "nationalist anthem" by Pavlo Chubyns'kyi, whose verses recall a Ukraine stretching from the San to the Don Rivers. Whereas in Soviet times it was obligatory to have at least one statue of Lenin in every town and city (many of which still remain, especially in eastern and southern Ukraine), the trend in independent Ukraine is to make the nineteenth-century Ukrainian bard, Taras Shevchenko, the obligatory icon in Ukraine's public spaces. Of particular symbolic importance are the monuments raised in the late 1990s in Kiev to the Ukrainian republic's first president Mykhailo Hrushevs'kyi and to the medieval Kievan ruler Iaroslav the Wise, and in L'viv to Galicia's medieval King Danylo. Enhancing historical memory through public statuary has not occurred without controversy, such as that which surrounded the statue in L'viv to the World War II Ukrainian underground leader Stepan Bandera (opposed by latent Soviet patriots, especially from the east of Ukraine), or the monuments in Odessa and Sevastopol' to Empress Catherine II (opposed by Ukrainian patriots who adamantly reject the epithet commonly given to her – "the Great").

The constitutional call for affirmative action on behalf of the Ukrainian language has been most evident in the educational system. During the Soviet era, especially since the 1930s, the Russian language enjoyed a privileged position in schools as either the dominant language of instruction throughout the country, or the exclusive language of instruction in eastern and southern Ukraine. Since 1991, government policy has attempted to reverse the Russian/Ukrainian language-of-instruction ratio. As the following table reveals, there has been a marked increase in the percentage of Ukrainian-language schools, in particular at the preschool and university levels. Over all, the Ukrainian-Russian ratio in 1991 was 1 to 1; by 2005 it stood at 3 to 1 in favor of Ukrainian.

Aggregate statistics for the country as a whole do not, however, reveal the disparities in language use among the country's regions and the status of the language outside the classroom. Whereas Ukrainian as a language of instruction has made remarkable progress, there are still parts of the country where it remains a "minority" language in the school system, in particular in the southern and eastern oblasts of Odessa (47 percent), Zaporizhzhia (45 percent), Luhans'k (17 percent),

TABLE 53.1
Language of instruction in Ukraine's schools, 1991–2008[8]

School year	Pre-schools		Primary and secondary		Higher	
	Ukrainian	Russian	Ukrainian	Russian	Ukrainian	Russian
1991–1992	51%	47%	49%	50%	37%	63%
1998–1999	76%	22%	70%	29%	69%	31%
2006–2007	85%	15%	79%	20%	85%	15%

Donets'k (14 percent), and the Autonomous Republic of Crimea (0.8 percent). Outside the classroom there has occurred what may be characterized as a psychological sea-change in public attitudes and perceptions. Still, in late Soviet times, the Ukrainian language was considered basically a peasant or even uncouth form of speech, which was inappropriate for serious discourse. Consequently, Russian (which often took the form of a bastardized mixture of Russian and Ukrainian known as *surzhyk)* was expected to be used as the "normal," "civilized" mode of communication, in particular in urbanized areas throughout Ukraine. Since independence, however, Ukrainian has gradually achieved a level of respect as the language of state, parliamentary discourse, and education, and in general it is no longer frowned upon in the public space, even by those cannot speak it properly or not at all.

Nonetheless, the government's promotion of Ukrainian still faces enormous challenges. The mass media, in particular, is dominated by Russian, whether it be the cinema (including DVDs), pop music (radio and CDs), or the Internet. The authorities have been somewhat more successful in promoting Ukrainian-language programming on state-owned television, although they can do little counteract easy access to Russian-language channels from neighboring Russia. The situation in the print media – still popular in Ukraine – also remains problematic. In fact, the proportion of newspapers printed in the Ukrainian language actually decreased between 1990 and 2000, from 68 percent to 35 percent, while the proportion of Ukrainian-language magazines declined even more so, from 90 to 12 percent during the same decade. The slack is taken up by a flood of Russian-language magazines on newsstands. Despite government efforts to assist Ukraine's publishing industry, by the outset of the twenty-first century a mere 10 percent of books available in Ukraine's stores were in the Ukrainian language. Ukrainian-language publishers simply cannot compete with Russia's vast publishing industry which, thanks to that to country's liberal tax laws on book production and export, continues to flood and dominate Ukraine's book market. All of these factors both reflect and contribute to the reality that a decade after Ukraine's independence (2001) more than half of country's inhabitants either use Russian (37 percent), or Russian and Ukrainian (26 percent) as their main "language of communication."[9] In other words, Russian remains the medium in which the majority of Ukraine's inhabitants most easily converse or speak most often, what some analysts have called their "language of convenience."

Religion

Despite its best efforts, the Soviet regime was unable to remove religion from Ukrainian society. In independent Ukraine religion has experienced a marked revival, in part because of a genuine spiritual transformation, and in part because religion acquired "prestige" for having been restricted or banned by the Communists. The Ukrainian government, moreover, has given its imprimatur and has welcomed the participation of religious institutions, especially the country's traditional Eastern-rite Christian churches, in the process of reawakening and restoration of

TABLE 53.2
Religions in Ukraine, ca. 2000[10]

Religious body	Parishes/ Communities	Churches/ Synagogues/ Mosques	Clerics
Ukrainian Orthodox – Moscow Patriarchate	7,996	6,590	6,568
Protestant*	4,030	–	–
Ukrainian Greek Catholic	3,212	2,877	2,161
Ukrainian Orthodox – Kiev Patriarchate	2,187	1,491	1,743
Ukrainian Autocephalous Orthodox	1,024	744	543
Roman Catholic	751	677	401
Islamic	281	112	273
Jewish	102	53	54
Other Christians**	1,237	–	–
Other***	74	–	–

*The Protestants are divided into several distinct orientations for which we only have data on the number of their communities: Union of Baptists (1,781); other Baptists (207); Pentecostals (1,313); Church of Full Gospel (191); other charismatics (137); Reformed Calvinists (100); Lutherans (45); other Protestants (256).
**These include communities of Seventh-Day Adventists (676); Jehovah Witnesses (514); and Mormons (47).
***These include communities of the neo-pagan *runvira* movement (42) and Krishnaites (32).

Ukrainian cultural values. Whereas Roman Catholicism (largely among Ukraine's Poles), Judaism (among Jews), Islam (among Crimean Tatars), and various Protestant sects (especially among ethnic Ukrainians and Russians) have all prospered under independent Ukraine's constitutional guarantees protecting freedom of religion, it is the various Eastern-rite Christian churches that remain the dominant religions of the country.

The biggest changes have perhaps occurred in the status of the Ukrainian Greek Catholic Church. Banned by the Soviet Union for close to four decades (see chapters 49 and 50), this church has once again became the dominant religion in its traditional territorial base, historic eastern Galicia, that is, western Ukraine's oblasts of L'viv, Ternopil', and Ivano-Frankivs'k. Of great symbolic importance has been the return to Ukraine in the early 1990s of the Greek Catholic hierarchy headed by then Metropolitan-Archbishop Myroslav Liubachivs'kyi, who since the late 1940s had been based in "temporary" exile in Rome. L'viv in western Ukraine again became the seat of the Greek Catholic Church in Ukraine, although for various reasons the Eparchy of Mukachevo (which coincides with the Transcarpathian oblast) remained apart and to this day is under the direct jurisdiction of the Holy See in Rome.

The restored Greek Catholic Church witnessed enormous growth in the 1990s, as a majority of parishes that had been forcibly made Orthodox during the Soviet period returned to the fold of Greek Catholicism. Monastic life was restored and religious instruction was again possible in public schools. In order to train a new generation of priests, the L'viv Theological Academy was reopened. Headed by distinguished church scholars from the ethnic Ukrainian diaspora in North America, in 2006 the academy was transformed into the Ukrainian Catholic University. Throughout the twentieth century the Greek Catholic Church had been closely associated with the Ukrainian national movement and, therefore, the restored institution remains an avid supporter of Ukrainian language use in its liturgies, sermons, publications, and educational institutions.

The restoration of the Greek Catholic Church that began in the very last years of Soviet rule has since then been fraught with challenges. Foremost among them is the question of church property, all of which technically was owned (expropriated) by the former Soviet state, but "on loan" to the Russian Orthodox Church. The Greek Catholics claimed their right to property restitution based on ownership in pre-Soviet times, and they expected the independent and democratic Ukrainian state to back their demands. In most cases the Greek Catholics have succeeded in securing the return of their former churches and monasteries, but not without opposition form the local Orthodox hierarchy and faithful, regardless of jurisdictional affiliation.

The restored and reinvigorated status of the Greek Catholic Church in Ukraine has also caused problems for Catholic-Orthodox ecumenical relations. The Moscow Patriarchate of the Russian Orthodox Church continues its historical rejection of the Greek Catholic Church as an uncanonical body, and therefore its leaders refuse to meet with the Roman Catholic representatives of the Vatican at any gathering in which the Greek Catholics may be present. Greek Catholic-Orthodox relations in Ukraine remained tense, especially after the decision in 2006 to move the metropolitan's seat from L'viv to Kiev. The Greek Catholic argument is that, as a "national church," its seat should be in the state's capital city; the Russian Orthodox Church – Moscow Patriarchate views the move as yet another example of the aggressive eastward proselytization of the Roman Catholic Church through its Greek Catholic minions.

Orthodoxy remains the largest religious orientation in Ukraine in terms of the number of adherents. The Orthodox are divided, however, among at least three jurisdictions, each with its own hierarchy and institutional structure. The divisions often have as much do with personality conflicts among ambitious leaders as they do with ideological matters, in particular the question of the church's attitude toward Ukraine as a state entity and distinct culture. At the same time, theological and liturgical differences between the various Orthodox jurisdictions are nonexistent. Consequently, the ordinary church-goer has no difficulty attending liturgy in any of the Orthodox churches, since from his or her perspective all of them are "ours" (*nashi pravoslavni*).

The largest and still the most influential of all religious bodies in Ukraine is the Ukrainian Orthodox Church jurisdictionally linked to the Moscow Patriarchate. In Soviet times the Moscow Patriarchal parishes in Ukraine were under the authority of an exarch, in the person of the metropolitan of Kiev. In an effort to adjust to changing political conditions, the Moscow Patriarchate enhanced the status of its Ukrainian Exarchate by renaming it in 1990 the Ukrainian Orthodox Church. The renamed body, which continued to be headed by the incumbent of what was now called the Metropolitan of Kiev and All Ukraine, at the time Filaret (Denysenko), was expected to obtain a greater degree of autonomy (ecclesiastic self-governance) or even autocephaly (jurisdictional independence). In fact, the nomenclature change proved to be largely cosmetic.

A very prominent feature of the Ukrainian Orthodox Church – Moscow Patriarchate remains its Russianness. Although Church Slavonic is the language of the liturgy, the sermons are usually in Russian and the entire religious culture of the Moscow Patriarchal parishes is Russian. Church publications are primarily in Russian; the saints who are venerated – including all those from the days of Kievan Rus' – are hailed as "Russians"; St Vladimir (Volodymyr the Great) is continually depicted as the grand prince who brought Christianity to Russia; and in recent years a veritable cult has grown up around the last tsar of Russia Nicholas II and his family, murdered by the Bolsheviks in 1918. The "Russian" orientation of the Moscow Patriarchal Ukrainian Orthodox Church is associated with the territorial sphere of the Commonwealth of Independent States (the putative successor of the Soviet Union and ultimately the imperial Russian Empire), and it is often accompanied by a dismissive attitude toward Ukraine and the Ukrainian language as inappropriate for serious and sacred church matters.

Opposition to the continued subordination of the Ukrainian Orthodox Church to the Moscow Patriarchate led to friction and the dismissal (and eventually to excommunication and an anathema) of its head Metropolitan, Filaret. In response, he helped spearhead the establishment in June 1992 of a new body called the Ukrainian Orthodox Church – Kiev Patriarchate. In an effort to distinguish itself from Ukraine's Moscow Patriarchal jurisdiction, the Kiev Patriarchate has prided itself on being a Ukrainian religious body. It uses the Ukrainian language alongside Church Slavonic in services and publications, and its head carries the title "Patriarch of Kiev and All Rus'-Ukraine," thereby claiming the inheritance of Orthodoxy in Ukraine since medieval Kievan Rus'. The two Orthodox jurisdictions, the Moscow Patriarchate and Kiev Patriarchate, immediately began a bitter struggle for control of individual parish churches, cathedrals, and monasteries throughout Ukraine, in particular the most venerated Orthodox holy places such as the Caves Monastery and St Sophia Cathedral in Kiev.

Yet a third jurisdiction is that of the Ukrainian Autocephalous Orthodox Church, the institution which was banned by the Soviet regime in 1930 but that survived in exile in the United States. In July 1992, the church's long-time head and self-styled patriarch, Mstyslav (Skrypnyk), returned to Ukraine. Initially, his parishes and hierarchy were part of the recently established Ukrainian Orthodox Church – Kiev Patriarchate. The unity between those two jurisdictions quickly broke down, however, and after the death of Mstyslav in 1993 the Ukrainian Autocephalous Orthodox Church elected a successor as patriarch.

Both before and after the return to Kiev of its exiled hierarchy, the Autocephalous Orthodox Church found its greatest strength (nearly 80 percent of its parishes) not in traditionally Orthodox central and eastern Ukraine, but rather in Galicia, the historic stronghold of Greek Catholicism. It is the deeply Ukrainian cultural nature of the Autocephalous Orthodox Church that has more likely attracted those Galician Ukrainians who, after four decades of being Orthodox under Soviet rule, were reluctant to become Greek Catholic but still wanted to be in a church that was Ukrainian in language and culture. Like the Ukrainian Orthodox Church – Kiev Patriarchate, the Ukrainian Autocephalous Orthodox Church remains uncanonical; that is, it is not yet recognized as part of the universal Orthodox community headed by the "first among equals," the ecumenical patriarch of Constantinople.

Like the governments of most other states that came into being since the early nineteenth century in the Balkan region and eastern Europe, Ukraine's political leaders have favored the idea of having for the country its own national Orthodox church. Initially, preference to one or another of the rival jurisdictions varied: President Kravchuk favored the Kiev Patriarchate, President Kuchma initially the Moscow Patriarchate. But since the adoption of Ukraine's constitution in 1996, which guarantees the separation of church and state, the government has supported the idea to create a single jurisdictionally independent church that would unite all the Orthodox faithful. Nevertheless, the country's three Orthodox churches – Moscow Patriarchate, Kiev Patriarchate, and Autocephalous – continue to remain divided over questions of jurisdictional authority, property, and canonical status.

All three Orthodox jurisdictions, and to a lesser degree the Greek Catholics, do seem to be in agreement, however, about one thing – what they consider the threat of Protestant "sects." Protestantism has existed in Ukraine since the sixteenth-century Reformation, although it soon died out. It was revived in the nineteenth century, whether in the form of the Baptist Church beginning in the 1860s, or even earlier in the form of various Protestant orientations associated with specific nationalities; for example, Lutheranism among ethnic Germans, Anabaptism among the Mennonites, or Reformed Calvinism among the Magyars in Transcarpathia. Since independence several other Christian bodies have expanded their influence in Ukraine, in particular Protestant Evangelicals (Pentecostals), Seventh-Day Adventists, and Jehovah Witnesses. Most of these groups are supported by evangelical activists in western Europe and, in particular, the United States. One aspect of such intervention proved to be particularly attractive during the economically difficult decade of the 1990s. These churches, or more precisely church communities, provided desperately needed social services (in particular soup kitchens, clothing, etc.) which clearly were a motivating factor in attracting adherents. It is interesting to note that virtually all the literature and services of these proselytizing evangelical groups is published and conducted in Russian.

National and ethnic diversity

Ukraine remains a multinational land, although the status and numerical size of its various peoples has changed since the country attained its independence in 1991. The overall size of the population has changed as well. As in many other

TABLE 53.3
Demographic change among the largest nationalities in Ukraine, 1989 and 2001[11]

Nationality	Number		Percentage of the total population		Percentage of absolute gain/loss
	1989	2001	1989	2001	
Ukrainians	37,419,000	37,542,000	72.7	77.8	+0.3
Russians	11,356,000	8,334,000	22.1	17.3	−26.6
Belarusans	440,000	276,000	0.8	0.6	−37.3
Moldovans	324,000	259,000	0.6	0.5	−20.1
Crimean Tatars	44,000	248,000	0.0	0.5	+ 463.6
Bulgarians	234,000	205,000	0.5	0.4	−12.4
Magyars/Hungarians	163,000	157,000	0.3	0.3	−3.7
Romanians	135,000	151,000	0.2	0.3	+11.9
Poles	219,000	144,000	0.4	0.3	−34.2
Jews	486,000	104,000	0.9	0.2	−78.7
Armenians	54,000	100,000	0.1	0.2	+85.1

former Communist-ruled states in central and eastern Europe, a declining birth rate has led to the stagnation or even decline in population. In the case of Ukraine the decline has been as high as 3 million, from 51.4 million inhabitants in 1989 to 48.4 million in 2001, and down even further to 46.2 million in 2008. Aside from a low birth rate, the other factor contributing to population decline is emigration. There could be as many as 7 million people who since independence have left Ukraine on a temporary or permanent basis in search of employment and a better life in Russia, the European Union, and North America.

With regard to the multinational composition of Ukraine's population, during the first decades of independence the general trend has been toward a decrease in the size of the country's numerically largest nationalities (see table 53.3).

The most dramatic decreases have occurred among Russians and Jews. The 26.6 percent decrease in Russians between the 1989 and 2001 censuses can be attributed to various factors, the most important of which are: (1) a change in identity of many citizens – often Russian-language speakers whose parents might be of mixed national background – from a Russian to a Ukrainian national identity; and (2) emigration, whether to neighboring Russia or to the European Union and North America. The decline in the number of Jews is due primarily to emigration largely to Israel and North America. At the same time the number of ethnic Ukrainians remained static, with losses because of birth rate and emigration being counterbalanced with the addition of a large number of former "Russians" who now declared themselves to be ethnic Ukrainians.

There are a few exceptions to the general trend of numerical decline, as among Armenians and Romanians. The increase among the latter is in part the result of a number of Moldovans now claiming Romanian national identity. But the most dramatic demographic change has occurred among the Crimean Tatars, who between 1989 and 2001 experienced a stunning 463 percent increase from 44,000 to

248,000. This is the result of the return of Crimean Tatars (forcibly expelled in May 1944), mostly from Uzbekistan, to their ancestral Crimean homeland, where they now comprise about 12 percent of population. Whereas return migration has reached its peak, the relatively higher-than-national birth rate among Crimean Tatars assures that their numbers are likely to increase in the future.

Ukraine's treatment of its various nationalities has been one of the more positive aspects of social development since independence. There have been incidents of violence against Russians, Jews, and ethnic Ukrainians, but these have, for the most part, been a few in number and isolated. The only exception is the Crimea, where clashes have occurred frequently between returning Crimean Tatars and East Slavic (especially Russian) inhabitants who fear they may lose their property and social status because of the demands of the returnees. Protests and at times harsh rhetoric, however, not physical clashes or death, have characterized interethnic relations in the Crimean Autonomous Republic.

If anything, the policies of Ukraine's various governments have worked in favor of Crimean Tatar interests. Kiev has made clear its opposition to those elements in Crimea's Autonomous Republic who have favored independence or unity with Russia. In any case, the Crimean Tatars were opposed to any kind of autonomous political entity that did not recognize Crimean Tatars as the peninsula's titular nationality. In order to pursue their own political agenda, they have created their own assembly, the Milli Meclis (People's Parliament), headed by the legendary Soviet dissident and long-time proponent of the Crimean Tatar return to the homeland, Mustafa Dzhemilev, who since 1998 has also been a deputy in the national parliament (Verkhovna Rada) in Kiev. Crimean Tatar discontent continues to be directed against Russians in the autonomous republic's administration, who are blamed for the lack of schools teaching the Crimean Tatar language, for the absence of guaranteed representation in the autonomous government and parliament, and for the ongoing difficulties in acquiring land lost during the 1944 deportation.

Whereas the central Ukrainian government is unable to provide any serious political or financial solutions to these problems, it does not hinder assistance that may come from local, private, or external sources. Crimean Tatars have received assistance from NGOs based in Europe and North America. In particular, the government of Turkey (where there is still a large Crimean Tatar diaspora) has been generous in supplying funds to build schools with Crimean Tatar as the language of instruction and to restore architectural monuments of historical significance. Among the latter are several mosques which have been reopened as part of a revival of the Islamic faith. Whereas the majority of Crimean Tatars maintain a distinction between their religion (a private matter) and their functioning in a secular society, there is a small percentage of the group – especially among young people – who have became enamored with Islamic fundamentalism. Their presence, made visible by wearing traditional dress, has prompted many local Russians to believe that the aim of all Crimean Tatars is to take back their land (that is, dispossess Russians) and to create an independent Islamic state. For the moment, the extremists on either side do not represent the norm in the Autonomous Republic of Crimea.

Table 53.4
Language of instruction in elementary and secondary schools,
2002–2003[13]

Language	Number of schools	Number of students	Percentage of students
Ukrainian	16,937	3,945,000	60.1
Russian	1,732	804,000	12.6
Romanian	94	25,000	0.3
Hungarian	69	16,500	0.2
Crimean Tatar	13	4,000	0.0
Moldovan	9	4,000	0.0
Polish	4	1,000	0.0
Bilingual	2,242	1,760,000	26.8

Ukraine's constitutional provisions to promote "the development of the ethnic, linguistic, and religious identity of all indigenous peoples and national minorities"[12] has indeed had a positive impact on most groups. The state allows for instruction at the elementary and secondary levels in various languages where a given group predominates, with Russians, Romanians, and Magyars/Hungarians having the largest number of "national minority" schools.

There are also bilingual schools in which one or more languages other than Ukrainian is taught as a subject. The largest number of students enrolled in schools where another language is available are: Russian (1.7 million), Crimean Tatar (32,500), and Bulgarian (13,400). All of the above mentioned groups as well as nineteen others – ranging from Azerbaijanis and Koreans to Uzbeks – each has its own cultural institutions and publications.

Despite their dramatic numerical decline, from 486,000 to 104,000 between 1989 and 2001, Jews in Ukraine have undergone a renaissance. Many urban centers where Jews once lived in high concentrations again have operating synagogues, even if their congregations are small. Like other national minorities, Jews receive financial assistance from abroad, from NGOs like the Joint organization or from wealthy Jewish philanthropists (some of whom are wealthy oligarchs currently living abroad), who are moved by the desire to contribute toward the preservation of the Jewish heritage in the land of their ancestors.

One group that has not fully benefitted from Ukraine's positive policies toward its various peoples are the Carpatho-Rusyns of the far western oblast of Transcarpathia. They officially number 10,000 (census of 2001), but group leaders claim their numbers could be as high as 800,000. The statistical discrepancies are in part the result of the Ukrainian government's refusal to recognize Carpatho-Rusyns as a distinct nationality. Nevertheless, organizations which promote the idea of Carpatho-Rusyn national distinctiveness are allowed to operate legally, and in March 2007 the locally elected regional assembly (Oblasna rada) virtually unanimously adopted a resolution declaring Carpatho-Rusyns to be a distinct nationality.

The identity question in Transcarpathia is complicated by the fact that some Carpatho-Rusyn activists have at various times formed parallel "governments" proclaiming the existence of an autonomous "republic" (1993) and subsequently a "sovereign" (2008) state of Subcarpathian Rus', arguing as precedent the status that the region had within Czechoslovakia before World War II. For their part, the Ukrainian authorities in Kiev may not oppose the existence of a Rusyn identity; they have remained adamant, however, in arguing that the ethnonym *Rusyn* is an older designation for Ukrainian and that the indigenous East Slavs living in Transcarpathia – whether Rusyns, Hutsuls, Boikos, and Lemkos – are only ethnic groups belonging to the Ukrainian nationality. Ukraine's position in this matter is in stark contrast to its European Union neighbors – Slovakia, Poland, Romania, Hungary – all of whom recognize Carpatho-Rusyns as a distinct fourth East Slavic nationality. While the "Rusyn question" has never gained national prominence, it does remain an unresolved issue that periodically is raised in domestic affairs, in Ukraine's foreign relations with its immediate neighbors to the west and with Russia, and by international human rights observers.

Much more problematic is the status and role in Ukrainian society of Russians. With the collapse of the Soviet Union, ethnic Russians outside the borders of the Russian Federation found themselves in an entirely new, and from their standpoint unenviable, position. As a former privileged people – the "most outstanding nation" and "leading force in the Soviet Union," to quote Stalin's 1945 war victory toast – Russians living in post-Soviet successor states such as Ukraine were transformed overnight. They continued to live in what they thought was their own homeland, but in fact they became members of a national minority, or at best part of a "diaspora" in Russia's "near abroad." Particularly galling for many Russians in former Soviet republics, including Ukraine, was that they were expected to learn the local, former "minority" language in order to function fully in the post-Soviet world.

The very concept *Russian* is complex and eludes easy definition in Ukraine. There are, according to the 2001 census, 8.3 million people who identify their nationality as Russian, as well as another 6.2 million persons of other nationalities (mostly ethnic Ukrainians) who indicate that their mother tongue is Russian. The vast majority of persons of Russian nationality reside in eastern and southern Ukraine, with particularly heavy concentrations in the urban heartland of the Dnieper-Donbas industrial triangle (cities like Dnipropetrovs'k, Donets'k, Luhans'k, Kharkiv, and Zaporizhzhia); in the southern Black Sea region cities of Odessa, Kherson, and Mykolaïv; and throughout the Crimea. In these same regions, as well as elsewhere in Ukraine, live over 5 million persons who identify their nationality as Ukrainian but whose native language, or language of convenience, is Russian.

Both ethnic Russians and many Russian-speaking self-identified ethnic Ukrainians embrace the Russian language and culture, and both groups have tended to act in the political sphere in similar ways. They form the background of constituents for the Ianukovych-led Party of Regions and they seem to welcome that leader's statement at a 2004 party congress that "Russia was, is, and will be for us a country tied to us by blood, history, religion, and spiritual values."[14] It is also they who sometimes listen with approval to local politicians who from time to time demand that Ukraine be transformed into a federal state, that an autonomous or an independent republic be formed in the southeast, or that that entire region be annexed to Russia.

Voting patterns and political pronouncements reflecting the above attitudes have prompted commentators within and outside Ukraine to speak of a deep division within the country between the European-oriented, Ukrainian nationalist, and Orange-supporting coalition forces in the western and central part of the country, versus the Eurasian-oriented, Russian-speaking eastern and southern regions. In other words, they emphasize the divide that was most evident in the 2004 presidential election that pitted Viktor Iushchenko and Viktor Ianukovych (ironically both "easterners") against each other. Perhaps too much, however, has been made of this alleged west-east divide. Regional differentiation, after all, is characteristic of many states, and in those that are democratic in orientation it is not uncommon to encounter extremist statements, especially during closely contested elections. Flanders in Belgium, Québec in Canada, and Lombardy in Italy are only a few of the many places like southern and eastern Ukraine in which feelings of alienation from a central government are sometimes expressed by regional activists in terms that seem, on the surface, to call into question the very existence of the larger state in which they live.

Moreover, Ukraine is no newcomer to internal differentiation. Historically, it was divided between a Polish and Habsburg-ruled west versus a Muscovite and Russian-ruled east. If anything, the idea of a unified Ukraine as the political norm has only really taken hold among an increasing percentage of the country's population – and most importantly among young generations – since the dawn of independence in 1991. Even the proverbial west-east divide has shifted, so that the center of the country (formerly part of "the east") is beginning to act politically more like "the west." As time progresses, the children of Russian-speaking Ukrainians are more and more likely to become culturally Ukrainian at the same time that Ukrainian becomes their language of convenience. While such a trend is likely to continue, there are other factors that will contribute to Ukraine's consolidation. Among these are Ukraine's very existence as a state, its integration into the global economy as a distinct national entity, and the recognition and respect accorded it by neighbors in the rest of Europe. Such external realities, together with the conviction of the majority of citizens that they deserve to have their own state, are the firmest guarantees for the future of Ukraine.

Notes

Chapter 1: Ukraine's Geographic and Ethnolinguistic Setting

1 Stephen Rudnytsky, *Ukraine: The Land and Its People* (New York 1918), p. 25.
2 http://www.ukrstat.gov.ua/Perepis/PidsPer.html
3 Data drawn from official statistical yearbooks from the Russian Federation, Moldova, Belarus, Slovakia, Romania, and Poland.
4 Data from ibid.; from statistical yearbooks from Latvia, Estonia, Lithuania; and from V. Kubijovyč et al., "Ukrainians," in *Encyclopedia of Ukraine*, Vol. V, ed. Danylo Husar Struk (Toronto, Buffalo, and London 1993), p. 460.

Chapter 2: Historical Perceptions

1 *Karamzin's Memoir on Ancient and Modern Russia*, translated by Richard Pipes (New York 1996), p. 112.
2 Bernard Lewis, *History Remembered, Recovered, Invented* (Princeton, N.J. 1975), p. 59.
3 From a pastoral letter by Filofei, dated 1524, cited in Vasyl' Hryshko, *Istorychno-pravne pidhruntia Teorïï III Rymu* (Munich 1953), p. 5.
4 S.M. Solov'ev, *Istoriia Rossii s drevnieishikh vremen*, Vol. IV, pt. 1 (St Petersburg 1894), p. 1343.
5 V. Kliuchevskii, *Kurs russkoi istorii*, Vol. II, 2nd ed. (Moscow 1915), p. 58.
6 Dmitrii S. Likhachev, *Reflections on Russia* (Boulder, Colo. 1991), p. 74.
7 From the Ukrainian text reproduced in Georges Luciani, *Le livre de la genèse du peuple ukrainien* (Paris 1956), pp. 124 and 126.
8 Konstantin F. Shteppa, "The 'Lesser Evil' Formula," in Cyril E. Black, ed., *Rewriting Russian History*, 2nd rev. ed. (New York 1962), pp. 105–106.
9 M. Iavors'kyi, *Istoriia Ukraïny v styslomu narysy* (Kharkiv 1928), p. 58.
10 A.M. Pankratov, ed., *Istoriia SSSR*, Vol. I (Moscow 1940), p. 189.
11 Ibid., 2nd ed. (1947) and subsequent editions.

Chapter 3: The Steppe Hinterland and the Black Sea Cities

1 Herodotus, *The History*, translated by George Rawlinson, Great Books of the Western World, Vol. VI (Chicago, London, and Toronto 1952), p. 133.

Chapter 4: The Slavs and the Khazars

1 *The Gothic History of Jordanes*, translated by Charles Christopher Mierow, 2nd ed. (Princeton, N.J. 1915), p. 60.
2 This and other quotations from *The Primary Chronicle: Laurentian Text* are taken from a translation by Horace G. Lunt of Harvard University. Manuscript (in possession of the author), PVL-B, p. 1.

Chapter 5: The Rise of Kievan Rus'

1 *The Primary Chronicle: Laurentian Text*, translated by Horace G. Lunt, manuscript, PVL-B, p. 1.
2 Ibid., PVL-B, p.2.
3 Ibid., PVL-B, p. 3.
4 Ibid., PVL-B, p. 5.
5 Constantine Porphyrogenitus, *De Administrando Imperio*, Vol. II: *Commentary*, by F. Dvornik, R.J.H. Jenkins, B. Lewis et al. (London 1962), p. 23.
6 *The Primary Chronicle*, PVL-B, p. 5.

Chapter 6: Political Consolidation and Disintegration

1 *The Primary Chronicle: Laurentian Text*, translated by Horace G. Lunt, manuscript, PVL-4e, p. 1.
2 Ibid., PVL-9, p. 5.
3 *The Nikonian Chronicle*, Vol. II, translated by Serge A. and Betty Jean Zenkovsky (Princeton, N.J. 1984), p. 216.

Chapter 7: Socioeconomic and Cultural Developments

1 Nikolai K. Gudzy, *History of Early Russian Literature* (New York 1949), p. 146.

Chapter 8: The Mongols and the Transformation of Rus' Political Life

1 René Grousset, *The Empire of the Steppes: A History of Central Asia* (New Brunswick, N.J. 1970), p. 248.
2 From the Novgorodian Chronicle, cited in Serge A. Zenkovsky, *Medieval Russia's Epics, Chronicles, and Tales*, 2nd rev. ed. (New York 1974), p. 196.
3 John Fennell, *The Crisis of Medieval Russia, 1200–1304* (London and New York 1983), p. 97.

Chapter 9: Galicia-Volhynia

1 *The Primary Chronicle: Laurentian Text*, translated by Horace G. Lunt, manuscript, PVL-4a1, p. 7.
2 *The Galician-Volhynian Chronicle: The Hypatian Codex*, pt. 2, translated by George A. Perfecky (Munich 1973), p. 58.

Chapter 10: Lithuania and the Union with Poland

1 Cited in Jaroslaw Pelenski, "The Contest for the 'Kievan Inheritance' in Russian-Ukrainian Relations,'" in Peter J. Potichnyj et al., *Ukraine and Russia in Their Historical Encounter* (Edmonton 1992), p. 7.

2 Cited in Omeljan Pritsak, "Kievan Rus' and Sixteenth–Seventeenth-Century Ukraine," in Ivan L. Rudnytsky, ed., *Rethinking Ukrainian History* (Edmonton 1981), p. 13.

3 Grand Duke Aleksander to his official in Vitsebsk (1495), in *Akty, otnosiashchiesia k istorii Zapadnoi Rossii*, Vol. I: *1340–1506*, ed. I. Grigorovich (St Petersburg 1846), p. 151.

Chapter 13: Reformation, Counter Reformation, and the Union of Brest

1 Cited in Mykhailo Hrushevs'kyi, *Istoriia Ukraïny-Rusy*, Vol. VI (Kiev 1907), p. 525.

2 Cited in Ivan Wlasowsky, *Outline History of the Ukrainian Orthodox Church*, Vol. I (New York and South Bound Brook, N.J. 1974), p. 255.

3 Cited in Russel P. Moroziuk, *Politics of a Church Union* (Chicago 1983), p. 35.

Chapter 14: The Tatars and the Crimean Khanate

1 Alan Fisher, *The Crimean Tatars* (Stanford, Calif. 1978), p. 25.

Chapter 15: The Cossacks and Ukraine

1 Cited in Dmytro Doroshenko, *Narys istoriï Ukraïny*, Vol. I, 2nd ed. (Munich 1966), p. 152.

2 Linda Gordon, *Cossack Rebellions* (Albany, N.Y. 1983), p. 87.

3 Cited in Mykhailo Hrushevs'kyi, *Istoriia Ukraïny-Rusy*, Vol. VII (Kiev 1909), pp. 391–392.

4 Ibid., p. 392.

Chapter 16: Khmel'nyts'kyi and the Uprising of 1648

1 Shaul Stampfer, "What Actually Happened to the Jews of Ukraine in 1648," *Jewish History*, XVII, 2 (Haifa 2003), p. 221.

2 Shmuel Ettinger, "Chmielnicki (Khmelnitski), Bogdan," in *Encyclopedia Judaica*, Vol. V (Jerusalem 1972), p. 481.

3 Cited in Mykhailo Hrushevs'kyi, *Iliustrovana istoriia Ukraïny*, 2nd ed. (Winnipeg [1923]), p. 303.

4 Cited in Mykhailo Hrushevskyi, *History of Ukraine-Rus'*, Vol. VIII (Edmonton and Toronto 2002), p. 535.

Chapter 17: Muscovy and the Agreement of Pereiaslav

1 K.V. Kharlampovich, *Malorossiiskoe vliianie na velikorusskuiu tserkovnuiu zhizn'*, Vol. I (Kazan 1914), p. 29.

2 Cited in Mykhailo Hrushevs'kyi, *Istoriia Ukraïny-Rusy*, Vol. IX, pt. 1 (Kiev 1928), p. 732.

Chapter 20: Mazepa and the Great Northern War

1 Michael T. Florinsky, *Russia: A History and Interpretation*, Vol. I (New York 1947), pp. 339–340.

2 V.A. Diadychenko, "Mazepa, Ivan Stepanovych," in *Radians'ka entsyklopediia istorii Ukraïny*, Vol. III, ed. A.D. Skaba (Kiev 1971), p. 67.

3 Iurii Iu. Kondufor, ed., *Istoriia Ukraïns'koï RSR*, Vol. II (Kiev 1979), p. 332.

4 Nataliia Polons'ka-Vasylenko, *Istoriia Ukraïny*, Vol. II (Munich 1976), p. 76.

Chapter 22: Ukraine's Autonomy and the Russian Empire

1 Cited in Michael T. Florinsky, *Russia: A History and Interpretation*, Vol. I (New York 1947), pp. 340–341n.1.

2 Cited in Zenon E. Kohut, *Russian Centralism and Ukrainian Autonomy* (Cambridge, Mass. 1988), p. 104.

Chapter 27: Socioeconomic Developments in Dnieper Ukraine

1 *Polnoe sobranie zakonov Rossiiskoi imperii*, Vol. XXI, No. 15724, cited in I.O. Hurzhii, ed., *Khrestomatiia z istorii Ukraïns'koï RSR* (Kiev 1970), p. 86.

2 Konstantyn Kononenko, *Ukraine and Russia: A History of the Economic Relations* (Milwaukee 1958), p. 49.

3 A.P. Ogloblin, *Ocherki istorii ukrainskoi fabriki: predkapitalisticheskaia fabrika* (Kiev 1925), p. 88.

4 Ibid., p. 47.

5 Ibid., p. 207.

6 Ibid., p. 89.

Chapter 28: The Peoples of Dnieper Ukraine

1 *Pervaia vseobshchaia perepis' naseleniia Rossiiskoi imperii 1897 goda*, Vols. 8, 13, 16, 32, 33, 41, 46–48 (St Petersburg 1899–1905).

2 Ibid.

3 A.P. Ogloblin, *Ocherki istorii ukrainskoi fabriki: predkapitalisticheskaia fabrika* (Kiev 1925), p. 88.

4 David G. Rempel, "The Mennonite Commonwealth in Russia, 1789–1919," *Mennonite Quarterly Review*, XLVIII, I (Goshen, Ind. 1974), p. 10.

5 Cited in George Vernadsky et al., eds., *A Source Book for Russian History from Early Times to 1917*, Vol. II (New Haven, Conn. 1972), p. 412.

Chapter 29: The Ukrainian National Awakening in Dnieper Ukraine before the 1860s

1 Johann Gottfried Herder, *Briefe zu Beförderung der Humanität*, No. 10, in his *Werke*, Vol. VII (Frankfurt am Main 1991), p. 65.

2 "Journal meiner Reise im Jahr 1769," *Herders sämtliche Werke*, Vol. IV (Berlin 1877), p. 402.

3 Letter to Denys Zubryts'kyi, cited in George S.N. Luckyj, *Between Gogol' and Ševčenko: Polarity in the Literary Ukraine, 1798–1847* (Munich 1971), p. 30.

4 Cited in Olexander Ohloblyn, "The Ethical and Political Principles of 'Istoriya Rusov'," *Annals of the Ukrainian Academy of Arts and Sciences*, II, 4 (New York 1952), p. 393.

5 Ibid., p. 396.

6 Luckyj, *Between Gogol' and Ševčenko*, p. 137.

7 Taras Shevchenko, *Songs Out of Darkness*, translated by Vera Rich (London 1961), p. 28.

8 From the poem "The Plundered Grave" (1843), ibid., p. 21.

9 From the Ukrainian text reproduced in Georges Luciani, *Le livre de la genèse du peuple ukrainien* (Paris 1956), p. 128.

10 Ibid., p. 134.

11 Ibid., p. 142.

12 Cited in Luckyj, *Between Gogol' and Ševčenko*, p. 186.

Chapter 30: The Ukrainian National Movement in Dnieper Ukraine after the Era of Reforms

1 Orest Pelech, "Toward a Historical Sociology of the Ukrainian Ideologues in the Russian Empire of the 1830s and 1840s" (unpublished PhD dissertation, Princeton University 1976), p. 93.

2 From the poem "Klevetnikam Rossii" (To the Slanderers of Russia, 1831), in *Pushkin Threefold* (New York 1972), p. 248.

3 From the archival title of the report as reprinted in Fedir Savchenko, *Zaborona ukraïnstva 1876 r.*, 2nd ed. (Munich 1970), p. 381.

4 Friedrich Engels, *Po und Rhein* (1915), cited in Richard Pipes, *The Formation of the Soviet Union*, 2nd rev. ed. (New York 1968), p. 21.

Chapter 31: The Administrative and Social Structure of Ukrainian Lands in the Austrian Empire before 1848

1 Hippolit Stupnicki, *Galicya pod względem topograficzno-geograficzno-historycznym* (L'viv 1849), p. 16.

Chapter 33: The Revolution of 1848

1 Cited in Kost' Levyts'kyi, *Istoriia politychnoï dumky halyts'kykh ukraïntsiv, 1848–1914*, Vol. 1 (L'viv 1926), p. 21.

2 Cited in C.A. Macartney, *The Habsburg Empire, 1790–1918* (New York 1969), p. 353.

Chapter 34: The Administrative and Socioeconomic Structure of Ukrainian Lands in the Austrian Empire, 1849–1914

1 Ivan L. Rudnytsky, "The Ukrainians in Galicia under Austrian Rule," *Austrian History Yearbook*, III, pt. 2 (Houston 1967), pp. 406–407.

2 Recalculated from census data in Adam Wandruszka and Peter Urbanitsch, eds., *Die Habsburgermonarchie, 1848–1918*, Vol. III: *Die Völker des Reiches* (Vienna 1980), tables 1 and 6.

Chapter 35: The Ukrainian National Movement in Austria-Hungary, 1849–1914

1 Cited in Vasyl' Lev, "Borot'ba za ukraïns'ku literaturnu movu v Halychyni ta kharakter ïï," *Naukovyi zbirnyk Ukraïns'koho naukovoho universytetu*, VII (Munich 1974), p. 73.
2 Ievhen Chykalenko, *Spohady, 1861–1907*, 2nd ed. (New York 1955), p. 336.
3 Kost' Levyts'kyi, *Istoriia politychnoï dumky halyts'kykh ukraïntsiv, 1848–1914*, Vol. II (L'viv 1927), p. 634.
4 Cited in C.A. Macartney, *The Habsburg Empire, 1790–1918* (New York 1969), p. 560.
5 As reported by Ivan A. Sil'vai, "Avtobiografiia" (1898), in his *Izbrannye proizvedeniia* (Bratislava 1957), p. 144.
6 *Mîsiatsoslov na 1909*, ed. Avhustyn Voloshyn (Uzhhorod 1908), p. 34.

Chapter 36: World War I and Western Ukraine

1 Omelian O. Popovych, *Vidrodzhennia Bukovyny* (L'viv 1933), p. 78.

Chapter 37: Revolutions in the Russian Empire

1 Cited in Dmytro Doroshenko, *Istoriia Ukraïny, 1917–1923 rr.*, Vol. I (Uzhhorod 1932), p. 95.
2 From the ultimatum signed by V. Ulianov (Lenin) and L. Trotskii, in ibid., p. 215.
3 *Texts of the Ukraine "Peace"* (Washington, D.C. 1918), p. 141.

Chapter 38: The Period of the Hetmanate

1 Volodymyr Vynnychenko, *Vidrodzhennia natsiia*, Vol. III (Vienna 1920), p. 16.
2 Dmytro Doroshenko, *Istoriia Ukraïny, 1917–1923 rr.*, Vol. II (Uzhhorod 1930), p. 110.

Chapter 39: The Directory, Civil War, and the Bolsheviks

1 Richard Pipes, *The Formation of the Soviet Union*, 2nd rev. ed. (New York 1968), p. 137.

Chapter 40: The Revolutionary Era and Ukraine's Other Peoples

1 Benzion Denur, "Ukraine," in *Encyclopedia Judaica*, Vol. XV (Jerusalem 1972), p. 1518.

Chapter 41: The West Ukrainian National Republic

1 Cited from the universal reprinted in Mykhailo Lozyns'kyi, *Halychyna v rr. 1918–1920* (Vienna 1922), pp. 68–69.
2 Cited in John S. Reshetar, Jr., *The Ukrainian Revolution, 1917–1920* (Princeton, N.J. 1952), p. 283.

Chapter 42: The Postwar Treaties and the Reconfiguration of Ukrainian Lands

1 Article 87, *La Paix de Versailles*, Vol. XII (Paris 1930), p. 358.

2 *Traité entre les Principales Puissances Alliées et Associées et la Tchécoslovaquie* (Paris 1919), p. 26.

Chapter 43: Soviet Ukraine: The Struggle for Autonomy

1 Taras Hunczak and Roman Sol'chanyk, eds., *Ukraïns'ka suspil'no-politychna dumka v 20 stolitti: dokumenty i materiialy*, Vol. II (New York 1983), p. 78.
2 Cited in Bohdan Krawchenko, *Social Change and National Consciousness in Twentieth-Century Ukraine* (New York 1985), p. 56.
3 The statistics in this paragraph are recalculated from data in George O. Liber, *Soviet Nationality Policy, Urban Growth, and Identity Change in the Ukrainian SSR, 1923–1934* (Cambridge 1992), p. 60.
4 Theses on the Plenum of the Central Committee of the CP(b)U on the Results of Ukrainianization (June 1926), cited in Robert S. Sullivant, *Soviet Politics and the Ukraine, 1917–1957* (New York and London 1962), pp. 113–114.

Chapter 44: Soviet Ukraine: Economic, Political, and Cultural Integration

1 I.S. Koropeckyj, "Industry," in *Encyclopedia of Ukraine*, Vol. II, ed. Volodymyr Kubijovyč (Toronto, Buffalo, and London 1988), p. 314.
2 Ivan Koshelivets', *Mykola Skrypnyk* (Munich 1972), p. 67.
3 The statistics are drawn from Bohdan Krawchenko, *Social Change and National Consciousness in Twentieth-Century Ukraine* (New York 1985), p. 134–140; and Terry Martin, *The Affirmative Action Empire: Nations and Nationalism in the Soviet Union, 1923–1939* (Ithaca and London 2001), p. 369.
4 P.P. Postyshev, *V borot'bi za lenins'ko-stalins'ku natsional'nu polityku partiia* (Kiev 1935), p. 19.
5 From a speech by the deputy minister of education Andrii Khvylia, cited in James E. Mace, *Communism and the Dilemmas of National Liberation* (Cambridge, Mass. 1983), p. 298.
6 From figures in Martin, *Affirmative Action Empire*, p. 369.
7 Cited in Robert S. Sullivant, *Soviet Politics and the Ukraine, 1917–1957* (New York and London 1962), p. 233.

Chapter 45: Other Peoples in Soviet Ukraine

1 Tsentral'noe statisticheskoe upravlenie, *Vsesoiuznaia perepis' naseleniia 1926 goda*, Vol. XII: *Ukrainskaia SSR* (Moscow 1929).
2 Calculations based on data in M.I. Panchuk, O.P. Koval'chuk, and B.V. Chyrko, eds., *Natsional'ni menshyny v Ukraïni v 1920–1930-ti roky: istoryko-kartohrafichnyi atlas* (Kiev 1996).
3 V.I. Lenin, *Sochineniia*, Vol. XX, 4th ed. (Moscow 1941), p. 12.
4 Andrzej Paczkowski, "Poland, the Enemy Nation," in Stéphane Courtois et al., *The Black Book of Communism: Crimes, Terror, Repression* (Cambridge, Mass., 1999), pp. 366–369.
5 Recalculated from data in Serhii Chornyi, *Natsional'nyi sklad naselennia Ukraïny v XX storichchi* (Kiev 2001), pp. 54–57.

Chapter 46: Ukrainian Lands in Interwar Poland

1 *Mały rocznik statystyczny* (Warsaw 1938), pp. 74–75.

2 *Ukraine: A Concise Encyclopedia*, Vol. II, ed. Volodymyr Kubijovyč (Toronto 1971), p. 374.

Chapter 47: Ukrainian Lands in Interwar Romania and Czechoslovakia

1 Cited in Volodymyr Kurylo et al., *Pivnichna Bukovyna, ïï mynule i suchasne* (Uzhhorod 1969), p. 91.
2 Article 8 of Romania's Primary Education Act of 1924, cited in C.A. Macartney, *Hungary and Her Successors: The Treaty of Trianon and Its Consequences, 1919–1937* (London 1937), p. 306.
3 *Školství na Podkarpatské Rusi v přítomnosti* (Prague 1932); Ievhen Iu. Pelens'kyi, "Shkil'nytstvo. Kul'turno-osvitne zhyttia," in *Karpats'ka Ukraïna* (L'viv 1939), pp. 125–127.

Chapter 49: World War II and Nazi German Rule

1 Cited in M. Suprunenko, "Ukraïna naperedodni i v vitchyznianii viini proty nimets'ko-fashystskykh zaharbnykiv," in *Borot'ba ukraïns'koho narodu proty nimets'kykh zaharbnykiv* (Ufa 1942), p. 33.
2 This formulation is partially that of Mark Mazower as paraphrased by Timothy Snyder, "Holocaust: The Ignored Reality," *New York Review of Books*, LVI, 12 (New York 2009), p. 15.
3 Cited in John A. Armstrong, *Ukrainian Nationalism*, 2nd ed. (Littleton, Colo. 1980), p. 87.
4 Cited in Alexander Dallin, *German Rule in Russia, 1941–1945* (New York 1957), p. 67.

Chapter 50: Postwar Soviet Ukraine under Stalin

1 Serhii Chornyi, *Natsional'nyi sklad naselennia Ukraïny v XX storichchi: dovidnyk* (Kiev 2001), pp. 81–82.
2 Cited in J. Otto Pohl, *Ethnic Cleansing in the USSR, 1937–1949* (Westport, Conn. 1999), p. 11.
3 Cited in É. Ozenbashly, *Krymtsy* (Akmesdzhit [Simferopol'] 1997), p. 21.
4 From a front page article in *Pravda* (Moscow), 25 May 1945, cited in Yaroslav Bilinsky, *The Second Soviet Republic: The Ukraine after World War II* (New Brunswick, N.J. 1964), p. 12.
5 Ibid.
6 From articles in *Pravda* (Moscow) and *Izvestiia* (Moscow), 12 January 1954, summarized in ibid., pp. 205–206.
7 "To the Pastors and Faithful of the Greek Catholic Church. Residents of the Western Oblasts of the Ukrainian SSR," cited in Bohdan Rostyslav Bociurkiw, *The Ukrainian Greek Catholic Church and the Soviet State, 1939–1950* (Edmonton and Toronto 1996), p. 119.

Chapter 51: Post-Stalinist Soviet Ukraine

1 N. Podgorny, "Sovetskaia Ukraina v bratskoi seme narodov SSR," *Kommunist*, No. 8 (Moscow 1954), p. 22.

2 Bohdan Krawchenko, *Social Change and National Consciousness in Twentieth-Century Ukraine* (New York 1985), pp. 173, 181, 194, and 205; Stephen Rapawy, *Ukraine and the Border Issues* (Washington, D.C. 1993), pp. 36 and 40.

3 Krawchenko, *Social Change*, p. 196.

Chapter 52: From Devolution to Independence

1 Interview with Serhii Odarych, secretary-general of Rukh, in the *Economist* (London), 17 April 1991.

2 *The Popular Movement of Ukraine for Restructuring – RUKH: Program and Charter* (Kiev 1989), p. 11.

Chapter 53: Independent Ukraine

1 The formulation is by Taras Kuzio, "Ukraine: Muddling Along," in Sharon Wolchik and Jane L. Curry, eds., *Central and East European Politics from Communism to Democracy* (Landham, Md. 2008), p. 361.

2 The figures are drawn from tables in Bohdan Harasymiv, *Post-Communist Ukraine* (Edmonton and Toronto 2002), p. 345; and George Thomas Kurian, ed., *The Illustrated Book of World Rankings,* 5th ed. (Armonk, N.Y. 2001), pp. 99–100.

3 Keith A. Darden, "Blackmail as a Tool of State Domination: Ukraine Under Kuchma," *East European Constitutional Review,* X, 2–3 (New York 2001), pp. 67–71.

4 *United Nations Statistical Yearbook,* 50th issue (New York 2006), pp. 138–154.

5 *Constitution of Ukraine,* Preamble (http://www.rada.gov.ua/const/conengl.htm), p. 1.

6 Article 10, p. 3.

7 Article 11, p. 3.

8 *Statystychnyi shchorichyk Ukraïny za 1998 rik/Statistical Yearbook of Ukraine for 1998* (Kiev 1999), pp. 434–436; ... *za /for 2000* (Kiev 2001), p. 447; ... za/for 2006 (Kiev 2007).

9 The figures are based on results from a sociological survey in which respondents were asked the question: Which language do you predominantly use at home? See Natalya Panina, *Ukrainian Society, 1994–2005: Sociological Monitoring* (Kiev 2005).

10 The figures are drawn from the data in John-Paul Himka, "Religious Communities in Ukraine," in Peter Jordan et al., eds., *Ukraine,* special issue of *Osthefte* (Vienna 2001), pp. 241–258.

11 Paul Robert Magocsi, *Ukraine: An Illustrated History* (Toronto 2007), p. 307.

12 *Constitution of Ukraine,* Article 11, p. 3.

13 The table is constructed from data in V. B. Ievtukh, V. P. Troshchyns'kyi, K. Iu. Halushko, and K. O. Chernova, *Etnonatsional'na struktura ukraïns'koho suspil'stva: dovidnyk* (Kiev 2004), p. 16.

14 *Ukraïns'ka pravda* (Kiev), July 5, 2004, cited in Taras Kuzio, "Nationalism, Identity, and Civil Society in Ukraine: Understanding the Orange Revolution," *Communist and Post-Communist Studies* XLIII (Berkeley, Calif. 2010), p. 291.

For Further Reading

The following is intended as an introductory guide to direct interested readers to other published materials about the subjects discussed in this book. It is not a comprehensive or even substantive bibliography; with very few exceptions, it is limited to English-language publications. Following the first section, which is devoted to reference works and general studies, the material is presented in sections that basically follow the chronological divisions used in the book.

1. Reference works and general studies
2. The pre-Kievan era
3. The Kievan period, circa 850–1350
4. The Lithuanian-Polish-Crimean period, circa 1350–1648
5. The Cossack state, 1648–1711
6. Ukrainian lands in the eighteenth century
7. Ukrainian lands in the Russian Empire, circa 1785–1914
8. Ukrainian lands in the Austrian Empire, circa 1772–1914
9. World War I, revolution, and civil war
10. The interwar years
11. World War II
12. The Soviet era, 1945–1991
13. Independent Ukraine

The following abbreviations are used:

AUAAS – Annals of the Ukrainian Academy of Arts and Sciences in the United States
HUS – Harvard Ukrainian Studies
JUS – Journal of Ukrainian Studies

1. Reference works and general studies

English-language readers are fortunate to have two comprehensive multivolume encyclopedias on all aspects of Ukraine: a thematic encyclopedia, *Ukraine: A Con-*

cise Encyclopedia, 2 vols., ed. Volodymyr Kubijovyč (Toronto, Buffalo, and London 1963–71); and an alphabetic encyclopedia, *Encyclopedia of Ukraine,* 5 vols., ed. Volodymyr Kubijovyč and Danylo Husar Struk (Toronto, Buffalo, and London 1984–93). In addition to thousands of entries on a whole host of personalia, organizations, and events, both encyclopedias include useful bibliographies following major sections and entries. Smaller in size but useful is the *Historical Dictionary of Ukraine,* ed. Zenon E. Kohut, Bohdan Y. Nebesio, and Myroslav Yurkevich (Lanham, Md., Toronto, and Oxford 2005). There is also a compre-hensive English-language encyclopedia for one region of Ukraine (Transcar-pathia) and immediately neighboring territories: *Encyclopedia of Rusyn History and Culture,* 2nd rev. ed., ed. Paul Robert Magocsi and Ivan Pop (Toronto, Buffalo, and London 2005). For the Soviet Marxist perspective, see the encyclopedic volume *Soviet Ukraine,* ed. M.P. Bazhan (Kiev 1969). Also useful is a translation of an earlier handbook produced during World War II: *Ukraine and Its People,* ed. Ivan Mirchuk (Munich 1949); and the visually informative Paul Robert Magocsi, *Ukraine: A Historical Atlas,* 2nd rev. ed. (Toronto 1987).

Readers interested in finding English-language works on various aspects of Ukraine have at their disposal several bibliographies and research guides. Among the most comprehensive and up-to-date annotated bibliographies (covering the period from the 1950s to 1999) are two volumes compiled by Bohdan S. Wynar, *Ukraine: A Bibliographic Guide to English-Language Publications* (Englewood, Colo. 1990) and *Independent Ukraine: A Bibliographic Guide to English-Language Publica-tions, 1989–1999* (Englewood, Colo. 2000) Also of value, especially for older publications, are Eugene J. Pelenskyj, *Ucrainica: Selected Bibliography on Ukraine in Western European Languages* (Munich 1948); and Roman Weres, *Ukraine: Selected References in the English Language,* 2nd rev. ed. (Chicago 1974). Bibliographical guides are available for the Cossack era, in Andrew Gregorovich, *Cossack Bibliog-raphy* (Toronto 2008), and for specific regions, in particular western Ukrainian lands: Paul Robert Magocsi, *Galicia: A Historical Survey and Bibliographic Guide* (Toronto 1983); Paul Robert Magocsi, "A Historiographical Guide to Subcar-pathian Rus'," *Austrian History Yearbook,* IX–X (Houston 1973–74), pp. 201–265 – revised with corrections and supplements in Paul Robert Magocsi, *Of the Making of Nationalities There Is No End,* Vol. II (New York 1999), pp. 323–485; Paul Robert Magocsi, *Carpatho-Rusyn Studies: An Annotated Bibliography,* Vol. I: *1975–1984* (New York 1988); Vol. II: *1985–1994* (New York 1998); Vol. III: *1995–1999* (New York 2004) and John-Paul Himka, "Bukovina," in his *Galicia and Bukovina: A Research Handbook about Western Ukraine, Late 19th and 20th Centuries,* Historic Sites Service Occasional Paper, No. 20 (Edmonton 1990), pp. 198–215. Informa-tion about all aspects of traditional Jewish life in Ukraine, with an emphasis on archival sources, is found in Miriam Weiner, *Jewish Roots in Ukraine and Moldova: Pages from the Past and Archival Inventories* (New York 1999).

There is a wide variety of articles about Ukrainian subjects that have appeared during the past half century in scholarly journals, access to which can be obtained by consulting the annual *American Bibliography of Slavic and East European Studies* (Bloomington, Ind. and Stanford, Calif. 1957–). This work includes separate sections titled "Ukraine" in each of the chapters that deals with history, government, law, politics, language and linguistics, and literature. There are, moreover, three scholarly journals that deal specifically with Ukraine, in particular in the fields of history and politics: *Annals of the Ukrainian Academy of Arts and Sciences in the United States – AUAAS* (New York 1951–); *The Journal of Ukrainian [Graduate] Studies – JUS* (Toronto and Edmonton 1976–); and *Harvard Ukrainian Studies – HUS* (Cambridge, Mass. 1977–). The Ukrainian language *Ukraïns'kyi istoryk / Ukrainian Historian* (Munich and New York 1963–) also includes some articles in English. Three other journals focus on Ukrainian topics: the *Ukrainian Quarterly* (New York 1944–) deals mainly with recent history and politics; *Logos* (Yorkton, Sask. 1950–83; Ottawa 1994–) primarily on Ukrainian religious studies; and the irregular *Studia Ucrainica* (Ottawa 1978–) with an emphasis on literature.

The development of Ukrainian historical writing from earliest times to 1956 is provided in a comprehensive survey by Dmytro Doroshenko (with a supplement covering the years 1917 to 1956 by Olexander Ohloblyn), *A Survey of Ukrainian Historiography*, in *AUAAS*, V–VI (1957). The manner in which a select number of Ukrainian historical issues have been treated in Polish and Russian as well as Ukrainian writings is surveyed in two volumes by Stephen Velychenko, *National History as Cultural Process: A Survey of the Interpretations of Ukraine's Past in Polish, Russian, and Ukrainian Historical Writing from Earliest Times to 1914* (Edmonton 1992); and *Shaping Identity in Eastern Europe and Russia: Soviet-Russian and Polish Accounts of Ukrainian History, 1914–1991* (New York 1993). Of interest in its own right is the polemical manner in which Soviet Ukrainian writers during the last years of Communist rule often dismissed Ukrainian scholarship in the West. A typical example of their politically motivated criticism is found in Nikolai N. Varvartsev, *Ukrainian History in the Distorting Mirror of Sovietology* (Kiev 1987). A wide-ranging discussion of Ukrainian historiography and how its proponents have, over several centuries, tried to carve out a Ukrainian national narrative distinct from that of Russia is found in Serhii Plokhy, *Ukraine and Russia: Representations of the Past* (Toronto, Buffalo, and London 2008). History writing and its politicization in Soviet and post-Soviet times continues to be a topic of concern as indicated in several studies discussed below in sections 12 and 13.

For readers interested in general surveys of Ukrainian history other than this one, there are several to choose from in English. In a class by itself is Mykhailo Hrushevs'kyi's monumental *Istoriia Ukraïny-Rusy* (History of Ukraine-Rus') , 10 vols. (Kiev 1898–1936; reprinted New York 1954–58 and Kiev 1991–). Based on a wide variety of primary sources, this study traces developments from prehistoric times to 1658. All ten volumes, entitled *History of Ukraine-Rus'*, are in the process of translation into English under the sponsorship of the Peter Jacyk Centre for Ukrainian Historical Research at the University of Alberta; those that have already appeared are noted in the appropriate sections below. Hrushevs'kyi himself and his enormous influence on the direction of Ukrainian historiography are the subject of critical essays by Frank E. Sysyn, Andrzej Poppe, and Serhii Plokhy in the form of introductions to each of the existing translated volumes of the *History of Ukraine-Rus'*, Vol. I (1997), pp. xxii–liv; Vol. VII (1999), pp. xxvii–lii;

Vol. VIII (2002), pp. xxxi–lxix; Vol. IX, Book 1 (2005), pp. xxix–lxiv; Vol. IX, Book 2, part 1 (2008), pp. xxvii–liv; Book 2, part 2 (2010), pp. lx–lxxviii; and in a comprehensive monograph by Serhii Plokhy, *Unmaking Imperial Russia: Mykhailo Hrushevsky and the Writing of Ukrainian History* (Toronto, Buffalo, and London 2005). Hrushevs'kyi's justification for treating Ukraine as a distinct historical entity is provided in a translation of his 1904 seminal article: Mychaylo Hrushevsky, "The Traditional Scheme of 'Russian' History and the Problems of a Rational Organization of the History of the East Slavs," *AUAAS*, I, 2 (1951), pp. 355–364, reprinted in *From Kievan Rus' to Modern Ukraine: Formation of the Ukrainian Nation* (Cambridge, Mass. 1984) and published separately (Winnipeg 1965). The whole question of the Ukrainian challenge to the traditional Russian view of the history of the East Slavs from earliest times to the eighteenth century is addressed in Serhii Plokhy, *The Origins of the Slavic Nations: Premodern Identities in Russia, Ukraine, and Belarus* (Cambridge 2006).

The earliest one-volume historical survey to appear in English, covering events from earliest times to World War I (originally published in Russian, 1911; updated 1921) is Michael Hrushevsky, *A History of Ukraine* (New Haven, Conn. 1941; reprinted 1970). More scholarly in nature is Dmytro Doroshenko, *A Survey of Ukrainian History* (Winnipeg 1975), originally covering the period from earliest times to 1914 with a supplement covering the years 1914–1975 by Oleh W. Gerus. Now dated is W.E.D. Allen, *The Ukraine* (Cambridge 1941), which concentrates on the modern period. Chronologically more comprehensive but often unreliable are Isidore Nahayevsky, *History of Ukraine* (Philadephia 1962); and Nicholas L. Chirovsky, *An Introduction to Ukrainian History*, 3 vols. (New York 1981–86). A modern one-volume survey that includes information on Ukrainians abroad as well as in the homeland is Orest Subtelny, *Ukraine: A History*, 3rd rev. ed. (Toronto 2000). Of particular interest is a survey which traces the idea of Ukrainian nationality as expressed through culture, myth, and politics from the medieval era to the present by Andrew Wilson, *The Ukrainians: Unexpected Nation* (New Haven and London 2000).

The aforementioned surveys are concerned primarily with the history of the Ukrainian people and not with a territory called Ukraine inhabited largely but not exclusively by the Ukrainians. Although the territorial approach was adopted by Soviet Ukrainian historians, they too largely ignored Ukraine's other peoples. This is the case even in the large-scale *Istoriia Ukraïns'koï RSR*, 8 vols., ed. Iurii Kondufor (Kiev 1977–79), produced during the last years of Communist rule. Although this work has never been – and is unlikely to be – translated into English, there is a concise one-volume version: Yuri Kondufor, ed., *A Short History of the Ukraine* (Kiev 1986). This and other Soviet Marxist accounts are useful for the emphasis they generally place on socioeconomic factors and for their attempt to cover developments in all regions within the boundaries of the post-1945 Ukrainian S.S.R. They suffer, however, from inadequate coverage or the elimination of persons and events that are not considered as belonging to the "progressive forces," and from the need to fit Ukrainian historical developments into a Soviet Marxist conceptual framework.

There are general historical surveys of Ukraine's traditional Eastern Christian churches: Ivan Wlasowsky, *Outline History of the Ukrainian Orthodox Church*, 2 vols. [earliest times to 1686] (New York and South Bound Brook, N.J. 1974–79); George Fedoriw, *History of the Church in Ukraine* (Toronto 1983); and, for the region of Transcarpathia and the immediately neighboring East Slavic-inhabited lands, Athanasius B. Pekar, *The History of the Church in Carpathian Rus'* (New York 1992). All three provide valuable factual data even if they are clearly apologetic in spirit and defensive of either the Orthodox (Wlasowsky) or the Greek Catholic (Fedoriw, Pekar) viewpoint. More balanced are the chronology of events compiled by Osyp Zinkewych and Andrew Sorokowski, *A Thousand Years of Christianity in Ukraine: An Encyclopedic Chronology* (New York, Baltimore, and Toronto 1988); and the projected four-volume work by Sophia Senyk, *A History of the Church in Ukraine*, the first volume of which (covering the period to the end of the thirteenth century) has appeared in the series, Orientalia Christiana Analecta, Vol. CCXLIII (Rome 1993).

Readers interested in Ukrainian history may need to consult basic surveys and reference works dealing with neighboring countries whose own development has often been intimately related to that of Ukraine. There are numerous English-language histories of Russia. The best of these, which incorporates the most recent findings of scholarship, is the three-volume work, *The Cambridge History of Russia*, Vol. I: *From Early Rus' to 1689*, ed. Maureen Derrie; Vol. II: *Imperial Russia, 1689–1917*, ed. Dominic Lieven; and Vol. III: *The Twentieth Century*, ed. Ronald Grigur Suny (Cambridge 2006–07). Earlier surveys of scholarly significance which present the Russian understanding of the history of eastern Europe include: Vasily O. Kluchevsky, *A History of Russia*, 5 vols. [to the 1850s] (New York 1960); George Vernadsky, *A History of Russia*, 5 vols. [to 1682] (New Haven and London 1943–69); Michael T. Florinsky, *Russia: A History and Interpretation*, 2 vols. [to 1917] (New York 1947); Nicholas V. Riasanovsky, *A History of Russia*, 6th rev. ed. (New York and Oxford 2000); and, for the twentieth century, Donald W. Treadgold, *Twentieth Century Russia*, 8th rev. ed. (Boulder, Colo. 1995). There are also surveys of the economy and culture of the former Russian Empire and Soviet Union which effectively deal with the lands of the East Slavs: Peter I. Lyashchenko, *History of the National Economy of Russia to the 1917 Revolution* (New York 1949); Jerome Blum, *Lord and Peasant in Russia* (New York 1964); and James H. Billington, *The Icon and the Axe* (New York 1967). Factual data on a wide range of historical events, organizations, and individuals (including many connected with Ukraine) are found in *The Modern Encyclopedia of Russian and Soviet History* (with *Supplements* and *Index*), 60 vols., edited by Joseph L. Wieczynski (Gulf Breeze, Fla. 1976–2000), and George N. Rhyne and Bruce F. Adams, eds. *The Supplement to the Modern Encyclopedia of Russian Soviet and Eurasian History*, Vols. 1–9 [A–E] (Gulf Breeze, Fla., 1995–2008).

For Poland, there is the older *Cambridge History of Poland*, 2 vols. (Cambridge 1950); as well as Norman Davies, *God's Playground: A History of Poland*, 2 vols. (New York 1982), and an encyclopedia of historical events and personages: George J. Lerski and Piotr Wróbel, *Historical Dictionary of Poland*, 2 vols: *966–1945* and *1945–1996* (Westport, Conn. and London 1996–98). A Polish perspective on the country's former eastern borderlands, with particular emphasis on eastern Galicia, is provided in a historical survey from earliest times to World War II by Adam Żołtowski, *Border of Europe: A Study of the Polish Eastern Provinces* (London 1950). Little known but extremely useful, and filled with extensive statistical data on Right Bank Ukraine and Galicia, is the *Polish Encyclopedia*, 3 vols. (Geneva 1922–26). On the Grand Duchy of Lithuania, in particular during the period when it ruled much of Ukraine, see Zigmantas Kiapa, Jūratė Kiaupienė, and Albinas Kuncevičius, *The History of Lithuania before 1975* (Vilnius 2000). The best introduction to the Ottoman Empire, in particular its early phases as an expanding state, is Paul Wittek, *The Rise of the Ottoman Empire* (London 1963). For the country's subsequent history, see Caroline Finkel, *Osman's Dream: The Story of the Ottoman Empire* (London 2005).

2. The pre-Kievan era

There is an extensive literature on the archaeology of lands north of the Black Sea and on the various nomadic and sedentary peoples who lived there before the beginning of the common era (BCE). Most of the works deal primarily, if not exclusively, with developments on Ukrainian territory. An introductory survey covering several millennia BCE as well as the first eight centuries of the Common Era to the eve of Kievan Rus' is provided in two works of George Vernadsky, *A History of Russia*, Vol. I: *Ancient Russia* (New Haven and London 1943) and *The Origins of Russia* (Oxford 1959); and in a shorter survey by Tadeusz Sulimirski, *Prehistoric Russia: An Outline* (London 1970). The results of recent archaeological research on these same millennia are found in Pavel M. Dolukhanov, *The Early Slavs: Eastern Europe from the Initial Settlements to the Kievan Rus* (London and New York 1996).

Particular attention has been given to the Trypillian culture, which flourished during the fourth and third millennia BCE. A short introductory survey of the topic is presented by Yaroslav Pasternak, "The Trypillian Culture in Ukraine," *Ukrainian Quarterly*, VI, 2 (New York 1950), pp. 112–133. More substantive discussions are available in Krzystof Ciuk, ed., *Mysteries of Ancient Ukraine: The Remarkable Trypilian Culture, 5400–2700 BC* (Toronto 2008); Linda Ellis, *The Cucuteni-Tripolye Culture: A Study in Technology and the Origins of a Complex Society*, B.A.R Series, Vol. 217 (Oxford 1984); Igor Manzura, "Steps to the Steppe: Or, How the North Pontic Region was Colonized," *Oxford Journal of Archaeology*, XXIV, 4 (Oxford 2005), pp. 313–338; Vladimir G. Zbenovich, "The Tripolye Culture: Centenary of Research," *Journal of World Prehistory*, X, 2 (1996), pp. 199–241; and in several works by Marija Gimbutas, the most prolific populariser of Trypillia as a highly advanced culture and matriarchal society: *The Civilization of the Goddess* (San Francisco 1991), with its numerous illustrations and ingenious reconstructions, and *The Slavs* (London 1971).

The classic studies on the interaction between the Greek settlements along the Black Sea coasts and the steppe hinterland is discussed in E. Minns, *Scythians and Greeks: A Survey of Ancient History and Archaeology on the North Coast of the Euxine from the Danube to the Caucasus* (Cambridge 1913); and Michael Rostovtzeff, *Iranians and Greeks in South Russia* (Oxford 1922), who surveys the interaction of the Cimmerians, Scythians, and Sarmatians with the Greek cities along the coast, including the Bosporan Kingdom during the period of Roman influence until the third century CE. The literature on the coastal and steppe hinterland relations has grown substantially, especially in the last few decades. Many of these works also include magnificent color reproductions of art works from the period: Marianna Koromila, *The Greeks in the Black Sea from the Bronze Age to the Early Twentieth Century* (Athens 1991), esp. chapters 3 and 4; Glenn R. Mack and Joseph Coleman Carter, eds., *Crimean Chersonesos: City, Chora, Museum, and Environs* (Austin, Tex. 2003); David Braund, ed., *Scythians and Greeks: Cultural Interactions in Scythia, Athens and the Early Roman Empire, 6th Century BC – 1st Century AD* (Exeter, UK 2005); and Anna A. Trofimova, ed., *Greeks on the Black Sea: Ancient Art from the Hermitage* (Los Angeles 2007). There are also monographs on individual nomadic tribal entities that dominated Ukrainian and surrounding lands: Tadeusz Sulimirski, *The Sarmatians* (New York 1970).

It is the Scythians, however, and in particular their art works, which have attracted the most attention: whose society and art are the subject of many works, including Tamara Rice, *The Scythians* (London 1957); Mikhail I. Artamanov, *The Splendor of Scythian Art: Treasures from Scythian Tombs* (New York 1969); Renata Rolle, *The World of the Scythians* (London 1989); Ellen D. Reeder, ed., *Scythian Gold: Treasures from Ancient Ukraine* (New York 1999); and Joan Aruz et al., eds., *The Golden Deer of Eurasia: Scythian and Sarmatian Treasures from the Russian Steppes* (New York 2000). Aside from their art and other physical remnants, our main source of information about Scythians comes from writings of the "father of history," the Greek writer Herodotus. His text about Scythia, with extensive commentary based on our current state of knowledge of the ancient world, is found in *The Landmark Herodotus: The Histories,* edited by Robert B. Strassler (New York 2007).

Studies on the first eight centuries of the common era before the establishment of Kievan Rus' deal either with invading nomadic peoples who made parts of Ukrainian territory their permanent home, or with the Slavs, whose original homeland is presumed to be centered in northwestern and north-central Ukraine. The relationships of these developments specifically to Ukrainian territory is surveyed in Mykhailo Hrushevsky, *History of Ukraine-Rus',* Vol. I (Edmonton and Toronto 1997), esp. chapters 3–6, although much of the author's information reflects the now-outdated state of archaeological research at the beginning of the twentieth century.

Monographs on individual groups and the civilizations they created include Alexander A. Vasiliev, *The Goths in the Crimea* (Cambridge, Mass. 1936). Particular attention has been accorded the Khazars and their "empire," which encompassed much of Ukraine, in the now classic introductory survey by D.M. Dunlop, *The History of the Jewish Khazars* (Princeton, N. J. 1954); in several essays by Peter B. Golden, *Khazar Studies: An Historico-Philological Inquiry into the Origins of the*

Khazars, esp. Vol. I (Budapest 1980); and in the more popular survey by Kevin Alan Brook, *The Jews of Khazaria,* 2nd ed. (Lanham, Md. 2006). The most recent scholarship is found in essays on the Khazar economy (by Thomas S. Noonan), on relations with Kievan Rus' (by Vladimir Petrukhin), and on the conversion to Judaism (by Peter B. Golden), among other related topics, in Peter B. Golden, Haggai Ben-Shammai, and András Róna-Tas, eds., *The World of the Khazars: New Perspectives* (Leiden and Boston 2007).

It is the Slavs, however, who have received the most attention, whether in works that focus on archaeological and historical evidence: Marija Gimbautas, *The Slavs* (London 1971); Zdeněk Váňa, *The World of the Ancient Slavs* (Detroit 1983); Bohuslav Chropovský, *The Slavs: Their Significance – Political and Cultural History* (Prague 1989); and Paul M. Barford, *The Early Slavs: Culture and Society in Early Medieval Eastern Europe* (Ithaca, N.Y. 2001); on linguistic data: Zbigniew Gołąb, *The Origins of the Slavs: A Linguist's View* (Columbus, Ohio 1992) and Alexander M. Schenker, *The Dawn of Slavic: An Introduction to Slavic Philology* (New Haven and London 1995); or on religious beliefs: Richard A.E. Mason, *The Ancient Religion of Kyivan Rus'* (Cleveland, L'viv, and Ulm 1994). Most of these works contain extensive information on the early developments in Kievan Rus'.

3. The Kievan Period, circa 850–1350

Because of its importance in the historiography of Russia and eastern Europe in general, the literature in English on Kievan Rus' is quite well developed. While general studies attempt to encompass the entire Kievan realm from the Baltic to the Black Sea, inevitably much attention is given to Kiev, the seat of the grand prince, and to the surrounding southern Rus'/Ukrainian territories.

Although by now dated, there is a still useful historiographic review of primary sources by Nora K. Chadwick, *The Beginnings of Russian History: An Inquiry into Sources* (Cambridge 1946; reprinted 1966). Several of the sources themselves have appeared in annotated English translations, including *The Russian Primary Chronicle: Laurentian Text* [to 1116], translated by Samuel Hazzard Cross and Olgerd P. Sherbowitz-Wetzor (Cambridge, Mass. 1953; reprinted 1973); *The Galician Volynian Chronicle* [to 1292], translated by George A. Perfecky, 2nd rev. ed. (Cambridge, Mass. 1994); *The Nikonian Chronicle,* 5 vols., translated by Serge A. and Betty Jean Zenkovsky (Princeton, NJ 1984–89), esp. Vols. I and II [to 1240]; *Medieval Russian Laws,* translated by George Vernadsky, 2nd ed. (New York 1969) – in particular the short and long versions of the *Pravda Russkaia;* and *A Source Book for Russian History from Early Times to 1917,* comp. Sergei Pushkarev (New Haven and London 1972), esp. chapter 2. The concrete manner in which law functioned in Kievan Rus' is discussed by Daniel H. Kaiser in *The Growth of the Law in Medieval Russia* (Princeton, N.J. 1980). A few documents and excerpts from some of the best secondary sources on aspects of Kievan Rus' are found in Daniel H. Kaiser and Gary Marker, comps., *Reinterpreting Russian History: Readings, 860–1860s* (New York and Oxford 1994), chapters 1–8. The invaluable report of the tenth-century Byzantine emperor Constantine Pophyrogenitus, with its detailed description of the Rus', the Khazars, and other peoples north of the Black Sea, is available in English translation: *De Administrando Imperio*, edited and translated by Gy. Moravcsik and R.J.H. Jenkins, 2nd rev. ed. (Washington, D.C. 1967), and Vol. II: *Commentary*, by F. Dvornik, R.J.H. Jenkins, B. Lewis, et al. (London 1962). The extensive commentary from volume II dealing with various aspects of the early Rus' is reprinted in Dimitrii Obolensky, *Byzantium and the Slavs: Collected Studies* (London 1971), chapter 5.

Introductory surveys on Kievan Rus' have appeared in several multi-volume histories of Russia, beginning with the pre-revolutionary classics of nineteenth-century Russian imperial historiography: Sergei M. Soloviev, *History of Russia*, Vol. II: *Early Russia, 1054–1157* (Gulf Breeze, Fla. 2002) and Vol. III: *The Shift Northward: Kievan Rus', 1154–1228* (Gulf Breeze, Fla. 2000); and are available in one-volume histories by the late nineteenth-century Russian historian Vasily O. Kluchevsky, *A History of Russia*, Vol. I (New York 1960); and continuing with the Russian émigré scholar George Vernadsky, *A History of Russia*, Vol. II: *Kievan Russia* (New Haven and London 1948). There are one-volume histories written from the Russian Marxist perspective: Boris Grekov, *Kiev Rus* (Moscow 1959) and Boris Rybakov, *Kievan Rus'* (Moscow 1984). Kievan Rus' also features prominently in Janet Martin, *Medieval Russia, 980–1584* (Cambridge 1995), esp. chapters 1–6, which is particularly useful for a concluding chapter on historiography and for the most comprehensive up-to-date bibliography of works on Kievan Rus' in western languages.

The economy and urban geography is surveyed in Mikhail Tikhomirov, *The Towns of Ancient Rus* (Moscow 1959). In addition to the often extensive discussion of economic developments in each of the aforementioned surveys, of importance are Daniel H. Kaiser, "The Economy of Kievan Rus': Evidence from the *Pravda Rus'skaia*"; Peter B. Golden, "Aspects of the Nomadic Factor in the Economic Development of Kievan Rus'" and Thomas S. Noonan, "The Flourishing of Kiev's International and Domestic Trade, ca. 1100-ca. 1240," in I.S. Koropeckyj, ed., *Ukrainian Economic History: Interpretive Essays* (Cambridge, Mass. 1991), pp. 37–146; David B. Miller, "Monumental Building and Its Patrons as Indicators of Economic and Political Trends in Rus', 900–1262," *Jahrbücher für Geschichte Osteuropas*, XXXVIII, 3 (Stuttgart 1990), pp. 321–355; and Vladimir I. Mezentsev, "The Territorial and Demographic Development of Medieval Kiev and Other Major Cities of Rus'," *Russian Review*, XLVIII, 2 (Columbus, Ohio 1989), pp. 145–170.

Most of the works noted above deal with the entire territorial extent of Kievan Rus', although they tend to end their narratives in the 1240s, with the Mongol invasions. By contrast, the first three volumes of Hrushevs'kyi's history not only provide great detail on developments specifically on Ukrainian territory, but also treat the principality/Kingdom of Galicia-Volhynia as a direct continuation of Kievan Rus' until its own demise in the 1340s: Mykhailo Hrushevsky, *History of Ukraine-Rus'*, Vol. I (Edmonton and Toronto, 1997) and Vols. II–III (forthcoming).

Of all the topics related to Kievan Rus', the one with perhaps the most extensive

literature in English as well as in other languages is the question of the origin of
Rus'. The most wide-ranging discussion of this issue as well as of the early settlement of eastern Europe in general and the evolution of and differentiation among
the East Slavs is found in two volumes by Henryk Paszkiewicz, *The Origin of Russia*
(London 1954; reprinted New York 1969); and *The Making of the Russian Nation*
(London 1963; reprinted Westport, Conn. 1977). The controversy over the possible Scandivanian origin of the Rus' – the so-called Normanist theory – is discussed
at length in Alexander Riasanovsky, *The Norman Theory of the Origin of the Russian
State: A Critical Analysis* (Stanford, Calif. 1960), while the actual arguments for and
against the theory appear in several works, including Vilhelm Thomsen, *The Relations between Ancient Russia and Scandinavia and the Origin of the Russian State* (Oxford
and London 1877; reprinted New York 1964); Adolf Stender-Petersen, *Varangica*
(Aarhus 1953); Imre Boba, *Nomads, Northmen and Slavs: Eastern Europe in the Ninth
Century* (The Hague 1967); Omeljan Pritsak, *The Origin of Rus'*, Vol. I (Cambridge,
Mass. 1981); Thomas S. Noonan, "Why the Vikings First Came to Russia," *Jahrbücher
für Geschichte Osteuropas*, XXXIV, 3 (Wiesbaden and Stuttgart 1986), pp. 321–348;
and Wladyslaw Duczko, *Viking Rus: Studies on the Presence of Scandinavians in Eastern
Europe* (Leiden and Boston 2004). The origin of Rus', the creation of the first state
structures, and the first centuries of Kievan Rus' history are treated in an authoritative manner by Simon Franklin and Jonathan Shepard, *The Emergence of Rus,
750–1200* (London and New York 1996).

The subsequent evolution of the term *Rus'/Rus' Land* to designate either relat-
ed ethnic groups, a geographic territory, or an ideological myth is, in part, dealt
with in the previously mentioned works on the origin of Rus', but specifically in
Paul Bushkovitch, "Rus' in the Ethnic Nomenclature of the *Povest vremennykh let*,"
Cahiers du monde russe et soviétique, XII, 1–2 (Paris 1971), pp. 296–306; Charles J.
Halperin, "The Concept of the Russian Land from the Ninth to the Fourteenth
Centuries," *Russian History*, II, 1 (Pittsburgh 1975), pp. 29–38; Charles Halperin,
"The Concept of the *Ruskaia zemlia* and Medieval National Consciousness from
the Tenth to the Fifteenth Centuries," *Nationalities Papers*, VII, 1 (Charleston, Ill.
1980), pp. 75–86; and Serhii Plokhy, *The Origins of the Slavic Nations* (Cambridge
2006), chapter 1.

There is as well an extensive body of scholarship in English on cultural life
in Kievan Rus'. Many works deal with what Russian historiography describes as
"Old Russian" culture and literature, as in a general collection of essays by Boris
D. Grekov, *The Culture of Kiev Rus* (Moscow 1947); an analysis of several literary
works, including the chronicles, by Dmitry Likhachev, *The Great Heritage: The Classical Literature of Old Rus* (Moscow 1981); and the initial chapters of descriptive
surveys by Nikolai K. Gudzy, *History of Early Russian Literature* (New York 1949),
and by J. Fennell and A. Stokes, *Early Russian Literature* (Berkeley, Calif. 1974). A
Ukrainian perspective on the same period is provided in the first half of Dmytro
Čyževs'kyj, *A History of Ukrainian Literature* (Littleton, Colo. 1975), esp. chapters
2–4.

Several of the literary works themselves from the Kievan period are available
in English translation, whether as part of collections: *Anthology of Old Russian*

Literature, compiled by Adolf Stender-Petersen (New York 1954); *Medieval Russia's Epics, Chronicles and Tales,* compiled by Serge A. Zenkovsky, 2nd rev. ed. (New York 1974); *The Hagiography of Kievan Rus',* translated by Paul Hollingsworth (Cambridge, Mass. 1992); *Sermons and Rhetoric of Kievan Rus',* translated by Simon Franklin (Cambridge, Mass. 1991); *The Edificatory Prose of Kievan Rus',* translated by William R. Veder (Cambridge, Mass. 1994); or as individual works: *The Paterik of the Kievan Caves Monastery,* translated by Muriel Heppell (Cambridge, Mass. 1989).

Special attention has been given to the *Lay of Prince Ihor's Campaign,* with at least two versions in English: *The Song of Ihor's Campaign,* translated by Vladimir Nabokov (Woodstock, N.Y. and New York 2003) and *The Tale of the Campaign of Ihor,* translated by Robert C. Howes (New York 1973). There exists a spirited scholarly debate around the question of whether it is an authentic literary work from the late twelfth century, as argued by Roman Jacobson, "The Puzzles of the Igor' Tale on the 150 Anniversary of its First Edition," in idem, *Selected Writings,* Vol. IV (The Hague 1971), pp. 380–410 and Omeljan Pritsak, "The Igor' Tale as a Historical Document," *AUAAS,* XII (1969–72), pp. 44–61; or a literary creation in medieval style from the late eighteenth century, as argued by André Mason, "Le Slovo d'Igor," *The Slavonic and East European Review,* XXVII [69] (London 1949), pp. 515–535 and Edward L. Keenan, *Josef Dobrovský and the Origins of the Igor' Tale* (Cambridge, Mass. 2003).

Monuments of architecture are treated in the early chapters of three works: George Heard Hamilton, *The Art and Architecture of Russia,* 3rd ed. (New York 1983); William C. Brumfield, *Gold in Azure* (Boston 1983); and William C. Brumfield, *A History of Russian Architecture* (Cambridge 1993). The cathedral of St Sophia has been given particular attention in Olexa Powstenko, *The Cathedral of St. Sophia in Kiev,* in *AUAAS,* III–IV [10–12] (1954); and in Andrzej Poppe, "The Building of the Church of St Sophia in Kiev," *Journal of Medieval History,* VII, 1 (Amsterdam 1981), pp. 15–66, reprinted in idem, *The Rise of Christian Russia* (London 1982), chapter 4.

The crucial relationship between the culture of Kievan Rus' and its spiritual source, Byzantium, is best explored in Dmitri Obolensky, *The Byzantine Commonwealth, 500–1453* (London 1971), esp. chapters 6 and 7. Particular attention has been given to Kiev's acceptance of Christianity and the organization of the Rus' church. These topics are covered in general histories of the church (see above, section I), in the historical surveys mentioned previously in this section, and in Yaroslav N. Shchapov, *State and Church in Early Russia, 10th–13th Centuries* (New Rochelle, N.Y., Athens, and Moscow 1993); A.P. Vlasto, *The Entry of the Slavs into Christendom* (Cambridge 1970), esp. chapter 5; Andrzej Poppe, *The Rise of Christian Russia* (London 1982), esp. chapters 2 and 3; John Fennell, *A History of the Russian Church to 1448* (New York 1995); and the extensive collection of essays by several specialists on the conversion, as well as a wide range of topics dealing with Byzantium's impact on Kievan Rus' in *Proceedings of the International Congress Commemorating the Millennium of Christianity in Rus'-Ukraine,* ed. Omeljan Pritsak and Ihor Ševčenko, special issue of *HUS,* XII–XIII (1988–89). The topic is also treated in several essays by Ihor Ševčenko, *Ukraine Between East and West* (Edmonton and Toronto 1996), esp. pp 12–111.

There is growing body of scholarship on the various nomadic peoples of the steppe who interacted with Kievan Rus'. For a general background on this wide-ranging topic, see Peter B. Golden, *An Introduction to the History of the Turkic Peoples* (Weisbaden 1992). There are also a few studies devoted to the Turkic Pechenegs in C.A. Macartney, "The Pechenegs," *Slavonic and East European Review*, VIII (London 1929–30), pp. 342–355; Omeljan Pritsak, "The Pečenegs: A Case Study of Social and Economic Transformation," *Archivum Eurasiae Medii Aevi*, I (Lisse, Netherlands 1975), pp. 211–235; and F. E. Wozniak, "Byzantium, the Pechenegs, and the Rus'," *ibid.*, pp. 299–316. Even more attention has been given to the steppe polity whose peoples are known variously as Polovcians/ Kipçaks/Cumans: Bruce A. Boswell, "The Kipchak Turks," *Slavonic and East European Review*, VI (London 1927–28), pp. 65–85; Omeljan Pritsak, "The Polovcians and Rus'," *Archivum Eurasiae Medii Aevi*, II (Lisse, Netherlands 1982), pp. 321– 380; and several articles on this group as well as on Kiev's close allies, the Chorni Klobuky, reprinted in Peter B. Golden, *Nomads and their Neighbours in the Russian Steppe: Turks, Khazars, and Qipchaqs* (Ashgate, U.K. and Burlington, Vt. 2003).

It is the Mongols, however, who have received the most extensive treatment, including a survey of their history both before and after their destruction of Kiev by George Vernadsky, *A History of Russia*, Vol. III: *The Mongols and Russia* (New Haven and London 1953). Much attention is given to Mongol military conquests toward the West (Kievan Rus' and Europe) in Timothy May, *The Mongol Art of War* (Yardley, Pa., 2007); Richard A. Gabriel, *Subotai the Valiant: Genghis Khan's Greatest General* (Westport, Conn. and London 2004); and the more popular survey by James Chambers, *The Devil's Horsemen: The Mongol Invasion in Europe* (London 1979). The creation of the Golden Horde in the second half of the thirteenth century and the subsequent Mongolo-Tatar impact on Kievan Rus' and its successor states, Lithuania and in particular Muscovy, is the topic of numerous studies, including the classic nineteenth century work by Sergei M. Soloviev, *History of Russia*, Vol. IV: *Russia under Tatar Yoke, 1228–1389* (Gulf Breeze, Fla. 2000); a well-illustrated monograph by German A. Fedorov-Davydov, *The Silk Road and the Cities of the Golden Horde* (Berkley, Calif. 1991); and popular surveys by Paul Harrison Silfen, *The Influence of the Mongols on Russia* (Hicksville, N.Y. 1974); and Leo de Hartog, *Russia and the Mongol Yoke: the History of the Russian Principalities and the Golden Horde, 1221–1502* (London and New York 1996). More interpretative and intellectually sophisticated in approach are several works by Charles J. Halperin, *Russia and the Golden Horde, 1221–1502* (Bloomington, Ind. 1985); Charles J. Halperin, *The Tatar Yoke* (Columbus, Ohio 1986); Charles J. Halperin, "Russia in the Mongol Empire in Comparative Prospective," *Harvard Journal of Asiatic Studies*, XLIII, 1 (Cambridge, Mass, 1983), pp. 239–261; and the comprehensive monograph by Donald Ostrowski, *Muscovy and the Mongols: Cross-Cultural Influences of the Steppe Frontier, 1304–1589* (Cambridge 1998). The Mongol relationship to the last independent principality in the southern Rus' lands is discussed in Michael B. Zdan, "The Dependence of Halych-Volyn' Rus' on the Golden Horde," *Slavonic and East European Review*, XXXV (London 1957), pp. 505–522.

Three of Kiev's grand princes have English-language biographies. Volodymyr "the Great" is the subject of a scholarly biography by Jukka Korpela, *Prince, Saint and Apostle: Prince Vladimir Svjatoslavovič of Kiev* (Wiesbaden, 2001); a popular but well-informed historical novel by Vladimir Volkoff, *Vladimir the Russian King* (London 1984); and an analysis of how the grand prince was viewed subsequently in Ukrainian and Russian society, by Francis Butler, *Enlightener of Rus': The Image of Vladimir Sviatoslavovich Across the Centuries* (Bloomington, Ind. 2002). The careers of two other Rus' rulers are analyzed by Dimitri Obolensky, "Vladimir Monomakh," in his *Six Byzantine Portraits* (Oxford 1988), pp. 83–114; and Martin Dimnik, *Mikhail, Prince of Chernigov and Grand Prince of Kiev, 1224–1246* (Toronto 1981), a work which provides a good picture of the status of the southern Rus' lands on the eve of the Mongol invasion. The principality of Chernihiv is given extensive attention in a two-volume study tracing its history from the death of Iaroslav I "the Wise" to the establishment of the Mongol Golden Horde, by Martin Dimnik, *The Dynasty of Chernigov, 1054–1146* (Toronto 1994) and *The Dynasty of Chernigov, 1146–1246* (Cambridge 2003). The subsequent decline of Kiev as a political and ecclesiastical center in eastern Europe and the struggle between Muscovy and Lithuania to replace it is presented in a masterful work by John Meyendorff, *Byzantium and the Rise of Russia: A Study of Byzantino-Russian Relations in the Fourteenth Century* (Crestwood, N.Y. 1989); and in two essays by Dimitri Obolensky: "Byzantium, Kiev and Moscow: A Study in Ecclesiastical Relations," *Dumbarton Oaks Papers*, XI (Washington, D.C. 1957), pp. 23–78, reprinted in his *Byzantium and the Slavs: Collected Studies* (London 1971), chapter 6; and "Metropolitan Cyprian of Kiev and Moscow," in his *Six Byzantine Portraits* (Oxford 1988), pp. 173–200.

4. The Lithuanian-Polish-Crimean period, circa 1350–1648

The most comprehensive treatment of the three centuries of Lithuanian and Polish rule are five volumes in Mykhailo Hrushevsky's *History of Ukraine-Rus'*. Among the topics covered in depth are political relations (Vol. IV, forthcoming); socioeconomic, cultural, and religious developments (Vols. V and VI, forthcoming); and the Cossack movement (see below). For an excellent introduction to the entire period and beyond, with an emphasis on Poland and its relationship to Lithuania (including Ukraine), see Daniel Stone, *The Polish-Lithuanian State, 1386–1795*, History of East Central Europe, Vol. IV (Seattle and London 2001). Excerpts of sixteen documents from this period dealing with the Union of Lublin, the Church Union of Brest, and the rise of the Cossacks are available in English translation in Sergei Pushkarev, *A Source Book for Russian History from Early Times to 1917*, Vol. I (New Haven and London 1972), esp. pp. 283–296.

Aside from Hrushevs'kyi, the available secondary literature in English deals with only a few topics. The rise of Lithuania and its rivalry with the Golden Horde for control of the southern lands of Kievan Rus' are reviewed by Henryk

Paszkiewicz, *The Origin of Russia* (London 1954), chapters 8–9; Jaroslaw Pelenski, "The Contest between Lithuania-Rus' and the Golden Horde in the Fourteenth Century for Supremacy over Eastern Europe,'" *Archivum Eurasiae Medii Aevi,* II (Wiesbaden 1982), pp. 300–320; Serhii Plokhy, "The Lithuanian Solution," in his *The Origins of the Slavic Nations* (Cambridge 2006), chapter 3; and more extensively in a monograph by S.C. Rowell, *Lithuania Ascending: A Pagan Empire within East-Central Europe, 1295–1345* (Cambridge 1994), which includes as well a detailed discussion of the "Lithuanian" Orthodox metropolitanate of Rus'.

The impact of Lithuanian and, later, Polish political institutions on Ukrainian lands is explored by Omeljan Pritsak, "Kievan Rus' and 16th-17th-Century Ukraine," in Ivan L. Rudnytsky, ed., *Rethinking Ukrainian History* (Edmonton 1981), pp. 1–28; and by Andrzej Kamiński, "The Polish-Lithuanian Commonwealth and Its Citizens: Was the Commonwealth a Stepmother for Cossacks and Ruthenians?" in Peter J. Potichnyj, ed., *Poland and Ukraine: Past and Present* (Edmonton and Toronto 1980), pp. 32–57. Poland's acquisition of the Rus' Kingdom of Galicia and the complex ethnic and religious composition of the region's population is discussed in a collection of essays: Thomas Wünsch and Andrzej Janeczek, eds., *On the Frontier of Latin Europe: Integration and Segregation in Red Ruthenia, 1350–1600* (Warsaw 2004). Polish expansion into neighboring Podolia is examined through the prism of that region's most important city and fortress in Adrian O. Mandzy, *A City on Europe's Steppe Frontier: An Urban History of Early Modern Kamianets-Podilsky, Origins to 1672* (New York 2004). The legal system of Lithuania, which was implemented in Ukrainian lands, is discussed (with legal texts) by Karl von Loewe, *The Lithuanian Statute of 1529* (London 1976); and Leo Okinshevich, *The Law of the Grand Duchy of Lithuania: Background and Bibliography* (New York 1953). Jaroslaw Pelenski, *The Contest for the Legacy of Kievan Rus'* (Boulder, Colo. and New York 1998), provides several studies concerning the ideological claims and political policies of Muscovy, Lithuania, the Golden Horde, and Poland for control of lands that once were within the sphere of Kievan Rus', including the background to the annexation of Ukrainian lands by Poland in 1569. The development of urban areas in Ukraine during the period of Polish-Lithuanian rule is surveyed in Vasyl P. Marochkin, *The Ukrainian City in the XV to mid XVII Centuries* (Toronto 2004), while the controversial question of the role of central Ukrainian lands in Poland's international trade is addressed by Stephen Velychenko, "Cossack Ukraine and Baltic Trade, *1600–1648:* Some Observations on an Unresolved Issue," in I.S. Koropeckyj, ed., *Ukrainian Economic History: Interpretive Essays* (Cambridge, Mass. 1991), pp. 151–171.

The question of the Ukrainian elite, its gradual absorption into the Polish sociopolitical structure, and the degree to which its members retained a sense of their political, religious, and national distinctiveness is explored in three studies by Frank E. Sysyn: "The Problem of Nobilities in the Ukrainian Past: The Polish Period, 1569–1648," in Ivan L. Rudnytsky, ed., *Rethinking Ukrainian History* (Edmonton 1981), pp. 29–102; "Ukrainian-Polish Relations in the 17th Century: The Role of National Consciousness and National Conflict in the Khmel'nyts'kyi Movement," in Peter J. Potichnyj, ed., *Poland and Ukraine: Past and Present* (Edmonton and Toronto 1980), pp. 52–82; and "Regionalism and Political Thought in 17th-Century Ukraine: The Nobility's Grievances at the Diet of 1641," *HUS*, VI, 2 (1982), pp. 167–190. Another approach to this topic is provided by Teresa Chynczewska-Hennel, "The National Consciousness of Ukrainian Nobles and Cossacks from the End of the 16th to the Mid 17th Century," *HUS*, X, 3–4 (1986), pp. 377–392.

The rise of the Zaporozhian Cossacks remains for many writers the most important aspect of Ukrainian history during the period of Lithuanian and Polish rule. The best and most comprehensive introduction to this topic remains Mykhailo Hrushevsky, *History of Ukraine-Rus'*, Vol. VII: *The Cossack Age to 1625* (Edmonton and Toronto 1999) and Vol. VIII: *The Cossack Age, 1626–1650* (Edmonton and Toronto 2002), esp. pt. 1, pp. 2–249. A more concise survey of developments among Zaporozhian Cossacks before 1648 from the perspective of Russian historiography is found in George Vernadsky, *A History of Russia*, Vol. V: *The Tsardom of Moscow, 1547–1682* (New Haven and London 1969), pp. 323–368. The early stages of the movement are treated in a monograph on the late sixteenth-century revolts by Linda Gordon, *Cossack Rebellions: Social Turmoil in the Sixteenth-Century Ukraine* (Albany, N.Y. 1983); and an interpretive essay by Władysław Serczyk, "The Commonwealth and the Cossacks in the First Quarter of the 17th Century," *HUS*, II, 1 (1978), pp. 73–93. How the Cossacks gradually came to be associated with the defense of the Orthodox Church and how their political and military actions were increasingly motivated by religious ideology are topics treated with sophistication in Serhii Plokhy, *The Cossacks and Religion in Early Modern Ukraine* (Oxford and New York 2001). The role of Zaporozhian Cossacks as Black Sea pirates and the manner in which their aggression was viewed by the Ottoman Empire is covered in great detail by Victor Ostapchuk, "The Human Landscape of the Ottoman Black Sea in the Face of the Cossack Naval Raids," *Oriente Moderno*, XX [LXXXI], 1 (Rome 2001), pp. 23–95. Of particular value are the contemporary accounts of Cossack life by Guillaume Le Vasseur, Sieur de Beauplan, *A Description of Ukraine* [1660] (Cambridge, Mass. 1993); and of the group's diplomatic activity: Lubomyr Wynar, ed., *Habsburgs and Zaporozhian Cossacks: The Diary of Erich Lassota von Steblau, 1594* (Littleton, Colo. 1975).

The formation of the Crimean Khanate in the mid-fifteenth century and its impact on Ukrainian lands farther north during the following two centuries is outlined in general histories about the state's ruling people: Alan Fisher, *The Crimean Tatars* (Stanford, Calif. 1978), esp. chapters 1–5; and Brian G. Williams, *The Crimean Tatars* (Leiden, Boston, and Köln 2001), esp. chapter 2. There are also studies on more specialized topics: on the particular relationship of the Crimean Khanate to its nominal overlord, the Ottoman Empire, in Halil Inalcik, "Power Relationships between Russia, the Crimea, and the Ottoman Empire, as Reflected in Titulature," in *Passé turco-tatar, présent soviétique: études offerts à Alexander Bennigson* (Louvain 1986), pp. 175–211, and Alan Fisher, "Crimean Separatism in the Ottoman Empire," in William W. Haddad and William Ochsenwald, eds., *Nationalism in Non-National States: The Dissolution of the Ottoman Empire* (Columbus, Ohio 1977), pp. 57–76; on the state's internal clan structure, in U.

Schamiloglu, "The *Qaraçi* Beys of the Golden Horde," in *Archivum Eurasiae Medii Aevi*, IV (Wiesbaden 1984), pp. 283–297; and Beatrice Forbes Manz, "The Clans of the Crimean Khanate, 1466–1532," *HUS*, II, 3 (1978), pp. 282–310; on the formation of a distinct, if heterogeneous, people, in Brian Glyn Williams, "The Ethnogenesis of the Crimean Tatars: Historical Reinterpretation," *Journal of the Royal Asiatic Society:* Series 3, XI, 3 (London 2001), pp. 329–348; and on the Crimean military and its closely related role in the slave trade, in L.J.D. Collins, "The Military Organization and Tactics of the Crimean Tatars, 16th-17th Centuries," in V.J. Parry and M.E. Yapp, eds., *War, Technology, and Society in the Middle East* (London 1975), pp. 257–276; Alan Fisher, "Muscovy and the Black Sea Slave Trade," *Canadian-American Slavic Studies*, VI, 4 (Pittsburgh 1972), pp. 575–594, and Gilles Veinstein, "From the Italians to the Ottomans: The Case of the Northern Black Sea Coast in the Sixteenth Century," *Mediterranean Historical Review*, I, 2 (London 1986), pp. 221–237. Ukrainian lands also figure prominently in a general history dealing with the military and social impact of the Crimean Tatars on the Slavic lands to the north: Brian L. Davies, *Warfare, State, and Society on the Black Sea Steppe, 1500–1700* (London and New York 2007), esp. pp. 1–114.

The best general introduction to the Jews of Poland-Lithuania, including Ukraine, is found is Salo Wittmayer Baron, *A Social and Religious History of the Jews,* Vol. XVI: *Poland-Lithuania 1500–1650* (New York and Philadelphia 1976). For emphasis on Ukraine, see Shmuel Ettinger, "The Legal and Social Status of the Jews of Ukraine from the 15th Century to the Cossack Uprising of 1648," *JUS,* XVII, 1–2 (1992), pp. 107–140. Eleonora Nadel-Golobič discusses the importance of Jews and Armenians in the economy of western Ukraine in "Armenians and Jews in Medieval Lvov: Their Role in Oriental Trade, 1400–1600," *Cahiers du monde russe et soviétique*, XX, 3–4 (Paris 1979), pp. 345–388. The influence of Greek merchants and scholars on schools and book printing is outlined by Iaroslav Isaievych, "Greek Culture in the Ukraine, 1550–1650," *Modern Greek Studies Yearbook*, VI (Minneapolis 1990), pp. 97–122.

Much more attention has been given to cultural developments, in particular religion and the role of churchmen during this period. A general introduction to the topic, with emphasis on the entire East Slavic/Orthodox world, is found in L.R. Lewitter, "Poland, the Ukraine and Russia in the 17th Century," *Slavonic and East European Review*, XXVII (London 1948-49), pp. 157–171 and 414–429; William K. Medlin and Christos G. Patrinelis, *Renaissance Influences and Religious Reforms in Russia: Western and Post-Byzantine Impacts on Culture and Education* (Geneva 1971); Georges Florovsky, *Ways of Russian Theology*, Pt. 1 (Belmont, Mass. 1979), esp. chapter 2; Frank E. Sysyn, "The Formation of Modern Ukrainian Religious Culture: The 16th and 17th Centuries," in Geoffrey A. Hosking, ed., *Church, Nation, and State in Russia and Ukraine* (Edmonton 1990), pp. 1–22 – revised version in Serhii Plokhy and Frank E. Sysyn, *Religion and Nation in Modern Ukraine* (Edmonton and Toronto 2003), pp. 1–22; and Iaroslav Isaievych, "Early Modern Belarus, Russia, and Ukraine: Culture and Cultural Relations," *JUS,* XVII, 1–2 (1992), pp. 17–28. Iaroslav Isaievych gives particular attention to the brotherhood schools and book printing in a comprehensive monograph, *Volun-*

tary Brotherhood Confraternities of Laymen in Early Modern Ukraine (Edmonton and Toronto 2006), and in two shorter studies: "Between Eastern Tradition and Influences from the West: Confraternities in Early Modern Ukraine and Byelorussia," *Richerche Slavistiche*, XXXVII (Rome 1990), pp. 269–293 (revised version in Jerzy Kloczowski and Henryk Gapski, eds., *Belarus, Lithuania, Poland, Ukraine* [Lublin and Rome 1994], pp. 175-198); and "Books and Book Printing in Ukraine in the 16th and First Half of the 17th Centuries," *Solanus,* N.S., VII (London 1993), pp. 69–95.

The efforts at Church Union (Unia) culminating in the Union of Brest of 1596 are surveyed in the classic study of Oscar Halecki, *From Florence to Brest, 1439–1596,* 2nd ed. (New York 1968). The broader context of these developments within the framework of an Orthodox spiritual and cultural reform in the face of challenges presented by the Protestant Reformation, the Catholic Counter-Reformation, and the ongoing relationship with the Ecumenical Patriarchate in Constantinople is addressed in a wide-ranging monograph by Borys A. Gudziak, *Crisis and Reform: The Kyivan Metropolitanate, the Patriarch of Constantinople, and the Genesis of the Union of Brest* (Cambridge, Mass. 1998), and in his shorter study, "The Kievan Hierarchy, the Patriarchate of Constantnople, and Union with Rome," in Bert Groen and Wil van den Bercken, eds., *Four Hundred Years of the Union of Brest (1596–1996): A Critical Reevaluation* (Leuven, 1998), pp. 17–56. Other studies on the events leading up to the Union of Brest and its immediate impact include: Taras Hunczak, "The Politics of Religion: The Union of Brest, 1596," *Ukraïns'kyi istoryk,* IX, 3–4 (New York 1972), pp. 97–106; Russel P. Moroziuk, *Politics of a Church Union* (Chicago 1983); Mikhail Dmitriev, "The Religious Programme of the Union of Brest in the Context of the Counter-Reformation in Eastern Europe," *JUS,* XVII, 1–2 (1992), pp. 29–44; and Sophia Senyk, "The Union of Brest: An Evaluation," in Groen and van den Bercken, *Four Hundred Years,* pp. 1–16. The widespread polemical literature from this period is surveyed by Ihor Ševčenko, "Religious Polemical Literature in the Ukrainian and Belarusian lands in the 16th and 17th Centuries," *ibid.,* pp. 45–58; and some of the texts are available in English translation: *Lev Krevza's "Defense of Church Unity" (1617) and Zaxarija Kopystens'kyi's "Palinodija or Book of Defense of the Holy Apostolic Eastern Catholic Church and Holy Patriarchs" (1620–1623),* translated by Bohdan Struminsky, 2 pts. (Cambridge, Mass. 1995); and *Rus' Restored: Selected Writings of Meletij Smotryc'kyj, 1610–1630,* translated by David A. Frick (Cambridge, Mass. 2003).

Several churchmen and intellectuals from the period are the subject of study. Particular attention has been given to Meletii Smotryts'kyi: David A. Frick, *Meletij Smotryc'kyj* (Cambridge, Mass. 1995); "Zyzanij and Smotryc'kyj (Moscow, Constantinople, and Kiev): Episodes in Cross-Cultural Misunderstanding," *JUS,* XVII, 1–2 (1992), pp. 67–94; David A. Frick, "Meletij Smotryc'kyj and the Ruthenian Question in the Early 17th Century," *HUS,* VIII, 3–4 (1984), pp. 351–375 and IX, 1–2 (1985), pp. 25–52; and Francis J. Thomson, "Meletius Smotritsky and Union with Rome: The Religious Dilemma in 17th Century Ruthenia," in Bert Groen and Wil van den Bercken, *Four Hundred Years of the Union of Brest* (Leuven 1998), pp. 55–126. Other figures whose careers are the subject of analysis include: Petro Mohyla – with essays by Ihor Ševčenko, Frank E. Sysyn, and Matei Cazacu in *HUS*, VIII, 1–2 (1984), pp. 9–44 and 155–222; Ivan Vyshens'kyi – with studies by Dmitry Čiževsky in *AUAAS*, I, 2 (1951), pp. 113–126, and by Harvey Goldblatt in *HUS*, XV, 1–2 and 3–4 (1991), pp. 7–34 and 354–382, and *HUS*, XVI, 1–2 (1992), pp. 37–66; David A. Frick on "Lazar Baranovych, 1680: The Union of Lech and Rus'," in Andreas Kappeler et al., eds., *Culture, Nation and Identity: The Ukrainian-Russian Encounter, 1600–1945* (Edmonton and Toronto 2003), pp. 19–56; and Sophia Senyk, "Rutskyj's Reform and Orthodox Monasticism: A Comparison of Eastern Rite Monasticism in the Polish-Lithuanian Commonwealth," *Orientalia Christiana Periodica*, XLVIII, 2 (Rome 1982), pp. 406–430. Finally, an otherwise little known aspect of religious life in Ukraine is explored in great detail by George H. Williams, "Protestants in the Ukraine during the Period of the Polish-Lithuanian Commonwealth," *HUS*, 11,1 and 2 (1978), pp. 41–72 and 184–210.

5. The Cossack state, 1648–1711

The uprising of 1648 and its leader Bohdan Khmel'nyts'kyi are of central concern to the historical literature on this period. An introductory survey outlining the uprising of 1648 and subsequent events that by the 1680s resulted in the division of Ukrainian lands between Poland and Muscovy is found in George Vernadsky, *A History of Russia*, Vol. V: *The Tsardom of Moscow, 1546–1682* (New Haven and London 1969), pp. 432–581 and 626–644. The most comprehensive survey of events, with coverage that begins with the decade before the 1648 uprising until the death of Khmel'nyts'kyi in 1657, is Mykhailo Hrushevsky, *History of Ukraine-Rus'*, Vol. VIII: *The Cossack Age, 1626–1650* (Edmonton and Toronto 2002), pts. 2 and 3 and Vol. IX, Book 1: *The Cossack Age, 1650–1653* (Edmonton and Toronto 2005), as well as Book 2: *The Cossack Age, 1654–1657*, Part One (Edmonton and Toronto 2008) and Part Two (forthcoming). There are also two biographies – the popular work by George Vernadsky, *Bohdan, Hetman of Ukraine* (New Haven, Conn. 1941); and the more sophisticated monograph by Frank E. Sysyn, *Between Poland and the Ukraine: The Dilemma of Adam Kysil, 1600–1653* (Cambridge, Mass. 1985) – which place the careers of Khmel'nyts'kyi and Kysil' in the broader context of developments just before and during the 1648 revolution.

Excerpts from documents and treaties among the Cossacks, Poland, and Muscovy between 1649 and 1686 are available in English translation in Sergei Pushkarev, *A Source Book for Russian History from Early Times to 1917*, Vol. I (New Haven and London 1972), esp. pp. 296–306. The structure of the Cossack state that came into being as a result of the uprising is outlined in Leo Okinshevich, *Ukrainian Society and Government, 1648–1781* (Munich 1978); and George Gajecky, *The Cossack Administration of the Hetmanate*, 2 vols. (Cambridge, Mass. 1978). The economic implications of the new Cossack regime in Dnieper Ukraine are reviewed briefly by Carol B. Stevens, "Trade and Muscovite Economic Policy toward the Ukraine: The Movement of Cereal Grains during the Second

Half of the 17th Century," in I.S. Koropeckyj, ed., *Ukrainian Economic History: Interpretive Essays* (Cambridge, Mass. 1991), pp. 172–185.

The status of the Jews of Ukraine during the Khmel'nyts'kyi era has attracted the attention of several authors. The graphic contemporary account by Nathan Hanover, *Abyss of Despair/Yeven Metzulah: The Famous 17th-Century Chronicle Depicting Jewish Life in Russia and Poland during the Chmielnicki Massacres of 1648–1649* (New Brunswick, N.J. and London 1983), is available in English translation. The questionable historical value of this and other accounts is discussed in three interpretive essays: Bernard D. Weinryb, "The Hebrew Chronicles on Bohdan Khmel'nyts'kyi and the Cossack-Polish War," *HUS*, I, 2 (1977), pp. 153–177; Jaroslaw Pelenski, "The Cossack Insurrections in Jewish-Ukrainian Relations," in Peter J. Potichnyj and Howard Aster, eds., *Ukrainian-Jewish Relations in Historical Perspective* (Edmonton 1988), pp. 31–42; and Frank Sysyn, "The Jewish Factor in Khmel'nyts'kyi's Uprising," ibid., pp. 43–56. The results of the most recent research on the topic are found in a special issue of *Jewish History*, XVII, 2 (Haifa 2003), pp. 105–255, devoted to "Jews, Cossacks, Poles, and Peasants in 1648 Ukraine," with studies by Shaul Stampfer, Frank E. Sysyn, Zenon E. Kohut, Natalia Yakovenko, Gershon Bacon, and Moshe Rosman. The otherwise little known presence and economic importance of the Armenians is discussed by Yaroslav Dashkevych, "Armenians in the Ukraine at the Time of Hetman Bohdan Xmel'nyc'kyj, 1648–1657," *HUS*, III–IV (1979–80), pp. 166–188.

Particular attention has been given to the 1654 Agreement of Pereiaslav. The controversial nature of the event and how it has been viewed in the writings of Russian and Ukrainian historians ever since the seventeenth century is surveyed by John Basarab, *Pereiaslav 1654: A Historiographical Study* (Edmonton 1982). The most detailed account of what actually took place during the negotiations is found in Mykhaylo Hrushevsky, *History of Ukraine-Rus'*, Vol. IX, Book 2, Pt. 1 (Edmonton and Toronto 2008), pp. 129–267. Other accounts, which tend to focus on the subsequent controversial relationship of Ukraine to Muscovy and Russia, whose roots go back to in the 1654 agreement, are found in Alexander Ohloblyn, *Treaty of Pereyaslav 1654* (Toronto and New York 1954); Mykhaylo I. Braichevskyi, *Annexation or Reunification: Critical Notes on One Conception* (Munich 1974); and Serhii Plokhy, "Was There a Reunification," in his *The Origins of the Slavic Nations* (Cambridge 2006), chapter 6. The place of the agreement and its aftermath in the larger historical framework of eastern Europe is provided by Hans-Joachim Torke, "The Unloved Alliance: Political Relations between Muscovy and Ukraine in the 17th Century," in Peter J. Potichnyj et al., eds., *Ukraine and Russia in Their Historical Encounter* (Edmonton 1992), pp. 39–66.

The status of Ukrainian lands as the object of rivalry between its powerful neighbors in the wake of the 1654 agreement is given extensive coverage in Mykhailo Hrushevsky, *History of Ukraine-Rus'*, Vol. IX, Book 2, Part 1 (Edmonton and Toronto 2008), esp. pp. 268–501, Vol. IX, Book 2, Pt. 2 (forthcoming), and Vol. X [1657–1659] (forthcoming); C. Bickford O'Brien, *Muscovy and the Ukraine from the Pereiaslav Agreement to the Truce of Andrusovo, 1654–1667* (Berkeley and Los Angeles 1963); Andrzej Sulima Kamiński, *Republic vs. Autocracy: Poland-*

Lithuania and Russia, 1686–1697 (Cambridge, Mass. 1993); Orest Subtelny, "Cossack Ukraine and the Turco-Islamic World," in Ivan L. Rudnytsky, ed., *Rethinking Ukrainian History* (Edmonton 1981), pp. 120–134; and Zbigniew Wójcik, "The Early Period of Pavlo Teterja's Hetmancy in the Right-Bank Ukraine 1661–1663," *HUS*, III–IV (1979–80), pp. 958–992. The last attempts to reach a political accommodation with Poland are given particular attention in Janusz Tazbir, "The Political Reversals of Jurij Nemyryč," *HUS*, V, 3 (1981), pp. 306–319; and Andrzej Kamiński, "The Cossack Experiment in Szlachta Democracy in the Polish-Lithuanian Commonwealth: The Hadiach (Hadziacz) Union," *HUS*, I, 2 (1977), pp. 178–197. The manner in which Cossack Ukraine and its elites accommodated and understood their new political relationship with Muscovy, and how "Ruthenian" values in turn influenced Muscovite cultural life are topics explored in essays by Zenon E. Kohut, Hans-Joachim Torke, and Frank E. Sysyn in Andreas Kappeler et al., eds., *Culture, Nation and Identity: The Ukrainian-Russian Encounter, 1600–1945* (Edmonton and Toronto 2003), pp. 57–143.

The Kievan-Mohyla Academy, Ukraine's leading cultural and educational institution during this period, is the subject of three works: Alexander Sydorenko, *The Kievan Academy in the Seventeenth Century* (Ottawa 1977); Frank B. Kortschmaryk, *The Kievan Academy and its Role in the Organization of Russia at the Turn of the Seventeenth Century* (New York 1976); and *The Kiev Mohyla Academy*, special issue of *HUS*, VIII, 1–2 (1984). The early career of one member of the Kiev Academy, Teofan Prokopovych, who is best known for his later ecclesiastical career in Muscovy/Russia, is described in James Cracraft, "Prokopovyč's Kiev Period Reconsidered," *HUS*, II, 2 (1978), pp. 138–157.

The degree to which the Khmel'nyts'kyi uprising was actually a national revolt and the question of how contemporary intellectuals viewed the Cossack leader, the state he created, and its relationship to their own national identity are subjects explored in several insightful studies by Frank E. Sysyn: "The Khmelnytsky Uprising and Ukrainian Nation-Building," *JUS*, XVII, 1–2 (1992), pp. 141–170; "Concepts of Nationhood in Ukrainian History Writing, 1620–1690," *HUS*, X, 3–4 (1986), pp. 393–423; 17th-Century Views on the Causes of the Khmel'nyts'kyi Uprising: An Examination of the "Discourse on the Present Cossack or Peasant War," *HUS*, V, 4 (1981), pp. 430–466, together with the text of the "Discourse" and a synopsis in *HUS*, V, 2 (1981), pp. 245–257; "The Cossack Chronicles and the Development of Modern Ukrainian Culture and National Identity," *HUS*, XIV, 3–4 (1990), pp. 592–607; and "Fatherland in Early 18th Century Ukrainian Political Culture," in Giovanna Siedina, ed., *Mazepa and His Time: History, Culture, Society* (Alessandria 2004), pp. 39–53. See also Serhii Plokhy, "The Symbol of Little Russia: The Pokrova Icon and Early Modern Ukrainian Political Ideology," *JUS*, XVII, 1–2 (1992), pp. 171–188.

The last important Cossack hetman from this period, Ivan Mazepa, has only limited literature in English. Clarence A. Manning wrote a popular biography, *Hetman of Ukraine Ivan Mazeppa* (New York 1957); more recently, Hubert F. Babinski, *The Mazeppa Legend in European Romanticism* (New York 1974) has surveyed how the Mazepa legend has been treated in European literature, painting, and music. Analytical studies on critical periods in Mazepa's career are provided by Orest Subtelny, "Mazepa, Peter I, and the Question of Treason," *HUS*, II, 2 (1978) pp. 158–183; and idem, ed., *On the Eve of Poltava: The Letters of Ivan Mazepa to Adam Sienawski, 1704–1708* (New York 1975). There is also a multilingual collection of essays in which those that are in English discuss Mazepa's relationship with Poland (by Teresa Chyńczewska-Hennel), his capital at Baturyn (by Volodymyr Mezentsev), and his relationship to the Orthodox Church (by Giovanna Brogi Bercoff), in Giovanna Siedina, ed., *Mazepa e il suo tempo: storia, cultura, società/Mazepa and His Time: History, Culture, Society* (Alessandria 2004).

6. Ukrainian lands in the eighteenth century

The structure and functioning of the Cossack state in the eighteenth century are discussed in the works by Okinshevich and Gajecky (above, section 5). Much attention has also been given to the efforts to retain Cossack autonomy within an expanding Russian Empire. The activity of the exiled Cossack hetman, Pylyp Orlyk, is the subject of articles by Borys Krupnytsky, Mykola Vasylenko, and Elie Borschak, in *AUAAS*, VI, 3–4 (1958), pp. 1247–1312; and of a monograph by Orest Subtelny, *The Mazepists: Ukrainian Separatism in the Early Eighteenth Century* (New York 1981). There is also a more popular biography by Elie Borschak, *Hryhor Orlyk: France's Cossack General* (Toronto 1956).

The final demise of Cossack autonomy within the Russian Empire, the adaptation of Ukraine's elite to Russian imperial society, and its efforts to retain a distinct regional/national identity are best described in four works by Zenon E. Kohut: *Russian Centralism and Ukrainian Autonomy: Imperial Absorption of the Hetmanate, 1760s–1830s* (Cambridge, Mass. 1988); "The Ukrainian Elite in the 18th Century and Its Integration into the Russian Nobility," in Ivo Banac and Paul Bushkovitch, eds., *The Nobility in Russia and Eastern Europe* (New Haven, Conn. 1983), pp. 65–98; "The Development of a Little Russian Identity and Ukrainian Nationbuilding," *HUS*, X, 3–4 (1986), pp. 559–576; and "The Problem of Ukrainian Orthodox Church Autonomy in the Hetmanate (1654–1780s)," ibid., XIV, 3–4 (1990), pp. 364–376. The end of autonomy in the Crimean Khanate is described by Alan W. Fisher, *The Russian Annexation of the Crimea, 1772–1783* (Cambridge 1970). The decline in Ukraine's cultural and social status after two centuries of Muscovite-Russian rule is the subject of Marc Raeff's essay, "Ukraine and Imperial Russia: Intellectual and Political Encounters from the 17th to 19th Century," in Peter J. Potichnyj et al., eds., *Ukraine and Russia in Their Historical Encounter* (Edmonton 1992), pp. 69–85. The last of the major uprisings against Polish rule in Ukraine is discussed by Jaroslaw Pelenski, "The Haidamak Insurrections and the Old Regimes in Eastern Europe," in *The American and European Revolutions, 1776–1848* (Iowa City 1980), pp. 228–242; and Barbara Skinner, "Borderlands of Faith: Reconsidering the Origins of a Ukrainian Tragedy," *Slavic Review*, LXIV, 1 (Champaign, Ill. 2005), pp. 88–116.

The economic transformation of Ukrainian lands under Russian imperial rule is described by Bohdan Krawchenko, "Petrine Mercantilist Economic Policies toward the Ukraine," in I.S. Koropeckyj, ed., *Ukrainian Economic History: Interpretive Essays* (Cambridge, Mass. 1991), pp. 186–209. The acquisition and early years of Russia's development of southern Ukraine (New Russia) and the establishment of new port cities along the Black Sea are topics that feature prominently in a comprehensive biography of Grigorii Potemkin, the imperial official responsible for the area; Simon Sebag Montefiore, *Prince of Princes: The Life of Potemkin* (London 2000). Sociodemographic and territorial changes are given much greater attention in monographs by N.D. Polons'ka-Vasylenko, *The Settlement of the Southern Ukraine, 1750–1775*, special issue of *AUAAS*, IV–V (1955); Roger P. Bartlett, *Human Capital: The Settlement of Foreigners in Russia, 1762–1804* (Cambridge 1980). The varied career of Ukraine's leading eighteenth-century intellectual is dealt with in a collection of essays edited by Richard H. Marshall, Jr., and Thomas E. Bird, *Hryhorij Savyč Skovoroda: An Anthology of Critical Articles* (Edmonton and Toronto 1994), and in a special issue of *JUS*, XXII, 1–2, ed. Michael M. Naydan (Toronto 1997), pp. 1–424, devoted to Hryhorii Skovoroda.

7. Ukrainian lands in the Russian Empire, circa 1785–1914

There is a relatively solid literature in English on the socioeconomic status of Ukrainian lands within the Russian Empire. A general survey of agrarian conditions and early industrial development is provided by Konstantyn Kononenko, *Ukraine and Russia: A History of the Economic Relations between Ukraine and Russia, 1654–1917* (Milwaukee 1958). Very useful, although more limited in chronological or territorial scope, are Daniel Beauvois, *The Polish Nobility between Tsarist Imperialism and the Ukrainian Masses, 1831–1863* (New York 1992); Leonard G. Friesen, *Rural Revolutions in Southern Ukraine: Peasants, Nobles, and Colonists, 1774–1905* (Cambridge, Mass. 2008); Charters Wynn, *Workers, Strikes, and Pogroms: The Donbass-Dnepr Bend in Late Imperial Russia, 1870-1905* (Princeton, N.J. 1992); and Robert Edelman, *Proletarian Peasants: The Revolution of 1905 in Russia's Southwest* [the Right Bank] (Ithaca and London 1987), esp. chapter 2.

Essays on more specific topics include: Robert E. Jones on the early nineteenth-century grain trade, Leonid Melnyk and Martin C. Spechler on industrial development, and Patricia Herlihy on southern Ukraine in I.S. Koropeckyj, ed., *Ukrainian Economic History: Interpretive Essays* (Cambridge, Mass. 1991), pp. 210–227, 246–276, and 310–338; and Bohdan Krawchenko, "The Social Structure of Ukraine at the Turn of the 20th Century," *East European Quarterly*, XVI (Boulder, Colo. 1982), pp. 171–181. Despite the recent advancements in many countries in women's studies, the literature on women in Dnieper Ukraine in the nineteenth century is limited to an introductory survey by Martha Bohachevsky-Chomiak, *Feminists Despite Themselves: Women in Ukrainian Community Life, 1884–1939* (Edmonton 1988), chapter 1; and an interpretive essay by Christine D. Worobec, "Temptress or Virgin? The Precarious Sexual Position of Women in Postemancipation Ukrainian Peasant Society," *Slavic Review*, XLIX, 2 (Austin 1990), pp. 227–238 – reprinted in Beatrice Farnsworth and Lynne Viola, eds., *Russian Peasant Women* (New York 1992), pp. 41–53. In a land traditionally associated with Eastern Christianity, the presence of other religions (Shalaputs, Stundists, Protestant sects) in Dnieper Ukraine has finally been given serious scholarly attention in Sergei I. Zhuk, *Russia's Lost Reformation: Peasants, Millennialism, and Radical Sects in Southern Russia and Ukraine, 1830–1917* (Washington, D.C., Baltimore, and London 2004).

Particular attention has been given to urbanization, both in general studies: Boris P. Balan, "Urbanization and the Ukrainian Economy in the Mid-19th Century," in I. S. Koropeckyj, ed., *Ukrainian Economic History* (Cambridge, Mass. 1991), pp. 277–309; Patricia Herlihy, "Ukrainian Cities in the 19th Century," in Ivan L. Rudnytsky, ed., *Rethinking Ukrainian History* (Edmonton 1981), pp. 135–155; Roger L. Theide on New Russia [southern Ukraine] and Frederick W. Skinner on Odessa, in Michael Hamm, ed., *The City in Russian History* (Lexington, Ky. 1976), pp. 125–149; and in "biographies" of three cities: Michael F. Hamm, *Kiev: A Portrait, 1800–1917* (Princeton, NJ 1993); Patricia Herlihy, *Odessa: A History, 1794–1914* (Cambridge, Mass. 1986); Anna Makolkin, *A History of Odessa: The Last Black Sea Colony* (Lewiston, N.Y. 2004); and Theodore H. Friedgut, *Yuzovka and Revolution: Life and Work/Politics and Revolution in Russia's Donbass, 1869–1924*, 2 vols. (Princeton, N.J. 1989–94). The manner in which peoples of various national backgrounds interacted in Ukraine's cities is discussed in each of the urban "biographies" noted above, as well as in Natan M. Meir, "Jews, Ukrainians, and Russians in Kiev: Intergroup Relations in Late Imperial Associational Life," *Slavic Review*, LXV, 3 (Champaign, Ill. 2006), pp. 475–501.

There is also material on developments among some of Ukraine's "other" (i.e., non-ethnic Ukrainian) peoples. The Crimean Tatars are discussed in several chapters covering the historic nineteenth century in Alan Fisher, *The Crimean Tatars* (Stanford, Calif. 1978), chapters 6–10; and Brian G. Williams, *The Crimean Tatars: The Diaspora Experience and the Forging of a Nation* (Leiden, Boston, and Köln 2001), chapters 3–10. On the impact of the Crimean War on Tatar life in the peninsula and the subsequent massive emigration to the Ottoman Empire, see Mara Kozelsky, "Casualties of Conflict: Crimean Tatars during the Crimean War," *Slavic Review*, LXVII, 4 (Cambridge, Mass. 2008), pp. 866–891; and Alan W. Fisher, "Emigration of Muslims from the Russian Empire in the Years after the Crimean War," *Jahrbücher für Geschichte Osteuropas*, XXXV, 3 (Wiesbaden 1987), pp. 356–371. Particular attention to the Crimean Tatar national awakening and the role of its leading activist, Ismail Gaspirali, is found in Hakan Kirimli, *National Movements and National Identity Among the Crimean Tatars, 1905–1916* (Leiden, Boston, and Köln, 2001); and in a portrait of the era's leading Crimean national leader, by Alan Fisher, "Ismail Gaspirali, Model Leader for Asia," in Edward Allworth, ed., *Tatars of the Crimea* (Durham, N.C. and London 1988), pp. 11–26. Essays by Detlef Brandes and Andreas Kappeler deal with German settlement and that group's relations with Ukrainians, in Hans-Joachim Torke and John-Paul Himka, eds., *German-Ukrainian Relations in Historical Perspective* (Edmonton and Toronto 1994), pp. 10–28 and 45–68. David G. Rempel focuses on the very last years of imperial rule in "The Expropriation of the German Colonists in South Russia during the Great War," *Journal of Modern History*, IV, 1 (Chicago 1932), pp.

49–67. A historic overview of the Czechs in Volhynia is found in Nad'a Valášková, Zdeněk Uherek, and Stanislav Broucek, *Aliens or One's Own People: Czech Immigrants from Ukraine in the Czech Republic* (Prague 1997), esp. pp. 9–31. Two communities in nineteenth-century Odessa are given special attention in John Athanasios Mazis, *The Greeks of Odessa: Diaspora Leadership in Late Imperial Russia* (New York 2004); and Anna Makolkin, *The Nineteenth Century in Odessa: One Hundred Years of Italian Culture on the Shores of the Black Sea, 1794–1894* (Lewiston N.Y. 2007).

The Jews in nineteenth-century Dnieper Ukraine have an extensive literature. The economic and cultural relations of Jews with Poles and Russians in the Right Bank, Kiev, and Odessa are discussed by Daniel Beauvois, "Polish-Jewish Relations in the Territories Annexed by the Russian Empire in the First Half of the 19th Century," in Chimen Abramsky et al., eds., *The Jews in Poland* (Oxford 1986), pp. 78–90; John Doyle Klier, *Imperial Russia's Jewish Question, 1855–1881* (Cambridge 1995), esp. chapters 8–9; and Steven J. Zipperstein, *The Jews of Odessa: A Cultural History, 1794–1881* (Stanford, Calif. 1985).

Two other topics have a rather extensive literature. The first concerns Jewish-Ukrainian political relations, with essays by Moshe Mishkinsky, Ivan L. Rudnytsky, Roman Serbyn, and Yury Boshyk, in Peter J. Potichnyj and Howard Aster, eds., *Ukrainian-Jewish Relations in Historical Perspective* (Edmonton 1988), pp. 57–110 and 173–202; Ivan L. Rudnytsky, "Mykhailo Drahomanov and the Problem of Ukrainian-Jewish Relations," *Canadian Slavonic Papers*, XI, 2 (Ottawa 1969), pp. 182–198; John D. Klier, "*Kievlianin* and the Jews: A Decade of Disillusionment, 1864–1873," *HUS*, V, 1 (1981), pp. 83–101; Olga Andriewsky, "*Medved' iz berlogi:* Vladimir Jabotinsky and the Ukrainian Question, 1904–1914," *HUS*, XIV, 3–4 (1990), pp. 249–267 and a monograph by Israel Kleiner, *From Nationalism to Universalism: Vladimir (Ze'ev) Jabotinsky and the Ukrainian Question* (Edmonton and Toronto 2000). The second topic concerns the pogroms that occurred in the early 1880s and again during the first decade of the twentieth century, which are treated from various perspectives by John D. Klier and Shlomo Lambroza, ed., *Pogroms: Anti-Jewish Violence in Modern Russian History* (Cambridge 1992), esp. chapters 3–5 and 8–9; J. Michael Aronson, "Geographical and Socio-economic Factors in the 1881 Anti-Jewish Pogroms in Russia," *Russian Review*, XXXIX, 1 (Cambridge, Mass. 1980), pp. 18–31; Omeljan Pritsak, "The Pogroms of 1881," *HUS*, XI, 1–2 (1987), pp. 8–43; and Erich Haberer, *Jews and Revolution in Nineteenth-Century Russia* (Cambridge 1995), esp. chapter 10. All aspects of the 1913 Beilis trial in Kiev are discussed in an eyewitness report by Arnold D. Margolin, *The Jews of Eastern Europe* (New York 1926), pp. 155–247; and in studies by Maurice Samuel, *Blood Accusation: The Strange History of the Beiliss Case* (New York 1966) and Ezekiel Leikin, *The Beilis Transcripts: The Anti-Semitic Trial That Shook the World* (London 1993).

Notwithstanding their small size, it is the Mennonites who among Dnieper Ukraine's other peoples have received extensive attention in English-language writings. The best introductions to the subject are by David G. Rempel, "The Mennonite Commonwealth in Russia: A Sketch of Its Founding and Endurance,

1789–1919," *Mennonite Quarterly Review,* XLVII, 4 (Goshen, Ind. 1973), pp. 259–308 and XLVIII, 1 (1974), pp. 5–54; and James Urry, *Mennonites, Politics, and Peoplehood: Europe – Russia – Canada, 1525 to 1980* (Winnipeg 2006). On the early settlement and socio-economic challenges faced by Mennonites, see John R. Staples, *Cross-Cultural Encounters on the Ukrainian Steppe: Settling the Molochna Basin, 1783–1861* (Toronto 2003). There is also the monumental 1911 compendium of Peter M. Friesen, *The Mennonite Brotherhood in Russia, 1789–1910* (Fresno, Calif, 1978); the synthetic history by James Urry, *None but Saints: The Transformation of Mennonite Life in Russia, 1789–1889* (Winnipeg 1989); articles by several authors on all aspects of Mennonite development in John Friesen, ed., *Mennonites in Russia, 1788–1988* (Winnipeg 1989), pp. 11–259 (including a historiographical survey by Peter J. Klassen, pp. 339–363); a biography of the leading Mennonite activist in Ukraine during the first half of the nineteenth century by David H. Epp, *Johann Cornies* (Winnipeg 1995); and a detailed memoir about Mennonite life with a scholarly introduction by Harvey L. Dyck that places the group within the larger imperial structure *A Mennonite in Russia: The Diaries of Jacob D. Epp, 1851–1880* (Toronto, Buffalo, and London 1991). There is a useful popular survey of Mennonite history in "Russia" (in fact, in Ukraine) that includes as well a discussion of the immigrant descendants of that group in Canada: Harry Loewen, *Road to Freedom: Mennonites Escape the Land of Suffering* (Kitchener, Ontario 2000).

Individual Mennonite communities, in particular those in south-central Ukraine, are described in great detail in *First Mennonite Villages in Russia, 1789–1943* (Vancouver 1981); and Heinrich Goerz, *The Molotschna Settlement* (Winnipeg 1993). Shorter studies describe the community's cultural life: John B. Toews, "Cultural and Intellectual Aspects of the Mennonite Experience in Russia," *Mennonite Quarterly Review,* LIII, 2 (Goshen, Ind. 1979), pp. 137–159, and David G. Rempel, "An Introduction to Russian Mennonite Historiography," ibid., XLVIII, 4 (1974), pp. 409–446; or its responses to the opportunities and restrictions of tsarist rule: James Urry, "Through the Eye of a Needle: Wealth and the Mennonite Experience in Imperial Russia," *Journal of Mennonite Studies,* III (Winnipeg 1985), pp. 7–35; Harvey L. Dyck, "Russian Mennonitism and the Challenge of Russian Nationalism, 1889," *Mennonite Quarterly Review,* LVI, 4 (Goshen, Ind. 1982), pp. 307–341; Leonard Friesen, "Mennonites in Russia and the Revolution of 1905," ibid., LXII, 1 (1988), pp. 42–55; and Helmut-Harry Loewen and James Urry, "Protecting Mammon: Some Dilemmas of Mennonite Non-Resistance in Late Imperial Russia and the Origins of the Selbstschutz," *Journal of Mennonite Studies,* IX (Winnipeg 1991), pp. 34–53. The problem of the relations – or lack of them – between Mennonites and Ukrainians is addressed by G.K. Epp, "Mennonite-Ukrainian Relations, 1789–1945," ibid., VII (1989), pp. 131–144; and Leonard G. Friesen, "Mennonites and Their Peasant Neighbours in Ukraine before 1900," ibid., X (1992), pp. 56–69.

The Ukrainian nationality question, in particular its relationship to socioeconomic and ideological factors, has an extensive literature. A conceptual introduction is provided by Paul Robert Magocsi, "The Ukrainian National Revival: A New

Analytical Framework," *Canadian Review of Studies in Nationalism*, XVI, 1–2 (Charlottetown, P.E.I. 1989), pp. 45–62. Roman Szporluk, "Ukraine: From Imperial Periphery to a Sovereign State," *Daedalus*, CXXVI, 3 (Boston 1997), pp.86–119 provides a sketch of the formation of the Ukrainian nationality in the context of concurrent developments among Russians in the Russian Empire and Poles in the Habsburg Empire. The manner in which the Ukrainian elites were absorbed into the Russian imperial social fabric while retaining a degree of regional/national distinctiveness is discussed in Zenon E. Kohut, *Russian Centralism and Ukrainian Autonomy: Imperial Absorption of the Hetmanate, 1760–1830s* (Cambridge, Mass. 1988), esp. chapter 6; David Saunders, *The Ukrainian Impact on Russian Culture, 1750–1850* (Edmonton 1985); Andreas Kappeler, "The Ukrainians of the Russian Empire, 1860–1914," in Andreas Kappeler, ed., *The Formation of National Elites*, Comparative Studies on Governments and Non-dominant Ethnic Groups in Europe, 1850–1940, Vol. VI (Aldershot, U.K. 1992), pp. 105–132; and Stephen Velychenko, "Identities, Loyalties, and Service in Imperial Russia: Who Administered the Borderlands?" *Russian Review*, LIV, 2 (Columbus, Ohio 1995), pp. 188–208. The attitude of the imperial government and its "use" of the Ukrainian national movement during the first half of the nineteenth century is treated by Orest Pelech, "The State and the Ukrainian Triumvirate in the Russian Empire, 1831–47," in Bohdan Krawchenko, ed., *Ukrainian Past, Ukrainian Present* (London and New York 1993), pp. 1–17. The participation of Ukrainians in the limited political structures of the Russian Empire in the decade before World War I is discussed in Oleh W. Gerus, "The Ukrainian Question in the Russian Duma, 1906–1917: An Overview," in *Studia Ucrainica*, Vol. II (Ottawa 1984), pp. 157–174; and Olga Andriewsky, "The Making of the Generation of 1917: Towards a Collective Biography," *JUS*, XXIX, 1–2 (Toronto 2004), pp. 19–37.

The use of history in the formulation of a Ukrainian national ideology is examined from various points of view by Mykhailo S. Hrushevskyi, *The Historical Evolution of the Ukrainian Problem* (Cleveland 1981); Natalia Polonska-Vasylenko, *Two Conceptions of the History of Ukraine and Russia* (London 1968); Omeljan Pritsak and John S. Reshetar, Jr., "The Ukraine and the Dialectics of Nationbuilding," *Slavic Review*, XXII, 2 (Seattle 1963), pp. 5–36, reprinted in Donald W. Treadgold, ed., *The Development of the USSR* (Seattle 1964), pp. 236–267; Ivan L. Rudnytsky and George G. Grabowicz, "Observations [and Further Observations] on the Problem of 'Historical' and 'Non-historical' Nations," *HUS*, V, 3 (1981), pp. 358–388; George G. Grabowicz, "Three Perspectives on the Cossack Past: Gogol', Ševčenko, Kuliš," *HUS*, V, 2 (1981), pp. 171–194; Stephen Velychenko, *National History as Cultural Process* (Edmonton 1992), esp. pt 3; and Serhii Plokhy, "Ukraine or Little Russia?: Revisiting an Early 19th-century Debate," *Canadian Slavonic Papers*, XLVIII, 3–4 (Edmonton 2006), pp. 335–353. The manner in which ethnic Ukrainians actually learned the history of their homeland is discussed by Serhy Yekelchyk, "The Grand Narrative and Its Discontents: Ukraine in Russian History Textbooks and Ukrainian Students' Minds, 1830s–1900s," in Andreas Kappeler et al., eds., *Culture, Nation, and Identity* (Edmonton 2003), pp. 229–255. For the dissenting Polish and Russian views that deny the very existence of a distinct Ukrainian polity, see Stephen Velychenko, *National History as Cultural Process* (Edmonton 1992), pts. 1 and 2; and Pierre Bregy and Serge Obolensky, *The Ukraine: A Russian Land* (London 1940). A provocative variant of the Russian interpretation, in which "all Russian" culture is considered to be primarily Ukrainian in origin following the reforms of the leading "Ukrainianizer," Tsar Peter I, is argued by Nikolai Sergeevich Trubetzkoy in "The Ukrainian Problem," in his *The Legacy of Genghis Khan and Other Essays on Russia's Identity* (Ann Arbor, Mich. 1991), pp. 245–267.

A useful overview of the work of intellectuals in the Ukrainian national revival is provided by Ivan Rudnytsky, "The Intellectual Origins of Modern Ukraine," *AUAAS*, VI, 3–4 (1958), pp. 1381–1405, reprinted in Ivan L. Rudnytsky, *Essays in Modern Ukrainian History* (Edmonton 1987), pp. 123–141. The best introduction to intellectual currents and practical cultural work during the early stages of the national revival is George S.N. Luckyj, *Between Gogol' and Ševčenko: Polarity in the Literary Ukraine, 1798–1847* (Munich 1971). On the ideology and limited practical activity of Dnieper Ukraine's first national organization, see Stefan Kozak, "On the Tradition of Cyril and Methodius in Ukraine," *JUS*, XIII, 2 [13] (1988), pp. 29–51; and George S.N. Luckyj, *Young Ukraine: The Brotherhood of Saints Cyril and Methodius in Kiev, 1845–1847* (Ottawa 1991). The importance of pan-Slavic ideology for that organization and for subsequent activists is discussed in Johannes Remy, "Panslavism in the Ukrainian National Movement from 1840s to the 1870s," *JUS*, XX, 2 (Edmonton 2005), pp. 27–50; the first call for Ukrainian independence is discussed in Zenon V. Wasyliw, "A Revolutionary Nationalist Declaration: Mykola Mikhnovsky's *Samostiina Ukraïna*," *East European Quarterly*, XXXIII, 3 (Boulder, Colo. 1999), pp. 371–384.

The question of literary and broader intellectual relations with Russian and Polish culture and society are addressed in the three essays by George G. Grabowicz: "Ukrainian-Russian Literary Relations in the 19th Century: A Formulation of the Problem," in Peter J. Potichnyj et al., eds., *Ukraine and Russia in Their Historical Encounter* (Edmonton 1992), pp. 214–244; "Between Subversion and Self-assertion: The Role of *Kotliarevshchyna* in Russian-Ukrainian Relations," in Andreas Kappeler et al. eds., *Culture, Nation, and Identity* (Edmonton and Toronto 2003), pp. 215–228; and "The History of Polish-Ukrainian Literary Relations: A Literary and Cultural Perspective," in Peter J. Potichnyj, ed., *Poland and Ukraine: Past and Present* (Edmonton and Toronto 1980), pp. 107–131. The problematic nature of Nikolai Gogol' and the relationship of this "Russian" writer to his origins and early interest and extensive writings about Ukrainian history and culture is given serious attention in Edyta M. Bojanowska, *Nikolai Gogol': Between Ukrainian and Russian Nationalism* (Cambridge, Mass. 2007).

Several of the leading national activists have biographies or substantive studies about them. Most attention has been given to Ukraine's "national bard": Volodymyr Mijakovs'kyj, ed., *Taras Ševčenko, 1814–1861: A Symposium* (The Hague 1962); George S.N. Luckyj, ed., *Shevchenko and the Critics 1861–1980* (Toronto, Buffalo, and London 1980); George G. Grabowicz, *The Poet as Mythmaker: A Study of Symbolic Meaning in Taras Ševčenko* (Cambridge, Mass. 1982); and Pavlo Zaitsev,

Taras Shevchenko: A Life (Toronto, Buffalo, and London 1988). There are also bio-graphical sketches of several writers (Hryhorii Osnovianenko, Panteleimon Kul-ish, Osyp Iurii Fed'kovych, Ivan Nechui-Levyts'kyi, Ivan Franko, Lesia Ukraïnka) by George S.N. Luckyj, *Seven Lives: Vignettes of Ukrainian Writers in the Nineteenth Century,* special issue of the *AUAAS,* XX (New York 1988–99); full-length biogra-phies of two figures: George S.N. Luckyj, *Panteleimon Kulish: A Sketch of His Life and Times* (Boulder, Colo. and New York 1983) and Thomas M. Prymak, *Mykola Kostomarov: A Biography* (Toronto, Buffalo, and London 1996); and a collection of essays by various authors on Mykhailo Drahomanov in a special issue edited by Ivan L. Rudnytsky of the *AUAAS,* II, 1 (1952). Rudnytsky's essay in this collection, "Drahomanov as a Political Theorist" is reprinted together with his "The First Ukrainian Political Program: Mykhailo Drahamanov's 'Introduction' to *Hroma-da,*" in Ivan L. Rudnytsky, *Essays in Modern Ukrainian History* (Edmonton 1987), pp. 203–282. Some of the key writings of these intellectual leaders are available in English, including several essays by Drahomanov in the special issue of the *AUAAS,* II, 1 (1952), pp. 141–218; and Nikolai Kostomarov, *Books of Genesis of the Ukrainian People* (New York 1954).

A useful introduction to Russian imperial policy toward its national minorities in the western part of the empire is found in Theodore R. Weeks, *Nation and State in Late Imperial Russia: Nationalism and Russification on the Western Frontier, 1863–1914* (De Kalb, Ill. 1996). Of particular use because of a comparative perspective is the work of Stephen Velychenko, "Empire Loyalism and Minority Nationalism in Great Britain and Imperial Russia, 1707 to 1914: Institutions, Law, and Nation-ality in Scotland and Ukraine," *Comparative Studies in Society and History,* XIX, 3 (Cambridge 1997), pp. 413–441 and his "Identities, Loyalties and Service in Imperial Russia: Who Administered the Borderlands?," *The Russian Review,* LIV, 1 (Columbus, Ohio 1995), pp. 188–208. On tsarist policy toward Poles, Czechs, and Jews in Ukraine, specifically in the Right Bank, Volhynia, see Valentyna Nadolska, "Volyn within the Russian Empire: Migratory Processes and Cultural Interaction," in Kimitaka Matsuzato, ed., *Imperiology: From Empirical Knowledge to Discussing the Russian Empire* (Sapporo, Japan 2007), pp. 85–110; and Kimitaka Matsuzato, "The Issue of Zemstvos in Right Bank Ukraine, 1864–1906: Russian Anti-Polonism under the Challenges of Modernization," *Jahrbücher für Geschichte Osteuropas, LI,* 2 (Stuttgart 2003), pp. 218–235. The restrictions directed specifically toward eth-nic Ukrainians are the subject of studies by Alexei Miller, *The Ukrainian Question: The Russian Empire and Nationalism in the Nineteenth Century* (Budapest 2003); Dav-id Saunders, "Russia and Ukraine under Alexander II: The Valuev Edict of 1863," *International History Review,* XVII, 1 (Burnaby, B.C. 1995), pp. 23–50; Johannes Remy, "The Valuev Circular and Censorship of Ukrainian Publications in the Russian Empire (1863–1876): Intention and Practice," *Canadian Slavonic Papers,* XLIX, 1–2 (Edmonton, 2007), pp. 87–110; George Y. Shevelov, *The Ukrainian Language in the First Half of the Twentieth Century (1900–1941): Its State and Status* (Cambridge, Mass. 1989), esp. chapters 1 and 2; and Stephen Velychenko, "Tsar-ist Censorship and Ukrainian Historiography, 1828–1906," *Canadian-American Slavic Studies,* XXIII, 4 (Bakersfield, Calif. 1989), pp. 385–408.

The attitudes of the Russian political and intellectual elite toward the Ukrainian movement and what forms the latter adopted in order to survive are discussed by Alexei Miller (noted in the previous paragraph); and in essays by Andreas Kappeler, "*Mazepintsy, Malorossy, Khokhly:* Ukrainians in the Ethnic Hierarchy of the Russian Empire," by Olga Andriewsky, "The Russian-Ukrainian Discourse and the Failure of the 'Little Russian Solution,' 1782–1917," and by Oleh S. Ilnytzkyj, "Modeling Culture in the Empire: Ukrainian Modernism and the Death of the all-Russian Idea," in Andreas Kappeler et al., eds., *Culture, Nation, and Identity* (Edmonton and Toronto 2003), pp. 162–214 and 298–324; David Saunders, "Russia's Ukrainian Policy (1847–1905): A Demographic Approach," *European History Quarterly,* XXV, 2 (London 1995), pp. 181–208; and David Saunders, "Contemporary Critics of Gogol's *Vechera* and the Debate about Russian *narodnost'*, 1831–1832," *HUS,* V, 1 (1981), pp. 66–82. More specific focus on individual Russian thinkers is found in Thomas M. Prymak, "Herzen on Poland and Ukraine," *JUS,* VII, 1 [12] (1982), pp. 31–40; Stephen Horak, "Alexander Herzen, Poles, and Ukrainians: A Dilemma in Unity and Conflict," *East European Quarterly,* XVII (Boulder, Colo. 1983), pp. 185–212; Andrea Rutherford, "Vissarion Belinskii and the Ukrainian National Movement," *The Russian Review,* LIV, 4 (Columbus, Ohio 1995), pp. 500–515; Alexis E. Pogorelskin, "A.N. Pypin's Defense of Ukraine: Sources and Motivation," in Bohdan Krawchenko, ed., *Ukrainian Past, Ukrainian Present* (London and New York 1993), pp. 35–54; and Richard Pipes, "Peter Struve and Ukrainian Nationalism," *HUS,* III–IV (1979–80), pp. 675–683. A good insight into Russian attitudes is found in the memoirs of one of Kiev's leading opponents of the Ukrainian movement: V.V. Shulgin, *The Years: Memoirs of a Member of the Russian Duma, 1906–1917* (New York 1984).

8. Ukrainian lands in the Austrian Empire, circa 1772–1914

The literature on Ukrainian developments in the Austrian Empire during the late eighteenth and the nineteenth centuries is differentiated according to the three regions where Ukrainians formed a majority population: eastern Galicia, northern Bukovina, and Transcarpathia. By far most of the material deals with the largest of these regions, Galicia. Still useful as a general introduction, with emphasis on politics and the nationality movement, is Ivan L. Rudnytsky, "The Ukrainians in Galicia under Austrian Rule," *Austrian History Yearbook,* III, pt. 2 (Houston 1967), pp. 394–429 – reprinted in a revised version in Andrei S. Markovits and Frank E. Sysyn, eds., *Nationbuilding and the Politics of Nationalism: Essays on Austrian Galicia* (Cambridge, Mass. 1982), pp. 23–93, and in Ivan L. Rudnytsky, *Essays in Modern Ukrainian History* (Edmonton 1987), pp. 315–352.

Of the studies available on Galicia's socioeconomic status, the best general introduction is found in the chapters by Francis Bujak, John Rozwadowski et al. in the *Polish Encyclopedia,* Vol. III: *Economic Life of Poland* (Geneva 1922), pp. 237–361. A focus on Ukrainian-inhabited eastern Galicia, in particular during the second half of the nineteenth century, is found in an introductory outline by John-Paul Himka, "The Background to Emigration: Ukrainians of Galicia and

Bukovina, 1848–1914," in Manoly R. Lupul, ed., *A Heritage in Transition* (Toronto 1982), pp. 11–31. The status of the peasantry is the subject of several studies. John-Paul Himka, "Serfdom in Galicia," *JUS,* IX, 2 (1984), pp. 3–28, emphasizes the long-term negative impact of serfdom even after it was abolished in 1848. A revisionist view, which argues that at least in some regions the economic outlook for peasants was steadily improving, is presented in a microeconomic analysis by Stella Hryniuk, *Peasants with Promise: Ukrainians in Southeastern Galicia, 1880–1900* (Edmonton 1991); and in a more interpretive essay by Hryniuk, "Polish Lords and Ukrainian Peasants: Conflict, Deference, and Accomodation in Eastern Galicia in the Late Nineteenth Century," *Austrian History Yearbook,* XXIV (Minneapolis 1993), pp. 119–132. Cottage industry is given extensive coverage in an essay by Richard L. Rudolph, "The East European Peasant Household and the Beginnings of Industry: East Galicia, 1786–1914," in I.S. Koropeckyj, ed., *Ukrainian Economic History: Interpretive Essays* (Cambridge, Mass. 1991), pp. 339–382. The industry for which Galicia became a major world producer during the half century before World War I is described in detail in Alison Fleig Frank, *Oil Empire: Visions of Prosperity in Austrian Galicia* (Cambrige, Mass and London 2005). Of particular value for understanding the administrative and governmental structures as well as the basic economic elements (weights, measures, currency) used in Ukrainian-inhabited Habsburg lands is John-Paul Himka, *Galicia and Bukovina: A Research Handbook about Western Ukraine, Late 19th and 20th Centuries,* Historic Sites Service Occasional Paper, No. 20 (Edmonton 1990).

A rather substantive literature exists on the nationality question in Galicia. The multicultural aspect of Habsburg Galicia as a land in which Poles, Ukrainians, Jews, and Austro-Germans interacted is discussed in a series of essays by various scholars in Christopher M. Hann and Paul Robert Magocsi, eds., *Galicia: A Multicultured Land* (Toronto, Buffalo, and London 2005). Particular attention has been given to the provincial capital of L'viv as a focal point for the development of differing national movements: John Czaplicka, ed., *Lviv: A City in the Crossroads of Culture,* special issue of *HUS,* XXIV (Cambridge, Mass. 2000) and separately (Cambridge, Mass. 2007), esp. pp. 13–170; and Harald Binder, "Making and Defending a Polish Town: 'Lwów' (Lemberg), 1848–1914," *Austrian History Yearbook,* XXXIV (Minneapolis 2003), pp. 57–81. For developments specifically among ethnic Ukrainians, see the comprehensive study on the earlier period, including events during the 1848 revolution, in Jan Kozik, *The Ukrainian National Movement in Galicia, 1815–1849* (Edmonton 1986). There is also a short narrative of the revolutionary year by Martha Bohachevsky-Chomiak, *The Spring of the Nation: The Ukrainians of Eastern Galicia in 1848* (Philadelphia 1967); an interpretive essay on the second half of the century by Iaroslav Isaievych, "Galicia and Problems of National Identity," in Ritchie Robertson and Edward Timms, eds., *The Habsburg Legacy: National Identity in Historical Perspective* (Edinburgh 1994), pp. 37–45; and a discussion of the first proposals for Ukrainian independence by John-Paul Himka, "Young Radicals and Independent Statehood: The Idea of a Ukrainian Nation-State, 1890–1895," *Slavic Review,* XLI, 2 (Urbana, Ill. 1982), pp. 219–235.

The manner in which national identity was understood by various factions of the Galician-Ukrainian intelligentsia and the population at large is dealt with in studies by Paul Robert Magocsi, "Old Ruthenianism and Russophilism: A New Conceptual Framework for Analyzing National Ideologies in Late 19th Century Eastern Galicia," in Paul Debreczyn, ed., *American Contributions to the Ninth International Congress of Slavists*, Vol. II (Columbus, Ohio 1983), pp. 305–324 – reprinted in Paul Robert Magocsi, *The Roots of Ukrainian Nationalism: Galicia as Ukraine's Piedmont* (Toronto, London, and Buffalo 2002), pp. 99–118; John-Paul Himka "The Construction of Nationality in Galician Rus': Icarean Flight in Almost All Directions," in Ronald Grigur Suny and Michael D. Kennedy, eds., *Intellectuals and the Articulation of the Nation* (Ann Arbor, Mich. 1999), pp. 109–164; Ostap Sereda, "Whom Shall We Be?: Public Debates over the National Identity of Galician Ruthenians in the 1860s," *Jahrbücher für Geschichte Osteuropa*, XLIX, 2 (Wiesbaden 2001), pp. 200–211; Ostap Sereda, "From Church-Based to Cultural Nationalism: Early Ukrainophiles, Ritual-Purification Movement, and the Emerging Cult of Taras Shevchenko in Austrian Eastern Galicia in the 1860s," *Canadian-American Slavic Studies*, XL, 1 (Idyllwild, Calif. 2006), pp. 21–47; and John-Paul Himka, *Religion and Nationality in Western Ukraine: The Greek Catholic Church and the Ruthenian National Movement in Galicia, 1867–1900* (Montreal and Kingston, Ont. 1999). There are also intellectual biographies of two national activists: Peter Brock, "Ivan Vahylevych (1811–1866) and the Ukrainian National Identity," *Canadian Slavonic Papers*, XIV, 2 (Ottawa 1972), pp. 153–190, reprinted in Markovits and Sysyn, *Nationbuilding and the Politics of Nationalism*, pp. 111–148, and by Ivan L. Rudnytsky, "Hipolit Vladimir Terlecki," in Rudnytsky, *Essays in Modern Ukrainian History*, pp. 143–172; and a detailed study of how history was used to create among Galicia's East Slavs a sense of national belonging: Andriy Zayarnyuk, "Obtaining History: The Case of Ukrainians in Habsburg Galicia, 1848–1900," *Austrian History Yearbook*, XXXVI (Minneapolis 2005), pp. 121–147.

John-Paul Himka describes in several studies the actual mechanisms by which nationalist ideologies were disseminated among the rural population: *Galician Villagers and the Ukrainian National Movement in the Nineteenth Century* (Edmonton 1988); and "Voluntary Artisan Associations and the Ukrainian National Movement in Galicia (1870s)," in Markovits and Sysyn, *Nationbuilding and the Politics of Nationalism*, pp. 178–195. He has given particular attention to the role of the Eastern-rite church in several articles: "The Greek Catholic Church in Galicia, 1848–1914," *Harvard Ukrainian Studies*, XXVI, 1–4 (Cambridge, Mass. 2002–03), pp. 245–260; "Priests and Peasants: The Greek Catholic Pastor and the Ukrainian National Movement in Austria, 1867–1900," *Canadian Slavonic Papers*, XXI, 1 (Ottawa 1979), pp. 1–14; "The Greek Catholic Church and Nation-Building in Galicia, 1772–1918," *HUS*, VIII, 3–4 (1984), pp. 426–452; "The Transformations and Formation of Social Strata and Their Place in the Ukrainian National Movement in Nineteenth-Century Galicia," *JUS*, XXIII, 2 (Toronto 1998), pp. 3–22; and "The Propagation of Orthodoxy in Galicia on the Eve of World War I," in *Ukraïna: kul'turna spadshchyna, natsional'na svidomist', derzhavnist'*, Vol. IX (L'viv, 2001), pp. 480–496. The role played by the leading Greek Catholic hierarch during the last two decades of Habsburg rule (until late 1918) in Galicia is discussed in Cyril Korolevskij, *Metropolitan Andrew, 1865–1944* (L'viv 1993), esp. chapters 3, 4, and 6; and in essays by Wolfdieter Bihl and John Paul Himka in Paul Robert Magocsi, ed., *Morality and Reality: The Life and Times of Andrei Sheptyts'kyi* (Edmonton 1989), pp. 15–46.

Other cultural and organizational mechanisms for Galician-Ukrainian nationality-building are described in a study about the role of one city in that process by Stanisław Stępen, "Borderland City: Przemyśl and the Ruthenian National Awakening in Galicia," in Hann and Magocsi, *Galicia: A Multicultured Land*, pp. 52–70; in three works by Paul Robert Magocsi: "The Language Question as a Factor in the National Movement in Eastern Galicia," in Markovits and Sysyn, *Nationbuilding and the Politics of Nationalism*, pp. 220–238; "Nationalism and National Bibliography: Ivan E. Levyts'kyi and 19th-Century Galicia," *Harvard Library Bulletin*, XXVIII, 1 (Cambridge, Mass. 1980), pp. 81–109; "The Kachkovs'kyi Society and the National Revival in 19th-Century East Galicia," *HUS*, XV, 1–2 (1991), pp. 48–87 – reprinted in Paul Robert Magocsi, *The Roots of Ukrainian Nationalism*, pp. 83–98 and 119–189; and in studies by Martha Bohachevsky-Chomiak, *Feminists Despite Themselves: Women in Ukrainian Community Life, 1884–1939* (Edmonton 1988), esp. chapter 59; Ann Sirka, *The Nationality Question in Austrian Education: The Case of Ukrainians in Galicia, 1867–1914* (Frankfurt-am-Main 1980); and Stephen M. Horak, "The Shevchenko Scientific Society, 1873–1973," *East European Quarterly*, VII, 3 (Boulder, Colo. 1973), pp. 249–264.

Political life among Galicia's Ukrainians varied in its attitude toward Habsburg rule. A discontented few hoped for salvation through annexation to the Russian Empire or in the changes that might be brought about at home by the socialist movement. Most of the populace and its leaders, however, remained to the end loyal subjects of the Austrian Habsburg monarch. These themes are discussed in John-Paul Himka, "Hope in the Tsar: Displaced Naive Monarchism among the Ukrainian Peasants of the Habsburg Empire," *Russian History*, VI, 1–2 (Tempe, Ariz. 1980), pp. 125–138; John-Paul Himka, *Socialism in Galicia: The Emergence of Polish Social Democracy and Ukrainian Radicalism, 1860–1890* (Cambridge, Mass. 1983); and Paul Robert Magocsi, *The Roots of Ukrainian Nationalism* (Toronto 2002), chapters 4 and 5. The achievements of the Ukrainian national movement in practical politics are described in three articles by Theodore Bohdan Ciuciura: "Ukrainian Deputies in the Old Austrian Parliament, 1861–1918," *Mitteilungen*, XIV (Munich 1977), pp. 38–56; "Galicia and Bukovina as Austrian Crown Provinces: Ukrainian Experience in Representative Institutions, 1861–1918," *Studia Ucrainica*, Vol. II (Ottawa 1984), pp. 175–195; and "Provincial Politics in the Habsburg Empire: The Case of Galicia and Bukovyna," *Nationalities Papers*, XIII, 2 (North York, Ont. 1985), pp. 247–273.

Among the other peoples of eastern Galicia, only the Jews have a literature on them in English. The intellectual currents during the first half century of Austrian rule are described in Raphael Mahler, *Hasidism and the Jewish Enlightenment* (Philadelphia, New York, and Jerusalem 1985), esp. chapters 1–6. The problems of identity, economic status, and political activism during the late nineteenth and early twentieth centuries are the subject of articles by Piotr Wróbel, "The Jews of Galicia under Austrian-Polish Rule, 1869–1918," *Austrian History Yearbook*, XXV (Minneapolis 1994), pp. 97–138; Ezra Mendelsohn, "Jewish Assimilation in Lvov: The Case of Wilhelm Feldman," *Slavic Review*, XXVIII (Seattle 1969), pp. 577–590, reprinted in Markovits and Sysyn, *Nationbuilding*, pp. 94–110; Raphael Mahler, "The Economic Background of Jewish Emigration from Galicia to the United States," *YIVO Annual of Jewish Social Science*, VIII (New York 1952), pp. 255–267; Jacob Bross, "The Beginnings of the Jewish Labor Movement in Galicia," ibid., V (1950), pp. 55–84; and Leila P. Everett, "The Rise of Jewish National Politics in Galicia, 1905–1907," in Markovits and Sysyn, *Nationbuilding*, pp. 149–177. There are also twelve essays on Jews in Austrian-ruled Galicia, with those by John-Paul Himka and Jaroslav Hrytsak focussing specifically on eastern Galicia, in *Polin: Studies in Polish Jewry*, Vol. XII: *Focussing on Galicia: Jews, Poles, and Ukrainians, 1772–1918* (London and Portland, Ore. 1999), esp. 3–176.

With regard to the other two Ukrainian-inhabited Habsburg lands, the literature on developments in northern Bukovina is limited. Aside from the handbook by Himka and studies on Austrian parliamentary life by Ciuciura mentioned above in which Bukovina is discussed along with Galicia, a popular description of national life is provided in the first part of I.M. Nowosiwsky, *Bukovinian Ukrainians: A Historical Background and Their Self Determination in 1918* (New York 1970), esp. pp. 23–89. Non-Ukrainian views of the last decades before World War I are provided in the section on Bukovina in the reliable work of Keith Hitchins, *Rumania, 1866–1917* (Oxford 1994), pp. 231–239; and in an essay by Fred Stambrook, "National and Other Identities in Bukovina in Late Austrian Times," *Austrian History Yearbook*, XXXV (Minneapolis 2004), pp. 185–203. For Transcarpathia, see Paul Robert Magocsi, *The Shaping of a National Identity: Subcarpathian Rus', 1848–1948* (Cambridge, Mass. 1978), esp. chapters 2–3, and Elaine Rusinko, *Straddling Borders: Literature and Identity in Subcarpathian Rus'* (Toronto, Buffalo, and London 2003), esp. chapters 1–4.

9. World War I, revolution, and civil war

The impact of military campaigns during the early years of the war, especially in Galicia, is covered in some detail in Norman Stone, *The Eastern Front, 1914–1917* (New York 1975), esp. chapters 4–6 and 11. Russian imperial policy before, during, and after its wartime rule in Galicia is discussed in Mark von Hagen, *War in a European Borderland: Occupations and Occupation Plans in Galicia and Ukraine, 1914–1918* (Seattle 2007). There are much more substantive studies of the German, Allied (French), and White Russian presence in eastern and southern Ukraine, in which the emphasis is on the diplomatic and political role of the foreign armies, not on their military activity: Oleh S. Fedyshyn, *Germany's Drive to the East and the Ukrainian Revolution, 1917–1918* (New Brunswick, N.J. 1971); George A. Brinkley, *The Volunteer Army and the Allied Intervention in South Russia, 1917–1921* (Notre Dame, Ind. 1966); Peter Kenez, *Civil War in South Russia, 1918: The First Year of the Volunteer Army* (Berkeley, Calif. 1971); Peter Kenez, *Civil*

War in South Russia, 1919–1920: The Defeat of the Whites (Berkeley, Calif. 1977); Anna Procyk, *Russian Nationalism and Ukraine: The Nationality Policy of the Volunteer Army during the Civil War* (Edmonton and Toronto 1995); and Aleksandr Ushakov and Vladimir Fediuk, "The Nationalities Policy of the Whites in the South of Russia in the Civil War Period," in John Morison, ed., *Ethnic and National Issues and East European History* (New York 2000), pp. 174–191.

The best introduction to the revolutionary era throughout the Russian Empire as a whole is in Richard Pipes, *A Concise History of the Russian Revolution* (New York 1995). For developments specifically in Ukraine, see in particular John S. Reshetar, Jr., *The Ukrainian Revolution, 1917–1920* (Princeton, N.J. 1952; reprinted New York 1972). Less satisfactory are Isidore Nahayewsky, *History of the Modern Ukrainian State, 1917–1923* (Munich 1966); and Matthew Stachiw, Peter G. Stercho, and Nicholas L.F. Chirovskyy, *Ukraine and the European Turmoil, 1917–1919*, 2 vols. (New York 1973). More reliable is a collection of essays on various aspects of the entire era, Taras Hunczak, ed., *The Ukraine, 1917–1921: A Study in Revolution* (Cambridge, Mass. 1977). Whereas this volume omits developments in western Ukraine, it does include translations of the Ukrainian government's four universals.

There are two substantive monographs on the revolution during its first two years, one written from the perspective of a professional historian and participant as minister of foreign affairs in the Hetmanate government: Dmytro Doroshenko, *History of Ukraine, 1917–1923*, Vol. II: *The Hetmanate* (Winnipeg, Toronto, and Detroit 1973); and the other from the perspective of a patriotic émigré: Oleh Semenovych Pidhainy, *The Formation of the Ukrainian Republic* (Toronto and New York 1966). The influential role of the first head of the Central Rada is outlined in an impartial biography by Thomas M. Prymak, *Mykhailo Hrushevsky: The Politics of National Culture* (Toronto, Buffalo, and London 1987), esp. chapters 6–8. The clauses dealing with Ukraine in the Treaty of Brest-Litovsk are translated into English in *Texts of the Ukraine "Peace,"* ed. Paul R. Magocsi, 2nd ed. (Cleveland 1981); and the treaty's significance is analyzed by Stephan M. Horak, *The First Treaty of World War I: Ukraine's Treaty with the Central Powers of February 9, 1918* (Boulder, Colo. 1988). The practical impact of the treaty on subsequent German-Ukrainian relations is discussed in Włodzimerz Mędrzecki, "Germany and Ukraine between the Start of Brest-Litovsk Peace Talks and Hetman Skoropads'kyi's Coup," *HUS*, XXIII, 1–2 (Cambridge, Mass. 1999), pp. 26–46; the complex ideological orientation and policies of the Hetmanate under Pavlo Skoropads'kyi are the subject of Mark von Hagen, "'I Love Russia, and/ but I Want Ukraine,' or How a Russian General became Hetman of Ukrainian State, 1917–1918," *JUS*, XXIX, 1–2 (Edmonton 2004), pp. 115–148. Finally, the attempt by Symon Peliura to save the Ukrainian National Republic by allying with the new state of Poland is covered in great detail by Michael Palij, *The Ukrainian-Polish Defensive Alliance, 1919–1921* (Edmonton and Toronto 1995). The current status of historiography on the Ukrainian revolutionary era is discussed by Vladyslav Verstiuk, "Conceptual Issues in Studying the History of Ukrainian Revolution," followed by extensive commentaries on his analysis by Marco Bojcun and Mark Baker, in *JUS*, XXIV, 1 (Toronto 1999), pp. 5–68.

There is much less literature on western Ukrainian lands during the revolutionary years. For Eastern Galicia the best work on the topic is Vasyl Kuchabsky, *Western Ukraine in Conflict with Poland and Bolshevism, 1918–1923* (Edmonton and Toronto 2009). Other studies that are uncritically sympathetic to one side or the other are, from Ukrainian perspective: Matthew Stachiw and Jaroslaw Sztendera, *Western Ukraine at the Turning Point of Europe's History, 1918–1923*, 2 vols. (New York 1969–71); and from the Polish perspective: Rosa Bailly, *A City Fights for Freedom: The Rising of Lwów in 1918–1919* (London 1956). The impact on the Jews in Galicia, in particular those in L'viv, of imperial Russia's occupation, the subsequent collapse of Habsburg rule, and the creation of independent Poland is discussed in Alexander Victor Prusin, *Nationalizing a Borderland: War, Ethnicity, and Anti-Jewish Violence in East Galicia, 1914–1920* (Tuscaloosa, Ala. 2005). The attempts of the Ukrainians to reach an accommodation with the Jews is reviewed in great detail by Nahum Michael Gelber, "The National Autonomy of Eastern Galician Jewry in the West Ukrainian Republic, 1918–1919," in Isaac Lewin, *A History of Polish Jewry during the Revival of Poland* (New York 1990), pp. 221–326. The little-known diplomatic background to Romania's eventual annexation of Bukovina is described in Leonid C. Sonevytsky, "Bukovina in the Diplomatic Negotiations of 1914," *AUAAS*, VII, 1–2 (1959), pp. 1586–1629. For Bukovina's role in the Ukrainian revolution and the Romanian annexation, see L. M. Nowosiwsky, *Bukovinian Ukrainians: A Historical Background and Their Self-Determination in 1918* (New York 1970). The Romanian understanding of these events is provided by Ion I. Nistor, *The Union of Bucovina with Romania* (Bucharest 1940). The unique developments in Transcarpathia are given detailed attention in two articles by Paul R. Magocsi, "The Political Activity of Rusyn-American Immigrants in 1918," *East European Quarterly*, X, 3 (Boulder, Colo. 1976), pp. 347–365; and "The Ruthenian Decision to Unite with Czechoslovakia," *Slavic Review*, XXXIV, 2 (Seattle 1975), pp. 360–381 – reprinted in Paul Robert Magocsi, *Of the Making of Nationalities There is No End*, Vol. I (New York 1999), pp. 124–146 and 394–415.

A few aspects of the revolutionary era have received particular attention. The sociodemographic structure of Ukrainian territory and the relationship of various social strata toward the Ukrainian revolution is analyzed by Steven L. Guthier, "The Popular Base of Ukrainian Nationalism in 1917," *Slavic Review*, XXXVIII, 1 (Columbus, Ohio 1979), pp. 30–47; by Bohdan Krawchenko, "The Social Structure of the Ukraine in 1917," *HUS*, XIV, 1–2 (1990), pp. 97–112; and by Rudolf A. Mark, "Social Questions and National Revolution: The Ukrainian National Republic in 1919–1920," ibid., pp. 113–131. The impact of events in eastern Ukraine are covered in great detail in Theodore H. Friedgut, *Iuzovka and Revolution*, Vol. II: *Politics and Revolution in Russia's Donbass, 1869–1924* (Princeton, N.J. 1994), esp. chapters 8–10. The reaction of the rural masses to the various governments that claimed to represent them is surveyed by Vsevolod Holubnychy, "The 1917 Agrarian Revolution in Ukraine," in *Selected Works of Vsevolod Holubnychy* (Edmonton 1982), pp. 3–65; and by Arthur E. Adams, "The Great Ukrainian Jacquerie," in Taras Hunczak, ed., *The Ukraine, 1917–1921: A Study in Revolution* (Cambridge Mass. 1977), pp. 247–270. Nestor Makhno, the leader who was most successful in mobilizing peasant discontent, is the subject of no fewer than five monographic studies: Peter Arshinov, *A History of the Makhnovist Movement, 1918–1921* (Detroit 1974); Michael Malet, *Nestor Makhno in the Russian Civil War* (London 1982); Michael Palij, *The Anarchism of Nestor Makhno, 1918–1921* (Seattle and London 1976); Victor Peters, *Nestor Makhno: The Life of an Anarchist* (Winnipeg 1970); and Frank Sysyn, "Nestor Makhno and the Ukrainian Revolution," in Hunczak, *Ukraine, 1917–1921*, pp. 271–304.

The attempts to create a national Orthodox Church are surveyed in several essays by Bohdan Bociurkiw: "The Church and the Ukrainian Revolution: The Central Rada Period," in Hunczak, *Ukraine, 1917–1921*, pp. 220–246; "The Issues of Ukrainianization and Autocephaly of the Orthodox Church in Ukrainian-Russian Relations, 1917–1921," in Peter J. Potichnyj et al., eds., *Ukraine and Russia in Their Historical Encounter* (Edmonton 1992), pp. 245–273; and "The Rise of the Ukrainian Autocephalous Orthodox Church, 1919–22," in Geoffrey A. Hosking, ed., *Church, Nation, and State in Russia and Ukraine* (Edmonton 1990), pp. 228–249. For information on the leading secular figure behind the movement, see Andre Partykevych, *Between Kyiv and Constantinople: Oleksander Lototsky and the Quest for Ukrainian Autocephaly* (Edmonton 1998).

The diplomatic interest of the Allied Powers was surveyed as early as 1921 by a former Ukrainian government official of non-ethnic Ukrainian background: Arnold Margolin, *Ukraine and Policy of the Entente*, 2nd ed. (n.p. 1977). His memoirs also deal in large part with events in Ukraine during the revolutionary era: Arnold Margolin, *From a Political Diary: Russia, Ukraine, and America, 1905–1945* (New York 1946). Specific aspects of the various Allied Powers have subsequently been studied by George A. Brinkley, "Allied Policy and French Intervention in the Ukraine, 1917–1920," in Hunczak, *Ukraine, 1917–1921*, pp. 323–351; Constantine Warvariv, "America and the Ukrainian National Cause, 1917–1920," in ibid., pp. 352–381; and by David Saunders, "Britain and the Ukrainian Question, 1912–1920," *English Historical Review*, CIII (London 1988), pp. 40–68.

The various attempts of the Bolsheviks to establish their regime in Ukrainian lands are also the subject of several studies. Developments in Ukraine as they relate to the larger context of other lands in the former Russian Empire are surveyed in Richard Pipes, *The Formation of the Soviet Union: Communism and Nationalism, 1917–1923*, 2nd rev. ed. (New York 1968), esp. chapters 1–3. More detail is provided by Arthur E. Adams, *Bolsheviks in the Ukraine: The Second Campaign, 1918–1919* (New Haven and London 1963); by Jurij Borys, *The Sovietization of Ukraine, 1917–1923*, 2nd rev. ed. (Edmonton 1980); and, in a memoiristic account, by two Bolshevik supporters of Ukrainian national communism, Serhii Mazlakh and Vasyl' Shakhrai, *On the Current Situation in the Ukraine* (Ann Arbor, Mich. 1970).

The general legal status of minorities is outlined by George Liber, "Ukrainian Nationalism and the 1918 Law on National-Personal Autonomy," *Nationalities Papers*, XV, 1 (New York 1987), pp. 22–42. The status specifically of Jews has been given particular attention in a collection of government documents and other contemporary materials in F. Pigido, ed., *Material Concerning Ukrainian Jewish Rela-*

tions during the Years of the Revolution, 1917–1921 (Munich 1956); and in three accounts by Jewish members of the Ukrainian government: Solomon I. Goldelman, *Jewish National Autonomy in Ukraine, 1917–1920* (Chicago 1968); Moses Silberfarb, *The Jewish Ministry and Jewish National Autonomy in Ukraine* (New York 1993); Abraham Revutsky, *Wrenching Times in Ukraine: Memoir of a Jewish Minister* (1924) (St. John's, Newfoundland 1998). Among several interpretive analyses by latter-day historians, the most comprehensive is by Henry Abramson, *A Prayer for the Government: Ukrainians and Jews in Revolutionary Times, 1917–1920* (Cambridge, Mass., 1999); others include: Joseph Schechtman, "Jewish Community Life in the Ukraine, 1917–1919," in Gregor Aronson et al., eds., *Russian Jewry, 1917–1967* (New York, South Brunswick, N.J., and London 1969), pp. 39–57; Henry Abramson, "Jewish Representation in the Independent Ukrainian Governments of 1917–1920," *Slavic Review,* L, 3 (Stanford, Calif. 1991), pp. 542–550; Mattityahu Minc, "Kiev Zionists and the Ukrainian National Movement," and Jonathan Frankel, "The Dilemmas of Jewish Autonomism: The Case of Ukraine, 1917–1920," in Peter J. Potichnyj and Howard Aster, eds., *Ukrainian Jewish Relations in Historical Perspective* (Edmonton 1988), pp. 247–280; and M. Mintz, "The Secretariat of Internationality Affairs *(Sekretariat mizhnatsional' nykh sprav)* of the Ukrainian General Secretariat, 1917–1918," *HUS,* VI, 1(1982), pp. 25–42.

The pogroms have received even more attention in the literature. A useful introduction to the controversy regarding their extent and the responsibility of the Ukrainian government is provided by Henry Abramson, "Historiography on the Jews and the Ukrainian Revolution," *JUS,* XV, 2 (1990), pp. 33–45. Some of the published material contains contemporary reports or analyses of concrete statistical data: Elias Heifetz, *The Slaughter of the Jews in the Ukraine in 1919* (New York 1921); Arnold D. Margolin, *The Jews of Eastern Europe* (New York 1926), esp. pp. 126–152; L. Motzkin, ed., *The Pogroms in the Ukraine 1917–1920 under the Ukrainian Governments: A Historical Survey* (London 1927); N. Gergel, "The Pogroms in the Ukraine in 1918–21," *YIVO Annual of Jewish Social Science,* Vol. VI (New York 1951), pp. 237–252; and Peter Kenez, "Pogroms and White Ideology in the Russian Civil War," in John D. Klier and Shlomo Lambroza, eds., *Pogroms: Anti-Jewish Violence in Modern Russian History* (Cambridge 1992), pp. 293–313. Other material is more polemical in nature, focusing on the Directory leader Symon Petliura and the question of his guilt or innocence with regard to the pogroms: Saul S. Friedman, *Pogromchik* (New York 1976); Taras Hunczak, "A Reappraisal of Simon Petliura and Jewish-Ukrainian Relations, 1917–1921"; Zosa Szajkowski, "A Rebuttal," *Jewish Social Studies,* XXXI (New York 1969), pp. 163–213; and Lars Fischer, "The *Pogromshchina* and the Directory: A New Historiographical Synthesis?," *Revolutionary Russia,* XVI, 2 (2003), pp. 47–93.

Like the Jews, the Mennonites view the revolutionary and civil war years as one of the most tragic periods in their history. Their plight worsened at the very outset of the war, when the Russian imperial government singled out all its ethnic Germans for deportation, as discussed in David Rempel, "The Expropriation of the German Colonists in South Russia during the Great War," *Journal of Modern*

History, IV, 1 (Chicago, 1932), pp. 49–67. The dilemmas encountered specifically by Mennonites, a community that professes non-violence but was faced with lawless and anarchic conditions, is discussed by John B. Toews, "The Origins and Activities of the Mennonite *Selbstschutz* in the Ukraine, 1918–1919," *Mennonite Quarterly Review*, XLVI, 1 (Goshen, Ind. 1972), pp. 5–40. There are also two memoirs from the period: Dietrich Neufeld, *A Russian Dance of Death: Revolution and Civil War in the Ukraine* (Winnipeg 1977); and a popular study of a specific community by Gerhard Lorenz, *Fire over Zagradovka* (Steinbach, Man. 1983). The effort of the Crimean Tatars toward their own national liberation is described by Alan Fisher, *The Crimean Tatars* (Stanford, Calif. 1978), pp. 109–129.

10. The interwar years

The literature on the interwar years of the twentieth century, like that on the nineteenth century, is basically divided between works dealing with eastern, by then Soviet Ukraine, and works dealing with the individual western Ukrainian lands of Galicia, Bukovina, and Transcarpathia. Several monographs are available that cover developments during the entire interwar period or a portion of it in Soviet Ukraine. Bohdan Krawchenko, *Social Change and National Consciousness in Twentieth-Century Ukraine* (New York 1985), esp. chapters 2–3; and George O. Liber, *Soviet Nationality Policy, Urban Growth, and Identity Change in the Ukrainian SSR 1923–1934* (Cambridge and New York 1992) concentrate on analyzing the available statistical data on demographic trends, Communist party membership, and state-driven cultural and educational activity. These and other topics are dealt with over a longer time period with focus on an important industrialized region of eastern Ukraine in Hiroaki Kuromiya, *Freedom and Terror in the Donbas: A Ukrainian-Russian Borderland, 1870s–1990s* (Cambridge 1999). Basil Dmytryshyn, *Moscow and the Ukraine 1918–1953* (New York 1956); Robert S. Sullivant, *Soviet Politics and the Ukraine, 1917–1957* (New York and London 1962), esp. chapters 3–5; and James E. Mace, *Communism and the Dilemmas of National Liberation: National Communism in Soviet Ukraine, 1918–1933* (Cambridge, Mass. 1983) are concerned with Bolshevik administrative policy and the ideological response of the defenders of Ukrainian particularism.

The very decision to create a Ukrainian Socialist Republic and the role played by the Bolsheviks in that matter is discussed by Stanislav Kulchytsky, "The Phenomenon of Soviet Statehood," in Andreas Kappeler et al., eds., *Culture, Nation, and Identity* (Edmonton and Toronto 2003), pp. 344–359. For the history of the party created by the Ukrainian Bolsheviks, see Vsevolod Holubnychy, "Outline History of the Communist Party of Ukraine," in *Selected Works of Vsevolod Holubnychy*, ed. Iwan S. Koropeckyj (Edmonton 1982), pp. 66–137. The abortive efforts by non-Bolshevik Marxists to gain political power are surveyed by Iwan Majstrenko, *Borotbism: A Chapter in the History of Ukrainian Communism* (New York 1954); and the ongoing post-civil war military resistance to Soviet rule is discussed by Bohdan Nahaylo, "Ukrainian National Resistance in Soviet Ukraine during the 1920s," *JUS*, XV, 2 (1990), pp. 1–18. Some of the writings of an early

Bolshevik government leader in Ukraine and defender of federalism in the Soviet Union have been translated: Christian Rakovsky, *Selected Writings on Opposition in the USSR, 1923–1930* (London and New York 1980).

Developments during the NEP period and under the new command economy are discussed by Bohdan Somchynsky, "National Communism and the Politics of Industrialization in Ukraine, 1923–1928," *JUS*, XIII, 2 [25] (1988), pp. 52–69; by I.S. Koropeckyj, *Location Problems in Soviet Industry before World War II: The Case of the Ukraine* (Chapel Hill, N.C. 1971); by Bohdan Krawchenko, "The Impact of Industrialization on the Social Structure of Ukraine," *Canadian Slavonic Papers,* XXII, 3 (Ottawa 1980), pp. 338–357; by Steven L. Guthier, "Ukrainian Cities during the Revolution and the Interwar Era," in Ivan L. Rudnytsky, ed., *Rethinking Ukrainian History* (Edmonton 1981), pp. 156–179; by Theodore H. Friedgut, *Iuzovka and Revolution,* Vol. II: *Politics and Revolution in Russia's Donbass, 1869–1924* (Princeton, N.J. 1994), esp. chapters 11–12; and by Vsevolod Holubnychy, "On the Rationale of the Soviet Collectivization of Agriculture in 1929," *AUAAS*, IX, 1–2 (1961), pp. 75–109.

The human cost of the radical political and socioeconomic changes put in place by the Bolshevik/Soviet regime, especially the suffering inflicted on the rural population, has received particular attention. The first crisis of the early 1920s is the subject of a monograph by Wasyl Veryha, *A Case Study of Genocide in the Ukrainian Famine of 1921–1923* (Lewiston, N.Y. 2007), and of several articles by Kazuo Nakai, "Soviet Agricultural Policies in the Ukraine and the 1921–1922 Famine," *HUS*, VI, (1982), pp. 43–61; Wasyl Veryha, "Famine in Ukraine in 1921–1923 and the Soviet Government's Countermeasures," *Nationalities Papers,* XII, 2 (Charleston, Ill. 1984), pp. 265–286; Roman Serbyn, "The Famine of 1921–1923: A Model for 1932–1933," in Roman Serbyn and Bohdan Krawchenko, eds., *Famine in Ukraine, 1932–1933* (Edmonton 1986), pp. 147–178; and of an earlier, more general monograph by H.H. Fisher, *The Famine in Soviet Russia, 1919–1923* (Stanford and London 1935).

It is the famine of 1932–1933, however, which has the most extensive literature. Some authors suggest that the tragedy was a natural disaster or the result of bureaucratic bungling; others argue that it was artificially created by the Soviet government in an effort to punish all peasants opposed to collectivization; still others maintain that it was an act of genocide directed specifically against Ukrainians. The first serious study of the subject was published as early as 1936 by a foreign observer and eyewitness: Ewald Ammende, *Human Life in Russia,* 2nd ed. (Cleveland 1984). It was followed by the publication of eyewitness accounts and documents: S.O. Pidhainy, V.I. Hryshko, and P.P. Pavlovych, eds., *The Black Deeds of the Kremlin: A White Book,* Vol. II: *The Great Famine in Ukraine in 1932–1933* (Toronto and Detroit 1955); D. Solovey, ed., *The Golgotha of Ukraine: Eyewitness Accounts of the Famine in Ukraine* (New York 1953); and of a scholarly analysis: Dana Dalrymple, "The Soviet Famine of 1932–1934," *Soviet Studies,* XV, 3 (London 1964), pp. 250–284.

But it was in conjunction with the fiftieth anniversary of the famine in 1983 that Ukrainianists in the West began to publish an exceedingly wide range of works on the subject. These include an extensive historiographical survey of all published sources on the subject by James Mace, in *Report to [the U.S.] Congress: Commission on the Ukraine Famine* (Washington, D.C. 1988), pp. 1–133, which forms the preface to a translation of select oral histories of eyewitnesses and of foreign diplomatic and consular dispatches from Ukraine during the early 1930s, ibid., pp. 237–523. Another volume of sources deals with the reaction of the Western powers: Marco Carynnyk, Lubomyr Y. Luciuk, and Bohdan S. Kordan, eds., *The Foreign Office and the Famine: British Documents on Ukraine and the Great Famine of 1932–1933* (Kingston, Ont. and Vestal, N.Y. 1988). Of the many recently published eyewitness accounts, particularly insightful are Wasyl Hryshko, *The Ukrainian Holocaust of 1933* (Toronto 1983); and Olexa Woropay, *The Ninth Circle* (Cambridge, Mass. 1983). The best scholarly studies are a monograph by Robert Conquest, *The Harvest of Sorrow: Soviet Collectivization and the Terror-Famine* (New York and Toronto 1986); an essay by James E. Mace, "The Famine of 1932–1933: A Watershed in the History of Soviet Nationality Policy," in Henry R. Huttenbach, ed., *Soviet Nationality Policies: Ruling Ethnic Groups in the USSR* (London 1990), pp. 177–205; and in collections of essays by various authors, in Roman Serbyn and Bohdan Krawchenko, eds., *Famine in Ukraine, 1932–1933* (Edmonton 1986); Lubomyr Haida, ed., "The Great Famine of 1932–1933," *HUS*, XXV, 3/4 (Cambridge, Mass. 2001), pp. 153–265 – reprinted in Halyna Hryn, ed., *Hunger by Design: The Great Famine and Its Soviet Context* (Cambridge, Mass. 2008); and Wsevolod W. Isajiw, ed., *Famine-Genocide in Ukraine, 1932–1933: Western Archives, Testimonies, and New Research* (Toronto 2003).

There are as well several studies which reveal how scholars interpret the new archival data that has become available. For an overall assessment, see Jacques Vallin, France Meslé, Serguei Adamets, and Serhii Pyrozhkov, "A New Estimate of Ukrainian Population Losses During the Crises of the 1930s and 1940s," *Population Studies*, LVI, 3 (London 2002), pp. 249–264. For the demographic impact specifically of the Great Famine, see Steven Rosefielde, "Excess Collectivization Deaths, 1929–1933: New Demographic Evidence," *Slavic Review*, XLIII, 1 (Stanford, Calif. 1984), pp. 83–88, with subsequent commentary and rejoinders by Stephen G. Wheatcroft, Steven S. Rosefielde, Barbara A. Anderson, and Brian D. Silver, ibid., XLIV, 3 (1985), pp. 505–536; Mark B. Tauger, "The 1932 Harvest and Famine of 1933," ibid., L, 1 (1991), pp. 70–89; Serhii Pirozhkov, "Population Loss in Ukraine in the 1930s and 1940s," in Bohdan Krawchenko, ed., *Ukrainian Past, Ukrainian Present* (London and New York 1993), pp. 84–96; R.W. Davies, M.B. Tauger, and S.G. Wheatcroft, "Stalin, Grain Stocks and the Famine of 1932–1933," *Slavic Review*, LIV, 3 (Cambridge, Mass. 1995), pp. 642–657; and R. W. Davies and Stephen G. Wheatcroft, eds., *The Years of Hunger: Soviet Agriculture, 1931–1933* (New York 2003). For a discussion of how the Great Famine is viewed in present-day Ukraine and elsewhere among scholars, see *The Holodomor of 1932–33: Papers From the 75th Anniversary Conference on the Ukrainian Famine-Genocide, University of Toronto*, special issue of the *Harriman Review*, XVI, 2 (New York 2008); Lubomyr Y. Luciuk, ed., *Holodomor: Reflections on the Great Famine of 1932–1933 in Soviet Ukraine* (Kingston, Ont. 2008); and Andrea Graziosi, "The Soviet

1931–1933 Famines and the Ukrainian Holodomor: Is a New Interpretation Possible, and What Would Its Consequences Be?," *HUS*, XXVII [2004–2005], 1–4 (Cambridge, Mass. 2008), pp. 97–115.

The best introduction to the Soviet Union's policy toward the various nationalities under its rule is Terry Martin, *The Affirmative Action Empire: Nations and Nationalism in the Soviet Union, 1923–1939* (Ithaca, N.Y. 2000). Martin provides an invaluable discussion of the policies of rooting or indigenization (*korenizatsiia*) and Ukrainianization. The latter phenomenon, in particular as it affected literary and intellectual currents, is treated systematically by George S.N. Luckyj, *Literary Politics in the Soviet Ukraine, 1917–1934*, 2nd rev. ed. (Durham, N.C. and London 1990); and Myroslav Shkandrij, *Modernists, Marxists and the Nation: The Ukrainian Literary Discussion of the 1920s* (Edmonton 1992). The impact of subsequent changes in Soviet policy are traced in a monograph by Hryhory Kostiuk, *Stalinist Rule in the Ukraine: A Study of a Decade of Terror, 1929–1939* (New York 1960); in a collection of 234 biographies of purged intellectuals by Borys Levytsky, *The Stalinist Terror in the Thirties: Documentation from the Soviet Press* (Stanford, Calif. 1974); in eyewitness recollections compiled by S.A. Pidhainy, ed., *The Black Deeds of the Kremlin*, Vol. I: *Book of Testimonies* (Toronto and Detroit 1953); in an analysis of secret police files on victims of Stalinist reprssion in Kiev, by Hiroaki Kuromiya, *The Voices of the Dead: Stalin's Great Terror in the 1930s* (New Haven 2007); in a study of the role played by the Soviet counter-intelligence services in undermining the Ukrainianization program, by Yuri Shapoval, "The GPU-NKVD as an Instrument of Counter-Ukrainization in the 1920s and 1930s," in Andreas Kappeler et al., eds., *Culture, Nation, and Identity* (Edmonton and Toronto 2003), pp. 325–343; and in a reassessment especially of the literary aspect of this period by Halyna Hryn, "The Executed Renaissance Paradigm Revisited," *HUS*, XXVII, 1–4 (Cambridge, Mass. 2004–05), pp. 67–96.

Several essays by a leading intellectual from the period have been translated into English: Mykola Khvylovy, *The Cultural Renaissance in Ukraine: Polemical Pamphlets, 1925–1926* (Edmonton 1986); and there are two biographies and a collection of articles devoted to Ukraine's influential practitioner of what was then the newest form of art and propaganda – film: Vance Kepley, Jr., *In the Service of the State: The Cinema of Alexander Dovzhenko* (Madison, Wis. 1986); George O. Liber, *Alexander Dovzhenko: A Life in Soviet Film* (London 2002); and Bohdan Y. Nebesio, ed., *The Cinema of Alexander Dovzhenko*, special issue of *JUS*, XIX, 1 (1994). The manner in which the authorities tried to manipulate historical memory in order to create loyal Soviet citizens among Ukrainians is discussed at length in Serhy Yekelchyk, *Stalin's Empire of Memory: Russian-Ukrainian Relations in the Soviet Historical Imagination* (Toronto, Buffalo, and London 2004).

Statistical data on the concrete mechanisms of cultural production are outlined by George O. Liber, "Language, Literacy, and Book Publishing in the Ukrainian SSR, 1923–1928," *Slavic Review*, XLI, 4 (Stanford, Calif. 1982), pp. 673-685. More attention is given to the use of language as an instrument of national development or of repression in George Y. Shevelov, *The Ukrainian Language in the First Half of the Twentieth Century (1900–1941): Its State and Status*

(Cambridge, Mass. 1989), esp. chapters 4–7; and Roman Solchanyk, "Language Politics in the Ukraine," in Isabelle T. Kreindler, ed., *Sociolinguistic Perspectives on Soviet National Languages* (Berlin, New York, and Amsterdam 1985), pp. 57–73.

There are a few studies about the impact of Soviet policies on other peoples in interwar Soviet Ukraine. For an insight into the fate of Poles and Germans living in the borderlands (*kresy*) on the Soviet side of the interwar border with Poland, see Kate Brown, *A Biography of No Place: From Ethnic Borderland to Soviet Hinterland* (Cambridge, Mass. and London 2003). Aspects of the Jewish experience are covered by Mordechai Altschuler, "Ukrainian-Jewish Relations in the Soviet Milieu in the Interwar Period," in Peter J. Potichnyj and Howard Aster, eds., *Ukrainian-Jewish Relations in Historical Perspective* (Edmonton 1988), pp. 281–305; Jonathan Dekel-Chen, *Farming the Red Land: Jewish Agricultural Colonization and Local Soviet Power* (New Haven 2005); Hillel Kazovsky, *Kultur-Lige: Artistic Avant-Garde of the 1910s and 1920s* (Kiev 2007); and Yohanan Petrovsky-Shtern, *The Anti-Imperial Choice: The Making of the Ukrainian Jew* (New Haven and London 2009). On the Crimean Tatars, see Alan Fisher, *The Crimean Tatars* (Stanford, Calif. 1978), esp. chapter 12; Brian Glyn Williams, *The Crimean Tatars* (Leiden 2001), chapter 11; and Edward Lazzerini, "Crimean Tatar: The Fate of a Severed Tongue," in Isabelle T. Kreindler, ed., *Sociolinguistic Perspectives on Soviet National Languages* (Berlin, New York, and Amsterdam 1985), pp. 109–124. On the Mennonites, see John B. Toews, "Early Communism and Russian Mennonite Peoplehood," in John Friesen, ed., *Mennonites in Russia, 1788–1988* (Winnipeg 1989), pp. 265–287; John B. Toews, "The Russian Mennonites and the Military Question, 1921–1927," *Mennonite Quarterly Review*, XLIII, 1 (Goshen, Ind. 1969), pp. 153–168; and Harry Loewen, "Anti-Menno: Introduction to Early Soviet-Mennonite Literature, 1920–1940," *Journal of Mennonite Studies*, XI (Winnipeg 1993), pp. 23–42.

The efforts to sustain a distinct Ukrainian Orthodox Church in the face of a generally antagonistic Soviet government are described in three studies by Bohdan Bociurkiw: "The Ukrainian Autocephalous Orthodox Church, 1920–1930," in Dennis Dunn, ed., *Religion and Modernization in the Soviet Union* (Boulder, Colo. 1977), pp. 310–347; "Ukrainianization Movements within the Russian Orthodox Church and the Ukrainian Autocephalous Orthodox Church," *HUS*, III–IV, pt. 1 (1979–80), pp. 92–111; and "The Soviet Destruction of the Ukrainian Orthodox Church, 1929–1936," *JUS*, XII, 1 [22] (Edmonton 1987), pp. 3–21. The largest and still most important Orthodox jurisdiction in Ukraine, that belonging to the Moscow Patriarchate, is surveyed by Bohdan R. Bociurkiw, "The Russian Orthodox Church in Ukraine: the Exarchate and Renovationists, and the 'Conciliar-Episcopal' Church, 1930–1939," *HUS*, XXVI, 1–4 (Cambridge, Mass. 2002–03), pp. 63–91.

There is less literature on western Ukrainian lands during the interwar period. A useful introductory overview of developments in Galicia, Bukovina, and Transcarpathia is provided by John-Paul Himka, "Western Ukraine in the Interwar Period," *Nationalities Papers*, XX, 2 (New York 1994), pp. 347–364. Ukrainians in Poland, in particular eastern Galicia, are given attention in a few general and specific works. General surveys of political, demographic, economic, and cultural developments are found in Bohdan Budurowycz, "Poland and the Ukrainian Problem, 1921–1939," *Canadian Slavonic Papers,* XXV, 4 (Toronto 1983), pp. 473–500; Stephen Horak, *Poland and Her National Minorities, 1919–1939* (New York 1961); Stephen Horak, "Belorussian and Ukrainian Peasants in Poland, 1919–1939," in Ivan Volgyes, ed., *The Peasantry of Eastern Europe,* Vol. I (New York 1979), pp. 133–156; Volodymyr Kubijovyč, *Western Ukraine within Poland, 1920–1939: Ethnic Relationships* (Chicago 1963); and Volodymyr Kubijovyč, *Ethnic Groups of the South-Western Ukraine: Halyčyna – Galicia I.I. 1939* (Wiesbaden 1983), with large-scale, detailed maps. The contemporary Polish perspective is provided by M. Feliński, *The Ukrainians in Poland* (London 1931); and Stanisław Łoś, "The Ukrainian Question in Poland," *Slavonic and East European Review,* IX [27] (London 1931), pp. 567–587. Twelve polemical pamphlets from the interwar years representing the Ukrainian and Polish views on Galicia are reprinted in *Seeds of Conflict Series I: Irredentist and National Questions in Central Europe, 1913–1939,* Vol. VIII: *Poland* (Nendeln, Liechtenstein 1973).

The fate of Galicia in diplomatic negotiations at the close of World War I is the subject of several studies: Laurence Orzell, "A 'Hotly Disputed' Issue: Eastern Galicia at the Paris Peace Conference," *Polish Review,* XXV, 1 (New York 1980), pp. 49–68; Leonid C. Sonevytsky, "The Ukrainian Question in R.H. Lord's Writings on the Paris Peace Conference," *AUAAS,* X, 1–2 (1962–63), pp. 65–84; Taras Hunczak, "Sir Lewis Namier and the Struggle for Eastern Galicia," *HUS,* I, 2 (1977), pp. 198–210; and Mark Baker, "Lewis Namier and the Problem of Eastern Galicia," *JUS,* XXIII, 2 (Toronto 1998), pp. 59–104. Subsequent problems related to Polish rule are outlined in a collection of accusatory eyewitness reports: Emil Revyuk, ed., *Polish Atrocities in Ukraine* (New York 1931); and in two impartial studies on the efforts to reach a modus vivendi and political compromise with Ukrainians: Mirosław Sycz, "Polish Policy toward the Ukrainian Cooperative Movement, 1920–1939," *HUS,* XXIII, 1–2 (Cambridge, Mass. 1999), pp. 25–46; and E. Wynot, Jr., "The Ukrainians and the Polish Regime, 1937–1939," *Ukraïns'kyi istoryk,* VII, 4 (New York 1970), pp. 44–60. The efforts to create in Volhynia an environment in which Ukrainians could accommodate to Polish rule is viewed through the career of that region's governor during the 1930s, Henryk Jozewski, in Timothy Snyder, *Sketches from a Secret War: A Polish Artist's Mission to Liberate Soviet Ukraine* (New Haven, Conn. 2005). A balanced view of the relations among Poles, Jews, and Ukrainians in the region's largest city is provided in essays by Liliana Hentosh, Wacław Wierzbreniec and Philip Thier in John Czaplicka, ed., *Lviv: A City in the Crosscurrents of Culture,* special issue of *HUS,* XXVI (Cambridge Mass. 2000), published separately (Cambridge Mass. 2007), pp. 171–204 and 223–284, and in two essays by Anna Veronika Wendland that focus on Polish-Ukrainian relations: "Post-Austrian Lemberg: War Commemoration, Interethnic Relations, and Urban Identity in L'viv, 1918–1939," *Austrian History Yearbook,* XXXIV (Minneapolis 2003), pp. 83–102; and her "Neighbors as Betrayers: Nationalization, Remembrence Policy, and the Urban Public Sphere in L'viv," in Christopher Hann and Paul Robert Magocsi, eds., *Galicia: A Multicultured Land* (Toronto 2005), pp. 139–159.

The Greek Catholic Church, which remained an important Ukrainian "national" institution in interwar Polish-ruled Galicia is given comprehensive coverage in Bohdan Budurowycz, "The Greek Catholic Church in Galicia, 1914–1944," *Harvard Ukrainian Studies,* XXVI, 1–4 (Cambridge, Mass. 2002–03), pp. 291–375. Particular attention has been accorded Metropolitan Sheptyts'kyi, the most important church and civic figure in eastern Galicia during the first half of the twentieth century. Aside from the comprehensive biography by Cyril Korolevskij, *Metropolitan Andrew (1865–1914)* (L'viv 1993), specific aspects of his career are treated in monographs by Andrii Krawchuk, *Christian Social Ethics in Ukraine: The Legacy of Andrei Sheptyst'kyi* (Edmonton, Ottawa, and Toronto 1997) and Peter Galadza, *The Theology and Liturgical Work of Andrei Sheptyst'kyi, 1865–1944* (Rome and Ottawa, 2004), and in essays by Bohdan Budurowycz (national movement), Ryszard Torzecki (Polish society), Ann Slusarczuk Sirka (education and philanthropy), and Myroslava M. Mudrak (art patronage) in Paul Robert Magocsi, ed., *Morality and Reality: The Life and Times of Andrei Sheptyts'kyi* (Edmonton 1989), esp. chapters 3, 4, 12, 13, and 14. The women's movement and the influence of the Greek Catholic Church are discussed in some detail in a monograph by Martha Bohachevsky-Chomiak, *Feminists Despite Themselves: Women in Ukrainian Community Life, 1884–1939* (Edmonton 1988), esp. chapters 12–18. Although of secondary importance during the interwar period, the Communist party, because of its subsequent significance, has been studied in detail by Roman Solchanyk, "The Foundation of the Communist Movement in Eastern Galicia, 1919–1921," *Slavic Review,* XXX, 4 (Columbus, Ohio 1971), pp. 774–794; and Janusz Radziejowski, *The Communist Party of Western Ukraine, 1919–1929* (Edmonton 1983).

A special topic that is linked only in part to that of eastern Galicia during the interwar period is Ukrainian political thought. A useful introductory survey is Ivan L. Rudnytsky, "Trends in Ukrainian Political Thought," in his *Essays in Modern Ukrainian History* (Edmonton 1987), pp. 91–122. The relationship between political thought and action is the subject of Alexander J. Motyl, *The Turn to the Right: The Ideological Origins and Development of Ukrainian Nationalism, 1919–1929* (New York 1980). One political thinker has received particular attention, in Jaroslaw Pelenski, ed., *The Political and Social Ideas of Vjačeslav Lypyns'kyj,* special issue of *HUS,* IX, 3–4 (1985); and in Alexander J. Motyl, "Viacheslav Lypyns'kyi and the Ideology and Politics of Ukrainian Monarchism," *Canadian Slavonic Papers,* XXVII, 1 (Toronto 1985), pp. 31–48; and the work by Rudnytsky above, pp. 437–462.

With regard to the other territories in western Ukraine, Bukovina during the interwar years is given only limited attention. Irina Livezeanu, *Cultural Politics in Great Romania: Regionalism, Nation Building, and Ethnic Struggle, 1918–1930* (Ithaca and London 1995), esp. chapter 2, provides a dispassionate account of the new school system established for both Ukrainians and Romanians; and David Shaary, "Jewish Culture in Multinational Bukovina between the World Wars," in *Shvut,* Vol. XVI, edited by Liviu Rotman (Tel Aviv 1993), pp. 281–296, surveys cultural developments among the region's third-largest minority.

In contrast, the literature about Transcarpathia is much more developed. The best general introductions are by C.A. Macartney, "Ruthenia," in his *Hungary*

and Her Successors: The Treaty of Trianon and Its Consequences, 1919–1937 (London
1937), pp. 200–250; and by Oscar Jaszi, "The Problem of Sub-Carpathian Ruthenia," in Robert J. Kerner, ed., *Czechoslovakia* (Berkeley, Calif. 1940), pp. 193–215.
Paul Robert Magocsi, *The Shaping of a National Identity: Subcarpathian Rus', 1848–
1948* (Cambridge, Mass. 1978), esp. chapters 5–11, deals with the political, cultural, and religious aspects of the nationality question; Elaine Rusinko, *Straddling
Borders: Literature and Identity in Subcarpathian Rus'* (Toronto, Buffalo, and London
2003), chapter 5, looks at the struggle between adherents of a Caryatho-Rusyn,
Russian, and Ukrainian national identity through the prism of literature; Peter
G. Stercho, *Diplomacy of Double Morality: Europe's Crossroads in Carpatho-Ukraine,
1919–1939* (New York 1971), esp. chapter 2, and Walter K. Hanak, *The Subcar-
pathian-Ruthenian Question, 1918–1945* (Munhall, Pa. 1962) both focus on efforts
to achieve autonomy. The economic, political, cultural, and religious life of Jews
in the region is treated in three essays by Aryeh Sole and Hugo Stransky in *The
Jews of Czechoslovakia* (Philadelphia and New York 1968), Vol. I, pp. 125-154 and
Vol. II, pp. 347–389 and 401–439; in a popular account by Herman Dicker, *Piety
and Perseverance: Jews from the Carpathian Mountains* (New York 1981); and in a
comprehensive monograph by Yeshayahu A. Jelinek, *The Carpathian Diaspora:
The Jews of Subcarpathian Rus' and Mukachevo, 1848–1948* (New York 2007), esp.
chapters 8–16.

11. World War II

General introductions on the war years are found in two collections of essays by
various authors: Yury Boshyk, ed., *Ukraine during World War II: History and Its Aftermath* (Edmonton 1986); and Taras Hunczak and Dmytro Shtohryn, eds., *Ukraine:
the Challenges of World War II* (Lanham, Md. 2003). The relationship of the war
to the national movement is best described in a detailed monograph by John
A. Armstrong, *Ukrainian Nationalism, 1939–1945* (New York 1955; 3rd rev. ed.,
Littleton, Colo. 1990); while the attitudes of Great Britain and the United States
toward Ukraine are traced in critical essays and a selection of diplomatic papers
in Lubomyr Y. Luciuk and Bohdan S. Kordan, eds., *Anglo-American Perspectives on
the Ukrainian Question, 1938–1951: A Documentary Collection* (Kingston, Ont. and
Vestal, N.Y. 1987). Of particular interest is the perspective on these years by the
head of the Communist Party of Ukraine at the time, as related in the *Memoirs of
Nikita Khrushchev,* Vol. I: *Commissar, 1918–1945* (University Park, Pa. 2004).

The "prewar" events that led to the creation of a Carpatho-Ukrainian autonomous state and its precarious position in the rapidly changing international setting are traced in Peter G. Stercho, *Diplomacy of Double Morality: Europe's Crossroads
in Carpatho-Ukraine, 1919–1939* (New York 1971), esp. chapters 3–8; and Bohdan
Budurowycz, "The Ukrainian Problem in International Politics, October 1938 to
March 1939," *Canadian Slavonic Papers,* III, 2 (Ottawa 1959), pp. 59–75. A view
of these events as well as of the wartime occupation of the region by Hungary
from local political leaders or eyewitnesses is provided by Augustin Stefan, Julian
Revay, Vincent Shandor, and Vasyl Markus in a special issue, *Carpatho-Ukraine's*

Struggle, of the *Ukrainian Quarterly*, X, 3 (New York 1954), pp. 219–256. On the same period from the perspective of an outsider, see Michael Winch, *Republic for a Day: An Eyewitness Account of the Carpatho-Ukraine Incident* (London 1939).

The first stage of the war – the Soviet invasion and annexation of eastern Galicia and western Volhynia – and its impact on Poles and Jews as well as Ukrainians is well documented in Jan T. Gross, *Revolution from Abroad: The Soviet Conquest of Poland's Western Ukraine and Western Belorussia* (Princeton, N.J. 1988); and in a collection of essays in Keith Sword, ed., *The Soviet Takeover of the Polish Eastern Provinces, 1939–1941* (London 1991). The broader context of Soviet policy toward what that country's leaders considered problematic social and national groups, including those in newly annexed lands from former eastern Poland is found in Pavel Polian, *Against Their Will: The History and Geography of Forced Migration to the USSR* (Budapest 2004). For more information about the specific impact on Ukrainians, see David R. Marples, "Western Ukraine and Western Belorussia under Soviet Occupation: The Development of Socialist Farming, 1939–1941," *Canadian Slavonic Papers*, XXVII, 2 (Toronto 1985), pp. 158–177 – reprinted in his *Stalinism in Ukraine in the 1940s* (Edmonton 1992), pp. 24–41. Soviet policy toward eastern Galicia's influential church is discussed in Bohdan Rostyslav Bociurkiw, *The Ukrainian Greek Catholic Church and the Soviet State, 1939–1950* (Edmonton and Toronto 1996), esp. pp. 32–61, and his shorter study "Sheptyts'kyi and the Ukrainian Greek Catholic Church under Soviet Occupation, 1939–1941," in Paul Robert Magocsi, ed., *Morality and Reality: The Life and Times of Andrei Sheptyts'kyi* (Edmonton 1989), pp. 101–124.

The war years are dealt with in great detail in several monographs. Good introductions to the military campaigns on Ukrainian territory by both the German and the Soviet armies are John Erickson, *The Road to Stalingrad: Stalin's War with Germany* (London 1975); John Erickson, *The Road to Berlin: Continuing the History of Stalin's War with Germany* (Boulder, Colo. 1983); and Joseph L. Wieczynski, ed., *Operation Barbarossa: The German Attack on the Soviet Union, June 22, 1941* (Salt Lake City, Utah 1993). Ukraine also figures prominently in general works on Nazi rule in eastern Europe: Alexander Dallin, *German Rule in Russia, 1941– 1945: A Study in Occupation Policies* (New York 1957; 2nd rev. ed., Boulder, Colo. 1981); Gerald Reitlinger, *The House Built on Sand: The Conflicts of German Policy in Russia, 1939–1945* (New York 1960); Ihor Kamenetsky, *Secret Nazi Plans for Eastern Europe: A Study of Lebensraum Policies* (New Haven, Conn. 1961); Theo Schulte, *The German Army and Nazi Policies in Occupied Russia* (New York 1989); and Timothy Patrick Mulligan, *The Politics of Illusion and Empire: German Occupation Policy in the Soviet Union, 1942–1943* (New York 1988), esp. chapters 5 and 7 on the Reichskommissariat Ukraine. The overall loss of life is documented by Stephan G. Prociuk, "Human Losses in the Ukraine in World War I and II," *AUAAS*, XIII (New York 1973–77), pp. 23–50.

Developments specifically in Ukraine are given attention in Ihor Kamenetsky, *Hitler's Occupation of Ukraine, 1941–1944* (Milwaukee 1956); Wolodymyr Kosyk, *The Third Reich and Ukraine* (New York 1993); Dieter Pohl, "Russians, Ukrainians, and German Occupation Policy 1941–43," in Andreas Kappeler et al., eds., *Culture,*

Nation, and Identity (Edmonton 2003), pp. 277–297; and Rudolf A. Mark, "The Ukrainians as Seen by Hitler, Rosenberg, and Koch," in Hunczak and Shtohryn, eds., *Ukraine: The Challenges of World War II*, pp. 23–36. The best work on daily life under the Nazi German rule in the Reichskommissariat Ukraine is Karel C. Berkhoff, *Harvest of Despair: Life and Death in Ukraine under Nazi Rule* (Cambridge, Mass. 2004). The same author has also produced a comprehensive guide to archival and secondary sources in "Ukraine Under Nazi Rule (1941–1944): Sources and Finding Aids," *Jahrbücher für Geschichte Osteuropas*, XLV, 1 and 2 (Wiesbaden, 1997), pp. 85–103 and 273–309. Coverage of Romanian wartime rule in Transnistria is available in Alexander Dallin, *Odessa, 1941–1944: A Case Study of Soviet Territory Under Foreign Rule*, 2nd ed. (Iaşi, Romania and Portland, Ore. 1998).

The status of Ukrainian churches is treated prominently in general works on the wartime religious revival: Wassilij Alexeev and Theofanis G. Stavrou, *The Great Revival: The Russian Church under German Occupation* (Minneapolis 1976), esp. chapter 5; Harvey Fireside, *Icon and Swastika: The Russian Orthodox Church under Nazi and Soviet Control* (Cambridge, Mass. 1971); and in studies focusing specifically on Ukraine: Hansjakob Stehle, "Sheptyts'kyi and the German Regime," in Magocsi, *Morality and Reality*, pp. 125–144; and Karel C. Berkhoff, "Was There a Religious Revival in the Soviet Union under the Nazi Regime?," *The Slavonic and East European Review*, LXXVIII, 3 (London 2000), pp. 536–567.

Many studies deal with Ukrainian military formations and their role in the nationalist struggle against the armies of both the Soviet Union and Nazi Germany. The Ukrainian Insurgent Army – UPA is perhaps the most controversial among these formations; a good introduction to the current state of knowledge is in Per Anders Rudling, "Theory and Practice: Historical Representation of the Wartime Accounts of the Activities of the OUN-UPA," *East European Jewish Affairs*, XXXVI, 2 (Oxon, U.K. 2006), pp. 163–189. Accounts of the UPA, how it derived from the Organization of Ukrainian Nationalists, and the changing relationship of both movements to the Nazi German authorities in Ukraine are reviewed in essays by Wolfdieter Bihl, Peter J. Potichnyj, and Taras Hunczak, in Hans-Joachim Torke and John-Paul Himka, eds., *German-Ukrainian Relations in Historical Perspective* (Edmonton and Toronto 1994), pp. 138–186; and by Myroslav Prokop, "Ukrainian Anti-Nazi Resistance, 1941–1944," in Hunczak and Shtohryn, *Ukraine: the Challenges of World War II*, pp. 63–88. Details on the UPA's military operations are found in: Y. Tys-Krokhmaliuk, *UPA Warfare in Ukraine: Strategical, Tactical, and Organizational Problems of Ukrainian Resistance in World War II* (New York 1972); Oleh Martowych [Lev Shankowsky], *The Ukrainian Insurgent Army* (Munich 1950); and Petro R. Sodol, *UPA: They Fought Hitler and Stalin: A Brief Overview of Military Aspects from the History of the Ukrainian Insurgent Army, 1942–1949* (New York 1987). On the role of the UPA in American foreign policy, see Jeffrey Burds, *The Early Cold War in Soviet West Ukraine, 1944–1948*, The Carl Beck Papers in Russian and East European Studies, No. 1505 (Pittsburgh 2001). The ideology of the movement is presented in an annotated collection of contemporary documents compiled by Peter J. Potichnyj and Yevhen Shtendera, eds., *Political Thought of the Ukrainian Underground, 1943–1951* (Edmonton 1986);

and in the writings of one of the movement's most prominent leaders: Yaroslav Stetsko, *Ukraine and the Subjugated Nations: Their Struggle for National Liberation – Selected Writings and Speeches by a Former Prime Minister of Ukraine* (New York 1989).

Ukrainian forces that fought on the side of Germany have been given particular attention in: Myroslav Yurkevich, "Galician Ukrainians in German Military Formations and in the German Administration," in Yuri Boshyk, ed., *Ukraine during World War II* (Edmonton 1986), pp. 67–88; Basil Dmytryshyn, "The SS Division Galicia, 1943–1945," in Hunczak and Shtohryn, *Ukraine: The Challenges of World War II*, pp. 209–230; Richard Landwehr, *Fighting for Freedom: The Ukrainian Volunteer Division of the Waffen-SS* (Silver Spring, Md. 1985); Michael O. Logosz, *The Waffen-SS 14th Grenadier Division, 1943–1945* (Atglen, Pa. 1997); Carlos Caballero Jurado, *Breaking the Chains: 14 Waffen-Grenadier Division der SS and Other Ukrainian Volunteer Formations, Eastern Front, 1941–45* (Halifax, United Kingdom 1998); Taras Hunczak, *On the Horns of a Dilemma: The Story of the Ukrainian Division "Halychyna"* (Lanham, Md. 2000); and Michael James Melnyk, *To Battle: The Formation and History of the 14th Galician Waffen-SS Division* (Solihull, U.K. 2002). There are also memoirs of German and Ukrainian officers connected with the Galicia Division: Wolf-Dietrich Heike, *The Ukrainian Division "Galicia": 1943–45: A Memoir* (Toronto, Paris, and Munich 1988); and Pavlo Shandruk, *Arms of Valor* (New York 1959).

Soviet writers and their sympathizers in the West also produced a wide body of accusatory polemics against what they described as "Ukrainian nationalist collaborators": V. Cherednychenko, *Collaborationists* (Kiev 1975); V. Cherednychenko, *Anatomy of Treason* (Kiev 1984); Yaroslav Halan, *Lest People Forget: Pamphlets, Articles, and Reports* (Kiev 1986); and Marko Terlytsia, *Here Is the Evidence* (Toronto 1984). To make the accusations sound more plausible, the Soviets published select documentary evidence: V.N. Denisov and G.I. Changuli, eds., *Nazi Crimes in Ukraine, 1941–1944: Documents and Materials* (Kiev 1987). The issue of wartime collaboration in scholarly as well as polemical writings is discussed by David R. Marples, *Stalinism in Ukraine in the 1940s*, esp. chapter 4 (Edmonton 1992). Collaboration of a different kind, that of leftist Czechoslovak and Soviet diplomats arranging for the acquisition of new territory south of the Carpathian Mountains, is the subject of a historical analysis and collection of documents from 1944–1945 in F. Nemec and V. Moudry, *The Soviet Seizure of Subcarpathian Ruthenia* (Toronto 1955).

The fate of Jews on Ukrainian lands during World War II is treated in several works. The transformation of their traditional life in western Ukraine in the wake of the Soviet annexation in late 1939 is discussed at some length in Ben-Cion Pinchuk, *Shtetl Jews under Soviet Rule: Eastern Poland on the Eve of the Holocaust* (Oxford 1990); Aharon Weiss, "Some Economic and Social Problems of the Jews of Eastern Galicia in the Period of Soviet Rule," in Norman Davies and Antony Polansky, eds., *Jews in Eastern Poland and the USSR, 1939–46* (Basingstoke, Hampshire, and London 1991), pp. 77–109; and by Jan Gross, "The Jewish Community in the Soviet-Annexed Territories on the Eve of the Holocaust," in Lucjan Dobroszycki and Jeffrey S. Gurock, eds., *The Holocaust in the Soviet Union* (Armonk, N.Y. and London 1993), pp. 155–172.

The impact of the German invasion and Nazi racial policy specifically on Jews is described in studies by Philip Friedman, "Ukrainian-Jewish Relations during the Nazi Occupation," *YIVO Annual of Jewish Social Science,* XII (New York 1958–59), pp. 259–296 – reprinted in Philip Friedman, *Roads to Extinction: Essays on the Holocaust* (New York and Philadelphia 1980), pp. 176–208; and in collection of essays about all Ukrainian lands: Roy Brandon and Wendy Lower, eds., *The Shoah in Ukraine: History, Testimony, Memorialization* (Bloomington and Indianapolis 2008). There are also studies of Nazi German policy in specific regions: Michael Gesin, *Nazi Genocide of Jews in Southern Ukraine* (Lewiston, N.Y. 2006), including a discussion of Transnistria and Crimea; Shmuel Spector, *The Holocaust of Volhynian Jews, 1941–1944* (Jerusalem 1990), and – with emphasis on the city of Zhytomyr – in Wendy Lower, *Nazi Empire-Building and the Holocaust in Ukraine* (Chapel Hill, N. C. 2005). There are also several contemporary recollections printed in Ilya Ehrenburg and Vasily Grossman, eds., *The Black Book: The Ruthless Murder of Jews by German-Fascist Invaders throughout the Temporarily-Occupied Regions of the Soviet Union and in the Death Camps of Poland during the War of 1941–1945* (New York 1981), esp. pt. 1: "The Ukraine," pp. 1–136.

The policy of the Soviet government toward Jews and its subsequent attitude toward the Holocaust are dealt with in essays by Zvi Gitelman, Lukasz Hirszowicz, William Korey, and Mordechai Altschuler in Lucjan Dobroszycki and Jeffrey S. Gurock, eds., *Holocaust in the Soviet Union* (Armonk, N.Y. and London 1993). The question of collaboration of the local non-Jewish population is treated with great care in John-Paul Himka, "Ukrainian Collaboration in the Extermination of the Jews during the Second World War: Sorting Out the Long-Term and Conjectural Factors," in Jonathan Frankel, ed., *The Fate of European Jews, 1939–1945/Studies in Contemporary Jewry: An Annual,* Vol. XIII (New York and Oxford 1997), pp. 170–189. Other aspects of this problem are discussed in Yaroslav Bilinsky, "Methodological Problems and Philosophical Issues in the Study of Jewish-Ukrainian Relations during the Second World War," in Peter J. Potichnyj and Howard Aster, eds., *Ukrainian-Jewish Relations in Historical Perspective* (Edmonton 1988), pp. 373-408; Taras Hunczak, "Ukrainian-Jewish Relations during the Soviet and Nazi Occupations," in Boshyk, *Ukraine during World War II,* pp. 39–57; Andrzej Zbikowski, "Local Anti-Jewish Pogroms in the Occupied Territories of Eastern Poland," in Dobroszycki and Gurock, *Holocaust in the Soviet Union,* pp. 173–180; Martin Dean, *Collaboration in the Holocaust: Crimes of the Local Police in Belorussia and Ukraine, 1941–44* (New York 2000); and Vladimir Melamed, "Organized and Unsolicited Collaboration in the Holocaust: The Multifaceted Ukrainian Context," *East European Affairs,* XXXVII, 2 (Oxon, U.K. 2007), pp. 217–248.

Jewish communities in western Ukrainian lands have been given particular attention. There are several memoirs of survivors: Leon Weliczker-Wells, *Janowska Road* (New York 1963); Joachim Schoenfeld, *Holocaust Memoirs: Jews in the Lwów Ghetto, the Janowski Concentration Camp, and as Deportees in Siberia* (Hoboken,

N.J. 1985); Yitzhak Sternberg, *Under Assumed Identity* (Jerusalem 1986); David Kahane, *Lvov Ghetto Diary* (Amherst, Mass. 1990); Robert Marshall, *In the Sewers of Lvov* (London 1990); Michael Diment, *The Lone Survivor: A Diary of the Lukacze Ghetto and Svyniukhy, Ukraine* (New York 1992); Nelly S. Toll, *Behind the Secret Window* (New York 1993); Kurt I. Lewin, *A Journey through Illusions* (Santa Barbara, Calif. 1994); and Ya. Khonigsman, *Janovska Hell: Brief Essay on the History of Janovska Concentration Camp in L'viv* (L'viv 2003).

There are also scholarly studies on the Jews in various western Ukrainian lands. On German-administered eastern Galicia, see Philip Friedman, "The Destruction of the Jews of Lwów," in his *Roads to Extinction,* pp. 244–321; Aharon Weiss, "Jewish-Ukrainian Relations in Western Ukraine during the Holocaust," in Potichnyj and Aster, *Ukrainian-Jewish Relations,* pp. 409–420; Shimon Redlich, "Sheptyts'kyi and the Jews," in Magocsi, *Morality and Reality,* pp. 145–162; Gabriel N. Finder and Alexander V. Prusin, "Collaboration in Eastern Galicia: The Ukrainian Police and the Holocaust," *Eastern European Jewish Affairs,* XXXIV, 2 (Oxon, U.K. 2004), pp. 95–118; and Simon Redlich, *Together and Apart in Brzezany: Poles, Jews, and Ukrainians, 1919–1945* (Bloomington, Ind. 2002). On Hungarian-ruled Transcarpathia, the most comprehensive treatment of the Holocaust is in Yeshayahu A. Jelinek, *The Carpathian Diaspora: The Jews of Subcarpathian Rus' and Mukachevo, 1848–1948* (New York 2007), esp. chapters 17–19. Other studies on the topic include Livia Rothkirchen, "Deep-Rooted Yet Alien: Some Aspects of the History of the Jews in Subcarpathian Ruthenia," *Yad Vashem Studies,* XII (Jerusalem 1977), pp. 147–191; and Randolph L. Braham, "The Destruction of the Jews of Carpatho-Ruthenia," in *Hungarian-Jewish Studies* (New York 1966), pp. 223–235. On Romanian- ruled Transnistria, the region between the Dniester and Southern Buh Rivers, see the series of essays in Randolf L. Braham, ed., *The Destruction of Romanian and Ukrainian Jews during the Antonescu Era* (Boulder, Colo. and New York 1997); Dalie Ofer, "The Holocaust in Transnistria," in Dobroszycki and Gurock, *Holocaust in the Soviet Union,* pp. 133–154; and Dennis Deletant, "Transnistria and the Romanian Solution to the 'Jewish Problem'," in Ray Brandon and and Wendy Lower, eds., *The Shoah in Ukraine: History, Testimony, Materialization* (Bloomington and Indianapolis 2008), pp. 159–189.

The fate of Poles, whether as a result of the first Soviet annexation or of the forced deportations and exchange of populations at the end of the war, is recorded in scholarly studies by Keith Sword, *Deportation and Exile: Poles in the Soviet Union, 1939–1948* (New York and London 1994); John J. Kulczycki, "The Soviet Union, Polish Communists, and the Creation of a Polish Nation-State," *Russian History,* XXIX, 2–4 (Idlewood, Calif. 2002), pp. 251–276; John J. Kulczycki, "'Repatriation': Bringing Poles from the Soviet Union Home after World War II," *Sprawy Narodowościowe: Seria nowa,* XXIII (Poznań 2003), pp. 7–41; and in an eyewitness report by Zygmunt Sobieski, "Reminiscences from Lwów, 1939–1944," *Journal of Central European Affairs,* VI, 4 (Boulder, Colo. 1947), pp. 350–374. The historiography on Polish-Ukrainian relations both during the war and the immediate postwar years is surveyed in short essays by Józef Lewandowski and John Basarab, in Peter J. Potichnyj, ed., *Poland and Ukraine: Past and Present* (Edmonton and Toronto 1980), pp. 231–270; and by Andrzej Zięba, "Sheptyts'kyi in Polish Public Opinion," in Magocsi, *Morality and Reality,* pp. 377–406.

The ongoing struggle between partisan and other armed forces representing both groups during the last years of World War II and the immediate postwar period is treated with great judiciousness by Timothy Snyder in "The Causes of Ukrainian-Polish Ethnic Cleansing 1943," *Past and Present,* No. 179 (Oxford 2003), pp. 197–234, and in his more wide-ranging monograph, *The Reconstruction of Nations: Poland, Ukraine, Lithuania, Belarus, 1569–1999* (New Haven and London 2003), in which there is also a discussion of the Poles and Ukrainians during the Communist and post-Communist eras. The wartime clashes are described in a partisan and often emotional manner in several individual works and in collections of memoirs: Mikolaj Terles, ed., *Ethnic Cleansing of Poles in Volhynia and East Galicia, 1942–1946* (Toronto 1993); Tadeusz Piotrowski, *Polish-Ukrainian Relations During World War II: Ethnic Cleansing in Volhynia and Eastern Galicia* (Toronto 1995); Tadeusz Piotrowski, *Vengeance of the Swallows: Memoir of a Polish Family's Ordeal under Soviet Aggression, Ukrainian Ethnic Cleansing and Nazi Enslavement, and Their Emigration to America* (Jefferson, N.C. 1994); Waldemar Lotnik, with Julian Preece, *Nine Lives: Ethnic Conflict in the Polish-Ukrainian Borderlands* (London 1999); Wladyslaw Dzemianczuk, *Polish Self Defence in Volhynia* (Toronto 1999); and in the best work in this genre, Tadeusz Piotrowski, ed., *Genocide and Rescue in Wołyń: Recollections of the Ukrainian Nationalist Ethnic Cleansing Campaign Against the Poles During World War II* (Jefferson, N. C. 2000).

The postwar years, when Ukrainian-Polish relations were determined by international agreements on "voluntarily" and forced population resettlement, are discussed by Bohdan Kordan, "Making Borders Stick: Population Transfer and Resettlement in the Trans-Curzon Territories, 1944–1949," *International Migration Review,* XXXI, 3 (Staten Island, N.Y. 1997), pp. 704–720; Tadeusz Piotrowski, "Akcja 'Wisła' – Operation 'Vistula', 1947: Background and Assessment," *Polish Review,* XLIII, 2 (New York, 1998), pp. 219–238; and by several Polish and Ukrainian authors in the collection, *The Lemko Region, 1939–1947: War, Occupation and Deportation,* ed., Paul Best and Jaroslaw Moklak (New Haven, Conn. 2002), esp. chapters 5–10. The ongoing friction between Poles and Ukrainians in borderland regions within Poland, especially among Roman Catholics and Greek Catholics in the city of Przemyśl, is the subject of several studies by the British anthropologist, Christopher M. Hann: "Ethnic Cleansing in Eastern Europe and Ukrainians beside the Curzon Line," *Nations and Nationalism,* II (Oxford, 1996), pp. 389–406; "Postsocialist Nationalism: Rediscovering the Past in Southeast Poland," *Slavic Review,* LVII, 4 (Cambridge, Mass. 1998), pp. 840–863; and "Religion, Trade, and Trust in South-East Poland," *Religion, State, and Society,* XXVI, 3–4 (Keston, U.K. 1998), pp. 235–249.

12. The Soviet era, 1945–1991

There is an extensive literature on the postwar years. Good introductions to the first two decades, with particular emphasis on administrative and ideological matters, are found in: Yaroslav Bilinsky, *The Second Soviet Republic: The Ukraine after World War II* (New Brunswick, N.J. 1964); and Robert S. Sullivant, *Soviet Politics and the Ukraine, 1917–1957* (New York and London 1962), esp. chapters 6–7. A description of developments until the end of the 1970s is provided by Borys Lewytzkyj, *Politics and Society in Soviet Ukraine, 1953–1980* (Edmonton 1984); Bohdan Krawchenko, *Social Change and National Consciousness in Twentieth-Century Ukraine* (New York 1985), esp. chapter 5; Peter J. Potichnyj, ed., *Ukraine in the Seventies* (Oakville, Ont. 1975); and Bohdan Krawchenko, ed., *Ukraine after Shelest* (Edmonton 1983). It is also useful to view this same period through the eyes of a former longtime first secretary of the Communist party of Ukraine: V.V. Shcherbitsky, *Soviet Ukraine* (Moscow 1985).

The manner in which the Communist party actually administered the country is described by John A. Armstrong, *The Soviet Bureaucratic Elite: A Case Study of the Ukrainian Apparatus* (New York 1959). The Ukrainian variant of Kremlinology – the attempt by western observers to determine by indirect evidence the reasons why Soviet leaders acted the way they did – produced a number of studies that tried to explain the motivations behind the changes in the Communist Ukrainian leadership: Grey Hodnett, "The Views of Petro Shelest," *AUAAS,* XIV (1978–80), pp. 209–243; Yaroslav Bilinsky "Mykola Skrypnyk and Petro Shelest: An Essay on the Persistence and Limits of Ukrainian National Communism," in Jeremy R. Azrael, ed., *Soviet Nationality Policies and Practices* (New York 1978), pp. 105–143; Lowell Tillett, "Ukrainian Nationalism and the Fall of Shelest," *Slavic Review,* XXXIV, 4 (Columbus, Ohio 1975), pp. 752–768; and Yaroslav Bilinsky, "Schcherbytsky, Ukraine and Kremlin Politics," *Problems of Communism,* XXXII, 4 (Washington, D.C. 1983), pp. 1–20.

The particular status of Soviet Ukraine as a "state within a state" also attracted the attention of several political and legal analyses. Theoretical issues are outlined in Theofil I. Kis, *Nationhood, Statehood, and the International Status of the Ukrainian SSR/Ukraine* (Ottawa, London, and Paris 1989). The manner in which the state functioned on the international scene is surveyed by Alexander J. Motyl, "The Foreign Relations of the Ukrainian SSR," *HUS,* VI, 1 (1982), pp. 62–78; and Yaroslav Bilinsky, "The Ukrainian SSR in International Affairs after World War II," *AUAAS,* IX, 1–2 (1961), pp. 147–166. The role of Soviet Ukraine in specific events is treated in great detail in Konstantin Sawczuk, *The Ukraine in the United Nations Organization: A Study in Soviet Foreign Policy, 1944–1950* (Boulder, Colo. 1975); and Grey Hodnett and Peter J. Potichnyj, *The Ukraine and the Czechoslovak Crisis* (Canberra 1970). Soviet Ukraine's economic and cultural relations with Poland as well as the status of Poles in postwar Soviet Ukraine are discussed by Vasyl Markus, Volodymyr N. Bandera, Georges Mond, Borys Lewytzkyj, and Roman Szporluk in Peter J. Potichnyj, ed., *Poland and Ukraine: Past and Present* (Edmonton and Toronto 1980), pp. 132–227.

Economic development in the decades after World War II is traced by several authors in I.S. Koropeckyj, ed., *The Ukraine within the USSR: An Economic Balance Sheet* (New York and London 1977); specifically in the 1970s, by Gennady Ozornoy, in Krawchenko, *Ukraine after Shelest,* pp. 73–100; and, specifically in agriculture, by Ihor Stebelsky, in Potichnyj, *Ukraine in the Seventies*, pp. 103–126. The question of Ukraine's economic integration in the Soviet Union is given particular attention in I.S. Koropeckyj, *Development in the Shadow: Studies in Ukrainian Economics* (Edmonton 1990); and I.S. Koropeckyj, "A Century of Moscow-Ukraine Economic Relations: An Interpretation," *HUS*, V, 4 (1981), pp. 467–496. Urban growth and its effect on society as a whole is discussed in great detail by Peter Woroby, "Effects of Urbanization in the Ukraine," *AUAAS*, XIII (1973–77), pp. 51–115; and by Roman Szporluk, "Urbanization in Ukraine since the Second World War," in Ivan Rudnytsky, ed., *Rethinking Ukrainian History* (Edmonton 1981), pp. 180–202. Particular attention is given to one urban environment in which Soviet-style socialism and Western cultural influencs successfully interacted: Sergei I. Zhuk, *Rock and Roll in the Rocket City: The West, Identity and Ideology in Soviet Dniepropetrovsk, 1960–1985* (Washington, D.C., Baltimore, and London 2009).

The newly annexed western Ukrainian lands, in particular Galicia, are the subject of several studies. The manner in which the Soviet system was implemented in concrete terms is discussed by David Marples, "The Kulak in Western Ukraine," *Soviet Studies*, XXXVI, 4 (Glasgow 1984), pp. 560–570, and "Collectivization in Western Ukraine, 1948–1949," *Nationalities Papers*, XIII, 1 (North York, Ont. 1985), pp. 24–44 – both articles reprinted, together with "Khrushchev and Mass Collectivization in Western Ukraine, 1950–1951," in David R. Marples, *Stalinism in Ukraine in the 1940s* (Edmonton 1992), pp. 97–160. The subsequent impact of the more nationally aware Galician Ukrainians on the rest of the country is treated by Yaroslav Bilinsky, "The Incorporation of Western Ukraine and Its Impact on Politics and Society in Soviet Ukraine," in Roman Szporluk, ed., *The Influence of East Europe and the Soviet West on the USSR* (New York 1976), pp. 180–228.

The destruction of the Greek Catholic Church has received special attention. An early description of events by church leaders, together with documents, that appeared in *First Victims of Communism: White Book of the Religious Persecution in Ukraine* (Rome 1953), was followed by three scholarly articles: Bohdan R. Bociurkiw, "The Uniate Church in the Soviet Ukraine: A Case Study in Soviet Church Policy," *Canadian Slavonic Papers*, VII (Ottawa 1965), pp. 89–115; D. Dirscherl, "The Soviet Destruction of the Greek Catholic Church," *Journal of Church and State*, XII (Waco, Tex. 1970), pp. 421–439; and Dennis J. Dunn, "The Disappearance of the Ukrainian Uniate Church: How and Why?" *Ukraïns'kyi istoryk*, IX, 1–2 (New York and Munich 1972), pp. 57–65; and in a general history of the destruction as well as survival of the "underground church" throughout the Soviet era in Serge Keleher, *Passion and Resurrection: The Greek Catholic Church in Soviet Ukraine, 1938–1989* (L'viv 1993). The Orthodox and approved Soviet view of these events is available in *Lvov Church Council: Documents and Materials, 1946–1981* (Moscow 1983). The most comprehensive analysis of the L'viv Sobor (council), based on extensive archival documentation from recently opened former Soviet archives, is Bohdan Rostyslav Bociurkiw, *The Ukrainian Greek Catholic Church and the Soviet State, 1939–1950* (Edmonton and Toronto 1996). A broader discussion, including the fate of the Greek Catholic Church in neighboring Communist countries, is provided by Dennis Dunn, *The Catholic Church and the Soviet Government, 1939–1949* (Boulder, Colo. 1977). The destruction of the church specifically in Transcarpathia and eastern Slovakia is discussed by Michael Lacko, "The Forced Liquidation of the Union of Užhorod," *Slovak Studies,* I (Rome 1961), pp. 145–185.

The various ways in which Ukrainian nationalism survived and evolved under the postwar Soviet regime is best described in Kenneth C. Farmer, *Ukrainian Nationalism in the Post-Stalin Era* (The Hague, Boston, and London 1980). Also of importance are extended essays by Yaroslav Bilinsky, "Assimilation and Ethnic Assertiveness among Ukrainians of the Soviet Union," in Eric Goldhagen, ed., *Ethnic Minorities in the Soviet Union* (New York 1968), pp. 147–184; and by Roman Szporluk, "The Ukraine and Russia," in Robert Conquest, ed., *The Last Empire: Nationality and the Soviet Future* (Stanford, Calif. 1986), pp. 151–182. The persistence of language as a political factor and as a barometer of national survival is discussed by Paul Wexler, *Purism and Language: A Study of Modern Ukrainian and Belorussian Nationalism, 1940–1967* (Bloomington, Ind. 1974); by Roman Solchanyk, "Language Politics in the Ukraine," in Isabelle T. Kreindler, ed., *Sociolinguistic Perspectives on Soviet National Languages* (Berlin, New York, and Amsterdam 1985), esp. pp. 73–105; and by Roman Szporluk, "West Ukraine and West Belorussia: Historical Tradition, Social Communication, and Linguistic Assimilation," *Soviet Studies,* XXXI, 1 (Glasgow 1979), pp. 76–98.

The experience of World War II and the manner in which the Soviet regime was able to use memories of those difficult years to bolster the allegiance and loyalty of the Ukrainian masses is the subject of a major monograph by Amir Weiner, *Making Sense of War: The Second World War and the Fate of the Bolshevik Revolution* (Princeton, N.J. 2001). The way in which the writing of Ukrainian history was used and misused by Soviet policy makers to justify and buttress their rule is the subject of several studies, including Stephen Velychenko, *Shaping Identity in Eastern Europe and Russia: Soviet Russian and Polish Accounts of Ukrainian History, 1914–1991* (New York 1993), esp. chapters 7–8; Stephen Velychenko, "The Origins of the Official Soviet Interpretation of Eastern Slavic History: A Case Study of Policy Formulation," *Forschungen zur osteuropäischen Geschichte,* XLVI (Berlin 1992), pp. 225–253; Roman Szporluk, "National History as a Political Battleground: The Case of Ukraine and Belorussia," in Michael S. Pap, ed., *Russian Empire: Some Aspects of Tsarist and Soviet Colonial Practices* (Cleveland 1985), pp. 131–150; Jaroslaw Pelenski, "Soviet Ukrainian Historiography after World War II," *Jahrbücher fur Geschichte Osteuropas,* N.S., XII (Wiesbaden 1964), pp. 375–418; Lubomyr R. Wynar, "The Present State of Ukrainian Historiography in Soviet Ukraine: A Brief Overview," *Nationalities Papers,* VII, 1 (Charleston, Ill. 1979), pp. 1–23; and Serhy Yelelchyk, "How the 'Iron Minister' Kaganovich Failed to Discipline Ukrainian Historians: A Stalinist Ideological Campaign Reconsidered," *Nationalities Papers,* XXVII, 4 (Oxfordshire, U.K. 1999), pp. 579–604.

Since the mid-1980s, during the decline and eventual end of Soviet rule, the historical past has again been used in an effort to help chart Ukraine's political future. The Cossack period, in particular, is emphasized, as in several essays by

Frank Sysyn, "The Reemergence of the Ukrainian Nation and Cossack Mythology," *Social Research*, LVIII, 4 (New York 1991), pp. 845–864; Zenon E. Kohut, "Russian-Ukrainian Relations and Historical Consciousness in Contemporary Ukraine" and Serhii M. Plokhy, "Cossack Mythology in the Russian-Ukrainian Border Dispute," in S. Frederick Starr, ed., *The Legacy of History in Russia and the New States of Eurasia* (Armonk, N.Y. and London 1994), pp. 123–146; and Karel C. Berkhoff, "'Brothers, We Are All of Cossack Stock': The Cossack Campaign in Ukrainian Newspapers on the Eve of Independence," *HUS*, XXI, 1–2 (Cambridge, Mass. 1997), pp. 119–140.

Scholars in the West, especially during the Cold War and the so-called era of détente, were anxious to uncover all forms of opposition, however limited or politically innocuous, against Soviet rule. A book-length bibliography of published literature on the subject is available: George Liber and Anna Mostovych, comp., *Nonconformity and Dissent in the Ukrainian SSR, 1955–1975: An Annotated Bibliography* (Cambridge, Mass. 1978). A good introduction to the sociodemographic background of dissidents and the response of the Soviet government is provided in Jaroslaw Bilocerkowycz, *Soviet Ukrainian Dissent: A Study of Political Alienation* (Boulder, Colo. and London 1988). For emphasis on ideological content, see Ivan L. Rudnytsky, "The Political Thought of Soviet Ukrainian Dissent," *JUS*, VI, 2 [11] (1981), pp. 3–16, reprinted in Ivan L. Rudnytsky, *Essays in Modern Ukrainian History* (Edmonton 1987), pp. 477–489; George S.N. Luckyj, "Polarity in Ukrainian Intellectual Dissent," *Canadian Slavonic Papers*, XIV, 2 (Ottawa 1972), pp. 269–279; and Victor Swoboda, "The Party Guidance of a Soviet Literature: The Case of the Ukraine, 1968–1975," in Evelyn Bristol, ed., *East European Literature: Selected Papers from the Second World Congress for Soviet and East European Studies* (Berkeley, Calif. 1982), pp. 85–106. The relationship of the dissident movement to Ukraine's other peoples is discussed in Yaroslav Bilinsky, "Political Relations between Russians and Ukrainians in the USSR: The 1970s and Beyond," in Peter J. Potichnyj et al., *Ukraine and Russia in Their Historical Encounter* (Edmonton 1992), pp. 165–198; Peter J. Potichnyj, "The Struggle of the Crimean Tatars," *Canadian Slavonic Papers*, XVII, 2–3 (Ottawa 1975), pp. 302–319; and Israel Kleiner, "The Present-Day Ukrainian National Movement in the USSR and the Jewish Question," *Soviet Jewish Affairs*, XI, 3 (London 1981), pp. 3–14.

Many of the writings of the dissidents from the period were translated into English. These exist as anthologies: Slava Stetsko, ed., *Revolutionary Voices: Ukrainian Political Prisoners Condemn Russian Colonialism*, 2nd rev. ed. (Munich 1971); Michael Browne, ed., *Ferment in the Ukraine: Documents by V. Chornovil, I. Kandyba, L. Lukyanenko, V. Moroz, and Others* (Woodhaven, N.Y. 1973); *The Ukrainian Herald*, issues 4–8 (Munich and Baltimore, 1972–77); Lesya Verba and Nina Strokata, eds., *The Human Rights Movement in Ukraine: Documents of the Ukrainian Helsinki Group, 1976–1980* (Baltimore 1980); or as individual works: Iurii Badzo, "An Open Letter to the Presidium of the Supreme Soviet of the USSR and the Central Committee of the CPSU," *JUS*, IX, 1 and 2 [16 and 17] (1984), pp. 74–94 and 47–70; Vyacheslav Chornovil, *The Chornovil Papers* (New York and Toronto 1968); Ivan Dzyuba, *Internationalism or Russification? A Study in the Soviet*

Nationalities Problem, 3rd ed. (New York 1974); *The Grigorenko Papers: Writings by General P.G. Grigorenko and Documents on His Case* (Boulder, Colo. 1976); Valentyn Moroz, *Report from the Beria Reserve* (Toronto 1974); Valentyn Moroz, *Boomerang: The Works of Valentyn Moroz* (Baltimore, Paris, and Toronto 1974); Mykhaylo Osadchy, *Cataract* (New York 1976); Leonid Plyushch, *History's Carnival: A Dissident's Autobiography* (New York 1979); Ivan Sverstiuk, *Clandestine Essays* (Cambridge, Mass. 1976); and Danylo Shumuk, *Life Sentence: Memoirs of a Ukrainian Political Prisoner* (Edmonton 1984).

A specific form of dissent against the Soviet system was related to religious belief and church life in Ukraine. This was discussed in two general studies: Bohdan Bociurkiw, "Religion and Nationalism in Contemporary Ukraine," in G. Simmonds, ed., *Nationalism in the USSR and Eastern Europe in the Era of Brezhnev and Kosygin* (Detroit 1977), pp. 81–93; and Bohdan Bociurkiw, "The Religious Situation in Soviet Ukraine," in Walter Dushnyk, ed., *Ukraine in the Changing World* (New York 1977), pp. 173–194. The specific status of Orthodoxy was reviewed by Bohdan R. Bociurkiw, "The Orthodox Church and the Soviet Regime in the Ukraine, 1953–1971," *Canadian Slavonic Papers,* XIV, 2 (Ottawa 1972), pp. 191–212; and Frank E. Sysyn, "The Ukrainian Orthodox Question in the USSR," *Religion in Communist Lands,* XI, 3 (Keston, U.K. 1983), pp. 251–263 – reprinted in Frank E. Sysyn, *The Ukrainian Orthodox Question in the USSR* (Cambridge, Mass. 1987), pp. 9–22. The suppressed Greek Catholic Church received much more attention, including articles by Bohdan Bociurkiw, "Religious Dissent and Soviet State," and Vasyl Markus, "Religion and Nationality: The Uniates in Ukraine," in Bohdan R. Bociurkiw and John Strong, eds., *Religion and Atheism in the USSR and Eastern Europe* (London 1975), pp. 58–90 and 101–122 – reprinted in Vasyl Markus, *Religion and Nationalism in Soviet Ukraine after 1945* (Cambridge, Mass. 1987); by Ivan Hvat, "The Ukrainian Catholic Church, the Vatican, and the Soviet Union during the Pontificate of Pope John Paul II," *Religion in Communist Lands,* XI, 3 (Keston, U.K. 1983), pp. 264–279 – reprinted in Ivan Hvat, *The Catacomb Ukrainian Catholic Church and Pope John Paul II* (Cambridge, Mass. 1984); and by Myroslaw Tataryn, "The Re-emergence of the Ukrainian (Greek) Catholic Church in the USSR," in Sabrina Petra Ramet, ed., *Religious Policy in the Soviet Union* (New York 1993), pp. 319–349. Also available is an intellectual biography of the church's imprisoned and later exiled metropolitan: Jaroslav Pelikan, *Confessor between East and West: A Portrait of Ukrainian Cardinal Josyf Slipyj* (Grand Rapids, Mich. 1990); and a memoir-like account of a leading dissident: Josyp Terelya, *Witness to Apparitions and Persecutions in the USSR* (Milford, Ohio 1991).

The last years of the Soviet era in Ukraine are discussed in a growing body of literature about the impact of Mikhail Gorbachev and his policies of *perestroika* and *glasnost* that began in 1985 and culminated in the collapse of the Soviet Union and the creation of an independent Ukraine in 1991. A useful chronicle-like introduction to the years just before and after independence is found in Bohdan Nahaylo, *The Ukrainian Resurgence* (Toronto and Buffalo 1999). More wide-range and interpretive are essays in Roman Szporluk, *Russia, Ukraine, and the Breakup of the Soviet Union* (Stanford 2000). For the specific impact of the Gorbachev era on Soviet Ukraine, see Taras Kuzio, *Ukraine: Perestroika to Independence*, 2nd ed. (London 2000), and the views of leading Ukrainian activists in their own words as presented in Roman Solchanyk, ed., *Ukraine: From Chernobyl' to Sovereignty: A Collection of Interviews* (Edmonton 1992) and Leonid Kravchuk, *Our Goal – Free Ukraine: Speeches, Interviews, Press-Conferences, Briefings* (Kiev 1993).

The ecological and political fallout from the 1986 nuclear disaster at Chornobyl' just north form Kiev has been accorded much attention. Among the more important works are three books by David R. Marples: *Chernobyl and Nuclear Power in the USSR* (Edmonton 1986); *The Social Impact of the Chernobyl Disaster* (New York 1988); and *Ukraine under Perestroika: Ecology, Economics, and the Workers' Revolt* (London 1991). Of the several other works on this topic, the best are by Victor Haynes and Marko Bojcun, *The Chornobyl Disaster* (London 1988); Grigorii Medvedev, *The Truth About Chernobyl* (New York 1991); Zhores Medvedev, *The Legacy of Chernobyl* (New York 1990); Yuri Scherbak, *Chernobyl: A Documentary Story* (London 1989); and Paul Read Piers, *Ablaze: The Story of Chernobyl* (New York 1993).

The legalization of several church bodies in Gorbachev's Soviet Union and the problem of ecclesiastical jurisdiction that has arisen in Ukraine both before and after independence, especially among the Orthodox, are discussed in several essays by Serhii Plokhy and Frank Sysyn, *Religion and Nation in Modern Ukraine* (Edmonton and Toronto 2003), esp. pp. 88–135. On the more general role of religion in independent Ukraine, see José Casanova, "Ethno-Linguistic and Religious Pluralism and Democratic Construction in Ukraine," in Barnett R. Rubin and Jack Snyder, eds., *Post-Soviet Political Order: Conflict and State Building* (London and New York 1998), pp. 81–103. The enormous increase in the number of Protestant Evangelicals, in particular Baptist and Pentecostals both on the eve of and after independence, is discussed at length in Catherine Wanner, *Communities of the Converted: Ukrainians and Global Evangelism* (Ithaca and London 2007).

13. Independent Ukraine

The so-called transitional period during the initial years of Ukrainian independence is discussed in several monographs. Among the earliest is an informed theoretical analysis that speculates on the possible evolution of the new state: Alexander J. Motyl, *Dilemmas of Independence: Ukraine after Totalitarianism* (New York 1993). A more traditional descriptive account of events during the first decade of independent Ukraine is provided by Bohdan Harasymiv, *Post-Communist Ukraine* (Edmonton and Toronto 2002). Various aspects and challenges faced by the newly sovereign country are dealt with in a series of recent books: Andrew Wilson, *Ukrainian Nationalism in the 1990s: A Minority Faith* (Cambridge 1997); Theofil Kis, Irena Makaryk et al., eds., *Toward a New Ukraine*, 3 vols. (Ottawa 1997–2001); Taras Kuzio, *Ukraine: State and Nation Building* (London and New York 1998); Taras Kuzio, ed., *Contemporary Ukraine: Dynamics of Post-Soviet Transformation* (Armonk, N.Y. 1998); Marta Dyczok, *Ukraine: Movement without Change, Change without Movement* (Amsterdam 2000); Robert S. Kravchuk, *Renaissance in*

Blue and Gold: Ukrainian Politics, Economics and Governance 1991–1996 (Basingstoke, U.K. 2000); Taras Kuzio, ed., *Ukraine: A Decade of Independence,* special issue of *JUS,* XXVI, 1–2 (Toronto 2001), pp. 1–324; Kataryna Wolczuk, *The Moulding of Ukraine: The Constitutional Politics of State Formation* (Budapest 2001); Wsewolod W. Isajiw, ed., *Society in Transition: Social Change in Ukraine in Western Perspectives* (Toronto 2003); Andrew Wilson, *Virtual Politics: Faking Democracy in the Post-Soviet World* (New Haven, Conn. 2005); Paul D'Anieri, *Understanding Ukrainian Politics: Power, Politics, and Institutional Design* (Armonk, N.Y. and London 2007). A useful overview of the period up until the Orange Revolution is Verena Fritz's, *State-Building: A Comparative Study of Ukraine, Lithuania, Belarus, and Russia* (Budapest and New York 2007), esp. pp. 109–209.

Particular attention has been given to Ukraine's economy and its international status. On the economy, see Axel Siedenberg and Lutz Hoffmann, eds., *Ukraine at the Crossroads: Economic Reforms in International Perspective* (Heidelberg 1999); King Banaian, *The Ukrainian Economy Since Independence* (Aldershot, U.K. 1999); Andrew Wilson and Igor Burakovsky, eds., *The Ukrainian Economy under Kuchma* (London 1996); and Hans von Zon, *The Political Economy of Independent Ukraine* (London and New York 2000). The country's international status, its relations with neighboring countries, and its national security are treated in Lubomyr A. Hajda, ed., *Ukraine in the World: Studies in the International Relations and Security Structure of a Newly Independent State,* special issue of *HUS,* XX (Cambridge, Mass. 1996); Sherman W. Ganett, *Keystone in the Arch: Ukraine in the Emerging Security Environment of Central and Eastern Europe* (Washington, D.C. 1997); Tor Bukkvol, *Ukraine and European Security* (London 1997); Yaroslav Bilinsky, *Endgame in NATO's Enlargement: The Baltic States and Ukraine* (Westport, Conn. 1999); Margarita M. Balmaceda, ed., *On the Edge: Ukrainian – Central European – Russian Security Triangle* (Budapest 2000); Roman Solchanyk, *Ukraine and Russia: The Post-Soviet Transition* (London, Md. 2001); Jennifer D. P. Moroney et al., eds., *Ukrainian Foreign and Security Policy: Theoretical and Comparative Perspectives* (Westport, Conn. 2002); and Roman Wolczuk, *Ukraine's Foreign and Security Policy, 1991–2000* (London and New York 2003).

As a newly independent country, Ukraine continues to face the challenge of creating in its citizenry an awareness and desire of belonging to a common civic political entity. This process, called nation-building, has focused on issues of language use, the educational system, and historical ideology. The theoretical and practical aspects of this topic are the subject of essays by various authors in Taras Kuzio and Paul D'Anieri, eds., *Dilemmas of State-Led Nation Building in Ukraine* (Westport, Conn. and London 2002). The relationship of historical ideology to national identity is the focus of a monograph by Catherine Wanner, *Burden of Dreams: History and Identity in Post-Soviet Ukraine* (University Park, Pa. 1998); and Kataryna Wolczuk, "History, Europe and the 'National Idea': The 'Official' Narrative of National Identity in Ukraine," *Nationalities Papers,* XXVIII, 4 (New York 2000), pp. 671–694.

For a general overview of challenges faced by the historical profession both in post-Communist Ukraine and abroad (mostly North America), see the monograph by Serhii Plokhy, *Ukraine and Russia: Representation of the Past* (Toronto, Buffalo, and London 2008), esp. chapters 9–16; and articles by Orest Subtelny, "The Current State of Ukrainian Historiography," *Journal of Ukrainian Studies*, XVIII, 1–2 (Edmonton 1993), pp. 33–54; by Mark von Hagen, "Does Ukraine Have a History?" with commentaries by George G. Grabowicz, Andreas Kappeler, Iaroslav Isaievych, Serhii Plokhy, and Yuri Slezkine, *Slavic Review*, LIV, 3 (Cambridge, Mass. 1995), pp. 658–719; by Taras Kuzio, "Post-Soviet Ukrainian Historiography in Ukraine," *International Textbook Research*, XXIII, 1 (Hannover 2001), pp. 27–42; and by Taras Kuzio, "Historiography and National Identity among the Eastern Slavs: Toward a New Framework," *National Identities*, III, 2 (Abingdon, U.K. 2001), pp. 109–132. One author has focused on how specific topics – the Great Famine of 1933, the Organization of Ukrainian Nationalists (OUN) and Ukrainian Insurgent Army (UPA), and the Ukrainian-Polish conflict – are dealt with by post-Communist Ukrainian scholars and publicists as well as some Ukrainianists in the West: David R. Marples, *Heroes and Villains: Creating National History in Contemporary Ukraine* (Budapest and New York 2007).

Scholars outside Ukraine, mostly political scientists, continue to be fascinated by the manner in which the new state has addressed the question of national identity. See in particular the collection of studies by Taras Kuzio, *Theoretical and Comparative Perspectives of Nationalism* (Stuttgart 2007), and the articles by Paul Kubicek, "Dynamics of Contemporary Ukrainian Nationalism: Empire Breaking to State Building," *Canadian Review of Studies in Nationalism* (Charlottetown, Prince Edward Is. 1996), pp. 39–50; Paul Kubicek "What Happened to the Nationalists in Ukraine?," *Nationalism and Ethnic Politics*, V, 1 (London and Portland, Ore. 1996), pp. 29–45; Paul Pirie, "National Identity and Politics in Southern and Eastern Ukraine," *Europe-Asia Studies*, XLVIII, 7 (Glasgow 1996), pp. 1079–1104; and Stephen Shulman, "Ukrainian Nation-Building under Kuchma," *Problems of Post-Communism*, LII, 5 (Armonk, N.Y., 2005), pp. 32–47.

The significance of the Ukrainian language as a factor of nation-building and identity is given particular attention in German Janmaat, *Nation-Building in Post-Soviet Ukraine: Educational Policy and the Response of the Russian Speaking Population* (Utrecht and Amsterdam 2000); and in Dominique Arel, "Language Politics in Independent Ukraine: Towards One or Two State Languages?," *Nationalities Papers*, XXIII, 3 (New York 1995), pp. 597–622; Dominique Arel, "Interpreting 'Nationality' and 'Language' in the 2001 Ukrainian Census," *Post-Soviet Affairs*, XVIII, 3 (Palm Beach, Fla. 2002), pp. 213–249; and Alexandra Hrycak, "Institutional Legacies and Language Revival in Ukraine," in Dominique Arel and Blair A. Ruble, eds., *Rebounding Identities: The Policies of Identity in Russia and Ukraine* (Washington, D.C. and Baltimore 2006), pp. 62–88.

Related to the nationality question is regionalism and the status of peoples other than ethnic Ukrainians. These factors, as potentially disruptive to Ukrainian state- and nationality-building, are viewed from the perspective of various regions and groups throughout the country. For a general introduction to the problem, see Dominique Arel, "The Hidden Face of the Orange Revolution: Ukraine in Denial Toward Its Regional Problem," (www.ukrainianstudies.uottawa.

ca), p. 41; and Gwendolyn Sasse, "The 'New' Ukraine: A State of Regions," in Gwendolyn Sasse and James Hughes, eds., *Ethnicity and Territory in the Former Soviet Union: Regions in Conflict* (London and Portland, Ore. 2002), pp. 69–100. Legal guarantees for national minorities, interethnic relations, and specific recent developments among Poles, Jews, and Crimean Tatars are the subject of several studies in Evgeniy Golovakha, Nataliya Panina, and Valeriy Vorona, eds., *Sociology in Ukraine: Selected Works Published During the 1990s* (Kiev 2000).

Although ever decreasing in numerical size, the status and treatment of the Jews is considered by many observers to be an important litmus test for the protection of human rights and democratic values in independent Ukraine. The best study on this topic is Aleksandr Burakovskiy, "The Characteristics and Transformation of Jewish-Ukrainian Relations During the Period of Ukraine's Independence, 1991–2008," *Nationalism and Ethnic Politics*, XV, 1 (London 2009), pp. 109–132. On the numerically larger ethnic Russian and Russian-speaking Ukrainian population of eastern Ukraine, see Paul Kolstoe, *Russians in Former Soviet Republics* (Bloomington and Indianapolis 1995), esp. pp. 170–199; Jan Bremmer, "The Politics of Ethnicity: Russians in the New Ukraine," *Europe-Asia Studies*, XLVI, 2 (Glasgow 1994), pp. 261–284; Andrew Wilson, "The Donbas between Ukraine and Russia: The Use of History in Political Disputes," *Journal of Contemporary History*, XX, 2 (London 1995), pp. 265–290; Roman Solchanyk, "Russians in Ukraine: Problems and Prospects," *HUS*, XXII (Cambridge, Mass. 1998), pp. 539–554; and Kateryna Stadniuk, "Inter-Ethnic Coexistence and Cultural Autonomy in Ukraine: the Case of the Donetsk Region," in Christopher Lord and Olga Strietska-Ilina, eds., *Parallel Cultures: Majority-Minority Relations in the Countries of the Former Eastern Bloc* (Aldershot, U.K. 2001), pp. 209–244.

Two other regions sought to achieve autonomy within Ukraine. The Crimea succeeded in its efforts, and the most comprehensive discussion of those developments following the collapse of the Soviet Union is found in Gwendolyn Sasse, *The Crimean Question: Identity, Transition, and Conflict* (Cambridge, Mass. 2007), esp. chapters 6–10. The role of the Crimea as a factor in relations between present-day Ukraine and Russia is explored in great detail in Taras Kuzio, *Ukraine – Crimea – Russia: Triangle of Conflict* (Stuttgart 2007). Other studies related to the political status of the Crimean Autonomous Republic and the separate issue of Crimean Tatars who have returned to their ancestral homeland include: David R. Marples and David F. Duke, "Ukraine, Russia, and the Question of Crimea," *Nationalities Papers*, XXIII, 2 (New York 1995), pp. 261–289; Edward A. Allworth, ed., *The Tatars of Crimea: Return to the Homeland* (Durham, N.C. 1998); Brian G. Williams, *The Crimean Tatars* (Leiden, Boston, and Köln 2001), esp. chapter 13; and Gwendolyn Sasse, "Conflict-Prevention in a Transition State: The Crimean Issue in Post-Soviet Ukraine," *Nationalism and Ethnic Politics*, VIII, 2 (London 2002), pp. 1–26. The 1944 deportation and the important role that the memory of that event has on Crimean Tatars who have returned to their homeland in 1990s is explored in Gretta Lynn Uehling, *Beyond Memory: The Crimean Tatars' Deportation and Return* (New York 2004).

The second region, Transcarpathia, did not achieve autonomous status. On its Rusyn and Hungarian inhabitants, see Paul Robert Magocsi, *Of the Making of Nationalities There is No End,* 2 vols. (New York 1999), and Ildikó Orosz and István Csernicskó, *The Hungarians in Transcarpathia* (Budapest 1999). Yet one more region, Galicia – otherwise considered the fount of Ukrainian nationalism – includes writers and civic activists who have toyed with the idea of separatism, even independence, from the rest of Ukraine: Lidia Stefanowska, "Back to the Golden Age: The Discourse of Nostalgia in Galicia in the 1990s," *HUS,* XXVII [2004–2005], 1–4 (Cambridge, Mass. 2008), pp. 181–193.

Finally, there is the topic which many observers consider to be the watershed event in the history of independent Ukraine: the controversial presidential elections of 2004 that led to what has become known as the Orange Revolution. The best introduction to this topic is by Andrew Wilson, *Ukraine's Orange Revolution* (New Haven and London 2005), and Anders Aslund, *Revolution in Orange: the Origins of Ukraine's Democratic Breakthrough* (Washington, D.C. 2006). Also available is a multivolume collection of articles by several scholars as well as documents and a chronology of events in Paul D'Anieri, Taras Kuzio, Bohdan Harasymiw, Ingmar Bredies et al., eds., *Aspects of the Orange Revolution* , 6 vols. (Stuttgart 2007).

Index

Third, 509, 510, 512, 518, 519; Fourth, 512, 537, 541
University: of Alberta, 455; of Chernivtsi/King Carol I University, 484, 644, 645; of Kam'ianets'-Podil's'kyi, 537; of Kiev (Ukrainian), 521, 578; of Königsberg, 168; of Manitoba, 464; of Toronto, 455; of Vilnius, 355, 382; of Waterloo, 464. *See also* Charles University; Columbia University; Ivan Franko University; Kharkiv University; L'viv University; Moscow University; Odessa University; Princeton University; Saint Clement Ukrainian Catholic University; Saint Petersburg University; Saint Vladimir University; Taurida University; Ukrainian Free University; Ukrainian Catholic University; Ukrainian Underground University; VUZ; Warsaw University; Yale University
UNRRA, 694
Untermenschen, 670, 675, 679
UPA. *See* Ukrainian Insurgent Army
Upper Austria, 414
Uppland, 56
Ural Mountains, 13, 387, 708, 730
Urbanik, Martin, 303
Urbanization: in pre-Kievan period, 25, 28–30, 32–36 *passim*; in Kievan Rus', 89, 125, 127, 129; in Mongol Crimea, 117–119, 177; in Poland-Lithuania, 156; in Ottoman Black Sea Lands, 179; the Cossack state/Hetmanate, 267, 295; in Dnieper Ukraine, 342–343, 353, 358; in Austrian Galicia, 420, 450; in Soviet Ukraine, 576–577, 684, 713–714; literature about, 783, 798, 813
Urumi. See Tatar Greeks
Uspens'kyi Sobor. *See* Church of the Holy Dormition (L'viv)
Utigurs, 29, 35, 36
Uvarov, Sergei S. (1786–1855), 382, 383
UVO. *See* Ukrainian Military Organization
Uzbek S.S.R., 562; Crimean Tatars in, 690–691

Uzbekistan, 746; ethnic Ukrainians in, 11, Uzbeks, 717, 747; in UPA, 681
Uzhhorod (city), 430, 445, 486, 553, 554, 647, 650, 658; (district), 441, 445; (seat of Greek Catholic eparchy), 441, 486
Uzhhorod, Union of, 175, 698–699

Vahylevych, Ivan (1811–1866), 428, 429, 435, 470, 472; literature about, 791
Val'nyts'kyi, Kyrylo (1889–193?), 636
Valuev, Petr (1814–1890), 393, 394
Valuev decree, 393–394; literature about, 788
Váňa, Zdeněk, 41
Vandalengau, 674
Vandals, 674
VAPLITE. *See* Free Academy of Proletarian Literature
Varangian Rus', 66, 68, 70, 76, 100, 102
Varangians, 51, 56, 57, 59, 60, 61, 62, 63, 66, 74, 82; "Varangians to the Greeks, from the" (waterway), 49, 60, 65, 67, 96, 97
Vasa/Wasa dynasty, 206
Vashkivtsi, 485
Vasilii III, 222
Vasmer, Max, 41
Vasyl'kiv, Osyp (Osyp Krilyk, 1898–1941), 636
Vasyl'ko Romanovych (1199–1271), 124
Vasyl'ko, Mykola (1868–1924), 485
Vatan. *See* Fatherland Society
Vatan Hâdimi (newpaper), 368
Vatican, 424, 638, 697, 698, 720, 721, 742
Vechernytsi (journal), 471
Vedel', Artem (1767–1808), 302
Veli Ibrahimovism, 623
Velikorossy. See Great Russians
Velychkivs'kyi, Mykola (1882–1976), 674
Velychko, Samiilo (1670–ca. 1728), 187, 305
Velychkovs'kyi, Ivan (d. 1726), 304
Venedi, 42
Venetia, 414, 433